The Handbook of Aging and Cognition

Second Edition

The Handbook
of Aging and Cognition

Second Edition

Edited by

Fergus I. M. Craik
University of Toronto

Timothy A. Salthouse
Georgia Institute of Technology

LAWRENCE ERLBAUM ASSOCIATES, PUBLISHERS
2000   Mahwah, New Jersey   London

Lawrence Erlbaum Associates, Inc., Publishers
10 Industrial Avenue
Mahwah, NJ 07430

Cover design by Kathryn Houghtaling Lacey

Library of Congress Cataloging-in-Publication Data

The handbook of aging and cognition / edited by Fergus I. M. Craik,
    Timothy A. Salthouse. — 2nd ed.
p.   cm.
        Includes bibliographical references and index.
ISBN 0-8058-2966-0 (alk. paper)
1. Cognition in old age. 2. Cognition—Age factors. I. Craik, Fergus
    I. M. II. Salthouse, Timothy A.
BF724.85.C64H36   1999
155.67'13—dc21   99-31065
                                                                CIP

Books published by Lawrence Erlbaum Associates are
printed on acid-free paper, and their bindings are chosen
for strength and durability.

Printed in the United States of America
10 9 8 7 6 5 4 3 2

Contents

Preface

The first edition of this handbook was published in 1992. Our idea at that time was to bring together a set of chapters on various topics in the field of cognitive aging, with the further notion that each chapter would be long enough to be able to treat its subject in some depth. So we settled on a modest number of chapters (10) and encouraged the authors to present a critical review of current findings and conceits in their specific area. The book was organized around some core topics in cognition—attention, memory, language, and reasoning—with additional sections on neuropsychology and on real-world applications. We were very pleased with the resulting collection, and this positive reaction was generally shared by researchers in the field.

Cognitive aging is a flourishing research area at present, with a growing number of journals and well-attended meetings. This activity has generated a lot of new data in the last 8 to 10 years, a number of new theoretical notions, and even some new research topics. In fact, the field is in some danger of emulating the flustered nobleman in Stephen Leacock's story and is beginning to "ride madly off in all directions"! So, two obvious purposes of the second edition are first, to review new findings and theories, and second, to enable the reader to assess where the field "is at" these days and to evaluate its points of growth.

To do this, we invited a completely new set of authors to review topics in the field. This is not in any sense an update or revision of the first edition but rather a completely new volume. The only exceptions to this principle were ourselves—exercising a sort of *droit des éditeurs*—but even here the topics have changed from the first edition, with Salthouse contributing a chapter on methodological assumptions in cognitive aging research and Salthouse and Craik providing a final chapter of closing comments. This latter contribution was an effort to respond to some reviewers of the first edition who liked the individual chapters, but criticized the absence of an overview chapter to provide some general integration and evaluation. We found this a rather daunting task because the chapters themselves cover a very wide range, and we ended up with some general comments on the field rather than with an attempt to truly summarize and integrate.

Otherwise, the chapters are organized to run from a consideration of the neural correlates of age-related changes in cognition, to the "mainstream" topics of perception, attention, memory, and language, to more applied areas, to reviews of cognitive changes in the contexts of emotion, motivation, and personality. The field of cognitive neuroscience is particularly active at present, and Naftali Raz provides an up-to-date review of structural and functional changes in the aging brain and how these changes may relate to changes in cognitive performance. This chapter is nicely complemented by the following one, which also deals with the cognitive neuroscience of cognitive aging but from a more neuro-psychological viewpoint. It is written by Matthew Prull, John Gabrieli, and Silvia Bunge.

Chapter 3 is by Bruce Schneider and Kathleen Pichora-Fuller. They deal with the relations between sensory and cognitive changes in the context of aging. For instance, does perceptual deterioration "cascade" through the processing sequence to cause cognitive problems, or do both sensory and cognitive changes reflect some third "common cause"? The next three chapters deal with some core topics in cognitive aging: Attention is reviewed by Joan McDowd and Raymond Shaw; memory by Rose Zacks, Lynn Hasher, and Karen Li; and language by Arthur Wingfield and Elizabeth Stine-Morrow. The three chapters give an excellent coverage and critique of recent work in these important areas. They are followed by a chapter on metacognition by Christopher Hertzog and David Hultsch, which examines to what extent older adults are aware of their cognitive problems, and whether they can use this knowledge strategically to compensate for their losses.

The next three chapters move into practical problems of aging and cognition. In chapter 8, Salthouse reviews some assumptions and methodological pitfalls inherent in cognitive aging research. We hope that new researchers will profit from his cautions and insights! Cognitive functioning in very old age is reviewed by Lars Bäckman and his colleagues from the Stockholm Gerontology Research Center: Brent Small, Åke Wahlin, and Maria Larsson. Next, Wendy Rogers and Arthur Fisk provide an assessment of how cognitive problems in older people can affect such real-life activities as driving, use of automatic teller machines, and computers. As they convincingly argue, human factors research can help to mitigate many of these problems. The next two chapters place cognitive changes in the context of concomitant changes in emotion and cognition (Derek Isaacowitz, Susan Turk Charles, and Laura Carstensen) and in the even broader context of age-related changes in personality and social interactions (Ursula Staudinger and Monisha Pasupathi). These two chapters place cognitive changes in the context of life-span growths and declines. Finally, the two editors provide some thoughts and reflections on the field as it is at present.

We feel that this second edition has an even broader scope than the first, running as it does from structural changes in the brain to a consideration of changes in the self-concept and changes in social cognition. We should also add that we are extremely pleased with the high caliber of all the chapters and are grateful to the authors for their sterling efforts. The book is aimed primarily at researchers in the field—from graduate students to senior investigators—but the material is also very understandable to senior undergraduates for whom we hope the handbook will provide an exciting introduction to the field.

We are grateful to a number of people for their help. In Toronto, we thank Jennie Sawula and Gena Argitis for their work on the manuscripts. We also thank Judi Amsel and the editors at Lawrence Erlbaum Associates for their help and encouragement. We are most grateful to the Natural Sciences and Engineering Research Council of Canada and the National Institute of Aging in the United States for grant support during the course of preparing the book for publication. Above all, we are extremely grateful to our outstanding group of authors who presented us with such excellent reviews of their fields. We hope you enjoy reading them all!

—Fergus I. M. Craik
—Timothy A. Salthouse

Aging of the Brain and Its Impact on Cognitive Performance: Integration of Structural and Functional Findings

Naftali Raz
University of Memphis

> *To old people dyspnea, catarrhs accompanied with coughs, dysuria, pains of the joints, nephritis, vertigo, apoplexy, cachexia, pruritus of the whole body, insomnolency, defluxions of the bowels, of the eyes, and of the nose, dimness of sight, cataract (glaucoma), and dullness of hearing.*
>
> —Hippocrates, *Aphorisms*

Aging is "a fundamental biological process that can be defined, measured, described, and manipulated" (Arking, 1991). On the one hand, it is deeply rooted in the genetic makeup and metabolic workings of the organism in toto and its every cell (Strehler, 1986; Yu & Yang, 1996). On the other hand, it is sensitive to many environmental influences that exert their effects through modulating events (Arking, 1991). So overwhelming are the transformations of the aging body and so pervasive are the changes in its basic functions that it may not be particularly surprising that the most famous of the ancient servants of Aesculapius did not find the brain and higher cognitive functions sufficiently important to be included in his list of geriatric troubles. Luckily, during the 20th century, and especially in the past 3 decades, this neglect has been more than adequately compensated through the efforts of many neuroscientists. The results of their labors have been periodically surveyed and summarized leaving an impressive body of scholarly reviews (e.g., Bourne, 1973; Esiri, 1994; Flood & Coleman, 1988; Kemper, 1994; Uylings, West, Coleman, de Brabander, & Flood, in press; for findings pertaining specifically to the aging of the hippocampal formation, see Geinisman, deToledo-Morell, Morell, & Heller, 1995, and Kadar, Dachir, Shukitt-Hale, & Levy, 1998). Although the cumulative record of in vivo exploration of the aging brain covers a substantially shorter period, it also has been reviewed and summarized in recent survey articles (e.g., Freedman, Knoefel, Naeser, & Levine, 1984, for computerized tomography [CT] studies; Raz, 1996, for structural magnetic resonance imaging [MRI]; Meyer, Kawamura, & Terayama, 1994, for cerebral blood flow [CBF]; Madden & Hoffman, 1997, and Waldemar, 1995, for CBF and metabolism). Therefore, to avoid redundancy and to save space, in this overview of the anatomical and physiological characteristics of the aging brain and their relation to cognitive aging, I will rely, whenever warranted, on the published reviews. However, the objective of this chapter is not only to update and augment the coverage of this rapidly expanding literature but also to provide a preliminary overview of the emerging discipline of cognitive neuroscience of aging, an area of research that has only now accumulated enough evidence to permit cautious generalizations. Although the bulk of the chapter is devoted to studies on humans, I provide relevant evidence from nonhuman primate and, sometimes, rodent models to place the discussion in the evolutionary context. Whenever possible, I furnish a quantitative assessment of the magnitude of age differences in brain structure and function.[1]

Understanding intricate and complex relationships between brain and behavior depends on the quality of measures in both realms. Thus, diverse methods used to assess structural and functional integrity of the brain should not be viewed as competing for the mantle of the best and most comprehensive probe designed to reveal all the brain mysteries at once. Rather, they are tools in a communal toolbox for scholars interested in answering specific scientific questions and integrating findings across multiple converging lines of inquiry. Each technique and experimental paradigm provides only a partial answer to comprehensive questions

---

[1]To quantify the findings, I use a product-moment correlation (Pearson r) between calendar age and a variety of measures as an index of the effect size (i.e., the magnitude of association between age and a given measure). Whenever other statistics are reported in the reviewed studies, they are converted into r for the sake of creating a common metric for comparison across multiple sources drawn from diverse domains of inquiry. Because most of the findings on the aging brain come from cross-sectional studies that used various measures, a dimensionless standardized sample-specific index of strength of association, such as Pearson r, is preferred to raw regression slopes and to estimates of percentage of decline that are more appropriate for longitudinal studies that use a relatively uniform set of measures. Because in many cases, the effect sizes were estimated from multiple studies conducted in the same laboratory, I tried to ascertain the independence of the samples, and when such ascertainment was not possible, I tried to err on the conservative side. When age effects observed in a set of studies are described by a single index, it is usually a median r. The median is preferred to the mean because it does not require Fisher's z transformation and because it is not sensitive to extreme values.

about the aging brain and its relations with cognitive functions. Thus, an understanding of the advantages and limitations of each tool used in neurogerontology is a necessary precursor of any attempt to integrate the findings from the growing literature.

The main features of commonly used methods, along with suggested sources containing more detailed accounts, are summarized in Table 1.1. The illustrations of typical images produced by techniques discussed in this chapter—MRI, positron-emission tomography (PET), and functional MRI (fMRI)—are presented in Fig. 1.1–1.3. A reader familiar with these methods can skip to the next section without interruption.

ANATOMICAL AND PHYSIOLOGICAL CHARACTERISTICS OF THE AGING BRAIN

Age-Related Differences in Global Measures of Neuroanatomy and Neurophysiology

A century-long cumulative record of postmortem studies of the aging brain indicates that aging is accompanied by a moderate linear reduction in the gross weight and volume of the brain. Postmortem investigations reveal persistent linear (albeit modest) age-related declines in brain weight and volume that amount to about 2% per decade (see Esiri, 1994, and Kemper, 1994, for a review). Similar, albeit milder, declines in brain weight have been observed in great apes (Herndon, Tigges, Anderson, Klumpp, & McClure, 1999) whereas examination of monkey brains revealed no age-related changes in weight (Herndon, Tigges, Klumpp, & Anderson, 1998).

CT studies have concluded that normal aging is associated with expansion of the cerebral ventricles (ventriculomegaly) and generalized enlargement of cerebral sulci (Stafford, Albert, Naeser, Sandor, & Garvey, 1988; see Freedman et al., 1984, for a review). More recently, studies on in vivo MRI volumetry have confirmed that there is age-related reduction in cerebral volume. Summaries of the literature reveal significant declines in the volume of cerebral hemispheres with age: median $r = -.40$ for studies that reported raw volume, and $r = -.60$ for those that reported volume adjusted for cranial size (see Raz, 1996, for a review; see also Blatter et al., 1995; Raz et al., 1997). However, in a recent study of 234 normal volunteers, I found lower estimates of brain volume–age association ($r = -.20$; Raz 1999a, 1999b). Because most studies report either a raw or an adjusted brain volume estimate, differences between the age effects across samples are not easy to interpret.

TABLE 1.1
Techniques for Investigation of the Human Brain

Technique and Study	What Is Measured?	Resolution		Major Advantages	Major Disadvantages
		Spatial	Temporal		
CT	Differential attenuation of X-rays passing through skull and brain tissue. Tissue is classified according to X-rays attenuation values.	Medium	Low (years)	Provides excellent differentiation of bone, cerebral tissue, and CSF; fast and relatively cheap.	Does not permit good differentiation among cerebral structures; does not allow experimental study of cognition; involves radiation.
MRR (Pettegrew, 1991)	Relaxation time constants (T1 and T2) of excited protons in water molecules that are subjected to radio frequency pulse irradiation in a static magnetic field are measured within different types of brain tissue. Physicochemical properties of the tissue (primarily the density of the protons and their interaction with the other molecules) determine the time constants of relaxation processes.	High	Low	Allows precise anatomical localization; completely non-invasive; does not involve radiation.	Very sensitive to partial voluming of several types of tissue within a location in which the time constants are estimated; does not allow experimental study of cognition.
MRI (Pettegrew, 1991)	Same as MRR, only the signal intensity calculated from time constants at each location is converted into gray-	Very high (up to $0.25 \times 0.25 \times 0.25$ mm)	Low (years)	As above, plus by varying the timing and the sequence of the exciting pulses, various aspects of brain tissues can be	Provides a static snapshot of the brain anatomy and pathology; does not allow experimental study of cognition.

Technique	Physiological/physical basis	Spatial resolution	Temporal resolution	Strengths	Limitations
	scale values. The latter are used to create maps that simulate the appearance of anatomical slices.			highlighted. Allows estimation of areas and volumes of cerebral regions and structures (but see Courchesne & Plante, 1997, for methodological critique).	
fMRI and perfusion imaging (Casey et al., 1996; Kraut et al., 1995; Prichard & Rosen, 1994; Turner & Jezzard, 1994)	Hemoglobin in deoxygenated state is paramagnetic and becomes less so during oxygenation, causing increase in signal intensity. The change in signal intensity can be measured to index stimulus-dependent changes in rCBF.	High (up to 1.25 × 1.25 × 5 mm^3)	High (ms)	Allows almost real-time experimental assessment of cognitive processes with high anatomic precision (event-related fMRI); reliable measure of changes in regional blood volume and blood flow; highly repeatable within participants; completely noninvasive; does not involve radiation; does not require injection or blood sampling.	Sensitive to motion artifacts; insensitive to neurochemical changes at the receptor level; more sensitive to changes in larger vessels only partially overlapping the ROI than in local capillaries; thus underestimating metabolic activity creates a high level of noise during acquisition; leaves little room within the confines of the magnet to study elaborate and realistic aspects of cognitive performance.
MRS	Nuclear resonance properties of atoms of a given chemical species (usually hydrogen, carbon, or phosphorus) within brain tissue.	Medium (cm^3)	Medium–high (min)	In vivo and almost real-time chemically specific assessment of cerebral energy metabolism; detects changes in lactate, glutamate, glucose, and creatine; completely noninvasive; does not involve radiation.	Relatively poor resolution (large voxel sampled); relatively low repeatability and high error.

(Continued)

TABLE 1.1
(Continued)

Technique and Study	What Is Measured?	Resolution — Spatial	Resolution — Temporal	Major Advantages	Major Disadvantages
SPECT (Waldemar, 1995)	Radioactive tracer (e.g., technetium-99-, xenon-133-, or iodine-123-labeled compounds) is inhaled or injected and is carried by the blood to the brain regions, where radioactive emissions are measured. Changes in rCBF are estimated. Ligand-labeled compound may be used to study neurotransmitter receptor activity.	Medium (9–10 mm, 5–7 mm in some cases)	Medium (min), depends on the tracer half-life	Provides a relatively cheap way to evaluate rCBF or receptor activity within relatively large but circumscribed cerebral regions; radioactive tracers can be selected to highlight a specific neurotransmitter system; dual tracers can be administered to track the activity in two neurotransmitter systems.	Resolution is too coarse for localization of function; scanning involves radiation, and higher sensitivity requires greater radiation exposure; unless there is arterial blood sampling, computation of absolute activation at given locations is impossible; only values relative to a specified ROI (i.e., the cerebellum) can be computed; photon scatter and attentuation may produce artifactual perfusion differences due to skull thickness and head position differences.
PET and rCMRglu or rCMRglc (Herscovitch, 1994)	Radioactive emissions generated in a reaction of annihilation between electrons and their positively charged	Medium (2 × 2-mm pixels can be acquired but are smoothed	Medium–low (30–45 min), depends on the tracer half-life	Allows to study in vivo energy (glucose) metabolism; allows testing of participants outside the confines of	Requires an assumption of constant glucose metabolism from the time of injection to the end of scanning and thus ig-

Technique	Description	Spatial resolution	Temporal resolution	Advantages	Disadvantages
	counterparts (positrons) as the latter are carried to the target organs in radio-labeled tracer (^{18}F-deoxy-glucose) injected into the blood stream. The tracer is metabolically trapped in the target tissue, especially axons and dendrites rather than neurons.	to 20 × 20-mm regions)		the scanner; allows correlations of cognitive performance integrated over time with brain energy metabolism.	nores habituation. Relatively slow for studying cognitive processes in real time; only slow and highly integrated cognitive activities can be studied because of a long half-life of the tracer (about 1.5 hr). PET image contains no neuroanatomical information; requires co-registration with an MR image. Involves radiation; requires injections and blood sampling; expensive.
PET and rCMRO$_2$ (Herscovitch, 1994)	Gamma rays generated in a reaction of annihilation between electrons and their positively charged counterparts (positrons) as the latter are carried to the target organs in radio-labeled tracer (usually with inhaled mixture with trace amounts of $C^{15}O$ or inhaled ^{15}O).	Medium–high, as above	Medium (1–2 min), depends on the tracer half-life	Allows assessment of brain oxygen consumption in vivo in conjunction with short-term cognitive activity, repeating scans every 10–12 min to cover multiple control conditions with a participant.	As above.
PET and rCBF (Kraut et al., 1995)	Same as above, usually with $H_2{}^{15}O$ water injected into the blood stream as a tracer.	Medium–high, as above	Medium (1–2 min), depends on the tracer half-life	As above, plus does not require arterial blood sampling.	As above, plus underestimates actual rCBF.

(Continued)

TABLE 1.1
(Continued)

Technique and Study	What Is Measured?	Resolution		Major Advantages	Major Disadvantages
		Spatial	Temporal		
PET and regional pharmacokinetics	As above, but a tracer is positron-labeled ligand with affinity to a specified type of receptor.	Medium–high	Medium–low, depends on the tracer half-life	Allows to study in vivo neurochemistry and pharmacokinetics.	Involves radiation and generation of positron-labeled ligands; expensive.
Postmortem (autopsy)	A variety of stain areas applied to thin brain tissue slices. Specific targets (neuron bodies, connections, dendritic trees, or myelinated axons) are stained. Receptors may be labeled by radioactive ligands.	Extremely high (μm)	None	Cellular and synaptic level.	No data on cognitive performance usually available; the effects of agonal state and diseases can confound the findings; tissue preparation methods may affect older brains differentially.

Note. CT = computerized tomography; MR = magnetic resonance; MRR = magnetic resonance relaxometry; MRI = magnetic resonance imaging; fMRI = functional magnetic resonance imaging; MRS = magnetic resonance spectroscopy; SPECT = single-photon emission computerized tomography; PET = positron-emission tomography; rCMRglu = regional cerebral metabolic rate of glucose; rCMRglc = regional cerebral metabolic rate of glucose; rCMRO$_2$ = regional cerebral metabolic rate of oxygen use; rCBF = regional cerebral blood flow; CSF = cerebrospinal fluid; ROI = region of interest.

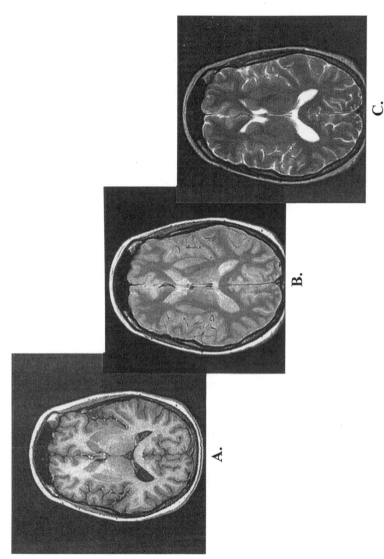

C.

B.

A.

FIG. 1.1. Examples of different structural magnetic resonance (MR) images of the same brain slice taken in the axial plane. (A) A T1-weighted MR image. Note good contrast between the gray and the white matter and excellent neuroanatomical demarcation of specific structures, such as the basal ganglia and of the cerebral ventricles. The cerebrospinal-fluid- (CSF-) producing choroid plexus is visible inside the occipital horns of the ventricles. (B) A proton-density-weighted MR image. Gray matter appears pale gray and white matter, dark gray. Note good delineation of the basal ganglia but somewhat fuzzy borders of the cerebral ventricles. (C) A T2-weighted MR image. Note that white matter appears dark, whereas the CSF-filled lateral ventricles appear bright. Note also the lack of white matter hyperintensities on this scan of a young person; compare with a T2-weighted scan of an older person in FIG. 1.4.

9

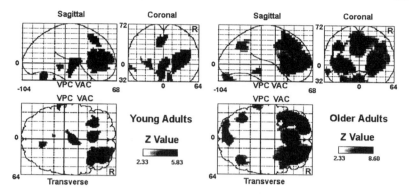

FIG. 1.2. An example of an $H_2^{15}O$ positron-emission tomography activation map in a recognition memory task produced after application of a statistical parametric mapping (SPM; Friston et al., 1995) analysis. On the left, a composite of 12 younger participants; on the right, a composite of 12 older participants. VAC and VPC refer to vertical planes passing through the anterior and posterior commissures (AC and PC), respectively. The activation values, which are transformed into z scores by SPM software, are mapped onto a coordinate grid in Talairach space anchored at the AC–PC line (Talairach & Tournoux, 1988). Note significant maxima of activation for younger adults covering the superior and middle frontal gyri (BA 10) in the right hemisphere versus extensive bilateral activation of the prefrontal cortex in older participants. In contrast to the almost exclusively prefrontal pattern of activation in the younger participants, significant bilateral maxima of activation were observed in the parietal lobe (BA 40) of the older participants. The images are provided courtesy of David J. Madden, Center for the Study of Aging and Human Development, Duke Medical Center.

Global changes in the aging brain can be found at almost any level of observation. Aging is accompanied by significant structural alterations in the basic elements of the central nervous system (CNS)—the neurons. Some of these changes are quite pervasive. For example, with age, a yellowish-brown lipid lipofuscin, dubbed "wear and tear pigment" (see Bourne, 1973, for a review), accumulates in the cells throughout the cerebellum and the cerebral cortex. Notably, the precise effects of lipofuscin on the workings of single neurons are unknown, and in the absence of behavioral and pathologic correlates, age-dependent accumulation of the pigment prompted speculations about its role as a "time keeper" (see Kemper, 1994, for a review). Neuritic plaques, pathological cellular changes of amyloid origin, are relatively infrequent in the brains of older individuals who died without signs of dementia (Troncoso, Martin, Dal Forno, & Kawas, 1996), and when they are found in that population, they are restricted to superficial cortical laminae (Esiri, 1994).

Whereas the existence of multiple age-related changes in neurons and their connections is widely agreed on, the question of age-related reduc-

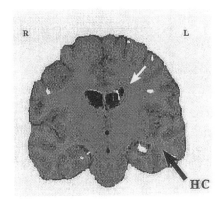

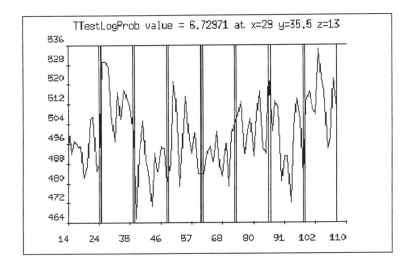

FIG. 1.3. An example of a functional magnetic resonance imaging activation study. The top panel depicts the foci of significant activation (white), which is evoked by the encoding of stimuli on a block design task. Note a substantial area of activation within the left hippocampus (HC). Also, note bilateral inferior parietal activation as well as increased drainage in a vein within the left lateral ventricle (white arrow). The bottom panel represents time-dependent changes in signal intensity during the block design task. R = right; L = left. The image and the graph are provided courtesy of Maija Pihlajamäki and Mikko P. Laakso, Department of Neurology, Kuopio University Hospital, Kuopio, Finland.

tion of the total population of neurons is still subject to lively debate. Although many studies have revealed an age-related attrition of neurons (see Kemper, 1994, for a review), the notion of inevitable and widespread neuronal loss in late adulthood is no longer a commonly accepted dictum. The evidence from more recent studies suggests that the magnitude of age-related neuronal loss might have been exaggerated by brain-processing artifacts and by inadequacies of measurement techniques (see Uylings et al., in press, for a review). It has been proposed that shrinkage of neurons may be a more decisive age-related change rather than their attrition (see Esiri, 1994, and Haug, 1985, for a review).

Neuronal connectivity is probably the most plastic aspect of the adult CNS. The neurons in the aging brain undergo systematic changes, such as "debranching" of the dendritic arborization (see Kemper, 1994, for a review; see also B. Anderson & Rutledge, 1996) and a decline in synaptogenesis (Bertoni-Freddari, Fattoretti, Casoli, Caselli, & Meier-Ruge, 1996). These differences, when present, are likely to be selective and regional (see Uylings et al., in press, for a review).[2]

Physiological indices of brain function also change with age. The preponderance of the findings suggests that aging is associated with a moderate reduction in regional CBF (rCBF) and regional cerebral metabolic rate of oxygen utilization (rCMRO^2). Significant reduction in these indices is observed in 65% and 80% of the examined samples, respectively (see Madden & Hoffman, 1997, for a review). Perfusion MRI studies have suggested that normal aging is associated with a reduction in the gray matter blood volume (Marchal et al., 1992; Rempp et al., 1994; Wenz et al., 1996). In contrast, the evidence concerning age effects on the total brain metabolism of glucose (CMRglu) is less clear, with slightly more than 50% of the samples yielding significant findings (see Madden & Hoffman, 1997, for a review; see also Baron et al., 1998; Loessner et al., 1995; Moeller et al., 1996; Petit-Taboué, Landeau, Desson, Desgranges, & Baron, 1998).

Heterogeneity of the studied samples and their small size may explain the lack of clarity in the findings. Some of the components of sample heterogeneity can be identified. For example, older adults who are at genetic risk for developing Alzheimer's disease (AD) show impairment of regional CMRglu (rCMRglu) similar to that found in people with AD (Reiman et al., 1998). Because aging is accompanied by a reduction in

---

[2]It is important to keep in mind that methodological difficulties in this type of study are substantial. In addition to the lack of information about critical aspects of participants' life history and events surrounding their demise, studies of age-related changes in synaptic density and dendritic structure also depend on the timing of autopsy, which must be kept rather short (from 6 to 24 hr, depending on the type of stain applied to the specimen). Hence, the difficulties in integrating the voluminous but rather disjointed body of literature on this topic.

brain volume and, probably, in the number of active neurons, the age-dependent drop in metabolic activity may be related to loss of working tissue. Thus, it is important to control for differences in tissue volume when considering age-related changes in brain metabolism. To date, only a small number of studies have attempted to estimate the effects of age on neurophysiological variables while taking into account age-related neuroanatomical alterations. Indeed, correction for reduction in volume of cerebral tissue and enlargement of cerebrospinal fluid (CSF) spaces results in a substantial increase in the estimated rCMRglu in normal elderly and AD patients alike, although it does not eliminate the metabolic deficits observed in AD (Labbé, Froment, Kennedy, Ashburner, & Cinotti, 1996; Meltzer et al., 1996). In addition, as further discussion shows, age-related differences in brain metabolism and blood flow are expressed not only in reduction but also in selective increases in the regional indices.

In sum, aging is associated with decline in several global properties of the brain, both structural and functional. Those changes must be considered in any theoretical account of age-related differences in cognitive perform-ance. However, against the backdrop of generalized age-related deterio-ration, numerous differential changes loom, like multiple islands of relative preservation and decline. Understanding the nature and the mechanisms of these differential effects may help to better understand age-related vulnerability and plasticity of cognition and its neural substrates.

Differential Aging of the Brain Components

Gray Versus White Matter.   The first and the clearest distinction among the brain components is between white and gray matter. The former represents tightly packed myelinated axons connecting the neurons of the cerebral cortex to each other and with the periphery, whereas the latter refers to cell bodies in the cortex and subcortical nuclei. Because of their structural, metabolic, and neurochemical differences, gray and white mat-ter may exhibit differential vulnerability to alterations of brain environment such as hypoxia and ischemia (Ginsberg, Hedley-Whyte, & Richardson, 1976; Pantoni, Garcia, & Gutierrez, 1996). Therefore, it is plausible that these compartments of the brain are differentially sensitive to the effects of aging.

At the time of this writing, it is unclear whether the gray or the white matter encounters the greatest impact of physiological aging. Postmortem studies (Double et al., 1996; see Esiri, 1994, and Kemper, 1994, for a review) have suggested that the age-related loss of the white matter (especially in the frontal lobes) is more extensive than the attrition of the gray matter. In contrast to the postmortem findings, the vast majority of the in vivo MRI investigations reveal no significant age-related differences in the volume of cerebral white matter (see Raz, 1996, for a review; see also Raz et al., 1997, and E. V. Sullivan, Marsh, Mathalon, Lim, & Pfefferbaum, 1995), with a possible exception of the prefrontal regions (Raz, 1998c; Raz et al., 1997; Salat, Kaye, & Janowsky, 1999). In one sample, however, only men evidenced modest declines in gross white matter volume (Blatter et al., 1995), and in another study age-related shrinkage of the total brain white matter exceeded the decline in gray matter volume (Guttmann et al., 1998). One factor usually not taken into account in MR segmentation and volumetry of the gray and white matter is the myeloarchitectonics of the cerebral cortex. Presence of myelinated fibers in laminae III, IV, and Vb and their differential genesis and attrition may bias the volumetric estimates of the two cerebral compartments by inflating or deflating the number of MR pixels classified as gray or white (see Courchesne & Plante, 1997, for a discussion).

The reduction in white matter volume is attributable in part to age-related loss and changes in myelin. Some postmortem studies have suggested that the loss of myelin is especially pronounced in the fibers projecting to and from the association and limbic cortices (see Kemper, 1994, for a review), whereas a more recent report indicated that the bulk of age-related loss of white matter is borne by small myelinated axons (Tang, Nyengaard, Pakkenberg, & Gundersen, 1997). Nonetheless, age differences in the area of the corpus callosum, one of the most heavily myelinated regions of the brain, are mild (median r = −.15; see Driesen & Raz, 1995, for a review).

One of the most striking features noted on the in vivo images of the aging brain is the spotty appearance of the white matter known as *leukoaraiosis* (when observed on CT scans) or *white matter hyperintensities* (WMHs, when observed on an MR image). Leukoaraiosis is defined as "diminution of density of representation of the white matter" (Hachinsky, Potter, & Merskey, 1987, p. 22) and was originally believed to represent pathological cerebrovascular aging. Subsequent research indicated, however, that nonvascular causes of the WMHs are also highly probable. As illustrated in Fig 1.4, WMHs appear in a variety of shapes: bright irregular patches in subcortical white matter, periventricular rims and caps, and distributed punctate spots. Despite their superficial resemblance, WMHs, located in different brain regions may reflect a multitude of pathological causes, both vascular and neural (see Pantoni & Garcia, 1997, for a review). Many factors were proposed to account for appearance of WMHs in asymptomatic elderly individuals,[3] but the most robust one is age itself.

---

[3]In examining the findings on cerebrovascular "lesions" in normal aging, it is important to take into account that some of the inconsistencies across the studies of WMHs in aging may be explained by a lack of uniformity in assessing the frequency and severity of the lesions. A recent survey of 13 rating scales widely used in research on WMHs and their correlates yielded only modest agreement across the instruments (Mäntyä et al., 1997).

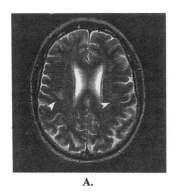 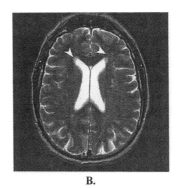

A.   B.

FIG. 1.4. An example of leukoaraiosis observed on T2-weighted axial magnetic resonance images in a healthy 62-year-old man. The arrows point to deep white matter hyperintensities (A) and periventricular caps (B).

In a quantitative review of 49 studies of WMHs in healthy adults, the magnitude of that effect was estimated bv a mean correlation between age and severity of WMHs (r = .37; Gunning-Dixon & Raz, 1996b).

The mammalian brain is a demanding consumer of blood supply, and throughout the adult part of the life span the cerebrovascular system experiences numerous structural changes (Akima, Nonaka, Hasegawa, & Tanaka, 1986; Marin, 1995). At least some types of leukoaraiosis may stem from transient cerebral ischemia (TIA), which induces incomplete infarction (Pantoni & Garcia, 1997). Indeed, in a quantitative summary of 10 studies, a history of TIA attacks or actual strokes emerges as the strongest cerebrovascular predictor of WMH burden: Correlation between positive history of TIA and WMH rating reaches r = .37 (Gunning-Dixon & Raz, 1996b). A prolonged history of hypertension may be detrimental to many brain structures, and studies of a rodent model of spontaneous hypertension revealed a significant reduction in brain volume and in the thickness of the cerebral cortex (Lehr, Browning, & Myers, 1980; Ritter & Dinh, 1986; Tajima, et al., 1993). However, in 24 human studies, the observed effect of hypertension on WMH ratings was mild (r =.20; Gunning-Dixon & Raz, 1999b). Advanced age and hypertension may serve as mutually reinforcing influences on WMH frequency and severity (Strassburger et al., 1997), and duration of hypertension may affect not only severity but also a pattern of WMH distribution in nondemented elderly individuals (de Leeuw et al., 1998). Even in normotensive adults, a relatively modest elevation of systolic blood pressure may be associated with increased frequency of WMHs (DeCarli et al., 1995; Goldstein, Bartzokis, Hance, & Shapiro, 1998). In contrast to the aforementioned risk factors, several predictors and correlates of cerebrovascular disease, such as diabetes mellitus, elevated blood cholesterol, smoking, and cardiovascular disease are not associated with WMHs (effect size r ranging from −.09 to .04; Gunning-Dixon & Raz, 1999b).

An additional factor that could affect brain aging in general and WMHs in particular is inheritance of a specific allele of apolipoprotein E (ApoE ε4), which has been hypothesized to play an important role in the maintenance and repair of neural circuits through influencing, among other things, the transport and uptake of cholesterol and the regulation of the levels of intracellular calcium (Masliah, Mallory, Veinbergs, Miller, & Samuel, 1996). An ApoE ε4/ε4 genotype has been implicated in some familial forms of AD, although it is not uniformly considered a specific and sensitive diagnostic marker of the disease (Mayeux et al., 1998). Asymptomatic carriers of ApoE ε4 genotypes (homo- and heterozygous) frequently exhibit significantly worse mnemonic skills than people with other ApoE genotypes (Bondi et al., 1995; Kuller et al., 1998; Reed et al., 1994; Reiman et al., 1998; H. Schmidt et al., 1996; but see G. E. Smith et al., 1998, for a counterexample). However, homozygocity for ApoE ε4 has not been consistently associated with an increased WMH burden (a positive link observed by Kuller et al., 1998; Plassman et al., 1997; Reiman et al., 1998; but see H. Schmidt et al., 1996, for negative findings). In other samples, trends toward such association has been reported. Moreover, increase in WMH burden may be linked to the ApoE ε2/ε3 genotype, despite the fact that the latter produces a lipid profile associated with low risk for cardiovascular disease (R. Schmidt et al., 1997). It is possible, however, that ApoE ε4 homozygocity, though not necessarily causal to WMH abnormalities, acts in synergy with them to increase individual risk for cognitive declines (Kuller et al., 1998). It is also possible that ApoE ε4 homozygocity increases individual susceptibility to ill effects of such known cerebrovascular risk factors as cigarette smoking and excessive alcohol consumption (Carmeli, Swan, Reed, Schellenberg, & Christan, 1999).

It has been suggested that WMH frequency and brain distribution may differ between the sexes, but data bearing on that question are still very scarce. A quantitative review of the literature (30 studies that reported the relevant data) showed that samples with a larger male-to-female ratio are less likely (r = −.33) to demonstrate the association between age and WMHs (Gunning-Dixon & Raz, 1999b). In postmenopausal women, WMH burden may be influenced by sex hormones, as women who receive estrogen supplements perform better than those who do not on a wide variety of neuropsychological tests and have a significantly lighter WMH burden (R. Schmidt et al., 1996). Notably, the total WMH area was inversely related to the duration of estrogen replacement therapy.

Some of the contradictions between the postmortem and in vivo studies may be more apparent than real and may be rooted in the very physical basis of MRI. Direct relaxometry (see Table 1.1 for a description) of the aging brain provides some insights into the differential aging of the white and the gray matter. Age-related prolongation of spin–lattice (T1) and spin–spin (T2) time constants is indicative of increases in intracellular and extracellular free water. Such prolongation has been observed in many regions of the brain, including the subcortical nuclei; the hippocampus; the frontal, temporal, parietal, and occipital white matter; optic radiation; and the genu of the corpus callosum (see Raz, 1996, for a review; see also Cho, Jones, Reddick, Ogg, & Steen, 1997). In vivo measures of the apparent diffusion coefficient of water in the subcortical white matter evidenced a substantial linear age-dependent increase, whereas no age-related changes were observed in the gray matter (Gideon, Thomsen, & Hendriksen, 1994). Thus, there is little doubt that both white and gray matter change with age. However, because different tools are sensitive to different aspects of age-related deterioration, claims of "intactness" of one or the other brain compartment are sometimes made.

The brain is hardly a monolithic organ, and the diversity of the cytoar-chitectonic appearance of the cerebral cortex is so impressive and bewil-dering that it has been translated into detailed maps. The most prominent and widely accepted cortical map is the one by German neuroanatomist Korbinian Brodmann (1909/1987). Brodmann's mapping of cortical areas (see Fig. 1.5) became a lingua franca of neuroanatomy, indispensable in communicating regional peculiarities in structural, functional, and neuro-chemical studies of the brain.

Regional differences in the magnitude of age effects on the brain may be subtle in comparison with the global deterioration, yet they are no-ticeable in white and gray matter alike. Although the gross appearance of the aging brain is characterized by generalized gyral atrophy, increased age sensitivity has been noted for the hippocampal formation; the frontal, temporal, and parietal convexities; and the parasagittal region, although the occipital lobe appears relatively spared (see Kemper, 1994, for a review). Furthermore, recent postmortem studies have suggested that age-related alterations in neurons and their connections may be limited to specific laminae of specific gyri (e.g., lamina V of the prefrontal cortex), with other regions and laminae being left relatively spared (Uylings et al., in press).

As the neurochemical makeup of the brain changes significantly throughout the life span, so do the distribution and concentration of important inorganic ions. Brain aging is accompanied by region-specific accumulation of iron, which causes shortening of T1 and T2 time con-stants, especially in the neostriatum, the deep cerebellar nuclei, and the motor cortex (Hallgren & Sourander, 1958; Hirai et al., 1996; Martin, Ye, & Allen, 1998; Ogg & Steen, 1998; Vymazal et al., 1995). In contrast, iron accumulation and T2 shortening are less pronounced in the visual cortex

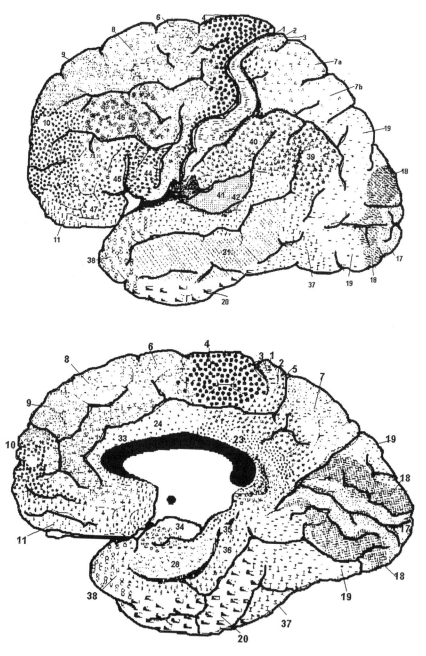

FIG. 1.5. A map of cytoarchitectonically defined cortical areas used in studies of localization of functions in the brain (after Brodmann, 1909/1987). Top panel, lateral view; bottom panel, midsagittal view. The numbers indicate distinct cytoarchitectonical regions, known as the Brodmann areas.

(Korogi, Hirai, Komohara, et al., 1997). The implication of this phenomenon for in vivo regional volumetry of the aging brain is that iron-related shortening of T2 is observed as decreased intensity of the cerebral cortex on T2-weighted images (Oba et al., 1996). Such alteration entails differences in appearance of cortical regions and a possibility of bias in their demarcation and measurement.

Limbic Regions. Postmortem studies of animal and human brains reveal age-related changes in the hippocampus (see Geinisman et al., 1995; and Kemper, 1994, for a review). Although some notable exceptions have been reported (see Raz, 1996, for a review; see also E. V. Sullivan et al., 1995), it is unlikely that in healthy humans this brain region completely escapes the ill effects of age. The hippocampus is a cytoarchitectonically complex structure; therefore, it is not surprising that its distinct subdivisions evidence differential aging rates. The magnitude of correlations between age and neuronal count in specific areas of the hippocampus may vary as widely within a sample as the findings obtained in multiple MRI investigations. For example, in one of the most comprehensive human postmortem studies, the correlations between neural counts and age ranged from $r = -.46$ for the subiculum to $r = -.11$ for the CA1 field, with a median value of $r = -.21$ (M. J. West, 1993). However, this pattern was not replicated in another study of age-related declines in the hippocampal formation, showing instead a steep age-related decrease in neuronal number within the CA1 sector (Simic, Kostovic, Winblad, & Bogdanovic, 1997). The results of several studies in rodents suggest that pyramidal neurons in CA3 sector are specifically vulnerable to aging (Kadar et al., 1998).

A close neighbor of the hippocampus and a component of the limbic system, the amygdala evidences age-related loss of neurons as well as neuronal atrophy (Navarro & Gonzalo, 1991). In addition to a selective loss of cell bodies, age-related synaptic loss in the hippocampus has also been documented (Geinisman et al., 1995).[4] It is worth noting that in monkeys, the hippocampus and its subdivisions exhibit no or very little change with age (Tigges, Herndon, & Rosene, 1995, 1996). Relative stability of the hippocampus has been observed in aging rodents as well (Rapp & Gallagher, 1996), although these findings may be strain-specific (Kadar et al., 1998). At any rate, the preponderance of postmortem evidence supports the notion that at least some of the limbic regions may be relatively spared by aging, whereas others are only mildly affected.

---

[4]Methodological problems outlined by Geinisman et al. (1995) call for caution in interpretation of the results reported before 1986, when the unbiased methodology was introduced (Brandgaard & Gundersen, 1986). Nonetheless, the two cited studies (Simic et al., 1997, and M. J. West, 1993), unlike most of the preceding investigations of neuronal counts in the hippocampus, used modern unbiased methodology.

Age affects the neuronal architecture in multiple ways, and some of these influences show well-defined regional predilections. Neurofibrillary tangles (NFTs), a hallmark of \D pathology, are believed to result from abnormal phosphorylation of the microtubule-associated protein. They can be found in the brain material long after neuronal death has occurred and are sometimes referred to as neuropathological "tombstones" (Kemper, 1994, for a review). Although not as rampant in the normal aging brain as in AD, the NFTs exhibit a similar characteristic regional distribution with affinity for the hippocampus, especially the CA 1 sector (see Kemper, 1994, for a review). The same area of the hippocampus is sensitive to other types of intracellular pathology—Hirano bodies and granulovacuolar degeneration that share it as a common target area despite their apparently dissimilar origins.

Thus, the hippocampus is a focal point of multiple pathological events associated with age and age-related diseases. However, the involvement of that area in physiological aging is uncertain. It must be noted, however, that the magnitude of these age-related effects is within the mild to moderate range. In accord with that assessment, in vivo neuroimaging reveals only mild age-related shrinkage of the broadly defined hippocampal formation (see Fig. 1.6).

Direct T1 and T2 relaxometry of the hippocampus has been conducted in a handful of samples. The results provide only weak evidence of age-related changes of molecular properties of water that may be indicative of atrophic processes (Campeau, Petersen, Felmlee, O'Brien, & Jack, 1997; Laakso et al., 1996; Raz, Millman, & Sarpel, 1990). In contrast, hippocampal volumetry h as been applied to more than a dozen samples of healthy adults. The results of cross-sectional studies of age differences in hippocampal volume are summarized in Table 1.2. These studies vary in methodological makeup (i.e., MR slice thickness, definition of the regions of interest [ROIs], type of MR sequences used in image acquisition, participants' age range, participant selection criteria, and type of correction for body size used in computation of the volumetric estimates). The connection between each and all of the listed factors and the magnitude of the observed age effect is not easily drawn.

Several factors, such as sampling differences and the definition of the ROI, may account for considerable variation between the studies. The nature of these differences cannot be divined from the sample descriptions provided in the studies. These samples may include different proportions of cases with preclinical AD, incipient cerebrovascular disease, or different proportions of persor s genetically at risk for various conditions known to affect the volume of the brain structures. The shape of age distribution rather than its parameters may play a critical role in determining the magnitude of the age effect. For example, if the distribution is badly skewed

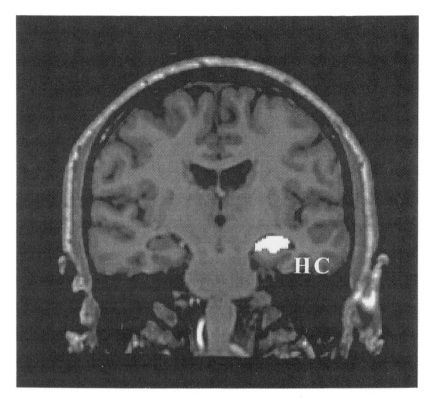

FIG. 1.6. A coronal slice from a reformatted 3D volume magnetic resonance scan aligned perpendicularly to the long axis of the right hippocampus shows the hippocampal formation (HC).

toward the younger age groups, the correlations with age is bound to be reduced. Studies that used extreme age groups (Convit et al., 1995, and Murphy et al., 1996) tend to show somewhat larger effects that are due to inflation of r values (but see Lim, Zipurski, Murphy, & Pfefferbaum, 1990). Unfortunately, it is impossible to evaluate what role the irregularities in the shape of age distribution actually play in modulating the magnitude of the age effects, as the shape of the distribution is rarely reported.

In studies that report results for both adjusted and unadjusted volumes, there is no difference between age effects on these indices of hippocampal size. I therefore combined the effects sizes for adjusted and unadjusted volumes to obtain a median effect of $r = -.30$, a modest yet not negligible effect. An effect of that magnitude, however, pales in comparison with the reported differences between normal elderly individuals and their age-matched peers afflicted by AD (Laakso et al., 1998) or major depression (Sheline & Gado, 1998).

TABLE 1.2
Effect of Age on the Limbic Regions Observed In Vivo

Study	N	Age (Years)	Effect Size (r)				
			Hippocampus	Parahippocampal Gyrus	Entorhinal Cortex	Amygdala	Cingulate Gyrus
Jernigan et al. (1991)	55	30–79	(-.38)				(-.13)
Lim et al. (1990)	15	24 vs. 73	(-.22)				
Coffey et al. (1992)	76	30–91	(-.27)				
Raz, Torres, Spencer, & Acker (1993)	29	18–78	-.03				-.18
Raz, Torres, Spencer, Baertschie, et al. (1993)	54	18–75	-.23	-.04			-.15
Golomb et al. (1994)	54	55–87	(-.46)				
Convit et al. (1995)	37	26 vs. 69	(-.60)	(.00)			
E. V. Sullivan et al. (1995)	72	21–70	-.05 (-.03)				
Murphy et al. (1996)	69	26 vs. 70	(-.63)	(-.50)		(-.48)	
Jack et al. (1997)	126	51–89	-.15 (-.15)	-.26 (-.25)		-.08 (-.08)	
Raz et al. (1997)	148	18–77	-.28 (-.30)	-.18			-.18
Bigler et al. (1997)	96	16–65	(-.33)				
Laakso et al. (1995, 1998)	102	21–81	(-.12)			(-.26)	
Raz et al. (1998c)	212	18–81	-.40 (-.38)	-.27			
Insausti et al. (1999)	52	28 vs. 72			(-.09)		
Mdn	69		-.19 (-.31)	-.22 (-.25)		(-.26)	-.17

Note. Values in parentheses are volumes adjusted for head size, intracranial volume, or height (i.e., ratio indices). Unpublished correlations for the studies by Jack et al. (1997) and Laakso et al. (1998) were kindly provided by Clifford R. Jack and Mikko P. Laakso, respectively (personal communication, June 1998).

The definition of the hippocampal ROI may be related to the age effect size observed in the studies. The results of some in vivo studies of the hippocampal formation suggest a possible anterior–posterior gradient of age-related vulnerability. Specifically, the anterior portion of the hippocampus (the head) may be less likely to show atrophy in normal elderly individuals with age-associated memory impairment and in early AD patients than the hippocampal body and the tail of the hippocampus (Petersen, Jack, Smith, Waring, & Ivnik, 1998). In addition, the volume of the anterior part of the hippocampus, unlike that of the body and the tail, does not distinguish between primary degenerative dementias (Laakso, Frisoni, Könönen, et al., 1999). This topographic distinction merits further consideration in light of recently published evidence regarding specialization of the anterior and posterior hippocampus in distinct mnemonic operations (Gabrieli, Brewer, Desmond, & Glover, 1997; Lepage, Habib, McIntosh, & Tulving, 1998). The implication for the cumulative record of hippocampal volumetry is that studies in which anterior hippocampus was not measured are more likely to show age-related declines in the hippocampal volume than those that include the anterior slices that are less vulnerable to age effects.

Regarding the paralimbic (entorhinal and parahippocampal) cortices, the picture of age-related changes is unclear, and the data bearing on that issue are very sparse. Postmortem investigations of the entorhinal cortex reveal age-related attrition of neurons (with effect magnitude ranging from $r = -.48$ to $r = -.67$, Heinsen et al., 1994) and a significant increase in amyloid deposits (Guillozet, Smiley, Mash, & Mesulam, 1995), although in nonhuman primates no comparable changes were noted (Gazzaley, Thakker, Hof, & Morrison, 1997). The results of in vivo volumetric studies of the limbic cortices are inconsistent. Most of the studies revealed minimal (or no) age related declines in the volume of entorhinal (deToledo-Morrell, Goncharova, Dickerson, & Wilson, 1998; Insausti et al., 1998) and parahippocampal (Raz et al., 1997, 1998c) cortices, with an exception of one sample (Murphy et al., 1996) in which substantial age differences in parahippocampal volume ($r = -.50$) were observed. In contrast to normal aging, AD is associated with considerable involvement of the entorhinal cortex from the very early stages of the malady, as indicated by both postmortem and in vivo MRI studies (Braak & Braak, 1991; Juottonen et al., 1998; Pearlson et al., 1992).

It is unclear whether ApoE ε4 status affects hippocampal volume. In some relatively large samples no differences in the volume of hippocampus (Jack, Petersen, Xu, O'Brien, Waring, et al., 1998; Reiman et al., 1998; H. Schmidt et al., 1996) or parahippocampal gyrus (H. Schmidt et al., 1996) have been found. In contrast, a number of studies reported trends toward smaller hippocampi in the carriers of the ε4 alleles (Kuller et al., 1998; Plassman et al., 1997; Tohgi et al., 1997).

Neocortex and Adjacent White Matter. Several lines of evidence converge on the notion of selective vulnerability of the association cortices to aging. When synaptic density and dendritic arborization of the cortical neurons is reduced with age, the reduction is especially significant in the prefrontal cortex (see Esiri, 1994, for a review; see also Liu, Erikson, & Brun, 1996). Moreover, in normal aging but not in confirmed AD, this effect may be especially pronounced in the large pyramidal cells and interneurons of the lamina V and less severe (although still significant) in the lamina III of the middle frontal gyrus populated by small and medium-size pyramidal neurons (de Brabander, Kramers, & Uylings, 1998; Uylings, de Brabander, & Kramers, 1998). Unlike neuritic plaques, NFTs show a propensity to accumulate in the frontal and temporal cortices, especially in the lamina V in which cortico-cortical and cortico-subcortical (cortico-striatal and cortico-thalamic) fibers originate (see Kemper, 1994, and Uylings et al., in press, for a review). Increased density of NFTs in temporal regions, especially Brodmann area (BA) 20, along with relative sparing of the sensory cortices, has been documented (Giannakopoulos et al., 1995; Hof, Giannakopoulos, & Bouras, 1996). Amyloid deposits, a hallmark of neuronal aging, are very mild in the primary motor and sensory cortices, moderate in visual and auditory cortices, and substantial (up to 25% of the total neuron area) in the association cortices (Guillozet et al., 1995; see Kemper, 1994, for a review). In nonhuman primates, some shrinkage of Betz cells in the primary motor cortex was noted, but no decline in the total of that region's neuronal population has been observed (Tigges, Herndon, & Peters, 1990, 1992).

Structural neuroimaging studies of the neocortex and adjacent white matter are summarized in Table 1.3 (see Fig. 1.7 for examples of the prefrontal regions of interest). Unlike the series of studies of aging hippocampal formation discussed above, the set of research reports on the age-related regional changes in the neocortical regions is rather sparse, and there is little consistency across laboratories in region selection and MR methods. To date, only five studies have examined age-related differences in the prefrontal cortex versus the prefrontal white matter in vivo. In four studies conducted in our laboratory (Raz, Torres, Spencer, & Acker, 1993; Raz, Torres, Spencer, Baertschie, et al., 1993b; Raz et al., 1997, 1998c), the results are quite consistent. They indicated that in participants between 18 and 81 years of age, the prefrontal gray matter shows stronger negative association with age than the prefrontal white matter. The median correlation between age and the gray matter volume was r $-.57$, a large effect (Cohen, 1988). For comparison, the median effect of age on the prefrontal white matter observed in the same studies was estimated at median $r = -.31$ (i.e., an effect identical to that observed for the hippocampal formation). The studies in which only the total volume

TABLE 1.3
Effect of Age on Cerebral Cortex Observed In Vivo: Regional Cortical Volumes

Study	N	Age (Years)	Effect Size (r) Frontal Total	Frontal Gray	Frontal White	Temporal Total	Temporal STG	Temporal Polar	Temporal ITG
Coffey et al. (1992)	76	30–91	(−.47)			(−.37)			
Raz, Torres, Spencer, & Acker (1993)	29	18–78		−.43 (−.29)	−.36				
Raz, Torres, Spencer, Baertschie (1993)	54	18–75		−.58 (−.61)	−.36		−.23 (−.14)		
Cowell et al. (1994)	130	25 vs. 62	−.26 (−.47)			−.16 (−.25)			
Golomb et al. (1994)	54	55–87				(−.27)			
Convit et al. (1995)	37	26 vs. 69							
E. V. Sullivan et al. (1995)	72	21–70				−.50 (−.39)			
Murphy et al. (1996)	69	26 vs. 70	(−.46)			(−.11)			
Raz et al. (1997)	148	18–77	−.39	−.55	−.22				
Raz et al. (1998c)	212	18–81	−.43	−.59	−.29				
Salat et al. (in press)	28	65–95	(−.47)	(−.26)	(−.54)				−.35
Insausti et al. (1998)	52	28 vs. 72						(−.39)	−.29
Mdn	61		−.39 (−.47)	−.57 (−.29)	−.32 (−.54)	−.35 (−.27)			−.32

(Continued)

TABLE 1.3
(Continued)

Study	N	Age (Years)	Effect Size (r)							
					Parietal				Occipital	
			FG	Total	White	SSC	SPL	IPL	Total	Gray
Coffey et al. (1992)	76	30–91								
Raz, Torres, Spencer, & Acker (1993)	29	18–78			−.31 (−.32)	−.19		−.42		−.28 (−.02)
Raz, Torres, Spencer, Baertschie (1993)	54	18–75				.02				−.14
Cowell et al. (1994)	130	25 vs. 62								
Golomb et al. (1994)	54	55–87								
Convit et al. (1995)	37	26 vs. 69	−.06							
E. V. Sullivan et al. (1995)	72	21–70								
Murphy et al. (1996)	69	26 vs. 70		(−.26)					(−.26)	
Raz et al. (1997)	148	18–77	−.36	−.27	−.16	−.26	−.36	−.18		−.19
Raz et al. (1998c)	212	18–81	−.35							−.17
Salat et al. (in press)	28	65–95								
Insausti et al. (1998)	52	28 vs. 72								
Mdn	61		−.35	−.29						−.18

Note. Correlations with volumes adjusted for cranial size or height are presented in parentheses. STG = superior temporal gyrus; ITG = inferior temporal gyrus; FG = fusiform gyrus gray matter; SSC = somatosensory cortex; SPL = superior parietal lobule; IPL = inferior parietal lobule.

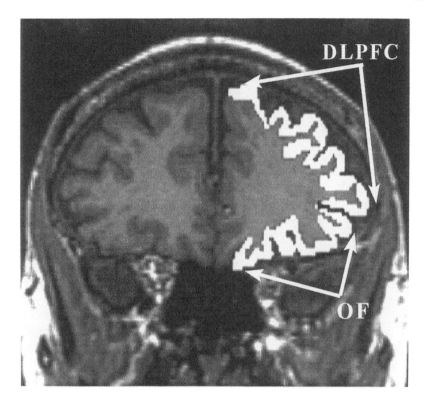

FIG. 1.7. A coronal slice through the rostral part of the brain (about 6 cm anterior to the genu of the corpus callosum) on a reformatted 3D volume magnetic resonance image. The volume was rotated and aligned along the anterior–posterior commissure plane to correct for head tilt, pitch, and rotation. The prefrontal structures shown are the dorsolateral prefrontal cortex (DLPFC) and the orbitofrontal cortex (OF).

of the prefrontal cerebral matter (gray and white) was reported show quite consistent, albeit somewhat attenuated, age differences at median r = −.47. The only study that shows a reversed pattern of prefrontal aging, suggesting greater vulnerability of the prefrontal white matter rather than the cortex (Salat et al., 1999), was conducted on a small sample of participants older than 65, including a few octa- and nonagenarians. Furthermore, it used measurement methods that could have resulted in differential reliability of gray matter volumes as well as introduction of additional error variance associated with the image appearance (T2- vs. Proton-density weighted).

Regardless of the issue of differential aging of prefrontal gray versus white matter, the evidence is clear that the latter is not spared by aging. In accord with the in vivo studies, the postmortem literature suggests that the fiber systems connecting the visual and the primary motor cortices are relatively insensitive to the effects of advancing age (see Kemper, 1994, for a review).

If studies of age effects on the prefrontal volume are scarce, the other cortical regions, by comparison, appear virtually neglected. Nevertheless, in a few studies that compared prefrontal volume to that of the other cortical regions (temporal, parietal, or occipital), the magnitude of the negative association between age and regional volume is consistently greater for the former than any of the latter. Three research groups (Coffey et al., 1992; Cowell et al., 1994; Murphy et al., 1996) have reported considerably smaller correlations between age and temporal lobe volumes (gray and white matter combined) than for the prefrontal regions. The median effect for the frontal lobes was $r = -.47$ compared with $r = -.25$ for the temporal lobes. In two studies (Raz et al., 1997, 1998c) that pattern has been replicated for the comparison of the prefrontal gray matter (mean $r = -.57$) versus the inferior temporal cortex ($r = -.32$). In another study, Raz, Torres, Spencer, Baertschie, et al. (1993) observed the same pattern for the prefrontal ($r = -.61$) versus the superior temporal cortex ($r = -.14$). In three additional studies (Golomb et al., 1994; Insausti et al., 1998; E. V. Sullivan et al., 1995), the volume of temporal regions was estimated without comparison with other cortical regions. The strength of association of temporal lobe volume with age did not differ from the one observed in the studies that involved interregional comparisons (median $r = -.32$).

Studies of brain aging that used other MR methods offer some convergent support to the idea of differential vulnerability of the prefrontal regions. In one sample of healthy elderly participants, the slope of the age-related trend for T1 time constant was steeper for the frontal lobe than for the occipital lobe (Agartz, Sääf, Wahlund, & Wetterberg, 1991). However, in two other samples (Kirsch, Jacobs, Butcher, & Beatty, 1992; Laakso et al., 1996), the prefrontal regions were not examined, and age-related T2 time prolongation was more pronounced in the posterior parietal white matter than in the hippocampus, the thalamus, and the temporal white matter. White matter abnormalities may be more prevalent in frontal regions than in other cortical regions of those who are "old-old" (age 75 and older; Kawamura et al., 1993). In one sample, frontal WMHs were specifically linked to an increase in arterial blood pressure (Yamashita et al., 1991).

In sum, the available evidence suggests that prefrontal cortices are more vulnerable to aging than all other cortical regions. Nonetheless, the sparsity of the data is troublesome and calls for further systematic investigation of differential cortical aging. Such comparisons are especially important in light of the longitudinal findings that suggest that prefrontal vulnerability to physiological aging notwithstanding, temporal cortex may be a more sensitive predictor of pathological cerebral changes in late adulthood. In a relatively short longitudinal follow-up, a small sample of comparatively young partipants evidenced significant shrinkage of the temporal lobes, although frontal lobe volumes remained stable (Gur et al., 1998). The short duration of the follow-up (fewer than 3 years), the young age of the participants (approximately 32 years old), and the substantial magnitude of shrinkage (7%) make this study especially intriguing, whereas its small sample size ($N = 17$) is a good reason for caution in interpretation. Changes in the volume of the temporal lobe (gray and white matter combined) predicted the onset of dementia, whereas changes in the volumes of the parahippocampal gyrus and the hippocampal formation did not (Kaye et al., 1997). In a 2.5-year longitudinal CT study of 35 healthy adults, the Sylvian fissure and the ventricular system showed the steepest deterioration (Shear et al., 1995). A 3- to 4-year longitudinal follow-up of older adults with mild memory deficits suggested that decline in the volume of the fusiform gyrus may be a better predictor of cognitive decline than changes in the hippocampal volume (Convit et al., 1998). A 1-year follow-up study in which an automated coregistration of sequential MRI scans was used showed that in contrast to dramatic deterioration of the hippocampal formation in AD patients, only minimal structural changes in the hippocampal formation (mean decline of 0.3 cm^3 per year) were observed in normal elderly participants (Fox, Freeborough, & Rossor, 1996). Another 1-year longitudinal comparison of hippocampal and temporal horn volumes in 24 cognitively normal elderly participants (70 to 89 years of age) revealed mild hippocampal volume loss ($-1.55\% \pm 1.38\%$ per year) and a more substantial temporal horns dilation ($6.15\% \pm 7.69\%$ per year; Jack, Peterson, Xu, O'Brien, Smith, et al., 1998). By comparison, demographically matched AD patients evidenced more than twice as fast rate of change. In a 3-year follow-up of AD patients and normal elderly individuals, a small but consistent shrinkage of the hippocampus (about 1% per year) was observed in the latter, whereas the AD patients evidenced an accelerated trend (almost 3% per year), with some of them reaching the pace of more than 5% per year (Laakso, Lehtovirta, Partanen, Riekkinen, & Soininen, 1999). One can conclude that in spite of their limited number and small samples involved, longitudinal studies of age-related changes in the brain support the notion of significant declines in regional volumes; that change may be differential with temporal lobe structures exhibiting steeper decline than prefrontal cortex; and that the rate of decline accelerates in older individuals harboring preclinical dementia.

Physiological neuroimaging of the aging brain in general corroborates the discussed findings from MR-based morphometry. The evidence from PET studies indicates that although age-related declines in glucose metabolism have been observed in less then 50% of the samples, when they are noted they tend to involve prefrontal and other association regions (about 90% of the samples) more than primary sensory areas (see Madden & Hoffman, 1997, for a review; see also Baron et al., 1998; Loessner et al., 1995; Moeller et al., 1996; Petit-Taboué et al., 1998). The findings in non-human primates are in accord with that trend (Eberling et al., 1995; Voytko et al., 1998). Findings from PET studies of resting oxygen use and rCBF, which have shown oxygen use and rCBF to decline more reliably with age, do not show a clear regional pattern (see Madden & Hoffman, 1997, for a review). However, a review of single-photon emission computerized tomography studies of rCBF suggests that aging is associated with dis-proportionate decrease in prefrontal flow (Waldemar, 1995), and primate data suggest that there are age-related reductions of rCBF in the prefrontal, inferior temporal, extrastriatal, and parietal cortices, as well as in the hippocampus and the neostriatal nuclei (Voytko et al., 1998).

Although the neurochemistry of the aging cerebral cortex is intricate and yet insufficiently understood, some regional distribution trends can be discerned. For example, density of noradrenergic α_2 receptors decline with age in the frontal and temporal cortex and, to a lesser extent, in the hippocampus; they are even less severe in the visual cortex (Pascual et al., 1991). In the rhesus monkey, dopamine synthesis and concentration are reduced in the prefrontal cortex, with parietal association areas show-ing smaller deficits and sensory cortices exhibiting no age-related effects at all (Creutzfeldt, 1995). The dopaminergic D_1 receptors in human pre-frontal cortex also decline with age (De Keyser, De Backer, Vauquelin, & Ebinger, 1990). A PET study of healthy volunteers revealed that while serotonergic receptor availability decreased significantly with age, the trend is stronger in the prefrontal cortex ($r = -.92$, $p < .001$) than in the occipital cortex ($r = -.62$, $p < .01$; Wang et al., 1995; Yonezawa et al., 1991). In another sample, a mild but significant loss of frontal but not cerebellar muscarinic receptors (relative to whole brain average receptor density) was found with advancing age (Lee et at., 1996).

Striatum, Thalamus, and Mammillary Body. Age effects on the striatum and diencephalon (see Fig. 1.8) are moderate. An update of a previously published quantitative review (Raz, Torres, & Acker, 1995), summarized in Table 1.4, reveals age effects of $r = -.47$ and $-.44$ for the caudate and the putamen, respectively. However, in the five studies in which both neostriatal nuclei were measured, there was a reversed trend (i.e., toward greater effects of age on the putamen rather than the caudate nucleus; $r = -.32$ for the caudate and $r = -.44$ for the putamen). Although only three studies considered the volume of the globus pallidus or its nuclei, the results consistently reveal smaller age effects than those observed in the

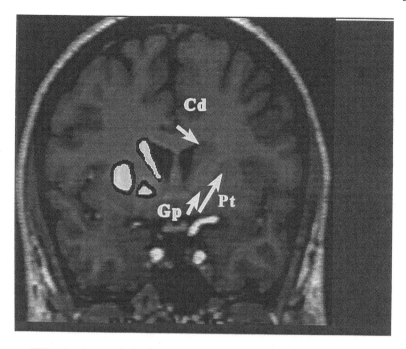

FIG. 1.8. A coronal slice of a reformatted 3D volume magnetic resonance image aligned perpendicular to the anterior–posterior commissure line showing the basal ganglia. Cd = caudate nucleus; Pt = putamen; and Gp = globus pallidus.

neostriatum (median $r = -.14$). In addition to the reviewed MRI studies, one CT study found age-related shrinkage of the caudate nucleus (Schwartz et al., 1985; $r = -.36$) and two postmortem investigations reported age-related volume loss in the putamen (Bugiani, Salvarini, Perdelli, Mancardi, & Leonardi, 1978; $r = -.76$) and the globus pallidus (Kooistra & Heilman 1988; $r = -.50$). Significant age-related shrinkage of the neostriatum has also been reported in nonhuman primates (Matochik et al., 1998).

The striatum (especially the neostriatal nuclei) tends to accumulate iron, and in some samples, the extent of iron deposits in the caudate nucleus and the putamen correlates with age (Martin et al., 1998; Steffens, McDonald, Tupler, Boyko, & Krishnan, 1996), although the relationship has not been observed in adults between the third and fifth decade of life (Vymazal et al., 1995). Notably, age-related accumulation of iron in the globus pallidus is relatively insubstantial (Martin et al., 1998), and in a rodent model, the globus pallidus was demonstrated to be far less sensitive than the neostriatal nuclei to some conditions that accompany normal aging, such as hypertension (Tajima et al., 1993).

TABLE 1.4
Age-Related Differences in the Volume of the Basal Ganglia and the Thalamus

Study	Age (Years)	N	Effect Size (r)				
			Caudate	Putamen	Globus Pallidus	Lenticular Nucleus	Thalamus
Jernigan et al. (1991)	30–79	55	-.49			-.24	-.12
Krishnan et al. (1992)	24–79	27	-.47				
Murphy et al. (1992)	19–92	27	-.48			-.51	
Harris et al. (1992)	29–72	19	-.52	-.53			
Hokama et al. (1995)[a]	38 ± 10	15	-.72	-.70	-.34		
Raz et al. (1995; Study 1)	18–78	29	-.52				
Women		12	-.52				
Men		17	-.60				
Raz et al. (1995; Study 2)	18–75	55	-.32	-.18			
Women		36	-.27	-.02			
Men		19	-.59	-.60			
Murphy et al. (1996)	26–70	69	-.18			-.38	-.23
Women		34	-.43			-.43	-.34
Men		35	-.08			-.38	-.23
Gunning-Dixon et al. (1998)	19–77	148	-.32	-.41	-.10		
Women		82	-.32	-.43	.06		
Men		66	-.35	-.45	-.33		
Schulz et al. (1999)	20–73	46	-.20	-.46			
Raz et al. (1999b)	19–81	212	-.29	-.41	-.14		
Women		125	-.24	-.39	-.20		
Men		87	-.34	-.45	-.07		
Mdn (total)		46	-.47	-.44	-.14		-.17
Mdn (men)			-.42	-.45	-.15		
Mdn (women)			-.32	-.39	.04		

[a]Effect size was estimated by Spearman ρ.

The neurochemistry of the striatum changes with age. Monoamine transport and dopamine receptor binding decline in the aging putamen at a rate of 0.6% to 0.8% per year (Antonini et al., 1993; Frey et al., 1996). Availability of D_2 receptors in the neostriatum, and especially in the caudate nucleus (Iyo & Yamasaki, 1993; Morgan & Finch, 1988; Rinne et al., 1993; Sahlberg, Marjamäki, & Rinne, 1998), also declines with age. In addition, accumulation of iron in the basal ganglia may promote cytotoxic activity of the free radical through increase in supply of the catalyst (Martin et al., 1998) and oxidative stress on dopaminergic neurons in the substantia nigra may be especially severe (Floor & Wetzel, 1998).

In contrast to the relative abundance of data on structural and functional aspects of the striatum, there is very little research on aging of human diencephalic structures. The importance of the thalamus in brain work notwithstanding, its response to aging is virtually unknown. In a few studies that attempted volumetry of this complex collection of nuclei, the thalamus evidences a considerably milder age-related shrinkage than the neostriatum ($r = -.17$). However, because of a high degree of functional specialization among the thalamic nuclei and clear-cut differences in their connections with the cortical regions, only limited interpretation can be given to the findings on the total thalamic volumetry.

Although the mammillary bodies (see Fig. 1.9) belong to the diencephalon (as does the thalamus), they are also frequently listed among the limbic structures. Age-related shrinkage in the mammillary bodies is moderate (median $r = -.39$ in three studies reviewed by Raz, 1996). A postmortem study revealed age-related changes in the nuclear area of the human mammillary body to be similar to those in the anterior thalamic nuclei to which it projects. The constant and gradual loss of neurons throughout the life span is accompanied by more complex changes in the area of nuclei. The latter decreases significantly until the age of 60 to 70 years, after which an increase up to the end of the life is observed. This increase is more intense in the mammillary nuclei than in the thalamus (Panadero & Gonzalo Sanz, 1988). In general, the findings from postmortem and in vivo studies of the basal ganglia and the diencephalon indicate that aging exerts moderate negative effects on the gross structure, as well as the neurochemical apparatus of the neostriatal nuclei and the mammillary bodies, while sparing the paleostriatum.

Cerebellum. Age-related loss of cerebellar tissue was first documented in a postmortem investigation by Ellis (1920) and replicated in later postmortem studies (Hall, Miller, & Corsellis, 1975; Torvik, Torp, & Lindboe, 1986). Two CT investigations of normal or neurologically normal participants revealed age-related sulcal enlargement in the vermis (Koller et al. 1981) and cerebellar hemispheres (Nishimiya, 1988). The results of in vivo studies of the cerebellum (see Fig. 1.9) are summarized in Table 1.5.

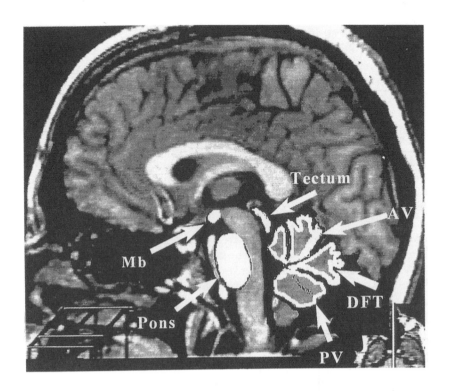

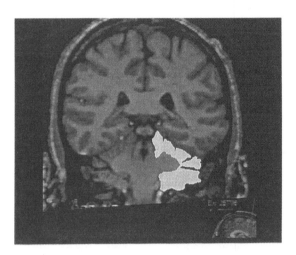

FIG. 1.9. Top panel: A midsagittal slice of a reformatted 3D volume magnetic resonance (MR) scan aligned by the middle of the vermis shows the cerebellar vermis (anterior [AV], posterior [PV], and declive-folium-tuber [DFT]), the tectum, the maminillary body (Mb), and the pons. Bottom panel: A coronal slice of a reformatted 3D volume MR image aligned perpendicular to the anterior–posterior commissure line, with a cerebellar hemisphere highlighted.

TABLE 1.5
Regional Volumes: Cerebellum, Midbrain, and Pons

Study	Age (Years)	N	Effect Size (r)						Tectum	Midbrain	Pons
				Vermis							
			Hemispheres	Total	Superior	DFT	Posterior				
Hayakawa et al. (1989)	16–60	49		-.12							.15
Schaeffer et al. (1991)	0.1–90	125		-.41	-.23	-.40	-.60				
Escalona et al. (1991)[a]	24–79	37	-.27 (-.32)								
Shah et al. (1991)	26–79	36		-.20	-.33		-.07				
Shah et al. (1992)	26–79	36									-.14
Raz, Torres, Spencer, et al. (1992)	18–78	82						-.08			
Raz, Torres, & Acker (1992)	18–78	59		-.54	-.29	-.50	-.33				.14
Doraiswami et al. (1992)	21–82	75							-.39		
Weis et al. (1993)	20–80	46		-.28					-.45		-.06
Raininko et al. (1994)	0.3–86	174		-.56							
Raz & Acker (1994); Raz (1999b)	18–80	159						-.27			
M. P. Sullivan et al. (1995)	27–70	64	-.56 (-.45)								
Murphy et al. (1996)	26–70	69	(-.26)								
Salat et al. (1997)	65–95	76		-.02							-.04
Deshmukh et al. (1997)	50 ± 16	10	-.28	-.67	-.57	-.76	-.35				
Raz, Dupuis, et al. (1998)	19–77	146	-.32	-.28	-.07	-.34	-.23				
Luft et al. (1998)	20–73	46	-.35 (-.10)	-.42	-.46	-.39	-.42				.11
Mdn		64	-.32 (-.29)	-.34	-.31	-.40	-.35	-.18	-.42		.07

Note. Values in parentheses indicate correlations for head-size- or height-adjusted volumes. DFT = declive-folium-tuber lobules of the cerebellar vermis.

[a]Correlations were Spearman ρ computed from a scatter plot.

35

The median age effect on the volume of cerebellar hemispheres is modest but not negligible (median $r = -.32$; $r = -.29$ when adjusted for height or cranial size). The pattern of regional sensitivity to aging reported by Raz and colleagues (Raz, Dupuis, Briggs, McGavran, & Acker, 1998; Raz, Torres, Spencer, White, & Acker, 1992) was not universally observed; however, across several samples, the cross-sectional area of superior lobules shows somewhat weaker association with age ($r = -.31$) than the posterior vermis ($r = -.35$) and, especially, the declive-folium-tuber ($r = -.40$).

Questions have been raised, however, about confounding the effects of age with the influence of alcohol to which cerebellum shows special sensitivity. Differences in alcohol consumption (even within the clearly nonpathological social drinking range) may produce sample-specific patterns of age-related cerebellar shrinkage by augmenting age-related attrition of Purkinje cells in the anterior vemis (Karhunen, Erkinjuntti, & Laippala, 1994). Thus, it is possible that the observed discrepancy between the samples may be due to the difference in alcohol consumption.

Midbrain, Pons, and Medulla. In contrast to age-related shrinkage observed in cortical and cerebellar structures, the ventral pons appears decidedly intact (median $r = .05$), with not a single study reporting significant age-related changes in that structure. In two studies, age effects on the cross-sectional area of the tectum also appear very small (median $r = -.18$), whereas the midbrain shows moderate sensitivity to aging (median $r = -.42$; see Luft et al., 1999; Raz, 1996, for a review). In another MR study, in which no statistical indices amenable to effect size calculations were reported, the midbrain was reported to shrink "slightly" with age, although no age-related differences in linear dimensions of the medulla and the pons were observed throughout the life span (Raininko et al., 1994). Notably, the medulla is not invulnerable to the effects of AD as it exhibits pathological changes that, by some accounts, may be responsible for the cardiovascular and pulmonary abnormalities that accompany the disease (Rüb, Braak, Braak, Schultz, & Ghebremedhin, et al., 1998).

The midbrain nuclei from which most of the monoaminergic projections of the brain originate—the locus coeruleus (LC), the substantia nigra, and the raphe dorsalis—exhibit significant age-related shrinkage and neuronal loss (McGeer & McGeer, 1989). The LC, a nucleus that serves as the major source of norepinephrine in the mammalian brain, presents an interesting example of differential aging. The neurons of the rostral part of the LC project to the forebrain and evidence substantial age-related attrition, whereas the caudal LC neurons send their axons to the spinal cord and remain virtually unaffected by age (Chan-Palay & Asan, 1989; Manaye, McIntire, Mann, & German, 1995). When the two compartments are lumped together, there are no significant age differences in neuronal number (Mouton, Pakkenberg, Gundersen, & Price, 1994).

Structural and Neurochemical Aspects of Brain Aging:
An Interim Summary and Discussion
of Possible Mechanisms

The findings reviewed in the preceding section indicate that in addition to global and pervasive changes in structure and physiology, the aging brain exhibits a patchwork pattern of differential declines and relative preservation. The negative impact of aging on the prefrontal cortex is greater than on other brain areas. Age effects on the neostriatum are less substantial, whereas the hippocampus, the cerebellum, and the temporal, parietal, and occipital cortices show somewhat greater resilience. Some regions, such as the pons and the tectum, appear insensitive to the impact of aging. Biological mechanisms that give rise to the emerging pattern of differential brain aging remain to be elucidated.

Given the complexity of the phenomena, it is unlikely that any single factor will account for all the accumulated data. Multiple neurochemical, cerebrovascular, and genetic determinants need to be reckoned with in any explanation of the observed tendency of phylogenetically newer (Armstrong, 1990) and ontogenetically less precocious (Koop, Rilling, Herrmann, & Kretschmann, 1986) brain structures, such as association cortices, to undergo age-related declines. It is possible that differential age-related vulnerability is absent in phylogenetically older species. Indeed, great apes show a more humanlike pattern of decline in brain weight with age than do monkeys (Herndon et al., 1998, 1999). The brains of older rhesus monkeys respond to the introduction of cytotoxic amyloid beta protein (Aβ) with a humanlike pattern of neural loss, whereas marmosets exhibit a considerably milder response; no effect at all is observed in mice (Geula et al., 1998). However, a systematic test of this evolutionary hypothesis will require a more extensive cross-species comparison.

The gradient of differential vulnerability suggested by the reviewed studies seems to follow the rule of "last (phylogenetically and ontogenetically) in, first out." Structures that evolved in more ancient species and those that mature early in the course of human development (i.e., the globus pallidus, the paleocerebellum, sensory cortices, and the pons) are less affected by age than the neocerebellar vermis, the neostriatum, and the association (especially prefrontal) cortex. For comparison, the following box plot (see Fig. 1.10) illustrates the difference among the effects of age on highly vulnerable (the prefrontal cortex), moderately vulnerable (the hippocampus), mildly vulnerable (the occipital cortex), and age-invariant (the pons) regions of the brain.

The correspondence between ontogenetic chronology and age-related vulnerability can be illustrated by the following observation. Figure 1.11 depicts a regression of the magnitude of the age effect on the volumes of 11 specific cortical regions (from Raz et al., 1997) on the precedence rank order

Age-Related Differences in Regional Brain Volumes

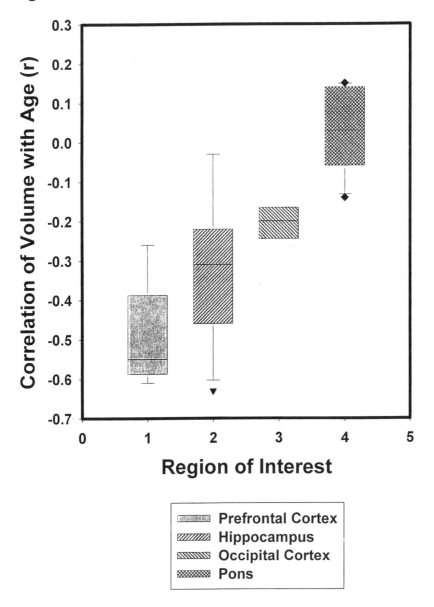

FIG. 1.10. Age-related differences in regional brain volumes: Comparison of age effects from different studies. The effects are expressed as a product–moment correlation (r) between volume/area and age. Four regions are compared: the prefrontal cortex (based on 5 samples), the hippocampus (based on 14 samples), the occipital cortex (based on 4 samples), and the pons (based on 6 samples).

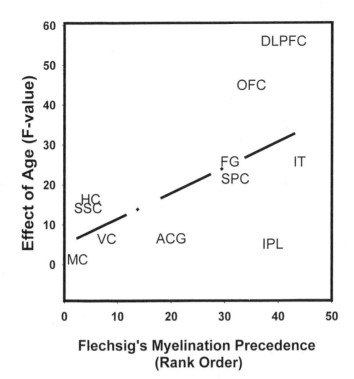

FIG. 1.11. Myelogenesis order predicts vulnerability of cortical regions to aging: Regression ($F = 5.06 + 0.64 \times$ Rank; $R^2 = .364$) of the magnitude of age effect on Flechsig's myelination precedence rank for 11 cortical regions measured by Raz et al. (1997). A greater rank corresponds to a later myelination of the region; a greater F value indicates a stronger association between age and the regional volume, controlling for gender and body size (height). DLPFC = dorsolateral prefrontal cortex; OFC = orbitofrontal cortex; IT = inferior temporal; IPL = inferior parietal lobule; SPC = superior parietal cortex; ACG = anterior cingulate gyrus; MC = motor cortex; VC = visual cortex; HC = hippocampus; SSC = somatosensory cortex; FG = fusiform gyrus.

of myelination of intracortical fibers in those regions according to Flechsig (1901). A higher rank signifies later completion of myelination, and the later a region completes its myelination, the greater age-related difference in volume it exhibits ($r = .60$, $p < .05$). This correlation also suggests that changes in cortical myeloarchitectonics may play a role in differential aging of the brain, as suggested by Courchesne and Plante (1997).

Age-related declines in specific brain neurotransmitter systems (cholinergic and dopaminergic) may account for some features of the regional distribution of age-sensitive and age-invariant areas (Bartus, Dean, Pontecorvo, & Flicker, 1985; McGeer et al., 1990). However, such proposals fall short of explaining the pattern of differential brain aging that emerges from postmortem and in vivo studies. Moreover, it is unclear whether the cholinergic system is significantly impaired in healthy elderly individuals (Namba et al., 1998), and when it is, the greatest impact of age on cholinergic function is observed in the areas that tend to exhibit few age-related declines (Wright, Geula, & Mesulam, 1993).

A possibility of an excitotoxic mechanism of differential vulnerability in the brain regions that are late to mature has been offered but remains highly speculative (Foster & Norris, 1997; Raz et al., 1997). Such a mechanism, if indeed established, may represent a dark side of neuronal plasticity, for both neuronal death and dendritic branching depend on calcium influx (Mattson, 1992). Change in calcium homeostasis has been proposed as the core mechanism of physiological and pathological aging (Khachaturian, 1984, 1994). A similar hypothesis has been advanced by Arendt, Bruckner, Gertz, and Marcova (1998), who found that brain regions known for their increased vulnerability to aging or AD pathology (entorhinal, prefrontal, fusiform, and inferior parietal cortices and the hippocampus) showed evidence of substantially more intense dendritic "remodeling" than sensory association areas, which in turn evidenced greater adult-life plasticity than the primary sensory and motor cortices. In rodents, a gradual increase in the density of calcium channels appears to be clearly associated with age-related loss of hippocampal neurons and may underpin the vulnerability of aged neurons to neurodegenerative age-related diseases (Landfield, 1996). However, in the realm of neurochemistry nothing is simple, and some evidence suggests that vulnerability of rodent hippocampus to an excitotoxic compound, kainate, may be even reduced with age (Kesslak, Yuan, Neeper, & Cotman, 1995). In addition, the very notion of alteration in calcium homeostasis as a cause of brain aging has been questioned: After all, it may be an adaptive response that accompanies physiological aging and causes cell loss only in Alzhiemer's disease.

Selective effects of aging of the association cortices and the limbic structures may be due to factors other than the alteration in distribution and activity of neurotransmitters. For example, 5-lipoxygenase (5-LO), the key enzyme in the synthesis of inflammatory eicosanoids that are capable of promoting neurodegeneration, is more abundant in the association and limbic structures of rodents (Uz, Pesold, Longone, & Manev, 1998). Thus, cumulative ill effects of subclinical inflamation may be more pronounced in those regions than in the primary cortices, thereby creating the observed pattern of differential vulnerability.

The cumulative influence of multiple pathogens throughout the life span may produce a pattern of selective vulnerability or, to use Vogt and

Vogt's (1951) term, *pathoclisis* of specific brain tissue if that tissue has increased susceptibility to pathogens, such as stress-induced release of glucocorticoids in the hippocampus (Sapolsky, 1990). Indeed, in a small sample of normal adults who were followed longitudinally for 6 years, high basal cortisol levels and steep cortisol elevation over time were associated with reduced hippacampal (but not temporal and fusiform cortex) volumes (Lupien et al., 1998). Response of regional hippocampal CMRglu to a hydrocortisone challenge is significantly reduced in comparison with a placebo (de Leon et al., 1997), and progressive increase in cortisol excretion may be associated with age-related memory declines in otherwise healthy elderly women (Seeman, McEwen, Singer, Albert, & Rowe, 1997). In rodents, chronic administration of corticosteroids results in hippocampal cell loss restricted to CA1 sector which may be relatively spared by normal aging (Kadar, Dachir, Shukitt-Hale, & Levy, 1998).

It is possible that high levels of lifelong stress produce hippocampal shrinkage in susceptible individuals. However, the glucocorticoid damage model does not account for the observed increase in vulnerability of the prefrontal cortex. In light of the detrimental effects of even mild hypertension on the brain, the interaction of cardio- and cerebrovascular factors merits special consideration in search of the reasons for the observed pattern of differential vulnerability. Notably, the evidence from a rodent model suggests that, in contrast to many cortical regions and the striatum, the tectum and the periaqueductal gray matter are insensitive to the effects of spontaneous hypertension (Tajima et al., 1993). Finally, a simple geometric explanation of the observed pattern of differential shrinkage cannot be completely ruled out. A possible reason for increased likelihood of detecting age-related changes in prefrontal and temporal cortices, rather than motor and primary visual cortices, may be the larger size and a more extensive gyrification in the former (Zilles, Armstrong, Schleicher, & Kretschmann, 1988).

It is important to keep in mind that relative macroscopic preservation of the primary sensory cortices with age does not necessarily imply lack of functional cellular changes. For example, single cell recordings in rhesus monkeys reveal no age-related effects in responses of layer 4c cells that receive input from the lateral geniculate nucleus of the thalamus (Schmolesky, Wang, & Leventhal, 1998). However, the cells of other layers of the primary visual cortex exhibited increased latency of response and decline in sensitivity.

A number of studies have suggested that the pace of cerebral aging may differ between men and women. However, there is no clear agreement as to which specific cerebral regions show sex differences in the magnitude of age effects (see Coffey et al., 1998, for a review). In general, men appear to be more vulnerable to the effects of age than do women, although some studies have shown the reverse pattern—that is, a greater vulnerability for women (Murphy et al., 1996; Raz, Torres, Spencer, & Acker, 1993, Study 1). When sex differences in brain aging are reported, they usually involve nonspecific neuroanatomical alterations, primarily expansion of the CSF cavities, such as the lateral ventricles. The likelihood of finding sex differences in the aging of the brain may depend on the criteria of sample selection. For example, in the largest sample in which sex differences were found (Coffey et al., 1998), 70% of the participants suffered from hypertension, ischemic heart disease. diabetes, or hypothyroidism—that is, age-associated disease that would preclude their participation in some other studies. Sampling criteria often preclude an unbiased examination of sex differences in brain aging. Because sex differences in longevity and in prevalence of diseases associated with brain changes usually favor women (Arking, 1991), application of identical screening criteria to both men and women may result in a skewed sex ratio and a bias against finding any disadvantage for men.

In discussing the phenomenon of brain aging, one cannot complain about a lack of interesting and intriguing questions. However, the fundamental importance of the surveyed neuroanatomical and neurophysiological findings is in their impact on our understanding of age-related changes in behavior and cognition. That enterprise, although still at its earliest stages, is reviewed in the remainder of this chapter.

COGNITIVE AGING: IN SEARCH OF NEURAL SUBSTRATES

Aging of cognitive skills mirrors the complex picture of brain aging by displaying a pattern of selective preservation and decline against the background of generalized changes. A cumulative record of research on cognitive aging shows that a large proportion of age-related variance in cognitive performance can be explained by one or two fundamental factors: generalized age-related slowing and reduction in working memory (Meyerson, Hale, Wagstaff, Poon, & Smith, 1990; Salthouse, 1996; Verhaeghen & Salthouse, 1997). Nonetheless, the examples of differential cognitive aging are plentiful. For example, functions associated with episodic memory and executive control are more sensitive to aging than semantic memory and verbal reasoning. Within the domain of episodic memory, age differences in free and cued recall are greater than in recognition memory, which in turn is more vulnerable to aging than repetition priming (see LaVoie & Light, 1994; Mitchell, 1993; and Verhaeghen, Marcoen, & Goosens, 1993, for a review). Thus, both brain and cognition age differentially as well as globally. Therefore, it is plausible that age-sensitive cognitive operations are supported by age-sensitive areas of the brain, whereas age-invariant cognitive abilities are maintained by brain circuits that are not particularly vulnerable to aging. By the same logic, the degree of preservation of general and complex cognitive skills would be related to the preservation of the brain in toto. An interesting exception to this pattern of brain–behavior relationships in aging may be cognitive expertise. Little is known about the impact of expertise acquisition on the brain. However, if development of expert performance in a narrow cognitive specialty is associated with alteration of brain representation of that skill, the impact of age on the brain would not necessarily produce the expected age-related changes in performance. Because this intriguing area of inquiry is still underdeveloped, it is excluded from the scope of this review.

Global Neuroanatomical Correlates of Cognitive Aging

The relationship between global indices of cognitive performance and generalized age-related alterations in brain structure has been examined in several studies. The early attempts to elucidate the neuroanatomical basis of cognitive aging used relatively coarse measures of brain structural integrity, such as CT, and revealed general associations between nonspecific age-related atrophy markers and performance on a battery of broad-range neuropsychological tests in healthy elderly individuals (e.g., Albert, Duffy, & Naeser, 1987).

Subsequent MRI studies have demonstrated that generalized changes such as reduction in the gross volume of the cerebral hemispheres and accumulation of cerebrovascular pathology markers (especially punctate lesions in the extraventricular regions) correlate with global measures of cognitive performance, with a z-transformed mean r of $-.22$ (see Gunning-Dixon & Ras, 1999a). Performance on age-sensitive nonverbal reasoning tasks correlated with prolongation of the white matter T1 time and reduction in gray–white ratio of T1 in medial temporal structures (Raz et al., 1990), as well as with the asymmetric loss of cerebral tissue (Raz, Torres, Spencer, Baertschie, et al., 1993). However, other studies in which similar measures of brain and behavior were used failed to find significant associations between apparent white matter pathology and cognition (Almkvist, Wahlund, Andersson-Lundman, Basun, & Bäckman, 1992; Hendrie, Farlow, Austrom, Edwards, & Williams, 1989; Hunt et al., 1989; O'Brien, Desmond, Ames, Schweitzer, & Tress, 1997; Rao, Mittenberg, Bernardin, Haughton, & Leo, 1989; Tupler, Coffey, Logue, Diang, & Fagan, 1992; Yamashita et al., 1991).

Boone et al. (1992) suggested that the association between cognition and the state of cerebral white matter was a threshold phenomenon. Their findings show that cognitive performance in asymptomatic elderly individuals drops precipitously when the white matter lesions accumulate above a certain critical level. The threshold hypothesis received further support in a study of healthy elderly adults by DeCarli et al. (1995).

If all expressions of cognitive aging are explained by deterioration of a single cognitive resource—that is, speed of processing (Meyerson et al., 1990; Salthouse, 1996)—it is possible that its neuropathological foundation is laid by generalized age-related declines in structural integrity of the cerebral white matter. Indeed, speed-of-processing declines are observed in demyelinating disease (Kail, 1998), and age-related slowing of mental processing has been associated with increase in the burden of white matter abnormalities (mean effect size for 16 studies, $r = .22$; $pr = .24$ for 9 studies in which age was controlled; Gunning-Dixon & Raz, 1999a).

Regional Measures of Brain Structure and Function and Cognitive Aging

Sensory Processes. Neuroimaging techniques based on assessment of task-related changes in rCBF or local blood oxygenation offer a multitude of exciting research opportunities. However, before embarking on an exploration of the neural substrates of cognitive aging with those techniques, it is prudent to inquire whether aging is associated with alteration of cerebral hemodynamics in response to simple sensory stimulation that evokes little if any cognitive activity. The need for examining these aspects of the aging brain appears even more urgent in light of reports of the association between age-related deficits in sensory information processing and declines in higher cognitive functions (Baltes & Lindenberger, 1997), and the dearth of neuroimaging research in this area is especially surprising.

To date, only one fMRI study that investigated the response of the aging brain to simple visual stimulation has been conducted. In a small sample of healthy adults, the amplitude of the visual cortex response to photic stimulation was significantly decreased in elderly participants compared with their younger counterparts (age effect $d = 1.18$, equivalent $r = -.50$; Ross et al., 1997). Whatever the mechanisms of these age-related deficits, they must be taken into account in drawing conclusions from the fMRI and PET investigations of information processing in older adults discussed below. The design and implementation of such a correction constitutes a challenge for future applications of functional neuroimaging to research on cognitive aging. It is unclear whether the observed dampening of response stems from reduction in neuronal activity, reduction in blood vessel responsiveness (see Marin, 1995, for a review), or an increase in noise that drowns the signal whose magnitude may be well preserved. In the latter case, it would be necessary to establish whether introduction of noise into the visual system occurs at the periphery or within the cortex.

A recent report of the role played by dopamine in the regulation of microvascular response of brain vessels (Krimer, Muly, Williams, & Goldman-Rakic, 1998), in conjunction with the age-related decline in the dopaminergic system (e.g., McGeer et al., 1990), suggested that, regardless of cognitive factors, the magnitude of response elicited from the aging brain can be attenuated or even distorted. Another complication in interpreting age-related differences in the patterns of rCBF comes from a recent PET study in which patients with cardiovascular disease displayed hyperactivation in the regions of the brain that were activated by the same task in normal controls (Soufer et al., 1998). Thus, the health problems frequently associated with aging impose constraints on interpreting observed brain activation patterns. Such constraints must be clearly explicated in studies of brain and cognition in aging participants.

Motor Functions. Aging is associated with multiple deficits in the planning, control, and execution of movements (Ingram, 1988; Mortimer, 1988; Spirduso & MacRae, 1990), only some of which are attributable to age-related changes in the musculoskeletal system (Arking, 1991). These deficits, however, are relatively mild and are significantly affected by individual differences in aerobic fitness and cardiovascular status (Spirduso & MacRae, 1990). Because of the involvement of dopaminergic pathways in the motor system and previous findings of age-related declines in dopaminergic functions (McGeer et al., 1990), this neurotransmitter system has been targeted in a recent in vivo PET study that used positron-labeled ^{11}C tracer raclopride to assess the function of dopamine D_2 receptors in healthy adults (Volkow et al., 1998). As expected, the availability of D_2 receptors in the neostriatum was negatively associated with age (range = 24 to 86 years). Moreover, performance on a standard finger-tapping task correlated with that index of dopaminergic activity in the caudate nucleus and the putamen (controlling for age, $pr = .56$). Thus, aging of the nigrostriatal dopaminergic system is associated with motor slowing, although the direction of causality responsible for this association is unclear.

As with sensory processing, the use of indices dependent on blood oxygenation and vascular response in assessment of age-related changes in motor performance must take into account the effects of age on the basic hemodynamic response. A recent fMRI study of healthy adults (range = 20 to 76 years) who performed a simple sequence of rhythmic grasping movements showed that age is associated with slowing of the buildup (but not of the dissipation) of task-dependent activation (Taoka et al., 1998). The age-dependent slowing of the hemodynamic response was significant (correlation between time and age, $r = -.38$ for buildup compared with $r = -.03$ for dissipation). It is unclear whether age differences in the hemodynamic response reflect alterations in the structure of the cerebral vessels, physiological regulation of blood flow, or neural metabolic demands.

Judging by their hemodynamic response on a simple sensorimotor task, the neural circuitry of healthy older adults may produce greater noise while keeping the signal at the same level of the younger people. As a result, a lower signal-to-noise ratio is observed in the elderly and fewer (by a factor of four) pixels on their fMRI images pass the threshold for activation (D'Esposito, Zarahn, Aguire, & Rypma, 1999). It is unclear whether age differences in hemodynamic response reflect alterations in the structure of the cerebral vessels and their spatial distribution, physiological regulation of blood flow, or neural metabolic demands. Nevertheless, the results of these investigations should provide a strong impetus to further examination of age-related differences in cerebral hemodynamics, their relation to senescent changes in cerebral cytoarchitecture, vasculature, and neurochemistry, and their effects on perfusion neuroimaging.

Perception. Beginning with a series of seminal experiments by Mishkin and Ungerleider (see Ungerleider & Haxby, 1994, and Ungerleider & Mishkin, 1982, for a review), a substantial amount of converging evidence established the existence of two main streams of visual information processing in the brain. According to the two-stream model, perception of objects depends on the ventral stream, incorporating the inferior temporal, the fusiform, and the inferior extrastriatal areas of the occipital lobe, whereas identification of spatial location is subserved by the dorsal stream anchored by the superior parietal lobule (e.g., Damasio, Tranel, & Damasio, 1989; Haxby et al., 1991; Köhler, Kapur, Moscovitch, Winocur, & Houle, 1995).

To date, age-related differences in neural substrates of visual perception have been examined in two PET investigations (Grady et al., 1992, 1994). In these studies, two groups of men (mean age of 27 vs. mean age of 72) were asked either to match unfamiliar framed faces or to locate a stimulus within a frame. Activation on a control task (viewing empty frames) was subtracted from the activation observed on the target tasks. In both studies, the patterns of incremental activation associated with face and location processing were similar in both age groups; that is, rCBF to the fusiform and prestriatal cortices (BA 37, BA 18, and BA 19) was increased in response to face stimuli, whereas processing of location information was associated with increases in parieto-occipital activation (BA 19 and BA 7). Thus, the double dissociation of ventral and dorsal streams of activation and face-location matching previously observed in young adults (Haxby et al., 1991) was replicated. However, despite an overall similarity in the activation patterns, several important differences were observed. Older participants evidenced increases in rCBF to the fusiform and the dorsolateral, inferior prefrontal, and anterior cingulate. Notably, they activated the fusiform gyrus (BA 37) more than did the younger participants and did so consistently for face and location matching. The younger participants showed greater activation than their older counterparts only in the prestriatal areas BA 18 and BA 19. Thus, both the configuration of cortical networks subserving visual perception and the amount of task-related work that specific circuits perform may vary with age. However, because the only available studies of neural bases of age differences in perception have used faces as stimuli, the generalization of these findings may be somewhat limited.

Attention. Attention is a major psychological construct that is easy to recognize although difficult to define (James, 1890/1952). The multiplicity of attention-related constructs and the importance of attention in cognitive performance (Kahneman, 1973) would suggest even to a naive observer that clarification of attention mechanisms must be important for an understanding of cognitive aging. Indeed, the questions of age-related differences in deployment and control of attention and their effect on cognitive performance have been raised and addressed in numerous experiments (see chap. 4, this volume, for a review).

The constructs included under the rubric of attention cover a wide range of cognitive tasks, from orienting responses to selective deployment of attention to a specific channel (selective attention), to maintaining attention on a specific target (focused attention) or keeping an above-average level of attention for a period of time in anticipation of specific targets (vigilance), to dividing attention between several targets or rapid switching of attention among the targets in a set. Because of its fundamental role in cognition, the construct of attention has attracted the interest of many experimental psychologists and theoreticians. Although an integration of the resulting body of empirical and theoretical literature is beyond the scope of this review, the following is a very brief synopsis of the current understanding of attention and its brain mechanisms.

The current view of the neural substrate of attention distinguishes between two major brain systems guiding deployment, maintenance, focusing, and division of attention: a posterior system mainly devoted to selective deployment and disengagement of visual attention and an anterior system that is responsible for division of attention among multiple cognitive processes (see Mesulam, 1981, and Posner & Petersen, 1990, for a review). The anterior cortical attentional system, which comprises the dorsolateral prefrontal cortex (DLPFC) and the anterior cingulate gyrus, largely overlaps with the proposed brain substrates of working memory (see Goldman-Rakic, 1987, for a review) or at least of its executive aspects (Kimberg & Farah, 1993). Whereas the prefrontal areas are critical for the executive control of attention, the anterior cingulate cortex is hypothesized to control the motivational aspects associated with the deployment of attention (Mesulam, 1981). The posterior attentional system involves a network of cortical and subcortical components. The former includes the superior and inferior parietal lobules and secondary association cortices in visual and auditory modalities. The latter consists of the tectopulvinar pathways and cerebellar circuits guiding saccadic eye movements. A dense network of neural connections between the two systems led to an understanding that they cannot operate in isolation; rather, they are parts of one interrelated system (Corbetta, Miezin, Shulman, & Petersen, 1993). In addition to these divisions, strong empirical evidence indicates that sustained attention and vigilance are almost exclusively right-hemisphere functions (see Cabeza & Nyberg, 1997, and Posner & Petersen, 1990, for a review).

Because putative substrates of selective and divided attention (the superior parietal lobule and the DLPFC) exhibit age-related structural deterioration (see Kemper, 1994, and Raz, 1996, for a review; see also Raz et al., 1997), it has been hypothesized that deficits in selective attention may lead to age-related declines in other cognitive functions (see Hartley, 1992, for a review). The evidence regarding age-related differences in attentional functions subserved by the posterior system (such as deployment of attention in space) is mixed. Some behavioral findings suggest that it is insensitive to aging (Hartley, 1993), whereas others show that under sufficiently challenging conditions age-related deficits can be observed even in simple attentional tasks geared to assess the posterior system (Faust & Balota, 1997; Thornton, Butler, McGavran, & Raz, 1998).

To date, two functional neuroimaging studies relevant to age-related differences in attentional systems of the brain have been conducted. In a series of visual attention tasks, elderly participants showed only right-hemisphere activation during sustained and divided attention tasks, with stronger prefrontal activation for divided attention and stronger parietal activation for sustained attention (Johannsen et al., 1997). In another comparison of healthy older and young adults, maintaining visual attention on a target letter surrounded by distractors evoked consistently weaker anterior cingulate and superior prefrontal activation in the older group than in the younger group (Madden et al., 1997). In addition, as they focused on a specific target (as compared with gazing at the matrix), the young participants showed significant reduction of the blood flow in the middle frontal gyrus (BA 8 and BA 9). No reduction of the rCBF was observed in older participants in the focused attention condition. When participants were asked to divide their attention among nine letters of the same matrix, the young adults showed relatively greater bilateral activation in the lingual gyrus (BA 18), whereas their older counterparts evidenced increased activation of the DLPFC (BA 6 and BA 8) and the anterior cingulate gyrus (BA 32). The switch from focused to divided attention also resulted in greater reduction of rCBF in the left middle frontal cortex (BA 8) of the younger participants, whereas the older participants showed greater deactivation of the insula.

In sum, age differences in focused and divided attention appear to stem not only from quantitative declines in the magnitude of cerebral activation but from discrepancies in the patterns of cortical activation as well. The younger participants activate the brain circuitry that subserves specific visual attention processing, whereas their older counterparts appear to increase engagement of the anterior and general attention system while failing to deactivate the regions usually not associated with attentional control.

Memory. Because the extant literature on cognitive aging emphasizes age-related differences in memory, and because mnemonic deficits frequently augur the onset of dementia (Bondi, Salmon, & Butters, 1994), most structural neuro-imaging studies have focused on a search for neural substrates of memory. It is generally believed that explicit (declarative) memory depends on two subdivisions of the CNS: the limbic-diencephalic system and the prefrontal cortex (for a review, see Nyberg, Cabeza, & Tulving, 1996; chap. 2, this volume; Squire, 1992). However, there is little agreement on the exact role played by specific limbic and anterior association structures in various memory functions.

Investigations of animal models and human brain lesions have suggested that the hippocampal formation and associated structures (such as the fornix, the entorhinal cortex, the medial dorsal thalamus, and the mammillary bodies) contribute to the formation and maintenance of memories (Squire, 1992). More recently, the view that holds the hippocampus to be the center of the mnemonic universe has been challenged and modified after a number of conflicting results failed to support the claims of exclusive importance of any single limbic structure for normal acquisition and retrieval of memories (see Tulving & Markowitsch, 1997, for a review). As the information from primate (especially human) studies accumulates, the importance of neocortical, specifically prefrontal areas, in mnemonic functions becomes clearer. Within the framework of the hemispheric encoding–retrieval asymmetry (HERA) model developed by Tulving and colleagues, multiple cortical networks participate in the mnemonic act. According to the HERA model, the left prefrontal cortex is viewed as preferentially involved in the encoding of episodic memories, whereas its counterpart on the right is considered dominant in the retrieval of episodically acquired information (see Nyberg et al., 1996, and

Tulving & Markowitsch, 1997, for a review). In young adults, retrieval, in addition to the right prefrontal cortex, activates the anterior cingulate, the cuneus–precuneus, the thalamus, and the brain stem. Encoding, on the average, produces less remarkable prefrontal activation in the left hemisphere and is associated with increased rCBF in temporal and entorhinal cortices (bilateral), the left fusiform gyrus, and the right parahippocampal gyrus (see Tulving & Markowitsch, 1997, for a review). It appears, therefore, that mnemonic processes depend on a wide network of prefrontal and limbic structures that are to various degrees affected by normal aging. The left and right hemispheres apparently interact by transferring across the corpus callosum information necessary for retrieval of memories stored in modality-specific cortices (Hasegawa, Fukushima, Ihara, & Miyashita, 1998).

In contrast to explicit memory that relies on effortful conscious processes, implicit memory involves retention of information without aid of conscious awareness and can be inferred only from changes in performance (rather than reported by the participant). Implicit memory requires virtually no limbic-diencephalic support and depends instead on multiple cortical and subcortical systems (see chap. 2, this volume, for a review). For example, repetition priming of visually presented stimuli produces a deactivation of the secondary visual cortex (BA 19, bilaterally or in the right hemisphere), whereas priming that depends on semantic search involves the inferior prefrontal cortex (see Cabeza & Nyberg, 1997, and chap. 2, this volume, for a review). Procedural learning, such as the acquisition of a motor or perceptual skill, depends on the integrity of premotor, supplementary motor, and secondary visual areas; the neostriatum; the cerebellum; and the connections among them (see Willingham, 1998, for a review).

The majority of studies that have addressed the issue of neuroanatomical correlates of age-related differences in mnemonic performance have concentrated on the hippocampus and adjacent limbic structures, although in some samples, global indices of brain aging, such as WMH ratings, predicted declines in delayed recall, with a mean r of $-.20$ in seven studies and an r of .18 in four studies that controlled for age (Gunning-Dixon & Raz, 1999). Soininen et al. (1994) examined a sample of healthy elderly (mean age = 69 years), half of whom exhibited sufficient memory difficulties to qualify for the diagnosis of age-associated memory impairment. They found that the volume of the right hippocampus correlated with the total score on the Benton Visual Retention Test ($r = .37$) and that the volume of the amygdala correlated ($r = .49$) with performance on another visual memory task (the Heaton Visual Retention Test), whereas verbal memory assessed by the Buschke-Fuld Selective Reminding Test was unrelated to any of the measured volumes.

In another group of carefully screened healthy older adults (range = 55–87 years, mean age = 69 years), the volume of the hippocampal formation, but not the volume of the superior temporal gyrus, predicted performance on delayed (30-min) recall (Golomb et al., 1994). The association between the hippocampal volume and the delayed recall composite measure was $r = .49$ and did not change significantly after controlling for age, sex, and vocabulary scores. A longitudinal follow-up (for about 3.8 years on the average) of healthy older adults (mean age = 68.4 years) drawn from the same population revealed that reduction of the hippocampal size predicted the decline in performance on age-sensitive memory tests (Golomb et a!., 1996). In another longitudinal study, a small sample of healthy middle-aged adults was followed up for 15 to 68 months. In that study, reduction of the whole brain volume predicted decline in verbal memory (correlation with age, $r = .53$), although no measures of the hippocampus were reported (Gur et al., 1998). Semiquantitative indices of hippocampal atrophy derived from MRI scans also predicted poor memory performance in healthy older adults (O'Brien et al., 1997).

Other studies in which similar measures of brain morphology and cognitive performances were used yielded contradictory results. In a sample of 72 healthy men (range = 21–70 years), the correlation between delayed verbal recall and hippocampal volume residualized on cranial size was $r = .17$, whereas the association with an immediate recall measure was somewhat stronger ($r = .25$; E. V. Sullivan et al., 1995). However, for nonverbal memory measures, the results were in the opposite direction ($r = -.21$ for immediate recall and $r = -.25$ for delayed recall). Such a reversal of the expected trend has been observed in one additional sample of 26 healthy elderly individuals (mean age = 71 years): Smaller hippocampi and smaller parahippocampal gyri predicted better verbal delayed free recall ($r = -.55$ and $-.20$, respectively; Köhler et al., 1998). The reasons for such findings are unclear, although it is possible that a sampling artifact cannot be ruled out: Within a very restricted age range, older participants with smaller hippocampi could have been more cognitively intact than their somewhat younger counterparts.

In a sample of 95 healthy adults (range = 19–77 years), who performed a number of tasks of verbal and nonverbal delayed recall and recognition, there was only a weak and statistically nonsignificant association between the composite of delayed explicit memory scores and the volume of the hippocampus ($r = -15$, ns), which was further reduced by controlling for age (standardized regression coefficient, $\beta = 0.07$, ns; Raz, Gunning-Dixon, Head, Dupuis, & Acker, 1998). The volume of prefrontal regions (dorsolateral and orbital) was not associated with explicit memory performance ($r = .08$, ns). A significant correlation between nonverbal explicit memory and prefrontal volume was observed ($r = .23$, $p < .05$), although adjusting for age virtually eliminated it (β = 0.05, *ns*). However, in the same study, the volume of the hippocampal formation emerged as an excellent predictor of memory performance in 8 participants who were older than 65 (r = −.85, p < .01). With addition of the parahippocampal gray matter volume the relationship between brain and cognitive measures grew even stronger (r = −.95, p < .001).

In a study of the effects of context and levels of processing on repetition priming and cued recall (Dorfman & Raz, 1998), 83 healthy adults (range = 18–81 years) were tested in a new association priming paradigm (Graf & Schacter, 1985). The participants studied unrelated word pairs under two elaborative encoding conditions (sentence generation and sentence rating) and then performed tests of word-stem completion and stem-cued recall of the words when the latter were paired with either their old associates or new words. Age-related reduction of performance was observed only in cued recall of the context words encoded under the generation (i.e., deep encoding) condition. This context recall index was associated with the volume of the hippocampus (r = .36, p < .001) and the DLPFC (r = .41, p < .001). Both associations remained significant after controlling for age (β = 0.33 for the DLPFC and β = 0.26 for the hippocampus, both *ps* < .05). However, in that sample, there was no significant correlation between the hippocampal volume and cued recall for 17 participants who were older than 65 (r = .19, *ns*). Performance on priming tasks was unrelated to age and regional brain volumes either in that sample or in the study by Raz, Gunning-Dixon, et al. (1998).

Structural neuroimaging studies provide insights into relations between long-term changes in the brain and cognitive declines. They indicate that significant deterioration of the limbic structures has a negative impact on various aspects of delayed recall and that performance on priming tasks is unrelated to normal age-dependent changes in the brain. These techniques cannot, however, shed light on the question of age-related differences in brain mechanisms underlying the observed cognitive changes. Functional neuroimaging, with its almost real-time capabilities, is better suited for examination of the impact of age-related changes in brain work on cognitive performance. A handful of activation studies have been conducted to investigate the neural underpinnings of age-related declines in memory. Some of these studies used a correlational approach in assessing strength of association between regional metabolic characteristics of the brain and performance on cognitive tasks in a way that is similar to structural neuroimaging investigations.

In one such study, age was shown to load on the same factors as memory for both verbal and pictorial stimuli and resting glucose metabolism indices for the prefrontal cortex and the thalamus (Riege, Metter, Kuhl, & Phelps, 1985). However, another study, which was very similar in its methodology (Haxby et al., 1986), revealed no association between visual memory and resting glucose metabolism in healthy men. In a more recent study, decline in performance on two memory tasks (paired-associate learning and the Brown-Peterson short-term memory task) conducted outside the scanner correlated with age-related declines in rCBF in the hippocampal formation and the thalamus (Eustache et al., 1995). A similar correlation between memory and the hippocampal glucose metabolism index was observed in rhesus monkeys (Eberling, Roberts, Rapp, Tuszynski, & Jagust, 1997).

The rest of the studies reviewed in this section examine the brain substrates of cognitive aging by examining differences in task-dependent activation in real-time cognitive experiments. These studies share several design features that facilitate comparison and integration of the findings. All used an extreme age-group design, with relatively small groups (N = 6–15) of highly cooperative and well-educated younger (mean age = 23–26 years) and older (mean age = 65–71 years) adults. In most of the studies, regional activation patterns were analyzed either with statistical parametric mapping (Friston et al., 1995), which is built on ordinary least squares estimates and general linear models, or latent variable analysis of regional patterns (McIntosh, Bookstein, Haxby, & Grady, 1996), which uses maximum likelihood estimates and a partial least squares approach. Verbal stimuli, minimally elaborative encoding instructions, and forced-choice recognition tests were used in the majority of the studies.

In spite of substantial variability in the observed patterns of activation, tentative conclusions can be drawn from 10 (7 PET, 3 fMRI) studies of encoding. The most consistent finding in the reviewed PET and fMRI studies is that older participants either show reduced activation in the left inferior prefrontal cortex (i.e. area 47; Cabeza, Grady, et al., 1997; Cabeza, McIntosh, Tulving, Nyberg, & Grady, 1997; Carillo et al., 1998; Grady, McIntosh, Rajah, Beig, & Craik, 1998) or fail to activate that area at all (Grady et al., 1995). Age-related reduction of the activation of the anterior cingulate gyrus was also observed (Cabeza, Grady, et al., 1997; Grady et al., 1995; Madden et al., 1996). These findings were relatively consistent across verbal and pictorial stimuli. It is important to note that, in contrast to episodic memory tasks used in the other studies reviewed in this section, Madden et al. (1996) studied encoding in a semantic recognition paradigm. Thus, lack of age differences in prefrontal activation in their study is consistent with the absence of semantic memory deficits in normal aging (Burke & Mackay, 1997; chap. 5, this volume). Madden et al.'s (1996) study is reviewed in greater detail in the section on language elsewhere in this chapter.

The evidence is less consistent and even less conclusive with regard to the role of medial temporal activation in age-related memory changes.

Although in two studies of memory for pictorial stimuli (Corkin et al., 1998; Grady et al., 1995) older participants evidenced a significantly weaker activation in the hippocampus and the parahippocampal gyrus, in another sample, words elicited comparable activation in the hippo-campi of the old and the young participants (Schacter, Savage, Alpert, Rauch, & Albert, 1996). In yet another sample, older participants displayed a significant increase in the medial temporal activation (especially in the right hemisphere), regardless of the level of processing (Grady et al., 1998). Verbal recognition in a forced-choice paradigm produced comparable ventromedial temporal activation in younger and older adults (Cabeza, Anderson, Mangels, Nyberg, & Houle, 1999). To complicate the picture even further, in a recent fMRI study of verbal-cued recall in healthy older adults who differed in genetic risk for AD (ApoE ε4 carriers vs. noncar-riers), the at-risk persons showed a considerably wider spread of medial temporal activation than did the controls (Bookheimer et al., 1998). Thus, one cannot conclude that aging brings with it decrease in task-related brain work. Older people in general and those predisposed to age-related pathology may use medial temporal structures in ways that are different from those of younger people.

In addition, age-related differences (mainly decreases) in activation were observed in dorsolateral prefrontal areas BA 6 (Cabeza, Grady, et al., 1997; Cabeza, McIntosh, et al., 1997), BA 10 (Madden et al., 1996), BA 45 (Grady et al., 1995), or BA 46 (Cabeza, Grady, et al., 1997). In some samples, older participants evidenced weaker activation of the visual association areas (i.e., the fusiform and/or the lingual gyrus; Cabeza, Grady, et al., 1997; Grady et al., 1995). Other studies, however, revealed equal activation across age groups in the same regions, BA 19 and BA 37 (Cabeza, McIntosh, et al., 1997; Corkin et al., 1998; Madden, Turkington, et al., 1999), as well as the dorsolateral prefrontal cortex, BA 10 and BA 45 (Madden, Turkington, et al., 1999).

Not all activation observed in a PET study reflects brain work beneficial to cognitive performance. Failure of older participants to show relative deactivation of the insula during encoding was first reported as an inci-dental finding (Madden et al., 1996) but was later replicated (Cabeza et al., 1997). In the latter study, the magnitude of activation in the insula during encoding was negatively correlated ($r = -.56$) with delayed recall in both age groups (Cabeza, Grady, et al., 1997).

The pattern of age-related differences in activation during recall and recognition of verbal and pictorial stimuli is less clear than the one observed during encoding. It appears that whereas the younger partici-pants, in accordance with the HERA model, show a consistent increase in rCBF in the right prefrontal regions (Cabeza, Grady, et al., 1997; Grady et al., 1995; Schacter et al., 1996), their older counterparts either activate the opposite hemisphere (Madden, Turkington, et al., 1999) or activate both prefrontal regions at once (Cabeza, Grady, et al., 1997; Grady et al., 1995). It is possible that greater involvement of the left prefrontal circuits in retrieval of information by older adults is due to the increase in perceived difficulty of the task in that age group. It has been shown that objectively more complex retrieval operations invoke more pronounced left prefrontal activation in young participants (Nolde, Johnson, & Raye, 1998).

Madden and colleagues reported an interesting insight into a possible mechanism of age-related differences in task-dependent brain activation. In recognition memory tasks, the distribution of the reaction time (RT) can be decomposed into Gaussian (basic feature-detection and response-selection process) and exponential (task-related decision processes) components (see Luce, 1986, for a review). A reanalysis of previously reported RT and rCBF data (Madden, Turkington, et al., 1999) suggests significant age differences in the deployment of brain resources. Specifically, in the younger participants engaged in retrieval of episodic information, activation of the DLPFC (BA 10) predicts the speed of basic processing (μ), whereas in the older people, the same region is also associated with task-specific decision processes (Madden, Gottlob, et al., in press). Thus, it appears that older brains have to recruit additional resources to manage the executive overhead of the task. It is unclear whether such an adjustment is of compensatory value, as it relies on the very circuitry (the prefrontal association cortex) that is hit the hardest by the adverse influences of aging.

Age-related differences in the distribution of activation may be influenced by task difficulty. In a verbal recall task, bilateral increases in rCBF in the anterior prefrontal cortex were observed only among the younger participants, whereas the older adults evidenced a more posterior frontal lobe activation focus (Schacter et al., 1996). These differences in topography of activation were more apparent when retrieval was difficult. In a task that produces small age differences, such as recognition of pictorial stimuli, equally substantial left and right prefrontal activation was observed, regardless of the participant's age (Corkin et al., 1998).

No age-related differences in hippocampal or parahippocampal activation during retrieval were observed in any of the reviewed studies. In some samples, recognition or recall of visually presented stimuli evoked activation of the ventral and posterior association areas 19, 20, 22, 37, 39, or 40 (Bäckman et al., 1997; Cabeza, Grady, et al., 1997; Madden et al., 1996), although there was little consistency across studies in the configuration of those posterior activation patterns.

Age-related differences in mnemonic performance may not stem exclusively from the underactivation of specific circuits but from the alteration in patterns of connectivity among them (Cabeza, McIntosh, et al.,

1997). In a study of paired-associate verbal learning, younger participants showed a cluster of positive interactions involving the left prefrontal cortex during encoding but evidenced a similar cluster of positive interactions involving the right prefrontal cortex during recall, as predicted by the HERA model. In the older participants, that pattern was less clear. They exhibited a mixture of left and right prefrontal interactions at encoding and bilaterally positive interactions during recall. A recent report from the same laboratory (Rajah, McIntosh, & Grady, 1998) suggests that at encoding, younger participants may establish more extensive bilateral positive inputs from ventral extrastriatal to medial temporal areas, whereas in elderly individuals, a similar pattern is observed only in the left hemisphere. Because virtually all functional neuroimaging studies of age-related differences in memory are conducted on extreme age groups, it is unclear how and at what part of the life span that pattern switch occurs.

In addition to these studies, which mostly focus on brain activation during episodic memory tasks, a recent study addressed the issue of differential aging of other mnemonic functions. It has been hypothesized that memory for source of information and the temporal–spatial context in which it was presented, is more sensitive to aging than the memory for the target information itself and that such differential mnemonic deficits are due to differential age-related declines in the prefrontal regions (see Spencer & Raz, 1995, for a review). Age-related differences in brain activation elicited by recognition of items in a visually presented word list and the retrieval of their relative temporal order (recency discrimination) were examined by Cabeza et al. (1999). In the younger participants of that study, recency discrimination (as opposed to item recognition) was accompanied by greater activation of the right prefrontal cortex (BA 10), the parieto-occipital cortex (BA 39), the precuneus (BA 19), and the cerebellum. When the same comparison was conducted in the older participants, these regions showed no significant blood flow changes. In contrast, the older participants showed greater activation of the left prefrontal cortex (BA 10) and the right cerebellum when they were engaged in item retrieval than when they performed recency discrimination. Thus, the older participants showed not only a more diffuse (bilateral prefrontal) activation at item recognition but also a lack of task-related increase in activation of the regions associated with temporal order memory (Petrides, 1991).

Two methodological factors—sample size and sample selection procedures—may need to be taken into account in interpreting the summarized findings. For example, in some samples, no age differences in rCBF during baseline were observed (Bäckman et al., 1997); other studies reported CBF differences but found no differences in the total cerebral volume (Madden et al., 1996; Madden, Turkington, et al., 1999). Because, as discussed elsewhere in this chapter, both blood flow and brain volume are typically reduced even in healthy elderly individuals, it appears that the participants in those samples could have been somewhat atypical, although the impact of their atypicality on the reported results is unclear.

Working Memory. Multiple studies have demonstrated that a significant proportion of age-related declines in cognitive performance can be explained by deterioration of working memory, the ability to process information while maintaining intermediate products, goals, and associated strategies of processing online (Moscovitch & Winocur, 1992; Salthouse, 1994). The notions of what constitutes working memory and how it should be measured are surprisingly diverse. A classic view of the construct holds that working memory is a system composed of a modality-free central executive and modality-specific subordinate modules: the articulatory loop and the visual–spatial sketch pad (Baddeley, 1994). Baddeley's model of working memory was developed and tested almost exclusively in dual-task experiments. In these studies, the index of working memory performance is the change in the primary task challenged by a concurrent secondary task, presumably competing for the same resources. In a typical cognitive aging study, different measures of working memory are used. Most of them are variations on a loaded span paradigm, in which participants are presented with progressively increasing sets of stimuli that they are asked to hold in mind for a relatively brief time while performing simple cognitive manipulations on the whole set or its members. In the animal literature, to add to the confusion, *working memory* is a term virtually identical to *short-term memory*, as used in the human cognitive literature. It presumes maintaining information across a delay that is not necessarily filled with any manipulation of the stored material (Goldman-Rakic, 1987). Finally, with the advent of functional neuroimaging, many studies on working memory were carried out within a framework of the "*n*-back" paradigm, in which a particpant is presented with a stream of stimuli and is asked, at designated trials, to report a stimulus presented *n* trials beforehand. The relations among all of the described indices of working memory in either college sophomores or healthy older adults is unknown, which limits the generalizability of the findings reported in specific studies.

Earlier models of working memory were derived from laboratory experiments in nonhuman primates, and human activation studies emphasized its almost exclusive dependence on polymodal prefrontal association areas (see Cabeza & Nyberg, 1997, and Goldman-Rakic, 1987, for a review). However, more recent data suggest that modality-specific secondary association cortices play an important role in supporting this resource (see Cabeza & Nyberg, 1997, for a review; see also Cohen et al.,

1994; D'Esposito et al., 1995; E. E. Smith, Jonides, & Koeppe, 1996) and that coactivation of anterior and posterior association cortices may be critical for maintaining performance during an increased load on working memory (Klingberg, O'Sullivan, & Roland, 1997).

Although older people consistently show moderate deficits on a variety of loaded span working memory tasks (Salthouse, 1994; Verhaeghen et al., 1993), the neurocognitive mechanisms underlying age differences in working memory are still unclear. In light of the central role of working memory in models of cognitive aging, the literature on cortical activation patterns associated with performance on working memory tasks is surprisingly sparse. Two structural MRI investigations of the neural substrates of age-related declines in working memory (Head, Raz, Gunning-Dixon, & Acker, 1999; Raz, Gunning-Dixon, et al., 1998) revealed significant, albeit weak, links between verbal working memory and the volume of the prefrontal cortex. In both samples, a composite of the absolute computation and listening spans (Salthouse, Mitchell, Skovronek, & Babcock, 1990) correlated with the volume of the DLPFC ($r = .27$, $p < .01$, and $r = .37$, $p < .001$, respectively). However, adjustment for age attenuated the strength of these associations to $\beta = 0.12$ and $\beta = 0.14$, respectively, both *ns*. In addition, age-related differences in nonverbal working memory operationalized by two tasks that required short-term storage and manipulation of visual images were associated with the volume of the fusiform gyros ($r = .25$, $p < .05$), and the prefrontal cortex ($r = .35$, $p < .001$). After adjustment for age, these associations were reduced to $\beta = .12$ and $\beta = 0.16$, respectively, both *ns*.

Four functional neuroimaging studies of brain substrates of age-related differences in working memory have been conducted. Hartley et al. (1998) examined age-related differences in performance on tasks that required maintaining online for a brief period information about either the identity or the location of an object. They found that as the load on working memory increased from one to two stimuli, performance declined. On the identity information task, the load-dependent decrement was equivalent in two age groups, whereas on location information tasks, older participants showed steeper load-dependent declines. The rCBF changes measured with PET revealed equivalent bilateral parietal activation during the identity task in both age groups; however, the prefrontal activation was greater in the elderly participants.

Rypma and D'Esposito (1998) used fMRI to investigate age-related differences in brain activation associated with working memory. Healthy adults performed a recognition task consisting of encoding of two- or six-letter sets, retention delay, and probe recognition. Both age groups showed activation of ventral and dorsal prefrontal, anterior cingulate, and posterior parietal cortices and the basal ganglia in all tasks. At encoding, activation was set size sensitive in the older but not the younger participants, whereas at other stages, activation was sensitive to memory set size in both groups. During retention of a larger set, activation extended into a larger region (posterior DLPFC) in the younger but not the older participants.

Only preliminary data are available on age differences in performance on an auditory *n*-back working memory task. In an fMRI study (Subaiya, Salat, Coshow, Nesbit, & Janowsky, 1998), two healthy elderly participants (aged 72 and 91) activated the same areas (BA 9 and BA 46), as did their younger counterparts. However, in the younger participants, the magnitude of activation in those areas increased in response to increased task load, whereas the older participants showed no detectable increase in regional perfusion.

Cortical mechanisms of age-related differences on a delayed matching to sample task were examined by Grady, McIntosh, Bookstein, et al. (1998). In both groups, increase in delay resulted in greater activation in the prefrontal cortex and reduction in rCBF to the extrastriatal cortex. However, hippocampal activation was observed only in the younger participants, and right prefrontal activation in older participants was smaller than in their younger counterparts. Task-related activation in the left prefrontal cortex and left visual association regions was weaker in the younger participants. When the relationship between cortical activation patterns and response speed was examined in both age groups, slower response times were associated with increased recruitment of posterior association areas, regardless of age. However, increased bilateral prefrontal activation predicted faster responses in the younger participants but slower responses in their older counterparts, with younger participants showing greater activation in the right prefrontal area and older participants activating the left hemispheric foci. Thus, different aspects of the delayed-response task appear to be reflected in activation patterns of younger and older people. Whereas activation patterns may reflect greater investment in stimulus-related aspects of the tasks in younger people, activation may signify recruitment of resources for keeping up with general attentional demands in older people.

As indicated by the studies discussed in the beginning of this section, multiple brain regions are involved in performance of even relatively simple working memory tasks. The size, location, and magnitude of activation of these regions varies across the life span, but no coherent pattern of age-related differences has been discerned. It must be noted that although the working memory tasks used in the three studies of activation and that although working memory in aging requires recruitment of working memory resources for maintaining the stimuli "off-line" during the delay, these requirements are probably weaker than those imposed on participants in working memory tasks that do show substantial age-related differences (Salthouse, 1994). The main difference among those tasks is in the emphasis on storage versus simultaneity of storage and processing. Tasks designed to tap into the latter aspect of working memory produce reliable age differences, whereas measures based on simple span retention and primary memory are less sensitive to aging (Verhaeghen et al., 1993).

If the central executive component of working memory is preferentially affected by aging, greater emphasis on that aspect of working memory in future neuroimaging studies may help to bring more coherence to this field of research. Age-related deficits in working memory may stem from declining function of the dopaminergic system, specifically the prefrontal D_1 receptors that are affected by aging (De Keyser et al., 1990). Such an association is especially plausible because activity of the dopaminergic receptors, both D_1 (U. Muller, von Cramon, & Pollmann, 1998) and D_2 (Kimberg, D'Esposito, & Farah, 1997; Luciana, Depue, Arbisi, & Leon, 1992; Zarahn et al., 1998), plays an important role in executive functions subserved by the prefrontal cortex. In aging monkeys, administration of low doses of D_1 agonists improves working memory (Cai & Arnsten, 1997). Furthermore, it has been suggested that optimal catecholaminergic (Arnsten, 1997) and cholinergic (Furey et al., 1997) activity in the prefrontal cortex may be the key to superior performance on executive and working memory tasks. Thus, impaired interaction between dopaminergic and noradrenergic systems (rather than a deficit in either of them) may cause age-related declines in working memory and in more complex cognitive activities that depend on it. This impairment may or may not be more acute in individuals who experience greater shrinkage of the prefrontal cortex and who show less efficient metabolism of glucose in the affected areas.

Executive Functions. Although the study of memory has been traditionally a central topic in cognitive gerontology, a growing body of research reveals that many age-related deficits in memory may stem from declines in the executive functions (see R. L. West, 1996 for a review). The term *executive* is somewhat amorphous and ill-defined. It encompasses a broad range of cognitive skills, such as monitoring one's recent and past performance, generating future goals, inhibiting prepotent overlearned responses, and alternating behavioral patterns in response to feedback.

A classic example of an executive task is the Wisconsin Card Sorting Test (WCST; Heaton, Chelune, Talley, Kay, & Curtis, 1993). In the WCST, participants are asked to classify and sort stimuli on one of three characteristics, to discover changes in sorting rules using feedback, and to alter their responses accordingly. Performance on the WCST is assessed by several indices, including the total number of errors, the number of perseverative errors (i.e., persisting in failed strategy in spite of negative feedback), and the number of classification categories successfully completed.

Age differences in WCST scores are comparable in magnitude with those observed in free recall. For example, in three independent samples (ns = 100–148) of healthy adults (range = 18–81 years), the strength of association between the indices of perseverative behavior on the WCST and age ranged from $r = .37$ to $r = .51$, corresponding to the effect size (d) of up to a full standard deviation (Raz, 1999a). Nonhuman primates also exhibit age-related increase in perseverative errors (Lai, Moss, Killiany, Rosene, & Herndon, 1995; Moore, Killiany, Rosene, & Moss, 1998).

Empirical evidence and computer models suggest that executive functions depend on the integrity of the prefrontal cortex (Kimberg & Farah, 1993; Stuss & Benson, 1984). Functional neuroimaging studies demonstrate the importance of the DLPFC and the inferior prefrontal cortex in performance on the WCST (e.g., Berman et al., 1995; Ragland et al., 1997; Tien, Schlaepfer, Orr, & Pearlson, 1998), whereas lesion studies indicate that intact orbitofrontal cortex is necessary for execution of cognitive operations involved in altering task strategies in response to feedback (Freedman & Oscar-Berman, 1986; Oscar-Berman, McNamara, & Freedman, 1991). Furthermore, a specific aspect of performance on the WCST (set shifting) activates almost exclusively the inferior regions of the DLPFC (BA 44 and BA 45), with the activation magnitude proportionate to the number of dimensions available for classification (Konishi et al., 1998). When multiple aspects of the executive tasks (e.g., the WCST)—such as inhibition of prepotent response, goal monitoring, and response shifting, as well as maintenance of instructions and strategic information in memory—are taken into account, it is hardly surprising that performance on those tasks depends on a widely distributed network of cortical circuits that cover the prefrontal association as well as the posterior association areas and the hippocampal formation (S. W. Anderson, Damasio, Jones, & Tranel, 1991; Berman et al., 1995; Corcoran & Upton, 1993; Eslinger & Grattan, 1993; Tien et al., 1998).

Structural neuroimaging investigations of age-related differences in executive functions have yielded inconclusive results. In a sample of 95 healthy adults (range = 19–77 years), a reduction in the volume of prefrontal gray matter (the DLPFC and the orbitofrontal regions) was associated with an increase in perseverative behavior on the WCST ($r = -.42$, $p < .001$; Raz, Gunning-Dixon, et al., 1998). After controlling for age, the association remained significant ($\beta = -0.26$, $p < .02$). In an independent sample of 138 healthy adults (range = 18–81 years), the relationship between the prefrontal volume and perseveration was observed again ($r = -.40$, $p < .001$). However, in that sample, adding age to the regression equation resulted in a weaker and statistically nonsignificant association ($\beta = -0.17$, $p < .10$; Head et al., 1999). In 10 studies of healthy aging, the mean correlation between assorted indices of executive functions and

WMH ratings was $r = -.30$; in 7 studies in which age was partialed out, the mean correlation was $r = -.35$ (Gunning-Dixon & Raz, 1999). Notably, participants with clinically significant leukoaraiosis were removed from Raz et al.'s (1998a) sample. Thus, it is possible that age-related alterations of white matter and age-related loss of gray matter volume are relatively independent in their contribution to the decline of the executive functions.

As discussed above, age-related declines in executive functions may stem from age-related neurochemical changes in the basal ganglia. In accordance with this hypothesis, a reduction in the availability of dopamine D_2 receptors predicts difficulties in inhibiting a prepotent response in the Stroop Color-Word Test and the total number of categories achieved on WCST (age-adjusted partial correlations, $pr = .38$ and $-.42$, respectively; Volkow et al., 1998).

The question of the neural basis of age-related differences in executive functions has been addressed in only one functional neuroimaging (PET) study (Nagahama et al., 1997). In that experiment, rCBF was assessed in 6 young (mean age = 22 years) and 6 older (mean age = 68 years) adults during the performance of a Modified Card Sorting Test (MCST), a task that is similar to the WCST in most respects, except for lesser uncertainty in cognitive demands. In a subtraction design, activation on the MCST was compared with that on the number-matching task, which features the cards of the MCST without the demands for formulation of rules and strategy shifting. As predicted, the comparison yielded significant activation foci in the left DLPFC (BA 9, BA 10, and BA 46) as well as the left angular gyros (BA 39) and the left cuneus (BA 18) in both age groups. In addition, the younger participants showed significant activation of the left-hemisphere regions: premotor cortex (BA 6), the posterior parietal cortex (BA 7 and BA 40), and the fusiform and lingual gyri (BA 19), as well as the left cerebellum.

A notable finding in this study was that in the areas of activation that were common to both age groups, the elderly participants evidenced lower magnitudes of activation than their younger counterparts, even after adjustment for individual differences in global CBF. Moreover, the magnitude of activation in the left DLPFC (BA 46/44), the right parahip-pocampal gyrus, and left prestriate cortex (BA 18 and BA 19) was negatively correlated with the number of perseverative errors (e.g., $r = -.71$ for the prefrontal focus of activation). However, in this sample, the number of perseverative errors was unusually highly correlated with age ($r = .77$). It is, therefore, unclear whether the association between perseveration and reduced activation was confounded by the age-related reduction of rCBF in the given ROIs.

Inhibition has been considered one of the key notions in discussions of age-related differences in working memory and higher cognitive functions (see chap. 5, this volume, for a review), and the prefrontal (chiefly, orbitofrontal) cortex has been widely considered the substrate of inhibitory control. Very few studies have addressed the question of brain correlates of age-related differences in inhibition. In a recent PET investigation, participants were required to inhibit a frequent and established "yes" response in a verbal recognition task in favor of a "no" response. Activation of the left DLPFC was associated with higher inhibitory demands in younger but not older participants (Marshuetz, Jonides, Smith, Reuter-Lorentz, & Koeppe, 1998).

The executive control of cognitive processes is a necessary component of virtually all cognitive activity, and its breakdown may underlie many of the age-related deficits in information processing when modality-specific functions are still intact. A good illustration of such a situation is the case of age-related differences in mental imagery. The ability to generate and manipulate mental images depends on multiple distributed cortical circuits, including the anterior cingulate, fusiform, inferior temporal, occipital, posterior parietal, and prefrontal cortices (Kosslyn, 1994). Most of the cognitive operations involved in mental imagery are negatively affected by aging (Briggs, Raz, & Marks, in press; Dror & Kosslyn, 1994; S. H. Johnson & Rybash, 1993), probably because of their reliance on age-sensitive cognitive resources such as working memory.

The relationship between performance on several mental imagery tasks and age-related differences in regional cortical volumes was examined in a sample of 60 healthy adults of a broad age range (Raz, in press). The participants performed a simple perception task and three imagery tasks with two-dimensional letter stimuli. The mental imagery tasks included image generation, mental rotation of the image, and a combination of image generation and rotation. The results revealed no associations between performance on the mental imagery tasks and volumes of the brain regions that are hypothesized to subserve image generation and manipulation (median $r = -.07$ for speed measures, median $r = -.09$ for accuracy measures). In contrast, the volume of the DLPFC was correlated with speed and accuracy of cognitive performance ($r = -.24$ to $-.42$ for speed measures, $r = .32$ to .41 for accuracy measures). An amalgamated index of speed and accuracy of mental imagery performance was significantly associated with the DLPFC volume after controlling for age ($\beta = -0.43$, $p < .001$). In addition, the path analyses showed that in that sample, age-related differences in working memory affected mental imagery performance independently from the effects of DLPFC shrinkage.

In summary, age-related shrinkage and reduced activation of the prefrontal cortical circuits are associated with a variety of errors in the executive control of cognitive performance. The mechanisms underlying these deficits and the relationship between executive functions, working memory, and their cortical substrates are yet to be elucidated.

Language. Verbal skills assessed by tests of word knowledge and verbal reasoning are considered virtually age invariant, although age-related differences have been reported in more subtle aspects of language processing (see chap. 6, this volume, for a review). Very little is known about neural substrates of age-related differences in linguistic functions. It is unclear whether declines in performance reflect changes in general resources such as speed and working memory or in specific deterioration of brain circuitry responsible for language processing. An optimistic belief in the lack of age effects on language may be responsible for the dearth of neuroimaging studies of age differences in that domain, although the results of recent investigations that used measures of linguistic competence may temper that optimism. For instance, a longitudinal study of a small sample of healthy middle-aged adults showed that reduction of temporal lobe volumes was associated with mild but statistically significant worsening of performance on language tests (Gur et al., 1998).

In a PET study of age differences in verbal memory discussed elsewhere in this chapter, Madden et al. (1996) also addressed age differences in neural response to some aspects of language processing. When the task required extraction of semantic information from visually presented words, all the participants exhibited a significant increase in rCBF in the extrastriate visual areas (BA 18 and BA 19). Introduction of visual noise into the stimuli resulted in equivalent rCBF increases in the lingual gyrus in both age groups. In contrast, only the younger participants exhibited increases in activation of the anterior cingulate, prefrontal, and inferior temporal cortices during encoding of word versus nonword letter strings.

These results suggest that neural mechanisms responsible for semantic processing and filtering of verbal information are unaffected by age, whereas older adults may experience difficulty in recruiting cortical resources for processing of novel pseudolinguistic stimuli. However, given the extreme shortage of data at the time of this writing, it would be highly imprudent to draw any conclusions about neural substrates of age-related differences in language.

BRAIN SUBSTRATES OF COGNITIVE AGING: SUMMARY AND CONCLUSIONS

Integration of information across relatively few studies in a rapidly developing field is an undertaking that challenges one's tolerance for uncertainty, for any new piece of evidence may lead to a radical change in conclusions. Nevertheless, I hope that a set of preliminary conclusions offered here will provide some guidance for future research on brain substrates of cognitive aging.

1. Aging is associated with numerous alterations of brain structure and function. Age-related changes that presumably affect the total volume of the brain and the integrity of the white matter predict global decline of cognitive functions. However, the shape of the described associations is unclear. It is possible that linearity is not a viable assumption and that age-related cognitive deficits are expressed only after a certain threshold of structural deterioration has been reached. Statistical tests of significance of nonlinear components are short on power and the samples used in neuroimaging research are notoriously small, hence the belief in linearity is rarely challenged. Nevertheless, at least for describing the association between white matter integrity, age, and cognition, a threshold model may be a preferred one.

2. Multiple neuroanatomical, neurochemical, and metabolic indicators converge on the notion that brain aging proceeds in selective fashion, taking the heaviest toll on the prefrontal cortex and on subcortical monoaminergic nuclei to which it is connected via a dense network of projections. The extent of age-related differences in the volume of the prefrontal cortex is comparable to the magnitude of other profound and well-established features of aging such as decreased lung capacity, reduced skin elasticity, drop in maximum oxygen uptake, and hearing loss (Balin, 1994). Lesser, though significant, deterioration occurs in the posterior association areas and the neostriatum, whereas the primary sensory regions remain largely spared. An interesting problem in the context of differential aging is presented by the hippocampal formation, which appears only mildly affected by normal aging. Because of a well-established role of the hippocampus as a reliable marker of AD pathology, it is plausible that the dissociation of prefrontal versus limbic declines lies in the distinction between physiologic and pathologic aging. Specifically, the deterioration of the prefrontal cortex may be characteristic of a normal aging process, whereas the atrophy of the hippocampus and the entorhinal cortex may be specific pathological features of early AD, especially of its genetic variant.

3. Age-related slowing of mental processing that has been posited as the most fundamental factor in cognitive aging may be associated with the deterioration of the white matter through demyelination and the increase in the burden of vascular lesions. Only two functional neuroimaging studies have addressed the question of the neural mechanisms of this important characteristic of the aging information-processing systems. Their findings lead to an intriguing possibility that age-related slowing may reflect the need of older brains to recruit additional resources to manage the executive overhead of otherwise simple and largely automatic tasks. Thus, a localized neural deficit in resource-managing brain circuits may be expressed as a generalized cognitive impairment.

4. The way the brain processes information to execute simple perception and attention allocation operations does not appear to vary with age. However, functional neuroimaging evidence suggests that the magnitude of the task-related hemodynamic response produced by the same cortical circuits may be lower in older persons in comparison with their younger counterparts.

5. Although structural and metabolic declines of the limbic regions and the prefrontal cortex are weakly associated with declines in performance on some memory tasks, this association may be more substantial in cases of significant memory impairment. Functional neuroimaging studies reveal that aging is associated with quantitative and qualitative differences in brain activation during encoding and retrieval stages of mnemonic processing. In general agreement with the HERA model, younger persons activate the inferior prefrontal–orbitofrontal cortex at encoding and the right prefrontal cortex during retrieval of episodic information. Nonetheless, healthy older persons usually fail to show such a well-defined pattern, exhibiting a more widespread task-related activation, sometimes of a lesser magnitude. Those expanded, less focused activation patterns may reflect age-related reorganization of system resource management (Grady et al., 1995). In addition to reduced and less focused activation in the areas necessary for specific information processing, older persons tend to activate cortical regions that are usually not activated or that are suppressed in younger adults during task performance.

Although the literature on the neural mechanisms of implicit memory in aging is very sparse, no differences in brain activity related to priming have been reported. In conjunction with the findings from structural MRI studies, we can conclude that when age-related deficits in priming are observed, they stem from factors unrelated to the specifics of information processing. Rather, they reflect a general failure of attentional or executive processes, such as reality monitoring and working memory management.

6. Surprisingly little attention has been paid to the fundamental age-sensitive domain of cognitive activity: working memory. Structural MRI data suggest that age-related shrinkage of the prefrontal cortex predicts reduction in working memory indices. However, activation studies suggest that older adults exhibit an increase rather than a decrease in prefrontal activation on working memory tasks. It is possible that older adults may have to recruit greater nonspecific or "domain-general" resources (Köhler, Moscovitch, Winocur, Houle, & McIntosh, 1998) to tackle an incrementally more difficult task.

7. Behavioral findings reveal negative effects of age on executive functions, yet data on the cerebral substrates of those declines are very scarce. Age-related shrinkage of the prefrontal cortex and deterioration of the dopaminergic system predict poor control of performance on tasks

that require inhibition of prepotent responses and planning and flexibility of strategic control. Older people show reduced blood flow in brain areas that are activated by executive tasks in younger people. Whether such a reduction is driven by specific aspects of executive tasks (e.g., inhibitory demands) remains to be seen. It appears, however, that age-related declines in various aspects of the prefrontal cortex are specifically related to well-established deficits in executive functions. Further examination of that relationship with a wider variety of psychometrically crafted measures will help determine the reliability of these intriguing findings. One can cautiously generalize from functional neuroimaging studies in various cognitive domains that the aging information-processing systems cope with decline in task-specific resources by broadening their recruitment base. Such an adjustment, however, may fall short of its projected compensatory value, as it relies on the very circuitry (the prefrontal association cortex) that is hit the hardest by the adverse influences of aging.

8. A survey of the efforts to understand the neural basis of age-related changes in cognition reveals that although providing interesting insights into the topic, neuroimaging investigations have been only modestly successful in explaining age-related variability in cognitive performance. Indeed, a substantial part of the variance in cognitive proficiency may be explained by calendar age alone. The meaning of age as a variable, however, varies among the studies because of the differences in criteria for selecting participants.

Because no two samples of human participants are identical, the general constraints and confounds imposed by these discrepancies must be explicitly treated in the studies of brain substrates of cognitive aging. Because changes in brain structure and function that characterize normal aging are also observed in age-related pathological conditions such as depression, hypertension, Parkinson's disease, diabetes mellitus, and cardiovascular disease, the validity of any study is limited by insufficiently rigorous screening. New confounding variables may appear as the investigations progress. For example, estrogen and progesterone supplements, unknown in the classic era of cognitive aging research, are now being administered to millions of postmenopausal women in developed countries (S. R. Johnson, 1998). The dosage, components, and duration of treatment, as well as women's adherence to the medication regimen, vary widely and are not easy to control. On the basis of studies in rodents, there is a certain degree of enthusiasm about estrogen as a neuroprotector, although experimental and clinical support in humans is still meager (Birge, 1996; van Duijn, 1997). Nonetheless, sex hormones have been demonstrated to affect the pattern of task-induced activation (Berman et al., 1997) and hormonal supplements may slow down age-related cognitive declines as well as age-related brain changes (R. Schmidt et al., 1996).

Studies on nonhuman primates show that in predicting cognitive declines, menopause status appears more important than calendar age. Post- and perimenopausal monkeys performed significantly worse than did age-matched premenopausal controls on a delayed-response task (Roberts, Gilardi, Lasley, & Rapp, 1997). It is clear that in spite of all the practical difficulties, the influence of hormonal therapy should be taken into account in studies concerned with age-related differences in neural bases of cognition.

An additional source of age-related variance that has not yet drawn full attention of researchers of cognitive aging is the influence of a host of variables associated with age-related alterations in the immune function. Recent findings highlighting the role of glucocorticoids in cognitive aging (Lupien et al., 1998) may be the harbingers of important developments in the understanding of age-related changes in cognition. Future research in the rapidly developing field of psychoneuroimmunology may produce important insights into yet-unexplained sources of age-related cognitive declines (Pierpaoli, 1998).

Because of the complexities of these confounding factors, research on the cognitive neuroscience of aging should seek exponents of healthy aging in its purest form, no matter how rare these persons are in the general population. In this sense, the goals of cognitive neuroscientists may diverge from those of the practitioners and researchers in the field of geriatric medicine who are interested in the typical elderly patient. Even in a carefully screened cohort, there will be people who are destined to develop one of the pathological age-related conditions and who enter the study while they are in a prodromal phase of their disease. Thus, it would be prudent to assume that the findings summarized in this chapter reflect a certain degree of negative overestimation.

9. Constraints on the application of functional neuroimaging techniques to the investigation of aging and cognition must be reexamined. These constraints include age-related changes in cerebral cytoarchitecture, vasculature, neurochemistry, and cerebral hemodynamics. Attention to these basic changes in brain physiology is especially crucial in studies that use neuroimaging techniques that depend on indices of blood flow. Although the effects of global and regional atrophy on "resting" cerebral metabolism have been demonstrated almost at the inception of modern functional neuroimaging (Chawluk et al., 1987, 1990; Schlageter et al., 1987) and have been successfully applied in some studies of cerebral metabolism (Meltzer et al., 1996), individual and age-related differences in regional volumes are simply ignored. Adjustment for total brain volume (Madden et al., 1996, 1997) is a step in the right direction but is still an inadequate solution to a problem that can be created by differential regional aging of the brain. It would be unrealistic, however, to expect a

simple linear relationship between age-related shrinkage of specific brain regions and complex differences in the patterns of activation observed in comparisons of extreme age groups. Reduction of hemodynamic response in a specific location may translate into a seemingly generalized deficit in brain work, and establishing well-defined connections in the maze of cortical and subcortical interactions is a daunting if not insurmountable challenge.

10. Reliance on the logic of cognitive subtraction on the basis of a questionable assumption of pure insertion of cognitive components is a serious problem in functional neuroimaging studies (Friston et al., 1996). Such an approach dictates blocking similar stimuli for each of the factors used in subtraction, integrating rCBF or oxygen use changes across several trials, and ignoring the interactions among the blocks of trials. Blocked presentation of stimuli similar to the one used in PET and fMRI studies may tap into cognitive processes that are different from those engaged in cognitive studies, in which trials are interspersed in a randomized fashion (M. K. Johnson et al., 1997). Although multivariate and univariate factorial designs were proposed to alleviate the latter problem in PET imaging (Friston et al., 1996; Fletcher et al., 1996), a recently introduced technique that takes full advantage of the almost real-time speed of fMRI can eliminate both types of problems. In a new approach, trial-based (or event-related) fMRI, regional hemodynamic response of the brain is time-locked to a single stimulus presentation without a need to integrate over multitrial blocks (Zarahn, Aguirre, & D'Esposito, 1997). As the randomized stimulus presentation becomes possible in trial-based fMRI, we may be able to resolve at least some of the discrepancies among the previously reported findings.

11. Finally, an important constraint on the validity of the offered conclusions lies in the design of the studies from which the evidence has been derived. The preponderance of the results summarized here were derived from cross-sectional investigations. Besides incidental and inevitable inclusion of participants who carry latent pathology, such studies are affected by cohort effects. Specifically, people born 60 years earlier have been exposed to a somewhat different biological environment since birth and probably in utero. Secular trends in stature, brain weight, onset of puberty, and many other biologic indices are well documented (e.g., Haug, 1987; Miller & Corsellis, 1977), although they are unlikely to account for a substantial part of observed age-related differences, especially for the differential ones (for a discussion of this issue, see Raz et al., 1997). Nonetheless, cohort effects present an acknowledged threat to the validity of cross-sectional studies and can be ruled out only by a longitudinal design. Because of the careful control of environment and standardized animal husbandry procedures, cohort effects are unlikely to occur in

nonhuman primates, thus making them a valuable model for cognitive aging research.

Significant progress has been made in the understanding of brain substrates of cognitive aging since the publication of the first edition of this handbook. The discipline of cognitive neuroscience of aging is now at the stage of initial data accumulation. The small number of studies and their methodological heterogeneity still preclude a rigorous quantitative evaluation (i.e., meta-analysis). The number of participants per study is so small that powerful statistical tools, customary in cognitive aging studies, cannot be applied. Nonetheless, with the spread of neuroimaging technology, it is easy to remain an optimist and to foster a hope that when the third edition of this handbook goes into print, we will be able to discuss the brain mechanisms behind the aging of cognition with much greater clarity. The old admonition that "more research is needed" has never been more appropriate.

ACKNOWLEDGMENTS

The work on this chapter was supported in part by Grant AG-11230 from the National Institutes of Health and by a Center of Excellence grant to the University of Memphis. I am grateful to Cheryl Grady, Jim Herndon, Stefan Kohler, Mikko Laakso, David Madden, and Eric Turkheimer for valuable comments on earlier versions of this work. All remaining errors are, of course, my responsibility. And let it be known that "these were the real facts I learnt at Memphis" (Herodotus, *The History*).

REFERENCES

Agartz, I., Sääf, J., Wahlund, L. -O., & Wetterberg, L. (1991). Tl and T2 relaxation time estimates in the normal human brain. *Radiology, 181,* 537–543.

Akima, M., Nonaka, H., Hasegawa, M., & Tanaka, K. (1986). A study on the microvasculature of the cerebral cortex: Fundamental architecture and its senile changes in the frontal cortex. *Laboratory Investigation, 55,* 482–489.

Albert, M., Duffy, F. H., & Naeser, M. (1987). Nonlinear changes in cognition with age and their neurophysiological correlates. *Canadian Journal of Psychology, 41,* 141–157.

Almkvist, O., Wahlund, L. -O., Andersson-Lundman, G., Basun, H., & Bäckman, L. (1992). White-matter hyperintensity and neuropsychological functions in dementia and healthy aging. *Archives of Neurology, 49,* 626–632.

Anderson, B., & Rutledge, V. (1996). Age and hemisphere effects on dendritic structure. *Brain, 119,* 1983–1990.

Anderson, S. W., Damasio, H., Jones, R. D., & Tranel, D. (1991). Wisconsin Card Sorting Test performance as a measure of frontal lobe damage. *Journal of Clinical and Consulting Psychology, 13,* 909–922.

Antonini, A., Leenders, K. L., Reist, H., Thomann, R., Beer, H. F., & Locher, J. (1993). Effect of age on D_2 dopamine receptors in normal human brain measured by positron emission tomography and ^{11}C-raclopride. *Archives of Neurology, 50*, 474–480.

Arendt, T., Bruckner, M. K., Gertz, H. J., & Marcova, L. (1998). Cortical distribution of neurofibrillary tangles in Alzheimer's disease matches the pattern of neurons that retain their capacity of plastic remodelling in the adult brain. *Neuroscience, 83*, 991–1002.

Arking, R. (1991). *Biology of aging: Observations and principles.* Englewood Cliffs, NJ: Prentice-Hall.

Armstrong, E. (1990). Evolution of the brain. In G. Paxinos (Ed.), *The human nervous system* (pp. 1–16). San Diego, CA: Academic Press.

Arnsten, A. F. (1997). Catecholamine regulation of the prefrontal cortex. *Journal of Psychopharmacology, 11*, 151–162.

Bäckman, L., Almkvist, O., Andersson, J., Norberg, A., Winblad, B., Reineck, R., & Långström, B. (1997). Brain activation in young and older adults during implicit and explicit retrieval. *Journal of Cognitive Neuroscience, 9*, 378–391.

Baddeley, A. (1994). Working memory: The interface between memory and cognition. In D.Schacter and E. Tulving (Eds.), *Memory systems 1994.* Cambridge, MA: MIT Press.

Balin, A. K. (Ed.). (1994). *Human biological age determination.* Boca Raton, FL: CRC Press.

Baltes, P. B., & Lindenberger, U. (1997). Emergence of a powerful connection between sensory and cognitive function across the adult life span: A new window to the study of cognitive aging? *Psychology and Aging, 12*, 12–21.

Baron, J. C., Godeau, C., Petit-Taboué, M. C., Landeau, B., Desgranges, B., Perchev, G., & Marchal, G. (1998). The brain metabolic effects of healthy aging in man: Mapping by 3-D PET and SPM. *Society for Neuroscience Abstracts, 24*(Part 2), 1764.

Bartus, R. T., Dean, R. L., Pontecorvo, M. J., & Flicker, C. (1985). The cholinergic hypothesis: A historical overview, current perspective, and future directions. *Annals of New York Academy of Sciences, 444*, 332–358.

Berman, K. F., Ostrem, J. L., Randolph, C., Gold, J., Goldberg, T. E., Copola, R., Carson, R. E., Herscovitch, P., & Weinberger, D. R. (1995). Physiological activation of a cortical network during performance on the Wisconsin Card Sorting Test: A positron emission tomography study. *Neuropsychologia, 33*, 1027–1046.

Berman, K. F., Schmidt, P. J., Rubinow, D. R., Danaceau, M. A., Van Horn, J. D., Esposito, G., Ostrem, J. L., & Weinberger, D. R. (1997). Modulation of cognition-specific cortical activity by gonadal steroids: A positron-emission tomography study in women. *Proceedings of the National Academy of Sciences of the USA, 94*, 8836–8841.

Bertoni-Freddari, C., Fattoretti, P., Casoli, T., Caselli, U., & Meier-Ruge, W. (1996). Deterioration threshold of synaptic morphology in aging and senile dementia of Alzheimer's type. *Annals of Quantitative Cytology and Histology, 18*, 209–213.

Bigler, E. D., Blatter, D. D., Anderson, C. V., Johnson, S. C., Gale, S. D., Hopkins, R. O., & Bennet, B. (1997). Hippocampal volume in normal aging and traumatic brain injury. *American Journal of Neuroradiology, 18*, 11–23.

Birge, S. J. (1996). Is there a role for estrogen replacement therapy in the prevention and treatment of dementia? *Journal of American Geriatric Society, 44*, 865–870.

Blatter, D. D., Bigler, E. D., Gale, S. D., Johnson, S. C., Anderson, C. V., Burnett, B. M., Parker, N., Kurth, S., & Horn, S. D. (1995). Quantitative volumetric analysis of brain MR: Normative database spanning 5 decades of life. *American Journal of Neuroradiology, 16*, 241–251.

Bondi, M. W., Salmon, D. P., & Butters, N. (1994). Neuropsychological features of memory disorders in Alzheimer disease. In R. D. Terry, R. Katzman, & L. Bick (Eds.), *Alzheimer Disease* (pp. 41–63). New York: Raven.

Bondi, M. W., Salmon, D. P., Monsch, A. U., Galasko, D., Butters, N., Klauber, M. R., Thal, L. J., & Saitoh, T. (1995). Episodic memory changes are associated with the APOE-epsilon 4 allele in nondemented older adults. *Neurology, 45*, 2203–2206.

Bookheimer, S., Strojwas, M., Ercoli, L., Felix, G., Zeineh, M., & Small, G. (1998). Differential patterns of memory activation during fMRI in genetically at-risk elderly volunteers. *Society for Neuroscience Abstracts, 24*(Part 2), 1269.

Boone, K. B., Miller, B. L., Lesser, I. M., Mehringer, M., Hill-Gutierrez, E., Goldberg, M. A., & Berman, N. G. (1992). Neuropsychological correlates of white-matter lesions in healthy elderly subjects: A threshold effect. *Archives of Neurology, 49,* 549–554.

Bourne, G. H. (1973). Lipofuscin. In D. H. Ford (Ed.), *Neurobiological aspects of maturation and aging* (pp. 189–201). Amsterdam: Elsevier.

Braak, H., & Braak, E. (1991). Neuropathological staging of Alzheimer-related changes. *Acta Neuropathologica, 82,* 239–259.

Brandgaard, H., & Gundersen, H. J. G. (1986). The impact of recent stereological advances on quantitative studies of nervous system. *Journal of Neuroscience Methods, 18,* 39–78.

Briggs, S. D., Raz, N., & Marks, W. (in press). Age-related deficits in generation and manipulation of mental images: I. The role of sensorimotor speed and working memory. *Psychology and Aging.*

Brodmann, K. (1987). Vergleichende Lokalisationslehre der Großhirnrinde in ihre Prinzipien dargestellt auf Grund des Zellenbaues. Leipzig: Barth. (Original work published 1909)

Bugiani, O., Salvarini, S., Perdelli, F., Mancardi, G. L., & Leonardi, A. (1978). Nerve cell loss with aging in the putamen. *European Neurology, 17,* 286–291.

Burke, D. M., & Mackay, D. G. (1997). Memory, language, and ageing. *Philosophical Transactions of Royal Society of London, B Biological Sciences, 352,* 1845–1856.

Cabeza, R., Anderson, N., Mangels, J., Nyberg, L., & Houle, S. (1999). *Age-related differences in neural activity during item and temporal-order memory retrieval: A positron emission tomography study.* Manuscript submitted for publication.

Cabeza, R., Grady, C. L., Nyberg, L., McIntosh, A. R., Tulving, E., Kapur, S., Jennings, J. M., Houle, S., & Craik, F. I. M. (1997). Age-related differences in neural activity during memory encoding and retrieval: A positron emission tomography study. *Journal of Neuroscience, 17,* 391–400.

Cabeza, R., McIntosh, A. R., Tulving, E., Nyberg, L., & Grady, C. L. (1997). Age-related differences in effective neural connectivity during encoding and recall. *NeuroReport, 8,* 3479–3483.

Cabeza, R., & Nyberg, L. (1997). Imaging cognition: An empirical review of PET studies with normal subjects. *Journal of Cognitive Neuroscience, 9,* 1–26.

Cai, J. X., & Arnsten, A. F. (1997). Dose-dependent effects of the dopamine D_1 receptor agonists A77636 or SKF81297 on spatial working memory in aged monkeys. *Journal of Pharmacology and Experimental Therapeutics, 283,* 183–189.

Campeau, N. G., Petersen, R. C., Felmlee, J. P., O'Brien, P. C., & Jack, C. R. (1997). Hippocampal transverse relaxation times in patients with Alzheimer disease. *Radiology, 205,* 197–201.

Carillo, M. C., Stebbins, G. T., Gabrieli, J. D. E., Desmond, J. E., Dirksen, C., Turner, D., & Glover, G. H. (1998). An fMRI study of the effects of aging on frontal activation during semantic encoding. *Cognitive Neuroscience Society Annual Meeting Abstract Program: A Supplement of the Journal of Cognitive Neuroscience,* 53.

Carmelli, D., Swan, G. E., Reed, T., Schellenberg, G. D., & Christian, J. C. (1999). The effect of apolipoptrotein E ε4 in the relationships of smoking and drinking to cognitive function. *Neuroepidemiology, 18,* 125–133.

Casey, B. J., Cohen, J. D., Nol, D. C., Schneider, W., Giedd, J. N., & Rapoport, J. L. (1996). Functional magnetic resonance imaging: Studies of cognition. In E. D. Bigler (Ed.), *Neuroimaging II: Clinical applications* (pp. 299–330). New York: Academic Press.

Chan-Palay, V., & Asan, E. (1989). Quantitation of catecholamine neurons in the locus coeruleus in human brains of normal young and older adults and in depression. *Journal of Comparative Neurology, 287,* 357–372.

Chawluk, J. B., Alavi, A., Dann, R., Hurtig, H. I., Bais, S., Kushner, M., Zimmerman, R. A., & Reivich, M. (1987). Positron emission tomography in aging and dementia: Effect of cerebral atrophy. *Journal of Nuclear Medicine, 28,* 431–437.

Chawluk, J. B., Dann, R., Alavi, A., Hurtig, H. I., Gur, R. E., Resnick, S., Zimmerman, R. A., & Reivich, M. (1990). Effect of focal cerebral atrophy in Positron Emission Tomographic studies of aging and dementia: *Nuclear Medicine and Biology, 17,* 797–804.

Cho, S., Jones, D., Reddick, W. E., Ogg, R. J., & Steen, R. G. (1997). Establishing norms for age-related changes in proton T1 of human brain tissue in vivo. *Magnetic Resonance Imaging, 15,* 1133–1143.

Coffey, C. E., Lucke, J. F., Saxton, J. A., Ratcliff, G., Unitas, L. J., Billig, B., & Bryan, R. N. (1998). Sex differences in brain aging: A quantitative magnetic resonance imaging study. *Archives of Neurology, 55,* 169–179.

Coffey, C. E., Wilkinson, W. E., Parashos, I. A., Soady, S. A. R., Sullivan, R. J., Patterson, L. J., Figiel, G. S., Webb, M. C., Spritzer, C. E., & Djang, W. T. (1992). Quantitative cerebral anatomy of the aging human brain: A cross-sectional study using magnetic resonance imaging. *Neurology, 42,* 527–536.

Cohen, J. (1988). *Statistical power analysis for the behavioral sciences.* Hillsdale, NJ: Lawrence Erlbaum Associates.

Cohen, J. D., Forman, S. D., Braver, T. S., Casey, B. J., Servan-Schreiber, D., & Noll, D. C. (1994). Activation of the prefrontal cortex in a nonspatial working memory task with functional MRI. *Human Brain Mapping, 1,* 293–304.

Convit, A., de Asis, J., de Leon, M. J., Tarshish, C., de Santi, S., Daisley, K., & Rusinek, H. (1998). The fusiform gyrus as the first neocortical site in AD? *Neurobiology of Aging, 19*(Suppl. 4S), Abstract No. 1286.

Convit, A., de Leon, M. J., Hoptman, M. J., Tarshish, C., De Santi, S., & Rusinek, H. (1995). Age-related changes in brain: I. Magnetic resonance imaging measures of temporal lobe volumes in normal subjects. *Psychiatric Quarterly, 66,* 343–355.

Corbetta, M., Miezin, F. M., Shulman, G. L., & Petersen, S. E. (1993). A PET study of visuospatial attention. *Journal of Neuroscience, 13,* 1202–1226.

Corcoran, R., & Upton, D. (1993). A role for the hippocampus in card sorting? *Cortex, 29,* 293–304.

Corkin, S., Kennedy, A. M., Bucci, J., Moore, C. I., Locascio, J. J., Stern, C. E., Rosen, B. R., & González, R. G. (1998). fMRI studies of episodic memory imaging and Alzheimer's disease. *Neurobiology of Aging, 19*(Suppl. 4S), Abstract No. 579.

Courchesne, E., & Plante, E. (1997). Measurement and analysis issues in neurodevelopmental magnetic resonance imaging. In R. W. Thatcher, G. R. Reid, M. Lyon, J. Rumsey, & N. Krasnegor (Eds.), *Developmental neuroimaging* (pp. 43–65). New York: Academic Press.

Cowell, P., Turetsky, B. I., Gur, R. C., Grossman, R. I., Shtasel, D. L., & Gur, R. E. (1994). Sex differences in aging of the human frontal and temporal lobes. *Journal of Neuroscience, 14,* 4748–4755.

Creutzfeldt, O. D. (1995). *Cortex cerebri: Performance, structural and functional organization of the cortex.* Oxford, England: Oxford University Press.

Damasio, A. R., Tranel, D., & Damasio, H. (1989). Disorders of visual recognition. In F. Boller & J. Grafman (Eds.), *Handbook of neuropsychology* (Vol. 2, pp. 317–332). Amsterdam: Elsevier.

de Brabander, J. M., Kramers, R. J. K., & Uylings, H. B. M. (1998). Layer-specific dendritic regression of pyramidal cells with ageing in the human prefrontal cortex. *European Journal of Neuroscience, 10,* 1261–1269.

DeCarli, C., Murphy, D. G. M., Tranh, M., Grady, C. L., Haxby, J. V., Gillette, J. A., Salerno, J. A., Gonzales-Aviles, A., Horwitz, B., Rapoport, S. I., & Schapiro, M. B. (1995). The effect of white matter hyperintensity volume on brain structure, cognitive performance, and cerebral metabolism of glucose in 51 healthy adults. *Neurology, 45,* 2077–2084.

de Groot, J. C., de Leeuw, F. E., Achten, E., Heijboer, R., Oudkerk, M., van Gijn, J., Hofman, A., Jolles, J., & Breteler, M. M. B. (1998). Cerebral white matter changes and cognitive functions—The Rotterdam Scan Study. *Neurobiology of Aging, 19*(Suppl. 4S), Abstract No. 277.

De Keyser, J., De Backer, J. -P., Vauquelin, G., & Ebinger, G. (1990). The effect of aging on the D_1 dopamine receptors in human frontal cortex. *Brain Research, 528*, 308–310.

de Leeuw, F. -E., de Groot, J. C., Achten, E., Heijboer, R., Oudkerk, M., van Gijn, J., Hofman, A., & Breteler, M. M. B. (1998). Duration of hypertension and cerebral white matter changes: The Rotterdam Scan Study. *Neurobiology of Aging, 19*(Suppl. 4S), Abstract No. 1018.

de Leon, M. J., McRae, T., Rusinek, H., Convit, A., De Santi, S., Tarshish, C., Golomb, J., Volkow, N., Daisley, K., Orentreich, N., & McEwen, R. (1997). Cortisol reduces hippocampal glucose metabolism in normal elderly, but not in Alzheimer's disease. *Journal of Clinical Endocrinology and Metabolism, 82*, 3251–3259.

Deshmukh, A. R., Desmond, J. E., Sullivan, E. V., Lane, B., Matsumoto, B., Marsh, L., Lim, K. O., & Pfefferbaum, A. (1997). Quantification of cerebellar structures with MRI. *Psychiatry Research: Neuroimaging, 75*, 159–171.

D'Esposito, M., Detre, J. A., Alsop, D. C., Shin, R. K., Atlas, S., & Grossman, M. (1995). The neural basis of the central executive system of working memory. *Nature, 378*, 279–281.

D'Esposito, M., Zarahn, E., Aguirre, J., & Rypma, B. (1999). The variability of BOLD hemodynamic responses in young and elderly subjects: Implications for fMRI studies of normal aging. *NeuroImage.*

de Toledo-Morrell, L., Goncharova, I., Dickerson, B., & Wilson, R. S. (1998). *In vivo* structural imaging demonstrates lack of entorhinal cortex atrophy in healthy aged humans. *Society for Neuroscience Abstracts, 24*(Part 1), 999.

Doraiswami, P. M., Na, C., Husain, M., Figiel, G. S., McDonald, W. M., Ellinwood, E. H., Boyko, O. B., & Krishnan, K. R. (1992). Morphometric changes in the human midbrain with normal aging: MR and stereologic findings. *American Journal of Neuroradiology, 13*, 383–386.

Dorfman, J., & Raz, N. (1998, April). *Neuroanatomical correlates of age-related differences in memory for new associations.* Paper presented at the Cognitive Aging Conference, Atlanta, GA.

Double, K. L., Halliday, G. M., Kril, J. J., Harasty, J. A., Cullen, K., Brooks, W. S., Creasy, H., & Broe, G. A. (1996). Topography of brain atrophy during normal aging and Alzheimer's disease. *Neurobiology of Aging, 17*, 513–521.

Driesen, N. R., & Raz, N. (1995). Sex-, age-, and handedness-related differences in human corpus callosum observed *in vivo*. *Psychobiology, 23*, 240–247.

Dror, I. E., & Kosslyn, S. M. (1994). Mental imagery and aging. *Psychology and Aging, 9*, 90–102.

Eberling, J. L., Roberts, J. A., De Manincor, D. J., Brennan, K. M., Hanrahan, S. M., Vanbrocklin, H. F., Roos, M. S., & Jagust, W. J. (1995). PET studies of cerebral glucose metabolism in conscious rhesus macaques. *Neurobiology of Aging, 16*, 825–832.

Eberling, J. L., Roberts, J. A., Rapp, P. R., Tuszynski, M. H., & Jagust, W. J. (1997). Cerebral glucose metabolism and memory in aged rhesus macaques. *Neurobiology of Aging, 18*, 437–443.

Ellis, R. S. (1920). Norms for some structural changes in human cerebellum from birth to old age. *Journal of Comparative Neurology, 32*, 1–33.

Escalona, P. R., McDonald, W. M., Doraiswamy, P. M., Boyko, O. B., Husain, M. M., Figiel, G. S., Laskowitz, D., Ellinwood, E. H., & Krishnan, K. R. R. (1991). In vivo stereological assessment of human cerebellar volume: Effects of gender and age. *American Journal of Neuroradiology, 12*, 927–929.

Esiri, M. (1994). Dementia and normal aging: Neuropathology. In F. A. Huppert, C. Brayne, & D. W. O'Connor (Eds.), *Dementia and normal aging* (pp. 385–436). Cambridge, England: Cambridge University Press.

Eslinger, P. L., & Grattan, L. M. (1993). Frontal lobe and frontal-striatal substrates for different forms of human cognitive flexibility. *Neuropsychologia, 31,* 17–28.

Eustache, P., Rioux, F., Desgranges, B., Marchal, G., Petit-Taboué, M. C., Dary, M., Lechevalier, B., & Baron, J. C. (1995). Healthy aging, memory subsystems and regional cerebral oxygen consumption. *Neuropsychologia, 33,* 867–887.

Faust, M. E., & Balota, D. A. (1997). Inhibition of return and visuospatial attention in healthy older adults and individuals with dementia of the Alzheimer type. *Neuropsychology, 11,* 13–29.

Flechsig, P. (1901, October 19). Developmental (myelogenetic) localisation of the cerebral cortex in the human subject. *The Lancet,* 1027–1029.

Fletcher, P. C., Dolan, R. J., Shallice, T., Frith, C. D., Frackowiak, R. S. J., & Friston, K. J. (1996). Is multivariate analysis of PET data more revealing than the univariate approach? Evidence from a study of episodic memory retrieval. *NeuroImage, 3,* 209–215.

Flood, D. G., & Coleman, P. D. (1988). Neuron numbers and size in aging brain: Comparison of human, monkey, and rodent data. *Neurobiology of Aging, 9,* 453–463.

Floor, E., & Wetzel, M. G. (1998). Increased protein oxidation in human substantia nigra pars compacta in comparison with basal ganglia and prefrontal cortex measured with an improved dinitrophenylhydrazine assay. *Journal of Neurochemistry, 70,* 268–275.

Foster, T. C., & Norris, C. M. (1997). Age-associated changes in Ca^{2+}-dependent processes: Relation to hippocampal synaptic plasticity. *Hippocampus, 7,* 602–612.

Fox, N., Freeborough, P. A., & Rossor, M. N. (1996). Visualisation and quantification of rates of atrophy in Alzheimer's disease. *The Lancet, 348,* 94–97.

Freedman, M., Knoefel, J., Naeser, M., & Levine, H. (1984). Computerized axial tomography in aging. In M. L. Albert (Ed.), *Clinical neurology of aging* (pp. 139–148). New York: Oxford University Press.

Freedman, M., & Oscar-Berman, M. (1986). Bilateral frontal lobe disease and selective delayed-response deficits in humans. *Behavioral Neuroscience, 100,* 337–342.

Frey, K. A., Koeppe, R. A., Kilbourn, M. R., Vander Borght, T. M., Albin, R. L., Gilman, S., & Kuhl, D. E. (1996). Presynaptic monoaminergic vesicles in Parkinson's disease and normal aging. *Annals of Neurology, 40,* 873–884.

Friston, K. J., Holmes, A. P., Worsley, K. J., Poline, J. P., Frith, C. D., & Frackowiak, R. S. J. (1995). Statistical parametric maps in functional imaging: A general linear approach. *Human Brain Mapping, 2,* 189–210.

Friston, K. J., Price, C. J., Fletcher, P., Moore, C., Frackowiak, R. S. J., & Dolan, R. J. (1996). The trouble with cognitive subtraction. *NeuroImage, 4,* 97–104.

Furey, M. L., Pietrini, P., Haxby, J. V., Alexander, G. E., Lee, H. C., VanMeter, J., Grady, C. L., Shetty, U., Rapoport, S. I., Schapiro, M. B., & Freo, U. (1997). Cholinergic stimulation alters performance and task-specific regional cerebral blood flow during working memory. *Proceedings of the National Academy of Science USA, 94,* 6512–6516.

Gabrieli, J. D. E., Brewer, J. E., Desmond, J. E., & Glover, G. H. (1997). Separate neural bases of two fundamental memory processes in the human medial temporal lobe. *Science, 276,* 264–266.

Gazzaley, A. H., Thakker, M. M., Hof, P. R., & Morrison, J. H. (1997). Preserved number of entorhinal cortex layer II neurons in aged macaque monkeys. *Neurobiology of Aging, 18,* 549–553.

Geinisman, Y., deToledo-Morell, L., Morell, F., & Heller, R. E. (1995). Hippocampal markers of age-related memory dysfunction: Behavioral, electrophysiological and morphological perspectives. *Progress in Neurobiology, 45,* 223–252.

Geula, C., Wu, C. K., Saroff, D., Lorenzo, A., Yuan, M., & Yankner, B. A. (1998). Aging renders the brain vulnerable to amyloid beta-protein neurotoxicity. *Nature Medicine, 4,* 827–831.

Giannakopoulos, P., Hof, P. R., Vallet, P. G., Giannakopoulos, A. S., Charnay, Y., & Bouras, C. (1995). Quantitative analysis of neuropathologic changes in the cerebral cortex of centenarians. *Progress in Neuropsychopharmacology and Biological Psychiatry, 19,* 577–592.

Gideon, P., Thomsen, C., & Hendriksen, O. (1994). Increased self-diffusion of brain water in normal aging. *Journal of Magnetic Resonance Imaging, 4,* 185–188.

Ginsberg, M. D., Hedley-Whyte, E. T., & Richardson, E. P., Jr. (1976). Hypoxic-ischemic leukoencephalopathy in man. *Archives of Neurology, 33,* 5–14.

Goldman-Rakic, P. S. (1987). Circuitry of primate prefrontal cortex and regulation of behavior by representational memory. In F. Plum & V. Mountcastle (Eds.), *Handbook of Physiology* (Vol. 5, pp. 373–417). Bethesda, MD: American Physiological Society.

Goldstein, I. B., Bartzokis, G., Hance, D. B., & Shapiro, D. (1998). Relationship between blood pressure and subcortical lesions in healthy elderly people. *Stroke, 29,* 765–772.

Golomb, J., Kluger, A., de Leon, M. J., Ferris, S. H., Convit, A., Mittelman, M., Cohen, J., Rusinek, H., De Santi, S., & George, A. E. (1994). Hippocampal formation size in normal human aging: A correlate of delayed secondary memory performance. *Learning and Memory, 1,* 45–54.

Golomb, J., Kluger, A., de Leon, M. J., Ferris, S. H., Mittelman, M., Cohen, J., & George, A. E. (1996). Hippocampal formation size predicts declining memory performance in normal aging. *Neurology, 47,* 810–813.

Grady, C. L., Haxby, J. V., Horwitz, B., Schapiro, M. B., Rapoport, S. I., Ungerleider, L. G., Mishkin, M., Carson, R. E., & Herskovitch, P. (1992). Dissociation of object and spatial vision in human extrastriate cortex: Age-related changes in activation of regional cerebral blood flow measured with [^{15}O] water and positron emission tomography. *Journal of Cognitive Neuroscience, 4,* 23–34.

Grady, C. L., Maisog, J. M., Horwitz, B., Ungerleider, L. G., Mentis, M. J., Salerno, J. A., Pietrini, P., Wagner, E., & Haxby, J. V. (1994). Age-related changes in cortical blood flow activation during visual processing of faces and location. *Journal of Neuroscience, 14,* 1450–1462.

Grady, C. L., McIntosh, A. R., Bookstein, F., Horwitz, B., Rapoport, S. I., & Haxby, J. V. (1998). Age-related changes in regional cerebral blood flow during working memory for faces. *NeuroImage, 8,* 409–425.

Grady, C. L., McIntosh, A. R., Horwitz, B., Maisog, J. M., Ungerleider, L. G., Mentis, M. J., Pietrini, P., Schapiro, M. B., & Haxby, J. V. (1995). Age-related reduction in human recognition memory due to impaired encoding. *Science, 269,* 218–221.

Grady, C. L., McIntosh, A. R., Rajah, M. N., Beig, S., & Craik, F. I. M. (1998, April). *The neural correlates of age-related differences in episodic memory for pictures and words.* Paper presented at the Cognitive Aging Conference, Atlanta, GA.

Graf, P., & Schacter, D. L. (1985). Implicit and explicit memory for new associations in normal and amnesic subjects. *Journal of Experimental Psychology: Learning, Memory, and Cognition, 11,* 501–518.

Guillozet, A., Smiley, J. F., Mash, D. C., & Mesulam, M. -M. (1995). The amyloid burden of the cerebral cortex in non-demented old age. *Society for Neuroscience Abstract, 21,* 1478.

Gunning-Dixon, F. M., Head, D., McQuain, J., Acker, J. D., & Raz, N. (1998). Differential aging of the human striatum: A prospective MR study. *American Journal of Neuroradiology, 19,* 1501–1507.

Gunning-Dixon, F. M., & Raz, N. (1999a). The cognitive correlates of white matter abnormalities in normal aging: A quantitative review. Manuscript submitted for publication.

Gunning-Dixon, F. M., & Raz, N. (1999b). Demographic and clinical correlates of white matter abnormalities in normal aging: A quantitative review. Manuscript submitted for publication.

Gur, R. E., Cowell, P., Turetsky, B. I., Gallagher, F., Cannon, T., Bilker, W., & Gur, R. C. (1998). A follow-up magnetic resonance imaging study of schizophrenia relationship of neuroanatomical changes to clinical and neurobehavioral measures. *Archives of General Psychiatry, 55,* 145–152.

Guttmann, C. R., Jolesz, F. A., Kikinis, R., Killiany, R. J., Moss, M. B., Sandor, T., & Albert, M. S. (1998). White matter changes with normal aging. *Neurology, 50,* 972–978.

Hachinsky, V. C., Potter, P., & Merskey, H. (1987). Leuko-araiosis. *Archives of Neurology, 44,* 21–23.

Hall, T. C., Miller, K. H., & Corsellis, J. A. N. (1975). Variations in human Purkinje cell population according to age and sex. *Neuropathology and Applied Neurobiology, 1,* 267–292.

Hallgren, B., & Sourander, P. (1958). The effect of age on the non-haemin iron in the human brain. *Journal of Neurochemistry, 3,* 41–51.

Harris, G. J., Pearlson, G. D., Peyser, C. E., Aylward, E. H., Roberts, J., Barta, P. E., Chase, G. A., & Folstein, S. E. (1992). Putamen volume reduction on magnetic resonance imaging exceeds caudate changes in mild Huntington's disease. *Annals of Neurology, 31,* 69–75.

Hartley, A. A. (1992). Attention. In F. I. M. Craik & T. A. Salthouse (Eds.), *The handbook of aging and cognition* (pp. 3–49). Hillsdale, NJ: Lawrence Erlbaum Associates.

Hartley, A. A. (1993). Evidence for the selective preservation of spatial selective attention in old age. *Psychology and Aging, 8,* 371–379.

Hartley, A. A., Speer, N., Jonides, J., Reuter-Lorenz, P., Smith, E. E., Marshuetz, C., Ciancicolo, A., Kia, M., & Koeppe, R. (1998). Do age-related impairments in specific working memory systems result in greater reliance on the central executive? *Cognitive Neuroscience Society Annual Meeting Abstract Program: A Supplement of the Journal of Cognitive Neuroscience,* 88.

Hasegawa, I., Fukushima, T., Ihara, T., & Miyashita, Y. (1998). Callosal window between prefrontal cortices: Cognitive interaction to retrieve long-term memory. *Science, 281,* 814–818.

Haug, H. (1985). Are neurons of the human cerebral cortex really lost during aging? A morphometric examination. In J. Tarber & W. H. Gispen (Eds.), *Senile dementia of Alzheimer type* (pp. 150–163). New York: Springer-Verlag.

Haug, H. (1987). Brain sizes, surfaces, and neuronal sizes of the cortex cerebri: A stereological investigation of man and his variability and a comparison with some mammals (primates, whales, marsupials, insectivores, and one elephant). *American Journal of Anatomy, 180,* 126–142.

Haxby, J. V., Grady, C. L., Duara, R., Robertson-Tchabo, E. A., Koziarz, B., Cutler, N. R., & Rapoport, S. I. (1986). Relations among age, visual memory, and resting cerebral metabolism in 40 healthy men. *Brain and Cognition, 5,* 412–427.

Haxby, J. V., Grady, C. L., Horwitz, B., Ungerleider, L. G., Mishkin, M., Carson, R. E., Herscovitch, P., Schapiro, M. B., & Rapoport, S. I. (1991). Dissociation of object and spatial visual processing pathways in human extrastriatal cortex. *Proceedings of the National Academy of Science USA, 88,* 1621–1625.

Hayakawa, K., Konishi, Y., Matsuda, T., Kuriyama, M., Konishi, K., Yamashita, K., Okumura, R., & Hamanaka, D. (1989). Development and aging of the brain midline structures: Assessment with MRI imaging. *Radiology, 172,* 171–177.

Head, D., Raz, N., Gunning-Dixon, F., & Acker, J. D. (1999, July). Contribution of the prefrontal cortex and working memory to age-related deficits in executive functions. To be presented at the VIIth European Congress of Psychology, Rome, Italy.

Heaton, R. K., Chelune, G. J., Talley, J. L., Kay, G. G., & Curtis, G. (1993). *Wisconsin Card Sorting Test manual: Revised and expanded.* Odessa, FL: Psychological Assessment Resources.

Heinsen, H., Henn, R., Eisenmenger, W., Gotz, M., Bohl, J., Bethke, B., Lockemann, U., & Puschel, K. (1994) Quantitative investigations on the human entorhinal area: Left–right asymmetry and age-related changes. *Anatomy and Embryology (Berlin), 190,* 181–194.

Hendrie, H. C., Farlow, M. R., Austrom, M. G., Edwards, M. K., & Williams, M. A. (1989). Foci of increased T2 signal intensity on brain MR scans of healthy elderly subjects. *American Journal of Neuroradiology, 10,* 703–707.

Herndon, J. G., Tigges, J., Anderson, D. C., Klumpp, S. A., & McClure, H. M. (1999). Brain weight throughout the life span of the chimpanzee. *Journal of Comparative Neurology.*

Herndon, J. G., Tigges, J., Klumpp, S. A., & Anderson, D. C. (1999). Brain weight does not decrease with age in adult rhesus monkeys. *Neurobiology of Aging, 19,* 267–272.

Herscovitch, P. (1994). Radiotracer techniques for functional neuroimaging with positron emission tomography. In R. W. Thatcher, M. Hallett, T. Zeffiro, E. R. John, & M. Huerta (Eds.), *Functional neuroimaging: Technical foundations* (pp. 29–46). New York: Academic Press.

Hirai, T., Korogi, Y., Sakamoto, Y., Hamatake, S., Ikushima, I., & Takahashi, M. (1996). T2 shortening in the motor cortex: Effect of aging and cerebrovascular diseases. *Radiology, 199,* 799–803.

Hof, P. R., Giannakopoulos, P., & Bouras, C. (1996). The neuropathological changes associated with normal brain aging. *Histology and Histopathology, 11,* 1075–1088.

Hokama, H., Shenton, M. E., Nestor, P. G., Kikinis, R., Levitt, J. J., Metcalf, D., Wible, C. G., O'Donnell, B. F., Jolesz, F. A., & McCarley, R. W. (1995). Caudate, putamen, and globus pallidus volume in schizophrenia: A quantitative MRI study. *Psychiatry Research: Neuroimaging, 61,* 209–229.

Hunt, A. L., Orrison, W. W., Yeo, R. A., Haaland, K. Y., Rhyne, R. L., Garry, P. J., & Rosenberg, G. A. (1989). Clinical significance of MRI white matter lesions in the elderly. *Neurology, 39,* 1470–1474.

Ingram, D. K. (1988). Motor performance variability during aging in rodents: Assessment of reliability and validity of individual differences. *Annals of New York Academy of Science, 515,* 70–96.

Insausti, R., Jouttonen, K., Soininen, H., Insausti, A. M., Partanen, K., Vainio, P., Laakso, M. P., & Pitkänen, A. (1998). MR volumetric analysis of the human entorhinal, perirhinal, and temporopolar cortices. *American Journal of Neuroradiology, 19,* 659–671.

Iyo, M., & Yamasaki, T. (1993). The detection of age-related decrease of dopamine D_1, D_2 and serotonin 5-HT_2 receptors in living human brain. *Progress in Neuropsychopharmacology and Biological Psychiatry, 17,* 415–421.

Jack, C. R., Jr., Petersen, R. C., Xu, Y., O'Brien, P. C., Smith, G. E., Ivnik, R. J., Tangalos, E. G., & Kokmen, E. (1998). Rate of medial temporal lobe atrophy in typical aging and Alzheimer's disease. *Neurology, 51,* 993–999.

Jack, C. R., Jr., Petersen, R. C., Xu, Y. C., O'Brien, P. C., Waring, S. C., Tangalos, E. G., Smith, G. E., Ivnik, R. J., Thibodeau, S. N., & Kokmen, E. (1998). Hippocampal atrophy and apolipoprotein E genotype are independently associated with Alzheimer's disease. *Annals of Neurology, 43,* 303–310.

Jack, C. R., Jr., Petersen, R. C., Xu, Y. C., Waring, S. C., O'Brien, P. C., Tangalos, E. G., Smith, G. E., Ivnik, R. J., & Kokmen, E. (1997). Medial temporal atrophy on MRI in normal aging and very mild Alzheimer's disease. *Neurology, 49,* 786–794.

James, W. (1952). *Principles of psychology.* Chicago: Encyclopedia Britannica. (Original work published 1890)

Jernigan, T. L., Archibald, S. L., Berhow, M. T., Sowell, E. R., Foster, D. S., & Hesselink, J. R. (1991). Cerebral structure on MRI: Part I. Localization of age-related changes. *Biological Psychiatry, 29,* 55–67.

Johannsen, P., Jakobsen, J., Bruhn, P., Hansen, S. B., Gee, A., Stodkilde-Jorgensen, H., & Gjedde, A. (1997). Cortical sites of sustained and divided attention in normal elderly humans. *NeuroImage, 6,* 145–155.

Johnson, M. K., Nolde, S. F., Mather, M., Kounios, J., Schacter, D. L., & Curran, T. (1997). The similarity of brain activity associated with true and false recognition memory depends on test format. *Psychological Science, 8,* 250–257.

Johnson, S. H., & Rybash, J. M. (1993). A cognitive neuroscience perspective on age-related slowing: Developmental changes in the functional architecture. In J. Cerella, J. Rybash, W. Hoyer, & M. L. Commons (Eds.), *Adult information processing: Limits on loss* (pp. 143–173). New York: Academic Press.

Johnson, S. R. (1998). Menopause and hormone replacement therapy. *Medical Clinics of North America, 82,* 297–320.

Juottonen, K., Laakso, M. P., Insausti, R., Lehtovirta, M., Pitkänen, A., Partanen, K., & Soininen, H. (1998). Volumes of the entorhinal and perirhinal cortices in Alzheimer's disease. *Neurobiology of Aging, 19,* 15–22.

Kadar, T., Dachir, S., Shukitt-Hale, B., & Levy, A. (1998). Sub-regional hippocampal vulnerability in various animal models leading to cognitive dysfunction. *Journal of Neural Transmission, 105,* 987–1004.

Kahneman, D. (1973). *Attention and effort.* Englewood Cliffs, NJ: Prentice-Hall.

Kail, R. (1998). Speed of information processing in patients with multiple sclerosis. *Journal of Clinical and Experimental Neuropsychology, 20,* 98–106.

Karhunen, P. J., Erkinjuntti, T., & Laippala, P. (1994). Moderate alcohol consumption and loss of cerebellar Purkinje cells. *British Medical Journal, 308,* 1663–1667.

Kawamura, J., Terayama, Y., Takashima, S., Obara, K., Pavol, M. A., Meyer, J. S., Mortel, K. F., & Weathers, S. (1993). Leuko-araiosis and cerebral perfusion in normal aging. *Experimental Aging Research, 19,* 225–240.

Kaye, J. A., Swihart, T., Howieson, D., Dame, A., Moore, M. M., Karnos, T., Camicioli, R., Ball, M., Oken, B., & Sexton, G. (1997). Volume loss of the hippocampus and temporal lobe in healthy elderly persons destined to develop dementia. *Neurology, 48,* 1297–1304.

Kemper, T. L. (1994). Neuroanatomical and neuropathological changes during aging and in dementia. In M. L. Albert & E. J. E. Knoepfel (Eds.), *Clinical neurology of aging* (2nd ed., pp. 3–67). New York: Oxford University Press.

Kesslak, J. P., Yuan, D., Neeper, S., & Cotman, C. W. (1995). Vulnerability of the hippocampus to kainate excitotoxicity in the aged, mature and young adult rat. *Neuroscience Letters, 188,* 117–120.

Khachaturian, Z. S. (1984). Towards theories of brain aging. In D. S. Kay & G. W. Borrows (Eds.), *Handbook of studies on psychiatry and old age* (pp. 7–30). Amsterdam: Elsevier.

Khachaturian, Z. S. (1994). Calcium hypothesis of Alzheimer's disease and brain aging. In J. F. Disterhoft, W. H. Gispen, J. Traber, & Z. S. Khachaturian (Eds.), Calcium hypothesis of aging and dementia. *Annals of New York Academy of Sciences, 747,* 1–11.

Kimberg, D. Y., D'Esposito, M., & Farah, M. J. (1997). Effects of bromocriptine on human subjects depend on working memory capacity. *NeuroReport, 8,* 3581–3585.

Kimberg, D. Y., & Farah, M. J. (1993). A unified account of cognitive impairments following frontal lobe damage: The role of working memory in complex, organized behavior. *Journal of Experimental Psychology: General, 122,* 411–428.

Kirsch, S. J., Jacobs, R. W., Butcher, L., & Beatty, J. (1992). Prolongation of magnetic resonance T_2 time in hippocampus of human patients marks the presence and severity of Alzheimer's disease. *Neuroscience Letters, 134,* 187–190.

Klingberg, T., O'Sullivan, B. T., & Roland, P. E. (1997). Bilateral activation of fronto-parietal network by incrementing demands in a working memory task. *Cerebral Cortex, 7,* 465–471.

Köhler, S., Black, S. E., Sinden, M., Szekely, C., Kidron, D., Parker, J. L., Foster, J. K., Moscovitch, M., Winocur, G., Szalai, J. P., & Bronskill, M. J. (1998). Hippocampal and parahippocampal gyrus atrophy in relation to distinct anterograde memory impairment in Alzheimer's disease: An MR volumetric study. *Neuropsychologia, 36,* 129–142.

Köhler, S., Kapur, S., Moscovitch, M., Winocur, G., & Houle, S. (1995). Dissociation of pathways for object and spatial vision: A PET study in humans. *NeuroReport, 6,* 1865–1868.

Köhler, S., Moscovitch, M., Winocur, G., Houle, S., & McIntosh, A. R. (1998). Networks of domain-specific and general regions involved in episodic memory for spatial location and object identity. *Neuropsychologia, 36,* 129–142.

Koller, W. C., Glatt, S. L., Fox, J. H., Kaszniak, A. W., Wilson, R. S., & Huckman, M. (1981). Cerebellar atrophy: Relationship to aging and cerebral atrophy. *Neurology, 31,* 1486–1488.

Konishi, S., Nakajima, K., Uchida, I., Kameyama, M., Nakahara, K., Sekihara, K., & Miyashita, Y. (1998). Transient activation of inferior prefrontal cortex during cognitive set shifting. *Nature Neuroscience, 1,* 80–84.

Kooistra, C. A., & Heilman, K. M. (1988). Motor dominance and lateral asymmetry of the globus pallidus. *Neurology, 38,* 388–390.

Koop, M., Rilling, G., Herrmann, A., & Kretschmann, H. -J. (1986). Volumetric development of the fetal telencephalon, cerebral cortex, diencephalon, and rhombencephalon including the cerebellum in man. *Bibliotheca Anatomica, 28,* 53–78.

Kosslyn, S. M. (1994). *Image and brain.* Cambridge, MA: MIT Press.

Kraut, M. A., Marenco, S., Soher, B. J., Wong, D. F., & Bryan, R. N. (1995). Comparison of functional MR and $H_2{}^{15}O$ Positron Emission Tomography in stimulation of the primary visual cortex. *American Journal of Neuroadiology, 16,* 2101–2107.

Krimer, L. S., Muly, E. C., Williams, G. V., & Goldman-Rakic, P. S. (1998). Dopaminergic regulation of cerebral cortical microcirculation. *Nature Neuroscience, 1,* 286–289.

Krishnan, R. R., McDonald, W. M., Escalona, P. R., Doraiswamy, P. M., Na, C., Husain, M., Figiel, G. S., Boyko, O. B., Ellinwood, E. H., & Nemeroff, C. B. (1992). Magnetic resonance imaging of the caudate nuclei in depression: Preliminary observations. *Archives of General Psychiatry, 49,* 553–557.

Kuller, L. H., Shemanski, L., Manolio, T., Haan, M., Fried, L., Bryan, N., Burke, G. L., Tracy, R., & Bhadelia, R. (1998). Relationship between ApoE, MRI findings, and cognitive function in the Cardiovascular Health Study. *Stroke, 29,* 388–398.

Laakso, M. P., Frisoni, G. B., Könönen, M., Mikkonen, M., Beltramello, A., Geroldi, C., Bianchetti, A., Trabucchi, M., Soininen, H., & Aronen, H. J. (1999). *Atrophy of the anterior hippocampus in frontotemporal dementia: An MRI study.* Manuscript submitted for publication.

Laakso, M. P., Lehtovirta, M., Partanen, K., Riekkinen, P. J., Sr., & Soininen, H. (1999). *Hippocampus in Alzheimer's disease—A three-year follow-up MRI study.* Manuscript submitted for publication.

Laakso, M. P., Partanen, K., Lehtovirta, M., Hallikainen, M., Hänninen, T., Vainio, P., Riekkinen, P., Sr., & Soininen, H. (1995). MRI of amygdala fails to diagnose early Alzheimer's disease. *NeuroReport, 6,* 2414–2418.

Laakso, M. P., Partanen, K., Soininen, H., Lehtovirta, M., Hallikainen, M., Hänninen, T., Heikalla, E. -L., Vainio, P., & Riekkinen, Sr., P. J. (1996). MR T_2 relaxometry in Alzheimer's disease and age-associated memory impairment. *Neurobiology of Aging, 17,* 535–540.

Laakso, M. P., Soininen, H., Partanen, K., Lehtovirta, M., Hallikainen, M., Hänninen T., Helkala, E. L., Vainio, P., & Riekkinen, P. J., Sr. (1998). MRI of the hippocampus in Alzheimer's disease: Sensitivity, specificity, and analysis of the incorrectly classified subjects. *Neurobiology of Aging 19,* 23–31.

Labbé, C., Froment, J. C., Kennedy, A., Ashburne, J., & Cinotti, L. (1996). Positron emission tomography metabolic data corrected for cortical atrophy using magnetic resonance imaging. *Alzheimer Disease and Associated Disorders, 10,* 141–170.

Landfield, P. W. (1996). Aging-related increase in hippocampal calcium channels. *Life Sciences, 56,* 399–404.

LaVoie, D., & Light, L. L. (1994). Adult age differences in repetition priming: A meta-analysis. *Psychology and Aging, 9,* 539–554.

Lee, K. S., Frey, K. A., Koeppe, R. A., Buck, A., Mulholland, G. K., & Kuhl, D. E. (1996). In vivo quantification of cerebral muscarinic receptors in normal human aging using positron emission tomography and [^{11}C]tropanyl benzilate. *Journal of Cerebral Blood Flow and Metabolism, 16,* 303–310.

Lehr, R. P., Jr., Browning, R. A., & Myers, J. H. (1980). Gross morphological brain differences between Wistar-Kyoto and spontaneously hypertensive rats. *Clinical and Experimental Hypertension, 2,* 123–127.

Lepage, M., Habib, R., McIntosh, A. R., & Tulving, E. (1998). Activation of the left anterior hippocampus covaries with semantic encoding of verbal information into episodic memory: A PET study. *Society for Neuroscience Abstracts, 24*(Part 1), 681.

Lim, K. O., Zipurski, R. B., Murphy, G. M., & Pfefferbaum, A. (1990). In vivo quantification of the limbic system using MRI: Effects of normal aging. *Psychiatry Research: Neuroimaging, 35,* 15–26.

Liu, X., Erikson, C., & Brun, A. (1996). Cortical synaptic changes and gliosis in normal aging, Alzheimer's disease and frontal lobe degeneration. *Dementia, 7,* 128–134.

Loessner, A., Alavi, A., Lewandrowski, K. U., Mozley, D., Souder, E., & Gur, R. E. (1995). Regional cerebral function determined by FDG-PET in healthy volunteers: Normal patterns and changes with age. *Journal of Nuclear Medicine, 36,* 1141–1149.

Luce, R. D. (1986). *Response times: Their role in inferring elementary mental organization.* New York: Oxford University Press.

Luciana, M., Depue, R. A., Arbisi, P., & Leon, A. (1992). Facilitation of working memory by a D_2 dopamine receptor agonist. *Journal of Cognitive Neuroscience, 4,* 58–68.

Luft, A., Skalej, M., Welte, D., Kolb, R., Bürk, K., Schultz, J., Klockgether, T., & Voigt, K. (1998). A new semi-automated three-dimensional technique allowing precise quantification of total and regional cerebellar volume using MRI. *Magnetic Resonance in Medicine, 40,* 143–151.

Luft, A., Skalej, M., Welte, D., Kolb, R., Schultz, J., Bürk, K., Klockgether, T., & Voigt, K. (1999). *Patterns of age-related shrinkage in cerebellum and brainstem observed* in vivo *using three-dimensional MRI volumetry.* Manuscript submitted for publication.

Lupien, S., de Leon, M. J., de Santi, S., Convit, A., Tarshish, C., Nair, N. P. V, Thakur, M., McEwen, B. S., Hauger, R. L., & Meaney, M. J. (1998). Cortisol levels during human aging predict hippocampal atrophy and memory deficits. *Nature Neuroscience, 1,* 69–73.

Madden, D. J., Gottlob, L. R., Denny, L. L., Turkington, T. G., Provenzale, J. M., Hawk, T. C., & Coleman, R. E. (in press). Aging and recognition memory: Changes in regional cerebral blood flow associated with components of reaction time distributions. *Journal of Cognitive Neuroscience.*

Madden, D. J., & Hoffman, J. M. (1997). Application of positron emission tomography to age-related cognitive changes. In K. R. R. Krishnan & P. M. Doraiswamy (Eds.), *Brain imaging in clinical psychiatry* (pp. 575–613). New York: Marcel Dekker.

Madden, D. J., Turkington, T. G., Coleman, R. E., Provenzale, J. M., DeGrado, T. R., & Hoffman, J. M. (1996). Adult age differences in regional cerebral blood flow during visual word identification: Evidence from $H_2^{15}O$ PET. *NeuroImage, 3,* 127–142.

Madden, D. J., Turkington, T. G., Provenzale, J. M., Denny, L. L., Hawk, T. C, Gottlob, L. R., & Coleman, R. E. (1999). Adult age differences in functional neuroanatomy of verbal recognition memory. *Human Brain Mapping, 7,* 115–135.

Madden, D. J., Turkington, T. G., Provenzale, J. M., Hawk, T. C., Hoffman J. M., & Coleman, R. E. (1997). Selective and divided visual attention: Age-related changes in regional cerebral blood flow measured by $H_2^{15}O$ PET. *Human Brain Mapping, 5,* 389–409.

Manaye, K. F., McIntire, D. D., Mann, D. M., & German, D. C. (1995). Locus coeruleus cell loss in the aging human brain: A non-random process. *Journal of Comparative Neurology, 358,* 79–87.

Mäntylä, R., Erkinjuntti, T., Salonen, O., Aronen, H., Peltonen, T., Pohjasvaara, T., & Standerskjöld-Nordenstam, C. -G. (1997). Variable agreement between visual rating scales for white matter hyperintensities on MRI. *Stroke, 28,* 1614–1623.

Marchal, G., Rioux, P., Petit-Taboué, M. C., Sette, G., Travère, J. M., LePoec, C., Courtheoux, P., Derlon, J. M., & Baron, J. C. (1992). Regional cerebral oxygen consumption, blood flow, and blood volume in healthy human aging. *Archives of Neurology, 49,* 1013–1020.

Marin, J. (1995). Age-related changes in vascular responses: A review. *Mechanisms of Aging and Development, 79,* 71–114.

Marshuetz, C., Jonides, J., Smith, E. E., Reuter-Lorentz, P. A., & Koeppe, R. A. (1998). PET evidence for age-related declines in inhibitory processes. *Cognitive Neuroscience Society Annual Meeting Abstract Program: A Supplement of the Journal of Cognitive Neuroscience,* 141.

Martin, W. R., Ye, F. Q., & Allen, P. S. (1998). Increasing striatal iron content associated with normal aging. *Movement Disorders, 13,* 281–286.

Masliah, E., Mallory, M., Veinbergs, I., Miller, A., & Samuel, W. (1996). Alterations in apolipoprotein E expression during aging and neurodegeneration. *Progress in Neurobiology, 50,* 493–503.

Matochik, J. A., Chefer, S. I., Morris, E. D., Lane, M. A., Ingram, D. K., Roth, G. S., & London, E. D. (1998). Age-related decline in striatal volume in monkeys as measured by MRI. *Society for Neuroscience Abstracts, 24*(Part 1), 999.

Mattson, M. P. (1992). Calcium as sculptor and destroyer of neural circuitry. *Experimental Gerontology, 27,* 29–49.

Mayeux, R., Saunders, A., Shea, S., Mirra, S., Evans, D., Roses, A. D., Hyman, B. T., Crain, B., Tang, M. -X., & Phelps, C. H. (1998). Utility of the apolipoprotein E genotype in the diagnosis of Alzheimer's disease. *New England Journal of Medicine, 338,* 506–511.

McGeer, P. L., & McGeer, E. G. (1989). Amino acid neurotransmitters. In G. J. Siegel, B. W. Agranoff, R. W. Albers, & P. W. Molinoff (Eds.), *Basic neurochemistry: Molecular, cellular, and medical aspects* (pp. 311–332). New York: Raven.

McGeer, P. L., McGeer, E. G., Akiyama, H., Itagaki, S., Harrop, R., & Peppard, R. (1990). Neuronal degeneration and memory loss in Alzheimer's disease and aging. In J. Eccles & O. Creutzfeldt (Eds.), *The principles of design and operation of the brain* (pp. 410–431). Berlin, Germany: Springer.

McIntosh, A. R., Bookstein, F. L., Haxby, J. V., & Grady, C. L. (1996). Spatial pattern analysis of functional brain images using partial least squares. *NeuroImage, 3,* 143–157.

Meltzer, C. C., Zubieta, J. K., Brandt, J., Tune, L. E., Mayberg, H. S., & Frost, J. J. (1996). Regional hypometabolism in Alzheimer's disease as measured by positron emission tomography after correction for effects of partial volume averaging. *Neurology, 47,* 454–461.

Mesulam, M. -M. (1981). A cortical network for directed attention and unilateral neglect. *Annals of Neurology, 10,* 309–325.

Meyer, J. S., Kawamura, J., & Terayama, Y. (1994). Cerebral blood flow and metabolism with normal and abnormal aging. In M. L. Albert & J. E. Knoefel (Eds.), *Clinical neurology of aging* (pp. 178–196). New York: Oxford University Press.

Meyerson, J., Hale, S., Wagstaff, D., Poon, L. W., & Smith, G. A. (1990). The information-loss model: A mathematical theory of age-related cognitive slowing. *Psychological Review, 97,* 475–487.

Miller, A. K. H., & Corsellis, J. A. N. (1977). Evidence for a secular increase in human brain weight during the past century. *Annals of Human Biology, 4,* 253–257.

Mitchell, D. B. (1993). Implicit and explicit memory for pictures: Multiple views across the lifespan. In P. Graf & M. E. J. Masson (Eds.), *Implicit memory: New directions in cognition, development, and neuropsychology* (pp. 171–190). Hillsdale, NJ: Lawrence Erlbaum Associates.

Moeller, J. R., Ishikawa, T., Dhawan, V., Spetsieris, P., Mandel, F., Alexander, G. E., Grady, C., Pietrini, P., & Eidelberg, D. (1996). The metabolic topography of normal aging. *Journal of Cerebral Blood Flow and Metabolism, 16,* 385–398.

Moore, T. L., Killiany, R. J., Rosene, D. L., & Moss, M. B. (1998). Executive system dysfunction in the aged rhesus monkey using an analog of the Wisconsin Card Sorting Test. *Society for Neuroscience Abstracts, 24*(Part 2), 1764.

Morgan, D. G., & Finch, C. E. (1988). Dopaminergic changes in the basal ganglia: A generalized phenomenon of aging in mammals. *Annals of New York Academy of Sciences, 515*, 145–160.

Mortimer, J. (1988). Human motor behavior & aging. *Annals of New York Academy of Sciences, 515*, 54–65.

Moscovitch, M., & Winocur, G. (1992). The neuropsychology of memory and aging. In F. I. M. Craik & T. A. Salthouse (Eds.), *The handbook of aging and cognition* (pp. 315–372). Hillsdale, NJ: Lawrence Erlbaum Associates.

Mouton, P. R., Pakkenberg, B., Gundersen, H. J., & Price, D. L. (1994). Absolute number and size of pigmented locus coeruleus neurons in young and aged individuals. *Journal of Chemical Neuroanatomy, 7*, 185–190.

Muller, U., von Cramon, D. Y., & Pollmann, S. (1998). D_1- versus D_2-receptor modulation of visuospatial working memory in humans. *Neuroscience, 18*, 2720–2728.

Murphy, D. G. M., DeCarli, C., McIntosh, A. R., Daly, E., Mentis, M. J., Pietrini, P., Szczepanik, J., Schapiro, M. B., Grady, C. L., Horwitz, B., & Rapoport, S. I. (1996). Age-related differences in volumes of subcortical nuclei, brain matter, and cerebro-spinal fluid in healthy men as measured with magnetic resonance imaging (MRI). *Archives of General Psychiatry, 53*, 585–594.

Murphy, D. G. M., DeCarli, C. S., Williams, W., Rapoport, S. I., Schapiro, M. B., & Horwitz, B. (1992). Age-related differences in volumes of subcortical nuclei, brain matter, and cerebro-spinal fluid in healthy men as measured with magnetic resonance imaging (MRI). *Archives of Neurology, 49*, 839–845.

Nagahama, Y., Fukuyama, H., Yamauchi, H., Katsumi, Y., Magata, Y., Shibasaki, H., & Kimura, J. (1997). Age-related changes in cerebral blood flow activation during a card sorting test. *Experimental Brain Research, 114*, 571–577.

Namba, H., Iyo, M., Shinotoh, H., Nagatsuka, S., Fukushi, K., & Irie, T. (1998). Preserved acetylcholinesterase activity in aged cerebral cortex. *The Lancet, 351*, 881–882.

Navarro, C., & Gonzalo, L. M. (1991). *Cambios en el complejo amigdalino humano debidos a la edad* [Changes in the human amygdaloid complex due to age]. *Revista Medica de Universidad de Navarra, 35*, 7–12.

Nishimiya, J. (1988). [CT evaluation of cerebellar atrophy with aging in healthy persons]. *No To Shinkei, 40*, 585–591.

Nolde, S. F., Johnson, M. K., & Raye, C. L. (1998). The role of prefrontal cortex during tests of episodic memory. *Trends in Cognitive Sciences, 2*, 399–406.

Nyberg, L., Cabeza, R., & Tulving, E. (1996). PET studies of encoding and retrieval: The HERA model. *Psychonomic Bulletin and Review, 3*, 135–148.

Oba, H., Ohtomo, K., Araki, T., Uchiyama, G., Monzawa, S., Nogata, Y., Kachi, K., Hussain, M. Z., Koizumi, K., & Shiozawa, Z. (1996). Decreased signal intensity of cerebral cortex on T2-weighted MR images. *Radiation Medicine, 14*, 19–23.

O'Brien, J. T., Desmond, P., Ames, D., Schweitzer, I., & Tress, B. (1997). Magnetic resonance imaging correlates of memory impairment in the healthy elderly: Association with medial temporal lobe atrophy but not white matter lesions. *International Journal of Geriatric Psychiatry, 12*, 369–374.

Ogg, R. J., & Steen, R. G. (1998). Age-related changes in brain T_1 are correlated with iron concentration. *Magnetic Resonance in Medicine, 40*, 749–753.

Oscar-Berman, M., McNamara, P., & Freedman, M. (1991). Delayed response tasks: Parallels between experimental ablation studies and findings in patients with frontal lesions. In H. E. Levine, H. M. Eisenberg, & A. L. Benton (Eds.), *Frontal lobe function and dysfunction* (pp. 230–255). New York: Oxford University Press.

Panadero, A., & Gonzalo Sanz, L. M. (1988). *Memoria y senescencia: cambios en el cuerpo mamilar y nucleos talamicos anteriores debidos a la edad* [Memory and aging: Changes in the mammillary body and anterior thalamic nuclei due to age]. *Revista Medica de Universidad de Navarra, 32,* 191–200.

Pantoni, L., & Garcia, J. H. (1997). Pathogenesis of leukoaraiosis: A review. *Stroke, 28,* 652–659.

Pantoni, L., Garcia, J. H., & Gutierrez, J. A. (1996). Cerebral white matter is highly vulnerable to ischemia. *Stroke, 27,* 1641–1646.

Pascual, J., del Arco, C., González, A. M., Díaz, A., del Olmo, E., & Pazos, A. (1991). Regionally specific age-dependent decline in α_2 receptors: An autoradiographic study in human brain. *Neuroscience Letters, 133,* 279–283.

Pearlson, G. D., Harris, G. J., Powers, R. E., Barta, P. E., Camargo, E. E., Chase, G. A., Noga, J. T., & Tune, L. E. (1992). Quantitative changes in mesial temporal volume, regional cerebral blood flow, and cognition in Alzheimer's disease. *Archives of General Psychiatry, 49,* 402–408.

Petersen, R. C., Jack, C. R., Smith, G. E., Waring, S. C., & Ivnik, R. J. (1998). MRI in the diagnosis of mild cognitive impairment and Alzheimer's disease [Abstract]. *Journal of the International Neuropsychological Society, 4,* 22.

Petit-Taboué, M. C., Landeau, B., Desson, J. F. Desgranges, B., & Baron, J. C. (1998). Effects of healthy aging on the regional cerebral metabolic rate of glucose assessed with statistical parametric mapping. *NeuroImage, 7,* 176–184.

Petrides, M. (1991). Functional specialization within the dorsolateral frontal cortex for serial order memory. *Proceedings of the Royal Society of London Series B, 246,* 299–306.

Pettegrew, J. W. (1991). Nuclear magnetic resonance: Principles and applications to neuroscience research. In F. Boller & J. Grafman (Eds.), *Handbook of neuropsychology* (Vol. 5, pp. 39–56). Amsterdam: Elsevier.

Pierpaoli, W. (1998). Neuroimmunomodulation of aging: A program in the pineal gland. *Annals of New York Academy of Science, 840,* 491–497.

Plassman, B. L., Welsh-Bohmer, K. A., Bigler, E. D., Johnson, S. C., Anderson, C. V., Helms, M. J., Saunders, A. M., & Breitner, J. C. (1997). Apolipoprotein E epsilon 4 allele and hippocampal volume in twins with normal cognition. *Neurology, 48,* 985–999.

Posner, M. I., & Petersen, S. E. (1990). The attention system of the human brain. *Annual Review of Neuroscience, 13,* 25–42.

Prichard, J. W., & Rosen, B. R. (1994). Functional study of the brain by NMR. *Journal of Cerebral Blood Flow and Metabolism, 14,* 365–372.

Ragland, J. D., Glahn, D. C., Gur, R. C., Centis, D. M., Smith, R. J., Mozley, P. D., Alavi, A., & Gur, R. E. (1997). PET regional cerebral blood flow change during working and declarative memory: Relationship with task performance. *Neuropsychology, 11,* 222–231.

Raininko, R., Autti, T., Vanhanen, S. L., Ylikoski, A., Erkinjuntti, T., & Santavuori, P. (1994). The normal brain stem from infancy to old age. *Neuroradiology, 36,* 364–368.

Rajah, M. N., McIntosh, A. R., & Grady, C. L. (1998). Age-related differences in networks for face encoding and recognition. *Cognitive Neuroscience Society Annual Meeting Abstract Program: A Supplement of the Journal of Cognitive Neuroscience, 37.*

Rao, S. M., Mittenberg, W., Bernardin, L., Haughton, V., & Leo, G. J. (1989). Neuropsychological test findings in subjects with leukoaraiosis. *Archives of Neurology, 46,* 40–44.

Rapp, P. R., Gallagher, M. (1996). Preserved neuron number in the hippocampus of aged rats with spatial learning deficits. *Proceedings of National Academy of Sciences USA, 93,* 9926–9930.

Raz, N. (1996). Neuroanatomy of aging brain: Evidence from structural MRI. In E. D. Bigler (Ed.), *Neuroimaging II: Clinical applications* (pp. 153–182). New York: Academic Press.

Raz, N. (1999a). [Age-related differences in cognition]. Unpublished raw data.

Raz, N. (1999b). [Age difference in striatal and cerebellar volume]. Unpublished raw data.

Raz, N., & Acker, J. D. (1994, September). *Differential aging of subcortical structures observed in vivo: A prospective study.* Paper presented at the annual meeting of the European Neuroscience Association, Vienna, Austria.

Raz, N., Briggs, S. D., Marks, W., & Acker, J. D. (in press). Age-related deficits in generation and manipulation of mental images: II. The role of dorsolateral prefrontal cortex. *Psychology and Aging*.

Raz, N., Dupuis, J. H., Briggs, S. D., McGavran, C., & Acker, J. D. (1998b). Differential effects of age and sex on the cerebellar hemispheres and the vermis: A prospective MR study. *American Journal of Neuroradiology, 19*, 65–71.

Raz, N., Gunning, F. M., Head, D., Dupuis, J. H., McQuain, J. M., Briggs, S. D., Thornton, A. E., Loken, W. J., & Acker, J. D. (1997). Selective aging of human cerebral cortex observed *in vivo*: Differential vulnerability of the prefrontal gray matter. *Cerebral Cortex, 7*, 268–282.

Raz, N., Gunning-Dixon, F. M., Head, D. P., Dupuis, J. H., & Acker, J. D. (1998a). Neuro-anatomical correlates of cognitive aging: Evidence from structural MRI. *Neuropsychology, 12*, 95–114.

Raz, N., Millman, D., & Sarpel, G. (1990). Cerebral correlates of cognitive aging: Grey–white matter differentiation in the medial temporal lobes, and fluid vs. crystallized abilities. *Psychobiology, 18*, 475–481.

Raz, N., Torres, I., & Acker, J. D. (1995). Age, gender, and hemispheric differences in human striatum: A quantitative review and new data from *in vivo* MRI morphometry. *Neurobiology of Learning and Memory, 63*, 133–142.

Raz, N., Torres, I. J., & Acker, J. D. (1992). Age-related shrinkage of the mammary bodies: Evidence from *in vivo* MRI. *NeuroReport, 3*, 713–716.

Raz, N., Torres, I. J., Spencer, W. D., & Acker, J. D. (1993). Pathoclysis in aging human cerebral cortex: Evidence from *in vivo* MRI morphometry. *Psychobiology, 21*, 151–160.

Raz, N., Torres, I. J., Spencer, W. D., Baertschie, J. C., Millman, D., & Sarpel, G. (1993). Neuroanatomical correlates of age-sensitive and age-invariant cognitive abilities: An *in vivo* MRI investigation. *Intelligence, 17*, 407–422.

Raz, N., Torres, I. J., Spencer, W. D., White, K., & Acker, J. D. (1992). Age-related regional differences in cerebellar vermis observed *in vivo*. *Archives of Neurology, 49*, 611–617.

Reed, T., Carmelli, D., Swan, G. E., Breitner, J. C., Welsh, K. A., Jarvik, G. P., Deeb, S., & Auwerx, J. (1994). Lower cognitive performance in normal older adult male twins carrying the apolipoprotein E epsilon 4 allele. *Archives of Neurology, 51*, 1189–1192.

Reiman, E. M., Uecker, A., Caselli, R. J., Lewis, S., Bandy, D., de Leon, M. J., De Santi, S., Convit, A., Osborne, D., Weaver, A., & Thibodeau, S. N. (1998). Hippocampal volumes in cognitively normal persons at genetic risk for Alzheimer's disease. *Annals of Neurology, 44*, 288–291.

Rempp, K., Brix, G., Wenz, F., Becker, C., Gückel, F., & Lorenz, W. J. (1994). Quantification of regional cerebral blood flow by dynamic susceptibility contrast enhanced MR imaging. *Radiology, 193*, 637–641.

Riege, W. H., Metter, E. J., Kuhl, D. E., & Phelps, M. E. (1985). Brain glucose metabolism and memory functions: Age decrease in factor scores. *Journal of Gerontology, 40*, 459–467.

Rinne, J., Hietala, H., Ruotsalainen, U., Säkö, E., Laihinen, A., Någren, K., Lehikoinen, P., Oikonen, V., & Syvälahti, E. (1993). Decrease in human striatal dopamine D2 receptor density with age: A PET study with [^{11}C]raclopride. *Journal of Cerebral Blood Flow and Metabolism, 13*, 310–314.

Ritter, S., & Dinh, T. T. (1986). Progressive postnatal dilation of brain ventricles in spontaneously hypertensive rats. *Brain Research, 370*, 327–332.

Roberts, J. A., Gilardi, K. V., Lasley, B., & Rapp, P. R. (1997). Reproductive senescence predicts cognitive decline in aged female monkeys. *NeuroReport, 8*, 2047–2051.

Ross, M. H., Yurgelun-Todd, D. A., Renshaw, P. F., Maas, L. C., Mendelson, J. H., Mello, N. K., Cohen, B. M., & Levin, J. M. (1997). Age-related reduction in functional MRI response to photic stimulation. *Neurology, 48*, 173–176.

Rüb, U., Braak, H., Braak, E., Schultz, C., & Ghebremedhin, E. (1998). Distinct nuclear groups in lower brainstem consistently develop Alzheimer's disease-associated neurofibrillary changes. *Neurobiology of Aging, 19*(Suppl. 4S), Abstract No. 1014.

Rypma, B., & D'Esposito, M. (1998). Age differences in components of working memory detected by event related fMRI. *Cognitive Neuroscience Society Annual Meeting Abstract Program: A Supplement of the Journal of Cognitive Neuroscience,* 88.

Sahlberg, N., Marjamäki, P., & Rinne, J. O. (1998). Different pattern of reduction of striatal dopamine reuptake sites in Alzheimer's disease and ageing: A post mortem study with [^{3}H]CFT. *Neurobiology of Aging, 19*(Suppl. 4S), Abstract No. 1015.

Salat, D. H., Kaye, J. A., & Janowsky, J. S. (1999). Prefrontal gray and white matter volumes in healthy aging and Alzheimer's disease. *Archives of Neurology, 56,* 338–344.

Salat, D. H., Ward, A., Kaye, J. A., & Janowsky, J. S. (1997). Sex differences in the corpus callosum with aging. *Neurobiology of Aging, 18,* 191–197.

Salthouse, T. A. (1994). The aging of working memory. *Neuropsychology, 8,* 535–543.

Salthouse, T. A. (1996). The processing-speed theory of adult age differences in cognition. *Psychological Review, 103,* 403–428.

Salthouse, T. A., Mitchell, D., Skovronek, E., & Babcock, R. (1990). Effects of adult age and working memory on reasoning and spatial abilities. *Journal of Experimental Psychology: Learning, Memory, and Cognition, 15,* 507–516.

Sapolsky, R. M. (1990). The adrenocortical axis. In E. L. Schneider & J. W. Rowe (Eds.), *Handbook of the biology of aging* (pp. 330–346). New York: Academic Press.

Schacter, D. L., Savage, C. R., Alpert, N. M., Rauch, S. L., & Albert, M. S. (1996). The role of hippocampus and frontal cortex in age-related memory changes: A PET study. *Neuro-Report, 7,* 1165–1169.

Schaefer, G. B., Thompson, J. N., Bodensteiner, J. B., Gingold, M., Wilson, M., & Wilson, D. (1991). Age-related changes in the relative growth of the posterior fossa. *Journal of Child Neurology, 6,* 15–19.

Schlageter, N. L., Horwitz, B., Creasey, H., Carson, R., Duara, R., Berg, G. W., & Rapoport, S. I. (1987). Relation of measured brain glucose utilisation and cerebral atrophy in man. *Journal of Neurology, Neurosurgery, and Psychiatry, 50,* 779–785.

Schmidt, H., Schmidt, R., Fazekas, F., Semmler, J., Kapeller, P., Reinhart, B., & Kostner, G. M. (1996). Apolipoprotein E e4 allele in the normal elderly: Neuropsychologic and brain MRI correlates. *Clinical Genetics, 50,* 293–299.

Schmidt, R., Fazekas, F., Reinhart, B., Kapeller, P., Fazekas, G., Offenbacher, H., Eber, B., Schumacher, M., & Freidl, W. (1996). Estrogen replacement therapy in older women: A neuropsychological and brain MRI study. *Journal of American Geriatric Society, 44,* 1307–1313.

Schmidt, R., Schmidt, H., Fazekas, F., Schumacher, M., Niederkorn, K., Kapeller, P., Weinrauch, V., & Kostner, G. M. (1997). Apolipoprotein E polymorphism and silent microangiopathy-related cerebral damage: Results of the Austrian Stroke Prevention Study. *Stroke, 28,* 951–956.

Schmolesky, M. T., Wang, Y. -C., & Leventhal, A. G. (1998). Effects of aging upon primary visual cortex of the rhesus macaque. *Society for Neuroscience Abstracts, 24*(Part 2), 1757.

Schulz, J. B., Skalej, M., Wedekind, D., Luft, A. R., Abele, M., Voigt, K., Dichgans, J., & Klockgether, T. (1999) MRI-based volumetry differentiates idiopathic Parkinson's syndrome from MSA and PSP. *Annals of Neurology, 45,* 65–74.

Schwartz, M., Creasey, H., Grady, C. M., DeLeo, J. A., Frederickson, H. A., Cutler, N. R., & Rapoport, S. I. (1985). Computerized tomographic analysis of brain morphometrics in 30 healthy men, aged 21 to 81 years. *Annals of Neurology, 17,* 146–153.

Seeman, T. E., McEwen, B. S., Singer, B. H., Albert, M. S., & Rowe, J. W. (1997). Increase in urinary cortisol excretion and memory declines: MacArthur studies of successful aging. *Journal of Clinical Endocrinology and Metabolism, 82,* 2458–2465.

Shah, S. A., Doraiswami, P. M., Husain, M. M., Escalona, P. R., Na, C., Figiel, G. S., Patterson, L. J., Ellinwood, E. H., McDonald, W. M., Boyko, O. B., Nemeroff, C. B., & Krishnan, K. R. R. (1992). Posterior fossa abnormalities in major depression: A controlled magnetic resonance imaging study. *Acta Psychiatrica Scandinavica, 85*, 474–479.

Shah, S. A., Doraiswami, P. M., Husain, M. M., Figiel, G. S., Boyko, O. B., McDonald, W. M., Ellinwood, E. H., & Krishnan, K. R. R. (1991). Assessment of posterior fossa structures with midsagittal MRI: The effects of age. *Neurobiology of Aging, 12*, 371–374.

Shear, P., Sullivan, E. V., Mathalon, D., Lim, K. O., Davis, L. F., Yesavege, J. A., Tinklenberg, J. R., & Pfefferbaum, A. (1995). Longitudinal volumetric computed tomographic analysis of regional brain changes in normal aging and Alzheimer's disease. *Archives of Neurology, 52*, 392–402.

Sheline, Y., & Gado, M. (1998). Duration of depression but not age accelerates with hippocampal volume loss in women. *Society for Neuroscience Abstracts, 24*(Part 1), 1237.

Simic, G., Kostovic, I., Winblad, B., & Bogdanovic, N. (1997). Volume and number of neurons of the human hippocampal formation in normal aging and Alzheimer's disease. *Journal of Comparative Neurology, 379*, 482–494.

Smith, E. E., Jonides, J., & Koeppe, R. A. (1996). Dissociating verbal and spatial working memory using PET. *Cerebral Cortex, 6*, 11–20.

Smith, G. E., Bohac, D. L., Waring, S. C., Kokmen, E., Tangalos, E. G., Ivnik, R. J., & Petersen, R. C. (1998). Apolipoprotein E genotype influences cognitive 'phenotype' in patients with Alzheimer's disease but not in healthy control subjects. *Neurology, 50*, 355–362.

Soininen, H. S., Partanen, K., Pitkänen, A., Vainio, P., Hänninen, T., Hallikainen, M., Koivisto, K., & Riekkinen, P. J., Sr. (1994). Volumetric MRI analysis of the amygdala and the hippocampus in subjects with age-associated memory impairment: Correlation to visual and verbal memory. *Neurology, 44*, 1660–1668.

Soufer, R., Bremner, J. D., Arrighi, J. A., Cohen, I., Zaret, B. L., Burg, M. M., & Goldman-Rakic, P. (1998) Cerebral cortical hyperactivation in response to mental stress in patients with coronary artery disease. *Proceedings of National Academy of Sciences USA, 95*, 6454–6459.

Spencer, W. D., & Raz, N. (1995). Differential age effects on memory for content and context: A meta-analysis. *Psychology and Aging, 10*, 527–539.

Spirduso, W. W., & MacRae, P. G. (1990). Motor performance and aging. In J. Birren & W. K. Schaie (Eds.), *Handbook of the psychology of aging* (pp. 183–200). New York: Academic Press.

Squire, L. R. (1992). Memory and the hippocampus: A synthesis from findings with rates, monkeys, and humans. *Psychological Review, 99*, 195–231.

Stafford, J. L., Albert, M., Naeser, M., Sandor, T., & Garvey, A. J. (1988). Age-related changes in computed tomographic scan measurements. *Archives of Neurology, 45*, 409–415.

Steffens, D. C., McDonald, W. M., Tupler, L. A., Boyko, O. B., & Krishnan, K. R. (1996). Magnetic resonance imaging changes in putamen nuclei iron content and distribution in normal subjects. *Psychiatry Research, 68*, 55–61.

Strassburger, T. L., Lee, H. C., Daly, E. M., Szczepanik, J., Krasuski, J. S., Mentis, M. J., Salerno, J. A., DeCarli, C., Schapiro, M. B., & Alexander, G. E. (1997). Interactive effects of age and hypertension on volumes of brain structures. *Stroke, 28*, 1410–1417.

Strehler, B. L. (1986). Genetic instability as the primary cause of human aging. *Experimental Gerontology, 21*, 283–319.

Stuss, D. T., & Benson, D. F. (1984). Neuropsychological studies of the frontal lobes. *Psychological Bulletin, 95*, 3–28.

Subaiya, I., Salat, D. H., Coshow, W., Nesbit, G., & Janowsky, J. S. (1998). FMRI of auditory working memory in the aged. *Society for Neuroscience Abstracts, 24*(Part 1), 1001.

Sullivan, E. V., Marsh, L., Mathalon, D. H., Lim, K. O., & Pfefferbaum, A. (1995) Age-related decline in MRI volumes of temporal lobe gray matter but not hippocampus. *Neurobiology of Aging, 16*, 591–606.

Sullivan, M. P., de Toledo-Morrell, L., & Morrell, F. (1995). MRI detected cerebellar atrophy during aging. *Society for Neuroscience Abstracts, 21,* 1708.

Tajima, A., Hans, F. -J., Livingstone, D., Wei, L., Finnegan, W., DeMaro, J., & Fenstermacher, J. (1993). Smaller local brain volumes and cerebral atrophy in spontaneously hypertensive rats. *Hypertension, 21,* 105–111.

Talairach, J., & Toumoux, P. (1988) *Co-planar stereotaxic atlas of the human brain.* Stuttgart, Germany: G. Thieme.

Tang, Y., Nyengaard, J. R., Pakkenberg, B., & Gundersen, J. G. (1997). Age-induced white matter changes in the human brain: A stereological investigation. *Neurobiology of Aging, 18,* 609–618.

Taoka, T., Iwasaki, S., Uchida, H., Fukusumi, A., Nakagawa, H., Kichikawa, K., Takayama, K., Yoshioka, T., Takewa, M., & Ohishi, H. (1998). Age correlation of the time lag in signal change on EPI-fMRI. *Journal of Computer Assisted Tomography, 22,* 514–517.

Thornton, W. J. L., Butler, P., McGavran, C., & Raz, N. (1998). *Working memory as a mediator of visuospatial attention: Evidence from normal aging.* Manuscript submitted for publication.

Tien, A. Y., Schlaepfer, T. E., Orr, W., & Pearlson, G. D. (1998). SPECT brain blood flow changes with continuous ligand infusion during previously learned WCST performance. *Psychiatry Research: Neuroimaging, 82,* 47–52.

Tigges, J., Herndon, J. G., & Peters, A. (1990). Neuronal population of Area 4 during the life span of the rhesus monkey. *Neurobiology of Aging, 11,* 201–208.

Tigges, J., Herndon, J. G., & Peters, A. (1992). Axon terminals on Betz cell somata of Area 4 in rhesus monkey throughout adulthood. *Anatomical Record, 232,* 305–315.

Tigges, J., Herndon, J. G., & Rosene, D. L. (1995). Mild age-related changes in the dentate gyrus of adult rhesus monkeys. *Acta Anatomica, 153,* 39–48.

Tigges, J., Herndon, J. G., & Rosene, D. L. (1996). Preservation into old age of synaptic number and size in the supragranular layer of the dentate gyrus in rhesus monkeys. *Acta Anatomica, 157,* 63–72.

Tohgi, H., Takahashi, S., Kato, E., Homma, A., Niina, R., Sasaki, K., Yonezawa, H., & Sasaki, M. (1997). Reduced size of right hippocampus in 39- to 80-year-old normal subjects carrying the apolipoprotein E epsilon 4 allele. *Neuroscience Letters, 236,* 21–24.

Torvik, A., Torp, S., & Lindboe, C. F. (1986). Atrophy of the cerebellar vermis in ageing: A morphometric and histological study. *Journal of Neurological Sciences, 76,* 283–294.

Troncoso, J. C., Martin, L. J., Dal Forno, G., & Kawas, C. H. (1996). Neuropathology in controls and demented subjects from the Baltimore Longitudinal Study of Aging. *Neurobiology of Aging, 17,* 365–371.

Tulving, E., & Markowitsch, H. J. (1997). Memory beyond hippocampus. *Current Opinion in Neurobiology, 7,* 209–216.

Tupler, L. A., Coffey, C. E., Logue, P. E., Djang, W. T., & Fagan, S. M. (1992). Neuropsychological importance of subcortical white matter hyperintensity. *Archives of Neurology, 49,* 1248–1252.

Turner, R., & Jezzard, P. (1994). Magnetic resonance studies of brain functional activation using echo-planar imaging. In R. W. Thatcher, M. Hallett, T. Zeffiro, E. R. John, & M. Huerta (Eds.), *Functional neuroimaging: Technical foundations* (pp. 69–78). New York: Academic Press.

Ungerleider, L. G., & Haxby, J. V. (1994). 'What' and 'where' in the human brain. *Current Opinion in Neurobiology, 4,* 157–165.

Ungerleider, L. G., & Mishkin, M. (1982). Two cortical visual systems. In D. J. Ingle, M. A. Goodale, & R. J. Mansfield (Eds.), *Analysis of visual behavior* (pp. 549–586). Cambridge, MA: MIT Press.

Uylings, H. B. M., de Brabander, J. M., & Kramers, R. J. K. (1998). Dendritic alterations in cerebral cortex related with Alzheimer's disease and normal aging. *Neurobiology of Aging, 19*(Suppl. 4S), Abstract No. 570.

Uylings, H. B. M., West, M. J., Coleman, P. D., de Brabander, J. M., & Flood, D. G. (in press). Neuronal and cellular changes in aging brain. In J. Trojanowski & C. Clark (Eds.), *Neurodegenerative dementias and pathological mechanisms*. New York: McGraw-Hill.

Uz, T., Pesold, C., Longone, P., & Manev, H. (1998). Aging-associated up-regulation of neuronal 5-lipoxygenase expression: Putative role in neuronal vulnerability. *FASEB Journal, 12*, 439–449.

van Duijn, C. M. (1997). Menopause and the brain. *Journal of Psychosomatic Obstetrics and Gynaecology, 18*, 121–125.

Verhaeghen, P., Marcoen, A., & Goosens, L. (1993). Facts and fiction about memory aging: A quantitative integration of research findings. *Journal of Gerontology: Psychological Sciences, 48*, P157–P171.

Verhaeghen, P., & Salthouse, T. A. (1997). Meta-analyses of age-cognition relations in adulthood: Estimates of linear and nonlinear age effects and structural models. *Psychological Bulletin, 122*, 231–249.

Vogt, C., & Vogt, O. (1951). Importance of neuroanatomy in the field of neuropathology. *Neurology, 1*, 205–218.

Volkow, N. D., Gur, R. C., Wang, G. J., Fowler, J. S., Moberg, P. J., Ding, Y. S., Hitzemann, R., Smith, G., & Logan, J. (1998). Association between decline in brain dopamine activity with age and cognitive and motor impairment in healthy individuals. *American Journal of Psychiatry, 155*, 344–349.

Voytko, M. L., Ehrenkaufer, R. L., Gage, H. D., Mach, R. H., Harkness, B. A., & Tobin, J. R. (1998). Changes in cerebral blood flow of aged rhesus monkeys. *Society for Neuroscience Abstracts, 24*(Part 2), 1496.

Vymazal, J., Hajek, M., Patronas, N., Giedd, J. N., Bulte, J. W. M., Baumgarner, C., Tran, V., & Brooks, R. A. (1995). The quantitative relation between T1-weighted and T2-weighted MRI of normal gray matter and iron concentration. *Journal of Magnetic Resonance Imaging, 5*, 554–560.

Waldemar, G. (1995). Functional brain imaging with SPECT in normal aging and dementia: Methodological, pathophysiological and diagnostic aspect. *Cerebrovascular and Brain Metabolism Reviews, 7*, 89–130.

Wang, G. J., Volkow, N. D., Logan, J., Fowler, J. S., Schlyer, D., MacGregor, R. R., Hitzemann, R. J., Gur, R. C., & Wolf, A. P. (1995). Evaluation of age-related changes in serotonin 5-HT$_2$ and dopamine D$_2$ receptor availability in healthy human subjects. *Life Sciences, 56*, 249–253.

Weis, S., Kimbacher, M., Wenger, E., & Neuhold, A. (1993). Morphometric analysis of the corpus callosum using MR: Correlation of measurements with aging in healthy individuals. *American Journal of Neuroradiology, 14*, 637–645.

Wenz, F., Rempp, K., Brix, G., Knopp, M. V., Gückel, F., Heβ, T., & van Kaick, G. (1996). Age dependency of the regional cerebral blood volume (rCBV) measured with dynamic susceptibility contrast MR imaging (DSC). *Magnetic Resonance Imaging, 14*, 157–162.

West, M. J. (1993). Regionally specific loss of neurons in the aging human hippocampus. *Neurobiology of Aging, 14*, 287–293.

West, R. L. (1996). An application of prefrontal cortex function theory to cognitive aging. *Psychological Bulletin, 120*, 272–292.

Willingham, D. B. (1998). A neuropsychological theory of motor skill learning. *Psychological Review, 105*, 559–589.

Wright, C. I., Geula, C., & Mesulam, M. M. (1993). Neurological cholinesterases in the normal brain and in Alzheimer's disease: Relationship to plaques, tangles, and patterns of selective vulnerability. *Annals of Neurology, 34*, 373–384.

Yamashita, K., Kobayashi, S., Fukuda, H., Koide, H., Okada, K., & Tsunematsu, T. (1991). Kenjou koureisha no dainou hakushitsu shougai to chiteki kinou, ketsu atsu no kanren nitsuite. [The relationship between cerebral white matter changes, mental function and blood pressure in normal elderly]. *Japanese Journal of Geriatrics, 28,* 546–550.

Yamashita, K., Kobayashi, S., Fukuda, H., Koide, H., Okada, K., & Tsunematsu, T. (1991). [The relationship between cerebral white matter changes, mental function and blood pressure in normal elderly]. *Japanese Journal of Geriatrics, 28,* 546–550.

Yonezawa, H., Iyo, M., Itoh, T., Fukuda, H., Yamasaki, T., Inoue, O., Suhara, T., Shinotoh, H., Nishio, M., & Tohgi, H. (1991). Effect of aging on in vivo binding of ^{11}C-N-methylpiperone in living human frontal cortex. *Kaku Igaku, 28,* 63–69.

Yu, B. P., & Yang, R. (1996). Critical evaluation of the free radical theory of aging: A proposal for the oxidative stress hypothesis. *Annals of New York Academy of Science, 786,* 1 –11.

Zarahn, E., Aguirre, G. K., & D'Esposito, M. (1997). A trial-based experimental design for the fMRI. *NeuroImage, 6,* 122–138.

Zarahn, E., D'Esposito, M., Aguirre, G. K., Armstrong, M., Lease, J., & Kimberg, D. Y. (1998, November). *Cortical effects of bromocriptine, a D-2 dopamine receptor agonist, on working memory and prefrontal function revealed by fMRI.* Paper presented at the 28th annual meeting of the Society for Neuroscience, Los Angeles, CA.

Zilles, K., Armstrong, E., Schleicher, A., & Kretschmann, H. -J. (1988). The human pattern of gyrification in the cerebral cortex. *Anatomy and Embryology, 179,* 173–179.

Age-Related Changes in Memory:
A Cognitive Neuroscience Perspective

Matthew W. Prull
John D. E. Gabrieli
Silvia A. Bunge
Stanford University

Everyday experiences and research studies converge on the observation that advancing age is often associated with a decline in recalling and recognizing new events and facts. Age-related changes in memory may reflect many factors, including changes in social activities, modifications of daily practices, and alterations of emotional functioning. It is likely, however, that they reflect, in large part, biological changes in the neural systems that mediate memory. It seems useful, therefore, to try to understand age-related changes in memory performance in terms of age-related changes in memory systems of the human brain. A *memory system* may be defined as a specific neural network that mediates a specific mnemonic process. Memory systems analyses have identified multiple forms of memory that depend on separable neural networks (Gabrieli, 1998).

A cognitive neuroscience approach has the potential to contribute to at least three issues in research on memory and aging. These issues are heterogeneity, covariation, and amelioration. *Heterogeneity* refers to observed dissociations between forms of memory that are compromised or relatively spared by aging. A cognitive neuroscience approach can determine whether heterogeneous changes in memory abilities that accompany normal aging are attributable to differential compromise or sparing of specific memory systems. *Covariation* refers to the observation that many memory abilities decline with aging in a correlated fashion. The knowledge of how memory systems mature in adulthood should help distinguish between memory difficulties that reflect the decline of a single process from other memory difficulties that reflect the correlated, but distinct, decline of other processes. *Amelioration* refers to the desire to understand how various patterns of age-related memory loss reflect various age-related changes in the brain and to the use of that knowledge to reduce or eliminate declines in memory abilities that diminish the quality of life for older people. Identifying the neural bases for age-related memory decline through memory systems analyses provides the initial step in developing biological interventions that target specific neural systems.

Studies of patients with focal lesions, or relatively focal degenerative lesions, have provided the evidence for identifying important components of memory systems. These findings are related in two ways to normal aging, which does not feature focal lesions. First, investigators can compare the profile of age-related changes in memory with the consequences of various focal lesions. To the extent that age-related changes in memory performance resemble those seen after focal damage to a particular memory system, age-related degenerative compromise of that same system may be hypothesized. Second, memory systems that are identified in studies of patients with focal lesions can be examined directly in older adults, either post-mortem by histological methods (e.g., cell counts) or in vivo by quantitative structural or functional neuroimaging methods. Structural neuroimaging in cognitive aging research attempts to measure age-related changes in the volume of certain brain regions; changes in memory that occur in aging can therefore be interpreted as reflecting anatomical changes in regional volume (see chap. 1, this volume). Functional neuroimaging methods, such as positron emission tomography (PET) and functional magnetic resonance imaging (fMRI), allow researchers to visualize brain regions that become more active during a memory task than during a baseline or comparison task. These methods also facilitate the direct comparison of brain regions that are active in young and older people performing memory tasks. A handful of studies has now applied these methods to adult participants of various ages, and we review these studies in later sections.

Functional neuroimaging methods hold the promise of relating age-related changes in memory performance to age-related changes in neural functioning. However, there are important factors to consider in the comparison of functional brain images from young and older adults. One factor is that both PET and fMRI derive their signals not from neural activity directly, but rather from local changes in blood flow or metabolism that are correlated with neural activity. Local vascular changes affect the distribution of an injected radionuclide (usually O^{15}) in PET or magnetic properties that are blood-oxygen level dependent (BOLD) in fMRI. The BOLD contrast reflects interactions among cerebral blood flow, cerebral blood volume, blood oxygen extraction, and local metabolism that occur as a consequence of neural activation. Thus, different brain activation patterns in young and older adults could reflect not only age-related changes in neural processes, but also age-related changes in vascular processes. A second factor to consider is that age-related changes in neural activation occur in the context of age-related atrophy of various brain structures. It seems important, therefore, to take into account normal, age-related differences in regional brain volume when interpreting functional activation differences between young and older adults. Finally, beyond these physiological issues, there remain additional important and unresolved psychological issues for the interpretation of age-related differences in functional images. For example, differences in brain activation between young and older adults may reflect the cause of the age-related memory difference, the compensatory consequence of that difference, or both. Therefore, functional neuroimaging techniques promise many new insights into the brain basis of age-related changes in memory, but the validity of those insights depends on the consideration of psychological and biological factors.

Our goals in the present chapter are threefold. In the previous edition of this handbook, the chapter on the neuropsychology of memory and aging interpreted age-related declines in recall and recognition in terms of age-related degeneration in medial-temporal lobe and frontal lobe regions (Moscovitch & Winocur, 1992). Our first goal, therefore, is to review the findings that support this interpretation in light of new evidence that has appeared subsequent to that chapter. The recent burst of functional neuroimaging studies is particularly relevant in this regard. Our second goal is to consider age-related changes in forms of memory that are mediated by regions other than the medial-temporal and frontal lobe areas implicated in recall and recognition. These include memory measures of skill learning, repetition priming, and conditioning, each of which are dissociable from recall and recognition. We ask whether these forms of memory, and their underlying neural bases, are relatively spared in aging or whether they too are compromised together with recall and recognition.

A third goal is to consider normal age-related changes in memory performance in relation to two common age-related neurological diseases, Alzheimer's disease (AD) and Parkinson's disease (PD). Although much cognitive aging research focuses on healthy older people, these two diseases account for a great deal of memory loss in people over age 60. Thus, aging itself is associated with a dramatic rise in the risk of acquiring a disease that affects memory. The analysis of memory loss in AD and PD is salient to understanding normal age-related memory decline in at least two ways. First, the chronic, degenerative, and age-related qualities of these diseases are more similar to healthy aging than are acute, focal lesions. These diseases may therefore offer clues about the non-focal etiology of age-associated memory loss. Second, because of the insidious and progressive nature of diseases such as AD, the boundary between healthy and unhealthy aging is not sharp. There is evidence that as many as 20% of older individuals in a given "normal" sample are in a transitional state between normal aging and AD (Sliwinski, Lipton, Buschke, & Stewart, 1996). Such diversity among nondemented older people, within and across study populations, may account for the remarkable diversity of results concerning the sparing or compromise of various kinds of memory in aging. Multiple factors likely contribute to such diverse outcomes, but variable inclusion among older adult samples of individuals who are in an early stage of an age-related degenerative disease may be a critical factor. The ability to identify and isolate early disease-specific effects on memory is likely to provide a more clear picture of normal, age-related effects on memory.

We review age-comparative studies of four forms of long-term memory: declarative memory, skill learning, repetition priming, and conditioning. For each form of memory, we begin by surveying the evidence from lesion data and imaging studies of young adults to outline the relevant memory system. We then examine behavioral studies of young and older adults to determine the extent to which normal age-related changes occur in that form of memory. Salient AD and PD studies are described and compared with studies of normal aging, and recent evidence from structural and functional neuroimaging methods applied to young and older adults are reviewed where appropriate. Our review is concluded with thoughts about the current state of knowledge about the cognitive neuroscience of memory and aging.

DECLARATIVE MEMORY

Medial-Temporal Lobe Lesions and Diencephalic Lesions

Declarative memory (N. J. Cohen & Squire, 1980), or explicit memory (Graf & Schacter, 1985), refers to conscious remembrance of past events and facts, and is tested by means of free or cued recall, or recognition. Two forms of declarative memory can be distinguished: episodic memory, which refers to conscious recollection of personally experienced events that occurred in a specific place and time, and semantic memory, which refers to the retrieval of factual information or general world knowledge (Tulving, 1983).

Critical components of the system underlying declarative memory are revealed by cases of amnesia, a syndrome characterized by a circumscribed inability to gain new long-term memories despite intact immediate memory, cognition, perception, and motivation. All amnesic patients have an anterograde amnesia (an inability to gain memories subsequent to the onset of the amnesia), but they vary considerably in the severity of their retrograde amnesia (i.e., the extent of time for which they cannot remember information that was acquired before the onset of the amnesia). Retrograde amnesias are temporally graded, with remote memories more likely to be spared than memories acquired more closely to the onset of the amnesia. Most cases of amnesia follow injury to the medial-temporal lobe or to regions of the diencephalon (N. J. Cohen & Squire, 1980; Scoville & Milner, 1957). Unilateral left or right medial-temporal lobe lesions can lead to material-specific deficits for verbal and nonverbal information, respectively (Milner, 1971). Bilateral medial-temporal lobe damage produces a global amnesia that encompasses all types of material, and impairs the ability to learn new events (episodic memories) and facts (semantic memories; Gabrieli, Cohen, & Corkin, 1988).

The medial-temporal lobe memory system consists of a number of structures, many of which can be classified as belonging to one of two regions (see Fig. 2.1). High-level unimodal and polymodal cortical inputs converge on the parahippocampal region, which consists of the parahippocampal and perirhinal cortices (Suzuki & Amaral, 1994). The parahippocampal region in turn provides inputs to the hippocampal region, which consists of the dentate gyrus, hippocampus proper (CA fields), and subiculum. Entorhinal cortex is variably classified as part of the parahippocampal region or part of the hippocampal region. A clinically significant anterograde amnesia can develop following lesions that are restricted to a small region of the hippocampus proper, the CA1 field (Zola-Morgan, Squire, & Amaral, 1986). Further damage that extends to other medial-temporal lobe structures exacerbates the severity of anterograde amnesia and increases the temporal extent of retrograde amnesia. For example, when lesions include the entorhinal and perirhinal cortices, retrograde amnesias can extend back 1 or 2 decades prior to injury (Corkin, Amaral, González, Johnson, & Hyman, 1997; Rempel-Clower, Zola, Squire, & Amaral, 1996).

Functional neuroimaging studies indicate that medial-temporal lobe structures participate during encoding and retrieval of declarative memories. Medial-temporal lobe activations that occur during encoding are linked to stimulus novelty: They are greater for stimuli seen initially than for stimuli seen repeatedly (Gabrieli, Brewer, Desmond, & Glover, 1997; Stern et al., 1996; Tulving, Markowitsch, Kapur, Habib, & Houle, 1994). Encoding activations are left-lateralized for verbal materials (words) and are right-lateralized for nonverbal materials (faces; Kelley et al., 1998). Studies using event-related fMRI, in which separate activation values are recorded for each stimulus, have found a positive correlation between the

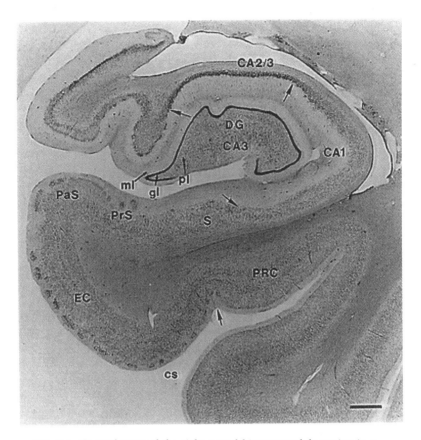

FIG. 2.1. Coronal view of the right rostral hippocampal formation in a normal adult. CA1 and CA2/3 refer to the CA fields of the hippocampus proper. Large arrows mark the boundaries between regions. Scale bar is 1 mm. DG = dentate gyrus; ml = molecular layer of the dentate gyrus; gl = granule cell layer; pl = polymorphic layer; S = subiculum; PrS = presubiculum; PaS = parasubiculum; EC = entorhinal cortex; PRC = perirhinal cortex; cs = collateral sulcus. From "Three Cases of Enduring Memory Impairment After Bilateral Damage Limited to the Hippocampal Formation," by N. L. Rempel-Clower, S. M. Zola, L. R. Squire, & D. G. Amaral, 1996, *Journal of Neuroscience*, 16, p. 5240. Copyright 1996 by Society for Neuroscience. Reprinted with permission.

magnitude of parahippocampal activation in response to a particular stimulus during encoding, and the likelihood of later remembering that stimulus (Brewer, Zhao, Desmond, Glover, & Gabrieli, 1998; Wagner, Schacter, et al., 1998).

Medial-temporal lobe activations observed during memory retrieval are associated with successful retrieval. For example, activations are greater when people make memory judgments for studied materials than for novel materials, and for well-remembered than for poorly-remembered materials (Schacter, Alpert, Savage, Rauch, & Albert, 1996; Schacter, Savage, Alpert, Rauch, & Albert, 1996; Squire et al., 1992). Additionally, across individuals, there is a positive correlation between the magnitude of anterior hippocampal activation and retrieval accuracy (Nyberg, McIntosh, Houle, Nilsson, & Tulving, 1996). The distinct roles of different medial-temporal lobe structures in the encoding and retrieval of declarative memories were demonstrated in an fMRI study showing separate encoding-related activations in the parahippocampal cortex and retrieval-related activations in the subiculum within individuals (Gabrieli, Brewer, et al., 1997). Neuroimaging studies, therefore, permit further specification of which particular declarative memory processes are mediated by which particular medial-temporal lobe structures.

Further evidence about the importance of medial-temporal lobe structures for declarative memory comes from AD. At present, the diagnosis of AD can only be validated at autopsy by the presence of characteristic neuropathological structures, such as amyloid plaques and neurofibrillary tangles (Khachaturian, 1985). However, a reliable antemortem diagnosis of AD can be made using a set of standard criteria adopted by the National Institute of Neurological and Communicative Disorders and Stroke (NINCDS) and the Alzheimer's Disease and Related Disorders Association (ADRDA) (McKhann et al., 1984). The initial damage in most cases of AD occurs in the medial-temporal lobe (Hyman, Van Hoesen, Damasio, & Barnes, 1984), and this may be why AD is associated with an initial and severe declarative memory deficit. Later stages of the disease are accompanied by dementia, as patients begin to suffer from multiple cognitive declines in language, attention, and reasoning that reflect additional compromise of association neocortices. Structural imaging studies have reported that the volume of the hippocampus is significantly reduced even in very mild AD relative to healthy, age-matched controls (e.g., deToledo-Morrell et al., 1997; Jack et al., 1997; Seab et al., 1988). However, AD also involves a regionally specific loss of cholinergic neurons in the basal forebrain (Arendt, Bigl, Arendt, & Tennstedt, 1983; Coyle, Price, & DeLong, 1983), and it is known that amnesia can develop following relatively restricted basal forebrain lesions (e.g., Morris, Bowers, Chatterjee, & Heilman, 1992). Thus, the AD-related declarative memory deficit cannot be attributed solely to medial-temporal lobe damage.

Diencephalic structures are also essential for normal declarative memory functioning. Patients with severe amnesia due to Korsakoff's syndrome (KS), a disorder caused by nutritional deficits associated with chronic alcoholism, typically do not sustain damage to medial-temporal lobe regions but do have damage to one or more structures of the diencephalon. These structures include the mammillary bodies and the dorsomedial nucleus of the thalamus (Squire, Amaral, & Press, 1990; Victor, Adams, & Collins, 1971). Direct lesions to these and other diencephalic regions, or to their projections, also compromise declarative memory (D'Esposito, Verfaellie, Alexander, & Katz, 1995; Graff-Radford, Tranel, Van Hoesen, & Brandt, 1990; Tanaka, Miyazawa, Akaoka, & Yamada, 1997; von Cramon, Hebel, & Schuri, 1990). Amnesias following medial-temporal lobe or diencephalic lesions are quite similar in nature, perhaps reflecting the extensive anatomical interconnections between these regions.

In sum, lesion evidence indicates that the medial-temporal lobe, the diencephalon, and the basal forebrain include critical components of the declarative memory system. Furthermore, functional neuroimaging evidence indicates that particular parts of the medial-temporal lobe mediate specific aspects of encoding and retrieving declarative memories.

Strategic Memory and Frontal Lesions

Declarative memory tasks vary in their strategic demands (i.e., how much planning, organization, evaluation, or manipulation is required to perform the task). Recognition tests, in which studied items are re-presented along with novel distractor items, typically require the least amount of strategy as responses can be guided relatively easily and quickly on the basis of stimulus familiarity. Free recall tests, on the other hand, require people to devise their own strategy for recollecting prior experiences without experimenter-supplied assistance. For example, free recall performance is often enhanced by the use of organizational strategies. Organizational strategies are revealed when semantically-related words are recalled together, even though the words may have been arranged randomly at study (Bousfield, 1953). They are also revealed when the same unrelated words are recalled together over several successive recall trials, indicating the use of subjective organization (unique, self-initiated strategies that are used for organizing information in memory; Tulving, 1962). Other strategic memory tests present the studied items to participants, but demand the retrieval of certain temporal or spatial properties of the episodes in which the stimuli were encountered. Such tests include memory for source (was the word BARREL originally heard in a male or female voice?), list discrimination (was BARREL presented in the first or second list?), frequency (how many times was the word BARREL presented?), and recency or temporal ordering (was BARREL presented after KITTEN?). These tests are inherently more difficult than tests of recognition, but difficult retrieval tasks are precisely where strategic operations are needed the most in order to complete them effectively.

There is considerable evidence that successful performance on strategic memory tasks depends on the integrity of the frontal lobes. Lesions to dorsolateral prefrontal and anterior frontal regions lead to specific impairments on tests of strategic memory. Impairments have been demonstrated on tests of source memory (Janowsky, Shimamura, & Squire, 1989), list discrimination (M. A. Butters, Kaszniak, Glisky, Eslinger, & Schacter, 1994), frequency of occurrence (Angeles Jurado, Junqué, Pujol, Oliver, & Vendrell, 1997; Smith & Milner, 1988), recency (Milner, Corsi, & Leonard, 1991), temporal ordering (Shimamura, Janowsky, & Squire, 1990), and recall relative to recognition (Wheeler, Stuss, & Tulving, 1995). Patients with frontal lobe lesions often exhibit specific deficits in the use of subjective organization (Gershberg & Shimamura, 1995; Stuss et al., 1994). These strategic memory deficits occur even when performance on corresponding recognition tests is normal. Convergent neuroimaging evidence has reported greater frontal lobe activation for recency judgments than for recognition memory judgments (Cabeza, Mangels, et al., 1997), and alterations in frontal lobe activation when retrieval strategies are manipulated through instructions (Wagner, Desmond, Glover, & Gabrieli, 1998).

Specific impairments in strategic declarative memory performance may be contrasted with those seen in amnesia. In most cases, amnesic patients do poorly on both strategic and nonstrategic memory tests. This strategic memory deficit in amnesic patients, however, is likely to reflect a consequence of their global declarative memory deficit. Consider, for example, the mnemonic demands of a source monitoring task. To identify the source of a learned fact, one must remember what the fact was in the first place. If the fact itself cannot be remembered, source identification will fail. What is needed to determine whether amnesic patients are disproportionately impaired on strategic memory tests is a situation in which amnesic patients and controls are first equated for their nonstrategic memory performance. Once equated, strategic memory can then be examined in the amnesic individuals to determine whether deficits in strategic memory remain. When such matching procedures were carried out for a mixed group of amnesic individuals with various etiologies (AD, anoxia, rupture of the anterior communicating artery, and closed-head injury), their deficits in a strategic memory task involving source monitoring were related to their performance on tests of frontal lobe function, not to the severity of their amnesia (Schacter, Harbluk, & McLachlan, 1984). Squire, Nadel, and Slater (1981) administered a strategic memory task involving list discrimination to the patient N.A., who suffered a severe amnesia following damage to the dorsomedial nucleus of the thalamus. N.A., however, performed normally on various tests that are sensitive to frontal lobe dysfunction (Squire, 1982). When N.A.'s nonstrategic memory performance was equated to that of healthy controls by testing the controls after long delays, N.A.'s performance on the list discrimination task was unimpaired. This suggests that amnesic patients without frontal lobe dysfunction exhibit deficits on strategic tasks that are proportional to their level of nonstrategic task performance. When frontal lobe dysfunction becomes evident, however, strategic memory performance becomes disproportionally impaired relative to nonstrategic task performance.

Strategic memory has also been examined in PD patients, who experience neural degeneration in the basal ganglia. The basal ganglia is a collection of subcortical structures including the caudate nucleus and putamen (together, the striatum), globus pallidus, subthalamic nucleus, and substantia nigra (see Fig. 2.2, for the location of these structures relative to the medial-temporal lobe). The primary pathology in PD is a loss of neurons in the substantia nigra pars compacta (about an 80% loss), resulting in a depletion of the neurotransmitter dopamine (DA) in the striatum (also about an 80% reduction). PD is best known for its movement disorders,

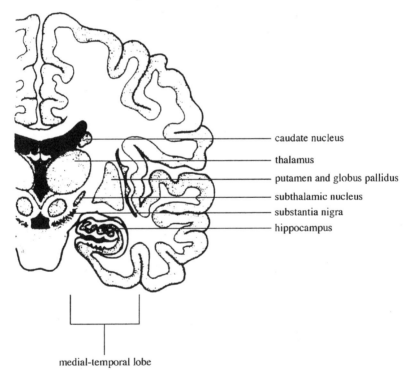

FIG. 2.2. Coronal view of basal ganglia relative to the hippocampus and medial-temporal lobe. From *Neuroanatomy: A conceptual approach* (p. 405), by C. Romero-Sierra: Churchill-Livingstone. Copyright 1986 by Churchill Livingstone, Inc. Adapted with permission.

such as resting tremor, cogwheel rigidity, inability to initiate spontaneous movement (akinesia), and slowness in executing movement (bradykinesia). In addition, PD patients have strategic memory impairments. Relative to healthy age-matched controls, PD patients have demonstrated impairments on tests of strategic memory involving list discrimination (Taylor, Saint-Cyr, & Lang, 1990), frequency of occurrence (Nichelli, Appollonio, Clark, & Grafman, 1994), recency (Sagar, Sullivan, Gabrieli, Corkin, & Growdon, 1988), temporal ordering (Vriezen & Moscovitch, 1990), recall relative to recognition (Gabrieli, Singh, Stebbins, & Goetz, 1996), and subjective organization in recall (Gabrieli, Singh, et al., 1996; Taylor et al., 1990).

PD and frontal lobe lesions both result in a specific declarative memory impairment on strategic memory tasks, and this similarity may occur for one or more reasons. One possibility is that PD patients sustain some degree of frontal lobe damage in addition to nigrostriatal damage. Indeed, there is evidence that damage occurs to the mesocortical dopaminergic projections from the ventral tegmental area to the frontal lobes (Javoy-Agid & Agid, 1980; Scatton, Rouquier, Javoy-Agid, & Agid, 1982). A second possibility arises from the extensive interconnectivity between the frontal cortex and the striatum; striatal damage may lead to deafferentation of corticostriatal circuits that results in frontal lobe dysfunction. Cerebral metabolic imaging studies have shown decreased frontal activity in PD patients relative to age-matched controls (Bès et al., 1983; Eidelberg et al., 1994; Wolfson, Leenders, Brown, & Jones, 1985). Thus, memory impairments associated with PD can be characterized as the result of disturbances in frontostriatal circuits, or "loops" (Alexander, DeLong, & Strick, 1986).

An important question is what processing deficit underlies the dissociation often observed in patients with frontal lobe lesions or PD between strategic memory tests and recognition memory tests? It is not recognition processes per se because extension of the study-test interval from a few minutes to 1 hr produces a recognition deficit for PD patients (Stebbins, Gabrieli, Masciari, Monti, & Goetz, 1999). Rather, it must be some capacity that is minimally taxed in standard recognition tests, but is maximally taxed when strategic operations become important for declarative memory performance.

A strong candidate for this capacity is the executive component of working memory (Gabrieli, Singh, et al., 1996). Working memory is a multicomponent cognitive system involved in the on-line processing and manipulation of currently relevant information. Baddeley (1986) proposed a fundamental distinction between domain-specific immediate memory stores for verbal (phonological loop) and visuospatial (visuospatial scratchpad) information, and a central executive that coordinates multiple mental processes. The executive component has a limited capacity that becomes increasingly taxed as a task becomes increasingly complex. Evidence that working memory depends critically on frontal cortices comes from many sources, including human and animal lesion studies (Goldman-Rakic, 1987; Owen, Morris, Sahakian, Polkey, & Robbins, 1996), single-cell recording studies (Funahashi, Bruce, & Goldman-Rakic, 1989), and neuroimaging studies (e.g., J. D. Cohen et al., 1994; Jonides et al., 1993). Functional neuroimaging studies indicate that executive processes in humans may be especially linked to dorsolateral prefrontal cortex (e.g., D'Esposito, Detre, et al., 1995; Petrides, Alivisatos, Meyer, & Evans, 1993). Furthermore, there is considerable evidence that dopamine plays a critical role in frontal lobe-mediated working memory processes from animal (Brozoski, Brown, Rosvold, & Goldman, 1979; Sawaguchi & Goldman-Rakic, 1991) and human (Luciana, Depue, Arbisi, & Leon, 1992; Müller, von Cramon, & Pollmann, 1998) drug studies. Severe dopamine depletion, therefore, likely accounts for reduced executive working memory capacity in PD (Gabrieli, 1996; Gabrieli, Singh, et al., 1996).

It may be hypothesized, therefore, that strategic memory tests tax the capacity of executive working memory stores. When the fronto-striatal basis of that capacity is reduced due to a focal lesion or a degenerative dopamine depletion, so is strategic memory performance. This hypothesis is supported by the finding that statistical control (analysis of covariance) of executive working memory deficits in PD renders multiple strategic memory deficits to be nonsignificant (Gabrieli, Singh, et al., 1996). Thus, it appears that strategic memory performance depends on the integrity of a fronto-striatal dopaminergic system that is an essential component of executive working memory.

Declarative Memory in Normal Aging

In studies of aging, the question arises as to whether older adults display a pattern of declarative and strategic memory impairment that is similar to the pattern exhibited by patients with focal lesions and/or degenerative disease. Because normal aging is not characterized by the extensive brain injuries that accompany these conditions, the memory deficits in normal aging are not expected to be as severe. Rather, it is the patterns of memory decline in aging, and the similarities of those patterns of decline to other neurological populations, that are of interest. The first question that we ask is whether normal aging is associated with memory difficulties for newly learned episodic and semantic information that are similar to the anterograde memory deficits that are observed in amnesia.

Episodic and Semantic Memory in Normal Aging. The considerable amount of data indicating that older adults perform less well than young adults on recall and recognition tests of newly learned information provides strong support for the reality of age-related changes in episodic memory (see chap. 5, this volume). These age-related changes are not peculiar to the artificial nature of memory tests that are administered in laboratory settings, because they also occur on batteries of tasks that are designed to emulate memory in everyday life (e.g., Kirasic, Allen, Dobson, & Binder, 1996) and because they occur in naturalistic settings that resemble everyday environments (e.g., Molander & Bäckman, 1990). Age-related declines in episodic memory tests are observed using materials that range from the meaningless (e.g., pictures of novel, unfamiliar objects; Schacter, Cooper, & Valdiserri, 1992) to the highly meaningful (e.g., information on labels of medicine bottles; Morrell, Park, & Poon, 1990). Age-dependent relationships in memory functioning have been documented primarily in studies that use cross-sectional designs (in which different groups of young and older individuals are compared), but they are also observed using longitudinal designs (in which the same individuals are compared at different points in time; e.g., Arenberg, 1983; Hultsch, Hertzog, Small, McDonald-Miszczak, & Dixon, 1992; Zelinski & Burnight, 1997).

Meta-analyses of studies that have examined recall and recognition in young and older adults have confirmed the results from individual experiments by reporting significant negative relationships between age and episodic memory test performance. In one such meta-analysis, for example, the average older adult above the age of 60 was situated between the 16th and 25th percentile of the young adult's performance distribution on various measures of recall. Such a result suggests that the recall performance level of the typical older individual is nearly 1 *SD* below the mean of the young adult's distribution (Verhaeghen, Marcoen, & Goossens, 1993). Additional meta-analyses of memory and aging also provide evidence for the superior performance of young adults relative to older adults on recall and recognition measures (LaVoie & Light, 1994; Spencer & Raz, 1995; Verhaeghen & Salthouse, 1997).

Although it is clear from these meta-analyses that aging is associated with a decline in declarative memory for recent episodic information, the decline does not appear to be restricted to such information. For example, it has also been observed that older adults are less able than young adults to deliberately retrieve novel factual information (e.g., McIntyre & Craik, 1987; Schacter, Osowiecki, Kaszniak, Kihlstrom, & Valdiserri, 1994). Thus, as is the case for amnesic patients, it appears that normal aging can be best described as being associated with a declarative memory deficit for new episodic (events) and semantic (facts) information.

A second question that can be asked is whether older adults exhibit retrograde memory losses that resemble the retrograde amnesia that variably occurs following medial-temporal lobe lesions. The assessment of retrograde memory losses in aging is of great interest, but the testing of remote memory is plagued with methodological problems because the original learning of events that occurred long ago is uncontrolled and the veracity of responses for personal experiences is difficult to ascertain. These difficulties probably underlie the inconsistent results that have been found in studies of remote memory in older adults (reviewed by Kausler, 1994).

Some sources of evidence, however, suggest that memory in old age is superior for information learned earlier rather than later in life. Research on autobiographical memory in older adults, for example, indicates that experiences from early in life (between 10 and 30 years of age) are reported more often than those occurring during middle adulthood (between 30 and 50 years of age; Fitzgerald & Lawrence, 1984; Rubin & Schulkind, 1997). Older adults have also demonstrated greater accuracy on factual memory tests of Academy Award winners, news stories, and teams that played in the World Series, if those events occurred earlier rather than later in life (Rubin, Rahhal, & Poon, 1998).

Also relevant to the question of whether a retrograde memory loss exists in old age are studies that test older adults on various words or pictures representing items that were either common in the years when elderly adults were young (dated material) or became more common in their later years (contemporary material). If older adults exhibit a retrograde memory loss, then memory should be superior for dated relative to contemporary materials, and such a pattern of performance should not be evident among young adults. Using word-frequency norms published in 1921 and 1967, one study found that older adults recalled more words that were high in frequency at the time when older adults were young (the 1921 words) than words that were later introduced into the English vocabulary and became highly frequent by 1967 (Worden & Sherman-Brown, 1983). Young adults, in contrast, showed exactly the reverse pattern: superior recall for contemporary words (highly frequent in 1967) than for dated words (highly frequent in 1921). Similar results were reported in a study of recognition memory for faces that represented contemporary or dated personalities (Bäckman, 1991). Also along these lines, Poon and Fozard (1978) found that older adults were faster to name pictures of objects that were believed to be common in their youth (e.g., a churn or a washboard) than pictures of objects that were currently in wide use (e.g., a hair dryer or a snowmobile). Young adults, in contrast, were faster to name the pictures corresponding to contemporary objects rather than dated objects.

Superior memory for episodic and semantic information acquired early in life could be considered as being similar to temporally graded retrograde amnesia, but there are other plausible explanations. First, cases of amnesia with acute onsets offer a distinct boundary between retrograde and anterograde amnesia. Aging, in contrast, does not have such a boundary, so it is difficult to know whether a memory difficulty in aging reflects a retrograde or anterograde memory impairment. For example, an older person may fail to remember events and facts from 20 years ago because of an anterograde memory decline that hindered the initial learning of that information, because of a retrograde memory decline that hinders the retrieval of that information, or both. Second, certain events and facts may procure a special status in memory when they are learned during critical periods of language development or personal development into adulthood. Third, memories acquired early in life will have an advantage of being recalled and used much more often than memories acquired later in life. At present, therefore, it is difficult to conclude that the inferiority of memories acquired later in life reflects a retrograde loss of information rather than an anterograde advantage for early memories.

The age-related decline in anterograde or new learning is clear-cut, however, and it is natural to ask whether this decline reflects degeneration in the medial-temporal lobe regions that are essential for declarative memory. Early post-mortem studies frequently reported widespread hippocampal cell loss with advancing age (reviewed by Coleman & Flood, 1987), but recent improvements in counting techniques suggest that this loss is minimal, being restricted to small subdivisions within the hippocampal region (see Morrison & Hof, 1997, for a review). In a sample of brains ranging from 13 to 85 years of age, M. J. West (1993) reported that age-related cell loss was evident in only two of five subdivisions of the hippocampal region, the hilus of the dentate gyrus and the subiculum. In another study, the number of neurons in the entorhinal cortex did not change significantly from 60 to 89 years of age (Gómez-Isla et al., 1996). However, there is some variability in these outcomes. A post-mortem study of brains ranging from 16 to 99 years of age reported robust age-related neuron loss in the CA1 field of the hippocampus proper (Simic, Kostovic, Winblad, & Bogdanovic, 1997). This result was not found by M. J. West (1993), who reported nonsignificant age-related declines in the number of CA1 neurons. Differences in counting methods or in participant characteristics may be responsible for the different results in these two studies. Nevertheless, recent studies have challenged previous beliefs that aging is associated with pervasive hippocampal cell loss, suggesting instead that aging has a limited effect on medial-temporal lobe cytoarchitecture. Whether such a limited effect has a significant influence on declarative memory, however, remains unknown.

Structural MRI methods have also been used to measure age-related changes in the volume of the hippocampal formation. Some studies have reported age-related declines in hippocampal volume (Coffey et al., 1992; Jack et al., 1997), but others have found that the volume of the hippocampus remains unchanged from young adulthood to old age (Sullivan,

Marsh, Mathalon, Lim, & Pfefferbaum, 1995). Furthermore, studies that have found age-related differences in hippocampal volume have asked whether significant relationships exist between the anatomical changes and declarative memory performance. Within a group of older adults (range = 55 to 87 years), Golomb et al. (1994) found that individuals with less hippocampal volume performed less well on a composite delayed recall measure than those with greater hippocampal volume. This relationship held even when various demographic variables and generalized cerebral volume estimates were statistically controlled (see Figs. 2.3 and 2.4). Similar relationships between recall performance and hippocampal volume have been found and reported elsewhere (O'Brien, Desmond, Ames, Schweitzer, & Tress, 1997; Raz, Gunning-Dixon, Head, Dupuis, & Acker, 1998), but they are not ubiquitous (Sullivan et al., 1995). Moreover, within older adults, volume estimates of the hippocampal formation (but not superior temporal gyrus) significantly predicted the magnitude of subsequent decline in paragraph memory after a test–retest interval of nearly 4 years (Golomb et al., 1996). Thus, hippocampal volume in old age is not only correlated with current memory performance, but also predicts the rate of further memory decline over time.

   PET studies have begun to examine the influence of age-related factors on the functional integrity of the medial-temporal region. Grady et al.

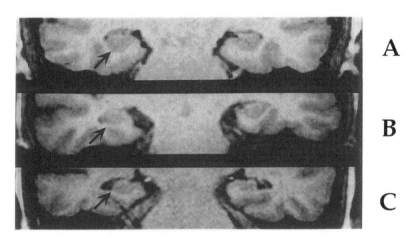

FIG. 2.3. Coronal MRI images focused on medial-temporal lobe regions in 3 older participants showing, from top to bottom (A through C), progressively increasing hippocampal atrophy. From "Hippocampal Formation Size in Normal Human Aging: A Correlate of Delayed Secondary Memory Performance," by J. Golomb, A. Kluger, M. J. de Leon, S. H. Ferris, A. Convit, M. S. Mittelman, J. Cohen, H. Rusinek, S. De Santi, & A. E. George, 1994, *Learning and Memory, 1*, p. 49. Copyright 1994 by Cold Spring Harbor Laboratory Press. Reprinted with permission.

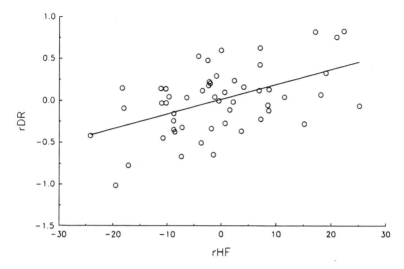

FIG. 2.4. Scatter plot depicting the relationship between a measure of hippocampal volume (rHF) and composite delayed recall performance (rDR) among healthy older adults. From "Hippocampal Formation Size in Normal Human Aging: A Correlate of Delayed Secondary Memory Performance," by J. Golomb, A. Kluger, M. J. de Leon, S. H. Ferris, A. Convit, M. S. Mittelman, J. Cohen, H. Rusinek, S. De Santi, & A. E. George, 1994, *Learning and Memory, 1*, p. 51. Copyright 1994 by Cold Spring Harbor Laboratory Press. Reprinted with permission.

(1995) reported that face encoding was associated with activity in the hippocampal region and parahippocampal gyrus for young adults but not for older adults. Together with additional evidence, the lack of me-dial-temporal lobe activity in older adults was interpreted as reflecting a difficulty among older people in engaging the neural systems necessary to establish durable memory traces. In contrast, another PET study re-ported equivalent hippocampal activation in young and older adults during successful recall of studied words (Schacter, Savage, et al., 1996; see also Bäckman et al., 1997). There are, of course, numerous differences in procedures, materials, and possibly participants, in these studies that may account for the different results (faces vs. words, encoding vs. re-trieval). By themselves, these results raise the possibility that medial-tem-poral structures involved in encoding are more affected by age-related processes than those involved in retrieving declarative memories. Studies that directly compare encoding and retrieval within the same individuals and with the same types of material will be needed to confirm this interesting possibility.

In a rapidly changing area of research, three tentative points may be made about the influence of aging on the medial-temporal region. First, there are currently very few studies that have examined memory-related activation in the medial-temporal lobe in young and older adults, and more research is needed to test the conclusions and suggestions that have been drawn from these initial studies. Second, improving histological and functional neuroimaging techniques have altered the research agenda from broad assumptions about widespread degeneration to much more specific inquiries about the relation of specific medial-temporal lobe structures to specific declarative memory processes. Third, and most speculatively, the variety of findings about the presence or absence of medial-temporal lobe degeneration raises the possibility that such degeneration may be quite variable across older people of the same age.

Strategic Memory in Normal Aging. Older adults consistently perform less well than young adults on tests of strategic declarative memory, including tests of memory for source (e.g., McIntyre & Craik, 1987; Schacter, Kaszniak, Kihlstrom, & Valdiserri, 1991; Spencer & Raz, 1994), list discrimination (Parkin, Walter, & Hunkin, 1995; McCormack, 1984), frequency (Freund & Witte, 1986; Kausler, Hakami, & Wright, 1982; Wiggs, 1993), recency (Fabiani & Friedman, 1997; McCormack, 1982), temporal ordering (Kausler, Salthouse, & Saults, 1988), recall relative to recognition (Craik & McDowd, 1987; LaVoie & Light, 1994), and subjective organization in recall (Stuss, Craik, Sayer, Franchi, & Alexander, 1996).

A critical question is whether older adults have a proportionate decline in strategic and nonstrategic memory performance, as seen in medial-temporal lobe amnesia, or whether they exhibit a disproportionate decline in strategic memory, as seen in patients with frontal lobe lesions and PD. Three sources of evidence suggest that age-related decline in strategic memory is disproportionately larger relative to declines in nonstrategic memory. First, as mentioned earlier, tests of recall frequently yield larger age differences than tests of recognition. Recall may demand more strategic operations than recognition. Second, even when young and older adult groups do not differ reliably on nonstrategic tests of memory, the same older adults perform less well than young adults on many strategic memory tasks (e.g., Fabiani & Friedman, 1997; Ferguson, Hashtroudi, & Johnson, 1992; Mark & Rugg, 1998; Parkin et al., 1995; Schacter et al., 1994). Third, in a meta-analysis of studies that examined young and older adults on memory tests that require the retrieval of various contextual features (e.g., source, case, color, and spatial position), the age effect size for these tests was larger (Cohen's $d = .87$) than for recognition memory tests that require fewer strategic demands (Cohen's $d = .57$; Spencer & Raz, 1995). Together, these results favor the view that older people show a disproportionate decline on strategic memory tests, the same pattern of memory impairment that occurs in frontal lobe and PD patients.

Two correlational approaches have been used to investigate whether age-related changes in strategic memory are associated specifically with age-related changes in frontal lobe functioning. First, investigators have asked whether significant correlations exist between strategic memory performance and scores on standardized, nonmnemonic neuropsychological tests sensitive to frontal dysfunction (e.g., the Wisconsin Card Sorting Test [WCST]). Although many studies have reported such correlations (Craik, Morris, Morris, & Loewen, 1990; Fabiani & Friedman, 1997; Schacter et al., 1991), sometimes these correlations do not reach statistical significance (e.g., Spencer & Raz, 1994). The failure to observe significant correlations could reflect a lack of overlap in the processes engaged by the strategic task and the processes engaged by the chosen neuropsychological measures.

Two studies have used this correlational approach to focus on the specificity of the relationship between age-related declines in strategic memory and performance on frontal lobe neuropsychological measures. In one (Glisky, Polster, & Routhieaux, 1995), older individuals were characterized as scoring relatively high or low on neuropsychological measures of either frontal lobe or medial-temporal lobe functioning. Some individuals scored particularly high on both measures, some scored low on both, and others scored high on one type of measure and low on the other. All were given two tests: a strategic memory test that involved source judgments (identify the voice in which sentences were originally spoken) and a nonstrategic declarative memory test (two-alternative forced-choice recognition of sentences). On the source judgment task, older people who scored well on the frontal lobe measures outperformed the older people who scored less well on the same measures. There was no difference between the two groups on recognition memory for the sentences (recognition performance, in contrast, was related to scores on the medial-temporal lobe tests but not the frontal lobe tests). This study lends further support to the specificity of the relation between age-related decline on nonmnemonic frontal lobe tests and strategic memory tests. Furthermore, it suggests that age-related declines in memory occur for different reasons in different people, perhaps reflecting variation in affected memory systems.

However, the specific relationship between source memory and frontal lobe functioning in older adults has been questioned by Henkel, Johnson, and De Leonardis (1998). These researchers used a source memory task in which participants had to decide whether studied pictures were previously seen or previously imagined (a type of source judgment that is commonly referred to as *reality monitoring*). Older adults were more likely than young adults to claim erroneously that pictures that were previously imagined were previously seen, particularly when the imagined pictures shared perceptual and conceptual features with the seen pictures. Older adults' source accuracy was correlated not only with composite scores of tests that are sensitive to frontal lobe functioning, but also with composite scores of tests that are sensitive to medial-temporal lobe functioning. These data are consistent with the view that strategic memory performance (in this case, source memory) depends on an interaction between processes mediated by the frontal lobe and on nonstrategic memory processes mediated by the medial-temporal lobe.

A second correlational approach involves comparing older adults directly to frontal lobe patients on certain memory tests that are thought to involve strategic memory operations. Using a word list recall paradigm, Stuss et al. (1996) compared healthy young, middle-aged, and older individuals to middle-age patients with unilateral-left, unilateral-right, or bilateral frontal lobe lesions. Participants were given three 16-word lists which consisted of unrelated words, related words that were grouped by category, or related words that were not grouped by category. Recalling unrelated words or related words that are not grouped by category may require more strategic search demands relative to recalling words that are grouped by semantic category. Each list was presented and recalled in four successive trials. Older adults were impaired in recall relative to young adults, particularly on the less structured word lists (i.e., unblocked and unrelated lists). The magnitude of the age-related impairment was not as large as the impairments exhibited by the patients with unilateral-left and bilateral frontal lobe damage (relative to the healthy middle-aged group), but was similar to the impairment displayed by patients with unilateral-right frontal lobe lesions (many of whom had dorsolateral lesions). A second similarity between older adults and patients with unilateral-right damage was observed in measures of subjective organization; each group displayed deficits in subjective organization that were similar in magnitude, whereas the patients with unilateral-left and bilateral frontal lobe lesions tended to have more severe deficits than the older adults and the unilateral-right group. Although patients with unilateral-right frontal lesions tended to make more recall errors and exhibited more inefficiencies in recall than older adults, the fact that there were several similarities between the two groups raises the possibility that at least part of the age-related decline in recall and subjective organization is attributable to normal, age-related dysfunction in a right dorsolateral frontal region. This right frontal region may be critically involved in certain executive capacities, and when its normal operation is affected, either by normal age-related processes or by a lesion, deficits of similar magnitude occur in recall and subjective organization.

A similar link between aging and right-frontal lesions can be found in studies of false memory. In some false memory studies, participants are presented with a study list of words that are all associated with a target word that is not presented; young participants tend to falsely recall and incorrectly recognize the target word, often maintaining a high degree of confidence that it was presented (Deese, 1959; Roediger & McDermott, 1995). A patient with a right-frontal lesion showed an exaggerated false memory effect under such conditions (Schacter, Curran, Galluccio, Milberg, & Bates, 1996). Older adults sometimes show an exaggeration of this false memory effect relative to young adults (Norman & Schacter, 1997; Tun, Wingfield, Rosen, & Blanchard, 1998). Amnesic patients, in contrast, have reduced memory for studied words but exhibit a reduced false memory effect that is proportionate to their memory deficit (Schacter, Verfaellie, & Pradere, 1996).

Thus, there is a striking correspondence between the pattern of strategic memory failure that occurs nearly ubiquitously in aging and selectively in patients with frontal lobe lesions. Indeed, there are many lines of evidence indicating that the frontal lobes are especially vulnerable in aging (reviewed by R. L. West, 1996). For example, relative to other cortical areas, frontal regions undergo a greater reduction of volume with age (e.g., Coffey et al., 1992; Haug & Eggers, 1991; Raz et al., 1997) and a greater reduction in resting cerebral blood flow (e.g., Shaw et al., 1984; Warren, Butler, Katholi, & Halsey, 1985). Frontal lobe regions also undergo declines in dendritic complexity (Scheibel, Lindsay, Tomiyasu, & Scheibel, 1975) and reductions of synaptic density (Masliah, Mallory, Hansen, De-Teresa, & Terry, 1993). Further, there is a trivariate correlation in aging between prefrontal cortical volume and performance on the WCST, a test sensitive to frontal lobe dysfunction that was used in many of the correlational studies described above (Raz et al., 1998). In the Raz et al. (1998) study, increased age was associated with decreased prefrontal volume and increased perseverative errors on the WCST. Whether such relationships exist between frontal lobe volume, age, and strategic forms of declarative memory per se has yet to be determined.

Frontal lobe activations are common in functional neuroimaging studies of memory, and there appear to be differences between young and older adults in the magnitude of these activations. Three studies have examined the encoding of words or faces, and all three have found a striking age-related reduction of left-frontal activations (Cabeza, Grady, et al., 1997; Carrillo et al., 1998; Grady et al., 1995). For example, one fMRI study compared semantic encoding of words (abstract vs. concrete judgments) with perceptual encoding (uppercase vs. lowercase judgments; Gabrieli, Desmond, et al., 1996). Semantic encoding, relative to perceptual encoding, enhances subsequent declarative memory (Craik & Lockhart, 1972) and results in left-frontal activation (see also Kapur et al., 1994). Older people showed a reduced extent of left-frontal fMRI activation for the semantic, relative to the perceptual, condition (see Fig. 2.5).

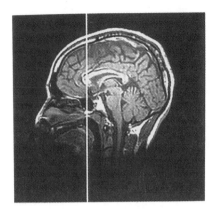

Young participants (n =15)   Older participants (n =15)

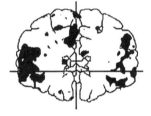   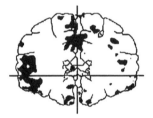

FIG. 2.5. Coronal view of encoding-related brain activity in young and older adults, as measured by functional magnetic resonance imaging. The left of the figure corresponds to the left side of the brain. Greater activation is seen following semantic encoding (judging whether words represent abstract or concrete entities) relative to perceptual encoding (judging whether words appear in uppercase or in lowercase). The vertical white line through the brain at the top of the figure refers to the approximate location at which the functional images were acquired. From "An fMRI study of the effect of aging on frontal activation during semantic encoding," by M. C. Carrillo, G. T. Stebbins, J. D. E. Gabrieli, J. E. Desmond, C. Dirksen, D. Turner, & G. H. Glover, 1998, *Cognitive Neuroscience Society 1998 Annual Meeting Abstract Program*, p. 53. Reprinted with permission.

Older people also show different patterns of frontal lobe activation during the retrieval of declarative memories, even when retrieval accuracy does not differ in young and older adults (Cabeza, Grady, et al., 1997; Schacter, Savage, et al., 1996). Parallels between the consequence of aging and of right-frontal lobe lesions were noted above, and the most common activation found during the retrieval of verbal and nonverbal memories in young people occurs in right-frontal lobe regions. This right-frontal lobe activation is sometimes, but not always, reduced in aging (Cabeza, Grady, et al., 1997; Schacter, Savage, et al., 1996; cf. Grady et al., 1995). Thus, functional neuroimaging studies concur with behavioral and anatomical studies in pointing toward deleterious age-related effects on the frontal lobes. Furthermore, they show that age-related frontal lobe dysfunction occurs not only when new memories are formed during encoding, but also when they are later retrieved.

The notable similarity between strategic memory deficits in aging and in PD points to degeneration of fronto-striatal dopamine systems as a potential basis for age-associated frontal dysfunction. Although less severe than PD, normal aging appears to be associated with declines in dopaminergic functioning. For example, post-mortem studies have documented age-related losses of dopamine-producing cells in the nigrostriatal dopamine system (Fearnley & Lees, 1991; McGeer, McGeer, & Suzuki, 1977). Because the striatum is heavily interconnected with the frontal lobes via thalamocortical pathways (Alexander et al., 1986), declines in the nigrostriatal dopamine system would likely lead to impoverished inputs to the frontal lobes. Additional post-mortem and imaging studies have reported evidence pointing to normal, age-related dopaminergic declines; these include reductions in the available levels of dopamine and declines in the number of dopamine receptor binding sites and dopamine transporters (a sample of such studies and their outcomes appears in Table 2.1). Some studies have reported nonlinear age-related declines in dopaminergic functioning (e.g., Mann, Yates, & Marcyniuk, 1984; Mozley et al., 1996; Suhara et al. 1991), but most have found linear, decade-by-decade reductions with advancing age. Age-related declines in fronto-striatal dopaminergic functioning may reduce the executive capacity of working memory, which in turn affects strategic memory. Age-related dopaminergic loss may be part of a broader decline in monoamine depletion that extends to norepinephrine (Arnsten, in press), but degeneration in fronto-striatal dopamingeric systems is a plausible etiology for the strategic memory declines that occur with advancing age.

Summary

Age-related deficits in declarative memory are typically disproportionately greater for strategic than for nonstrategic declarative memory tasks. This pattern of memory decline resembles that seen in patients with frontal lobe lesions or PD and is correlated with nonmnemonic tests sensitive to frontal lobe lesions and PD. Histological, structural imaging, functional imaging, and receptor binding studies provide convergent evidence that the frontal lobes and fronto-striatal dopaminergic pathways are especially affected by age-related processes. In accord with the parallel finding that

TABLE 2.1
Age-Related Declines in Dopaminergic Functioning

Brain Region and Observation	Method	Age Range (Years)	N	Reduction/ Decade	Citation
Substantia nigra					
Linear reduction of pigmented cells	PM	5–90[a]	28	6.0[a]	McGeer et al. (1977)
Linear reduction of pigmented cells	PM	21–91	36	4.7	Fearnley & Lees (1991)
Linear reduction of D2 receptors	PM	4–93	78	6.5	Rinne (1987)
Striatum					
Linear reduction of DA levels in caudate nucleus	PM	45–95	28	12.8	Riederer & Wuketich (1976)
Linear reduction of DA levels in striatum	PET	22–80	10	9.1[a]	Martin et al. (1989)
Linear reduction of DA levels in striatum	PET	18–80	24	3.5	Cordes et al. (1994)
Linear reduction of DA levels in striatum	PM	65–95	49	7.4	Scherman et al. (1989)
Linear reduction of D2 receptors in putamen	PM	4–93	78	6.3	Rinne (1987)
Linear reduction of D2 receptors in striatum	PET	20–81	21	4.6	Rinne et al. (1993)
Linear reduction of D1 and D2 receptors in striatum	PET	6–93	65	4.2	Rinne et al. (1990)
Linear reduction of D2 receptors in striatum	PET	37–68	15	5.0	Antonini et al. (1993)
Linear reduction of D1 and D2 receptors in striatum	PM	20–93	150[a]	2.7	Seeman et al. (1987)
Linear reduction of DA binding sites in caudate	PM	2–94	44	7.5	Severson et al. (1982)
Linear reduction of DA transporters in striatum	SPECT	18–83	28	8.0	van Dyck et al. (1995)
Linear reduction of DA transporters in basal ganglia	PET	21–63	26	3.3[a]	Volkow et al. (1994)
Frontal lobes					
Negatively accelerated reduction of D1 receptors in frontal cortex	PET	20–72	17	7.5[a]	Suhara et al. (1991)
Linear reduction of D1 receptors in frontal cortex	PM	19–88	32	4.8[a]	DeKeyser et al. (1990)

Note. PM = post-mortem; PET = positron emission tomography; SPECT = single photon emission computerized tomography.
[a] Estimated from graph or from other reported data.

the frontal lobes and fronto-striatal dopaminergic pathways are essential for executive working memory, it may be proposed that aging consistently, and throughout the life span, diminishes the ability of the fronto-striatal system to "work with" capacities mediated by other brain regions in the service of strategic memory (Moscovitch & Winocur, 1992).

Medial-temporal dysfunction appears to occur more variably in old age, and it is not evident in many studies. When it occurs, it is accompanied by nonstrategic memory deficits. It remains to be determined whether such medial-temporal dysfunction is an inevitable precursor of AD, or whether some percentage of older people have medial-temporal degeneration that is not a precursor of AD.

In many cases, strategic and nonstrategic forms of memory failure must interact (Henkel et al., 1998). A potential example of this interaction is given in the strategic task of self-ordered pointing. In this task, participants are given a series of displays, each one consisting of an array of stimuli (different pictures, patterns, etc.). The same stimuli appear on all displays, but the positions of the stimuli vary from display to display. The task is to point to a different stimulus on each display. Therefore, performance on the self-ordered pointing task requires a number of strategic memory operations, as participants must constantly compare those responses that have already been made with those that have yet to be carried out. Deficits in self-ordered pointing are apparent in patients with frontal lobe damage (Petrides & Milner, 1982), which may reflect a heightened sensitivity to proactive interference (e.g., Shimamura, Jurica, Mangels, Gershberg, & Knight, 1995). Self-ordered pointing deficits are also evident in patients with PD (Gabrieli, Singh, et al., 1996), who likely experience frontal lobe dysfunction.

Although strategic memory processes are critical for the self-ordered pointing task, it is likely that the task also depends on nonstrategic processes that are involved in recognizing the previously seen stimuli. This view was proposed by Shimamura and Jurica (1994), who administered a self-ordered pointing task to young, old, and very old participants (mean ages of 19.8, 66.5, and 75.4 years, respectively). Participants performed the task twice in two successive blocks of trials using the same set of stimuli. The young and old group performed similarly on the first block of trials, but the old adults made more errors than the young adults on the second block. The old adults were less able than the young adults to distinguish between responses made during the first block from those made during the second block of trials. This pattern cannot be explained by an age-related deficit in recognition memory, because it is likely that declines in recognition memory would affect performance on the first *and* the second block of trials. Instead, the pattern of results suggests that the old adults were impaired in the strategic operations that are used to overcome the effects of proactive interference. The very old participants, in contrast, made more errors on both the first and second block of trials, but showed no proactive interference (i.e., equal number of errors in both blocks). Thus, their memory impairment appears to reflect a nonstrategic memory failure in simply remembering the items to which they had pointed; they did not experience proactive interference because they forgot the potentially interfering information. These results are consistent with the idea that frontal lobe regions, which are critical for strategic memory processes, are disproportionately affected in aging. They are also consistent with the idea that increasingly advanced age, which is correlated with increasing risk of AD, is associated with a great rise in risk for medial-temporal dysfunction.

NONDECLARATIVE MEMORY

Nondeclarative memory refers to all forms of learning that are not dependent on the medial-temporal lobe or other brain regions essential for declarative memory. Nondeclarative memory is measured indirectly or implicitly by changes in behavior due to prior experience without any direct or explicit reference to that experience. Not all implicit tests measure only nondeclarative memory—some implicit tests regularly invoke declarative memory (reviewed by Gabrieli, 1999). Other implicit tests, however, do not invoke declarative memory. Perhaps the most impressive evidence that a form of learning is nondeclarative comes from studies with amnesic patients showing completely normal learning despite their severe declarative memory deficit.

Nondeclarative memory encompasses many different forms of learning that have different neural substrates. The three most studied classes of nondeclarative memory are skill learning, repetition priming, and conditioning. First, we review the brain basis of each type of nondeclarative memory, then we examine how each type of nondeclarative memory is affected in aging.

Skill Learning

In skill learning, participants perform a challenging task on repeated trials in one or more sessions. The indirect or implicit measure of learning is the improvement in speed or accuracy achieved by a participant across trials and sessions. Preservation of sensorimotor, perceptual, and cognitive skill learning in amnesia indicates that learning these skills is not dependent on declarative memory. Amnesic patients have shown intact sensorimotor skill learning on tasks of rotary pursuit, in which a small revolving target the size of a nickel is tracked with a hand-held stylus more accurately across trials (Corkin, 1968); mirror tracing, in which a geometric pattern is traced more accurately and quickly with practice while viewing the figure and the drawing hand through a mirror (Gabrieli, Corkin, Mickel, & Growdon, 1993; Milner, 1962); and serial reaction time (SRT), in which a specific sequence of key presses is executed more rapidly across trials (Nissen & Bullemer, 1987; although see Curran, 1997b, for evidence that some aspects of SRT learning are impaired). In the SRT task, sequence-specific learning is measured by faster RTs for patterned sequences relative to RTs for random key presses. Amnesic patients have shown normal perceptual skill learning by reading mirror-reversed words more quickly and accurately across trials (N. J. Cohen & Squire, 1980). These patients have also exhibited intact learning on a variety of cognitive skill learning tasks, including solving the Tower of Hanoi puzzle (N. J. Cohen, Eichenbaum, DeAcedo, & Corkin, 1985; Saint-Cyr, Taylor, & Lang, 1988; but see N. Butters, Wolfe, Martone, Granholm, & Cermak, 1985), learning and applying an algorithm for squaring numbers (Charness, Milberg, & Alexander, 1988), and classifying stimuli on the basis of probabilistic information (during early but not later stages of learning; Knowlton, Squire, & Gluck, 1994).

Brain Basis of Skill Learning. Patient and neuroimaging studies are beginning to identify the neural substrates of nondeclarative skill learning. Patient studies have pointed to the basal ganglia as being critical for a wide range of skill learning. For example, individuals with Huntington's disease (HD), which affects primarily the caudate nucleus in the basal ganglia, are impaired at learning the sensorimotor skills of rotary pursuit (Heindel, Butters, & Salmon, 1988) and SRT (Willingham & Koroshetz, 1993), the perceptual skill of reading mirror-reversed words (Martone, Butters, Payne, Becker, & Sax, 1984), and the cognitive skills involved in the Tower of Hanoi puzzle (Saint-Cyr et al., 1988) and in probabilistic classification tasks (early and late stages; Knowlton, Squire, et al., 1996).

PD patients typically have less severe basal ganglia damage than patients with HD, and their skill learning deficits are more variable. PD patients usually show less sequence-specific learning in SRT paradigms relative to age-matched controls (e.g., Ferraro, Balota, & Connor, 1993; Jackson, Jackson, Harrison, Henderson, & Kennard, 1995; but see Selco, Cohen, Stebbins, & Goetz, 1997). PD patients are also impaired at learning a computer-administered mirror tracking skill, one that is similar to the skill learned in standard mirror tracing paradigms (Frith, Bloxham, & Carpenter, 1986). Rotary pursuit skill learning impairments, however, vary depending on the severity of the disease and on the nature of the pursuit task. Deficits have been observed in advanced stages of PD or when dementia is present (Harrington, Haaland, Yeo, & Marder, 1990;

Heindel, Salmon, Shults, Walicke, & Butters, 1989), or when tracking speeds vary from trial to trial (Haaland, Harrington, O'Brien, & Hermanowicz, 1997). Nondemented PD patients are normal on pursuit tasks when tracking speed is held constant (Bondi & Kaszniak 1991; Haaland et al., 1997; Heindel et al., 1989). The perceptual skill of mirror reading often develops normally in PD (Bondi & Kaszniak, 1991; Harrington et al., 1990), although again, occasional deficits are found (Yamadori, Yoshida, Mori, & Yamashita, 1996). PD patients have also shown impaired learning of various cognitive skills; they are impaired, for example, on various Tower tasks (Daum et al., 1995; Saint-Cyr et al., 1988) and on probabilistic classification tasks (Knowlton, Mangels, & Squire, 1996).

The cerebellum is also important for some kinds of skill learning. For example, patients with early HD show apparently intact skill learning for mirror tracing (Gabrieli, Stebbins, Singh, Willingham, & Goetz, 1997), but patients with cerebellar atrophy are impaired on this skill (Sanes, Dimitrov, & Hallett, 1990). Individuals with cerebellar lesions acquire mirror-reading skills normally (Daum, Ackermann, et al., 1993). Thus, some processes that are involved in acquiring a new skill are dependent on the basal ganglia, whereas others appear to involve the cerebellum.

Functional neuroimaging studies support the roles of the basal ganglia and the cerebellum in sensorimotor skill learning, and also reveal the important role of neocortical areas in such learning. In addition, imaging studies show that skill learning is associated with changes in the extent of regional activations and with shifts of activation from one region to another as skill is acquired. For example, activity in basal ganglia has been reported in SRT skill learning (Doyon, Owen, Petrides, Sziklas, & Evans, 1996; Hazeltine, Grafton, & Ivry, 1997). Learning finger movement sequences has also been associated with decreases in cerebellar activation (Friston, Frith, Passingham, Liddle, & Frackowiack, 1992) and increases in primary motor cortex (Karni et al., 1995) as well as supplementary motor cortex (Grafton, Hazeltine, & Ivry, 1995). Additionally, activity in the cerebellum was positively correlated with the number of errors in a perceptual-motor task (Flament, Ellermann, Kim, Ugurbil, & Ebner, 1996), consistent with the possibility that cerebellar activation reflects error-correction processes. The importance of the basal ganglia in normal skill learning is indicated by studies reporting caudate activation during perceptual skill learning in the mirror-reading task (Poldrack, Hsieh, & Gabrieli, 1998) and cognitive skill learning in probabilistic classification tasks (Poldrack, Prabhakaran, Seger, & Gabrieli, in press). Further, skill learning for mirror reading is associated with increasing activity in the left inferior temporal cortex and decreasing activity in occipital and right superior parietal regions (Poldrack, Desmond, Glover, & Gabrieli, 1998). One interpretation of the observed changes in cortical activity in the latter study is that participants progressed from performing visuospatial transformations early in mirror reading skill development (the right superior parietal region) to using a more direct reading strategy in later stages of development (the left inferior temporal region).

Skill Learning in Normal Aging. Two approaches have been taken to assess whether skill learning changes with age. One approach addresses the question of how older adults who are experts in domains such as chess, bridge, or transcription typing develop strategies to maintain their high levels of skilled performance when declarative memory and speed of processing decline (Charness, 1981; Salthouse, 1984). A second approach (which is the one that we emphasize in this review) asks whether the initial development of a new skill proceeds similarly in young and older adults. This latter set of studies paints a rather mixed picture as to whether skill learning is intact or impaired in normal aging. Here, we focus on studies of age-related changes in skill learning that have used the same sensorimotor, perceptual, and cognitive tasks that have yielded intact learning in amnesic patients and therefore do not appear to involve declarative memory.

Sensorimotor skills have been assessed using rotary pursuit, mirror tracing, and SRT tasks. In studies that have examined the development of sensorimotor skills in young and older adults, two studies reported age differences favoring young adults on the development of a rotary pursuit skill (Ruch, 1934; Wright & Payne, 1985). However, in another study that included multiple sessions lasting over several days, older adults developed this skill normally (Durkin, Prescott, Furchtgott, Cantor, & Powell, 1995). Age differences favoring young adults were reported for the acquisition of a mirror tracing skill (Ruch, 1934; Snoddy, 1926; Wright & Payne, 1985). Similar age differences were also found in a computerized line-tracing task in which the movement of a drawing stylus and the movement of a cursor was transformed by 90°, so that a leftward or rightward movement of the stylus made the cursor move up or down on the screen, respectively (McNay & Willingham, 1998; see also Breitenstein, Daum, & Schugens, 1996, for age differences in a tracking task that used a similar movement transformation). Of interest in the McNay and Willingham study was the absence of an age affect when study participants were transferred to a normal tracing task and had to unlearn aftereffects. This dissociation raised the possibility that the age difference in the transformed line-tracing condition reflected deficient selection or use of strategies (such as mental rotation of the visual input); normal tracing removed the need for any use of strategies.

Older adults sometimes learn a repeating sequence of key presses in SRT tasks at the same rate as young adults (D. V. Howard & Howard,

1989, 1992), but sometimes they do not. For example, older adults learned pattern-specific sequences less well than young adults when the older adults were tested under dual-task conditions (Frensch & Miner, 1994), were less well educated (Cherry & Stadler, 1995), were tested with particularly complex sequences (Curran, 1997a), or when the key presses alternated between a random and a repeating pattern, thereby requiring the learning of higher order information (J. H. Howard & Howard, 1997). Older adults also learned a repeating pattern of hand postures less well than young adults (Harrington & Haaland, 1992). The observations with mirror tracing, rotary pursuit, and SRT tasks therefore suggests that older adults can demonstrate normal learning of sensorimotor skills under some circumstances but not others.

A mixed pattern of results also holds for perceptual skills. Older adults were impaired relative to young adults in a study of inverted-word reading skill and word-fragment identification skill, although group differences disappeared when older adults were given additional exposure time in the word reading task or were given more perceptual information in the fragment identification task (Hashtroudi, Chrosniak, & Schwartz, 1991). Improvements in reading geometrically transformed script appeared smaller for older adults than for young adults, although the results of a direct comparison between young versus older adults were not reported (Moscovitch, Winocur, & McLachlan, 1986). In contrast, two studies reported no deficit in the ability of older adults to acquire a mirror reading skill (Durkin et al., 1995; Schugens, Daum, Spindler, & Birbaumer, 1997). Salthouse and Somberg (1982) gave young and older adults extensive practice at a video game that required a number of perceptual skills; although the older adults' performance never met the level of young adults' performance after equal amounts of practice, the development of these skills was normal. Thus, as with sensorimotor skills, the outcomes in age-comparative studies of perceptual skill acquisition appear quite variable.

Few studies have administered to young and older adults the same tasks used to assess cognitive skill learning in amnesia. Although small in number, these indicate that healthy older adults can acquire cognitive skills normally. For example, older adults developed skill at solving the Tower of Hanoi puzzle at a rate that was similar to that of young adults (Vakil & Agmon-Ashkenazi, 1997; but see Davis & Bernstein, 1992). Young and older adults were also equally proficient in learning to use an algorithm to square numbers (Charness & Campbell, 1988).

Summary. Older adults can certainly improve their performance with practice on several sensorimotor, perceptual, and cognitive skills, but relative to young adults, the rate of skill learning is sometimes impaired. In many cases, age-related reductions in skill learning cannot be explained by declarative memory declines because such skill learning is intact in amnesia. Rather, the deficits could reflect age-associated changes in the fronto-striatal system or in the cerebellum, on which skill learning tasks may depend. Imaging studies of young and older adults may provide further clues about the brain basis of age-related declines in some forms of skill learning.

Repetition Priming

Repetition priming refers to a change in the speed, accuracy, or bias with which previously studied material is processed relative to baseline material in a task that does not invoke conscious recollection of the earlier study episode. A standard repetition priming experiment begins with a study phase that involves processing a set of stimuli, usually words or pictures. In a later test phase, the identical or related stimuli are reprocessed (old items), along with stimuli that were not processed earlier (new items). The difference in processing old items relative to the new item baseline reflects the degree of repetition priming (hereinafter referred to as *priming*). Old items are often processed faster, are identified more accurately, or come to mind more frequently than new items. In the past 20 years, a great deal of effort has been directed toward understanding how the psychological characteristics of repetition priming differ from those of declarative memory.

Priming can be either perceptual or conceptual in nature, depending on whether it is modulated by factors that affect stimulus form or stimulus meaning (e.g., Roediger, Weldon, & Challis, 1989). Perceptual priming is maximized when stimuli in study and test phases are identical in form; it is reduced when physical characteristics of stimuli are changed (auditory to visual presentation, or uppercase to lowercase presentation). Perceptual priming typically does not vary substantially with study-phase manipulations that enhance or suppress the analysis of stimulus meaning (i.e., manufactured or natural decisions vs. uppercase or lowercase judgments). Examples of perceptual priming include word-fragment completion (e.g., complete the fragment with a word: T_U_K), word-stem completion (e.g., complete TRU___ with the first word that comes to mind), and identification of words shown at visual threshold. In contrast, conceptual priming does not vary following a change in stimulus form, but it is maximized by study-phase manipulations that encourage the analysis of stimulus meaning. Examples of conceptual priming include category exemplar generation (e.g., what are the first five VEHICLES that come to mind?), word association (e.g., what word goes with CAR?), and answering questions about general knowledge (what is a "lorry"?). Although many priming tasks are well characterized as predominantly perceptual or conceptual, some tasks possess qualities that make them difficult to classify. For example, category verification priming (e.g., is this a vehicle? TRUCK) clearly requires access to stimulus meaning, and thus is logically classified as a conceptually-driven test of memory. However, unlike other conceptually-driven tests, category verification priming is unaffected by study-phase manipulations that enhance or suppress analysis of stimulus meaning (Vaidya et al., 1997).

Many forms of priming are dissociable from declarative memory, both in normal individuals (reviewed by Roediger & McDermott, 1993) and in amnesic patients (reviewed by Gabrieli, 1998). Indeed, amnesic patients show fully intact priming on many perceptual priming tasks (including word-stem completion and word identification) and conceptual priming tasks (including category exemplar generation and word association; e.g., Cermak, Talbot, Chandler, & Wolbarst, 1985; Graf, Shimamura, & Squire, 1985; Graf, Squire, & Mandler, 1984; Keane et al., 1997; Shimamura & Squire, 1984; Vaidya, Gabrieli, Keane, & Monti, 1995). Thus, repetition priming does not depend on medial-temporal lobe structures that are damaged in amnesia. Amnesic patients are, however, impaired on other priming tasks that probably invoke declarative memory processes, such as answering general knowledge questions (Vaidya, Gabrieli, Demb, Keane, & Wetzel, 1996; other priming impairments in amnesia are reviewed by Gabrieli, in press). Priming is also intact in HD patients (e.g., Heindel et al., 1989), so repetition priming does not depend on basal ganglia structures that are critical for skill learning. The analysis of priming in AD patients, however, offers clues about the neural basis of repetition priming.

Brain Basis of Repetition Priming. Neuropsychological and neuro-imaging evidence converge to point to the cerebral neocortex as the basis for repetition priming. Initial evidence for this notion came from the fact that many studies reported reduced word-stem completion priming in AD patients relative to age-matched controls (Heindel et al., 1989; Shimamura, Salmon, Squire, & Butters, 1987; for a review, see Fleischman & Gabrieli, 1998). This priming deficit in AD cannot be attributed to a declarative memory impairment because amnesic patients show fully intact priming on the same test (e.g., Graf et al., 1984). Comparison of the regional pathology of AD with amnesia offers a candidate neural basis of priming: AD is similar to amnesia in that both disorders are associated with disruptions in medial-temporal lobe functioning, but only AD is associated with further degeneration in frontal, parietal, and temporal association neocortices. Thus, the AD results on these tasks and on conceptual priming tasks (e.g., Monti et al., 1996) point to a neocortical basis for priming.

Patient and imaging studies have subsequently indicated that visual neocortical (occipital) areas are important for visual perceptual priming.

Patients with right-occipital lesions have shown reduced perceptual priming despite intact declarative memory (the double dissociation to amnesia; Gabrieli, Fleischman, Keane, Reminger, & Morrell, 1995; Keane, Gabrieli, Mapstone, Johnson, & Corkin, 1995). PET and fMRI studies have reported reduced activation in extrastriate occipital cortex for old, relative to new, visual stimuli (Blaxton et al., 1996; Buckner et al., 1995; Schacter, Alpert, et al., 1996; Squire et al., 1992). Reduced activation for primed items is interpreted as reflecting enhanced psychological and neural efficiency in visually processing primed stimuli relative to baseline stimuli. Conceptual priming, in contrast, appears to be associated with amodal cortical association areas located near regions important for language. Reduced activations for conceptual priming have been most consistently observed in left frontal lobe and left temporal lobe regions (Blaxton et al., 1996; Demb et al., 1995; Gabrieli, Desmond, et al., 1996; Raichle et al., 1994; Wagner, Desmond, Demb, Glover, & Gabrieli, 1997).

Repetition Priming in Normal Aging.   Initial studies of repetition priming in young and older adults were quite clear in their outcome: Young and older adults displayed similar magnitudes of priming, although older adults performed less well on declarative memory tests of recall and recognition (e.g., Light & Singh, 1987; Mitchell, 1989). A functional neuroimaging study corroborated these early findings by showing similar patterns of brain activity in young and older adults for word-stem completion priming (Bäckman et al., 1997). These results paralleled the findings with amnesia and suggested that age-related decline in the declarative memory system leaves priming unaffected. As the number of priming studies of young and older adults has grown, however, there have been many reports in which older adults show significantly less priming than young adults (e.g., Abbenhuis, Raaijmakers, Raaijmakers, & van Woerden, 1990; Chiarello & Hoyer, 1988; Davis et al., 1990; Hultsch, Masson, & Small, 1991; Rose, Yesavage, Hill, & Bower, 1986; Titov & Knight, 1997). However, equivalent priming effects across young and older adult groups continue to be demonstrated (e.g., Java, 1996; Monti et al., 1996; Nyberg, Bäckman, Erngrund, Olofsson, & Nilsson, 1996; Rastle & Burke, 1996). At present, the majority of studies have reported that the magnitude of priming in young and older adults is not significantly different, but the fact that some studies have reported significantly reduced priming effects in older adults raises the question of when age-related changes in priming are most likely, and least likely, to occur.

One possibility is that significant age differences in priming are found only when the power of the experimental design to detect such differences is high (Chiarello & Hoyer, 1988). It is conceivable, therefore, that studies with relatively few participants per age group lack the statistical power necessary to detect significant age-related reductions in priming. However, increasing power by increasing sample size does not guarantee that age differences in priming will be found. Significantly reduced priming in older people has been reported in studies with as few as 11 participants per age group (e.g., Abbenhuis et al., 1990), and nonsignificant age differences in priming have been documented in studies that contain over 140 participants per group (e.g., Park & Shaw, 1992; see also Nyberg et al., 1996). Certainly, variations in statistical power can lead to variations in outcomes, but it appears unlikely that the diversity of results across studies can be accounted for solely by differences in power.

This state of affairs led to a meta-analysis of age-related changes in priming (LaVoie & Light, 1994). When effect sizes from 39 individual experiments were aggregated and analyzed, LaVoie and Light concluded that age-related reductions in priming were statistically significant. The age-related effect size for priming was not as large as the age-related effect size for recognition or recall (Cohen's $d = .304$ vs. $.497$ and $.968$, respectively). This observation could be interpreted as indicating that age-related declines in the systems mediating repetition priming are less severe than in those mediating declarative memory. Alternatively, because priming magnitudes are usually smaller than declarative memory scores, the differences could reflect measurement sensitivity rather than differential decline.

The 1994 meta-analysis was useful in documenting the extent to which aging was associated with changes in priming, yet the criteria for including studies in that analysis was relatively focused. Omitted were priming tasks that were conceptual in nature or that involved pictorial or nonverbal stimuli. Infrequently used tasks for which only one experiment had been reported in the literature were also excluded. There have also been many age-comparative studies of priming that have been published since 1994 that may alter the conclusions drawn from this meta-analysis. Thus, in 1998 the LaVoie and Light meta-analysis was updated, taking advantage of the additional published studies to explore potential explanations for when age-related changes in priming are most and least likely to be observed (Light, Prull, LaVoie, & Healy, in press).

One possibility that was considered was whether aging affects conceptual priming more than perceptual priming (suggested by Jelicic, 1995; Rybash, 1996). This proposal, however, does not seem to account for variation in findings. Many studies have reported no age differences on conceptual priming tasks (Isingrini, Vazou, & Leroy, 1995; Light & Albertson, 1989; Maki & Knopman, 1996; Monti et al., 1996), and some studies have demonstrated significant age differences on perceptual priming tasks (e.g., Abbenhuis et al., 1990). One large-scale study that administered perceptual and conceptual tests to the same individuals reported the exact opposite pattern of findings: age-related differences on perceptual, but not conceptual, tests of priming (Small, Hultsch, & Masson, 1995). Indeed, in the revision of LaVoie and Light's (1994) meta-analysis, the age-related effect size for conceptual priming tests was not significantly greater than the corresponding effect size for perceptual priming tests (Light et al., in press).

Also examined was the difference between studies that used item priming and associative priming. Associative priming may be measured by first presenting pairs of unrelated words in an initial study phase (i.e., CHANNEL–PASTURE, FORTUNE–SPINDLE, MUSTARD–SATELLITE). At test, three types of items are presented: (a) intact items, in which the original pairing is preserved (CHANNEL–PASTURE), (b) recombined items, in which the pairings are broken and individual studied items are rearranged (FORTUNE–SATELLITE, MUSTARD–SPINDLE), and (c) new baseline items that were not seen in the original study phase (AMAZE–VOTER). Associative priming occurs to the extent that processing is superior for intact items relative to recombined items, representing priming of a new association that was formed in memory.

Amnesic patients have shown impaired associative priming for some tasks on which they showed intact item priming (e.g., for word-stem completion: Cermak, Bleich, & Blackford, 1988; Schacter & Graf, 1986). This raises the possibility that assocative priming invokes declarative memory. Indeed, age differences in associative priming have been reported (D. V. Howard, Fry, & Brune, 1991; Spieler & Balota, 1996), although equivalent associative priming effects in young and older adults have also been demonstrated (e.g., Light, Kennison, Prull, LaVoie, & Zuellig, 1996; Light, LaVoie, & Kennison, 1995; Moscovitch et al., 1986; Rabinowitz, 1986). D. V. Howard (1988) suggested that under challenging study conditions, young but not older adults are able to perform the elaborative encoding processes necessary to show associative priming (Graf & Schacter, 1985). Thus, age differences should occur following study conditions that do not foster elaborative encoding among stimulus pairs (i.e., limited exposure or time constraints), but should not occur under study conditions that permit elaborative encoding to take place. Consistent with this view, age differences in associative priming were reported when participants were given limited (albeit generous) exposure to study materials (e.g., 8 s), but not when presentation of study items was self-paced (D. V. Howard et al., 1991). Age differences were also observed when study items were presented once but not twice (D. V. Howard, Heisey, & Shaw, 1986). Conflicting with this view, however, are reports of equivalent associative priming in young and older adults following single presentations of study items and/or study conditions in which elaborative processing would have been unlikely (Hasher & Zacks,

1988; Light et al., 1995, 1996; Moscovitch et al., 1986; Rabinowitz, 1986). There are many variations across these priming tasks in terms of materials and performance measures, and these may account for the variable findings. Overall, however, support for the view that aging affects associative priming more than item priming is not strong. In two meta-analyses, the age effect size for associative priming was not significantly greater than the age effect size for item priming (LaVoie & Light, 1994; Light et al., in press).

Two related hypotheses have been inspired by the observation that many studies that have reported age differences in priming used one particular task: word-stem completion (e.g., Chiarello & Hoyer, 1988; Davis et al., 1990; Titov & Knight, 1997). Moscovitch and Winocur (1992) and Winocur, Moscovitch, and Stuss (1996) suggested that this task relies on strategic memory processes involved in retrieving responses to word stems, and that strategic processes are often mediated by the frontal lobes.[1] They administered this task, as well as word-fragment completion (which may require fewer strategic demands), to young adults, community-dwelling older adults, and institutionalized older adults. The institutionalized older adults exhibited reduced priming on the word-stem task, but showed intact priming on the word-fragment task (Winocur et al., 1996). Further, for all older adults, word-stem completion priming, but not word-fragment completion priming, correlated with other measures sensitive to frontal lobe dysfunction (WCST and verbal fluency; see also Davis et al., 1990). These findings suggest that age-related declines in frontal lobe functioning selectively reduce priming on tests demanding strategic search. What remains to be explained, however, is why patients with direct lesions to the frontal lobes, and patients with frontal lobe dysfunction (PD and HD), are unimpaired on word-stem completion priming (e.g., Bondi & Kaszniak, 1991; Heindel et al., 1989; Shimamura, Gershberg, Jurica, Mangels, & Knight, 1992).

The second hypothesis distinguishes between priming tasks that involve identifying a stimulus or one of its attributes and the production of one of many possible responses when given a partial cue (the *identification/production distinction*; Fleischman & Gabrieli, 1998; Gabrieli et al.,

---

[1]Although the processes governing word-stem priming are described in these studies as "strategic" and are thought to be mediated by frontal lobe regions, they are not considered to be the same conscious retrieval processes that are involved in strategic declarative memory tasks. The strategic processes involved in word-stem completion priming have been thought to include search, bias detection, and retrieval mechanisms that take place at a nonconscious level, and operate on items in the lexicon that are activated in response to word stems. In contrast, the processes involved in strategic memory tasks occur at a conscious level and function on contextually-bound episodic memory representations, rather than on entries in the lexicon (see Nyberg, Winocur, & Moscovitch, 1997, for further elaboration of this viewpoint).

1994). On this view, identification tasks include identification of words shown at visual threshold, lexical decision, and semantic verification. Production tasks include word-stem completion and category exemplar generation—tasks in which participants do not attempt to identify the test cue but rather must use that cue to retrieve a response. This distinction explains dissociations in AD, such as intact word-identification priming (an identification task) and impaired word-stem completion priming (a production task; Keane, Gabrieli, Fennema, Growdon, & Corkin, 1991) that are not accounted for by perceptual/conceptual or item/associative distinctions. It may also apply to the dissociation between intact word-fragment completion priming and impaired word-stem completion that was reported in young versus older adults (Moscovitch & Winocur, 1992). Although word-fragment and word-stem completion both involve producing a response on the basis of a partial cue, word-fragment completion may depend more heavily on processes involved in analyzing letter patterns rather than on processes that are required in producing a response (Fleischman & Gabrieli, 1998). The identification/production distinction has some support in the 1998 meta-analysis, as the age effect size in priming was significantly larger for tasks that required production of a response from a cue than for tasks that did not involve production (Light et al., in press). There are, however, multiple reports of undiminished priming in older adults in category exemplar generation, a test that is clearly one requiring stimulus production (Isingrini et al., 1995; Light & Albertson, 1989; Monti et al., 1996; however, see Jelicic, Craik, & Moscovitch, 1996, for a different outcome). The identification/production distinction predicts an age-related diminution of priming on this test. Thus, the identification/production distinction cannot currently explain all patterns of age-related change in priming.

Summary. The status of repetition priming is replete with contradictory findings. Many studies report no influence of age on priming, but many others report reduced priming in older adults. The reductions cannot be explained as a consequence of diminished declarative memory, because they often occur on tests that yield intact priming in amnesic patients. The contradictions are not explained by variations in statistical power or by perceptual/conceptual or item/associative distinctions. Some results favor the idea that production forms of priming are more vulnerable to age-related processes than identification forms of priming, although other results (i.e., category exemplar generation data) conflict with this idea. Variations in tasks, procedures, and participant characteristics may underlie the variable outcomes. The view that certain participant characteristics influence priming has some support in studies suggesting that word-stem priming is reduced in healthy older adults who are in their late 70s or 80s relative to adults in their 60s (Davis et al., 1990), and reduced in some conditions among healthy older adults with low, relative to high, scores on the Mini-Mental State Examination (MMSE; Fleischman et al., 1999). The MMSE is a short examination that broadly reflects cognitive status; lower scores indicate greater compromise in cognitive abilities.

These individual differences in word-stem completion priming suggest a plausible explanation for the inconsistencies across studies in whether priming is or is not affected in old age. Perhaps the studies that documented age-related differences in priming inadvertently included a subgroup of old adults who exhibited early signs of an age-related degenerative disease. Including such individuals would lower the magnitude of priming for the older group as a whole, thereby increasing the likelihood of detecting statistically significant differences in priming across young and old groups. Future work should therefore be directed toward examining the role of participant and task characteristics to determine which conditions govern age differences in priming.

Conditioning

A third nondeclarative form of memory is some, but not all, kinds of conditioning. The neural circuitry underlying eyeblink classical conditioning (EBCC) has been especially well delineated in studies of rabbits and rats. An advantage of EBCC is that it can be administered in an almost identical fashion to humans and other mammals, so that insights from invasive animal studies can be used to interpret findings in humans.

Most studies in humans have examined either delay or trace EBCC. In the delay paradigm, participants hear a 250- to 500-ms tone (the conditioned stimulus [CS]), which is repeatedly followed by a puff of air to the eye (the unconditioned stimulus [US]). The air puff elicits an eyeblink response (the unconditioned response [UR]), and the tone and air puff coterminate. With time, participants form an association in memory between the tone and the air puff, and begin to elicit conditioned responses (CRs) in which an eyeblink occurs after the tone is heard, but before the air puff is delivered. The CR overlaps with the US, so that the conditioned eyeblink response provides the organism with an adaptive and protective response to the puff of air. The trace paradigm is virtually identical, except that a brief interval (less than 1,000 ms) occurs between the offset of the CS tone and the onset of the US air puff.

Brain Basis of Conditioning. In the rabbit, electrophysiological activity in the cerebellum (McCormick & Thompson, 1987) and in the hippocampus (Disterhoft, Coulter, & Alkon, 1986) parallels the development of CRs in the delay paradigm. Lesions to the cerebellar dentate-interpositus nuclei prevent acquisition or eliminate the retention of the conditioned association. This effect is ipsilesional (e.g., a unilateral lesion affects only the eye on the same side) because of the ipsilateral connectivity of the cerebellum and eyelid responses. However, hippocampal lesions do not impair delay conditioning in the rabbit (Schmalz & Theios, 1972). Thus, electrophysiological activity in the hippocampus may reflect a parallel learning circuit that does not mediate delay conditioning.

The neural circuitry in EBCC has been specified with a high level of precision in the rabbit. A simplified model of the cerebellar circuit is displayed in Fig. 2.6. Air puff information (US) is carried to the cerebellum via climbing fiber inputs and auditory information (CS) is transmitted to the cerebellum through mossy fiber inputs. These inputs ultimately converge on two cerebellar sites, the anterior cerebellar cortex and the interpositus nucleus. Plasticity in these two sites is associated with normal learning of the CS–US association, and each site may serve different functions. The conditioned eyeblink response (CR) is then transmitted from the interpositus nucleus to the motor system through the red nucleus and the descending rubral pathway (Desmond & Moore, 1991; Raymond, Lisberger, & Mauk, 1996; Thompson, 1990).

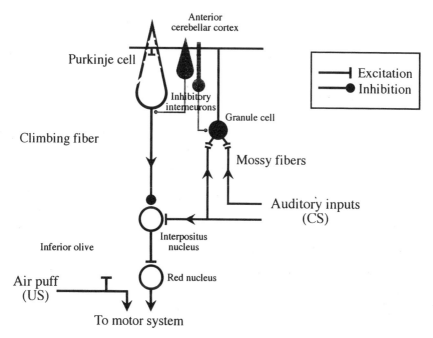

FIG. 2.6. Depiction of cerebellar circuit involved in eyeblink classical conditioning. US = unconditioned stimulus; CS = conditioned stimulus. From "The Cerebellum: A Neuronal Learning Machine?" by J. L. Raymond, S. G. Lisberger, & M. D. Mauk, 1996, *Science, 272*, p. 1126. Copyright 1996 by the American Association for the Advancement of Science. Adapted with permission.

There are many similarities between humans and rabbits in delay EBCC. First, cerebellar lesions in humans impair delay EBCC (Daum, Schugens, et al., 1993). Unilateral lesions to the cerebellum lead to EBCC deficits only in the ipsilesional eye (Woodruff-Pak, Papka, & Ivry, 1996). Second, delay eyeblink conditioning is intact in amnesic patients with medial-temporal lobe damage (Gabrieli, McGlinchey-Berroth, et al., 1995). This form of conditioning is impaired in the well-known amnesic patient H.M. (Woodruff-Pak, 1993), and in amnesic KS patients (McGlinchey-Berroth et al., 1995), but these impairments likely reflect cerebellar damage associated with anticonvulsant drug treatments or long-term alcohol consumption, respectively. Third, PET studies of delay conditioning have reported activity in the cerebellum and the hippocampus that parallels the development of CRs (Blaxton et al., 1996; Logan & Grafton, 1995).

Although hippocampal activity does not appear to mediate delay EBCC, the hippocampus does appear to be essential for trace EBCC. In rabbits, medial-temporal lobe lesions impair trace eyeblink conditioning (Solomon, Vander Schaaf, Thompson, & Weisz, 1986). In humans, amnesic patients with medial-temporal lobe damage who are intact on delay conditioning are impaired on trace conditioning with CS–US intervals as short as 500 ms (McGlinchey-Berroth, Carrillo, Gabrieli, Brawn, & Disterhoft, 1997). Successful trace conditioning may depend on declarative memory for a temporal relationship between the CS and the US. In one study, trace conditioning was acquired in healthy individuals only if they had de-clarative memory for the temporal contingency between the CS and the US (amnesic patients never had such declarative memory; Clark & Squire, 1998). Altogether, it appears that the neural circuitry underlying delay and trace EBCC is remarkably conserved across mammalian species.

These findings from studies in humans and rabbits suggest that (a) the cerebellum is important for the normal acquisition of delay and trace EBCC, and (b) the hippocampal formation is additionally important for the normal acquisition of trace EBCC. Although EBCC may be considered a form of skill learning, delay EBCC does not appear to depend on the basal ganglia because it is unimpaired in HD (Woodruff-Pak & Papka, 1996b) and in PD (Daum, Schugens, Breitenstein, Topka, & Spieker, 1996).

Conditioning in Normal Aging and in AD. Normal aging is associated with a decline in EBCC. Indeed, an age-related decline in EBCC has been documented in a number of mammalian species, including rabbits, cats, and humans (Woodruff-Pak, 1990). Early studies of humans demonstrated significant age-related impairments in acquiring eyeblink CRs in the delay paradigm (Braun & Geiselhart, 1959; Gakkel & Zinna, as described by Jerome, 1959; Kimble & Pennypacker, 1963; Solyom & Barik, 1965). These findings were subsequently replicated and extended using both delay and trace paradigms (Durkin, Prescott, Furchtgott, Cantor, & Powell, 1993; Finkbiner & Woodruff-Pak, 1991; Solomon, Pomerleau, Bennett, James, & Morse, 1989; Woodruff-Pak & Finkbiner, 1995; Woodruff-Pak & Thompson, 1988). The age-related decline in acquiring eyeblink CRs appears quite robust; many studies have included participants from each decade of adult life and have reported steady, decade-by-decade declines (e.g., Solomon et al., 1989; Woodruff-Pak & Thompson, 1988). This decline can be detected even when people in their 30s are compared with people in their 20s (Woodruff-Pak & Jaeger, 1998). Additionally, recent studies have reported that older adults retain the eyeblink CR less well over time relative to young people, a result that is revealed when participants are retested with the tone CS after a retention period of approximately 5 years (Solomon et al., 1998). Age-related deficits in EBCC do not appear to reflect differences in peripheral or sensory processes, such as corneal sensitivity, hearing loss, or rates of random or voluntary blinking. It is more likely that these deficits reflect age-related changes within the central nervous system.

The essential role of the cerebellum in EBCC has been supported by lesion evidence, and this evidence has motivated investigations of age-associated alterations in the cerebellum. In the rabbit, there is a close relationship between the number of Purkinje cells in the cerebellum and EBCC. Older rabbits that were impaired on trace EBCC had fewer cerebellar Purkinje cells than young rabbits at post-mortem examination (Woodruff-Pak, Cronholm, & Sheffield, 1990); the positive correlation between Purkinje cell number and EBCC held even among young rabbits. Post-mortem studies in humans have also revealed normal, age-related losses of cerebellar Purkinje cells (Hall, Miller, & Corsellis, 1975; Torvik, Torp, & Lindboe, 1986). Age-related decline in the volume of the cerebellar vermis has also been found using structural MRI (Raz, Torres, Spencer, White, & Acker, 1992). Thus, age-related changes in the integrity of the cerebellum may limit the degree to which an older organism can be conditioned. Future developments in this area may include attempts to relate age-related changes in cerebellar volume or activity with age-related changes in EBCC.

Patients with AD exhibit deficits in delay and trace EBCC paradigms that are more severe than those exhibited by healthy elderly adults (Solomon, Levine, Bein, & Pendlebury, 1991; Woodruff-Pak, Finkbiner, & Sasse, 1990; Woodruff-Pak & Papka, 1996a). The AD-specific deficit may be attributable to the hippocampal pathology that accompanies AD. This is counterintuitive because amnesic patients with extensive medial-temporal lesions are intact in delay EBCC. However, delay EBCC is affected by the presence of a hippocampus whose normal functioning has been altered, even though delay EBCC may not be affected when the entire hippocampus is destroyed or removed (Solomon, Solomon, Vander Schaaf, & Perry, 1983). Therefore, AD may be associated with alterations in hippocampal functioning, which, in turn, disrupt EBCC. One candidate mechanism for altering hippocampal function in AD is the characteristic severe compromise of the cholinergic neurotransmitter system. Patients with AD incur a loss of cholinergic neurons in the basal forebrain, a structure that provides a major source of the neurotransmitter acetylcholine to the hippocampus (Arendt et al., 1983; Coyle et al., 1983). In rabbits, lesions of the medial septum that interfere with hippocampal activity (Berry & Thompson, 1979) or alterations of septo-hippocampal functioning following injections of scopolomine (Salvatierra & Berry, 1989) reduce the acquisition of EBCC. Humans are also impaired in EBCC following the administration of scopolomine (Solomon et al., 1993). Thus, the AD results are consistent with the possibility that alterations in hippocampal functioning prevent the normal acquisition of EBCC.

Summary. Studies of conditioning in young and older adults are quite uniform in showing that normal aging is associated with deficits in delay and trace EBCC. Such deficits are consistent with the normal, age-related changes that occur in the cerebellum and in the hippocampus. AD, however, is associated with further declines in EBCC, which may be attributable to the normal age-related changes in the cerebellum and in the hippocampus, compounded by a disease-specific alteration of hippocampal functioning. Unlike studies of age-related changes in skill learning and repetition priming, which tend to yield variable outcomes, the studies of EBCC in young and older adults indicate a clear and consistent age-related decline in a nondeclarative form of memory.

SUMMARY: PATTERNS OF AGE-RELATED
DECLINE IN MEMORY

Age-related changes in memory often resemble the kinds of impairments that are sustained by patients with various lesions or with certain neurodegenerative diseases, although the impairments that are observed in aging are usually less severe than those seen in patients. Despite this quantitative difference, comparing normal age-related changes in memory to various diseases of memory suggests what age-related alterations in specific memory systems may account for specific memory failures. In summary, our review suggests that aging is associated with (a) episodic and semantic memory deficits for newly learned information that are also exhibited by amnesic patients with medial-temporal or diencephalic damage and by patients with AD, (b) disproportionate strategic memory deficits that are also exhibited by patients with frontal lobe lesions and by patients with

PD, (c) occasional declines in skill learning that are more commonly observed in patients with HD, PD, and cerebellar damage, (d) occasional priming deficits that may reflect changes in the neocortical systems mediating priming-related phenomena, and (e) EBCC deficits that are shown by patients with cerebellar lesions and by patients with AD.

We touch on two issues in the remainder of this chapter. First, the study of memory in certain neurological populations has led to the development of multiple distinctions between spared and impaired memory processes. We therefore ask whether two of these distinctions, declarative versus nondeclarative and strategic versus nonstrategic, which account for the memory performance of patients with amnesia and frontal lobe damage, respectively, can also account for the observed patterns of age-related memory change. Second, we discuss the possibility that the development of long-term memory in adulthood follows one of two distinct trajectories, each reflecting different developmental changes in individual memory systems. We sketch the types of long-term memory that appear to belong to each type of developmental category. Future directions are then discussed.

Declarative/Nondeclarative
and Strategic/Nonstrategic Distinctions

Many studies of aging have been inspired by the dissociation between impaired declarative memory and intact nondeclarative memory that is seen in amnesic patients with bilateral medial-temporal or diencephalic lesions. Aging certainly features a decline in declarative memory for new episodic and semantic information. However, aging does not spare the range of nondeclarative forms of memory that are intact in amnesia. In aging, unlike amnesia, classical conditioning is routinely affected, and there is variable compromise of multiple forms of skill learning and repetition priming. It is still of interest that when forms of memory are equivalent in young and older people, such as those measured in various skill learning and repetition priming paradigms, those forms of memory are usually nondeclarative in nature and are intact in amnesia. Thus, appreciation of the independent psychological and neural bases of nondeclarative memory has revealed forms of long-term memory that can be spared in aging, but the declarative/nondeclarative distinction is limited in its ability to explain age-related changes in memory. In part, this reflects the fact that nondeclarative memory refers to many different kinds of learning supported by different memory systems, and that these multiple nondeclarative systems may be variably affected by aging.

Other studies of aging have been motivated by the distinction between impaired strategic and intact nonstrategic memory shown by patients with frontal lobe lesions or with PD. Indeed, a great deal of evidence reviewed above does support the view that aging is characterized by a disproportionate decline in strategic memory. The strategic/nonstrategic distinction, however, does not account for the additional nonstrategic (recognition) memory failures common among older people or the compromise of various forms of nondeclarative memory. It appears, therefore, that age-related changes in long-term memory are not accounted for by these distinctions and perhaps may not be well accounted for by any one dichotomy. Rather, it will require the consideration of multiple kinds of changes across multiple memory systems.

Two Developmental Trajectories
of Age-Related Mnemonic Decline

Instead of interpreting various age-related memory changes in terms of declarative/nondeclarative or strategic/nonstrategic distinctions, perhaps they may be best understood in the context of two separate developmental patterns that reflect two different trajectories in memory systems that occur from young adulthood to old age. One developmental path may be characterized by virtually inevitable declines that appear to occur throughout the life span. Forms of memory that seem to follow this path of unavoidable decline across the life span are strategic declarative memory and EBCC. Virtually every cross-sectional study reports reduced strategic declarative memory and reduced EBCC in older relative to young adults. Moreover, studies that measure EBCC across the adult life span report reduced performance on a nearly decade-by-decade basis from age 20 onward (e.g., Solomon et al., 1989; Woodruff-Pak & Jaeger, 1998). The cumulative degeneration of the relevant memory systems makes these forms of memory reliably reduced in older adults.

Strategic memory decline may be a consequence of degeneration in a dopaminergic fronto-striatal memory system. Damage to this system, either because of focal lesions or because of degeneration, results in strategic memory failure in patients. In HD and PD, the strategic memory failure may reflect a consequence of reduced executive working memory capacity. Both executive working memory capacity (e.g., Salthouse & Babcock, 1991) and fronto-striatal dopamine systems (reviewed earlier) exhibit steady, lifelong declines in normal aging. More research, however, needs to be done to directly link dopamine systems, working memory, and strategic memory across the life span. One promising direction is the ability to measure dopamine function in vivo via PET or SPECT (single photon emission computerized tomography) with the use of radioligands. These techniques could be used to measure the strength and specificity of the relation between dopamine function and strategic memory performance.

Damage to the fronto-striatal system could also account for the frequent, but not universal, reduction in skill learning observed in older adults on tasks such as mirror tracing and SRT. Perhaps skill learning, as typically measured in aging, does not demand as many fronto-striatal resources as strategic memory tasks. This would explain the variability in skill learning deficits observed in aging and in PD. There is no evidence at present, however, that fronto-striatal damage can account for the delay classical conditioning decline associated with aging. Studies examining cerebellar degeneration may provide some insight into the neural basis of this mnemonic decline.

A second pattern of memory development is characterized by more variable declines that appear to occur especially late in life, after about 60 or 70 years of age. For example, there is great variation in the reported status of repetition priming in older adults. With advancing old age, there is also an increased likelihood of nonstrategic declarative memory decline. A critical but currently unresolved question is whether these variable memory declines reflect, in part, the unintentional inclusion of older individuals who are in the early stages of an age-related degenerative disease such as AD. The separation of those who possess nascent symptoms of AD from those who do not should provide a more accurate estimate of how normal aging affects repetition priming and other nonstrategic measures of memory.

Future Directions

Memory systems analyses of aging is a new endeavor. It is clear that although much recent data have begun to shed light on the neural basis of age-related memory change, there is still much more work to be done and there are several important issues to address. A particularly important issue is to identify sources of variability in age-related memory change, especially in domains such as skill learning and repetition priming. One potential source of variance—heterogeneity of older adult samples—has already been suggested. Many experimental studies of memory treat older people homogeneously when they compare young and older groups of people, but some older people may be in early stages of AD. Some older people may be on less favorable developmental paths and consequently suffer more decline than others in some memory systems. The composition of groups of older adults may, therefore, vary considerably from study to study.

However, a second source of variance comes not from aging per se but from the modest understanding of human cognitive neuroscience. Although there has been a great deal of progress in the nearly 50 years since the case of H.M. revealed the importance of the medial-temporal region in everyday memory, we still have little knowledge about the specific proc-esses—and their underlying neural substrates—that make memories. Thus, we and other researchers group tasks into taxonomic categories, such as sensorimotor skill learning or conceptual repetition priming. These taxo-nomic categories are helpful for thinking and for communication, but we are far from understanding the extent to which tasks that are grouped together reflect shared and unshared memory systems.

The difference between task categories, the current basis of theorizing, and memory systems is illustrated powerfully in EBCC. The mere inser-tion of a 500-ms silent gap between the tone (CS) and the air puff (US) makes such conditioning become dependent on the declarative memory system (Clark & Squire, 1998; McGlinchey-Berroth et al., 1997). Thus, a small quantitative manipulation results in a large qualitative difference in terms of which memory systems mediate learning. This difference between delay and trace conditioning in humans was examined because of similar findings in animals. For other categories of human memory, however, the discovery of memory systems progresses in a more unpre-dictable and opportunistic fashion. For example, there are proposals in domains such as repetition priming (identification vs. production; Gabrieli et al., 1994; Vaidya et al., 1997) and skill learning (open-loop vs. closed-loop learning; Gabrieli, Stebbins, et al., 1997) that have been offered to explain patterns of results observed in AD and HD patients, respectively. Whether these proposals are correct or incorrect, it is safe to posit that future research will define the psychological properties and neural iden-tities of an increasing number of memory systems.

Our modest knowledge about the memory systems of the human brain consequently makes it unclear whether aging studies truly contradict one another. What appear to be immaterial differences in procedures across two studies may actually serve to dissociate the mental and neural basis of two similar tasks, just as 500 ms does for delay versus trace conditioning. There are probably many other important processing distinctions in repetition priming than perceptual versus conceptual or identification versus produc-tion, for example, and many more in skill learning. As cognitive neurosci-ence matures and better identifies memory systems, it may be that many current contradictions in aging will not be contradictions at all.

There is a steady advance in the techniques available to cognitive neuroscience and especially in techniques such as fMRI that can be used with older adults. By gradually improving our ability to measure the structure and function of the brain, we will simultaneously develop more precise understandings of the functional neural architecture of human memory and appreciate how that architecture is affected in aging. The apparently contradictory findings that are currently inscrutable now set the agenda for future progress.

ACKNOWLEDGMENTS

Preparation of this chapter was supported in part by a National Research Service Award (AG05750) from the National Institute on Aging (NIA), as well as by NIA Grants AG11121 and AG12995. We thank Fergus I. M. Craik, Leah Light, Alison Preston, Allyson Rosen, Bart Rypma, Timothy A. Salthouse, and Daniel Spieler for their comments on earlier versions of this chapter. Additional thanks go to Guillén Fernández and Eric Fine for their assistance.

REFERENCES

Abbenhuis, M. A., Raaijmakers, W. G. M., Raaijmakers, J. G. W., & van Woerden, G. J. M. (1990). Episodic memory in dementia of the Alzheimer type and in normal ageing: Similar impairment of automatic processing. *Quarterly Journal of Experimental Psychology, 42A,* 569–583.

Alexander, G. E., DeLong, M. R., & Strick, P. L. (1986). Parallel organization of functionally segregated circuits linking basal ganglia and cortex. *Annual Review of Neuroscience, 9,* 357–381.

Angeles Jurado, M., Junqué, C., Pujol, J., Oliver, B., & Vendrell, P. (1997). Impaired estimation of word occurrence frequency in frontal lobe patients. *Neuropsychologia, 35,* 635–641.

Antonini, A., Leenders, K. L., Reist, H., Thomann, R., Beer, H. -F., & Locher, J. (1993). Effect of age on D_2 dopamine receptors in normal human brain measured by positron emission tomography and ^{11}C-raclopride. *Archives of Neurology, 50,* 474–480.

Arenberg, D. (1983). Memory and learning do decline late in life. In J. E. Birren, J. M. A. Munnichs, H. Thomae, & M. Marios (Eds.), *Aging: A challenge to science and society: Volume 3. Behavioural sciences and conclusions* (pp. 312–322). Oxford, England: Oxford University Press.

Arendt, T., Bigl, V., Arendt, A., & Tennstedt, A. (1983). Loss of neurons in the nucleus basalis of meynert in Alzheimer's disease, paralysis agitans and Korsakoff's disease. *Acta Neuropathologica (Berl.), 61,* 101–108.

Arnsten, A. F. T. (1999). Age-related cognitive deficits and neurotransmitters: The role of catecholamine mechanisms in prefrontal cortical cognitive decline. In A. Peters & J. Morrison (Eds.), *Neurodegenerative and age-related changes in structure and function of cerebral cortex (Cerebral cortex, Vol. 14;* pp. 89–110). New York: Plenum Press.

Bäckman, L. (1991). Recognition memory across the adult life span: The role of prior knowledge. *Memory and Cognition, 19,* 63–71.

Bäckman, L., Almkvist, O., Andersson, J., Nordberg, A., Winblad, B., Reineck, R., & Lång-ström, B. (1997). Brain activation in young and older adults during implicit and explicit retrieval. *Journal of Cognitive Neuroscience, 9,* 378–391.

Baddeley, A. D. (1986). *Working memory.* New York: Oxford University Press.

Berry, S. D., & Thompson, R. F. (1979). Medial septal lesions retard classical conditioning of the nictitating membrane response in rabbits. *Science, 205,* 209–211.

Bès, A., Güell, A., Fabre, N., Dupui, P., Victor, G., & Géraud, G. (1983). Cerebral blood flow studied by xenon-133 inhalation technique in Parkinsonism: Loss of hyperfrontal pattern. *Journal of Cerebral Blood Flow and Metabolism, 3,* 33–37.

Blaxton, T. A., Bookheimer, S. Y., Zeffiro, T. A., Figlozzi, C. M., Gaillard, W. D., & Theodore, W. H. (1996). Functional mapping of human memory using PET: Comparisons of conceptual and perceptual tasks. *Canadian Journal of Experimental Psychology, 50*, 42–56.

Bondi, M. W., & Kaszniak, A. W. (1991). Implicit and explicit memory in Alzheimer's disease and Parkinson's disease. *Journal of Clinical and Experimental Neuropsychology, 13*, 339–358.

Bousfield, W. A. (1953). The occurrence of clustering in the recall of randomly arranged associates. *Journal of General Psychology, 49*, 229–240.

Braun, H. W., & Geiselhart, R. (1959). Age differences in the acquisition and extinction of the conditioned eyelid response. *Journal of Experimental Psychology, 57*, 386–388.

Breitenstein, C., Daum, I., & Schugens, M. M. (1996). Altersunterschiede beim motorischen lernen. *Zeitschrift für Gerontopsychologie und -psychiatrie, 1*, 33–41.

Brewer, J. B., Zhao, Z., Desmond, J. E., Glover, G. H., & Gabrieli, J. D. E. (1998). Making memories: Brain activity that predicts how well visual experience will be remembered. *Science, 281*, 1185–1187.

Brozoski, T. J., Brown, R. M., Rosvold, H. E., & Goldman, P. S. (1979). Cognitive deficit caused by regional depletion of dopamine in prefrontal cortex of rhesus monkey. *Science, 205*, 929–932.

Buckner, R. L., Petersen, S. E., Ojemann, J. G., Miezin, F. M., Squire, L. R., & Raichle, M. E. (1995). Functional anatomical studies of explicit and implicit memory retrieval tasks. *Journal of Neuroscience, 15*, 12–29.

Butters, M. A., Kaszniak, A. W., Glisky, E. L., Eslinger, P. J., & Schacter, D. L. (1994). Recency discrimination deficits in frontal lobe patients. *Neuropsychology, 8*, 343–353.

Butters, N., Wolfe, J., Martone, M., Granholm, E., & Cermak, L. S. (1985). Memory disorders associated with Huntington's disease: Verbal recall, verbal recognition and procedural memory. *Neuropsychologia, 23*, 729–743.

Cabeza, R., Grady, C. L., Nyberg, L., McIntosh, A. R., Tulving, E., Kapur, S., Jennings, J. M., Houle, S., & Craik, F. I. M. (1997). Age-related differences in neural activity during memory encoding and retrieval: A positron emission tomography study. *Journal of Neuroscience, 17*, 391–400.

Cabeza, R., Mangels, J., Nyberg, L., Habib, R., Houle, S., McIntosh, A. R., & Tulving, E. (1997). Brain regions differentially involved in remembering what and when: A PET study. *Neuron, 19*, 863–870.

Carrillo, M. C., Stebbins, G. T., Gabrieli, J. D. E., Desmond, J. E., Dirksen, C., Turner, D., Glover, G. H. (1998). An fMRI study of the effect of aging on frontal activation during semantic encoding. *Cognitive Neuroscience Society 1998 Annual Meeting Abstract Program*, 53.

Cermak, L. S., Bleich, R. P., & Blackford, S. P. (1988). Deficits in the implicit retention of new associations by alcoholic Korsakoff's patients. *Brain and Language, 7*, 312–323.

Cermak, L. S., Talbot, N., Chandler, K., & Wolbarst, L. R. (1985). The perceptual priming phenomenon in amnesia. *Neuropsychologia, 23*, 615–622.

Charness, N. (1981). Aging and skilled problem solving. *Journal of Experimental Psychology: General, 110*, 21–38.

Charness, N., & Campbell, J. I. D. (1988). Acquiring skill at mental calculation in adulthood: A task decomposition. *Journal of Experimental Psychology: General, 117*, 115–129.

Charness, N., Milberg, W., & Alexander, M. P. (1988). Teaching an amnesic a complex cognitive skill. *Brain and Cognition, 8*, 253–272.

Cherry, K. E., & Stadler, M. A. (1995). Implicit learning of a nonverbal sequence in younger and older adults. *Psychology and Aging, 10*, 379–394.

Chiarello, C., & Hoyer, W. J. (1988). Adult age differences in implicit and explicit memory: Time course and encoding effects. *Psychology and Aging, 3*, 358–366.

Clark, R. E., & Squire, L. R. (1998). Classical conditioning and brain systems: The role of awareness. *Science, 280*, 77–81.

Coffey, C. E., Wilkinson, W. E., Parashos, I. A., Soady, S. A. R., Sullivan, R. J., Patterson, L. J., Figiel, G. S., Webb, M. C., Spritzer, C. E., & Djang, W. T. (1992). Quantitative cerebral anatomy of the aging human brain: A cross-sectional study using magnetic resonance imaging. *Neurology, 42,* 527–536.

Cohen, J. D., Forman, S. D., Braver, T. S., Casey, B. J., Servan-Schreiber, D., & Noll, D. C. (1994). Activation of the prefrontal cortex in a nonspatial working memory task with functional MRI. *Human Brain Mapping, 1,* 293–304.

Cohen, N. J., Eichenbaum, H., DeAcedo, B. S., & Corkin, S. (1985). Different memory systems underlying acquisition of procedural and declarative knowledge. In D. S. Olton, E. Gamzu, & S. Corkin (Eds.), *Annals of the New York Academy of Sciences: Vol. 444. Memory dysfunctions: An integration of animal and human research from preclinical and clinical perspectives* (pp. 54–71). New York: New York Academy of Sciences.

Cohen, N. J., & Squire, L. R. (1980). Preserved learning and retention of pattern-analyzing skill in amnesia: Dissociation of knowing how and knowing that. *Science, 210,* 207–210.

Coleman, P. D., & Flood, D. G. (1987). Neuron numbers and dendritic extent in normal aging and Alzheimer's disease. *Neurobiology of Aging, 8,* 521–545.

Cordes, M., Snow, B. J., Cooper, S., Schulzer, M., Pate, B. D., Ruth, T. J., & Calne, D. B. (1994). Age-dependent decline of nigrostriatal dopamineric function: A positron emission tomographic study of grandparents and their grandchildren. *Annals of Neurology, 36,* 667–670.

Corkin, S. (1968). Acquisition of motor skill after bilateral medial temporal-lobe excision. *Neuropsychologia, 6,* 255–265.

Corkin, S., Amaral, D. G., González, R. G., Johnson, K. A., & Hyman, B. T. (1997). H.M.'s medial temporal lobe lesion: Findings from magnetic resonance imaging. *Journal of Neuroscience, 17,* 3964–3979.

Coyle, J. T., Price, D. L., & DeLong, M. R. (1983). Alzheimer's disease: A disorder of cortical cholinergic innervation. *Science, 219,* 1184–1189.

Craik, F. I. M., & Lockhart, R. S. (1972). Levels of processing: A framework for memory research. *Journal of Verbal Learning and Verbal Behavior, 11,* 671–684.

Craik, F. I. M., & McDowd, J. M. (1987). Age differences in recall and recognition. *Journal of Experimental Psychology: Learning, Memory, and Cognition, 13,* 474–479.

Craik, F. I. M., Morris, L. W., Morris, R. G., & Loewen, E. R. (1990). Relations between source amnesia and frontal lobe functioning in older adults. *Psychology and Aging, 5,* 148–151.

Curran, T. (1997a). Effects of aging on implicit sequence learning: Accounting for sequence structure and explicit knowledge. *Psychological Research, 60,* 24–41.

Curran, T. (1997b). Higher-order associative learning in amnesia: Evidence from the serial reaction time task. *Journal of Cognitive Neuroscience, 9,* 522–533.

Daum, I., Ackermann, H., Schugens, M. M., Reimold, C., Dichgans, J., & Birbaumer, N. (1993). The cerebellum and cognitive functions in humans. *Behavioral Neuroscience, 107,* 411–419.

Daum, I., Schugens, M. M., Ackermann, H., Lutzenberger, W., Dichgans, J., & Birbaumer, N. (1993). Classical conditioning after cerebellar lesions in humans. *Behavioral Neuroscience, 107,* 748–756.

Daum, I., Schugens, M. M., Breitenstein, C., Topka, H., & Spieker, S. (1996). Classical eyeblink conditioning in Parkinson's disease. *Movement Disorders, 11,* 639–646.

Daum, I., Schugens, M. M., Spieker, S., Poser, U., Schönle, P. W., & Birbaumer, N. (1995). Memory and skill acquisition in Parkinson's disease and frontal lobe dysfunction. *Cortex, 31,* 413–432.

Davis, H., & Bernstein, P. A. (1992). Age-related changes in explicit and implicit memory. In L. R. Squire & N. Butters (Eds.), *Neuropsychology of memory* (2nd ed., pp. 249–261). New York: Guilford.

Davis, H., Cohen, A., Gandy, M., Colombo, P., VanDusseldorp, G., Simolke, N., & Romano, J. (1990). Lexical priming deficits as a function of age. *Behavioral Neuroscience, 104*, 288–297.

Deese, J. (1959). On the prediction of occurrence of particular verbal intrusions in immediate recall. *Journal of Experimental Psychology, 58*, 17–22.

DeKeyser, J., De Backer, J. -P., Vauquelin, G., & Ebinger, G. (1990). The effect of aging on the D1 dopamine receptors in human frontal cortex. *Brain Research, 528*, 308–310.

Demb, J. B., Desmond, J. E., Wagner, A. D., Vaidya, C. J., Glover, G. H., & Gabrieli, J. D. E. (1995). Semantic encoding and retrieval in the left inferior prefrontal cortex: A functional MRI study of task difficulty and process specificity. *Journal of Neuroscience, 15*, 5870–5878.

Desmond, J. E., & Moore, J. W. (1991). Single-unit activity in red nucleus during the classically conditioned rabbit nictitating membrane response. *Neuroscience Research, 10*, 260–279.

D'Esposito, M., Detre, J. A., Alsop, D. C., Shin, R. K., Atlas, S., & Grossman, M. (1995). The neural basis of the central executive system of working memory. *Nature, 378*, 279–281.

D'Esposito, M., Verfaellie, M., Alexander, M. P., & Katz, D. I. (1995). Amnesia following traumatic bilateral fornix transection. *Neurology, 45*, 1546–1550.

deToledo-Morrell, L., Sullivan, M. P., Morrell, F., Wilson, R. S., Bennett, D. A., & Spencer, S. (1997). Alzheimer's disease: In vivo detection of differential vulnerability of brain regions. *Neurobiology of Aging, 18*, 463–468.

Disterhoft, J. F., Coulter, D. A., & Alkon, D. L. (1986). Conditioning-specific membrane changes of rabbit hippocampal neurons measured in vitro. *Proceedings of the National Academy of Sciences USA, 83*, 2733–2737.

Doyon, J., Owen, A. M., Petrides, M., Sziklas, V., & Evans, A. C. (1996). Functional anatomy of visuomotor skill learning in human subjects examined with positron emission tomography. *European Journal of Neuroscience, 8*, 637–648.

Durkin, M., Prescott, L., Furchtgott, E., Cantor, J., & Powell, D. A. (1993). Concomitant eyeblink and heart rate classical conditioning in young, middle-aged, and elderly human subjects. *Psychology and Aging, 8*, 571–581.

Durkin, M., Prescott, L., Furchtgott, E., Cantor, J., & Powell, D. A. (1995). Performance but not acquisition of skill learning is severely impaired in the elderly. *Archives of Gerontology and Geriatrics, 20*, 167–183.

Eidelberg, D., Moeller, J. R., Dhawan, V., Spetsieris, P., Takikawa, S., Ishikawa, T., Chaly, T., Robeson, W., Margouleff, D., Przedborski, S., & Fahn, S. (1994). The metabolic topography of parkinsonism. *Journal of Cerebral Blood Flow and Metabolism, 14*, 783–801.

Fabiani, M., & Friedman, D. (1997). Dissociations between memory for temporal order and recognition memory in aging. *Neuropsychologia, 35*, 129–141.

Fearnley, J. M., & Lees, A. J. (1991). Ageing and Parkinson's disease: Substantia nigra regional selectivity. *Brain, 114*, 2283–2301.

Ferguson, S., Hashtroudi, S., & Johnson, M. K. (1992). Age differences in using source-relevant cues. *Psychology and Aging, 7*, 443–452.

Ferraro, F. R., Balota, D. A., & Connor, T. (1993). Implicit memory and the formation of new associations in nondemented Parkinson's disease individuals and individuals with senile dementia of the Alzheimer type: A serial reaction time (SRT) investigation. *Brain and Cognition, 21*, 163–180.

Finkbiner, R. G., & Woodruff-Pak, D. S. (1991). Classical eyeblink conditioning in adulthood: Effects of age and interstimulus interval on acquisition in the trace paradigm. *Psychology and Aging, 6*, 109–117.

Fitzgerald, J. M., & Lawrence, R. L. (1984). Autobiographical memory across the life-span. *Journal of Gerontology, 39*, 692–698.

Flament, D., Ellermann, J. M., Kim, S. -G., Ugurbil, K., & Ebner, T. J. (1996). Functional magnetic resonance imaging of cerebellar activation during the learning of a visuomotor dissociation task. *Human Brain Mapping, 4*, 210–226.

Fleischman, D. A., & Gabrieli, J. D. E. (1998). Repetition priming in normal aging and Alzheimer's disease: A review of findings and theories. *Psychology and Aging, 13,* 88–119.

Fleischman, D. A., Gabrieli, J. D. E., Gilley, D. W., Hauser, J. D., Lange, K. L., Dwornik, L. M., Bennett, D. A., & Wilson, R. S. (1999). Word-stem completion priming in healthy aging and Alzheimer's disease: The effects of age, cognitive status, and encoding. *Neuropsychology, 13,* 22–30.

Frensch, P. A., & Miner, C. S. (1994). Effects of presentation rate and individual differences in short-term memory capacity and on an indirect measure of serial learning. *Memory and Cognition, 22,* 95–110.

Freund, J. S., & Witte, K. L. (1986). Recognition and frequency judgments in young and elderly adults. *American Journal of Psychology, 99,* 81–102.

Friston, K. J., Frith, C. D., Passingham, R. E., Liddle, P. F., & Frackowiak, R. S. J. (1992). Motor practice and neurophysiological adaptation in the cerebellum: A positron emission tomography study. *Proceedings of the Royal Society of London, Series B, 248,* 223–228.

Frith, C. D., Bloxham, C. A., & Carpenter, K. N. (1986). Impairments in the learning and performance of a new manual skill in patients with Parkinson's disease. *Journal of Neurology, Neurosurgery, and Psychiatry, 49,* 661–668.

Funahashi, S., Bruce, C. J., & Goldman-Rakic, P. S. (1989). Mnemonic encoding of visual space in the monkey's dorsolateral prefrontal cortex. *Journal of Neurophysiology, 61,* 331–349.

Gabrieli, J. D. E. (1996). Memory systems analyses of mnemonic disorders in aging and age-related disease. *Proceedings of the National Academy of Sciences USA, 93,* 13534–13540.

Gabrieli, J. D. E. (1998). Cognitive neuroscience of human memory. *Annual Review of Psychology, 49,* 87–115.

Gabrieli, J. D. E. (1999). The architecture of human memory. In J. K. Foster & M. Jelicic (Eds.), *Memory: Systems, process, or function?* (pp. 205–231). New York: Oxford University Press.

Gabrieli, J. D. E., Brewer, J. B., Desmond, J. E., & Glover, G. H. (1997). Separate neural bases of two fundamental memory processes in the human medial temporal lobe. *Science, 276,* 264–266.

Gabrieli, J. D. E., Cohen, N. J., & Corkin, S. (1988). The impaired learning of semantic knowledge following bilateral medial temporal-lobe resection. *Brain and Cognition, 7,* 157–177.

Gabrieli, J. D. E., Corkin, S., Mickel, S. F., & Growdon, J. H. (1993). Intact acquisition and long-term retention of mirror-tracing skill in Alzheimer's disease and in global amnesia. *Behavioral Neuroscience, 107,* 899–910.

Gabrieli, J. D. E., Desmond, J. E., Demb, J. B., Wagner, A. D., Stone, M. V., Vaidya, C. J., & Glover, G. H. (1996). Functional magnetic resonance imaging of semantic memory processes in the frontal lobes. *Psychological Science, 7,* 278–283.

Gabrieli, J. D. E., Fleischman, D. A., Keane, M. M., Reminger, S. L., & Morrell, F. (1995). Double dissociation between memory systems underlying explicit and implicit memory in the human brain. *Psychological Science, 6,* 76–82.

Gabrieli, J. D. E., Keane, M. M., Stanger, B. Z., Kjelgaard, M. M., Corkin, S., & Growdon, J. H. (1994). Dissociations among structural–perceptual, lexical–semantic, and event–fact memory systems in Alzheimer, amnesic, and normal subjects. *Cortex, 30,* 75–103.

Gabrieli, J. D. E., McGlinchey-Berroth, R., Carrillo, M. C., Gluck, M. A., Cermak, L. S., & Disterhoft, J. F. (1995). Intact delay-eyeblink classical conditioning in amnesia. *Behavioral Neuroscience, 109,* 819–827.

Gabrieli, J. D. E., Singh, J., Stebbins, G. T., & Goetz, C. G. (1996). Reduced working memory span in Parkinson's disease: Evidence for the role of a frontostriatal system in working and strategic memory. *Neuropsychology, 10,* 322–332.

Gabrieli, J. D. E., Stebbins, G. T., Singh, J., Willingham, D. B., & Goetz, C. G. (1997). Intact mirror-tracing and impaired rotary pursuit skill learning in patients with Huntington's disease: Evidence for dissociable memory systems in skill learning. *Neuropsychology, 11,* 272–281.

Gershberg, F. B., & Shimamura, A. P. (1995). Impaired use of organizational strategies in free recall following frontal lobe damage. *Neuropsychologia, 33,* 1305–1333.

Glisky, E. L., Polster, M. R., & Routhieaux, B. C. (1995). Double dissociation between item and source memory. *Neuropsychology, 9,* 229–235.

Goldman-Rakic, P. S. (1987). Circuitry of primate prefrontal cortex and regulation of behavior by representational memory. In F. Plum (Ed.), *Handbook of physiology—The nervous system* (Vol. 5, pp. 373–417). New York: Oxford University Press.

Golomb, J., Kluger, A., de Leon, M. J., Ferris, S. H., Convit, A., Mittelman, M. S., Cohen, J., Rusinek, H., De Santi, S., & George, A. E. (1994). Hippocampal formation size in normal human aging: A correlate of delayed secondary memory performance. *Learning and Memory, 1,* 45–54.

Golomb, J., Kluger, A., de Leon, M. J., Ferris, S. H., Mittelman, M., Cohen, J., & George, A. E. (1996). Hippocampal formation size predicts declining memory performance in normal aging. *Neurology, 47,* 810–813.

Gómez-Isla, T., Price, J. L., McKeel, D. W., Jr., Morris, J. C., Growdon, J. H., & Hyman, B. T. (1996). Profound loss of layer II entorhinal cortex neurons occurs in very mild Alzheimer's disease. *Journal of Neuroscience, 16,* 4491–4500.

Grady, C. L., McIntosh, A. R., Horwitz, B., Maisog, J. M., Ungerleider, L. G., Mentis, M. J., Pietrini, P., Schapiro, M. B., & Haxby, J. V. (1995). Age-related reductions in human recognition memory due to impaired encoding. *Science, 269,* 218–221.

Graf, P., & Schacter, D. L. (1985). Implicit and explicit memory for new associations in normal and amnesic patients. *Journal of Experimental Psychology: Learning, Memory, and Cognition, 11,* 501–518.

Graf, P., Shimamura, A. P., & Squire, L. R. (1985). Priming across modalities and priming across category levels: Extending the domain of preserved function in amnesia. *Journal of Experimental Psychology: Learning, Memory, and Cognition, 11,* 386–396.

Graf, P., Squire, L. R., & Mandler, G. (1984). The information that amnesic patients do not forget. *Journal of Experimental Psychology: Learning, Memory, and Cognition, 10,* 164–178.

Graff-Radford, N. R., Tranel, D., Van Hoesen, G. W., & Brandt, J. P. (1990). Diencephalic amnesia. *Brain, 113,* 1–25.

Grafton, S. T., Hazeltine, E., & Ivry, R. (1995). Functional mapping of sequence learning in normal humans. *Journal of Cognitive Neuroscience, 7,* 497–510.

Haaland, K. Y., Harrington, D. L., O'Brien, S., & Hermanowicz, N. (1997). Cognitive–motor learning in Parkinson's disease. *Neuropsychology, 11,* 180–186.

Hall, T. C., Miller, A. K. H., & Corsellis, J. A. N. (1975). Variations in the human Purkinje cell population according to age and sex. *Neuropathology and Applied Neurobiology, 1,* 267–292.

Harrington, D. L., & Haaland, K. Y. (1992). Skill learning in the elderly: Diminished implicit and explicit memory for a motor sequence. *Psychology and Aging, 7,* 425–434.

Harrington, D. L., Haaland, K. Y., Yeo, R. A., & Marder, E. (1990). Procedural memory in Parkinson's disease: Impaired motor but not visuoperceptual learning. *Journal of Clinical and Experimental Neuropsychology, 12,* 323–339.

Hasher, L., & Zacks, R. T. (1988). Working memory, comprehension, and aging: A review and a new view. *Psychology of Learning and Motivation, 22,* 193–225.

Hashtroudi, S., Chrosniak, L. D., & Schwartz, B. L. (1991). Effects of aging on priming and skill learning. *Psychology and Aging, 6,* 605–615.

Haug, H., & Eggers, R. (1991). Morphometry of the human cortex cerebri and corpus striatum during aging. *Neurobiology of Aging, 12,* 336–338.

Hazeltine, E., Grafton, S. T., & Ivry, R. (1997). Attention and stimulus characteristics determine the locus of motor-sequence encoding: A PET study. *Brain, 120*, 123–140.

Heindel, W. C., Butters, N., & Salmon, D. P. (1988). Impaired learning of a motor skill in patients with Huntington's disease. *Behavioral Neuroscience, 102*, 141–147.

Heindel, W. C., Salmon, D. P., Shults, C. W., Walicke, P. A., & Butters, N. (1989). Neuropsychological evidence for multiple implicit memory systems: A comparison of Alzheimer's, Huntington's, and Parkinson's disease patients. *Journal of Neuroscience, 9*, 582–587.

Henkel, L. A., Johnson, M. K., & De Leonardis, D. M. (1998). Aging and source monitoring: Cognitive processes and neuropsychological correlates. *Journal of Experimental Psychology: General, 127*, 251–268.

Howard, D. V. (1988). Implicit and explicit assessment of cognitive aging. In M. L. Howe & C. J. Brainerd (Eds.), *Cognitive development in adulthood: Progress in cognitive development research* (pp. 3–37). New York: Springer-Verlag.

Howard, D. V., Fry, A. F., & Brune, C. M. (1991). Aging and memory for new associations: Direct versus indirect measures. *Journal of Experimental Psychology: Learning, Memory, and Cognition, 17*, 779–792.

Howard, D. V., Heisey, J. G., & Shaw, R. J. (1986). Aging and the priming of newly learned associations. *Developmental Psychology, 22*, 78–85.

Howard, D. V., & Howard, J. H., Jr. (1989). Age differences in learning serial patterns: Direct versus indirect measures. *Psychology and Aging, 4*, 357–364.

Howard, D. V., & Howard J. H., Jr. (1992). Adult age differences in the rate of learning serial patterns: Evidence from direct and indirect tests. *Psychology and Aging, 7*, 232–241.

Howard, J. H., Jr., & Howard, D. V. (1997). Age differences in implicit learning of higher order dependencies in serial patterns. *Psychology and Aging, 12*, 634–656.

Hultsch, D. F., Hertzog, C., Small, B. J., McDonald-Miszczak, L., & Dixon, R. A. (1992). Short-term longitudinal change in cognitive performance in later life. *Psychology and Aging, 7*, 571–584.

Hultsch, D. F., Masson, M. E. J., & Small, B. J. (1991). Adult age differences in direct and indirect tests of memory. *Journal of Gerontology: Psychological Sciences, 46*, P22–P30.

Hyman, B. T., Van Hoesen, G. W., Damasio, A. R., & Barnes, C. L. (1984). Alzheimer's disease: Cell-specific pathology isolates the hippocampal formation. *Science, 225*, 1168–1170.

Isingrini, M., Vazou, F., & Leroy, P. (1995). Dissociation of implicit and explicit memory tests: Effect of age and divided attention on category exemplar generation and cued recall. *Memory and Cognition, 23*, 462–467.

Jack, C. R., Petersen, R. C., Xu, Y. C., Waring, S. C., O'Brien, P. C., Tangalos, E. G., Smith, G. E., Ivnik, R. J., & Kokmen, E. (1997). Medial temporal atrophy on MRI in normal aging and very mild Alzheimer's disease. *Neurology, 49*, 786–794.

Jackson, G. M., Jackson, S. R., Harrison, J., Henderson, L., & Kennard, C. (1995). Serial reaction time learning and Parkinson's disease: Evidence for a procedural learning deficit. *Neuropsychologia, 33*, 577–593.

Janowsky, J. S., Shimamura, A. P., & Squire, L. R. (1989). Source memory impairment in patients with frontal lobe lesions. *Neuropsychologia, 27*, 1043–1056.

Java, R. I. (1996). Effects of age on state of awareness following implicit and explicit word-association tasks. *Psychology and Aging, 11*, 108–111.

Javoy-Agid, F., & Agid, Y. (1980). Is the mesocortical dopaminergic system involved in Parkinson disease? *Neurology, 30*, 1326–1330.

Jelicic, M. (1995). Aging and performance on implicit memory tasks: A brief review. *International Journal of Neuroscience, 82*, 155–161.

Jelicic, M., Craik, F. I. M., & Moscovitch, M. (1996). Effects of ageing on different explicit and implicit memory tasks. *European Journal of Cognitive Psychology, 8*, 225–234.

Jerome, E. A. (1959). Age and learning—Experimental studies. In J. E. Birren (Ed.), *Handbook of aging and the individual* (pp. 655–699). Chicago: University of Chicago Press.

Jonides, J., Smith, E. E., Koeppe, R. A., Awh, E., Minoshima, S., & Mintun, M. A. (1993). Spatial working memory in humans as revealed by PET. *Nature, 363,* 623–625.

Kapur, S., Craik, F. I. M., Tulving, E., Wilson, A. A., Houle, S., & Brown, G. M. (1994). Neuroanatomical correlates of encoding in episodic memory: Levels of processing effect. *Proceedings of the National Academy of Sciences USA, 91,* 2008–2011.

Karni, A., Meyer, G., Jezzard, P., Adams, M. M., Turner, R., & Ungerleider, L. G. (1995). Functional MRI evidence for adult motor cortex plasticity during motor skill learning. *Nature, 377,* 155–158.

Kausler, D. H. (1994). *Learning and memory in normal aging.* San Diego, CA: Academic Press.

Kausler, D. H., Hakami, M. K., & Wright, R. E. (1982). Adult age differences in frequency judgments of categorical representations. *Journal of Gerontology, 37,* 365–371.

Kausler, D. H., Salthouse, T. A., & Saults, J. S. (1988). Temporal memory over the adult lifespan. *American Journal of Psychology, 101,* 207–215.

Keane, M. M., Gabrieli, J. D. E., Fennema, A. C., Growdon, J. H., & Corkin, S. (1991). Evidence for a dissociation between perceptual and conceptual priming in Alzheimer's disease. *Behavioral Neuroscience, 105,* 326–342.

Keane, M. M., Gabrieli, J. D. E., Mapstone, H. C., Johnson, K. A., & Corkin, S. (1995). Double dissociation of memory capacities after bilateral occipital-lobe or medial temporal-lobe lesions. *Brain, 118,* 1129–1148.

Keane, M. M., Gabrieli, J. D. E., Monti, L. A., Fleischman, D. A., Cantor, J. M., & Noland, J. S. (1997). Intact and impaired conceptual memory processes in amnesia. *Neuropsychology, 11,* 59–69.

Kelley, W. M., Miezin, F. M., McDermott, K. B., Buckner, R. L., Raichle, M. E., Cohen, N. J., Ollinger, J. M., Akbudak, E., Conturo, T. E., Snyder, A. Z., & Petersen, S. E. (1998). Hemispheric specialization in human dorsal frontal cortex and medial temporal lobe for verbal and nonverbal memory encoding. *Neuron, 20,* 927–936.

Khachaturian, Z. S. (1985). Diagnosis of Alzheimer's disease. *Archives of Neurology, 42,* 1097–1104.

Kimble, G. A., & Pennypacker, H. S. (1963). Eyelid conditioning in young and aged subjects. *Journal of Genetic Psychology, 103,* 283–289.

Kirasic, K. C., Allen, G. L., Dobson, S. H., & Binder, K. S. (1996). Aging, cognitive resources, and declarative learning. *Psychology and Aging, 11,* 658–670.

Knowlton, B. J., Mangels, J. A., & Squire, L. R. (1996). A neostriatal habit learning system in humans. *Science, 273,* 1399–1402.

Knowlton, B. J., Squire, L. R., & Gluck, M. A. (1994). Probabilistic classification learning in amnesia. *Learning and Memory, 1,* 106–120.

Knowlton, B. J., Squire, L. R., Paulsen, J. S., Swerdlow, N. R., Swenson, M., & Butters, N. (1996). Dissociations within nondeclarative memory in Huntington's disease. *Neuropsychology, 10,* 538–548.

LaVoie, D., & Light, L. L. (1994). Adult age differences in repetition priming: A meta-analysis. *Psychology and Aging, 9,* 539–553.

Light, L. L., & Albertson, S. A. (1989). Direct and indirect tests of memory for category exemplars in young and older adults. *Psychology and Aging, 4,* 487–492.

Light, L. L., Kennison, R., Prull, M. W., LaVoie, D., & Zuellig, A. (1996). One-trial associative priming of nonwords in young and older adults. *Psychology and Aging, 11,* 417–430.

Light, L. L., LaVoie, D., & Kennison, R. (1995). Repetition priming of nonwords in young and older adults. *Journal of Experimental Psychology: Learning, Memory, and Cognition, 21,* 327–346.

Light, L. L., Prull, M. W., LaVoie, D. J., & Healy, M. R. (in press). Dual process theories of memory in old age. In T. J. Perfect & E. A. Maylor (Eds.), *Models of cognitive aging.* New York: Oxford University Press.

Light, L. L., & Singh, A. (1987). Implicit and explicit memory in young and older adults. *Journal of Experimental Psychology: Learning, Memory, and Cognition, 13,* 531–541.

Logan, C. G., & Grafton, S. T. (1995). Functional anatomy of human eyeblink conditioning determined with regional cerebral glucose metabolism and positron-emission tomography. *Proceedings of the National Academy of Sciences USA, 92,* 7500–7504.

Luciana, M., Depue, R. A., Arbisi, P., & Leon, A. (1992). Facilitation of working memory in humans by a D_2 dopamine receptor agonist. *Journal of Cognitive Neuroscience, 4,* 58–68.

Maki, P. M., & Knopman, D. S. (1996). Limitations of the distinction between conceptual and perceptual implicit memory: A study of Alzheimer's disease. *Neuropsychology, 10,* 464–474.

Mann, D. M. A., Yates, P. O., & Marcyniuk, B. (1984). Monoaminergic neurotransmitter systems in presenile Alzheimer's disease and in senile dementia of Alzheimer type. *Clinical Neuropathology, 3,* 199–205.

Mark, R. E., & Rugg, M. D. (1998). Age effects on brain activity associated with episodic memory retrieval: An electrophysiological study. *Brain, 121,* 861–873.

Martin, W. R. W., Palmer, M. R., Patlak, C. S., & Calne, D. B. (1989). Nigrostriatal function in humans studied with positron emission tomography. *Annals of Neurology, 26,* 535–542.

Martone, M., Butters, N., Payne, M., Becker, J. T., & Sax, D. S. (1984). Dissociations between skill learning and verbal recognition in amnesia and dementia. *Archives of Neurology, 41,* 965–970.

Masliah, E., Mallory, M., Hansen, L., DeTeresa, R., & Terry, R. D. (1993). Quantitative synaptic alterations in the human neocortex during normal aging. *Neurology, 43,* 192–197.

McCormack, P. D. (1982). Temporal coding and study-phase retrieval in young and elderly adults. *Bulletin of the Psychonomic Society, 20,* 242–244.

McCormack, P. D. (1984). Temporal coding by young and elderly adults in a list-discrimination setting. *Bulletin of the Psychonomic Society, 22,* 401–402.

McCormick, D. A., & Thompson, R. F. (1987). Neuronal responses of the rabbit cerebellum during acquisition and performance of a classically conditioned nictitating membrane-eyelid response. *Journal of Neuroscience, 4,* 2811–2822.

McGeer, P. L., McGeer, E. G., & Suzuki, J. S. (1977). Aging and extrapyramidal function. *Archives of Neurology, 34,* 33–35.

McGlinchey-Berroth, R., Cermak, L. S., Carrillo, M. C., Armfield, S., Gabrieli, J. D. E., & Disterhoft, J. F. (1995). Impaired delay eyeblink conditioning in amnesic Korsakoff's patients and recovered alcoholics. *Alcoholism: Clinical and Experimental Research, 19,* 1127–1132.

McGlinchey-Berroth, R., Carrillo, M. C., Gabrieli, J. D. E., Brawn, C. M., & Disterhoft, J. F. (1997). Impaired trace eyeblink conditioning in bilateral, medial-temporal lobe amnesia. *Behavioral Neuroscience, 111,* 873–882.

McIntyre, J. S., & Craik, F. I. M. (1987). Age differences in memory for item and source information. *Canadian Journal of Psychology, 41,* 175–192.

McKhann, G., Drachman, D., Folstein, M., Katzman, R., Price, D., & Stadlan, E. M. (1984). Clinical diagnosis of Alzheimer's disease: Report of the NINCDS–ADRDA work group under the auspices of Department of Health and Human Services Task Force on Alzheimer's disease. *Neurology, 34,* 939–944.

McNay, E. C., & Willingham, D. B. (1998). Deficit in learning of a motor skill requiring strategy, but not of perceptuomotor recalibration, with aging. *Learning and Memory, 4,* 411–420.

Milner, B. (1962). Les troubles de la memoire accompagnant des lesions hippocampiques bilaterales. In P. Passouant (Ed.), *Physiologie de l'hippocampe* (pp. 257–272). Paris: Centre de la Recherche Scientifique.

Milner, B. (1971). Interhemispheric differences in the localization of psychological processes in man. *British Medial Journal, 27,* 272–277.

Milner, B., Corsi, P., & Leonard, G. (1991). Frontal-lobe contribution to recency judgements. *Neuropsychologia, 29,* 601–618.

Mitchell, D. B. (1989). How many memory systems? Evidence from aging. *Journal of Experimental Psychology: Learning, Memory, and Cognition, 15,* 31–49.

Molander, B., & Bäckman, L. (1990). Age differences in the effects of background noise on motor and memory performance in a precision sport. *Experimental Aging Research, 16,* 55–60.

Monti, L. A., Gabrieli, J. D. E., Reminger, S. L., Rinaldi, J. A., Wilson, R. S., & Fleischman, D. A. (1996). Differential effects of aging and Alzheimer's disease on conceptual implicit and explicit memory. *Neuropsychology, 10,* 101–112.

Morrell, R. W., Park, D. C., & Poon, L. W. (1990). Effects of labeling techniques on memory and comprehension of prescription information in young and old adults. *Journals of Gerontology, 45,* P166–P172.

Morris, M. K., Bowers, D., Chatterjee, A., & Heilman, K. M. (1992). Amnesia following a discrete basal forebrain lesion. *Brain, 115,* 1827–1847.

Morrison, J. H., & Hof, P. R. (1997). Life and death of neurons in the aging brain. *Science, 278,* 412–419.

Moscovitch, M., & Winocur, G. (1992). The neuropsychology of memory and aging. In F. I. M. Craik & T. A. Salthouse (Eds.), *The handbook of aging and cognition* (pp. 315–372). Hillsdale, NJ: Lawrence Erlbaum Associates.

Moscovitch, M., Winocur, G., & McLachlan, D. (1986). Memory as assessed by recognition and reading time in normal and memory-impaired people with Alzheimer's disease and other neurological disorders. *Journal of Experimental Psychology: General, 115,* 331–347.

Mozley, P. D., Kim, H. -J., Gur, R. C., Tatsch, K., Muenz, L. R., McElgin, W. T., Kung, M. -P., Mu, M., Myers, A. M., & Kung, H. F. (1996). Iodine-123-IPT SPECT imaging of CNS dopamine transporters: Nonlinear effects of normal aging on striatal uptake values. *Journal of Nuclear Medicine, 37,* 1965–1970.

Müller, U., von Cramon, D. Y., & Pollmann, S. (1998). D1- versus D2-receptor modulation of visuospatial working memory in humans. *Journal of Neuroscience, 18,* 2720–2728.

Nichelli, P., Appollonio, I., Clark, K., & Grafman, J. (1994). Word frequency monitoring in Parkinson's disease: An analysis of accuracy and precision. *Neuropsychiatry, Neuropsychology, and Behavioral Neurology, 7,* 289–294.

Nissen, M. J., & Bullemer, P. (1987). Attentional requirements of learning: Evidence from performance measures. *Cognitive Psychology, 19,* 1–32.

Norman, K. A., & Schacter, D. L. (1997). False recognition in younger and older adults: Exploring the characteristics of illusory memories. *Memory and Cognition, 25,* 838–848.

Nyberg, L., Bäckman, L., Erngrund, K., Olofsson, U., & Nilsson, L.-G. (1996). Age differences in episodic memory, semantic memory, and priming: Relationships to demographic, intellectual, and biological factors. *Journal of Gerontology: Psychological Sciences, 51B,* P234–P240.

Nyberg, L., McIntosh, A. R., Houle, S., Nilsson, L. -G., & Tulving, E. (1996). Activation of medial temporal structures during episodic memory retrieval. *Nature, 380,* 715–717.

Nyberg, L., Winocur, G., & Moscovitch, M. (1997). Correlation between frontal lobe functions and explicit and implicit stem completion in healthy elderly. *Neuropsychology, 11,* 70–76.

O'Brien, J. T., Desmond, P., Ames, D., Schweitzer, I., & Tress, B. (1997). Magnetic resonance imaging correlates of memory impairment in the healthy elderly: Association with medial temporal lobe atrophy but not white matter lesions. *International Journal of Geriatric Psychiatry, 12,* 369–374.

Owen, A. M., Morris, R. G., Sahakian, B. J., Polkey, C. E., & Robbins, T. W. (1996). Double dissociations of memory and executive functions in working memory tasks following frontal lobe excisions, temporal lobe excisions or amygdalo-hippocampectomy in man. *Brain, 119,* 1597–1615.

Park, D. C., & Shaw, R. J. (1992). Effect of environmental support on implicit and explicit memory in younger and older adults. *Psychology and Aging, 7*, 632–642.

Parkin, A. J., Walter, B. M., & Hunkin, N. M. (1995). Relationships between normal aging, frontal lobe function, and memory for temporal and spatial information. *Neuropsychology, 9*, 304–312.

Petrides, M., Alivisatos, B., Meyer, E., & Evans, A. C. (1993). Functional activation of the human frontal cortex during the performance of verbal working memory tasks. *Proceedings of the National Academy of Sciences USA, 90*, 878–882.

Petrides, M., & Milner, B. (1982). Deficits on subject-ordered tasks after frontal- and temporal-lobe lesions in man. *Neuropsychologia, 20*, 249–262.

Poldrack, R. A., Desmond, J. E., Glover, G. H., & Gabrieli, J. D. E. (1998). The neural basis of visual skill learning: An fMRI study of mirror reading. *Cerebral Cortex, 8*, 1–10.

Poldrack, R. A., Hsieh, J. C., & Gabrieli, J. D. E. (1998). Striatal activation associated with visual skill learning and repetition priming examined using fMRI. *Society for Neuroscience Abstracts, 24*, 408.5.

Poldrack, R. A., Prabhakaran, V., Seger, C. A., & Gabrieli, J. D. E. (in press). Striatal activation during cognitive skill learning. *Neuropsychology.*

Poon, L. W., & Fozard, J. L. (1978). Speed of retrieval from long-term memory in relation to age, familiarity, and datedness of information. *Journal of Gerontology, 33*, 711–717.

Rabinowitz, J. C. (1986). Priming in episodic memory. *Journal of Gerontology, 41*, 204–213.

Raichle, M. E., Fiez, J. A., Videen, T. O., MacLeod, A. K., Pardo, J. V., Fox, P. T., & Petersen, S. E. (1994). Practice-related changes in human brain functional anatomy during non-motor learning. *Cerebral Cortex, 4*, 8–26.

Rastle, K. G., & Burke, D. M. (1996). Priming the tip of the tongue: Effects of prior processing on word retrieval in young and older adults. *Journal of Memory and Language, 35*, 586–605.

Raymond, J. L., Lisberger, S. G., & Mauk, M. D. (1996). The cerebellum: A neuronal learning machine? *Science, 272*, 1126–1131.

Raz, N., Gunning, F. M., Head, D., Dupuis, J. H., McQuain, J., Briggs, S. D., Loken, W. J., Thornton, A. E., & Acker, J. D. (1997). Selective aging of the human cerebral cortex observed in vivo: Differential vulnerability of the prefrontal gray matter. *Cerebral Cortex, 7*, 268–282.

Raz, N., Gunning-Dixon, F. M., Head, D., Dupuis, J. H., & Acker, J. D. (1998). Neuroanatomical correlates of cognitive aging: Evidence from structural magnetic resonance imaging. *Neuropsychology, 12*, 95–114.

Raz, N., Torres, I. J., Spencer, W. D., White, K., & Acker, J. D. (1992). Age-related regional differences in cerebellar vermis observed in vivo. *Archives of Neurology, 49*, 412–416.

Rempel-Clower, N. L., Zola, S. M., Squire, L. R., & Amaral, D. G. (1996). Three cases of enduring memory impairment after bilateral damage limited to the hippocampal formation. *Journal of Neuroscience, 16*, 5233–5255.

Riederer, P., & Wuketich, S. (1976). Time course of nigrostriatal degeneration in Parkinson's disease. *Journal of Neural Transmission, 38*, 277–301.

Rinne, J. O. (1987). Muscarinic and dopaminergic receptors in the aging human brain. *Brain Research, 404*, 162–168.

Rinne, J. O., Hietala, J., Ruotsalainen, U., Säkö, E., Laihinen, A., Någren, K., Lehikoinen, P., Oikonen, V., & Syvälahti, E. (1993). Decrease in human striatal dopamine D_2 receptor density with age: A PET study with [^{11}C]Raclopride. *Journal of Cerebral Blood Flow and Metabolism, 13*, 310–314.

Rinne, J. O., Lönnberg, P., & Marjamäki, P. (1990). Age-dependent decline in human brain dopamine D_1 and D_2 receptors. *Brain Research, 508*, 349–352.

Roediger, H. L., III, & McDermott, K. B. (1993). Implicit memory in normal human subjects. In F. Boller & J. Grafman (Eds.), *Handbook of neuropsychology* (Vol. 8, pp. 63–131). New York: Elsevier.

Roediger, H. L., III, & McDermott, K. B. (1995). Creating false memories: Remembering words not presented in lists. *Journal of Experimental Psychology: Learning, Memory, and Cognition, 21,* 803–814.

Roediger, H. L., III, Weldon, M. S., & Challis, B. H. (1989). Explaining dissociations between implicit and explicit measures of retention: A processing account. In H. L. Roediger III & F. I. M. Craik (Eds.), *Varieties of memory and consciousness: Essays in honour of Endel Tulving* (pp. 3–41). Hillsdale, NJ: Lawrence Erlbaum Associates.

Romero-Sierra, C. (1986). *Neuroanatomy: A conceptual approach.* New York: Churchill Livingstone.

Rose, T. L., Yesavage, J. A., Hill, R. D., & Bower, G. H. (1986). Priming effects and recognition memory in young and elderly adults. *Experimental Aging Research, 12,* 31–37.

Rubin, D. C., Rahhal, T. A., & Poon, L. W. (1998). Things learned in early adulthood are remembered best. *Memory and Cognition, 26,* 3–19.

Rubin, D. C., & Schulkind, M. D. (1997). The distribution of autobiographical memories across the lifespan. *Memory and Cognition, 25,* 859–866.

Ruch, F. L. (1934). The differentiative effects of age upon human learning. *Journal of General Psychology, 11,* 261–286.

Rybash, J. M. (1996). Implicit memory and aging: A cognitive neuropsychological perspective. *Developmental Neuropsychology, 12,* 127–179.

Sagar, H. J., Sullivan, E. V., Gabrieli, J. D. E., Corkin, S., & Growdon, J. H. (1988). Temporal ordering and short-term memory deficits in Parkinson's disease. *Brain, 111,* 525–539.

Saint-Cyr, J. A., Taylor, A. E., & Lang, A. E. (1988). Procedural learning and neostriatal dysfunction in man. *Brain, 111,* 941–959.

Salthouse, T. A. (1984). Effects of age and skill in typing. *Journal of Experimental Psychology: General, 113,* 345–371.

Salthouse, T. A., & Babcock, R. L. (1991). Decomposing adult age differences in working memory. *Developmental Psychology, 27,* 763–776.

Salthouse, T. A., & Somberg, B. L. (1982). Skilled performance: Effects of adult age and experience on elementary processes. *Journal of Experimental Psychology: General, 111,* 176–207.

Salvatierra, A. T., & Berry, S. D. (1989). Scopolomine disruption of septo-hippocampal activity and classical conditioning. *Behavioral Neuroscience, 103,* 715–721.

Sanes, J. N., Dimitrov, B., & Hallett, M. (1990). Motor learning in patients with cerebellar dysfunction. *Brain, 113,* 103–120.

Sawaguchi, T., & Goldman-Rakic, P. S. (1991). D1 dopamine receptors in prefrontal cortex: Involvement in working memory. *Science, 251,* 947–950.

Scatton, B., Rouquier, L., Javoy-Agid, F., & Agid, Y. (1982). Dopamine deficiency in the cerebral cortex in Parkinson disease. *Neurology, 32,* 1039–1040.

Schacter, D. L., Alpert, N. M., Savage, C. R., Rauch, S. L., & Albert, M. S. (1996). Conscious recollection and the human hippocampal formation: Evidence from positron emission tomography. *Proceedings of the National Academy of Sciences USA, 93,* 321–325.

Schacter, D. L., Cooper, L. A., & Valdiserri, M. (1992). Implicit and explicit memory for novel visual objects in older and younger adults. *Psychology and Aging, 7,* 299–308.

Schacter, D. L., Curran, T., Galluccio, L., Milberg, W. P., & Bates, J. F. (1996). False recognition and the right frontal lobe: A case study. *Neuropsychologia, 34,* 793–808.

Schacter, D. L., & Graf, P. (1986). Preserved learning in amnesic patients: Perspectives from research on direct priming. *Journal of Clinical and Experimental Neuropsychology, 8,* 727–743.

Schacter, D. L., Harbluk, J. L., & McLachlan, D. R. (1984). Retrieval without recollection: An experimental analysis of source amnesia. *Journal of Verbal Learning and Verbal Behavior, 23,* 593–611.

Schacter, D. L., Kaszniak, A. W., Kihlstrom, J. F., & Valdiserri, M. (1991). The relation between source memory and aging. *Psychology and Aging, 6,* 559–568.

Schacter, D. L., Osowiecki, D., Kaszniak, A. W., Kihlstrom, J. F., & Valdiserri, M. (1994). Source memory: Extending the boundaries of age-related deficits. *Psychology and Aging, 9*, 81–89.

Schacter, D. L., Savage, C. R., Alpert, N. M., Rauch, S. L., & Albert, M. S. (1996). The role of hippocampus and frontal cortex in age-related memory changes: A PET study. *NeuroReport, 7*, 1165–1169.

Schacter, D. L., Verfaellie, M., & Pradere, A. (1996). The neuropsychology of memory illusions: False recall and recognition in amnesic patients. *Journal of Memory and Language, 35*, 319–334.

Scheibel, M. E., Lindsay, R. D., Tomiyasu, U., & Scheibel, A. B. (1975). Progressive dendritic changes in aging human cortex. *Experimental Neurology, 47*, 392–403.

Scherman, D., Desnos, C., Darchen, F., Pollak, P., Javoy-Agid, F., & Agid, Y. (1989). Striatal dopamine deficiency in Parkinson's disease: Role of aging. *Annals of Neurology, 26*, 551–557.

Schmalz, L. W., & Theios, J. (1972). Acquisition and extinction of a classically conditioned response in hippocampectomized rabbits (*Oryctolagus cuniculus*). *Journal of Comparative and Physiological Psychology, 79*, 328–333.

Schugens, M. M., Daum, I., Spindler, M., & Birbaumer, N. (1997). Differential effects of aging on explicit and implicit memory. *Aging, Neuropsychology, and Cognition, 4*, 33–44.

Scoville, W. B., & Milner, B. (1957). Loss of recent memory after bilateral hippocampal lesions. *Journal of Neurology, Neurosurgery, and Psychiatry, 20*, 11–21.

Seab, J. P., Jagust, W. J., Wong, S. T. S., Roos, M. S., Reed, B. R., & Budinger, T. F. (1988). Quantitative NMR measurements of hippocampal atrophy in Alzheimer's disease. *Magnetic Resonance in Medicine, 8*, 200–208.

Seeman, P., Bzowej, N. H., Guan, H. -C., Bergeron, C., Becker, L. E., Reynolds, G. P., Bird, E. D., Riederer, P., Jellinger, K., Watanabe, S., & Tourtellotte, W. W. (1987). Human brain dopamine receptors in children and aging adults. *Synapse, 1*, 399–404.

Selco, S. L., Cohen, N. J., Stebbins, G. T., & Goetz, C. G. (1997). Motor sequence learning in Parkinson's disease: A direct comparison between two tasks using two response modes. *Society for Neuroscience Abstracts, 23*, 553.3.

Severson, J. A., Marcusson, J., Winblad, B., & Finch, C. E. (1982). Age-correlated loss of dopaminergic binding sites in human basal ganglia. *Journal of Neurochemistry, 39*, 1623–1631.

Shaw, T. G., Mortel, K. F., Meyer, J. S., Rogers, R. L., Hardenberg, J., & Cutaia, M. M. (1984). Cerebral blood flow changes in benign aging and cerebrovascular disease. *Neurology, 34*, 855–862.

Shimamura, A. P., Gershberg, F. B., Jurica, P. J., Mangels, J. A., & Knight, R. T. (1992). Intact implicit memory in patients with frontal lobe lesions. *Neuropsychologia, 30*, 931–937.

Shimamura, A. P., Janowsky, J. S., & Squire, L. R. (1990). Memory for the temporal order of events in patients with frontal lobe lesions and amnesic patients. *Neuropsychologia, 28*, 803–813.

Shimamura, A. P., & Jurica, P. J. (1994). Memory interference effects and aging: Findings from a test of frontal lobe function. *Neuropsychology, 8*, 408–412.

Shimamura, A. P., Jurica, P. J., Mangels, J. A., Gershberg, F. B., & Knight, R. T. (1995). Susceptibility to memory interference effects following frontal lobe damage: Findings from tests of paired-associate learning. *Journal of Cognitive Neuroscience, 7*, 144–152.

Shimamura, A. P., Salmon, D. P., Squire, L. R., & Butters, N. (1987). Memory dysfunction and word priming in dementia and amnesia. *Behavioral Neuroscience, 101*, 347–351.

Shimamura, A. P., & Squire, L. R. (1984). Paired-associate learning and priming effects in amnesia: A neuropsychological study. *Journal of Experimental Psychology: General, 113*, 556–570.

Simic, G., Kostovic, I., Winblad, B., & Bogdanovic, N. (1997). Volume and number of neurons of the human hippocampal formation in normal aging and Alzheimer's disease. *Journal of Comparative Neurology, 379*, 482–494.

Sliwinski, M., Lipton, R. B., Buschke, H., & Stewart, W. (1996). The effects of preclinical dementia on estimates of normal cognitive functioning in aging. *Journals of Gerontology: Series B. Psychological Sciences and Social Sciences, 51B*, P217–P225.

Small, B. J., Hultsch, D. F., & Masson, M. E. J. (1995). Adult age differences in perceptually based, but not conceptually based implicit tests of memory. *Journal of Gerontology: Psychological Sciences, 50B*, P162–P170.

Smith, M. L., & Milner, B. (1988). Estimation of frequency of occurrence of abstract designs after frontal or temporal lobectomy. *Neuropsychologia, 26*, 297–306.

Snoddy, G. S. (1926). Learning and stability: A psychophysiological analysis of a case of motor learning with clinical applications. *Journal of Applied Psychology, 10*, 1–36.

Solomon, P. R., Flynn, D., Mirak, J., Brett, M., Coslov, N., & Groccia, M. (1998). Five-year retention of the classically conditioned eyeblink response in young adult, middle-aged, and older humans. *Psychology and Aging, 13*, 186–192.

Solomon, P. R., Groccia-Ellison, M., Flynn, D., Mirak, J., Edwards, K. R., Dunehew, A., & Stanton, M. E. (1993). Disruption of human eyeblink conditioning after central cholinergic blockade with scopolamine. *Behavioral Neuroscience, 107*, 271–279.

Solomon, P. R., Levine, E., Bein, T., & Pendlebury, W. W. (1991). Disruption of classical conditioning in patients with Alzheimer's disease. *Neurobiology of Aging, 12*, 283–287.

Solomon, P. R., Pomerleau, D., Bennett, L., James, J., & Morse, D. L. (1989). Acquisition of the classically conditioned eyeblink response in humans over the life span. *Psychology and Aging, 4*, 34–41.

Solomon, P. R., Solomon, S. D., Vander Schaaf, E., & Perry, H. E. (1983). Altered activity in the hippocampus is more detrimental to classical conditioning than removing the structure. *Science, 220*, 329–331.

Solomon, P. R., Vander Schaaf, E. R., Thompson, R. F., & Weisz, D. J. (1986). Hippocampus and trace conditioning of the rabbit's classically conditioned nictitating membrane response. *Behavioral Neuroscience, 100*, 729–744.

Solyom, L. S., & Barik, H. C. (1965). Conditioning in senescence and senility. *Journal of Gerontology, 20*, 483–488.

Spencer, W. D., & Raz, N. (1994). Memory for facts, source, and context: Can frontal lobe dysfunction explain age-related differences? *Psychology and Aging, 9*, 149–159.

Spencer, W. D., & Raz, N. (1995). Differential effects of aging on memory for content and context: A meta-analysis. *Psychology and Aging, 10*, 527–539.

Spieler, D. H., & Balota, D. A. (1996). Characteristics of associative learning in younger and older adults: Evidence from an episodic priming paradigm. *Psychology and Aging, 11*, 607–620.

Squire, L. R. (1982). Comparisons between forms of amnesia: Some deficits are unique to Korsakoff's syndrome. *Journal of Experimental Psychology: Learning, Memory, and Cognition, 8*, 560–571.

Squire, L. R., Amaral, D. G., & Press, G. A. (1990). Magnetic resonance imaging of the hippocampal formation and mammillary nuclei distinguish medial temporal lobe and diencephalic amnesia. *Journal of Neuroscience, 10*, 3106–3117.

Squire, L. R., Nadel, L., & Slater, P. C. (1981). Anterograde amnesia and memory for temporal order. *Neuropsychologia, 19*, 141–145.

Squire, L. R., Ojemann, J. G., Miezin, F. M., Petersen, S. E., Videen, T. O., & Raichle, M. E. (1992). Activation of the hippocampus in normal humans: A functional anatomical study of memory. *Proceedings of the National Academy of Sciences USA, 89*, 1837–1841.

Stebbins, G. T., Gabrieli, J. D. E., Masciari, F., Monti, L., & Goetz, C. G. (1999). Delayed recognition memory in Parkinson's disease: A role for working memory? *Neuropsychologia, 37*, 503–510.

Stern, C. E., Corkin, S., González, R. G., Guimaraes, A. R., Baker, J. R., Jennings, P. J., Carr, C. A., Sugiura, R. M., Vedantham, V., & Rosen, B. R. (1996). The hippocampal formation participates in novel picture encoding: Evidence from functional magnetic resonance imaging. *Proceedings of the National Academy of Sciences USA, 93*, 8660–8665.

Stuss, D. T., Alexander, M. P., Palumbo, C. L., Buckle, L., Sayer, L., & Pogue, J. (1994). Organizational strategies of patients with unilateral or bilateral frontal lobe injury in word list learning tasks. *Neuropsychology, 8*, 355–373.

Stuss, D. T., Craik, F. I. M., Sayer, L., Franchi, D., & Alexander, M. P. (1996). Comparison of older people and patients with frontal lesions: Evidence from word list learning. *Psychology and Aging, 11*, 387–395.

Suhara, T., Fukuda, H., Inoue, O., Itoh, T., Suzuki, K., Yamasaki, T., & Tateno, Y. (1991). Age-related changes in human D1 dopamine receptors measured by positron emission tomography. *Psychopharmacology, 103*, 41–45.

Sullivan, E. V., Marsh, L., Mathalon, D. H., Lim, K. O., & Pfefferbaum, A. (1995). Age-related decline in MRI volumes of temporal lobe gray matter but not hippocampus. *Neurobiology of Aging, 16*, 591–606.

Suzuki, W. A., & Amaral, D. G. (1994). Perirhinal and parahippocampal cortices of the macaque monkey: Cortical afferents. *Journal of Comparative Neurology, 350*, 497–533.

Tanaka, Y., Miyazawa, Y., Akaoka, F., & Yamada, T. (1997). Amnesia following damage to the mammillary bodies. *Neurology, 48*, 160–165.

Taylor, A. E., Saint-Cyr, J. A., & Lang, A. E. (1990). Memory and learning in early Parkinson's disease: Evidence for a "frontal lobe syndrome." *Brain and Cognition, 13*, 211–232.

Thompson, R. F. (1990). Neural mechanisms of classical conditioning in mammals. *Philosophical Transactions of the Royal Society of London, Series B, 329*, 161–170.

Titov, N., & Knight, R. G. (1997). Adult age differences in controlled and automatic memory processing. *Psychology and Aging, 12*, 565–573.

Torvik, A., Torp, S., & Lindboe, C. F. (1986). Atrophy of the cerebellar vermis in ageing: A morphometric and histologic study. *Journal of the Neurological Sciences, 76*, 283–294.

Tulving, E. (1962). Subjective organization in free recall of "unrelated" words. *Psychological Review, 69*, 344–354.

Tulving, E. (1983). *Elements of episodic memory.* New York: Oxford University Press.

Tulving, E., Markowitsch, H. J., Kapur, S., Habib, R., & Houle, S. (1994). Novelty encoding networks in the human brain: Positron emission tomography data. *NeuroReport, 5*, 2525–2528.

Tun, P. A., Wingfield, A., Rosen, M. J., & Blanchard, L. (1998). Response latencies for false memories: Gist-based processes in normal aging. *Psychology and Aging, 13*, 230–241.

Vaidya, C. J., Gabrieli, J. D. E., Demb, J. B., Keane, M. M., & Wetzel, L. C. (1996). Impaired priming on the general knowledge task in amnesia. *Neuropsychology, 10*, 529–537.

Vaidya, C. J., Gabrieli, J. D. E., Keane, M. M., & Monti, L. A. (1995). Perceptual and conceptual memory processes in global amnesia. *Neuropsychology, 9*, 580–591.

Vaidya, C. J., Gabrieli, J. D. E., Keane, M. M., Monti, L. A., Gutiérrez-Rivas, H., & Zarella, M. M. (1997). Evidence for multiple mechanisms of conceptual priming on implicit memory tests. *Journal of Experimental Psychology: Learning, Memory, and Cognition, 23*, 1324–1343.

Vakil, E., & Agmon-Ashkenazi, D. (1997). Baseline performance and learning rate of procedural and declarative memory tasks: Younger versus older adults. *Journal of Gerontology: Psychological Sciences, 52B*, P229–P234.

van Dyck, C. H., Seibyl, J. P., Malison, R. T., Laruelle, M., Wallace, E., Zoghbi, S. S., Zea-Ponce, Y., Baldwin, R. M., Charney, D. S., Hoffer, P. B., & Innis, R. B. (1995). Age–related decline in striatal dopamine transporter binding with iodine-123-β-CIT SPECT. *Journal of Nuclear Medicine, 36*, 1175–1181.

Verhaeghen, P., Marcoen, A., & Goossens, L. (1993). Facts and fiction about memory aging: A quantitative integration of research findings. *Journal of Gerontology: Psychological Sciences, 48,* P157–P171.

Verhaeghen, P., & Salthouse, T. A. (1997). Meta-analyses of age–cognition relations in adulthood: Estimates of linear and nonlinear age effects and structural models. *Psychological Bulletin, 122,* 231–249.

Victor, M., Adams, R. D., & Collins, G. H. (1971). *The Wernicke-Korsakoff's syndrome.* Philadelphia: Davis.

Volkow, N. D., Fowler, J. S., Wang, G. J., Logan, J., Schlyer, D., MacGregor, R., Hitzemann, R., & Wolf, A. P. (1994). Decreased dopamine transporters with age in healthy human subjects. *Annals of Neurology, 36,* 237–239.

von Cramon, D. Y., Hebel, N., & Schuri, U. (1990). A contribution to the anatomical basis of thalamic amnesia. *Brain, 108,* 993–1008.

Vriezen, E. R., & Moscovitch, M. (1990). Memory for temporal order and conditional associative-learning in patients with Parkinson's disease. *Neuropsychologia, 28,* 1283–1293.

Wagner, A. D., Desmond, J. E., Demb, J. B., Glover, G. H., & Gabrieli, J. D. E. (1997). Semantic repetition priming for verbal and pictorial knowledge: A functional MRI study of left inferior prefrontal cortex. *Journal of Cognitive Neuroscience, 9,* 714–726.

Wagner, A. D., Desmond, J. E., Glover, G. H., & Gabrieli, J. D. E. (1998). Prefrontal cortex and recognition memory: Functional-MRI evidence for context-dependent retrieval processes. *Brain, 121,* 1985–2002.

Wagner, A. D., Schacter, D. L., Rotte, M., Koutstaal, W., Maril, A., Dale, A. M., Rosen, B. R., & Buckner, R. L. (1998). Building memories: Remembering and forgetting of verbal experiences as predicted by brain activity. *Science, 281,* 1188–1191.

Warren, L. R., Butler, R. W., Katholi, C. R., & Halsey, J. H., Jr. (1985). Age differences in cerebral blood flow during rest and during mental activation measurements with and without monetary incentive. *Journal of Gerontology, 40,* 53–59.

West, M. J. (1993). Regionally specific loss of neurons in the aging human hippocampus. *Neurobiology of Aging, 14,* 287–293.

West, R. L. (1996). An application of prefrontal cortex function theory to cognitive aging. *Psychological Bulletin, 120,* 272–292.

Wheeler, M. A., Stuss, D. T., & Tulving, E. (1995). Frontal lobe damage produces episodic memory impairment. *Journal of the International Neuropsychological Society, 1,* 525–536.

Wiggs, C. L. (1993). Aging and memory for frequency of occurrence of novel, visual stimuli: Direct and indirect measures. *Psychology and Aging, 8,* 400–410.

Willingham, D. B., & Koroshetz, W. J. (1993). Evidence for dissociable motor skills in Huntington's disease patients. *Psychobiology, 21,* 173–182.

Winocur, G., Moscovitch, M., & Stuss, D. T. (1996). Explicit and implicit memory in the elderly: Evidence for double dissociation involving medial temporal- and frontal-lobe functions. *Neuropsychology, 10,* 57–65.

Wolfson, L. I., Leenders, K. L., Brown, L. L., & Jones, T. (1985). Alterations of regional cerebral blood flow and oxygen metabolism in Parkinson's disease. *Neurology, 35,* 1399–1405.

Woodruff-Pak, D. S. (1990). Mammalian models of learning, memory, and aging. In J. E. Birren & K. W. Schaie (Eds.), *Handbook of the psychology of aging* (3rd ed., pp. 234–257). San Diego, CA: Academic Press.

Woodruff-Pak, D. S. (1993). Eyeblink classical conditioning in H.M.: Delay and trace paradigms. *Behavioral Neuroscience, 107,* 911–925.

Woodruff-Pak, D. S., Cronholm, J. F., & Sheffield, J. B. (1990). Purkinje cell number related to rate of classical conditioning. *NeuroReport, 1,* 165–168.

Woodruff-Pak, D. S., & Finkbiner, R. G. (1995). Larger nondeclarative than declarative deficits in learning and memory in human aging. *Psychology and Aging, 10,* 416–426.

Woodruff-Pak, D. S., Finkbiner, R. G., & Sasse, D. K. (1990). Eyeblink conditioning discriminates Alzheimer's patients from non-demented aged. *NeuroReport, 1,* 45–49.

Woodruff-Pak, D. S., & Jaeger, M. E. (1998). Predictors of eyeblink classical conditioning over the adult age span. *Psychology and Aging, 13,* 193–205.

Woodruff-Pak, D. S., & Papka, M. (1996a). Alzheimer's disease and eyeblink conditioning: 750 ms trace vs. 400 ms delay paradigm. *Neurobiology of Aging, 17,* 397–404.

Woodruff-Pak, D. S., & Papka, M. (1996b). Huntington's disease and eyeblink classical conditioning: Normal learning but abnormal timing. *Journal of the International Neuropsychological Society, 2,* 323–334.

Woodruff-Pak, D. S., Papka, M., & Ivry, R. B. (1996). Cerebellar involvement in eyeblink classical conditioning in humans. *Neuropsychology, 10,* 443–458.

Woodruff-Pak, D. S., & Thompson, R. F. (1988). Classical conditioning of the eyeblink response in the delay paradigm in adults aged 18–83 years. *Psychology and Aging, 3,* 219–229.

Worden, P. E., & Sherman-Brown, S. (1983). A word-frequency cohort effect in young versus elderly adults' memory for words. *Developmental Psychology, 19,* 521–530.

Wright, B. M., & Payne, R. B. (1985). Effects of aging on sex differences in psychomotor reminiscence and tracking proficiency. *Journal of Gerontology, 40,* 179–184.

Yamadori, A., Yoshida, T., Mori, E., & Yamashita, H. (1996). Neurological basis of skill learning. *Cognitive Brain Research, 5,* 49–54.

Zelinski, E. M., & Burnight, K. P. (1997). Sixteen-year longitudinal and time lag changes in memory and cognition in older adults. *Psychology and Aging, 12,* 503–513.

Zola-Morgan, S., Squire, L. R., & Amaral, D. G. (1986). Human amnesia and the medial temporal region: Enduring memory impairment following a bilateral lesion limited to field CA1 of the hippocampus. *Journal of Neuroscience, 6,* 2950–2967.

3

Implications of Perceptual Deterioration for Cognitive Aging Research

Bruce A. Schneider
University of Toronto at Mississauga

M. Kathleen Pichora-Fuller
University of British Columbia

Information-processing approaches argue for an intimate relationship between perceptual and cognitive processing.[1] Nevertheless, rather than

---

[1]From an information-processing point of view, the boundaries between sensation, perception, and cognition are fuzzy. In this chapter, we reserve the word *sensory* to refer to receptor cells and their functions, which may be indexed in a variety of ways. Measures that involve detection (whether or not there is a response to the presence of a stimulus) but not the discrimination, identification, and interpretation of stimuli can be thought of as accessing the sensitivity of sensory organs. For example, pure-tone thresholds or visual grating contrast thresholds may be thought of as primarily sensory measures. On the other hand, Snellen acuity or auditory word-recognition tests, although dependent on sensory processes, require a certain degree of cognitive involvement because they rely on linguistic knowledge. However, to the extent that the cognitive components of the task are overlearned, one could argue that performance on these tasks primarily reflects the status of the sensory system. Tasks that require relational judgments (e.g., is Stimulus A in front of or behind Stimuli B, C, or D?) can be considered as primarily perceptual. They do not necessarily require that stimuli be identified, and they may not be "conscious." Tasks that require observers to identify, remember, or categorize stimuli are primarily cognitive in nature. For example, tasks that require the observer to classify a particular pictorial representation as a bird or a mammal require higher order processes for successful completion. The boundaries between sensation, perception, and cognition are necessarily fuzzy when viewed from an information-processing point of view. As we make clear later, from an information-processing point of view, given the existence of both bottom-up and top-down processing, it is virtually impossible and perhaps misleading to distinguish perceptual from cognitive processing; however, for the purposes of this chapter, we follow the usual practice of the researchers whose work we review. Those processes that occur relatively early and depend heavily on signal properties are referred to as *perceptual*, whereas those that occur relatively late and depend heavily on semantic and linguistic knowledge are referred to as *cognitive*.

treating the perceptual and cognitive systems as an integrated whole, researchers have usually attempted to isolate perceptual processes from cognitive processes. On the one hand, most perception researchers try to minimize the contribution of cognitive factors in their experiments; on the other hand, most cognition researchers have assumed that the contribution of sensory or perceptual factors has been minimal in their experiments. Both of these assumptions may well be true when the participant population is young. However, over the past decade there has been mounting interest in the effects of aging on perception and cognition, and assumptions about the separability of the two domains are being called into question. Perception researchers can no longer be sure that age-related differences, either between groups or individuals, reflect only perceptual factors. Correspondingly, cognitive researchers cannot assume that perceptual input to the cognitive system is invariant with age. Researchers are now compelled to examine more closely the relationship between perception and cognition.

Within the cognitive literature, a large body of evidence points to losses of cognitive function with age, but "sensory functioning and its relationship to complex intellectual functioning has rarely been part of the research agenda" (P. B. Baltes & Lindenberger, 1997, p. 12). Within the perception literature, it is also true that a large body of evidence points to a considerable degree of auditory and visual degeneration with age, but the role of cognition in perceptual function has rarely been taken into account (e.g., Committee on Hearing, Bioacoustics, and Biomechanics [CHABA], 1988). The coexistence of these two kinds of age-related changes raises important questions about the relationship between early and later stages in information processing, that is, between perceptual and cognitive processes, which have now been shown to have "a powerful inter-systemic connection" (P. B. Baltes & Lindenberger, 1997, p. 16). In this chapter, we argue that perception and cognition must be considered as parts of an integrated system if we are to understand how they are affected by age.

Given that both perception and cognition decline with age, it is important to determine the factor or factors responsible for this covariation. There are at least four logical possibilities. The first possibility is that perceptual decline causes cognitive decline (the sensory deprivation hypothesis; Lindenberger & Baltes, 1994; R. Sekuler & Blake, 1987). The second possibility is that both perceptual and cognitive declines reflect either widespread degeneration in the central nervous system or changes in specific functions or circuitry that have systemwide consequences (the common-cause hypothesis; P. B. Baltes & Lindenberger, 1997; Lindenberger & Baltes, 1994; Marsiske, Klumb, & Baltes, 1997; Salthouse, Hancock, Meinz, & Hambrick, 1996). Third, cognitive declines could contribute to age-related differences in sensory measures (the cognitive load on perception hypothesis; Lindenberger & Baltes, 1994; Salthouse et al., 1996). A fourth possibility is that there is a decline in cognitive performance because unclear and distorted perceptual information is delivered to the cognitive systems, thereby compromising cognitive performance (the information-degradation hypothesis; Pichora-Fuller, Schneider, & Daneman, 1995; Salthouse et al., 1996; Schneider, Daneman, Murphy, & Kwong-See, in press). In this chapter, we review evidence relevant to the evaluation of these hypotheses. We begin by reviewing recent evidence showing that age-related perceptual deterioration is more extensive than the already well-known loss of auditory sensitivity and visual acuity. Next, we consider how such losses might affect long- and short-term cognitive functioning by examining the emerging literature on the interrelations between perception, cognition, and aging. Finally, we discuss theoretical and practical implications of age-related differences in perception for cognitive aging research.

DESCRIPTION OF AGE-RELATED CHANGES IN HEARING AND VISION

Demography

The prevalence of clinically significant auditory and visual deficits increases markedly with age, beginning in the fourth decade (Willott, 1991). Although corrective lenses largely overcome most kinds of vision loss, in almost all cases hearing aids are of limited benefit in correcting for hearing loss (Lubinski & Higginbotham, 1997). It is noteworthy that the prevalence of noncorrectable vision and hearing losses increases with age. Furthermore, subclinical reductions in hearing and vision are also common in older adults. Consequently, it must be assumed that the everyday perceptual function of most older adults is reduced compared with the everyday perceptual function of younger adults and that it may not be possible to restore perceptual performance to normal through surgery or the use of prostheses, such as lenses or hearing aids.

Hearing loss is the third most prevalent chronic disability among older adults, exceeded only by arthritis and hypertension (e.g., Binnie, 1994; Haber, 1994). Age-related hearing loss, presbycusis, progresses over time until there are measurable and clinically significant changes in threshold sensitivity. As many as half of adults aged 75 to 79 years have some degree of audiometrically measurable threshold hearing loss (for a review, see Willott, 1991). Although clinically significant elevations in high-frequency pure-tone thresholds are the hallmark of presbycusis, other auditory processing deficits, including those involving the central auditory nervous system, may exist independent of, or in combination with, threshold elevation. Estimates suggest that only about one fourth of older adults who might benefit from hearing aids have one (Gabbard, 1994; Gallup, 1980), and few who have one find that it overcomes all their hearing problems (Holmes, 1995; Pichora-Fuller, 1997). The amplification provided by hearing aids is beneficial when important low-intensity information, such as consonants in speech, would otherwise be inaudible. However, hearing aids also amplify unwanted background or competing sounds, and they do not yet offer sufficiently sophisticated signal processing to mimic the processing performed by an intact auditory system (Levitt, 1993; Plomp, 1978). Thus, it is not surprising that almost a third of older hearing-aid users report that they have difficulties in everyday situations where there are multiple signals (e.g., group conversation) or background noise (Smedley & Schow, 1994). Overall, considering the number with hearing loss who do not own hearing aids, the number who use a hearing aid but continue to experience difficulty, and the number who have central auditory processing problems, either in conjunction with or in the absence of clinically significant threshold elevation, it can be assumed that hearing aids overcome the hearing problems of less than 10% of older adults.

Refractive errors in the optics of the eye are ubiquitous in humans and, if uncorrected, would produce moderate to severe reductions in visual acuity in over 50% of the population. The most common measure of visual acuity is Snellen acuity, in which the patient is asked to identify letters of varying size (visual angle) on an eye chart placed at a known distance from the observer. A number of cross-sectional studies have shown that visual acuity, after correction for refractive errors, starts to decline after 45 years of age. Undoubtedly, some of this loss of visual acuity may be attributable to various pathologies in the eyes of these older adults. However, acuity losses have also been observed in older adults with good eye health (Frisen & Frisen, 1981; Owsley, Sekuler, & Siemsen, 1983; Weale, 1987). In addition to the obvious age-related changes in visual acuity, other aspects of visual function (e.g., contrast sensitivity, contrast discrimination, dark adaptation, perimetric fields, color, and stereopsis) are not usually measured in the clinic but do decline with age. Thus, as in audition, there may be various kinds of losses in visual function other than acuity that may affect perceptual processing.

Consequently, matching for auditory sensitivity and visual acuity across age groups does not guarantee equivalence with respect to the kinds of auditory and visual processing that are required in everyday life when complex, suprathreshold stimuli must be not only detected but also identified, attended to, comprehended, and remembered. Moreover, although losses in acuity can be corrected to some extent (especially in vision), it is difficult if not impossible to correct for losses in other relevant perceptual abilities. In this review, we focus on recent findings that suggest that the effects of aging are more pervasive than previously thought, and we show that these age-related changes can have a dramatic effect on the kind and quality of information available for cognitive processing.

Auditory System

Age-related changes in the anatomy, biomechanics, and physiology of the subcortical auditory system affect an individual's ability to process sounds. Older listeners find it more difficult to detect simple, low-intensity stimuli, discriminate small changes in frequency or intensity, filter out background noise, or precisely locate the source of a target in space. These processing difficulties compromise listening and the encoding of information in many everyday situations. Therefore, it is important to determine the nature and extent of these processing difficulties and how they are related to changes in the anatomy and physiology of subcortical structures.

Age-Related Changes in the Outer and Middle Ears

Anatomical changes due to aging in the outer and middle ears have little effect on hearing in everyday listening conditions (Marshall, 1981; Willott, 1991). Unless there is outer ear blockage or middle ear disease, it is relatively safe to assume that age-related changes in outer and middle ear structures do not produce significant hearing loss. Nevertheless, because of softening of the cartilage in the ear canal, when standard earphones are worn, in about one third of older listeners, the pressure exerted by the earphones will collapse the ear canal (Marshall, 1981). When the ear canal is collapsed by an earphone, a significant amount of high-frequency speech information can be lost, such that the quality of the sound delivered to the eardrum is poorer than it would be if earphones were not worn. To determine whether or not the ear canal is likely to collapse when earphones are worn, the tester simply presses a finger on the listener's outer ear, as if the earphone were pressing on it, and observes whether or not the ear canal remains open. If the opening of the listener's ear canal closes, then the tester should anticipate that sound emitted from the earphone will be blocked in the ear canal, resulting in reduced transmission of the signal. The problem of collapsing ear canals may be avoided if circumaural or insert earphones are used instead of standard earphones or if sound is presented over loudspeakers.

Age-Related Changes in the Inner Ear
and in the Auditory Nerve

It is crucial to recognize that within the past 2 decades there has been
a major reconceptualization of how the cochlea works (for a review, see
Pickles, 1988). In the cochlea, along the length of the basilar membrane,
there is one row of inner hair cells and three rows of outer hair cells. The
afferent fibers innervating the inner hair cells convey information about
sounds to the brain. In contrast, the outer hair cells are primarily inner-
vated by efferent fibers. (The relatively small number of afferent fibers
servicing the outer hair cells do not appear to play a major role in
conveying information about sound to the brain.) Thus, the inner hair
cells are the true sensory receptors. It follows from the coding of frequency
by place along the basilar membrane that a loss of inner hair cells in the
basal region will result in the loss of high-frequency hearing sensitivity,
whereas a loss of inner hair cells in the apical region will result in the
loss of low-frequency hearing sensitivity.

The function of the outer hair cells is quite different. They are motile
and can contract to increase the degree to which the basilar membrane
vibrates in response to a low-intensity input. In other words, they act as
a gain control for low-intensity signals, with the efferent fibers controlling
the extent of the gain (Dulon & Schacht, 1992). Therefore, even a total
loss of outer hair cells would not eliminate hearing, even though such a
loss would destroy many of the nonlinear mechanisms that enhance the
detection and processing of low-intensity signals. Note that most speech
spoken at quiet or normal conversational levels (less than 65 dB sound
pressure level [SPL]) would be in the low-intensity range, where signals
are boosted by the outer hair cells in normal ears. Thus, outer hair cell
loss could affect the processing of speech signals without necessarily producing a hearing loss.

In aging, the pattern of outer and inner hair cell loss differs. Inner hair
cell loss is concentrated in the basal region of the basilar membrane,
whereas outer hair cell loss is more widely distributed, with the outer
rows being the most severely affected. Therefore, the common age-related
finding of extensive loss of inner hair cells in the basal region of the
cochlea most likely accounts for the high-frequency hearing loss observed
in older adults. The more generalized loss of outer hair cells suggests a
diminution of the degree of gain control and thus less efficient processing
of low-intensity signals.

In addition to hair cell loss in the cochlea, there is also some evidence
of age-related changes in the mechanics of cochlear membranes and even
stronger evidence indicating that cochlear blood supply and metabolism
change with age. However, no convincing evidence has yet been found
that relates such changes to specific perceptual problems (Willott, 1991).

As is the case for inner hair cell loss, there is also an age-related loss of ganglion cells (cell bodies of the cochlear neurons housed in the modiolus or core of the cochlea), which is typically greatest near the base of the cochlea. Ganglion cell loss has been observed in the absence of hair cell loss and vice versa, so that hair cell loss is neither a necessary nor a sufficient condition for ganglion cell degeneration. It is very important to note that audiometric thresholds can remain relatively normal in the presence of either considerable hair cell loss or spiral ganglion degeneration.

Individuals with cochlear pathologies resulting in threshold elevation are known to have other associated auditory impairments, including reduced frequency selectivity (broadened critical bandwidths), recruitment (abnormal growth of loudness as signal intensity level increases), and reduced speech discrimination (Moore, 1989; Pickles, 1988). Consequently, we would expect that those older adults in the later stages of presbycusis whose audiograms show clinically significant threshold elevations would experience a number of auditory processing deficits known to be associated with cochlear pathology (for a review, see Schneider, 1997). These deficits would go a long way in explaining the difficulties that the large number of older adults with clinically significant threshold hearing loss may have understanding language spoken in ideal, quiet conditions (see Humes, 1996, for a review).

Unfortunately, the performance of presbycusic individuals in quiet conditions is poorly correlated with their performance in noisy conditions (Plomp, 1986), and we still need to account for the finding that older listeners with hearing sensitivity thresholds within normal clinical limits, who have no trouble listening in quiet conditions, often have more trouble than their younger counterparts when listening in noisy conditions (for reviews see CHABA, 1988, and Willott, 1991). This observation suggests that there are age-related changes in auditory processing even when older adults continue to have hearing sensitivity thresholds within normal clinical limits.

Age-related changes in auditory brain-stem responses (ABRs) suggest that there are age-related changes in auditory processing that are independent of changes in auditory sensitivity. Hellstrom and Schmiedt (1990) suggested that age-related changes in the compound action potential (CAP) in quiet-reared gerbils could be interpreted as indicating a loss in synchrony in nerve firing. ABRs measured by Boettcher, Mills, and Norton (1993) in quiet-reared aged gerbils were also found to be consistent with this interpretation. Synchrony in auditory processing is presently receiving increasing attention in auditory aging research and has been recognized as a deficit distinct from the previously identified high-frequency hearing loss associated with basal hair cell loss.

Age-related subcortical changes in the auditory system have various consequences for processing of auditory stimuli. The first and most obvious consequence is that damage can result in significant threshold elevation. However, the fact that an elderly individual has a clinically normal audiogram is no guarantee that there has not been a significant amount of sensory, neural, or sensorineural degeneration leading to abnormal auditory functioning. Indeed, the effect of degenerative changes may not become evident until older listeners are perceptually stressed, such as when they are required to listen to speech or other complex signals in noisy environments where more complex auditory processing is required. For example, if, as suggested by Hellstrom and Schmiedt (1990), there is a loss of synchrony in neural firing, we would expect that any auditory processes strongly dependent on neural synchrony (such as frequency discrimination, temporal discrimination, localization, binaural unmasking, or speech perception) might be adversely affected, even though pure-tone thresholds remain unaffected. Below, we examine those perceptual abilities most likely to be affected by a loss of neural synchrony in the auditory system. For a more detailed consideration of age-related changes that are associated with cochlear hearing loss, but that are unlikely to be affected by a loss of neural synchrony (e.g., frequency selectivity; intensity discrimination; and forward, simultaneous, and backward masking), see Schneider (1997).

The Effect of Anatomical and Physiological Changes on Temporal Processing Abilities

Age-related changes in auditory temporal processing are of special interest because slowing in aging is a topic that has received much attention in the literature on cognitive aging. In particular, changes in hearing have been shown to be highly correlated with measures of speed of processing in older adults (Lindenberger & Baltes, 1994). More generally, the role of neural synchrony is a topic of great interest in neuroscience today. Therefore, for the purposes of this chapter, we focus on those age-related changes in auditory processing, such as frequency discrimination, monaural temporal resolution, and binaural processing, which are thought to rely on neural synchrony.

Frequency Discrimination. Konig (1957) found that frequency discrimination declined with age at all frequencies. Increased difference limens at the high frequencies could be attributed to sensorineural hearing loss; however, older participants whose audiometric thresholds were only slightly elevated in the low-frequency region (10–20 dB from 125–500 Hz) showed over a fivefold greater difference limen at 125 Hz than did younger adults. Because this large change in the difference limen was associated with such a small change in absolute threshold at this frequency, Konig's data suggest that age-related increases in frequency difference limens occur even in the absence of any significant threshold hearing loss. Further evidence confirming this possibility has been provided by recent studies in which the degree of threshold hearing loss was carefully controlled. S. M. Abel, Krever, and Alberti (1990) found clear indications of increased frequency difference limens at both 500 Hz and 4,000 Hz for middle-aged listeners (40–57 years old) whose audiometric thresholds were within the normal range (≤20 dB hearing level [HL] at 4,000 Hz; ≤15 dB HL at lower frequencies). Moreover, Moore and Peters (1992) reported that some older listeners with clinically normal audiometric thresholds had very large frequency difference limens at low frequencies. Poorer frequency discrimination in the high-frequency region might be due to high-frequency hearing loss in older adults. However, even larger losses in frequency discrimination are observed at low frequencies where the audiometric thresholds of older adults are only slightly elevated over those of younger adults.

Why is the loss in frequency discrimination more severe at low rather than at high frequencies? First of all, it should be noted that frequency discrimination in young participants at low frequencies (Δf = 1–2 Hz) is much better than at high frequencies, where Δf can vary between 10 Hz and 50 Hz. It is unlikely that the excellent frequency discrimination found at low frequencies results from the coding of different loci of maximal vibration on the basilar membrane; rather, it is most likely based on discrimination of differences in interspike times (for a review, see Pickles, 1988). Because the degree of phase locking decreases with increasing signal frequency, any loss of synchrony based on phase locking should not have a dramatic effect on frequency difference limens for high-frequency tones. Thus, the effects of age on frequency discrimination are consistent with the notion that there is a loss of synchrony in the aged auditory system.

Monaural Temporal Resolution. A recent study by Shannon, Zeng, Kamath, Wygonski, and Ekelid (1995) illustrates the importance of temporal envelope information in speech perception. In one of their conditions, the speech signal was divided into three spectral regions (0–500 Hz, 500–1,500 Hz, and 1,500–4,000 Hz) and the amplitude envelope of the filtered speech was determined in each region. The amplitude envelope of the speech in the low-frequency spectral region was then used to modulate a band-limited noise (0–500 Hz); the amplitude envelope of the speech in the middle-frequency region was used to modulate a band-passed noise (500–1,500 Hz); and the amplitude envelope of the speech from the high-frequency region was used to amplitude-modulate a high-frequency band-passed noise (1,500–4,000 Hz). These three amplitude-modulated noises were then added together to produce a signal that retained only the temporal properties of the speech envelope in these three broad frequency regions. Surprisingly, speech recognition for sentences processed in this way exceeded 90%. Clearly, a large amount of information in the speech signal is conveyed by the temporal pattern of the speech envelope (see also Drullman, 1995a, 1995b).

Given the importance of temporal information in speech perception (e.g., Tyler, Summerfield, Wood, & Fernandes, 1982), any loss of temporal resolving abilities with age is likely to affect speech processing. The two most common ways to measure temporal resolution are to (a) determine the minimal duration of a gap in a continuous tone or noise that can just be detected or (b) determine the smallest increase in the duration of a tone or a gap that can just be detected. (Other ways of measuring temporal resolution are reviewed by Schneider, 1997).

With respect to gap detection, a number of studies (e.g., Buus & Florentine, 1985; Moore, Glasberg, Donaldson, McPherson, & Plack, 1989) have reported that hearing-impaired listeners have larger gap-detection thresholds than listeners with normal audiometric thresholds. Many of the hearing-impaired listeners who participated in these experiments were older adults. Only in later studies did researchers try to determine whether temporal resolution covaries directly with age or is mediated by hearing loss. Moore, Peters, and Glasberg (1992) determined the minimal gap that could be detected in a long-duration tonal signal for a group of young normals, a group of older adults with good hearing, and a group of older adults with threshold hearing loss. The first finding of interest was that gap-detection thresholds in the older groups did not appear to be related to hearing loss. Moreover, the average gap-detection thresholds of the older listeners were larger than those of the young listeners. However, the investigators attributed this apparent age effect to the inclusion in the older group of some individuals who had rather large gap-detection thresholds.

Schneider, Pichora-Fuller, Kowalchuk, and Lamb (1994) had younger and older adults discriminate a gap between two Gaussian-modulated 2-kHz tone pips from a short 2-kHz continuous tone of the same total energy (Fig. 3.1). Gap-detection thresholds in the older group were, on average, twice as large as those in the younger group. Moreover, gap-detection thresholds appeared to be independent of the degree of hearing loss in the older group, a result later confirmed by Schneider, Speranza, and Pichora-Fuller (1998). In summary, the studies on gap detection in older listeners suggest that (a) gap-detection ability is independent of hearing loss in older adults and (b) gap-detection thresholds increase with age.

Schneider et al. (1994), using very short tonal markers to define a gap, found a much larger age difference in gap-detection thresholds than did Moore et al. (1992), who used tonal markers of a much longer duration.

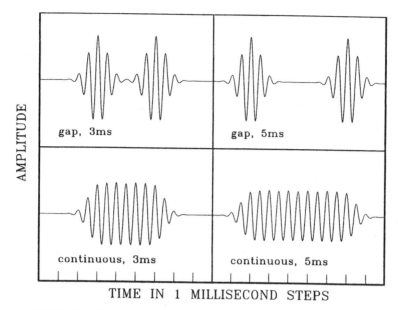

FIG. 3.1. Top left: Two Gaussian-enveloped, 2-kHz tones whose peaks are separated by a 3-ms gap. The Gaussian envelope for these tone pips has a standard deviation of 0.5 ms. Bottom left: A 3-ms, continuous (no-gap) 2-kHz tone with the same total duration and energy as the two tones immediately above it. Top right: Two Gaussian-enveloped, 2-kHz tones whose peaks are separated by a 5-ms gap. The Gaussian envelope for these tone pips also has a standard deviation of 0.5 ms. Bottom right: A 5-ms, continuous (no-gap), 2-kHz tone with the same total duration and energy as the two tone pips separated by a 5-ms gap. From "Gap Detection and the Precedence Effect in Young and Old Adults" by B. A. Schneider, M. K. Pichora-Fuller, D. Kowalchuk, & M. Lamb, 1994, *Journal of the Acoustical Society of America, 95*, p. 981. Copyright © 1994 by the American Institute of Physics. Reprinted with permission.

Thus, it is possible that the size of the age effect on gap detection threshold depends on the duration of the tonal markers that precede and follow the gap. To explore this possibility, Schneider and Hamstra (1999) varied the duration of the tonal markers (f = 2kHz) while holding the onset and offset characteristics of the tones constant. They found that there was a substantial age effect at the shorter durations that disappeared completely when the duration of the markers approached 500 ms. Thus, older listeners are considerably disadvantaged relative to younger listeners when marker durations are less than 100 ms.

In addition to detecting gaps in the auditory stream, a listener processing speech often has to discriminate among temporal intervals. S. M. Abel et al. (1990) studied the difference limen for changes in stimulus duration at two reference durations (20 ms and 200 ms) in young and old listeners. Duration discrimination was poorer in older listeners and appeared to be unrelated to hearing loss. Fitzgibbons and Gordon-Salant (1994) found that older listeners (both normal hearing and hearing impaired) had higher duration discrimination thresholds than younger listeners (both normal hearing and hearing impaired). These two studies suggest that there is an age-related deficit in duration discrimination that is independent of hearing loss.

This brief survey indicates fairly clearly that there is a loss of monaural temporal resolving power in older adults that is not necessarily related to degree of threshold elevation and may affect higher order processes, such as the encoding of spoken language (see also Strouse, Ashmead, Ohde, & Grantham, 1998).

Binaural Processing. In everyday listening situations, the sound waves impinging on the left and right eardrums would be identical (diotic) if the sound source were located directly in front of the listener and if the details of the contours of the outer ear and ear canal of the two ears were identical. However, the anatomical details of the two outer ears usually differ, and sounds often originate off midline. Consequently, the sound waves arriving at the left and right ears are usually nonidentical (dichotic). The direct sound emitted by a source off midline will take longer to reach the far ear than the near ear, and it will be more attenuated by the head as it travels to the far ear, resulting in interaural time and intensity cues. In rooms, direct sound waves are also reflected off objects or walls, resulting in echo or reverberation. Listeners rely primarily on interaural time cues to locate low-frequency signals and on interaural intensity cues to locate high-frequency sounds. The ability of the listener to use these interaural time and intensity-difference cues is amply demonstrated by a consideration of the so-called "cocktail party effect" (e.g., by comparing how well a listener can understand binaural and monaural tape recordings of language spoken by a target talker at a noisy party in a highly reverberant room). The binaural stimuli are recorded from two microphones, with one positioned in each of the listener's ears. For the binaural stimuli, the listener's perception is reasonably close to what it would have been in the original conditions—sound sources appear to have specifiable and different locations, and the listener is able to concentrate on one source to the exclusion of others. For monaurally recorded stimuli, however, all sound sources appear to originate at the stimulated ear, and the listener finds it much more difficult to attend to a single source. Clearly, a loss of binaural information will have a deleterious effect on speech understanding in informationally complex and noisy situations such as those encountered in daily life. Whereas high-frequency threshold hearing loss would clearly interfere with the coding of high-frequency interaural intensity cues, use of low-frequency interaural time cues should remain available. However, if there is loss of neural synchrony with age, then the low-frequency interaural time cues would also be affected.

Although localization is an important binaural phenomenon, very little is known about sound localization in older adults other than that the ability to localize sounds is affected by hearing loss. Noble, Byrne, and Lepage (1994) found sound localization to be poorer in the hearing-impaired group (whose members were also older) relative to the young normal-hearing controls, with the degree and kind of localization problem depending on the type and severity of hearing loss; however, the investigators also noted that variation in the ability to localize sounds in the older group was only partly explained by the nature and degree of hearing loss. Therefore, we might expect normal-hearing older adults to also be impaired with respect to sound localization.

Binaural unmasking is measured by comparing how well a signal is detected in noise when interaural difference cues help the listener to isolate the signal from the noise (such as when the signal and the noise originate from different locations), as opposed to when there are no useful interaural difference cues (such as when only one ear is used or when the signal and noise originate from the same location). For example, laboratory experiments have shown that the detectability of a monaural signal in an ipsilateral monaural masker (S_mN_m) can be enhanced by simultaneously presenting the identical masking noise and no signal to the other ear (S_mN_0). This shows that the intact auditory system is capable of comparing binaural inputs in such a way that the masking effects of a noise in one ear are partially canceled, or "unmasked," by the presence of the identical noise in the opposite ear. The difference in threshold between these two conditions ($S_mN_m - S_mN_0$) is a measure of the binaural masking-level difference (MLD). In addition to the comparison between S_mN_m and S_mN_0, several other methods of measuring the MLD have been used (for reviews, see Durlach, 1972, and Durlach & Colburn, 1978). Binaural unmasking enhances a young, normal-hearing listener's ability to detect a low-frequency tonal signal in broadband background noise by as much as 15 dB. Young adults may be able to perform better than older adults in noisy situations because they make more effective use of interaural cues to unmask signals. For this reason, it is important to determine whether or not aging affects binaural unmasking ability.

Pichora-Fuller and Schneider (1991) found the size of the MLD to be significantly larger for younger listeners than for older listeners, with the extent of the difference being dependent on the particular dichotic comparison condition that was tested. Grose, Poth, and Peters (1994) conducted a study on younger and older listeners in which the target signals were two-syllable spondee words and the masking noise was speech-shaped (for basic information about speech MLDs, see Levitt & Rabiner, 1967). A comparison of performance between diotic and dichotic conditions indicated that there were no differences between young and elderly adults in diotic conditions but that young listeners were significantly better at recognizing words under dichotic listening conditions. Thus, consistent with the age-related differences in MLDs found when using tonal signals, binaural processing differences between young and older adults were also found to significantly affect speech recognition. Because diotic thresholds were comparable for both young and old listeners (Grose et al., 1994; Pichora-Fuller & Schneider, 1991, 1992), one cannot attribute the older adult's poorer performance in dichotic conditions to a general decline in ability to extract signals from noise. Rather, there appears to be a loss that is specific to the binaural processing of stimuli. Such a loss would be consistent with the hypothesis that there is an age-related loss in neural synchrony that begins to appear in the very early stages of presbycusis. Under dichotic conditions, a high degree of neural synchrony is required if low-frequency signals are to be unmasked. The same is not true for either monaural or diotic signal detection. The degree of age-related loss in synchrony was tested and incorporated into a model in a subsequent study (Pichora-Fuller & Schneider, 1992).

In summary, recent research on hearing and aging has provided us with a fuller understanding of age-related changes in the anatomy and physiology of the subcortical auditory system and how these changes relate to the well-known high-frequency hearing loss that typically accompanies aging. Experimental designs controlling for degree of hearing loss and age as separate variables have clarified that there are age-related changes in some aspects of auditory processing that are largely independent of degree of hearing loss, with changes in auditory temporal processing being the most potentially interesting of these for cognitive aging researchers.

Vision

Specific pathologies of the eye, such as cataracts, glaucoma, and macular degeneration, occur more frequently as we age (see Michaels, 1993, for a review), and researchers interested in cognitive aging usually exclude participants with these pathologies. However, screening for eye pathology does not guarantee perfect vision. There are also declines in visual processing abilities that occur in the absence of any observable pathology and persist even after correction for optical abnormalities (see Kline, 1991, Owsley & Burton, 1991, and Sturr & Hannon, 1991, for reviews). Some of these declines may result from subclinical deterioration in the structure and function of the eye or may be a consequence of subclinical deterioration in the early visual pathways. Such deterioration of the visual system inevitably leads to a less accurate and more noisy representation of the visual world in the aging observer, especially in those instances in which the lighting is poor or the stimulus contrast is low.

Age-Related Changes in the Eye and Their Consequences for Basic Visual Abilities

The structures of the eye (cornea, iris, lens, and the vitreous and aqueous humours), when functioning correctly, produce a relatively sharp and clear image on the retina over a wide range of distances and viewing conditions. Age-related changes in these structures will adversely affect the quality of this retinal image. Age-related changes in the layers of the cornea increase light scatter (Michaels, 1993), thereby reducing retinal image quality. As we age, the crystalline lens increases in size and weight, loses its elasticity (presbyopia), and absorbs more light (because of its increased thickness), especially at the short wavelengths (Morgan, 1993). The stiffening of the lens means that we lose the ability to accommodate (bring objects into focus at different distances). The iris of the eye also loses its full range of motility as we age (senile miosis; Weale, 1963), with the result that pupil size becomes smaller at all levels of illumination (Feinberg & Podolak, 1965), such that all other factors being equal, less light falls on the retinas of old viewers than on the retinas of young viewers of the same visual scene. There are also age-related changes in the retinal layers. The thickness of the choroid, which contains the arteries serving the retina, decreases with age because of arteriosclerosis, even in the absence of vascular disease (Michaels, 1993). Presumably, continued thinning of the choroid could reduce the blood supply to a point where it might interfere with the efficient transduction of light to neural impulses in an anatomically intact retina. There is also evidence of an age-related decline in the number of rods (but not in the number of cones) in central vision (Curcio, Millican, Allen, & Kalina, 1993; Dorey, Wu, Ebenstein, Garsd, & Weiter, 1989) and in the number of retinal ganglion cells, although the relatively large amount of intersubject variability can sometimes obscure this ganglion cell loss (Balazsi, Rootman, Drasnce, Schulzer, & Douglas, 1984; Dolman, McCormick, & Drance, 1980; Jonas, Müller-Bergh, Scholtzer-Schrehardt, & Naumann, 1990; Jonas, Schmidt, Müller-Bergh, Schlotzer-Schrehardt, & Naumann, 1992).

As a result of these changes, the aging eye will be less efficient at processing visual input. The loss in lens elasticity reduces accommodative power, with the result that by age 65, only objects at a fixed distance from the observer can be in sharp focus on the retina. The distance at which objects are in focus can differ between the two eyes and can be changed using corrective lenses (such as reading glasses or the lower portion of bifocals). However, any task that requires the processing of visual stimuli that are not located at this distance might be impaired in the elderly because the image is out of focus on the retina. For example, when material is presented on a computer screen, the use of glasses does not guarantee that the objects or letters in question are in focus for the viewer, unless they are presented at the optimal distance for which the eyes have been optically corrected.

The age-related reduction in pupil size and the increased optical density of the lens reduce the amount of light falling on the retina of a normal 60-year-old by about two thirds (Weale, 1961). This will, of course, raise the thresholds for rod and cone vision. Rod sensitivity declines by approximately 2 log units between 20 and 80 years of age (primarily because of the differential absorption of the short wavelengths by the lens), whereas cone sensitivity declines by a little less than 1 log unit (Gunkel & Gouras, 1963; Pitts, 1982). Pitts (1982) has argued that most of this loss reflects the reduction in the amount of light falling on the receptors, with the remainder (approximately 0.5 log units) being attributed either to metabolic decay in the aging eye or to changes in the neural system. McFarland, Domey, Warren, and Ward (1960) have shown that visual thresholds are increased when there is a decrease in blood sugar level and/or under conditions of hypoxia. Hence, reductions in circulatory capacity in the retina or the loss of rods may contribute to losses in light sensitivity.

It is worth noting that transmission losses in the eye mean that the luminance boundaries between "nighttime" (scotopic) and "daytime" (photopic) vision and the region between these two (mesopic) are raised by a factor of 3 or more in the older viewer. The greater absorption of shorter wavelengths by the aging lens, coupled with loss of receptor sensitivity to these wavelengths (Birch et al., 1979; Werner & Steele, 1988), also may lead to blue-yellow confusions so that the color vision of an older person approaches that of an anomalous tritanope.

Another consequence of structural changes is that retinal blurring in the older eye is likely to be greater because optical aberrations are more severe. The effect of age on subclinical retinal blurring was studied by Artal, Ferro, Miranda, and Navarro (1993). These investigators measured the retinal image of a point in young and old eyes with corrected visual acuity of 20/20 or better. Thus, by the usual clinical standards, all of the young and old participants had excellent vision. Measurements were obtained under conditions of paralyzed accommodation, using an artificial pupil to control for senile miosis, with the image centered to control astigmatism and with appropriate refraction to provide the least blurred image. Figure 3.2 shows the sharpness of the retinal image for two young

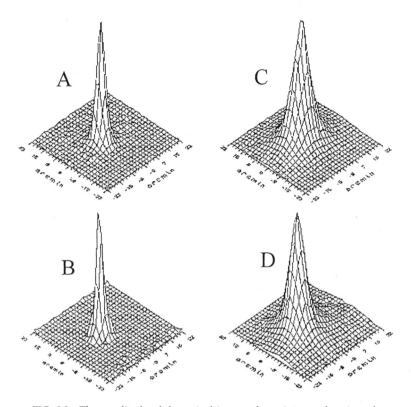

FIG. 3.2. The amplitude of the retinal image of a point as a function of retinal location for two young eyes (A and B) and two old eyes (C and D). Note that there is greater blurring for the older eyes. From "Effects of Aging in Retinal Image Quality," by P. Artal, M. Ferro, I. Miranda, & R. Navarro, 1993, *Journal of the Optical Society of America A, 10,* p. 1659. Copyright 1993 by the Optical Society of America. Reprinted with permission.

eyes and two old eyes. (A perfect image would be represented by a single narrow line or cylinder emerging from the surface.) Figure 3.2 indicates that the retinal image is more blurred for older participants because of cumulative optical defects that cannot be corrected. This increased blurring may explain why there are losses in visual acuity even after the eye is optically corrected. A number of studies (e.g., Frisen & Frisen, 1981; Yang, Elliott, & Whitaker, 1993) have shown that corrected Snellen acuity or its equivalent declines from about 20/12 to 20/16 in young adults to about 20/20 to 20/30 in 80-year-old adults.

Increase in the amount of light scatter in the aging eye will also produce a decrease in retinal contrast. If scattering is virtually complete (as is the case when the cornea becomes completely clouded), no image can be formed because scattering disperses the light rays in all directions so that the retina becomes uniformly illuminated. If only a small amount of light is scattered, an image will be formed, but there will be a reduction in retinal contrast. Contrast sensitivity in older observers has been studied using sinusoidal gratings. The contrast between the grating's light and dark bars (difference between peak and trough luminance divided by their sum) is varied until the observer can just detect a difference between a display containing the grating and one that contains a uniform background having the same space-average luminance. A number of studies (e.g., Crassini, Brown, & Bowman, 1988; Sloane, Owsley, & Jackson, 1988) have found a loss of sensitivity with age that is frequency dependent, with the loss being more severe at higher spatial frequencies. Not all of this loss in contrast sensitivity can be attributed to optical factors. Age-related differences at medium and high spatial frequencies remain even after removal of the lens and its replacement with an artificial intraocular lens, which should reduce the amount of intraocular scattering (Morrison & McGrath, 1985; Owsley, Gardner, R. Sekuler, & Liberman, 1985). These age-related differences also remain even when laser interference fringes are used to image gratings directly on the retina, thereby bypassing the optics of the eye (Morrison & McGrath, 1985; Nameda, Kawara, & Ohzu, 1989; but see Burton, Owsley, & Sloane, 1993; Dressler & Rassow, 1981). Thus, the existing evidence suggests that there is either a retinal and/or a neural component to lowered contrast sensitivity in older observers.

It is worth noting that contrast sensitivity is a good predictor of discrimination performance. For example, Owsley and Sloane (1987) have shown that the detection and recognition of common objects is more highly correlated with contrast sensitivity than with visual acuity, and Evans and Ginsburg (1985) have shown that the discriminability of highway signs is more closely associated with contrast sensitivity than with visual acuity. Moreover, contrast discrimination at suprathreshold levels in older observers is strongly correlated with contrast thresholds (Beard, Yager, & Neufeld, 1994; Tulunay-Keesey, Ver Hoeve, & Terkla-McGrane, 1988). It would seem, therefore, that contrast discrimination measures or contrast sensitivity measures would be a more sensitive indicator of the visual system's ability to identify and discriminate among objects in visual space than measures of visual acuity.

Age-Related Changes in the Visual Pathways and Their Effect on Vision

In studies comparing the lateral geniculate nuclei (LGNs) of young and old rhesus monkeys, no significant differences were found in the number of neurons in young and old monkeys, although the neuron soma-size was greater in the older monkeys, with a correspondingly slight increase in the size of the LGN (Ahmad & Spear, 1993). The response properties of the LGN cells also did not differ with age (Spear, Moore, Yim, Xue, & Tumosa, 1994). In essence, the extensive studies of Spear and colleagues indicate that LGN structure and function is not greatly affected by age. However, as Spear (1993) noted, these studies were conducted under photopic conditions. Given that the rods are more severely affected by aging, it is possible that functional differences in the LGN, because of the reduced input of the rods, will be restricted to lower levels of illumination.

In recent studies in humans (Haug, Kuhl, Mecke, Sass, & Wasner, 1984; Leuba & Garey, 1987) and rhesus monkeys (Vincent, Peters, & Tigges, 1989) no differences in neuron density were found in the striate cortex. Relatively little is known about changes in the dendritic trees in the striate cortex (Spear, 1993). Thus, there is relatively little evidence of anatomical changes in the early visual pathways.

In general, we find that (a) even after optical correction, age-related structural changes in the eye lead to a more blurred, lower contrast and less bright retinal image; (b) there is an age-related decrease in vascular density and the number of rods; (c) the anatomy of the early visual pathways beyond the retina appears to remain intact with age; and (d) there is some evidence for neural involvement with respect to loss of high-spatial frequency sensitivity with age. We would expect, then, that these various anatomical and physiological changes would have multiple consequences for perceptual function. A greater blurring of the image would lead to loss of high-spatial frequency information. Decreased vascularization may have an adverse effect on both spatial and temporal processing. Loss of rods may be expected to affect vision under low levels of illumination and reduce the effective field of view. Finally, physiological changes in the early visual pathways would lead to a number of subsequent difficulties in image processing by the visual system.

Visual Perception

Having reviewed age-related changes in the optics, anatomy, and physiology of the early visual system and their effects on basic visual abilities, such as light sensitivity, visual acuity, color vision, and contrast sensitivity, we now consider how these changes might affect higher order visual functions, such as the effective field of view, motion, and binocular processes. All of these functions are important for the location, detection, recognition and identification of objects in the visual world. Moreover, these functions are prerequisite for many higher order cognitive processes. For example, a reduction of the effective visual field, combined with a loss of peripheral sensitivity, would seriously disrupt visual search. An examination of the nature of age-related changes in early visual function, therefore, will help us to identify the cognitive processes most likely to be affected.

In everyday situations and in visual search tasks, it is often necessary for an observer to respond to objects in the periphery. Older observers find it more difficult to detect and discriminate between peripheral targets. Johnson (1986) showed the effective limits of the visual field declined from 180° for young adults to about 140° at age 70. Recently, many investigators have become interested in age-related declines in the "useful" visual field. The useful visual field limits are considered to be reached when observers can no longer identify or locate objects or targets in the visual field. Not surprisingly, the extent of the useful visual field in older adults depends on such factors as the presence or absence of background distractors, the similarity of distractors and targets, and the presence or absence of a secondary task (Ball, Beard, Roenker, Miller, & Griggs, 1988; R. Sekuler & Ball, 1986; Treisman & Gelade, 1980). For example, A. B. Sekuler, Bennett, and Mamelak (in press) studied the effect of divided attention on the useful field of view using three tasks. In the first task, observers had to identify a letter presented centrally. In the second task, they had to specify the location of a target presented peripherally. In the third task they had to do both simultaneously. They found a uniform decrease in performance in central letter identification at all ages but an age-related decline on the peripheral task when both tasks were done simultaneously; however, the extent of the decrement in performance increased with age when a central task was added to the peripheral location task. Thus, there was an age effect in the periphery, but not in the fovea, when going from focused to divided attention, indicating that the useful field of view is more severely constricted in older participants by the addition of a foveal task. Depending on the situation, an older adult's useful visual field can be only one third that of a younger adult, even when foveal visual acuity is in the normal range. Such restrictions in the useful field of view have obvious implications for real-world situations, such as driving, where people routinely have to divide their attention between central and peripheral vision.

Up to this point, we have considered only static (nonmoving) visual displays. In everyday situations, objects and observers move, and this information must be processed by the visual system. A number of studies (e.g., Coppinger, 1955; Huntington & Simonsen, 1965; Kim & Mayer, 1994; McFarland, Warren, & Karis, 1958) have shown that the frequency at which a flickering light appears to stop flickering declines with age. In addition to losses in temporal resolution, older observers also appear to be less sensitive to object movement (Elliott, Whitaker, & Thompson, 1989; Kline, Culham, Bartel, & Lynk, 1994). Motion perception has been investigated using a motion coherence paradigm. In these studies, a subset of elements in an array of moving elements move in a coherent direction. The experimenter varies the proportion of elements moving together until the observer detects coherent motion in a particular direction. Older observers have higher thresholds for the detection of this kind of motion than do younger observers (Trick & Silverman, 1991; Wojciechowski, Trick, & Steinman, 1995). Thus, older observers are not as sensitive as younger observers to temporally modulated, stationary patterns and to motion of one or more objects against a background.

In real-world situations, observers have to be able to locate objects in depth. It seems sensible, then, to determine whether older observers have poorer depth perception because of a loss of stereopsis. Stereoscopic detection threshold appears to increase with age in some studies (Bell, Wolf, & Bernholtz, 1972; Jani, 1966; Speranza, Moraglia, & Schneider, 1995) but not others (Gittings & Fozard, 1986; Greene & Madden, 1987; Yekta, Pickwell, & Jenkins, 1989). Thus, it is not clear that there is much of an age-related decline in stereoacuity. Binocular processing, in addition to placing objects in depth, is also useful in camouflage breaking (Julesz, 1971; Schneider & Moraglia, 1994), in the sense that interocular disparity differences between target and background can be used to unmask targets. Thus, a visual signal can be much easier to detect in a noisy background when viewing is binocular than when it is monocular. However, Speranza et al. (1995) found that young and old participants with good visual acuity did not differ with respect to the amount of binocular unmasking. Thus, the available evidence suggests very little decline in static binocular mechanisms.

Efficient processing of visual stimulation in search paradigms requires an intact oculomotor system. A number of studies concerned with oculomotor control indicate that latencies for saccades increase with age but that accuracy is not affected (L. Abel, Troost, & Dell'Osso, 1983; Spooner, Sakala, & Baloh, 1980; Warabi, Kase, & Kato, 1964). Older observers are also not able to track moving targets smoothly when target velocities are high (Sharpe & Sylvester, 1978). As a consequence, they are unable to keep the target centered on the fovea for higher target velocities. Correspondingly, older observers are not as good as younger observers in processing target information when there is a high degree of relative motion between the target and observer (Scialfa et al., 1988), and this decline is probably related to smearing of the retinal image caused by inadequate pursuit movements.

General Characteristics and Current Conceptions of Aging in Audition and Vision

Although researchers have acknowledged that age differences in audition and vision occur both at the sensory end organs and in more central neural pathways (e.g., Fozard, 1990), cognitive aging researchers, nonetheless, have emphasized age-related differences in central rather than peripheral information processing (Cerella, 1990; Lindenberger & Baltes, 1994; Meyerson, Hale, Wagstaff, Poon, & Smith, 1990; Salthouse, 1985). Because of this emphasis in the cognitive aging literature, there has been a lack of research on the relation between perceptual and cognitive aging, especially with respect to more peripheral changes. There has also been an accompanying lack of applied research on how age-related differences in hearing and vision might account for age-related variance in everyday activity (Marsiske et al., 1997). The need for new theoretical and experimental efforts to study the relationship between sensory and cognitive aging has emerged from recent correlational studies (Lindenberger & Baltes, 1994; Marsiske et al., 1997; Salthouse et al., 1996). To be able to effectively examine the interconnections between perceptual and cognitive changes in aging, we must first characterize perceptual changes. Having done this, we will have highlighted those changes that are most likely to be relevant to cognitive aging.

In the auditory system, the most commonly measured and well-known change is a loss of high-frequency sensitivity. Moreover, the degree of threshold loss is predictive of decline in some but not all aspects of suprathreshold auditory processing. For example, threshold sensitivity is highly correlated with frequency selectivity, whereas it is not significantly correlated with other measures, such as gap detection. One consequence of this relative independence of different auditory processes is that older listeners whose hearing thresholds are within normal clinical limits may nonetheless have auditory processing deficits. In the visual domain, the most commonly measured visual ability is Snellen acuity. However, Snellen acuity is often not a good predictor of other kinds of visual declines because it only measures acuity under static, high-contrast conditions. For example, an older observer could have good Snellen acuity but perform poorly under low-contrast conditions. Moreover, Snellen acuity is not strongly correlated with other aspects of processing, such as temporal resolution or effective field of view. Thus, it follows that people who have corrected Snellen acuities in the normal range may nonetheless experience declines in other visual functions, such as loss of discriminative capacity under low levels of illumination, restricted field of view, impaired temporal processing, and slower eye movement in search or pursuit tasks.

Can we then characterize the auditory and visual processing capabilities of older people who satisfy clinical standards with respect to audiometric thresholds and visual acuity? The average of pure-tone thresholds at 0.5 kHz, 1 kHz, and 2 kHz is often considered when screening for hearing. Even if this average falls in the normal range (<20–25 dB HL), it is quite likely that the older listener has a significant high-frequency hearing loss. Although most of the content of the speech signal would be available to such a person, and they would judge a voice to be comfortably loud, some of the fine detail (which is conveyed by the high frequencies) would be lost. Furthermore, these difficulties would be exacerbated in background noise, which tends to mask the low frequencies. Loss of high frequencies would also hamper sound localization. In addition, temporal processing in the older listener may be disrupted. Even if most of the speech signal was audible, a loss of synchrony in the auditory nerve would likely disrupt speech perception, especially in noisy or reverberant conditions or at fast speech rates. Such an asynchrony would also reduce the normal advantage of listening with two ears over monaural listening.

The standard criterion that appears to be used in the vision cognition literature is a corrected Snellen acuity of 20/40 or less. Thus, some older viewers may experience some difficulty in encoding the fine detail in a visual display even if the display is presented at high contrast. If older and younger viewers are tested under the same lighting condition, the effective retinal illumination for older viewers may be as much as 0.5 log units fewer than that for younger viewers. Because loss of contrast sensitivity at the middle- and high-spatial frequencies is greater the lower the average luminance, even older viewers with good visual acuity may have lost high-spatial frequency information. Older viewers are also likely to be more severely affected by low lighting conditions or low-contrast displays. All of these visual deficits may be more pronounced in peripheral vision, and the effective visual field might be severely reduced in search tasks. Finally, the ability to detect, locate, identify, or follow flickering or moving stimuli will be reduced, and if the visual display includes color, there is likely to be reduction in the ability to discriminate blues from yellows.

Obviously, there are a large number of older individuals who will not be able to pass either or both of the auditory and visual screening tests. The degree of the above-mentioned problems could be substantially worse in these individuals. Finally, for those with clinically significant hearing or visual loss, there would also be additional kinds of deficits that would vary with degree of loss. Thus, it is risky to assume, on the basis of simple clinical screening measures, that perceptual processing is equivalent for younger and older adults. It is even riskier to assume age equivalences in perceptual processing when screening consists of subjective reports by older persons as to whether they have visual or auditory problems or whether they can hear or see the stimuli that are to be used. Perhaps most important of all, we have now identified other measures of perceptual processing that may be even more directly related to higher order cognitive processing (e.g. auditory temporal resolution or visual contrast sensitivity) than are the more basic measures of perceptual status. Further research on the relationship between these perceptual measures and higher order cognitive processes should be undertaken.

RELATIONSHIPS BETWEEN PERCEPTUAL STATUS AND COGNITIVE AGING

Literature Search

In an attempt to find out how frequently researchers in cognitive aging actually assessed the auditory and visual acuities of their participant populations, we used PsycLIT to conduct a literature search for all articles published from 1990 to 1997 that satisfied the conditions "aged and (attention, memory, inhibition, or cognition)." The initial search yielded over 2,800 articles. We narrowed our selection to articles published in 34 major journals.[2] From these, we selected 288 articles, eliminating studies that targeted older adults with pathological conditions (e.g., dementia), did not include both younger and older participants, did not involve auditory or visual presentation of material, and were reviews or meta-analyses that did not report original data. Of the selected studies, 24 used auditory-only presentation, 174 used visual-only presentation, 83 used both modalities, and 7 could not be classified because of insufficient information (e.g., "lists" were presented). Audiometric thresholds were measured in 18% of the studies using auditory materials, and visual acuity was measured in 21% of the studies using visual materials. In all but one of these studies, these acuity measures were used in participant selection. In only 6 of the 288 studies (all auditory) was acuity used as a covariate in an analysis of variance.

In the 16 auditory studies in which audiometric thresholds were used to select participants, criteria for inclusion of older participants varied from very strict criteria for normal hearing to general statements that the hearing was adequate (or hearing loss was not excessive), without specifying the criteria for inclusion or quantitatively describing the audiometric thresholds of the participants. The Snellen acuity criterion used for inclusion of older participants in the vision studies also varied widely, ranging from 20/20 to 20/40. Actual tests for differences in visual acuity between young and old groups were conducted in eight of the studies, with only four studies reporting that there were no significant differences in visual acuity between the groups.

In most of the recent studies of cognitive performance in aging, the basic hearing and visual abilities of their participants has not been meas-

---

[2]A list of these journals can be obtained from the authors.

ured. If perceptual status is importantly related to cognitive performance, then some of the findings could, in part, reflect the contributions of vision and hearing to performance. Such potential contributions remain largely undetermined, but recent large-scale correlational studies suggest that this matter needs to be evaluated in future research. In the next sections, we examine correlational and experimental studies of the relationship between perception and cognition in older adults.

Correlational Studies of the Interdependence of Perception and Cognition

Prior to the present decade, there were very few studies of the relationship between perceptual and cognitive measures in aging adults. The relationship between auditory and cognitive status was found to be moderate in some studies (Birren, Botwinick, Weiss, & Morrison, 1963; Granick, Kleban, & Weiss, 1976; O'Neill & Calhoun, 1975; Schaie, Baltes, & Strother, 1964) and small or insignificant in other studies (Colsher & Wallace, 1990; Era, Jokela, Qvarnberg & Heikkinen, 1986; Gilholme Herbst & Humphrey, 1980; Jones, Victor, & Vetter, 1984; Ohta, Carlin, & Harmon, 1981; Schaie et al., 1964; Thomas et al., 1983). Studies of the relationship between visual and cognitive measures in older adults are even more limited. Salthouse et al. (1996) reanalyzed the data of Clark (1960) and found that vision accounted for about half of the age-related variance in two cognitive measures. They also reanalyzed the data of Heron and Chown (1967) and found that vision accounted for a third of the age-related variance in scores on the Raven's Progressive Matrices (RPM).

In contrast to the limited research conducted previously on the relationship between perceptual and cognitive abilities of older adults, in the present decade this topic has received considerable attention. Since 1988, there have been two major correlational studies conducted by cognitive aging researchers to examine the contributions of perceptual and cognitive factors to intellectual functioning in aging adults. One research group worked in Berlin (P. B. Baltes & Lindenberger, 1997; Lindenberger & Baltes, 1994; Marsiske et al., 1997) and the other in Atlanta (Salthouse et al., 1996). Around the same time, correlational studies undertaken by a hearing research group in Amsterdam to investigate the contributions of auditory and cognitive factors to word recognition also provided some evidence of the link between auditory and cognitive status in a community sample of aging adults (van Rooij & Plomp, 1992) but not in a laboratory sample (van Rooij & Plomp, 1990; see also Humes, 1996; Humes et al., 1994).

Results from the Berlin Aging Study (BASE; 1988–1993) reported by Lindenberger and Baltes (1994), which indicated that there was a strong connection between basic measures of auditory and visual functioning

and intelligence in old age, sparked the interest of cognitive aging researchers in examining this connection. Their initial report was framed
with reference to the theoretical issue of life-span continuity versus discontinuity (P. B. Baltes, 1973; Herzog & Schaie, 1986, 1988; Rabbitt, 1990).
Within this framework, the continuity view holds that interindividual
differences are largely stable throughout middle and old age, whereas
the discontinuity view credits the possibility that new determinants of
interindividual differences (e.g., changes in auditory or visual sensitivity)
might arise in old age. Larger correlations between auditory and visual
sensitivity and cognitive measures in older adults than in younger adults
would be consistent with the discontinuity view, and it was suggested
that such age-related increases in the correlations between auditory and
visual sensitivity and cognition could be understood either in terms of
the deprivation or the common cause hypothesis.

Subsequently, a number of replications and extensions by both the
Berlin group and the Atlanta group provided additional evidence of an
important relationship between auditory and visual functioning and complex intellectual functioning. The research groups conducted correlational
studies incorporating age, perceptual measures, and cognitive measures
and developed structural models of the relationships between these factors. By examining the pattern of intercorrelations among variables such
as vision, hearing, balance–gait, education, and general health and by
determining the extent to which these variables could account for age-related variations in intelligence, they hoped to be able to distinguish
between continuity and discontinuity models of intellectual function and
to explore the merits of various hypotheses, including the deprivation
hypothesis and the common-cause hypothesis. According to P. B. Baltes
and Lindenberger (1997), "the present findings open a new window to
the investigation of negative age differences in adult cognition by redi-
recting the explanatory search. The strong connection between audi-
tory/visual functioning and intellectual functioning in old age points to
inquiries into sources, factors, and mechanisms that are common to both
domains" (p. 20). These works have challenged cognitive researchers to
consider new hypotheses as they have confronted new and unexpected
findings. The findings of these research groups are summarized below.

A heterogeneous sample of adults aged 70 to 103 years participated in
the study by Lindenberger and Baltes (1994). The BASE sample was
stratified by gender and by age in 5-year groups. Visual acuity was based
on three measurements taken with the best optical correction available:
binocular distance acuity and right- and left-eye close visual acuity. Consistent with prior characterizations of age-related visual acuity levels
(Pitts, 1982), the average corrected visual acuity (.33 or 20/60) was well
below normal and the vast majority of the participants owned glasses

(over 90% in the entire BASE sample; P. B. Baltes & Lindenberger, 1997). Three indicator variables for auditory sensitivity were constructed: right- and left-ear composites of the frequencies from .25 kHz to 4 kHz and a log-transformed cross-ear score for 6 kHz and 8 kHz. Consistent with prior characterizations of age-related hearing loss (Willott, 1991), the average hearing level in the BASE sample was in the moderate hearing loss range (46.3 dB HL); that is, half the sample had a hearing loss that would render much of normal conversational speech inaudible. Also consistent with prior characterizations of hearing-aid use by older adults (Holmes, 1995), 16.7% of the BASE sample had hearing aids. Fourteen cognitive tests were administered representing five abilities: speed (Digit Letter Test, Digit Symbol Substitution, and Identical Pictures), reasoning (Figural Analogies, Letter Series, and Practical Problems), knowledge (Practical Knowledge, Spot-a-Word, and Vocabulary), memory (Activity Recall, Memory for Text, and Paired Associates), and fluency (Animals and Letter S). Reasoning, memory, and speed are assumed to reflect the fluid domain, and knowledge and fluency are assumed to reflect the crystallized domain of intelligence. A hierarchical model with the five cognitive abilities as first-order factors and general intelligence as a second-order factor was shown to provide a good characterization of the cognitive test battery. All five first-order factors and the general intelligence factor correlated negatively with aging.

The structural model that provided the best fit was one in which age effects on intelligence were mediated by age effects on auditory and visual functioning. Taken together, vision and hearing accounted for 49.2% of the total and 93.1% of the age-related variance. Importantly, the model fitted the younger half of the sample as well as it fitted the older half, and excluding those with clinical diagnoses of dementia or with severe hearing or visual loss did not alter the results. Furthermore, whereas speed mediated age effects on the remaining intellectual abilities in previous models that did not include auditory or visual factors (Lindenberger, Mayr, & Kliegl, 1993; see also Salthouse, 1993, 1996), in Lindenberger and Baltes' 1994 model, speed failed to explain all of the age-related variance in vision and hearing, but vision and hearing mediated all of the age-related variance in both speed and the other cognitive components of intelligence. Thus, auditory and visual sensitivity were more powerful predictors of negative age effects than was speed.

Further analyses conducted by Lindenberger and Baltes (1994) showed that as a predictor of intelligence, balance–gait was comparable with vision and hearing in its predictive power. In contrast, general somatic health and education were less powerful predictors of intelligence. The fact that balance–gait accounted for almost the same amount of age-related variance in intelligence as did vision and hearing is consistent with a common-cause interpretation. Widespread neural degeneration could affect the cerebellum and interfere with balance and gait. Furthermore, neural degeneration affecting the vestibular sensory system or the visuomotor system could compromise balance–gait. Other alternative hypotheses were suggested, including the hypothesis that there could be a cognitive load effect on sensory measures whereby age-related cognitive changes in decision or attention may contaminate measures of sensory performance.· Another suggested hypothesis was that "decrements in sensory functioning may require aging individuals to invest an increasing amount of cognitive resources (e.g., attention) into the ongoing coordination and compensatory management of sensori-motor behavior." (Lindenberger & Baltes, 1994, p. 353). Directions for future research were also suggested including (a) longitudinal work on the relationship between sensory and intellectual functioning, (b) age-comparative studies across the life span, (c) examination of the cognitive demand during acuity testing, and (d) experimental simulations of sensory system age effects.

Responding to the need for age-comparative studies, the Atlanta group (Salthouse et al., 1996) undertook three studies using large independent samples of adults in good to excellent health. The first two studies used data collected previously for adults between 18 and 80 years of age ($N =$ 127 and 77, respectively). The foci of the first two studies were to examine the correlations between age, vision, and a limited set of cognitive variables (two perceptual speed measures and two reaction time measures) using commonality and quasi-partial correlation analyses and, in particular, to investigate the role of vision in the relationship between age and speed of processing. The third study was conducted on adults between 18 and 92 years of age ($N = 197$) to examine the relationship between age, vision, speed, and performance on other higher order cognitive tasks. In all three studies, there were significant negative correlations between vision and age; these were not mediated by education in any of the three studies or by self-reported health factors in the first two studies, although in the third study there was some reduction in this relation when health variables were controlled. There were also strong correlations between speed and age. In all three studies, most of the shared variance between vision and speed was attributable to age. In other words, older participants were slower and had poorer vision. It was noted that there was little or no relation between vision measures and either speed or cognitive measures independent of age.

In a sequel to the original BASE study, P. B. Baltes and Lindenberger (1997) repeated the original study with an expanded sample consisting of 687 adults ranging in age from 25 to 103 years. It was argued that age-related increases in the correlations between sensory and intellectual measures would support the common-cause hypothesis insofar as both sets of measures are an expression of the physiological architecture of the aging brain (P. B. Baltes & Lindenberger, 1997; Lindenberger & Baltes, 1994). The goals of the sequel study were to replicate the original finding of a link between sensory and intellectual functioning and to determine if the strength of the link varied across the adult life span. It was found that age-related individual differences in cognitive functioning were no longer significant after controlling for hearing alone or for hearing and vision. Furthermore, controlling for vision and hearing reduced age-related individual differences about as well as controlling for perceptual speed. Vision, hearing, or both accounted for 67.7% of the total variance and 94.7% of the age-related variance. The five major conclusions were as follows: (a) The magnitudes of the slopes relating hearing and vision measures to age were substantial in the age-comparative sample; (b) the slopes of other measures as a function of age were extremely well predicted by measures of hearing and vision; (c) the magnitude of the link between sensory and intellectual function increased from young to old adulthood; (d) in young and old adults, the proportion of age-related variance in cognition accounted for by sensory variables was similar; and (e) intercorrelations within the cognitive domain were higher in older adults than in younger adults. The overall implications were that "the mechanisms underlying the connection between sensory and cognitive functioning are similar across the entire adult life span, but that their expression is amplified in old and very old age" (P. B. Baltes & Lindenberger, 1997, p. 19). Although "the present results do not allow for a conclusive distinction among the three hypotheses [sensory deprivation, aging-induced cognitive load on sensory performance, and common cause] and do not allow for the specification of underlying mechanisms" (p. 19), the favored hypothesis was "the common cause hypothesis, according to which negative age differences in sensory and cognitive domains are the outcome of a third common factor or ensemble of factors, namely, the integrity of brain structure and function and its aging-induced changes" (p. 19), even though "the common cause hypothesis in its current form is both theoretically and empirically under-identified" (P. B. Baltes & Lindenberger, 1997, p. 19). The investigators identified the need for future research in three areas: (a) longitudinal studies; (b) more fine-grained and comprehensive sensory assessments; and (c) componential analyses of relevant cognitive and sensory tasks, using psychophysical and neuroscience approaches. Specifically, it was argued that the common-cause hypothesis would be supported if simulated sensory losses in younger adults do not result in generalized cognitive decrements "because such treatments do not alter the neurophysiological status of the brain" (P. B. Baltes & Lindenberger, 1997, p. 19) and if cognitive tasks with relatively high sensory demands or sensory specificity do not exhibit a stronger or more modality-specific relation to sensory function than tests with low or less specific sensory demands.

The investigation of the connection between sensory and cognitive functioning in aging adults was later extended in a study by other members of the Berlin group, which examined the contributions of sensory and cognitive measures to variance in basic and discretionary activities of everyday living (Marsiske et al., 1997). Two categories of functioning in everyday activities were measured: (a) perceived competence in performing basic activities of daily living (BADLs; bathing, grooming, dressing, toileting, stair climbing, walking, bed transfers, eating, bladder control, bowel control) and (b) advanced activities of daily living (AADLs; total time reported to have been spent in the previous day in household chores, physical activities and exercise, intellectual activities, television watching, or social activities but excluding time spent in self-care, resting, and sleeping activities). Previous work (M. M. Baltes, Mayr, Borchelt, Maas, & Wilms, 1993) has shown that individual differences in health largely determine how well BADLs were performed, whereas AADLs were more influenced by preferences, motivation, skill, and intellectual and personality factors. Viewing sensory loss as a health factor, the predicted result was that sensory status should affect performance in BADLs, which would in turn affect AADLs, with there being no direct relationship between sensory status and AADLs. However, experts in hearing and vision have argued for a direct relation between hearing and vision and AADLs. Reductions in participation in AADLs have been reported to accompany both vision loss (e.g., Heinemann, Colorez, Frank, & Taylor, 1988) and hearing loss (e.g. Bess, Lichtenstein, Logan, Burger, & Nelson, 1989; Pichora-Fuller & Robertson, 1994). Models have been constructed that relate hearing loss to AADLs (e.g., Hyde & Riko, 1994), and rehabilitation programs for hard-of-hearing adults have been developed and shown to be effective in improving performance in AADLs (for a review, see Lubinski & Higginbotham, 1997).

The final model retained the important features of the earlier model fit by the Berlin group: The effects of age on intelligence were mediated by vision, hearing, and balance–gait (P. B. Baltes & Lindenberger, 1997; Lindenberger & Baltes, 1994), performance on BADLs was mediated by depressivity and balance–gait, and performance on AADLs was mediated by performance on BADLs and intelligence (M. M. Baltes et al., 1993). No direct paths emerged between vision or hearing and either BADLs or AADLs. There were effects of vision, hearing, and balance–gait on AADLs, but these effects were mediated by intelligence. "Substantively, these results suggest that sensory acuity may influence the physical and psychological resources that more directly undergird activity participation" (Marsiske et al., 1997, pp. 453–454). The researchers endorsed the common-cause hypothesis but commented that "the common cause, if it exists, is not univariate in its effects—its commonality lies in its complexity and its ability to touch many different aspects of individual functioning" (Marsiske et al., 1997, p. 454) and that "the actual processes by which sensory aging may influence other domains may be complex" (Marsiske et al., 1997, p. 455). In our opinion, it seems reasonable that vision and hearing make a significant, although indirect, contribution to AADLs because the selected activities (e.g., interpersonal communication) do rely crucially on hearing or vision.

Another extension of the initial research on the relation between sensory and cognitive factors was to expand the set of variables to include nonsensory factors, as well as cognitive and sensory and perceptual factors. The main nonsensory factors have been blood pressure, grip strength, and lower limb strength (Anstey, Lord, & Williams, 1997; Anstey, Stankov, & Lord, 1993; Cook et al., 1995; Elias, D'Agostino, Elias, & Wolf, 1995; Salthouse, Hambrick, & McGuthry, 1998), and all have been found to be correlated with age and, in turn, cognitive performance. Salthouse et al. (1998) explored the nature of these relationships by first determining a common factor underlying test performance on nonsensory, sensory, and cognitive tests. When the effect of age was partialed out or the age range was restricted, the correlation between nonsensory variables and the common factor became nonsignificant; the correlation between vision and the common factor, although considerably reduced, remained significant; and the correlations between cognitive tests and the common factor were only marginally reduced (Salthouse et al., 1998). With regard to the nonsensory variables, this is what we would expect if blood pressure and grip strength had no direct effect on cognitive performance. The fact that the correlation between vision and the common factor remained significant (although reduced to a greater extent than the correlations between the common factor and the cognitive tests), suggests a direct relationship between vision and cognitive performance that is weaker than that which exists among the cognitive tests.

The correlational evidence that there is a powerful connection between perceptual and cognitive factors in aging compels us to develop a model of the nature of this connection. Experiments provide another source of evidence that needs to be considered in developing or evaluating such a model. We turn now to consider this type of evidence.

Experimental Approaches to the Interdependence of Perception and Cognition

To control for any effect that age-related differences in perception might have on cognitive performance, researchers might (a) equate young and old participants with respect to performance on all relevant perceptual measures, (b) simulate perceptual deficits in younger participants to mimic those found in older participants, or (c) "correct" perceptual deficits in older participants and look for improvements in cognitive performance.

Experimental Studies of the Interdependence of Auditory Acuity and Cognition

Hearing researchers, attempting to recreate the effects of cochlear hearing loss, have shown that the most successful method to date for accomplishing this is to use spectrally shaped masking noise (see Humes, 1996, for a review). In this simulation, the level of masking noise at each frequency was adjusted to produce a threshold elevation in normal participants that matched the threshold elevation of individuals with presbycusis. This simulation method has the advantage that it also mimics sensorineural hearing loss with respect to loudness recruitment and level-specific changes in frequency resolution (Humes, 1996; Humes, Espinoza-Varas, & Watson, 1988; Humes & Jesteadt, 1991), even though it does not mimic other aspects of hearing loss, such as reduced temporal resolution. Presbycusic listeners and young listeners with matched simulated hearing losses were found to perform equivalently on monaural identification of closed-set nonsense syllables in conditions of reverberation (room echo), background noise, and both reverberation and background noise (Humes & Roberts, 1990) and when the nonsense syllables were degraded spectrally using bandpass filtering from 500 Hz to 2,000 Hz or temporally when a reverberation time of 0.8 s was used (Humes & Christopherson, 1991). It was also found that young-old listeners (63–74 years old) performed better on the syllable identification test than old-old listeners (75–83 years old) when cognitive status was not controlled, suggesting that there might be age-related differences within the old-old group. However, these differences between young-old and old-old listeners were eliminated when audiometric and cognitive status (IQ and digit-span memory) were matched (Lee & Humes, 1992), suggesting that both hearing status and cognitive status contributed to word-recognition performance, regardless of age.

The work of other researchers has focused on how hearing difficulty may affect cognitive performance (for a discussion, see Cohen, 1987, and chap. 6, this volume). As noted in chapter 6, the most widely used construct in research on language processing is that of working memory. According to the typical working memory explanation of age-related differences in comprehension, whereas older adults have well-preserved internally stored linguistic, social, and general world knowledge (e.g., Kemper, 1992; Kwong See & Ryan, 1996), they are less successful than younger listeners in executing multiple operations within a limited capacity or time or with sufficiently precise timing. For example, according to Carpenter, Miyake, and Just (1994), "results suggest that reduced working memory resources in elderly adults may limit their capabilities to simultaneously retain, monitor, and manipulate structurally complex sentences in working memory" (p. 1104). In ideal perceptual conditions, external and internal information sources are rich and readily accessed, multiple processing operations are executed with no difficulty, and storage and comprehension are highly accurate and relatively effortless. Under these conditions, the limited capacity of working memory is not exceeded. In contrast, when external cues are impoverished or perceived less accurately, when activation thresholds are achieved slowly, when it becomes difficult to execute some processing operations either because the required input is reduced or because the operations themselves are compromised, or when there are too many operations required in too short a time, then the limited capacity of working memory becomes overloaded. In such conditions, resampling or reallocation of working memory resources must occur or else processing will fail. On the one hand, it is conceivable that processing is stressed because perceptual input is poorer for older listeners than for younger listeners; they have difficulty hearing speech cues, and, in everyday life, communication partners may alter speech cues, further reducing the quality and quantity of useable perceptual input (e.g., Ryan, Giles, Bartolucci, & Henwood, 1986). On the other hand, higher level linguistic and cognitive processing may also be slower or less efficient in older adults compared with younger adults (for reviews, see Kemper, 1992, and Wingfield, 1996). Furthermore, the consequences of processing difficulties at the perceptual level may cascade, resulting in additional negative effects on processing at higher levels (Pichora-Fuller et al., 1995). In the model of language comprehension presented in chapter 6, Wingfield and Stine-Morrow describe the different computational components involved in language processing spanning segregation of the input sound stream to construction and updating of a situation model. In their chapter, they explore the effects of poorer or slower processing in higher level computational components in older adults, whereas we concentrate on age-related changes in perceptual-level computational components.

To explore the extent to which perceptual stress consumes working memory resources, it is useful to assume that there are three different zones of listening conditions: (a) effortless listening (working memory capacity is not saturated by processing demands), (b) effortful but still largely error-free listening (errors would occur unless processing is slowed or resources are reallocated from less critical or nontaxed component processes), and (c) error-prone listening (time-consuming operations that exceed the duration or capacity of the stored memory, insufficient resources available for reallocation, or the use of nonoptimal reallocation schemes). Psychophysical experiments can be designed to test performance across this range of listening zones. Two ways to alter auditory input are to vary the speed of presentation or to vary the S:N (for a review, see Pichora-Fuller, 1997).

The three zones of listening conditions are captured to some extent in experiments using time-compressed speech (for a review, see Wingfield, 1996). In the first zone, at normal speech rates (140–180 words per minute [wpm]), listeners with near-normal audiograms experience effortless listening; they recognize words with a high degree of accuracy without reliance on contextual support beyond the target word. In the second zone, with rates varying from 275 to 425 wpm, word recognition relies more and more heavily on supportive context as speed increases. In the third zone, at extremely fast speech rates, word recognition would no doubt totally fail, but these limits are not usually tested.

The time-compression manipulation is accomplished by deleting a chosen percentage of the samples of the speech wave that are digitally recorded in a computer sound file. This manipulation of the auditory signal can result in two different kinds of stress on processing. For the most part, Wingfield and his colleagues have been interested in the kind of stress resulting from increasing the rate at which linguistic and cognitive operations must be executed (see chap. 6, this volume). In recent work, they have also tried to differentiate the role played by stress due to the speeding of linguistic–cognitive operations from perceptual stress due to distortion of the signal by compression (Wingfield, Tun, Koh, & Rosen, in press). They tested young and old listeners using uncompressed sentences, compressed sentences, and compressed sentences with pauses inserted so that the total duration of the sentence was restored to its original uncompressed duration. As in earlier studies, the performance of both age groups declined as compression was increased. Although the insertion of pauses resulted in improvements in the performance of both age groups, the restoration was totally successful for young adults but only partially successful for older adults. The finding that pause insertion helped both groups indicates that linguistic–cognitive operations were stressed by speeding speech; the finding that older adults demonstrated a residual deficit even when pauses were inserted suggests that their performance was also affected by perceptual stress related to subtle distortions of the signal created by the time-compression manipulation.

Experiments in which the S:N condition is manipulated provide further evidence of how perceptual stress affects word recognition and memory. In these experiments (Pichora-Fuller et al., 1995), the Daneman and Carpenter (1980) working memory span procedure was used with the materials of the Speech Perception in Noise (SPIN) test (Bilger, Nuetzel, Rabinowitz, & Rzeczkowski, 1984). The materials of the SPIN test consist of eight equivalent lists of 50 sentences with accompanying multitalker babble background noise. Half of the sentences provide supportive context for the sentence-final word (e.g., "The witness took a solemn oath") and half do not (e.g., "John hadn't discussed the oath"). The word-recognition task requires the listener to repeat the sentence-final word, and the working-memory span task requires that the recognized words from a set of sentences be recalled. Over a range of S:N conditions, older adults with near-normal audiometric thresholds were able to achieve the same word recognition scores as younger listeners but they needed an S:N advantage to do so. With low supportive context, word recognition reached 50% correct at a S:N 6 dB higher for old compared to young listeners (see Fig. 3.3). Therefore, apparent age-related differences in word recognition are largely eliminated by providing older listeners with an S:N advantage. When the S:N condition is unfavorable, older listeners benefitted more than younger listeners from prior sentence or discourse context. For presbycusic listeners, without supportive context, word recognition never reaches 100% in any S:N condition; however, with the benefit of supportive context, they can achieve perfect performance if the S:N condition is sufficiently favorable.

Consistent with the findings for speeded speech, even when words heard in noisy conditions are recognized, they are remembered less well. In one study, young adults recalled fewer correctly perceived digits and they remembered fewer details of short passages of discourse when materials were presented in a noisy condition compared with when they were presented in a quiet condition (Rabbitt, 1968). In the Pichora-Fuller et al. (1995) study, working memory span decreased for both young and old adults as S:N decreased. A subsequent study of how words heard in a noisy condition are recognized and remembered, with and without supportive visual speech cues (speech reading), replicated the original finding of a decline in recall with increased perceptual stress, and it also demonstrated how bimodal perceptual support offsets the declines in recall observed in conditions of competing noise (Pichora-Fuller, 1996).

To further investigate whether some of the memory deficits of older adults could be related to poorer perceptual status, Craik, Murphy, and Schneider (1998) tested younger and older adults in a paired-associates memory task modeled after the Madigan and McCabe (1971) study. In this task, the listener hears sets of five paired associates. After each set, the first member of one of the paired associates is presented to the listener, who is then supposed to supply the other word in the pair. When the tested paired associate is the last from the set of five, performance is very good. However, when paired associates from earlier in the set are presented, listeners often fail to recall the second member of the pair. Figure 3.4 plots the percentage of items correctly recalled as a function of their serial position in the set for three groups: younger and older adults tested under quiet conditions and young adults tested under conditions of background babble. Note that recall is equivalent for young adults tested in babble conditions and older adults tested in quiet conditions at all five

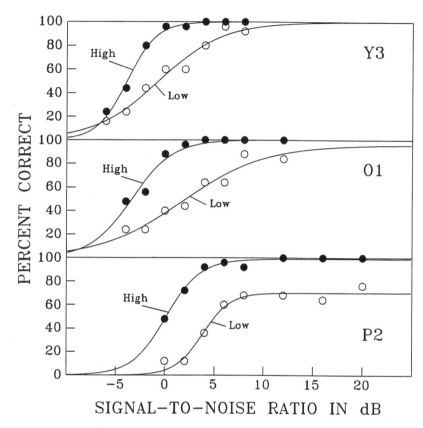

FIG. 3.3. The percentage of high-context and low-context words correctly identified as a function of signal-to-noise ratio for three adults. The top panel shows the performance of a young adult (Y3). The middle panel shows the performance of an older adult with good hearing (O1). The bottom panel shows the performance of a presbycusic individual (P2). Note that for signal-to-noise ratios greater than 10 dB, all 3 listeners were able to correctly identify 100% of the high-context words. However, whereas the younger and older normal-hearing participants appear to be able to identify all or nearly all of the low-context words at the higher signal-to-noise ratios, the presbycusic listener is still missing some of the low-context words, even at the highest signal-to-noise ratio tested. From "How Young and Old Adults Listen to and Remember Speech in Noise," by M. K. Pichora-Fuller, B. A. Schneider, & M. Daneman, 1995, *Journal of the Acoustic Society of America, 97*, p. 598. Copyright 1995 by the American Institute of Physics. Reprinted with permission.

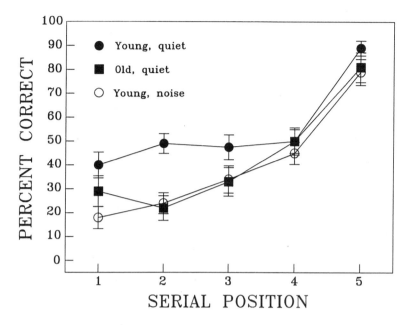

FIG. 3.4. The percentage of words correctly recalled as a function of their serial position for three groups of participants: young normal-hearing adults tested under quiet conditions, older normal-hearing adults tested under quiet conditions, and young normal-hearing adults tested under a condition of a background babble. Adapted from "Comparing the Effects of Aging and Background Noise on Short-Term Memory Performance," by F. I. M. Craik, D. Murphy, & B. Schneider, 1998.

serial positions. Notice, however, that when young adults are tested in quiet conditions, they perform significantly better for the first three serial positions but are equivalent to older adults in quiet conditions and younger adults in noisy conditions in the latter two serial positions. This study shows that, for young adults, the addition of background noise can change their serial position curve so that it matches that of older adults in quiet conditions. Thus, adding a perceptual processing load to young adults makes their performance look like that of older adults in this memory experiment. It is important to note that adding noise affects only the first three serial positions. That the last two positions are not affected indicates that the younger adults in noisy conditions still recognize the words, although listening is more effortful. A greater perceptual processing load induced by noise reduces recall in young adults. Similarly, a greater perceptual processing load in older adults resulting from changes in the auditory system may contribute to their poorer performance in the early serial positions.

Rabbitt (1991) proposed that effortful listening affected memory by undermining rehearsal, elaborative encoding, and deep processing of material heard in noisy conditions by those who are hard of hearing, even when word recognition was highly accurate. Thus, if processing resources must be allocated to the processing of a speech signal that is difficult to encode, there could be fewer resources available for storage. In such effortful listening conditions, listeners are often able to overcome signal ambiguity by relying on contextual redundancies derived from prior input or from world knowledge. Importantly, a variety of successful solutions or routes to map signal to meaning may be manifested. The acceptability and availability of different solutions to the problem of mapping ambiguous input to meaning will also be governed by the purpose or goal of the communication and be related to the task and the participants themselves (for a discussion of the importance of text, task, and comprehender factors in discourse processing, see Ska & Joannette, 1996). It is necessary to begin to specify how processing resources can be economically reallocated to different processing options when comprehension or other higher order cognitive processes are at risk because the demands of disambiguation may exceed the listener's working memory capacity. Perceptual stress is one of the factors that may lead to reallocation.

One of the demands of disambiguation is that unwanted alternative solutions must be inhibited. A number of studies have suggested that older adults find it more difficult than younger adults to inhibit the processing of irrelevant visual material (Hasher & Zacks, 1988; see also chap. 4, this volume). Murphy, McDowd, and Wilcox (1999) conducted three experiments to evaluate the extent to which irrelevant auditory material influenced performance on a variety of tasks using speech stimuli. As a partial control for auditory declines in older adults, they presented all of the auditory stimuli at a fixed number of decibels above each individual's speech reception threshold. Across all of their experiments, the amount of irrelevant information processed by younger and older adults did not differ.

If cognitive factors affect comprehension, why haven't the studies of age-related differences in word recognition conducted by the hearing researchers (for a review, see Humes, 1996) identified a significant cognitive component? There are three possible reasons that come immediately to mind: (a) The variation in perceptual status was so large that it tended to overwhelm or obscure the contribution of cognitive variables; (b) declines in auditory sensitivity and cognitive ability are both strongly related to declines in speech detection, discrimination, and recognition, but lack of precision in the cognitive measures substantially weakens the observed correlations with cognitive performance relative to those observed with pure-tone thresholds; and (c) the speech tests that were used did not fully engage the linguistic and cognitive processes needed for comprehension in everyday listening situations. Listeners in these speech tasks typically were required to either discriminate between speech sounds or recognize words in quiet or noisy listening situations. They did not have to integrate heard information with past knowledge, store it in memory for future use, or formulate a reply based on the content of the signal. However, all these higher order processing abilities are required if a person is to engage in spoken communication with another individual, and age-related declines in any of these abilities might result in difficulties in comprehension but not necessarily in speech detection, speech discrimination, or word recognition.

To engage a fuller range of cognitive abilities, Schneider et al. (1999) asked participants to listen to stories or lectures and to answer multiple-choice questions concerning the material they had just heard. The answers to these questions required the listener either to recall specific details or to integrate information over several sentences. Participants were screened to ensure that they all had relatively good hearing. They listened to the stories in three different listening conditions (quiet, moderate level of noise, and high level of noise), with the presentation levels individually adjusted so that listeners were equally likely to recognize words in noisy conditions. If older listeners had more trouble comprehending connected discourse in these conditions than younger listeners, this would indicate a cognitive problem such as a decline in working memory or a failure to inhibit irrelevant information. Alternatively, if no age differences were found, this would suggest either that age differences in cognition had little effect on comprehension once auditory factors were taken into account or that older listeners with good hearing had little or no cognitive decline with respect to the factors required for comprehension.

The number of correctly answered questions declined with increasing noise level for both types of questions. Both younger and older adults performed better on the detail questions than on the integrative questions. For integrative questions, there were no significant age differences, regardless of listening condition, perhaps because the older listeners were more able to benefit from context. For detail questions, younger and older adults performed equivalently in the quiet and moderate-noise conditions, but younger adults performed better than older adults in the high-noise condition. This study indicates that when the test conditions were adjusted so that both young and old adults experienced comparable perceptual stress, they differed only in their ability to extract detailed information in the highest noise condition. It is noteworthy that when younger and older listeners were tested without customizing the noise level and without adjusting the story levels to compensate for hearing difficulties, the performance of older adults on detail questions was significantly worse than the performance of younger adults in both the quiet and noisy conditions.

These studies indicate that when the listening situation is altered to produce comparable perceptual stress in younger and older adults, age-related performance differences in cognition are minimized. In contrast, age-related performance differences in cognition were not reduced in a study by Lindenberger, Scherer, and Baltes (1999) when ear protectors were used to simulate presbycusis in younger adults. This result may not be surprising, given that this simulation method only mimics threshold elevation but not any of the other aspects of auditory changes that are known to accompany cochlear hearing loss. To more fully simulate cochlear hearing loss, one would have to use another simulation method, such as the one used by Humes (1996).

In summary, experimental studies of the relationship between audition and cognition in aging adults provide evidence that the apparent age-related differences on cognitive measures, such as word recognition, immediate recall, inhibition and discourse comprehension, that are observed when conditions are not adjusted in accordance with hearing status can be significantly reduced when listening conditions are adjusted to equate for perceptual stress. These findings are consistent with a working memory model in which perceptual stress consumes resources.

Experimental Studies of the Interdependence of Visual Acuity and Cognition

In our survey of studies relating visual acuity to cognitive performance, we found only four studies in which there were no statistically significant differences in Snellen acuity between young and old adults. To increase the number of studies, we relaxed the criterion to include all studies in which the mean, median, or modal near-visual acuity was 20/25 or less in both age groups. There were nine studies that met this relaxed criterion. All nine of these studies were concerned with some aspect of visual attention, most of them with visual search and how attentional resources are allocated. The results of these nine studies suggest that, when foveal visual acuity is controlled, the distribution of attentional resources is nearly identical in young and old populations.

Mouloua and Parasuraman (1995) varied spatial uncertainty and trial presentation rate in a visual vigilance task. A trial consisted of the presentation of a string of letters whose spatial location could vary. The task was to detect the presence of a lowercase letter in a string of uppercase letters (string length varied between one and four characters). The results showed that d', a measure of signal detectability, was smaller for older observers and that it decreased with increasing event rate (increasing number of trials per minute), spatial uncertainty, and trial block. Under conditions of medium and high spatial uncertainty, but not low spatial uncertainty, older adults showed a slightly smaller decline in vigilance over time than did younger adults, resulting in a significant interaction between age, spatial uncertainty, and trial block. This interaction suggests that older adults were slightly better at maintaining vigilance over time when spatial uncertainty was relatively high but not when it was low. Thus, the performance of older adults on a vigilance task seemed to be essentially equivalent to that of younger adults, once age-related differences in signal detectability were taken into account.

In the low-spatial-uncertainty condition used in the Mouloua and Parasuraman (1995) study, a trial consisted of the presentation of a single letter at the screen's center such that attention would be focused. In contrast, attention would be more widely distributed in the high-spatial-uncertainty condition because the position of the target letter varied from trial to trial. Age differences in how attention is distributed should produce an interaction between age and spatial uncertainty. However, Mouloua and Parasuraman found that age differences were comparable across uncertainty conditions, suggesting that younger and older adults tend to allocate attentional resources in the same way. A similar conclusion was reached by Hartley, Kieley, and McKenzie (1992), who manipulated the degree of focus by changing the task demands and found no essential difference in the ability of younger and older participants to change their attentional focus. Using a different paradigm, Madden (1992) also concluded that shifts in attentional focus were essentially identical in younger and older adults.

Madden, Pierce, and Allen (1992) investigated the effects of a nonpositional cue in which the task was to discriminate whether the stimulus was either an F or a D (Category 1) or a 3 or a 7 (Category 2). The cue, which preceded the probe and whose validity was varied, was either a member of the letter category or the numeral category. They argued that the greater the validity of the cue, the more likely it would be that observers would allocate attention to the appropriate category (number or letter). The reaction time data suggested that both younger and older adults adjusted their attentional focus with changes in cue validity but that older adults tended to use focused attention more frequently than younger adults when the cue was less than 100% valid.

Hahn and Kramer (1995) examined whether younger and older adults were able to attend to noncontinuous locations in the visual field when the intervening space was filled with visual distractors. A narrow attentional focus would require a sequential search of the two locations. If attentional focus were broadened so that both targets could be simultaneously processed, the presence of intervening distracting stimuli might adversely affect performance. However, if the attentional beam could be split into two, the presence of intervening stimuli might not have such an adverse affect on performance. Hahn and Kramer found that the performance of both younger and older adults was unaffected by distractor type (compatible or incompatible) so long as there were no sudden stimulus onsets, suggesting that older observers can split their visual attention as well as younger observers.

The results described so far indicate that when the visual acuity of older adults is similar to that of younger adults, age-related differences in attentional processes are negligible. The possibility remains, however, that the presence or absence of an age effect is dependent on the particular stimulus parameters that are used. Hartley and McKenzie (1991) tested younger and older adults in two conditions, with the primary task in one of the conditions designed to focus attention more than the other. They found that reaction time in the secondary task varied more with retinal eccentricity in the focused condition than in the unfocused condition and that the reaction times of older adults were longer than those of younger adults. In addition, the effect of retinal eccentricity was greater for older adults than for younger adults and the amount by which the slope of the function relating reaction time to retinal eccentricity changed when going from the focused to unfocused condition did depend on age. However, in a second experiment, in which the duration of the stimuli was increased, the interaction effects disappeared, indicating that when older adults are given sufficient time for processing the stimuli, age-related differences in the functions relating reaction time to eccentricity disappear.

The six studies just discussed indicate that younger and older adults allocate their attentional resources in equivalent ways; that is, older adults are as good as younger adults at narrowing, broadening, or splitting their attentional focus. The only age-related differences are that older adults generally take longer than younger adults to react in these tasks and that they may need additional viewing time to process the stimuli as efficiently as younger adults.

The remaining three studies in which the visual acuities of younger and older adults were equated consider a broader range of tasks. Kramer, Humphrey, Larish, Logan, and Strayer (1994) examined the performance of younger and older adults on a variety of tasks in an attempt to determine whether older adults were less able to inhibit the processing of irrelevant information (the inhibitory deficit hypothesis; Hasher & Zacks, 1988). These tasks included (a) negative priming, (b) response compatibility, (c) response stopping, and (d) the Wisconsin Card Sorting Test. In general, reaction times were longer for the older participants on the first three tests, but there were no interactions of age with any of the experimental manipulations. Because the WCST is less likely to be dependent on visual acuity than the other tasks, it is not discussed here, other than to note that the number of trials required to solve the first sort was essentially the same for younger and older adults and there were no age differences on the concept-level response measure.

Using the negative priming paradigm, a number of studies (see chap. 4, this volume) have failed to find an inhibitory effect for older adults, suggesting that older adults do not build up inhibition to the priming stimulus. These previous studies did not control for visual acuity in the older participants. Hence, it is possible that buildup of inhibition to the prime did not occur or was considerably weaker in older adults because of poorer visual processing of the stimuli. Interestingly, when visual acuity was controlled in the Kramer et al. (1994) study, equal amounts of negative priming were found for younger and older adults.

Furthermore, Kramer et al. (1994) did not find any age-related differences in response compatibility. In this response-compatibility study, a letter target always appeared in the same location surrounded by other letters. Sometimes the surrounding letters were selected from a set associated with the same response as the target (response compatible), sometimes from a set associated with a second response (response incompatible), and sometimes from a neutral set. In this paradigm, the compatibility (or lack thereof) of the surrounding letters affected performance in a similar way for both younger and older adults.

Cerella (1985) attributed the smaller response-compatibility effect in older adults to the fact that the surrounding maskers were located in the periphery. He argued that because the surrounding letters were in the periphery, the smaller effect could be attributed to the more rapid falloff in visual acuity with retinal eccentricity in older adults. In support of this point, Cerella showed that the response-compatibility effect was larger for older adults than for younger adults when the distractors were close to the fovea but that the effect was reversed in the periphery. This would indicate that when the presentation was foveal, the incompatibility of the surrounding distractors had a greater inhibitory effect on older adults. However, there are two major differences between the Cerella study and the Kramer et al. (1994) study that may account for this difference. First, Cerella used a shorter display time (200 ms) than Kramer et al. As Hartley and McKenzie (1991) showed, age differences in this type of response paradigm can be eliminated by increasing target duration. In the Kramer et al. study the target remained on for 1,000 ms and was not followed by a mask. Second, there were significant age-related differences in visual acuity in Cerella's study but not in Kramer et al.'s study. Thus, Kramer et al.'s study shows that when foveal acuity is equivalent and targets and maskers are presented close to the fovea (the distractors were 0.58° from the fixation point) for a sufficiently long duration (1,000 ms), there are no age differences with respect to the size of the response-compatibility effect.

Kramer et al. (1994) also found that there were no age differences with respect to the size of the response-compatibility effect when a response-stopping task was added to the response-compatibility task. On response-stopping trials (25% of total trials), a tone was sounded, which was to signal the participants to withhold or stop their response. There were no age effects on the probability of stopping. Older adults had significantly longer stopping reaction times (stopping reaction times were estimated using the race model of Logan & Cowan, 1984), but age did not interact with response compatibility or tone delay.

In the eight studies discussed so far, the reaction times of older adults were significantly longer than those of younger adults in all conditions. It is important to note that the longer reaction times of older adults in these studies cannot be attributed easily to generalized slowing as it is usually modeled. According to the generalized slowing hypothesis, when comparisons are made across tasks or different levels of task difficulty, the reaction times of older adults should be a monotonic function of the reaction times of younger adults. Typically, it is argued that this function is linear with a slope of 1.5. Note that if this function were to characterize reaction time in the experiments discussed above, we would expect to see age interact with the different task manipulations. In none of the eight studies discussed so far, in which visual acuity was controlled and stimulus duration was reasonably long, were there any interactions of task manipulations with age for reaction time measures. This implies that the function relating the reaction times of older adults to those of younger adults would have to be linear with a slope of 1.0 in each of these experiments.

Kramer, Martin-Emerson, Larish, and Andersen (1996) compared the performance of younger and older adults searching for a target defined by a conjunction of movement and form. For example, the observer might have to search for a moving "O" embedded in a display that might contain other stationary Os and Xs, which might or might not be stationary. In general, the search behavior of older adults was very much like that of younger adults. As a result, Kramer et al. concluded that the processes responsible for the segregation of moving and stationary objects in the visual field, as well as those processes underlying dynamic search behavior, were equivalent for younger and older adults.

The final study in which visual acuity was controlled (Kramer, Larish, & Strayer, 1995) compared the effects of training on performance in single- and dual-task situations. The results from this study were mixed in that the increase in reaction time in going from a single to a dual task was larger for older adults than for younger adults on the training tasks but equal on the transfer tasks. Both sets of tasks involved monitoring visual stimuli over a 15° × 20° area; however, the first set of tasks involved forced pacing, whereas the second set of tasks did not. Because a relatively large visual field and range of eye movements were involved, it is difficult to know the extent to which other age-related visual differences may have contributed to these effects. For example, a number of studies have shown that the effective size of the visual field can depend on the nature of the task. Hence, it is not possible to determine the extent, if any, that differences in other visual processes may have contributed to differences in performance in this study.

These studies show that when visual acuity is controlled and when stimulus duration is sufficiently long, younger and older adults allocate their attentional resources in a similar fashion. Moreover, when visual acuity and stimulus duration are controlled, inhibiting stimuli seem to have the same effect on performance in younger and older adults. By way of contrast, many of the studies of negative priming (see chap. 4, this volume), which do not control for visual acuity, demonstrate inhibitory effects in younger adults but not in older adults. Of course, when studies use different methods (as they do in the negative priming literature), it is not possible to determine whether differences across studies are due to differences in methodology or to differences in the visual acuities of the older participants in the different studies. To determine whether the observed age effects are a consequence of visual status, at least three groups are required: young adults with good vision, older adults with good vision, and older adults with poor vision. If in the identical experimental paradigm an age effect is observed when comparing young adults with older adults with poor vision, but not when comparing young adults with older adults with good vision, then it is reasonable to attribute the age effect to reduced visual functioning. To our knowledge, such experiments have not been conducted. Finally, the fact that age effects are not found when visual acuity is controlled in experiments on attention or inhibition does not imply that younger and older adults are equivalent with respect to other cognitive processes.

We turn now to consider how visual stress might impact cognitive processing. We have seen that the perceptual systems of older adults are not functioning as well as those of younger adults. In particular, corrected visual acuity and contrast sensitivity are reduced. In certain neural pathologies, such as Alzheimer's disease (AD), perceptual declines are accentuated. For example, Gilmore, Thomas, Koss, and Townsend (1994) have shown that the contrast sensitivity of AD patients is about 0.5 log units lower than that of a group of healthy older adults. Similar results have been reported by other investigators (Cronin-Golomb et al., 1991; Gilmore & Levy, 1991; Nissen et al., 1985; but see Schlotterer, Moscovitich, & Crapper-McLachlan, 1984). As we have argued, such visual deficits should reduce performance in cognitive tasks that depend heavily on visual processing.

If the poorer cognitive performance of healthy older adults or AD patients is solely a product of their reduced contrast sensitivity, then it should be possible to produce equivalent short-term cognitive deficits in healthy young adults by reducing stimulus contrast by an amount that would simulate the contrast-sensitivity deficit of the older adult or AD patient. Gilmore (1995) has reviewed a number of studies indicating that a simulation of the contrast deficit experienced by AD patients results in poorer performance in picture naming, letter naming, and word reading by normal young and old adults. However, even with this degraded stimulus, younger and older adults still perform better on these tasks than AD patients. Conversely, these studies have also shown that under some conditions the performance of AD patients can be significantly improved by increasing contrast to compensate for their loss in contrast sensitivity. Hence, it is clear that part of the deficit observed in AD patients on these cognitive tasks is likely to be due to a loss in contrast sensitivity (see Gilmore, 1995, for a discussion of this issue).

Spinks, Gilmore, and Thomas (1996) also have simulated the effect that a contrast deficit characteristic of an 80-year-old adult would have on a young adult's performance on the Symbol Digit Substitution Task and on the Raven's Advanced Progressive Matrices (RAPM). They modified the stimuli in these tasks to mimic the contrast deficit experienced by a typical 80-year-old participant. Half the young adults were tested under normal contrast conditions, whereas the other half were tested under the age-simulated reduced contrast conditions. Participants who were tested under degraded conditions performed more poorly on both tests. Moreover, in both cases the reduced contrast condition caused young adults to perform the cognitive task like normal older adults who were 50–55 years of age. Thus, these studies indicate that a portion of the age-related and AD-related deficits in performance observed on cognitive tests can be attributed to reduced contrast sensitivity in these participants. Of course, contrast sensitivity is only one of the visual deficits experienced by older adults. It is possible that simulating more of the age-related perceptual deficits would further reduce the performance of younger participants to be even more like that of older adults.

Echt and Pollack (1998) evaluated the extent to which age-related contrast differences and age-related differences in the amount of retinal illumination affected cognitive performance. They found that increasing contrast improved cognitive performance in all age groups and that when age-related visual differences were taken into account, age-related cognitive differences disappeared. However, using goggles to mimic the wavelength-dependent reduction in retinal illumination did not produce performance decrements in young participants on cognitive tasks. A similar finding was reported by Lindenberger et al. (1999). Goggles, however, only simulate one aspect of the age-related changes in vision that are known to occur. These studies help to sort out which specific perceptual processing deficits affect cognitive processing.

The possibility that a reversal of a contrast sensitivity deficit in older adults might enhance cognitive performance has been investigated by Owsley, Berry, Sloane, Stalvey, and Wells (1998), who found significant improvement on tests of explicit memory following cataract surgery compared to preoperative performance. This sort of improvement would be expected if cognitive performance directly depended on the quality of the visual input, but it is interesting to note that this improvement occurred in a memory paradigm in which the quality of the visual input would primarily affect encoding. It is also important to note that cataract surgery improves contrast sensitivity, which has been shown to be a critical variable in simulating agelike cognitive decrements in young viewers. Unfortunately, there is no auditory equivalent to cataract surgery at present. Hearing aids amplify sound but do not improve S:N. Hence, failure to observe improvements in cognitive performance after hearing-aid fitting (Tesch-Romer, 1997) is likely due to the inadequacy of this treatment (see also Chmiel & Jerger, 1996).

We have seen that reducing stimulus contrast can make younger adults perform more like older adults on a number of cognitive tests. Another way of producing a visual processing load in younger adults is to add noise to the visual stimulus. Speranza, Daneman, and Schneider (in press) asked younger and older participants to report the last word in a sentence presented visually when that sentence was masked by varying degrees of band-limited white noise (the visual equivalent of adding a band-limited white noise to an auditory speech signal). Printed versions of the SPIN sentences were used and tested under eight different S:N conditions. As found previously for the auditory modality (Pichora-Fuller et al., 1995), younger adults tolerated a lower S:N than did older adults and both younger and older adults benefitted from context, with older adults benefitting more from context than younger adults.

In summary, the experimental research provides evidence that age-related differences on measures of visual attention are not observed when the visual acuity of participants is carefully controlled. Simulation of vision loss or increasing perceptual stress in viewing conditions renders the performance of young adults more like that of older adults on cognitive measures. There is also some evidence that reversing a visual deficit in older adults can improve cognitive performance. Finally, it has been shown that older adults use context to greater advantage than younger adults when perceptual conditions are unfavorable.

THEORETICAL IMPLICATIONS FOR COGNITIVE AGING RESEARCH

Our review of aging and perception has documented many changes in perceptual processing. Recent studies have also documented a strong relationship between a person's perceptual and cognitive abilities over the life span. A goal of this chapter has been to review changes in specific aspects of perceptual processing as they might relate to changes in cognitive processing, with a view toward evaluating four hypotheses concerning this relationship.

The Deprivation/"Sensory Underload" Hypothesis

The deprivation hypothesis is that prolonged lack of adequate sensory input will result in permanent deterioration of more central functions. The model in the left-hand side of Fig. 3.5 schematically represents this hypothesis. In this model, the perceptual and cognitive systems are represented as separate modules. The rightward-pointing arrow connecting the two modules indicates that information is passed from the perceptual system to the cognitive system, and the leftward-pointing arrow indicates that there is central control over perceptual processing. Within the model,

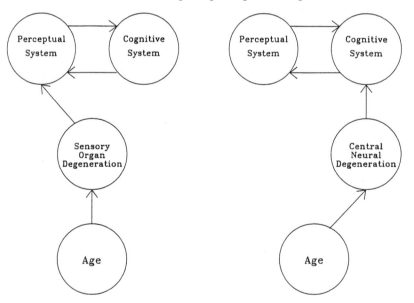

FIG. 3.5. Left: A modular representation of the perceptual and cognitive systems in which sensory degeneration affects only the perceptual system. Right: A modular representation of the perceptual and cognitive systems in which central neural degeneration affects only the cognitive module.

it is assumed that age leads to sensory organ deterioration that affects the kind and quality of information delivered by the perceptual system to the cognitive system. Ultimately, a reduction in both the quality and quantity of input would result in cognitive deterioration due to atrophy. Neuroanatomical studies in both the auditory and visual system, however, provide evidence that age-related sensory cell loss does not inevitably lead to neural loss (Spear, 1993; Willott, 1991). This evidence does not seem to be consistent with the deprivation hypothesis; neither is it sufficiently strong to enable us to reject the deprivation hypothesis. The ideal experiment to resolve this issue would be to restore perceptual input to older individuals who have been suffering from prolonged sensory deprivation to see whether this restoration would improve cognitive performance. No improvement in cognitive performance would support the deprivation hypothesis, and restoration of cognitive function would be evidence against it. Owsley et al. (1998) have shown that cataract removal can improve performance on cognitive tests, providing evidence against the deprivation hypothesis.

The Effect of Cognitive Load on Sensory Performance

Another logical possibility is that cognitive deterioration adversely affects performance on tests of basic sensory abilities. This hypothesis is illustrated on the right-hand side of Fig. 3.5. In this illustration, age leads to central nervous system degeneration that directly affects the cognitive system. Because the cognitive system exerts top-down control over the perceptual system, a loss of integrity in the cognitive system could lead to less efficient control over the perceptual system, reducing perceptual function. For example, inability to maintain focused attention on a task could result in reduced measures of sensitivity.

If age-related differences in cognitive abilities are responsible for age-related differences in perceptual performance, then age-related differences should be observed for all perceptual abilities so long as task demands are held constant. For example, Pichora-Fuller and Schneider (1991) have determined absolute noise-masked monaural and noise-masked binaural thresholds for the same pure tones, using an identical two-interval, forced-choice procedure. Therefore, any task demands introduced by the procedure were constant. It is unlikely that a change from absolute to masked monaural pure tones decreased cognitive load. Nevertheless, an age-effect was found for absolute thresholds and masked binaural thresholds but not for masked monaural thresholds. Because task demands were unchanged, all three conditions should have produced comparable age effects if cognitive declines are responsible for performance differences on perceptual tests. That they did not suggests that the factors responsible for the age differences, when present, were sensory and not cognitive.

Common Cause, Multiple Causes, or Perceptual Degradation?

The common-cause hypothesis attributes the strong correlation between sensory and cognitive measures to a third variable with widespread systemic consequences (e.g., neural degeneration, decrements in the vascular system, or loss of temporal synchrony). Of course, it is also possible that deficits in the cognition and perception modules are caused by different processes (i.e., multiple causes). These two alternatives are illustrated in the top half of Fig. 3.6. In the left-hand model, age leads to widespread systemic disruption, which, in turn, affects both perceptual and cognitive processes. In the multiple-cause model, one age-related cause leads to central neural problems and another age-related cause leads to peripheral sense organ degeneration, with the former affecting cognitive processes and the latter affecting perceptual processes and with both correlated with each other (because each is correlated with age). Thus, both the common-cause and the multiple-cause models would result in a correlation between perceptual and cognitive processes.

The perceptual degradation hypothesis states that errors in perceptual processing cascade upward to disrupt cognitive processing. Hence, performance on cognitive and perceptual tasks could be correlated without any degeneration in the cognitive system per se. Schematically, it resembles the sensory deprivation hypothesis (see Fig. 3.5, left). However, it attributes disruption in cognitive function to immediate misinformation being delivered to the cognitive system rather than to the effects of sensory disruption producing long-term changes in cognitive function. Therefore, in theory, apparent cognitive declines would not be observed if distortions and degradation introduced by sensory degeneration were corrected. The improved performance on a variety of cognitive tests in AD patients when stimulus contrast was increased (Gilmore, 1995) and a similar improvement in cognitive performance when cataracts in normal older adults were removed (Owsley et al., 1998) support this hypothesis.

An implicit assumption in both the common-cause and multiple-cause models is that a distinction can be made between perception and cognition (i.e., that the systems are somehow autonomous or modular). If perception and cognition were, indeed, totally compartmentalized, then either a common cause (third variable) or two independent causes would mean that changes in the perception module would not directly affect the functioning of the cognition module or vice versa. Thus, an observed correlation between measures on perceptual and cognitive tests would

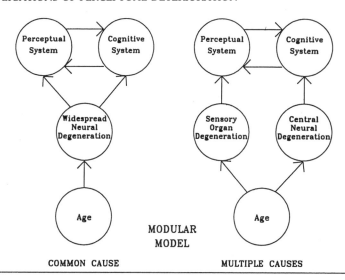

MODULAR
MODEL

COMMON CAUSE   MULTIPLE CAUSES

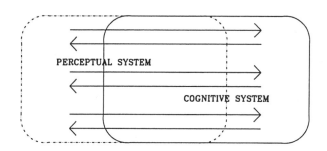

INTEGRATED SYSTEM

FIG. 3.6. Top left: A modular representation of the perceptual and cognitive systems in which widespead neural degeneration has a direct effect on both systems (a common cause). Top right: A modular representation of the perceptual and cognitive systems in which age-related sensory degeneration directly affects the functioning of the perception module, whereas central nervous system degeneration affects the cognitive module (multiple-cause hypothesis). Bottom: An integrated model of perception and cognition in which both the perception and cognition components are highly interconnected and may even share some overlapping resources.

simply reflect that both systems were affected by neural degeneration or some other factor. However, as indicated in Fig. 3.6, perceptual information still feeds into the cognitive system (bottom-up processing) and cognitive information still feeds into the perceptual system (top-down processing). This means that changes in one of the systems could influence the efficiency of the other. Therefore, if a common cause or multiple causes were operating to disrupt both systems, correlations between perceptual tasks and cognitive tasks would reflect a mixture of effects. On the one hand, degeneration in both the cognition and perception modules would lead to performance deficits in both domains, leading to a correlation between perceptual measures and cognitive measures that is independent of any interactions between the two modules. On the other hand, a perceptual deficit resulting from this common cause could exacerbate a cognitive performance deficit because the perceptual system is delivering erroneous or degraded information to the cognitive system. Conversely, deterioration in the cognitive system due to this common cause could contribute to perceptual processing difficulties because the top-down control mechanisms are disrupted or disabled. Another way of looking at the problem is that the correlation between perception and cognition could reflect the joint operation of three or four different processes: a common cause, multiple causes, stimulus degradation, and loss of top-down control due to cognitive degeneration. These mutual influences make it difficult to disconfirm the common-cause hypothesis unless additional assumptions are made.

If we assume a high degree of modularity, then the common-cause hypothesis can be tested by simulating a perceptual deficit in young or middle-aged adults. This method of disproving the common-cause hypothesis has been suggested by P. B. Baltes and Lindenberger (1997), who argued that "according to the common cause hypothesis, simulated reductions of peripheral input should not result in major and generalized performance decrements in middle-aged adults because such treatments do not alter the neurophysiological status of the brain" (p. 19). Accordingly, this would suggest that there is, in effect, a "fire wall" between the perceptual system and the cognitive system that prevents disruptions in the perceptual system from influencing performance in the cognitive system. Only if the two systems were highly modular or encapsulated would a reduction or degradation of peripheral input have no effect on the cognitive system.

A high degree of encapsulation between the two systems is unlikely with respect to certain cognitive processes. For example, it would be hard to imagine that visual search and visual attention functions would not be affected by peripheral degradation of the stimulus. We would, however, expect a greater degree of encapsulation on other cognitive tasks, such as fluency tasks involving the generation of information from semantic memory. For example, instructing participants to name as many birds beginning with the letter S as they can in a limited period of time is likely to be relatively immune from stimulus degradation. However, Lindenberger and Baltes (1994) found correlations between vision and audition and measures of fluency and naming words that were nearly as strong as those found for cognitive measures with a more obvious relation to vision or audition. These findings are consistent with either the multiple-cause or common-cause hypothesis but do not preclude a direct relationship between sensory and cognitive performance.

To evaluate the common-cause hypothesis, we first must determine the extent to which there is a fire wall between perception and cognition. Existing experimental evidence suggests that the cognitive system is compromised by faulty perceptual information. The work of Gilmore and his associates shows that AD patients suffer from a loss of contrast sensitivity as well as from a number of central nervous system disorders. When Gilmore simulated this loss in contrast sensitivity in older observers, he was able to show that the healthy older observers with the simulated loss performed more like AD patients on a number of tasks. Thus, reductions in perceptual input do result in decrements of performance on cognitive tests administered to healthy adults, even to the point of mimicking pathology. Similarly, there are a number of studies in the auditory domain that suggest that when younger and older adults are tested under conditions of comparable perceptual stress, older adults are at least as good as younger adults at speech recognition and comprehension of spoken language. Furthermore, Craik, Murphy, and Schneider (1998) found that adding noise to the stimuli presented to young adults made them remember like older adults. Finally, there are a number of studies in the visual attention literature that suggest that when younger and older adults are equated for visual acuity, they are equally affected by distracting stimuli and deploy their attentional resources in a similar fashion. Overall, there is a fair amount of evidence in support of the stimulus degradation hypothesis and against the notion that the cognitive module is immune to perceptual disruption.

An Integrated Approach to Perceptual and Cognitive Aging

The permeability of the wall between the perceptual and cognitive systems suggests that they are both part of a highly integrated information-processing system. Indeed, in audition the two systems are interconnected neurally between the hair cells and the cortex via numerous afferent and efferent pathways, and in the visual system reafferent stimulation is commonplace. Furthermore, intermodal connections between vision and audition exist from the brain stem to the cortex. The diagram in the top of Fig. 3.6 is somewhat misleading in the sense that it gives the impression that changes in one of the systems may not be of consequence to the functioning of the other system. We have seen that degradation of the perceptual input leads to poorer performance on a number of cognitive tasks, indicating a strong interaction between perception and cognition. A more reasonable way in which to view the system is shown in the bottom half of Fig. 3.6 in which the perceptual and cognitive functions are represented as part of an integrated system, with connections running in both directions, and as sharing a number of processing resources (see also chap. 6, this volume). It should also be clear that losses in any part of the system will stress other parts of the system, especially when informationally complex operations are performed because such operations will involve a number of ascending and descending pathways.

It is important to note that the sharing of resources between the perceptual and cognitive systems can only occur if the two systems are integrated, and strong evidence of their integration now exists. Depending on the task, it appears that resources can be reallocated from either perception to cognition, or vice versa. We have already given many examples of how perceptual processing influences cognitive processing. Conversely, cognitive processing can also influence perceptual processing. For example, in an auditory detection experiment in which most of the trials consist of the presentation of a 1-kHz tone, listeners are less able to detect an occasional presentation of a 970-Hz tone than they are to detect this tone when it is the only one presented (see Dai, Scharf, & Buus, 1991; Hafter & Schlauch, 1991). When attention is focused on a narrow frequency region, the audibility of tones in other regions is reduced. This reduction in audibility may be accomplished by a place-specific, short-term adjustment of cochlear mechanics, presumably by efferent control of the outer hair cells. Indeed, Schneider and Parker (1990) and Parker and Schneider (1994) have suggested that the degree of change in loudness with changes in intensity is under cognitive control.

Reallocation of resources becomes necessary when task demands are high and require an integrated system. This has been nicely illustrated in a recent brain imaging study showing that when processing is relatively effortless, less of the brain is activated but that as the same task is made effortful, more of the brain is activated, presumably because more processing resources are engaged when a person "thinks hard" (Just, Carpenter, Keller, Eddy, & Thulborn, 1996).

The availability of a common pool of resources also suggests that age-related changes in either perceptual or cognitive functions may result in a more or less stable reallocation of resources that would permit the individual to compensate for these deficits. Thus, we might expect to find a greater degree of individual variation in the way in which a particular task is performed in an aging population. In contrast to the deprivation hypothesis, which assumes that deterioration in one area leads to deterioration in another, studies of neural plasticity suggest that the brain reorganizes so that functions that are usually performed by the damaged area are assumed by areas that would normally make a secondary contribution (e.g., Jenkins, Merzenich, & Recanzone, 1990). Thus, the individual might very well be able to carry out the functions originally performed by the damaged area but at a cost—the area that has assumed the functions now has a heavier processing load and may not be as available as it previously was for other tasks.

Within an integrated information processing model, widespread or even local neural degeneration would result in correlated age-related declines in both perceptual and cognitive measures. At one extreme, if there is localized degeneration (e.g., loss of hair cells in the cochlea), then correlations should only be observed between auditory perception measures and performance on cognitive tasks that rely on high-quality auditory input. At the other extreme, if there is widespread degeneration, then correlations should be observed on a much wider range of tasks. In either case, any age-related change that degrades the representation of the stimulus will result in performance decrements in any cognitive task dependent on this input. Conversely, a loss in a cognitive function that lessens the degree of top-down control over the perceptual apparatus will also result in performance decrements in any perceptual task dependent on that control. Rather than seeing a conflict between the perceptual degradation hypothesis and the common-cause hypothesis, both are accommodated within an integrated system model. The interesting questions then become how information is processed, how resources are reallocated within this integrated system, and how age-related changes in this system affect processing.

PRACTICAL IMPLICATIONS FOR COGNITIVE AGING RESEARCH

It is clear from this review that it is crucial for cognitive aging researchers to test the perceptual status of research participants and equate participants in terms of perceptual status whenever possible. Tests of basic auditory sensitivity and visual acuity are a good beginning, but tests of other aspects of auditory and visual processing (such as temporal processing, detection of signals in noise, or contrast sensitivity) may be even more highly related to the apparent age-related changes in cognitive tasks. When participants cannot be matched for perceptual status, psychophysical methods offer an important way to determine how perceptual conditions or simulations of perceptual loss affect the performance of both young and old adults on cognitive measures. Test stimuli and ambient environmental conditions must also be specified fully so that factors such as S:N and contrast can be considered when experiments are compared.

ACKNOWLEDGMENTS

This work was supported by grants from the Natural Sciences and Engineering Research Council of Canada and the Medical Research Council of Canada. We thank Paul Baltes, Ulman Lindenberger, Dana Murphy, and Scott Parker for their comments on earlier versions of this chapter.

REFERENCES

Abel, L. A., Troost, B. T., & Dell'Osso, L. F. (1983). The effects of age on normal saccadic characterstics and their variability. *Vision Research, 23,* 33–37.

Abel, S. M., Krever, E. M., & Alberti, P. W. (1990). Auditory detection, discrimination and speech processing in ageing, noise-sensitive and hearing-impaired listeners. *Scandinavian Audiology, 19,* 43–54.

Ahmad, A., & Spear, P. D. (1993). Effects of aging on the size, density, and number of rhesus monkey lateral geniculate neurons. *Journal of Comparative Neurology, 334,* 631–643.

Anstey, K. J., Lord, S. R., & Williams, P. (1997). Strength in the lower limbs, visual contrast sensitivity, and simple reaction time predict cognition in older women. *Psychology and Aging, 12,* 137–144.

Anstey, K. J., Stankov, L., & Lord, S. (1993). Primary aging, secondary aging, and intelligence. *Psychology and Aging, 8,* 562–570.

Artal, P., Ferro, M., Miranda, I., & Navarro, R. (1993). Effects of aging in retinal image quality. *Journal of the Optical Society of America A, 10,* 1656–1662.

Balazsi, A. G., Rootman, J., Drasnce, S. M., Schulzer, M., & Douglas, G. R. (1984). The effect of age on the nerve fiber population of the human optic nerve. *American Journal of Ophthalmology, 97,* 760–766.

Ball, K. K., Beard, B. L., Roenker, D. L., Miller, R. L., & Griggs, D. S. (1988). Age and visual search: Expanding the useful field of view. *Journal of the Optical Society of America A, 5,* 2210–2219.

Baltes, M. M., Mayr, U., Borchelt, M., Maas, I., & Wilms, H. -U. (1993). Everyday competence in old and very old age: An interdisciplinary perspective. *Ageing and Society, 13,* 657–680.

Baltes, P. B. (1973). Prototypical paradigms and questions in life-span research on development and aging. *Gerontologist, 13,* 458–467.

Baltes, P. B., & Lindenberger, U. (1997). Emergence of a powerful connection between sensory and cognitive functions across the adult life span: A new window to the study of cognitive aging? *Psychology and Aging, 12,* 12–21.

Beard, B. L., Yager, D., & Neufeld, S. (1994). Contrast detection and discrimination in young and older adults. *Optometry and Vision Science, 71,* 783–791.

Bell, B., Wolf, E., & Bernholtz, C. D. (1972). Depth perception as a function of age. *Aging and Human Development, 3,* 77–81.

Bess, F. H., Lichtenstein, M. J., Logan, S. A., Burger, M. C., & Nelson, E. (1989). Hearing impairment as a determinant of function in the elderly. *Journal of the American Geriatrics Society, 37,* 123–128.

Bilger, R. C., Nuetzel, M. J., Rabinowitz, W. M., & Rzeczkowski, C. (1984). Standardization of a test of speech perception in noise. *Journal of Speech and Hearing Research, 27,* 32–48.

Binnie, C. A. (1994). The future of audiologic rehabilitation: Overview and forecast. *Journal of the Academy of Rehabilitative Audiology Monographs, 27,* 13–24.

Birch, J., Chisholm, I. A., Kinnear, P., Marre, M., Pinckers, A. J. L. G., Pokorny, J., Smith, V. C., & Verriest, G. (1979). Acquired color vision defects. In J. Pokorny, V. C. Smith, G.

Verriest, & A. J. L. G. Pinckers (Eds.), *Congenital and acquired color vision defects* (pp. 243–348). New York: Grune & Stratton.

Birren, J. E., Botwinick, J., Weiss, A. D., & Morrison, D. F. (1963). Interrelations of mental and perceptual tests given to healthy elderly men. In J. E. Birren, R. N. Butler, S. W. Greenhouse, & M. R. Yarrow (Eds.), *Human aging: A biological and behavioral study* (pp. 143–156). Washington, DC: U.S. Government Printing Office.

Boettcher, F. A., Mills, J. H., & Norton, B. L. (1993). Age-related changes in auditory evoked potentials of gerbils: I. Response amplitudes. *Hearing Research, 71*, 137–145.

Burton, K. B., Owsley, C., & Sloane, M. E. (1993). Aging and neural spatial contrast sensitivity: Photopic vision. *Vision Research, 33*, 939–946.

Buus, S., & Florentine, M. (1985). Gap detection in normal and impaired listeners: The effect of level and frequency. In A. Michelson (Ed.), *Time resolution in auditory systems* (pp. 159–179). London: Springer-Verlag.

Carpenter, P. A., Miyake, A., & Just, M. A. (1994). Working memory contraints in comprehension: Evidence from individual differences, aphasia, and aging. In M. A. Gernsbacher (Ed.), *Handbook of psycholinguistics* (pp. 1075–1122). San Diego, CA: Academic Press.

Cerella, J. (1985). Age-related decline in extrafoveal letter perception. *Journal of Gerontology, 40*, 727–736.

Cerella, J. (1990). Aging and information-processing rate. In J. E. Birren & K. W. Schaie (Eds.), *Handbook of the psychology of aging* (3rd ed., pp. 201–221). San Diego, CA: Academic Press.

Chmiel, R., & Jerger, J. (1996). Hearing aid use, central auditory disorder, and hearing handicap in elderly persons. *Journal of the American Academy of Audiology, 7*, 190–202.

Clark, J. W. (1960). The aging dimension: A factorial analysis of individual differences with age on psychological and physiological measurements. *Journal of Gerontology, 15*, 183–187.

Cohen, G. (1987). Speech comprehension in the elderly: The effects of cognitive changes. *British Journal of Audiology, 21*, 221–226.

Colsher, P. L., & Wallace, R. B. (1990). Are hearing and visual dysfunction associated with cognitive impairment? A population-based approach. *The Journal of Applied Gerontology, 9*, 91–105.

Committee on Hearing, Bioacoustics, and Biomechanics. (1988). Speech understanding and aging. *Journal of the Acoustical Society of America, 83*, 859–895.

Cook, N. R., Albert, M. S., Berkman, L. F., Blazer, D., Taylor, J. O., & Hennekens, C. H. (1995). Interrelationships of peak expiratory flow rate with physical and cognitive function in the elderly: MacArthur Foundation Studies of Aging. *Journal of Gerontology: Medical Sciences, 50A*, 317–323.

Coppinger, N. W. (1955). The relationship between critical flicker frequency and chronologic age for varying levels of stimulus brightness. *Journal of Gerontology, 10*, 48–52.

Craik, F. I. M., Murphy, D. R., & Schneider, B. A. (1998, April). *Comparing the effects of aging and background noise on short-term memory performance.* Poster session presented at the Cognitive Aging Conference, Atlanta, GA.

Crassini, B., Brown, B., & Bowman, K. (1988). Age-related changes in contrast sensitivity in central and peripheral retina. *Perception, 17*, 315–332.

Cronin-Golomb, A., Corkin, S., Rizzo, J. F., Cohen, J., Growdon, J. H., & Banks, K. S. (1991). Visual dysfunction in Alzheimer's disease: Relation to normal aging. *Annals of Neurology, 29*, 41–52.

Curcio, C. A., Millican, C. L., Allen, K. A., & Kalina, R. E. (1993). Aging of the human photoreceptor mosaic: Evidence for selective vulnerability of rods in central retina. *Investigative Ophthalmology & Visual Science, 34*, 3278–3296.

Dai, H., Scharf, B., & Buus, S. (1991). Effective attenuation of signals in noise under focused attention. *Journal of the Acoustical Society of America, 89*, 2837–2842.

Daneman, M., & Carpenter, P. A. (1980). Individual differences in working memory and reading. *Journal of Verbal Learning and Verbal Behavior, 19,* 450–466.

Dolman, C. L., McCormick, A. Q., & Drance, S. M. (1980). Aging of the optic nerve. *Archives of Ophthalmology, 98,* 2053–2058.

Dorey, C. K., Wu, G., Ebenstein, D., Garsd, A., & Weiter, J. J. (1989). Cell loss in the aging retina: Relationship to lipofuscin accumulation and macular degeneration. *Investigative Ophthalmology and Visual Science, 30,* 1691–1699.

Dressler, M., & Rassow, B. (1981). Neural contrast sensitivity measurements with a laser interference system for clinical screening application. *Investigative Ophthalmology and Visual Science, 21,* 737–744.

Drullman, R. (1995a). Speech intelligibility in noise: Relative contribution of speech elements above and below the noise level. *Journal of the Acoustical Society of America, 98,* 1796–1798.

Drullman, R. (1995b). Temporal envelope and fine structure cues for speech intelligibility. *Journal of the Acoustical Society of America, 97,* 585–592.

Dulon, D., & Schacht, J. (1992). Motility of cochlear outer hair cells. *American Journal of Otolaryngology, 13,* 108–112.

Durlach, N. I. (1972). Binaural signal detection: Equalization and cancellation theory. In J. V. Tobias (Ed.), *Foundations of modern auditory theory* (Vol. 2, pp. 369–462). New York: Academic Press.

Durlach, N. I., & Colburn, H. S. (1978). Binaural phenomena. In E. C. Carterette & M. P. Friedman (Eds.), *Handbook of perception: Hearing* (Vol. 4, pp. 365–466). London: Academic Press.

Echt, K. V., & Pollack, R. H. (1998, April). *The effect of illumination, contrast, and age on text comprehension performance.* Poster session presented at the Cognitive Aging Conference, Atlanta, GA.

Elias, M. F., D'Agostino, R. B., Elias, P. K., & Wolf, P. A. (1995). Neuropsychological test performance, cognitive functioning, blood pressure, and age: The Framingham Heart Study. *Experimental Aging Research, 21,* 369–391.

Elliott, D. B., Whitaker, D., & Thompson, P. (1989). Use of displacement threshold hyperacuity to isolate the neural component of senile vision loss. *Applied Optics, 28,* 1914–1918.

Era, P., Jokela, J., Qvarnberg, Y., & Heikkinen, E. (1986). Pure-tone thresholds, speech understanding, and their correlates in samples of men of different ages. *Audiology, 25,* 338–352.

Evans, D., & Ginsberg, A. P. (1985). Contrast sensitivity predicts age-related differences in highway sign discriminability. *Human Factors, 17,* 637–642.

Feinberg, R., & Podolak, E. (1965). Latency of pupillary reflex to light stimulation and its relationship to aging. In A. T. Welford & J. E. Birren (Eds.), *Behavior, aging and the nervous systems.* Springfield, IL: Thomas.

Fitzgibbons, P. J., & Gordon-Salant, S. (1994). Age effects on measures of auditory duration discrimination. *Journal of Speech and Hearing Research, 37,* 662–670.

Fozard, J. L. (1990). Vision and hearing in aging. In J. E. Birren & K. W. Schaie (Eds.), *Handbook of the psychology of aging* (3rd ed., pp. 150–170). San Diego, CA: Academic Press.

Frisen, L., & Frisen, M. (1981). How good is normal acuity? A study of letter acuity thresholds as a function of age. *Albrecht Von Graefes Arch für klinische und experimentelle Ophthalmologie, 215,* 149–157.

Gabbard, S. A. (1994). AARP's report on hearing aids. *Audiology Today, 6,* 15.

Gallup. (1980). *A survey concerning hearing problems and hearing aids in the United States.* Princeton, NJ: Author.

Gilholme Herbst, K., & Humphrey, C. (1980). Hearing impairment and mental state in the elderly living at home. *British Medical Journal, 281,* 903–905.

Gilmore, G. C. (1995). Stimulus encoding in Alzheimer's disease: A multichannel view. In P. Allen & T. R. Bashore (Eds.), *Age differences in word and language processing* (pp. 199–219). New York: Elsevier.

Gilmore, G. C., & Levy, J. (1991). Spatial contrast sensitivity in Alzheimer's disease: A comparison of two methods. *Optometry and Vision Science, 68,* 790–794.

Gilmore, G. C., Thomas, C. W., Koss, E., & Townsend, L. (1994). *Impact of Alzheimer-type contrast filter on picture naming and memory in healthy adults.* Poster session presented at the annual meeting of the Optical Society of America, Dallas, TX.

Gittings, N. S., & Fozard, J. L. (1986). Age-related changes in visual acuity. *Experimental Gerontology, 21,* 423–433.

Granick, S., Kleban, M. H., & Weiss, A. D. (1976). Relationships between hearing loss and cognition in normally hearing aged persons. *Journal of Gerontology, 31,* 434–440.

Greene, H. A., & Madden, D. J. (1987). Adult age differences in visual acuity, stereopsis, and contrast sensitivity. *American Journal of Optometry and Physiological Optics, 64,* 749–753.

Grose, J. H., Poth, E. A., & Peters, R. W. (1994). Masking level differences for tones and speech in elderly listeners with relatively normal audiograms. *Journal of Speech and Hearing Research, 37,* 422–428.

Gunkel, R. D., & Gouras, P. (1963). Changes in scotopic visibility thresholds with age. *Archives of Ophthalmology, 69,* 4–9.

Haber, D. (1994). *Health promotion and aging.* New York: Springer.

Hafter, E. R., & Schlauch, R. S. (1991). Cognitive factors and selection of auditory listening bands. In A. L. Dancer, D. Henderson, R. J. Salvi, & R. P. Hammernik (Eds.), *Noise-induced hearing loss* (pp. 303–310). Philadelphia: Decker.

Hahn, S., & Kramer, A. F. (1995). Attentional flexibility and aging: You don't need to be 20 years of age to split the beam. *Psychology and Aging, 10,* 597–609.

Hartley, A. A., Kieley, J., & McKenzie, C. R. (1992). Allocation of visual attention in younger and older adults. *Perception & Psychophysics, 52,* 175–185.

Hartley, A. A., & McKenzie, C. R. M. (1991). Attentional and perceptual contributions to the identification of extrafoveal stimuli: Adult age comparisons. *Journal of Gerontology: Psychological Sciences, 46,* 202–206.

Hasher, L., & Zacks, R. T. (1988). Working memory, comprehension, and aging: A review and a new view. In G. H. Bower (Ed.), *The psychology of learning and motivation* (Vol. 22, pp. 193–225). New York: Academic Press.

Haug, H., Kuhl, S., Mecke, E., Sass, N. -L., & Wasner, K. (1984). The significance of morphometric procedures in the investigation of age changes in cytoarchitectonic structures of human brain. *Journal für Hirnforschung, 25,* 353–374.

Heinemann, A. W., Colorez, A., Frank, S., & Taylor, D. (1988). Leisure activity participation of elderly individuals with low vision. *Gerontologist, 28,* 181–184.

Hellstrom, L. I., & Schmiedt, R. A. (1990). Compound action potential input/output functions in young and quiet-aged gerbils. *Hearing Research, 50,* 163–174.

Heron, A., & Chown, S. M. (1967). *Age and function.* Boston: Little, Brown.

Herzog, C., & Schaie, K. W. (1986). Stability and change in adult intelligence: 1. Analysis of longitudinal covariance structures. *Psychology and Aging, 1,* 159–171.

Herzog, C., & Schaie, K. W. (1988). Stability and change in adult intelligence: 2. Simultaneous analysis of longitudinal means and covariance structures. *Psychology and Aging, 3,* 122–130.

Holmes, A. E. (1995). Hearing aids and the older adult. In P. B. Kricos & S. A. Lesner (Eds.), *Hearing care for the older adult: Audiologic rehabilitation* (pp. 59–74). Boston: Butterworth-Heinemann.

Humes, L. E. (1996). Speech understanding in the elderly. *Journal of the American Academy of Audiology, 7,* 161–167.

Humes, L. E., & Christopherson, L. (1991). Speech identification difficulties of hearing-impaired elderly persons: The contributions of auditory-processing deficits. *Journal of Speech and Hearing Research, 34,* 686–693.

Humes, L. E., Espinoza-Varas, B., & Watson C. S. (1988). Modeling sensorineural hearing loss: I. Model and retrospective evaluation. *Journal of the Acoustical Society of America, 83,* 188–202.

Humes, L. E., & Jesteadt, W. (1991). Models of the effects of threshold on loudness growth and summation. *Journal of the Acoustical Society of America, 90,* 1933–1943.

Humes, L. E., & Roberts, L. (1990). Speech-recognition difficulties of the hearing-impaired elderly: The contributions of audibility. *Journal of Speech and Hearing Research, 33,* 726–735.

Humes, L. E., Watson, B. U., Christensen, L. A., Cokely, C. G., Halling, D. C., & Lee, L. (1994). Factors associated with individual differences in clinical measures of speech recognition among the elderly. *Journal of Speech and Hearing Research, 37,* 465–474.

Huntington, J. M., & Simonsen, E. (1965). Critical flicker fusion frequency as a function of exposure time in two different age groups. *Journal of Gerontology, 20,* 527–529.

Hyde, M. L., & Riko, K. (1994). A decision-analytic approach to audiological rehabilitation. In J. -P. Gagné & N. Tye-Murray (Eds.), Research in audiological rehabilitation: Current trends and future directions. *Journal of the Academy of Rehabilitative Audiology Supplement, 27,* 337–374.

Jani, S. N. (1966). The age factor in stereopsis screening. *American Journal of Optometry and Archives of the American Academy of Optometry, 43,* 653–657.

Jenkins, W. M., Merzenich, M. M., & Recanzone, G. (1990). Neocortical representational dynamics in adult primates: Implications for neuropsychology. *Neuropsychologia, 28,* 573–584.

Johnson, C. A. (1986, February). *Peripheral visual fields and driving in an aging population.* Paper presented at the meeting of the Invitational Conference on Work, Aging, and Vision, National Research Council, National Academy of Science, Committee on Vision, Washington, DC.

Jonas, J. B., Müller-Bergh, J. A., Scholtzer-Schrehardt, U. M., & Naumann, G. O. (1990). Histomorphometry of the human optic nerve. *Investigative Ophthalmology and Visual Science, 31,* 736–744.

Jonas, J. B., Schmidt, A. M., Müller-Bergh, J. A., Scholtzer-Schredardt, U. M., & Naumann, G. O. H. (1992). Human optic nerve fiber count and optic disc size. *Investigative Ophthalmology and Visual Science, 33,* 2012–2018.

Jones, D. A., Victor, C. R., & Vetter, N. J. (1984). Hearing difficulty and its psychological implications for the elderly. *Journal of Epidemiology and Community Health, 38,* 75–78.

Julesz, B. (1971). *Foundations of cyclopean perception.* Chicago: University of Chicago Press.

Just, M. A., Carpenter, P. A., Keller, T. A., Eddy, W. F., & Thulborn, K. R. (1996). Brain activation modulated by sentence comprehension. *Science, 274,* 114–116.

Kemper, S. (1992). Language and aging. In F. I. M. Craik & T. A. Salthouse (Eds.), *The handbook of aging and cognition* (pp. 213–270). Hillsdale, NJ: Lawrence Erlbaum Associates.

Kim, C. B. Y., & Mayer, M. J. (1994). Foveal flicker sensitivity in healthy aging eyes: II. Cross-sectional aging trends from 18 through 77 years of age. *Journal of the Optical Society of America, 11,* 1958–1969.

Kline, D. W. (1991). Light, ageing and visual performance. In J. Marshall & J. R. Cronly-Dillon (Eds.), *Vision and visual dysfunction: Vol 16. The susceptible visual apparatus* (pp. 150–161). London: Macmillan.

Kline, D. W., Culham, J., Bartel, P., & Lynk, L. (1994). Aging and hyperacuity thresholds as a function of contrast and oscillation rate. *Canadian Psychology, 35*(2a), 14.

Konig, E. (1957). Pitch discrimination and age. *Acta Otolaryngologica, 48,* 475–489.

Kramer, A. F., Humphrey, D. G., Larish, J. F., Logan, G. D., & Strayer, D. L. (1994). Aging and inhibition: Beyond a unitary view of inhibitory processing in attention. *Psychology and Aging, 9,* 491–512.

Kramer, A. F., Larish, J. F., & Strayer, D. L. (1995). Training for attentional control in dual task settings: A comparison of young and old adults. *Journal of Experimental Psychology: Applied, 1,* 50–76.

Kramer, A. F., Martin-Emerson, R., Larish, J. F., & Andersen G. J. (1996). Aging and filtering by movement in visual search. *Journal of Gerontology: Psychological Sciences, 51B*, 201–216.

Kwong See, S., & Ryan, E. B. (1996). Cognitive mediation of discourse processing in later life. *Journal of Speech–Language Pathology and Audiology, 20*, 109–117.

Lee, L. W., & Humes, L. E. (1992). Factors associated with speech-recognition ability of the hearing-impaired elderly. *Asha, 34*(10), 212.

Leuba, G., & Garey, L. J. (1987). Evolution of neuronal numerical density in the developing and aging human visual cortex. *Human Neurobiology, 6*, 11–18.

Levitt, H. (1993). Digital hearing aids. In G. A. Studebaker & I. Hochberg (Eds.), *Acoustical factors affecting hearing aid performance* (2nd ed., pp. 317–335). Boston: Allyn & Bacon.

Levitt, H., & Rabiner, L. R. (1967). Binaural release from masking for speech and gain in intelligibility. *Journal of the Acoustical Society of America, 42*, 601–608.

Lindenberger, U., & Baltes, P. B. (1994). Sensory functioning and intelligence in old age: A strong connection. *Psychology and Aging, 9*, 339–355.

Lindenberger, U., Scherer, H., & Baltes, P. B. (1999). The strong association between sensory and cognitive performance in old age: Not due to sensory acuity reductions operating during cognitive assessment. Unpublished manuscript, Max Planck Institute for Human Development, Berlin.

Lindenberger, U., Mayr, U., & Kliegl, R. (1993). Speed and intelligence in old age. *Psychology and Aging, 8*, 207–220.

Logan, G. B., & Cowan, W. B. (1984). On the ability to inhibit thought and action: A theory of an act of control. *Psychological Review, 91*, 295–327.

Lubinski, R., & Higginbotham, J. (1997). *Communication technologies for the elderly: Hearing, speech, and vision.* San Diego, CA: Singular.

Madden, D. J., Pierce, T. W., & Allen, P. (1992). Adult age differences in attentional allocation during memory search. *Psychology and Aging, 7*, 594–601.

Madden, D. J. (1992). Selective attention and visual search: Revision of an allocation model and application to age differences. *Journal of Experimental Psychology: Human Perception & Performance, 18*, 821–836.

Madigan, S. A.., & McCabe, L. (1971). Perfect recall and total forgetting: A problem for models of short-term memory. *Journal of Verbal Learning and Verbal Behavior, 10*, 101–106.

Marshall, L. (1981). Auditory processing in aging listeners. *Journal of Speech and Hearing Disorders, 46*, 226–240.

Marsiske, M., Klumb, P., & Baltes, M. M. (1997). Everyday activity patterns and sensory functioning in old age. *Psychology and Aging, 12*, 444–457.

McFarland, R. A., Domey, R. C., Warren, A. B., & Ward, D. C. (1960). Dark adaptation as a function of age: I. A statistical analysis. *Journal of Gerontology, 15*, 149–154.

McFarland, R. A., Warren, B., & Karis, C. (1958). Alterations in critical flicker frequency as a function of age and light:dark ratio. *Journal of Experimental Psychology, 56*, 529–538.

Meyerson, J., Hale, S., Wagstaff, D., Poon, L. W., & Smith, G. A. (1990). The information-loss model: A mathematical theory of age-related cognitive slowing. *Psychological Review, 97*, 475-487.

Michaels, D. D. (1993). Ocular disease in the elderly. In A. A. Rosenbloom & M. W. Morgan (Eds.), *Vision and aging* (pp. 111–159). Boston: Butterworth-Heinemann.

Moore, B. C. J. (1989). *An introduction to the psychology of hearing.* London: Academic Press.

Moore, B. C. J., Glasberg, B. R., Donaldson, E., McPherson, T., & Plack, C. J. (1989). Detection of temporal gaps in sinusoids by normally hearing and hearing-impaired subjects. *Journal of the Acoustical Society of America, 85*, 1266–1275.

Moore, B. C. J., & Peters, R. W. (1992). Pitch discrimination and phase sensitivity in young and elderly subjects and its relationship to frequency selectivity. *Journal of the Acoustical Society of America, 91*, 2881–2893.

Moore, B. C. J., Peters, R. W., & Glasberg, B. R. (1992). Detection of temporal gaps in sinusoids by elderly subjects with and without hearing loss. *Journal of the Acoustical Society of America, 92,* 1923–1932.

Morgan, M. W. (1993). Normal age related vision changes. In A. A.. Rosenbloom & M. W. Morgan (Eds.) *Vision and aging* (pp 178–199). Boston: Butterworth-Heinemann.

Morrison, J. D., & McGrath, C. (1985). Assessment of the optical contributions to the age-related deterioration in vision. *Quarterly Journal of Experimental Physiology, 70,* 249–269.

Mouloua, M., & Parasuraman, R. (1995). Aging and cognitive vigilance: Effects of spatial uncertainty and event rate. *Experimental Aging Research, 21,* 17–32.

Murphy, D., McDowd, J., & Wilcox, K. (1999). Inhibition and aging: Similarities between younger and older adults as revealed by the processing of unattended auditory information. *Psychology and Aging, 14,* 44–59.

Nameda, N., Kawara, T., & Ohzu, H. (1989). Human visual spatio-temporal frequency performance as a function of age. *Optometry and Vision Science, 66,* 760–765.

Nissen, M. J., Corkin, S., Buonanno, F. S., Growdon, J. H., Wray, S. H., & Bauer, J. (1985). Spatial vision in Alzheimer's disease. *Archives of Neurology, 42,* 667–671.

Noble, W., Byrne, D., & Lepage, B. (1994). Effects on sound localization of configuration and type of hearing impairment. *Journal of the Acoustical Society of America, 95,* 992–1005.

Ohta, R. J., Carlin, M. F., & Harmon, B. M. (1981). Auditory acuity and performance on the Mental Status Questionnaire in the elderly. *Journal of the American Geriatrics Society, 29,* 476–478.

O'Neill, P. M., & Calhoun, K. S. (1975). Sensory deficits and behavioral deterioration in senescence. *Journal of Abnormal Psychology, 84,* 579–582.

Owsley, C., Berry, B., Sloane, M., Stalvey, B., & Wells, J. (1998, April). *Improved vision enhances explicit memory capabilities in older adults.* Poster session presented at the Cognitive Aging Conference, Atlanta, GA.

Owsley, C., & Burton, K. B. (1991). Aging and spatial contrast sensitivity: Underlying mechanisms and implications for everyday life. In P. Gagnoli & W. Hodos (Eds.), *The changing visual system* (pp. 119–136). New York: Plenum.

Owsley, C., Gardner, T., Sekuler, R., & Liberman, H. (1985). Role of the crystalline lens in the spatial vision loss of the elderly. *Investigative Ophthalmology and Visual Science, 26,* 1165–1170.

Owsley, C., Sekuler, R., & Siemsen, D. (1983). Contrast sensitivity throughout adulthood. *Vision Research, 23,* 689–699.

Owsley, C., & Sloane, M. E. (1987). Contrast sensitivity, acuity and the perception of 'real world' targets. *British Journal of Ophthalmology, 71,* 791–796.

Parker, S., & Schneider, B. (1994). The stimulus range effect: Evidence for top-down control of sensory intensity in audition. *Perception & Psychophysics, 56,* 1–11.

Pichora-Fuller, M. K. (1996). Speechreading and working memory. In D. G. Stork & M. E. Hennecke (Eds.), *Speechreading by humans and machines: Models, systems, and applications* (pp. 257–274). Berlin, Germany: Springer-Verlag.

Pichora-Fuller, M. K. (1997). Language comprehension in older listeners. *Journal of Speech Language Pathology and Audiology, 21,* 125–142.

Pichora-Fuller, M. K., & Robertson, L. F. (1994). Hard of hearing residents in a home for the aged. *Journal of Speech Language Pathology and Audiology, 18,* 278–288.

Pichora-Fuller, M. K., & Schneider, B. A. (1991). Masking-level differences in the elderly: A comparison of antiphasic and time-delay dichotic conditions. *Journal of Speech and Hearing Research, 34,* 1410–1422.

Pichora-Fuller, M. K., & Schneider, B. A. (1992). The effect of interaural delay of the masker on masking-level differences in young and old adults. *Journal of the Acoustical Society of America, 91,* 2129–2135.

Pichora-Fuller, M. K., Schneider, B. A., & Daneman, M. (1995). How young and old adults listen to and remember speech in noise. *Journal of the Acoustical Society of America, 97,* 593–608.

Pickles, J. O. (1988). *An introduction to the physiology of hearing* (2nd ed.). San Diego, CA: Academic Press.

Pitts, D. G. (1982). The effects of aging on selected visual functions: Dark adaptation, visual acuity, stereopsis, and brightness contrast. In R. Sekuler, D. Kline, & K. Dismukes (Eds.), *Aging and human visual function* (pp. 131–159). New York: Liss.

Plomp, R. (1978). Auditory handicap of hearing impairment and the limited benefit of hearing aids. *Journal of the Acoustical Society of America, 63,* 533–549.

Plomp, R. (1986). A signal-to-noise ratio model for the speech reception threshold of the hearing impaired. *Journal of Speech and Hearing Research, 29,* 146–154.

Rabbitt, P. M. (1990). Applied cognitive gerontology: Some problems, methodologies, and data. *Applied Cognitive Psychology, 4,* 225–246.

Rabbitt, P. M. (1991). Mild hearing loss can cause apparent memory failures which increase with age and reduce with IQ. *Acta Otolaryngologica, 476*(Suppl.), 167–176.

Rabbitt, P. M. (1968). Channel capacity, intelligibility and immediate memory. *Quarterly Journal of Experimental Psychology, 20,* 241–248.

Ryan, E. B., Giles, H., Bartolucci, G., & Henwood, K. (1986). Psycholinguistic and social psychological components of communication by and with the elderly. *Language and Communication, 6,* 1–24.

Salthouse, T. A. (1985). *A theory of cognitive aging.* Amsterdam: North-Holland.

Salthouse, T. A. (1993). Speed mediation of adult age differences in cognition. *Developmental Psychology, 29,* 722–738.

Salthouse, T. A. (1996). The processing speed theory of adult age differences in cognition. *Psychological Review, 103,* 403–428.

Salthouse, T. A., Hambrick, D. Z., & McGuthry, K. E. (1998). Shared age-related influences on cognitive and non-cognitive variables. *Psychology and Aging, 13,* 486–500.

Salthouse, T. A., Hancock, H. E., Meinz, E. J., & Hambrick, D. Z. (1996). Interrelations of age, visual acuity, and cognitive functioning. *Journal of Gerontology: Psychological Sciences, 51B,* P317–P330.

Schaie, K. W., Baltes, P. B., & Strother, C. R. (1964). A study of auditory sensitivity in advanced age. *Journal of Geronotology, 19,* 453–457.

Schlotterer, G., Moscovitch, M., & Crapper-McLachlan, D. (1984). Visual processing deficits as assessed by spatial frequency contrast sensitivity and backward masking in normal aging and Alzheimer's disease. *Brain, 107,* 309–325.

Schneider, B. A. (1997). Psychoacoustics and aging: Implications for everyday listening. *Journal of Speech–Language Pathology and Audiology, 21,* 111–124.

Schneider, B. A., Daneman, M., Murphy, D. R., & Kwong-See, S., (in press). Listening to discourse in distracting settings: The effects of aging. *Psychology and Aging.*

Schneider, B. A., & Hsamstra, S. J. (1999). Gap detection thresholds as a function of tonal duration for younger and older listeners. *Journal of the Acoustical Society of America, 106,* 371–380.

Schneider, B. A., & Moraglia, G. (1994). Binocular vision enhances target detection by filtering the background. *Perception, 23,* 1267–1286.

Schneider, B. A., & Parker, S. (1990). Does stimulus context affect loudness or only loudness judgments? *Perception & Psychophysics, 48,* 409–418.

Schneider, B. A., Pichora-Fuller, M. K., Kowalchuk, D., & Lamb, M. (1994). Gap detection and the precedence effect in young and old adults. *Journal of the Acoustical Society of America, 95,* 980–991.

Schneider, B. A., Speranza, F., & Pichora-Fuller, M. K. (1998). Age-related changes in temporal resolution: Envelope and intensity effects. *Canadian Journal of Experimental Psychology, 52,* 184–191.

Scialfa, C. T., Garvey, P. M., Gish, K. W., Deering, L. M., Leibowitz, H. W., & Goebel, C. G. (1988). Relationships among measures of static and dynamic visual sensitivity. *Human Factors, 30,* 677–687.

Sekuler, A. B., Bennett, P. J., & Mamelak, M. (in press). The effects of aging on the useful field of view. *Experimental Aging Research.*

Sekuler, R., & Ball, K. (1986). Visual localization: Age and practice. *Journal of the Optical Society of America A, 3,* 864–867.

Sekuler, R., & Blake, R. (1987). Sensory underload. *Psychology Today, 21,* 48–51.

Shannon, R. V., Zeng, F. -G., Kamath, V., Wygonski, J., & Ekelid, M. (1995). Speech recognition with primarily temporal cues. *Science, 270,* 303–304.

Sharpe, J. A., & Sylvester, T. O. (1978). Effect of aging on horizontal smooth pursuit. *Investigative Ophthalmology and Visual Science, 17,* 465–468.

Ska, B., & Joannette, Y. (1996). Discourse in older adults: Influence of text, task, and participant characteristics. *Journal of Speech–Language Pathology and Audiology, 20,* 101–108.

Sloane, M. E., Owsley, C., & Jackson, C. A. (1988). Aging and luminance-adaptation effects on spatial contrast sensitivity. *Journal of the Optical Society of America, 5,* 2181–2190.

Smedley, T. C., & Schow, R. (1994). Frustrations with hearing aid use: Candid observations from the elderly. *Hearing Instruments, 43,* 21–27.

Spear, P. D. (1993). Neural bases of visual deficits during aging. *Vision Research, 33,* 2589–2609.

Spear, P. D., Moore, R. J., Kim, C. B. Y., Xue, J. -T., & Tumosa, N. (1994). Effects of aging on the primate visual system: Spatial and temporal processing by lateral geniculate neurons in young adult and old rhesus monkeys. *Journal of Neurophysiology, 72,* 402–420.

Speranza, F., Daneman, M., & Schneider, B. A. (in press). How aging affects the reading of words in noisy backgrounds. *Psychology and Aging.*

Speranza, F., Moraglia, G., & Schneider, B. A. (1995). Age-related changes in binocular vision: Detection of noise-masked targets in young and old observers. *Journal of Gerontology: Psychological Sciences, 50B,* P114–P123.

Spinks, R., Gilmore, G. C., & Thomas, C. (1996, April). *Age simulation of a sensory deficit does impair cognitive test performance.* Poster session presented at the Cognitive Aging Conference, Atlanta, GA.

Spooner, J. W., Sakala, S. M., & Baloh, R. W. (1980). Effect of aging on eye tracking. *Archives of Neurology, 37,* 575–576.

Strouse, A., Ashmead, D. H., Ohde, R. N., & Grantham, D. W. (1998). Temporal processing in the aging auditory system. *Journal of the Acoustical Society of America, 104,* 2385–2399.

Sturr, J. F., & Hannon, D. J. (1991). Methods and models for specifying sites and mechanisms of sensitivity regulation in the aging visual system. In P. Bagnoli & W. Hodos (Eds.), *The changing visual system* (pp. 219–232). New York: Plenum.

Tesch-Romer, C. (1997). Psychological effects of hearing aid use in older adults. *Journal of Gerontology: Psychological Sciences, 52B,* 127–138.

Thomas, P. D., Hunt, W. C., Garry, P. J., Hood, R. B., Goodwin, J. M., & Goodwin, J. S. (1983). Hearing acuity in a healthy elderly population: Effects on emotional, cognitive, and social status. *Journal of Gerontology, 38,* 321–325.

Treisman, A. M., & Gelade, G. (1980). A feature-integration theory of attention. *Cognitive Psychology, 12,* 97–136.

Trick, G. L., & Silverman, S. E. (1991). Visual sensitivity to motion: Age-related changes and deficits in senile dementia of the Alzheimer type. *Neurology, 41,* 1437–1440.

Tulunay-Keesey, U., Ver Hoeve, J. N., & Terkla-McGrane, C. (1988). Threshold and supra-threshold spatiotemporal response throughout adulthood. *Journal of the Optical Society of America A, 5,* 2191–2200.

Tyler, R. S., Summerfield, Q., Wood, E. J., & Fernandes, M. A. (1982). Psychoacoustic and phonetic temporal processing in normal and hearing-impaired listeners. *Journal of the Acoustical Society of America, 72,* 740–752.

van Rooij, J. C. G. M., & Plomp, R. (1990). Auditive and cognitive factors in speech perception by elderly listeners: II. Multivariate analyses. *Journal of the Acoustical Society of America, 88*, 2611–2624.

van Rooij, J. C. G. M., & Plomp, R. (1992). Auditive and cognitive factors in speech perception by elderly listeners: III. Additional data and final discussion. *Journal of the Acoustical Society of America, 91*, 1028–1033.

Vincent, S. L., Peters, A., & Tigges, J. (1989). Effects of aging on the neurons within Area 17 of rhesus monkey cerebral cortex. *Anatomical Record, 223*, 329–341.

Warabi, T., Kase, M., & Kato, T. (1964). Effect of aging on the accuracy of visually guided saccadic eye movement. *Annals of Neurology, 16*, 449–454.

Weale, R. A. (1961). Retinal illumination and age. *Transactions of the Illuminating Engineering Society, 26*, 95–100.

Weale, R. A. (1963). *The aging eye.* London: Lewis.

Weale, R. A. (1987). Senescent vision: Is it all the fault of the lens? *Eye, 1*, 217–221.

Werner, J. S., & Steele, V. G. (1988). Sensitivity of human foveal color mechanisms through the lifespan. *Journal of the Optical Society of America A, 5*, 2122–2130.

Willott, J. F. (1991). *Aging and the auditory system: Anatomy, physiology, and psychophysics.* San Diego, CA: Singular.

Wingfield, A. (1996). Cognitive factors in auditory performance: Context, speed of processing, and constraints of memory. *Journal of the American Academy of Audiology, 7*, 175–182.

Wingfield, A., Tun, P., Koh, C. K., & Rosen, M. J. (in press). Regaining lost time: Adult aging and the effect of time restoration on recall of time-compressed speech. *Psychology and Aging.*

Wojciechowski, R., Trick, G. L., & Steinman, S. B. (1995). Topography of the age-related decline in motion sensitivity. *Optometry and Vision Science, 72*, 67–74.

Yang, K. C. H., Elliott, D. B., & Whitaker, D. (1993). Does logMAR VA change linearly with age? *Investigative Ophthalmology and Visual Science, 24*, 1422.

Yekta, A. A., Pickwell, L. D., & Jenkins, T. C. A. (1989). Binocular vision, age and symptoms. *Ophthalmic and Physiological Optics, 9*, 115–120.

4

Attention and Aging:
A Functional Perspective

Joan M. McDowd
University of Kansas Medical Center

Raymond J. Shaw
Merrimack College

In the psychologist's search for the cause of age-related cognitive changes, there is frequently an expectation that there will be a single underlying mechanism responsible for many, if not all, observable developmental changes. Age-related changes in attention have been cited as the basis for a variety of age-related behavioral inefficiencies and have been the focus of both empirical and theoretical work designed to understand these inefficiencies. The goal of the present chapter is to review data related to age differences in attentional competence (primarily those data that have been published since the previous edition of this handbook; see Hartley, 1992), to discuss the functional consequences of such differences, and to consider the theoretical constructs hypothesized to account for the findings.

Attention is a term used to describe a variety of cognitive phenomena, and the literature pertaining to its study could be organized in a variety of ways. Here, we follow the lead of Woodrow (1914), who stated that even though "the intimate nature" of attention was not completely understood, attention could be "known by certain of its functions" (p. 6). For example, processing one source of information at the expense of others is the "selective" function of attention, simultaneous processing of two or more sources of information is the function of "divided attention," alternately processing one source and then another is the "switching" function of attention, and maintaining a consistent focus on one source of information over time is the function of "sustained attention." These functions provide a framework here for organizing and presenting recent work on aging and attention (for other recent reviews, see Hartley, 1992; Klein, 1997; Madden, 1990; Madden & Allen, 1996; Madden & Plude, 1993; Plude, Enns, & Brodeur, 1994). Our "functional perspective" thus refers to our approach to attention as composed of separable dimensions serving different functions. We believe that this approach provides a useful way to understand the variety of attentional phenomena that have been studied in the context of adult aging, although we also recognize that this organization can sometimes produce an artificial division of attentional phenomena. That is, complex tasks may require more than one attentional function. In addition, the theoretical approaches to understanding attention and aging that we consider here are not limited to particular functions but tend to cut across them. For example, attentional capacity or resources (the terms *capacity* and *resources* are used interchangeably here) are conceptualized as the limited supply of fuel that permits most cognitive processes to be performed. Similarly, age-related decline in speed of processing is hypothesized to be a fundamental component in most age-related changes in cognitive functioning. The role of inhibition in cognition is not limited to a single domain. Thus, the role of each of these theoretical constructs is mentioned in more than one section on the functions of attention, although we defer any extended discussion of such notions to the section on theoretical approaches.

What follows are separate sections covering recent research related to selective, divided, switching, and sustained attention. After considering the relevant data in the initial sections of this chapter, we move on to discuss the consequences of age-related attentional impairments, then conclude with theoretical considerations.

EMPIRICAL APPROACHES TO ATTENTION IN AGING

Selective Attention

The ability to attend selectively is generally considered a prerequisite for efficient behavior; individuals must be able to attend to relevant information and ignore irrelevant information in order to meet effectively most task requirements, as in driving an automobile, conversing in noisy environments, reading on the subway, or searching for a friend in a crowd. Laboratory analogues of tasks such as these have been developed and studied in some detail in an effort to understand age-related changes in underlying attentional abilities. In general, tasks designed to assess selective attention have created situations in which multiple sources of information are available for processing, but only a subset are relevant to the primary task and the others are considered distractors. Performance in a control condition without distractors is typically compared with performance in the presence of distractors; decreases in speed or accuracy in the latter condition are attributed to difficulty in filtering out the distractors. For example, Connelly, Hasher, and Zacks (1991) observed that reading times of older adults were more negatively affected by the presence of distracting information than those of young adults. Earles et al. (1997) reported a similar finding. A follow-up study by Carlson, Hasher, Connelly, and Zacks (1995) indicated that the magnitude of the age-related distraction effect in the reading task was reduced when target and distractor information occupied different and predictable locations in space. This finding fits well with earlier work showing that advance knowledge about target location can reduce the negative impact of distractors for older adults (e.g., Wright & Elias, 1979; see Plude & Hoyer, 1985, for a review of earlier work). We now consider a variety of specific paradigms that have been used to examine selective attention in aging.

Visual Search. Deficits in selective attention abilities among older adults were identified by Rabbitt (1965) in a paradigm involving a search for targets among distractors; these deficits were said to be due to a reduced ability to ignore irrelevant information. Much of the work since then has been carried out in an effort to understand the factors that account for age differences in visual search performance. For example, Madden (1992) asked whether focused attention was best described as a spotlight that moves around visual space in a search task or as a gradient of attention distributed across visual space and whether the performance of young and old adults could be characterized by the same or different models. His findings suggest that a processing gradient model of attention best characterizes the performance of both young and old adults, although processing speed was slower for old adults than for young adults. That is, both young and old adults appear to adjust the breadth of their attentional focus according to task demands rather than maintain a single narrow focus of attention that is used to carry out a serial search process. Madden noted that the age-related slowing of processing speed observed in his study is not necessarily limited to selective attention tasks but may be symptomatic of an age-related generalized slowing of cognitive processes (cf. Cerella, 1990; Salthouse, 1985). That is, across tasks or task conditions, older adults may be slowed relative to young adults by a constant proportion, regardless of the nature of any specific task. Madden tested this possibility in his data and found that the relation between response speed in young and old adults could be well described by a linear function (96% of the variance was accounted for by this linear model of age-related slowing). Although this simple quantitative function can predict the performance of older adults on the basis of only young adults' performance speed, Madden (1992) concluded that his work in characterizing attentional allocation performance in young and old adults is still useful for understanding age differences beyond a simple slowing account "because the specific forms of attentional allocation that potentially contribute to age-related slowing can be defined quantitatively" (p. 835).

McCalley, Bouwhuis, and Juola (1995) examined spotlight, zoom lens, and ring models of attentional allocation with regard to their fit to the attentional performance of young and old adults. A spotlight model assumes that attention is allocated in search of a target in a serial fashion; items outside the spotlight are not processed. A zoom lens model holds that attention can be expanded and contracted around a central point and that items within the beam can be searched in parallel. Finally, a ring model assumes that attention can be separated from a central point and spread out over regions that do not contain fixation. McCalley et al. devised a task and an analysis strategy that allowed them to fit these models to the performance data produced by young and old adults and to decide which model fit best. Their task required participants to indicate which of two possible target characters was present in a display containing similar distractors. Stimuli were arranged in rings around a central fixation point; location cues indicated whether the target was likely to appear in a solid central circle, a middle ringlike area surrounding the central circle, or an outer ring surrounding the middle ring. After controlling for age differences in acuity and target eccentricity, McCalley et al. observed that a ring model gave the best fit to the data of both young and old adults. They found that older adults incurred lower costs from invalid cues and greater benefits from valid cues than did young adults and suggested that this may reflect a decreased ability to inhibit uncued areas of the display and a greater reliance on excitatory processes in selection. These latter effects may play an important role in increased susceptibility to distraction in visual search tasks among older adults.

Allen and colleagues investigated the possibility that greater internal noise among older adults contributed to age-related slowing in visual search tasks. Allen, Madden, Groth, and Crozier (1992) argued that previous accounts of age differences in visual search in terms of an age-related difficulty with ignoring irrelevant stimuli might not tell the whole story. Allen et al. offered a model in which older adults are characterized by greater internal noise than are young adults as an account of age differences in selectivity. They suggested that increased spurious internal noise present in the nervous systems of older adults impairs their ability to distinguish target information from distractor information because the presence of noise decreases processing resolution. So when both targets and distractors are present in a display, older adults will take longer and perhaps be more prone to errors because the internal noise makes it more difficult to discriminate between target and distractor items. They have tested this model in a series of studies using a redundancy gain paradigm. Redundancy gain is the empirical observation of faster response times when two or three instances of a target are presented compared with trials containing only one target (e.g., Grice & Canham, 1990). Allen et al. reasoned that if age differences in visual search are due to older adults' greater difficulty in selecting targets from distractors, the age differences should vary as a function of redundancy in target-only (TO) versus target-plus-noise (TPN) conditions. Specifically, both age groups should show comparable redundancy gains in the TO condition because there are no irrelevant items to interfere with target processing. In contrast, older adults should show a greater redundancy gain than young adults in the TPN condition because the target redundancy should reduce the interfering effects of internal noise in differentiating target from distractor(s).

The data are mixed with regard to these predictions. Allen et al. (1992) reported results that supported an internal noise hypothesis, but Allen, Groth, Weber, and Madden (1993) reported data that contradicted predictions. Allen et al. (1993) went on to test the possibility that target–distractor similarity and number of distractors present in the display might be responsible for the observed discrepancy. Results indicated that a single distractor may not be sufficient to put older adults at a significant disadvantage from increased internal noise. However, perceptual similarity of target and distractors did not affect age differences in redundancy gain, contrary to the predictions of an internal noise model of age differences in target–distractor discrimination in selective attention. Thus, an internal noise model of age differences in redundancy gain cannot account for all of the observed results.

Allen, Weber, and Madden (1994) further investigated redundancy gain in aging with an experiment designed to identify a locus for the observed age differences. Their experiment examined three possible factors that could be responsible for age differences: (a) filtering processes, those that allow an individual to ignore or inhibit irrelevant information; (b) search processes, also called "activation" by Allen et al. and described as those processes that excite or activate the relevant target information; and (c) sensory–perceptual processes that may produce a decrement in the rate at which older adults accumulate information at stimulus detection stages. Across two experiments, they replicated the finding that older adults showed greater redundancy gains than did young adults. However, this difference did not interact with the other manipulated variables: response type (two choice vs. go/no go); display type (TO vs. TPN), or distractor type (similar vs. dissimilar). If age differences in redundancy gains were due to decrements in filtering, older adults should have committed more errors in the go/no-go task or they should have shown greater redundancy gains in the TPN condition than in the TO condition or greater redundancy gains with increasing target–distractor similarity. None of these predictions were observed in the data. The data also showed that reducing luminance level for young adults had very little effect on performance, indicating that less efficient information accumulation among older adults was not responsible for their greater redundancy gains. From this pattern of results, Allen et al. concluded that the larger redundancy gain for older adults was due to an activation decrement at the identification stage of processing. That is, older adults apparently have more difficulty associated with activating or selecting the targets. According to Allen et al. (1994), older adults "had more difficulty in activating the attentional selection process during the identification stage of the visual search task than in filtering nontarget stimuli" (p. 221). This conclusion was based in large part on the failure to find any evidence for the other accounts of age-related superiority in redundancy gains, such as age-related increased internal noise or decreased inhibitory functioning.

It appears that Salthouse's (1985) warning that age-related noise hypotheses must be well specified, as not all versions are tenable, holds true here. Certainly more information on the role of task variables in producing susceptibility to noise is needed to fully evaluate this hypothesis regarding attentional functioning in older age. Part of the difficulty comes in specifying the locus and nature of the "noise." Theories postulating greater internal noise generated in the aging nervous system often are tested with tasks involving different levels of externally generated perceptual noise (e.g., distractors). Sorting out the role and effect of these different sources of noise remains a conceptual challenge that has yet to be met.

The work of Kotary and Hoyer (1995) might be interpreted as another approach to understanding the role of noise in visual selective attention tasks. They varied the nature of distracting information while keeping the number of distractors constant across conditions in an effort to discover the processing level at which interfering noise was produced. Participants were required to count the number of targets (the letter Q) present in a display; distractors were either categorically or conceptually related to the targets. Categorically related distractors were other letters of the alphabet. Conceptually related distractors were numbers, representing either the number of targets present in the display or another number. In the conditions of interest, (a) either three or four targets were present or (b) either no distractors or eight distractors were present.

Kotary and Hoyer (1995) hypothesized that if distractor interference, or noise, is largely due to perceptual aspects of searching the display, then performance should not vary as function of distractor type. If semantic processing of distractor information also produces interference or noise, and if participants process distractors at a semantic level, then performance might be expected to be more negatively affected by the conceptually related distractors. Kotary and Hoyer's data revealed the typical pattern of results in which older adults were more slowed in the presence of distractors than were young adults. In addition, when only three targets were present, the type of distractor made no difference to performance for either young or old adults. However, with four targets, the pattern of results indicated that the identity of distractors was apparently processed by both young and old adults as performance was more disrupted when distractor identities were numbers different from the correct number of targets than in either of the other distractor conditions. This greater disruption in the case where distractor identity specified a number different from the correct target number suggests that the activation of two different numbers under these circumstances may have introduced response conflict that led to the additional slowing. Although this response conflict slowed performance more than the simple presence of distractors, the magnitude of this slowing was equivalent for young and old adults. In addition, the magnitude of interference produced by categorically related distractors (other letters) and conceptually related distractors (numbers) having the same identity as the target response did not differ for young and old adults, although the overall magnitude of interference was greater for older adults. On the basis of these findings, Kotary and Hoyer (1995) concluded that "there was no evidence to suggest an age difference in the effects of type of distractor on selective attention performance" (p. 169).

Madden, Pierce, and Allen (1996) also examined distractor characteristics in a study of age differences in visual search. Their task was to search for the presence of a target upright L among a field of distractor rotated Ls. The distractors were either homogeneous relative to each other (all rotated 90° in the same direction) or heterogeneous (half rotated 90° to the right and half rotated 90° to the left). Across two experiments in which display size and distractor type were manipulated, Madden et al. observed faster search times in the homogeneous versus heterogeneous distractor conditions for both young and old adults, suggesting that both age groups respond similarly to changes in distractor type. In an analysis of ratios composed of slopes of response time on display size in the presence of homogeneous distractors and heterogeneous distractors, they found the ratios to be smaller for young adults than for old adults. Thus, the magnitude of the homogeneous benefit was somewhat greater for young adults than for old adults. Again these results suggest that both young and old adults are sensitive to the nature of the distractors; however, on the basis of the finding that young adults were better able to improve performance in the homogeneous distractor condition relative to the heterogeneous distractor condition, Madden et al. (1996) suggested that their data are consistent with the claim that young adults are "more efficient than older adults in the inhibition of nontarget information during visual search" (p. 471).

Madden et al. (1996) also noted that a generalized slowing model of cognitive aging could account for many of their findings, but they stopped short of concluding that task-specific effects were not useful for understanding performance. Perhaps most notable was their finding that although statistical control of perceptual speed significantly attenuated age-related effects, the degree of attenuation varied across task conditions, suggesting that "the degree of age-related slowing may be influenced by task-specific processes" (Madden et al., 1996, p. 473). They concluded that these task-specific processes may be useful in informing our understanding of selective attention performance in aging.

Humphrey and Kramer (1997) examined the role of top-down processes in determining age differences in visual search. Their search conditions involved feature search, in which the target is defined by a single feature (e.g., color); conjunction search, in which the target is defined by two features (e.g., color and size); and triple-conjunction search, in which the target is defined by the combination of three features (e.g., color, size, and orientation). Recent theorizing about performance under these conditions suggests that performance is a function of both top-down processes (e.g., activation of relevant feature combinations and inhibition of irrelevant features) and bottom-up processes (e.g., feature identification and perceptual grouping). Previous work (e.g., Plude & Doussard-Roosevelt, 1989) has shown older adults to be comparable to young adults on single-feature, bottom-up search but less able than young adults to perform efficiently in conjunction search conditions. Humphrey and Kramer endeavored to examine whether older adults could make use of top-down guidance of attentional processing in triple-conjunction search conditions. Triple-conjunction search may be speeded relative to conjunction search by top-down processes if an individual can use the added information made available by defining a third target feature to guide attentional processes in the search field. Like Plude and Doussard-Roosevelt, Humphrey and Kramer found age equivalence in feature search and age deficits in conjunction search. They interpreted the latter deficit as suggesting that there are "age-related differences in the ability to use successfully top-down activation to either facilitate the conjunction targets or inhibit the distractors" (Humphrey & Kramer, 1997, p. 711). However, improvement in search performance in triple-conjunction conditions relative to conjunction conditions was comparable for old and young adults, suggesting that both age groups were able to use the added information supplied by the additional defining target feature to guide attention during the search process. Whether the mechanism of this improved performance among older adults is better explained by improved activation or improved in-hibition remains to be seen. In either case, older adults may require more information than young adults to support top-down processes and effec-tively guide attention in conjunction search conditions.

On the basis of the data described in this section, the following general observations regarding age-related performance similarities and differ-ences in search tasks can be made. Models of attention as a processing gradient characterizes both young and old adults (Madden, 1992), but a ring model of attention also appears to characterize both young and old adults (McCalley et al., 1995). The important point may be that with either model, attentional performance is similar in young adults and old adults. In tasks with small display sizes, attentional filtering is comparable in young and old adults (Allen et al., 1994). Old and young adults process distractor identities in a similar manner (Kotary & Hoyer, 1995). Specify-ing targets with three instead of just two variables improves performance of old and young adults to a comparable extent (Humphrey & Kramer, 1997). However, older adults are slower than young adults to allocate attention (Madden, 1992); internal noise may be greater in old adults than in young adults (Allen et al., 1992, 1993); and distractor homogeneity facilitates performance more for young adults than for old adults (Madden et al., 1996).

The Stroop Task. The Stroop color-word task has long been used as a measure of selective attention (see MacLeod, 1991, for a review), requir-ing as it does processing one aspect of a stimulus word (the color in which it is printed) and ignoring another aspect of the same stimulus (the word itself). Results from this task have typically shown greater susceptibility to interference among older adults than among younger adults (e.g., Cohn, Dustman, & Bradford, 1984; Comalli, Wapner, & Werner, 1962; Dulaney & Rogers, 1994; Earles et al., 1997; Hartley, 1993; Houx, Jolles, & Vreeling, 1993; Klein, Ponds, Houx, & Jolles, 1997), a finding that has been inter-preted to indicate an age-related decline in selective attention abilities. Other recent work, however, has called into question the conclusions regarding poorer selective attention among older adults on the basis of the Stroop task. Salthouse and Meinz (1995) found that age-related vari-ance in Stroop interference scores largely overlapped the variance asso-ciated with other measures of processing speed, indicating that the Stroop interference is not a pure measure of selective attention abilities but may reflect basic processing speed. Salthouse, Toth, Hancock, and Woodard (1997) reported a similar finding in a spatial variant of the Stroop task. Instead of colors and color words, their task stimuli were left- and right-pointing arrows presented on the left, right, or center of a display. Par-ticipants were to respond with their left or right hand to the direction of the arrow; Stroop trials were those in which the direction of the arrow did not match the side of the display on which it was presented. In a regression analysis involving congruent, incongruent, and neutral trials, Salthouse et al. found that age was not significantly associated with either facilitation effects from congruent trials or interference effects from incongruent trials after overall response speed in the neutral condition was controlled. They concluded, then, that the influence of age on selective attention is not unique to selective attention but is the same influence that affects a variety of other cognitive processes.

Verhaeghen and De Meersman (1998) reached a conclusion similar to that of Salthouse and colleagues in a meta-analytic study of Stroop interference in aging. Using data from 20 relevant studies, Verhaeghen and De Meersman found no age differences in interference effects expressed as mean standardized differences. In addition, regression analysis (e.g., Cerella, 1990) and application of the information loss model of age-related slowing (Myerson, Hale, Wagstaff, Poon, & Smith, 1990) showed no evidence of age interactions. Verhaeghen and De Meersman (1998) concluded that "the presumed age relatedness of the Stroop interference effect is merely an artifact of general slowing" (p. 125). However, Spieler, Balota, and Faust (1996) reached a different conclusion regarding aging and Stroop interference effects. They recognized that general slowing may play a role in the magnitude of the Stroop effect but argued that a proportional transformation was both theoretically and empirically justified as a way to deal with group differences in baseline speed of performance. They observed larger proportional Stroop interference scores among old adults compared with young adults in their sample and concluded that this difference "was not simply a scaling effect resulting from differences in overall speed of processing" (Spieler et al., 1996, p. 475). In contrast, Verhaeghen and De Meersman argued that proportional models give less good fits to data than does either Cerella's multilayered slowing model or Myerson et al.'s information loss model, which they used in reaching their conclusion about Stroop effects in aging. Thus, there remains some controversy regarding the appropriate way to handle age differences in baseline speed of behavior (see also Cerella, 1994; Fisk & Fisher, 1994; Myerson, Wagstaff, & Hale, 1994; and Perfect, 1994, for more on this controversy).

Spieler et al. (1996) also used both process dissociation methods (Jacoby, 1991) and ex-Gaussian analyses (e.g., Hockley, 1984; Ratcliff, 1979) to further analyze age differences in Stroop performance. On the basis of the work of Lindsay and Jacoby (1994) that shows that Stroop performance is made up of separable processes involving word information and color information, Spieler et al. predicted that selective attention deficits would affect word process estimates and not color process estimates because it is presumably word processing that produces interference and slowing. Their analysis revealed that the only reliable age difference was larger word process estimates for old adults than for young adults. They interpreted this finding in terms of an age-related selective attention deficit; efficient selective attention on the Stroop task would limit word information processing in favor of color information processing, and the process estimates indicated that older adults had a more difficult time with this than did young adults.

Ex-Gaussian analyses of reaction time distributions are designed to reveal qualitative differences in these distributions between age groups. Differences between age groups in mean interference scores could result from differences in the modal part of the distribution or from differences in the skew of the distribution (or a combination of both). Spieler et al.'s (1996) analysis indicated that the age groups in their study produced response time distributions that differed in skew. That is, on most trials older and young adults showed comparable levels of interference, but for a subset of trials, older adults showed considerably more interference than did young adults. They concluded that "disproportionate age effects may arise from an increase in the tail of the distribution rather than simply from a shift in the entire distribution, as might be predicted by some generalized slowing accounts of aging effects" (Spieler et al., 1996, p. 476). Again, the primacy of general slowing or task-specific attentional processes in determining age differences in performance appears to be a matter of some controversy. The unsettled issue is whether the purported attentional differences are the cause of performance differences or slowing or are themselves a consequence of general slowing. For example, Earles et al. (1997) designed a study to examine relations between age, perceptual speed, inhibitory function, susceptibility to interference, and working memory. Their data led them to take one side of the cause–consequence controversy, concluding that their results did not support the claim that age-related attentional deficiencies produced age-related increases in susceptibility to interference but that the "consequences of the slower and less efficient processing system possessed by older adults are an impaired ability to inhibit previously relevant information and an increase in susceptibility to interference" (Earles et al., 1997, p. 56). Spieler et al. took the other side.

Hartley (1993) also took the other side in his study involving two different versions of the Stroop task. In addition to the standard Stroop stimuli, Hartley used a task version that required participants to name the color of a colored block and ignore a color word that appeared above or below the block. In this color block condition, target and distractor information were thus separated in space. His findings revealed comparable Stroop effects among old and young adults in the color block version of the task but significant age-related slowing among old adults compared with young adults in the color word version of the task. Hartley concluded that spatial filtering is intact in older adults but that when spatial filtering is not possible, as in the color word task version, older adults show greater negative effects of distracting information. He also reported analyses of proportional slowing in the color word task versions compared with the color block task versions. The pattern of results obtained in these analyses indicate that older adults were not simply proportionately slower than young adults; rather, "for older adults, but not for younger adults, the Stroop effect was disproportionately exaggerated by combining the color and the word in the same location" (Hartley, 1993, p. 376). Thus, notions of general slowing are not adequate to account for this age-related decline in attentional functioning.

There appears to be no definitive answer regarding the source of age-related performance differences in the Stroop task. Attentional interpretations cite increased age-related distractibility as the source of performance differences, particularly when target and distractor are different features of the same object occupying the same location in space. Processing speed accounts suggest that age-related slowing alone can account for observed age differences, although at issue is the best way to assess the source of the slowing, whether by process dissociation, ex-Gaussian analyses, Brinley analyses, or regression analyses. More empirical work may help answer the relevant questions, but more theoretical work may also be required to identify the best approach for explaining the observed age differences.

Negative Priming. One critical issue in understanding selective attention concerns the fate of distractor information in the information-processing system. The negative priming paradigm was initially designed to provide some insight into this issue. In this task, a target and a distractor item (e.g., pictures or words), usually distinguishable on the basis of color, are presented and the task requires that some response (e.g., naming) be made to the target item while ignoring the distractor item. On some proportion of trials, the next pair of items includes the just-previous distractor item now presented as the target, along with a unique distractor. On these trials, responses to the distractor-become-target are slower than on trials in which items are not repeated from the previous trial. This slowing has been interpreted as resulting from inhibitory processes directed against that item when it was presented as a distractor (but see more recent interpretations of negative priming, e.g., May, Kane, & Hasher, 1995; Neill & Valdes, 1992; J. Park & Kanwisher, 1994). According to the inhibition view of negative priming, when an item is re-presented as a target, the effects of the just-previous inhibition or suppression must be overcome in order for a response to be made and that response is slowed. The magnitude of slowing has also been taken as an index of the degree or extent of inhibition directed to the item in the distractor trial.

Connelly and Hasher (1993) devised a set of manipulations that illustrate two main classes of negative priming tasks: those involving identity suppression and those involving location suppression. Their task required participants to name a target red letter and ignore a green letter, or vice versa, each presented in one of four locations. Identity negative priming was indexed by slowing on trials when the to-be-named target had the same identity as the to-be-suppressed distractor on the just-previous trial. Location negative priming was indexed by a slowing on trials in which a target stimulus appeared in the same location as the to-be-suppressed distractor on the just-previous trial. Examining the pattern of age differences in location suppression and identity suppression, both separately and in combination, Connelly and Hasher found that in the location suppression condition, both age groups showed response slowing (negative priming). However, when a target letter shared the identity but not the location of the distractor letter from the previous trial, young adults but not older adults showed response slowing (negative priming). In addition, when both the identity and location of distractor information were repeated in the target stimulus, the effect of identity and location suppression appeared additive for young adults, whereas older adults were not significantly more slowed than they were for location suppression alone. They concluded that there appears to be a dissociation in the inhibitory function of older adults: Age deficits are apparent in identity suppression (see also Hasher, Stoltzfus, Zacks, & Rypma, 1991; McDowd & Oseas-Kreger, 1991; Tipper, 1991), whereas age equivalence is observed in location suppression (see McDowd & Filion, 1995, for an exception).

On the hypothesis that inhibitory processes take more time to develop and reach peak efficiency in older adults, Hasher et al. (1991) varied the interval between the pairs of letters. The first experiment had an interval of 500 ms between the participant's response to one display and the presentation of the next display. A second experiment increased that interval to 1,200 ms. In follow-up work, Stoltzfus, Hasher, Zacks, Ulivi, and Goldstein (1993) reported two more experiments using the same letter naming task, with intervals both shorter (300 ms) and longer (1,700) than used previously. Still, the results from both of these studies did not differ from the first Hasher et al. finding: Young adults but not old adults showed evidence of negative priming.

Kane, Hasher, Stoltzfus, Zacks, and Connelly (1994) tested the notion that stimulus display duration in previous work was too brief for the inhibitory processes of older adults to be brought to bear. They presented displays containing two words arranged vertically, one printed in red ink and one printed in green. The participant's task was simply to read aloud the red target word and to ignore the green word. With display durations of 300 ms (and interstimulus intervals [ISIs] of 2,150 ms), they observed significant negative priming in young adults but not in older adults. In a second experiment involving only older adults that increased display duration to 500 ms (and the same ISI of 2,150 ms), still no negative priming was observed in older adults. Kane et al. concluded that their results supported the claim that inhibitory processes directed at distractor identity operate less well in older adults.

Counter to these initial findings, several recent studies have reported age equivalence in identity negative priming tasks. Sullivan and Faust's (1993) task required naming one of two superimposed line drawings—one red and one green. In this case, significant negative priming was observed both in young adults and in two samples of older adults. This finding was also replicated in a subsequent study (Sullivan, Faust, & Balota, 1995) using the same task. Age equivalence in identity negative priming has also been reported by Kramer, Humphrey, Larish, and Logan (1994). Kieley and Hartley (1997) found equivalent identity suppression between young and old adults in a negative priming task using Stroop color word stimuli. Together, these studies call into question the existence of any age-related inhibitory deficit.

In their review of the negative priming and aging literature, May et al. (1995) suggested that an alternative account of negative priming in terms of episodic retrieval processes (Neill & Valdes, 1992; Neill, Valdes, Terry, & Gorfein, 1992) can explain the apparently discrepant findings, without abandoning the hypothesis of an age-related inhibitory decline. Under certain conditions the probe stimulus may elicit memory for previous instances of its presentation, and if the response tags ("respond" or "do not respond") associated with these instances do not match, performance will be slowed. This is just the case in negative priming conditions, so if episodic memory is consulted, memory processes, rather than inhibitory processes, will produce the slowing. May et al. suggested that episodic retrieval is more likely to occur in experimental contexts in which targets are repeated from prime to probe, which is true of the Sullivan and Faust (1993) and Sullivan et al. (1995) studies. Thus, May et al. concluded that the findings of Sullivan and Faust did not affect their claims about inhibitory function in aging because their task did not measure inhibitory function.

Recent work by Schooler, Neumann, Caplan, and Roberts (1997) was designed to test the age-related inhibitory deficit hypothesis in a task that was not subject to an episodic retrieval explanation of negative priming. They devised an identity negative priming task that did not involve characteristics likely to induce episodic retrieval. In two experiments, target and distractor were pictures on the prime trial and words on the probe trial. In the second experiment, the condition in which the same target was repeated across prime and probe trials was eliminated in a further effort to reduce the likelihood of episodic retrieval processes contributing to performance. Across both experiments, both old and young adults were observed to produce identity negative priming. The fact that this pattern of results occurred in a task designed to discourage episodic retrieval processes is inconsistent with the episodic retrieval explanation of age equivalence in negative priming offered by May et al. (1995). Together with the studies just described, these data do not fit neatly into performance models that cite age differences in inhibitory function as underlying age differences in selective attention.

One approach to integrating these negative priming data is to identify a theoretical framework that can explain them in terms of relevant task parameters that produce performance similarities and differences. However, Verhaeghen and De Meersman (1998) have conducted a meta-analysis of 21 studies examining negative priming in young and old adults and found no evidence that moderating variables (i.e., task parameters, such as overlapping or nonoverlapping stimuli, preparatory interval, or exposure duration) were necessary to account for the patterns of results. In addition, they found that both young and old adults produced significant negative priming effects for both identity and location suppression tasks, although there was evidence that the effect size is smaller among older adults than among young adults in the identity tasks. However, Brinley analyses of identity task data also showed that a multilayered slowing model (Cerella, 1990) provided a good fit to the data ($R^2 = .95$), indicating that general slowing can account for the pattern of results. Verhaeghen and De Meersman cited insufficient power as a possible source for sometimes conflicting patterns of results between individual studies in the literature and suggested that the meta-analytic approach can overcome such difficulties and provide a more accurate picture of the pattern of results across studies.

The findings with regard to negative priming and aging are somewhat muddled. The various findings described above illustrate some of the reasons why the negative priming paradigm has recently been called into question as the best measure of inhibitory function in selective attention and aging (e.g., Kieley & Hartley, 1997; McDowd, 1997; McDowd & Filion, 1995). Also called into question is the notion that declining inhibitory function is the best way to describe age-related decrements in selective attention; further discussion of this point is taken up in the section on theoretical considerations.

Divided Attention

In 1977, Craik wrote that "one of the clearest results in the experimental psychology of aging is the finding that older subjects are more penalized when they must divide their attention, either between two input sources, input and holding, or holding and responding" (p. 391). More recently, Kramer and Larish (1996) wrote that "one of the best examplars of a mental activity in which large and robust age-related differences have been consistently obtained is dual-task processing" (p. 83). Although this is generally the case, there have been exceptions. For example, a recent study by Hahn and Kramer (1995) examined the ability of young and old adults to divide attention between two separate locations in visual space. Participants in this study were required to decide whether two letters presented in precued, nonadjacent locations were the same. Coincident with the presentation of target letters, two distractor letters were presented between the two locations by removing a premask. Distractor letters either matched or did not match each other and matched or did not match the targets. If distractor type did not affect target performance, then it could be inferred that attention was successfully and separately allocated to two different spatial locations. With a cue–target interval of 600 ms, Hahn and Kramer observed a pattern of results suggesting that both old and young adults could divide their attention between separate spatial locations. The authors conducted a second experiment in which the cue–target interval was reduced to 150 ms to eliminate the possible confound of eye movements and a serial search of target locations, but the results did not change. Hahn and Kramer concluded that age does not affect the ability to divide attention between multiple nonadjacent locations. Interestingly, when targets and distractors are presented in previously empty space (rather than by removing a premask), both old and young adults are affected by distractor type: Neither age group can maintain attention to separate locations in this onset presentation condition. These data suggest that the ability to divide attention varies with stimulus parameters.

   One difficulty in trying to synthesize the literature on age differences in divided attention or dual-task performance stems from the fact that each study typically involves some idiosyncratic combination of tasks that participants are asked to perform simultaneously. The lack of any over-arching theory of task parameters within which to organize empirical findings complicates the task of understanding which parameters may produce age differences in dual-task performance. It may be moot anyway, as Hartley (1992) concluded on the basis of his review of the literature that "the processes involved in doing two things concurrently are probably qualitatively quite similar in younger and older adults. The differences are caused by the fact that each of the component processes is affected by aging" (p. 32).

Salthouse, Fristoe, Lineweaver, and Coon (1995) reached a similar conclusion in their study of divided attention in aging. Instead of attempting a systematic evaluation of the many task parameters that may contribute to age differences in divided attention ability, Salthouse et al. asked whether age differences in dual-task performance might be predicted from age differences in the component tasks. They asked young and old adults to perform a reaction time task during the retention interval of a letter memory task. In this way, attention was divided between maintaining the target letters in memory and performing the reaction time task. Across two experiments, they varied the memory load in the letter memory task and the amount of processing required in the reaction time task. Their analysis strategy was to attempt to account for age-related variance in dual-task conditions across the various task combinations with age-related variance in the component tasks. They generally succeeded in this attempt. In all cases, the age-related variance attributable to divided attention was significantly reduced or eliminated when variance attributable to single-task performance was taken into account first. However, because there were instances of unique age-related variance remaining after single-task variance was removed, Salthouse et al. (1995) concluded that "an important priority for future research should be to determine the identity of cognitive processes associated with unique or independent age-related influences, and to specify the factors responsible for those influences as well as for the shared or common influences" (p. 70).

Kramer and Larish (1996) agreed that age-related general slowing alone cannot account for all of the observed age differences in divided-attention performance. In their review of the dual-task literature, they cited evidence that illustrates the shortcomings of the general slowing hypothesis for understanding aging and dual-task performance: disproportionate age-related divided-attention costs, larger age differences in the less complex than in more complex task combinations, and specific rather than general deficits in divided-attention situations. Kramer and Larish (1996) noted that accounts of age differences in terms of slowing are "descriptive rather than explanatory" (p. 86), but like Salthouse et al., they concluded that "much remains to be discovered about the mechanisms and strategies" (p. 106) responsible for age differences in divided-attention performance.

Tsang and Shaner (1998) made a systematic attempt to identify factors relevant to age-related declines in dual-task performance. They examined the role of age and expertise in dual-task performance in the context of Wickens' (1984) structure-specific model of dual-task interference. Wickens proposed that tasks will produce dual-task decrements to the extent that the two tasks require the same stages of processing, codes of processing, or input–output modalities. Tsang and Shaner applied this model to a group of 90 individuals aged 20 to 79 years that included both experienced pilots and nonpilots. Across a series of six sessions, participants performed a vertical-axis tracking task; an easy and difficult spatial orientation task; and two Sternberg tasks, one requiring a manual response and one requiring a vocal response. Each task was performed individually and in combination with a horizontal-axis tracking task. The dual-task combinations varied in their structural similarity based on Wickens' model, and so varied in the extent of interference they were predicted to produce. In addition, participants were required to perform task combinations under different emphasis conditions in order to assess potential age differences in the ability to flexibly allocate attention among tasks.

Tsang and Shaner (1998) presented a detailed series of analyses involving both raw performance scores and single- to dual-task difference scores. They concluded from their data that there is an age-related decline in dual-task abilities beyond that observed for the separate tasks performed on their own. These authors suggested that earlier conclusions indicating that adequate control of allocation strategies and single-task performance levels would eliminate an age-related dual-task performance deficit (e.g., Somberg & Salthouse, 1982; Wickens, Braune, & Stokes, 1987) may have been based on relatively easier single tasks. Tsang and Shaner suggested that age-related decrements in time sharing may be observed only when attentional demands are very high. They also observed that older adults were less able to produce dual-task performance trade-offs with instructions to vary task priority and concluded that older adults experience a decreased flexibility of attentional control. Finally, although expertise did not eliminate age-related performance decrements, it did, in some instances, reduce the dual-task decrement.

One advantage of studies such as Tsang and Shaner's (1998) comes from the use of a performance model that guides task selection and data interpretation. This approach makes it possible to generalize to other tasks or situations because a theoretical rationale provided the basis for the choice of task and interpretation of results. This approach is advantageous for the application of empirical data to practical problems; knowing that older adults are generally slower than young adults doesn't tell us which design features to use or avoid in creating environments, road signs, kitchen appliances, automobile dashboards, or computer software.

Kramer, Larish, and Strayer (1995) conducted a study to examine the effect of extended practice on age differences in divided-attention performance. They used two different training approaches: (a) fixed priority (FP), in which the two tasks were always to be emphasized equally in divided-attention performance, and (b) variable priority (VP), where, in addition to equal emphasis conditions, participants were instructed to emphasize one task more or less than the other across different blocks of trials. The tasks were a visual display-monitoring task (in which participants had to watch a series of gauges and reset each gauge as it reached some criterion state) and an alphabet–arithmetic task (in which the problem "K + 2 = ?" was presented, and the correct response was "M"). Speed and accuracy of response was measured for both tasks. Young and old adults performed these tasks across five sessions, for a total of 50 min of practice on the single tasks and 80 min of practice under divided-attention conditions. Following this training, participants' dual-task performance was assessed in two subsequent sessions involving a combination of new tasks. These latter sessions were designed to determine whether practice-related improvement was due to improvement with the component tasks or to improvement in the ability to divide attention between the tasks.

Results from the Kramer et al. (1995) study indicate that although practice improved performance for all groups overall, VP training led to better performance than FP training for both young and old adults. However, older adults did not achieve a performance level comparable with that of young adults; an age-related divided-attention deficit remained even after considerable practice. It is interesting to note, however, that both young and old adults in the VP training condition showed more improvement under dual-task than single-task conditions. This was not true for the adults in the FP training condition; their improvement was limited to improvement on the single tasks. In addition, the sessions in which participants' ability to transfer the benefits of practice to a new combination of tasks revealed that VP training resulted in a generalizable dual-task processing ability; both old and young VP participants showed less of a dual-task decrement with the new task combination than did the FP participants. These results indicated that training can improve divided-attention performance for older adults as well as for young adults, although the age difference in performance was not eliminated.

Kramer, Larish, Weber, and Bardell (in press) conducted a follow-up study in which practice under dual-task conditions was doubled relative to the Kramer et al. (1995) study. The initial task combination involved a target-canceling task and a one-dimensional pursuit-tracking task. Transfer to a novel set of tasks was also assessed. In addition, a subsequent retention session was included that followed initial training by 45 to 60 days. As in the earlier study, both FP and VP training conditions were included with separate groups of young and old adults. As in the earlier study, results indicated that VP training resulted in better performance than did FP training. Especially interesting was the finding that extended VP training reduced the age-related deficit in divided-attention performance, whereas FP training did not affect the magnitude of the age difference. VP and FP participants improved comparably on the single tasks, but VP participants improved at a faster rate under dual-task conditions. The transfer sessions also indicated that the VP participants were better able to generalize their divided-attention ability to a new set of tasks than were the FP participants. Finally, the VP participants showed significant retention of ability across 45 to 60 days, whereas the FP participants showed a decline in dual-task performance across the same retention interval. Together, these findings indicate that training can improve divided-attention abilities among older (and younger) adults, but the type of training also makes a difference. The varied experience obtained in performing concurrent tasks under different emphasis conditions appears to lead to the most improvement in performance among older adults, as well as to the development of a lasting and generalizable ability.

Another factor relevant to divided-attention performance among older adults was examined by Hawkins, Kramer, and Capaldi (1992). They tested two groups of older adults on a divided-attention task requiring responses to simultaneously presented auditory and visual stimuli. One group of older adults received a 10-week course in aquatic exercise and the second group served as a no-exercise control. Results indicated that the divided-attention performance of the exercise group improved significantly following the aquatic course, whereas the no-exercise group's divided-attention performance did not change across a similar time frame. Hawkins et al. hypothesized that the exercise improved cerebrovascular sufficiency, which improved frontal lobe functioning, which in turn improved attentional performance; at the present time, this hypothesis has not been tested directly.

An alternative approach to understanding age differences in dual-task performance is to simply ask older adults how they would rate their ability in such circumstances. Tun and Wingfield (1995) did just that; they developed the Divided Attention Questionnaire (DAQ) to investigate possible age differences in individuals' beliefs about their own divided-attention abilities. The DAQ is composed of items varying in difficulty and representing three domains of performance: routine activities, such as walking and doing chores; speech activities, such as talking while playing cards; and monitoring activities, such as driving while looking for a particular exit or road sign. Tun and Wingfield reported that older adults perceived all types of tasks as being more difficult than did young adults. In addition, the difficulty ratings assigned to monitoring activities increased in the older adult sample: old-old adults (aged 82–91 years) rated these types of tasks as more difficult than did the old group (aged 72–81 years), who in turn rated the activities as more difficult than the young-old group (aged 60–71 years). Tun and Wingfield suggested that these monitoring tasks involve greater levels of novelty in their performance and that this increasing difficulty rating may be consistent with other findings indicating that novel tasks are more demanding for older adults. Older adults also rated the divided-attention tasks as having become more difficult in the past 10 years. These results are consistent with other findings that divided-attention tasks are performed less well by old adults than by young adults. One question that remains concerns the issue of whether an individual's perceptions of ability are correlated with actual performance measures. Also interesting was Tun and Wingfield's finding that perceived difficulty was negatively related to the frequency with which older adults performed divided-attention tasks. The authors suggested that beliefs about attentional ability may be related to beliefs about self-efficacy and that this association may have important implications for behavior, affecting the types of activities in which older adults are likely to engage. The relation between self-efficacy and attentional behavior is deserving of further study, both for the knowledge it will generate and for potential practical outcomes it may produce that encourage challenging activities well into old age.

Other studies of dual-task performance are undertaken not to understand dual-task ability per se, but to examine the effect of processing load (combining two tasks) on some other aspect of information processing (e.g., Light & Prull, 1995; Perfect & Rabbitt, 1993; Tun & Wingfield, 1994; Tun, Wingfield, Stine, & Mecsas, 1992). These studies are typically motivated by the notion that the processing resources that fuel cognition are limited, especially in older adults, and that these resource limitations may be responsible for differences in cognitive performance. For a given combination of tasks, it is probably reasonable to compare performance by young and old adults in these types of studies. It is difficult to integrate findings across studies, however, because different task combinations may produce different patterns of age effects for different reasons, such as level of novelty, levels of processing overlap between tasks, or individual expertise. In addition, the general usefulness of capacity notions for understanding age differences has been questioned; further discussion of this point is presented in the section on theoretical approaches.

Once again, a central issue in the experimental literature concerns the question of whether attentional variables or simple slowing can best account for age differences in complex tasks, such as divided-attention situations. The studies reviewed here that bear on that question suggest that task-specific factors may indeed have a role in addition to generalized slowing. Salthouse et al. (1995) reported that although single-task performance can account for most of the variance observed in dual tasks, it cannot account for all of it. Kramer and Larish (1996) came to a similar conclusion. Tsang and Shaner (1998) made a stronger statement in favor of task-specific factors. Although not exactly providing a consensus, these studies suggest some agreement about a role for task-specific factors in determining age differences in attentional performance; these factors include task difficulty (e.g., memory load; Salthouse et al., 1995), task similarity (e.g., shared response mode; Tsang & Shaner, 1998), and task novelty (Tun & Wingfield, 1995). In addition, aerobic fitness (Hawkins et al., 1992) and extended training (Kramer et al., 1995) may be important and manipulable factors in determining the presence or absence of age deficits in attentional performance.

Switching Attention

Meeting the demands of interacting with a dynamic environment often requires that attentional focus be switched from one location to another, from one task to another, or from one component process to another. With regard to aging, switching attention has most often been studied in the context of visual–spatial locations, but recent work has also considered age differences in switching attention between different tasks. Findings with regard to aging and these two types of attention switching are considered in turn below.

Switching Between Spatial Locations. Studies designed to examine attention switching between spatial locations typically involve a cue that specifies a certain location as likely to contain target information. The extent to which individuals of different ages use this information to switch attention from fixation to the likely target location has been examined, as has the efficiency with which attention can be switched to another location when the target is presented elsewhere in the display. These studies are reviewed in the present section.

A typical task in visual–spatial switching studies involves the presentation of a cue to the likely location of a target followed by a variable interval, and then the presentation of the target. The cue may be accurate regarding the location of the subsequent target with varying frequency (e.g., 75% valid); the remaining 25% of the trials are referred to as invalid. The participant's task may be to locate the target as rapidly as possible (detection task) or to indicate the identity of the target as rapidly as possible (discrimination task). The nature of the cue can also be varied. Central cues are typically arrows or some other symbol that indicates direction; the information contained in central cues must be interpreted by the observer and then used to guide a voluntary switch of attention. Peripheral cues are typically abrupt onset stimuli that occur in one of the possible target locations; these cues are said to direct attention to that location automatically (e.g., Yantis & Jonides, 1984, 1990).

Folk and Hoyer (1992) asked whether age differences in the allocation and switching of attention would vary as a function of central or peripheral cues. They predicted that age differences would be slight or nonexistent in the automatic allocation of attention following peripheral cues but that age differences might be apparent following cues requiring voluntary, effortful attention shifts. Their two-choice discrimination task required participants to identify one of two targets that appeared in one of four possible locations. The array of possible locations in their task was created with a set of four boxes located immediately above, below, to the left, and to the right of a central fixation box. A peripheral cue consisted of the abrupt onset of four small circles surrounding one of the four location boxes. With peripheral cues, Folk and Hoyer did indeed find comparable performance for the two age groups. However, the presence or absence of age effects in the central cue condition varied with the nature of the central cue. When the cue was a directional arrow presented in the central fixation box, older adults were slower (relative to a no-cue condition) to identify the target, regardless of whether the cue was valid or invalid. That is, the presence of the central cue actually hindered the performance of older adults, whereas only the invalid cue slowed the performance of young adults relative to the neutral cue condition. In a follow-up experiment, Folk and Hoyer altered the nature of the central cue, replacing the central arrow with a larger arrowhead that appeared just outside the center box, on the same side as the direction indicated by the cue. Using this type of central cue, older adults were found to be just as efficient as young adults in shifting attention to a cued location. Folk and Hoyer interpreted the difference in age effects in their two central cue conditions as reflecting age differences in the efficiency with which central cues can be encoded, but not in the efficiency with which voluntary attention shifts are accomplished once the cue is encoded (see Allen et al., 1994, for a similar conclusion). It seems likely, however, that there is some nonsymbolic location information carried by the cues appearing outside of the central fixation box; perhaps this is what makes them easier to use for older adults. If it is this location information that assists the shift of attention in older adults, it still may be that shifts based on purely symbolic information are impaired in aging.

Greenwood and colleagues (Greenwood & Parasuraman, 1994; Greenwood, Parasuraman, & Haxby, 1993) examined the effect of central and peripheral cues on the time course of voluntary and involuntary attentional shifting in a discrimination task among adults aged 17 to 85 years. Their findings suggest that up to age 75, peripheral cues eliciting involuntary shifts of attention do not differ as a function of age, whereas central cues eliciting voluntary shifts of attention do produce an age-related increase in combined costs and benefits related to valid and invalid cues. After the age of 75, however, both voluntary and involuntary attention shifts show age-related effects (Greenwood & Parasuraman, 1994). This older group showed equivalent benefit to younger groups from valid cues, indicating that the initial allocation of attention appears not to be affected by age, but showed greater costs of invalid cues, suggesting that the subsequent requirement to disengage and switch attention to another location is impaired in advanced age. Although the age of 75 years is somewhat arbitrary as a cutoff for the presence or absence of attention allocation effects, these results suggest that the age composition of samples has a role in the outcome regarding age effects.

Lincourt, Folk, and Hoyer (1997) compared the time course of attentional allocation among young and old adults in response to central and peripheral cues. Part of their interest in comparing the role of central and peripheral cues was to evaluate single-factor accounts of aging and attention against mechanism-specific models. Their task involved cue–target intervals ranging between 0 ms and 300 ms, employed both peripheral and central cues using a within-subject design, and required a speeded two-choice target identification decision. They found that the cuing effects indicated a similar time course of attention shifts following central cues, but not following peripheral cues. The magnitude of peripheral cuing effects was larger for old adults than for young adults, particularly at the longer cue–target intervals. Lincourt et al. noted that this finding is consistent with others (e.g., Greenwood & Parasuraman, 1994; Juola, Koshino, & Warner, 1996) showing that the effects of automatic allocation of attention believed to follow peripheral cues are typically larger for old adults than for young adults. Interpretation of these differences in the Lincourt et al. study is complicated, however, by the absence of any cuing effects among young adults in the peripheral cue conditions. Lincourt et al. suggested that this may be due to the display conditions used in their study to produce acceptable levels of accuracy among older adults; these conditions differed from previous studies in which peripheral cuing effects had been observed among young adults. The question of general versus specific deficits in aging is left unanswered by this study; although the pattern of results suggests differential effects as a function of cue type, the absence of peripheral cue effects among young adults prevents any strong conclusion.

Yamaguchi, Tsuchiya, and Kobayashi (1995) examined electrophysiological correlates of attention shifting in young and old adults in a target detection task that included both peripheral and central cue conditions. They varied cue–target intervals between 200 ms and 800 ms. Eighty percent of the cues were valid; 20% were invalid. In addition to target detection times, electrophysiological activity in the interval between cue and target was measured to assess age differences in neural activity during attentional shifts. The pattern of target detection times they observed did not differ as a function of age, although older adults were slower overall; for both young and old adults, validly cued trials were faster than invalidly cued trials and longer cue–target intervals produced short detection times. These age similarities held for both central and peripheral cue types. However, Yamaguchi et al. observed different patterns of event-related potentials (ERPs) produced in the brain in the two cue conditions; older adults were more like young adults in the peripheral cue conditions than in the central cue condition. On the basis of the differing patterns of brain activity following central cues among the two age groups, they concluded from their data that electrophysiological components of voluntary attention shifts are affected by age. Age similarities in brain activity following peripheral cues suggest that the components of involuntary shifts are not affected by age. According to Yamaguchi et al. (1995), these "different effects of age on ERPs generated by voluntary and reflexive shift mechanisms appear to support the notion that these two attentional mechanisms involve distinct neural systems with differential vulnerability to aging" (p. 48). However, the assumption that dissociation implies distinct mechanisms is not supported by any direct evidence in this study. In addition, the performance data did not show any evidence for age differences as a function of cue type. Thus, more work is required before any conclusions can be made regarding brain mechanisms underlying age differences in attention switching.

In his review of the literature on the time course of attention switching in cuing tasks, Hartley (1992) concluded that "the presence or absence of age differences in the time course of cue utilization is still an open question" (p. 18). Studies conducted subsequent to Hartley's review have attempted to identify relevant task parameters that affect the time course of attentional allocation, with the goal of perhaps bringing some order to the previous findings. For example, Gottlob and Madden (1998) examined the contribution of age-related sensory differences to possible differences in the time course of switching attention following peripheral cues. They used accuracy as a dependent measure in order to eliminate the possible confounding of nonattentional factors, such as motor processes or response selection processes, and varied stimulus duration individually for each participant in order to equate baseline performance levels across age groups. The task involved the presentation of a peripheral location cue (valid on 75% of the trials) and then a target, which was the letter T presented in one of four orientations (upright, upside down, rotated 90° to the left, rotated 90° to the right). The participant's task was to indicate in which of the four orientations the target was presented. The interval between cue and target was variable; accuracy levels plotted against interval describe the time course of attentional allocation. Their analyses indicated that the attentional processes examined in this study were age invariant, showing a similar time course across age groups. The authors suggested that the allocation of attention does not suffer any age-related slowing, but they recognized that this conclusion was based on a study using abrupt onset peripheral cues, only two potential target locations, and no near distractors. Other combinations of task parameters might produce a different pattern of results.

Atchley and Kramer (1998) used a spatial cuing paradigm to look at attention switching between depths in three-dimensional space. They used luminance cues to indicate the probable location of a target in a four-location display; in each trial, two of the locations were further in depth relative to the fixation point than the other two locations. Response times to indicate which of two targets were presented were measured following valid, invalid, and neutral cues. In addition, on a subset of the invalid cues (requiring a switch of attention), the target appeared at a different depth than had the cue. Results indicated that both young and old adults were slowed by switching attention between depths (for both closer to farther depths and farther to closer depths), and the magnitude of this cost was the same in the two age groups, suggesting that three-dimensional attention does not change as a function of adult age.

Madden, Connelly, and Pierce (1994) examined attention switching in the presence of nontarget information. In an earlier study using peripheral location cues, Madden (1992) had reported that the time required to shift attention between display locations was longer for old adults than for young adults. However, nontarget distractor stimuli were always present in that study; the Madden et al. study included a condition in which no distractor information was present. This condition also used a peripheral cue and permitted a purer estimate of the time required to shift attention from one display location to another. Results indicated that in the absence of distractors, this shift time was essentially zero for both young and old adults. A second experiment addressed whether the nature of the distractor information was relevant to the age differences observed by Madden. In that study, the distractors were letters of the alphabet and the task was to indicate the identity of the target letter. Madden et al. used asterisks as distractors to examine shifting time in the presence of distractors that could elicit little processing. Results indicated that the time to shift attention was significantly greater than zero and was significantly greater for old adults than for young adults. Thus, whether or not age differences in the time taken to switch attention among locations in visual space will be observed depends on the visual context. The presence of distracting nontarget information appears to slow older adults more than young adults, but estimates of pure switching time do not seem to vary as a function of adult age.

A recent study by Madden and Gottlob (1997) examined age differences in the ability to switch attention between a narrow and broad focus using a flanker task. In their task (based on that developed by LaBerge, Brown, Carter, Bash, & Hartley, 1991), the identity of a letter located in the middle of a 17-character display determined whether a response was required to a second 17-item display in which the central target letter was flanked by response-compatible letters or response-incompatible letters. LaBerge et al. had varied the interval between onset of the first display and onset of the second display (SOA) between blocks and observed that the flanker compatibility effect (difference in response times when flankers were compatible with the appropriate response compared with trials on which flankers were incompatible with the appropriate response) was greater when the SOA was greater. They hypothesized that the longer time spent waiting for the second display led to an increase in the breadth of attention and thus greater opportunity for flankers to have their effect. Madden and Gottlob's analysis of this finding was that there is apparently an involuntary broadening of attention with increasing SOA, and they altered the task to examine this phenomenon on a trial-by-trial basis in young and older adults. In their first experiment, they varied within blocks the interval between onset of the first display and the SOA to assess the possibility of a dynamic switching of attention from a narrow focus to a broad focus. Their results indicated that an increased broadening of attention does accompany increased SOA, as evidenced by greater compatibility effects with increased SOA. With regard to aging, they found that the magnitude of compatibility effects as a function of SOA was comparable for young and old adults, indicating no age differences in focusing or broadening of attention or in the distracting effect of flankers.

A second experiment was designed to provide more of a challenge to presumably preserved attentional functioning in age. The experimental task was basically the same as in the first experiment just described, but the location of the target in the second display was varied unpredictably among five possible locations. Madden and Gottlob (1997) hypothesized that spatial uncertainty might alter the ability of older adults to avoid differential negative effects of the flanking distractors. What they found, however, was that young adults were more negatively affected by flankers in the second experiment than were old adults. This finding suggests that young adults were more likely to switch to a broad attentional focus to include a range of possible target locations when target location was uncertain, although they paid the price for this in terms of greater slowing in the presence of incompatible flankers. Older adults did not broaden their attentional focus, even when target location was uncertain. Madden and Gottlob interpreted this age difference in susceptibility to disruption by flankers as reflecting a strategic difference in the allocation of attention. They suggested that older adults apparently preferred the more conservative strategy of maintaining a narrow focus, thereby minimizing all effects of flanker information, and concluded that there appear to be age differences in strategic components of attentional control.

Another study designed to examine age differences (between young-old and old-old adults) in narrowing and broadening the focus of attention during visual search was reported by Greenwood, Parasuraman, and Alexander (1997). Their visual search task involved a 2 × 5 or 3 × 5 array of letters and required participants to decide whether the target letter, a pink *T*, was present or absent in the display. The entire display was made up of green, blue, or pink letters (*N*s, *G*s, and *T*s). An outline precue varying in size indicated the probable location of the target, with cue size ranging from surrounding the entire array, to one column of the array, to a single element in the array. The search task was carried out under three conditions: (a) color only, in which the display contained only one pink item; (b) color + letter, in which equal numbers of pink items and *T*s appeared in the display; and (c) confined search, in which only two display items were pink. Participants were young-old adults (aged 63–74 years), old-old adults (aged 75–81 years), and a sample of individuals with early dementia of the Alzheimer type (DAT; aged 50–84). Overall, search performance was fairly similar for the three groups in the color-only condition, with response time little affected by either display size or cue size. In both the color + letter condition and the confined-search condition, search performance differed more among the three groups with smaller, as opposed to larger, cue sizes in a way that indicates that any search advantage offered by increased cue precision was diminished in the old-old and DAT groups relative to the young-old group. Greenwood et al. (1997) concluded that old-old adults and individuals with DAT "have difficulties in controlling the spatial focus of attention"; because the extent of cuing effects was greatest among young-old adults, less among old-old adults, and least among individuals with DAT, Greenwood et al. also concluded that "these results point to a continuum of efficiency in the modulation of spatial attention" (p. 11).

Cuing effects appear to be comparable in young and old adults, at least with peripheral, exogenous cues (Folk & Hoyer, 1992; Greenwood & Parasuraman, 1994; Madden et al., 1994; Yamaguchi et al., 1995). Factors that produce age differences in favor of young adults include the presence of distractors (Madden et al., 1994) and the use of central, endogenous cues (Folk & Hoyer, 1992; Greenwood & Parasuraman, 1994; Yamaguchi et al., 1995). Attempts to measure the manner, time course, and flexibility with which attention is allocated indicate age equivalence (Atchley & Kramer, 1998; Gottlob & Madden, 1998; Madden & Gottlob, 1997), at least until later old age (Greenwood et al., 1997).

Switching Between Tasks. Attention switching has also been examined in terms of alternating performance between separate tasks. For example, Hawkins et al. (1992) had young and old adults perform a two-choice response time task to auditory stimuli, a two-choice response time task to visual stimuli, and a two-choice response time task that alternated between visual and auditory stimuli. All participants were slower on the alternating-task version compared with either the auditory or the visual task alone, and older adults were more slowed than were young adults. This greater slowing among older adults held even when single-task response speed was taken into account. As part of the same experiment discussed earlier in the context of divided attention, Hawkins et al. examined the possibility that increased aerobic fitness might improve the ability of older adults on the attention-switching task. A group of older adults participated in an aquatic exercise program of three weekly exercise sessions across 10 weeks. At the conclusion of this program, the older adults in the exercise program and an age-matched comparison group that had not participated in the exercise activities were compared on their performance abilities in the switching task. The exercise group's performance in the switching task improved significantly following the exercise program, whereas the control group's switching performance did not change. Hawkins et al. (1992) suggested that the mechanism of this effect may be improved cerebrovascular sufficiency and concluded that their results "indicate that a short-term program of mild aerobic exercise can have beneficial effects on attentional capacity in the healthy aging population" (p. 651).

In another study of attention switching among young and old adults, Kramer, Hahn, and Gopher (in press) reported a series of experiments in which they measured the time required to switch from performing one task to performing a second task. In their first experiment, a stimulus display contained between 1 and 10 instances of the digits 1 through 10. Participants performed one of two two-choice response time tasks. In the "digit identity" task, responses were to be made on the basis of whether the digit identity was less than 5 or greater than 5 (the number 5 was never presented). In the "digit quantity" task, responses were made on the basis of whether greater than five instances were present in the display or less than five instances were present (exactly five instances were never presented). The tasks were performed in single-task blocks, in which only one or the other task was required, or in switch blocks, in which a signal to switch to the other task was presented at unpredictable intervals within a block of trials. Participants in the Kramer et al. study performed these tasks across three 90-min sessions. Kramer et al. reasoned that the time required to accomplish the switch to a different task reflected the time to carry out the relevant processes required to abandon one task and begin the other. Their results showed that switch costs (slowing of response time just following an attention switch relative to no-switch response times) were greater for old adults than for young adults in the initial sessions but that by the end of the third session, switch costs were equivalent for old and young adults. These findings suggest that attention-switching ability is comparable in young and old adults if sufficient practice is provided.

Kramer et al. (in press) followed up this finding with another experiment designed to test the hypothesis that response–stimulus interval (RSI) and working memory load might produce age differences in attention switching, even with substantial practice. They examined both short and long ISIs (200 ms, 400 ms, 800 ms, and 1,600 ms) on the hypothesis that older adults may require more time to prepare and execute a switch that longer ISIs could hide. In addition, instead of an external signal to switch from one task to the other, the subsequent experiment required participants to switch attention after every five responses. This manipulation increases memory load because participants had to keep track of how many responses they had made in order to correctly switch at five-response intervals. Under these task conditions, older adults had significantly greater switch costs, and this age difference in switch costs was maintained over a number of trials comparable with that of the first experiment. RSI did not significantly affect switch costs. Kramer et al. (in press) concluded that "increased working memory load that resulted from the requirement to keep track of the trial sequence in the present study served to diminish the abililty of the older adults to capitalize on practice to reduce switch costs" (p. 30). Together, the two experiments described here begin to identify boundaries for age equivalence and age deficits in attention switching: Extended practice and low memory load allow age equivalence; increased memory load produces an age deficit. Thus, although attention-switching ability per se can be equivalent in old and young adults, an added memory load serves to slow switching more in old adults than in young adults.

Kramer et al. (in press) conducted further analyses on their data to test (a) whether the processes underlying the separate tasks were different from those required to accomplish a switch between tasks and (b) whether aging affected the separate tasks and the switching processes in similar or different ways. They concluded from an analysis of residuals following a regression of switch times and single-task response times that task-switching processes are distinct from the processes subserving the individual tasks. Two additional analyses led them to the conclusion that aging affects attention switching differently than it affects component task processes: A regression of old and young adults' response times was not well fit by a single, linear function, suggesting differential effects of aging on the two types of processes, and a hierarchical regression identified unique, age-related variance in attention-switching speed even after component task variance was removed. These findings suggest that aging affects the two types of processes differently and that "general slowing in and of itself is not sufficient to account for age related performance differences in switch and non-switch performance" (Kramer et al., in press, p. 34).

A recent study by Salthouse, Fristoe, McGuthry, and Hambrick (1998) also examined attention switching between separate tasks in a sample of adults between the ages of 18 and 80 years. Their study was designed to examine attention switching as a possible "cognitive primitive" that may underlie a variety of age differences in other cognitive processes. They administered three sets of tasks under conditions that required either (a) the repeated performance of one or the other of the component tasks or (b) the switching of attention between tasks. The tasks all involved the presentation of digits; the first task set involved two digits presented in a row and required a response based on either the digit on the right or on the left, the second task set involved a single digit and required assessing the digit for odd or even values or values greater or less than 5, and the third set required that two presented digits be either added or subtracted. The signal to switch attention was a rectangle surrounding the digit(s) and was presented simultaneously with a stimulus display at unpredictable intervals during a sequence of trials. The response time results showed that attention switching was slower among older adults compared with young adults, both in the first half and the second half of trials. Similar to the finding reported by Kramer et al. (in press), factor analyses conducted by Salthouse et al. indicated that attention switching is a distinct construct, separate from component task processes. However, structural equation modeling and single common factor analysis led Salthouse et al. to a different conclusion than that reached by Kramer et al. with regard to the role of aging in component task and attention-switching processes. That is, the analyses conducted by Salthouse et al. indicated that although attention switching is a meaningful theoretical construct that is related to age, it is not unique in its relation to other cognitive processes. Thus, attention switching does not appear to be a cognitive primitive. Rather, the relations between attention switching and aging and between attention switching and other cognitive processes appear to be mediated by another construct, such as overall speed of processing.

As was the case for divided attention, aerobic fitness (Hawkins et al., 1992) and extended training (Kramer et al., in press) may be important factors in determining age-related differences in performance. Increasing component task demands (Kramer et al., in press) tends to increase age deficits in performance. The most parsimonious model of age differences suggests that general slowing mediates much of the age-related deficit in attention switching (Salthouse et al., 1998).

Sustained Attention

Sustained attention is the ability to maintain concentration or focus over time. The term *vigilance* is often used to describe this mode of attentional functioning, as well as to describe tasks that assess sustained attention abilities. The literature contains relatively few investigations of age differences in vigilance task performance, and those studies that do exist show little evidence for age-related declines in performance across time (see Giambra, 1993, for a review). However, a study by Mouloua and Parasuraman (1995) identified some conditions in which age differences are observed. They manipulated event rate (low, high) and target location certainty (low, moderate, high) in a vigilance task requiring target identification across 30-min sessions. They found that task performance deteriorated across time at a faster rate for old adults than for young adults when event rate was high and target location certainty was low. These results suggest that sustained attention performance does change with age, at least when demands on visual attention are great.

Two other recent studies suggest that fitness level may affect sustained attention, particularly for older adults. Bunce, Warr, and Cochrane (1993) examined sustained attention on a trial-by-trial basis in a four-choice reaction time task. They were interested in the occurrence of performance blocks, defined as occasional very long response times, apparently due to breaks in concentration (Bills, 1931). They had 116 male white-collar workers between the ages of 17 and 63 years perform 400 trials of the choice response time task and counted the number of blocks, defined as responses on which response time exceeded 1,000 ms (average response time was 580 ms). Overall, age was positively correlated with the frequency of blocks, but this association was moderated by fitness level. After subdividing the participants by aerobic fitness level (measured by a composite score based on body mass, body fat, and lung function), analyses showed that fitness was unrelated to blocks in young adults, but among older adults, the unfit men produced a particularly large number of blocks. Bunce et al. interpreted this finding as suggesting an age-related vulnerability to inhibitory failures that affect concentration and sustained attention, particularly for less fit individuals.

A subsequent study by Bunce, Barrowclough, and Morris (1996) used the same choice response time task as in the study just described, as well as a sustained attention task in which a long series of degraded digit stimuli were visually presented at a rate of one per second over the course of 10 min and participants were required to make a keypress when they detected a 0 (Neuchterlein, Parasuraman, & Jiang, 1983). Participants were 90 postal workers: 48 men and women between the ages of 18 and 30 years (the young group) and 42 men and women between the ages of 43 and 62 (the older group). Bunce et al. reported more attentional blocks (again defined as response times exceeding 1,000 ms) on the choice response time task among older and less fit individuals. Indeed, the age and fitness factors produced an interaction such that the older, less fit individuals produced more blocks than any of the other three groups. They wanted to conclude that increased blocks among the older, less fit individuals represent a failure to maintain attention to task allowing "intrusions into information processing" (Bunce et al., 1996, p. 676). However, their conclusion had to be tempered by the finding that mean response time was correlated with block frequency, indicating that the two measures are related. When they reanalyzed the block data with mean response time as a covariate, the Age × Fitness interaction was no longer significant, leading to their conclusion that processing speed can account for much of the variance in the block data.

Data from the sustained attention task included A' (a nonparametric index of sensitivity). The A' analyses showed an Age × Fitness interaction, indicating that older adults, particularly older, less fit individuals, showed reduced target detection levels. However, the vigilance decrement (change in detection accuracy over time) did not vary as a function of age. This finding fits with earlier work on sustained attention and aging, suggesting maintained abilities across the adult life span, although it is important to note again that these findings are based on a sample of relatively young working people. Bunce et al.'s (1996) findings also suggest that aerobic fitness may be an important moderator variable, at least for age-related response slowing. As will be described below, the interpretation of blocks as failures of attention is not uncontested.

The conclusions of Bunce and colleagues with regard to sustained attention are related to the question of attention as cause or consequence in understanding behavior. Clearly, their assumption is that lapses of attention cause slower and less efficient behavior among older adults. Salthouse (1993) deduced a series of testable predictions about response time distributions from this view of slowing and tested them using response time data young and old adults had produced in the performance of the Digit Symbol task and the Digit Digit task. The Digit Symbol task requires participants to indicate as rapidly as possible whether a digit and a symbol presented on a computer display match any digit–symbol pairs presented in a code table. The Digit Digit task is similar but requires participants to indicate simply whether two presented digits are the same or different. Salthouse observed that older adults responded more slowly than did young adults, but he also reported a pattern of results that was not consistent with an attentional blocking view of age-related slowing. For example, in regression analyses, he observed that age differences in the slowest responses were largely mediated through age-related effects on the fastest responses. In other words, no support was found for the attentional blocking prediction that the slowest response times would be produced by a unique age-related (attentional) influence. Salthouse (1993) concluded that attentional blocks as described by Bunce and colleagues were "a consequence, rather than a cause, of the age-related slowing phenomenon" (p. P269). This conclusion appears to contradict Spieler et al.'s (1996) ex-Gaussian analysis of age differences in Stroop response time distributions (discussed previously); the difference may be due to differences in analysis methods or in the tasks that produced the data. In support of the latter possibility, Salthouse found little or no age-related influence on skewness, whereas Spieler et al. based their conclusion regarding qualitative age differences in performance on their observed differences in skewness. It may be that in some cases attention is a cause in age-related speed of behavior, but it appears that more work with sophisticated analysis techniques will be required to resolve that question.

Evidence related to sustained attention indicates age equivalence in vigilance task performance (Bunce et al., 1996; Giambra, 1993). There is some evidence to suggest that increasing vigilance task difficulty by increasing event rate or target location uncertainty does produce age-related decrements in performance relative to young adults.

FUNCTIONAL CONSEQUENCES OF AGING AND ATTENTION

Attentional processes are involved in a variety of other cognitive functions; therefore, any attentional deficits will have a variety of functional consequences. A number of broad theories of cognitive aging in the information-processing tradition have pointed to attentional deficits as the source of all or most age-related changes in cognition. Notable among these are the inhibition-deficit view (e.g., Hasher & Zacks, 1988) and the variety of processing resource views, particularly those based on attention or effort as the primary resource (e.g., Craik & Byrd, 1982; Hasher & Zacks, 1979). Some specific topics that have seen recent work from those perspectives are comprehension, memory, and intelligence. (Other chapters in this volume also address some of these topics and at least touch on the role of attentional theory in accounting for age-related change; e.g., chap. 5 on memory and chap. 6 on language.) In addition to these theoretical accounts of attention in higher order cognitive processes, a number of researchers have examined the direct (and indirect) consequences of attentional deficits on daily living, in such domains as learning, driving, safety, and problem solving (see chap. 10, this volume, for a review of applied work on aging). In the sections that follow, we examine some selected areas of research to illustrate the ways in which the role of attention in other behaviors has been considered, reviewing briefly the major findings. The review focuses on language and memory as representative of the cognitive consequences of attentional dysfunction, then driving and problem solving as representative of more applied concerns.

Cognitive Consequences

Language. Language comprehension often takes place in the context of multiple sources competing for attention. Attending to one source and maintaining that focus represents a classic illustration of focusing on relevant information and inhibiting irrelevant information (cf. Stoltzfus et al., 1993). In addition, as a conversation proceeds, a person may find multiple associations to the content of the speech of the other participants in the conversation, some of which will become a part of the person's own input to the conversation and others of which will be suppressed. Likewise, conversations often include moments when the speaker is unclear, and one interpretation may persist for a while, but then be altered; the first interpretation needs to be suppressed (at least in part) for a coherent conversation to proceed. Such processing can also be described as relying heavily on attentional resources. Language processing, of course, refers to a broad range of specific activities: Comprehension of text and speech are two topics that have been studied in recent years from the perspective of attentional deficits. Because a more comprehensive review of language can be found elsewhere in this volume, only highlights of that research are discussed here. A recent analysis of language processing focusing on the role of attention can also be found in the exchange between Zacks and Hasher (1997) and Burke (1997).

A number of recent studies have examined the role of selective attention in determining the ability of older and younger adults to comprehend text in the presence of irrelevant information. A frequently cited series of studies has made use of a reading with distraction task (Carlson et al., 1995; Connelly et al., 1991; Dywan & Murphy, 1996). Those studies demonstrated that older adults have a greater difficulty ignoring distractors embedded in text (as indexed by increased reading times) and are particularly negatively affected by semantically related distractors. These results have been taken as evidence in favor of an inhibitory deficit (e.g., Zacks & Hasher, 1994, 1997).

Dywan and Murphy (1996), in an extension of the work by Carlson et al. (1995) and Connelly et al. (1991), also reported results in which text comprehension was negatively affected by the presence of distractors, especially for older adults. Dywan and Murphy used the same arrangement of materials as Connelly et al., with target words of a passage interrupted unpredictably by irrelevant phrases in italics. Connelly et al. had found that when the irrelevant phrases were semantically related to the target text, older but not younger adults read more slowly than when the irrelevant phrases were semantically unrelated. Dywan and Murphy extended the exploration of the meaningfulness of the distraction. Rather than using simply related words as distractors, Dywan and Murphy's distractors, if read, altered the meaning of the passage. For example, in one passage, the target text described a brutal sea captain with few redeeming characteristics. The distractors included such phrases as *fair minded, bravely rescued,* and *heroism.* Reading times replicated earlier work, but older adults were significantly more likely to confuse distractors in a multiple-choice recognition test for phrases from the text (e.g., they might choose *fair minded* instead of *brutal*). Thus, the failure of selective attention among older adults had, as a consequence, reduced comprehension. The finding of poorer selective attention among older adults is consistent with the basic inhibition-deficit view. However, the unexpected result occurred in a surprise recognition test for the distractor phrases: Younger adults were more accurate than the older adults. The younger adults supposedly had suppressed the distractors, and thus should not have remembered them; the older adults supposedly had not suppressed the distractors, and thus should have remembered them well. In an effort to account for these results, Dywan and Murphy provided a source-monitoring interpretation (see also Burke, 1997): For both younger and older adults, the targets and distractors were available, but only the younger adults could discriminate, for example, which word to respond with in the memory test (on the basis of its "source" as target or distractor).

A similar analysis has been made (Burke, 1997) of some related work by Hartman (1995) and Hartman and Hasher (1991). Hartman and Hasher encouraged participants to anticipate endings to sentences such as "She ladled the soup into her ____," and then provided either the expected ending (*bowl*) or an unexpected ending (*lap*). Participants were told to remember the provided ending; later they were given an opportunity to produce either word as endings to other sentences. Older adults, but not younger adults, showed an increased likelihood of producing nonpresented but expected words (like *bowl*), demonstrating that such words were maintained even when they were disconfirmed. Burke argued that this could be interpreted as evidence that older adults failed to discriminate which word (expected or unexpected ending) was presented versus which was generated; that is, they could not remember the source. However, a source-monitoring explanation seems incomplete. Such an explanation fails to account for the online difficulties for older adults in these experiments (e.g., disproportionately increased reading time in the presence of distractors). A discrimination difficulty combined with a failure to inhibit may be relevant. Hartman found that when the status of an item as target or distractor (unexpected vs. expected ending when the unexpected ending was to be remembered) was sufficiently ambigous, younger adults demonstrated the same pattern as did older adults in the Hartman and Hasher's study. Age differences were most apparent with the greatest amount of ambiguity (e.g., when both words were presented and the participant had to select the unexpected one). Likewise, in the reading with distraction studies, age differences were moderated by physical and semantic distinctions between targets and distractors, to the point of disappearing with sufficient support for discriminating (e.g., Carlson et al., 1995). Thus, the difficulty appears to lie in discriminating distractors from targets at the time of presentation, a relatively long-standing idea in aging and selective attention (e.g., Farkas & Hoyer, 1980; Nebes & Madden, 1983). This failure to discriminate and then suppress alters interpretations and increases processing time (e.g., Dywan & Murphy, 1996), leads to the maintenance of irrelevant interpretations (e.g., Hamm & Hasher, 1992; Hartman & Hasher, 1991), and leads to errors in memory subsequently.

Research on text comprehension, then, is generally in line with the inhibition-deficit theory and demonstrates nicely the role of attention in this domain of cognitive aging. However, it is also clear that such an interpretation is controversial (Burke, 1997; Zacks & Hasher, 1997) and that further methodological and theoretical work is needed to clarify the collection of results (cf. McDowd, 1997).

Another area of research on language and aging that is relevant to attention is speech comprehension. Tun and Wingfield and their colleagues have conducted a program of research focused primarily on the role of processing resources in producing age differences in performance (see chap. 6, this volume). As Tun and Wingfield (1993) noted in their review of research on speech perception in older adults, the characteristics of speech clearly lead to a prediction of an age deficit in comprehension: Speech, they noted, is fast, with the rate controlled by the speaker; it requires extensive use of working memory resources; and it involves auditory processes that decline regularly with age. All of these factors relate to cognitive skills noted consistently in other contexts to show age-related deficits (Tun & Wingfield, 1993). However, despite deficits in those component processes or skill domains older adults do quite well in studies of speech comprehension (Tun & Wingfield, 1993; chap. 6, this volume). They accounted for the paradox between expectations from age differences in the underlying processes and the data on age-equivalence in speech comprehension by reference primarily to attentional-resource-relevant notions. They suggested that language skills are automatic, encapsulated, and an area of expertise in older adults. The lifetime experience of older adults allows them "to exploit whatever linguistic context is available, using the redundancy and predictability of language to compensate for deficits in lower-level cognitive skills" (Tun & Wingfield, 1993, p. 449).

Nevertheless, Tun and Wingfield (1994) noted that "one might question how far language processing abilities in the elderly hold up under the stress of increases in processing load" (p. 29). Much of the research program of the Brandeis group in recent years can be characterized as addressing that question, when the limits are pushed beyond normal speech situations (e.g., Tun & Stanko, 1997; Tun, Wingfield, & Stine, 1991; Tun et al., 1992; Wingfield, Aberdeen, & Stine, 1991; Wingfield, Tun, & Rosen, 1995). Some of the results of that work include greater age decrements in performance of a secondary task in a divided-attention context (e.g., Tun et al., 1991), greater memory deficits (for detail but not for gist) when text passages contained less redundancy or predictability (e.g., Tun & Wingfield, 1994), and greater difficulty with faster speech (e.g., Tun et al., 1992). Thus, speech comprehension under certain demanding circumstances is sensitive to aging, and researchers have attributed the effects to the aging of attentional resources.

Memory. Information-processing psychology generally posits at least three ways in which attention is relevant to remembering: proper selection of what should be remembered, concentration or maintenance of attention to what should be remembered (or the corollary ability to avoid distraction), and the resources to accomplish more complex processing of information. Thus, attribution of memory deficits in old age to attentional deficits of some sort has a long-standing tradition in cognitive aging theory (e.g., Craik, 1977). Light (1991) noted that reduced processing resources was one of the four major classes of hypotheses about aging and memory; attentional capacity was one of three resource-based explanations (along with working memory and slowing). Specifically, attentional capacity was considered relevant to encoding and retrieval strategies (because strategies are effortful and demand resources) and to different memory processes that differ in resource demands (e.g., Craik & McDowd, 1987). Light reviewed the findings in two primary domains of memory with respect to attentional capacity: working memory and long-term memory. The dominant method for examining attentional capacity is examining the consequences of divided attention on memory performance. She noted that there was conflicting evidence of the impact of divided attention in both of these domains. More pointedly, Light (1991) noted that progress in this area was hampered by "a lack of clarity as to the nature of the concepts of attention or effort" and because "the precise manner in which attention might affect the operation of mechanisms responsible for storage and retrieval of information has not been specified" (p. 363).

Since Light's (1991) review, a number of researchers have investigated the impact of divided attention on memory (e.g., Einstein, Smith, McDaniel, & Shaw, 1997; Light & Prull, 1995; Mäntylä & Bäckman, 1992; Nyberg, Nilsson, Olofsson, & Bäckman, 1997; Whiting & Smith, 1997; see chap. 5, this volume, for a summary of the findings in this area). These researchers have demonstrated that a wide variety of memory functions are sensitive to aging when attention is drawn away from them by a secondary task. For example, Einstein et al. found that older adults showed a deficit in prospective memory tasks when there is an increase in other activities (simulated in their study with a digit-monitoring task). Whiting and Smith extended the work of Craik and McDowd (1987) by dividing the attention of younger and older adults during recognition and recall, finding that recall was more effortful than recognition and more effortful for older than for younger adults. Mäntylä and Bäckman successfully simulated aging effects in younger adults by requiring them to count backward during encoding. However, Light and Prull found no evidence of differential effects of divided attention for older adults in repetition priming (word naming), recognition, or recall, despite clear age decrements in all three tasks under divided attention and age differences in recall and recognition. However, interpretation of their results is complicated by an age difference in performance on the secondary task in divided attention. Performance on that task was not assessed in isolation, so it is not clear whether the lack of age differences in memory is due to differential emphasis with age; older adults might have had a larger negative effect in memory performance if they had performed equally to young adults on the secondary task.

Another approach to exploring the role of attention in memory, of course, is the inhibition view, which has consistently considered memory performance deficits as a central consequence of the inhibitory deficit (Hasher & Zacks, 1988; Hasher, Zacks, & May, in press). By this view, irrelevant information will enter working memory (through deficient access and deficient restraint of strong responses—in Zacks & Hasher's, 1997, terms) and stay there when it should not (deficient deletion). Two memorial consequences should be demonstrable: First, because working memory contains extra information, memory for the relevant information should be poorer because it must share time with the irrelevant information, and second, memory for irrelevant information should be better than expected. However, the extent to which this pattern of results has been obtained is controversial (e.g., Burke, 1997; Hasher et al., in press; Zacks & Hasher, 1997); much of the work relevant to this controversy is considered elsewhere in this chapter (in evaluating the theory and in the review of text comprehension, above).

Finally, recent work by May, Hasher, and Kane (cited in Zacks & Hasher, 1997) suggested that some of the age differences in memory generally may be caused by an inhibitory deficit. These researchers demonstrated that items from the early trials in a standard span-measurement procedure interfere with performance on later trials (because of a failure to delete these items efficiently from working memory, according to the theory). Because older adults are more prone to interference of this kind, they are at a disadvantage on later trials, which are used to measure higher levels of memory span. Thus, traditional measures of memory span may underestimate the ability of older adults. To the extent that memory span serves as a resource for episodic memory (e.g., D. C. Park et al., 1996), age differences in memory may, in fact, be related to age differences in attention.

Applied Consequences

Driving. Research exploring driving behavior among older adults has produced a reasonably large literature on the role of visual attention in older drivers (e.g., Ball, Owsley, Sloane, Roenker, & Bruni, 1993; Ball & Rebok, 1994; Barr & Eberhard, 1994; Holland & Rabbitt, 1994; Owsley, Ball, Sloane, Roenker, & Bruni, 1991; Parasuraman & Nestor, 1991). Owsley et al. (1991) characterized the driving task as involving "a visually cluttered array, both primary and secondary visual tasks, and simultaneous use of central and peripheral vision. In addition, the driver is usually uncertain as to when and where an important visual event may occur" (p. 404). There is, consequently, strong agreement in the literature that some aspect of attention is related to such variables as the probability or frequency of motor vehicle accidents (e.g., Ball et al., 1993; Holland & Rabbitt, 1994; Owsley et al., 1991; Parasuraman & Nestor, 1991). A primary candidate seems to be the ability to switch attention (e.g., Lerner, 1994; Parasuraman & Nestor, 1991); others have discussed vigilance (e.g., Holland & Rabbitt, 1994) and divided attention (e.g., Crook, West, & Larrabee, 1993; Holland & Rabbitt, 1994; Parasuraman & Nestor, 1991). Together, these results suggest that inefficient or disordered attention in the context of driving has important and potentially life-threatening consequences.

One very successful model for characterizing the role of attention in age differences in driving is the work on useful field of view (UFOV) by Ball and colleagues (e.g., Ball et al., 1993; Ball & Rebok, 1994; Owsley et al., 1991). The UFOV refers to the extent of the visual field available to an individual in performing a particular visual task. Work by Ball and colleagues has demonstrated that the UFOV is not simply a measure of peripheral sensory functioning. Owsley et al. reviewed research showing that the size of the UFOV varies not only across individuals but also across situations within persons and is reduced under dual-task conditions, in the presence of distractors, with increased target–distractor similarity, and with short target duration. They concluded that when the UFOV is particularly restricted in older adults, three factors are involved: speed of processing, divided-attention ability, and susceptibility to distraction (Ball, Roenker, & Bruni, 1990). These are all clear indicators that attention is involved as much or more than simple sensory processes.

A study by Owsley et al. (1991) illustrates the usefulness of this approach. Three different variants of the UFOV task were used to assess the basic ability to identify the location of a peripheral target, the ability to identify location in the presence of distractors, and the ability to perform the task along with another visual task (a divided-attention condition). Participants were categorized on a pass–fail basis (where *fail* meant having failed to meet minimum performance criteria in all three tasks and *pass* meant having met the criteria in at least one task). Although Owsley et al. used this crude measure of UFOV in their analysis, when combined with a mental status score, UFOV status accounted for 20% of the variance in all types of traffic accidents (as reported by state records for the participants in the study) and 29% of the variance in intersection accidents. Further, the group of individuals who failed the UFOV tasks had 4.2 times more accidents than the group of those who passed and 15.6 times more accidents at intersections. This composite measure of early attentional function has been shown to be an excellent basis for predicting accidents, and attention turns out to be the major predictor of driving safety.

Crook et al. (1993) explored the nature of attentional functioning involved in driving in a laboratory simulation. Young and old adults participated in a simulated driving task in which they pressed an "accelerator pedal" on a touch-screen display when a traffic light on the display was green and a "brake pedal" when the light was red. Participants were instructed to switch back and forth as quickly as possible with changes in the traffic light. Response times were decomposed into lift time (stimulus onset to release of the current pedal) and travel time (release of one pedal to the pressing of the other pedal). According to Crook et al., lift time is related to attention, concentration, and vigilance, whereas travel time is a measure only of psychomotor speed. A dual-task condition was also used; participants were told to listen to a taped weather report and a traffic report for a later memory test. The participants in the study represented a continuous age sample from 18 to 85 years of age. Regression analyses showed that both lift time and travel time increased with age in the single-task condition. A regression of dual-task performance on age with single-task performance partialed out showed that aging had a negative effect on lift time but not on travel time under dual-task conditions. Thus, the dual-task cost was associated only with the attention-demanding part of the task; that is, the age difference in performance due to attention was exaggerated under dual-task conditions, which were somewhat more representative of actual driving. However, given the simplified character of the simulation (the traffic light was the only stimulus and stayed lit on the display continuously) and the complexity of driving as described by Owsley et al. (1991) above, it would be useful to conduct further studies decomposing attentional processes more specifically in more realistic situations.

Problem Solving. Although there is much literature on problem-solving in older adults (e.g., Denney, 1990; Lachman & Burack, 1993; Willis, 1996), the role of attention in problem solving has typically been considered only peripherally. Walsh and Hershey (1993), for example, noted only that attentional capacity limits in older adults may play a role in their finding that older adults generally considered fewer parameters in their problem-solving task. However, one research program that directly considered attentional variables in a task that also involved problem solving is the work on aging and miniature golf by Molander and Bäckman (1993). Molander and Bäckman (1989, 1990) examined concentration and selective attention in miniature-golf players, using highly skilled older and younger adults. A concentration phase of play occurs when a player plans a shot, addresses, and strikes the ball. They noted that this phase of play is a "complex self-paced decision task, in which the player focuses attention on internal and external stimuli" (Molander & Bäckman, 1993, p. 242). They cited other research showing that in similar sports, young adults primarily direct their attention externally (on the basis of a pattern of heart rate changes indicative of the focus of attention; see, e.g., Lacey & Lacey, 1970). Molander and Bäckman (1989) confirmed this external focusing pattern in their young adult participants, both in a laboratory setting and in a competitive setting with the same individuals. The older adults exhibited an internal focus of attention in the laboratory but no clear internal or external focus in competition. Thus, older adults' attentional strategy was lost in the stress of competition; younger adults showed an enhancement of their strategy in competition. The attentional weakness of the older adults was also accompanied by poorer performance during competition, whereas young adults' performance was unaffected by the setting.

In another study, Molander and Bäckman (1990) examined selective aspects of attention by playing two kinds of noise in the background while monitoring players' performance, heart rate, and memory for shots made. One noise condition was meaningless traffic noise; the other was a radio broadcast of a soccer game. Whereas younger adults were unaffected by noise type, older adults did less well with the soccer game than the traffic noise, which was reminiscent of the results of the reading with distraction task of Connelly et al. (1991), such that meaningful information is more distracting than meaningless noise. Thus, attentional differences between young and older adults clearly have consequences related to performance in this complex task.

A more traditional problem-solving study recently examined attention effects. Martin and Ewert (1997) gave participants a trip-planning task and examined attentional flexibility and inhibitory functioning as determinants of performance in older adults. Martin and Ewert argued that planning (i.e., "the implementation and/or elaboration of schematic and/or hierarchical representations whose function is to guide activity" [Hoc, 1988, p. 84]) is influenced by working memory capacity, the ability to inhibit irrelevant information, and the flexibility of focusing attention on various aspects of a task. They noted that in problem-solving tasks such as planning, there is usually more information than is needed, the information varies in relevance, and there are multiple paths to the solution (which influences the relevance of various parts of the information). In line with inhibition-deficit theory, Martin and Ewert (1997) noted that "deficient inhibitory mechanisms could result in an increased number of task irrelevant information or intentions maintained in the working memory system . . . [resulting] in an increase in the time to solve a task and the number of errors" (p. 580). A second characteristic of planning tasks relates to attentional flexibility. Martin and Ewert noted that what is relevant at one stage can become irrelevant later (e.g., comparison information across car models before and after a decision about which model to buy). They argued that planning requires flexibility and that overly efficient inhibition (rejection of momentarily irrelevant information) can be detrimental to planning performance in later stages.

Flexibility of attention was measured with a prospective memory task concurrent with the planning task; inhibitory functioning was measured in two ways. First, performance on a typical Stroop task served as an external, context-free measure. Second, the difference in memory for relevant and irrelevant information presented during the early part of the task served as an internal, context-specific measure. The context-specific measure was significantly correlated ($r = .53$) with a measure of the quality of performance. The context-free measure was not. The measure of flexibility was not directly related to performance; however, for participants with low working memory capacity, if inhibitory efficiency (on the Stroop task) and flexibility were high, performance improved relative to those participants who scored low on these measures. Thus, the ability to inhibit irrelevant information enhanced performance in this planning task and was more important for older adults with lower working memory performance (Martin & Ewert, 1997).

Information-processing models typically place some variety of attention as an early part of the sequence of mental operations involved in cognitive tasks. In these models, the amount, content, and quality of information available for processing is determined by attentional processes. Attention has also served as the focal point of several general theories of cognitive aging (e.g., Craik & Byrd, 1982; Hasher & Zacks, 1979, 1988). It is common in cognitive aging research that attention is not only an object of study in itself but also a cause of cognitive performance. The preceding overview highlighted some areas that have explicitly explored the role of age differences in attention in more complex cognitive tasks. We turn now to a consideration of theories of attention in aging.

THEORETICAL APPROACHES TO ATTENTION AND AGING

How do we integrate all these findings? A number of theoretical constructs have been offered as accounts of age differences in attentional functioning. At the level of theory, the goal has typically been to identify a single construct as responsible for the widest possible range of phenomena. In the sections that follow, the strengths and weaknesses of the most encompassing of these explanatory constructs are outlined and their underlying assumptions are examined.

Cognitive Resources

Kahneman's (1973) influential work provided a conceptualization of attention as a fuel or processing resource for other cognitive processes. Attention could be understood in economic terms: A limited supply of attentional resources could be allocated to any number of tasks as long as task demands did not exceed available supply. In the context of aging, researchers such as Hasher and Zacks (1979) and Craik and Byrd (1982) suggested that older adults are characterized by a reduction in attentional capacity. Age-related performance differences in attention-demanding situations, such as divided attention or sustained attention, have been cited as evidence for an age-related reduction in processing resources. However, dissatisfaction with the resource concept soon surfaced as difficulties in definition and measurement emerged. Salthouse (1988, 1991) has provided a critical analysis of the concept in the context of aging; O. Neumann (1996) has provided a recent analysis of the resource notion in the context of a historical overview of the development of theories of attention. Both concluded that the usefulness of the resource construct is severely limited in the absence of any precision in specifying exactly what resources are (either physiologically or in terms of some information-processing component) and how they might be measured (without resorting to circular logic).

In his review, O. Neumann (1996) cited the cognitive–energetical model of Sanders (1983; Gopher & Sanders, 1984) as one tenable conceptualization of attentional resources, in part because it combines both psychological and physiological considerations, leading to a conceptualization of resources as "intervening variables that relate independent variables to dependent variables, and do not therefore suffer from the danger of circularity" (p. 409). Other researchers have also appreciated the value of identifying a physiological index of resources. For example, Stankov and Dunn (1993) identified "neural efficiency" as a characteristic of the central nervous system corresponding to mental energy or attentional resources. Dujardin, Derambure, Bourriez, Jacquesson, and Guieu (1993) examined brain ERPs as an index of attentional resources. They observed an age-related decrease in amplitude of the P300 component of event-related brain activity and suggested that this reflects reduced processing resources among older adults. Lorist, Snel, Mulder, and Kok (1995) conducted an ERP analysis of selective attention in young and old adults. Their hypothesis regarding a reduction in the energetic component of attention was tested in two ways. First, they assessed P300 amplitude in young and old adults as an index of attentional resources. Second, they administered caffeine as a simulant for the energetic processes of attention on the hypothesis that if these processes were reponsible for age differences, caffeine might reduce these differences. Caffeine speeded the performance of both young and old adults as measured by response time and P300 latency. In addition, ERP analyses reflecting selective attention showed that caffeine also increased the resources available to both young and old adults. Lorist et al. (1995) concluded that "caffeine seems to improve selective attention to environmental stimuli in both young and old participants by changing the availability of energy resources" (p. 465). These studies are mentioned here as examples of the way in which the concept of resources continues to be used and to make the point that if the concept of resources can be defined and measured in a precise way, the notion may continue to be useful in understanding age differences in performance. However, even though psychophysiological indices of resources may provide some precision in measurement, underlying mechanisms remain to be identified if the resource concept is to offer something beyond redescription of data.

Processing Speed

One attempt to preserve the notion of resources as useful in theories of cognitive aging is to specify processing components that might be considered as resources rather than assuming that resources constitute some additional input required by processing components. Along these lines Salthouse (1991), for example, has suggested processing speed as a resource for information processing. Indeed, one common characteristic of older adults is that they are slower than young adults. The notion that a single factor, processing speed, can explain a significant proportion of age-related variance in cognitive processes suggests that this construct may offer considerable parsimony for theories of aging and cognition. However, this notion has not met with universal acceptance (e.g., Bashore, van der Molen, Maurits, Ridderinkhof, & Wylie, 1997; Fisk & Fisher, 1994; Hartley, 1992; Perfect, 1994). Controversy has centered on the related issues of (a) whether age differences in cognition are best explained by the single, general factor of processing speed or by process-specific factors and (b) how best to decide between general and specific factors in aging and cognition.

Fisk and Fisher (1994) suggested that the dichotomy between general and specific factors had become something of a straw man as accumulating evidence made strong versions of either position untenable. That is, a number of studies reported patterns of data that were not compatible with single-factor accounts of age differences in performance (see Bashore et al., 1997, Fisk & Fisher, 1994; Hartley, 1992; Kramer & Larish, 1996), and Brinley plots were shown to be inadequate on their own to rule out a role for process-specific factors in age-related performance deficits (Fisk & Fisher, 1994; Hartley, 1992; Salthouse, 1996). Birren and Fisher (1995) provided an overview of some of the issues related to the general–specific controversy; they concluded that "sufficient research has been conducted to indicate that there are specific factors as well as a general process associated with the slowing of behavior with advancing age" (p. 349). In addition, Salthouse has recently stated that although his processing-speed theory of age differences in cognition holds that age-related slowing is fundamental in explaining age differences in cognitive functioning, the theory also allows for process-specific mechanisms to have a role in determining cognitive function.

Support for the processing-speed theory as articulated by Salthouse (1996) comes from a number of studies showing that a large proportion of age-related variance across a variety of tasks is shared with measures of processing speed. That is, when performance is measured on a variety of tasks, including some basic measures of processing speed, age-related variance in criterion task performance is reduced or eliminated when variance in processing speed is controlled. Thus, processing speed would appear "to be a major contributor to the adult age differences in many measures of cognition" (Salthouse, 1996, p. 404). However, studies that explicitly ask whether slowing is the cause of other cognitive deficits observed in aging or the consequence of some more basic age-related change have been few. In the context of attention, the question amounts to asking whether slowing leads to declines in attentional function or declines in attentional functioning lead to age-related slowing. Salthouse, Fristoe, McGuthry, and Hambrick (1998) examined attention switching as a possible cause of age-related variability in processing speed but found that a model in which processing speed accounted for age-related variability in attention provided a better fit to the data. In contrast, Cohen and Servan-Schreiber (1992) reported a computational study in which variations in attention parameters gave a better fit to slowing data than did variations in speed-of-processing parameters. More studies along these lines will continue to elucidate the relations among attention, speed of processing, and aging.

Many of the studies reviewed in the present chapter have attempted to rule out slowing as an account for any age differences in attentional performance they observed; some succeeded and some did not. These attempts may reflect concern about the same straw man referred to above. Clearly a single slowing factor is not sufficient to explain all aspects of cognition in aging. In this vein, Madden and Gottlob (1997) have suggested that general process and process-specific conceptualizations of underlying causes are actually complementary; analyses supporting task-specific mechanisms "can identify exceptions to generalized slowing and provide a basis for interpreting those exceptions as either strategic or dynamic aspects of attentional focusing" (Madden & Gottlob, 1997, p. 24).

Even though they do allow for the existence of process-specific factors, explanations of age-related attentional deficits in terms of a general slowing factor are still subject to criticisms. For example, Kramer and Larish (1996) have suggested that general slowing explanations are "descriptive rather than explanatory" (p. 86). Collins (1994) made a similar point in reference to Salthouse's (1994a) analyses that identified a limited number of dimensions of age-related variabililty (including processing speed) across a variety of tasks. Collins took exception to Salthouse's suggestion that processing speed is a "cause" of many age-related declines in cognitive functioning. Rather, Collins (1994) stated that the dimensions underlying age-related variability "are the result of data reduction, and provide a parsimonious way of expressing age-related variance in a large set of variables" (p. 442). She suggested that identifying the factors that lead to age-related slowing is a more appropriate goal for theory. That is, even if general slowing can account for the lion's share of age-related variance, that variance may not be entirely explained because the question of what causes slowing remains unanswered. In his reply, Salthouse (1994b) recognized the importance of identifying the factors that contribute to slowing but defended his approach with the argument that "if research reveals that only three or four factors are sufficient to account for a large percentage of age-related variance in 100 or more distinct cognitive variables, then the task for other levels of explanation should be considerably easier" (p. 446). Birren and Fisher (1995) advocated theory building that incorporates hierarchical levels of explanation and identified the need to create links from one level of analysis to another in order to have a truly general theory of cognitive aging. The "complementary" contributions of specific and general factors, when recognized, would seem to be represent progress toward Birren and Fisher's vision of a general theory of cognitive aging.

Inhibition

In 1988, Hasher and Zacks suggested that age-related changes in inhibitory function may be responsible for a variety of age-related cognitive deficits. Inhibitory processes serve to keep information processing and responding focused on relevant information and so are essentially attentional processes that serve a selective function. A number of studies have been conducted in an attempt to evaluate the inhibitory-deficit hypothesis (see Burke, 1997; McDowd, 1997; and McDowd, Oseas-Kreger, & Filion, 1995, for a review), with mixed results. By way of illustration, consider the data on negative priming and aging. Available data definitely do not support the notion of a general age-related inhibitory decline, and although the original hypothesis of a general decline has been modified (e.g., Connelly & Hasher, 1993; Stoltzfus, Hasher, & Zacks, 1996) to account for data suggesting differential decline (e.g., Earles et al., 1997; Kramer et al., 1994; Sullivan & Faust, 1993), not all evidence points to altered inhibitory function as underlying age differences in selective attention.

Other paradigms besides negative priming have also produced mixed evidence regarding age-related inhibitory dysfunction. For example, Balota and Ferraro (1993) argued that pronunciation of irregular words requires that the regular (but incorrect) pronunciation, which may be activated initially, be inhibited in favor of the irregular (but correct) pronunciation. They observed increased regularization errors (e.g., pronouncing *pint* the same way as *hint*) among older adults compared with young adults in their pronunciation task and suggested that this finding may reflect a breakdown in inhibitory control of activated or partially activated information. Balota and Black (1997) used the phenomenon of semantic satiation to assess inhibitory function in young and old adults. Semantic satiation is a phenomenon whereby repeated exposure to a word reduces that word's meaningfulness. They described this satiation as a type of habituation process involving the inhibition of attention to repeated, unchanging information. Balota and Black observed less semantic satiation among old than young adults and suggested that it may be due to an age-related reduction in inhibitory function. Lindfield, Wingfield, and Bowles (1994) administered a picture fragment naming task to young and old adults in which progressively more visual information was provided until the participant could correctly identify the picture. Older adults required more visual information than young adults to correctly identify the picture. After young and old adults were equated for accuracy of picture identification on the progressive information version of this task, they were asked to identify a picture fragment presented at a single, intermediate level of degradation on the basis of their performance in the progressive version. Findings indicated that older adults were faster and better able to identify the pictures in the latter condition. Lindfield et al. interpreted this pattern of results in terms of declining inhibitory function among older adults. They reasoned that early in the progressive information sequence, both old and young adults generated guesses about what the fragment might be but that older adults were less able to abandon these guesses when told they were wrong because of deficient inhibitory function. Because they were less able to abandon incorrect guesses, older adults required more information to overcome these guesses and arrive at a correct identification. So older adults were presented with more information than were young adults when they equated for accuracy with young adults, allowing older adults to then be faster and more accurate on the subsequent single presentation of a picture fragment.

At the same time, MacKay, Miller, and Schuster (1994) tested an inhibitory-deficit explanation for age differences in the phenomenon of repetition blindness, defined as "the reduced probability of encoding and recalling a word or letter because of prior occurrence of the same word (or letter) in a rapidly presented list or sentence" (MacKay et al., 1994, p. 251). One theoretical explanation of repetition blindness that has been offered is that once the lexical phonological nodes associated with a word have been activated by an initial presentation, inhibitory processes prevent reactivation at very short delays (e.g., Hochhaus & Marohn, 1991). An inhibitory deficit among older adults would predict less repetition blindness among old adults than among young adults. Mackay et al. presented sentences one word at a time at a very rapid rate (50, 70, 90, 100, and 200 ms per word) to young and old adults and asked them to repeat the sentence verbatim. Sentences either involved a repeated word (e.g., "He is the one who one day will be famous") or had no repeated words (e.g., "He is the man who one day will be famous"). Performance measures included accuracy in recalling the sentences; repetition blindness was defined as the difference in accuracy between the two sentence types. Contrary to the pattern of results predicted by an inhibition model of repetition blindness and an age-related inhibitory deficit, MacKay et al. observed greater repetition blindness in old adults than in young adults.

Although they conceded that the type of inhibitory process involved in repetition blindness may not be the same as the types that have led to the inhibitory-deficit hypothesis of aging, they suggested that their finding is not explained by any parsimonious version of an inhibition model.

Stine and Wingfield (1994) used a speech recognition task and observed that older adults were no more disrupted by distractor information than were young adults, contrary to notions of age-related inhibitory decline. Rouleau and Belleville (1996) found that older adults were no more distracted by irrelevant auditory information in an auditory span task than were young adults, again contrary to inhibitory-deficit accounts of cognitive aging. Einstein and McDaniel (1997) looked for evidence of age-related decline in inhibitory function in a study assessing mind wandering. They found comparable levels of mind wandering in both young and old adults and thus no support for age differences in inhibition. Finally, Dywan and Murphy (1996) reported mixed evidence in the same study: In a reading task, older adults' reading times were more slowed in the presence of distraction than were young adults' reading times, but young adults were more likely to recognize words they apparently had ignored. In summary, it is difficult to summarize these findings! It would seem that there is much work to be done to develop the inhibitory-deficit hypothesis in sufficient detail to be able to account for these seemingly disparate findings.

Hasher et al. (in press) have begun to flesh out their notions about inhibitory processes. In one approach, they identified three functions of inhibition, which they called access, deletion, and restraint. The access function acts to prevent irrelevant information from receiving further processing, the deletion function acts to suppress information that is no longer relevant to the task at hand, and the restraint function keeps habitual responses from always getting precedence in behavior. One possibility is that age differences might vary as a function of these separate inhibitory functions. Although it is not immediately obvious how well such a taxonomy would work for existing data, careful task analysis might support such a possibility.

Another approach was to identify potential boundary conditions for an age-related inhibitory deficit. Hasher, Quig, and May (1997) explicitly adopted this approach in their reexamination of the finding reported by Hartman and Hasher (1991). Hartman and Hasher had observed sustained activation of no-longer-relevant words among older but not younger adults performing a garden-path sentence-processing task; they concluded that diminished inhibition among older adults was responsible for the sustained but irrelevant activation. On the hypothesis that additional semantic information and/or additional processing time might allow older adults to more effectively inhibit the irrelevant information, Hasher et al. modified the Hartman and Hasher task to provide both additional contextual information and extra processing time. Their goal with the added contextual support following a garden-path sentence was to constrain activation of irrelevant information and, in so doing, ameliorate the hypothesized age-related inhibitory deficit. The manipulation involving extra processing time was necessary to test the possibility that the added contextual information simply provided additional time for the activation of irrelevant information to dissipate or be inhibited. The data reported by Hasher et al. indicate that the contextual support, and not merely extra time, was necessary to eliminate the age deficit in inhibitory function. They concluded that the presence or absence of such contextual support constitutes a boundary condition for observing age differences in inhibitory function.

Another finding relevant to the notion of boundary conditions in age-related inhibitory dysfunction was reported by Duchek, Balota, Faust, and Ferraro (1995). Their study involved selective attention to pictures or words in displays containing pictures and words. On a given trial in their task, a context display was first presented that included a picture and a word. Participants were instructed to attend to either the picture or the word. This display was followed by a test display that contained a picture or a word. The task was to indicate by saying "yes" or "no" whether the target in the test display was related to the target in the context display. Critical trials were those that required a "no" response; the relevant comparison was between (a) trials in which neither the picture nor the word in the context display was related to the test display and (b) trials in which the to-be-ignored item in the context display was related to the target item in the test display. If individuals have difficulty filtering out the to-be-ignored item in the the context display, then their response time to the test display might be slowed by yes–no response conflict induced by having processed the distractor. Overall, Duchek et al. found that, in general, older adults were slower than young adults and that older adults were slower when they were required to identify and name pictures rather than comparable word trials. This pattern of slowing supports their claim that older adults are more fluent in processing words than in processing pictures. In addition, they observed that older adults showed a larger relatedness effect (the difference between Conditions a and b described above) than young adults only on word trials; picture trials produced age equivalence. These results indicate that older adults were less able to ignore those stimuli that they process more fluently (i.e., words) than they were to ignore the less-fluent stimuli (i.e., pictures). They interpreted this finding in terms of differential fluency in the processing routes for pictures and words; age differences in inhibitory strength are apparent in the more fluent lexical-processing route than the less fluent picture-coding route.

Thus, processing fluency appears to be relevant to age differences in inhibitory function and may constitute another boundary condition for observing age-related effects.

An alternative to searching for boundary conditions for an age-related inhibitory deficit is to propose multiple mechanisms of inhibition. Myerson, Hale, and colleagues (Hale, Myerson, Rhee, Weiss, & Abrams, 1996; Jenkins, Myerson, Hale, & Fry, 1999; Myerson, Hale, Rhee, & Jenkins, in press) examined patterns of verbal and spatial interference in verbal and spatial working memory tasks. They observed that interference was specific rather than general; that is, verbal distractors disrupted the verbal working memory task, and spatial distractors disrupted the spatial working memory task, but cross-modal interference did not occur. They concluded that inhibitory mechanisms acting on interfering information must be specific rather than general. However, the proliferation of inhibitory mechanisms is no more palatable now than the proliferation of specific resources has been in the past (e.g., Navon, 1984); proliferation reduces explanatory power in both cases. In addition, Jenkins et al. found that the magnitude of interference effects did not vary systematically with adult age. Again, these findings are not consistent with any simple version of an inhibitiory-deficit hypothesis.

Hasher and Zacks (1988) initially offered the inhibitory framework as a replacement for a resource view of cognitive aging, which they suggested had outlived its usefulness. However, McDowd (1997) pointed out that the inhibition view is not immune to criticisms similar to those leveled against resources. Indeed, none of the theories of age-changes in attention have really moved beyond a resourcelike conceptualization of attention. Inhibition is itself a resource-limited process (Engle, Conway, Tuholski, & Shisler, 1995; E. Neumann & DeSchepper, 1992) and, like earlier resource models of attention, currently leaves unanswered fundamental questions of mechanism, measurement, specificity, and circularity (see Burke, 1997, and Zacks & Hasher, 1997, for further discussion of these issues).

Environmental Support

Shaw (1990, 1991) has argued that Craik's (1983, 1986) environmental support perspective on memory could also be a useful way to describe age differences in selective attention. The environmental support perspective suggests that remembering depends on the interaction of environmental (bottom-up) characteristics (e.g., the stimulus and its context, retrieval cues) and internally driven, top-down, "self-initiated" retrieval processes. The self-initiated processes, in this view, are effortful, and older adults have reduced resources to carry out such processes. Older adults, therefore, are relatively more dependent on the contextual or environmental support for remembering and are expected to have more difficulty when environmental support is weak (see Craik & Jennings, 1992, and chap. 5, this volume, for a review of the success of this perspective in memory and aging).

In the context of attention, Shaw (1991) argued that attentional tasks frequently involve the combination of behavioral goals and a complex, distraction-laden environmental context. The daily environments through which we navigate contain stimuli that help us reach our goals, stimuli that are irrelevant to our goals, and stimuli that can encourage mental processes that are inconsistent with our goals. If older adults rely more on environmental context than on self-initiated processes, then in the regular interplay of process and context, the distracting elements of the context may win out, and older adults will exhibit difficulties with maintaining attention to goal-relevant activities.

Shaw (1991) and Shaw, Rypma, and Toffle (1992) reported several investigations of selective attention in older adults from this perspective. In each set of studies, experimental conditions varied the amount of environmental or contextual support for a target task. For example, Shaw examined people's ability to avoid distraction in the flanker task (e.g., Eriksen & Eriksen, 1974). Shaw used a version of the flanker task developed by Shaffer and LaBerge (1979; see also Mitchell & Perlmutter, 1986), in which participants indicated the category of a word that was presented with another word printed both above and below the target word. The flanking word could be from the same category as the target or from a different category. Because of the difficulty of ignoring the flankers in this task, response times were particularly slowed when the flanking words induced response competition. Shaw contrasted the standard condition with a condition in which the flanker was either brighter than (Experiment 1) or appeared 620 ms earlier than the target (Experiment 2). Both of these manipulations made it easier for participants to discriminate target and flanking words; they provided support for focusing only on the target, in environmental support terms. Both younger and older adults were able to benefit from this support, suggesting that environmental support can facilitate attentional processes as well as memory processes.

Several studies examining people's ability to avoid distraction while reading also illustrate the role of environmental support in determining age differences. Connelly et al. (1991), Carlson et al. (1995), and Shaw et al. (1992) reported a collection of experiments exploring people's ability to read text with embedded distraction. Each experiment (or contrast between experiments) contained a variation between different degrees of support for ignoring the distraction. In general, participants read text with to-be-ignored words interleaved among the target words. For example, participants might encounter "IT it WAS was A the COLD silent GRAY time DAY before" with the instruction to read aloud only the words in capital letters. Across conditions or studies, the to-be-ignored words were indicated by font changes, capitalization, and relative or absolute position, with some of these cues occurring alone or in combination. Overall, age differences were reduced when environmental conditions were supportive of reading the target text and ignoring the distraction and magnified when no such external support was provided. Age differences were eliminated when target and distracting text were distinguished on both font and predictable position (Carlson et al., 1995). Such results are also consistent with a substantial literature on the efficacy of cues in reducing age differences in selective attention (as reviewed earlier in this chapter).

It is worth noting that support for selection need not consist solely of physical cues. In the reading tasks described above (Carlson et al., 1995; Connelly et al., 1991; Shaw, 1990; Shaw et al., 1992), for example, the meaningfulness of the distraction was important as well. Nonwords produced smaller age differences than words as distraction (Shaw et al., 1992), related words exaggerated age differences over unrelated words (e.g., Connelly et al., 1991), and the "false words" created by changing the spaces between letters and words in a phrase were primarily responsible for the age differences in the research by Shaw. Likewise, in the various versions of the flanker task (with words or letters), the distraction created by flankers varied as a function of their relation to the target. According to the environmental support perspective, semantic characteristics vary in the level of support provided to the extent that they affect the amount of self-initiated processing required to perform the task.

Other recent work is consistent with this perspective. For example, the work by Madden et al. (1994) on attention switching showed that the visual context (distractor presence) was the primary determinant of age differences in estimated time to switch attention between display locations. Older adults were more dependent on a distraction-free context for fast switching. Also, Humphrey and Kramer (1999) interpreted their results in a study of perceptual organization and selective attention as consistent with environmental support. Visual displays of letter sequences were presented as a monochrome, unsegmented string; as two strings separated by a space; or as an unsegmented string with letters in two colors. Older adults benefitted more when selective attention was supported by segmentation or color cues than did younger adults, again suggesting that the visual context, or environment, can support efficient selective attention. Finally, Wingfield et al. (1995) showed that older adults could be more distracted than younger adults by pauses introduced randomly in speech rather than at syntactic boundaries. Pauses in speech normally guide selective attention for processing speech, and this study showed that older adults depend more on this guidance than do younger adults (as Shaw, 1990, demonstrated with distorted text). Older adults' greater difficulty with recall under this condition was further exacerbated by increased speech rate.

From a theoretical standpoint, the strength of the environmental support approach lies in its usefulness for post hoc summaries and for organizing research findings. As a basis for making predictions, it falls short unless a process-oriented characterization (Shaw, 1991; see also Light, 1991; D. C. Park & Shaw, 1992) is developed of how environmental context supports cognitive operations or processes. In other words, what is needed is a clear specification of what kind of support will be useful for what cognitive operations, whether older adults need support for those operations, and whether older adults can make use of the support provided. For example, Shaw (1990) found that physically de-emphasizing the salience of false words, which was expected to increase support for ignoring them, decreased reading times equally for younger and older adults. Without a thorough understanding of the processes involved, one could not have predicted that outcome. Thus, productive work from the environmental support approach requires the prior development of process models, although the environmental support approach is not unique in this way.

Executive Control of Attention

A final theoretical approach is based on notions of executive processes in the control of attention. In this view, a superordinate, executive mechanism controls the changing allocation of attention in complex tasks, such as dividing attention between two inputs, or in dynamically switching between two tasks (e.g., Shallice's Supervisory Attentional System [Shallice & Burgess, 1993]; see also Kramer, Larish, et al., in press). Models that specify a controller, according to Shallice and Burgess (1993), have not been popular in traditional cognitive psychology because such a supervisory system can be criticized as "a controlling homunculus" (p. 173). However, they noted that such systems are popular in cognitive science and artificial intelligence models and in cognitive neuropsychology. In addition, one similar theoretical construct from traditional cognitive psychology is the central executive in Baddeley's (1986, 1993; Baddeley & Hitch, 1974) working memory model. Recently, Baddeley (1993) has characterized the purpose of the central executive as coordinating the processing of information to marshall the relevant cognitive processes and procedures for meeting task or situational demands. The essence of executive control, in Baddeley's (1993) words, is "the *integration* of information and the *control* of action" (p. 155).

Although there has been extensive research on aging and working memory, relatively little of it has been directed at the central executive specifically (see Belleville, Rouleau, & Caza, 1998, for an exception). However, several researchers have recently begun to apply the notion of executive control to understanding attention and aging (e.g., Kramer, Hahn, & Gopher, in press; Kramer et al., 1995; Kramer, Larish, et al., in press; Rogers & Monsell, 1995; Tsang & Shaner, 1998). An important influence on executive control work in aging is the growing interest in the frontal lobe hypothesis of aging (see West, 1996, and Woodruff-Pak, 1997, for a review). Cognitive functions believed to be subserved by frontal regions of the brain, such as those involved in both working memory and inhibition tasks, are known to be strongly affected by aging. Executive control is believed to be closely associated with frontal lobe functioning as well (e.g., Luria, 1980; Shallice & Burgess, 1993; West, 1996). West made the link between frontal lobe functioning, executive control, and aging by applying his theory of frontal lobe functioning to a variety of age-related differences in cognition (specifically, aging and proactive interference, Stroop, and vigilance). His model characterized the primary role of the prefrontal cortex as supporting "the integration, formation, and execution of complex, novel behavioral structures . . . which support the direction of behavior in an orderly, purposeful manner" (West, 1996, p. 282). This could also be a model of executive control, and the success with which he applied it to age-related attentional phenomena suggests that understanding frontal lobe functioning and executive control may contribute importantly to understanding attentional functioning in aging (see also Klein, 1997).

Two research methods for studying executive control are task switching (e.g., Kramer, Hahn, & Gopher, in press; Salthouse et al., 1998) and divided attention (e.g., Kramer et al., 1995; Kramer, Larish, et al., in press; Tsang & Shaner, 1998). Researchers have argued that task switching requires executive control because the cognitive system must be reset—the procedures required to perform the first task must be abandoned, and those required for the new task must be set up. Evidence for these control processes comes from the switch costs (slowed responding on the first trial of a new task compared with nonswitch trials on that task), which persist with practice. Work by Kramer, Hahn, and Gopher (reviewed above in the section on task switching) showed that although switch costs were greater for older adults, age differences were eliminated with practice. However, when working memory load was increased, age differences were not eliminated with practice, suggesting a clear relationship between executive functions in working memory and in attention and a potential weakness with increased age. Kramer, Hahn, and Gopher also showed through regression analysis that age-related slowing was different on switch and nonswitch trials, suggesting differential aging of component processes and executive control processes (see Salthouse et al., 1998, for a different result).

Divided-attention performance is also controlled by a processing executive, according to this theoretical perspective. The executive mechanism allocates attention between the two tasks and manages the flow of input and output from the two tasks. Typically, older adults perform less well under dual-task conditions than do young adults (see the section on divided attention), suggesting an age-related deficit in executive function. However, work by Kramer and colleagues (Kramer et al., 1995; Kramer, Larish, et al., in press; see the section on divided attention for details) indicates that training can improve divided-attention performance; Kramer, Larish, et al. showed that practice with differently allocating attention between two tasks reduced the age decrement in dual-task performance (see also Tsang & Shaner, 1998). Additionally, as further evidence for a superordinate executive control mechanism, Kramer, Larish, et al. found that the improved performance acquired with one pair of tasks generalized to a new, unrelated pair of tasks in a divided-attention situation for both younger and older adults.

In summary, conceptualizing attentional functioning in terms of executive control may offer a more fruitful way to explore age difference in the dynamic control of action. That is, although traditional work on divided attention is frustrated by the complexities of unpredictable interactions among component tasks, exploration of executive control may provide more consistent results (given the generalization of skill observed above).

Kliegl and colleagues (e.g., Mayr & Kliegl, 1993; Mayr, Kliegl, & Krampe, 1996; Verhaegen, Kliegl, & Mayr, 1997) have been working on a related theoretical perspective, distinguishing coordinative and sequential complexity. They have argued that an inadequacy of general slowing models is that complex cognitive tasks require that participants coordinate basic processes as well as perform them. For example, Verhaeghen et al. (1997) wrote that "two fundamentally distinct factors are operating in cognitive aging, the first referring to the speed of basic components, the other to the coordination of basic process components in working memory" (p. 560). The heart of the distinction lies in the "coordination of information exchange between processing steps" (Mayr & Kliegl, 1993, p. 1298). This coordination takes place in working memory, according to the theory. This theory has not been applied directly to attention research, but it is argued to be a general theory of complex cognition relevant to aging (e.g., Verhaeghen et al., 1997). Presumably, then, it would apply to complex attentional tasks (e.g., divided attention or attention switching) and to complex tasks involving attentional processes (e.g., driving). These researchers characterized it as an addition to general slowing and, in combination with executive control notions, it has real promise.

Finally, in further support of the merit of an executive control approach, some recent neuroimaging work (Madden et al., 1997) found that, under divided-attention conditions, older but not younger adults showed increased activation in prefrontal regions. Madden et al. (1997) concluded from their results that "aging is associated with a change in the pattern in cortical activation rather than with an overall decline in the magnitude of activation" (p. 407). Such a result speaks clearly to the benefits of an executive control over generalized resource notions. This is clearly an area for further important findings. Interestingly, however, Belleville et al. (1998) provided a cautionary note. They found that when older and younger adults were tested on an alphabetic span task (in which participants must reorganize the presented words into alphabetic order), no age differences were found when older and younger adults were working at their own memory span, determined in a straight word span task. The reorganization of words presumably uses executive control, yet age differences were not found. They concluded that a generalized frontal deficit theory of aging may be premature.

CONCLUSIONS

In the final paragraph of Hartley's (1992) review, he concluded that in order to make progress toward a better understanding of attention in aging, "we need more data, we need innovative techniques to measure performance and innovative perspectives on the organization of the results, and we need more rigorous theoretical accounts of our findings" (p. 41). If we use these stated needs as criteria against which to judge progress since then, what conclusions can we draw?

Data and Measurement Techniques

With regard to the first criterion, we can certainly say that we have more data! So much so that it is nearly impossible to do an exhaustive review, as the literature on aging and attention has grown significantly in recent years. Some of these data also come out of the development of new techniques for measuring performance, although judging progress against this criterion is less straightforward, primarily because studies outside of the typical reaction time design are few. For example, neuroscience offers a variety of techniques and dependent measures to assess brain function in attentional behavior. The chapters on aging and neuropsychology by Raz (see chap. 1, this volume) and by Prull, Gabrieli, and Bunge (see chap. 2, this volume) discuss the important developments in this area. One of the areas of neuropsychology of particular interest to attention is the differential aging of the frontal lobes (see West, 1996; Woodruff-Pak, 1997). West and Bell (1997) illustrated the potential of this approach in a study that showed Stroop task performance to be related to prefrontal cortex activation. Both empirical and theoretical work has pointed to central roles in attentional processes for functions that are presumed to be sub-served by the frontal lobes, such as working memory, inhibition, and executive or strategic control. Linking neuropsychological work with ex-isting theoretical perspectives in the context of aging promises to be a productive avenue for future work. Although the application of these techniques and measures in aging is not yet widespread, it is likely that neuroscientific studies of attention in aging will grow in number, espe-cially in light of the recent interest in executive control theories that implicate frontal lobe functioning in attentional behavior. Progress has been slow, however, in part because of the expense and technical skill required by these methods.

Organizational Strategies

Another important benchmark of progress is the development of new ways to organize the relevant data. We have tried to provide here a functional organization for existing data on attention and aging, although this has not proved to be entirely satisfactory, in part because it requires an artificial separation of data into a single category of attentional behavior and in part because the categories we have identified are not specific enough to allow any single generalization about age-related performance. Presumably, some different, as-yet-unidentified organization would allow such generalizations to be made. Typically we look to theories to provide such an organization, which leads to the final criterion for progress iden-tified by Hartley (1992).

Rigorous Theories

Limited progress in the development of increasingly rigorous theories has been made in recent years. Probably the most promising are inhibitory-deficit theory and executive control theory. Progress in inhibitory-deficit theory has come from identifying boundary conditions for expecting age-related attentional effects and from identifying subprocesses of the more global concept of inhibition (e.g., access, deletion, and restraint). These developments constitute progress because identifying boundary conditions can make a theory falsifiable and because identifying subproc-esses can increase the specificity of underlying mechanisms required by the theory. Executive control theory also represents progress in theory development at least in part because of its ties to (brain) mechanisms as an explanation for age-related attentional deficits. The assumption here is that a rigorous theory is one that that specifies a mechanism for the phenomena it purports to explain. This sort of rigor is absent in early versions of resource theory and contributed to much of the dissatisfaction with that theory. It is also relatively weak in speed-of-processing theory. Although Salthouse (1996) offered two possible mechanisms to account for the relation between processing speed and cognition (the limited time mechanism and the simultaneity mechanism), these mechanisms represent the aftermath of some unspecified age-related slowing process and not the underlying age-related process that produces the slowing. However, that theory may be being held to an unfair standard in this case. That is, Salthouse (1994b) stated that processing speed is a proximal factor in accounting for age differences in attentional behavior; the search for a mechanism represents a distal level of analysis. Such a distinction is important to keep in mind, especially when processing speed is sometimes offered as a "cause" for age-related attentional deficits (e.g., Salthouse, 1994a).

The notion of mechanism is essentially irrelevant to environmental support theory. Although this irrelevancy makes the theory less rigorous, as we have defined rigor here, the merit of the environmental support approach lies in its ability to organize findings and predict functional outcomes. By taking a functional approach, age differences can often be reduced or eliminated, regardless of the cognitive mechanisms involved, by providing support for achieving the task requirements (e.g., suppressing distractors and responding more quickly). It also can serve as an organizing principle for applied research aimed at ameliorating age-related functional deficits. Research on medication adherence, for example, is designed to determine the cognitive processes involved, identify the relevant age-related deficits, and restructure labeling and instructional information to minimize reliance on deficient processes (e.g., D. C. Park, 1992). When attentional deficits are relevant to daily tasks, a functional analysis of the role of the environmental context can lead to suggestions about how to enhance the ability of the environment to support functioning. In short, if one starts from the point of view that older adults rely more on support from the environment for attaining behavioral goals, the reasons why this is so are of somewhat less interest than understanding the conditions that support cognitive processes.

All of the theories described in the foregoing sections vary both in the extent to which they can account for the data on attention and aging and the specificity with which they suggest mechanisms to account for these data. Across all of them, however, the implicit goal is to identify a single construct that can account for all age-related attentional phenomena. McDowd (1997) has argued previously that it may be premature to expect the young science of cognitive aging to produce a single, parsimonious theory to explain a diversity of findings. Rather than just premature, O. Neumann's (1987, 1996) work suggests that it is simply a mistake to try to identify a single cause underlying age changes in attentional function. He claims that attentional behavior results from the operation of a number of neural mechanisms, so "there is no point in seeking a unified theory of attention in the style of Capacity theories. What we need to understand are the different mechanisms that subserve selection functions and thereby produce capacity limitations" (O. Neumann, 1987, p. 375). Thus, this view suggests a different approach to theory development in the study of attention and aging; the goal of parsimony is replaced with the goal of understanding the multiple mechanisms of attention in the context of the control of behavior.

O. Neumann's (1987, 1996) functional approach also embodies a radically different conceptualization of attention. In his view, information-processing limits are not due to any deficit in the cognitive system (e.g., insufficient speed or capacity or inhibitory strength) but are in fact the desired outcome for a system whose goal is the control of action (see also Allport, 1987; van der Heijden, 1992). That is, although there is no physiological evidence establishing the limits of the brain's capacity for information processing, behavioral chaos would result from processing and responding to all possible stimuli and performing all associated actions. O. Neumann argued that there are processing mechanisms designed to prevent this chaos, and these mechanisms also produce the phenomena that have been attributed to a limited-capacity system.

With regard to understanding aging and attention, O. Neumann's model suggests that such understanding will be advanced by identifying and examining the mechanisms of behavioral control rather than by trying to identify and measure capacity. The question that remains, however, is how this view helps us understand age-related changes in attentional behavior. The answer to this question may relate to the general approach it engenders rather than to a specific empirical contribution. That is, O. Neumann's functional view requires multiple mechanisms to account for attentional behavior and, in so doing, relieves the search for a single cause of age-related attentional differences. It also represents a fundamental reconceptualization regarding how attentional phenomena are produced, which, together with the notion of multiple mechanisms, may prove fruitful in ways previous attempts to identify a single causal factor have not.

Applications of Theory and Data

Another criterion for progress not stated explicitly by Hartley (1992) is the extent to which theory and data have contributed to improving quality of life among older adults. Like much of cognitive aging research, research on attention and aging continues to grow in volume and extent and has the potential to be usefully applied in a variety of domains. For example, understanding attention in aging may help us to understand and solve real-world problems, support the needs of daily living, and enhance the functionality of the human interface with technology. Rogers and Fisk (see chap. 10, this volume) provide an excellent review of work in the area of human factors and ergonomics. Salthouse, Hambrick, Lukas, and Dell (1996) illustrated one way in which a theoretical approach can be applied to practical issues in their research on synthetic work performance. Clearly, the consequences of attentional deficits are many because of the central gate-keeping role of attentional processes. More applied work is essential to understand how older adults interact with their environments. Such work will require clear models of the cognitive processes involved in various tasks (Light, 1991; Zacks & Hasher, 1997) for accurate and sensible applications of relevant theories of attention; and, as D. C. Park (1992) noted, such work must also take into account the real-world context in which cognition takes place.

In summary, evaluation of progress in understanding attentional function in aging depends on one's criteria for progress. From a scientific point of view, more work is required to continue to develop and test rigorous and falsifiable theories of attentional function in aging. From a functional approach, knowing what works to support efficient attentional behavior may be sufficient to consititute progress without worrying about underlying mechanisms or distal levels of explanation. It is likely that active discourse between investigators working from each approach will be the most productive in solving both scientific and practical problems related to attention and aging.

ACKNOWLEDGMENTS

Preparation of this chapter was supported in part by Grant AG07991 from the National Institute on Aging to Joan M. McDowd and by a Merrimack College Faculty Development Grant to Raymond J. Shaw.

REFERENCES

Allen, P. A., Groth, K. E., Weber, T. A., & Madden, D. J. (1993). Influence of response selection and noise similarity on age differences in the redundancy gain. *Journal of Gerontology, 48,* 189–198.

Allen, P. A., Madden, D. J., Groth, K. E., & Crozier, L. C. (1992). Impact of age, redundancy, and perceptual noise on visual search. *Journal of Gerontology: Psychological Sciences, 47,* 69–74.

Allen, P. A., Weber, T. A., & Madden, D. J. (1994). Adult age differences in attention: Filtering or selection? *Journal of Gerontology: Psychological Sciences, 49,* 213–222.

Allport, A. (1987). Selection for action: Some behavioral and neurophysiological considerations of attention and action. In H. Heuer & A. F. Sanders (Eds.), *Perspectives on perception and action* (pp. 395–419). Hillsdale, NJ: Lawrence Erlbaum Associates.

Atchley, P., & Kramer, A. F. (1998). Spatial cuing in a stereoscopic display: Attention remains "depth-aware" with age. *Journal of Gerontology, 53B.*

Baddeley, A., & Hitch, G. (1974). Working memory. In G. Bower (Ed.), *The psychology of learning and motivation* (pp. 47–90). New York: Academic Press.

Baddeley, A. D. (1986). *Working memory.* New York: Oxford University Press.

Baddeley, A. D. (1993). Working memory or working attention? In A. Baddeley & L. Weiskrantz (Eds.), *Attention: Selection, awareness and control* (pp. 152–170). New York: Oxford University Press.

Ball, K., Owsley, C., Sloane, M. E., Roenker, D. L., & Bruni, J. R. (1993). Visual attention problems as a predictor of vehicle crashes among older drivers. *Investigative Ophthalmology & Visual Science, 34,* 3110–3123.

Ball, K., & Rebok, G. (1994). Evaluating the driving ability of older adults. *Journal of Applied Gerontology, 13,* 20–38.

Ball, K., Roenker, D. L., & Bruni, J. R. (1990). Developmental changes in attention and visual search throughout adulthood. *Advances in Psychology, 69,* 489–508.

Balota, D. A., & Black, S. (1997). Semantic satiation in healthy young and older adults. *Memory and Cognition, 25,* 190–202.

Balota, D. A., & Ferraro, F. R. (1993). A dissociation of frequency and regularity effects in pronunciation performance across young adults, older adults, and individuals with senile dementia of the Alzheimer type. *Journal of Memory and Language, 32,* 573–592.

Barr, R. A., & Eberhard, J. (1994). Older drivers: A different problem, a different solution? *Alcohol, Drugs, and Driving, 10,* 93–100.

Bashore, T. R., van der Molen, M. W., Maurits, W., Ridderinkhof, K., & Wylie, S. A. (1997). Is the complexity effect mediated by reductions in a general processing resource? *Biological Psychology, 45,* 263–282.

Belleville, S., Rouleau, N., & Caza, N. (1998). Effect of normal aging on the manipulation of information in working memory. *Memory and Cognition, 26,* 572–583.

Bills, A. G. (1931). Blocking: A new principle of mental fatigue. *American Journal of Psychology, 43,* 230–245.

Birren, J. E., & Fisher, L. M. (1995). Aging and speed of behavior: Possible consequences for psychological functioning. *Annual Review of Psychology, 46,* 329–353.

Bunce, D. J., Barrowclough, A., & Morris, I. (1996). The moderating influence of physical fitness on age gradients in vigilance and serial choice responding tasks. *Psychology and Aging, 11,* 671–682.

Bunce, D. J., Warr, P. B., & Cochrane, T. (1993). Blocks in choice responding as a function of age and physical fitness. *Psychology and Aging, 8,* 26–33.

Burke, D. M. (1997). Language, aging and inhibitory deficits: Evaluation of a theory. *Journal of Gerontology: Psychological Sciences, 52B,* P254–P264.

Carlson, M. C., Hasher, L., Connelly, S. L., & Zacks, R. T. (1995). Aging, distraction, and the benefits of predictable location. *Psychology and Aging, 10,* 427–436.

Cerella, J. (1990). Aging and information-processing rate. In J. E. Birren & K. W. Schaie (Eds.), *Handbook of the psychology of aging* (3rd ed., pp. 201–221). San Diego, CA: Academic Press.

Cerella, J. (1994). Generalized slowing in Brinley plots. *Journal of Gerontology: Psychological Sciences, 49,* P65–P71.

Cohen, J. D., & Servan-Schreiber, D. (1992). Context, cortex, and dopamine: A connectionist approach to behavior and biology in schizophrenia. *Psychological Review, 99,* 45–77.

Cohn, N. B., Dustman, R. E., & Bradford, D. C. (1984). Age-related decrements in Stroop color test performance. *Journal of Clinical Psychology, 40,* 1244–1250.

Collins, L. M. (1994). Comment on "How many causes are there of aging-related decrements in cognitive functioning?" *Developmental Review, 14*, 438–443.

Comalli, P. E., Wapner, S., & Werner, H. (1962). Interference effects of Stroop color-word test on childhood, adulthood, and aging. *Journal of Genetic Psychology, 100*, 47–53.

Connelly, S. L., & Hasher, L. (1993). Aging and inhibition of spatial location. *Journal of Experimental Psychology: Human Perception and Performance, 19*, 1238–1250.

Connelly, S. L., Hasher, L., & Zacks, R. T. (1991). Age and reading: The impact of distraction. *Psychology and Aging, 6*, 533–541.

Craik, F. I. M. (1977). Age differences in human memory. In J. E. Birren & K. W. Schaie (Eds.), *Handbook of the psychology of aging* (pp. 384–420). New York: Van Nostrand Reinhold.

Craik, F. I. M. (1983). On the transfer of information from temporary to permanent memory. *Philosophical Transactions of the Royal Society, London, B302*, 341–359.

Craik, F. I. M. (1986). A functional account of age differences in memory. In F. Klix & H. Hagendorf (Eds.), *Human memory and cognitive capabilities: Mechanisms and performances* (pp. 409–422). Amsterdam: Elsevier.

Craik, F. I. M., & Byrd, M. (1982). Aging and cognitive deficits: The role of attentional resources. In F. I. M. Craik & S. Trehub (Eds.), *Aging and cognitive processes* (pp. 191–211). New York: Plenum.

Craik, F. I. M., & Jennings, J. M. (1992). Human memory. In F. I. M. Craik & T. A. Salthouse (Eds.), *Handbook of cognition and aging* (pp. 51–110). Hillsdale, NJ: Lawrence Erlbaum Associates.

Craik, F. I. M., & McDowd, J. M. (1987). Age differences in recall and recognition. *Journal of Experimental Psychology: Learning, Memory, and Cognition, 13*, 474–479.

Crook, T. H., West, R. L., & Larrabee, G. J. (1993). The driving-reaction time test: Assessing age declines in dual-task performance. *Developmental Neuropsychology, 9*, 31–39.

Denney, N. W. (1990). Adult age differences in traditional and practical problem solving. In E. A. Lovelace (Ed.), *Aging and cognition: Mental processes, self awareness, and interventions* (pp. 329–349). Amsterdam: North-Holland.

Duchek, J. M., Balota, D. A., Faust, M. E., & Ferraro, F. R. (1995). Inhibitory processes in young and older adults in a picture–word task. *Aging & Cognition, 2*, 1–11.

Dujardin, K., Derambure, P., Bourriez, J. L., Jacquesson, J. M., & Guieu, J. D. (1993). P300 component of the even-related potentials (ERP) during an attention task: Effects of age, stimulus modality and event probability. *International Journal of Psychophysiology, 14*, 255–267.

Dulaney, C. L., & Rogers, W. A. (1994). Mechanisms underlying reduction in Stroop interference with practice for young and old adults. *Journal of Experimental Psychology: Learning, Memory, and Cognition, 20*, 470–484.

Dywan, J., & Murphy, W. E. (1996). Aging and inhibitory control in text comprehension. *Psychology and Aging, 11*, 199–206.

Earles, J. L., Connor, L. T., Frieske, D., Park, D. C., Smith, A. D., & Zwahr, M. (1997). Age differences in inhibition: Possible causes and consequences. *Aging, Neuropsychology, and Cognition, 4*, 45–57.

Einstein, G. O., & McDaniel, M. A. (1997). Aging and mind wandering: Reduced inhibition in older adults? *Experimental Aging Research, 23*, 343–354.

Einstein, G. O., Smith, R. E., McDaniel, M. A., & Shaw, P. (1997). Aging and prospective memory: The influence of increased task demands at encoding and retrieval. *Psychology and Aging, 12*, 479–488.

Engle, R. W., Conway, A. R., Tuholski, S. W., & Shisler, R. J. (1995). A resource account of inhibition. *Psychological Science, 6*, 122–125.

Eriksen, B. A., & Eriksen, C. W. (1974). Effects of noise letters upon the identification of a target letter in a nonsearch task. *Perception and Psychophysics, 16*, 143–149.

Farkas, M. S., & Hoyer, W. J. (1980). Processing consequences of perceptual grouping in selective attention. *Journal of Gerontology, 35,* 207–216.

Fisk, A. D., & Fisher, D. L. (1994). Brinley plots and theories of aging: The explicit, muddled, and implicit debates. *Journal of Gerontology: Psychological Sciences, 49,* P81–P89.

Folk, C. L., & Hoyer, W. J. (1992). Aging and shifts of visual spatial attention. *Psychology and Aging, 7,* 453–465.

Giambra, L. M. (1993). Sustained attention in older adults: Performance and processes. In J. Cerella, J. Rybash, W. Hoyer, & M. L. Commons (Eds.), *Adult information processing: Limits on loss* (pp. 259–272). San Diego, CA: Academic Press.

Gopher, D., & Sanders, A. F. (1984). 'S-Oh-R': Oh stages! Oh resources! In W. Prinz & A. F. Sanders (Eds.), *Cognition and motor processes* (pp. 231–253). Berlin, Germany: Springer.

Gottlob, L. R., & Madden, D. J. (1998). Time course of allocation of visual attention after equating for sensory differences: An age-related perspective. *Psychology and Aging, 13,* 138–149.

Greenwood, P. M., & Parasuraman, R. (1994). Attentional disengagement deficit in nondemented elderly over 75 years of age. *Aging and Cognition, 1,* 188–202.

Greenwood, P. M., Parasuraman, R., & Alexander, G. E. (1997). Controlling the focus of spatial attention during visual search: Effects of advanced aging and Alzheimer disease. *Neuropsychology, 11,* 3–12.

Greenwood, P. M., Parasuraman, R., & Haxby, J. V. (1993). Changes in visuospatial attention over the adult lifespan. *Neuropsychologia, 31,* 471–485.

Grice, G. R., & Canham, L. (1990). Redundancy phenomena are affected by response requirements. *Perception & Psychophysics, 48,* 209–213.

Hahn, S., & Kramer, A. F. (1995). Attentional flexibility and aging: You don't need to be 20 years of age to split the beam. *Psychology and Aging, 10,* 597–609.

Hale, S., Myerson, J., Rhee, S. H., Weiss, C. S., & Abrams, R. A. (1996). Selective interference with the maintenance of location information in working memory. *Neuropsychology, 10,* 228–240.

Hamm, V. P., & Hasher, L. (1992). Age and the availability of inferences. *Psychology and Aging, 7,* 56–64.

Hartley, A. A. (1992). Attention. In F. I. M. Craik & T. A. Salthouse (Eds.), *The handbook of aging and cognition* (pp. 3–49). Hillsdale, NJ: Lawrence Erlbaum Associates.

Hartley, A. A. (1993). Evidence for the selective preservation of spatial selective attention in old age. *Psychology and Aging, 3,* 371–379.

Hartman, M. (1995). Aging and interference: Evidence from indirect memory tests. *Psychology and Aging, 10,* 659–669.

Hartman, M., & Hasher, L. (1991). Aging and suppression: Memory for previously relevant information. *Psychology and Aging, 6,* 587–594.

Hasher, L., Quig, M. B., & May, C. P. (1997). Inhibitory control over no longer relevant information: Adult age differences. *Memory and Cognition, 25,* 286–295.

Hasher, L., Stoltzfus, E. R., Zacks, R. T., & Rypma, B. (1991). Age and inhibition. *Journal of Experimental Psychology: Learning, Memory, and Cognition, 17,* 163–169.

Hasher, L., & Zacks, R. T. (1979). Automatic and effortful processes in memory. *Journal of Experimental Psychology: General, 108,* 356–388.

Hasher, L., & Zacks, R. T. (1988). Working memory, comprehension, and aging: A review and a new view. In G. H. Bower (Ed.), *The psychology of learning and motivation* (Vol. 22, pp. 193–225). Orlando, FL: Academic Press.

Hasher, L., Zacks, R. T., & May, C. P. (in press). Inhibitory control, circadian arousal, and age. In D. Gopher & A. Koriat (Eds.), *Attention and performance: XVII. Cognitive regulation of performance: Interaction of theory and application.* Cambridge, MA: MIT Press.

Hawkins, H. L., Kramer, A. F., & Capaldi, D. (1992). Aging, exercise, and attention. *Psychology and Aging, 7,* 643–653.

Hoc, J. (1988). *Cognitive psychology of planning.* London: Harcourt Brace.

Hochhaus, L., & Marohn, K. M. (1991). Repetition blindness depends on perceptual capture and token individuation failure. *Journal of Experimental Psychology: Human Perception and Performance, 17,* 422–432.

Hockley, W. E. (1984). Analysis of response time distributions in the study of cognitive processes. *Journal of Experimental Psychology: Learning, Memory, and Cognition, 10,* 598–615.

Holland, C. A., & Rabbitt, P. M. A. (1994). The problems of being an older driver: Comparing the perspectives of an expert group and older drivers. *Applied Ergonomics, 25,* 17–27.

Houx, P. J., Jolles, J., & Vreeling, F. W. (1993). Stroop interference: Aging effects assessed with Stroop color-word test. *Experimental Aging Research, 19,* 209–224.

Humphrey, D. G., & Kramer, A. F. (1997). Age differences in visual search for feature, conjunction, and triple-conjunction targets. *Psychology and Aging, 12,* 704–717.

Humphrey, D. G., & Kramer, A. F. (1999). Age-related differences in perceptual organization and selective attention: Implications for display segmentation and recall performance. *Experimental Aging Research, 25,* 1–26.

Jacoby, L. L. (1991). A process dissociation framework: Separating automatic from intentional uses of memory. *Journal of Memory and Language, 30,* 513–541.

Jenkins, L., Myerson, J., Hale, S., & Fry, A. F. (1999). Lifespan developmental differences in interference with verbal and spatial working memory. *Psychonomic Bulletin & Review, 6,* 28–40.

Juola, J. F., Koshino, H., & Warner, C. B. (1996). *Automatic and voluntary control of attention in young and elderly adults.* Unpublished manuscript.

Kahneman, D. (1973). *Attention and effort.* Englewood Cliffs, NJ: Lawrence Erlbaum Associates.

Kane, M. J., Hasher, L., Stoltzfus, E. R., Zacks, R. T., & Connelly, S. L. (1994). Inhibitory attentional mechanisms and aging. *Psychology and Aging, 9,* 103–112.

Kieley, J. M., & Hartley, A. A. (1997). Age-related equivalence of identity suppression in the Stroop color-word task. *Psychology and Aging, 12,* 22–29.

Klein, M. (1997). *Cognitive aging, attention, and mild traumatic brain injury.* Maastricht, The Netherlands: Neuropsych Publishers.

Klein, M., Ponds, R. W. H. M., Houx, P. J., & Jolles, J. (1997). Effect of test duration on age-related differences in Stroop interference. *Journal of Clinical and Experimental Neuropsychology, 19,* 77–82.

Kotary, L., & Hoyer, W. (1995). Age and the ability to inhibit distractor information in visual selective attention. *Experimental Aging Research, 21,* 159–171.

Kramer, A. F., Hahn, S., & Gopher, D. (in press). Task coordination and aging: Explorations of executive control processes in the task switching paradigm. *Acta Psychologica.*

Kramer, A. F., Humphrey, D. G., Larish, J. F., & Logan, G. D. (1994). Aging and inhibition: Beyond a unitary view of inhibitory processing in attention. *Psychology and Aging, 9,* 491–512.

Kramer, A. F., & Larish, J. (1996). Aging and dual-task performance. In W. R. Rogers, A. D. Fisk, & N. Walker (Eds.), *Aging and skilled performance* (pp. 83–112). Hillsdale, NJ: Lawrence Erlbaum Associates.

Kramer, A. F., Larish, J. F., & Strayer, D. L. (1995). Training for attentional control in dual task settings: A comparison of young and old adults. *Journal of Experimental Psychology: Applied, 1,* 50–76.

Kramer, A. F., Larish, J. F., Weber, T. A., & Bardell, L. (in press). Training for executive control: Task coordination strategies and aging. In D. Gopher & A. Koriat (Eds.), *Attention and Performance: XVIII.* New York: Academic Press.

LaBerge, D., Brown, V., Carter, M., Bash, D., & Hartley, A. (1991). Reducing the effects of adjacent distractors by narrowing attention. *Journal of Experimental Psychology: Human Perception and Performance, 17,* 65–76.

Lacey, J. I., & Lacey, B. C. (1970). Some autonomic–central nervous system interrelationships. In P. Black (Ed.), *Physiological correlates of emotion* (pp. 205–227). New York: Academic Press.

Lachman, M. E., & Burack, O. R. (1993). Planning and control processes across the life span. *International Journal of Behavioral Development, 16,* 131–143.

Lerner, N. (1994). Giving the older driver enough perception–reaction time. *Experimental Aging Research, 20,* 25–33.

Light, L. L. (1991). Memory and aging: Four hypotheses in search of data. *Annual Review of Psychology, 42,* 333–376.

Light, L. L., & Prull, M. (1995). Aging, divided attention, and repetition priming. *Swiss Journal of Psychology, 54,* 87–101.

Lincourt, A. E., Folk, C. L., & Hoyer, W. J. (1997). Effects of aging on voluntary and involuntary shifts of attention. *Aging, Neuropsychology, and Cognition, 4,* 1.

Lindfield, K. C., Wingfield, A., & Bowles, N. L. (1994). Identification of fragmented pictures under ascending versus fixed presentation in young and elderly adults: Evidence for the inhibition-deficit hypothesis. *Aging and Cognition, 1,* 282–291.

Lindsay, D. S., & Jacoby, L. L. (1994). Stroop process dissociations: The relation between facilitation and interference. *Journal of Experimental Psychology: Human Perception and Performance, 20,* 219–234.

Lorist, M. M., Snel, J., Mulder, G., & Kok, A. (1995). Aging, caffeine, and information processing: An event-related potential analysis. *Electroencephalography and Clinical Neurophysiology, 96,* 453–467.

Luria, A. R. (1980). *Higher cortical function in man.* New York: Basic Books.

MacKay, D. G., Miller, M. D., & Schuster, S. P. (1994). Repetition blindness and aging: Evidence for a binding deficit involving a single, theoretically specified connection. *Psychology and Aging, 9,* 251–258.

Madden, D. J. (1990). Adult age differences in attentional selectivity and capacity. *European Journal of Cognitive Psychology, 2,* 229–252.

Madden, D. J. (1992). Selective attention and visual search: Revision of an allocation model and application to age differences. *Journal of Experimental Psychology: Human Perception and Performance, 18,* 821–836.

Madden, D. J., & Allen, P. A. (1996). Attention. In J. E. Birren (Ed.), *Encyclopedia of Gerontology* (pp. 131–140). San Diego, CA: Academic Press.

Madden, D. J., Connelly, S. L., & Pierce, T. W. (1994). Adult age differences in shifting focused attention. *Psychology and Aging, 9,* 528–538.

Madden, D. J., & Gottlob, L. R. (1997). Adult age differences in strategic and dynamic components of focusing visual attention. *Aging, Neuropsychology, and Cognition, 4,* 185–210.

Madden, D. J., Pierce, T. W., & Allen, P. A. (1996). Adult age differences in the use of distractor homogeneity during visual search. *Psychology and Aging, 11,* 454–474.

Madden, D. J., & Plude, D. J. (1993). Selective preservation of selective attention. In J. Cerella, J. M. Rybash, W. Hoyer, & M. L. Commons (Eds.), *Adult information processing: Limits on loss* (pp. 273–300). San Diego, CA: Academic Press.

Madden, D. J., Turkington, T. G., Provenzale, J. M., Hawk, T. C., Hoffman, J. M., & Coleman, R. E. (1997). Selective and divided visual attention: Age-related changes in regional cerebral blood flow measured by H_2 ^{15}O PET. *Human Brain Mapping, 5,* 389–409.

Mäntylä, T., & Bäckman, L. (1992). Aging and memory for expected and unexpected objects in real-world settings. *Journal of Experimental Psychology: Learning, Memory, and Cognition, 18,* 1298–1309.

Martin, M., & Ewert, O. (1997). Attention and planning in older adults. *International Journal of Behavioral Development, 20,* 577–594.

May, C. P., Kane, M., & Hasher, L. (1995). Determinants of negative priming. *Psychological Bulletin, 118,* 35–54.

Mayr, U., & Kliegl, R. (1993). Sequential and coordinative complexity: Age-based processing limitations in figural transformations. *Journal of Experimental Psychology: Learning, Memory, and Cognition, 19,* 1297–1320.

Mayr, U., Kliegl, R., & Krampe, R. T. (1996). Sequential and coordinative processing dynamics in figural transformations across the life span. *Cognition, 59,* 61–90.

McCalley, L. T., Bouwhuis, D. G., & Juola, J. F. (1995). Age changes in the distribution of visual attention. *Journal of Gerontology: Psychological Sciences, 50B,* P316–P331.

McDowd, J. M. (1997). Inhibition in attention and aging. *Journal of Gerontology: Psychological Sciences, 52B,* 265–273.

McDowd, J. M., & Filion, D. L. (1995). Aging and negative priming in a location suppression task: The long and short of it. *Psychology and Aging, 10,* 34–47.

McDowd, J. M., & Oseas-Kreger, D. M. (1991). Aging, inhibitory processes, and negative priming. *Journal of Gerontology: Psychology Sciences, 46,* 340–345.

McDowd, J. M., Oseas-Kreger, D. M. & Filion, D. L. (1995). Inhibitory processes in cognition and aging. In F. N. Dempster & C. J. Brainerd (Eds.), *Interference and inhibition in cognition* (pp. 363–400). San Diego, CA: Academic Press.

Mitchell, D. B., & Perlmutter, M. (1986). Semantic activation and episodic memory: Age similarities and differences. *Developmental Psychology, 22,* 86–94.

Molander, B., & Bäckman, L. (1989). Age differences in heart rate patterns during concentration in a precision sport: Implications for attentional functioning. *Journal of Gerontology: Psychological Sciences, 44,* 80–87.

Molander, B., & Bäckman, L. (1990). Age differences in the effects of background noise on motor and memory performance in a precision sport. *Experimental Aging Research, 16,* 55–60.

Molander, B., & Bäckman, L. (1993). Performance of a complex motor skill across the life-span: General trends and qualifications. In J. Cerella, J. Rybash, W. Hoyer, & M. L. Commons (Eds.), *Adult information processing: Limits on loss* (pp. 231–257). San Diego: Academic Press.

Mouloua, M., & Parasuraman, R. (1995). Aging and cognitive vigilance: Effects of spatial uncertainty and event rate. *Experimental Aging Research, 21,* 17–32.

Myerson, J., Hale, S., Rhee, S. H., & Jenkins, L. (in press). Age and selective interference with the maintenance of information in working memory. *Memory & Cognition.*

Myerson, J., Hale, S., Wagstaff, D., Poon, L. W., & Smith, G. A. (1990). The information-loss model: A mathematical theory of age-related cognitive slowing. *Psychological Review, 97,* 475–487.

Myerson, J., Wagstaff, D., & Hale, S. (1994). Brinley plots, explained variance, and the analysis of age differences in response latencies. *Journal of Gerontology: Psychological Sciences, 49,* P72–P80.

Navon, D. (1984). Resources—A theoretical soupstone? *Psychological Review, 91,* 216–234.

Nebes, R. D., & Madden, D. J. (1983). The use of focussed attention in visual search by young and old adults. *Experimental Aging Research, 9,* 139–143.

Neill, W. T., & Valdes, L. A. (1992). The persistence of negative priming: Steady state or decay? *Journal of Experimental Psychology: Learning, Memory, and Cognition, 18,* 565–576.

Neill, W. T., Valdes, L. A., Terry, K. M., & Gorfein, D. S. (1992). The persistence of negative priming: II. Evidence for episodic trace retrieval. *Journal of Experimental Psychology: Learning, Memory, and Cognition, 18,* 993–1000.

Neumann, E., & DeSchepper, B. G. (1992). An inhibition-based fan effect: Evidence for an action suppression mechanism for selective attention. *Canadian Journal of Psychology, 46,* 1–40.

Neumann, O. (1987). Beyond capacity: A functional view of attention. In H. Heuer & A. F. Sanders (Eds.), *Perspectives on perception and action* (pp. 361–394). Hillsdale, NJ: Lawrence Erlbaum Associates.

Neumann, O. (1996). Theories of attention. In O. Neumann & A. F. Sanders (Eds.), *Handbook of perception and action* (Vol. 3, pp. 389–446). New York: Academic Press.

Neuchterlein, K. H., Parasuraman, R., & Jiang, Q. (1983). Visual sustained attention: Image degradation produces rapid sensitivity decrement over time. *Science, 220,* 327–329.

Nyberg, L., Nilsson, L. -G., Olofsson, U., & Bäckman, L. (1997). Effects of division of attention during encoding and retrieval on age differences in episodic memory. *Experimental Aging Research, 23,* 137–143.

Owsley, C., Ball, K., Sloane, M. E., Roenker, D. L., & Bruni, J. R. (1991). Visual/cognitive correlates of vehicle accidents in older drivers. *Psychology and Aging, 6,* 403–415.

Parasuraman, R., & Nestor, P. G. (1991). Attention and driving skills in aging and Alzheimer's disease. *Human Factors, 33,* 539–557.

Park, D. C. (1992). Applied cognitive aging research. In F. I. M. Craik & T. A. Salthouse (Eds.), *Handbook of cognitive aging* (pp. 449–494). Hillsdale, NJ: Lawrence Erlbaum Associates.

Park, D. C., & Shaw, R. J. (1992). Effect of environmental support on implicit and explicit memory in younger and older adults. *Psychology and Aging, 7,* 632–642.

Park, D. C., Smith, A. D., Lautenschlager, G., Earles, J. L., Frieske, D., Zwahr, M., & Gaines, C. L. (1996). Mediators of long-term memory performance across the life span. *Psychology and Aging, 11,* 621–637.

Park, J., & Kanwisher, N. (1994). Negative priming for spatial location: Identity mismatching, not distractor inhibition. *Journal of Experimental Psychology: Human Perception and Performance, 20,* 613–623.

Perfect, T. J. (1994). What can Brinley plots tell us about cognitive aging? *Journal of Gerontology: Psychological Sciences, 49,* P60–P64.

Perfect, T. J., & Rabbitt, P. M. (1993). Age and the divided attention costs of category exemplar generation. *British Journal of Developmental Psychology, 11,* 131–142.

Plude, D. J., & Doussard-Roosevelt, J. A. (1989). Aging, selective attention, and feature integration. *Psychology and Aging, 4,* 98–105.

Plude, D. J., Enns, J. T., & Brodeur, D. (1994). The development of selective attention: A life-span overview [Special issue]. *Acta Psychologica, 86,* 227–272.

Plude, D. J., & Hoyer, W. J. (1985). Attention and performance: Identifying and localizing age deficits. In N. Charness (Ed.), *Aging and performance* (pp. 47–99). New York: Wiley.

Rabbitt, P. M. A. (1965). An age decrement in the ability to ignore irrelevant information. *Journal of Gerontology, 20,* 233–238.

Ratcliff, R. (1979). Group reaction time distributions and an analysis of distribution statistics. *Psychological Review, 86,* 446–461.

Rogers, D. R., & Monsell, S. (1995). Costs of a predictable switch between simple cognitive tasks. *Journal of Experimental Psychology: General, 124,* 207–231.

Rouleau, N., & Belleville, S. (1996). Irrelevant speech effect in aging: An assessment of inhibitory processes in working memory. *Journal of Gerontology: Psychological Sciences, 51B,* P356–P363.

Salthouse, T. A. (1985). Speed of behavior and its implications for cognition. In J. E. Birren & K. W. Schiaie (Eds.), *Handbook of the psychology of aging* (2nd ed., pp. 400–426). New York: Van Nostrand Reinhold.

Salthouse, T. A. (1988). Resource-reduction interpretations of cognitive aging. *Developmental Review, 8,* 238–272.

Salthouse, T. A. (1991). *Theoretical perspectives on cognitive aging.* Hillsdale, NJ: Lawrence Erlbaum Associates.

Salthouse, T. A. (1993). Attentional blocks are not responsible for age-related slowing. *Journal of Gerontology: Psychological Sciences, 48*, P265–P270.

Salthouse, T. A. (1994a). How many causes are there of aging-related decrements in cognitive functioning? *Developmental Review, 14*, 413–437.

Salthouse, T. A. (1994b). Reply to commentary by Collins: Distinguishing proximal and distal levels of explanation. *Developmental Review, 14*, 444–446.

Salthouse, T. A. (1996). The processing-speed theory of adult age differences in cognition. *Psychological Review, 103*, 403–428.

Salthouse, T. A., Fristoe, N., McGuthry, K. E., & Hambrick, D. Z. (1998). Relation of task switching to speed, age, and fluid intelligence. *Psychology and Aging, 13*, 445–461.

Salthouse, T. A., Fristoe, N. M., Lineweaver, T. T., & Coon, V. E. (1995). Aging of attention: Does the ability to divide decline? *Memory and Cognition, 23*, 59–71.

Salthouse, T. A., Hambrick, D. Z., Lukas, K. E., & Dell, T. C. (1996). Determinants of adult age differences on synthetic work performance. *Journal of Experimental Psychology: Applied, 2*, 305–329.

Salthouse, T. A., & Meinz, E. J. (1995). Aging, inhibition, working memory, and speed. *Journal of Gerontology: Psychological Sciences, 50*, 297–306.

Salthouse, T. A., Toth, J. P., Hancock, H. E., & Woodard, J. L. (1997). Controlled and automatic forms of memory and attention: Process purity and the uniqueness of age-related influences. *Journal of Gerontology: Psychological Sciences, 52B*, P216–P228.

Sanders, A. F. (1983). Towards a model of stress and human performance. *Acta Psychologica, 53*, 61–97.

Schooler, C., Neumann, E., Caplan, L. J., & Roberts, B. R. (1997). Continued inhibitory capacity throughout adulthood: Conceptual negative priming in younger and older adults. *Psychology and Aging, 12*, 667–674.

Shaffer, W. O., & LaBerge, D. (1979). Automatic semantic processing of unattended words. *Journal of Verbal Learning and Verbal Behavior, 18*, 413–426.

Shallice, T., & Burgess, P. (1993). Supervisory control of action and thought selection. In A. Baddeley & L. Weiskrantz (Eds.), *Attention: Selection, awareness and control* (pp. 171–187). New York: Oxford University Press.

Shaw, R. J. (1990). Older adults sometimes benefit from environmental support: Evidence from reading distorted text. *Proceedings of the Human Factors Society, 34*, 168–172.

Shaw, R. J. (1991). Age-related increases in the effects of automatic semantic activation. *Psychology and Aging, 6*, 595–604.

Shaw, R. J., Rypma, B., & Toffle, C. E. (1992, April). *The effects of environmental support on age differences in ignoring distraction in reading.* Paper presented at the Fourth Cognitive Aging Conference, Atlanta, GA.

Somberg, B. L., & Salthouse, T. A. (1982). Divided attention abilities in young and old adults. *Journal of Experimental Psychology: Human Perception and Performance, 8*, 651–663.

Spieler, D. H., Balota, D. A., & Faust, M. E. (1996). Stroop performance in healthy younger and older adults and in individuals with dementia of the Alzheimer's type. *Journal of Experimental Psychology: Human Perception and Performance, 22*, 461–479.

Stankov, L. & Dunn, S. (1993). Physical substrata of mental energy: Brain capacity and efficiency of cerebral metabolism. *Learning and Individual Differences, 5*, 241–257.

Stine, E. A. L., & Wingfield, A. (1994). Older adults can inhibit high-probability competitors in speech recognition. *Aging and Cognition, 1*, 152–157.

Stoltzfus, E. R., Hasher, L., & Zacks, R. T. (1996). Working memory and aging: Current status of the inhibitory view. In J. T. E. Richardson, R. W. Engle, L. Hasher, R. H. Logie, E. R. Stoltzfus, & R. T. Zacks (Eds.), *Working memory and human cognition* (pp. 66–88). New York: Oxford University Press.

Stoltzfus, E. R., Hasher, L., Zacks, R. T., Ulivi, M. S., & Goldstein, D. (1993). Investigations of inhibition and interference in younger and older adults. *Journal of Gerontology: Psychological Sciences, 48*, 179–188.

Sullivan, M. P., & Faust, M. E. (1993). Evidence for identity inhibition during selective attention in old adults. *Psychology and Aging, 8,* 589–598.

Sullivan, M. P., Faust, M. E., & Balota, D. A. (1995). Identity negative priming in older adults and individuals with dementia of the Alzheimer type. *Neuropsychology, 9,* 537–555.

Tipper, S. P. (1991). Less attentional selectivity as a result of declining inhibition in old adults. *Bulletin of the Psychonomics Society, 29,* 45–47.

Tsang, P. S., & Shaner, T. L. (1998). Age, attention, expertise, and time-sharing performance. *Psychology and Aging, 13,* 323–347.

Tun, P. A., & Wingfield, A. (1993). Is speech special? Perception and recall of spoken language in complex environments. In J. Cerella, J. Rybash, W. Hoyer, & M. L. Commons (Eds.), *Adult information processing: Limits on loss* (pp. 425–457). San Diego, CA: Academic Press.

Tun, P. A., & Wingfield, A. (1994). Speech recall under heavy load conditions: Age, predictability, and limits on dual-task interference. *Aging, Neuropsychology, and Cognition, 1,* 29–44.

Tun, P. A., & Wingfield, A. (1995). Does dividing attention become harder with age? Findings from the Divided Attention Questionnaire. *Aging and Cognition, 2,* 39–66.

Tun, P. A., Wingfield, A., & Stine, E. A. L. (1991). Speech processing capacity in young and older adults: A dual task study. *Psychology and Aging, 6,* 3–9.

Tun, P. A., Wingfield, A., Stine, E. A. L., & Mecsas, C. (1992). Rapid speech processing and divided attention: Processing rate versus processing resources as an explanation of age effects. *Psychology and Aging, 7,* 546–550.

van der Heijden, A. H. C. (1992). *Selective attention in vision.* London: Routledge & Kegan Paul.

Verhaeghen, P., & De Meersman, L. (1998). Aging and the Stroop effect: A meta-analysis. *Psychology and Aging, 13,* 120–129.

Verhaeghen, P., & De Meersman, L. (1998). Aging and the negative priming effect: A meta-analysis. *Psychology and Aging, 13,* 435–444.

Verhaeghen, P., Kliegl, R., & Mayr, U. (1997). Sequential and coordinative complexity in time-accuracy functions for mental arithmetic. *Psychology and Aging, 12,* 555–564.

Walsh, D. A., & Hershey, D. A. (1993). Mental models and the maintenance of complex problem-solving skills in old age. In J. Cerella, J. Rybash, W. Hoyer, & M. L. Commons (Eds.), *Adult information processing: Limits on loss* (pp. 553–584). San Diego, CA: Academic Press.

West, R. L. (1996). An application of prefrontal cortex function theory to cognitive aging. *Psychological Bulletin, 120,* 272–292.

West, R., & Bell, M. A. (1997). Stroop color-word interference and electroencephalogram activation: Evidence for age-related decline of the anterior attention system. *Neuropsychology, 11,* 421–427.

Whiting, W. L., IV, & Smith, A. D. (1997). Differential age-related processing limitations in recall and recognition tasks. *Psychology and Aging, 12,* 216–224.

Wickens, C. D. (1984). Processing resources in attention. In R. Parasuraman & D. R. Davies (Eds.), *Varieties of attention* (pp. 63–102). Orlando, FL: Academic Press.

Wickens, C. D., Braune, R., & Stokes, A. (1987). Age differences in the speed and capacity of information processing: I. A dual-task approach. *Psychology and Aging, 2,* 70–78.

Willis, S. (1996). Everyday problem solving. In J. E. Birren & K. W. Schaie (Eds.), *Handbook of the psychology of aging* (4th ed., pp. 287–307). San Diego, CA: Academic Press.

Wingfield, A., Aberdeen, J. S., & Stine, E. A. L. (1991). Word onset gating and linguistic context in spoken word recognition by young and elderly adults. *Journal of Gerontology: Psychological Sciences, 46,* P127–P129.

Wingfield, A., Tun, P. A., & Rosen, M. J. (1995). Age differences in veridical and reconstructive recall of syntactically and randomly segmented speech. *Journal of Gerontology: Psychological Sciences, 50B,* P257–P266.

Woodrow, H. (1914). The measurement of attention. *The Psychological Monographs, XVII* (Whole No. 76).

Woodruff-Pak, D. S. (1997). *The neuropsychology of aging.* Malden, MA: Blackwell.

Wright, L. L., & Elias, J. W. (1979). Age differences in the effects of perceptual noise. *Journal of Gerontology, 34,* 704–708.

Yamaguchi, S., Tsuchiya, H., & Kobayashi, S. (1995). Electrophysiologic correlates of age effects on visuospatial attention shift. *Cognitive Brain Research, 3,* 41–49.

Yantis, S., & Jonides, J. (1984). Abrupt visual onsets and selective attention: Evidence from visual search. *Journal of Experimental Psychology: Human Perception and Performance, 10,* 601–620.

Yantis, S., & Jonides, J. (1990). Abrupt visual onsets and selective attention: Voluntary versus automatic allocation. *Journal of Experimental Psychology: Human Perception and Performance, 16,* 121–134.

Zacks, R. T., & Hasher, L. (1994). Directed ignoring: Inhibitory regulation of working memory. In D. Dagenbach & T. H. Carr (Eds.), *Inhibitory processes in attention, memory, and language* (pp. 241–264). San Diego, CA: Academic Press.

Zacks, R. T., & Hasher, L. (1997). Cognitive gerontology and attentional inhibition: A reply to Burke (1997) and McDowd (1997). *Journal of Gerontology: Psychological Sciences, 52B,* P274–P283.

5

Human Memory

Rose T. Zacks
Michigan State University

Lynn Hasher
Duke University

Karen Z. H. Li
Max Planck Institute for Human Development

Certain broad points of consensus are highlighted in previous reviews of the aging and memory literature (e.g., Craik, 1977; Craik, Anderson, Kerr, & Li, 1995; Craik & Jennings, 1992; Kausler, 1994; Light, 1991; A. D. Smith, 1996). For one, it is agreed that experimental and psychometric findings indicate age-related decrements in the ability to learn and remember. It is also agreed that not all types of memory show equal age deficits. Memories that were well established earlier in life and that are regularly retrieved (i.e., semantic memories and significant autobiographical memories) frequently show minimal decrease in retrieval probability or even in retrieval efficiency (speed) in old age. Even some forms of new memory formation (e.g., implicit learning and memory) are relatively spared from aging decrements. Furthermore, there is consensus that certain noncognitive and situational factors can modulate the degree to which age decrements are seen in particular memory tasks (see the section on memory and its moderators).

As a quick scan through aging journals and certain cognitive journals reveals, publications on aging and memory have been appearing at an accelerating rate over the past 10 to 15 years. In this work, aging and memory researchers have encompassed and built on theoretical concepts and methodologies that originate in cognitive gerontology, as well as in mainstream cognitive research, psychometric–individual difference work, and, increasingly, cognitive neuropsychology. Not surprisingly, this gives rise to diverse methods and to alternative explanatory frameworks. Although this is a sign of the health and vibrancy of the field, it means that it is not possible to attempt anything close to a comprehensive review of the literature. Nor is it necessary. Several excellent summaries of the literature have been published in recent years (see above citations). This chapter presents a selective review emphasizing recent work on topics of current major interest in the field. Our survey addresses age-related differences in memory performance in healthy individuals: Neuroimaging findings and patient data (e.g., from patients with Alzheimer's disease) are mentioned only as they might illuminate the "normal" aging of memory performance (discussions of neuroimaging findings and of findings on memory in brain-damaged older adults can be found, respectively, in chap. 1 and 2, this volume).

We begin with a brief overview of several important theoretical–methodological approaches to the study of aging and memory. The main section of the chapter is organized into sections on immediate and long-term memory, with the latter including subdivisions on unintentional remembering (implicit memory and learning) and deliberate remembering (episodic and prospective memory). Following the long-term memory section is one that addresses a number of biological and social factors that may have moderating influences on age differences in memory.

THEORETICAL ORIENTATIONS

Limited Resources and Self-Initiated Processing

One general approach to aging and memory proposes that age-related differences in memory are a consequence of age deficits in an essential processing resource, such as attentional or working memory capacity (e.g., Craik, 1986; Craik & Byrd, 1982; Hasher & Zacks, 1979; see Light, 1991, for a review). The viewpoint developed by Craik and colleagues (Craik, 1983, 1986; Craik et al., 1995; Craik & Byrd, 1982) has been especially influential in recent years, and we use it to represent theoretical approaches that formulate accounts of age differences in memory in terms of limited resources.[1] Craik's viewpoint is a functional account of memory that considers memory performance to result from an interaction between external and internal factors. The external factors include the amount of

---

[1]Speed of processing is sometimes considered a resource in the cognitive aging literature (e.g., Light, 1991). We treat speed-of-processing views separately from resource views because capacity-based and speed- or time-based constraints on performance seem quite different to us. For example, a capacity-based view suggests that decline in the capacity of working memory is a *direct* effect of aging, whereas a time-based view suggests that it is an *indirect* effect of slowed processing.

environmental support provided by the encoding and retrieval situations and by the form of the task. Environmental support is a broad notion that includes such dimensions as the amount of guidance provided as to how information should be encoded, the availability of relevant prior knowledge that might foster rich encoding of information, and the presence or absence at retrieval of external cues that might lead to direct access to memory traces. A major internal factor is the processing resources the person has available for memory encoding and retrieval. The presumed age-related decline in processing resources (e.g., Craik, 1983, 1986; Craik & Byrd, 1982; Hasher & Zacks, 1979) means that older adults are less able to carry out resource-demanding encoding and retrieval operations than are younger adults. The resource-demanding operations include *self-initiated* encoding and retrieval processes, such as the generation of novel connections among items or the construction of retrieval plans. These processes are most likely to come into play when materials are unfamiliar and thus are not readily interpreted or organized by the learner and when the environment provides few retrieval cues, as occurs when unrelated words are presented in the context of a free-recall task. On the other hand, strong environmental support in the form of familiar tasks and materials and the availability of external reminders and other cues for retrieval can compensate for the age-related reductions in the ability to carry out self-initiated processing.

Various types of findings from the aging and memory literature are consistent with this viewpoint. Among the strongest findings are those that relate to age effects on different types of memory tasks. In particular, in conformity with the differences among recognition, cued recall, and free-recall tasks in the cues that they provide for retrieval of target memories (and therefore in the demands they place on self-initiated processing), age differences are smallest in recognition tasks and largest in free-recall tasks, with cued recall falling in between (e.g., Craik, 1986; Craik & Anderson, 1999). Also, a study by Craik and McDowd (1987) that used secondary-task performance as a measure of the resource demands of recognition versus free recall found that the resource demands of the recall task as compared with the recognition task were differentially greater for older adults. These kinds of findings, and their general face validity, contribute to the continued viability of the Craik viewpoint and of reduced-resources views in general.

Speed of Processing

If there is any cognitive change with aging that is more apparent to casual observation than memory changes, it is the slowing of mental processing. That slowed processing might have a broad impact on the cognitive functioning of older adults has been proposed by a number of theorists, including Cerella (1985); Myerson, Hale, Wagstaff, Poon, and Smith (1990); and Salthouse (1991, 1996). For example, Salthouse and colleagues (e.g., Salthouse, 1991, 1992, 1996; Verhaeghen & Salthouse, 1997) have explored the implications of age-related slowing for working memory, episodic memory, and various fluid-intelligence functions, such as inferential reasoning.[2] This work has produced an impressive body of findings showing that (a) slowing of processing (as measured on simple perceptual tasks) accounts for a considerable portion of the age-related variance on a large number of cognitive tasks and (b) the amount of age-related variance accounted for by the speed factor is generally much greater than that accounted for by other possible mechanisms of age decline in cognitive function, in particular, working memory capacity (e.g., Park et al., 1996; Salthouse & Meinz, 1995; Verhaeghen & Salthouse, 1997). However, there are indications (Park et al., 1996) that working memory capacity increases in importance relative to speed as a predictor of cognitive performance as the memory task places greater demands on self-initiated processing (e.g., recognition vs. free recall).

In a recent article, Salthouse (1996) suggested that two mechanisms underlie the pattern of relations between speed and age-related changes in cognition. According to the *limited time mechanism*, the cognitive processes needed to complete tasks of any complexity may not occur when time is restricted because much of the available time is taken up with early processes. According to the *simultaneity mechanism*, the outcomes of early processes may be lost before they can be used by later processes. These are promising ideas that are likely to foster research examining the operation of the proposed mechanisms in the context of specific cognitive tasks.

Inhibitory Control

This view (Hasher & Zacks, 1988; Hasher, Zacks, & May, 1999; Zacks & Hasher, 1994, 1997; see also McDowd, Oseas-Kreger, & Filion, 1995) attributes age-related differences in memory and other cognitive functions to a decline in attentional inhibitory control over the contents of working memory. Hasher et al. (1999) proposed that there are three aspects to

---

[2]We note that there is a difference in typical research strategy between the work associated with the slowing approach versus other theoretical approaches to aging and cognition. Studies deriving from a slowing framework commonly administer a battery of cognitive tasks (often including a selection of standardized psychometric and neuropsychological measures) to a large sample of individuals from across the adult age range and make use of various regression and quantitative modeling techniques to analyze the data. By contrast, the typical research strategy used in the work associated with other approaches involves the administration of specially designed tasks to groups of younger and older adults (or sometimes also middle-aged adults) and the use of hypothesis-testing statistical techniques (e.g., analysis of variance) to analyze the data.

inhibitory control: access, deletion, and restraint. Working together, the *access* function, by hindering access to working memory of goal-irrelevant information that may be partially activated, and the *deletion* function, by suppressing the activation of any inadvertently activated extraneous and no-longer-relevant information, help ensure that the momentarily most active mental representations form a coherent set related only to the current goal(s) of cognitive function. The *restraint* function serves to prevent strong but situationally inappropriate responses from gaining control over thought and/or action, thereby allowing consideration of weaker but potentially more relevant responses.

When inhibitory control is deficient (as the Hasher–Zacks view suggests it is in older adults), the result is a kind of "mental clutter" in which extraneous thoughts and plans can interfere with, and possibly crowd out, goal-relevant thoughts and plans. This momentary increase in clutter is proposed to have subsequent consequences for long-term memory encoding and retrieval (e.g., Hasher et al., 1999; Zacks & Hasher, 1994; Zacks, Radvansky, & Hasher, 1996). Specifically, inhibitory failures to limit the presence of extraneous information in working memory during encoding results in the formation of associations between extraneous and goal-relevant thoughts. These "enriched" or "cluttered" memory structures will later result in slower and more error-prone retrieval of specific target information. One demonstration of this is the finding of age-related increases in the "fan effect" (Cohen, 1990; Gerard, Zacks, Hasher, & Radvansky, 1991), the finding that the more associations that are linked to a concept (the greater the "fan"), the slower and more error prone is the retrieval of any one of those associations. Also relevant are findings from "directed forgetting" tasks (Zacks et al., 1996) indicating that older adults are less able than younger adults to suppress the continued processing and retrieval of already-studied items cued as to be forgotten; these items can then produce more interference with the retrieval of to-be-remembered items than is true for younger adults. The retrieval problems of older adults may, in turn, promote increased reliance on schematic knowledge and other prepotent associations and responses to incoming information and retrieval cues. In general, this view suggests that an important consequence of increased mental clutter in working memory is an elevated sensitivity to potential sources of interference, both at encoding and retrieval. (For recent critiques of this view, see Burke, 1997; McDowd, 1997; for a rejoinder, see Zacks & Hasher, 1997).

Contextual Features and Source Memory

Relative to younger adults, older adults have been found to remember less about the contextual features of prior experiences (e.g., Spencer & Raz, 1995) and so less about the sources of their memories (e.g., Hashtroudi,

Johnson, & Chrosniak, 1989; McIntyre & Craik, 1987). In addition, older adults have been found to make more memory errors of various sorts (see the section on memory errors). A theoretical approach that potentially accounts for all these trends is Johnson's source-monitoring framework (Johnson, Hashtroudi, & Lindsay, 1993; Johnson & Raye, 1981; see also Schacter, Norman, & Koutstaal, 1998). This framework proposes that memory for any given event consists of a bundle of attributes or features of that event (cf. Underwood, 1983). These attributes can be more cognitive in nature—for example, attributes that refer to the kinds of operations (e.g., imagining and inferring) that were used to think about an item, or to the meaning of the item and its relation to other ideas, or to other aspects of the environment. Or the attributes can be more perceptual and contextual in nature—for example, attributes that specify the color, shape, size, or sound of an object and its spatial and temporal location. Memory for such information is critical for determining the "source" of a memory: Did I read that fact, did I hear it, or did I make it up?

The perceptual and cognitive features encoded about an event can either be strongly or weakly encoded, and they can either be strongly or weakly "bound" or integrated with each other. Both these aspects of encoding are thought to be important for later accurate retrieval of source. Factors that promote weak feature encoding and binding, and that may play a role in the weaker integration of target and contextual memory in older adults (Chalfonte & Johnson, 1996; Henkel, Johnson, & De Leonardis, 1998), include distraction in the environment or in thought; a tendency to pay attention to the emotional, interpretive qualities of input rather than to factual qualities (e.g., Hashtroudi, Johnson, Vnek, & Ferguson, 1994); or a tendency to pay attention to one's own emotional responses rather than to events in the environment (Johnson, Nolde, & De Leonardis, 1996). At retrieval, other factors come into play: In particular, because retrieval is conceived of as a reconstructive process, changes in external cues and internal cues (goals) can influence what is reactivated. Additionally, whatever is reactivated at retrieval also goes through an evaluation process that can be set along a continuum from heuristic to systematic. When set toward the heuristic end, decisions about cues can be made quickly on the basis of rules about features that co-occur with different types of memories. For example, if a memory carries with it many perceptual features and few mental features (e.g., cognitive operations), it is likely to be the product of observation, whereas if it carries with it many mental features and few perceptual features, it is likely to be the product of thought. More systematic evaluation of memories may occur if, for example, the cost of an error in a given situation is high or if other related information is assessed about plausibility of source. Older adults may be less likely than young adults to engage in such systematic evaluation processes of retrieved information in making source attributions. This, in combination with weaker encoding of contextual attributes and weaker integration of those attributes that are encoded, could account for older adults' poorer source-monitoring performance.

Summary

This brief summary of theories is not exhaustive (e.g., minimal reference was made to frameworks that have a strong neurocognitive basis). Even so, it should be apparent that the theoretical ideas that motivate research on age differences in memory are wide-ranging. Because the different theories tend to speak to different empirical issues, the above review of theories was intended to serve as a background for situating some of the research questions we subsequently address, rather than to set the stage for a systematic evaluation of each viewpoint against the others. Nonetheless, our survey of findings on age differences in memory should reveal that each of the theories under consideration has some major strengths, particularly in its areas of primary application, but also some limitations.

IMMEDIATE MEMORY AND GENERAL CAPACITY

The idea of span as a basic measure of mental capacity, and particularly of immediate-memory capacity, has been central to the individual differences tradition in psychology since its earliest days. The idea of a limited span of primary or short-term memory became important to the field of memory in the late 1950s (e.g., Miller, 1956) and was included in multistore memory models, such as Atkinson and Shiffrin's (1968). In earlier studies, most span data were collected using "simple" span measures (see below) that ostensibly emphasized passive storage of verbal information. Since the 1980 publication of Daneman and Carpenter's landmark paper, a large body of evidence has also accumulated using more complex "working memory" measures (see also below) that impose simultaneous processing and storage demands. The popularity of the latter type of measure reflects, in part, a shift in the conception of short-term memory. In particular, current views emphasize that immediate memory functions as a system in which processing and storage demands trade off for capacity (hence the currently more popular term, *working memory*).

In the general cognitive literature, the capacities measured by simple span and working memory span have been implicated in a broad range of cognitive activities, including encoding of new information into long-term memory, retrieval of information from long-term memory, syntactic processing and language comprehension, and reasoning (see, e.g., Daneman & Carpenter, 1980; Daneman & Merikle, 1996; Engle, Cantor, & Carullo, 1992; Just & Carpenter, 1992; Salthouse, 1993). Given these findings, it is not surprising that evidence also suggests that age-related declines in span, and particularly in working memory span, play a role in age differences in episodic memory and fluid cognition (cf. Verhaeghen & Salthouse, 1997). Examples come from studies investigating language comprehension and production (e.g., J. T. Hartley, 1988; Kemtes & Kemper, 1997; Light, Capps, Singh, & Albertson-Owens, 1994; Stine & Wingfield, 1987), reasoning (e.g., Salthouse, 1993, 1994), and episodic memory tasks (e.g., Cherry & Park, 1993; Hultsch, Hertzog, & Dixon, 1990; Park et al., 1996; for a review, see Park et al., 1996; Verhaeghen & Salthouse, 1997; but see also J. T. Hartley, 1988, 1993; Hasher & Zacks, 1988). We begin our discussion of age patterns in immediate memory with the simple span.

Simple Memory Span Measures

The digit span is an example of a simple span measure. The forward span version of the test measures the longest series of digits that a person can recall immediately after presentation and in the order in which the items were presented. This test (whether digits, letters, or words were used as materials) was once taken as a pure measure of short-term memory capacity.

Although individual studies have frequently reported small and nonsignificant age differences on simple span measures (e.g., see Craik, 1977), a recent meta-analysis (Verhaeghen, Marcoen, & Goosens, 1993) suggested that older adults are reliably poorer on simple span tasks than are younger adults. For example, the 13 young–old comparisons of forward digit span included in the meta-analysis showed an average effect size for age of –.53 compared with an effect size of –.91 for age on paired-associate recall. Such span differences are unlikely to be due entirely to basic differences in short-term memory capacity, however, because it has long been known that there is a contribution of long-term memory to these measures (e.g., see Craik, 1977). If so, the age difference in span may in part be due to age-sensitive factors affecting long-term memory processes: One such possibility is less rehearsal of the items by older adults (Kausler, 1994); another is discussed in the section below on working memory.

Baddeley's (1986) working memory model suggests another type of account of age differences in simple span. According to this viewpoint, working memory is not a unitary entity but is composed of multiple components. These include two "buffer" stores, the phonological loop for holding phonologically based verbal representations and the visuospatial sketchpad for holding visual and spatial representations, and a central executive that has monitoring, coordinating, and controlling functions in the service of ongoing processing. In the context of this model, it can be argued that simple span performance may primarily rely on the phonological loop rather than on the entire working memory system (cf. Baddeley, 1986). If so, and given that the presumed capacity of the phonological loop roughly corresponds to the number of items that can be subvocally articulated in 2 s, it becomes important to consider age differences in articulation rate. There is some evidence that the slower articulation rate of older adults contributes to their reduced span measures (Multhaup, Balota, & Cowan, 1996).

Working Memory Span Measures

The working memory span measure introduced by Daneman and Carpenter (1980) attempts to assess the individual's capacity to simultaneously store recently presented information (as simple span presumably does) while engaging in ongoing processing. Their basic task requires participants to read and comprehend a series of sentences while also remembering the final word of each. The test requires recall of the final words immediately following the last sentence of each set. Series lengths typically range from two to seven sentences, and starting with the shortest length, participants are given three to five sets of sentences before continuing on to the next set length. Working memory capacity (here specifically "reading span") is defined as the largest set for which the individual is able to both accurately comprehend the sentences and recall their final words. Daneman and Carpenter's initial measure has spawned many variations, including ones that use listening comprehension tasks instead of reading ("listening span") and ones that use arithmetic tasks along with recall of numbers from the arithmetic problems or randomly paired words ("computation" or "operation span"; see, e.g., Daneman & Merikle, 1996; Engle et al., 1992; Salthouse & Babcock, 1991).

As is the case for simple span measures, the research on complex measures is not entirely straightforward; most studies show age differences, some do not (see Light, 1991). The Verhaeghen et al. (1993) meta-analysis does, however, show a clear age effect of −.81. Note that part of the inconsistency in age differences across individual studies may stem from the contribution of vocabulary (and its correlates) to working memory span measures. In view of the fact that age differences in vocabulary, if present, generally favor older adults and that there is a positive correlation between vocabulary and span (Daneman & Carpenter, 1980), age differences in working memory span may be underestimated.

Interpretations

Older adults appear to have smaller span measures whether measured by simple or complex measures, and individual differences in span are important predictors of performance on other tasks, including language comprehension and reasoning tasks (e.g., Just & Carpenter, 1992). As we indicate in the following several paragraphs, a variety of theoretical viewpoints can potentially provide insight regarding the mechanisms underlying these important findings.

Baddeley's Working Memory Model

Although the Baddeley (1986) working memory model has stimulated considerable research on span and its determinants, including age differences, there is no easy meshing of these findings with the specifics of Baddeley's model. The strongest connection is the one that has already been mentioned, between the simple span data and the phonological loop, and even that connection is somewhat indirect. The working memory span measures that have gained so much attention in recent years do not precisely match any of the specific components of Baddeley's model, although the closest connection is the central executive: In requiring coordination between simultaneous processing and storage demands, the Daneman–Carpenter (1980) procedure seems to capture at least one essential feature of Baddeley's (1986) central executive, its role in coordinating among different processes (in the working memory span measures, between processing of new information and rehearsing a subset of previous information). To the degree that this proposed connection has validity,[3] it is of interest to consider a theoretical viewpoint that Baddeley (1986, 1996) has pointed to as having a strong influence on his concept of the central executive, namely, the viewpoint of D. A. Norman and Shallice (1986) regarding the "supervisory attentional system." This limited-capacity mechanism, which is presumed to be localized in the frontal lobes, is involved in strategic control of processing (i.e., planning, decision making, and coordination of resources) during the performance of nonroutine tasks.

Hasher and Zacks' Inhibition-Deficit View

Hasher and colleagues (Hasher & Zacks, 1988; Hasher et al., 1999; Zacks & Hasher, 1994) have also built on the work of D. A. Norman and Shallice (1986) and, more generally, on the work of attention theorists who have

---

[3]One factor that makes this connection tentative is that the conceptualization of the central executive is still under development, as Baddeley (1986, 1996) has readily acknowledged.

a selection-for-action focus (e.g., Navon, 1989a, 1989b; Tipper, 1992) in their analysis of working memory. One of their three inhibitory processes is critical to thinking about age differences in span measures: the deletion process. This is a mechanism responsible for clearing from working memory information that is no longer relevant to a current task. Because of the efficient operation of this mechanism, younger adults can readily suppress no-longer-relevant information, sometimes to below its preexperimental baseline level of availability. By contrast, because of less efficient operation of this mechanism, older adults have difficulty suppressing no-longer-relevant information (see also the section on circadian rhythms). What impact might this have on span tasks? As May, Hasher, and Kane (in press) pointed out, span tasks are actually a series of recall tests on lists that increase in length from the shortest to the longest. On each test trial, only the most recently presented string of items (digits, letters, words, or sentences) is relevant to the recall task. To accomplish focusing on only the current list, suppression of previous input (study lists) and outputs (retrievals) is required. If older adults are less able to do this than younger adults (see Hasher et al., 1999; Zacks & Hasher, 1994), items from previous lists will be more accessible in memory than they should be, creating larger sets of items to be searched through to produce the correct items from the current test list. In other words, the functional list length for those with poor inhibitory control will be longer than the functional length for those with efficient suppression. A large literature in memory confirms that list length[4] is a major determinant of the proportion recalled; and the typical explanation of this finding is based in interference theory: With longer lists, there is greater competition at retrieval among potential candidates for response (e.g., Watkins & Watkins, 1975). We note that larger search sets are known to have two effects on retrieval, one on amount recalled (reducing it) and one on speed of recall (slowing it). Hence, older adults may show smaller spans because of deficient inhibitory control over deleting no-longer-relevant information from working memory.

The evidence in support of this line of reasoning is not extensive, but it is encouraging. In a recent study, reading span materials from Daneman and Carpenter's (1980) study were presented in their standard, ascending list length order (as described above) or in a nonstandard, descending list length order (i.e., starting with the largest set size and going backward

---

[4]We use the term *list-length difficulty effect* to refer to a group of phenomena that go by various names, including the *fan effect* and the *cue overload effect*. In our view, these are all examples of the competition at retrieval induced by larger search sets, that is, by increases in the number of potential targets that are activated by a retrieval cue. It should also be noted that competition at retrieval is the major mechanism that classic interference theory used to explain proactive interference (cf. Baddeley, 1990).

through the series; May, Hasher, & Kane, in press). This manipulation was intended to reduce carryover (or proactive interference) effects from short lists to long lists, and it was indeed successful: Working memory span estimates were as large for older adults as for younger adults when span was measured in a descending manner. When measured in an ascending manner (with proactive interference effects increasing as list length increases), younger adults had their usual advantage in span.

Salthouse's Slowing View

A final viewpoint on the mechanisms underlying the aging and span findings is the speed of processing hypothesis (e.g., Salthouse, 1994, 1996; Salthouse & Meinz, 1995). According to the speed hypothesis, the age-related decline in span is mediated by slowing of processing, which somehow limits the amount of information that can be held or processed in immediate memory. Support for this account comes from the following pattern of findings (see recent reviews by Park et al., 1996; Salthouse, 1996; and Verhaeghen & Salthouse, 1997): First, there is the basic finding that measures of speed of processing show pervasive slowing with increasing age. Second, age-related declines in speed of processing share considerable variance with age-related differences in measures of short-term memory and working memory capacity. Third, age-related declines in speed of processing also share considerable variance with age differences in episodic memory and fluid-intelligence measures. Finally, structural equation modeling and other statistical and quantitative modeling procedures frequently show that speed is a stronger mediator of age-related variance on memory, reasoning, and language tasks than is working memory capacity. This pattern has been taken to suggest that slowing of processing is a "fundamental" underlying mediator of age deficits in a broad range of cognitive tasks and that it is relatively more fundamental than changes in working memory capacity (e.g., see Park et al., 1996, p. 634).

However, there are complications to this picture. Most important, factors beyond speed frequently emerge as significant mediators of age-related deficits in episodic memory and fluid-intelligence tasks. Of these additional factors, short-term memory, or working memory, is the most common (cf. Park et al., 1996; Salthouse, 1993, 1994; Verhaeghen & Salthouse, 1997). As Verhaeghen and Salthouse noted in discussing the mediational model generated from their meta-analysis of a large number of adult developmental studies, "age-related declines in speed *and* working memory capacity, efficiency, or both appear to be involved in the age-related decline in more complex aspects of cognition" (p. 246, italics added). Another issue is the limitations of the available data: The evidence supporting the speed hypothesis primarily comes from individual difference or statistical control methods and only some potential mediators of age deficits in complex cognition have been systematically studied (cf. Verhaeghen & Salthouse, 1997). For example, according to the inhibitory view, slowing could be due to increased mental clutter engendered by inefficient suppression processes. Finally, it can be noted that the mechanisms by which slowing might negatively impact on performance remain to be clearly specified and tested for many cognitive tasks (cf. Craik & Anderson, 1999).

This lack of theoretical resolution should not detract from the fact that the study of age differences in simple and complex span measures has presented us with some compelling findings, both about age differences and about how those differences might relate to performance on more complex cognitive tasks.

LONG-TERM MEMORY

Long-term memory includes vastly different sorts of memories, from remembering where one put one's key a few minutes ago and what one ate for breakfast a few hours ago to remembering how to shift gears, even though one has driven only automatic transmission cars for many years. In response to this diversity, Tulving (1972) proposed that long-term memory is not a unitary entity but is composed of distinct systems (originally, episodic and semantic memory) that have different functional properties and that are served by different brain structures. Almost 30 years later, memory researchers still debate whether it is best to consider long-term memory a unitary system or not, and if nonunitary, what the important subdivisions are (e.g., Schacter & Tulving, 1994; see chap. 2, this volume). Even though the theoretical issues are not settled, much of current research on long-term memory focuses on the properties of different types of long-term memory rather than on questions common to all of long-term memory. Nowhere is this trend more salient than in research on implicit memory.

Implicit Memory

By contrast with *explicit memory*, which is measured by tests including deliberate reference to a previous event, the term *implicit memory* refers to memory for a prior experience that is revealed by performance effects in the absence of deliberate recollection. Thus, implicit or indirect memory tests (Johnson & Hasher, 1987) measure the residue of previous stimulus exposure through changes in response accuracy, reaction time, or response bias (transfer effects or "priming"). Many of the most commonly used implicit memory tests involve measures of *repetition priming*. In repetition priming procedures, individuals first participate in a study phase in which they are exposed to a set of stimuli under the guise of some orienting task. This is followed by a test phase in which processing of the studied or related stimuli is compared with processing of unstudied, baseline stimuli. For example, in the test phase of a *fragment completion test*, participants are asked to complete word fragments (e.g., _ol_ _ _r) with the first word that comes to mind. Repetition priming is indicated by the increased likelihood of completing the fragments with words that had been studied (e.g., *soldier*) relative to a baseline unstudied condition. Other examples of repetition priming measures include stem completion (in which the test items are the first two or three letters of the target words), latency of word and picture naming, and lexical decision speed, among others.

Similar to research comparing amnesic patients to age-matched normal controls (e.g., Graf, Squire, & Mandler, 1984), research comparing healthy older adults with younger adults frequently shows a striking dissociation between explicit and implicit memory tests. For example, in an early study modeled after the one performed by Graf et al., Light and Singh (1987, Experiment 2) found a significant age deficit on word-stem cued recall but only a small and nonsignificant age difference on word-stem completion. Adding to the salience of these results is the fact that the only difference between the word-stem completion and the explicit cued-recall tests was the instructions: For the explicit test, participants were told to use the cues (three-letter stems) to help them retrieve words from the study list; for the implicit test, they were told to complete the stems with the first word that came to mind. It appears from these findings, and many others, that implicit memory tests provide an exception to the general finding of an age-related deficit in long-term memory for new information. This exciting possibility has generated a considerable body of research on adult age differences in implicit memory, which has been the subject of several recent reviews (Fleischman & Gabrieli, 1998; La Voie & Light, 1994; Light & La Voie, 1993; Rybash, 1996).

These reviews reach similar empirical conclusions about age effects on implicit memory tasks. The most general conclusions are that older adults show robust repetition priming effects across a wide variety of implicit memory tasks and that age effects on implicit memory tests are either nonsignificant in individual experiments or notably smaller than age effects on explicit memory tests (Fleischman & Gabrieli, 1998; La Voie & Light, 1994; Light & La Voie, 1993; see also Graf, 1990; D. V. Howard, 1988; Light, 1991; Rybash, 1996). However, the occasional significant age difference almost always favors the young group, as do the majority of nonsignificant trends (Fleischman & Gabrieli, 1998); and La Voie and

Light's (1994) meta-analysis indicates a reliable age decrement in implicit memory, although the age effect size (.30) is smaller than for explicit memory tests (.97 and .50 for recall and recognition, respectively). Other important but slightly more tentative findings relate to different kinds of repetition priming. One question that has received some study is whether aging patterns are similar for *perceptual* and *conceptual* priming tasks (see Roediger & McDermott, 1993). The perceptual priming category includes tasks (e.g., perceptual identification and picture naming) that are presumed to rely heavily on analysis of the perceptual features of inputs, whereas the conceptual priming category includes tasks (e.g., answering general information questions and retrieval of category instances) that appear to be sensitive to analysis of conceptual or meaning features of inputs. Comparisons of age effects on these two types of priming tasks have produced some divergent findings: For example, Small, Hultsch, and Masson (1995) found no age deficit on a conceptual priming task and a significant age deficit on a perceptual priming task, whereas Jelicic, Craik, and Moscovitch (1996) found the reverse pattern of age effects. In addition, other data (Multhaup, Hasher, & Zacks, 1998) suggest that there are circumstances in which older adults show reliable conceptual priming, whereas younger adults do not. However, despite these divergent findings in individual studies, the literature as a whole suggests equal age effects in the two types of priming paradigms (Fleischman & Gabrieli, 1998; La Voie & Light, 1994).

At this time at least, it appears that a similar conclusion applies to comparisons between *item* and *associative* priming, the former referring to facilitation from the repetition of familiar individual stimuli and the latter to facilitation from the repetition of novel connections between stimuli. Also included in the category of associative priming tasks by Light and colleagues (La Voie & Light, 1994; Light, Kennison, Prull, La Voie, & Zuellig, 1996; Light, La Voie, & Kennison, 1995) are tests of repetition priming using novel stimuli, such as nonwords (*kensess, obnel*) constructed by swapping syllables from words (*kennel, obsess*) or novel compound words (*fishdust, waygirl*). La Voie and Light's meta-analysis indicates that the age effects are roughly equivalent on associative and item priming measures (see also Fleischman & Gabrieli, 1998).

Given that older adults show clear deficits in learning new associations when such learning is measured on explicit retrieval tasks (see Kausler, 1994, for a comprehensive review), it is surprising that indirect tests measuring priming for new associations should show as modest an age deficit as item priming tests. This outcome suggests that clear age deficits in memory for new associations seen on explicit tests are due to retrieval rather than encoding or binding problems (cf. La Voie & Light, 1994). However, such conclusions should be treated with caution until there are more aging studies of associative priming, particularly ones using tasks tapping the formation of novel associations between distinct stimuli as contrasted with the more ambiguous cases of novel nonwords or compound words. It would also be useful to have more experiments that involve dependent measures other than reading speed because this measure may be sensitive to associations formed at a presemantic level, namely, to connections between elements of an output or motor program (i.e., motor fluency effects) rather than to the kinds of associative, semantic level connections that are the primary basis of performance on most deliberate memory tests (Spieler & Balota, 1996; see also Monti et al., 1997; Poldrack & Cohen, 1997). Further discussion of the theoretical interpretation of implicit memory findings follows a brief summary of research on a closely related phenomenon, implicit learning.

Implicit Learning

Seger (1994) defined *implicit learning* as the "learning [of] complex information without complete verbalizable knowledge of what is learned" (p. 163). Although there are clear similarities between implicit learning and implicit memory (diminished involvement of conscious mechanisms of memory retrieval and relative lack of impairment in individuals with amnesia; Nissen, Willingham, & Hartman, 1989), the two phenomena are demonstrated under quite different learning conditions (Seger, 1994). In particular, whereas most repetition priming tests measure memory for single stimuli or novel associations after a single study trial, implicit learning procedures generally measure learning of novel patterns or rules involving complex stimulus arrays over many trials. Almost all the studies comparing implicit learning in younger and older adults have used variants of the *serial reaction time (SRT) task* (Nissen & Bullemer, 1987). In this task, participants respond (e.g., by pressing a corresponding button) to each stimulus (e.g., onset of one of several lights) in a long series. Learning is shown by faster responding in a condition in which the stimuli appear in a repeating sequence (typically 8 to 12 elements long) versus a condition in which the stimuli appear in a random order. The random versus repeating sequence conditions are sometimes compared between subjects. More often, the comparison is within subjects through the use of random sequence blocks intermixed with repeating sequence blocks. The learning effect reflected in reaction time facilitation is not dependent on explicit awareness of the repeating sequence: Individuals with amnesia (e.g., Nissen et al., 1989), older adults (e.g., D. V. Howard & Howard, 1989), and a subgroup of young adults who demonstrate little or no explicit knowledge of the sequence can show as much reaction time speedup as individuals who become aware of the repeating sequence and can report what it is.

With few exceptions, the literature on aging and implicit learning has found robust learning of novel patterns in older adults when that learning is measured indirectly through improvements in performance of the required responses. For example, in the D. V. Howard and Howard (1989, 1992) studies, both younger and older participants showed more rapid responding for the repeating sequence than in the random condition of a SRT task and more rapid responding for both 10- and 16-element sequences. Furthermore, initial indications of learning emerged after a comparable number of repetitions (<20) of the sequence for the two age groups.

Although older adults generally show reliable implicit learning, there are sometimes age differences in the amount of learning seen in indirect as well as direct measures. In particular, whereas D. V. Howard and Howard (1989, 1992) reported no age differences on the reaction time measures of implicit learning, other investigators have reported age deficits under certain training conditions (i.e., dual-task demands; Frensch & Miner, 1994), for certain types of sequences (i.e., sequences of greater "complexity"; Curran, 1997; Harrington & Haaland, 1992), and for specific subgroups of older adults (i.e., lower ability older adults; Cherry & Stadler, 1995). It also appears that younger and older adults can show differences in what is learned, with older adults showing less implicit knowledge of higher order statistical dependencies in the repeating sequence (J. H. Howard & Howard, 1997). On the other hand, explicit knowledge of the sequence (as assessed by posttraining ability to recall, recognize, or consciously generate the sequence) has been found to show clear age deficits (e.g., D. V. Howard & Howard, 1989, 1992).

Theoretical Interpretations

The similarity between implicit memory and implicit learning does not end with the basic results; they also share a number of issues that complicate theoretical analysis of the findings. One of these issues is the interpretation of the frequent null age effects, particularly in cases involving reaction time measures of priming (e.g., picture or word naming) or implicit learning (SRT task): Specifically, given age-related general slowing, similar absolute reaction time benefits for younger and older adults have been interpreted by some investigators as indicating less priming or less implicit learning for the slower older group (cf. Fleischman & Gabrieli, 1998; Rybash, 1996). In line with this possibility, some investigators (e.g., Cherry & Stadler, 1995) have used proportional priming or learning scores (amount of speedup relative to a baseline reaction time) to adjust for general slowing. Others disagree with this procedure, citing questions about assumptions underlying the proportional slowing correction and other statistical issues (Curran, 1997; D. V. Howard & Howard, 1992; J. H. Howard & Howard, 1997).

Another complication is the possibility that *explicit contamination*, the use of explicit retrieval strategies to bolster performance on ostensibly implicit tests, could account for the intermittent findings of significant age decrements on implicit memory (e.g., Habib, Jelicic, & Craik, 1996) or implicit learning tasks (J. H. Howard & Howard, 1997): Younger adults' better explicit memory of the studied materials means that this group has a greater potential for conscious recollection to benefit their performance on implicit tasks. Alternatively, or additionally, young adults may be more likely than older individuals to use self-initiated conscious retrieval strategies (cf. Craik, 1986) when performing the implicit task.[5] In the case of implicit memory, a number of different approaches have been used to measure or eliminate explicit contamination: interviewing participants on strategies used on the implicit test, demonstrating that variables (e.g., level of processing) known to affect explicit memory do not affect implicit memory, and using individuals with amnesia as a comparison group lacking explicit memory (e.g., Fleischman & Gabrieli, 1998; Habib et al., 1996; La Voie & Light, 1994; Light & La Voie, 1993). Although each of these approaches is acknowledged to have limitations,[6] the results of their application generally support the conclusion that the small but persistent age differences in implicit memory are real and not merely an artifact of explicit contamination.[7]

So where does this leave us theoretically? Given the similarity between the aging and amnesia data in the early research on implicit memory and on implicit learning, a multiple brain systems approach seemed to be gaining ascendancy. In general, this approach claims that there is differential age-related deterioration in the brain structures underlying explicit memory versus those underlying implicit memory and learning (e.g., Squire, 1987; Tulving & Schacter, 1990). Chapter 2 describes this approach

---

[5]Explicit contamination has also been suggested as an explanation for the indications that, despite being superficially similar, implicit stem completion and fragment completion tasks show different age patterns, namely, frequent reports of age differences on stem completion but not on fragment completion (e. g., Winocur, Moscovitch, & Stuss, 1996). However, some findings support an alternative explanation in terms of the differential involvement of strategic processing dependent on the frontal lobes (Winocur et al., 1996) for stem completion but not for fragment completion.

[6]For example, the use of null effects of variables known to affect explicit memory helps rule out explicit contamination only for perceptual priming tasks (Fleischman & Gabrieli, 1998). For conceptual implicit tests, level of processing and similar variables are expected to have effects that parallel those seen on explicit tests.

[7]Issues relating to the experimental tasks are also of concern. The almost exclusive use of the SRT task to study implicit learning in older adults is problematic. Although the aging and implicit memory literature includes a much broader range of tasks, how to categorize some of them has turned out to be controversial. For example, usually stem completion is considered a perceptual task, but on occasion (e. g., Rybash, 1996), it has been categorized as a conceptual priming task.

in much greater detail, including an assessment of its current status among cognitive neuroscience researchers. For more behaviorally oriented investigators, it is our impression that the increasingly complex patterns of findings in the area seem to be leading to more of a reserve-judgment stance. As La Voie and Light (1994) have pointed out, the pattern that emerged from their meta-analysis (smaller age-related decrements on implicit memory tasks than on explicit memory tasks) is an example of what Shimamura (1993) called a "partial dissociation," a pattern that has ambiguous theoretical implications. It could be consistent with views assuming that there are qualitative differences between implicit and explicit memory, either in the processes or in the brain systems involved, and that there is age sparing in the process (system) that serves implicit memory but not in the one that serves explicit memory. Or it could be consistent with alternative interpretations, including ones that suggest only quantitative differences between younger and older adults coupled with tasks differing in difficulty (see La Voie & Light, 1994, pp. 547–551). Or, as we suggest in the final segment of this chapter, there may be a number of moderating variables whose roles on implicit memory tasks remain to be explained before final conclusions can be drawn. It is our judgment that further investigation of age differences in associative priming using tasks where priming effects are not tied to facilitation of motor-output mechanisms will be essential to the resolution of theoretical questions about implicit memory and implicit learning. We also note that two recent studies suggest that, at least with respect to stimuli that were designated as distractors at encoding, older adults' implicit retrieval of such information can leave them at an advantage relative to young adults (May, 1999; Multhaup et al., 1998).

Deliberate Remembering: Encoding and Retrieval Processes

The findings from tasks in which participants are asked to deliberately remember specific information contrast sharply with those from implicit memory and implicit learning tasks on which age-related differences are small and sometimes nonexistent. Older adults typically perform more poorly than younger adults on direct or explicit tests of memory. In recall, older adults omit more of the originally occurring information than do younger adults, include more never-presented items (intrusions), and repeat more previously recalled items. On recognition tests, older adults are more likely than younger adults to accept as old never-presented items (called *foils* or *lures*), especially if those lures share a conceptual, schematic, or perceptual resemblance to the presented items. There are exceptions to these general findings (see the later discussion on narrative recall; see also, e.g., Craik, Byrd, & Swanson, 1987; Rahhal & Hasher,

1998), and these exceptions suggest the presence of moderating variables that might prove to be deeply important, both practically and theoretically (as is outlined in the final major section of this chapter).

Despite the exceptions, reduced recollection, coupled with heightened errors, is at the focus of much work in aging and memory. Of particular interest is the pattern of high levels of omission for presented items coupled with intrusions bearing a systematic relation to presented information. Note that this is precisely the pattern that stimulated work on schema or constructivist theories of memory in the 1970s and 1980s; in many ways, the return of interest in such errors in the explicit memory tradition heralds the renaissance of a constructivist view of memory (see Johnson & Raye, in press ; Schacter et al., 1998).[8] Before considering errors in detail, we begin with general attempts to explain the most striking findings in aging and deliberate memory, the poorer overall retrieval of older adults as compared with younger adults.

Some earlier attempts to account for the poorer deliberate memory of older adults have emphasized processes occurring either at encoding or at retrieval. Such views have generally met with mixed success (e.g., Light, 1991). One example is the hypothesis that older adults engage in shallower, less elaborate processing at encoding than do younger adults (Craik & Byrd, 1982; Rabinowitz, Craik, & Ackerman, 1982). Tests of this hypothesis have involved procedures (instructions and orienting tasks) that control how participants process inputs at encoding, with the idea that age differences will be eliminated, or at least reduced, if younger and older adults encode in the same way. Studies using such procedures have produced a conflicting and confusing array of findings (Craik & Jennings, 1992; A. D. Smith, 1996), even among studies carried out by the same group of investigators. For example, Park and colleagues have used encoding conditions that promote increased elaboration of memory targets in a number of experiments and have found that such conditions produce (a) greater benefits for older adults (Park, Smith, Morrell, Puglisi, & Dudley, 1990), (b) equal benefits for older and younger adults (Park, Puglisi, & Smith, 1986), and (c) smaller benefits for older adults (Puglisi & Park, 1987).

It is likely that some of the divergence in findings is due to differences in the retrieval tests that were used, among other factors. If so, one has to consider that differences in encoding can typically be observed only on a retrieval test of some sort and that encoding differences are known to interact with differences in the retrieval demands of different types of

---

[8]See Alba and Hasher (1983) for a review of the earlier work on schema theory and for a criticism of the overextension of conclusions from that work—a criticism with relevance to some of the current work as well. By contrast, see Brewer and Nakamura (1984).

memory tests (Baddeley, 1990; Craik, 1977). These considerations suggest that it can be difficult to draw sharp distinctions between encoding and retrieval factors as sources of age-related deficits in deliberate remembering. Indeed, in contrast to the past, there has recently been relatively less work with older adults on traditional encoding and retrieval variables (e.g., acoustic vs. semantic encoding tasks and recall vs. recognition tests). In addition, more recent theoretical viewpoints, including those described earlier, tend to attribute age deficits in deliberate remembering to factors that are presumed to operate at both encoding and retrieval. For example, in the absence of explicit guidance from the environment or strong support from the learning materials, the reduced-resources/reduced self-initiated processing view (Craik, 1986; Craik et al., 1995) predicts that older adults are less likely to engage in effective strategic processing, both at encoding and at retrieval. Likewise, the inhibitory-deficit view (Hasher & Zacks, 1988; Hasher et al., 1999) argues that inefficient suppression mechanisms not only impede effective encoding (e.g., more extraneous associations are formed) but also impede retrieval through (a) the reactivation of enriched memory bundles that include extraneous associations and (b) the slowed suppression of any nontarget associations that are activated.

Given this situation, we make no attempt to maintain a strong separation between encoding and retrieval processes in the following discussion. Furthermore, in order not to repeat the thorough and excellent reviews of explicit memory work in previous reviews of the aging and memory literature (e.g., Craik et al., 1995; Craik & Jennings, 1992; Light, 1991; A. D. Smith, 1996), we deal with a limited set of topics of current interest. We begin with a task variable, divided attention, that is known to have a major impact at encoding but has also been investigated for its effects at retrieval.

Divided Attention

Possibly because of the widespread belief that older people are especially impaired when doing two things at once, the study of age-related differences in divided-attention costs on cognitive performance has been an active research domain. Studies investigating divided-attention costs on episodic memory commonly use procedures in which a "secondary" reaction time or short-term memory task is paired with the encoding or retrieval phase of a "primary" episodic memory task (e.g., see Craik, Govoni, Naveh-Benjamin, & Anderson, 1996). For example, in a recent study by Anderson, Craik, and Naveh-Benjamin (1998) involving groups of younger and older adults, a continuous reaction time task was combined with either encoding or retrieval for a free-recall or cued-recall test. In such experiments, divided-attention costs are revealed by poorer performance (lower accuracy on the memory test, slower responding on the reaction time task) in either or both the primary and secondary tasks when they are performed together versus separately.

Reduced-resources approaches to cognitive aging predict that divided-attention costs will be larger in older adults than in younger adults, except perhaps when the tasks being combined are both distinctive and relatively automatic tasks. Experimental situations involving online performance measures (e.g., reaction times) generally provide support for this prediction (e.g., A. A. Hartley, 1992), although there are exceptions (e.g., Somberg & Salthouse, 1982; Tun & Wingfield, 1994). In addition, questions have been raised about how to best account for age differences in baseline or single-task control conditions in measuring divided-attention costs (Naveh-Benjamin & Craik, 1998; Salthouse, 1991; Salthouse, Fristoe, Lineweaver, & Coon, 1995).

With respect to the specific question of whether older adults show larger divided-attention costs on explicit memory tasks than do younger adults, there are different findings depending on whether one looks at costs on the primary or the secondary task. To be specific, as predicted by reduced-resource views, the secondary task measures typically indicate greater costs for older adults at both encoding and retrieval (especially the latter) and particularly when the memory task is one that is presumed to involve greater self-initiated processing (free recall vs. cued recall or recognition; Anderson et al., 1998; Craik & McDowd, 1987; Whiting & Smith, 1997; but see Park, Smith, Dudley, & Lafronza, 1989). By contrast, the most common finding on the primary episodic memory task is that younger and older adults show equivalent divided-attention costs that are substantially greater when a secondary task is performed during encoding rather than at retrieval (Anderson et al., 1998; Nyberg, Nilsson, Olofsson, & Bäckman, 1997; Park, Puglisi, Smith, & Dudley, 1987; Whiting & Smith, 1997; but see Park et al., 1989). The pattern of greater divided-attention costs for older adults on the secondary task along with equivalent disruption of primary task performance provides mixed support for a reduced-resources view. However, it might be possible to fully reconcile these data to a reduced-resources view if it could be shown through instructional manipulation that the pattern of results reflects participants' strategic inclinations to protect performance on the primary memory task at the expense of the secondary task. (See also the later discussion on automatic retrieval.)

Effects of Structure and Prior Knowledge on Deliberate Remembering

Memory for structured materials that relate to prior knowledge is generally better than memory for materials that either are unstructured or make little contact with what the individual already knows. But how do these types of effects come about, and, especially important in the current context, are there age-related differences in the effects of structure and prior knowledge on memory? (Because of the close relationship between structure and prior knowledge—i.e., prior knowledge frequently determines whether inputs are seen as structured or not—we treat them together in the following discussion.)

Much of the early research in this domain used lists of words or pictures containing groups of related items, for example, several instances from each of several different taxonomic categories. In general, such lists produce better memory performance than lists of unrelated items, but the size of the benefit is known to be influenced by other variables, including the typicality of the category instances, the list presentation format (random order or blocked by category), and the type of memory test (free recall, cued recall, or recognition). At a global level at least, all these variables have similar effects for younger and older adults (cf. Kausler, 1994). That is, for both age groups, memory is enhanced by the presence of a categorical structure in the list; and for categorized lists, memory is better when the list is presented in a blocked-by-category fashion rather than a random fashion and when recall is cued by the category labels rather than when no cues are provided. Also, when a free-recall memory test is used, both younger and older adults show grouping or clustering of items from the same category in their recall orders. Like young adults, older adults' recall is also affected by other types of list structure, including the presence of sets of rhyming words (Mueller, Rankin, & Carlomusto, 1979) or the inclusion of groups of items relating to different scripted activities (Hess, Flanagan, & Tate, 1993).

Our emphasis on the global similarity of structural effects for younger and older adults should not be taken to mean that there are no age differences. Kausler's (1994) summary of the relevant literature documents the frequent findings of quantitative differences between younger and older adults (e.g., lower clustering scores or smaller cuing effects in older adults). But these differences do not detract from the fact that older adults show robust effects of the structure that may be present in a memory list, indicating that they reliably encode the structure and use it in retrieving list items. The same basic sensitivity to structure in the input and prior knowledge is seen in findings on older adults' memory for sentences and prose passages (cf. Light, 1992).

Effects of Different Levels of Linguistic Structure

Sentences and longer segments of prose contain structure at several hierarchical levels, some relating to individual sentences (phrase, clause, or proposition) and others relating to the connections among propositions and sentences. In theories of text processing (e.g., Kintsch, 1988; Kintsch & van Dijk, 1978), the structural components of larger text units include the *microstructure* of a discourse (the structure relating individual propositions to each other) and its *macrostructure* (the structure of the major themes of a discourse). On top of these more or less text-based levels of structure, Kintsch and others (e.g., Zwaan & Radvansky, 1998) have argued that deep comprehension of a prose passage involves the construction of a *situation model*, a high-level representation that captures the gist of the situation described by the text. Recent work has produced interesting findings regarding effects of these different levels of structure on older adults' comprehension of and memory for prose. (For more details on this literature, see chap. 6, this volume.)

Text-Based Levels. As an example of research investigating lower structural levels, we consider findings from a paradigm that has been used in several studies by Wingfield and colleagues. This paradigm involves the use of prerecorded speech passages that are presented in segments of either the participant's or the experimenter's choosing, with each segment being followed by immediate recall of the preceding unit of speech. When participants are allowed to select their own segments by stopping the tape recorder as often as they would like, younger and older adults show similar segmentation and recall patterns. Both age groups tend to interrupt the tape at syntactic (i.e., phrase, clause, or sentence) boundaries, and both age groups show excellent recall of the selected segments (Wingfield & Butterworth, 1984; Wingfield, Lahar, & Stine, 1989). This pattern holds even for relatively unpredictable text (Wingfield & Lindfield, 1995) and for relatively fast speech rates (Wingfield & Stine, 1986). On the other hand, when the speech segments are predetermined by the experimenter, age differences are affected by the location of the interruptions. When the speech is segmented at syntactic boundaries, the age deficit is smaller than when it is segmented at random intervals (Wingfield, Tun, & Rosen, 1995). Furthermore, in contrast to what is true for syntactic segments and self-selected segments, fast presentation rates result in greatly impaired recall by older adults in the random segment condition. This pattern of results is interpreted as indicating that older adults are efficient online processors of the syntactic and prosodic structure of speech and that they can use these levels of structure to parse the speech into coherent units and to guide their recall. Wingfield and colleagues (e.g., Wingfield et al., 1995) also suggested that because of the availability of different types of structure (i.e., syntactic or prosodic) in speech, at least the early stages of speech processing appear to be relatively free of short-term memory capacity constraints.

Research on the *levels effect*, the finding that the central propositions of a text are more likely to be recalled than less important propositions, likewise shows that younger and older adults are, with some qualifications, similar in their processing of text-based levels of linguistic structure (J. T. Hartley, 1993). This conclusion also applies to higher level structures to which we now turn.

Situation Models. As has already been indicated, a situation (or mental) model of a prose passage is a high-level representation of the state of affairs described by the text (rather than a representation of the text itself; cf. Zwaan & Radvansky, 1998). The creation of situation models involves the conjoining of information retrieved from general knowledge to text-based information. The result is a representation that incorporates inferences about such features as characters' predispositions, their emotional states, and their goals, as well as about the spatial relationships among the people, objects, and events that are described (Morrow, Stine-Morrow, Leirer, Andrassy, & Kahn, 1997; Zwaan & Radvansky, 1998). Consequently, the construction of a situation model and the updating of that model as new information is encountered result in a richer understanding of a text than would be possible from text-based representations alone.

In an early demonstration of the importance of situation models, Garnham (1981) showed that if distractor and originally processed sentences describe the same situation, young adults have difficulty discriminating between them on a recognition test. For example, the original sentence "The hostess bought the mink coat from the furrier" is likely to be confused with a distractor sentence consistent with the same situation, namely, "The hostess bought the mink coat at the furrier's." The suggestion is that a situation model had encoded the description, and because both sentences satisfy the model, each is acceptable. By contrast, fewer confusions occur for another pair of sentences that, at text-based levels, are as similar to each other as the first pair but that are unlikely to refer to the same situation model (e.g., "The hostess received a telegram from the furrier" vs. "The hostess received a telegram at the furrier's"). Using lists of sentences structurally similar to the examples, Radvansky, Gerard, Zacks, and Hasher (1990) found that although older adults made more errors overall than younger adults, the pattern of those errors was very similar: Both groups made many more false alarms to same-situation distractors as compared with different-situation distractors, suggesting similar use of mental models across age groups.

Other studies have investigated not only older adults' ability to construct a situation model of a text but also their ability to update the model. For example, in two studies by Morrow and colleagues (Morrow, Leirer, Altieri, & Fitzsimmons, 1994a; Morrow et al., 1997), participants first memorized a map of a building (e.g., a research center) in which there were several rooms, each of which contained several objects. They then read narratives that included statements about the protagonist moving from one room to another. Such circumstances are thought to elicit the construction of a spatially organized situation model centered on the protagonist and her or his current location. Movement of the protagonist to a new location elicits updating of the situation model to maintain the centered position of the protagonist (Morrow et al., 1997).

In the study by Morrow et al. (1994a), reading of the narratives was interrupted at various points with probe questions about objects that were near or far from the protagonist's current location. For both younger and older adults, answers to probes were more accurate and faster the closer the probed object was to the protagonist. Morrow et al.'s (1997) study produced similar findings with a more direct measure, reading time. This was assessed for target sentences that referred to objects that were in the room the protagonist had just entered or to objects that were in other rooms at various distances from the current location of the protagonist. Like younger adults, older participants took longer to read target sentences that mentioned more distant objects. Both age groups also showed a benefit when the target sentence explicitly mentioned the room location of the critical object. These results suggest that the two age groups are similar in their use of the memorized map and other background information to create a situation model of the narrative that centers on the protagonist and his or her current location and that is updated as the protagonist moves through space. The data could also be taken to suggest that implicit use of spatial context is spared with aging.

Note that both of the Morrow et al. studies found that older adults took longer than younger adults to memorize the maps. In addition, older adults were not only slower overall on the critical dependent measures (probe answering time in the Morrow et al., 1994a, study; target sentence reading time in the Morrow et al., 1997, study), but they also showed a larger distance effect than did younger adults. Morrow et al. (1997) interpreted their findings as indicating that "older and younger adults used qualitatively similar strategies to update situation models from narratives" (p. P78) but that the updating process was more effortful, or at least took longer, for older adults.

An additional set of findings confirming age invariant use of spatial situation models comes from the fan effect literature. Although it is generally the case that fact retrieval is slower and more error prone as the number of responses associated with a particular cue gets larger and that these effects are larger for older adults than for younger adults (Cohen, 1990; Gerard et al., 1991; see also previous discussion), there are situations in which fan effects can be eliminated. One such situation occurs when a spatial mental model is provided to organize information. For example, the facts "The potted palm is in the hotel lobby" and "The pay phone is in the hotel lobby" can be readily integrated into a single situation model of the "hotel lobby." For sets of facts that permit integration through such a mental model, the fan effect is largely and equally eliminated for both younger and older adults (Radvansky, Zacks, & Hasher, 1996). Again, spatial models prove useful for older adults. In addition, Radvansksy and Curiel (1998) recently showed that the representation of protagonists' goals is another aspect of situation model processing that differs little between younger and older adults.

Thus, across several paradigms, younger and older adults are similar with respect to the construction, updating, and use of situation models (at least ones organized around space and goals) in representing text. To be sure, there are subtle age differences suggesting that use of such models may be more demanding for older adults (Morrow et al., 1994a, 1997), but this finding is not uniform (cf. Radvansky & Curiel, 1998; Radvansky et al., 1996). In general, it seems clear that the findings on situation models are consistent with the data from studies of other encoding processes (organization and schema use) that suggest similarity in encoding between younger and older adults, coupled with some quantitative differences. There are even instances (e.g., Adams, Smith, Nyquist, & Perlmutter, 1997; see the section on social contexts) in which older adults appear to encode more of the deep and symbolic meaning of a text than do younger adults.

Expertise. Before leaving the topic of memory for structured materials, we briefly consider whether there are age differences in memory performance for domain-specific knowledge such as is possessed by experts in an area but not by nonexperts. It has been known for some time (e.g., Chase & Simon, 1973) that because of their superior domain knowledge, experts more quickly and more effectively encode the underlying structure of new inputs in their area of expertise than do novices, and consequently, they remember these inputs better on both immediate- and delayed-retention tests. Not much research has specifically addressed the impact of expertise on the memory ability of older adults, but the studies that have been done show memory benefits of expertise in older as well as younger adults. For example, Morrow, Leirer, and Altieri (1992) compared young and older pilots with young and older novices on their memory for narrative passages concerning aviation or nonaviation themes. For both ages, expertise was associated with increased memory for the aviation-related narrative, but the pilots and nonpilots showed similar age deficits in performance whether they were recalling the aviation or the nonaviation passage. In a more recent study, Morrow, Leirer, Altieri, and Fitzsimmons (1994b) compared younger and older pilots and nonpilots on short-term recall of heading, altitude, speed, and frequency commands in a simulated air-traffic control communication situation. Short-term memory tasks were also used by Halpern, Bartlett, and Dowling (1995) in their investigation of effects of musical experience on auditory recognition of transposed melodies and by Meinz and Salthouse (1998) in their study of recall of visually presented musical melodies. With minor exceptions (recall of heading commands in the Morrow et al., 1994b, study and one of four experiments in the Halpern et al., 1995, study), the pattern of findings in these other studies is similar to the pattern demonstrated in the narrative recall results of the Morrow et al. (1992) study. Specifically, all ages showed a benefit of expertise on memory for domain-relevant information, but expertise was not associated with reliable attenuation of age differences in performance. Morrow et al. (1994b) claimed that their exception to this trend, the finding that old pilots recalled heading commands as well as young pilots, is meaningful. They suggested that of all the types of information they tested, recalling the heading commands may be most relevant to pilots' expertise, thus allowing expertise to compensate for age-related cognitive deficits. Aside from this suggestive finding, the literature on expertise effects on memory in older adults joins the other findings described in this section of the chapter in snowing that structure and prior knowledge in various forms have similar effects on younger and older adults' memory performance; however, these effects do not reliably attenuate the age difference in deliberate memory.

Retrieval Phenomena

We now shift to topics that focus more heavily on retrieval than encoding processes. The first topic in this category deals with an aspect of retrieval for which there is intriguing evidence of relative insensitivity to age effects.

Automatic Retrieval

The notion that at least one aspect of retrieval is obligatory or automatic comes from several recent lines of work. Consider first aspect of the work we previously mentioned by Craik and colleagues (Anderson et al., 1998; Craik et al., 1996; see also Jennings & Jacoby, 1993; Moscovitch, 1994; Nyberg et al., 1997) on the memory effects of divided attention manipulations. That work shows that divided-attention costs at retrieval primarily impact on the secondary task (and more so for older adults), with little impact on the memory task itself. An implication of this pattern of findings is that retrieval processes are effortful but obligatory. Work of this sort is exciting because it dovetails nicely with two other lines of research, one behavioral and the other more neuropsychological.

One of the lines of work supporting the ideas that aspects of retrieval can be automatic and equivalent for older and younger adults is that of Jacoby and colleagues (Jacoby, 1991; Jacoby, Yonelinas, & Jennings, 1997). On the basis of the claim that all memory tasks involve a combination of automatic and deliberate processes (none are "process pure"), Jacoby developed a research strategy, the "process–dissociation paradigm," in which conscious recollection and automatic retrieval are pitted against each other.

One example of the implementation of this strategy is in a series of experiments on the "false-fame effect" (e.g., Dywan & Jacoby, 1990; Jennings & Jacoby, 1993). For example, in the Dywan and Jacoby study, participants first read a list of nonfamous names. Then they were given a new list consisting of three types of names: those from the first list, additional nonfamous names, and moderately famous names. Their task was to indicate which of the names were famous. Participants were informed that the names on the original study list were nonfamous, and so any names that were recognized from that list could be excluded from consideration. The rationale behind this design is as follows: Studying a nonfamous name increases its familiarity (and familiarity mediates automatic retrieval), and unless this enhanced familiarity response is counteracted by the conscious recollection that the name had appeared on the original study list, the individual is likely to misinterpret familiarity as fame (the false-fame effect). Dywan and Jacoby found a larger false-fame effect for older adults as compared with younger adults.

A later experiment (Jennings & Jacoby, 1993) compared the condition just described with one in which participants were told that the names that they had read previously were actually obscure famous names; in this case, it was appropriate to label a familiar name as famous whether or not the individual had a specific recollection of having studied it previously. The condition included in the Dywan and Jacoby (1990) study is termed an *exclusion condition* (exclude any names recollected from the initial list). The condition added in the Jennings and Jacoby study is termed an *inclusion condition* (include any names whether recollected or only familiar). The data from experiments that include both of these conditions can be analyzed to provide quantitative estimates of conscious recollection and automatic retrieval (e.g., Jacoby, 1991). In the Jennings and Jacoby study, the estimates of conscious recollection were lower for older adults than for younger adults, but the estimates for the automatic retrieval component did not differ across age groups. This suggests that being old impairs conscious recollection while leaving automatic retrieval (familiarity) unchanged.

The age findings in the false-fame studies have been confirmed in studies using other implementations of the process–dissociation procedure. For example, Jennings and Jacoby (1997b) used a procedure in which participants first learned a list of words and then were given a recognition test in which the distractor words were repeated at varying lags. In the exclusion condition, participants were instructed to respond "no" to repeated distractors (which presumably should be somewhat familiar because of their prior occurrence). In the inclusion condition, they were told to respond "no" only to entirely new distractors; any familiar item could legitimately receive a "yes" response. Once again, the estimates from the process–dissociation analysis showed lower recollection for older adults, along with no age difference in automatic retrieval (see also Jennings & Jacoby, 1997a; Salthouse, Toth, Hancock, & Woodward, 1997; Titov & Knight, 1997). Thus, the pattern of age-related decline in conscious recollection and age constancy in automatic retrieval appears to be robust. However, it should be noted that the process–dissociation paradigm is not without its critics (Curran & Hintzman, 1995; Dodson & Johnson, 1996; Graf & Komatsu, 1994). Of particular concern for aging studies is the possibility that older adults may have greater difficulty than younger adults switching retrieval strategies in response to the instructions for the inclusion versus the exclusion condition. Final interpretation of the aging data derived from the Jacoby paradigm will have to await resolution of these criticisms.

In addition, the work of Moscovitch and colleagues suggests (along with Schacter et al., 1998) that some aspects of retrieval are obligatory responses to cues, whereas others require more (frontally mediated) control. Older adults may be particularly impaired at the latter processes, which Moscovitch and Winocur (1992) termed "working with memory." Work of this sort dovetails nicely with work in the process–dissociation tradition.

Errors in Memory

We return now to an observation made at the beginning of our discussion of deliberate remembering—that there is currently a heightened interest in errors. This can probably be traced to three lines of work: (a) research investigating the highly predictable errors produced in recall and recognition in the Deese–Roediger–McDermott (DRM) paradigm (Deese, 1959; Roediger & McDermott, 1995), (b) research in the memory for source tradition (Johnson et al., 1993; Schacter et al., 1998), and (c) research on the misinformation effect (e.g., Loftus, 1992). We primarily focus on the first two because of their substantial link to the current aging and memory literature.

Misrecall and Misrecognition of Related Items

Consider Reder, Wible, and Martin's (1986) landmark investigation of the patterns of errors made by older and younger adults. In Experiment 1, participants read a series of stories and subsequently were asked to identify which sentences had or had not been presented. The critical foil sentences were either highly or moderately plausible inferences from the text. Older adults were far more likely than younger adults to falsely recognize sentences that were related to the original story. This general finding has since been replicated several times (e.g., May, Hasher, & Stoltzfus, 1993; Yoon, 1997). Reder et al. focused on retrieval strategies to explain their findings. In particular, they suggested that relative to younger adults, older adults were more likely to use a plausibility criterion ("If it is consistent with the story, call it old") rather than a direct retrieval strategy when they judged items as old. Other data support the idea that older adults are more likely than younger adults to rely on plausibility or heuristic decision rules (as compared with analytic rules) at retrieval rather than on direct retrieval (Stine & Wingfield, 1987; Tun, 1989; Wingfield et al., 1995). As Reder et al. pointed out, if relatedness helps performance, older and younger adults will do equally well; if it does not, differences will arise (see their Experiment 2).

The general finding that predictable errors in recall and recognition are more common for older adults than for younger adults has been repeatedly demonstrated in a task specifically implemented to show high rates of such errors, the DRM paradigm (Deese, 1959; Roediger & McDermott, 1995). In this task, participants typically hear a series of lists (or sublists, if one long series is used) of words (e.g., *thread, pin, eye, sew*), each of which is composed of the associates of a particular, never-presented lure (e.g., *needle*). When tested at the end of the presentation series, lures are highly likely to be produced in recall or accepted as old in recognition (Roediger & McDermott, 1995; see review by Schacter, Koutstaal, & Norman, 1997).[9] Recent studies have found that acceptance of lures, even weakly associated ones, as old is more common for older adults than for younger adults. Acceptance of lures as old is also more common for older adults even when their recognition of old items does not differ from that of younger adults (e.g., K. A. Norman & Schacter, 1997; Tun, Wingfield, Rosen, & Blanchard, 1998). Tun et al. also found that lures are actually termed "old" *more quickly* by older adults than by

---

[9]In the current literature, these errors are referred to as "false memories" rather than as false alarms or more generally as errors. We use the more neutral terms because of the politically charged debate over false and recovered memories and because of the tenuous relationship we see between most laboratory studies and critical real-life issues (but see Christianson, 1992).

younger adults, which is consistent with the suggestion from Reder et al. (1986) that different decision criteria are used by the two age groups, with older adults relying more frequently than younger adults on plausibility or similarity.

In the general memory literature, and particularly in the DRM paradigm, another explanation for errors is tied to the elaborative or associative encoding people are thought to engage in as each item is presented (see Underwood's, 1965, notion of implicit associative responses). If a self-generated item then occurs at test, people may call it old because it occurred in the context of the experiment (see the next section on source errors). However, if older adults are somewhat less likely than younger adults to use elaborative encoding (or self-initiated processing) in the first place (Craik, 1986; A. D. Smith, Park, Earles, Shaw, & Whiting, 1998), they should be less likely to generate at encoding the lures that subsequently occur at test. This would then result in reduced rates of errors for older adults rather than in the actually observed heightened rates. As a direct test of the lure-generation hypothesis, Koutstaal and Schacter (1997) presented photographs of category instances (e.g., shoes) selected in such a way as to preclude the possibility that participants would generate during encoding the exact instance that then served as a lure during testing. Even with such materials, older adults still showed higher rates of false alarms than did younger adults. A plausibility or gistlike retrieval criterion, and age differences in reliance on this criterion, seems strongly implicated in these error patterns.

Other evidence suggests that testing circumstances can substantially alter the degree to which schematic retrieval plans or heuristic decision rules, on the one hand, versus direct retrieval plans or analytic decision rules, on the other, are used at test by both younger and older adults (Dodson & Johnson, 1993; Multhaup, 1995; Multhaup, De Leonardis, & Johnson, 1999). These studies are discussed below. We note here, however, that a key finding in the schema theory literature in the 1970s is that the pattern of retrieval will vary as a function of the instructions given at test, with some instructions encouraging gist- or schema-level recall and others encouraging more reproductive strategies (see Alba & Hasher, 1983; Brainerd & Reyna, 1990). Thus, even though much current work suggests that older adults are more likely than younger adults to use low-demand retrieval strategies (e.g., gist- or schema-based ones), and low-demand decision rules (heuristic ones such as plausibility), their use is not inevitable, even by older adults.

One additional encoding process might play a role in producing errors in the DRM paradigm. Note that even for younger adults, the greatest numbers of errors occur when sets of related items are grouped in a series rather than distributed throughout the presentation list (McDermott, 1996).

A blocked series of related items is thought to encourage *relational* encoding rather than *item-specific* or distinctive encoding (Hunt & McDaniel, 1993). Recent work suggests that encouraging young adults (R. E. Smith & Hunt, 1998) and both younger and older adults (Weichmann & Hasher, 1998) to engage in item-specific encoding radically reduces the overall rate of intrusions of lures at recall (see also Israel & Schacter, 1997). Thus, it is possible that older adults are more likely than younger adults to engage in relational encoding processes unless the encoding circumstances dictate otherwise. Without item-specific information available, and with little press for analytic decisions at test, many related items will be judged old. If so, these findings suggest that although relational or gist coding can be and often is used by participants in DRM paradigm tasks, it is not inevitably used. As is also suggested above, although heuristic decision rules can be, and often are, used in DRM paradigm and other tasks, these too are not inevitable—for either younger or older adults.

Source Errors

As was indicated earlier, the theoretical frameworks of Johnson et al. (1993; Johnson & Raye, 1981) and of Schacter et al. (1998) argue that events are encoded as bundles of conceptual and perceptual features and that the properties of these bundles of features (how strongly different features are encoded, how well the features are bound together), along with processes occurring at retrieval, determine the ability to judge the source of a memory (among other important uses of memory). This approach has stimulated a number of lines of research, including work on age differences in source memory; and that work has joined with an existing line of work on age differences in context versus content memory. For present purposes, these two topics are intermixed.

Findings on Age Differences in Memory for Source. Research on memory for contextual features and source typically uses deliberate memory tasks and, with a few notable exceptions (see below), shows that older adults are less accurate at recalling and recognizing contextual features of events than are younger adults (see Spencer & Raz, 1995, for a meta-analysis). For example, older adults are at a disadvantage relative to younger adults in remembering various perceptual details, such as the color, case, or font, in which target items occurred (e.g., Kausler & Puckett, 1981; Naveh-Benjamin & Craik, 1995; Park & Puglisi, 1985); their locations (e.g., Chalfonte & Johnson, 1996; Cherry & Park, 1993; Light & Zelinski, 1983; Park, Puglisi, & Lutz, 1982; Uttl & Graf, 1993); their temporal sequence (Kausler, Salthouse, & Saults, 1988); and even seemingly potentially more salient characteristics, such as whether the speaker was male or female (Bayen & Murnane, 1996; Kausler & Puckett, 1981), whether the items were presented in a video or photo format (Schacter, Koutstaal, Johnson, Gross, & Angell, 1997), and whether items were presented auditorially or visually (Light, La Voie, Valencia-Laver, Albertson-Owens, & Mead, 1992).

Older adults are also at a disadvantage in remembering attributes that code for differences in enactment, such as actually saying or doing something versus merely imagining doing so (Cohen & Faulkner, 1989; Guttentag & Hunt, 1988; Hashtroudi et al., 1989, 1994; Hashtroudi, Johnson, & Chrosniak, 1990) and actually reading or hearing something versus generating it on the basis of cues (Brown, Jones, & Davis, 1995; K. A. Norman & Schacter, 1997). Indeed, some have suggested that heightened false memories in the DRM paradigm itself can be taken as evidence of confusion between seen (old items) and imagined events (lures). Several investigators have noted that even when event memory is equivalent between younger and older adults, the latter can be at a disadvantage in remembering source (Chalfonte & Johnson, 1996; Henkel et al., 1998; Johnson, De Leonardis, Hashtroudi, & Ferguson, 1995; Schacter et al., 1997; Schacter, Kaszniak, Kihlstrom, & Valdiserri, 1991). These findings are taken to suggest that either the encoding of attributes or their binding together with items is generally poorer for older adults than for younger adults (e.g., Chalfonte & Johnson, 1996; Johnson, 1997). It is also taken as evidence that older adults have even greater memory problems with context information than they do with content.

One novel way of studying recollection of the features of items is to use a task developed by Johnson and colleagues (e.g., Johnson, Foley, Suengas, & Raye, 1988), the Memory Characteristics Questionnaire. Versions of this task require participants to indicate the characteristics they recollect for each item or event judged as old (e.g., spatial arrangement of objects and associated feelings). Variants of the questionnaire have been used with younger and older adults in both source-monitoring and DRM paradigm tasks, with the findings generally showing age differences in the characteristics that are remembered. For both younger and older adults, items that were presented and are recognized have more sensory (e.g., color) and contextual (e.g., list position) information than do nonpresented lures that are misrecognized as old. Of special note, however, is the finding that for items judged as old, the differences in reported features between actual old items and lures are smaller for older adults than for younger adults (Hashtroudi et al., 1990; K. A. Norman & Schacter, 1997). Presumably, then, older adults have less detailed information in memory to distinguish between types of events than do younger adults. It is no surprise, then, that older adults have more difficulty distinguishing between sources originating in the same general domain (e.g., two voices in the perceptual world or a thought and an image in the conceptual world) than in distinguishing between sources that cross these domains (a speaker and a thought; Johnson et al., 1993).

The evidence we have reviewed so far suggests that one "source" of the age-related increase in source errors is the reduced discriminability of old items and lures. It remains to be learned what the cause is of the reduced discriminability. Because different features take different amounts of time to recover once retrieval is initiated (see Johnson et al., 1993) and because older adults say "yes" faster to lures than do younger adults (Tun et al., 1998), it is possible that older adults respond with less information than younger adults and so answer questions differently. It is also possible that older adults have slowed or reduced access to features in experiments because the features of different items in a list may be quite similar and because the retrieval costs of similarity are greater for older adults (e.g., because they have created functionally larger search sets for themselves and so greater competition at retrieval). Relevant here are findings indicating that similarity between and among features is a critical variable in determining source-monitoring difficulties (Johnson et al., 1993). One recent experiment in the source memory tradition asked younger and older adults to look at versus imagine a series of pictures (Henkel et al., 1998). Among the imagined items were some that were perceptually similar to seen objects (e.g., a lollipop and a magnifying glass) and others that were conceptually similar to seen objects (e.g., a banana and an apple). In addition to the expected finding that older adults were less able to discriminate between seen and imagined objects than were younger adults, the findings also showed that both perceptual and conceptual featural similarity between imagined and seen objects were differentially disruptive to older adults (see Bayen & Murnane, 1996; Bayen, Murnane, & Erdfelder, 1996). Given the well-established role of similarity in causing retrieval difficulties (i.e., interference in memory), this finding could also be taken to point toward retrieval problems. If so, the finding is consistent with the view that older adults are more vulnerable to sources of interference than are younger adults (see Kane & Hasher, 1995).

This differential vulnerability to interference among similarly featured events could also play a role in the "reminiscence bump," the elevated levels of recall shown by older adults for memories from their 10th to their 30th years relative to other time periods. Rubin, Rahhal, and Poon (1998) reviewed research showing that this bump is present for personal or autobiographical memories and for memories judged as most important or most vivid. Similar bumps (albeit with different overall life-span curves as well as slightly different age ranges for the bump) are also seen for questionnaire research using historical events and people as targets (e.g., Botwinick & Storandt, 1980; Rubin et al., 1998). Thus, more of the events that older adults recollect come from a time in their lives (late adolescence and early adulthood) that probably offered more unique events than any other time period.[10] This argument claims that distinctiveness insulates memories from interfering with each other, thereby potentially helping to preserve these early memories. Of course, multiple interpretations have been offered for these patterns of recollection (see Burke & MacKay, 1997; Rubin et al., 1998).

"Remember–Know" Paradigm. To return to the issue of memory for source, we turn to findings from the "remember–know" paradigm (Gardiner & Java, 1993; Tulving, 1985) findings, which are also suggestive of reduced availability of contextual features for older adults. The remember–know paradigm explores the difference between episodic recognition judgments that are accompanied by recollection of contextual details present at the time of encoding and ones that are empty of such details, with recognition being based on decontextualized familiarity of the target. The procedures involve variants of standard recognition memory tests in which participants decide, for each item recognized as old, whether they consciously recollect having previously studied that item (remember judgment) or merely find the item familiar (know judgment). In general, remember–know studies comparing younger and older adults have found a lower proportion of remember responses for the older group but equal or greater know responses for older adults than for younger adults (e.g., Java, 1996; Mäntylä, 1993; Parkin & Walter, 1992; Perfect & Dasgupta, 1997). In other words, even for items that are recognized as coming from the study list, older adults are less likely to have clear source information than are younger adults.

Incidental Tests of Memory for Source. So far, we have considered deliberate tests of source memory. Memory for source can also be tested incidentally—that is, the ostensible task relies on the use of some information whose importance is not deliberately noted at encoding, at retrieval, or both. Consider the "misinformation" paradigm (e.g., Loftus, 1992) by which two successive, related events occur with the second event providing (or not providing in the control condition) a critical fact or observation that contradicts information in the first event. At test, participants are asked to choose between items they saw in Phase 1 and new items. Included in this list is a lure containing the Phase 2 error. Partici-

---

[10]A typical procedure in the autobiographical memory tradition is to provide participants with a long series of cue words used to retrieve personal memories. The memories are then self-dated. The bumps are found within the 50% of memories that do not come from the most recent year (see Rubin et al., 1998).

pants can potentially discriminate between the two sets on the basis of temporal information (which came first), modality information (if, for example, the first were presented as a film and the second as a written description of the film's incident), or any other contextual cues that distinguish the two sources. If contextual features are less accessible to older adults than to younger adults, they might be expected to make more such errors than younger adults, and they do (Cohen & Faulkner, 1989). Among related findings, we include the false-fame findings mentioned earlier (e.g., Dywan & Jacoby, 1990; see also Bartlett, Strater, & Fulton, 1991). Lack of access to temporal attributes may also lie behind other patterns of errors shown by older adults (e.g., Jennings & Jacoby, 1997b).

By contrast, however, it is also worth noting that the provision of contextual cues that might otherwise be difficult to retrieve (e.g., location) appears to help older adults at least as much as younger adults (e.g., Cherry & Park, 1993; Cherry, Park, & Donaldson, 1993; Earles, Smith, & Park, 1994; Naveh-Benjamin & Craik, 1995). There are also reports that context actually helps older adults more than younger adults (e.g., Park et al., 1990). This suggests that features may be coded but difficult to retrieve. Other evidence further suggests that age differences in context memory are substantially reduced when testing is implicit rather than explicit (Light et al., 1992; Vakil, Melamed, & Even, 1996; see also the section on situation models). Together, such evidence seems to point toward deliberate retrieval problems rather than encoding problems.

Moderating Factors. Are older adults inevitably worse on source memory tasks than younger adults? There is, in fact, some suggestive work that might be taken as evidence for boundary effects for source deficiencies. For one thing, the nature of the stimulus materials may well influence the degree to which older adults show source deficits. Several studies suggest smaller age deficits (or even nonexistent ones) when the materials are engaging and well-known to the older adults (Brown et al. 1995; McIntyre & Friesen, 1998). Roles in social contexts may also influence the size of source errors shown by older adults (Brown et al., 1995), with better memory when older adults are active participants rather than (as is the case in most studies) passive observers. Instructions to older adults to focus on facts rather than on affect while listening to a play being read will also reduce source differences (Hashtroudi et al., 1994).

Coupling interesting materials (facts) with the use of instructions that emphasize the acquisition and use of *knowledge* rather than *memory* for that information also appears to eliminate age differences in memory for source (Rahhal & Hasher, 1998). Changing decision criteria from loose (or gistlike ones) to tight, reasoned ones will also influence source-based errors and can even eliminate age differences (Multhaup, 1995; Multhaup et al., 1999).

Encoding Factors and Age Differences in Source Memory. As we have seen, the findings on age differences in memory for contextual features and source are complex. There generally is an age deficit, but the size of the deficit and the overall performance of younger and older adults are a function of numerous factors. That both ages are more accurate under some instructions than others, with some materials than others, and that age differences can even be eliminated (even if rarely) seems particularly important both to our understanding of source memory and to our understanding of memory more generally. Here, we try to draw out the theoretical implications of the variability of source memory and age differences therein for viewpoints on age differences in source errors that emphasize encoding factors. Such viewpoints might claim that fewer features were encoded in the first place or that those features that were encoded were insufficiently "bound" or associated, so that the retrieval of one or more features does not succeed in retrieving others. Both of these types of explanations are called into question by the powerful effects of retrieval conditions (e.g., instructions) and materials. If a particular feature were not encoded, no retrieval manipulations could induce its recollection or its use. Likewise, effects of retrieval manipulations also challenge at least the strong form of the view that age deficits are the result of weaker binding or integrating of features by older adults. In terms of broad implications, we note that very different views of retrieval accuracy will be the result of assumptions that suggest encoding processes that leave inaccurate traces or incomplete features in memory once the episode is encoded versus processes that leave traces that may or may not be retrieved in detail. Herein lies the contrast between constructivist views (with inevitable errors; e.g., Brewer & Nakamura, 1984; Schacter et al., 1998) and flexible views of memory, views that suggest that a number of variables can influence performance, with retrieval looking more or less detailed, depending on circumstances (e.g., Alba & Hasher, 1983; Johnson & Raye, in press).

This is not to say that encoding processes play no role in the ultimate success of retrieval. One view (Hasher et al., 1999; Zacks & Hasher, 1994) proposes that the speed and accuracy of retrieval will be partly determined by encoding processes that influence the size of the "fan" stemming from a cue. If the fan includes relevant information only, retrieval will be faster and more accurate than if the fan includes relevant and irrelevant information. Thus, control over access of relevant and irrelevant information to working memory at encoding is part of what determines retrieval (Hasher et al., 1999; Zacks & Hasher, 1994). Older adults may have less control over working memory and so have far less ability to ignore distraction in the environment (see, e.g., May, 1999; Multhaup et al., 1998), in thought (see below), or from the recent past (May et al., in press).

Furthermore, from the perspective of a young or middle-aged experimenter, older adults may have goals that are different from those set by the instructions and so have a greater tendency than younger adults to pay attention to the emotional and interpretive qualities of input along with or rather than the factual qualities (e.g., Adams et al., 1997; Hashtroudi et al., 1994). Or they may attend more to their own emotional responses to a situation and less to the events in the environment than do younger adults (Hasher & Zacks, 1988; Johnson et al., 1996; see also chap. 11, this volume; Johnson & Raye, in press). Thus, age differences in goals and in control over working memory can influence retrieval efficiency (see Burke & MacKay, 1997, for a different view).

Prospective Memory

Regardless of the participant population involved, most research on deliberate memory has been concerned with *retrospective remembering*, recall or recognition of experiences that occurred in the past. We end our discussion of explicit memory with another category of deliberate memory functions—*prospective remembering*, or remembering to perform a planned action sometime in the future. Prospective memory is critical to the accomplishment of everyday social and personal goals. A person who chronically forgets dates with family and friends, who misses appointments with health professionals, and who forgets to carry out intended household chores is likely to both suffer from and cause numerous problems in everyday life.

Despite its obvious importance, memory researchers have only recently engaged in a concerted effort to study prospective memory. One factor contributing to this situation is the difficulty of defining the unique characteristics and essential components of prospective memory so that appropriate experimental tasks can be designed. A number of authors have commented that prospective memory situations are multidimensional and involve several qualitatively different components, including retrospective memory elements (e.g., remembering what the required action is) and elements such as compliance and motivation that are rarely considered in research on retrospective memory (Dobbs & Reeves, 1996; Maylor, 1996). Given this situation, it is not surprising that there is some divergence among authors as to what are the critical components of prospective memory tasks. For example, Maylor focused on remembering an intention to carry out a specified action in the absence of external prompting. Although Craik and Kerr (1996) agreed that prospective memory involves the retrieval of intentions, they also focused on the planning and monitoring components of prospective memory tasks (cf. Dobbs & Reeves, 1996). Another characteristic that is frequently mentioned in relation to prospective memory is the use of dual-task situations in which the participant is required to interrupt an ongoing or primary task to carry out the prospective action, as often occurs outside of the lab (e.g., Einstein, Smith, McDaniel, & Shaw, 1997; Maylor, 1996; Park, Hertzog, Kidder, Morrell, & Mayhorn, 1997).

Much of the theorizing in prospective memory has been grounded in Craik's (1986) views, which argue that the magnitude of age deficits will be a joint function of the reduced processing resources of older adults, environmental support for effective encoding and retrieval strategies, and task demands. In this view, a critical factor is the amount of self-initiated processing the memory task requires. On the basis that retrieval in a prospective memory task occurs on the individual's own initiative rather than being initiated by the experimenter, Craik had predicted large age deficits in prospective memory, even relative to other deliberate memory tasks, such as cued recall. Reviews of aging and prospective memory research (e.g., Dobbs & Reeves, 1996; Einstein & McDaniel, 1996; Maylor, 1996) indicate only partial support for this prediction. In fact, there is considerable variation across studies in the magnitude and even in the occurrence of age deficits in prospective memory. To a degree at least, these variations may be generally consistent with Craik's viewpoint.

Consider, for example, the difference between two nominally distinct types of prospective memory tasks, those in which the prospective action is to be performed at a *particular time* (time-based tasks) versus those in which the prospective action is to be performed in conjunction *with a particular external event* (event-based tasks). The importance of this distinction was signaled by the unexpectedly good prospective memory performance of older adults in a series of studies conducted by Einstein, McDaniel, and colleagues (Einstein, Holland, McDaniel, & Guynn, 1992; Einstein & McDaniel, 1990). Einstein and McDaniel hypothesized that the absence of a prospective memory age deficit in their experiments was due to the use of an event-based prospective memory task requiring relatively little self-initiated processing (a keypress was required on the presentation of a particular target word). They also predicted, and later found (e.g., Einstein, McDaniel, Richardson, Guynn, & Cunfer, 1995), significant age deficits on a time-based prospective memory task for which there was not a specific external trigger to cue the required action (a keypress was required every 5 or 10 min). The latter study also found that older adults engaged in less monitoring behavior (checking the clock) than younger adults when performing a time-based prospective memory task (see also Park et al., 1997).

The difference between time-based and event-based prospective memory situations is not the only factor determining the size of age differences in this type of memory. One important factor relating to the dual-task nature of most prospective memory situations is the processing load of the nonprospective or primary task. Einstein et al. (1997) recently reported findings indicating that more demanding primary tasks are associated with larger age deficits in prospective memory. Another aspect of the dual-task context of prospective memory tasks is the degree to which the prospective memory and primary tasks are related or unrelated in terms of cognitive process and/or relevant stimuli (Maylor, 1996). For example, in the Einstein and McDaniel (1990) procedure, the prospective cues were words that were presented as part of the ongoing short-term memory task. By contrast, the event-based cues in the Park et al. (1997) study were irrelevant background patterns on the video monitor. Although both experiments involved event-based tasks, the prospective cues were much more embedded in the primary task in the Einstein and McDaniel study than in the Park et al. procedure. This fact may in part account for the contrasting results of the two studies: no age differences in the former versus a significant age deficit in the latter. Other properties of the cues used in event-based tasks have been investigated as well: Age differences are more likely when multiple rather than single prospective cues are designated (Einstein et al., 1992; Kidder, Park, Hertzog, & Morrell, 1997) and when less typical instances of category-defined cues are used (e.g., *milk* vs. *ink* given as cues when participants are told to respond to instances of the category liquid; Mäntylä, 1994).

Another point is that although the distinction between event-based and time-based prospective memory tasks may appear to be fairly clear-cut, this is only true in tightly controlled circumstances. In less controlled circumstances, indications are that at least some individuals turn time-based tasks into event-based tasks. For example, a number of "naturalistic" studies have used nominally time-based tasks in which participants are asked to mail postcards and/or make phone calls to the experimenter at specified future times. These studies have generally not imposed any restrictions on the way participants go about remembering how to carry out the prospective tasks. For the most part, age differences are minimal in these studies. For example, in Maylor's (1990) study, 222 women between the ages of 52 and 95 years were asked to call the experimenter once a day from Monday to Friday, either between two times or at an exact time. They were also asked to complete a questionnaire at the end of the week and to mail it in as soon as possible. Overall, there was a weak trend toward the older participants performing better on the prospective memory tasks than the younger adults, but this trend was limited to individuals using self-initiated strategies in which the prospective action was linked to some external trigger (e.g., performing it in conjunction with a routine daily activity, such as morning coffee, or using a calendar notation). In effect, these strategies turned a nominally time-based task into an event-based task. Among individuals who tried to rely only on internal time cues, poorer performance was associated with greater age.

As this summary of age differences in prospective memory suggests, prospective memory is similar to other forms of deliberate remembering, both in the fact that age deficits are frequently obtained and in the fact that the magnitude of age differences is variable. As a first approximation at least, the pattern of findings is generally consistent with Craik's (1986) hypotheses regarding reduced self-initiated processing in older adults. There are some recent arguments, however, that Craik's viewpoint may provide an incomplete account of prospective memory findings. For example, on the basis of participant reports that the prospective action seems to "pop into mind," Einstein et al. (1997) have recently suggested that retrieval of a prospective action seems to be relatively spontaneous and to not rely heavily on self-initiated processes. Note that age differences in prospective memory would be tied to differences in the ability to maintain activation of the intended action in working memory. Such ideas are consistent with earlier discussed automatic retrieval mechanisms being spared with age.

MEMORY AND ITS MODERATORS

To a large degree, the study of both basic memory processes and age differences in those basic processes takes the approach that these phenomena can be studied in isolation from other aspects of cognitive, social, and biological functioning. This "isolationist" approach to the study of memory and its aging seems to be changing, in part because of large-scale cross-disciplinary longitudinal studies of aging (e.g., Lindenberger & Baltes, 1997; McDonald-Miszczak, Hertzog, & Hultsch, 1995; Nilsson et al., 1997) and also because of developments in cognitive neuropsychology, including a productive line of work connecting age differences in memory to changes in brain function (see chap. 1 and 2, this volume; see also Johnson & Raye, in press; Moscovitch & Winocur, 1992; Perfect, 1997; Schacter et al., 1998; Stuss, Craik, Sayer, Franchi, & Alexander, 1996). However, other developments are also contributing to the breaking down of this isolationist approach. Here, we consider several that have special relevance to aging and memory. In general, the work suggests that the study of basic memory processes might benefit greatly from situating them into their social as well as their biological contexts (see also chap. 11, this volume). We begin with some biological issues.

Biological Contexts

Here, we consider several issues, including general and circadian arousal and health changes associated with aging and their impact on age differences in memory.

General and Circadian Arousal

Although the relationship between general arousal and memory performance is extremely complex (e.g., Christianson, 1992), there is reason to consider the role that this variable (and others, such as self-efficacy and stereotype vulnerability, which may themselves operate through heightened arousal) might play in influencing age differences in memory. Consider the study of competitive-level miniature golfers (Bäckman & Molander, 1986a, 1986b) in which age was associated with different patterns of arousal and these differences were especially notable on measures taken on practice versus competition days. For young adults, measures did not change much across the two types of days. For older adults, performance declined from practice to test days, suggesting that arousal differences can impact negatively on well-learned motor skills and on the thoughts needed to maintain those skills (see also Boutcher & Stocker, 1996).

Suppose arousal level for older adults in experimental situations is elevated more so than for younger adults (Fisk & Warr, 1996; McDowd & Birren, 1990; but see Levenson, Carstensen, & Gottman, 1994). Or suppose that arousal is better controlled by most younger adults than by most older adults (e.g., in novel situations it returns to baseline more quickly). What might one expect to see in memory performance? Age differences in performance should be reduced when arousal is statistically controlled, and some evidence suggests it is, at least for a computer-based associative learning task (Fisk & Warr, 1996). Age differences also should be reduced when instructions are used that de-emphasize more threatening aspects of a task, and this expectation is also confirmed (Rahhal & Hasher, 1998).

It is possible, as Christianson (1992) has argued is true for people in highly arousing situations, that content (or central) information will be encoded at the expense of context (or peripheral) information. Insofar as the source memory literature suggests age differences in context information as compared with content information (or the differential binding of those attributes), is it possible that age differences in arousal are moderating variables (see, e.g., Johnson et al., 1996)?

Eysenck and Calvo's (1996) processing efficiency theory suggests that increased anxiety will enable task-irrelevant, worrisome thoughts to enter working memory, thereby reducing its capacity for task-relevant information processing. This view overlaps with the notions of Hasher and Zacks (1988; Hasher et al., 1999) regarding inhibitory control over working memory. It is conceivable, then, that the impact of arousal on memory, including on memory-based language comprehension tasks, will be very similar to those suggested by the inhibitory framework, a topic we consider next.

Casual observation and interaction with younger and older research participants (i.e., college students and community-dwelling older adults) suggest that these two groups of people are on different circadian schedules. Of particular importance here is the suggestion in recent work that these differences in temporal schedules are real; impact on aspects of cognition including both explicit and implicit memory tasks; and can, depending on when testing occurs, influence conclusions arrived at regarding the magnitude of age differences in memory performance.

Work on circadian arousal patterns is not, of course, new to some areas of psychology (e.g., human performance), although it is relatively new to work in mainstream cognition. A substantial literature suggests that circadian patterns can be measured in a number of ways, but perhaps most easily with a valid and reliable paper-and-pencil inventory introduced by Horne and Östberg (1976, 1977; see Intons-Peterson, Rocchi, West, McLellan, & Hackney, 1998; May et al., 1993). A series of normative studies using this inventory shows that peak times of functioning for young adults tend toward midday and later, whereas peak times for older adults center on early to midmorning (see, e.g., Hoch et al., 1992; Intons-Peterson et al., 1998; May et al., 1993; Yoon, 1997). According to U.S. norms (May & Hasher, 1998), only a small proportion of older adults (<3%) are evening-type people, with 75% or so falling into the morning-type category. By contrast, only around 5% to 6% of young-adult college students are morning types, with approximately 35% being evening-type people. Depending, of course, on the degree to which a cognitive process is influenced by circadian arousal, as well as on when in the day testing actually occurs, different conclusions may be reached if these general age trends are ignored. Is this a worrisome matter for the memory literature and for conclusions about age differences in memory? A tentative answer is yes.

It was known in 1990 (Bodenhausen, 1990) that young adults are more likely to rely on schematic or heuristic judgment principles at their nonoptimal times of day than at their optimal times, when they are more likely to rely on individual evidence or analytic decision rules. As we saw earlier (in the section on memory errors), older adults rely more heavily on schematic or heuristic retrieval principles than younger adults (Reder et al., 1986). In an initial study, May et al. (1993) considered whether reliance on schematic memories (acceptance of foil sentences that are meaningfully related to those in the story but that were never actually presented; see Reder et al., 1986) would vary across the day. In that study, as in several others in this tradition (but see Intons-Peterson et al., 1998), morning-type older adults and evening-type younger adults were tested early in the morning or late in the afternoon. In addition to confirming the Bodenhausen finding that reliance on schematic information increased at nonoptimal times of day, the pattern of performance on a recognition task varied across the day for both older and younger adults but did so differently for the two age groups (May et al., 1993). Young adults' recognition performance increased from morning to afternoon, whereas older adults' performance declined across the same time frame. Thus, recognition (a task with substantial contextual support; see Craik, 1986) can be impacted by time of testing, and the patterns of performance from morning to afternoon are different for older and younger adults.

Other evidence suggests that even implicit memory performance can vary across the day in patterns that are different for older and younger adults. In particular, May and Hasher (1998) showed that there were implicit memory differences following an encoding task that required suppression of highly probable but no-longer-relevant information along with the acquisition of new, relevant information. Participants' ability to suppress the no-longer-relevant information was measured by their tendency to later use that information in generating completions for incomplete sentence frames. Consistent with earlier findings (Hartman & Hasher, 1991; Hasher, Quig, & May, 1997), the data indicate that older adults were generally less able to suppress no-longer-relevant information than were younger adults. Both age groups, however, showed strong synchrony effects, with suppression greater at optimal than at nonoptimal times. Of special note was the startlingly poorer performance of older adults tested late in the afternoon, performance that left them showing no implicit access to newly acquired information. These data suggest the possibility that the acquisition of new information is impaired for older adults when a new response needs to be learned in the presence of a well-established response, particularly when the learning occurs at nonoptimal times. The data also suggest that both the suppression of irrelevant information and the "binding" of new information are processes influenced by circadian arousal levels.

There is some suggestion that prospective memory may also show a circadian pattern for groups of older adults such that compliance with a drug-taking regimen and with appointment keeping is greater in the morning than at other times of day (Leirer, Tanke, & Morrow, 1994). Additionally, there is the suggestion that some classic neuropsychological tests (Stroop and Trail Making) may also show circadian patterns, particularly for older adults who show larger Stroop and Trail Making effects in the afternoon than in the morning (May & Hasher, 1998; but see Davidson & Zacks, 1998).

To our knowledge, there is little evidence on any number of other tasks and processes that are relevant to memory researchers. However, work with younger adults does suggest that circadian patterns can influence their recall of newly learned information (Petros, Beckwith, & Anderson, 1990), and there seems to be every reason to suggest that similar effects would be seen with older adults. Still other work shows circadian effects on some attentional cognitive-control tasks (Intons-Peterson et al., 1998; May, 1999).

Not all tasks show circadian patterns, for either younger or older adults for that matter. On the basis of current evidence, very well-learned skills and tasks tapping semantic memory appear to show equivalent performance across the day (see, e.g., Hasher et al., 1999; Li, Hasher, Jonas, Rahhal, & May, 1998; Yoon, May, & Hasher, 1999).

To date, evidence suggests circadian synchrony effects in the acquisition of new information, in the implicit and explicit use of that information, and in those tasks requiring inhibitory control over physically present distraction (May, 1999) and possibly over strongly activated responses (e.g., Intons-Peterson et al., 1998). On the basis of current findings, including the fact that approximately 75% of older adults are morning-type people, it no longer seems appropriate to treat time of testing as a noise factor in studies of aging and memory. Failures to take this into account can increase (or decrease) estimates of age differences, depending on the task or processes studied and on the testing times used for younger and older participants.

General Health

Aging is associated with increasing health problems, and these in turn are associated with higher use of medications. It is possible that some portion of the age differences seen on a variety of memory and cognitive tasks is associated with health factors. Research on these factors presents a mixed picture, but one we believe bears watching. (For a discussion of the related topic of associations between age-related changes in perceptual and intellectual functioning, see chap. 3, this volume.)

Work on health factors has been done using both subjective measures (self-ratings of health status) and more objective indicators, including physiological data, number of hospitalizations, and number of chronic illnesses. Although the two types of indicators show significant correlations, there are reasons to be cautious about data involving subjective ratings (see Salthouse, 1991). For one thing, subjective ratings of health tend to be more optimistic than objective measures. Additionally, there are potential age differences in how subjective instruments are interpreted (e.g., whether the reference group used in making subjective ratings consists of age peers or, in the case of older adults, consists of younger adults). In any event, subjective indicators do not strongly support the idea that health predicts performance. For example, in two studies conducted by Salthouse and colleagues (Salthouse, Kausler, & Saults, 1988; Salthouse & Mitchell, 1990), those individuals who rated their health status as "excellent" were compared with the entire sample. Health status did not predict cognitive performance in either study, either as a main effect or in interaction with age (see also Earles & Salthouse, 1995;

Salthouse & Babcock, 1991). There are some indications, however, that health ratings may show a stronger relationship to more basic cognitive tasks (Hultsch, Hammer, & Small, 1993).

The literature using more objective measures is also mixed in terms of what health status does predict. For example, work on physical fitness suggests that long-term fitness programs may improve certain aspects of attention and memory performance (e.g., Kramer et al., 1998), but this is not always found to be the case (Blumenthal et al., 1991; Hill, Storandt, & Malley, 1993). Similarly, work on current fitness levels also shows a mixed pattern of findings (Bunce, Barrowclough, & Morris, 1996). Work on "biological life events" (which include exposure to organic solvents, anesthesia, mild head injuries, and the presence vs. absence of birth complications) does suggest some impact on measures of choice reaction time, movement speed, and Stroop color naming (Houx & Jolles, 1993; Houx, Jolles, & Vreeling, 1993). In addition, chronic smokers have been found to show lower scores than nonsmokers on tests of fluid intelligence (Hill, Nilsson, & Nyberg, 1998). By contrast, several studies have also suggested that the contribution of health factors to cognitive functioning is not large (e.g., Lindenberger & Baltes, 1997; Luszcz, Bryan, & Kent, 1997; Nilsson et al., 1997). We note that recent work from a longitudinal study (Small, Viitanen, & Bäckman, 1997) suggests that older adults whose performance on memory tasks is particularly poor at one time (and who are symptom free by standard measures of AD) are far more likely to show AD symptoms at a subsequent testing than are other older adults (see also Sliwinski, Lipton, Buschke, & Stewart, 1996). In this way, health, or at least undetected AD, may well contribute to the widely reported increases in variability of performance associated with aging and may also lead to overestimates of age differences, ones that may be greater the older the sample of older adults (Sliwinski et al., 1996).

Social Contexts

The concept of self-efficacy refers to beliefs about one's abilities to exercise control over cognitive and motivational resources so as to be responsive to both local and more global task demands (Bandura, 1986, 1997; Cavanaugh, 1996; see also chap. 7, this volume). This concept has played an influential role in the literature on social development, where it has been shown to be a powerful variable determining a broad range of behaviors from classroom learning to condom use (e.g., Bandura, 1997). In general, people with higher levels of self-efficacy show greater effort across a broad range of tasks than do people with lower levels of self-efficacy. However, self-efficacy beliefs can be manipulated in the context of an experimental setting, even in groups that begin a task at equal levels of performance. As an example, consider a study in which Stanford University MBA students played a managerial simulation game under high versus low self-efficacy instructions (Wood & Bandura, 1989). The two groups showed equivalent performance initially but rapidly diverged, with those under high self-efficacy instructions improving their performance and those under low self-efficacy instructions showing a considerable decline.

With respect to aging and self-efficacy, or lack thereof, there is a substantial literature showing that across all adult ages, North Americans hold negative stereotypes about cognition and aging in general and about memory and aging in particular (e.g., Bieman-Copland & Ryan, 1998; Erber, 1989; Heckhausen, Dixon, & Baltes, 1989; Ryan, 1992). If older adults are more likely to hold such views about themselves than are younger adults (see, e.g., Cavanaugh & Green, 1990; Hertzog, Dixon, & Hultsch, 1990; West & Berry, 1994), it would be no surprise that relative to younger adults, older adults might be less motivated to perform well in memory tasks, to consider strategies appropriate for the tasks, and to use any feedback that is provided to modify their behavior so as to improve performance. In other words, it would be no surprise if older adults behaved as if they had lower self-efficacy than younger adults.

However, the literature on self-efficacy and memory does not strongly support the conclusion that this variable is correlated with memory performance or that changes in individuals' self-efficacy will result in associated changes in memory performance (see, e.g., Cavanaugh, 1996; Cavanaugh, Feldman, & Hertzog, 1998; Hultsch, Hertzog, Dixon, & Davidson, 1988; Lachman, Weaver, Bandura, Elliott, & Lewkowicz, 1992; Ryan, 1992; Welch & West, 1995).

A related literature considers the memory performance of groups of younger and older adults who differ in their stereotypes about aging. Levy (1996) demonstrated that implicit activation (through "subliminal" presentation of words, such as *senile* and *wisdom*) decreased the subsequent memory performance of older adults and increased the subsequent memory performance of younger adults. An earlier study (Levy & Langer, 1994) compared younger and older adults sampled from mainland Chinese residents, members of the American Sign Language (ASL) community, and U.S. residents. Stereotypes regarding aging and cognition are more positive among the first two groups than among the last group; and consistent with the view that stereotypes (and attendant self-efficacy) mediate performance, no age differences on memory and other cognitive tasks were found for Chinese participants, small age differences were found for ASL participants, and larger age differences were found for Americans. Dramatic as these findings are, they were limited to a small number of participants in each group ($ns = 10$). In a replication comparing younger and older recent Hong Kong Chinese immigrants to Toronto with younger and older nonimmigrants (ns = 24–28 per group), the usual age differences were found (Yoon, Hasher, Rahhal, & Winocur, 1998), with little suggestion that negative stereotypes (which did differ between the two cultural groups) mediated performance.

A final study in this series is particularly interesting with respect to stereotypes, self-efficacy beliefs, and their possible impact on source memory tasks (Rahhal & Hasher, 1998). In this instance, trivia statements, selected so as to not be in the knowledge base of either younger or older adults, were presented with immediate feedback as to their truth or falseness. Afterward, the original trivia statements were presented amidst a series of new ones and participants were asked to indicate the status of items: Were they old or new, and if old, were they true or false? Half the participants in each age group were given instructions that emphasized the memory nature of the task, whereas the other half were given instructions that emphasized the knowledge acquisition aspect of the task. Although both instructional groups were told about an upcoming test, performance patterns varied with instructions. With memory instructions, the usual age differences were present; with knowledge instructions, they were not (see also McIntyre & Friesen, 1998). A related set of findings has been reported by Earles and Kersten (1998), who showed that after performing a series of tasks (five each from the categories of memory, speed, knowledge, and problem-solving tasks), younger adults were more likely to remember the ones they rated as difficult, whereas older adults were more likely to remember the ones they rated as relatively easy. Taken together, these findings suggest that task perception can be quite different for younger and older adults and that performance differences may sometimes be tied to beliefs and concerns about skill levels.

We note that the Rahhal and Hasher (1998) findings are generally consistent with the notion of "stereotype vulnerability" (e.g., Steele, 1997), such that performance on the very same task will vary as a function of whether it is framed (or spoken about) in such a way as to evoke a negative stereotype (which may reduce self-efficacy or heighten arousal) or not. Note in particular that all implicit or indirect memory tasks avoid reference to a memory task. As we indicated previously, older adults frequently show as much priming on implicit tasks, and occasionally even more (Multhaup et al., 1998), than do younger adults. Of course, the pattern of findings on explicit tasks is quite different, an outcome which might partly be due to the tendency for deliberate memory instructions to activate negative stereotypes in older adults.

More generally, however, these findings raise questions about the social situational variables that differentially alter performance of older adults relative to younger adults (see, e.g., Hess & Pullen, 1996). Such issues take on special importance in light of recent findings in the storytelling literature in which older adults' production and reproduction of stories are judged as being better than those produced by younger adults (e.g., Pratt & Robins, 1991). The goal of older adults is to tell interesting stories, and there is the possibility that in story recall tasks, there is a greater match between the objectives of the experimenter and those of the older participants than may be the case in other areas of the experimental study of memory (see, e.g., Dixon & Gould, 1996). Other considerations also suggest that goals may have a general role in determining memory performance (see, e.g., Blanchard-Fields & Abeles, 1996).

An interesting alternative interpretation of these findings fits nicely, however, with the age invariance seen in the situation model findings reviewed earlier. If we assume (see Adams et al., 1997) that in comprehending a text, individuals may construct a high level of representation that codes its symbolic or interpretive meaning, then on this dimension there may be an advantage in recall for older adults as compared with younger adults. Except for the situation model research, there has not been much emphasis in the literature on such levels of text representation, but it may be that older adults prefer encoding at deep, interpretive levels (see, e.g., Carstensen & Turk-Charles, 1994; Labouvie-Vief, 1990) and so they pay less attention to those levels closer to the more factual, propositional levels that permit the detailed recall most often assessed in experiments (Hashtroudi et al., 1994). As previously mentioned, in many situations (including in experiments), older adults may pay relatively more attention to their own and others' emotional responses than to events in the environment (see chap. 11, this volume; Johnson et al., 1996). All attentional control theories have as a basic assumption that goals control allocation of attention (e.g., Duncan, Emslie, Williams, Johnson, & Freer, 1996; Hasher & Zacks, 1988; D. A. Norman & Shallice, 1986). If young adults are more likely to share the goals of the experimenters than are older adults, instructions may constrain the processing of the younger participants more than they constrain the processing of the older participants. In any event, research on the interrelated sets of variables of arousal, self-efficacy, stereotypes, and goals would be most valuable; our understanding of age patterns in memory abilities would likely be enriched.

CONCLUSIONS

The study of the aging of human memory continues to be a vital domain of investigation, with recent work reinforcing, adding to, and modifying our understanding. It is clear that there are no simple rules that allow us to predict when age differences in memory will and will not occur, and if they do occur, whether the differences will be small, modest, or large.

The work reviewed here joins other reviews to suggest that a number of factors are involved in this determination. As a field, we have known about some of these factors for a while (e.g., the importance of environmental support for task performance, the difference between indirect and direct memory tasks), with more recent work confirming their importance. We have been reminded of the impact of other factors (e.g., the amount of interference present in the materials and tasks, the goals of individuals involved, and constructive processes in recall), with recent work suggesting some of the sources of age differences. We are learning more about still other factors (e.g., the impact of higher order structure inherent in to-be-remembered materials), with the exciting suggestion that older and younger adults may be able to use and update such structures equally well. Other factors appear to be relatively new (e.g., the importance of decision strategies induced or adopted at retrieval, the framing of the task itself, the minimal age differences found under more automatically driven retrieval circumstances, and substantial age differences in source memory). These lines of work will enrich the picture of age differences and similarities in memory. Additionally, there are new trends in the literature that are directed toward integrating memory in its larger cognitive, biological, and social contexts, trends that seem likely to improve our understanding of basic memory phenomena.

ACKNOWLEDGMENTS

The writing of this chapter and some of the research described in it were supported by Grants AGO4306 and AGO2753 from the National Institute on Aging. Rose T. Zacks is grateful for the sabbatical home provided by the University of California, Berkeley, and Karen Z. H. Li is grateful for postdoctoral support from the Max Planck Institute for Human Development while working on the chapter. We also wish to thank Cindi May, Tammy Rahhal, and Carolyn Yoon for their suggestions and comments on earlier versions of the chapter; Neil Smith and Carrick Williams for help with the references; and David Goldstein and Jim Zacks for their general helpfulness.

REFERENCES

Adams, C., Smith, M. C., Nyquist, L., & Perlmutter, M. (1997). Adult age-group differences in recall for the literal and interpretive meanings of narrative text. *Journal of Gerontology: Psychological Sciences, 52B*, P187–P195.

Alba, J. W., & Hasher, L. (1983). Is memory schematic? *Psychological Bulletin, 93*, 203–231.

Anderson, N. D., Craik, F. I. M., & Naveh-Benjamin, M. (1998). The attentional demands of encoding and retrieval in younger and older adults: Evidence from divided attention costs. *Psychology and Aging, 13,* 405–423.

Atkinson, R. C., & Shiffrin, R. M. (1968). Human memory: A proposed system and its control processes. In K. W. Spence & J. T. Spence (Eds.), *The psychology of learning and motivation* (Vol. 2, pp. 89–195). New York: Academic Press.

Bäckman, L., & Molander, B. (1986a). Adult age differences in the ability to cope with situations of high arousal in a precision sport. *Psychology and Aging, 1,* 133–139.

Bäckman, L., & Molander, B. (1986b). Effects of adult age and level of skill on the ability to cope with high-stress conditions in a precision sport. *Psychology and Aging, 1,* 334–336.

Baddeley, A. D. (1986). *Working memory.* Oxford, England: Oxford University Press.

Baddeley, A. D. (1990). *Human memory: Theory and practice.* Hove, United Kingdom: Lawrence Erlbaum Associates.

Baddeley, A. D. (1996). Exploring the central executive. *Quarterly Journal of Experimental Psychology: Human Experimental Psychology, 49A,* 5–28.

Bandura, A. (1986). *Social foundations of thought and action: A social cognitive theory.* Englewood Cliffs, NJ: Prentice-Hall.

Bandura, A. (1997). *Self-efficacy: The exercise of control.* New York: Freeman.

Bartlett, J. C., Strater, L., & Fulton, A. (1991). False recency and false fame of faces in young adulthood and old age. *Memory & Cognition, 19,* 177–188.

Bayen, U. J., & Murnane, K. (1996). Aging and the use of perceptual and temporal information in source memory tasks. *Psychology and Aging, 11,* 293–303.

Bayen, U. J., Murnane, K., & Erdfelder, E. (1996). Source discrimination, item detection, and multinomial models of source monitoring. *Journal of Experimental Psychology: Learning, Memory, and Cognition, 22,* 197–215.

Bieman-Copland, S., & Ryan, E. B. (1998). Age-biased interpretation of memory successes and failures in adulthood. *Journal of Gerontology: Psychological Sciences, 53B,* P105–P111.

Blanchard-Fields, F., & Abeles, R. P. (1996). Social cognition and aging. In J. E. Birren & K. W. Schaie (Eds.), *Handbook of the psychology of aging* (4th ed., pp. 150–161). San Diego, CA: Academic Press.

Blumenthal, J. A., Emery, C. F., Madden, D. J., Schiebolk, S., Walsh-Riddle, M., George, L. K., McKee, D. C., Higginbotham, M. B., Cobb, F. R., & Coleman, R. E. (1991). Long-term effects of exercise on psychological functioning in older men and women. *Journal of Gerontology: Psychological Sciences, 46,* P352–P361.

Bodenhausen, G. V. (1990). Stereotypes as judgmental heuristics: Evidence of circadian variations in discrimination. *Psychological Science, 1,* 319–322.

Botwinick, J., & Storandt, M. (1980). Recall and recognition of old information in relation to age and sex. *Journal of Gerontology, 35,* 70–76.

Boutcher, S. H., & Stocker, D. (1996). Cardiovascular response of young and older males to mental challenge. *Journal of Gerontology: Psychological Sciences, 51B,* P261–P267.

Brainerd, C. J., & Reyna, V. F. (1990). Gist is the grist: Fuzzy-trace theory and the new intuitionism. *Developmental Review, 10,* 3–47.

Brewer, W. F., & Nakamura, G. V. (1984). The nature and function of schemas. In R. S. Wyer, Jr. & T. K. Srull (Eds.), *Handbook of social cognition* (Vol. 1, pp. 119–160). Hillsdale, NJ: Lawrence Erlbaum Associates.

Brown, A. S., Jones, E. M., & Davis, T. L. (1995). Age differences in conversational source monitoring. *Psychology and Aging, 10,* 111–122.

Bunce, D., Barrowclough, A., & Morris, I. (1996). The moderating influence of physical fitness on age gradients in vigilance and serial choice responding tasks. *Psychology and Aging, 11,* 671–682.

Burke, D. M. (1997). Language, aging, and inhibitory deficits: Evaluation of a theory. *Journal of Gerontology: Psychological Sciences, 52B,* P254–P264.

Burke, D. M., & MacKay, D. G. (1997). Memory, language, and ageing. *Philosophical Translations of the Royal Society of London, B352*, 1845–1856.

Carstensen, L., & Turk-Charles, S. (1994). The salience of emotion across the adult lifespan. *Psychology and Aging, 9*, 259–264.

Cavanaugh, J. C. (1996). Memory self-efficacy as a moderator of memory change. In F. Blanchard-Fields & T. M. Hess (Eds.), *Perspectives on cognitive change in adulthood and aging* (pp. 488–507). New York: McGraw-Hill.

Cavanaugh, J. C., Feldman, J. M., & Hertzog, C. (1998). Memory beliefs as social cognition: A reconceptualization of what memory questionnaires assess. *Review of General Psychology, 2*, 48–65.

Cavanaugh, J. C., & Green, E. E. (1990). I believe, therefore I can: Self efficacy beliefs in memory aging. In E. A. Lovelace (Ed.), *Aging and cognition: Mental processes, self-awareness and interventions* (pp. 189–230). Amsterdam: North-Holland.

Cerella, L. (1985). Information processing rates in the elderly. *Psychological Bulletin, 98*, 67–83.

Chalfonte, B. L., & Johnson, M. K. (1996). Feature memory and binding in young and older adults. *Memory & Cognition, 24*, 403–416.

Chase, W. G., & Simon, H. A. (1973). The mind's eye in chess. In W. G. Chase (Ed.), *Visual information processing* (pp. 215–281). New York: Academic Press.

Cherry, K. E., & Park, D. C. (1993). Individual differences and contextual variables influence spatial memory in younger and older adults. *Psychology and Aging, 8*, 517–526.

Cherry, K. E., Park, D. C., & Donaldson, H. (1993). Adult age differences in spatial memory: Effects of structural context and practice. *Experimental Aging Research, 19*, 333–350.

Cherry, K. E., & Stadler, M. A. (1995). Implicit learning of a nonverbal sequence in younger and older adults. *Psychology and Aging, 10*, 379–394.

Christianson, S. A. (1992). Emotional stress and eyewitness memory: A critical review. *Psychological Bulletin, 112*, 284–309.

Cohen, G. (1990). Recognition and retrieval of proper names: Age differences in the fan effect. *European Journal of Cognitive Psychology, 2*, 193–204.

Cohen, G., & Faulkner, D. (1989). Age differences in source forgetting: Effects on reality monitoring and eyewitness testimony. *Psychology and Aging, 4*, 10–17.

Craik, F. I. M. (1977). Age differences in human memory. In J. E. Birren & K. W. Schaie (Eds.), *Handbook of the psychology of aging* (pp. 384–420). New York: Von Nostrand Reinhold.

Craik, F. I. M. (1983). On the transfer of information from temporary to permanent memory. *Philosophical Transactions of the Royal Society of London, B302*, 341–359.

Craik, F. I. M. (1986). A functional account of age differences in memory. In F. Klix & H. Hagendorf (Eds.), *Human memory and cognitive capabilities* (pp. 409–422). Amsterdam: Elsevier.

Craik, F. I. M., & Anderson, N. D. (1999). Applying cognitive research to problems of aging. In D. Gopher & A. Koriat (Eds.), *Attention and performance XVII. Cognitive regulation of performance: Interactions of theory and application* (pp. 583–615). Cambridge, MA: MIT Press.

Craik, F. I. M., Anderson, N. D., Kerr, S. A., & Li, K. Z. H. (1995). Memory changes in normal ageing. In A. D. Baddeley, B. A. Wilson, & F. N. Watts (Eds.), *Handbook of memory disorders* (pp. 211–241). New York: Wiley.

Craik, F. I. M., & Byrd, M. (1982). Aging and cognitive deficits: The role of attentional resources. In F. I. M. Craik & S. Trehub (Eds.), *Aging and cognitive processes* (pp. 191–211). New York: Plenum.

Craik, F. I. M., Byrd, M., & Swanson, J. M. (1987). Patterns of memory loss in three elderly samples. *Psychology and Aging, 2*, 79–86.

Craik, F. I. M., Govoni, R., Naveh-Benjamin, M., & Anderson, N. D. (1996). The effects of divided attention on encoding and retrieval processes in human memory. *Journal of Experimental Psychology: General, 125*, 159–180.

Craik, F. I. M., & Jennings, J. M. (1992). Human memory. In F. I. M. Craik & T. A. Salthouse (Eds.), *The handbook of aging and cognition* (pp. 51–110). Hillsdale, NJ: Lawrence Erlbaum Associates.

Craik, F. I. M., & Kerr, S. A. (1996). Prospective memory, aging, and lapses of intention. In M. Brandimonte, G. O. Einstein, & M. A. McDaniel (Eds.), *Prospective memory: Theory and applications* (pp. 227–237). Hillsdale, NJ: Lawrence Erlbaum Associates.

Craik, F. I. M., & McDowd, J. M. (1987). Age differences in recall and recognition. *Journal of Experimental Psychology: Learning, Memory, and Cognition, 13,* 474–479.

Curran, T. (1997). Effects of aging on implicit sequence learning: Accounting for sequence structure and explicit knowledge. *Psychological Research, 60,* 24–41.

Curran, T., & Hintzman, D. L. (1995). Violations of the independence assumption in process dissociation. *Journal of Experimental Psychology: Learning, Memory, and Cognition, 21,* 531–547.

Daneman, M., & Carpenter, P. A. (1980). Individual differences in working memory and reading. *Journal of Verbal Learning and Verbal Behavior, 19,* 450–466.

Daneman, M., & Merikle, P. M. (1996). Working memory and language comprehension: A meta-analysis. *Psychonomic Bulletin & Review, 3,* 422–433.

Davidson, D., & Zacks, R. T. (1998, April). *Practice, time of day, and Stroop interference in older adults.* Poster session presented at the Cognitive Aging Conference, Atlanta, GA.

Deese, J. (1959). On the prediction of occurrence of particular verbal intrusions in immediate recall. *Journal of Experimental Psychology, 58,* 17–22.

Dixon, R. A., & Gould, O. N. (1996). Adults telling and retelling stories collaboratively. In P. B. Baltes & U. M. Staudinger (Eds.), *Interactive minds: Life-span perspectives on the social foundation of cognition* (pp. 221–241). Cambridge, England: Cambridge University Press.

Dobbs, A. R., & Reeves, M. B. (1996). Prospective memory: More than memory. In M. Brandimonte, G. O. Einstein, & M. A. McDaniel (Eds.), *Prospective memory: Theory and applications* (pp. 199–225). Hillsdale, NJ: Lawrence Erlbaum Associates.

Dodson, C. S., & Johnson, M. K. (1993). Rate of false source attributions depends on how questions are asked. *American Journal of Psychology, 106,* 541–557.

Dodson, C. S., & Johnson, M. K. (1996). Some problems with the process-dissociation approach to memory. *Journal of Experimental Psychology: General, 125,* 181–194.

Duncan, J., Emslie, H. Y., Williams, P., Johnson, R., & Freer, C. (1996). Intelligence and the frontal lobe: The organization of goal-directed behavior. *Cognitive Psychology, 30,* 257–303.

Dywan, J., & Jacoby, L. L. (1990). Effects of aging on source monitoring: Differences in susceptibility to false fame. *Psychology and Aging, 5,* 379–387.

Earles, J. L., & Kersten, A. (1998). Influences of age and perceived activity difficulty differences on activity recall. *Journal of Gerontology: Psychological Sciences, 53B,* P324–P328.

Earles, J. L., & Salthouse, T. A. (1995). Interrelations of age, health, and speed. *Journal of Gerontology: Psychological Sciences, 50B,* P33–P41.

Earles, J. L., Smith, A. D., & Park, D. C. (1994). Age differences in the effects of facilitating and distracting context on recall. *Aging and Cognition, 1,* 141–151.

Einstein, G. O., Holland, L. J., McDaniel, M. A., & Guynn, M. J. (1992). Age-related deficits in prospective memory: The influence of task complexity. *Psychology and Aging, 7,* 471–478.

Einstein, G. O., & McDaniel, M. A. (1990). Normal aging and prospective memory. *Journal of Experimental Psychology: Learning, Memory, and Cognition, 16,* 717–726.

Einstein, G. O., & McDaniel, M. A. (1996). Retrieval processes in prospective memory: Theoretical approaches and some new empirical findings. In M. Brandimonte, G. O. Einstein, & M. A. McDaniel (Eds.), *Prospective memory: Theory and applications* (pp. 115–142). Hillsdale, NJ: Lawrence Erlbaum Associates.

Einstein, G. O., McDaniel, M. A., Richardson, S. L., Guynn, M. J., & Cunfer, A. R. (1995). Aging and prospective memory: Examining the influences of self-initiated retrieval processes. *Journal of Experimental Psychology: Learning, Memory, and Cognition, 21,* 996–1007.

Einstein, G. O., Smith, R. E., McDaniel, M. A., & Shaw, P. (1997). Aging and prospective memory: The influence of increased task demands at encoding and retrieval. *Psychology and Aging, 12,* 479–488.

Engle, R. W., Cantor, J., & Carullo, J. J. (1992). Individual differences in working memory and comprehension: A test of four hypotheses. *Journal of Experimental Psychology: Learning, Memory, and Cognition, 18,* 972–992.

Erber, J. T. (1989). Young and older adults' appraisal of memory failure in young and older target persons. *Journal of Gerontology: Psychological Sciences, 44,* P170–P175.

Eysenck, M. W., & Calvo, M. G. (1996). Anxiety and performance: The processing efficiency theory. *Cognition and Emotion, 6,* 409–434.

Fisk, J. E., & Warr, P. (1996). Age-related impairment in associative learning: The role of anxiety, arousal and learning self-efficacy. *Personality and Individual Differences, 21,* 675–686.

Fleischman, D. A., & Gabrieli, J. D. E. (1998). Repetition priming in normal aging and Alzheimer's disease: A review of findings and theories. *Psychology and Aging, 13,* 88–119.

Frensch, P. A., & Miner, C. S. (1994). Effects of presentation rate and individual differences in short-term memory capacity on an indirect measure of serial learning. *Memory & Cognition, 22,* 95–110.

Gardiner, J. M., & Java, R. I. (1993). Recognition memory and awareness: An experiential approach. *European Journal of Cognitive Psychology, 5,* 337–346.

Garnham, A. (1981). Mental models as representations of text. *Memory & Cognition, 9,* 560–565.

Gerard, L. D., Zacks, R. T., Hasher, L., & Radvansky, G. A. (1991). Age deficits in retrieval: The fan effect. *Journal of Gerontology: Psychological Sciences, 46,* P131–P146.

Graf, P. (1990). Life span changes in implicit and explicit memory. *Bulletin of the Psychonomic Society, 28,* 353–358.

Graf, P., & Komatsu, S. (1994). Process dissociation procedure: Handle with caution! *European Journal of Cognitive Psychology, 6,* 113–129.

Graf, P., Squire, L. R., & Mandler, G. (1984). Information that amnesic patients do not forget. *Journal of Experimental Psychology: Learning, Memory, and Cognition, 10,* 164–178.

Guttentag, R. E., & Hunt, R. R. (1988). Adult age differences in memory for imagined and performed actions. *Journal of Gerontology: Psychological Sciences, 43,* P107–P108.

Habib, R., Jelicic, M., & Craik, F. I. M. (1996). Are implicit memory deficits in the elderly due to differences in explicit memory processes? *Aging, Neuropsychology, and Cognition, 3,* 264–271.

Halpern, A. R., Bartlett, J. C., & Dowling, W. J. (1995). Aging and experience in the recognition of musical transpositions. *Psychology and Aging, 10,* 325–342.

Harrington, D. L., & Haaland, K. Y. (1992). Skill learning in the elderly: Diminished implicit and explicit memory for a motor sequence. *Psychology and Aging, 7,* 425–434.

Hartley, A. A. (1992). Attention. In F. I. M. Craik & T. A. Salthouse (Eds.), *The handbook of aging and cognition* (pp. 3–49). Hillsdale, NJ: Lawrence Erlbaum Associates.

Hartley, J. T. (1988). Aging and individual differences in memory for written discourse. In L. L. Light & D. M. Burke (Eds.), *Language, memory, and aging* (pp. 36–57). New York: Cambridge University Press.

Hartley, J. T. (1993). Aging and prose memory: Tests of the resource-deficit hypothesis. *Psychology and Aging, 8,* 538–551.

Hartman, M., & Hasher, L. (1991). Aging and suppression: Memory for previously relevant information. *Psychology and Aging, 6,* 587–594.

Hasher, L., Quig, M. B., & May, C. P. (1997). Inhibitory control over no-longer–relevant information: Adult age differences. *Memory & Cognition, 25,* 286–295.

Hasher, L., & Zacks, R. T. (1979). Automatic and effortful processes in memory. *Journal of Experimental Psychology: General, 108,* 356–388.

Hasher, L., & Zacks, R. T. (1988). Working memory, comprehension, and aging: A review and a new view. In G. Bower (Ed.), *The psychology of learning and motivation* (Vol. 22, pp. 193–225). New York: Academic Press.

Hasher, L., Zacks, R. T., & May, C. P. (1999). Inhibitory control, circadian arousal, and age. In D. Gopher & A. Koriat (Eds.), *Attention and performance XVII. Cognitive regulation of performance: Interaction of theory and application* (pp. 653–675). Cambridge, MA: MIT Press.

Hashtroudi, S., Johnson, M. K., & Chrosniak, L. D. (1989). Aging and source monitoring. *Psychology and Aging, 4,* 106–112.

Hashtroudi, S., Johnson, M. K., & Chrosniak, L. D. (1990). Aging and qualitative characteristics of memories for perceived and imagined complex events. *Psychology and Aging, 5,* 119–126.

Hashtroudi, S., Johnson, M. K., Vnek, N., & Ferguson, S. A. (1994). Aging and effects of affective and factual focus on source monitoring and recall. *Psychology and Aging, 9,* 160–170.

Heckhausen, J., Dixon, R. A., & Baltes, P. B. (1989). Gains and losses in development throughout adulthood as perceived by different adult age groups. *Developmental Psychology, 25,* 109–121.

Henkel, L. A., Johnson, M. K., & De Leonardis, D. M. (1998). *Aging and source monitoring: Cognitive processes and neuropsychological correlates.* Manuscript submitted for publication.

Hertzog, C., Dixon, R. A., & Hultsch, D. F. (1990). Metamemory in adulthood: Differentiating knowledge, belief and behavior. In T. M. Hess (Ed.), *Aging and cognition: Knowledge, organization and utilization* (pp. 161–212). Amsterdam: North-Holland.

Hess, T. M., Flanagan, D. A., & Tate, C. S. (1993). Aging and memory for schematically vs. taxonomically organized verbal materials. *Journal of Gerontology: Psychological Sciences, 48,* P37–P44.

Hess, T. M., & Pullen, S. M. (1996). Memory in context. In F. Blanchard-Fields & T. M. Hess (Eds.), *Perspectives on cognitive change in adulthood and aging* (pp. 387–427). New York: McGraw-Hill.

Hill, R. D., Nilsson, L. -G., & Nyberg, L. (1998, April). *The relationship between chronic smoking and cognitive functioning across age cohorts.* Poster session presented at the Cognitive Aging Conference, Atlanta, ᴧ ʴ.

Hill, R. D., Storandt, M., & Malley, M. (1993). The impact of long-term exercise training on psychological function in older adults. *Journal of Gerontology: Psychological Sciences, 48,* P12–P17.

Hoch, C. C., Reynolds, C. F., Jennings, J. R., Monk, T. H., Buysse, D. J., Machen, M. A., & Kupler, D. J. (1992). Daytime sleepiness and performance among healthy 80 and 20 year olds. *Neurobiology of Aging, 13,* 353–356.

Horne, J., & Östberg, O. (1976). A self-assessment questionnaire to determine morningness–eveningness in human circadian rhythms. *International Journal of Chronobiology, 4,* 97–110.

Horne, J., & Östberg, O. (1977). Individual differences in human circadian rhythms. *Biological Psychology, 5,* 179–190.

Houx, P. J., & Jolles, J. (1993). Age-related decline of psychomotor speed: Effects of age, brain health, sex, and education. *Perceptual and Motor Skills, 76,* 195–211.

Houx, P. J., Jolles, J., & Vreeling, F. W. (1993). Stroop interference: Aging effects assessed with the Stroop color-word test. *Experimental Aging Research, 19,* 209–224.

Howard, D. V. (1988). Implicit and explicit assessment of cognitive aging. In M. L. Howe & C. J. Brainerd (Eds.), *Cognitive development in adulthood: Progress in cognitive development research* (pp. 3–37). New York: Springer-Verlag.

Howard, D. V., & Howard, J. H., Jr. (1989). Age differences in learning serial patterns: Direct versus indirect measures. *Psychology and Aging, 4,* 357–364.

Howard, D. V., & Howard, J. H., Jr. (1992). Adult age differences in the rate of learning serial patterns: Evidence from direct and indirect tests. *Psychology and Aging, 7*, 232–241.

Howard, J. H., Jr., & Howard, D. V. (1997). Age differences in implicit learning of higher order dependencies in serial patterns. *Psychology and Aging, 12*, 634–656.

Hultsch, D. F., Hammer, M., & Small, B. J. (1993). Age differences in cognitive performance in later life: Relationships to self-reported health and activity lifestyle. *Journal of Gerontology: Psychological Sciences, 48*, P1–P11.

Hultsch, D. F., Hertzog, C., & Dixon, R. A. (1990). Ability correlates of memory performance in adulthood and aging. *Psychology and Aging, 5*, 356–368.

Hultsch, D. F., Hertzog, C., Dixon, R. A., & Davidson, H. (1988). Memory, self-knowledge, and self-efficacy in the aged. In M. L. Howe & C. J. Brainerd (Eds.), *Cognitive development in adulthood: Progress in cognitive development research* (pp. 65–93). New York: Springer-Verlag.

Hunt, R. R., & McDaniel, M. A. (1993). The enigma of organization and distinctiveness. *Journal of Memory and Language, 32*, 421–445.

Intons-Peterson, M. J., Rocchi, P., West, T., McLellan, K., & Hackney, A. (1998). Aging, optimal testing times, and negative priming. *Journal of Experimental Psychology: Learning, Memory, and Cognition, 24*, 362–376.

Israel, L., & Schacter, D. L. (1997). Pictorial encoding reduces false recognition of semantic associates. *Psychonomic Bulletin & Review, 4*, 577–581.

Jacoby, L. L. (1991). A process dissociation framework: Separating automatic from intentional uses of memory. *Journal of Memory and Language, 30*, 513–541.

Jacoby, L. L., Yonelinas, A. P., & Jennings, J. M. (1997). The relation between conscious and unconscious (automatic) influences: A declaration of independence. In J. Cohen & J. W. Schooler (Eds.), *Scientific approaches to consciousness* (pp. 13–47). Mahwah, NJ: Lawrence Erlbaum Associates.

Java, R. I. (1996). Effects of age on state of awareness following implicit and explicit word-association tasks. *Psychology and Aging, 11*, 108–111.

Jelicic, M., Craik, F. I. M., & Moscovitch, M. (1996). Effects of ageing on different explicit and implicit memory tasks. *European Journal of Cognitive Psychology, 8*, 225–234.

Jennings, J. M., & Jacoby, L. L. (1993). Automatic versus intentional uses of memory: Aging, attention, and control. *Psychology and Aging, 8*, 283–293.

Jennings, J. M., & Jacoby, L. L. (1997a). Improving age-related deficits in recollection: Application of an opposition procedure. *Brain and Cognition, 35*, 403–406.

Jennings, J. M., & Jacoby, L. L. (1997b). An opposition procedure for detecting age-related deficits in recollection: Telling effects of repetition. *Psychology and Aging, 12*, 352–361.

Johnson, M. K. (1997). Identifying the origin of mental experience. In M. S. Myslobodsky (Ed.), *The mythomanias: The nature of deception and self-deception* (pp. 133–180). Mahwah, NJ: Lawrence Erlbaum Associates.

Johnson, M. K., De Leonardis, D. M., Hashtroudi, S., & Ferguson, S. A. (1995). Aging and single versus multiple cues in source monitoring. *Psychology and Aging, 10*, 507–517.

Johnson, M. K., Foley, M. A., Suengas, A. G., & Raye, C. L. (1988). Phenomenal characteristics of memories for perceived and imagined autobiographical events. *Journal of Experimental Psychology: General, 117*, 371–376.

Johnson, M. K., & Hasher, L. (1987). Human learning and memory. *Annual Review of Psychology, 38*, 631–638.

Johnson, M. K., Hashtroudi, S., & Lindsay, D. S. (1993). Source monitoring. *Psychological Bulletin, 114*, 3–28.

Johnson, M. K., Nolde, S. F., & De Leonardis, D. M. (1996). Emotional focus and source monitoring. *Journal of Memory and Language, 35*, 135–156.

Johnson, M. K., & Raye, C. L. (1981). Reality monitoring. *Psychological Review, 88*, 67–85.

Johnson, M. K., & Raye, C. L. (in press). Cognitive and brain mechanisms of false memories and beliefs. In D. L. Schacter & E. Scarry (Eds.), *Memory, brain, and belief.* Cambridge, MA: Harvard University Press.

Just, M. A., & Carpenter, P. A. (1992). A capacity theory of comprehension: Individual differences in working memory. *Psychological Review, 99*, 122–149.

Kane, M. J., & Hasher, L. (1995). Interference. In G. L. Maddox (Ed.), *Encyclopedia of aging* (2nd ed., pp. 514–516). New York: Springer-Verlag.

Kausler, D. H. (1994). *Learning and memory in normal aging.* San Diego, CA: Academic Press.

Kausler, D. H., & Puckett, J. M. (1981). Adult age differences in memory for sex of voice. *Journal of Gerontology, 36*, 44–50.

Kausler, D. H., Salthouse, T. A., & Saults, J. S. (1988). Temporal memory over the adult lifespan. *American Journal of Psychology, 101*, 207–215.

Kemtes, K. A., & Kemper, S. (1997). Younger and older adults' on-line processing of syntactically ambiguous sentences. *Psychology and Aging, 12*, 362–371.

Kidder, D. P., Park, D. C., Hertzog, C., & Morrell, R. (1997). Prospective memory and aging: The effects working memory and prospective memory task load. *Aging, Neuropsychology, and Cognition, 4*, 93–112.

Kintsch, W. (1988). The role of knowledge in discourse comprehension: A construction–integration model. *Psychological Review, 95*, 163–182.

Kintsch, W., & van Dijk, T. A. (1978). Toward a model of text comprehension and production. *Psychological Review, 85*, 363–394.

Koutstaal, W., & Schacter, D. L. (1997). Gist-based false recognition of pictures in older and younger adults. *Journal of Memory and Language, 37*, 555–583.

Kramer, A., Hahn, S., Banich, M., Cohen, N., McAuley, E., Bardell, L., Harrison, C., Chason, J., Vakil, E., Prioux, H., Glass, A., Minear, M., & Nash, C. (1998, April). *Influence of aerobic fitness on the neurocognitive function of sedentary older adults.* Poster session presented at the Cognitive Aging Conference, Atlanta, GA.

Labouvie-Vief, G. (1990). Modes of knowledge and the organization of development. In M. L. Commons, C. Armon, L. Kohlberg, F. A. Richards, T. A. Grotzer, & J. Sinnott (Eds.), *Adult development: Models and methods in the study of adolescent and adult thought* (Vol. 2, pp. 43–62). New York: Praeger.

Lachman, M. E., Weaver, S. L., Bandura, M., Elliot, E., & Lewkowicz, C. J. (1992). Improving memory and control beliefs through cognitive restructuring and self-generated strategies. *Journal of Gerontology: Psychological Sciences, 47*, P293–P299.

La Voie, D., & Light, L. L. (1994). Adult age differences in repetition priming. A meta-analysis. *Psychology and Aging, 4*, 539–553.

Leirer, V. O., Tanke, E. D., & Morrow, D. G. (1994). Time of day and naturalistic prospective memory. *Experimental Aging Research, 20*, 127–134.

Levenson, R. W., Carstensen, L. L., & Gottman, J. M. (1994). Influence of age and gender on affect, physiology, and their interrelations: A study of long-term marriages. *Journal of Personality and Social Psychology, 67*, 56–68.

Levy, B. (1996). Improving memory in old age through implicit self-stereotyping. *Journal of Personality and Social Psychology, 71*, 1092–1107.

Levy, B., & Langer, E. (1994). Aging free from negative stereotypes: Successful memory in China and among American deaf. *Journal of Personality and Social Psychology, 66*, 989–997.

Li, K. Z. H., Hasher, L., Jonas, D., Rahhal, T. A., & May, C. P. (1998). Distractibility, circadian arousal, and aging: A boundary condition? *Psychology and Aging, 13*, 574–583.

Light, L. L. (1991). Memory and aging: Four hypotheses in search of data. *Annual Review of Psychology, 42*, 333–376.

Light, L. L. (1992). The organization of memory in old age. In F. I. M. Craik & T. A. Salthouse (Eds.), *The handbook of aging and cognition* (pp. 111–165). Hillsdale, NJ: Lawrence Erlbaum Associates.

Light, L. L., Capps, J. L., Singh, A. O., & Albertson-Owens, S. A. (1994). Comprehension and use of anaphoric devices in young and older adults. *Discourse Processes*, *18*, 77–103.

Light, L. L., Kennison, R., Prull, M. W., La Voie, D., & Zuellig, A. (1996). One-trial associative priming of nonwords in young and older adults. *Psychology and Aging*, *11*, 417–430.

Light, L. L., & La Voie, D. (1993). Direct and indirect measures of memory in old age. In P. Graf & M. E. J. Masson (Eds.), *Implicit memory: New directions in cognition, development, and neuropsychology* (pp. 207–230). Hillsdale, NJ: Lawrence Erlbaum Associates.

Light, L. L., La Voie, D., & Kennison, R. (1995). Repetition priming of nonwords in young and older adults. *Journal of Experimental Psychology: Learning, Memory, and Cognition*, *21*, 327–346.

Light, L. L., La Voie, D., Valencia-Laver, D., Albertson-Owens, S. A., & Mead, G. (1992). Direct and indirect measures of memory for modality in young and older adults. *Journal of Experimental Psychology: Learning, Memory, and Cognition*, *18*, 1284–1297.

Light, L. L., & Singh, A. (1987). Implicit and explicit memory in young and older adults. *Journal of Experimental Psychology: Learning, Memory, and Cognition*, *13*, 531–541.

Light, L. L., & Zelinski, E. M. (1983). Memory for spatial information in young and old adults. *Developmental Psychology*, *19*, 901–906.

Lindenberger, U., & Baltes, P. B. (1997). Intellectual functioning and intelligence in old and very old age: Cross-sectional results from the Berlin Aging Study. *Psychology and Aging*, *12*, 410–432.

Loftus, E. F. (1992). When a lie becomes memory's truth: Memory distortion after exposure to misinformation. *Current Directions in Psychological Science*, *1*, 121–123.

Luszcz, M. A., Bryan, J., & Kent, P. (1997). Predicting episodic memory performance of very old men and women: Contributions from age, depression, activity, cognitive ability, and speed. *Psychology and Aging*, *12*, 340–351.

Mäntylä, T. (1993). Knowing but not remembering: Adult age differences in recollective experience. *Memory & Cognition*, *21*, 379–388.

Mäntylä, T. (1994). Remembering to remember: Adult age differences in prospective memory. *Journal of Gerontology: Psychological Sciences*, *49*, P276–P282.

May, C. P. (1999). Synchrony effects in cognition: The costs and a benefit. *Psychonomic Bulletin & Review*, *6*, 142–147.

May, C. P., & Hasher, L. (1998). Synchrony effects in inhibitory control over thought and action. *Journal of Experimental Psychology: Human Perception and Performance*, *24*, 363–379.

May, C. P., Hasher, L., & Kane, M. (in press). The role of interference in memory span. *Memory & Cognition*.

May, C. P., Hasher, L., & Stoltzfus, E. R. (1993). Optimal time of day and the magnitude of age differences in memory. *Psychological Science*, *4*, 326–330.

Maylor, E. A. (1990). Age and prospective memory. *Quarterly Journal of Experimental Psychology*, *42A*, 471–493.

Maylor, E. A. (1996). Does prospective memory decline with age? In M. Brandimonte, G. O. Einstein, & M. A. McDaniel (Eds.), *Prospective memory: Theory and applications* (pp. 173–198). Hillsdale, NJ: Lawrence Erlbaum Associates.

McDermott, K. B. (1996). The persistence of false memories in list recall. *Journal of Memory and Language*, *35*, 212–230.

McDonald-Miszczak, L., Hertzog, C., & Hultsch, D. F. (1995). Stability and accuracy of metamemory in adulthood and aging: A longitudinal analysis. *Psychology and Aging*, *10*, 553–564.

McDowd, J. M. (1997). Inhibition in attention and aging. *Journal of Gerontology: Psychological Sciences*, *52B*, P265–P273.

McDowd, J. M., & Birren, J. E. (1990). Aging and attentional processes. In J. E. Birren & K. W. Schaie (Eds.), *Handbook of the psychology of aging* (3rd ed., pp. 222–233). San Diego, CA: Academic Press.

McDowd, J. M., Oseas-Kreger, D. M., & Filion, D. L. (1995). Inhibitory processes in cognition and aging. In F. N. Dempster & C. J. Brainerd (Eds.), *Interference and inhibition in cognition* (pp. 363–400). San Diego, CA: Academic Press.

McIntyre, J. S., & Craik, F. I. M. (1987). Age differences in memory for item and source information. *Canadian Journal of Psychology, 41,* 175–192.

McIntyre, J. S., & Friesen, I. C. (1998, March). *Effects of source manipulations on fact and source memory in young and old adults.* Poster session presented at the Rotman Research Institute Conference, Toronto, Ontario, Canada.

Meinz, E. J., & Salthouse, T. A. (1998). The effects of age and experience on memory for visually presented music. *Journal of Gerontology: Psychological Sciences, 53B,* P60–P69.

Miller, G. A. (1956). The magical number seven plus or minus two. Some limits on our capacity for processing information. *Psychological Review, 63,* 81–97.

Monti, L. A., Gabrieli, J. D. E., Rinaldi, J. A., Wilson, R. S., Beckett, L. A., Grinnell, E., Lange, K. L., & Reminger, S. L. (1997). Sources of priming in text rereading: Intact implicit memory for new associations in older adults and in patients with Alzheimer's disease. *Psychology and Aging, 12,* 536–547.

Morrow, D. G., Leirer, V. O., & Altieri, P. A. (1992). Aging, expertise, and narrative processing. *Psychology and Aging, 7,* 376–388.

Morrow, D. G., Leirer, V. O., Altieri, P. A., & Fitzsimmons, C. (1994a). Age differences in creating spatial mental models from narratives. *Language and Cognitive Processes, 9,* 203–220.

Morrow, D. G., Leirer, V. O., Altieri, P. A., & Fitzsimmons, C. (1994b). When expertise reduces age differences in performance. *Psychology and Aging, 9,* 134–148.

Morrow, D. G., Stine-Morrow, E. A. L., Leirer, V. O., Andrassy, J. M., & Kahn, J. (1997). The role of reader age and focus of attention in creating situation models from narratives. *Journal of Gerontology: Psychological Sciences, 52B,* P73–P80.

Moscovitch, M. (1994). Cognitive resources and dual-task interference effects at retrieval in normal people: The role of the frontal lobes and medial temporal cortex. *Neuropsychology, 8,* 524–534.

Moscovitch, M., & Winocur, G. (1992). The neuropsychology of memory and aging. In F. I. M. Craik & T. A. Salthouse (Eds.), *The handbook of aging and cognition* (pp. 315–372). Hillsdale, NJ: Lawrence Erlbaum Associates.

Mueller, J. H., Rankin, J. L., & Carlomusto, M. (1979). Adult age differences in free recall as a function of basis of organization and method of presentation. *Journal of Gerontology, 34,* 375–380.

Multhaup, K. S. (1995). Aging, source, and decision criteria: When false fame errors do and do not occur. *Psychology and Aging, 10,* 492–497.

Multhaup, K. S., Balota, D. A., & Cowan, N. (1996). Implications of aging, lexicality, and item length for the mechanisms underlying memory span. *Psychonomic Bulletin & Review, 3,* 112–120.

Multhaup, K. S., De Leonardis, D. M., & Johnson, M. K. (1999). Source memory and eyewitness suggestibility in older adults. *Journal of General Psychology, 126,* 74–84.

Multhaup, K. S., Hasher, L., & Zacks, R. T. (1998). *Age and memory for distracting information: A double dissociation.* Manuscript submitted for publication.

Myerson, J., Hale, S., Wagstaff, D., Poon, L. W., & Smith, G. A. (1990). The information-loss model: A mathematical theory of age-related cognitive slowing. *Psychological Review, 97,* 475–487.

Naveh-Benjamin, M., & Craik, F. I. M. (1995). Memory for context and its use in item memory: Comparisons of younger and older persons. *Psychology and Aging, 10,* 284–293.

Naveh-Benjamin, M., & Craik, F. I. M. (1998). Presenting and analyzing results in aging research: A methodological note. *Experimental Aging Research, 24,* 83–98.

Navon, D. (1989a). The importance of being visible: On the role of attention in a mind viewed as an anarchic intelligence system. I: Basic tenets. *European Journal of Cognitive Psychology, 1,* 191–213.

Navon, D. (1989b). The importance of being visible: On the role of attention in a mind viewed as an anarchic intelligence system. II: Application to the field of attention. *European Journal of Cognitive Psychology, 1,* 215–238.

Nilsson, L. -G., Bäckman, L., Erngrund, K., Nyberg, L., Adolfsson, R., Bucht, G., Karlsson, S., Widing, M., & Winblad, B. (1997). The Betula prospective cohort study: Memory, health, and aging. *Aging, Neuropsychology, and Cognition, 4,* 1–32.

Nissen, M. J., & Bullemer, P. (1987). Attentional requirements of learning: Evidence from performance measures. *Cognitive Psychology, 19,* 1–32.

Nissen, M. J., Willingham, D., & Hartman, M. (1989). Explicit and implicit remembering: When is learning preserved in amnesia? *Neuropsychologica, 27,* 341–352.

Norman, D. A., & Shallice, T. (1986). Attention to action: Willed and automatic control of behavior. In R. J. Davidson, G. E. Schwartz, & D. Shapiro (Eds.), *Consciousness and self-regulation: Advances in theory and research* (Vol. 4, pp. 1–18). New York: Plenum.

Norman, K. A., & Schacter, D. L. (1997). False recognition in younger and older adults: Exploring the characteristics of illusory memories. *Memory & Cognition, 25,* 838–848.

Nyberg, L., Nilsson, L. -G., Olofsson, U., & Bäckman, L. (1997). Effects of division of attention during encoding and retrieval on age differences in episodic memory. *Experimental Aging Research, 23,* 137–143.

Park, D. C., Hertzog, C., Kidder, D., Morrell, R., & Mayhorn, C. (1997). The effect of age on event-based and time-based prospective memory. *Psychology and Aging, 12,* 314–327.

Park, D. C., & Puglisi, J. T. (1985). Older adults' memory for the color of pictures and words. *Journal of Gerontology, 40,* 198–204.

Park, D. C., Puglisi, J. T., & Lutz, R. (1982). Spatial memory in older adults: Effects of intentionality. *Journal of Gerontology, 37,* 330–335.

Park, D. C., Puglisi, J. T., & Smith, A. D. (1986). Memory for pictures: Does an age-related decline exist? *Psychology and Aging, 5,* 250–255.

Park, D. C., Puglisi, J. T., Smith, A. D., & Dudley, W. N. (1987). Cue utilization and encoding specificity in picture recognition by older adults. *Journal of Gerontology, 42,* 423–425.

Park, D. C., Smith, A. D., Dudley, W. N., & Lafronza, V. N. (1989). Effects of age and a divided attention task presented during encoding and retrieval on memory. *Journal of Experimental Psychology: Learning, Memory, and Cognition, 15,* 1185–1191.

Park, D. C., Smith, A. D., Lautenschlager, G., Earles, J. L., Frieske, D., Zwahr, M., & Gaines, C. L. (1996). Mediators of long-term memory performance across the life span. *Psychology and Aging, 11,* 621–637.

Park, D. C., Smith, A. D., Morrell, R. W., Puglisi, J. T., & Dudley, W. N. (1990). Effects of contextual integration on recall of pictures by older adults. *Journal of Gerontology: Psychological Sciences, 45,* P52–P57.

Parkin, A. J., & Walter, B. (1992). Recollective experience, normal aging, and frontal dysfunction. *Psychology and Aging, 7,* 290–298.

Perfect, T. (1997). Memory aging as a frontal lobe dysfunction. In M. A. Conway (Ed.), *Cognitive models of memory* (pp. 315–339). Hove, United Kingdom: Psychology Press.

Perfect, T. J., & Dasgupta, Z. R. R. (1997). What underlies the deficit in reported recollective experience with age? *Memory & Cognition, 25,* 849–858.

Petros, T. V., Beckwith, B. E., & Anderson, M. (1990). Individual differences in the effects of time of day and passage difficulty on prose memory in adults. *British Journal of Psychology, 81,* 63–72.

Poldrack, R. A., & Cohen, N. J. (1997). Priming of new associations in reading time: What is learned? *Psychonomic Bulletin & Review, 4,* 398–402.

Pratt, M. W., & Robins, S. L. (1991). That's the way it was: Age differences in structure and quality of adults' personal narratives. *Discourse Processes, 14*, 73–85.

Puglisi, J. T., & Park, D. C. (1987). Perceptual elaboration and memory in older adults. *Journal of Gerontology, 42*, 160–162.

Rabinowitz, J. C., Craik, F. I. M., & Ackerman, B. P. (1982). A processing resource account of age differences in recall. *Canadian Journal of Psychology, 36*, 325–344.

Radvansky, G. A., & Curiel, J. M. (1998). Narrative comprehension and aging: The fate of completed goal information. *Psychology and Aging, 13*, 69–79.

Radvansky, G. A., Gerard, L. D., Zacks, R. T., & Hasher, L. (1990). Younger and older adults use of mental models. *Psychology and Aging, 5*, 209–214.

Radvansky, G. A., Zacks, R. T., & Hasher, L. (1996). Fact retrieval in younger and older adults: The role of mental models. *Psychology and Aging, 11*, 258–271.

Rahhal, T. A., & Hasher, L. (1998, April). *It's not all downhill: Age differences in explicit memory performance can be eliminated by instructions.* Poster session presented at the Cognitive Aging Conference, Atlanta, GA.

Reder, L. M., Wible, C., & Martin, J. (1986). Differential memory changes with age: Exact retrieval versus plausible inference. *Journal of Experimental Psychology: Learning, Memory, and Cognition, 12*, 72–81.

Roediger, H. L., III, & McDermott, K. B. (1993). Implicit memory in normal human subjects. In F. Boller & J. Grafman (Eds.), *Handbook of neuropsychology* (Vol. 8, pp. 63–131). Amsterdam: Elsevier.

Roediger, H. L., III, & McDermott, K. B. (1995). Creating false memories: Remembering words not presented in lists. *Journal of Experimental Psychology: Learning, Memory, and Cognition, 21*, 803–814.

Rubin, D. C., Rahhal, T. A., & Poon, L. W. (1998). Things learned in early adulthood are remembered best. *Memory & Cognition, 26*, 3–19.

Ryan, E. B. (1992). Beliefs about memory changes across the adult lifespan. *Journal of Gerontology: Psychological Sciences, 47*, P41–P46.

Rybash, J. M. (1996). Implicit memory and aging: A cognitive neuropsychological perspective. *Developmental Neuropsychology, 12*, 127–179.

Salthouse, T. A. (1991). *Theoretical perspectives on cognitive aging.* Hillsdale, NJ: Lawrence Erlbaum Associates.

Salthouse, T. A. (1992). Influences of processing speed on adult age differences in working memory. *Acta Psychologica, 79*, 155–170.

Salthouse, T. A. (1993). Influence of working memory on adult age differences in matrix reasoning. *British Journal of Psychology, 84*, 171–199.

Salthouse, T. A. (1994). The aging of working memory. *Neuropsychology, 8*, 535–543.

Salthouse, T. A. (1996). The processing speed theory of adult age differences in cognition. *Psychological Review, 103*, 403–428.

Salthouse, T. A., & Babcock, R. L. (1991). Decomposing adult age differences in working memory. *Developmental Psychology, 27*, 763–776.

Salthouse, T. A., Fristoe, N. M., Lineweaver, T. T., & Coon, V. E. (1995). Aging of attention: Does the ability to divide decline? *Memory & Cognition, 23*, 59–71.

Salthouse, T. A., Kausler, D. H., & Saults, J. S. (1988). Investigation of student status, background variables, and the feasibility of standard tasks in cognitive aging research. *Psychology and Aging, 3*, 29–37.

Salthouse, T. A., & Meinz, E. J. (1995). Aging, inhibition, working memory, and speed. *Journal of Gerontology: Psychological Sciences, 50B*, P297–P306.

Salthouse, T. A., & Mitchell, D. R. (1990). Effects of age and naturally occurring experience on spatial visualization performance. *Developmental Psychology, 26*, 845–854.

Salthouse, T. A., Toth, J. P., Hancock, H. E., & Woodard, J. L. (1997). Controlled and automatic forms of memory and attention: Process purity and the uniqueness of age-related influences. *Journal of Gerontology: Psychological Sciences, 52B,* P216–P228.

Schacter, D. L., Kaszniak, A. W., Kihlstrom, J. F., & Valdiserri, M. (1991). The relation between source memory and aging. *Psychology and Aging, 6,* 559–568.

Schacter, D. L., Koutstaal, W., Johnson, M. K., Gross, M. S., & Angell, K. E. (1997). False recollection induced via photographs: A comparison of older and younger adults. *Psychology and Aging, 12,* 203–215.

Schacter, D. L., Koutstaal, W., & Norman, K. A. (1997). False memories and aging. *Trends in Cognitive Sciences, 1,* 229–236.

Schacter, D. L., Norman, K. A., & Koutstaal, W. (1998). The cognitive neuroscience of constructive memory. *Annual Review of Psychology, 49,* 289–318.

Schacter, D. L., & Tulving, E. (1994). What are the memory systems of 1994? In D. L. Schacter & E. Tulving (Eds.), *Memory systems 1994* (pp. 1–38). Cambridge, MA: MIT Press.

Seger, C. A. (1994). Implicit learning. *Psychological Bulletin, 115,* 163–196.

Shimamura, A. P. (1993). Neuropsychological analyses of implicit memory: History, methodology, and theoretical interpretations. In P. Graf & M. E. J. Masson (Eds.), *Implicit memory: New directions in cognition, development, and neuropsychology* (pp. 265–285). Hillsdale, NJ: Lawrence Erlbaum Associates.

Sliwinski, M., Lipton, R. B., Buschke, H., & Stewart, W. (1996). The effects of preclinical dementia on estimates of normal cognitive functioning in aging. *Journal of Gerontology: Psychological Sciences, 51B,* P217–P225.

Small, B. J., Hultsch, D. F., & Masson, M. E. (1995). Adult age differences in perceptually based, but not conceptually based implicit tests of memory. *Journal of Gerontology: Psychological Sciences, 50B,* P162–P170.

Small, B. J., Viitanen, M., & Bäckman, L. (1997). Mini-Mental State Examination item scores as predictors of Alzheimer's disease: Incidence data from the Kungsholmen Project, Stockholm. *Journal of Gerontology: Medical Sciences, 52A,* M299–M304.

Smith, A. D. (1996). Memory. In J. E. Birren & K. W. Schaie (Eds.), *Handbook of the psychology of aging* (4th ed., pp. 236–250). San Diego, CA: Academic Press.

Smith, A. D., Park, D. C., Earles, J. L. K., Shaw, R. J., & Whiting, W. L., IV. (1998). Age differences in context integration in memory. *Psychology and Aging, 13,* 21–28.

Smith, R. E., & Hunt R. R. (1998). Presentation modality affects false memory. *Psychonomic Bulletin & Review, 5,* 710–715.

Somberg, B. L., & Salthouse, T. A. (1982). Divided attention abilities in young and old adults. *Journal of Experimental Psychology: Human Perception and Performance, 8,* 651–663.

Spencer, W. D., & Raz, N. (1995). Differential effects of aging on memory for content and context: A meta-analysis. *Psychology and Aging, 10,* 527–539.

Spieler, D. H., & Balota, D. A. (1996). Characteristics of associative learning in younger and older adults: Evidence from an episodic priming paradigm. *Psychology and Aging, 11,* 607–620.

Squire, L. R. (1987). *Memory and brain.* New York: Oxford University Press.

Steele, C. M. (1997). A threat in the air: How stereotypes shape intellectual identity and performance. *American Psychologist, 52,* 613–629.

Stine, E. A. L., & Wingfield, A. (1987). Process and strategy in memory for speech among younger and older adults. *Psychology and Aging, 2,* 272–279.

Stuss, D. T., Craik, F. I. M., Sayer, L., Franchi, D., & Alexander, M. P. (1996). Comparisons of older people and patients with frontal lesions: Evidence from word list learning. *Psychology and Aging, 11,* 387–395.

Tipper, S. P. (1992). Selection for action: The role of inhibitory mechanisms. *Current Directions in Psychological Science, 1,* 105–109.

Titov, N., & Knight, R. G. (1997). Adult age differences in controlled and automatic memory processing. *Psychology and Aging, 12,* 565–573.

Tulving, E. (1972). Episodic and semantic memory. In E. Tulving & W. Donaldson (Eds.), *Organization of memory* (pp. 381–403). New York: Academic Press.

Tulving, E. (1985). Memory and consciousness. *Canadian Psychology, 26,* 1–12.

Tulving, E., & Schacter, D. L. (1990). Priming and human memory systems. *Science, 247,* 301–306.

Tun, P. A. (1989). Age differences in processing expository and narrative text. *Journal of Gerontology: Psychological Sciences, 44,* P9–P15.

Tun, P. A., & Wingfield, A. (1994). Speech recall under heavy load conditions: Age, predictability, and limits on dual-task interference. *Aging and Cognition, 1,* 29–44.

Tun, P. A., Wingfield, A., Rosen, M. J., & Blanchard, L. (1998). Response latencies for false memories: Gist-based processes in normal aging. *Psychology and Aging, 13,* 230–241.

Underwood, B. J. (1965). False recognition produced by implicit verbal responses. *Journal of Experimental Psychology, 70,* 122–129.

Underwood, B. J. (1983). *Attributes of memory.* Glenview, IL: Scott, Foresman.

Uttl, B., & Graf, P. (1993). Episodic spatial memory in adulthood. *Psychology and Aging, 8,* 257–273.

Vakil, E., Melamed, M., & Even, N. (1996). Direct and indirect measures of contextual information: Older versus young adults. *Aging, Neuropsychology, and Cognition, 3,* 30–36.

Verhaeghen, P., Marcoen, A., & Goosens, L. (1993). Facts and fiction about memory aging: A quantitative integration of research findings. *Journal of Gerontology: Psychological Sciences, 48,* P157–P171.

Verhaeghen, P., & Salthouse, T. A. (1997). Meta-analyses of age-cognition relations in adulthood: Estimates of linear and nonlinear age effects and structural models. *Psychological Bulletin, 122,* 231–249.

Watkins, O. C., & Watkins, M. J. (1975). Build up of proactive inhibition as a cue-overload effect. *Journal of Experimental Psychology: Learning, Memory, and Cognition, 104,* 442–452.

Weichmann, D. J., & Hasher, L. (1998). *Item-specific encoding and false memory effects.* Manuscript in preparation.

Welch, D. C., & West, R. L. (1995). Self-efficacy and mastery: Its application to issues of environmental control, cognition, and aging. *Developmental Review, 15,* 150–171.

West, R. L., & Berry, J. M. (1994). Age declines in memory self-efficacy: General or limited to particular tasks and measures? In J. D. Sinnott (Ed.), *Interdisciplinary handbook of adult lifespan learning* (pp. 426–445). Westport, CT: Greenwood.

Whiting, W. L., IV, & Smith, A. D. (1997). Differential age-related processing limitations in recall and recognition tasks. *Psychology and Aging, 12,* 216–224.

Wingfield, A., & Butterworth, B. (1984). Running memory for sentences and parts of sentences: Syntactic parsing as a control function in working memory. In H. Bouma & D. G. Bouwhuis (Eds.), *Attention and performance X* (pp. 351–363). New York: Academic Press.

Wingfield, A., Lahar, C. J., & Stine, E. A. L. (1989). Age and decision strategies in running memory for speech: Effects of prosody and linguistic structure. *Journal of Gerontology: Psychological Sciences, 44,* P106–P113.

Wingfield, A., & Lindfield, K. C. (1995). Multiple memory systems in the processing of speech: Evidence from aging. *Experimental Aging Research, 21,* 101–121.

Wingfield, A., & Stine, E. A. L. (1986). Organizational strategies in immediate recall of rapid speech by young and elderly adults. *Experimental Aging Research, 12,* 79–83.

Wingfield, A., Tun, P. A., & Rosen, M. J. (1995). Age differences in veridical and reconstructive recall of syntactically and randomly segmented speech. *Journal of Gerontology: Psychological Sciences, 50B,* P257–P266.

Winocur, G., Moscovitch, M., & Stuss, D. T. (1996). Explicit and implicit memory in the elderly: Evidence for double dissociation involving medial temporal- and frontal-lobe functions. *Neuropsychology, 10,* 57–65.

Wood, R. W., & Bandura, A. (1989). Impact of conceptions of ability on self-regulatory mechanisms and complex decision making. *Journal of Personality and Social Psychology, 56,* 407–415.

Yoon, C. (1997). Age differences in consumers' processing strategies: An investigation of moderating influences. *Journal of Consumer Research, 24,* 329–342.

Yoon, C., Hasher, L., Rahhal, T., & Winocur, G. (1998, April). *Cross-cultural differences in memory performance between younger and older adults: The role of culture-based stereotypes about aging.* Poster session presented at the Cognitive Aging Conference, Atlanta, GA.

Yoon, C., May, C. P., & Hasher, L. (1999). Aging, circadian arousal, and cognition. In N. Schwartz, D. Park, B. Knäuper, & S. Sudman (Eds.), *Aging, cognition and self reports* (pp. 117–143). Washington, DC: Psychological Press.

Zacks, R. T., & Hasher, L. (1994). Directed ignoring: Inhibitory regulation of working memory. In D. Dagenbach & T. H. Carr (Eds.), *Inhibitory mechanisms in attention, memory, and language* (pp. 241–264). San Diego, CA: Academic Press.

Zacks, R. T., & Hasher, L. (1997). Cognitive gerontology and attentional inhibition: A reply to Burke and McDowd. *Journal of Gerontology: Psychological Sciences, 52B,* P274–P283.

Zacks, R. T., Radvansky, G. A., & Hasher, L. (1996). Studies of directed forgetting in older adults. *Journal of Experimental Psychology: Learning, Memory, and Cognition, 22,* 143–156.

Zwaan, R. A., & Radvansky, G. A. (1998). Situation models in language comprehension and memory. *Psychological Bulletin, 123,* 162–185.

6

Language and Speech

Arthur Wingfield
Brandeis University

Elizabeth A. L. Stine-Morrow
University of New Hampshire

All languages have certain structural features in common. They have a *lexicon* (a vocabulary keyed to specific concepts) and a *syntax* (rules that represent the relationships between vocabulary elements). Within the lexicon, elements are distinguished by whether they refer to objects and concepts (nouns), actions (verbs), or modifiers of nouns and verbs. The details of these systems may vary from one language to another, but the presence of a structured language is common to all societies on earth. Humans are unique both in their natural drive to communicate with others and in their cognitive power to develop sophisticated language structures to fulfill this need. This fact of human nature is central to our understanding of the special place of language in adult aging and cognition.

The comprehension and production of language cannot be understood independently of the limitations in processing resources of the language perceiver and language producer. The characterization of the limited-capacity system has evolved over the years from early references to "psychic energy," to the engineering metaphor of a limited channel capacity (Broadbent, 1971), to the concept of a cognitive system with limited attentional or processing resources (Kahneman, 1973). Currently, the most widely used construct in the literature on language processing is that of working memory. As distinct from earlier notions of a simple short-term buffer store (Atkinson & Shiffrin, 1968), the term *working memory* has been used to refer to a limited-capacity cognitive system that both holds recent information and provides computational space in which the stored materials can be monitored and manipulated (Baddeley, 1986). Working memory has also been conceptualized as the finite quantity of activation available to the individual for storage and computation (Just & Carpenter, 1992). Other resource-limiting factors may also constrain language processing. These include upper limits on speed of processing (Foulke, 1971), the effectiveness with which one's limited resources may be allocated among competing tasks (Kahneman, 1973), and the effectiveness of inhibiting irrelevant information (Hasher & Zacks, 1988). Because language is often processed in complex, noisy, and distracting environments (Tun, 1998), such limitations can have special implications for the elderly adult.

In the following section, we outline the basic processes involved in language comprehension, highlighting the ways in which limited resources constrain language-processing capability in young and elderly adults. We then move to a discussion of the special resource limitations in the elderly adult and present the implications of these limitations for language processing in the aging adult. We then describe factors that ameliorate what might otherwise be far more serious consequences of these declines. Finally, we end with a discussion of language use in a broader societal setting.

BASIC PROCESSES: MODELS
OF LANGUAGE PROCESSING

To comprehend spoken language, a number of operations must be performed on the speech signal as it is arriving. An important element in this processing is the rapidity of natural speech. In ordinary conversation, speech can run from as slow as 90 words per minute (wpm) for individuals engaged in thoughtful conversation to rates in excess of 210 wpm for a person attempting to read naturally from a prepared script. Whether speech rates are on average fast or slow, the rate of speech varies considerably from moment to moment in people's speech, with the speech arriving in rhythmic clusters separated by periodic pauses. Studies have shown that the pauses in speech tend to occur before words of low probability in the context (Goldman-Eisler, 1968). Some estimates suggest that as much as 40% to 50% of speaking time is occupied by pauses that are determined by the way speakers group their thoughts and the time taken to select the words they wish to say. These pauses are also used by listeners to perceptually "chunk" the speech as it is being heard.

The way in which readers approach text in allocating time shows the evolutionary footprint of speech understanding. Readers are remarkably reliable in pausing momentarily between linguistic constituents, exactly in the locations at which speakers pause (Aaronson & Scarborough, 1976; Just

& Carpenter, 1980). This phenomenon has been called "wrap-up." As in speech, the durations of the pauses in reading depend on the complexity of the content (Aaronson & Scarborough, 1976; Haberlandt, Graesser, Schneider, & Kiely, 1986). The implication is that these natural pauses are as much a part of the linguistic input as the words themselves.

Regardless of the modality, the task of the perceiver is a demanding one. As language comprehenders, we must perceptually encode the input, identify the lexical elements, determine the syntactic and semantic relations between them, and, finally, develop an understanding of the message at the discourse level. In speech, this must be done with the input arriving at a rate of two to three new words each second. Although in reading one can control the rate of input and reread sections as needed, in actuality adults tend to read at a fairly rapid rate. Carver (1982) estimated that 300 wpm is an optimal reading rate, with faster rates resulting in insufficient processing and slower rates increasing the burden of integration across a fading trace. However, B. J. F. Meyer and Talbot (1998) reported reading rates of 105 to 180 wpm for young adult readers and 75 to 200 wpm for elderly readers, with comprehension declining when readers are forced to keep up with a 300-wpm march. In summary, although the rate of information flow varies considerably in both listening and reading, rarely does it drop below 120 wpm.

Listening and Reading: Phonological Analysis and Segregation of the Speech Stream Versus Orthographic Analysis

Figure 6.1 illustrates the constellation of processes needed to understand a simple sentence. There is an important distinction to be made in the way in which these processes operate. *Bottom-up processing* refers, in the case of speech, to the way in which a listener's sensory apparatus processes the acoustic signal "upward" from the level of the acoustic waveform, to the level of recognition of *phonemes* (individual speech sounds), syllables, words, sentence structure, and, finally, to the recognition of the semantic relations between the sentence elements that give the sentence its meaning. In reading, the bottom-up information is supplied by the letters and words on the printed page. Language comprehension, however, also reflects a continual interaction between the information being derived from bottom-up processing and higher level knowledge available from both linguistic context and real-world knowledge. These latter sources are referred to as *top-down information*. We use bidirectional arrows in many places in Fig. 6.1 to indicate the influence top-down knowledge can have on lower level processing.

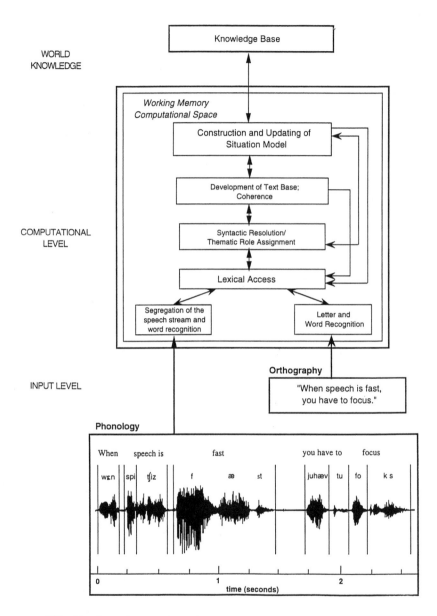

FIG. 6.1. Operations performed in the comprehension of spoken and written language.

At the bottom of Fig. 6.1, we show the acoustic waveform (i.e., the phonology) of the spoken sentence *When speech is fast, you have to focus*, as well as its written counterpart (i.e., the orthography). The vertical displacements along the horizontal line represent the changes in energy level, or *amplitude*, of the speech signal over time. Directly above the waveform, we have written a phonetic transcription of the words as the listener would hear them. Unlike written text, in which words are neatly separated by spaces, in this typical sample of speech words run together (e.g., *speechis*). The fact is that the word boundaries that listeners hear in speech must often be imposed by the listener on the basis of the linguistic context. The process of segregating the speech stream into words represents one of the first challenges facing the listener in comprehending a speech message.

Our sample sentence consists of a dependent clause (*When speech is fast*) and an independent clause (*you have to focus*). As is typical of sentences of this form, the speaker paused for a beat between the first and the second clauses. This can be seen on the sentence waveform by the flattening of the energy track between the words *fast* and *you*. (In the case of reading, the eyes will typically rest for an extra 100 ms or so at this point, mimicking the temporal input pattern of speech.) It can be seen in this example that the speaker has also done something common in speech, which is to lengthen the word immediately prior to the clause boundary.

It cannot be seen in this waveform, but speakers also vary the melody pattern across sentences. This melody pattern, the *intonation contour* of a sentence, is measured as the change in fundamental frequency ($f_\emptyset$) of the voice over the course of the sentence. Most noticeable to listeners is the way in which a rising pitch can indicate that the speaker is asking a question or the way some words may be given extra stress to indicate the semantic focus of a sentence. Pitch changes can also help signal that a clause boundary is about to occur. *Prosody* is the collective term used to refer to the full array of suprasegmental features that overlay spoken sentences and discourse: the pitch contour (intonation pattern) of the sentence, word stress, pauses that sometimes occur between major linguistic elements of a sentence, and the lengthening of words immediately prior to a clause boundary (Shattuck-Hufnagel & Turk, 1996). Word stress, it should be noted, is in itself a complex subjective variable that is based on amplitude, pitch, and duration of the stressed word relative to other words in the sentence.

Although speech may sound clear, it is rare that the individual speech sounds are fully articulated in natural speech. This is partly due to the natural dynamics of speech movements, such that the production movements for one sound often merge into the production movements for the next sound. This is referred to as *coarticulation*, and it results in the fact that the same phoneme may be uttered somewhat differently depending on the particular phonemes that surround it. Listeners can detect these subtle differences in the acoustic coloring of sounds, and these coarticulatory cues can aid in speech perception. Phonemes are also uttered differently by different individuals, requiring the listener to calibrate perception to different speakers (Mullennix, Pisoni, & Martin, 1989). This requires normalizing the speech input so that the acoustic signal is "cleaned up" to take into account speaker variability and thus allow for speech perception to be speaker independent.

In some cases, prosodic features, such as intonation and timing, can help the listener determine correct perceptual segmentation (e.g., "He saw the *car go*" vs. "He saw the *cargo*") (Gow & Gordon, 1995). In other cases, there may be no acoustic distinction at all, and one must use the linguistic or real-world context to indicate the correct way to segregate the acoustic stream. In these cases, and in cases in which words are poorly articulated, listeners sometimes cannot identify particular words until more of the downstream speech is heard (Grosjean, 1985; Wingfield, Alexander, & Cavigelli, 1994). For this to be accomplished, there needs to be a transient memory representation of the phonological input until the downstream clarifying information has been heard (cf. Mattys, 1997).

Evolving from spoken language, orthographies (i.e., written representations) are of three types: *logographic*, in which characters correspond to morphemes (i.e., units of meaning, such as words, suffixes, and prefixes); *syllabic*, in which characters correspond to vowel–consonant combinations; and *alphabetic*, in which characters correspond to phonemes (Just & Carpenter, 1987). The segregation problem in reading must therefore be solved somewhat differently depending on the language. English, of course, has an alphabetic orthography in which words are segmented for the reader by spaces (in contrast with Thai, for example, in which all of the words within a sentence are run together).

Phonological representations of words are also presumed to be activated during reading (Just & Carpenter, 1987). Access to the sounds of the words in reading becomes obvious when a text becomes difficult conceptually, or sometimes orthographically, such as attempting to read the following: JUSTTRYTOUNDERSTANDTHISWITHOUTREADINGITALOUD. Activation of the phonological code has been demonstrated in the laboratory, for example, by showing that the naming time for a target word can be facilitated by prior processing of a homophone of a semantic associate, such as the prime–target pair *dough–deer* (Lesch & Pollatsek, 1993). Some researchers argue that this "inner speech" represents prelexical processing that is necessary to access word meaning (Lesch & Pollatsek, 1993; Van Orden, Johnston, & Hale, 1988). Others argue that it is postlexical, an epiphenomenon of lexical access (Fleming, 1993).

Analogous to the processes in speech perception, orthographic decoding does not arise strictly letter by letter. There are also influences of word-level context. In a classic demonstration, Reicher (1969) presented participants with a letter string that either formed a word or didn't (e.g., WORD vs. ORWD), after which participants made a choice about whether a particular letter occurred in the string (e.g., D or K). Participants were more accurate at choosing the correct letter in the context of a real word, even though the word itself did not constrain the choice of letters. Data such as these suggest that orthographic decoding depends on an interaction between letter-level and word-level codes (cf. Allen, Madden, & Slane, 1995), not unlike the contextual influences that affect speech perception.

Word Recognition and Lexical Access

Because of the lack of articulatory invariance, spoken word recognition must be based on a "best-fit" principle, in which recognition comes about when the input features of the stimulus come closer to the features of one lexical alternative than to others. The *cohort model* of word recognition can give a feeling for the processes involved (Marslen-Wilson, 1987, 1990). According to this model, at the moment the initial phonemes of a word are heard, all words in the lexicon that share those initial phonemes are automatically activated. Hearing the "ca" (/kæ/) of the word *camera*, for example, will activate all words sharing this initial sound (not only *camera*, but also *camel*, *cactus*, *castle*, and so forth). This is referred to as the word-initial cohort. As the amount of the word onset increases to include the "m" sound (i.e., "cam") words that no longer fit this pattern, such as *cactus* or *castle*, are eliminated as possibilities.

As more and more of the word is heard as it unfolds in time, the size of this initial cohort becomes progressively trimmed until no other words remain that fit this pattern. This point, called the *isolation point*, is often reached before the full word has been heard. For example, on hearing *eleph*—, one does not have to hear any more to know that the word must be *elephant*, or some derivative of it (although for some, *Ella Fitzgerald* may yet remain in the cohort). The rate of decline of word possibilities shrinks at a dramatic rate as more and more of the word is heard (Tyler, 1984; Wayland, Wingfield, & Goodglass, 1989), especially when the stress patterns of words are taken into account (Wingfield, Goodglass, & Lindfield, 1997). Some theorists have argued that linguistic context will lower the threshold of likely alternatives even before any part of the word is heard (Morton, 1969), whereas others have argued that context can eliminate unlikely alternatives only after the initial cohort has been activated (Marslen-Wilson, 1990).

In contrast with the cohort model, in which the word-initial cohort has primacy in the perceptual decision, overall goodness-of-fit models hold that words are recognized on the basis of an overall fit between the features of the stimulus and the perceptual alternatives. In these models, *neighborhood density*, which is based on the number of words in the lexicon that share phonemes with the stimulus word, is the critical variable controlling word recognition. The higher the density and the activation levels of the neighbors, the more difficult word recognition will be (Luce, Pisoni, & Goldinger, 1990). That is, words with high-density, high-frequency neighbors will be less easy to recognize than words with low-density, low-frequency neighbors. Thus, this neighborhood activation model shares many of the same features as the cohort model, differing most importantly on its de-emphasis of the beginnings of words in favor of an overall goodness of fit.

Although word recognition implies knowledge of the identity of a word, lexical access also includes activation of the word's meaning. Activation of word meanings (*semantic activation*) can be shown in *semantic priming tasks* in which a word like *doctor* is presented, followed by either a related word (e.g., *nurse*), an unrelated word (e.g., *house*), or a nonword (e.g., *surne*), with the participant's task being to press a key or say aloud whether the letter string is a word or a nonword. This is referred to as making a *lexical decision*. Studies of semantic priming show that following the presentation of *doctor*, lexical decisions are faster for *nurse* than for an unrelated word (*house*). This is because the word *nurse* was activated, or *primed*, by the semantically related word (*doctor*) that had preceded it (D. E. Meyer & Schvaneveldt, 1971). One can also use a *naming task*, in which the participant is asked to pronounce the target words as quickly as possible. In this case, it is the speed of naming words that have been preceded by related or unrelated words that serves as the evidence for priming.

Although in ordinary discourse word recognition occurs in a rich semantic context, some operations, such as lexical access, are accomplished so rapidly that the activation of word meanings can be completed before a prior linguistic context can come into play (Swinney, 1979). Findings such as these have suggested "modular" operations in rapid sentence comprehension as well as interactive ones.

Syntactic Resolution and Determination of Thematic Roles

To understand a sentence, the listener or reader must determine the syntactic structure of the sentence. In this process the perceiver determines which are the main nouns and verbs, their modifiers, connectives, and so forth. For example, even though the sentences *The man sold the car to the woman* and *The woman sold the car to the man* have the same words, we understand them to have different meanings. This is so because of the way in which different words are assigned to the thematic roles of direct and indirect objects in the two sentences.

The complexity of syntax can vary a great deal in natural language and hence can place a varying burden on one's working memory or processing resources. Generally speaking, sentences with left-branching structures (e.g., *Having sold the car to the man, the woman collected her commission*) are more difficult to process than right-branching sentences (e.g., *The woman collected her commission after selling the car to the man*). Also difficult are sentences with embedded clauses (e.g., *The man who sold the car to the woman had red hair*). One feature of most models of sentence processing is the presumption that the surface form of an utterance is held in a brief short-term or working memory system and discarded once the meaning, or "deep structure," of the sentence has been determined. Difficult or time-consuming sentence operations that would exceed the capacity or duration of this store could thus produce errors in sentence comprehension (Carpenter, Miyaki, & Just, 1994; Daneman & Merikle, 1996).

There are numerous examples in sentence processing in which resource limitations have an effect, not merely on the accuracy with which a sentence is processed but also on *how* it is processed. Although listeners and readers are usually not consciously aware of it, there are many regions of spoken and written sentences that contain temporary *syntactic ambiguities*. These are cases in which the representation of the underlying linguistic structure of the utterance (how to *parse* the sentence), remains temporarily ambiguous until it is later clarified.

Consider, for example, the following two sentences:

1. "Although the two friends pushed/the car wouldn't move."
2. "Although the two friends pushed the car/it wouldn't move."

Both sentences share the same first seven words, but in the first sentence the clause boundary comes between the words *pushed* and *the car* and in the second sentence the boundary comes between the words *the car* and *it*. This illustrates a temporary closure ambiguity, an ambiguity about where the first clause ends (closes) that is quickly resolved as more of the sentence is heard or read.

Frazier (1987) has argued that, in the presence of a temporary syntactic ambiguity, memory resources are conserved by a strategy that maintains only a single syntactic representation rather than multiple alternatives. Memory resources are also conserved by using a default strategy that selects the syntactic interpretation that is more easily computed. Studies of online reading time have suggested that participants use a default strategy that attempts to interpret sentences such as these as having a late-closure structure, in which the reader attempts to close the clause boundary at the later point (after the noun phrase *the car*) rather than the earlier point (after the verb *pushed*). This is considered to be less computationally demanding because it does not require the construction of a new syntactic clause at the point of the syntactic ambiguity (linguists refer to this as the "minimal attachment principle").

The consequence of this bias toward assuming the computationally less-demanding late-closure structure means that sentences like Sentence 1 will initially be misparsed, with the parsing error having to be corrected when the second verb *wouldn't* is encountered and the error is discovered. Evidence consistent with such a reanalysis comes from studies that show longer reading times for early closure sentences at the point of disambiguation and more eye-movement backtracking to that region (Frazier, 1987).

The proposal that only one structure is computed by the reader or listener can be contrasted with a model in which other possible interpretations are also computed, even though they remain inaccessible to conscious awareness (Just & Carpenter, 1992). Both possibilities, of course, accept that only a single interpretation of the sentence is consciously available to the listener or reader, and hence both make the similar prediction that a disruption in the flow of processing will occur when a parsing error is discovered. Indeed, it has been suggested that the first possibility, that only a single structure is computed at points of syntactic ambiguity, may be true for readers with small working memory spans. By contrast, the second possibility, that multiple interpretations are computed at the points of ambiguity, may be true for readers with larger working memory spans (Just & Carpenter, 1992; MacDonald, Just, & Carpenter, 1992; but see also Waters & Caplan, 1996).

Unlike reading, where local ambiguity can be resolved only by reading what follows in the text, in spoken language ambiguity can be averted or quickly repaired because of the prosodic pattern in which the sentence is uttered (Ferreira, Henderson, Anes, Weeks, & McFarlane, 1996; Kjelgaard, Titone, & Wingfield, 1999). The question of whether comprehension shares resources with other verbal operations or whether it draws from a specific sentence-processing resource is currently under debate (cf. Caplan & Waters, 1999; Waters & Caplan, 1996; Wingfield, Waters, & Tun, 1998).

Representing Meaning: Construction of the Text Base

To understand the meaning of discourse, readers and listeners must not only access the meanings of the individual words and the syntactic relations between them. They must also develop an integrated representation of the ideas expressed in the text. This representation is constructed within syntactically coherent segments, which Kintsch and van Dijk (1978) have called *input cycles*. As the representation of the semantic content is constructed, the verbatim trace of the acoustic or orthographic representation is assumed to fade so as to free working memory capacity for the processing of the next input cycle (Glanzer, Dorfman, & Kaplan, 1981; Jarvella, 1971). Thus, at each input cycle, readers and listeners must organize meaning within the current cycle as well as form an integrative representation of meaning across cycles.

In the Kintsch and van Dijk (1978) model, the representation of the explicit text content is given by *propositions*, or "idea units." A proposition represents the relationship between two or more concepts and is thus the smallest particle of text meaning. For example, to understand the sentence *The woman's mauve handbag was stolen by the podiatrist*, we must represent three ideas: that the woman owned a handbag, that it was mauve, and that the podiatrist stole it. In the Kintsch and van Dijk model, this would be represented as follows:

P1 (OWN WOMAN HANDBAG)
P2 (MODIFY HANDBAG MAUVE)
P3 (STEAL PODIATRIST HANDBAG).

A further assumption of the model is that propositions are organized so as to discriminate among idea units on the basis of their relative importance. For example, we would generally agree that P3 is more central to the sentence meaning than P1, which in turn is more central than P2. Thus, in the face of working memory limits, P1 or P3 might not be retained. Suppose now that the story continued as follows: *He had slipped it under the table with a subtle movement*. It is presumed that as the propositional content of this new segment (or input cycle) is being encoded, the residual semantic representation of the first sentence is retained in working memory, allowing for the propositional representation of the second input cycle to be integrated into it. The surface form of the propositional content at the end of the second input cycle might be comparable with *The podiatrist stole the handbag, slipping it under the table*.

All else being equal, reading time increases (cf. Kintsch & van Dijk, 1978) and listening accuracy decreases (Stine, Wingfield, & Poon, 1986) as the density of propositions increases in a text, supporting the representational assumption of this model. As the number of propositions encoded in the network increases, there is also an increase in the time to verify any particular proposition and an increase in the probability of making an error. This latter phenomenon is called the *fan effect* (Anderson, 1983). The fan effect implies that once encoded, search through a propositional network takes time.

The pauses we have previously noted in reading and listening seem to correspond to the ends of input cycles. In reading, their duration is directly related to the complexity of the preceding text (Aaronson & Scarborough, 1976; Haberlandt et al., 1986) and memory for particular propositions can be predicted by the number of times they are held over across input cycles by virtue of their positions in the coherence graph (cf. van Dijk & Kintsch, 1983). This phenomenon of better recall for main ideas than for less important detail as derived from a text's coherence graph has been termed the "levels effect" in recall.

Construction of a Situation Model

In text processing, the text-based representation that we have been considering is elaborated with world knowledge to create a more global understanding of what the text is about. This representation is called a *situation model* (van Dijk & Kintsch, 1983), or a *mental model* (Johnson-Laird, 1983). Illustrating the importance of the situation model to comprehension of a text, Garnham (1981) showed that even though participants had trouble discriminating in memory between *The woman was given a pedicure at the podiatrist's* and *The woman was given a pedicure by the podiatrist*, they had no difficulty discriminating between the sentences *The woman's handbag was stolen at the podiatrist's* and *The woman's handbag was stolen by the podiatrist*. Because these sentence pairs differ by only one proposition, it would be hard to explain these results in terms of differences in the complexity or discriminability of the text bases. Rather, the difference rests in the situations represented by the sentences.

In an attempt to formalize this concept, Zwann, Langston, and Graesser (1995) have proposed an event-indexing model to account for the construction of the situation model. They argued that the reader (or listener) monitors and updates the situation model on five dimensions: temporality, spatiality, protagonist involvement, causality, and intentionality. In support of this model, they found that the greater the extent to which a story's verbs share these dimensions, the more likely participants are to group them together in a clustering task after reading.

Perhaps the most well-studied aspect of situation models has been the "sense of place" that one constructs in understanding narratives. When one is truly engaged by a narrative, one is apt to have the phenomenal experience of moving with the protagonist through the fictional world. This has been captured in the laboratory through the *distance effect*. This is a decrease in processing time, measured as either verification or reading time, as the information to be accessed is spatially close to the protagonist (Morrow, Greenspan, & Bower, 1987). In a typical experiment, the reader encounters a sentence describing the movement of a character through a known setting from one place (the "source") to another place (the "goal") through an unmentioned "path" room. In the next sentence, the character is described as thinking about an object residing in the goal, path, source, or some other room. The distance effect describes the fact that reading time, taken as a measure of processing time, is faster for objects in the goal room than for objects in the path room, which in turn is faster than for objects in the source room, and so on (Rinck & Bower, 1995).

Another aspect of situation models that has received considerable attention is the structure of causal connections (Myers & Duffy, 1990; van den Broek, 1990). Generally speaking, propositions from narratives are more likely to be recalled if they are part of a causal chain of events that connects the beginning of the story to its end. By contrast, "dead-end statements" that have no stated consequences are less likely to be recalled, especially after a delay (van den Broek, 1990). Because causal connections are not always explicitly given in a text, elaborative processing is needed to establish these connections, and this elaborative processing can enhance memory. Consider the following examples from Myers and Duffy: *Jimmy's big brother beat him up. The next day he was covered with bruises* versus *Jimmy spent the night in his brother's room. The next day he was covered with bruises.* In the first case, the cause of the bruises is explicit, whereas in the second case, the causal connection between the statements is vague and must be inferred. Myers and Duffy showed that the stronger and more explicit the causal connection, the faster participants were at reading the second sentence. Memory, however, showed a curvilinear relationship to causal relatedness, such that cued recall for the second sentence from the first was best at intermediate levels of relatedness. Myers and Duffy argued that at an intermediate level of relatedness, elaborative inference is invited; by contrast, no inference is required when cause is explicit, and no inference is possible without some constraints. They assumed that the additional retrieval routes created by the elaboration of the intermediate-relatedness cases was responsible for the good levels of recall. Indeed, such curvilinear relationships between memory and contextual connections may be a general property of encoding and recall (cf. Perry & Wingfield, 1994).

Another facet of situation models is the *goal structure* of a narrative (Suh & Trabasso 1993). Narratives are most often built around an account of a protagonist attempting to reach a series of goals. Narrative understanding depends on the reader or listener keeping track of these goals that provide coherence to the narrative as a whole. Suh and Trabasso showed that failed-goal information was more available to readers than was completed-goal information, suggesting that the activation of completed goals does indeed help to guide narrative understanding.

There are two reasons why the representation of the situation model in discourse is of special importance in aging. First, until very recently, the construction and updating of situation models has largely been neglected in the study of language and aging. Given the degree to which this level of discourse comprehension contributes to the experiential value of a text, what Gerrig (1993) called the "discourse world," as well as the use of a text for problem solving (Kintsch, 1994), we may have been systematically neglecting a critically important function of text among older adults. Second, situation models are most easily constructed when the reader or listener has a high level of knowledge relevant to the domain represented by the text (cf. Kintsch, 1994). To the extent that older adults often have an advantage over their younger counterparts in this regard, we may have been neglecting an aspect of language processing in which elderly adults may well excel.

Language Production

There is a very tight theoretical and conceptual bond between the production and comprehension of language. Although the detail in number of functional elements may vary, most models of language production follow the same general scheme shown in Fig. 6.1, but with the operations running in the reverse order (Levelt, 1989). In these models, the speaker begins at a conceptual level where the motivation begins for the generation of the utterance: the broad ideas one wishes to convey in one's message. At the next level, one formulates the utterance in terms of retrieving the lexical items for the message and organizing the syntactic frame in which the information will be conveyed. For speech, the final stage is represented by accessing the phonology of the words to be uttered and the specification of the motor programming for articulation of the speech itself. For writers, retrieval of orthography and specification of the motor programming for the specific writing movements complete the sequence.

The temporal pattern of speech production, with its rapid bursts of speech and periodic pauses, is one window we have on the way speech is organized from the conceptual level through the planning stages for the utterance itself. Another window on this process has been the study of speech errors as a way of determining how far ahead one plans when one speaks. For example, it is not uncommon for a hurried or distracted speaker to exchange one word with another in an utterance, as when "I like milk in my coffee" comes out as "I like coffee in my milk." Most of the time, such word exchanges take place within a single clause, suggesting that linguistic clauses are units of production just as they are units in perception (Fromkin & Ratner, 1998). As Fromkin and Ratner added, however, approximately 15% to 21% of exchange errors do run across clauses, suggesting that speakers often plan far in advance when organizing a message. To the extent that such long-term planning depends on working memory, one might expect adaptive productions by elderly adults with more limited working memory spans to be typified by simpler syntax.

AGE-RELATED CONSTRAINTS

Data Limitations: Auditory and Visual Processing

When most people think of age and spoken language comprehension they think of the declines in sensory acuity that accompany the aging auditory system. The decline in auditory acuity with age is referred to as *presbycusis*, and it has two important elements related to speech perception. The first is a sensory loss in the *high-frequency range* of hearing. A second area of concern is *phonemic regression*, in which the perception of speech sounds is affected to a greater degree than would be predicted from pure-tone audiometry alone. These changes are outlined elsewhere in chapter 3.

In any consideration of speech comprehension, however, it is important to remember that although such declines may be a natural part of the aging process, there are wide individual differences in the appearance and rate of these declines. That is, although age-related hearing declines do occur, in many elderly adults such declines may be quite minimal (U.S. Congress, Office of Technology Assessment, 1986).

Declines in visual processing are also relevant. In particular, age-related declines in visual acuity (e.g., contrast sensitivity) and increased susceptibility to glare can make reading difficult. This is especially the case under conditions of low luminance and low contrast (Scheiber & Baldwin, 1996). However, as long as the text is not too small (less than 0.3° of visual angle; for reference, viewing your index fingernail at arm's length casts an image of approximately 1° of visual angle) or too large (greater than 1°), there does not appear to be an age-related decline in maximum reading rate (Akutsu, Legge, Ross, & Schuebel, 1991).

We are only beginning to understand the complex interactions between sensory decline and cognitive efficacy. On the one hand, perception of a weakened bottom-up signal can be facilitated by its interaction with top-down knowledge, such as the use of linguistic context. On the other hand, there is a concern that the extra effort required to process these impoverished signals may draw resources that would otherwise be available for higher level interpretive operations and memory (Pichora-Fuller, Schneider, & Daneman, 1995).

Resource Limitations: Working Memory, Speed, and Inhibition

In addition to visual and auditory processing deficits that limit the quality of data entering the system, there are also age-related resource limitations that may impact on language processing. These have been modeled alternatively as reductions in working memory capacity (Baddeley, 1986), a slowing in component processes (Salthouse, 1996), or an inhibition deficit that allows off-task information to consume otherwise available memory or processing capacity (Hasher & Zacks, 1988; chap. 5, this volume). Nor are these mutually exclusive. The more important points here are that there are age-related declines across a wide range of tasks and that these declines may only become apparent when processing resources are taxed.

IMPLICATIONS OF AGE-RELATED DECLINES IN BASIC PROCESSES FOR LANGUAGE COMPREHENSION AND RECALL

It would not be surprising to find that the age-related changes in sensory and cognitive function have an impact on the ability of elderly adults to perform many of the basic functions required for comprehension and memory for language. This is indeed the case. As we will also see, however, selective preservation in many important areas of language knowledge helps most elderly adults maintain a very high level of functioning in day-to-day discourse processing. That is, what in an experiment might be referred to as a "ceiling effect" (i.e., two groups performing at near-perfect levels) is the nature of language.

Word-Level Processing

Adult aging brings with it increasing complaints of an inability to remember the names of people, places, and objects. Experimental studies of word retrieval support this subjective experience.

Confrontation Naming and Tip-of-the-Tongue (TOT) Studies. One method used to study word retrieval has been the study of confrontation naming, in which participants are asked to name pictures of common and rare objects. These studies show a decease in naming ability with age, although the decrease is slight until participants are in their 70s (Au et al., 1995). Age differences can also be found in studies of naming latencies. Thomas, Fozard, and Waugh (1977) measured latencies to naming pictures of common and rare objects and showed that elderly adults are as sensitive to word frequency as are young adults (Wingfield, 1968). Interestingly, Thomas et al. failed to find an Age × Word Frequency interaction in these naming latencies (see Nicholas, Barth, Obler, Au, & Albert, 1997, for a review).

   A second source of data on lexical retrieval and aging has come from studies of the TOT phenomenon. The TOT phenomenon refers to the feeling one often has of knowing the name of an object, person, or place, although the word itself remains elusive. This sense of having a word on the tip of the tongue was described vividly over 100 years ago by William James (1893):

> It feels as if there is a gap that is intensely active. A sort of wraith of the name is in it, beckoning us in a given direction, making us at moments tingle with the sense of our closeness and then letting us sink back without the longed-for term. (p. 251)

R. Brown and McNeill (1966), who first examined the TOT state experimentally, referred to the feeling as analogous to being on the brink of a sneeze: a sense of mild torment, followed by considerable relief when the act is finally accomplished. The implication underlying the TOT phenomenon is that the target words are known to the individual but not readily accessible.

As typically studied, participants are given definitions designed to put the average participant into a TOT state, such as *A seemingly self-contradictory statement that may, nevertheless, be true* or *Transformation from one form to another as from a caterpillar to butterfly*. Participants in a TOT state often report a sense of a "search," in which one feels that the elusive word can be found through a combination of mental effort and the appropriate retrieval strategy (Kohn et al., 1987; see A. S. Brown, 1991, for a good review).

Studies using both diary keeping (Burke, MacKay, Worthley, & Wade, 1991; Cohen & Faulkner, 1986b) and experimentally induced TOTs (Burke et al., 1991) confirm elderly adults' general impression that the incidence of TOTs increases with age and that they generally have less access to partial information about the elusive words than do young adults (Burke et al., 1991; Cohen & Faulkner, 1986b; Maylor, 1990). Diary studies have reported a significant difference in the number of TOTs reported between college-age participants and participants in their late 30s, with the number increasing more markedly into old age (Burke et al., 1991). Experimental studies suggest that elderly adults are slower and less successful in retrieving words from definitions than are young adults, especially for low- and moderate-frequency words (Bowles & Poon, 1985). In addition to age differences in single-word retrieval, when asked to describe pictured scenes and events, elderly adults tend to show longer pauses than do young adults and a higher incidence of indefinite words such as *thing* in place of specific words that would be more appropriate (Cooper, 1990; Heller & Dobbs, 1993). Proper name retrieval has been reported to be a special difficulty for older adults (Burke et al., 1991; Stanhope, Cohen, & Conway, 1993), although Maylor (1997) suggested that the effect may be partly attributable to a functional ceiling for young adults in naming. When Maylor used a more difficult task of voice recognition, she found that younger and older adults were similarly disadvantaged in retrieving speakers' names relative to other information.

The word retrieval difficulties associated with normal aging can be contrasted with the serious anomia in dementia of the Alzheimer type. In patients with probable Alzheimer's disease (AD), some naming errors may be due to perceptual failures resulting from visual deficits associated with the disease (Cronin-Golomb, Corkin, & Rizzo, 1991). Analyses of error types, however, suggest that misrecognition of pictures to be named accounts for only a small proportion of the naming errors (LaBerge, Balota, Storandt, & Smith, 1992). Unlike healthy aging, there is a good possibility in AD patients that the semantic system itself is disrupted (Nicholas et al., 1997). Others have argued that the failure is primarily an access problem from an otherwise intact lexical semantic system, at least in the earlier stages of the disease (Nebes & Brady, 1990).

Gating and Word Recognition. In describing the cohort model of word recognition, we noted that words can often be recognized before their full acoustic duration has been completed. This has been demonstrated with the "gating technique," in which the first 50 ms of a word is presented to the participant, who is asked to identify the word. If the participant is unable to recognize the word (which is most likely with a "gate" this small), the participant is then allowed to hear the first 100 ms of the word and again attempts identification. This procedure is continued over a sequence of presentations, with the total amount of word onset being increased by 50-ms increments until the word can be correctly identified. Using this technique, Grosjean (1980) found that words can often be identified when only the first half, or less, of the word has been heard. The size of the gate needed for recognition is even smaller when the word is presented in a linguistic context (see Grosjean, 1996, for a review).

Because of both sensory and higher level auditory processing deficits, elderly adults with age-normal hearing generally require a larger word-onset gate to recognize a spoken word than do young adults (Wingfield, Aberdeen, & Stine, 1991), an effect that is further marked in patients with AD (Marshall, Duke & Walley, 1996). In cases of normal adults, this age difference progressively diminishes when words are presented in moderately to highly constraining linguistic contexts (Craig, Kim, Rhyner, & Chirillo, 1993; Perry & Wingfield, 1994; Stine & Wingfield, 1994; Wingfield et al., 1991). This latter finding would be expected from our earlier presentation that word recognition can be facilitated by top-down information in combination with the bottom-up input. It is partly for this reason that, barring serious sensory loss or neuropathology, spoken language comprehension remains typically well preserved in adult aging (Wingfield & Stine, 1992).

Focusing on words spoken in isolation from a constraining context, Sommers (1996), noted the importance of findings, such as those by Craig (1992), that the age difference in recognition of gated words is not a simple correlate of age-related hearing impairment. Sommers' particular focus was on the neighborhood density of the spoken words, the number of words that share phonemes with the stimulus word. Sommers demonstrated that high-density words with high-frequency neighbors ("difficult" words) were more difficult to recognize for both young and elderly adults than low-density words from low-frequency neighborhoods ("easy" words), although the difficulty was differentially greater for elderly adults than for young adults.

As Sommers (1996) was able to show, these results were independent of age-related differences in hearing acuity (Experiment 1) and were still obtained even when white-noise masking was used to equate baseline performance levels of young and elderly listeners (Experiment 2). This differential age effect of lexical difficulty could be due to a reduction in the ability to inhibit activation of close lexical candidates, to a slowing in the speed with which lexical candidates are eliminated, or to some degradation of the acoustic input related to a reduced effectiveness of auditory processing in elderly listeners. We agree with Sommers that this is a fruitful area for future research.

Perhaps the most interesting of Sommers' (1996) findings was the demonstration (Experiment 3) of a three-way interaction between age, lexical difficulty, and stimulus variability. This last factor was varied by having stimulus words spoken by a single speaker or a number of different speakers. That is, the increased effects of lexical difficulty for elderly listeners was further amplified in the presence of speaker variability. Assuming that speaker variability requires extra effort because of increased perceptual normalizing demands, Sommers interpreted his findings as demonstrating that the need to divert cognitive resources to meet these demands reduced the resources available for distinguishing the stimulus from other words in the lexical neighborhood. To the extent that elderly adults begin the task with reduced resources, this added drain would be likely to impair their speech perception to a greater degree than it would for young adults.

As in spoken word recognition, aging also brings difficulty in the extraction of feature-level information from the printed word. Older adults, for example, are particularly slowed in word identification when the stimulus is degraded (e.g., Allen, Madden, Weber, & Groth, 1993; Madden, 1988, 1992; see Allen et al., 1995, for a review). There is some debate about whether this difficulty in word decoding is best explained as a result of generalized (e.g., Madden, 1992) or localized slowing (Allen et al., 1995). There is general agreement, however, that these deficits cannot be completely accounted for in terms of age-related declines in visual acuity (e.g., Madden, 1992).

Studies of Semantic Priming and Lexical Access. The question has been raised as to whether age-related word retrieval difficulties are due to a problem of accessing the lexical information or whether there is a loss of structure or richness of this information in semantic memory. The weight of the evidence seems to support the presumption that the lexical system and its semantic associations remain intact in normal aging. For example, both cross-sectional and longitudinal studies have reported that vocabulary knowledge, as measured by the ability to define words, remains constant or even increases with age (Botwinick, 1977; Bowles & Poon, 1985).

Studies of semantic priming have shown that elderly adults are as influenced by the semantic relatedness of the two words as are young adults (Burke & Peters, 1986; Burke, White, & Diaz, 1987; Howard, 1983; Madden, Pierce & Allen, 1993). Young and elderly adults are also similar in the semantic associations they give (A. S. Brown & Mitchell, 1991; Howard, 1980). Also, in word recognition, older adults show the same effects of word frequency as do young adults (Allen et al., 1993). Indeed, in a meta-analysis of priming studies, Laver and Burke (1993) concluded that older adults showed no less priming than young adults in either lexical decision or word-naming tasks. To the extent that age differences appeared, they were in the form of greater priming effects for older adults than for younger adults. A good review of age and priming can be found in the work by Duchek and Balota (1993).

In spite of this preservation in the spread of activation, there may be age differences in the ability to suppress activation. When younger adults are exposed to the same word a number of times, it ceases to act as a prime, a phenomenon known as "semantic satiation." This is thought to have evolutionary significance, demonstrating a preference in the attentional system for new and changing information. In a series of experiments by Balota and Black (1997), older adults did not show semantic satiation, which may be taken as an expression of an age-related inhibition failure.

A finding that older adults may not show priming at very short interstimulus intervals (e.g., less than 200 ms) has led to speculation that the spread of activation may be slower in later adulthood (Howard, Shaw, & Heisey, 1986). Madden, Pierce, and Allen (1993), who among others did not find data to support this finding (e.g., Balota, Black, & Cheney, 1992; Balota & Duchek, 1988; Burke et al., 1987), offered a good discussion of factors that can affect results in primed lexical decision and primed naming tasks. Thus, the evidence for slower activation in normal aging has received, at best, mixed support.

Syntactic Processing

Older adults have been reported to show reduced performance in imitating sentences that are syntactically complex (Kemper, 1986) and in the recall of prose when it contains more complex left-branching constructions (Kemper, 1987b). In diary studies, longitudinal changes have also been found in syntactic complexity of productions (Kemper, 1987a). Older adults may also be less accurate in successfully resolving the meaning of sentences with a temporary closure ambiguity (Kemtes & Kemper, 1997). Finally, elderly adults have more difficulty than young adults in determining the antecedents of pronouns when the distance between the two is larger (Light & Capps, 1986). This distance factor has also been shown for referent trace activation in online sentence comprehension (Zurif, Swinney, Prather, Wingfield, & Brownell, 1995). By contrast, age differences in language comprehension and recall are generally minimal or absent when the stimuli consist of simpler, more canonical sentence forms (Kemper, 1986, 1992; Light, 1991). Because such forms predominate in everyday discourse, age differences in everyday sentence processing are minimal, with effects appearing primarily in real-life and laboratory studies when the system is stressed.

Studies in which independent estimates of working memory capacity have been obtained suggest that age-related difficulties in the processing of complex syntax can be accounted for by working memory changes in adult aging (Norman, Kemper, & Kynette, 1992). That is, it is currently believed that it is not the competence for syntactic processing per se that deteriorates. Rather, there is a decline in performance in the face of heavy working memory demands imposed by complex syntax. Although this conclusion fairly represents the consensus position in the field, it should be noted that a number of questions remain regarding the role of working memory at different levels of language processing and how working memory should best be measured (Waters & Caplan, 1996; Wingfield et al., 1998).

We cited earlier a suggestion by MacDonald et al. (1992) that individuals with small working memory spans may compute and maintain only one interpretation of a sentence with a temporary closure ambiguity, whereas individuals with high working memory spans may be able to compute and maintain multiple interpretations. For this reason, high-span individuals should paradoxically show slower reading times in a syntactically ambiguous region of a sentence (because multiple alternatives are being constructed) than low-span individuals (who are constructing only a single default structure). Kemtes and Kemper (1997) examined this hypothesis directly in a study of word-by-word reading times with young and elderly adults with high and low working memory spans. They found that older adults generally had slower reading times than young adults, but contrary to the results of MacDonald et al., the differential slowing of reading times for high-span participants in the ambiguous regions of sentences relative to low-span participants did not appear within either age group. Although these authors were careful to point out that these results do not rule out the multiple-interpretation possibility for high-span participants, the issue must remain open at this time.

A general picture of relatively spared linguistic knowledge combined with performance constraints also appears for syntactic processing ability in AD (Kempler & Zelinski, 1994). For example, Kemper (1997) asked groups of healthy young and elderly adults and a group of elderly adults with a diagnosis of probable AD to judge the acceptability of grammatical sentences, ungrammatical sentences, and random word strings. Even though the elderly adults with probable AD were less confident in their judgments, all three groups judged the random word strings as unacceptable, suggesting that they could all recognize when word strings adhered to grammatical rules. By contrast, for sentences that had complex syntactic forms (e.g., having embedded clauses, such as *Plots by many conspirators who work for the government have been hatched*), both healthy elderly adults and elderly adults with probable AD were more likely than the healthy young adults to rate these as unacceptable, suggesting that they could not parse the syntax when working memory demands were high. In fact, the older adults with probable AD showed no statistical difference in their ratings between the acceptability of sentences with such embeddings and randomized word strings, providing insight into just how incomprehensible complex syntax can be to AD patients. By contrast, when sentences required the processing of less demanding transformations, like the passive form of the verb (e.g., *The bed was slept on by George Washington*), all three groups rated them as acceptable. As with normal aging, disruption of syntactic processing in AD appears to arise from a severe reduction in working memory resources, whereas general procedural knowledge of linguistic rules and their application remain preserved.

AD is also characterized by simplification in production. Kemper et al. (1993) have reported that in a sentence-formulation task, sentences became shorter, less syntactically complex, and less informationally dense as the clinical rating of AD increased, suggesting to Kemper et al. that "syntactic simplifications in written language may be an early marker of the onset of Alzheimer's Disease" (p. 86).

In an even more dramatic demonstration of this effect, Snowdon et al. (1996) coded autobiographical statements that had been written by Notre

Dame nuns at the end of their novitiate (at about age 22) for propositional density and syntactic complexity. They then correlated these measures with performance on a cognitive test battery about 60 years later, when the nuns were 75 to 87 years old. Generally there was a reliable relationship. After partialing out the effects of age, average grammatical complexity of the statements made in young adulthood accounted for 19% of the variance in a mini-mental status exam 60 years later and propositional density accounted for 36% of the variance. Autopsies conducted on the 14 nuns who had died revealed AD for 5 of them. All five with confirmed AD had scored in the lower third of the distribution on propositional density at age 22, whereas none of the remaining nine did. Snowdon et al. saw this as support for the position that linguistic simplification may be a marker of AD that can be manifested well in advance of its more devastating symptoms.

Although these findings might suggest a potential for early diagnosis in AD, the causal status of this relationship is far from clear. It may be, for example, that linguistic simplification is a consequence of subtle neuropathic changes related to the development of the disease, or it may be that high cognitive ability enables a chain of life-span events (e.g., choices of intellectual stimulation) that buffers against the disease. Another open question is the extent to which these early cognitive markers are purely linguistic. That is, to the extent that the linguistic simplification associated with AD is a working memory phenomenon, or some other generalized deficit , one might expect to observe early poor performance on a range of cognitive tasks. These are important issues for future research.

Constructing and Using the Text-Base Representation

There are many similarities in the way in which text factors affect young and elderly adults. For example, as texts increase in propositional density, both young and elderly adults show slower reading speed (Stine & Hindman, 1994) and a decrease in text recall (Stine et al., 1986). These results suggest that young and old adults alike are sensitive to the propositional structure of discourse. Both are sensitive to the introduction of new conceptual arguments (Dixon, Hultsch, Simon, & von Eye, 1984). Both show a levels effect in recall, reflecting an ability to discriminate between major and minor points of a text (Dixon, Simon, Nowak, & Hultsch, 1982; Stine & Wingfield, 1990a). Both activate word meanings that are contextually appropriate to the text base (Burke & Harrold, 1988; Light, Valencia-Laver, & Zavis, 1991). Both show sensitivity to pragmatic constraints in making anaphoric inferences (Light & Capps, 1986; Light, Capps, Singh, & Owens, 1994). Finally, both can effectively integrate information when the anaphoric distance is short to achieve coherence (Zelinski, 1988).

In spite of this demonstrated competence, processing deficits may put limits on absolute measures of performance. There have been several large-scale individual-difference studies in recent years designed to account for age differences in cognitive performance, including text memory, in terms of indicators of basic processing mechanisms. These have included differences in working memory, speed, and inhibition (Hultsch, Hertzog, Small, McDonald-Miszczak, & Dixon, 1992; Kwong See & Ryan, 1995; Van der Linden et al., 1999). Their general approach has been to administer a large battery of cognitive measures representing these constructs of interest to a large number of participants and then to use structural equation modeling to determine the best-fitting causal model that accounts for age-related differences in performance.

A study by Van der Linden et al. (1999) represents an excellent example of this approach, which focuses exclusively on language-processing performance using multiple estimates of working memory, speed, and inhibition. Their measurements of text processing included comprehension questions for expository texts, recall of sentences varying in propositional density, narrative recall, and verbal list learning, with intercorrelations among these measures ranging from .40 to .60. They argued that age-related variance in language processing could be completely accounted for by working memory processing, which in turn could be accounted for by speed and inhibition. This issue, however, is far from closed. For example, the importance of these three different mechanisms for age-related change in language processing may vary as a function of the text and task demands (e.g., Park et al., 1996). At the present time, experimental studies have implicated all three factors as contributors to age differences in language comprehension and recall.

Many results have highlighted the role of declining processing speed in the aging of language processing (Salthouse, 1996). For example, in reading studies, older adults have been found to require more time per proposition for accurate recall (Hartley, Stojack, Mushaney, Annon, & Lee, 1994), with the age difference exaggerated for low-span elderly adults (Stine & Hindman, 1994). Older adults may also have differential difficulty in the recall of propositionally dense speech (Stine & Wingfield, 1990b), when speech has low predictability (Wingfield & Lindfield, 1995), or when the speech rate is very fast (Stine & Wingfield, 1987; Stine et al., 1986).

The most common way to study speech-rate effects is to time-compress speech on a computer. This allows one to increase speech rates while still maintaining the same relative word-to-pause durations and without disturbing the intonation pattern of the speech. Elderly adults, like young adults, show little performance effects on comprehension or recall with moderate increases in speech rate, up to about 200 wpm (Small, Kemper, & Lyons, 1997). Beyond this point, however, both age groups show performance declines with increasing speech rates, with elderly listeners typically showing a steeper rate of decline than young adults, reflected by a significant Age × Speech Rate interaction (Stine et al., 1986; Wingfield, Poon, Lombardi, & Lowe, 1985).

Three points should be made with regard to this special difficulty elderly adults have with rapid speech. The first is that this special difficulty is not due simply to age differences in peripheral acuity, as this Age × Speech Rate interaction appears even when young and elderly adults are carefully matched for hearing acuity (Gordon-Salant & Fitzgibbons, 1993). Second, older adults' speech recall is most compromised when lists of unrelated words are presented at rapid speech rates, with the age difference reduced when the words are combined into meaningful sentences, and even when meaningless words strings are presented with grammatical endings that mimic normal sentences (Wingfield et al., 1985). It is presumed that the structure provided by meaningful speech provides a predictive context that facilitates recognition and adds support for recall (Gordon-Salant & Fitzgibbons, 1997; Wingfield, 1996). The final point relates to reports that age differences in recall of linguistic materials are often smaller for elderly adults with good levels of general verbal ability (West, Crook, & Barron, 1992; Zelinski & Gilewski, 1988). Whether it is the case that verbal ability per se drives these results or whether verbal ability is acting as a surrogate for general intellectual ability, similar results are found for elderly adults' recall of time-compressed speech. Although high verbal ability reduces age differences in overall levels of recall for rapid speech, it does not, however, eliminate the Age × Speech Rate interaction (Stine et al., 1986).

Rapid speech rate is not the only factor that puts elderly adults at a disadvantage at the text-base level; other difficulties can be accounted for in terms of reduced working memory resources. One of these is the previously noted difficulty older adults have in making the correct pronominal inference when the distance between the referent and anaphor is increased or when working memory is otherwise taxed (Light & Capps, 1986). Older adults may also be less thorough in processing causal inferences (Hess, 1995). Whereas younger adults show reading time patterns that reflect integration at the ends of input cycles (Aaronson & Ferres, 1984), the average older adult may not (Stine, 1990). Nor do they seem to integrate conceptual arguments as thoroughly as do young adults at the ends of sentences, suggesting that concepts introduced earlier in the text may decay later in the sentence (Stine, 1990; Stine, Cheung, & Henderson, 1995).

Other difficulties seem most compatible with an inhibition-deficit notion. For example, older adults have been reported to be disproportionately slowed in their reading when distracting material is embedded in the text at unpredictable locations, especially when the embedded material is meaningful text (Carlson, Hasher, Connelly, & Zacks, 1995; Connelly, Hasher, & Zacks, 1991). Older adults, however, were not particularly hindered when the distracting material was nonlinguistic (i.e., a string of *x*s). This control condition would suggest that it was the proposition-based content of the distracting material that the elderly readers were not effectively inhibiting. Nor were older adults hindered when the linguistic material was in a predictable location, further suggesting that the inhibition failure resided at the text-based level that could only be overcome by effective inhibition of location.

Other evidence of an age-related difficulty in effective inhibition at the text-base level comes from studies of the fan effect described earlier (Gerard, Zacks, Hasher, & Radvansky, 1991; Zacks & Hasher, 1994). So, for example, it takes longer for participants to verify that they have read *The pay phone is in the laundromat* when they have also read *The pay phone is in city hall* and *The pay phone is in the barber shop*. Older adults demonstrate a larger fan effect than do young adults, suggesting that the number of propositions creates difficulty for older adults in retrieval from the text base. This can be interpreted as demonstrating that they have more difficulty in inhibiting the propositions that are irrelevant to the target judgment. Alternatively, it could be argued that older adults take differentially longer to search the network surrounding the critical concept.

Generally speaking, the inhibition-deficit theory has been a highly successful tool for generating interesting experimental work in language and aging. It has come under fire lately for its failure to discriminate between inhibition at the theoretical and behavioral levels (i.e., a lack of computational specificity) and its failure to account for age-related preservation in many aspects of language processing (Burke, 1997). Its proponents, however, have noted the theory's success and have defended the value of a conceptual processing model that can be more successful than a computational model in describing behavior across a wider range of domains (Zacks & Hasher, 1997).

Regardless of how these processing limits are modeled, they can also have an impact on the ability of older adults to effectively organize text. As we have noted, older adults have been repeatedly shown to demonstrate a levels effect in their recall protocols (Stine et al., 1986; Zelinski, Light, & Gilewski, 1984), showing that they are capable of distinguishing between major ideas that constitute the gist of the text and the expendable minor details (cf. Stine & Wingfield, 1990a). However, even though older adults show competence in their ability to organize text, they are more likely than young adults to remember a disproportionate number of the generally less memorable idea units (i.e., typically, details) as the text becomes more propositionally dense (Stine & Wingfield, 1988), faster

(Hartley, 1993), or less familiar (Hartley, 1993). Thus, as there is more information to organize per unit time, or as there is less support for organization within the text, older adults have a relatively more difficult time than do young adults in identifying or inhibiting the less important idea units. This finding could be accounted for in terms of an age-related decline in the effectiveness of inhibitory mechanisms that would allow less relevant propositions to persist across input cycles (cf. Kintsch, 1988), in terms of a reduced working memory capacity that might allow fewer propositions to be considered for carryover within a single input cycle (Kintsch & van Dijk, 1978), or in terms of an organizational deficit (Stine & Wingfield, 1990a).

Constructing and Updating the Situation Model

In many ways, older adults show a qualitative similarity to young adults in building and updating situation models in discourse understanding (for an explicit discussion of the implications of this level of representation for memory, see chap. 5, this volume). In a replication of the Garnham (1981) "podiatrist" study, Radvansky, Gerard, Zacks, and Hasher (1990) found that elderly readers showed the same ease as younger adults in distinguishing propositionally similar sentences that described different situation models. So at least when the situation is conveyed by simple linguistic cues, like prepositions, it appears that older adults are just as likely as young adults to create an appropriate representation of the situation model.

Older adults also seem to represent the relative spatial locations of a narrative and to update this representation as the protagonist moves through a spatial array. Both probe verification and reading time studies have shown older adults to manifest a distance effect, processing information about objects in the text more quickly when they are closer to the current location of the protagonist than when they are farther away (Morrow, Leirer, Altieri, & Fitzsimmons, 1994; Morrow, Stine-Morrow, Leirer, Andrassy, & Kahn, 1997). The use of goal structure also appears to be preserved with aging. Radvansky and Curiel (1998) asked younger and older adults to read narratives in which the protagonist had a goal (e.g., *Roy wanted to buy his boss a retirement gift*) that was either completed (e.g., *Roy went shopping and bought a big screen TV*) or not (e.g., *Roy went shopping but couldn't find anything*). The protagonist then engaged in an activity that was relevant to the goal (e.g., *Roy comes across an ad for a Caribbean cruise*), after which the participant was presented a probe about the goal (e.g., *Had Roy wanted to buy his boss a gift?*).

Both young and elderly readers keep "open" goal information active so as to readily interpret the protagonist's actions (e.g., Suh & Trabasso, 1993; Zwann, Langston, & Graesser, 1995). Both age groups answered the probes more quickly when the protagonist had not completed the goal, suggesting that they updated the situation model of the story by inhibiting the goal information once it was no longer relevant.

Finally, the ability to represent the situation conveyed by metaphors appears to be preserved with age. In a series of experiments, Light, Owens, Mahoney, and LaVoie (1993) showed that older adults construct metaphorical meaning much as younger adults do. In a sentence verification task ("Is this sentence literally true?"), both younger and older adults were relatively slow to reject false statements that were metaphors (e.g., Some jobs are jails), suggesting that metaphorical meaning was activated for both groups. In another experiment, they presented participants with novel metaphors (e.g., Billboards are warts on the landscape vs. Billboards are yellow pages of the highway) followed by a statement of the metaphoric reference, or "ground" (e.g., Billboards are ugly protrusions vs. Billboards help to find businesses). Both younger and older adults were faster to verify the ground activated by the metaphor, again suggesting age preservation in the construction of the situation presented by the metaphor. Indeed, some researchers have suggested that metaphoric interpretation becomes more central to discourse understanding in later life, with young adults more reproductive and elderly adults more metaphorical or interpretive in their recall (Adams, 1991; Adams, Smith, Nyquist, & Perlmutter, 1997).

In spite of apparent age constancy in the online processing of the situation model, its construction and updating can be resource-consuming, and thus the consequent memory representation may not always be comparable in the two groups. For instance, in the Light et al. (1993, Experiment 2) study of metaphor, even though younger and older adults were equally facilitated in verifying the metaphoric ground, in a subsequent memory experiment, the ground was a differentially better retrieval cue for the young. This would imply that the ground was not as fully elaborated among the elderly adults.

Another example of this principle is provided by Hess (1995) in a study of age differences in the processing of causal connections in text. Using the Myers and Duffy (1990) paradigm we described earlier, Hess presented younger and older adults with pairs of sentences varying in their degree of causal relatedness. Older adults showed the same facilitation in reading time for the second sentence as younger adults as relatedness to the first sentence was increased, showing that older adults were processing causal aspects of the situation model. In the cued-recall test, however, although younger adults showed the same quadratic function in recall shown by Myers and Duffy, older adults' recall was linearly related to, and much less improved by, causal relatedness. This could suggest that the network of causal elaborations among the older adults had been less well developed.

Online measures have also provided evidence that situation model updating is resource-consuming. In a probe verification study in which participants' reading is periodically interrupted to verify the locations of objects, older adults have been found to show an exaggerated distance effect for correct verifications (Morrow et al., 1994). Although the older adults produced more errors in verification, the latency measures excluded those trials, suggesting that older adults had to allocate more time to achieve the same level of accuracy as young adults. Reading time has also been found to show an exaggerated distance effect for elderly participants, even when comprehension accuracy was similar across the two groups (Morrow et al., 1997).

Another area in which older adults have been found to show diminished capability in situation model processing is the case in which the text suggests an inference that is incorrect. Hamm and Hasher (1992) had participants read a series of passages that at first implied a certain situation (e.g., *Carol is ill, she calls a friend who is a nurse, and then enters a large building*, a series of events that suggests that Carol has entered a hospital). Subsequently, however, new information is provided that is inconsistent with that situation (e.g., *Carol goes to the desk to check out a book*, suggesting that the building is not a hospital but rather a library). When explicitly asked about the location at the end of the passage, younger adults were likely to have updated their situation model (i.e., they report that Carol is in the library), whereas older adults were equally likely to report the original as well as the revised situation (e.g., that Carol is in a library and a hospital).

Even though the construction and updating of the situation model is resource-consuming and apparently subject to disruption by inhibition failure, there may, nevertheless, be advantages to relying on this level of representation as we age. Provided the situation model is not so resource-consuming that it cannot be constructed at all, it may provide contextual support so that processing of the text base is ultimately less resource-consuming. The implication of this line of reasoning is that the availability of a situation model, once constructed, may reduce age differences in language processing.

There is some evidence for this proposal. For example, working memory is a stronger predictor of age decrements for shorter texts than for longer texts that provoke a more elaborated situation model (Stine & Wingfield, 1990b). A situation model may also reduce age-related effects of propositional density by providing an easy way to integrate information. Radvansky, Zacks, and Hasher (1996) compared age differences in the fan effect when the same object was in multiple locations (ML; as in the Gerard et al., 1991, study) with age differences in the fan effect when multiple objects were in the same location (SL; e.g., *The pay phone is in the barber shop, The potted palm is in the barber shop*, and *The ceiling fan is in the barber shop*). Even though the ML and SL conditions are identical in the number of propositions involved and the number of new concepts introduced, they differ in that the SL condition allows for the propositions to be represented within a single situation, which, of course, the ML condition does not. Figure 6.2 shows error data in the Radvansky et al. experiment for trials in which the proposition was in the original studied set ("yes" trials, left panel) and those in which it was not ("no" trials, right panel). Consistent with the Gerard et al. study, the older adults showed an exaggerated fan effect in the ML condition. In the SL condition, however, the older adults showed the same null fan effect as young adults, regardless of the trial type. These data demonstrate that the older adults were effectively integrating the propositional content into a situation model, thereby eliminating the effects of age-related processing limitations.

Another example of this principle is provided in a study by Miller and Stine-Morrow (1998), in which younger and older adults read passages for which a situation model was difficult to construct. For example, the following passage is in itself incomprehensible: *The strength and flexibility of this equipment is remarkable. Keep in mind that all the components must be carefully controlled to prevent injury or even death.* However, when a title that provides a situation model (e.g., "Driving a Car") is presented prior to reading, comprehension is greatly facilitated, in part because the situation model guides the reader toward correct referential assignment (e.g., to what does *components* refer?) and cues about conceptual integration (e.g., how does the control of the components prevent injury?). This is empirically demonstrated by the fact that the time taken for wrap-up in word-by-word

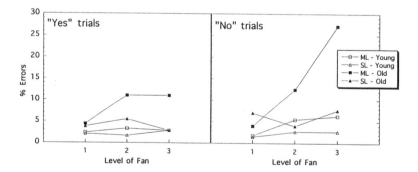

FIG. 6.2. Percentage of errors in verifying accuracy of encoded propositions for "Yes" trials (left panel) and "No" trials (right panel) as a function of the number of propositions encoded (i.e., the "fan"), number of target locations (multiple locations [ML] vs. single location [SL]), and age. From "Fact Retrieval in Younger and Older Adults: The Role of Mental Models," by G. A. Radvansky, R. T. Zacks, & L. Hasher, 1996, *Psychology and Aging, 11,* 258–271. Copyright 1996 by the American Psychological Association. Reprinted with permission.

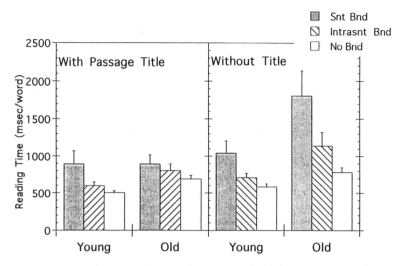

FIG. 6.3. Reading time allocation for young and elderly participants with above-average recall as a function of passage location. Snt Bnd = sentence boundary; Intrasnt Bnd = intrasentence boundary; No Bnd = no important syntactic boundary; Error bars represent one standard error. Reprinted with permission of the Gerontological Society of America, 1030 15th Street, NW, Suite 250, Washington, DC 20005. *Aging and the Effects of Knowledge on On-line Reading Strategies* (Figure), L. M. S. Miller & E. A. L. Stine-Morrow, Journal of Gerontology: Psychological Sciences, 1998, 53B. Reproduced by permission of the publisher via Copyright Clearance Center, Inc.

reading is greatly reduced when titles are available. In Fig. 6.3, we present the data only for those participants who were effective in processing the text as measured by subsequent above-average levels of recall performance (participants who were below average generally showed very little wrap-up at all). Thus, the data in Fig. 6.3 illustrate what younger and elderly readers had to do in order to effectively recall the passages. These data show that although older readers without a title took differentially longer than younger readers to integrate new concepts at the ends of input cycles (see Fig. 6.3, right panel), they showed virtually the identical pattern of resource allocation as younger readers when provided a title (see Fig. 6.3, left panel). These results support the notion that the availability of a situation model can facilitate text-base integration among older adults.

WHY LANGUAGE PROCESSING
IN LATE LIFE IS SO GOOD

To this point, we have argued that normal aging brings little change in the structures and knowledge base that support language processing, such as the structure of semantic memory, mechanisms for syntactic parsing, propositional coding, and situation model construction and updating. By contrast, age-related change in processing capacity (e.g., working memory, processing rate, and inhibition) does occur. It is this change, we believe, that underlies those differences observed in language performance. The question arises, then, how is it that language processing so often shows relative preservation in advanced age.

Recent theoretical models of compensation provide some guidance in approaching this question (Bäckman & Dixon, 1992; Dixon & Bäckman, 1995; Salthouse, 1995). There seems to be general agreement that compensation can be said to exist when behavior is altered in some way so as to produce effective performance in a given domain in spite of the existence of a deficit relevant to the performance—the very situation we have been describing with respect to language processing. Nevertheless, there is some debate as to how inclusive this term should be. Bäckman and Dixon and Dixon and Bäckman, for example, used the term *compensation* broadly to include a variety of mechanisms used to overcome deficits, such as (a) allocating more time or effort to the deficit skill, (b) relying on a latent skill as a replacement for the one showing the deficit, (c) learning a new skill to replace the deficit, or even (d) resetting one's goals or expectations.

Salthouse (1995), on the other hand, argued that the term *compensation* should be reserved strictly for the situation in which "the same (or higher) level of criterion functioning is achieved by means of different processes or mechanisms" (p. 24), so as to include only b and c above. By contrast, he argued that allocating more resources to the deficient skill can eradicate the deficit, thereby reducing the need for compensation ("remediation"), or it can create a new skill so that the deficient component is no longer important to performance ("compilation" or "elimination"). Similarly, adjusting one's goals would not be considered compensation but rather "accommodation" because the performance goal itself is altered. Further issues are whether the demonstration of true compensation depends on showing (a) a causal relationship between the deficit and the compensatory process, (b) the existence of awareness of the deficit and attempts at correction, (c) the uniqueness of the compensatory mechanism among individuals with the deficit, and (d) a qualitative shift in importance among a set of processes for performance rather than just a relative increase in the presumed compensatory process itself.

Even though there is much theoretical development to be done on this issue, these arguments highlight the many different mechanisms through which older adults may achieve proficiency in language performance, irrespective of whether one calls it compensation. In the discussion below, we describe three basic reasons why language processing is so well maintained in late life, noting instances of remediation, elimination, and, perhaps, compensation.

Older Adults Benefit From the Contextual Support Inherent in Language

As a rule, age differences in memory performance are greatest in cases in which there is little in the way of contextual support. Because language by its nature is richly structured and highly redundant, age differences are greatest when verbal materials are least like real language. So, for example, older adults have difficulty recognizing words in isolation, but as we have already noted, when the words are embedded in the context of natural speech, older listeners can do nearly as well as their younger counterparts (Pichora-Fuller et al., 1995; Wingfield et al., 1991). Although this last point is an important one, the use of context in speech processing may be constrained by working memory limits. For example, especially for elderly adults, the context following the target word is much less useful than the context preceding it (Wingfield et al., 1994). This is presumably because in order to use the context following a word, the phonological trace must be maintained in working memory for a longer period of time, a factor that may put the elderly adult at a disadvantage.

Older listeners also make good use of the contextual constraints of language in construction of a text base in comprehension. For example, even though older adults show very poor recall for random word lists, especially at fast speech rates, they can perform nearly at the level of young adults for text with strong semantic constraints (Wingfield & Lindfield, 1995; Wingfield et al., 1985). Such mitigation of age deficits by contextual constraint is not always reported (e.g., Holtzman, Familitant, Deptula, & Hoyer, 1986), reinforcing the suggestion that contextual support can be used effectively only in conditions that are not resource-consuming (Holtzman et al., 1986; Wingfield et al., 1994). The exact nature of these conditions remains to be specified.

Older adults also seem to take good advantage of the prosodic contour of sentences to aid syntactic parsing and comprehension. Older adults are differentially likely to recall the stressed information from text (Cohen & Faulkner, 1986a) and to show greater deterioration in their immediate-recall performance as the speech is deprived of prosodic contour (Stine & Wingfield, 1987). Older adults appear to rely on the prosodic contour not only as an indicator of important elements of the speech but also as a guide to parsing syntactic elements (Kjelgaard et al., 1999; Wingfield, Wayland, & Stine, 1992).

Older adults also may take exceptional advantage when the text as a whole is well structured. For example, older adults can show recall performance at similar levels to young adults when the events of a narrative are presented in canonical order, but they lose this advantage if events are interleaved with another story (Smith, Rebok, Smith, Hall, & Alvin, 1983). Age differences are also less likely to be apparent when texts are narrative rather than expository (Stine & Wingfield, 1990a; Tun, 1989). This may be attributable in part to the more predictable structure of the narrative form (e.g., setting, goal or conflict, and resolution). Other structural factors, such as the integration of emotional content and the strong sense of place inherent in narratives, may contribute as well.

B. J. F. Meyer (1999) has noted that many texts can be classified as following one of five basic writing plans: description, temporal sequence, causation, problem leading to a solution, and comparison. These structures are more likely in certain types of text and are likely to contain tell-tale signals. For example, sequences are likely to be found in recipes and other procedures and to contain signals like "to begin with," "next," and so on. When readers are trained to identify these plans, prose recall is improved regardless of age.

In summary, there is now a fairly large body of literature showing that the language performance of older adults is often differentially benefited by the structural and contextual constraints of natural language, suggesting that declines in bottom-up processing are offset by attention to the broader context. Although this may provide an example of compensation, there are a number of issues that remain to be resolved (cf. Salthouse, 1995). For example, there is no one who would argue that the use of contextual support is unique to aged individuals; rather, the argument is that there is an age-related shift in the usefulness of contextual support. Under what circumstances is the use of context an effective strategy, and under what circumstances do younger adults also adopt it? Also, does benefit arise from more thorough processing of the context among elderly adults, or do elderly adults perform the same computations as do younger adults but simply give them more weight? Finally, do processing deficits cause the reliance on contextual support, or is it that a habitual reliance on the broader context weakens bottom-up processing ability? These are important questions that remain to be explored.

Older Adults Reconstruct Ambiguous or Missing Elements to Restore Meaning to a Message

Because of the fleeting and perceptually ambiguous nature of the speech stream, effective memory for speech often depends on regeneration of the surface form from whatever semantic representations can be constructed on the fly (Potter, 1993). This is true for both young and elderly adults, although there are some reports in the literature that older adults show more reconstructions in memory for linguistic materials than do young adults (e.g., Smith et al., 1983; Stine & Wingfield, 1987). For both age groups, when participants fail to recall sentences or prose with total word-for-word accuracy (*veridical recall*) their responses are invariably coherent and consistent with the constraints induced by what has been remembered. For a discussion of memory processes that could give rise to reconstructions, see chapter 5.

Figure 6.4 shows a plot of data taken from a study by Wingfield, Tun, and Rosen (1995), who presented paragraph-length speech passages to young and elderly adults for recall. The passages were presented to participants in short segments (8 to 12 words) composed of grammatical sentences or clauses. The participants' task was to recall each of the speech segments as accurately as possible as they were presented. Although the recall segments themselves were short, they not only had their own internal linguistic structure, but they were also heard within a larger narrative context. In addition, the speech rate was manipulated to vary the encoding difficulty of the speech. As might be expected, verbatim recall performance (percentage of words correct) was poorer for the elderly participants than for the young participants and the detrimental effects of increasing speech rates were especially great among the elderly adults. Of present interest, however, was that when the participants in either age group failed to recall a segment perfectly, an average of 97% of all of their responses remained meaningful and syntactically coherent. This was accomplished by reconstructing missing elements.

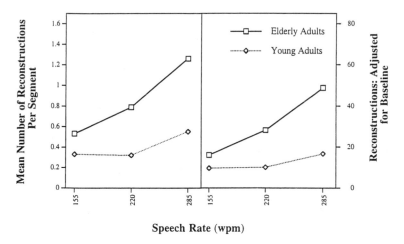

FIG. 6.4. Left panel: The mean number of reconstructions in the recall of speech segments presented to young and elderly adults at three speech rates in words per minute (wpm). Right panel: Data adjusted for participants' baseline accuracy levels. [Data from Wingfield, Tun, & Rosen, 1995].

For the purposes of scoring, a reconstruction was defined as the addition or substitution of a word or phrase that was not contained in the original stimulus but that nevertheless left the response semantically and syntactically coherent. In the left panel of Fig. 6.4, we can see that the elderly participants produced more reconstructions than did the young participants and that for both age groups the number of reconstructions increased with increasing speech rates. We can also see that there was a sharper increase in the number of reconstructions with speech rate for the elderly participants for the young participants. These age differences were not simply due to the poorer recall levels among old adults, which would allow more room for reconstructions. The right panel in Fig. 6.4 shows these data adjusted for baseline accuracy (number of reconstructions divided by number of errors). The pattern is identical for these adjusted scores.

These findings are consistent with other reports of a higher incidence of additions, reconstructions, and elaboration in elderly participants' recall (Hultsch & Dixon, 1983; Smith et al., 1983; Stine & Wingfield, 1987; Tun, 1989). Most interesting, they show that these reconstructions can occur at the sentence and clause level just as they have long been known to occur at the larger, narrative level.

One is bound to ask whether this high incidence of reconstructions reflects a failure to inhibit meaningfully related responses or whether these reconstructions should be seen as an adaptive response to a diminishing recall capacity. It is our view that elderly adults are applying reconstruction in an adaptive fashion. For example, when in another condition segments were delivered to participants at a rapid rate in nonsyntactically determined groupings (thus making them very difficult to follow), elderly adults reduced their attempts at reconstruction. That is, elderly adults did not make additions and changes in their recall to produce meaningful utterances without a sufficient base on which to build (Wingfield et al., 1995).

Reports in the literature that older adults are more metaphor-driven or interpretive in their text recall (Adams, 1991; Adams et al., 1997) and more reliant on plausibility judgment than on exact retrieval in sentence recognition (Reder, Wible, & Martin, 1986) may also be instances of this principle. As in the examples of reconstruction in recall, such responses may be construed as errors that derive from participants' attempts to generate a coherent surface form from an impoverished representation of the text base. There is also a possibility that older adults may be more skilled in reconstruction because of an advantage in world knowledge, schema-based processing (Hess, 1990), or attention to the situation model level of discourse (Adams, 1991; Stine-Morrow, Loveless, & Soederberg, 1996).

Even though regeneration may produce errors at the text-base level, to the extent that it is based on intact knowledge or an accurate situation model, the recall may be broadly accurate (Neisser, 1982). On the whole, there is evidence for a positive relationship between performance level and occurrence of reconstructions that is greater for older adults. For example, older participants (but not younger ones) in an auditory lexical decision task showed a positive correlation between B (a nonparametric measure of bias toward reporting the signal to be a word) and response time for hits (Stine-Morrow, Miller, & Nevin, 1999). That is, older adults, who were more likely to reconstruct ambiguous auditory signals into lexical items, were faster at recognizing real words. Overall, there was a robust age difference in B, with older adults showing larger parameters; the relationship between B and response time among older adults suggests that there was a special adaptive function in this bias. Similar findings have been reported with narrative recall (Smith et al., 1983) and in the recall of anomalous sentences (Stine & Wingfield, 1987).

Collectively, these data demonstrate that older adults show a greater tendency toward reconstruction at the lexical and text-base levels than do young adults. We argue that this is not simply random error but rather meaning-based regeneration (possibly derived from the situation model) that can offset for age-related processing and veridical memory limitations. As in the case of contextual processing, we view this as an age-related shift in the balance of processing, although questions remain with respect to uniqueness, the direction of causation, and the exact quality of the computations.

Older Adults Can Mitigate Processing Declines by Adapting Their Patterns of Resource Allocation in the Online Processing of Language

The general model of language processing we have described assumes that limited resources must be allocated to word, syntactic, text-base, and situation model representations. Discourse theorists often put such processes on a continuum, ranging from automatic processes that are done obligatorily without consumption of resources to effortful processes that are implemented strategically at some cost to the available pool of processing resources. However, in principle, at any level in the system, from lexical access to situation model updating, processing may vary in its demands on resources depending on the context, the characteristics of the reader or listener, the inherent difficulty of the operation itself, and competing demands relative to the goals of the reader or listener. It has been argued, for example, that even lexical access in reading, which is often cited as the prototypical automatic process, may be conducted more or less thoroughly, depending on whether the task gives priority to comprehension or to a memory task that is irrelevant to sentence comprehension (Carpenter & Just, 1989). There is also the claim that syntactic processing may vary in its complexity depending on the working memory capacity of the individual (Just & Carpenter, 1992) and that the extent of processing flexibility may also be related to working memory span (Carpenter & Just; 1989; Just & Carpenter, 1992).

Processes not only vary in the resources they consume but also in their priority. There is some intuitive appeal for a cumulative notion of resource allocation in which one constructs the text base by first accessing words, builds a mental model by first building a text base, and so on. However, depending on task demands, any one of these levels of representation can be given priority, and the construction of a detailed text base may actually detract from the construction of the situation model (Kintsch, 1994). Even though some processes may generally have priority over other processes (e.g., lexical access must be completed before inferences about causal consequence), the system is highly flexible in how resources are allocated to these domains. For example, readers told that they will have to recall the text allocate less time to processing coherence breaks that would be important for situation model construction than when participants were told simply to read the text for comprehension (Zwann, Magliano, & Graesser, 1995). Thus, rather than reinforcing the situation model, under some circumstances a meticulously constructed text-base may actually draw resources away from it. To the extent that older adults direct resources to the situation model (e.g., Adams et al., 1997), this could have implications for the thoroughness of the text-base representation.

Even though aging is accompanied by slowing in a wide variety of tasks (Salthouse, 1996), reading times are not always longer among old adults than among young adults (Ratner, Schell, Crimmins, Mittelman, & Baldinelli, 1987; Stine, 1995). Because these comparable reading times are often accompanied by memory differences, it is probably not the case that language-processing operations are exempt from slowing. Rather, it may be that comparable operations are not being completed by young and elderly readers.

In a compelling demonstration of the difference between the minimal time required to complete a set of processing operations and the actual time allocated to it, Hartley et al. (1994) measured reading time using three different methods: threshold reading time (the minimum amount of time needed per proposition to accurately recall a single sentence), text-based reading time (based on self-paced reading for comprehension), and self-paced memory reading time (based on self-paced reading for recall). These measures were moderately but not highly related (correlations of .44 to .55). More important, they showed stability over repeated test, suggesting that these measures represented reliable individual differences.

There were interesting differences among the measures, however. Older adults were slower on the threshold estimate but not for either self-paced estimate; so even though older adults needed more time to effectively process the information, they did not, on average, allocate more time when given the opportunity to do so. In a regression analysis, recall performance was negatively related to threshold reading time and positively related to self-paced reading time. This suggests that memory is optimal when processing is fast, but resources are nevertheless effectively allocated.

A more fine-grained way to examine the allocation of time to different aspects of language processing is to measure the time allocated at each unit of text (e.g., a word, clause, or sentence) and then use a regression analysis to decompose this time to that allocated for word decoding (e.g., time per syllable), for text-base construction (e.g., time per proposition or new concept introduced), for situation model updating (e.g., time allocation in the face of a temporal or causal coherence break), and so on (Zwann, Magliano, & Graesser, 1995). This can be accomplished either with self-paced reading (Aaronson & Scarborough, 1976) or listening (Ferreira et al., 1996; Titone, Prentice, & Wingfield, 1996). In the latter case, a digitized speech stream is presented in segments with the rate of presentation controlled by the listener.

Such techniques have been used to examine age differences in resource allocation in both reading (Stine, 1990; Stine-Morrow et al., 1996) and listening (Titone et al., 1996). These studies show that older adults are in many ways quite similar to younger adults in the way they distribute processing time across a text. For example, young and elderly adults show the same pattern in the relative amount of time they allocate for orthographic or phonological coding, lexical access, and syntactic processing (Stine, 1990; Stine et al., 1995; Stine-Morrow et al., 1996; Titone et al., 1996), even though age differences in subsequent memory performance often appear.

In spite of considerable similarity, there are also important differences in the manner in which young and elderly participants allocate attentional resources. Older adults, on average, are less likely to allocate time at the ends of sentences for conceptual integration (Stine, 1990; Stine et al., 1995). Zabrucky and Moore (1994) also found that older readers are less likely to allocate time to reread text so as to resolve inconsistency than are younger adults, a difference in process that accounted for age differences in subsequent recall performance. Titone et al. (1996) found that elderly listeners slow the speech input in the second half of a passage rather than take time at the beginning of a passage to build up a coherence structure that might facilitate later processing, an adaptive allocation policy that is used by young listeners.

Consistent with research on age differences in memory monitoring (Dunlosky & Connor, 1997), this pattern of data suggests that age-related deficits in text recall may arise in part because of a failure of the average older adult to successfully gauge the need for resource allocation in online language comprehension. This is not universal, however. Age differences in reading time allocation are especially likely to emerge when younger and older adults with high levels of recall are compared. In this case, older adults with good memory for what they have read are likely to have allocated relatively more time for conceptual integration at intrasentence boundaries (Stine, 1990; Stine et al., 1995), representing what Salthouse (1995) would call "remediation." Also, whereas younger adults who have high levels of subsequent recall seem to allocate extra time to text-based features, older adults allocate extra time early in the text to set up the situation model (Stine-Morrow et al., 1996). Indicative of more thorough situation model processing, older adults with above-average narrative comprehension scores have been found to allocate differentially more time to process sentences that refer to objects without explicit locations (Morrow et al., 1997). These shifts in the balance of processes used in the online processing of discourse may represent examples of compensation. Thus, these data suggest that high levels of comprehension and memory among elderly adults is engendered by flexible patterns of resource allocation that are sensitive to limitations in basic processes.

LANGUAGE IN EVERYDAY LIFE

To this point, we have explored the effects of age on the basic processes that give rise to language comprehension and memory. In doing this, we have shown that age effects can change drastically depending on the task, the structure of the linguistic materials, and the individual's goals in processing the text. Thus, it is of considerable theoretical and practical importance to consider how language is actually used in the discourse world of the elderly adult.

The Social Function of Language

One important function of language is that it serves as a conduit to the social world, allowing us to build and maintain a network that provides information about the world and about ourselves and helps us to regulate our emotional experience. According to "socioemotional selectivity" theory (Carstensen, 1995), the emotion regulation functions of social interaction take on greater importance as we age, given that as we begin to anticipate endings, there is more to be gained from effective modulation of the emotional climate than there is from increasing the complexity of our informational array. There is now a small but growing literature on aging and discourse focused on the social and affective functions of language use. Overall, this research suggests that older adults are at least as sensitive as younger adults to the emotional tone of discourse and that they are often found to be even more finely tuned than younger adults to the interpersonal dynamic in communication.

Emotion and Storytelling. In studies of online language comprehension and memory, older readers have been shown to be responsive to emotionally provocative texts. Their reading times show similar facilitation by consistent emotional tone as those of younger readers (Soederberg & Stine, 1995). Older readers have also been found to show disproportionately high recall for the emotionally salient information from mystery stories (Carstensen & Turk-Charles, 1994). Overall, older adults seem to be very good storytellers. Early research showed that even when stories are simply read, younger adults prefer older adults' telling to younger adults' telling (Mergler, Faust, & Goldstein, 1985). It is not clear what it is about how older adults read that makes the difference: It could be something as basic as a slower speech rate or the use of a prosodic pattern that is more compelling. To be sure, on some dimensions, it appears that older storytellers produce stories that could be more difficult to understand. For example, Pratt, Boyes, Robins, and Manchester (1989) found that their older storytellers made more referential errors and were less likely to use proper names, factors that would presumably make a story more difficult to follow.

Other research suggests, however, that older storytellers have an advantage in terms of the structural aspects of the storytelling. Pratt and Robins (1991) had young, middle-aged, and older participants generate personal narratives that were rated by an age-diverse sample on a variety of dimensions (e.g., "good story" and "interesting"). Story grammar analysis was used to analyze the total number of episodes and the percentages of completed and linked episodes. Narratives by older adults were rated more highly and were more likely to have a classic high-point structure (i.e., one that builds toward a climax that is resolved). A partial correlation analysis showed that older adults' advantage in ratings could be completely accounted for by their more consistent use of the high-point form, suggesting that structure was what made their narratives more compelling. In a similar vein, Kemper, Rash, Kynette, and Norman (1990) studied the structural complexity of narrative form and of the text-base in stories told by adults ranging in age from 60 to 90 years. Older adults' stories showed greater structural complexity with respect to the narrative. Clausal density, syntactic complexity, and cohesion declined with age but only for the more narratively complex stories, suggesting that the decline in the quality of the text-based presentation could be the result of a trade-off within a limited-capacity working memory.

Another feature of effective storytelling is engaging the listener by varying the affective tone and, Dear Reader, by directly addressing the person to whom the story is being told. One recent study suggests that older adults may be particularly adept at such strategies. Carstensen (1998) described a study conducted by Pasupathi, Carstensen, and Henry in which they observed younger and older adults telling stories to a child. Older adults were more likely than younger adults to use more "together" pronouns (e.g., "we" and "let's") and to directly address the child during the story. Some older adults showed more attention to the emotional aspects of the story than did the younger adults, but this was restricted by ethnic group, thus providing only partial support for the emotionality hypothesis.

In a sense, one could think about telling a story as a multitask situation, in which the teller must do three things at once: produce a compelling narrative structure, convey this structure in understandable prose that is syntactically parsable and referentially coherent, and monitor the listener and make adjustments so as to keep the listener involved. Given the age-related declines in processing capacity considered above, the older storyteller faces a choice about how to allocate limited resources among these aspects of telling the story. This fledgling literature to date suggests that we may become more effective storytellers as we age because we reallocate resources from text-base aspects of production (which, within a normal range, are less essential for a good story) to the structural aspects of the narrative and the interpersonal connection with the listener—elements that are critical to effective storytelling.

Collaborative Communication. Another blossoming area of research on age differences in the social interactive function of discourse deals with how people work together to effectively communicate. The classic paradigm for studying collaborative communication between two individuals is the referential communication task. In one version of this task, a dyad is separated by a partition; one member is given an array of ambiguous shapes in a particular arrangement and must communicate to the other member (who is given the same objects) so that he or she can re-create the same arrangement on the other side of the partition. The ability to accomplish this task depends on the participants developing a common set of references for the ambiguous objects, so that an arrangement can then be conveyed (e.g., "the waiter goes on top of the boat" instead of "the thingy goes on top of the doohickey"). The establishment of common referential ground is measured as a decrease in word length and in the number of conversational turns across trials.

Hupet, Chantraine, and Nef (1993) used this paradigm to compare young and elderly dyads' communication. The older adults, who started with more and longer turns than the young adults, showed a parallel decrease across trials to the young adults, but their dialogue never reached the same level of efficiency. Older adults were less likely to adopt the reference of the partner and were more idiosyncratic in proposing references. This suggested to Hupet et al. that the age difference in efficiency was attributable to the older adults' inability to inhibit ineffective and personally generated references.

Another variety of collaborative communication is that which occurs when individuals work together to convey a story or a memory to a third party (Dixon & Gould, 1996). Perhaps the most basic question that one could have from such a situation is whether the age deficits in discourse memory often observed among individuals are reduced in a collaborative situation. There is some evidence that this may be the case when the collaborators know each other very well (Dixon & Gould, 1996; Gould, Kurzman, & Dixon, 1994). Gould et al. had younger and older adults recall novel stories in dyads, with half the dyads being married couples and the other half being newly acquainted for the experiment. Gould et al. not only scored total propositional recall of the texts but also the quantity of dialogue used for reporting recall, discussing task and strategy, and providing support or indicating sociability.

All four groups in this study started sessions with strong bursts of individual recall; as individual recall declined, the proportion of dialogue devoted to task–strategy and sociability–support increased. The increase in task–strategy discussion was greater for married couples (from both age groups), which is interesting because it suggests that people with a common history are better able to devote resources to developing strategy toward problem solution. Also, older adults, especially those from the unacquainted dyads, increased the amount of dialogue devoted to sociability and support.

What makes this off-the-story dialogue interesting is that it seemed to be functional for the elderly adults but not for the young adults. First, the overall amount of extranarrative dialogue was positively related to recall performance among the old adults but not among the young adults, suggesting that it served a supportive function for older collaborators. Second, among the old adults, the quantity of task–strategy dialogue was positively related to recall, but the quantity of sociability–support dialogue was negatively related to performance. Thus, older married couples were unique in terms of both allocating their resources to the type of dialogue that can optimize performance (task–strategy discussion) and being able to take advantage of it. So it seems that collaboration may either be helpful or detrimental for older adults, depending on the quality of the relationship between the collaborators.

The Cognitive Function of Language

Even though the function of language may shift in later adulthood in service to social emotional goals, the cognitive function of language is still critical to survival. We consider how age differences in language processing can affec: ~ur ability to follow instructions and to make decisions.

Understanding Instructions. It is not uncommon for any reasonably intelligent adult to feel as though the limits of one's cognitive capacity have been reached in assembling objects using the accompanying instructions. A familiar object like a barbecue grill, a computer desk, or a bicycle can become an unrecognizable morass of parts as one tries to join the long side of Part B to the short side of Part C while making sure the unfinished side of Part B faces away from the predrilled holes of Part A. Sometimes such instructions are accompanied by pictures, and sometimes they are not. It has been shown that for younger adults, pictures that accompany text can facilitate building a mental model (Glenberg & Langston, 1992), the essential element often sorely lacking as we struggle with the assembly.

Age differences in the ability to construct objects from procedural texts and the effects of accompanying pictures have been explored by Morrell and Park (1993). They found that older adults made more errors during assembly, with these age differences exacerbated for more difficult constructions. For young and old adults alike, however, the number of errors was reduced when the instructions were presented in both text and pictorial form, suggesting that both age groups took advantage of the pictorial representation to facilitate mental model building.

A serious concern is that older adults may not always adhere to instructions for taking medication (Park & Jones, 1997). Because comprehension is a necessary precondition for adherence, several recent studies have focused on the conditions that enhance comprehension and memory for medical instructions. These studies have shown that younger and older adults share the same schema for medication instructions (e.g., name and purpose of medication grouped together, side effects grouped together), and they benefit similarly when medication instructions are organized so as to be consistent with this schema (Morrow, Leirer, Andrassy, Tanke, & Stine-Morrow, 1996). The literature on the usefulness of icons is somewhat more complicated. Whereas some research has shown that younger adults benefit more from icons than do older adults (Morrell, Park, & Poon, 1990), other research has demonstrated that both age groups benefit equally (Morrow, Hier, Menard, & Leirer, 1998).

An important factor mediating the icon effect may be the extent to which icon information is easily integrated. To the extent that icon information is cohesive (e.g., a time line depicting the times and doses of medication; Morrow et al., 1998) and easily integrated with written instructions, it may promote the construction of a situation model for the daily medication regimen and, hence, be more useful to older adults. Such icons appear to be useful when they make explicit some information that is only implicit in the text (e.g., total daily dose).

Problem Solving. Adulthood is said to be a time of reasoning in the face of uncertainty (Baltes & Staudinger, 1993). Selecting the appropriate day-care arrangements for one's children or one's parents, making wise career moves, making financial arrangements for a secure retirement, and selecting treatment options in the face of a grave illness all require that the individual consider information about different options and then make a choice. Very often this information is presented in the format of text. Several studies have explored age differences in this process. For example, B. J. F. Meyer and colleagues (B. J. F. Meyer, Russo, & Talbot, 1995; Meyer & Talbot, 1998) have reported that in using texts about breast cancer to make a decision about treatment, older adults spent less time processing the information in the text than the young adults, and yet individuals from the different age groups arrived at qualitatively similar decisions. A similar sort of finding has been reported by Walsh and Hershey (1993) in regard to financial planning. Meyer and Talbot (1998) argued that this is attributable to a greater top-down processing among old adults, who rely more on what they already know and so attend less thoroughly to the new information presented. This is an interesting hypothesis that deserves further testing.

Speech Adjustments to Elders: Elderspeak

A research topic that cuts across both social and the cognitive uses of language concerns the extent to which speakers modulate their language in their encounters with elderly adults. The term *elderspeak* was coined by Cohen and Faulkner (1986a), who noted that elderly adults are often spoken to in a manner that is often used with young children. As shown in data from a study by Kemper (1994) (see Table 6.1), this is a speech pattern characterized by, among other things, an exaggerated intonation, slower speech rate, shortened utterances, and simplified vocabulary. In this study, Kemper examined how service providers (who had histories of working with healthy community-dwelling elderly adults) and care providers (who had histories of working with frail elderly adults) addressed young and older adults. She found that regardless of the type of elderly adults with whom the speakers had previous experience, they simplified their speech to a similar extent.

Elderspeak is something of a double-edged sword. On the one hand, such speech accommodations can sometimes facilitate comprehension

TABLE 6.1
Characteristics of Elderspeak (adapted from Kemper, 1994)

Characteristic	Audience	
	Younger	Older
No. of clauses (per utterance)	1.7	1.0
Length of utterance (words)	16.5	8.6
Left-branching constructions (% utterances)	19.5	10.0
Fillers (no. per 100 words)	18.0	31.0
Fragments (% utterances)	21.5	28.0
Cohesive ties (no. per 100 words)	23.0	13.5
Long words (% words)	6.0	<1.0
Repetitions (% utterances)	13.0	32.0
Speech rate (wpm)	122.0	99.0
Total duration of all pauses (s/min)	13.0	25.5

Note. wpm = words per minute.

among older adults in the face of processing declines. As we have shown, older adults take special advantage of stress patterns in memory for speech (Cohen & Faulkner, 1986a) and of prosodic contour in parsing sentences (Wingfield et al., 1992). Finally, they also differentially benefit as speech rate is decreased (Stine et al., 1986). On the other hand, speech that crosses the line of simplicity and exaggerated prosody can be perceived as patronizing, reflecting negative stereotypes about aging that often provoke speakers to communicate in a way that makes these negative inferences painfully clear (Ryan, Giles, Bartolucci, & Henwood, 1986). Indeed, these kinds of speech adjustments are judged to be less respectful (Ryan, Bourhis, & Knops, 1991). Furthermore, to the extent that the elderly adult is chronically faced with simplified speech, there may be less of an environmental demand (or "press") for more sophisticated dialogue. It has been suggested that the internalization of negative stereotypes and the very real reduction in environmental press magnifies declines in communicative competence. This conflict between the benefits and pitfalls of linguistic accommodation has been termed the *communicative predicament of aging* (Ryan et al., 1986). The balance between accommodating speech patterns to the listener and the risk of introducing a demeaning or patronizing tone is thus a delicate one.

DIRECTIONS FOR FUTURE RESEARCH

There are many areas in which research on language and aging needs to be done for both practical and theoretical ends. We would like to highlight several examples.

Research on age differences at the stimulus input level as cited in this chapter has begun to show how resources devoted to stimulus recognition may deplete resources necessary for higher level functions, just as resources dedicated to higher level functions may lead to reduced effectiveness in initial stimulus encoding. We see the need for continued progress in understanding how sensory loss may interact with these factors and the ways in which contextual and structural support may help in remediation.

There is need for further exploration of the mechanisms underlying the ways in which contextual and structural support can minimize age differences. Older adults take good, and sometimes better, advantage of such supports when available; however, in many cases, such as in construction of a causal network, the availability of such supports depends on the expenditure of processing resources. We need to know the factors that may promote the productive allocation of resources for construction of situation models that can, in turn, promote comprehension and problem solving from spoken or written text.

As indicated in our review, the bulk of studies conducted on age differences in discourse processing and the development of situation models have used reading times to measure resource allocation and processing differences among young and elderly adults. A distinguishing feature of spoken language is the presence of prosody, a feature that has been shown to aid young and elderly adults in detecting speech structure at the sentence and text-base level. There has been little research on the use of prosodic information as it may be used to aid in higher level comprehension processes, such as the development and updating of situation models. We encourage the use of self-paced reading and analogous self-paced listening studies to explore parallels and contrasts between processing for comprehension and memory in these two input domains.

There is a further need in aging research for studies of the causal links between the appearance of simplified language in early adulthood and severe cognitive declines that appear in later adulthood. Specifically, it is important to determine whether simplified language use in young adulthood may be a marker for global processing declines that are already under way or whether there is an environmental press or a "habit of mind" in youth that leads to preservation or deterioration of cognitive efficacy in later life.

Although there is general agreement in the literature that transient memory traces are necessary for effective language comprehension, less is known about the kinds of representations that may be involved. There is a need for continued efforts in delineating the nature of the memory representations that arise at different levels of the processing hierarchy and determining which of these are more or less vulnerable in adult aging. We believe that continued study of language processing in neurological patients with dissociable memory deficits may be especially useful in this regard. Our last point expresses our belief in the need to move beyond global accounts of processing limitations to a more careful specification of cognitive systems that underlie language processing in the aging adult.

ACKNOWLEDGMENTS

The authors acknowledge support from Grants R37 AG04517 and RO1 AG13935 from the National Institute on Aging. The authors also acknowledge support from the W. M. Keck Foundation.

REFERENCES

Aaronson, D., & Ferres, S. (1984). The word-by-word reading paradigm: An experimental and theoretical approach. In D. E. Kieras & M. A. Just (Eds.), *New methods in reading comprehension research* (pp. 31–68). Hillsdale, NJ: Lawrence Erlbaum Associates.

Aaronson, D., & Scarborough, H. S. (1976). Performance theories for sentence coding: Some qualitative evidence. *Journal of Experimental Psychology: Human Perception and Performance, 2,* 56–70.

Adams, C. (1991). Qualitative age differences in memory for text: A life-span developmental perspective. *Psychology and Aging, 6,* 323–336.

Adams, C., Smith, M. C., Nyquist, L., & Perlmutter, M. (1997). Adult age-group differences in recall for the literal and interpretive meanings of narrative text. *Journal of Gerontology: Psychological Sciences, 52B,* P187–P195.

Akutsu, H., Legge, G. E., Ross, J. A., & Schuebel, K. J. (1991). Psychophysics of reading X. Effects of age related changes in vision. *Journal of Gerontology: Psychological Science, 46,* P325–P331.

Allen, P. A., Madden, D. J., & Slane, S. (1995). Visual word encoding and the effect of adult age and word frequency. In P. A. Allen & T. R. Bashore (Eds.), *Age differences in word and language processing* (pp. 30–71). New York: Elsevier.

Allen, P. A., Madden, D. J., Weber, T. A., & Groth, K. E. (1993). Influence of age and processing stage on visual word recognition. *Psychology and Aging, 8,* 274–282.

Anderson, J. R. (1983). *The architecture of cognition.* Cambridge, MA: Harvard University Press.

Atkinson, R. C., & Shiffrin, R. M. (1968). Human memory: A proposed system and its control processes. In K. W. Spence & J. T. Spence (Eds.), *The psychology of learning and motivation: Advances in research and theory* (Vol. 2, pp. 89–195). New York: Academic Press.

Au, R., Joung, P., Nicholas, M., Kass, R., Obler, L. K., & Albert, M. L. (1995). Naming ability across the lifespan. *Aging and Cognition, 2,* 300–311.

Bäckman, L., & Dixon, R. A. (1992). Psychological compensation: A theoretical framework. *Psychological Bulletin, 112,* 259–283.

Baddeley, A. D. (1986). *Working memory.* Oxford, England: Oxford University Press.

Balota, D. A., & Black, S. (1997). Semantic satiation in healthy young and older adults. *Memory and Cognition, 25,* 190–202.

Balota, D. A., Black, S. R., & Cheney, M. (1992). Automatic and attentional priming in young and older adults: Reevaluation of the two-process model. *Journal of Experimental Psychology: Human Perception and Performance, 18,* 485–502.

Balota, D. A., & Duchek, J. M. (1988). Age-related differences in lexical access, spreading activation, and simple pronunciation. *Psychology and Aging, 3,* 84–93.

Baltes, P. B., & Staudinger, U. M. (1993). The search for a psychology of wisdom. *Current Directions in Psychological Science, 2,* 75–80.

Botwinick, J. (1977). Intellectual abilities. In J. Birren & K. W. Schaie (Eds.), *Handbook of the psychology of aging* (pp. 580–605). New York: Van Nostrand Reinhold.

Bowles, N. L., & Poon, L. W. (1985). Aging and retrieval of words in semantic memory. *Journal of Gerontology, 40,* 71–77.

Broadbent, D. E. (1971). *Decision and stress.* New York: Academic Press.

Brown, A. S. (1991). A review of the tip-of-the-tongue experience. *Psychological Review, 9,* 204–223.

Brown, A. S., & Mitchell, D. B. (1991). Age differences in retrieval consistency and response dominance. *Journal of Gerontology, 46,* 332–339.

Brown, R., & McNeill, D. (1966). The "tip of the tongue" phenomenon. *Journal of Verbal Learning and Verbal Behavior, 5,* 325–337.

Burke, D. M. (1997). Language, aging, and inhibitory deficits: Evaluation of a theory. *Journal of Gerontology: Psychological Sciences, 52B,* P254–P264.

Burke, D. M., & Harrold, R. M. (1988). Approaches to the study of memory and language in old age. In L. L. Light & D. M. Burke (Eds.), *Language, memory, and aging* (pp. 100–116). New York: Cambridge University Press.

Burke, D. M., MacKay, D. G., Worthley, J. B., & Wade, E. D. (1991). On the tip of the tongue: What causes word-finding failure in young and older adults? *Journal of Memory and Language, 30,* 237–246.

Burke, D. M., & Peters, L. (1986). Word associations in old age: Evidence for consistency in semantic encoding during adulthood. *Psychology and Aging, 1,* 283–292.

Burke, D. M., White, H., & Diaz, D. (1987). Semantic priming in younger and older adults: Evidence for age consistency in automatic and attentional processes. *Journal of Experimental Psychology: Human Perception and Performance, 13,* 79–88.

Caplan, D., & Waters, G. S. (1999). Verbal working memory and sentence comprehension. *Behavioral and Brain Sciences, 22,* 77–126.

Carlson, M. C., Hasher, L., Connelly, S. L., & Zacks, R. T. (1995). Aging, distraction and the benefits of predictable location. *Psychology and Aging, 10,* 427–436.

Carpenter, P. A., & Just, M. A. (1989). The role of working memory in language comprehension. In D. Klahr & K. Kotovsky (Eds.), *Complex information processing: The impact of Herbert A. Simon* (pp. 31–68). Hillsdale, NJ: Lawrence Erlbaum Associates.

Carpenter, P. A., Miyaki, A., & Just, M. A. (1994). Working memory constraints in comprehension: Evidence from individual differences, aphasia, and aging. In M. Gernsbacher (Ed.), *Handbook of psycholinguistics* (pp. 1075–1122). San Diego, CA: Academic Press.

Carstensen, L. L. (1995). Evidence for a life-span theory of socioemotional selectivity. *Current Directions in Psychological Science, 4,* 151–156.

Carstensen, L. L. (1998). A life-span approach to social motivation. In J. Heckhausen & C. Dweck (Eds.), *Motivation and self-regulation across the life span* (pp. 341–364). New York: Cambridge University Press.

Carstensen, L. L., & Turk-Charles, S. (1994). The salience of emotion across the adult life-span. *Psychology and Aging, 9,* 259–264.

Carver, R. P. (1982). Optimal rate of reading prose. *Reading Research Quarterly, 18,* 56–58.

Cohen, G., & Faulkner, D. (1986a). Does "elderspeak" work? The effect of intonation and stress on comprehension and recall of spoken discourse in old age. *Language and Communication, 6,* 91–98.

Cohen, G., & Faulkner, D. (1986b). Memory for proper names: Age differences in retrieval. *British Journal of Developmental Psychology, 4,* 187–197.

Connelly, S. L., Hasher, L., & Zacks, R. T. (1991). Age and reading: The impact of distraction. *Psychology and Aging, 6*, 533–541.

Cooper, P. V. (1990). Discourse production and normal aging: Performance on oral picture description tasks. *Journal of Gerontology, 45*, 210–214.

Craig, C. H. (1992). Effects of aging on time-gated isolated word-recognition performance. *Journal of Speech and Hearing Research, 35*, 234–238.

Craig, C. H., Kim, B. W., Rhyner, P. M. P., & Chirillo, T. K. B. (1993). Effects of word predictability, child development, and aging on time-gated speech recognition performance. *Journal of Speech and Hearing Research, 36*, 832–841.

Cronin-Golomb, A., Corkin, S., & Rizzo, J. F. (1991). Visual dysfunction in Alzheimer's disease: Relation to normal aging. *Annals of Neurology, 29*, 41–52.

Daneman, M., & Merikle, P. M. (1996). Working memory and language comprehension: A meta-analysis. *Psychonomic Bulletin and Review, 3*, 422–433.

Dixon, R. A., & Bäckman, L. (1995). Concepts of compensation: Integrated, differentiated, and Janus-faced. In R. A. Dixon & L. Bäckman (Eds.), *Compensating for psychological deficits and declines: Managing losses and promoting gains* (pp. 3–19). Mahwah, NJ: Lawrence Erlbaum Associates.

Dixon, R. A., & Gould, O. N. (1996). Adults telling and retelling stories collaboratively. In P. B. Baltes & U. M. Staudinger (Eds.), *Interactive minds: Life-span perspectives on the social foundation of cognition* (pp. 221–241). Cambridge, England: Cambridge University Press.

Dixon, R. A., Hultsch, D. F., Simon, E. W., & von Eye, A. (1984). Verbal ability and text structure effects on age differences in text recall. *Journal of Verbal Learning and Verbal Behavior, 37*, 358–364.

Dixon, R. A., Simon, E. W., Nowak, C. A., & Hultsch, D. F. (1982). Text recall in adulthood as a function of level of information, input modality, and delay interval. *Journal of Gerontology, 37*, 358–364.

Duchek, J. M., & Balota, D. A. (1993). Sparing activation processes in older adults. In J. Cerella, J. Rybash, W. Hoyer, & M. L. Commons (Eds.), *Adult information processing: Limits on loss* (pp. 383–406). San Diego, CA: Academic Press.

Dunlosky, J., & Connor, L. T. (1997). Age differences in the allocation of study time account for age differences in memory performance. *Memory and Cognition, 25*, 691–700.

Ferreira, F., Henderson, J. M., Anes, M. D., Weeks, P. A., & McFarlane, M. D. (1996). Effects of lexical frequency and syntactic complexity in spoken-language comprehension: Evidence from the auditory moving-window technique. *Journal of Experimental Psychology: Learning, Memory, and Cognition, 22*, 324–335.

Fleming, K. K. (1993). Phonologically mediated priming in spoken and printed word recognition. *Journal of Experimental Psychology: Learning, Memory, and Cognition, 19*, 272–284.

Foulke, E. (1971). The perception of time compressed speech. In D. L. Horton & J. J. Jenkins (Eds.), *The perception of language* (pp. 79–107). Columbus, OH: Merrill.

Frazier, L. (1987). Sentence processing: A tutorial review. In M. Coltheart (Ed.), *Attention and performance: XII* (pp. 559–586). Hillsdale, NJ: Lawrence Erlbaum Associates.

Fromkin, V., & Ratner, N. B. (1998). Speech production. In J. B. Gleason & N. B. Ratner (Eds.), *Psycholinguistics* (2nd ed., pp. 309–346). Forth Worth, TX: Harcourt Brace.

Garnham, A. (1981). Mental models as representations of text. *Memory and Cognition, 9*, 560–565.

Gerard, L. D., Zacks, R. T., Hasher, R. T., & Radvansky, G. A. (1991). Age deficits in retrieval: The fan effect. *Journal of Gerontology, 46*, 131–136.

Gerrig, R. J. (1993). *Experiencing narrative worlds.* New Haven, CT: Yale University Press.

Glanzer, M., Dorfman, D., & Kaplan, B. (1981). Short-term storage in the processing of text. *Journal of Verbal Learning and Verbal Behavior, 20*, 656–670.

Glenberg, A. M., & Langston, W. (1992). Comprehension of illustrated text: Pictures help to build mental models. *Journal of Memory and Language, 31*, 129–151.

Goldman-Eisler, F. (1968). *Psycholinguistics: Experiments in spontaneous speech.* New York: Academic Press.

Gordon-Salant, S., & Fitzgibbons, P. J. (1993). Temporal factors and speech recognition performance in young and elderly listeners. *Journal of Speech and Hearing Research, 36,* 1276–1285.

Gordon-Salant, S., & Fitzgibbons, P. J. (1997). Selected cognitive factors and speech recognition performance among young and elderly listeners. *Journal of Speech, Language, and Hearing Research, 40,* 423–431.

Gould, O. N., Kurzman, D., & Dixon, R. A. (1994). Communication during prose recall conversations by young and old dyads. *Discourse Processes, 17,* 149–165.

Gow, D. W., & Gordon, P. C. (1995). Lexical and prelexical influences on word segmentation: Evidence from priming. *Journal of Experimental Psychology: Human Perception and Performance, 21,* 344–359.

Grosjean, F. (1980). Spoken word recognition processes and the gating paradigm. *Perception and Psychophysics, 38,* 299–310.

Grosjean, F. (1985). The recognition of words after their acoustic offset: Evidence and implications. *Perception and Psychophysics, 38,* 299–310.

Grosjean, F. (1996). Gating. *Language and Cognitive Processes, 11,* 597–604.

Haberlandt, K. F., Graesser, A. C., Schneider, N. J., & Kiely, J. (1986). Effects of task and new arguments on word reading times. *Journal of Memory and Language, 25,* 314–322.

Hamm, V. P., & Hasher, L. (1992). Age and the availability of inferences. *Psychology and Aging, 7,* 56–64.

Hartley, J. T. (1993). Aging and prose memory: Tests of the resource-deficit hypothesis. *Psychology and Aging, 8,* 538–551.

Hartley, J. T., Stojack, C. C., Mushaney, T. J., Annon, T. A. K., & Lee, D. W. (1994). Reading speed and prose memory in older and younger adults. *Psychology and Aging, 9,* 216–223.

Hasher, L., & Zacks, R. T. (1988). Working memory, comprehension, and aging: A review and a new view. In G. H. Bower (Ed.), *The psychology of learning and motivation: Advances in research and theory* (Vol. 22, pp. 193–225). San Diego, CA: Academic Press.

Heller, R. B., & Dobbs, A. R. (1993). Age differences in word finding in discourse and nondiscourse situations. *Psychology and Aging, 8,* 443–450.

Hess, T. M. (1990). Aging and schematic influences on memory. In T. M. Hess (Ed.), *Aging and cognition: Knowledge organization and utilization* (pp. 93–160). Amsterdam: North-Holland.

Hess, T. M. (1995). Aging and the impact of causal connections on text comprehension and memory. *Aging and Cognition, 2,* 216–230.

Holtzman, R. E., Familitant, E., Deptula, P., & Hoyer, W. J. (1986). Aging and the use of sentential structure to facilitate word recognition. *Experimental Aging Research, 12,* 85–88.

Howard, D. V. (1980). Category norms: A comparison of the Battig and Montague (1969) norms with the responses of adults between the ages of 20 and 80. *Journal of Gerontology, 35,* 225–231.

Howard, D. V. (1983). The effects of aging and degree of association on the semantic priming of lexical decisions. *Experimental Aging Research, 9,* 145–151.

Howard, D. V., Shaw, R. J., & Heisey, J. J. (1986). Aging and the time course of semantic activation. *Journal of Gerontology, 41,* 195–203.

Hultsch, D. F., & Dixon, R. A. (1983). The role of pre-experimental knowledge in text processing in adulthood. *Experimental Aging Research, 9,* 17–22.

Hultsch, D. F., Hertzog, C., Small, B. J., McDonald-Miszczak, L., & Dixon, R. A. (1992). Short-term longitudinal change in cognitive performance in later life. *Psychology and Aging, 7,* 571–584.

Hupet, M., Chantraine, Y., & Nef, F. (1993). References in conversation between young and old normal adults. *Psychology and Aging, 8,* 339–346.

James, W. (1893). *The principles of psychology: Vol. 1.* New York: Holt.

Jarvella, R. J. (1971). Syntactic processing of connected speech. *Journal of Verbal Learning and Verbal Behavior, 10,* 409–416.

Johnson-Laird, P. N. (1983). *Mental models.* Cambridge, MA: Harvard University Press.

Just, M. A., & Carpenter, P. A. (1980). A theory of reading: From eye fixations to comprehension. *Psychological Review, 87,* 329–354.

Just, M. A., & Carpenter, P. A. (1987). *The psychology of reading and language comprehension.* Boston: Allyn & Bacon.

Just, M. A., & Carpenter, P. A. (1992). A capacity theory of comprehension: Individual differences in working memory. *Psychological Review, 99,* 122–149.

Kahneman, D. (1973). *Attention and effort.* Englewood Cliffs, NJ: Prentice-Hall.

Kemper, S. (1986). Imitation of complex syntactic constructions by elderly adults. *Applied Psycholinguistics, 7,* 277–288.

Kemper, S. (1987a). Life span changes in syntactic complexity. *Journal of Gerontology, 42,* 323–328.

Kemper, S. (1987b). Syntactic complexity and elderly adults' prose recall. *Experimental Aging Research, 13,* 47–52.

Kemper, S. (1992). Language and aging. In F. I. M. Craik & T. A. Salthouse (Eds.), *Handbook of aging and cognition* (pp. 213–270). Hillsdale, NJ: Lawrence Erlbaum Associates.

Kemper, S. (1994). Elderspeak: Speech accommodations to older adults. *Aging and Cognition, 1,* 17–28.

Kemper, S. (1997). Metalinguistic judgments in normal aging and Alzheimer's disease. *Journal of Gerontology: Psychological Sciences, 52B,* P147–P155.

Kemper, S., LaBerge, E., Ferraro, R., Cheung, H. T., Cheung, H., & Storandt, M. (1993). On the preservation of syntax in Alzheimer's disease: Evidence from written sentences. *Archives of Neurology, 50,* 81–86.

Kemper, S., Rash, S., Kynette, D., & Norman, S. (1990). Telling stories: The structure of adults' narratives. *European Journal of Cognitive Psychology, 2,* 205–228.

Kempler, D., & Zelinski, E. M. (1994). Language in dementia and normal aging. In F. A. Huppert, C. Brayne, & D. W. O'Connor (Eds.), *Dementia and normal aging* (pp. 331–365). New York: Cambridge University Press.

Kemtes, K. A., & Kemper, S. (1997). Younger and older adults' on-line processing of syntactically ambiguous sentences. *Psychology and Aging, 12,* 362–371.

Kintsch, W. (1988). The role of knowledge in discourse comprehension: A construction–integration model. *Psychological Review, 95,* 163–182.

Kintsch, W. (1994). Text comprehension, memory, and learning. *American Psychologist, 49,* 294–303.

Kintsch, W., & van Dijk, T. A. (1978). Toward a model of text comprehension and production. *Psychological Review, 85,* 363–394.

Kjelgaard, M. M., Titone, D., & Wingfield, A. (1999). The influence of prosodic structure on the interpretation of temporary syntactic ambiguity by young and elderly listeners. *Experimental Aging Research, 25,* 1–21.

Kohn, S. E., Wingfield, A., Menn, L., Goodglass, H., Gleason, J. B., & Hyde, M. (1987). Lexical retrieval: The tip-of-the-tongue phenomenon. *Applied Psycholinguistics, 8,* 245–266.

Kwong See, S. T., & Ryan, E. (1995). Cognitive mediation of adult age differences in language performance. *Psychology and Aging, 10,* 458–468.

LaBerge, E., Balota, D. A., Storandt, M., & Smith, D. S. (1992). An analysis of confrontation naming errors in senile dementia of the Alzheimer type. *Neuropsychology, 6,* 77–95.

Laver, G., & Burke, D. (1993). Why do semantic priming effects increase in old age? A meta-analysis. *Psychology and Aging, 8,* 34–43.

Lesch, M. F., & Pollatsek, A. (1993). Automatic access of semantic information by phonological codes in visual word recognition. *Journal of Experimental Psychology: Learning, Memory, and Cognition, 19,* 285–294.

Levelt, W. J. M. (1989). *Speaking: From intention to articulation.* Cambridge, MA: MIT Press.

Light, L. L. (1991). Memory and aging: Four hypotheses in search of data. *Annual Review of Psychology, 42,* 333–376.

Light, L. L., & Capps, J. L. (1986). Comprehension of pronouns in young and older adults. *Developmental Psychology, 22,* 580–585.

Light, L. L., Capps, J. L., Singh, A., & Owens, S. A. A. (1994). Comprehension and use of anaphoric devices in young and older adults. *Discourse Processes, 18,* 77–104.

Light, L. L., Owens, S. A., Mahoney, P. G., & LaVoie, D. (1993). Comprehension of metaphors by young and older adults. In J. Cerella, W. Hoyer, J. Rybash, & M. L. Commons (Eds.), *Adult information processing: Limits on loss* (pp. 459–488). New York: Academic Press.

Light, L. L., Valencia-Laver, D., & Zavis, D. (1991). Instantiation of general terms in young and old adults. *Psychology and Aging, 6,* 337–351.

Luce, P. A., Pisoni, D. B., & Goldinger, S. D. (1990). Similarity neighborhoods of spoken words. In G. T. Altmann (Ed.), *Cognitive models of speech processing: Psycholinguistic and computational perspectives* (pp. 122–147). Cambridge, MA: MIT Press.

MacDonald, M. C., Just, M. A., & Carpenter, P. A. (1992). Working memory constraints on the processing of syntactic ambiguity. *Cognitive Psychology, 24,* 56–98.

Madden, D. J. (1988). Adult age differences in the effects of sentence context and stimulus degradation during visual word recognition. *Psychology and Aging, 3,* 167–172.

Madden, D. J. (1992). Four to ten milliseconds per year: Age-related slowing of visual word identification. *Journal of Gerontology: Psychological Sciences, 47,* P59–P68.

Madden, D. J., Pierce, T., & Allen, P. A. (1993). Age-related slowing and the time course of semantic priming in visual word identification. *Psychology and Aging, 8,* 490–507.

Marshall, N. B., Duke, L. W., & Walley, A. C. (1996). Effects of age and Alzheimer's disease on recognition of gated spoken words. *Journal of Speech and Hearing Research, 39,* 724–733.

Marslen-Wilson, W. D. (1987). Functional parallelism in spoken word recognition. *Cognition, 25,* 71–102.

Marslen-Wilson, W. D. (1990). Activation, competition, and frequency in lexical access. In G. T. M. Altmann (Ed.), *Cognitive models of speech processing* (pp. 148–172). Cambridge, MA: MIT Press.

Mattys, S. L. (1997). The use of time during lexical processing and segmentation: A review. *Psychonomic Bulletin and Review, 4,* 310–329.

Maylor, E. A. (1990). Recognizing and naming faces: Aging, memory retrieval, and the tip of the tongue state. *Journal of Gerontology, 45,* 215–226.

Maylor, E. A. (1997). Proper name retrieval in old age: Converging evidence against disproportionate impairment. *Aging and Cognition, 4,* 211–226.

Mergler, N., Faust, M., & Goldstein, M. (1985). Storytelling as an age-dependent skill. *International Journal of Aging and Human Development, 20,* 205–228.

Meyer, B. J. F. (1999). Importance of text structure in everyday reading. In A. Ram & K. Moorman (Eds.), *Understanding language understanding: Computational models of reading* (pp. 227–253). Cambridge, MA: MIT Press.

Meyer, B. J. F., Russo, C., & Talbot, A. (1995). Discourse comprehension and problem solving: Decisions about the treatment of breast cancer by women across the life-span. *Psychology and Aging, 10,* 84–103.

Meyer, B. J. F., & Talbot, A. P. (1998). Adult age differences in reading and remembering text and using this information to make decisions in everyday life. In M. C. Smith & T. Pourchot (Eds.), *Adult learning and development: Perspectives from educational psychology* (pp. 179–200). Hillsdale, NJ: Lawrence Erlbaum Associates.

Meyer, D. E., & Schvaneveldt, R. W. (1971). Facilitation in recognizing pairs of words: Evidence of a dependence between retrieval operations. *Journal of Experimental Psychology, 90*, 227–234.

Miller, L. M. S., & Stine-Morrow, E. A. L. (1998). Aging and the effects of knowledge on on-line reading strategies. *Journal of Gerontology: Psychological Sciences, 53B*, 223–233.

Morrell, R. W., & Park, D. C. (1993). The effects of age, illustrations, and task variables on the performance of procedural assembly tasks. *Psychology and Aging, 8*, 389–399.

Morrell, R. W., Park, D. C., & Poon, L. W. (1990). Effects of labeling techniques on memory and comprehension of prescription information in young and old adults. *Journal of Gerontology: Psychological Sciences, 45*, P166–P172.

Morrow, D. G., Greenspan, S. L., & Bower, G. H. (1987). Accessibility and situation models in narrative comprehension. *Journal of Memory and Language, 26*, 165–187.

Morrow, D. G., Hier, C. M., Menard, W. E., & Leirer, V. O. (1998). Icons improve older and younger adult comprehension of medication information. *Journal of Gerontology: Psychological Sciences, 53B*, 240–254.

Morrow, D. G., Leirer, V., Altieri, P., & Fitzsimmons, P. (1994). Age differences in updating situation models from narratives. *Language and Cognitive Processes, 9*, 203–220.

Morrow, D. G., Leirer, V. O., Andrassy, J. M., Tanke, E. D., & Stine-Morrow, E. A. L. (1996). Medication instruction design: Younger and older adult schemas for taking medication. *Human Factors, 38*, 556–573.

Morrow, D. G., Stine-Morrow, E. A. L., Leirer, V. O., Andrassy, J. M., & Kahn, J. (1997). The role of reader age and focus of attention in creating situation models from narratives. *Journal of Gerontology: Psychological Sciences, 52B*, P73–P80.

Morton, J. (1969). Interaction of information in word recognition. *Psychological Review, 76*, 165–178.

Mullennix, J. W., Pisoni, D. B., & Martin, C. S. (1989). Some effects of talker variability on spoken word recognition. *Journal of the Acoustical Society of America, 85*, 365–372.

Myers, J. L., & Duffy, S. A. (1990). Causal inferences and text memory. In A. C. Graesser & G. H. Bower (Eds.), *Inferences and text comprehension* (pp. 159–173). New York: Academic Press.

Nebes, R. D., & Brady, C. B. (1990). Preserved organization of semantic attributes in Alzheimer's disease. *Psychology and Aging, 5*, 574–579.

Neisser, U. (1982). John Dean's memory: A case study. In U. Neisser (Ed.), *Memory observed: Remembering in natural contexts* (pp. 139–159). New York: Freeman.

Nicholas, M., Barth, C., Obler, L. K., Au, R., & Albert, M. L. (1997). Naming in normal aging and dementia of the Alzheimer's type. In H. Goodglass & A. Wingfield (Eds.), *Anomia: Neuroanatomical and cognitive correlates* (pp. 166–188). San Diego, CA: Academic Press.

Norman, S., Kemper, S., & Kynette, D. (1992). Adults' reading comprehension: Effects of syntactic complexity and working memory. *Journal of Gerontology: Psychological Sciences, 47*, P258–P265.

Park, D. C., & Jones, T. R. (1997). Medication adherence and aging. In A. D. Fisk & W. A. Rogers (Eds.), *Handbook of human factors and the older adult* (pp. 257–287). New York: Academic Press.

Park, D. C., Smith, A. D., Lautenschlager, G., Earles, J. L., Frieski, D., Zwahr, M., & Gaines, C. L. (1996). Mediators of long-term memory performance across the life span. *Psychology and Aging, 11*, 621–637.

Perry, A. R., & Wingfield, A. (1994). Contextual encoding by young and elderly adults as revealed by cued and free recall. *Aging and Cognition, 1*, 120–139.

Pichora-Fuller, M. K., Schneider, B. A., & Daneman, M. (1995). How young and old adults listen to and remember speech in noise. *Journal of the Acoustical Society of America, 97*, 593–607.

Potter, M. C. (1993). Very short-term conceptual memory. *Memory and Cognition, 21*, 156–161.

Pratt, M. W., Boyes, C., Robins, S., & Manchester, J. (1989). Telling tales: Aging, working memory, and the narrative cohesion of story retellings. *Developmental Psychology, 25,* 628–635.

Pratt, M. W., & Robins, S. L. (1991). That's the way it was: Age differences in the structure and quality of adults' personal narratives. *Discourse Processes, 14,* 73–85.

Radvansky, G. A., & Curiel, J. M. (1998). Narrative comprehension and aging: The fact of completed goal information. *Psychology and Aging, 13,* 69–79.

Radvansky, G. A., Gerard, L., Zacks, R., & Hasher, L. (1990). Younger and older adults' use of mental models as representations for text materials. *Psychology and Aging, 5,* 209–214.

Radvansky, G. A., Zacks, R. T., & Hasher, L. (1996). Fact retrieval in younger and older adults: The role of mental models. *Psychology and Aging, 11,* 258–271.

Ratner, H. H., Schell, D., Crimmins, A., Mittelman, D., & Baldinelli, L. (1987). Changes in adults' prose recall: Aging or cognitive demand? *Developmental Psychology, 23,* 521–525.

Reder, L. M., Wible, C., & Martin, J. (1986). Differential memory changes with age: Exact retrieval versus plausible inference. *Journal of Experimental Psychology: Learning, Memory, and Cognition, 12,* 72–81.

Reicher, G. M. (1969). Perceptual recognition as a function of meaningfulness of stimulus material. *Journal of Experimental Psychology, 81,* 274–280.

Rinck, M., & Bower, G. H. (1995). Anaphora resolution and the focus of attention in situation models. *Journal of Memory and Language, 34,* 110–131.

Ryan, E. B., Bourhis, R. Y., & Knops, U. (1991). Evaluative perceptions of patronizing speech addressed to elders. *Psychology and Aging, 6,* 442–450.

Ryan, E. B., Giles, H., Bartolucci, G., & Henwood, K. (1986). Psycholinguistic and social psychological components of communication by and with the elderly. *Language and Communication, 6,* 1–24.

Salthouse, T. A. (1995). Refining the concept of psychological compensation. In R. A. Dixon & L. Bäckman (Eds.), *Compensating for psychological deficits and declines: Managing losses and promoting gains* (pp. 21–34). Mahwah, NJ: Lawrence Erlbaum Associates.

Salthouse, T. A. (1996). The processing-speed theory of adult age differences in cognition. *Psychological Review, 103,* 403–428.

Scheiber, F., & Baldwin, C. L. (1996). Vision, audition, and aging research. In F. Blanchard-Fields & T. M. Hess (Eds.), *Perspectives on cognitive change in adulthood and aging* (pp. 122–162). New York: McGraw-Hill.

Shattuck-Hufnagel, S., & Turk, A. E. (1996). A prosody tutorial for investigators of auditory sentence processing. *Journal of Psycholinguistic Research, 25,* 193–247.

Small, J. A., Kemper, S., & Lyons, K. (1997). Sentence comprehension in Alzheimer's disease: Effects of grammatical complexity, speech rate, and repetition. *Psychology and Aging, 12,* 3–11.

Smith, S., Rebok, G., Smith, W., Hall, S. E., & Alvin, M. (1983). Adult age differences in the use of story structure in delayed free recall. *Experimental Aging Research, 9,* 191–195.

Snowdon, D. A., Kemper, S. J., Mortimer, J. A., Greiner, L. H., Wekstein, D. R., & Markesebery, W. R. (1996). Linguistic ability in early life and cognitive function and Alzheimer's in late life. *JAMA: Journal of the American Medical Association, 275,* 528–532.

Soederberg, L. M., & Stine, E. A. L. (1995). Activation of emotion information in text among younger and older adults. *Journal of Adult Development, 2,* 253–270.

Sommers, M. S. (1996). The structural organization of the mental lexicon and its contribution to age-related declines in spoken-word recognition. *Psychology and Aging, 11,* 333–341.

Stanhope, N., Cohen, G., & Conway, M. (1993). Very long-term retention of a novel. *Applied Cognitive Psychology, 7,* 239–256.

Stine, E. A. L. (1990). On-line processing of written text by younger and older adults. *Psychology and Aging, 5,* 68–78.

Stine, E. A. L. (1995). Aging and the distribution of resources in working memory. In P. Allen & T. Bashore (Eds.), *Age differences in word and language processing* (pp. 171–186). Amsterdam: North-Holland.

Stine, E. A. L., Cheung, H., & Henderson, D. T. (1995). Adult age differences in the on-line processing of new concepts in discourse. *Aging and Cognition, 2,* 1–18.

Stine, E. A. L., & Hindman, J. (1994). Age differences in reading time allocation for propositionally dense sentences. *Aging and Cognition, 1,* 2–16.

Stine, E. A. L., & Wingfield, A. (1987). Process and strategy in memory for speech among younger and older adults. *Psychology and Aging, 2,* 272–279.

Stine, E. A. L., & Wingfield, A. (1988). Memorability functions as an indicator of qualitative age differences in text recall. *Psychology and Aging, 3,* 179–183.

Stine, E. A. L., & Wingfield, A. (1990a). The assessment of qualitative age differences in discourse processing. In T. M. Hess (Ed.), *Aging and cognition: Knowledge organization and utilization* (pp. 33–92). New York: Elsevier.

Stine, E. A. L., & Wingfield, A. (1990b). How much do working memory deficits contribute to age differences in discourse memory? *European Journal of Cognitive Psychology, 2,* 289–304.

Stine, E. A. L., & Wingfield, A. (1994). Older adults can inhibit high-probability competitors in speech recognition. *Aging and Cognition, 1,* 152–157.

Stine, E. A. L., Wingfield, A., & Poon, L. W. (1986). How much and how fast: Rapid processing of spoken language in later adulthood. *Psychology and Aging, 1,* 303–311.

Stine-Morrow, E. A. L., Loveless, M. K., & Soederberg, L. M. (1996). Resource allocation in on-line reading by younger and older adults. *Psychology and Aging, 11,* 475–486.

Stine-Morrow, E. A. L., Miller, L. M. S., & Nevin, J. A. (1999). The effects of context and feedback on age differences in spoken word recognition. *Journal of Gerontology: Psychological Sciences, 54B,* 125–134.

Suh, S., & Trabasso, T. (1993). Inferencing during reading: Converging evidence from discourse analysis, talk-aloud protocols, and recognition priming. *Journal of Memory and Language, 32,* 279–300.

Swinney, D. (1979). Lexical access during sentence comprehension: (Re)consideration of context effects. *Journal of Verbal Learning and Verbal Behavior, 18,* 645–659.

Thomas, J., Fozard, J., & Waugh, N. C. (1977). Age-related differences in naming latency. *American Journal of Psychology, 90,* 499–509.

Titone, D., Prentice, K., & Wingfield, A. (1996, November). *Self-paced listening and discourse comprehension: Speech rate, passage complexity, and age.* Paper presented at the 37th annual meeting of the Psychonomics Society, Chicago, IL.

Tun, P. A. (1989). Age differences in processing expository and narrative texts. *Journal of Gerontology: Psychological Sciences, 44,* P9–P15.

Tun, P. A. (1998). Fast noisy speech: Age differences in processing rapid speech with background noise. *Psychology and Aging, 13,* 424–434.

Tyler, L. (1984). The structure of the initial cohort: Evidence from gating. *Perception and Psychophysics, 36,* 417–427.

U.S. Congress, Office of Technology Assessment. (1986). *Hearing impairment and elderly people—A background paper* (Publication No. OTA-BP-BA-30). Washington, DC: U.S. Government Printing Office.

van den Broek, P. (1990). Causal inferences and the comprehension of narrative texts. In A. C. Graesser & G. H. Bower (Eds.), *Inferences and text comprehension* (pp. 155–196). New York: Academic Press.

Van der Linden, M., Hupet, M., Ahmadi, A. E., Feyereisen, P., Schelstraete, M., Bestgen, Y., Bruyer, R., Lories, G., & Seron, X. (1999). Cognitive mediators of age-related differences in language comprehension and verbal memory performance. *Aging, Neuropsychology and Cognition, 6,* 32–55.

van Dijk, T. A., & Kintsch, W. (1983). *Strategies of discourse comprehension*. New York: Academic Press.

Van Orden, G. C., Johnston, J. C., & Hale, B. L. (1988). Word identification in reading proceeds from spelling to sound to meaning. *Journal of Experimental Psychology: Learning, Memory, and Cognition, 14*, 371–386.

Walsh, D. A., & Hershey, D. A. (1993). Mental models and the maintenance of complex problem-solving skills in old age. In J. Cerella, J. Rybash, W. J. Hoyer, & M. L. Commons (Eds.), *Adult information processing: Limits on loss* (pp. 553–584). New York: Academic Press.

Waters, G., & Caplan, D. (1996). The capacity theory of sentence comprehension: Critique of Just and Carpenter (1992). *Psychological Review, 103*, 761–772.

Wayland, S. C., Wingfield, A., & Goodglass, H. (1989). Recognition of isolated words: The dynamics of cohort reduction. *Applied Psycholinguistics, 10*, 475–487.

West, R. L., Crook, T. H., & Barron, K. L. (1992). Everyday memory performance across the lifespan: Effects of age and noncognitive individual differences. *Psychology and Aging, 7*, 72–82.

Wingfield, A. (1968). Effects of frequency on the identification and naming of objects. *American Journal of Psychology, 81*, 226–234.

Wingfield, A. (1996). Cognitive factors in auditory performance: Context, speed of processing and constraints of memory. *Journal of the American Academy of Audiology, 7*, 175–182.

Wingfield, A., Aberdeen, J. S., & Stine, E. A. L. (1991). Word onset gating and linguistic context in spoken word recognition by young and elderly adults. *Journal of Gerontology: Psychological Sciences, 46*, P127–P129.

Wingfield, A., Alexander, A. H., & Cavigelli, S. (1994). Does memory constrain utilization of top-down information in spoken word recognition? Evidence from normal aging. *Language and Speech, 37*, 221–235.

Wingfield, A., Goodglass, H., & Lindfield, K. C. (1997). Word recognition from acoustic onsets and acoustic offsets: Effects of cohort size and syllabic stress. *Applied Psycholinguistics, 18*, 85–100.

Wingfield, A., & Lindfield, K. C. (1995). Multiple memory systems in the processing of speech: Evidence from aging. *Experimental Aging Research, 21*, 101–121.

Wingfield, A., Poon, L. W., Lombardi, L., & Lowe, D. (1985). Speed of processing in normal aging: Effects of speech rate, linguistic structure, and processing time. *Journal of Gerontology, 40*, 579–585.

Wingfield, A., & Stine, E. A. L. (1992). Age differences in perceptual processing and memory for spoken language. In R. L. West & J. D. Sinnott (Eds.), *Everyday memory and aging: Current research and methodology* (pp. 101–123). New York: Springer-Verlag.

Wingfield, A., Tun, P. A., & Rosen, M. J. (1995). Age differences in veridical and reconstructive recall of syntactically and randomly segmented speech. *Journal of Gerontology: Psychological Sciences, 50*, P257–P266.

Wingfield, A., Waters, G. S., & Tun, P. A. (1998). Does working memory work in language comprehension? Evidence from behavioral neuroscience. In N. Raz (Ed.), *The other side of the error term: Aging and development as model systems in cognitive neuroscience* (pp. 319–393). Amsterdam: Elsevier.

Wingfield, A., Wayland, S. C., & Stine, E. A. L. (1992). Adult age differences in the use of prosody for syntactic parsing and recall of spoken sentences. *Journal of Gerontology: Psychological Sciences, 47*, P350–P356.

Zabrucky, K., & Moore, D. (1994). Contributions of working memory and evaluation and regulation of understanding to adults' recall of texts. *Journal of Gerontology: Psychological Sciences, 49*, P201–P212.

Zacks, R., & Hasher, L. (1997). Cognitive gerontology and attentional inhibition: A reply to Burke and McDowd. *Journal of Gerontology: Psychological Sciences, 52B*, P274–P283.

Zacks, R. T., & Hasher, L. (1994). Directed ignoring: Inhibitory regulation of working memory. In D. Dagenbach & T. H. Carr (Eds.), *Inhibitory mechanisms in attention, memory, and language* (pp. 241–264). New York: Academic Press.

Zelinski, E. M. (1988). Integrating information from discourse: Do older adults show deficits? In L. L. Light & D. M. Burke (Eds.), *Language, memory, and aging* (pp. 117–132). New York: Cambridge University Press.

Zelinski, E. M., & Gilewski, M. J. (1988). Memory for prose and aging: A meta-analysis. In M. L. Howe, & C. J. Brainerd (Eds.), *Cognitive development in adulthood* (pp. 133–158). New York: Springer-Verlag.

Zelinski, E. M., Light, L. L., & Gilewski, M. J. (1984). Adult age differences in memory for prose: The question of sensitivity to passage structure. *Developmental Psychology, 20,* 1181–1192.

Zurif, E. B., Swinney, D., Prather, P., Wingfield, A., & Brownell, H. (1995). The allocation of memory resources during sentence comprehension: Evidence from the elderly. *Journal of Psycholinguistic Research, 24,* 165–182.

Zwann, R. A., Langston, M. C., & Graesser, A. C. (1995). The construction of situation models in narrative comprehension: An event-indexing model. *Psychological Science, 6,* 292–297.

Zwann, R. A., Magliano, J. P., & Graesser, A. C. (1995). Dimensions of situation model construction in narrative comprehension. *Journal of Experimental Psychology: Learning, Memory, and Cognition, 21,* 386–397.

7

Metacognition in Adulthood and Old Age

Christopher Hertzog
Georgia Institute of Technology

David F. Hultsch
University of Victoria

This chapter reviews the literature on aging and metacognition. Metacognition can be defined as cognitions about cognition (Wellman, 1983), and a wide variety of concepts have been included under this rather broad umbrella. We identify and treat three major categories of metacognitions: (a) knowledge about cognition and cognitive functions, (b) the monitoring of the current state of the cognitive system, and (c) beliefs about cognition (including beliefs about aging and cognition and beliefs about one's own cognition).

For a variety of reasons, much of the work on aging and metacognition has focused on the domain of episodic memory, particularly verbal memory. Historically, metacognitive research arose from developmental psychology and the focus was largely on memory and metamemory development (Schneider & Pressley, 1989). Perlmutter's (1978) seminal article on aging and metamemory initiated much of the gerontological work on metacognition, including studies using questionnaire measures of metamemory and experimental analyses of memory predictions and performance. Much of the early interest in aging and metacognition focused on the hypothesis that deficits in metacognition might explain age differences in memory performance, as measured by standard laboratory tasks, such as free recall and paired-associate recall. In general, this hypothesis has not been supported by experimental data (see Hertzog, Dixon, & Hultsch, 1990a, for a review), but more subtle and varied forms of the general hypothesis survive and continue to be evaluated in the literature we review. Arguably, the incorporation of empirical methods for measuring metacognition into experimental learning and memory tasks provided a scaffold on which to erect a structure of scientific, empirical evidence regarding awareness and self-regulation. Otherwise, metacognition might have been branded as little more than introspectionism rediscovered (see Nelson, 1996). Hence, our emphasis is on treatments of metacognition in the domains of learning and memory, although we do, to a degree, cover other domains of cognition as well. Our view is that many of the issues regarding metacognition can be framed in terms of what is known about verbal learning and memory and that the limits on generalization from the existing literature to other aspects of metacognition are undoubtedly real but are for the most part still unexplored.

There are a number of reviews of these and related topics in the existing literature (Berry & West, 1993; Cavanaugh, 1996; Cavanaugh, Feldman, & Hertzog, 1998; Dixon, 1989; Gilewski & Zelinski, 1986; Hertzog & Dixon, 1994; Hertzog et al., 1990a), most of which emphasize metacognitive phenomena revealed by questionnaire data (e.g., memory self-efficacy and use of external aids). We review these topics as well but give more emphasis to the domain of monitoring, which has received less attention in the secondary literature.

KNOWLEDGE ABOUT COGNITION

Knowledge has often been considered a defining concept or metaphor for metacognition (Wellman, 1983; see also Hertzog et al., 1990a). Here, we restrict the definition of metacognitive knowledge to refer to *declarative knowledge* about the nature of memory and cognition. Metacognitive knowledge was conceptualized through a "library" metaphor by Nelson and Narens (1990). That is, individuals are regarded as having a library of stored experiences regarding cognition and situations requiring cognition. Knowledge about situations and corresponding situational constraints, task requirements, and possible strategies for encoding and retrieval can be of tremendous benefit for learning and remembering, provided that this knowledge is retrieved and used in the performance situation.

Of course, such knowledge could be gained from taking classes about memory or cognition, conducting Internet searches, reading independently, watching media coverage of related issues, and accessing or using a variety of other sources. Presumably, personal experience plays a role as well. Knowledge undoubtedly accrues over a lifetime, if for no other reason than age-related changes themselves may create changing conditions that generate new challenges to learning. It is reasonable to assume that knowledge about memory and cognition would behave much like any other kind of information held in semantic memory. That is, it is unlikely that such knowledge, once gained, would be lost, but it may become more or less accessible, depending on a number of factors. There is only limited empirical data regarding knowledge about cognition, including memory, and how it changes over the life span. One source of information is the Metamemory in Adulthood (MIA) Questionnaire Task scale (Dixon & Hultsch, 1983). It asks individuals to give preferred answers to statements about memory, stated as possible facts (e.g., "Most people find it easier to remember concrete things than abstract things"). Age differences in the MIA Task scale have been reported in several, but not all, samples (Dixon, Hertzog, & Hultsch, 1986; Dixon & Hultsch, 1983; Hultsch, Hertzog, & Dixon, 1987). Studies with findings of superior knowledge about memory and cognition by younger adults often use college undergraduates and may reflect the beneficial experiences of undergraduate psychology study for knowledge about cognition rather than any developmental loss of knowledge by older adults.

An interesting issue for any knowledge dimension is the possible influence of social change (including scientific advances) on knowledge, reflected either as period effects or as cohort effects on amount of knowledge in different domains. The domain of aging and cognition is certainly one that has undergone profound changes in both scientific knowledge and societal interest over the past 3 decades. Public awareness of a number of issues concerning aging, including the problem of Alzheimer's disease (AD) and related disorders, has increased dramatically. These kinds of temporal trends in public attitudes and awareness could, in principle, produce generational differences in knowledge about aging, memory, and age-related disorders.

Not all of the ramifications of increasing knowledge about aging and cognition are positive. Increased awareness of the debilitating nature of AD and its increasing prevalence after age 70 may have an adverse impact on the subjective well-being of middle-aged and older adults who fear developing the disease. For example, Cutler and Hodgson (1996) surveyed fear of age-related cognitive loss and dementia. Some of their respondents were highly concerned about future impairments, some because they had parents or grandparents who had developed dementing illnesses. Some middle-aged respondents interpreted memory failures as evidence that AD had already begun to affect them, even though such an early age of onset was highly improbable.

MONITORING COGNITION

Cognitive psychologists, most notably Nelson (1996; Nelson & Narens, 1990), have argued for some time that the ability to monitor processes and products associated with learning and memory plays a critical role in the learning process itself (see also Borkowski, Carr, & Pressley, 1987; A. L. Brown, 1978). Monitoring is seen as an essential part of the process of adapting control behavior in order to optimize learning. Some developmental psychologists have argued strongly that the development of metacognitive awareness and the ability to monitor performance play a key role in the development of learning skills during childhood (e.g., Schneider & Pressley, 1989). It can be argued that young adult maturity is characterized by efficient and effective central executive functioning (i.e., optimal allocation of limited central resources and effective selection of processing strategies and algorithms), especially relative to performance at earlier levels of development. According to this view, metacognitive development matters for the ultimate attainment of central executive skills.

Monitoring provides the evidence about ongoing learning that an individual needs to either maintain or change a particular strategic approach to learning. For example, an individual who perceives that a particular strategy for learning new information (e.g., relating multiple items in a word list by means of forming sentences using the words) is not proving useful could switch to a new and perhaps more effective strategy.

To set the stage for our discussion of monitoring, we briefly cover three sets of conceptual and methodological issues: types of monitoring, types of metacognitive judgments, and evaluation criteria.

Types of Monitoring

It is possible to distinguish between several different aspects of monitoring. Nelson and Narens (1990) discussed the monitoring and control processes involved in a typical memory task involving phases of acquisition (learning), retention, and retrieval (performance). Their treatment of the problem is shown in Fig. 7.1. The control and monitoring processes depicted in Fig. 7.1 should be considered illustrative, not exhaustive. The psychologist's goal is to create tasks that translate the internal process of monitoring into overt behaviors that can be empirically measured. Usually this is accomplished by asking individuals to make discriminative judgments about the stimuli they are processing as part of the cognitive task, under the assumption that monitoring is required to make such judgments. Nelson and Narens identified four different types of monitoring, which they defined in terms of four different types of judgments that individuals could make: ease-of-learning judgments, judgments of learning (JOLs), feeling-of-knowing (FOK) judgments, and confidence in retrieved answers.

The Nelson and Narens (1990) framework closely identifies types of monitoring with the types of judgments used to operationally define them.

MONITORING

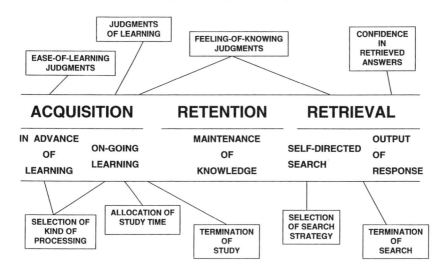

CONTROL

FIG. 7.1. Nelson-Narens framework for the relations of metacognitive monitoring and control during stages of learning and memory. Memory stages are shown inside the horizontal bars. Examples of monitoring components are shown above the memory stages; examples of control components are shown below the memory stages. Adapted from Nelson & Narens, 1990. Reprinted with permission of Academic Press.

Another way of thinking about types of monitoring is in terms of the types of control processes that are required in cognitive tasks. For example, monitoring during learning might involve monitoring various aspects of the encoding process itself, including monitoring the rate with which strategies are executed, the quality of an implemented strategy, the difficulty of using a specific strategy for a given to-be-learned item, and so on. Monitoring retrieval processes would be important at testing (e.g., for evaluating whether the information that has been retrieved is actually the information sought) but might also be an important part of rehearsal (e.g., when individuals test themselves to determine whether the information can be successfully accessed). From this point of view, the challenge to experimental psychologists is to design tasks that assess the varied kinds of monitoring that may occur during cognitive task performance, and the kinds of judgment tasks currently in use may eventually be supplanted by other measurement approaches. Nevertheless, the critical point for this review is that there are, in theory, multiple types of metacognitive monitoring and that there could be age differences in some types but not others.

Types of Metacognitive Judgments. The general method for evaluating metacognitive monitoring is to have individuals judge or rate stimuli and then to evaluate either (a) variables that influence these judgements or (b) the relationship of judgments to criterion variables, most notably cognitive task performance. In the case of monitoring learning, psychologists often ask participants in an experiment to make predictions of future performance. Prediction accuracy can then be assessed by a variety of criteria (see below). The two major types of predictions are global (or aggregated) predictions and item-level judgments of learning. Global predictions require a performance prediction for a set (e.g., an entire word list or test) or subset (e.g., all words studied with a particular strategy) of information. These predictions can be, but need not be, numerical estimates (e.g., predicting that 10 words will be recalled from a 30-word list). The item-level predictions are called JOLs. They are often obtained by asking individuals to rate their relative confidence that a particular item will be recalled at a later point in time. For example, given a list of concrete paired associates, individuals might be asked to study an item (e.g., *TICK–SPOON*) and, after study, rate their confidence (on a 0%-to-100% scale) that they will recall the paired word when presented at test with the stimulus word (e.g., TICK–???).

A major issue for any metacognitive judgment is how the response is scaled. Multiple techniques are possible (e.g., single-item ratings vs. comparative judgments) and multiple response scales can be considered. In the preceding example, and much of the experimental literature, JOLs are scaled in terms of percentage confidence (0% to 100%). Given a conception of probability as subjective confidence, one could argue that it is reasonable to expect a close correspondence between rated confidence and probability of recall, given accurate monitoring. On the other hand, if one were to scale the JOLs as an ordinal 1- to 5-point Likert rating, (say, from *definitely will recall* to *definitely will not recall*), then the mapping of the metacognitive judgment to probability of item recall is considerably more problematic (see below). In general, little attention has been paid in the aging literature to issues of how adults of different ages differ in their use of rating scales and what impact (if any) this would have on inferences about age differences in monitoring. In short, experimental psychologists typically assume and rarely evaluate measurement equivalence in rating scale behavior for different age groups.

Evaluation Criteria. Experimental studies often focus on understanding the sources of information that affect various metacognitive judgments. At issue is the *sensitivity* of these judgments to other experimentally manipulated variables, such as study time, type of encoding process (e.g., use of intentional learning strategies such as categorization), and item characteristics (e.g., concreteness and word frequency). For example, Benjamin and Bjork (1996) argued that JOLs are influenced by retrieval fluency—the ease with which information comes to mind (see also Kelley & Jacoby, 1996). Likewise, Koriat (1993; Koriat & Goldsmith, 1996) argued that FOK judgments were often based on accessibility of information that might be related to the information being sought. Reder and Ritter (1992) argued that feeling of knowing judgments are often influenced by familiarity with the topic of the information, independent of whether the information is actually in memory.

A critical issue for metacognitive monitoring is the accuracy of the judgments. For example, when an individual reports an FOK judgment for information that has not yet been retrieved, how accurate is that judgment? Or when individuals predict that they will recall a specific item at a later test, to what degree is that true? Are individuals more likely to recall information they previously rated as likely to be recalled?

Sensitivity of metacognitive judgments to experimental variables may enhance or suppress the accuracy of the judgments, depending on whether the variable is actually diagnostic of performance. Benjamin and Bjork (1996) argued that the influence of retrieval fluency on metacognitive judgments can actually impair their accuracy because fluency at the time of the judgment may not be associated with the likelihood of later recall.

When prediction accuracy is at issue, there are multiple ways to conceptualize and measure accuracy. *Absolute accuracy* (also known as *under/overconfidence* in the human judgment and decision-making literature) refers to the degree of discrepancy between predicted and actual performance, scaled in the units of to-be-learned information. For global predictions, absolute accuracy can be easily measured by the arithmetic difference, prediction minus recall. Underestimation is reflected in negative differences, overestimation in positive differences. For item-level judgments, absolute accuracy can be measured as the difference between the arithmetic means of the judgments and recall. Some scientists have argued that the absolute value of the difference, not the simple arithmetic difference, should be used to assess prediction accuracy (Devolder, Brigham, & Pressley, 1990). The rationale is that the age-group mean of simple difference averages overpredictions and underpredictions, so that on aggregate a group could appear to have good absolute accuracy when there was considerable variability in the difference scores. The mean absolute difference captures the average discrepancy between prediction and recall. Attention to both the mean and the variance of the simple differences would, in principle, capture both phenomena, but psychologists often ignore group differences in variances. In any case, absolute accuracy refers to the quantitative difference between prediction and recall, and the magnitude of the difference is taken as a measure of monitoring accuracy.

Relative accuracy refers to the extent to which increases in predicted performance are associated with increases in the probability of actual performance. Relative accuracy ignores the means of both judgments and recall, instead focusing on correlational indices of association between the two variables. In the decision-making literature, relative accuracy is often referred to as *resolution*. Nelson (1984) argued that the best index of metacognitive accuracy was the Goodman–Kruskal gamma correlation, which is an index of the rank order agreement of metacognitive judgments with recall. As with a Pearson product–moment correlation, a gamma of 1.0 indicates perfect agreement, a gamma of 0 indicates independence of judgments and probability of recall, and a gamma of −1.0 indicates a perfect inverse relationship. In this case, the correlation between JOL ratings and the binary outcome of ("yes" or "no") recall is computed for each individual, summing concordances and discordances over the set of rated items. Each person, then, contributes a gamma, a measure of metacognitive accuracy in the sample data, to the between-persons (individual differences) dimension of relative accuracy of the JOLs. Although gamma can be argued to be unaffected by the overall mean levels of recall and ratings, it is sensitive to extreme marginal distributions of either judgments or recall (e.g., ceiling or floor effects in recall).

Another important criterion for metacognitive accuracy is the *calibration* of judgments to recall, defined in terms of the conditional probabilities of recall, given different values of the judgments. Calibration curves plot the probability of recall for different values of the metacognitive judgment. For example, one might assign judgments of learning to grouped intervals of rated confidence (0%–9%, 10%–19%, and so on) and then compute the probability of recall for each grouping. Judgments with perfect relative accuracy should show a monotonic increase in the probability of recall as a function of increasing confidence. The judgments of learning would also be well calibrated to the extent that the predicted probability of recall for each grouped interval (defined by the interval midpoints of 5%, 15%, and so on) equals the actual probability of recall for the items receiving that rating. There are several issues with calibration curves, including variability in the frequency with which different rating scale values are used by raters and whether the nature of the rating scale provides a valid basis for determining calibration (see Keren, 1991, for an extended discussion). With respect to the latter issue, it is an open question whether ratings of percentage confidence in later recall (as in the JOL method described earlier) can validly be expressed as a predicted probability of recall (which depends, in part, on the implicit theory of probability adopted by both rater and experimenter; Gigerenzer, Hoffrage, & Kleinbolting, 1991).

To the extent that individuals have only indirect access to information in memory (i.e., through what is accessible to conscious awareness through retrieval mechanisms), metacognitive judgments require that the information that is accessible be translated or mapped into the rating scale required by the judgment. This process of accessing information, and then mapping that information into the response scale (see N. R. Brown & Siegler, 1993), may introduce inaccuracy in the judgments because of idiosyncracies in the mapping function and the criterion thresholds used by raters. For this reason, among others, scientists interested in metacognitive accuracy have argued that primary attention should be given to measures of relative accuracy rather than absolute accuracy or calibration (Nelson, 1984).

Age Differences in Memory Monitoring

We focus first on item-level judgments as methods of measuring memory monitoring at different stages of the learning process. In terms of the four types of judgments identified by Nelson and Narens (1990), there have been, to our knowledge, no studies of age differences in ease-of-learning judgments. Moreover, there are few metacognitively oriented studies of confidence ratings of recognition or recall at test (but see Lovelace & Marsh, 1985). The most commonly studied metacognitive judgments in the aging literature are JOLs and FOKs.

FOKs. The literature on feelings of knowing suggests that both younger and older adults can make accurate FOK judgments (Anooshian, Mammarella, & Hertel, 1989; Butterfield, Nelson, & Peck, 1988; J. L. Lachman, Lachman, & Thronesbery, 1979). The study by Butterfield et al. (Experiment 2) provides compelling evidence that aging does not change the accuracy of FOK judgments. They used gamma correlations to evaluate relative accuracy of FOKs and found equivalent accuracy for both younger and older adults.

A tip-of-the-tongue (TOT) state is a special type of FOK. It refers to a particular kind of retrieval block—a temporary inaccessibility of information held in memory—often accompanied by access to some features of the information. Frequently a TOT state is associated with the inability to retrieve the name of a person, place, or thing, even though individuals experiencing the retrieval block are often able to describe the target and provide partial information about it (e.g., starts with the letter S). Research on this phenomenon has indicated that both older and younger adults experience TOT states that can later be overcome (Burke, MacKay, Worthley, & Wade, 1991; Cohen & Faulkner, 1986; Maylor, 1990). Older adults tend to report more TOT states than do younger adults, although these reports are not as frequently accompanied by accurate reports of partial information about information being sought. One of the best strategies for resolving these retrieval blocks is to cease searching for the information, suggesting that the act of deliberate retrieval search may contribute to the interference effects (Cohen & Faulkner, 1986). Burke et al. argued that TOT states can often be attributed to spreading activation to multiple, competing phonological codes from the semantic concept held in memory and that older adults were especially vulnerable to a deficit in transmission of information from the semantic to the phonological level. The important point regarding metacognition is that it appears that there are no age differences in the accuracy of TOT reports or in the ability to monitor retrieval operations when in that state. Admittedly, however, additional work assessing age differences in the accuracy of FOK judgments when individuals are in a TOT state are needed before definitive conclusions can be drawn.

JOLs. Two early studies of JOLs and aging suggested little age difference in the accuracy of these judgments. Lovelace and Marsh (1985) had groups of old and young adults learn 60 high-frequency paired associates with self-paced study. JOLs were obtained as Likert-scaled confidence judgments of subsequent recall, and in both age groups higher JOL confidence was associated with higher probability of recall. Lovelace and Marsh concluded that there were no age differences in memory monitoring during learning.

Rabinowitz, Ackerman, Craik, and Hinchley (1982) studied JOLs for paired associates in the context of different instruction conditions (instructions to use interactive imagery or instructions to learn by any method) while also manipulating the semantic relatedness of the pairs. JOLs were made on a 1- to 10-point scale ranging from 1 (*sure not to remember*) to 10 (*sure to remember*). JOLs were strongly influenced by semantic relatedness, as was paired-associate recall, for both age groups (see Fig. 7.2, Panels A and B). Imagery instructions produced higher recall than generic instructions to learn, but this effect was not as pronounced for the JOLs.

Rabinowitz et al. (1982) also assessed metacognitive accuracy by grouping JOLs into three levels (high, medium, and low confidence) and evaluating probability of recall at each level (see Fig. 7.2, Panel C). In terms of the criteria for evaluating JOL accuracy, this method is perhaps most closely akin to a calibration curve; it is certainly not a pure measure of relative accuracy. Older and younger adults given intentional learning instructions showed stronger relationships of JOLs to recall than did adults in the imagery instruction condition. Perhaps more important, there were no age differences in these relationships. Rabinowitz et al. concluded that adults can monitor the effects of stimulus characteristics on learning but not the differential effectiveness of processing strategies.

Shaw and Craik (1989) found that item-level predictions were not greatly influenced by the types of cues provided to participants. Indi-

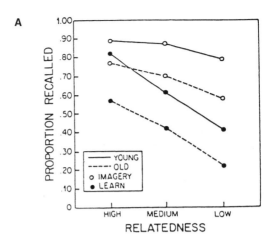

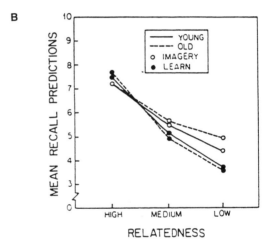

FIG. 7.2. Data from Rabinowitz et al., 1982, on mean recall and recall predictions for related and unrelated word pairs under different encoding conditions. Reprinted with permission from the Gerontological Society of America. (A) Proportion of items recalled as a function of age, encoding condition, and relatedness. (B) Mean recall predictions as a function of age, encoding condition, and relatedness. (C) Probability of recall as a function of age, encoding condition, and prediction level.

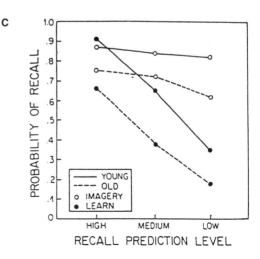

viduals were given concrete nouns paired with one of three different kinds of cues: syntactic (e.g., "starts with *ic*: *ice*"), rhyme (e.g., "rhymes with *dice*: *ice*"), and semantic (e.g., "something slippery: *ice*"). They made item-level predictions after studying each cue–target pair. The different kinds of cues strongly influenced recall because of levels-of-processing effects (semantic processing results in better retention than rhyme processing for both older and younger adults; see Craik & Jennings, 1992). There were effects of cue type on prediction, but the magnitude of the relationship was much smaller for predictions than for recall (12% of the variance in predictions, but 53% of the variance in recall, was associated with type of cue). There were no age differences in predictions or in prediction accuracy.

Bieman-Copeland and Charness (1994) criticized Shaw and Craik's (1989) semantic cues as being too closely related to the target words and replicated the experiment with a different set of semantic stimuli. Predictions were sensitive to the cue conditions, although the mean predictions ranged from 4 to 6 on a 0- to 10-point scale, whereas cued recall varied from roughly 0.3 to 0.9 for younger adults and from roughly 0.2 to 0.6 for older adults (see Fig. 7.3).

Findings such as these led Lovelace (1990) to conclude, in agreement with both Rabinowitz et al. (1982) and Shaw and Craik (1989), that adults of all ages were less likely to monitor the effects of processing strategies and their effects on recall than they were to monitor possible influences of stimulus characteristics like semantic relatedness or word concreteness. The data plotted in Fig. 7.2 and 7.3 illustrate a problem with this logic, however. Inherently, the predictions are scaled in a different metric than is recall, and it is not clear exactly what the conversion of ordinal Likert ratings to expected percentage of recall should be. If one treats ratings as containing only ordinal, and not interval, information (see Nelson, 1984), then it is not clear that one should interpret the data in Fig. 7.2 and 7.3 as indicating that item-level predictions are relatively insensitive to effects of strategies or knowledge about cue benefits. In fact, predictions varied reliably as a function of these experimental variables, but when the data are plotted on common axes where Likert scales are juxtaposed against proportion recall, it appears that item predictions are less influenced by the experimental variables than is item recall. It is not clear, however, that the interval-scaling assumptions required for interpreting differences in absolute accuracy (as is implied, at least, in the contrasting functions plotted in Fig. 7.3) are warranted. Moreover, the data as reported in Fig. 7.2 and 7.3 cannot be used to assess relative accuracy. That is, even though group mean JOLs varied, on average, between 0.4 and 0.6, it could well be the case that the ordinal intraindividual correlation of each person's JOLs with observed item recall would be relatively high.

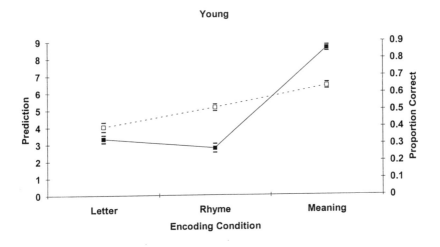

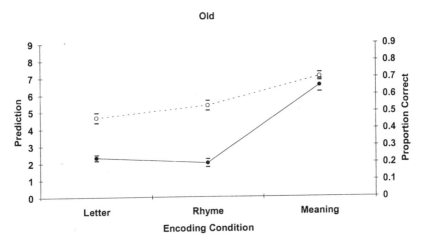

FIG. 7.3. Mean predicted performance (0–10 scale, plotted with dotted lines) and mean proportion correct for cued recall (plotted with solid lines) for young and old adults in three encoding conditions. From Bieman-Copeland & Charness, 1994. Reprinted with permission from the American Psychological Association.

None of the studies just cited used gamma correlations to evaluate relative accuracy of the JOLs. Connor, Dunlosky, and Hertzog (1997) conducted a study that explicitly evaluated both absolute and relative accuracy of JOLs. Table 7.1 provides relevant gamma correlations from three experiments, all of which presented 60 concrete paired associates to groups of younger and older adults. The first column from the table

TABLE 7.1
Accuracy of Monitoring Learning in Three Experiments: Gamma
Correlations of Judgments of Learning With Paired-Associate Recall

Experiment and Group	Immediate Recall	Delayed Recall
Experiment 1		
Young	.29	.88
Old	.44	.88
Experiment 2		
Young	.51	.82
Old	.50	.83
Experiment 3		
Young	.55	.82
Old	.49	.78

Note. Entries are mean intraindividual gamma correlations within each group. From "Age-Related Differences in Absolute but Not Relative Metamemory Accuracy," by L. T. Connor, J. D. Dunlosky, & C. Hertzog, 1997, Psychology and Aging, 12, p. 59. Copyright 1997 by the American Psychological Association. Reprinted with permission.

reports JOLs obtained immediately after the item pairs were studied. As can be seen, there were no systematic age differences in the gamma correlations.

Connor et al. (1997) also evaluated absolute accuracy and calibration of the JOLs. Their three experiments produced different levels of paired-associate recall, ranging from relatively low (Experiment 1; unrelated word pairs, no strategy instructions) to intermediate (Experiment 3; mixed related and unrelated word pairs, explicit instructions to use mediators) to high (Experiment 2; two study trials with explicit instructions to learn mediators). The results suggested that one of the influences on absolute accuracy and calibration is the level of recall. In Experiment 1, older adults had low levels of recall and appeared to be overconfident, whereas younger adults had better absolute accuracy. They also demonstrated better calibration of JOLs relative to older adults. However, in Experiment 2, younger adults had high levels of recall and appeared to be underconfident; they also exhibited poorer calibration. Connor et al. argued that JOLs are influenced by a tendency to anchor judgments at the midpoint of the rating scale (50% confidence), independent of level of recall, and that this effect could artifactually inflate or minimize age differences in absolute accuracy. Given that studies of metacognition typically have not equated the age groups on level of recall performance, this finding raises questions about whether age differences in absolute accuracy are an artifact of group differences in level of recall (see below).

Connor et al. (1997) also evaluated age differences in the delayed-JOL effect first reported by Nelson and Dunlosky (1991). A delayed JOL is obtained by deferring the JOL for some items until after some intervening delay (often with other items being studied before the JOL is obtained).

When JOLs are provided by presenting only the cue (the stimulus word, as in Fig. 7.2), JOL accuracy is greatly enhanced. This effect can be observed in Table 7.1; delayed JOLs (the right-hand column) are much more accurate than JOLs obtained immediately after study. Note that both older adults and younger adults show this delayed-JOL effect. Moreover, delayed JOLs are much better calibrated than are immediate JOLs (Connor et al., 1997). When both words are presented at the time the JOL is made, there are no appreciable differences in accuracy between the two types of JOLs (Connor et al., 1997).

Why are delayed JOLs more accurate? Although there is some debate on this issue (Spellman & Bjork, 1992), a plausible explanation is that presentation of the stimulus triggers a covert retrieval attempt. Successful retrieval at the time of the JOL is highly predictive of recall at testing, and hence the accuracy of the delayed JOL is enhanced relative to the immediate JOL. Retrieval is not an all-or-none phenomenon, of course, and retrieved information may vary on dimensions that influence the JOLs. Moreover, as noted earlier, failure to retrieve may be accompanied by partial information or FOKs that could also be used to predict some nonzero probability of later recall. If this explanation is accurate, then one could argue that the equivalent delayed-JOL effect, combined with the age equivalence in immediate JOLs, suggests no age differences in the relative accuracy of monitoring both encoding and retrieval processes.

Given these results, it is clear that monitoring accuracy per se is not a viable explanatory variable for age differences in learning and memory. Indeed, quite to the contrary, metacognitive monitoring ability appears to be spared even when learning and memory are impaired by aging. The simple hypothesis of deficits in monitoring ability accounting for age differences in cognition can be rejected on the basis of available data.

Nevertheless, a number of interesting issues regarding aging, monitoring, and cognitive performance remain. For example, an important direction for future research on aging and metacognitive monitoring will be to evaluate the influence of different sources of information on the metacognitive judgments of older and younger adults. Given the prevailing view that JOLs are potentially influenced by multiple sources of information that are accessed at the time of judgment (see Koriat, 1997), it may be the case that certain sources of information are more salient than others. In principle, attending to different dimensions of information could change JOL accuracy, provided that these dimensions vary in their diagnostic value for future recall. The conditions under which individuals of different ages attend to and use multiple sources of information when making a JOL may shed additional light on their monitoring skills. Such research may prove important because older adults may be able to monitor but may not spontaneously do so and because older adults may not monitor the aspects of encoding and retrieval that are most critical for optimizing learning (see below).

Global Predictions. These measures have been the most frequently used indices of metacognitive accuracy in the developmental literature (see Cavanaugh & Green, 1990; Hertzog & Dixon, 1994; and Lovelace, 1990, for a review). Global predictions have been used, in varying accounts, as operational definitions of self-knowledge, monitoring accuracy, task-specific memory self-efficacy (Berry & West, 1993; Berry, West, & Dennehey, 1989), and more (Hertzog, Saylor, Fleece, & Dixon, 1994).

Most often, predictions have been obtained after task instructions but before items are studied. The classic finding in the literature is "overconfidence" by older adults—that is, predicted memory performance is greater than actual memory performance for older adults (e.g., Bruce, Coyne, & Botwinick, 1982; Perlmutter, 1978). However, this outcome is not always obtained (see Hertzog et al., 1994), perhaps because the levels of recall are not typically controlled. Connor et al. (1997) showed that, like mean JOLs, global predictions' absolute accuracy in a paired-associate task depended on level of recall.

One of the major differences between studies using global predictions is whether they use a measure of absolute accuracy (such as the simple or absolute difference between predicted and actual recall) or whether they use a measure of relative accuracy. For global predictions, in which a single judgment is obtained, the typical measure of relative accuracy is actually a correlation (between persons) of individual differences in predictions with individual differences in recall (which is clearly not comparable with relative accuracy of item-level predictions using intraindividual correlations, as discussed earlier). Nevertheless, there are some interesting, parallel discrepancies between absolute and relative accuracy.

One major discrepancy involves shifts in accuracy as a function of the timing of the prediction. Predictions can be obtained before task instructions and practice, after practice but before study, after study, or immediately prior to recall (given an appreciable delay between study and recall). Correlations of predictions with recall increase from before to after study of the materials for free recall (Hertzog et al., 1994; Lineweaver & Hertzog, 1998), paired-associate recall (Connor et al., 1997), and recognition memory (Hertzog et al., 1994). Table 7.2 illustrates the phenomenon for a categorized free-recall task. Note that at both recall trials the correlation of predictions and recall increases after the materials have been studied. Although Table 7.2 might suggest the magnitude of this increase is smaller for older adults (which indeed was true in these data; Hertzog et al., 1994), older adults have been found to have equivalent increases in the studies by Connor et al. and Lineweaver and Hertzog and in other recent unpublished studies.

TABLE 7.2
Correlations of Global Predictions and Postdictions
With Free Recall Across Two Recall Trials

	Group	
Trial	Young	Old
Trial 1		
Prediction 1	.15	.13
Prediction 2	.49	.30
Postdiction	.94	.92
Trial 2		
Prediction 1	.35	.45
Prediction 2	.53	.53
Postdiction	.95	.92

Note. $n = 261$ for each age group. Correlations are weighted averages (using *r*-to-*z* transformations) of correlations from Experiments 2 and 3 of Hertzog, Saylor, Fleece, and Dixon (1994). From Hertzog and Dixon (1994), p. 247, In J. Metcalfe & A. P. Shimamura (Eds.), *Metacognition: Knowing about knowing.* Cambridge, MA: MIT Press. Copyright 1994 by MIT Press. Reprinted with permission.

One can argue that the upgrading in prediction–recall correlations reflects the benefit of monitoring learning during study for improving prediction accuracy. Connor et al. (1997) provided some data that were consistent with this hypothesis. Mean JOLs during paired-associate study correlated higher with the second global prediction than with the first global prediction, suggesting that the degree of confidence, averaged over items, may have influenced the second global prediction.

What about absolute accuracy? In the studies by Hertzog et al. (1994) and Connor et al., (1997), the simple differences (prediction–recall) did not decrease—and in some cases actually increased—after study in the same individuals who exhibited an increase in the prediction–recall correlations. In our view, this disassociation of absolute and relative accuracy does not bode well for arguments that absolute accuracy is the best way of conceptualizing metacognitive monitoring. An alternative view is that global predictions and item-level predictions are both subject to judgment and scaling processes that are unrelated to metacognitive monitoring per se. Additional research will be needed to evaluate alternative explanations of the phenomena, but at present it appears that much of the literature on monitoring accuracy—often based on absolute accuracy of global predictions—may be vulnerable to the devastating methodological criticism that failure to equate level of recall for age groups, combined with scaling behaviors common to adults of all ages, artifactually produce the appearance of monitoring differences in different age groups (see Connor et al., 1997, for further discussion).

One area where absolute and relative accuracy indices appear to converge concerns monitoring of task performance, as measured by global performance postdictions (estimates of level of performance [e.g., number of items recalled] made after testing). The literature suggests strongly that there are no age differences in the ability to monitor performance because postdictions tend to have high absolute accuracy and high between-person correlations with recall (Connor et al., 1997; Devolder et al., 1990; Hertzog et al., 1994). This result appears to contradict Koriat, Ben-Zur, and Sheffer's (1988) argument that older adults experience impaired output monitoring by older adults in free recall (on the basis of increased repetition errors; see also Stuss, Craik, Sayer, Franchi, & Alexander, 1996).

The correlations of initial predictions with recall are often surprisingly low (as in Table 7.2). Another indication of accurate performance monitoring is the fact that correlations of predictions made before study with recall increase across multiple recall tests for individuals of all ages (Hertzog, Dixon, & Hultsch, 1990b; Hertzog et al., 1994; M. E. Lachman, Steinberg, & Trotter, 1987; see Table 7.2).

In summary, recent evidence from global performance predictions and postdictions reinforces earlier research in suggesting sparing of ability to monitor multiple aspects of memory functioning even in persons showing impaired memory functioning.

RELATIONS OF METAMEMORY TO STRATEGY USE

The evidence just reviewed indicates that when an experimental task requires it, older adults can monitor different aspects of cognition as well as younger adults. Such findings do not speak to the issue of whether older adults spontaneously use monitoring to guide and control learning. Indeed, there is some evidence that this may not be the case (but see Dunlosky & Hertzog, 1997). Murphy, Sanders, Gabriesheski, and Schmitt (1981) assessed age differences in the extent to which individuals monitored readiness for serial recall of pictures. Young adults were better at serial recall, perhaps because they took longer to study the items during self-paced study. Forcing older adults to study longer improved their performance. Murphy, Schmitt, Caruso, and Sanders (1987) tested the hypothesis that the age deficit was attributable to older adults not using self-testing to determine if they were ready for the recall test. Under remember instructions, younger adults studied longer, rehearsed more, and were more likely than older adults to test their recall by practice retrievals. The study also included groups either forced to take more time to study or instructed to use self-testing. Both conditions improved older adults serial recall performance, although older adults' self-testing increased only under explicit instructions to do so. Murphy et al. (1987)

argued that age-related metacognitive deficits will arise when the task requires use of monitoring for strategic self-regulation.

Additional evidence that older adults may not use monitoring as effectively comes from a recent study by Dunlosky and Connor (1997). They administered three learning trials for a set of paired associates. To maximize rates of learning, individuals should concentrate more effort to learn items that they had not recalled at earlier trials (Nelson et al., 1994). Dunlosky and Connor computed intraindividual gamma correlations between item recall at trial N and time taken to study items at trial $N + 1$. To the extent that individuals allocate more study time to items they had not already recalled, there should be a negative gamma correlation between prior recall and study time. Table 7.3 summarizes the findings. Both older and younger adults produce negative correlations that are significantly different from zero; hence, both age groups apparently use performance monitoring at the item level to guide subsequent study. However, there was a significant age difference in the magnitude of the gamma correlations, suggesting that older adults were not allocating study as optimally as younger adults. The difference cannot be attributed to impaired retrieval monitoring; the same individuals showed equivalent accuracy in delayed JOLs measured during study. Moreover, in a second experiment, Dunlosky and Connor actually provided their participants with explicit information about whether the to-be-studied item had been recalled on the previous trial. Age differences in gamma correlations persisted. These results are consistent with the argument that older adults do not spontaneously utilize monitoring as effectively, although there can be other interpretations (e.g., a strategic goal to protect against forgetting items already learned by allocating extra study time to them, at the cost of slower learning of new items).

Other studies have suggested that older adults do not use monitoring of performance to update their metacognitive knowledge about learning strategies that are effective for specific learning tasks. Brigham and

TABLE 7.3
Relationship Between Recall Performance
and Self-Paced Study at Next Trial

	Trial		
Group	2	3	4
Young	−.74	−.82	−.73
Old	−.54	−.56	−.47

Note. Entries are mean intraindividual gamma correlations. Adapted from "Age Differences in the Allocation of Study Time Account for Age Differences in Memory Performance," by J. Dunlosky & L. T. Connor, 1997, *Memory and Cognition, 25.*

Pressley (1988) required old and young adults to learn new, esoteric vocabulary words after instructions exposing them to two mnemonic strategies to assist in learning: key-word generation and semantic context generation. The key-word method generally produces superior learning. They collected predictions and performance postdictions and also asked individuals to indicate which strategy they would choose if asked to learn additional vocabulary items. Younger adults' postdictions were somewhat more influenced by the differences in strategy effectiveness, and they were more likely to indicate future use of the superior key-word method. Older adults were apparently less aware of the relative superiority of the key-word strategy, even after using it. There are some potential problems with the Brigham and Pressley study, including the fact that the key-word method was not definitively a superior method for older adults (see also Salthouse, 1991, for other concerns).

Bieman-Copeland and Charness (1994) had their participants make a second set of item recall predictions after performance on the cued-recall task described in the preceding section. The purpose was to determine whether both age groups improved the accuracy of their second recall predictions after having monitored recall performance. They argued that older adults improved prediction accuracy generically for all three types of cues but that younger adults differentially improved prediction accuracy for nonsemantic cues. They inferred that younger adults, but not older adults, had monitored the differential effectiveness of the cues and used that information to adjust their prediction accuracy. Given that Bieman-Copeland and Charness restricted their analysis to absolute accuracy of the predictions and did not measure performance monitoring directly, their conclusions are open to criticism. Nevertheless, both studies just cited raise the possibility that intact performance monitoring (as could be measured by global postdictions and/or confidence judgments during retrieval) by older adults does not necessarily imply equivalent utilization of performance monitoring to learn about the task and to adapt learning strategies for the task. Indeed, Bieman-Copeland and Charness explicitly argued that the problem lies in central executive control because of limited processing resources of older adults. That is, they suggested that older adults' resources were more engaged by the cued-recall task, making it more difficult for them to monitor performance.

Utilization of monitoring is, of course, only one aspect of executive control required to guide learning. Another critical issue is whether individuals choose effective initial strategies in intentional learning situations. For example, in paired-associate learning, it is highly beneficial to use a strategy to form a mediating link between the two stimuli (e.g., by using sentence generation or interactive imagery to associate word pairs). A critical issue is whether older adults behave strategically in such tasks, and if not, whether deficient metacognitive knowledge or deficient use of metacognitive monitoring contributes to deficient strategic behavior.

There have been a number of demonstrations that older adults do not spontaneously generate and use effective mediational strategies to the same extent that younger adults do (e.g., Hulicka, Sterns, & Grossman, 1967; Treat & Reese, 1976). Kausler (1994), in his review of the available evidence, concluded that a production deficiency (failure to produce mediational strategies) contributes to age differences in associative learning. Likewise, Devolder and Pressley (1992) argued that age differences in strategy use, perhaps related to differences in metacognitive knowledge and negative perceptions of their ability to control memory performance (see below), influence age differences in episodic memory tasks, including free recall. Certainly, there are frequent reports that older adults are not as likely to use effective organizational strategies in such tasks (e.g., Hultsch, 1969; Luszcz, Roberts, & Mattiske, 1990; Sanders, Murphy, Schmitt, & Walsh, 1980; Witte, Freund, & Sebby, 1990).

The available evidence suggests that deficient production of effective strategies is not a sufficient account of age differences in episodic recall performance (Light, 1996; Salthouse, 1991). Recent results by Hertzog, McGuire, and Lineweaver (1998) reinforce this view. They obtained retrospective attributions for task performance and used these self-reports to code for strategy use. This method avoided the demand characteristics of explicitly asking which strategies, if any, had been used. They classified young, middle-aged, and older individuals according to whether they used optimal strategies (usually, relational strategies like semantic categorization of like items; Luszcz et al., 1990). Other strategies, such as serial (rote) rehearsal, were identified as marginally effective. Individuals reporting no strategies during encoding were placed in the no-strategy group. There were age differences in the likelihood of producing optimal strategies; only 35% of older adults reported using optimal strategies at encoding compared with 49% of younger adults and with 58% of middle-aged adults. However, there were large age differences in recall for all three strategy groups (see Fig. 7.4). When strategies were ignored, age differences in recall were inflated slightly relative to the differences shown in Fig. 7.4. A path analysis showed that age and strategy production had significant, independent direct effects on recall (−.39 and .36, respectively). The indirect effect of age on recall mediated by strategy production was only −.09. Thus, age differences in strategy production had a relatively modest contribution to the total age differences in recall.

Recently, Dunlosky and Hertzog (1998a) reevaluated the argument that age differences in strategy production influence paired-associate performance. They instructed adults to try to use a mediational strategy and provided illustrations of two effective strategies, interactive imagery and

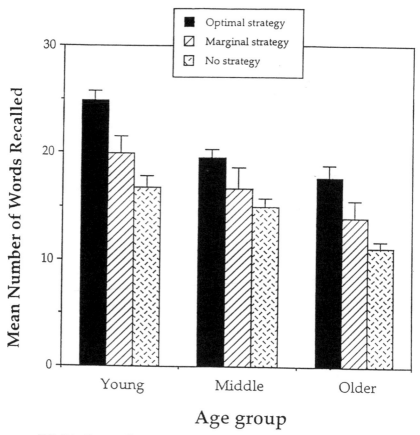

FIG. 7.4. Free recall performance by three age groups classified by level of strategy utilized (optimal, marginal, and none). From Hertzog, McGuire, & Lineweaver, 1998. Reprinted with permission from Swets & Zeitlinger, Inc.

sentence generation, and one less effective strategy, rote repetition. Participants were not informed of the differential effectiveness of the illustrated strategies. Dunlosky and Hertzog obtained strategy reports at the item level by having older and younger participants respond immediately after studying each pair. Individuals tended to use multiple strategies, even when explicitly instructed to try to use interactive imagery. There were no major age differences in proportion of trials in which the effective strategies were used, and yet age differences in recall were still observed. Thus, Dunlosky and Hertzog showed that robust age differences in recall occur even when older adults produce potentially effective strategies, which demonstrates that the production deficiency hypothesis is not a sufficient explanation of age differences in paired-associate recall. Larger age differences in recall may be observed without strategy instructions because of an age-related production deficiency but by merely instructing older individuals to use strategies is sufficient to overcome any production deficiency (see also Kausler, 1994).

Producing a strategy does not necessarily imply that the strategy is used effectively. Hence, it could be the case that age differences in the quality of strategy implementation influences age differences in memory task performance. Currently, it is difficult to evaluate the quality of implementation of strategies, as opposed to their production. An important area for future research will be to develop methods for obtaining valid indices of strategy quality. Marshall et al. (1978) and A. D. Smith et al. (1998) provided evidence that older adults generate verbal mediators (e.g., sentences) that are of comparable quality with those of younger adults, but more work is needed in this area. For example, it could be the case that older adults' sentence mediators generated at encoding for cued recall are of high quality with regard to the associational link between cue and target words. However, they may be of poor functional quality in the sense of lower likelihood of sentence retrieval on presentation of the cue at test. Moreover, little is known about age differences in the quality of image mediators that are generated under imagery strategy instructions (but see Craik & Dirkx, 1992). This issue is important because monitoring the quality of mediators generated during encoding could be critical for adaptive study behavior. For example, an individual who attempts but is unable to generate a high-quality interactive image might decide to shift to a secondary mediational strategy for that item, such as sentence generation.

In summary, the available evidence suggests that there may be, under certain circumstances, age differences in strategic behavior during learning and that deficient utilization of metacognitive processes during learning may contribute to the age differences in strategy use. Admittedly, these mechanisms probably cannot account for age differences in episodic memory. Nevertheless, utilization of monitoring as part of strategic self-regulation represents a largely unexplored area where older adults' functional use of memory could be enhanced by training or instruction. This is especially true because it appears that the ability to monitor cognitive processes is relatively unimpaired, even in individuals with deficient memory task performance. Training individuals of any age to use monitoring to regulate learning may have tangible benefits, but given normative age declines in incidental learning and memory, the benefits of such training may be an important vehicle for maintaining cognitive competence in late adulthood (Dunlosky & Hertzog, 1998b; Murphy et al., 1987).

METACOGNITION AS A SOCIAL-PSYCHOLOGICAL CONSTRUCT

To this point, we have been considering metacognition primarily as a cognitive construct—knowledge about and monitoring of cognitive processes. Metacognition may also be profitably considered as a social psychological construct. From this perspective, individuals' thinking about cognition is associated with beliefs about cognition rather than with knowledge or awareness of cognitive functioning. For purposes of this discussion, we differentiate two classes of beliefs about cognitive functioning: (a) implicit theories of cognition, which reflect largely unconscious and untested beliefs about the nature of cognitive functioning, including central characteristics such as its developmental course (Greenwald & Banaji, 1995; Sternberg, 1987), and (b) self-referent beliefs, which consist of an individual's beliefs about efficacy, control, and perceived changes related to their own cognitive functioning (e.g., Bandura, 1977, 1986; Berry & West, 1993). Researchers have hypothesized that at least some of the age differences in cognitive performance might be attributable to beliefs about cognition rather than to age differences in ability (e.g., Berry & West, 1993; Cavanaugh, 1996). Importantly, however, beliefs about cognition are also potentially relevant in other ways. Implicit theories about cognition may influence our judgments about the cognitive capability of others or our recall of our past standing on personal attributes and characteristics (e.g., Erber, 1989; Ross, 1989). Beliefs about cognitive efficacy may affect not only performance but also other aspects of behavior, such as the decision to engage or avoid cognitively demanding situations or contexts.

Implicit Theories of Aging and Cognition

Implicit theories have been defined as informal constructions held by individuals about psychological phenomena, such as memory or intelligence (Sternberg, 1987). In contrast to explicit theories, which are based on systematically collected and analyzed data, implicit theories are the result of earlier experiences that are typically unexamined, or at least not examined systematically (e.g., Chanowitz & Langer, 1981). Implicit theories are often widely shared within a culture or subculture, contributing to stereotypes about characteristic traits or behaviors of members of a certain group. In addition to dimensions such as gender and race, chronological age represents a fundamental characteristic of persons around which implicit theories are often constructed. Indeed, Kite, Deaux, and Miele (1991) reported results suggesting that age stereotypes are more pronounced than gender stereotypes. These researchers found that when asked to freely generate attributes of persons, respondents categorize others more readily on the basis of age compared with gender.

Implicit theories about the developmental course of various behaviors and characteristics probably reflect the influence of multiple factors, including age stratification and socialization processes that influence opportunities, timing of events, and normative values within a given culture. Given this, it is reasonable to anticipate that implicit theories about change and the causes of change will vary across cultures or even across subcultures within a given society (Morris & Peng, 1994). It is also reasonable to anticipate that implicit theories may have their greatest impact on perceived functioning in the absence of more specific information about a given target person or task. For example, differences in the evaluation of younger and older adults tend to be minimized when individual information in addition to age is provided about the target (Kite & Johnson, 1988). Similarly, for some types of judgments, differences between younger and older targets appear to be minimized when ratings are made in isolation (rating a single age target) in contrast to ratings made in a comparative context (rating multiple age targets; Knox & Gekoski, 1989).

Despite such contextual effects, belief systems about age show substantial consistency within a culture. For example, Heckhausen, Dixon, and Baltes (1989) found that younger, middle-aged, and older adults shared a substantial set of beliefs about the degree, desirability, and timing of developmental changes across the adult life span. Of particular interest for the present discussion is the question of adults' beliefs about the trajectory and timing of cognitive changes over the adult life span. Overall, there is an expectation that undesirable characteristics will increase with aging, whereas desirable characteristics will decrease (Heckhausen et al., 1989; Kite & Johnson, 1988). However, Heckhausen et al. noted that perceived gains continue to exist even in very late life. Expectations related to cognitive competence appear to be more negative than those associated with personality (Kite & Johnson, 1988). However, even within the cognitive domain, there appears to be substantial variation in belief systems across different domains. In particular, relatively early losses are expected in domains such as speed and memory in contrast to gains in areas such as wisdom (Heckhausen et al., 1989).

Implicit Theories of Memory Change. Although implicit theories about aging and cognition appear to suggest trajectories of both gains and losses, research attention has been focused largely on behaviors that are expected to decline in later life. Perhaps the most widely examined domain is memory. In general, adults in Western cultures appear to expect that memory functioning will show a loss trajectory with increasing age, with the onset of difficulties occurring as early as middle age. For example, Heckhausen et al. (1989) found that participants anticipated that forgetfulness would increase over adulthood with an average age of onset of 55 years. Similarly, Ryan (1992) found that both younger and older adults expected memory failures to increase from young adulthood to middle age and again from middle age to late life. A later study using a different measure of memory beliefs revealed an expectation of decline in memory ability between the two younger target ages (25 years and 45 years) and the two older target ages (65 years and 85 years). There was also an expectation of intraindividual decline in memory functioning between the 25-year-olds and 45-year olds and also from 45-year olds to the two oldest target ages. (Ryan & Kwong See, 1993).

Lineweaver and Hertzog (1998) recently developed an instrument designed to allow participants to express their beliefs about aging and memory across the entire life span rather than to focus on a few target ages. The General Beliefs About Memory instrument uses a graphic rating scale on which participants are asked to draw a line representing the expected trajectory for a given aspect of memory over the age range of 20 to 90 years. Multiple items examining the adequacy and effectiveness of memory functioning (efficacy) and the degree to which individuals can influence memory ability and functioning (control) are used. A companion instrument (Personal Beliefs About Memory) is designed to assess the individual's beliefs about his or her own memory functioning.

The results of an initial study of 307 adults aged 18 to 93 years reported by Lineweaver and Hertzog (1998) suggest that implicit theories about memory and aging in our culture reveal a general expectation of loss. However, they also found substantial diversity across different aspects of memory and evidence that beliefs change as individuals become older and begin to experience actual changes in memory functioning. For example, Fig. 7.5 shows aggregate functions for several memory efficacy and control scales or items calculated for three separate age groups of respondents (18–25 years, 26–55 years, and 56–93 years). Consistent with other studies, all of the trajectories reveal a general expectation of decline with increasing target age, both in terms of memory efficacy and memory control. Expectations of decline are not uniform across different aspects of memory functioning, however. In some cases, specific efficacy beliefs (e.g., memory for faces) are quite similar to global efficacy beliefs, whereas in other specific cases they are somewhat more (e.g., memory for things that happened long ago) or less (e.g., names) optimistic. Lineweaver and Hertzog's analyses also suggest that there are significant differences in beliefs across different age groups of respondents (despite the fact that the overall pattern is similar across respondent age). There were significant Target Age × Respondent Age interactions for 20 of the 27 items

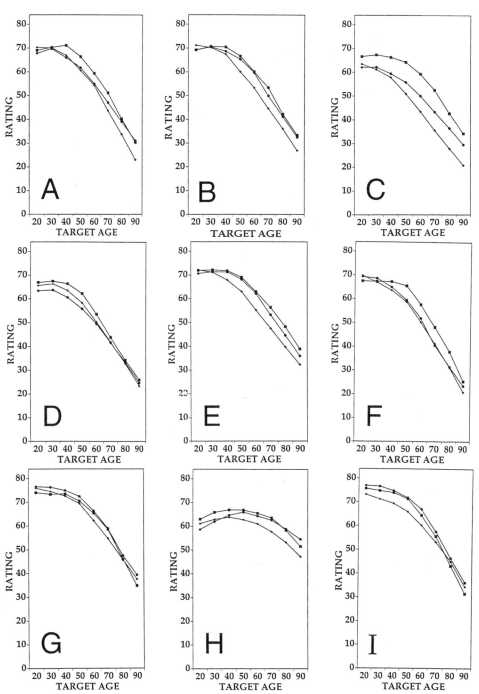

FIG. 7.5. Average perceived developmental curves for the average adult on different types of memory (in different panels) by three respondent age groups (young, middle-age, and old). From Lineweaver & Hertzog, 1998. Reprinted with permission from Swets & Zeitlinger, Inc. (A) Global Memory Efficacy (B) Control over Memory Functioning (C) Future Control over Memory Functioning (D) Names (E) Faces (F) Telephone Number, Just Checked (G) Telephone Number, Frequently Used (H) Remote Memory (I) Recent Memory.

presented. Although the patterns differed across items, a common finding was that younger respondents rated the 20-year-old target higher than the middle-aged and older respondents. Compared with the two younger groups, the older respondents often rated the 30- and 40-year-old targets the highest, suggesting older adults may believe peak performance occurs somewhat later in the life span than do younger adults. However, on about half of the items, they also tended to rate the oldest targets the lowest, suggesting an expectation of greater ultimate loss in certain areas (e.g., people met in the past and appointments). Older respondents, then, may have somewhat more differentiated beliefs, perhaps as a function of experience with the effects of aging on memory in self, friends, and family. In contrast, younger adults' beliefs may be shaped largely by stereotypes about aging.

Dixon, Gagnon, and Crow (1998) also report findings that suggest older respondents may hold more elaborate conceptions about memory functioning in adulthood than do younger respondents. They explored adults' beliefs related to collaborative cognition (cognitive activity that occurs in the context of more than one individual). Participants were asked to rank the effectiveness of memory performance under six recall conditions: working (a) alone, (b) with a spouse, (c) with a friend (same gender), (d) with a friend (other gender), (e) with a stranger (same gender), and (f) with a stranger (other gender). Both age groups believed working with a spouse would be most effective and working with a stranger of the other gender would be least effective, with the other groups ranked in between in the order noted above. However, the profile of responses suggested that younger adults effectively distinguish between two levels of collaborative effectiveness: (a) working with a spouse or friend (same or other gender) and (b) working alone or with a stranger (same or other gender). In contrast, older adults appeared to distinguish among three levels of collaborative effectiveness: (a) working with a spouse, (b) working alone or with a friend (same or other gender), and (c) working with a stranger (same or other gender). Qualitative analyses suggested that the complementarity and familiarity achieved by many years of working together has heightened the sense of self-efficacy associated with collaboration with a spouse for older adults.

Implicit Theories of Other Cognitive Processes. Research examining implicit theories about aging-related changes in other domains of cognitive functioning has also generally revealed expectations of loss. Older adults are typically perceived as less competent than younger adults (e.g., Kite & Johnson, 1988; Ryan & Heaven, 1988). Although respondents seem to expect greater change in the domain of memory than in domains such as intelligence and language (e.g., Heckhausen et al., 1989), the overall expectation is that losses will occur with increasing age in these areas as well (e.g., Rubin & Brown, 1975; Ryan, Kwong See, Meneer, & Trovato, 1992). For example, Ryan et al. found that both younger and older respondents generally expected more receptive and expressive language problems for 75-year-old targets than for 25-year-old targets. However, again beliefs varied substantially as a function of the specific language task. Thus, older adults were expected to perform more poorly than younger adults on tasks that involve memory or speed (e.g., lose track of what talking about and hard to speak if pressed for time). In contrast, some enhancement was expected in some social aspects of language functioning (e.g., telling interesting stories and sincerity in conversation).

A similar differentiated perspective emerges in the domain of intelligence. In general, elementary intellectual abilities and the speed of their execution are expected to decline with age, whereas intellectual tasks that rely on experience or common sense are expected to show continued gains through later life (e.g., Heckhausen et al., 1989; Hendrick, Gekoski, & Knox, 1991; Hendrick, Knox, Gekoski, & Dyne, 1988; Orwoll & Perlmutter, 1990). For example, Hendrick et al. (1988) showed younger adults items from some subtests of the Wechsler Adult Intelligence Scale and asked them to estimate how younger and older adults would perform on these tasks. Older targets were seen as less cognitively able than older targets to perform subtests involving memory and psychomotor speed. In contrast, older targets were seen as more cognitively able than younger targets on subtests that assessed practical judgment and common sense. Several studies have found that adults in our culture expect wisdom to increase with age well into later life (Heckhausen et al., 1989; Orwoll & Perlmutter, 1990).

Relation of Implicit Theories of Cognition to Behavior. The literature reviewed above suggests that adults in our culture hold multidimensional and multidirectional beliefs about aging and cognition. Implicit theories of both loss and gain are held, although theories that postulate increasing losses in cognition with increasing age tend to be more predominant. Such belief systems constitute an important source of information for making judgments about the behavior of others and for recalling past personal status on various attributes and characteristics. Expectations derived from implicit theory beliefs may also influence performance on cognitive tasks.

In the case of judgments about the behavior of others, studies using person–perception paradigms suggest that individuals use an age-based double standard in evaluating memory failures. Memory failures exhibited by older adults are viewed as signifying greater mental difficulties and greater need for intervention than memory failures exhibited by younger adults (Erber, 1989; Erber, Szuchman, & Rothberg, 1990a). Moreover, memory failures on the part of older adults are more likely to be attributed to internal, stable, and uncontrollable causes (e.g., lack of ability and age-related mental problems), whereas the same behaviors exhibited by younger adults are more likely to be attributed to internal, unstable, and controllable causes (e.g., lack of attention and lack of effort; Erber & Rothberg, 1991; Erber, Szuchman, & Rothberg, 1990b; Parr & Siegert, 1993). Perhaps because memory failures are seen to be an inevitable part of growing older, people appear to be more forgiving of memory lapses on the part of older adults, at least if other information does not conflict with the perception that the person in question is a typical older adult (Erber, Caiola, & Pupo, 1994; Erber, Szuchman, & Prager, 1997).

Implicit theories have also been hypothesized to be central to individuals' constructions of their own personal histories (Ross, 1989). This perspective suggests that recalling "the way we were" is determined substantially by active, constructive, schema-driven processes rather than by detailed veridical recall of events. Specifically, Ross argued that long-term recall of personal attributes involves two major steps. First, individuals access information about their present status on the attribute in question. Presumably, this information is more salient and more accessible than their status at some time in the past. Second, in attempting to determine whether there has been any change on the attribute in question, individuals may invoke an implicit theory of stability or change to guide their reconstruction of the past. These beliefs may influence both the information retrieved from memory as well as its interpretation. If specific information cannot be recalled, the theory may be used to construct a likely scenario. An implicit theory that contains a strongly held belief of gains or losses over time may lead to constructions of the past that are consistent with these beliefs.

Empirical evidence supporting the role of implicit theories of change in people's recall of their past standing on personal attributes is available in a number of domains (e.g., McFarland, Ross, & DeCourville, 1989; McFarland, Ross, & Giltrow, 1992). For example, McFarland et al. (1992) reported that implicit theories of age-related gain and loss were important determinants of how older adults recall the characteristics they possessed at an earlier age. For attributes expected to increase with age (e.g., kindness and physical problems), older adults recalled possessing less of the attribute when they were younger than younger adults reported currently. For attributes expected to show decreases with age (memory for names and activity), older adults recalled possessing more of the attribute when they were younger than younger adults did currently.

Cross-sectional results of this sort are limited by the possibility of cohort and selection effects. However, recent longitudinal analyses also offer some support for the role of implicit theories in the reconstruction of personal past. McDonald-Miszczak, Hertzog, and Hultsch (1995) reported that a sample ranging in age from middle age to old age and tested three times over 6 years showed significant changes on measures of both perceived memory functioning and actual memory performance. However, they observed only weak relationships between longitudinal changes in memory performance and retrospective perceptions of memory change at the end of the longitudinal period. Although such relationships suggest that adults may monitor changes in their memory ability to some extent, other findings were consistent with an implicit theory perspective. Specifically, within-occasion correlations of perceived level of memory efficacy and perceived retrospective change were high and changed together. This result is consistent with the hypothesis that current perceptions of efficacy level drive current perceptions of how memory has changed over time.

Some investigators have also suggested that negative stereotypes about aging may contribute directly to age-related declines in memory performance. Levy and Langer (1994) postulated that negative expectations (what they term *premature cognitive commitments*) about memory loss and aging in our culture may become a self-fulfilling prophecy through a variety of indirect mechanisms. To examine the general hypothesis that implicit theories influence performance, they examined general beliefs about aging and memory performance in three cultural groups. Younger and older American hearing adults were contrasted with younger and older adults from the American deaf and mainland Chinese cultures. Consistent with their hypotheses, Levy and Langer reported that the American deaf and Chinese groups held more positive attitudes toward aging than the American hearing groups. In addition, the results indicated the expected significant interaction between cultural group and age on a composite measure of episodic memory. Among the younger participants, there were no significant cultural group differences, whereas among the older participants the Chinese group performed significantly better than the American deaf group, who, in turn, performed significantly better than the American hearing group. These provocative results require replication because they are limited by a number of factors, such as the cross-sectional design, small sample sizes, and the use of a spatial memory task that may have favored Chinese participants. Nevertheless, they point to the potential influence of implicit beliefs on cognitive performance in later life.

Levy (1996) conducted a study that was, she argued, evidence that subliminal activation of negative age stereotypes impaired the memory performance of older adults. She used a visual masking paradigm to present words like *senile* and *Alzheimer's* to young and old adults below the threshold of conscious awareness (see Greenwald & Banaji, 1995, for a review of methods and data on unconscious activation of implicit beliefs and stereotypes). Results indicated poorer performance by older adults primed with the negative stereotype words at posttest on two of four memory tasks. There are some potential concerns with the Levy study, including no direct evidence of priming effects and inadequate checks to ensure that participants did not perceive some of the words, leading to resentful demoralization. Given some of the methodological difficulties with subliminal priming, the study certainly needs replication. Moreover, the mechanisms mediating the effects of age stereotype activation on memory performance have yet to be identified. Although it can be construed in the context of the self-fulfilling culturally based expectations of poor memory (as in the Levy & Langer, 1994, study), it could also be the case that the unconscious activation of the negative implicit theory about aging and memory leads to heightened performance anxiety, which impairs performance. Nevertheless, this is an intriguing study with important implications regarding the impact of beliefs about aging and memory.

Self-Referent Beliefs About Cognition

Implicit theories of cognition may be contrasted with self-referent beliefs about cognition. The former focus on beliefs about the nature of cognition and its characteristics as they apply to most people, whereas the latter focus on assessments and expectations about one's own cognitive functioning. Of course, as we have implied earlier, these two types of beliefs are not necessarily unrelated. For example, implicit theories of age-related change may influence beliefs related to the self as well as generalized or specific others. In fact, some studies have suggested that there is substantial correspondence between beliefs about others and beliefs about the self. Ryan and Kwong See (1993) asked people to complete ratings of memory ability, intraindividual change, and personal control for both typical adults and themselves at several target ages. They found no significant differences in ratings of self and others for any of the measures. Although self-referent beliefs and generalized beliefs about others within a given domain are significantly related, personal beliefs are not necessarily age-relevant application of general beliefs to the self. Several studies suggest that this may be the case (Camp & Pignatiello, 1988; Lineweaver & Hertzog, 1998; Ryan et al., 1992). For example, Lineweaver and Hertzog did find that there were substantial correlations between the predicted score for a person of a given age on his or her own general beliefs age curve for memory efficacy and control (see Fig. 7.5) and their personal belief about current efficacy and control over memory. However, the correlations were not so high as to argue that the two beliefs were interchangeable, suggesting that there is heuristic value in distinguishing between general and personal beliefs about memory.

Theorists have suggested that self-referent beliefs about cognition are most profitably considered to be multidimensional and domain specific (Cavanaugh, 1996; Cavanaugh & Green, 1990; Dixon & Hertzog, 1988; Hertzog & Dixon, 1994; Hertzog et al., 1990a; Hultsch, Hertzog, Dixon, & Davidson, 1988; M. E. Lachman, 1983; Wellman, 1983). From our perspective, three dimensions focused on the effectiveness, causes, and changes in one's own behavior have been salient in the literature. The concept of *self-efficacy* focuses on the beliefs about the effectiveness of one's own behavior. Briefly, self-efficacy may be defined as the belief in one's ability, broadly defined to include motivation, cognitive knowledge and resources, and behaviors and skills, to meet a set of task demands. It may be assessed with reference to a general domain of functioning or a specific task. The issue of the causes of behavior is captured in the concept of *personal control*. Here, the focus is on individuals' beliefs about whether outcomes are contingent on their own behaviors as opposed to external influences, such as chance or the actions of other individuals or entities. Finally, the issue of *perceived change* focuses on individuals' beliefs about whether their cognitive functioning has been or will be characterized by gains, stability, or losses over some period of time. Although these three constructs are related, they are differentiable from one another, both conceptually and empirically. At the conceptual level, consider a person's beliefs related to the task of recalling the names of a dozen people to whom they have just been introduced. Self-efficacy beliefs would influence the person's assessment of the number of names they could retrieve and their confidence in this assessment. Their sense of personal control would manifest itself in beliefs about the extent to which they could do something that would affect the probability of successfully recalling the names. Finally, their perceptions of change would be reflected in their beliefs about the developmental trajectory of their ability to perform this task. Although these beliefs may coincide, they also may diverge. Thus, a person may assess their current efficacy to be relatively low but believe that it could be substantially increased if they learned a mnemonic system for remembering names.

In addition to the three central dimensions of self-efficacy, personal control, and perceived change, several investigators have suggested that individuals' representations about the ways in which they react emotionally to cognitively demanding situations may also be an important aspect of metacognition (e.g., Hertzog & Dixon, 1994; Hultsch et al., 1988; M. E. Lachman, 1983). Such beliefs may include (a) the expectation that being asked to perform a cognitively demanding task will produce affective states, such as anxiety, or (b) achievement motivation with respect to a given cognitive domain.

Measurement of Self-Referent Beliefs. Over the past 20 years, investigators have developed a multitude of measures of self-referent beliefs about cognition. Much of the effort has been aimed at developing paper-and-pencil questionnaires. Although generic measures of constructs such as efficacy and control are available (e.g., Levenson, 1974; Scherer et al., 1982), it has been argued that examination of the relationship between beliefs and actual behavior requires a domain-specific or task-specific approach (M. E. Lachman, 1983). Since the early 1980s, a number of psychometrically sound multidimensional scales have been developed focused on several domains, such as attention (e.g., Tun & Wingfield, 1995), memory (e.g., Berry et al., 1989; Dixon & Hultsch, 1983; Dixon, Hultsch, & Hertzog, 1989; Gilewski, Zelinski, & Schaie, 1990; M. E. Lachman, Bandura, Weaver, & Elliott, 1995; Winterling, Crook, Salama, & Gobert, 1986), intelligence (e.g., M. E. Lachman, Baltes, Nesselroade, & Willis 1982), and language (e.g., Ryan et al., 1992). Many of these questionnaires are multidimensional in that they address more than one of the constructs central to self-referent beliefs about cognition described previously. The great bulk of them measure beliefs about memory functioning. More detailed reviews of the conceptual and psychometric characteristics of these measures are available elsewhere (e.g., Cavanaugh, 1996; Dixon, 1989; Gilewski & Zelinski, 1986).

One general approach to the measurement of self-referent beliefs about cognition has emphasized relatively global assessments of functioning across a wide range of everyday situations. Some of these global measures have a central focus on problems or complaints within a given domain (e.g., Chaffin & Herrmann, 1983; Gilewski et al., 1990; Sunderland, Harris, & Baddeley, 1983; Ryan et al., 1992; Tun & Wingfield, 1995). The most widely used of these instruments is Gilewski et al.'s Memory Functioning Questionnaire (MFQ). This instrument contains 64 items defining four factors: general frequency of forgetting (how often the person experiences problems with specific types of everyday memory tasks), seriousness of forgetting (rating of the seriousness of the problems created by incidents of forgetting), retrospective functioning (rating of current compared with past memory ability), and mnemonics usage (frequency of the use of techniques to aid remembering).

Other global measures have focused on asking people to assess their cognitive abilities within a domain rather than on emphasizing the frequency of cognitive problems or failures (e.g., Dixon et al., 1989; M. E. Lachman et al., 1982, 1995). One of the most widely used measures of this type is the MIA instrument (Dixon & Hultsch, 1983; Dixon et al., 1989). This 108-item questionnaire contains eight subscales: Capacity (assessment of memory ability on everyday tasks), Change (perception of change in memory ability over time), Locus (perceived control over memory ability), Anxiety (anxiety evoked by memory-demanding tasks), Achievement (perceived importance of having a good memory), Strategy (use of strategies for facilitating performance), and Knowledge (knowledge of basic memory processes). Recent analyses have indicated the Strategy subscale can be divided into internal (mental mnemonics) and external (physical reminders) strategies (McDonald-Miszczak et al., 1995).

Both the MIA and the MFQ show high levels of internal consistency and factorial validity of their respective subscales (Dixon & Hultsch, 1983; Gilewski et al., 1990; Hultsch et al., 1987). The MIA and the MFQ show convergent validity as indicators of memory self-efficacy (as indicated principally by the MIA Capacity subscale and the MFQ General Frequency of Forgetting subscale) and strategy (as indicated principally by the MIA Strategy subscale and the MFQ Mnemonics Usage subscale; Hertzog, Hultsch, & Dixon, 1989). There is also evidence that measures of memory self-efficacy and memory control may be discriminated from other constructs, such as global self-efficacy and personal control, personality traits, personality states, and social desirability (Hertzog et al., 1990a).

Some measures combine an emphasis on rating problems and assessing ability. In particular, the Memory Assessment Clinics Self-Rating Scale (Crook & Larrabee, 1990; Winterling et al., 1986) consists of 49 items that measure individuals' self-assessments of their ability to remember specific types of information (e.g., "the name of a person just introduced to you") and how often they experience specific types of memory problems (e.g., "forget what you intended to buy at a grocery store or pharmacy"). Each of these two sets of items has been shown to be composed of five factors: for ability factors, remote personal memory, numeric recall, everyday task oriented memory, word recall/semantic memory, and spatial and topographical memory; for problem frequency factors, word/fact recall, attention/concentration, everyday task-oriented memory, general forgetfulness, and facial recognition (Crook & Larrabee, 1990).

Questionnaires such as the MFQ and the MIA tap multiple dimensions of individuals' self-assessments of cognitive functioning. More recently, several questionnaires focusing on one aspect of metacognition have been developed. For example, M. E. Lachman et al. (1995) developed the Memory Controllability Inventory, which emphasizes several facets of the personal control construct. The 12-item instrument consists of four subscales: Present Ability (current memory ability), Potential Improvement (confidence that strategies can be found to improve memory), Effort/Utility (degree to which memory can be improved through expenditure of effort), and Inevitable Decrement (belief that memory inevitably deteriorates with age). Similarly, a scale designed to measure self-assessed difficulty in dividing attention between two activities has been developed (the Divided Attention Questionnaire; Tun & Wingfield, 1995).

A second broad approach to measuring self-referent beliefs about cognition focuses on assessing self-efficacy with reference to a specific task. The previously discussed prediction paradigm, in which participants are asked to predict their expected level of performance on a specific task prior to performing the task, is frequently used to assess the impact of individuals' self-efficacy on their expectations for success on a given task. Depending on the study, participants may receive only a description of the task or they may complete several sample items before making their predictions. The paradigm may be extended to include postdictions of performance following completion of the task.

A more sophisticated approach, derived specifically from Bandura's (1986) theory of self-efficacy, establishes a hierarchy of levels of performance in relation to an overall goal. Participants provide predictions of the level of the task that they can successfully achieve (self-efficacy level) and assessments of their confidence in achieving these levels (self-efficacy strength). This approach is the basis for the Memory Self-Efficacy Questionnaire (MSEQ; Berry et al., 1989). Rather than asking participants to make a single prediction, the MSEQ identifies a task hierarchy of increasing difficulty and asks participants to make multiple predictions in reference to an overall goal (the highest level of task performance). The MSEQ asks people to rate 10 memory tasks, 5 of which represent laboratory-type tasks (e.g., remembering unrelated pairs of words) and 5 of which represent everyday-type tasks (e.g., recalling a shopping list). For each task, participants are asked to indicate whether they would be able to perform the task at each of five levels of difficulty, ranging from relatively minimal performance to perfect performance (e.g., for a list of 18 items on a shopping list: 2 of 18, 6 of 18, 10 of 18, 14 of 18, or 18 of 18). For each level at which they indicate they can accomplish the task, participants are also asked to rate their degree of confidence that they will be able to complete the task (from 10% to 100%). Of the several measures that may be derived from the MSEQ, the most common are the number of "yes" responses (with at least 20% confidence), which is taken as an indicator of self-efficacy level, and the average confidence rating, which is taken as an indicator of self-efficacy strength. This measure has good psychometric properties, and several alternative forms have been developed (Berry et al., 1989).

Age Differences and Changes in Self-Referent Cognitive Beliefs. Researchers interested in self-referent beliefs about cognition have devoted considerable attention to the question of age differences and age changes in these beliefs. Given that there is a general expectation of cognitive loss in our culture and actual performance on many cognitive tasks shows a decline with increasing age, it is reasonable to expect that individuals' assessments of their own cognitive performance may decline as well. However, as noted earlier, self-referent beliefs may diverge from general beliefs. Moreover, as was the case with studies examining implicit theories of cognition, the results vary as a function of the types of questions asked and the cognitive domain on which they focus.

Perhaps as a result of available instruments, most studies have been directed toward self-referent beliefs about memory. Although there are inconsistencies across studies, the literature tends to point to both cross-sectional age differences and longitudinal age changes in multiple aspects of metamemory. Older adults report lower levels of memory efficacy (Berry et al., 1989; Gilewski et al., 1990; Hultsch et al., 1987; Zelinski, Gilewski, & Thompson, 1980), believe their memory has declined more over time (Gilewski et al., 1990; Hultsch et al., 1987; G. E. Smith, Petersen, Ivnik, Malec, & Tangalos, 1996; Taylor, Miller, & Tinklenberg, 1992), and report less control over their memory functioning (e.g., Hultsch et al., 1987; M. E. Lachman et al., 1995) than do younger adults. There are studies that show little or no evidence of age differences in self-referent beliefs about memory (e.g., Crook & Larrabee, 1992; Devolder & Pressley, 1991), but these findings are in the minority.

Data from longitudinal studies are particularly important because they examine changes in beliefs directly. McDonald-Miszczak et al. (1995), for example, reported significant changes on several subscales of the MIA for a sample of adults ranging in age from 55 to 86 years measured three times over 6 years. Participants reported significant changes in rated memory capacity (lower), perceived stability of memory (more decline), personal control (lower), anxiety about memory (higher), and external strategy use (greater) over the period. It should be noted, however, that the effect sizes for perceived change over the 6 years were relatively modest (range = −0.15 SDs to 0.26 SDs) and did not vary much across the young-old (ages 55–70) and old-old (ages 71–86) groups. These effect sizes are somewhat smaller than those observed for measures of actual memory performance for word recall (−0.30 SDs) and fact recall (−0.39 SDs) obtained over the same interval in the old-old group (Hultsch, Hertzog, Dixon, & Small, 1998).

The report by McDonald-Miszczak et al. (1995) covers the longest longitudinal span currently available on beliefs about memory. Other studies covering shorter spans have also reported evidence of change, but the findings across shorter intervals are more inconsistent. For example, in an examination of an adult sample ranging in age from 22 to 78 years tested twice over 2 years, McDonald-Miszczak et al. did not find significant changes on any of the MIA subscales other than internal strategy use (increase). However, they did observe significant change on two subscales of the MFQ, indicating an increase in reports that memory was getting worse and memory failures were increasing. Taylor et al. (1992) also found significant changes on the MFQ Retrospective Functioning subscale over the same interval.

Longitudinal data also provide important information at the level of individual differences. One finding is that indicators of self-referent cognitive beliefs show very high stability over time. McDonald-Miszczak et al. (1995) reported 6-year disattenuated stability coefficients for the subscales of the MIA ranging from .87 to .99. Although there were some individual differences in change in beliefs, roughly 80% to 90% of the true scale variance is associated with stable individual differences. Thus, beliefs about memory functioning and change in memory functioning appear to be relatively stable and enduring characteristics of the individual.

Information about the relative durability of self-referent cognitive beliefs may also be derived from examining the impact of cognitive training on such beliefs. There is substantial evidence supporting the conclusion that cognitive training can lead to substantial improvements in domains such as intelligence and memory, even late in life (Verhaeghen, Marcoen, & Goossens, 1992; Willis, 1989). However, self-referent beliefs about cognition may be somewhat resistant to modification. A recent meta-analysis of 27 studies conducted by Floyd and Scogin (1997) indicated that the impact of training (effect size) was considerably higher for objective measures of performance than for subjective memory assessments. In general, experiences that result in improvement or success appear to be more likely to affect judgments of self-efficacy related to the specific task on which training occurred (e.g., Dittmann-Kohli, Lachman, Kliegl, & Baltes, 1991) in contrast to judgments about of self-efficacy related to memory functioning in general (Rebok & Balcerak, 1989). It may also be the case that mastery experiences alone are not sufficient to modify self-referent beliefs in the face of an implicit theory of decline. M. E. Lachman, Weaver, Bandura, Elliott, and Lewkowicz (1992) examined the impact of memory training and cognitive restructuring designed to promote adaptive beliefs about memory on individuals' perceptions of memory control. Their results indicated that enhancing memory skills alone did not change control beliefs. Cognitive restructuring did lead to more favorable beliefs about the contribution of effort to performance, the possibility of memory improvement, and the inevitability of memory loss. The greatest gains were observed when memory skill training was combined with cognitive restructuring. However, Lachman et al. also found that there was a trend for the treatment effects to regress toward baseline at long-term follow-up.

Another consideration in judging the evidence of age differences and change are the base rates of beliefs and changes in beliefs across persons. That is, although older persons, on average, may rate their memory efficacy or control as lower than that of younger adults (or than they rated these characteristics at an earlier point it time), it is not clear whether these perceptions are typical of most older adults. Cross-sectional surveys of representative samples attempting to assess such base rates suggest that negative beliefs about cognitive functioning may not be characteristic of the majority of older adults (e.g., Cutler & Grams, 1989; Herzog & Rodgers, 1989). For example, Cutler and Grams reported the results of a brief survey of memory problems obtained from a representative sample of over 14,000 adults aged 55 and over. Respondents were asked whether they had experienced problems remembering things during the past year, and if so, whether the frequency of such problems had changed during the past year. For the total sample, only 15% of respondents indicated they had frequent trouble remembering in contrast to 46% who said they rarely or never had trouble. Even within the oldest group (85+ years), only about 23% indicated frequent trouble remembering. Similarly, only about 18% of the sample reported they experienced an increase in trouble remembering over the past year. These results are mirrored in a recent longitudinal study reported by G. E. Smith et al. (1996), in which two questions from the MFQ ("How would you rate your memory in terms of the kinds of problems you have?" and "How is your memory compared to the way it was 5 years ago?") were presented to a representative sample of 394 adults aged 55 to 97 years. Only 12% of the sample reported that they experienced no memory problems. However, less than 3% reported major problems. About half the respondents indicated their memory was relatively stable. Nearly 25% reported their memory was actually better currently than 5 years ago, whereas only 5% reported it to be worse or much worse.

It is possible that these types of general questions about memory problems underestimate self-perceived decline in memory functioning. Hertzog et al. (1989) suggested that questionnaires designed to measure memory problems or difficulties may show smaller age differences than questionnaires that ask people to assess their memory ability, either in general or with respect to a range of tasks. It is possible that although individuals perceive that their memory ability has declined, they do not view this loss as a problem for their everyday functioning. Nevertheless, the results do suggest that perceived memory loss is not uniform across respondents.

Perhaps even more diversity is observed in the domain of intellectual functioning. Using data from the Seattle Longitudinal Study, Schaie, Willis, and O'Hanlon (1994) examined actual and self-perceived change in a sample of 837 adults aged 25 to 94 years tested on the subscales of the Primary Mental Abilities Test in 1977 and again in 1984. At the second testing, participants were asked to rate how their performance on the tests just completed compared with their performance 7 years ago. The percentage of people indicating their performance was worse on the later occasion compared with the earlier occasion was higher for older than middle-aged and younger respondents in most cases. An exception was Number, for which younger and middle-aged participants were more likely than older participants to report that their performance had deteriorated. However, critical for our purposes is the finding that, for virtually all abilities, a majority of respondents indicated that their performance was either better or the same as previously. The percentage of participants indicating their more recent performance was worse was substantial (ranging from 17% for vocabulary to 48% for spatial orientation). However, it is clear that not all participants believed in cognitive decline. Moreover, older adults were less likely to see decline than middle-aged and younger adults on at least one ability.

Relation of Self-Referent Beliefs to Performance. A central issue facing researchers interested in metacognition concerns the relationship between beliefs about cognition and actual cognitive functioning. Initially, investigators made the straightforward assumption that individuals' self-reports about their abilities in a cognitive domain such as memory would mirror their actual performance on tasks in that domain (e.g., Herrmann & Neisser, 1978). However, subsequent work has clearly shown that this assumption is anything but straightforward.

There is now a substantial body of work examining the relationship between self-reports of ability and performance, particularly in the domain of memory. This research supports the conclusion that self-referent beliefs about cognitive functioning are often inaccurate. The finding of relatively modest correlations between questionnaire measures of beliefs and performance led to questions about the reliability and construct validity of the self-report scales (e.g., Herrmann, 1982). However, research on the psychometric properties of these instruments has shown that they demonstrate more than adequate internal consistency, factorial validity, convergent validity, and discriminant validity (e.g., Crook & Larrabee, 1992; Gilewski et al., 1990; Hertzog et al., 1989, 1990a).

A specific issue that has been addressed in some detail is the question of whether self-reports of memory or other cognitive problems are actually the product of depressive affect (e.g., Gilewski & Zelinski, 1986) or of personality traits such as neuroticism (e.g., McCrae & Costa, 1990) that are associated with negative self-assessments about many aspects of the self. Some studies have suggested that memory complaints are more likely to be related to depressive affect than to actual memory performance (Bolla, Lindgren, Bonaccorsy, & Bleecker, 1991; Hanninen et al., 1994; Kahn, Zarit, Hilbert, & Niederehe, 1975; G. E. Smith et al., 1996). Although it is clear that there is a relationship between affective states and personality traits on the one hand, and memory complaints and other self-assessments of cognitive functioning on the other, the small size of the relationship cannot explain age differences in perceived memory ability or the modest correlation between memory beliefs and memory performance. At least some studies indicate that when the effects of depression and other variables are partialed out, self-reports of memory still account for statistically significant amounts of variance in memory performance (Zelinski, Gilewski, & Anthony-Bergstone, 1990).

The zero-order correlations between indicators of memory self-efficacy and memory performance vary considerably across studies but tend to be in the range of 0.2 to 0.3 in both normal and mildly cognitively impaired adults (e.g., Cavanaugh & Poon, 1989; Rabbitt & Abson, 1990; Sunderland, Watts, Baddeley, & Harris, 1986; Zelinski et al., 1990). For those experiencing more pronounced symptoms of dementia, concurrent assessments of memory ability show little relationship to actual memory performance (e.g., Kaszniak, 1996; Reisberg, Ferris, de Leon, & Crook, 1985).

The magnitude of the relationship between beliefs and performance may be influenced by a number of factors, including correspondence between the context in which self-efficacy is assessed and performance is measured on the one hand and the familiarity of the memory task on the other. For example, Berry, West, and Dennehey (1989) found a stronger relationship between indicators of self-efficacy and performance for familiar everyday tasks (e.g., recalling phone numbers) than for more traditional laboratory tasks (e.g., recalling unrelated words). More recently, West, Dennehey-Basile, and Norris (1996) examined age differences in the relationship between memory self-efficacy and memory performance for a set of laboratory and everyday tasks. They found that older adults showed less correspondence between self-efficacy judgments and performance than did younger adults and that this difference was larger for unfamiliar laboratory tasks than for more familiar everyday tasks.

It is of particular interest to examine the relationship between beliefs and performance in a longitudinal context. Assessment of the relationship at a single point in time may be complicated by individual differences in interpretation of the anchors and scales used to assess beliefs. Some people may demand few or no memory failures before they are willing to indicate that they have a good memory for names, whereas other people may decide that their ability is quite good if their assessment suggests that they remember the names of those most important to them most of the time. With longitudinal data, the focus is on changes in beliefs, with the result that individual differences in absolute criteria may be minimized. However, it is also possible that the interpretation of what constitutes good or poor performance will change over time.

In general, longitudinal data also suggest modest relationships between perceived change in memory beliefs and changes in performance. For example, McDonald-Miszczak et al. (1995) found small but significant relationships between retrospective perceptions of memory change (taken at the last longitudinal occasion) and changes in memory performance over 6 years on three memory tasks: word recall (.16), fact recall (.26), and text recall (.21). These relationships are of the same moderate sort seen in the concurrent relationship of beliefs and performance and suggest that individuals are capable of some degree of accuracy in monitoring changes in their memory ability. Similar evidence was reported recently by Johansson, Allen-Burge, and Zarit (1997) for a sample of very old adults from four birth cohorts (aged 84, 86, 88, and 90 years at initial testing) retested twice at intervals of 2 years. Reported decline in memory was significantly related to actual decline on three of five memory tests. In addition, self-evaluations obtained at Time 1 were predictive of a diagnosis of dementia at Times 2 and 3. As with previous research findings, the relationships were significant but of modest magnitude. It must be noted that some studies have failed to find significant linkage between perceived and actual changes in memory (e.g., G. E. Smith et al., 1996; Taylor et al., 1992; Zelinski, Gilewski, & Schaie, 1993). However, there are many factors that may explain this discrepancy, including differences in measures and limited evidence for cognitive change in some studies.

CONCLUSIONS

Metacognition is a multidimensional construct, which is reflected in the pattern of age relationships with different metacognitive constructs. It appears to be the case that older adults have relatively intact monitoring skills, although they may not always use monitoring effectively to control learning and cognition and to update knowledge about effective strategies for cognitive performance. Older adults may be less likely to use effective strategies spontaneously, although their behavior improves with specific instructions. Having said that, it appears that many of the salient age changes in metacognition are associated with beliefs about cognitive ability and control over cognition. As individuals grow old, they are likely to perceive that their cognitive ability has declined. Adults of all ages believe that there are declines after early middle age in memory and cognition and also in control over cognition. Negative beliefs about aging and cognition appear to develop early and to persist across the life span. Although these beliefs may be normatively accurate, individual differences in rated memory self-efficacy are not highly correlated with memory performance, nor are perceived changes highly correlated with actual cognitive changes. Such findings underscore the importance of treating beliefs about one's own memory as possibly inaccurate beliefs that can have consequences for subjective well-being and everyday behavior in cognitively demanding situations, not just cognitive tasks.

These conclusions should be treated as tentative statements about an area of research on aging and cognition that is growing in its methodological sophistication and in the kinds of research questions being tackled. Research on metacognition has advanced beyond the point of testing the idea that metacognitive deficits are the sole or even primary cause of age changes in cognition. Instead, research is increasingly asking when, how, and under what conditions metacognition is utilized effectively in service of learning, whether beliefs about self and other are differentiated and adaptive, whether memory self-efficacy is a cause of performance limitations (and if so, by what mechanism), and so on. There is reason to be optimistic about what can and will be learned in the future, although we decline to make specific predictions, lest we be accused of overconfidence.

ACKNOWLEDGMENTS

Work on this chapter was supported in part by Grant R01 AG08235 from the National Institute on Aging (NIA). Christopher Hertzog was also supported by NIA Grant R01 AG13148. We thank John Dunlosky for his helpful comments on an earlier version of this chapter and Christy McGuire and Jennifer Hertzog for their assistance in the preparation of the final manuscript.

REFERENCES

Anooshian, L. J., Mammarella, S. L., & Hertel, P. T. (1989). Adult age differences in knowledge of retrieval processes. *International Journal of Aging and Human Development, 29*, 39–52.

Bandura, A. (1977). Self-efficacy: Toward a unifying theory of behavioral change. *Psychological Review, 84*, 191–215.

Bandura, A. (1986). *Social foundations of thought and action: A social cognitive theory.* Englewood Cliffs, NJ: Prentice-Hall.

Benjamin, A. S., & Bjork, R. A. (1996). Retrieval fluency as a metacognitive index. In L. M. Reder (Ed.), *Implicit memory and metacognition* (pp. 309–338). Mahwah, NJ: Lawrence Erlbaum Associates.

Berry, J. M., & West, R. L. (1993). Cognitive self-efficacy in relation to personal mastery and goal setting across the life span. *International Journal of Behavioral Development, 16,* 351–379.

Berry, J. M., West, R. L., & Dennehey, D. M. (1989). Reliability and validity of the Memory Self-Efficacy Questionnaire. *Developmental Psychology, 5,* 701–713.

Bieman-Copeland, S., & Charness, N. (1994). Memory knowledge and memory monitoring in adulthood. *Psychology and Aging, 9,* 287–302.

Bolla, K. I., Lindgren, K. N., Bonaccorsy, C., & Bleecker, M. L. (1991). Memory complaints in older adults: Fact or fiction? *Archives of Neurology, 48,* 61–64.

Borkowski, J. G., Carr, M., & Pressley, M. (1987). Spontaneous strategy use: Perspectives from metacognitive theory. *Intelligence, 11,* 61–75.

Brigham, M. C., & Pressley, M. (1988). Cognitive monitoring and strategy choice in younger and older adults. *Psychology and Aging, 3,* 249–257.

Brown, A. L. (1978). Knowing when, where, and how to remember: A problem of metacognition. In R. Glaser (Ed.), *Advances in instructional psychology* (pp. 367–406). Hillsdale, NJ: Lawrence Erlbaum Associates.

Brown, N. R., & Siegler, R. S. (1993). Metrics and mappings: A framework for understanding real-world quantitative estimation. *Psychological Review, 100,* 511–534.

Bruce, P. R., Coyne, A. C., & Botwinick, J. (1982). Age differences in metamemory. *Journal of Gerontology, 37,* 354–357.

Burke, D. M., MacKay, D. G., Worthley, J. S., & Wade, E. (1991). On the tip of the tongue: What causes word finding failures in young and older adults? *Journal of Memory and Language, 30,* 542–579.

Butterfield, E. C., Nelson, T. O., & Peck, V. (1988). Developmental aspects of the feeling of knowing. *Developmental Psychology, 24,* 654–663.

Camp, C. J., & Pignatiello, M. F. (1988). Beliefs about fact retrieval and inferential reasoning across the adult lifespan. *Experimental Aging Research, 14,* 89–97.

Cavanaugh, J. C. (1996). Memory self-efficacy as a moderator of memory change. In F. Blanchard-Fields & T. M. Hess (Eds.), *Perspectives on cognitive change in adulthood* (pp. 488–507). New York: McGraw-Hill.

Cavanaugh, J. C., Feldman, J., & Hertzog, C. (1998). Memory beliefs as social cognition: A reconceptualization of what memory questionnaires assess. *Review of General Psychology, 2,* 48–65.

Cavanaugh, J. C., & Green, E. E. (1990). I believe, therefore I can: Personal beliefs and memory aging. In E. A. Lovelace (Ed.), *Aging and cognition: Mental processes, self-awareness, and interventions* (pp. 189–230). Amsterdam: North-Holland.

Cavanaugh, J. C., & Poon, L. W. (1989). Metamemorial predictors of memory performance in young and older adults. *Psychology and Aging, 4,* 365–368.

Chaffin, R., & Herrmann, D. J. (1983). Self reports of memory abilities by old and young adults. *Human Learning, 2,* 17–28.

Chanowitz, B., & Langer, E. (1981). Premature cognitive commitment. *Journal of Personality and Social Psychology, 41,* 1051–1063.

Cohen, G., & Faulkner, D. (1986). Memory for proper names: Age differences in retrieval. *British Journal of Developmental Psychology, 4,* 187–197.

Connor, L. T., Dunlosky, J. D., & Hertzog, C. (1997). Age-related differences in absolute but not relative metamemory accuracy. *Psychology and Aging, 12,* 50–71.

Craik, F. I. M., & Dirkx, E. (1992). Age-related differences in three tests of visual imagery. *Psychology and Aging, 7,* 661–665.

Craik, F. I. M., & Jennings, J. M. (1992). Human memory. In F. I. M. Craik & T. A. Salthouse (Eds.), *The Handbook of Aging and Cognition* (pp. 51–110). Hillsdale, NJ: Lawrence Erlbaum Associates.

Crook, T. H., III, & Larrabee, G. J. (1990). A self-rating scale for evaluating memory in everyday life. *Psychology and Aging, 5,* 48–57.

Crook, T. H., III, & Larrabee, G. J. (1992). Normative data on a self-rating scale for evaluating memory in everyday life. *Archives of Clinical Neuropsychology, 7*, 41–51.

Cutler, S. J., & Grams, A. E. (1988). Correlates of self-reported everyday memory problems. *Journal of Gerontology: Social Sciences, 43*, S82–S90.

Cutler, S. J., & Hodgson, L. G. (1996). Anticipatory dementia: A link between memory appraisals and concerns about developing Alzheimer's disease. *The Gerontologist, 36*, 657–664.

Devolder, P. A., Brigham, M. C., & Pressley, M. (1990). Memory performance awareness in younger and older adults. *Psychology and Aging, 5*, 291–303.

Devolder, P. A., & Pressley, M. (1991). Memory complaints in younger and older adults. *Applied Cognitive Psychology, 5*, 443–454.

Devolder, P. A., & Pressley, M. (1992). Causal attributions and strategy use in relation to memory performance differences in younger and older adults. *Applied Cognitive Psychology, 6*, 629–642.

Dittmann-Kohli, F., Lachman, M. E., Kliegl, R., & Baltes, P. B. (1991). Effects of cognitive training and testing on intellectual efficacy beliefs in elderly adults. *Journal of Gerontology: Psychological Sciences, 46*, P162–P164.

Dixon, R. A. (1989). Questionnaire research on metamemory and aging: Issues of structure and function. In L. W. Poon, D. C. Rubin, & B. A. Wilson (Eds.), *Everyday cognition in adulthood and old age* (pp. 394–415). New York: Cambridge University Press.

Dixon, R. A., Gagnon, L. M., & Crow, C. B. (1998). Collaborative memory accuracy and distortion: Performance and beliefs. In M. J. Intons-Peterson & D. Best (Eds.), *Memory distortions and their prevention* (pp. 63–68). Mahwah, NJ: Lawrence Erlbaum Associates.

Dixon, R. A., & Hertzog, C. (1988). A functional approach to memory and metamemory development in adulthood. In F. E. Weinert & M. Perlmutter (Eds.), *Memory development: Universal changes and individual differences* (pp. 293–330). Hillsdale, NJ: Lawrence Erlbaum Associates.

Dixon, R. A., & Hultsch, D. F. (1983). Structure and development of metamemory in adulthood. *Journal of Gerontology, 38*, 682–688.

Dixon, R. A., Hultsch, D. F., & Hertzog, C. (1989). The Metamemory in Adulthood (MIA) Questionnaire. *Psychopharmacology Bulletin, 24*, 671–688.

Dunlosky, J. & Connor, L. T. (1997). Age differences in the allocation of study time account for age differences in memory performance. *Memory and Cognition, 25*, 691–700.

Dunlosky, J., & Hertzog, C. (1997). Older and younger adults use a functionally identical algorithm to select items for restudy during multi-trial learning. *Journal of Gerontology: Psychological Sciences, 52*, P178–P186.

Dunlosky, J., & Hertzog, C. (1998a). Aging and deficits in associative memory: What is the role of strategy production? *Psychology and Aging, 13*, 597–607.

Dunlosky, J., & Hertzog, C. (1998b). Training programs to improve learning in later adulthood: Helping older adults educate themselves. In D. J. Hacker, J. Dunlosky, & A. C. Graesser (Eds.), *Metacognition in educational theory and practice* (pp. 251–277). Mahwah, NJ: Lawrence Erlbaum Associates.

Erber, J. T. (1989). Young and older adults' appraisal of memory failures in young and older adult target persons. *Journal of Gerontology: Psychological Sciences, 44*, P170–P175.

Erber, J. T., Caiola, M. A., & Pupo, F. A. (1994). Age and forgetfulness: Managing perceivers' impressions of targets' capability. *Psychology and Aging, 9*, 554–561.

Erber, J. T., & Rothberg, S. T. (1991). Here's looking at you: The relative effect of age and attractiveness on judgements about memory failure. *Journal of Gerontology: Psychological Sciences, 46*, P116–P123.

Erber, J. T., Szuchman, L. T., & Prager, I. G. (1997). Forgetful but forgiven: How age and life style affect perceptions of memory failure. *Journal of Gerontology: Psychological Sciences, 52B*, P303–P307.

Erber, J. T., Szuchman, L. T., & Rothberg, S. T. (1990a). Age, gender, and individual differences in memory failure appraisal. *Psychology and Aging, 5,* 600–603.

Erber, J. T., Szuchman, L. T., & Rothberg, S. T. (1990b). Everyday memory failure: Age differences in appraisal and attribution. *Psychology and Aging, 5,* 236–241.

Floyd, M., & Scogin, F. (1997). Effects of memory training on the subjective memory functioning and mental health of older adults: A meta-analysis. *Psychology and Aging, 12,* 150–161.

Gigerenzer, G., Hoffrage, U., & Kleinbolting, H. (1991). Probabilistic mental models: A Brunswikian theory of confidence. *Psychological Review, 98,* 506–528.

Gilewski, M. J., & Zelinski, E. M. (1986). Questionnaire assessment of memory complaints. In L. W. Poon, T. Crook, K. L. Davis, C. Eisdorfer, B. J. Gurland, A. W. Kaszniak, & L. W. Thompson (Eds.), *Handbook for clinical memory assessment of older adults* (pp. 93–107). Washington, DC: American Psychological Association.

Gilewski, M. J., Zelinski, E. M., & Schaie, K. W. (1990). The Memory Functioning Questionnaire for assessment of memory complaints in adulthood and old age. *Psychology and Aging, 5,* 482–490.

Greenwald, A. G., & Banaji, M. R. (1995). Implicit social cognition: Attitudes, self-esteem, and stereotypes. *Psychological Review, 102,* 4–27.

Hanninen, T., Reinkainen, K. J., Helkala, E., Koivisto, K., Mykkanen, L., Laakso, M., Pyorala, K., & Riekkinen, P. J. (1994). Subjective memory complaints and personality traits in normal elderly subjects. *Journal of the American Geriatrics Society, 42,* 1–4.

Heckhausen, J., Dixon, R. A., & Baltes, P. B. (1989). Gains and losses in development throughout adulthood as perceived by different adult age groups. *Developmental Psychology, 25,* 109–121.

Hendrick, J. J., Gekoski, W. L., & Knox, V. J. (1991). Accuracy of young adults' perceptions of cognitive ability across adulthood. *Canadian Journal on Aging, 10,* 165–176.

Hendrick, J. J., Knox, V. J., Gekoski, W. L., & Dyne, K. J. (1988). Perceived cognitive ability in young and old targets. *Canadian Journal on Aging, 7,* 192–203.

Herrmann, D. J. (1982). Know thy memory: The use of questionnaires to assess and study memory. *Psychological Bulletin, 92,* 434–452.

Herrmann, D. J., & Neisser, U. (1978). An inventory of everyday memory experiences. In M. M. Gruenberg, P. E. Morris, & N. Sykes (Eds.), *Practical aspects of memory* (pp. 35–51). New York: Academic Press.

Hertzog, C., & Dixon, R. A. (1994). Metacognitive development in adulthood and old age. In J. Metcalf & A. P. Shimamura (Eds.), *Metacognition: Knowing about knowing* (pp. 227–251). Cambridge, MA: MIT Press.

Hertzog, C., Dixon, R. A., & Hultsch, D. F. (1990a). Metamemory in adulthood: Differentiating knowledge, belief, and behavior. In T. M. Hess (Ed.), *Aging and cognition: Knowledge organization and utilization* (pp. 161–212). Amsterdam: Elsevier.

Hertzog, C., Dixon, R. A., & Hultsch, D. F. (1990b). Relationships between metamemory, memory predictions, and memory task performance in adults. *Psychology and Aging, 5,* 217–227.

Hertzog, C., Hultsch, D. F., & Dixon, R. A. (1989). Evidence for the convergent validity of two self-report metamemory questionnaires. *Developmental Psychology, 25,* 687–700.

Hertzog, C., McGuire, C. L., & Lineweaver, T. T. (1998). Aging, attributions, perceived control, and strategy use in a free recall task. *Aging, Neuropsychology, and Cognition, 5,* 85–106.

Hertzog, C., Saylor, L. L., Fleece, A. M., & Dixon, R. A. (1994). Metamemory and aging: Relations between predicted, actual, and perceived memory task performance. *Aging and Cognition, 1,* 203–237.

Herzog, A. R., & Rodgers, W. L. (1989). Age differences in memory performance and memory ratings as measured in a sample survey. *Psychology and Aging, 4,* 173–182.

Hulicka, I. M., Sterns, H., & Grossman, J. L. (1967). Age-group comparisons for the use of mediators in paired associate learning. *Journal of Gerontology, 22*, 46–51.

Hultsch, D. F. (1969). Adult age differences in the organization of free recall. *Developmental Psychology, 1*, 673–678.

Hultsch, D. F., Hertzog, C., & Dixon, R. A. (1987). Age differences in metamemory: Resolving the inconsistencies [Special issue]. *Canadian Journal of Psychology, 41*, 193–208.

Hultsch, D. F., Hertzog, C., Dixon, R. A., & Davidson, H. (1988). Memory self-knowledge and self-efficacy in the aged. In M. L. Howe & C. J. Brainerd (Eds.), *Cognitive development in adulthood: Progress in cognitive development research* (pp. 65–92). New York: Springer-Verlag.

Hultsch, D. F., Hertzog, C., Dixon, R. A., & Small, B. J. (1998). *Memory change in the aged.* New York: Cambridge University Press.

Johansson, B., Allen-Burge, R., & Zarit, S. H. (1997). Self-reports on memory functioning in a longitudinal study of the oldest old: Relation to current, prospective, and retrospective performance. *Journal of Gerontology: Psychological Sciences, 52B*, P139–P136.

Kahn, R. L., Zarit, S. H., Hilbert, N. M., & Niederehe, G. (1975). Memory complaint and impairment in the aged. *Archives of General Psychiatry, 32*, 1569–1573.

Kaszniak, A. W. (1996). Preparing for treatment of the elderly: Assessment. In S. H. Zarit & B. Knight (Eds.), *A guide to psychotherapy and aging: Effective interventions in a life stage context* (pp. 163–220). Washington, DC: American Psychological Association.

Kausler, D. H. (1994). *Learning and memory in normal aging.* New York: Academic Press.

Kelley, C. M., & Jacoby, L. L. (1996). Memory attributions: Remembering, knowing, and feeling of knowing. In L. M. Reder (Ed.), *Implicit memory and metacognition* (pp. 287–308). Mahwah, NJ: Lawrence Erlbaum Associates.

Keren, G. (1991). Calibration and probability judgments: Conceptual and methodological issues. *Acta Psychologica, 77*, 217–273.

Kite, M. E., Deaux, K., & Miele, M. (1991). Stereotypes of young and old: Does age outweigh gender? *Psychology and Aging, 6*, 19–27.

Kite, M. E., & Johnson, B. T. (1988). Attitudes toward older and younger adults: A meta-analysis. *Psychology and Aging, 3*, 233–244.

Knox, V. J., & Gekoski, W. L. (1989). The effect of judgement context on assessments of age groups. *Canadian Journal on Aging, 8*, 244–254.

Koriat, A. (1993). How do we know that we know? The accessibility model of the feeling of knowing. *Psychological Review, 100*, 609–639.

Koriat, A. (1997). Monitoring one's own knowledge during study: A cue-utilization approach to judgments of learning. *Journal of Experimental Psychology: General, 126*, 349–370.

Koriat, A., Ben-Zur, H., & Sheffer, D. (1988). Telling the same story twice: Output monitoring and age. *Journal of Memory and Language, 27*, 23–39.

Koriat, A., & Goldsmith, M. (1996). Monitoring and control processes in the strategic regulation of memory accuracy. *Psychological Review, 103*, 490–517.

Lachman, J. L., Lachman, R., & Thronesbery, C. (1979). Metamemory through the adult life span. *Developmental Psychology, 15*, 543–551.

Lachman, M. E. (1983). Perceptions of intellectual aging: Antecedent or consequence of intellectual functioning? *Developmental Psychology, 19*, 482–498.

Lachman, M. E., Baltes, P. B., Nesselroade, J. R., & Willis, S. L. (1982). Examination of personality–ability relationships in the elderly: The role of the contextual (interface) assessment mode. *Journal of Research in Personality, 16*, 485–501.

Lachman, M. E., Bandura, M., Weaver, S. L., & Elliott, E. (1995). Assessing memory control beliefs: The Memory Controllability Inventory. *Aging and Cognition, 2*, 67–84.

Lachman, M. E., Steinberg, E. S., & Trotter, S. D. (1987). Effects of control beliefs and attributions on memory self-assessments and performance. *Psychology and Aging, 2*, 266–271.

464   HERTZOG AND HULTSCH

Lachman, M. E., Weaver, S. L., Bandura, M., Elliott, E., & Lewkowicz, C. J. (1992). Improving memory and control beliefs through cognitive restructuring and self-generated strategies. *Journal of Gerontology: Psychological Sciences, 47*, P293–P299.

Levenson, H. (1974). Activism and powerful others: Distinctions within the concept of internal–external locus of control. *Journal of Personality Assessment, 38*, 377–383.

Levy, B. (1996). Improving memory in old age through implicit self-stereotyping. *Journal of Personality and Social Psychology, 71*, 1092–1107.

Levy, B., & Langer, E. (1994). Aging free from negative stereotypes: Successful memory in China and among the American deaf. *Journal of Personality and Social Psychology, 66*, 989–997.

Light, L. L. (1996). Memory and aging. In E. L. Bjork & R. A. Bjork (Eds.), *Memory* (pp. 443–490). New York: Academic Press.

Lineweaver, T. T., & Hertzog, C. (1998). Adults' efficacy and control beliefs regarding memory and aging: Separating general from personal beliefs. *Aging, Neuropsychology, and Cognition, 5*, 264–296.

Lovelace, E. A. (1990). Aging and metacognitions concerning memory function. In E. A. Lovelace (Ed.), *Aging and cognition: Mental processes, self awareness, and interventions* (pp. 157–188). Amsterdam: North-Holland.

Lovelace, E. A., & Marsh, G. (1985). Predictions and evaluation of memory performance by young and old adults. *Journal of Gerontology, 40*, 197.

Luszcz, M. A., Roberts, T. H., & Mattiske, J. (1990). Use of relational and item-specific information in remembering by older and younger adults. *Psychology and Aging, 5*, 242–249.

Marshall, P. H., Elias, J. W., Webber, S. M., Gist, B. A., Winn, F. J., & King, P. (1978). Age differences in verbal mediation: A structural and functional analysis. *Experimental Aging Research, 4*, 175–193.

Maylor, E. A. (1990). Recognizing and naming faces: Aging, memory retrieval and the tip of the tongue state. *Journal of Gerontology: Psychological Sciences, 45*, P215–P225.

McCrae, R. R., & Costa, P. T., Jr. (1990). *Personality in adulthood.* New York: Guilford.

McDonald-Miszczak, L., Hertzog, C., & Hultsch, D. F. (1995). Stability and accuracy of metamemory in adulthood and aging: A longitudinal analysis. *Psychology and Aging, 10*, 553–564.

McFarland, C., Ross, M., & DeCourville, N. (1989). Women's theories of menstruation and biases in recall of menstrual symptoms. *Journal of Personality and Social Psychology, 57*, 522–531.

McFarland, C., Ross, M., & Giltrow, M. (1992). Biased recollections in older adults: The role of implicit theories of aging. *Journal of Personality and Social Psychology, 62*, 837–850.

Morris, M. W., & Peng, K. (1994). Culture and cause: American and Chinese attributions for social and physical events. *Journal of Personality and Social Psychology, 67*, 949–971.

Murphy, M. D., Sanders, R. E., Gabriesheski, A. S., & Schmitt, F. A. (1981). Metamemory in the aged. *Journal of Gerontology, 36*, 185–193.

Murphy, M. D., Schmitt, E. A., Caruso, M. J., & Sanders, R. E. (1987). Metamemory in older adults: The role of monitoring in serial recall. *Psychology and Aging, 2*, 331–339.

Nelson, T. O. (1984). A comparison of current measures of the accuracy of feeling-of-knowing predictions. *Psychological Bulletin, 84*, 93–116.

Nelson, T. O. (1996). Consciousness and metacognition. *American Psychologist, 51*, 102–116.

Nelson, T. O., & Dunlosky, J. (1991). When people's judgments of learning (JOLs) are extremely accurate at predicting subsequent recall: The "delayed-JOL effect." *Psychological Science, 2*, 267–270.

Nelson, T. O., Dunlosky, J., Graf, A., & Narens, L. (1994). Utilization of metacognitive judgments in the allocation of study during multitrial learning. *Psychological Science, 5*, 207–213.

Nelson, T. O., & Narens, L. (1990). Metamemory: A theoretical framework and new findings. In G. Bower (Ed.), *The psychology of learning and motivation* (Vol. 26, pp. 125–173). New York: Academic Press.

Orwoll, L., & Perlmutter, M. (1990). The study of wise persons: Integrating a personality perspective. In R. Sternberg (Ed.), *Wisdom: Its nature, origins, and development* (pp. 160–180). New York: Cambridge University Press.

Parr, W. V., & Siegert, R. (1993). Adults' conceptions of everyday memory failure in others: Factors that mediate the effects of target age. *Psychology and Aging, 8,* 599–605.

Perlmutter, M. (1978). What is memory aging the aging of? *Developmental Psychology, 14,* 330–345.

Rabbitt, P., & Abson, V. (1990). 'Lost and Found': Some logical and methodological limitations of self-report questionnaires as tools to study cognitive ageing. *British Journal of Psychology, 81,* 1–16.

Rabinowitz, J. C., Ackerman, B. P., Craik, F. I. M., & Hinchley, J. L. (1982). Aging and metamemory: The roles of relatedness and imagery. *Journal of Gerontology, 37,* 688–695.

Rebok, G. W., & Balcerak, L. J. (1989). Memory self-efficacy and performance differences in young and old adults: The effect of mnemonic training. *Developmental Psychology, 25,* 714–721.

Reder, L. M., & Ritter, F. E. (1992). What determines initial feeling of knowing? Familiarity with question terms, not with the answer. *Journal of Experimental Psychology: Learning, Memory, and Cognition, 18,* 435–451.

Reisberg, B., Ferris, S. H., de Leon, M. J., & Crook, T. (1985). Age-associated cognitive decline and Alzheimer's disease: Implications for assessment and treatment. In M. Berenger, M. Ermini, & H. Stahelin (Eds.), *Thresholds in aging* (pp. 255–292). London: Academic Press.

Ross, M. (1989). Relation of implicit theories to the construction of personal histories. *Psychological Review, 96,* 341–357.

Rubin, K. H., & Brown, I. D. R. (1975). A life-span look at person perception and its relationship to communicative interaction. *Journal of Gerontology, 30,* 461–468.

Ryan, E. B. (1992). Beliefs about memory changes across the adult life span. *Journal of Gerontology: Psychological Sciences, 47,* P41–P46.

Ryan, E. B., & Heaven, K. B. (1988). The impact of situational context on age-based attitudes. *Social Behavior, 3,* 105–117.

Ryan, E. B., & Kwong See, S. (1993). Age-based beliefs about memory changes for self and others across adulthood. *Journal of Gerontology: Psychological Sciences, 48,* P199–P201.

Ryan, E. B., Kwong See, S., Meneer, W. B., & Trovato, D. (1992). Age-based perceptions of language performance among younger and older adults. *Communication Research, 19,* 423–443.

Salthouse, T. A. (1991). *Theoretical perspectives on cognitive aging.* Hillsdale, NJ: Lawrence Erlbaum Associates.

Sanders, R. E., Murphy, M. D., Schmitt, F. A., & Walsh, K. K. (1980). Age differences in free recall rehearsal strategies. *Journal of Gerontology, 35,* 550–558.

Schaie, K. W., Willis, S. L., & O'Hanlon, A. M. (1994). Perceived intellectual performance change over seven years. *Journal of Gerontology: Psychological Sciences, 49,* P108–P118.

Scherer, M., Maddux, J. E., Mercandante, B., Prentice-Dunn, S., Jacobs, B., & Rogers, R. W. (1982). The Self-Efficacy Scale: Construction and validation. *Psychological Reports, 51,* 663–671.

Schneider, W., & Pressley, M. (1989). *Memory development between 2 and 20.* New York: Springer.

Shaw, R. J., & Craik, F. I. M. (1989). Age differences in predictions and performance on a cued recall task. *Psychology and Aging, 4,* 131–135.

Smith, A. D., Park, D. C., Earles, J. L., Shaw, R. J., & Whiting, W. L., IV. (1998). Age differences in context integration in memory. *Psychology and Aging, 13,* 21–28.

Smith, G. E., Petersen, R. C., Ivnik, R. J., Malec, J. F., & Tangalos, E. G. (1996). Subjective memory complaints, psychological distress, and longitudinal change in objective memory performance. *Psychology and Aging, 2*, 272–279.

Spellman, B. A., & Bjork, R. A. (1992). When predictions create reality: Judgments of learning may alter what they are intended to access. *Psychological Science, 3*, 315–316.

Sternberg, R. J. (1987). Implicit theories: An alternative to modeling cognition and its development. In J. Bisanz, C. J. Brainerd, & R. Karl (Eds.), *Formal methods in developmental psychology: Progress in cognitive developmental research* (pp. 155–192). New York: Springer.

Stuss, D. T., Craik, F. I. M., Sayer, L., Franchi, D., & Alexander, M. P. (1996). Comparison of older people and patients with frontal lesions: Evidence from word list learning. *Psychology and Aging, 11*, 387–395.

Sunderland, A., Harris, J. E., & Baddeley, A. D. (1983). Do laboratory tests predict everyday ...·· iory? A neuropsychological study. *Journal of Verbal Learning and Verbal Behavior, 22*, 341–357.

Sunderland, A., Watts, K., Baddeley, A. D., & Harris, J. E. (1986). Subjective memory assessment and test performance in elderly adults. *Journal of Gerontology, 41*, 376–384.

Taylor, J. L., Miller, T. P., & Tinklenberg, J. R. (1992). Correlates of memory decline: A 4-year longitudinal study of older adults with memory complaints. *Psychology and Aging, 7*, 185–193.

Treat, N. J., & Reese, H. W. (1976). Age, imagery, and pacing in paired-associate learning. *Developmental Psychology, 12*, 119–124.

Tun, P. A., & Wingfield, A. (1995). Does dividing attention become harder with age? Findings from the Divided Attention Questionnaire. *Aging and Cognition, 2*, 39–66.

Verhaeghen, P., Marcoen, A., & Goossens, L. (1992). Improving memory performance in the aged through mnemonic training: A meta-analytic study. *Psychology and Aging, 7*, 242–251.

Wellman, H. M. (1983). Metamemory revisited. In M. T. H. Chi (Ed.), *Trends in memory development research* (pp. 31–51). Basel, Switzerland: Karger.

West, R. L., Dennehey-Basile, D., & Norris, M. P. (1996). Memory self-evaluation: The effects of age and experience. *Aging, Neuropsychology, and Cognition, 3*, 67–83.

Willis, S. L. (1989). Cognitive training in later adulthood: Remediation vs. new learning. In L. W. Poon, D. C. Rubin, & B. A. Wilson (Eds.), *Everyday cognition in adulthood and old age* (pp. 545–569). New York: Cambridge University Press.

Winterling, D., Crook, T., Salama, M., & Gobert, J. (1986). A self-rating scale for assessing memory loss. In A. Bes, J. Cahn, S. Hoyer, J. P. Marc-Vergnes, & H. M. Wisniewski (Eds.), *Senile dementias: Early detection* (pp. 482–486). London: John Libbey Eurotext.

Witte, K. L., Freund, J. S., & Sebby, R. A. (1990). Age differences in free recall and subjective organization. *Psychology and Aging, 5*, 307–309.

Zelinski, E. M., Gilewski, M. J., & Anthony-Bergstone, C. R. (1990). Memory Functioning Questionnaire: Concurrent validity with memory performance and self-reported memory failures. *Psychology and Aging, 5*, 388–399.

Zelinski, E. M., Gilewski, M. J., & Schaie, K. W. (1993). Individual differences in cross-sectional and 3-year longitudinal memory performance across the adult life span. *Psychology and Aging, 8*, 176–186.

Zelinski, E. M., Gilewski, M. J., & Thompson, L. W. (1980). Do labratory tests relate to self-assessment of memory ability in the young and old? In L. W. Poon, J. L. Fozard, L. S. Cermak, D. Arenberg, & L. W. Thompson (Eds.), *New directions in memory and aging: Proceedings of the George A. Talland Memorial Conference* (pp. 519–544). Hillsdale, NJ: Lawrence Erlbaum Associates.

8

Methodological Assumptions in Cognitive Aging Research

Timothy A. Salthouse
Georgia Institute of Technology

Consider the characteristics of a prototypical study in the area of cognitive aging: 20 young adults recruited from a pool of college students are contrasted with 20 older adults with a mean age of between 60 and 75 years, often recruited from a pool of individuals who have participated in prior studies; a single task is administered with two (or more) conditions assumed to differ with respect to one or more theoretically interesting components; a single measure of performance is obtained in each condition, usually with no indication of its reliability; and the results are analyzed with an analysis of variance (ANOVA), with the greatest interest in the Age × Condition interaction. If the interaction is statistically significant, then the researcher usually infers that the age effects are especially pronounced on the theoretical component corresponding to the variable with the largest age difference. Frequently the researcher concludes that there are no age differences in a component in which the age difference in the relevant measure was not statistically significant (i.e., the null hypothesis is accepted).

Each aspect of the design, analysis, and interpretation in this prototypical approach involves numerous important, but often unrecognized, assumptions. The primary goal of this chapter is to examine assumptions implicit in current research practices in cognitive aging. In the process, possible consequences of violations of the assumptions will be identified, as well as ways in which the validity of the assumptions can be investigated.

Methodological issues will be considered from a mixture of perspectives in this chapter. Cognitive researchers sometimes view psychometric and experimental approaches to cognition as corresponding to fundamentally different subdisciplines, but this is a misleading and short-sighted attitude, particularly when it leads to the neglect of valuable analytical principles and tools. The failure to capitalize on potentially useful analytical procedures can be especially problematic in research in aging. That is, because people who differ in age are also likely to differ in other respects, it is always possible that the observed results are attributable to some variable other than age. In a "true" experiment, the research participants are assigned randomly to the groups to ensure that they do not differ systematically, except with respect to the treatment or condition of primary interest. However, because age is a naturally occurring "treatment" that cannot be randomly assigned, studies involving age comparisons are, strictly speaking, not true experiments. Research involving relations between variables that have not been manipulated is usually classified as correlational, and because age cannot be manipulated, in many respects studies of aging are more similar to correlational than to experimental research. For this reason if no other, then, it is important that a broader range of analytical methods be considered than merely those typically used within the field of experimental psychology where more complete control over the independent variables can be exercised.

CROSS-SECTIONAL VERSUS LONGITUDINAL DESIGNS

The two major data-collection strategies used in the investigation of developmental issues are cross-sectional and longitudinal designs. The vast majority of research has been conducted with cross-sectional designs because they are considerably more efficient (i.e., quicker and less expensive) than longitudinal designs. They are also valuable for investigating the detailed nature of age-related differences apparent at a given period in time. That is, cross-sectional comparisons can be useful for determining whether age-related differences exist in certain variables and in specifying their proximal determinants (i.e., correlates of the differences observed at the time of assessment).

There currently appears to be some ambivalence about the value of cross-sectional designs in research on aging, and a number of researchers seem to dismiss them as always inferior to longitudinal designs. This attitude is understandable if the only interest is in identifying and investigating age-related changes. That is, to make inferences about age changes from cross-sectional data, the researcher must assume that in all relevant respects the current young adults will resemble the old adults when they reach that age or that when the current old adults were younger they resembled the young adults. Because these assumptions could easily be wrong, and because their validity is very difficult to evaluate, cross-sectional research provides a weak basis for investigating processes of change. It is largely for this reason that some researchers have suggested that the term *changes* only be used with reference to longitudinal comparisons.

Because change can be directly studied, instead of merely inferred, only if the same individual is followed over a period of time, longitudinal designs are clearly essential for investigating correlates of change. However, it is important to note that the changes observed from longitudinal comparisons are not necessarily attributable to intrinsic or endogenous (i.e., "pure age") processes unless it is additionally assumed (a) that the physical and social environment has not changed over time in ways that might affect the variables of interest, (b) that reactive effects associated with prior participation are minimal, and (c) that any attrition across the retest interval was not selective. These are very strong assumptions, and they all seem to be at least partially contradicted by empirical evidence (e.g., Flynn, 1987; Neisser, 1997; Schaie, 1996).

It is sometimes suggested that different patterns of results from cross-sectional and longitudinal designs reflect the influence of extrinsic factors on development. That is, longitudinal comparisons are occasionally claimed to provide purer estimates of maturational effects because they are argued to be less influenced by sociocultural factors or "cohort effects." However, neither the cross-sectional nor the longitudinal method is ideal for distinguishing between intrinsic (endogenous) and extrinsic (exogenous) determinants of the observed differences or changes. This is the case because potentially relevant aspects of the environment are changing as the individual is aging, and consequently it is very difficult to separate the two types of influences without more elaborate sequential designs, which essentially involve repetitions of cross-sectional and longitudinal studies at different periods in time (e.g., Baltes, 1968; Schaie, 1965). Moreover, for comparisons of the results from the two types of designs to be meaningful, it is important to ensure that the data are equivalent with respect to (a) the variables under consideration (which was not always the case in some early comparisons in which measures of crystallized or knowledge aspects of cognition were emphasized in longitudinal studies and in which measures of fluid or processing aspects of cognition were emphasized in cross-sectional studies), (b) the retest intervals or age ranges (because, for example, it is not appropriate to contrast a 40-year cross-sectional effect with a 7-year longitudinal effect; cf. Botwinick & Arenberg, 1976), (c) the effects of practice or repeated exposures to the testing situation (which are frequently confounded with age in longitudinal studies), (d) the effects of selective attrition (which can result in a positively biased sample in longitudinal studies), and (e) the effects of time of measurement (which are confounded with age in longitudinal studies but not in cross-sectional studies).

The second of these points is not always appreciated and deserves some elaboration in light of the growing number of short-term longitudinal studies that are being reported. Data from reaction times in the same task across four different cross-sectional studies reported by Salthouse (1993) can be used for purposes of illustration. If all of the relations between the variable and age are linear, then the best estimate of the annual age-related difference in a cross-sectional sample is the slope of a linear regression equation relating the variable to age. A strong linear relation between age and reaction time was evident in each of the studies analyzed by Salthouse, with an average correlation above .60. The average slope of the median reaction times was 16.6 ms per year, the average intraindividual standard deviation (i.e., the variability of an individual's reaction times around his or her own mean) was 672 ms, and the average interindividual standard deviation (i.e., the variability of the medians of the individuals around the mean of the sample) was 460 ms.

Now consider the expected reaction time differences across either a 5- or 10-year age range expressed in units of intraindividual and interindividual standard deviation. These estimates are computed by multiplying the slope by the number of years and then dividing by the relevant standard deviation. The resulting values for 5 and 10 years in intraindividual standard deviation units are 0.12 and 0.24, respectively, and those in interindividual standard deviation units are 0.18 and 0.36, respectively.

Notice that in both types of comparisons—the difference relative to within-person variability and the difference relative to between-person variability—the expected cross-sectional effects over short time periods are rather small. Because effect sizes are commonly expressed as differences relative to units of standard deviation, these values can be considered analogous to effect sizes. Thus, these results indicate that even with the 10-year difference, the statistical power would be less than .30 with a two-tailed alpha of .05 and samples of 50 in each age group (Cohen, 1988, Table 2.3.5). In other words, a difference of about 0.30 SD units would be detected as statistically significant less than one third of the time with samples of 50 in each group, and samples of over 300 would be needed in each group to have a .95 probability of detecting a cross-sectional difference of this magnitude.

Similar outcomes occur if the estimates of annual age-related differences are derived from other types of information, such as meta-analyses of effect sizes. For example, if earlier research revealed that the total effect size in comparisons of cognitive variables in 20-year-olds and 70-year-olds is 1.25 *SD* units, then the expected annual cross-sectional difference would be 0.025 *SD* units. Alternatively, if prior research indicated that the correlation between age and the cognitive variable is .45 and the standard deviation for age is 18 years (a reasonable value in a sample with a nearly rectangular distribution of ages between 18 and 80), then the same estimate of about 0.025 *SD* units per year would be obtained. If this difference is accumulated across 8 years, it will lead to a total difference of 0.20 *SD* units. Approximately 400 participants per group would be needed to have a .80 probability that an effect of this magnitude would be detected as significant, and 600 participants per group would be needed to detect an effect of this magnitude as significant with a probability of .95. The point of these computations is that with relatively small age ranges (corresponding to short longitudinal retest intervals), it is highly unlikely that age-related differences in most cognitive variables would be detected as statistically significant with conventional sample sizes in cross-sectional designs. It may therefore be very misleading to conclude that results from longitudinal and cross-sectional comparisons are inconsistent when the longitudinal data are based on retest intervals of less than 10 years and the cross-sectional data are based on intervals of 30 or more years.

Two recent comparisons involving cognitive variables are relevant to this issue. First, Zelinski and Burnight (1997) reported that there were few significant differences in the estimates from longitudinal and cross-sectional comparisons when both sets of results were expressed in terms of change or difference per year. And second, reanalyses reported by Salthouse (1991) of data from Schaie's (1996) Seattle Longitudinal Study revealed that the estimates of the age-related differences for independent-groups same-cohort and cross-sectional comparisons were virtually identical when influences associated with attrition, practice, and time of measurement were taken into consideration. The estimates of the age-related changes from longitudinal comparisons were smaller and appeared to start later in life than the estimates from the cross-sectional and independent-groups same-cohort comparisons. However, the observed differences with the longitudinal results may be attributable to effects of practice and selective attrition rather than to effects related to cohort membership, given that these factors were not operating in the independent-groups same-cohort condition in which the age change or difference estimates were nearly identical to those from the between-cohort cross-sectional comparisons.

To summarize, both cross-sectional and longitudinal designs require that a number of assumptions be accepted in order for the results of the comparisons to be interpreted as reflecting the operation of intrinsic or endogenous processes of aging. Because it is seldom possible to completely rule out the influence of historical changes in the physical and social environment on the observed differences or changes, it is probably advisable to use the term *age-related* when referring to results from both cross-sectional and longitudinal designs. Nevertheless, there are distinct advantages and disadvantages of each type of design, and the choice of a particular design should always be based on the specific question under investigation rather than on a priori biases. A recent suggestion by Hertzog (1996) with respect to the optimum sequence for research on aging and cognition is particularly appropriate in this context. In Hertzog's scheme, the first type of study that should usually be conducted is an extreme-group cross-sectional study to establish the existence of age differences. Studies with larger cross-sectional samples involving a continuous range of ages should be conducted next to estimate the adult life-span trajectories in potentially more representative samples. Finally, longitudinal and sequential studies should be conducted to investigate age-related changes in the relevant variables and predictors of those changes.

SAMPLES

A fundamental assumption of virtually all age-comparative research is that the results from samples of adults of different ages will be informative about the age relations in the general population. However, there are a number of current practices that may limit the extent to which this is true.

Selection

Of course, for most research studies, the ideal sample is one that is fully representative of the general population. Unfortunately, this is almost never achieved because it would not only require quota sampling or some other type of recruitment strategy to ensure coverage of relevant groups (as in the samples used to establish the norms for standardized tests), but it would also involve procedures to maximize participation of all targeted individuals rather than exclusive reliance on volunteers. Age-related differences observed in the type of convenience samples most often used in cognitive aging research may therefore not accurately reflect the true age-related differences in the population, with the direction of the distortion depending on the extent of bias in each age group.

Although truly representative samples may not be feasible for most studies of cognitive aging, there is a relatively simple means by which the representativeness of a sample can be determined once it has been recruited. This involves administering one or more standardized tests to all members of the sample, and then referring to the published norms of the tests to determine the relative position (e.g., percentile) of each age group in the relevant distributions from the normative sample. That is, because the normative data for standardized tests are usually based on a large nationally representative sample, an indication of the representativeness of the samples of participants in a particular study can often be determined by reporting the average percentiles at each age relative to the normative distribution (e.g., Salthouse, Fristoe, & Rhee, 1996).

Participant Pools

As noted earlier, a common practice in contemporary cognitive aging research is to rely on college students as the source of the young research participants in extreme-group designs. To the extent that college students are not typical of their age group in terms of, for example, intellectual ability, socioeconomic status, or personality characteristics (such as openness to experience), the results from studies involving college students may have limited generalizability. This is a legitimate concern, but there is some evidence that the effects of student status are relatively small or possibly even completely nonexistent for several types of cognitive variables. For example, in one study, the regression equations predicting cognitive performance from age in a sample of nonstudent adults across a wide age range were used to predict the performance of a sample of college students (Salthouse, Kausler, & Saults, 1988). The results of the analyses revealed that, across a wide range of variables, the performance of college students was accurately predicted on the basis of the regression equation derived from the nonstudent adults. These findings imply that although college students could obviously differ from nonstudents in many respects, their level of performance in a number of different cognitive variables seems generally consistent with what one would expect among individuals of that age.

Because of the difficulty associated with locating and recruiting nonstudent adults, many researchers in cognitive aging have established participant pools of older adults who can be contacted to participate in multiple studies. Although this practice can save considerable time and energy that would otherwise have to be devoted to locating and recruiting potential participants, there are several implications of this practice that are not always recognized.

First, the results from these types of participant pools may be even less representative of the general population than those from other convenience samples because the participants are partially "selected" on the basis of a willingness to participate in multiple studies. In other words, results from such samples may have limited generalizability to a broader population if these "professional" participants differ in important characteristics (such as level of cognitive ability, altruism, and extroversion) from the target population. It is also possible that reactive effects may be operating, such that participation in one study or task influences performance in subsequent studies or tasks. This possibility is difficult to evaluate at the present time because records of the prior testing history of the research participants are often incomplete and seldom systematically examined. However, to the extent that reactive effects do occur, then generalizability of the results would be even further restricted.

Second, if the same individuals contribute data in different studies then there will be a lack of independence of the results across studies. A common assumption underlying most statistical procedures is that if there are independent samples of moderate size, then factors unrelated to the variable of primary interest (e.g., age in studies concerned with aging) will cancel one another out. However, if the same individuals participate in several studies, even if the studies focus on what are assumed to be different abilities or characteristics, then some of the same individual-specific factors may be operating in each study.

One way to think about this issue is to consider what would happen if the target variable was included in the same report with other variables obtained from the same research participants. Under circumstances such as these, that variable would almost certainly be treated differently because of awareness of the problem of capitalization on chance and an inflated probability of committing a Type I error when there are multiple comparisons on nonindependent observations. Merely because the variable is reported in a separate article, or was obtained at a different time from the other variables, does not mean that the problem is eliminated.

Finally, use of the same individuals in multiple studies creates a problem in later meta-analyses because if the samples are not independent, then complications arise in aggregating effect sizes for comparisons across different types of variables. For example, consider what would happen if many of the same individuals were used in a study on memory and in a study on reasoning, and both the memory and reasoning variables were later included in a meta-analysis comparing effect sizes across different categories of cognitive variables. The lack of independence of the estimates from the two studies greatly complicates the analyses, and subsequent interpretations, of these types of research integrations. It is quite true that research should not be designed simply for the convenience of subsequent meta-analysis, but a potential problem nevertheless exists with respect to how the results from repeat participants should be interpreted. What is easiest for the individual investigator is not always best for the progress of the field.

There are no easy solutions to the issues just mentioned because in many situations it may be impractical to avoid testing the same individual more than once. However, it is probably desirable when describing the samples in a study to report the recent testing history of the participants (e.g., over an interval of 3 to 5 years). This could be in the form of a table summarizing the number of individuals in each prior study or merely in terms of a statement to the effect that $X\%$ of the older adults also participated Y months earlier in a study investigating Z (the broad topic of the study), which was reported in A (giving the citation). Ultimately, of course, research should be conducted to investigate the effects of prior participation as a function of factors such as similarity of the tasks and interval between tests.

Continuous Versus Extreme Groups

A large majority of cross-sectional studies in aging and cognition consist of comparisons of samples of young and old adults. Extreme-group designs (i.e., consisting of just young and old adults) are clearly efficient if the researcher is only interested in linear age-related effects (e.g., McClelland, 1997) or if he or she wants maximum power for detecting interactions of age and some other variable (e.g., McClelland & Judd, 1993). However, the implicit assumption that middle-aged adults will perform at a level intermediate between that of the two extreme groups cannot be tested unless the sample consists of a continuous distribution of ages. Some evidence for statistically significant nonlinear age–cognition relations has been reported in a recent meta-analysis (Verhaeghen & Salthouse, 1997) and in analyses of large data sets from nationally representative samples (e.g., Avolio & Waldman, 1994; Salthouse, 1998). However, at least in the range from 18 to 70 years of age, the nonlinear effects in those analyses were typically small relative to the linear effects, and thus the assumption of linearity is probably reasonable as a first approximation in many situations.

Nevertheless, if data are available from adults across the complete age range, then the researcher may be in a better position to separate the effects of variables that partially covary with age or do so only within certain age ranges. This, in turn, may be helpful in distinguishing between theoretical interpretations postulating abrupt versus continuous age-related influences. For example, if retirement, menopause, or other events usually restricted to particular ages are hypothesized to be important influences on cognition, then when the complete age distribution is represented it would be possible to determine whether there are discontinuities in the age–cognition relations corresponding to the occurrence of these other factors.

Finally, if one of the goals of the research is to describe the magnitude of age relations across the entire age range, then continuous samples are preferable because the estimates of the age-related effects are inflated when only extreme groups are used. That is, when the variability associated with scores in the middle of the age range is not represented in the computation of the proportions of variance associated with age, then the resulting variance proportions tend to overestimate the true magnitude of the age relations.

Sample Size and Statistical Power

Because aging is associated with statistically significant effects on many cognitive variables, a finding of no age-related difference is often considered theoretically interesting. However, before such a null result can be meaningfully interpreted, it is important to consider whether the power in a given study was sufficient to detect small or moderate effects.

As an illustration, assume that a researcher conducts a study and finds a small nonsignificant age difference, which he or she would like to interpret as evidence that there really is no difference associated with age in that variable. If confronted with potentially embarrassing questions about statistical power, one strategy the researcher might consider is to compute the sample size that would be needed for the observed difference to be statistically significant. If this number is very large, then the researcher might use the information as support for the claim that there was no real difference. As an example, the following statement appeared in a recent article: "It would take approximately 2000 subjects to achieve a .80 power level with the .12 effect size in this experiment" (Allen, Smith, Jerge, & Vires-Collins, 1997, p. P86).

Unfortunately, interpretations of power are often misleading because of confusion between the observed effect and an effect that is specified a priori. Before a study is conducted, researchers would like to know the probability of being able to detect an effect of a specified magnitude, and it is this type of information that is provided by typical power analyses (e.g., Cohen, 1988). However, after the study has been conducted, more information is available and a different question can be asked. Namely, given the observed results, what is the likely range within which the true effect will occur? There is seldom any interest in determining the power to detect an effect that has already been observed, but it is informative to determine the confidence interval around the observed value as a means of estimating the range within which the true effect is likely to fall.

Two questions related to statistical power should therefore be distinguished: (a) a priori power concerning the probability of detecting an effect of a given magnitude (e.g., an effect equivalent to 0.5 SDs) and (b) precision relating to the size of the confidence interval for the effect that was actually observed. This latter question does not refer to the probability of detecting an effect of a particular magnitude because the results are already known, and thus those types of probabilities are no longer relevant. However, the researcher (and the research community) typically is interested in the likelihood of replication of the results, and this can be estimated from the confidence interval around the observed effect. The region within which the true difference would likely fall can be estimated from the confidence interval around the observed difference, and if this region is small and includes zero, then the researcher is justified in concluding that the effect was very small or possibly even nonexistent. In contrast, if the confidence interval is very large, and encompasses effect sizes in the moderate range, then a conclusion of no difference would be very tenuous. Few impartial observers would likely have much confidence in a conclusion of no difference if the a priori probability of detecting moderate-sized effects was small or if the post hoc confidence interval around the observed effect was large.

With respect to a priori power, if there are 20 individuals in each of two age groups, there will only be about a 1 in 3 chance (i.e., power of .34) to detect significance with a two-tailed alpha of .05, what Cohen (1988) referred to as a medium effect (i.e., approximately 0.50 pooled SD units). In other words, a finding of no age-related difference in a prototypical study would be difficult to interpret because under these conditions it would have been unlikely that even a medium-sized effect could have been detected had it existed.

Figure 8.1 portrays the power (with a two-tailed alpha of .05) to detect different effect sizes with varying numbers of individuals in each age group. Notice that even with 60 people per group the power is not very high unless the effect size is quite large. It is sometimes recommended that power of .80 is a minimally acceptable value. Although in certain areas of research it may be reasonable to have the probability of a Type II error that is four times more likely than the probability of a Type I error, it should be recognized that adoption of this guideline in aging research results in a strong bias against detecting age-related differences when they really exist. It could therefore be argued that a more reasonable goal is to attempt to obtain the same probability of erroneously concluding that there is no difference (Type II error) as erroneously concluding that there is a difference (Type I error). Under these circumstances, and with an alpha of .05, the power should be .95, which corresponds to the dotted line in Fig. 8.1.

Inspection of Fig. 8.1 reveals that samples much larger than 60 individuals per group would be needed to have the same probability of a Type II error as a Type I error for all but the largest effect sizes. Therefore, the use of relatively small samples results in a systematic bias toward accepting the null hypothesis and claiming that there are no age differences when they may in fact exist. Because small-sample studies have

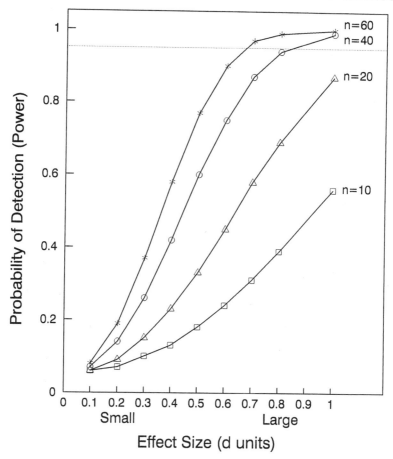

FIG. 8.1. Relation between effect size (Cohen's, 1988, d) and statistical power for different sample sizes in each age group. The dotted line represents power of .95, corresponding to the same probability of making a Type II error as a Type I error with an alpha of .05.

been the norm for many years in the area of cognitive aging, it is quite possible that the research literature is distorted because of the acceptance of claims that no differences exist when the likelihood of detecting small or moderate-sized differences has been very low.

One potential illustration of this phenomenon is evident in studies of the relation between age and measures of implicit memory. Many studies have reported nonsignificant age differences in measures of implicit memory, leading a number of researchers to conclude that there were little or no effects of aging on memory assessed without deliberate attempts at conscious recollection. However, later meta-analyses (e.g., LaVoie & Light, 1994) revealed that older adults are actually somewhat impaired in measures of implicit memory relative to young adults but that the effects were simply too small to be detected in single studies with small sample sizes. Unfortunately, in relatively few areas of research have there been enough studies such that sensitive meta-analyses could be conducted to allow more powerful and accurate assessments of the true effects than what is available in the typical small-sample study.

What can be done to improve the power of individual studies in the area of aging and cognition? As is well-known, statistical significance is jointly determined by (a) sample size, (b) alpha level, (c) between-groups difference, (d) within-group variability, and (e) power. (This list is actually somewhat out-of-date because it has recently been pointed out that statistical significance is also affected by deviations from normality in the sample distributions and unequal variances across groups [Wilcox, 1998] and by the distribution of observations on the independent variable and the relations among independent variables [McClelland, 1997].)

One strategy for increasing power may be to try to reduce within-person variability by more precise assessment, addition of practice or training, collection of more observations or trials, and so on. Moreover, when multiple measures are available, they may be combined to minimize measurement error, thereby reducing effective variability. However, although it is always desirable to obtain the most sensitive possible assessment of an individual, manipulations of this type directly affect only the estimates of within-person variability. To increase statistical power, it is also important to consider how to reduce across-person variability among people within each age group or to increase the across-age (i.e., between-groups) variability. If the factors contributing to within-person variability are differentially represented in the various age groups, then reducing their influence will remove a confounding and will likely improve the internal validity of the comparison. However, statistical power could either increase or decrease depending on the relative effects of these manipulations on within-person, within-group, and between-groups (i.e., between-age) variability.

It is useful to consider an extreme situation in which, for example, a sample consists of only two individuals, one aged 25 and the other aged 65, with very extensive and precise information about each. Given sufficient information from each individual, a researcher could construct confidence intervals around the means of the variables for each person and probably have some assurance that the two individuals differed significantly from one another. However, the difference between these two people could not necessarily be attributed to factors related to age as opposed to other characteristics that differed between the two people. To be confident that age was the critical factor, it is necessary to collect data from samples of people of different ages and then to assume that with large enough samples individual difference characteristics unrelated to age will cancel one another out. To the extent that this assumption is valid, the remaining differences between the groups could be attributed to the major factor that distinguishes them, which in this case would be age. The critical point to note, however, is that moderately large samples are typically required to allow these other characteristics to cancel one another out. It is for this reason that increasing the sample size is often the most feasible method of increasing power in studies involving age comparisons.

Although the preceding discussion has focused on the issue of power in traditional significance tests, a practice that should probably be encouraged in future research in cognitive aging is to shift the emphasis from null hypothesis significance tests to the generation of confidence intervals (e.g., Cohen, 1994; Humphreys, 1985; Lipsey, 1990; Loftus, 1996; Schmidt, 1996). Not only is it generally more informative to specify the magnitude, and precision, of the estimate of the effect than merely to report that it is not zero, but confidence intervals are also helpful in predicting the likelihood of replicating results that have already been obtained. That is, if the confidence interval is very large, then the results may have a low probability of replication, regardless whether they were statistically significant.

Many cognitive researchers assume that the results of their studies would be very similar, if not identical, if the study were to be repeated with a new sample. Largely because of this assumption, a great deal of effort is often invested in investigating the role of methodological differences when two studies appear to yield somewhat different results. Although the strategy of trying to identify the factors responsible for variation in results is clearly valuable, it is much more likely to be successful when one can be confident that the variation across samples is systematic. However, when sample sizes are small, the confidence intervals are frequently so large that a very wide range of results could be expected in a replication. Only when the confidence intervals around the estimates of the effects are fairly small, which usually requires moderately large samples, will the strategy of identifying factors responsible for discrepancies between studies likely be productive.

To summarize, on the basis of current practices, it appears that many researchers seem to assume that relatively small samples of young and old adults, many of whom have participated in prior studies, provide an adequate basis for achieving generalizable results. The impact of the use of participant pools is difficult to assess, but it is possible that repeat participants are positively biased in a variety of relevant characteristics in a manner analogous to what has been found among returning participants in longitudinal studies. The use of extreme groups, instead of continuous samples, can be justified in many situations, and some indication of the representativeness of the samples may be obtained from percentile scores on standardized tests with nationally representative samples. However, the use of relatively small samples may have had a major impact on the research literature because of the low likelihood of detecting effects of moderate or small magnitude. Furthermore, even when the results from a study with small samples are statistically significant, the confidence interval around the observed difference is likely to be so large as to preclude an accurate estimate of the true effect size, which can complicate the interpretation of subsequent attempts at replication. Future research should therefore be based on larger samples than in the past, and confidence intervals or other indications of the precision of the estimates should be provided whenever possible.

MULTIVARIATE VERSUS UNIVARIATE RESEARCH

Most research studies in aging and cognition have focused on single variables, but there are at least four reasons why a multivariate approach is often superior: (a) It allows for a more complete characterization of the samples, (b) it is valuable for investigating construct validity, (c) it helps to minimize measurement error, and (d) it serves to place the results in a broader context. Each of these reasons is elaborated in the following paragraphs.

Characterization of Samples

An essential prerequisite for evaluating the likely generalizability of the results of a research study is an adequate description of the samples, and the sample can be characterized more precisely and completely if additional variables are obtained from the participants. People of different ages almost certainly also differ in numerous characteristics besides age; consequently, it is desirable to be as explicit as possible in describing the samples used in a particular study to ensure the most appropriate level of generalization. Many contemporary researchers report the mean levels of the participants on a number of variables, such as amount of education or score on a vocabulary test, but the rationale for the selection of these particular variables is seldom provided, nor is there typically any reference to published norms to indicate the representativeness of the samples. A more desirable practice might consist of reporting the mean and range of percentiles from national norms on variables representing at least the two major categories of intellectual ability, namely, fluid and crystallized intelligence.

Construct Validity

Extensive debates frequently occur within cognitive psychology about whether a particular variable is a good measure of a given theoretical construct. The approach often used to try to resolve these debates involves attempting to refine or purify the assessment to minimize other influences on the variable. This can be effective in eliminating extraneous variance, but it may also result in a very narrow construct that has limited generalizability. Furthermore, when only this approach is used it is not possible to determine whether, and if so to what extent, that particular operational definition of the construct is related to other possible operational definitions of the construct. Considerable confusion can occur if the same term is used in different ways and if there are no attempts to determine whether what are postulated to be different constructs are really distinct from one another.

The multivariate approach to research acknowledges that any single variable confounds the theoretical construct of interest with a particular operationalization of it (based on specific methods, materials, and measures); consequently, it relies on multiple variables in an attempt to average out the specific, construct-irrelevant aspects. When a researcher uses a single variable to represent a theoretical construct, he or she is effectively assuming that it perfectly reflects the entire construct and nothing but the construct. Unfortunately, this assumption is almost certainly false for nearly all variables in psychology because most behavioral measures are influenced by multiple factors, and not merely by the theoretical construct of primary interest. Furthermore, it is probably also the case that most variables represent only a few limited aspects of a theoretical construct. The use of multiple variables can thus cancel out construct-irrelevant aspects by aggregating across multiple indicators and in the process also more completely assess the breadth of the construct.

It is somewhat ironic that experimental psychology tends to pride itself on its methodological rigor when the typical practice within that subdiscipline of relying on single variables to assess constructs has been subject to severe criticism. For example, Cook and Campbell (1979) warned against "mono-operation bias," stating, "Since single operations both underrepresent constructs and contain irrelevancies, construct validity will be lower in single exemplar research than in research where each construct is multiply operationalized in order to triangulate on the referent" (p. 65). Horn (1979) also argued that a manifest-variable focus was undesirable because no manifest (directly observable) variables are pure indicators of a construct, and Cliff (1983) cautioned against what he termed the *nominalistic fallacy,* or the belief that merely because a variable can be named it accurately reflects the complete theoretical construct, with no surplus and no error. Although discussions of construct validity have largely been found within the psychometric literature, the basic ideas are very similar to the notion of converging operations described in a classic article by three experimental psychologists, Garner, Hake, and Eriksen (1956).

A key issue with respect to construct validity is that although constructs are of primary interest, they are almost always evaluated by indicators (i.e., variables) that are specific and unreliable to varying degrees. It is therefore important to attempt to unconfound the construct from its method of assessment because a single observed (manifest) variable can be thought of as being filtered through a particular combination of methods, materials, and measurements. In other words, when only a single variable is used, it is impossible to separate the contribution of the theoretical construct of interest from what is attributable to the particular way in which it is being assessed.

When multiple variables are available, it becomes possible to examine construct validity in terms of the patterns of intercorrelations among variables. That is, to the extent that the variables are moderately correlated with one another, they can be inferred to be measuring the same or similar constructs (and exhibit convergent validity). In contrast, if the variables have little or no correlations with one another, they can be inferred to be measuring different constructs (and exhibit discriminant validity). Both convergent and discriminant validity information is needed to establish the meaning of a construct because there are many possible reasons for the presence of correlations between variables (e.g., the existence of a general factor) and for the absence of correlations between variables (e.g., low reliability in one or more variables). Valuable information relevant to the meaning of a construct can therefore be obtained by determining the constructs to which the target construct is, and is not, related.

When the data are obtained from members of several groups, such as people of different ages, the existence of multivariate data can also be used to test for measurement equivalence. It is sometimes speculated that, perhaps because of variations in strategy, relevant knowledge, and so on, the same variable might measure different things in people of different ages. This is a potentially important concern because, to the extent that the variables reflect different aspects of functioning in different groups of people, quantitative comparisons may be meaningless. One of the most powerful ways of investigating measurement equivalence consists of using multivariate methods, such as multiple-group confirmatory factor analysis, to examine the pattern of correlations between the target variable and other variables across different groups of individuals. These types of procedures provide an objective means of evaluating the extent to which measurement equivalence exists across groups and, if there is no measurement equivalence, of indicating exactly how the groups differ (e.g., in the constructs the variables reflect, in the quantitative relation between variable and construct, and in the strength of the relations between constructs).

It is encouraging that several comparisons have suggested that there is a moderately high level of measurement equivalence and factor structure across adulthood (e.g., Babcock & Laguna, 1996; Babcock, Laguna, & Roesch, 1997; Salthouse, McGuthry, & Hambrick, 1998; Schaie, Maitland, Willis, & Intrieri, 1998; Schaie, Willis, Jay, & Chipuer, 1989; Verhaeghen & Salthouse, 1997). However, it is also important to realize that the issue of measurement equivalence will never be definitively resolved because new variables continue to be introduced and questions can always be raised with respect to whether they have the same meaning across the life span.

Reduction of Measurement Error

The variance in a variable can be assumed to consist, at a minimum, of systematic variance and unsystematic or error variance. The error variance in the variable therefore needs to be taken into consideration to obtain an accurate estimate of the magnitude of the true relation between the target variable and other variables, such as the age of the research participants.

Although most researchers are primarily interested in the relations between theoretical constructs, only the correlation between two manifest variables can be directly observed. However, the relation between the manifest variables is a function not only of the relation between the constructs but also of the relation of the variables to the constructs (i.e., the epistemic correlations). As a consequence, to the extent that the construct–variable relations are low, the correlation between the variables will underestimate the true relation between the constructs. This point can be clarified by reference to Fig. 8.2, in which the circles correspond to theoretical constructs, the boxes correspond to manifest or observed variables, and E represents error variance. Notice that the correlation between the two observed variables (V_1 and V_2) will underestimate the correlation between the two constructs (C_1 and C_2) by the degree to which each variable contains measurement error (i.e., the extent to which the C-V relations are less than 1.0 in standardized units).

For the reason just described, analyses can be closer to the theoretical issues if the relations among constructs are examined independent of their measurement error or unreliability. An advantage of the availability of multiple variables is that the analyses can be shifted to the level of theoretical constructs that are postulated to be responsible for the observed variables. In other words, when multiple variables are available, it is possible to distinguish between the variance in the variable that is

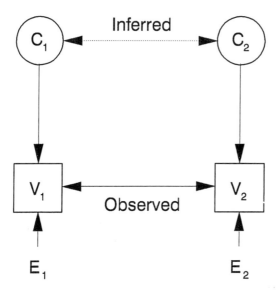

FIG 8.2. Illustration of the distinction between observed correlations (between manifest variables) and inferred correlations (between theoretical constructs). C = construct; V = observed variable; E = error variance.

attributable to the construct and that which is attributable to error. Furthermore, by focusing on the construct variance, one can conduct the analyses at a level in which there is no measurement error. This possibility is represented in Fig. 8.3, in which the constructs can be assumed to be assessed without measurement error because they correspond to the systematic variance that the relevant variables have in common. Procedures such as structural equation modeling make it possible to derive separate estimates of the unique and shared aspects of each variable and then to examine relations only among the shared aspects that can be presumed to reflect the relevant theoretical constructs.

Providing a Broader Context for the Results

A fundamental but largely neglected question in any emerging scientific field is the extent to which the results with a given variable are unique or merely another manifestation of a broader phenomenon. There is still little understanding of the level at which age-related influences on cognition operate (Salthouse, 1998). However, if that level is fairly high or broad, then many of the age-related effects on specific variables may simply be a consequence of more fundamental influences. Another advantage of multivariate research is that it provides a means of investigating age-related effects on one variable in the context of age-related effects

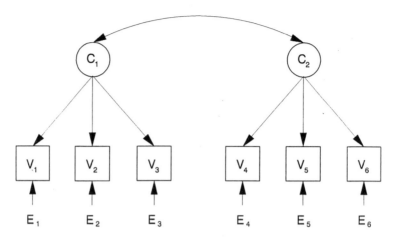

FIG. 8.3. Representation of the relations between theoretical constructs defined in terms of several observed variables. C = construct; V = observed variable; E = error variance.

on other variables. For example, Fig. 8.4 illustrates several possibilities for the relation between age and variable X. The top panel (A) is the age-variable relation in isolation and independent of any other variables. The middle panel (B) portrays the relation with potential mediators, and the bottom panel (C) portrays the relation with other variables that share age-related influences with variable X. Because of their focus on single variables, most contemporary cognitive researchers seem to implicitly assume that the situation represented in the top panel is the most accurate characterization of the relations between age and the cognitive variables they are investigating. However, this assumption cannot be evaluated and distinguished from the other possibilities portrayed in Fig. 8.4, unless additional variables are included in the analyses. Moreover, to the extent that one of the other possibilities is plausible, then the theoretical interpretations could be very misleading when the focus is restricted to a single variable.

To summarize, despite its reputation for methodological rigor, experimental research based on single variables is actually quite limited in several respects. When only a single variable is examined, the description of the sample is often crude, the focus is typically quite narrow and may only represent limited aspects of the relevant theoretical constructs, estimates of the relations among constructs are distorted by the neglect of measurement error, and age-related effects on variables are considered in isolation and interpreted as though they were completely independent of the effects on other variables. All of these limitations could be overcome by the sophisticated use of multivariate data.

(A)

(B)

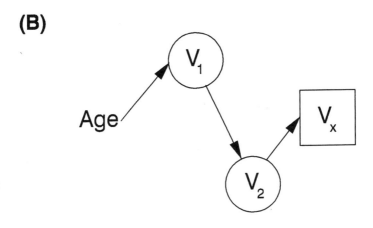

(C)

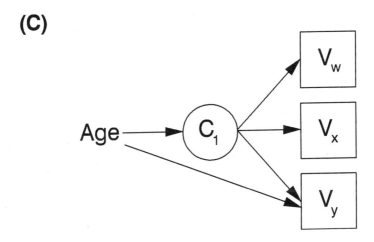

FIG. 8.4. Three representations of how age might be related to variable X. In A the relation is direct, in B the relation is mediated, and in C the relation is shared with the age-related effects on other variables. C = construct; V = observed variable.

ANALYTICAL METHODS

It could be argued that two of the most fundamental questions in research concerned with aging are which variables are related to age and which variables are not related to age. That is, to have an accurate characterization of the nature of age-related differences, it is important to determine not only which variables exhibit patterns of association with age but also which variables exhibit patterns of dissociation in the form of the absence of relations. Two different analytical approaches have been used to investigate this question in research on cognitive aging.

Statistical Interactions

Tests of interactions in an ANOVA are sometimes considered to be the most informative analytical procedure available in individual difference research because of the assumption that an interaction implies that at least some specific influences are present (cf. Kausler, 1982). However, the interpretation of interactions can be quite complicated for several reasons. Figure 8.5 schematically portrays three ways in which interactions involving age could emerge even when there were no selective or specific age-related influences on the relevant constructs. The top panel illustrates the possibility of nonlinear relations between construct and variable, the middle panel illustrates the consequences of variations in reliability of the variables, and the bottom panel represents a situation in which there is differential dependence of the variables on a common factor. Each of these possibilities is briefly discussed in the following paragraphs.

First, interpretations can be ambiguous unless the interactions are true crossover (disordinal) interactions because otherwise they may not be robust across transformations of scale (Loftus, 1978). That is, because the true relation between construct and variable is typically not known, it is often impossible to determine whether the original variables, or some transformation of them, provide the best reflection of variations in the underlying construct. An example of the consequences of a nonlinear construct–variable relation is illustrated in the two graphs in the top panel of Fig. 8.5. Assume that the construct–variable relation is nonlinear (as in the top left panel) and that two groups are operating at different levels of the construct (perhaps with older adults corresponding to the two left points and with young adults corresponding to the two right points). Under circumstances such as these, a manipulation that has equivalent effects at the construct level could have quite different effects at the level of observed variables, thereby resulting in spurious interactions. That is, because the difference between points D and C for young adults is much smaller than the difference between points B and A for older adults (top

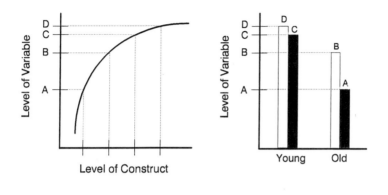

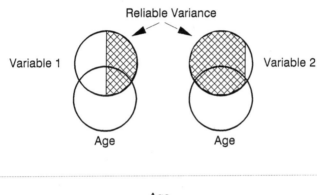

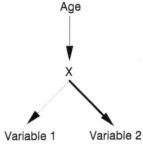

FIG. 8.5. Schematic illustration of three possible ways in which Age × Condition interactions could be misleading. See text for details.

right panel), a significant statistical interaction between age and variable would likely be evident despite equivalent differences at the level of the construct (top left panel). Because it is seldom possible to evaluate the validity of assumptions about the linearity of the relation between construct and variable, and the invariance of that relation across age groups, most interactions need to be interpreted very cautiously.

Second, interactions may not be meaningful if the variables being compared are not equivalent in what Chapman and Chapman (1973) referred to as *discriminating power*. One of the most important determinants of discriminating power is reliability because high relations with other variables (such as age) cannot be expected if the variable does not even have a high relation with itself. In other words, because a reliability coefficient reflects the proportion of true score or systematic variance in a variable, its value (more precisely the square root of the reliability coefficient) sets the upper bound of the correlation of that variable with any other variable. Therefore, if the variables being examined in an ANOVA do not have similar reliabilities, then it may be impossible to determine whether any interactions they might have with age reflect true differences in susceptibility to age-related influences or whether they merely indicate that the variables are not equally capable of exhibiting a relation with other variables. This possibility is illustrated in the middle panel of Fig. 8.5, in which variable 2 has a much larger proportion of systematic variance available for association with age than variable 1 and hence may have a stronger relation to age than variable 1 simply because of its greater reliability.

A third issue that needs to be considered when interpreting interactions is whether the primary interest is in the relative magnitude of the age-related effects or in the independence of those effects (Salthouse & Coon, 1994). That is, there are at least two distinct questions that can be asked in developmental comparisons involving two or more variables. One question is whether the age-related effects in certain variables or conditions are larger in absolute magnitude than those in other variables or conditions. The other question is to what extent are the age-related effects in some variables or conditions independent and distinct from the age-related effects in other variables or conditions.

ANOVA and other traditional analytical procedures focus on the former question, but in some circumstances the latter question may be at least as interesting and important. As an example, consider a study designed to determine whether there are age differences in the effects of priming. A researcher could use an ANOVA to compare young and old adults on variables with and without the presence of a prime, which would be informative about whether there are age-related differences in the absolute magnitude of priming. However, an alternative question is whether there are significant unique age-related effects in the priming condition distinct from those that are evident in the no-priming condition. One way in which this second question could be investigated is to use hierarchical regression analysis to control the variation in one variable (e.g., the variable without priming) when examining the age-related influences on the second variable (e.g., the variable with priming). If there is no evidence of independent or unique age-related effects in this analysis, then the most reasonable inference may be that the priming and no-priming variables overlap completely with respect to their age-related influences, even though those influences may be manifested to a greater extent in one variable than in another.

A relevant analogy in this situation might be that of an energy shortage that affects several different industries. A single event (e.g., the closure of all nuclear reactors) could be responsible for the energy shortage, but the impact of the shortage might nevertheless be greater in some industries, such as manufacturing, than in others, such as agriculture. An ANOVA of measures of productivity before and after the shortage would likely reveal an interaction of time of assessment and industry, but an inference that different causal factors were responsible for the observed effects in the two industries would be incorrect. In contrast, if measures of the changes in productivity in one industry were examined after controlling for measures of the changes in productivity in another industry, the results might more accurately reflect the fact that the two effects were not independent. That is, if both effects are attributable to a common third variable, then using the effects on one of the variables to control for the influence of the third variable will likely also reduce or eliminate its effects on the other variable.

The bottom panel of Fig. 8.5 illustrates how selective age-related effects on two variables might not reflect the operation of distinct age-related influences. Note that because both variables are related to age through a common construct, labeled X in the figure, they would share exactly the same age-related determinants. Despite complete overlap of the age-related influences, however, the magnitude of the age-related effects could be greater on variable 2 than on variable 1 because it is more strongly related to the critical causal factor. That is, the total age-related effect in this type of path diagram is determined by the product of the paths between age and X and between X and the variable; thus, the age-related effects will be larger for the variable with the stronger relation from the critical (X) factor.

Traditional statistical procedures, such as ANOVAs, are extremely useful for many types of comparisons. However, they have limitations when used to identify selective or specific age-related influences. Researchers using these procedures should therefore recognize that the interpretation of interactions depends on the following assumptions: (a) that the relation between the variable and the construct is correctly specified and is invariant across the age range and that transformations that might eliminate the interaction would not be meaningful, (b) that the variables are equivalent in discriminating power or in the ability to exhibit relations with other variables, and (c) that the primary interest is in the absolute magnitude of the group differences in the observed variables and not in the relative independence of the age-related influences on the relevant theoretical constructs. It is worth noting that these assumptions are generally less critical when multivariate methods are used because multiple variables minimize the importance of any single variable–construct relation, reduce measurement error (and increase reliability) at the level of constructs, and, as elaborated below, are easily amenable to analyses examining independence of relations among variables.

Mediational Hypotheses

A major advantage of multivariate analytical methods over more traditional univariate methods is that they provide a powerful means of investigating mediational hypotheses in which it is postulated that some variables contribute to the relations of age with other variables. For example, it might be hypothesized that factor X (e.g., the capacity of working memory or the efficiency of an aspect of attention, such as inhibition) is important in contributing to the age-related differences in certain variables because prior research has established that age-related differences exist in measures of X. The argument could even be extended with a speculation about how X could affect the critical target variable. However, it is not sufficient merely to establish a relation of age to the hypothesized mediator or of the hypothesized mediator to the target variable. It is also important to simultaneously examine relations among age, the mediator, and the target variable to evaluate the relative contribution of the hypothesized mediator to the relation between age and the target variable. If the hypothesized mediator is related to age but does not exhibit a strong mediational pattern in simultaneous analyses, then it would not be convincing as a mediator. At the present time, the only feasible method of examining these types of relations is with correlational procedures.

Researchers trained within the experimental tradition often object that procedures based on correlations provide a very weak basis for inferring causality. There are two major responses to this concern. The first is to acknowledge that because age, the variable of primary interest in studies of aging, cannot be randomly assigned to individuals, age-comparative research can never be truly experimental and will always be fundamentally correlational in nature. Therefore, any causal inferences involving the variable of age will necessarily be weak because people of different ages are likely to differ from one another in potentially important characteristics besides age. Experimental research is extremely valuable for examining causal linkages between manipulated and observed variables, but it is not particularly useful for determining whether an observed variable is actually attributable to differences in a preexisting variable such as age rather than to differences in other variables that happen to be correlated with age.

The second response to the concern about weak causal inferences is to point out that although it is true that correlation does not imply causality, it is also true that causality does imply correlation. In other words, although correlation-based methods do not provide strong tests of causality, they do provide a means of examining whether the data are consistent with causal theoretical assumptions. That is, if the available measures are reliable and the observed results are inconsistent with the predictions from a theoretical hypothesis, then the hypothesis would be called into question. On the other hand, if the results are consistent with the implications of the hypothesis, then it can be concluded that the mediational hypothesis, and an unknown number of other hypotheses that could also lead to the same results, is still plausible. (It is important to note that a discovery that one hypothesis is consistent with the data does not mean that it is the *only* hypothesis that could be consistent.)

One way of thinking about mediational hypotheses is that they provide a means of fractionating or decomposing the relation between two variables. Just as there is interest in unpacking the processes involved in a particular variable, it is also valuable to identify the relative contribution of different possible determinants to the relation between two variables. This is only possible if variables representing other influences are available so that their effects can be partialed out when examining the relations between the two variables of primary interest.

There are several ways in which mediational hypotheses can be investigated with multivariate methods. If the hypothesis is fairly simple, then hierarchical regression methods could be used. For example, if the goal is to determine the role of a variable as a potential mediator of the age relations on the target variable, then hierarchical regression methods could be used in which the variance of the hypothesized mediating variable is held constant before examining the relation of age to the target variable. If the assumptions of multiple regression procedures (e.g., Cohen & Cohen, 1983) are met, then the results will indicate what the age–variable relations would look like if there was little or no variation in the variable hypothesized to function as the mediator.

More complex hypotheses can be investigated with structural equation models, which have the added advantage of adjusting for measurement error. These procedures can be thought of as multiple regression involving several sets of dependent or criterion variables, with the analyses conducted at the level of latent constructs instead of only at the level of manifest variables. Not only do structural equation models provide a powerful means of testing theoretical predictions while adjusting for measurement error, but because they involve multiple variables they also yield information relevant to the validity of the major constructs. A brief overview of structural equation procedures is available in the article by

McArdle (1996), a more extensive but still quite readable coverage is available in a recent book by Kline (1998), and useful guidelines for reporting results from such analyses are contained in articles by Raykov, Tomer, and Nesselroade (1991) and by Thompson and Daniel (1996). However, a few additional points should be noted about the use of structural equation models in research in cognitive aging.

First, if the fit of the model is good, then it is reasonable to conclude that the model is plausible but not that it is correct. A good fit means that the results are consistent with the postulated structure, but it does not mean that only that particular hypothesized set of causal relations is plausible (e.g., Cliff, 1983; MacCallum, Roznowski, & Necowitz, 1992; MacCallum, Wegener, Uchino, & Fabrigar, 1993). In part for this reason, some authors have suggested that rather than focusing on a single model, it is often more valuable to compare several alternative models to determine which ones are *not* plausible. Furthermore, because not all plausible models can be known a priori, it is frequently recommended that the correlation matrix, along with the standard deviations, be reported so that other researchers can reconstruct the covariance matrix and use it to examine as-yet-unspecified alternative models.

Second, when age comparisons are of primary interest, it is often desirable to include age as an exogenous variable in the model in order to examine the manner in which it exerts its influence on the variables. It is important to recognize that use of age in this fashion does not mean that the researcher is analyzing only intrinsic or endogenous aspects of development but rather that the age variable is serving as a convenient index of the time-ordered relations among variables. Some researchers have objected to any use of structural models based on cross-sectional data because of the belief that this use conveys an impression of causality that is unwarranted. Although it is quite true that structural models can be easily misinterpreted, they can nevertheless be very informative in decomposing correlational patterns, regardless of whether the correlations are based on cross-sectional or longitudinal data.

Third, if separate models are formed for each age group, then the various models should be tested simultaneously, and directly compared, to determine which relations are significantly different from one another. Humphreys (1985) discussed this problem in the following passage in the context of correlations, but it is also applicable to these more complex types of analyses because they are also based on essentially correlational information:

> Ability to reject a zero relationship in one sample and inability to do so in a second sample does not constitute evidence for a difference in outcomes. Failure to compare the two relationships with each other is probably the most common logical–statistical error. (p. 7)

Extension of this reasoning to structural equation models means that researchers should not conclude that different models apply to samples of different ages unless the models have been directly compared with one another to determine which relations cannot be constrained to be equal across the two groups without a significant loss in fit. Fortunately, tests such as these can now be performed fairly easily with computer programs, such as EQS (e.g., Byrne, 1994; Kline, 1998).

Fourth, sample size is relevant in structural equation analyses because, if it is small, then there will be large confidence intervals around the estimates of the relations and consequently low power to detect deviations of the data from the model. The recommended minimum numbers vary, but a number of authors have suggested that samples of 200 or more individuals are needed to have meaningful results in structural equation analyses. Furthermore, MacCallum, Browne, and Sugawara (1996) have reported that power for a test of close fit depends on both the degrees of freedom and the sample size but that with few degrees of freedom (e.g., 10), power may be only .612 with a sample of 500 and even with 50 degrees of freedom, the power with a sample of 200 might only be .769.

Finally, if the model has been modified on the basis of the data, then it should be replicated or cross-validated in a new sample before accepting the model (Cliff, 1983; MacCallum et al., 1992). The problem here is that data-based modifications capitalize on chance and on sample-specific characteristics, which increases the likelihood of a Type II error in which the model is accepted when it is false. MacCallum et al. also pointed out that post hoc modifications often do not replicate with small samples (which in some circumstances may mean less than 1,200 individuals!).

If it is assumed that the original sample was completely representative of the population in all important respects, then the researcher may be justified in concluding that the modified model provides a good description of the true relations among the variables. However, only the most arrogant researchers are likely to feel confident of that assumption, and thus the outcomes of data-based modifications are likely to reflect at least some sample-specific characteristics. It is therefore prudent to treat a model based on empirical modifications as an informed hypothesis (i.e., derived from a description of one set of data), which should then be tested with an independent set of data before it is accepted as a generalizable model of the true situation.

To summarize, although the majority of the current research in cognitive aging has been analyzed with traditional procedures, such as t tests and ANOVAs, there are numerous advantages of more sophisticated multivariate procedures. Not only are these techniques often more powerful than univariate techniques because of the ability to control extraneous variables and minimize measurement error, but they also provide methods of investigating the implications of theoretical hypotheses that are simply impossible with univariate analytical procedures.

CONCLUSIONS

In light of the numerous untested assumptions that have been discussed, it is clear that researchers in the area of cognitive aging need to be cautious in reaching conclusions on the basis of their empirical results. Greater emphasis should therefore be placed on replication and on the importance of converging evidence, and systematic meta-analytic integrations of the research literature should be encouraged to provide more powerful analyses of the data than that available in single small-sample studies.

Several changes in research practices are probably also desirable. First, the practice of using the same individuals in multiple studies should either be avoided or, if it is continued, researchers should consider reporting the testing history of the participants in order to document the degree of overlap of samples in different studies. Second, larger samples should be included in each age group to increase statistical power and to reduce the bias against detecting small but potentially theoretically important age differences. Third, confidence intervals around the estimates for both significant and nonsignificant results should be reported as an indication of the precision of the results, instead of only describing the outcomes of null hypothesis significance tests. Finally, the typical study should include more variables and capitalize on the advantages of powerful multivariate analytical methods that are currently available.

REFERENCES

Allen, P. A., Smith, A. F., Jerge, K. A., & Vires-Collins, H. (1997). Age differences in mental multiplication: Evidence for peripheral but not central decrements. *Journal of Gerontology: Psychological Sciences, 52B*, P81–P90.

Avolio, B. J., & Waldman, D. A. (1994). Variations in cognitive, perceptual, and psychomotor abilities across the working lifespan: Examining the effects of race, sex, experience, education, and occupational type. *Psychology and Aging, 9*, 430–442.

Babcock, R. L., & Laguna, K. D. (1996). An examination of the adult age-related differences on the Raven's advanced progresive matrices: A structural equations approach. *Aging, Neuropsychology, and Cognition, 3*, 187–200.

Babcock, R. L., Laguna, K. D., & Roesch, S. C. (1997). A comparison of the factor structure of processing speed for younger and older adults: Testing the assumptions of measurement equivalence across age groups. *Psychology and Aging, 12*, 268–276.

Baltes, P. B. (1968). Longitudinal and cross-sectional sequences in the study of age and generation effects. *Human Development, 11*, 145–171.

Botwinick, J., & Arenberg, D. (1976). Disparate time spans in sequential studies of aging. *Experimental Aging Research, 2*, 55–61.

Byrne, B. (1994). *Structural equation modeling with EQS and EQS/Windows*. Beverly Hills, CA: Sage.

Chapman, L. J., & Chapman, J. P. (1973). Problems in the measurement of differential deficit. *Psychological Bulletin, 79*, 380–385.

Cliff, N. (1983). Some cautions concerning the application of causal modeling methods. *Multivariate Behavioral Research, 18*, 115–126.

Cohen, J. (1988). *Statistical power analysis for the behavioral sciences*. Hillsdale, NJ: Lawrence Erlbaum Associates.

Cohen, J. (1994). The earth is round ($p < .05$). *American Psychologist, 49*, 997–1003.

Cohen, J., & Cohen, P. (1983). *Applied multiple regression/correlation analysis for the behavioral sciences*. Hillsdale, NJ: Lawrence Erlbaum Associates.

Cook, T. D., & Campbell, D. T. (1979). *Quasi-experimentation: Design and analysis issues for field settings*. Skokie, IL: Rand McNally.

Flynn, J. R. (1987). Massive IQ gains in 14 nations: What IQ tests really measure. *Psychological Bulletin, 101*, 171–191.

Garner, W. H., Hake, H. W., & Eriksen, C. W. (1956). Operationism and the concept of perception. *Psychological Review, 63*, 149–159.

Hertzog, C. (1996). Research design in studies of aging and cognition. In J. E. Birren & K. W. Schaie (Eds.), *Handbook of the psychology of aging* (4th ed., pp. 24–37). San Diego, CA: Academic Press.

Horn, J. L. (1979). Some correctable defects in research on intelligence. *Intelligence, 3*, 307–322.

Humphreys, L. G. (1985). Correlations in psychological research. In D. K. Detterman (Ed.), *Current topics in human intelligence* (Vol. I, pp. 3–24). Norwood, NJ: Ablex.

Kausler, D. H. (1982). *Experimental psychology and human aging*. New York: Wiley.

Kline, R. B. (1998). *Principles and practice of structural equation Modeling*. New York: Guilford.

LaVoie, D., & Light, L. L. (1994). Adult age differences in repetition priming: A meta-analysis. *Psychology and Aging, 9*, 539–553.

Lipsey, M. W. (1990). *Design sensitivity: Statistical power for experimental research*. Newbury Park, CA: Sage.

Loftus, G. R. (1978). On the interpretation of interactions. *Memory & Cognition, 6*, 312–319.

Loftus, G. R. (1996). Psychology will be a much better science when we change the way we analyze data. *Current Directions in Psychological Science, 5*, 161–171.

MacCallum, R. C., Browne, M. W., & Sugawara, H. M. (1996). Power analysis and determination of sample size for covariance structure modeling. *Psychological Methods, 1*, 130–149.

MacCallum, R. C., Roznowski, M., & Necowitz, L. B. (1992). Model modifications in covariance structure analysis: The problem of capitalization on chance. *Psychological Bulletin, 111*, 490–504.

MacCallum, R. C., Wegener, D. T., Uchino, B. N., & Fabrigar, L. R. (1993). The problem of equivalent models in applications of covariance structure analysis. *Psychological Bulletin, 114*, 185–199.

McArdle, J. J. (1996). Current directions in statistical factor analysis. *Current Directions in Psychological Science, 5*, 11–18.

McClelland, G. H. (1997). Optimal design in psychological research. *Psychological Methods, 2*, 3–19.

McClelland, G. H., & Judd, C. M. (1993). Statistical difficulties of detecting interactions and moderator effects. *Psychological Bulletin, 114*, 376–390.

Neisser, U. (1997). Rising scores on intelligence tests. *American Scientist, 85*, 440–447.

Raykov, T., Tomer, A., & Nesselroade, J.R. (1991). Reporting structural equation modeling results in *Psychology and Aging*: Some proposed guidelines. *Psychology and Aging, 6*, 499–503.

Salthouse, T. A. (1991). *Theoretical perspectives on cognitive aging*. Hillsdale, NJ: Lawrence Erlbaum Associates.

Salthouse, T. A. (1993). Attentional blocks are not responsible for age-related slowing. *Journal of Gerontology: Psychological Sciences, 48,* P263–P270.

Salthouse, T. A. (1998). Independence of age-related influences on cognitive abilities across the life span. *Developmental Psychology, 34,* 851–864.

Salthouse, T. A., & Coon, V. E. (1994). Interpretation of differential deficits: The case of aging and mental arithmetic. *Journal of Experimental Psychology: Learning, Memory, and Cognition, 20,* 1172–1182.

Salthouse, T. A., Fristoe, N., & Rhee, S. H. (1996). How localized are age-related effects on neuropsychological measures? *Neuropsychology, 10,* 272–285.

Salthouse, T. A., Kausler, D. H., & Saults, J. S. (1988). Investigation of student status, background variables, and the feasibility of standard tasks in cognitive aging research. *Psychology and Aging, 3,* 29–37.

Salthouse, T. A., McGuthry, K., & Hambrick, D. Z. (1998). Shared age-related influences on cognitive and non-cognitive variables. *Psychology and Aging, 13,* 486–500.

Schaie, K. W. (1965). A general model for the study of developmental problems. *Psychological Bulletin, 64,* 92–107.

Schaie, K. W. (1996). *Intellectual development in adulthood: The Seattle Longitudinal Study.* New York: Cambridge University Press.

Schaie, K. W., Maitland, S. B., Willis, S. L., & Intrieri, R. C. (1998). Longitudinal invariance of adult psychometric ability factor structures across 7 years. *Psychology and Aging, 13,* 8–20.

Schaie, K. W., Willis, S. L., Jay, G., & Chipuer, H. (1989). Structural invariance of cognitive abilities across the adult life span: A cross-sectional study. *Developmental Psychology, 25,* 652–662.

Schmidt, F. L. (1996). Statistical significance testing and cumulative knowledge in psychology: Implications for training of researchers. *Psychological Methods, 2,* 115–129.

Thompson, B., & Daniel, L. G. (1996). Factor analytic evidence for the construct validity of scores: A historical overview and some guidelines. *Educational and Psychological Measurement, 56,* 197–208.

Verhaeghen, P., & Salthouse, T. A. (1997). Meta-analyses of age–cognition relations in adulthood: Estimates of linear and non-linear age effects and structural models. *Psychological Bulletin, 122,* 231–249.

Wilcox, R. R. (1998). How many discoveries have been lost by ignoring modern statistical methods? *American Psychologist, 53,* 300–314.

Zelinski, E. M., & Burnight, K. P. (1997). Sixteen-year longitudinal and time lag changes in memory and cognition in older adults. *Psychology and Aging, 12,* 503–513.

9

Cognitive Functioning in Very Old Age

Lars Bäckman
Uppsala University
Karolinska Institute Stockholm

Brent J. Small
Karolinska Institute Stockholm
University of South Florida

Åke Wahlin
Maria Larsson
Karolinska Institute Stockholm

In this chapter, we focus on the changes in cognitive functioning that occur in very late life. Thus, unlike many other chapters in this volume, the basic criterion which we have used to select research articles deals with the nature of the participants, rather than the characteristics of the outcome measures.

Obviously, the definition of what constitutes very old age is arbitrary. Neugarten (1974) was one of the first to distinguish among specific segments of the aging population. She viewed 55- to 74-year-olds as "young-old," whereas those 75 years and above were considered as "old-old." More recently, authors have begun to refer to individuals 85 years and older as the "oldest-old" (e.g., Lindenberger & Baltes, 1997; Suzman, Willis, & Manton, 1992), and centenarians, those who are 100 years and older, have received some empirical attention in recent years (Poon, Sweaney, Clayton, & Merriam, 1992). To be sure, terms such as *young-old*, *old-old*, and *oldest-old* are not static entities. Their meaning varies across time and cultures. As the expected life expectancy continues to increase due to changes in medical technology and lifestyle behaviors (e.g., Taeuber & Rosenwaike, 1992), and with the advent of possible means to extend the human life span through chromosomal modification (e.g., Telomerase; see Bodnar et al., 1998), the definition of very old age is likely to be altered in the near future.

Those who are very old represent the fastest growing segment of the older adult population in Western societies today. For example, in the United States from the period of 1990 to 2010, the number of individuals between the ages of 65 and 74 years is expected to increase by 16%. By contrast, the expected increase for persons 75 years of age and older is close to 50%. Further, if we just focus on those individuals who are 85 years and older, the prediction is that this segment of the population will almost double (97%) across the same 20-year interval (U.S. Bureau of the Census, 1996). This selective increase in the number of very old adults is not unique to the United States, as similar changes are expected in Sweden (Statistiska Centralbyrån, 1994) and Canada (Statistics Canada, 1996), to mention just two examples.

Despite these ongoing demographic changes, individuals in late senescence have been largely neglected by cognitive aging researchers. For example, a literature search in *Psychology and Aging* and the *Journal of Gerontology: Psychological Sciences* revealed that less than 10% of the articles with a cognitive orientation that were published between 1990 and 1997 targeted very old adults or included this group for comparative purposes. The striking absence of relevant research, when faced with the dramatic increase in the number of persons living to very old age, warrants a detailed examination of these persons.

Acknowledging that what defines very old age is a relativistic matter, in the present chapter we focus on individuals who are 75 years and older. Thus, research focusing exclusively on the 75+ population and studies that have compared this group with younger age cohorts are the primary objects of study.

The general objective of this chapter is to provide an overview of current research on cognitive functioning among very old adults, with particular emphasis on memory functioning. Of special interest is whether empirical regularities derived from traditional cognitive aging research generalize to persons in late senescence. The issue of continuity versus discontinuity of cognitive functioning in late life is addressed from the perspective of general performance trajectories. Here, an important goal is to identify factors that may determine whether cognitive decline in very old age is gradual, accelerated, or attenuated.

In addition, we discuss the extent to which the effects of various types of individual-difference variables on cognitive performance may change in very old age. A critical point to be made is that the prevalence and incidence of various diseases related to cognitive functioning (e.g., dementia, circulatory disease [CD], and diabetes) increase greatly with advancing age. This fact calls our attention to the issue of what should define "normal aging" in very late life. Of further interest is that the influence of various concomitant conditions (e.g., sensory deficits, depression, and vitamin deficiency) on cognitive performance may be magnified, reduced, or unchanged in very old age. Delineating conditions that follow these patterns is another way of addressing the issue of continuity versus discontinuity of cognitive functioning across the adult life span.

EMPIRICAL GENERALIZATIONS IN COGNITIVE AGING

Most research on cognitive aging involves comparisons between one group of young adults (often in their 20s) and one group of older adults (often ranging from the late 60s to the 80s). To accomplish the goals of the present chapter, it is imperative to relate the body of knowledge on cognition in very old age to empirical generalizations from traditional cognitive aging research. Thus, in this section, we summarize key findings and explanatory concepts from the general literature on cognitive aging, with special reference to memory functioning. We also highlight salient individual-difference variables found to be related to cognitive performance in adulthood and aging.

A striking observation from cognitive aging research is that no form of memory appears to be fully resistant to the negative influence of human aging. Thus, age-related deficits may be observed in tasks assessing implicit memory (e.g., Hultsch, Masson, & Small, 1991; Jelicic, Craik, & Moscovitch, 1996), semantic memory (e.g., Albert, Heller, & Milberg, 1988; Crook & West, 1990), primary memory (e.g., Botwinick & Storandt, 1974; Parkinson, 1982), working memory (Craik & Rabinowitz, 1984; Salthouse & Babcock, 1991), and episodic memory (Craik & Jennings, 1992; Kausler, 1994). However, it is important to note that the size of age-related deficits and the consistency with which such deficits are observed varies systematically across different forms of memory. Specifically, age deficits tend to be large and robust for measures of episodic memory and working memory, smaller and more contingent on demand characteristics in tasks assessing implicit and semantic memory, and even smaller in primary memory tasks (e.g., Bäckman, Small, & Larsson, in press; Craik & Jennings, 1992).

Attempts to (a) understand the sources of age-related memory deficits, (b) delineate memory-relevant individual-difference variables in aging, and (c) improve memory in old age through training or other forms of support have mostly been concerned with episodic memory. This is likely due to the highly systematic age–performance relationship observed for this form of memory. Two processing resources, speed of processing (Bryan & Luszcz, 1996; Hultsch, Hertzog, & Dixon, 1990; Salthouse, 1991) and working memory capacity (Hartley, 1986; Morrell & Park, 1993; Stine

& Wingfield, 1990), have been found to account for a sizable proportion of the age-related performance variation in episodic memory, although residual age-related variance typically remains after measures of these constructs have been partialed out. At the same time, it is important to recognize that age-related deficits in various memorial processes, such as distinctiveness of encoding (Mäntylä & Bäckman, 1990; Rabinowitz, Craik, & Ackerman, 1982) and contextual integration (Mäntylä & Bäckman, 1992; Park, Smith, Morrell, Puglisi, & Dudley, 1990) may contribute to deteriorating memory capabilities in old age. The relationship between such processes and more general abilities, including speed and working memory capacity, is not fully understood.

Despite the overall pattern of age-related decline, memory functioning in late life is characterized by substantial individual differences. Participant-related factors within demographic (e.g., education and gender), cognitive (e.g., speed and working memory), lifestyle (e.g., social activity and exercise habits), and biological (e.g., vitamin B_{12} and folic acid) domains greatly influence level of memory functioning in older cohorts (Bäckman et al., in press). In addition, normal aging is marked by a cognitive reserve capacity—a potential for improving performance. Evidence for older adults' ability to improve memory performance has been documented, both in experimental work varying the degree of cognitive support (e.g., through manipulation of factors such as organizational structure, richness of the stimulus input, and retrieval cues; Bäckman, Mäntylä, & Herlitz, 1990; Craik & Jennings, 1992) and in training research focusing on the use of memory strategies (Stigsdotter Neely & Bäckman, 1995; Verhaeghen, Marcoen, & Goossens, 1992).

Cognitive aging research addressing functions other than memory also reveals systematic variability across different domains with regard to the magnitude of the age-related impairment. Psychometric tests of intelligence represent a case in point and one that is particularly relevant to the present purpose of examining whether established patterns of performance in the cognitive aging literature generalizes into very old age.

There is substantial evidence that tests that are termed "verbal" and are assumed to reflect crystallized intelligence show relatively modest age-related changes from early to late adulthood. Such results have been documented using the Wechsler Adult Intelligence Scale (WAIS; Kaufman, Reynolds, & McLean, 1989), the Army Alpha (Jones & Conrad, 1933), and the Primary Mental Abilities (PMA) battery (Schaie, 1985). Tests subsumed under these rubrics (e.g., Vocabulary and Comprehension) assess world knowledge in a broad sense, draw on prior experience, and have rather limited speed demands.

These findings contrast with the results from performance tests in intelligence batteries that are thought to reflect fluid aspects of intelligence.

Such tests (e.g., Digit Symbol and Block Design) involve relatively unfamiliar material and require fast and efficient solutions to novel problems. Age-related decline in tests of fluid intelligence are robust and gradual across the adult life span (for a review, see Kausler, 1991; Salthouse, 1991). Tasks derived from the experimental literature that tap related abilities (e.g., fact retrieval and object-naming tasks vs. perceptual closure and syllogistic reasoning tasks) show similar performance trajectories from early to late adulthood (e.g., Bäckman & Nilsson, 1996; Mitchell, 1989; Salthouse, 1992).

There is an interesting parallel in the patterns of age changes between tasks assessing semantic memory and crystallized intelligence, on the one hand, and tasks assessing episodic memory and fluid intelligence, on the other. Whereas the former categories of tasks exhibit relative stability across the adult life span, the onset of age-related deterioration occurs early in life for the latter categories of tasks. There are also interesting parallels with regard to the cognitive processes involved during task performance, with semantic memory and crystallized intelligence drawing largely on prior knowledge and episodic memory and fluid intelligence requiring new learning and flexible adjustments to new situational demands (Kinsbourne, 1980). At a general level, then, these patterns appear to reflect the fact that older adults are quite efficient in using preexisting knowledge structures but not when fast and efficient processing of novel information is required.

COGNITIVE FUNCTIONING IN VERY OLD AGE

In this section, we describe general performance trends as well as individual differences in late-life cognitive functioning. The perspective on individual differences is broad and encompasses demographic, lifestyle, cognitive, health-related, and genetic factors. Two diseases, dementia and depression, are treated in separate subsections because in work on normal aging participants are typically excluded if they suffer from these conditions. Although we focus on the way in which different forms of memory are affected in very old age, we begin by presenting relevant research on intelligence in late senescence. This is because most systematic research on cognitive functioning in very old age has dealt with intelligence.

Intelligence

In our brief review of psychometric intelligence, we noted that age-related deficits on tests of fluid abilities are typically observed, although tests of crystallized skills show relative stability from early to late adulthood.

However, as individuals enter very old age, deficits in intelligence may be more global in nature.

Results from the Seattle Longitudinal Study (SLS; Schaie, 1996) provide relevant information regarding the onset of negative changes in intelligence. Schaie reported 21-year changes in the five PMA scales and observed different points of departure for negative age changes in performance. For inductive reasoning and number ability, decline began at age 60, for spatial orientation and word fluency it was 67 years, and age 74 was the point of decline for verbal meaning, a measure of crystallized intelligence. Further analyses revealed that age 74 was also the point at which decline in a measure of practical intelligence became evident. Thus, from these analyses, it appears that the pattern of trajectory for multiple domains of intelligence, including fluid abilities, crystallized abilities, and practical skills, is one of decrements after age 74.

Additional evidence on the nature of age differences in intelligence can be derived from the Berlin Aging Study (BASE; Baltes & Mayer, 1999). In this study, cross-sectional relationships among tests of intelligence were examined in 70- to 103-year-old adults. Lindenberger and Baltes (1997) reported that the performance trajectory for multiple domains of intelligence was one of "generalized linear decline" (p. 429). For example, among the three tests of fluid intelligence, the average age–ability correlation was −.53, whereas the corresponding correlation for the two crystallized-intelligence tests was −.44. Thus, consistent with other reports (e.g., Schaie, 1996), although the performance trajectory is one of decline in very old age, there is partial evidence that this decline is attenuated among tests of crystallized abilities (see also Howieson, Holm, Kaye, Oken, & Howieson, 1993; Koss et al., 1991; Rabbitt, Donlan, Watson, McInnes, & Bent, 1995).

In general, it appears that although the conceptual distinction between fluid and crystallized abilities is maintained in studies that examine intelligence test performance among very old adults (e.g., Lindenberger & Baltes, 1997), the differential preservation of crystallized abilities seen in young-old adults does not generalize to very advanced age. It should be noted that although the research programs from the SLS and the BASE figure prominently in this review, similar patterns of results, indicating decline in all aspects of intelligence in very old age, have also been seen in other studies, including the Duke Longitudinal Study (Busse & Maddox, 1985) and recent reports from a population-based study of Australians (Christensen et al., 1994).

In addition to attempts to describe the nature of age-related changes in intelligence, several studies have tried to identify the source of these changes. Perhaps the most interesting explanatory concept in recent years relates to sensory functioning (e.g., vision and hearing). Lindenberger and Baltes (1994, 1997) reported that over 90% of the age-related variance in intellectual performance in two samples of very old adults could be accounted for by individual differences in vision and hearing (see also Salthouse, Hancock, Meinz, & Hambrick, 1996, for similar findings in a younger cohort of adults).

Although neither Lindenberger and Baltes (1994) nor Salthouse et al. (1996) addressed potential age × sensory capacity interaction effects, comparing the absolute magnitude of the relationships across these studies suggests that sensory variables are more strongly related to cognitive performance in old age than in early adulthood. Indeed, Baltes and Lindenberger (1997) addressed this issue in a sample ranging in age from 25 to 103 years. The results showed that although the variance shared by age and sensory functioning was similar across the studied age span, the total amount of variance in cognitive performance accounted for by sensory functioning was larger in the older (70–103 years) than in the younger (25–69 years) sample. However, Salthouse, Hambrick, and McGuthry (1998) recently reported interactions of age and sensory capacity in the direction of larger sensory effects for younger adults than for older adults. Thus, although the relationship between sensory and cognitive variables is well established across the life span, the way in which the magnitude of this relationship may change with increasing age remains unclear.

The strong link between sensory integrity and cognitive functioning has led investigators to posit a common-cause hypothesis for the observed predictive relationships (e.g., Lindenberger & Baltes, 1994; Salthouse et al., 1996). Put simply, this hypothesis states that there is a common cause that is related to age-associated variance in cognitive measures, as well as to variance in more basic biological parameters, such as vision and hearing. However, although sensory measures may do an excellent job in accounting for age-related variance in cognitive functioning, the theoretical value of this account is debatable. Rather than focusing on yet another surrogate variable that does a good job in accounting for a great deal of age-related cognitive variance, future research should explore what this common factor actually represents. Such an enterprise would benefit from the inclusion of brain-based indices (e.g., morphological parameters, cerebral blood flow, and receptor density).

In summary, the pattern of age-related differences in intelligence test performance of very old adults is one of generalized decline. There is some evidence that this decline is less pronounced for tests of crystallized abilities, but in general the trajectory of performance is downward.

Memory

In comparison with the domain of psychometric intelligence, there is less systematic information available on changes in memory functioning in very old age. Much of the relevant information is gathered within large-scale multidisciplinary studies in which memory performance is assessed along with other indices of cognitive functioning, as well as various social and biological variables. Analytical experimental work that targets very old adults is essentially lacking. This section is organized according to research findings on episodic memory, semantic memory, short-term memory, and implicit memory, respectively. The purpose is to evaluate whether these different forms of memory exhibit differential patterns of change in very old age.

Episodic Memory

In a study addressing episodic memory changes in older adults (65+ years), Colsher and Wallace (1991) reported an age deterioration in immediate and delayed recall, as well as in delayed recognition, across a 6-year period. The size of the age-related decline was invariant across age in delayed recall and recognition, although the older participants (75+ years) experienced greater decline than the younger participants (65–74 years) in immediate recall. Further evidence of a differential age trend in episodic memory was reported by Giambra, Arenberg, Kawas, Zonderman, and Costa (1995). They studied a large sample of healthy participants from the late teens through the 100s using the Benton Visual Retention Test, which assesses immediate memory for geometric designs. The results demonstrated a more precipitous decline in visual retention from the mid-60s than earlier in the adult life span.

Hultsch, Hertzog, Small, McDonald-Miszczak, and Dixon (1992) followed samples of young-old (55–70 years) and old-old (71–86 years) adults across a 3-year period in a number of cognitive tasks, including measures of episodic memory (word and text recall). Although no reliable age changes were observed for the two episodic memory tasks, the Age × Time of Testing interaction was just below conventional significance for text recall. This reflected that the young-old cohort showed stability over the test interval, whereas the old-old cohort showed a slight, but not statistically reliable, deterioration.

One reason for the nonsignificant change in episodic memory in the Hultsch et al. (1992) study may have been that longer test intervals are needed to detect reliable age decline. Shorter retest intervals may increase the possibility of drawing from recent task-relevant experience, thereby counteracting the decline process. For example, Zelinski and Burnight (1997) suggested that 6 years is the minimal test interval required to ensure that age-related decline in episodic memory is reliable. Indeed, when the Hultsch et al. sample was examined 6 years after baseline, significant decrements in word recall were observed for both age groups (Small, Dixon, Hultsch, & Hertzog, 1999).

Evidence of accelerated decline of episodic memory in very old age was recently provided by Korten et al. (1997). Using participants ranging in age from 70 to 102 years who were tested on two occasions 3 years apart, these authors found a more pronounced rate of decline with advancing age for tests of verbal and nonverbal recall and face recognition, as well as for a test of global cognitive skill. Crook and Larrabee (1992) reported a gradual age-related decrement in episodic face recognition among individuals ranging in age from 18 to 80 years. However, the most pronounced age deterioration was observed after 70 years of age. Further evidence for a selective drop in episodic memory performance for visually presented information (i.e., words and objects) was reported by Bäckman and Larsson (1992) and by Hall, Pinkston, Szalda-Petree, and Coronis (1996). The results from these studies showed no differences in memory performance between participants in their 60s and those in their 70s, although both these groups outperformed participants in their 80s.

In contrast to the findings of disproportionate deficits in episodic memory in very old age, Zelinski and Burnight (1997) demonstrated continuous decline in text and word recall after age 55. Their study revealed no evidence for accelerated decline in very old age over a 16-year test interval, although the sample ranged from 71 to 97 years of age at follow-up. Cross-sectional evidence for a continuous age deterioration in episodic memory was recently presented from the Betula Prospective Cohort Study (Nilsson et al., 1997). One hundred participants in each of 10 age cohorts (35 to 80 years, in intervals of 5 years) participated. Across a comprehensive battery of episodic memory tasks (i.e., free recall of words; free recall, cued recall, and recognition of sentences and actions; face and name recognition; activity memory; and fact recall and source recall), a very consistent pattern emerged: For all these tasks, there was a continuous drop in memory performance with increasing adult age.

Further support for a continuous decline in memory performance through very old age was provided in a series of studies from the Kungsholmen project, which targets the 75+ population. In these studies, Wahlin and colleagues (Bäckman & Wahlin, 1995; Hill, Wahlin, Winblad, & Bäckman, 1995; Wahlin et al., 1993; Wahlin, Bäckman, & Winblad, 1995) observed a gradual performance decrement in normally aged samples between 75 and 96 years of age in tasks assessing free and cued recall of words, as well as in word and face recognition (see also Corey-Bloom et al., 1996).

However, very old age may not necessarily be characterized by a decline in episodic memory. Evidence for age invariance in episodic memory functioning was recently demonstrated both cross-sectionally (Hill, Grut, et al., 1995) and longitudinally (Bäckman et al., 1998; Hill, Stigsdotter Neely, & Bäckman, 1997) using samples of optimally healthy participants between 76 and 87 years of age. These studies examined verbal and nonverbal memory as well as performance on the Fuld Object Memory Evaluation Test. In the longitudinal assessment, participants were tested at baseline and after 1 and 2 years.

The lack of age-related decline in these studies is consistent with other research in which the samples have been optimally healthy or assessed within a a short time frame (Albert et al., 1995; Johansson, Zarit, & Berg, 1992; Lachman, 1983; Zelinski & Burnight, 1997). It is noteworthy that the pattern of age equivalence found in the studies by Hill and colleagues was seen also in cross-sectional comparisons (Hill, Grut, et al., 1995). This suggests that the lack of age-related change in the longitudinal assessment may not only reflect practice effects.

One reason why older adults have episodic memory problems may be that they treat contextual information differently than do their younger counterparts (e.g., Burke & Light, 1981; Mäntylä & Bäckman, 1990). The tendency of older participants to encode information in a rather general and prototypical manner may cause particular difficulties in remembering the source of an event. Indeed, a number of studies have reported that older adults are selectively impaired in source memory relative to item memory (e.g., Hashtroudi, Johnson, & Chrosniak, 1989, 1990; Larsson & Bäckman, 1998; Spencer & Raz, 1994).

To examine whether very old age takes an additional toll on source memory functioning, Erngrund, Mäntylä, and Nilsson (1996) and Erngrund, Mäntylä, and Rönnlund (1996) compared healthy participants between 35 and 80 years in different item and source memory tasks. These studies demonstrated a linear age-related deterioration for both item and source memory. However, the linear age trend remained when source memory was conditionalized on item memory. This suggests that source memory may be more affected by the normal aging process than item memory and that source memory deficits occur gradually across the adult life span.

Episodic memory performance may be conceived of as a context-sensitive phenomenon that involves consideration of acquisition factors, test factors, the nature of the materials, characteristics unique to the rememberer, and multiple interactions among these factors (e.g., Bäckman et al., 1990; Craik & Jennings, 1992; Jenkins, 1979). The lack of a simple relationship among the variables involved is perhaps particularly notable with respect to the interplay among adult age, level of cognitive support, and memory performance. For example, in some situations, older people benefit more from supportive conditions than do their younger counterparts (e.g., Craik & McDowd, 1987); in other situations, old and young participants benefit to the same extent from cognitive support (e.g., Park, Cherry, Smith, & Lafronza, 1990); and in still other situations, younger adults benefit more than older adults from cognitive support (e.g., Puglisi & Park, 1987).

Two patterns of data can be seen in research that has examined the relationship between cognitive support and episodic memory in older adults of different ages. First, it is clear that very old adults possess the ability to utilize cognitive support for improving memory. Several forms of cognitive support appear to be utilized as efficiently by very old adults as compared with younger elderly persons. This includes motor activity at learning (Karlsson et al., 1989), more study time (Wahlin et al., 1995), prior knowledge (Wahlin et al., 1993), and retrieval cues (Bäckman & Wahlin, 1995). In the work by Wahlin and colleagues, it is noteworthy that the beneficial effects from cognitive support were equally large for participants in their 70s and for those in their 90s.

However, there is also evidence that the facilitative effects from some forms of cognitive support are reduced in very old age. Hill, Wahlin, et al. (1995) found that the effect of item organizability on word recall decreased from the 70s through the 90s. Similarly, Bäckman (1991) demonstrated that although very old adults could use general aspects of prior knowledge to enhance face recognition much like young-old adults, very old adults showed deficits in using subtler aspects of prior knowledge in this task situation. This result suggests that very old adults may require a higher level of cognitive support than their younger counterparts to demonstrate memory improvement. Bäckman and Larsson (1992) obtained direct evidence for this hypothesis. In their study, young, young-old, old, and old-old adults were assessed in free and cued recall of words and objects. The main finding was a three-way interaction involving age, richness of encoding (words vs. objects), and retrieval support (free vs. cued recall). There was a parallel decrease for free and cued recall of words with increasing age. For objects, the free-recall data again revealed a gradual decrease in performance across age. However, in cued recall of objects, age differences were relatively small, indicating an age-related increase in cue benefits. The overall pattern of results from this study suggests that the degree of support required at encoding for optimal cue utilization may increase in very old age.

Additional evidence for a reduction in cognitive reserve capacity in very old age comes from intervention research. Training studies focusing on both episodic memory (Yesavage, Sheikh, Friedman, & Tanke, 1990) and fluid intelligence (Baltes, Dittmann-Kohli, & Kliegl, 1986) show that the magnitude of intervention-related gains is smaller for old-old adults than for younger elderly persons.

Thus, work on the effects of cognitive support in late senescence suggests a correlation between overall ability and the potential for improvement: Performance decreases and so does the ability to utilize supportive conditions. In this way, very old age represents one among many instances in which a condition that is negatively related to cognitive functioning is also associated with a reduced reserve capacity in late life. Other examples include low education (Hill, Wahlin, et al., 1995), low verbal ability (Craik, Byrd, & Swanson, 1987), slow information processing (Kliegl, Smith, & Baltes, 1990), and low intelligence (Bäckman et al., 1998). Still other examples are discussed in subsequent sections in this chapter dealing with dementia and depression.

Semantic Memory

Although age-related deficits may be observed in semantic memory performance, particularly when lexical information has to be accessed rapidly (e.g., Albert et al., 1988; Howard, Heisey, & Shaw, 1986), the dominant pattern in the literature is that semantic memory shows little variation from early adulthood to earlier portions of the late adult life span (Bäckman et al., in press; Craik & Jennings, 1992). As seen below, this pattern of stability of semantic memory functioning appears to change in very old age.

Bäckman and Nilsson (1996) examined vocabulary, verbal fluency (four tests), and fact retrieval performance in a sample ranging from 35 to 80 years. Controlling for age-related differences in education, they found that the middle-aged adults performed at the highest level and, with the exception of one fluency test, they observed no aging-related deterioration before age 75. In a similar vein, Gilinsky and Judd (1994) reported that vocabulary scores increased with age up to the 40s and then remained stable until very old age (>80 years). A comparable pattern of results for vocabulary was found by Giambra et al. (1995). Somewhat contradictory findings were reported by Hultsch et al. (1992), who found significant decline across 3 years in measures of fact retrieval and verbal fluency in both young-old and old-old adults. The fact that a similar decline was not observed for vocabulary suggests that retrieval problems may have been the source of the age-related declines observed.

An important aspect of semantic memory is naming ability. Au et al. (1995) evaluated performance on the Boston Naming Test in participants aged 30 to 79 years who were tested three times over a 7-year span. With years of education partialed out, naming performance declined from the initial assessment to the third testing, and the rate of negative change was particularly pronounced in the oldest participants. Taken together, these longitudinal findings are in agreement with cross-sectional data (e.g., LaBarge, Edwards, & Knesevich, 1986; Mitrushina & Satz, 1995), suggesting that participants in their 70s exhibit a faster drop in naming performance than do participants in younger cohorts.

Although significant decline in semantic memory may typically not be seen until the mid-70s, there is evidence that further decline in very old age is systematic and gradual. In BASE, participants between 70 and 103 years were assessed in tests assessing vocabulary and lexical decision (Lindenberger & Baltes, 1994). The results indicated a negative linear age gradient for all measures, and the quadratic age trend did not differ significantly from zero.

Taken together, it appears that like measures of crystallized intelligence, the relative preservation of semantic memory seen among young-old adults, does not generalize to late senescence. The general shape of the downward trend in very old age is one of gradual loss.

Short-Term Memory

In this section, we discuss work addressing working memory and primary memory. Both these types of memory may be considered as indices of short-term memory because they deal with information that resides in consciousness (Baddeley, 1986). Within this domain of cognitive functioning, evidence suggests that the well-established patterns of pronounced age-related deficits in working memory and relative preservation of primary memory in late adulthood (Bäckman et al., in press; Brébion, Ehrlich, & Tardieu, 1995; Salthouse, 1991) continue into very old age.

Gilinsky and Judd (1994) studied performance in several working memory tests (e.g., computational span and reading span) in persons ranging from 19 to 96 years of age. A composite working memory measure indicated a systematic decrement in working memory performance with increasing age, with a slight decrement over each decade. However, a steeper decline in performance was observed in the oldest age group (>80 years). Norman, Kemper, and Kynette (1992) found similar results with pronounced deficits in working memory for a subsample in their 90s compared with samples from earlier decades in life.

Additional evidence for decline in working memory performance among very old adults was reported by Hultsch et al. (1992). In this study, although there were significant longitudinal changes for both age groups, very old adults (71–86 years) declined by almost 0.50 SDs over the 3-year follow-up interval, whereas the younger age group (55–70 years) declined by less than 0.20 SDs. Finally, Nyberg, Nilsson, Olofsson, and Bäckman (1997) observed a linear age-related deterioration from 35 through 80 years of age in a word recall task where working memory was taxed at encoding, retrieval, or both.

The pattern of results seen for working memory may be contrasted against that seen in tasks assessing primary memory. A number of studies have indicated that primary memory performance remains relatively stable through very old age (e.g., Corey-Bloom et al. 1996; Howieson et al., 1993). Wahlin et al. (1993, 1995) found no age-related differences from the mid-70s through the mid-90s for different indices of primary memory (i.e., digit span and scores derived by means of the Tulving-Colotla lag method). This is perhaps not surprising considering that measures indexing temporary holding of information in consciousness are little affected even by neurodegenerative diseases such as Alzheimer's disease (AD; e.g., Morris, 1996; Simon, Leach, Winocur, & Moscovitch, 1995).

Thus, although measures of primary memory may be relatively well preserved in very old age, the performance patterns on tests that assess working memory suggest otherwise. If anything, the negative age-related trends observed in younger groups of elderly persons appear to accelerate when individuals older than 70 years are examined in tests of working memory.

Implicit Memory

In recent years, there has been a great deal of interest in implicit tests of memory (see Graf & Masson, 1993, for a review). Whereas performance on explicit tests, such as recall and recognition, typically show robust age deficits, results from implicit tests show only a small advantage in favor of younger adults. Often these differences are not reliable (e.g., Light & Singh, 1987; Russo & Parkin, 1993), but in some studies they are statistically significant (e.g., Hultsch et al., 1991; Jelicic et al., 1996).

Small, Hultsch, and Masson (1995) examined implicit test performance in three groups of participants (19–34 years, 58–73 years, and 74–89 years). They noted that although the young-old group exhibited significantly less priming on a test of word-stem completion as compared with the youngest age group, their performance did not differ from that of the very old group. In addition, all three age groups performed similarly on another test of implicit memory (fact completion), which emphasized conceptual processing of information. In another study using 1,000 participants from 35 to 80 years of age (Nilsson et al., 1997), there was no evidence for age differences in word-stem completion priming across the age range examined.

Two additional studies have examined implicit test performance among very old adults. Isingrini, Vazou, and Leroy (1995) reported no significant age group differences on a test of implicit category generation for persons aged 20–35, 40–55, 60–75, and 76–90 years. Likewise, Vakil, Melamed, and Even (1996) found no differences between 18- to 27-year-olds and 77- to 93-year-olds on a test of implicit memory for contextual information.

Taken together, the results of these studies suggest that performance on implicit tests of memory for individuals over 75 years of age is as good as that of young-old persons and may be as good as persons in their 20s. Future studies using very old persons as the criterion group should allow conclusions to be made regarding whether this data pattern generalizes across additional tests of implicit memory.

In conclusion, the overall pattern of results from research on intelligence and memory functioning in aging suggests that tasks tapping fluid intelligence, episodic memory, and working memory are associated with a robust age deterioration, characterized by a relatively early onset of decline that continues into very old age. In contrast, tasks tapping crystallized intelligence and semantic memory typically demonstrate stability across much of the adult life span, with the onset of deterioration occurring in later stages of life. Finally, tasks assessing primary memory and implicit memory show the least consistent age deficits from early to late adulthood and show relative preservation even in very old age.

Individual Differences in the Normal Population

Individual differences within multiple domains (e.g., demographic, lifestyle, cognitive, and health) are known to affect cognitive performance across the life span (e.g., Bäckman et al., in press; Hultsch, Hertzog, Dixon, & Small, 1998). In this section, we review studies addressing the influence of individual-difference variables on cognitive performance in very old age. Our goal is to determine whether the importance of individual-difference variables observed in younger cohorts remains unchanged in very old age. Obviously, a major class of individual-difference variables in late life concerns health-related factors. This is reflected in the present discussion.

Demographic Factors

It is well established that women typically outperform men in tasks assessing verbal skill, whereas men are superior to women in tasks assessing spatial abilities (e.g., Maccoby & Jacklin, 1974). A more recent observation is that there appears to be a small, but often statistically reliable, female advantage in episodic memory (e.g., Herlitz, Nilsson, & Bäckman, 1997; Larabee & Crook, 1993; Zelinski, Gilewski, & Schaie, 1993). Social, hormonal, and evolutionary factors have been proposed to account for these patterns of gender differences in cognitive functioning (e.g., Halpern, 1992; Herlitz, Nilsson, Bäckman, 1997).

To the extent that hormonal factors play an important role in gender-related cognitive differences, one would expect an attenuation of gender differences in late life, as a result of age-related hormonal changes. From a different perspective, it has been demonstrated that men exhibit greater losses in brain volume than do women in old age (Gur et al., 1991), suggesting that the pattern and magnitude of gender differences in cognitive functioning may change in late life. However, none of these views are supported by recent evidence, which indicates that the typical pattern of gender differences in verbal and spatial performance generalizes from early adulthood to very old age (Herlitz, Nilsson, Bäckman, 1997; Meinz & Salthouse, 1998; Wiederholt et al., 1993). Moreover, several studies have demonstrated that the female superiority in episodic memory performance is of equal magnitude from the mid-30s through the late 90s (e.g., Herlitz, Nilsson, Bäckman, 1997; Hill, Grut, et al., 1995; Lindenberger & Baltes, 1997; Rabbitt et al., 1995; Wahlin et al., 1993; West, Crook, & Barron, 1992).

Another demographic characteristic, years of education, has been shown to exert a positive influence on cognitive performance, and this influence extends into very old age (e.g., Hill, Wahlin, et al., 1995; Inouye, Albert, Mohs, Sun, & Berkman, 1993; Nilsson et al., 1997; Wiederholt et al., 1993). Educational status may be linked to a variety of factors, including genetic selection, neuronal growth during critical periods in life, cognitive stimulation during active work period, physical health, and use of memory strategies (e.g., Hill, Wahlin, et al., 1995; Mortimer & Graves, 1993).

However, some research has suggested that demographic characteristics may have a reduced impact on cognitive functioning in both octogenarians (Hill, Grut et al., 1995) and nonagenarians (Hassing, Wahlin, & Bäckman, 1998) who are carefully screened for physical health. Such findings may reflect that health and other biological factors become increasingly important to cognitive functioning in late life, possibly at the expense of sociodemographic characteristics (Lindenberger & Baltes, 1997). Thus, when participants are both very old and in optimal physical health, the effect of education on cognitive performance may be lessened.

Lifestyle Factors

Lifestyle activities constitute another class of factors of interest. Much of this research has dealt with social activities, such as visiting friends, going to parties and public meetings, preparing meals, and shopping. Participation in social activities has been shown to share variance with performance in memory tasks, such as text recall and word recall in both middle and old age (e.g., Christensen et al., 1996; Cockburn & Smith, 1991; Hultsch, Hammer, & Small, 1993).

In a sample ranging from 75 to 96 years of age, Hill, Wahlin, et al. (1995) found that not only was social activity positively associated with word-recall performance, but it was also related to the ability to benefit from cognitive support for remembering. Hill, Wahlin, et al. also demonstrated a positive relationship between physical exercise and memory performance. However, the effects of both social activity and exercise on word recall did not interact with age in this study. A somewhat different pattern of results was reported by Hultsch et al. (1993). They found that although social activity was related to semantic memory performance in both young-old and old-old adults, the size of the relationship was larger in the older group. Thus, activity patterns appear to constitute a reliable correlate of late-life cognitive functioning, and the strength of this relationship may increase in very old age.

It should be noted, however, that the causal direction of the relationship between activity and cognitive performance is unclear. As much as social activities may be beneficial to intellectual functioning, it may also be the case that persons who are cognitively adept tend to engage more in social activities than those who have lower cognitive functioning.

Cognitive Factors

A great deal of effort in cognitive aging research has been invested in examining whether basic cognitive abilities (e.g., processing speed) can account for age-related and general variation in the criterion measures of interest (e.g., episodic memory). To a large extent, this research has focused on indices of perceptual speed and working memory as predictors of memory performance, but indices of fluid intelligence, verbal ability, and world knowledge have also been examined (e.g., Cockburn & Smith, 1991; Hultsch et al., 1990; Park et al., 1996; Salthouse, 1991).

A consistent finding from studies using this analytical strategy is that processing speed and working memory account for substantial portions of the variance in episodic memory performance and that statistical control of speed or working memory greatly reduces the amount of age-related variation (e.g., Hartley, 1986; Park et al., 1996; Salthouse & Babcock, 1991).

Overall, research suggests that these predictive patterns generalize into very old age. In a population-based study of very old adults, Bryan and Luszcz (1996) found sizable reductions of the age-related variance in episodic memory, once measures of perceptual speed were partialed out (see also Luszcz, Bryan, & Kent, 1997). Similar results in samples of young-old and old-old adults were reported by Hultsch et al. (1992) using measures of both speed and working memory as predictors of text and word recall. An interesting finding in the Hultsch et al. study was that the age-related variance in episodic memory was not only reduced but eliminated when measures of verbal ability and world knowledge were added to the prediction model.

Finally, a series of studies targeting samples in the 70s and 80s (Bäckman et al., 1998; Hill, Grut, et al., 1995; Hill et al., 1997) has demonstrated that composite scores of tests assessing fluid intelligence (which draw heavily on cognitive speed) account for a substantial proportion of the variance in both verbal and nonverbal episodic recall, clearly overshadowing demographic variables as predictors of performance.

Although few studies have specifically addressed Age × Predictor interactions, the available evidence suggests that the majority of individual-difference variables within the demographic, lifestyle, and cognitive domains are as important in very old age as they are in earlier parts of life. A possible change in the predictor space in late life may occur such that demographic variables become gradually less important, whereas health-related and biological variables become gradually more important. This pattern is manifested in research demonstrating that the impact of demographics (e.g., age and education) on cognitive performance among very old adults is negligible when participants are rigorously screened for health. In addition, some work on intelligence suggests that sensory variables become increasingly important as predictors of performance in very old age. However, as shown in the next section, for some health conditions the relationship to cognitive performance appears to remain invariant in very old age.

Health-Related Factors

A major factor to consider in research with older participants is the increase in physiological pathology and related mortality. Indeed, it is well-known that age is associated with an increased prevalence of a variety of diseases that may affect cognitive fuctioning (e.g., Brody & Schneider, 1986; Fries & Crapo, 1981). Among persons over 65, more than 80% have at least one chronic illness and many individuals have multiple conditions (Fozard, Metter, & Brant, 1990). Increased health problems likely contribute to the increased variability in cognitive performance among older people, and it has been argued that the presence of cognitive deficits that are secondary to physiological pathology may not signify true age-normative change (e.g., Abrahams, 1976).

Comprehensive health screening is rarely performed in cognitive aging studies, which is perhaps not surprising given the financial costs associated with the inclusion of a proper medical examination. However, large-scale multidisciplinary projects examining age-related effects on memory and other cognitive functions have tended to screen for potentially critical aspects of physical health (e.g., Fratiglioni, Viitanen, Bäckman, Sandman, & Winblad, 1992; Nilsson et al., 1997; Steinhagen-Thiessen & Borchelt, 1993). Typically, studies emanating from such projects indicate that age-related decline in cognitive functioning continues into very old age, although the effects may be smaller than expected when participants are adequately screened for various health-related factors (e.g., Koss et al., 1991; Wahlin et al., 1993).

Self-Reported Health. Cognitive aging studies often include self-report indicators of health as predictors of performance (e.g., Earles & Salthouse, 1995; M. Perlmutter & Nyquist, 1990). However, these are typically self-ratings of global assessments of subjective health and may not provide any detail as to specific conditions. In addition, the correspondence between self-report measures of physical health and objective indicators of disease has been reported to range from absent (e.g., Nilsson et al., 1997) to moderate (e.g., Elias, Elias, & Elias, 1990) to high (e.g., Schultz et al., 1994). Although self-report measures of health may be less than ideal, some studies have found a relationship between self-reported health and self-reported memory problems (Bazargan & Barbre, 1994), actual memory performance (e.g., Hultsch et al., 1993), and mortality (e.g., Schoenfeld, Malmrose, Blazer, Gold, & Seeman, 1994).

Given that self-reports of health may reflect an unknown combination of subjective and objective factors (e.g., Costa & McCrae, 1985), the existing evidence on the relation between self-reported health and cognitive performance is somewhat difficult to interpret (e.g., Earles, Connor, Smith, & Park, 1997). An alternative approach is to examine the relationship between specific diseases (or disease categories) and cognitive performance. Such an approach may be particularly useful in very old age, considering the age-related increases in prevalence rates for a variety of conditions that affect cognitive functioning. In the following sections, we describe the effects of a select number of health conditions on cognitive performance in very old age. Although not exhaustive, the coverage attempts to illustrate the extent to which some conditions that are relatively common in very old age, and that may not be routinely screened for in cognitive aging research, influence cognitive functioning.

CD. Diseases related to the circulatory system are very common among elderly adults in the Western world and constitute a major cause of death and disability in old age (Wenger, 1988). CD encompasses a cluster of conditions, including hypertension, hypotension, and coronary heart disease. The most extreme effects of circulatory changes on cognitive functioning are seen in the pathogenesis of vascular dementia (VaD; e.g., Sulkava & Erkinjuntti, 1987).

CD-related cognitive deficits are also evident among nondemented elderly persons. In a study involving all persons aged 55 years and older in a suburb of Rotterdam (Breteler, Claus, Grobbee, & Hofman, 1994), it was found that although CD may result in relatively small cognitive deficits at the individual level, at the population level it accounts for a considerable proportion of age-related cognitive deficits.

Most research on the effects of CD on cognitive functioning in old age has focused on hypertension, a condition that is found in more than 25%

of the 70+ population (Uemura, 1988). Hypertensive groups of older individuals have been found to perform less well than groups of normotensive individuals across a variety of cognitive tests (e.g., Elias & Elias, 1993; Starr, Whalley, Inch, & Shering, 1993). Further, high blood pressure is associated with increased risk of vascular disease and related complications, where marked cognitive deficits constitute cardinal symptoms (e.g., Bots, Grobbee, & Hofman, 1991; Bush, 1991). Some evidence indicates that episodic memory is especially vulnerable to hypertension in old age (Waldstein, 1995).

It has been suggested that the effects of hypertension on cognitive performance may be especially pronounced in very old adults (Elias & Robbins, 1991). Although some studies support this hypothesis (Launer, Masaki, Petrovitch, Foley, & Havlik, 1995; Wilkie & Eisdorfer, 1980), most recent research fails to confirm that cognitive performance of very old adults is more affected by hypertension than that of younger elderly adults (e.g., Elias, D'Agostino, Elias, & Wolf, 1995; Elias, Wolf, D'Agostino, Cobb, & White, 1993; Scherr, Hebert, Smith, & Evans, 1991), and some research even shows greater negative effects of hypertension on cognitive functioning in younger than in older samples (Madden & Blumenthal, 1998; Waldstein et al., 1996). Although hypertension is typically associated with cognitive deficits in old age, negative effects of hypotension on cognitive performance have also been documented in both young-old (Sands & Meredith, 1992) and very old (e.g., Guo, Viitanen, & Winblad, 1997) adults. Thus, there is some evidence that the relationship between blood pressure and cognitive performance in old age may be described as an inverted U-shaped function.

A serious cerebral accident resulting from circulatory disturbances is a stroke. Old age is associated with an increased incidence of stroke, which is a leading cause of disability among elderly adults (e.g., Walker, Robins, & Weinfeld, 1981). Recovery from cognitive deficits can be expected within 6 months after the stroke incident, the level of improvement depending on the amount of brain tissue destroyed (e.g., Jongbloed, 1986). However, full recovery may not be possible; evidence suggests that stroke victims may experience many of the problems reported in the earlier stages of recovery even 3 years after the incident, despite continued functional improvement (e.g., Greveson, Gray, French, & James, 1991; Langton-Hewer, 1990).

It is important to note that mortality resulting from stroke, as well as problems in the rehabilitation process, increases in late life. Recent evidence indicates that such problems are particularly prevalent among persons above 75 years of age (Falconer, Naughton, Strasser, & Sinacore, 1994), possibly reflecting decreases in brain reserve capacity in very old age. Note also that because residual stroke-related cognitive deficits may be focal and domain specific (Bowler, Hadar, & Wade, 1994; Wade, Wood, & Hewer, 1988), such deficits may easily be missed if the cognitive assessment focuses on a narrow range of abilities.

Finally, cognitive deficits resulting from neurologically "silent" cerebral infarctions have been documented among very old adults (e.g., Meyer, Obara, Muramatsu, Mortel, & Shirai, 1995; Price et al., 1997). As opposed to more severe cerebrovascular conditions, this condition often passes without clinical recognition (O'Brien, 1994).

Diabetes. Diabetes mellitus also increases in very old age, with prevalence rates around 20% among persons who are 80 years and older (Worrall, Moulton, & Briffett, 1993). Diabetes may cause cognitive impairment regardless of age, and deficits have been documented even in small children and adolescents (Rovet, Ehrlich, & Hope, 1988; Ryan, Vega, & Drash, 1985).

There has been debate as to whether the aging process is accelerated in diabetes (Croxon & Jagger, 1995; Kent, 1976). If this is the case, exacerbated cognitive deficits would be expected among very old diabetic individuals. However, recent research indicates that the duration of disease, rather than chronological age, determines the size of diabetes-related cognitive deficits (Croxon, & Jagger, 1995; Dornan, Peek, Dow, & Tattersall, 1992).

Nevertheless, the bulk of empirical evidence indicates that elderly diabetic individuals show cognitive deficits as compared with their nondiabetic age peers (e.g., Croxon & Jagger, 1995; Dornan et al., 1992; L. C. Perlmuter et al., 1984; Prirart, 1978). In a population-based study of elderly adults ranging in age from 69 to 89 years (Kalmijn, Feskens, Launer, Stijnen, & Kromhout, 1995), nondiabetic participants with impaired glucose tolerance and hyperinsulinaemia showed cognitive deficits as compared with normal controls, although the magnitude of the cognitive impairment was even larger in diabetic patients. Interestingly, these effects remained after controlling for age, occupation, smoking, previous stroke, and insulin treatment. These results suggest that there may be a continuum of diabetes-related cognitive deficits that progresses from the subclinical to the clinical state.

Thyroid Disease. The prevalence of thyroid disease in the elderly population is approximately twice as high as in younger individuals. Hypothyroidism and hyperthyroidism each affect around 4% of the older population (Levy, 1991). Subclinical hypothyroidism, which is characterized by elevated levels of thyrotropin (thyroid-stimulating hormone [TSH]) and normal levels of thyroid hormones, is even more common in old age, with prevalence estimates ranging from 4% to 14% (Greenspan & Resnick,

1991). Effects of hypothyroidism include slowness in thinking, increased response latency, and a decrement in mood level. Low levels of thyroid hormones may disrupt brain systems that support episodic memory, concentration, and problem solving (Denicoff, Joffe, Lakshmanan, Robbins, & Rubinow, 1990; Whybrow, Prange, & Treadway, 1969).

Hyperthyroidism, on the other hand, is often accompanied by emotional lability, anxiety, overactiveness, restlessness, tremor, and sleep disturbance (G. M. Brown, 1980). Diagnosis of hypo- or hyperfunction of the thyroid gland may be particularly difficult in older participants (Lazarus, 1997; Lindsay & Toft, 1997). Although these diseases may lead to serious complications (e.g., dementia) if left untreated over extended time periods, symptoms may be mistakenly interpreted as expressions of normal aging or other diseases (e.g., Griffin & Solomon, 1986).

Even within normal ranges, thyroid functioning appears to be related to cognitive performance. In a recent population-based study of very old adults, Wahlin, Robins-Wahlin, Small, and Bäckman (1998) found that TSH was positively related to performance on a variety of episodic memory tasks. TSH levels accounted for roughly 10% of the total variation in memory performance, independent of age and other demographic factors.

Vitamin Deficiency. Low vitamin levels also become more prevalent in very old age (Bell et al., 1990; van Goor, Woiski, Lagaay, Meinders, & Tak, 1995). Thus, it may be especially important to consider the relationship between vitamin status and cognitive functioning among very old adults. Two vitamins known to be related to brain functioning are vitamin B_{12} and folic acid (D. C. Martin, 1988). In particular, these vitamins play an important role in protein synthesis in the brain (e.g., Robinson, 1966; Venkataraman, Walerych, & Johnson, 1967), a process known to be critical to memory consolidation (e.g., Davis & Squire, 1984).

The relationship between vitamin status and cognitive functioning in old age has been addressed in several recent studies. These studies vary both in terms of the cognitive abilities assessed and in the definition of what constitutes vitamin deficiency, resulting in somewhat equivocal patterns of results. Typically, however, a positive relationship has been documented between levels of vitamin B_{12}, folic acid, or both and performance in various cognitive tasks, including spatial copying (Riggs, Spiro, Tucker, & Ruh, 1996), Stroop test performance (Bohnen, Jolles, & Degenaar, 1992), word recall and recognition (Wahlin, Hill, Winblad, & Bäckman, 1996), and object recall (Hassing, Wahlin, Winblad, & Bäckman, 1999).

An interesting finding in the Wahlin et al. (1996) study was that the effects of B_{12} and folic acid levels on memory were quadratic rather than linear, suggesting that there may be a critical threshold above which the relationship disappears. Hassing et al. (1999) and Wahlin et al. also tested for potential Age × Vitamin Deficiency effects, but these were found to be nonsignificant. Thus, although the prevalence of vitamin deficiency increases in late senescence, very old persons may not be selectively penalized by this condition.

Medication. Given that the prevalence of disease increases in very old age, this is also the period in life when medications are taken most frequently. For example, benzodiazepines are widely used by older adults in many countries (Ashton & Golding, 1989). It has been suggested that the aging brain may be particularly sensitive to benzodiazepines and other common drugs (Closser, 1991). Although several authors have argued that it is important to consider psychotropic drugs in studies of age-related cognitive changes (e.g., Berg & Dellasega, 1996; Dealberto, Mcavay, Seeman, & Berkman, 1997), participants are rarely excluded from cognitive aging studies as a result of being on such medications.

Nevertheless, several studies have documented that benzodiazepines may result in cognitive deficits among elderly persons (e.g., Foy et al., 1995), particularly in tasks assessing episodic memory (e.g., Kruse, 1990), and that anticholinergic medication could have dramatic negative effects on cognitive performance in older adults (e.g., Kurlan & Como, 1988).

In addition, side effects of a number of other drugs may mimic age-related cognitive deficits, two pertinent examples being digitalis and antihypertensives (e.g., Blass & Plum, 1983). Although older adults are thought to be more sensitive to the adverse effects of specific medications because of somatic changes (e.g., diminished kidney function; Rudorfer, 1993) leading to an accumulation of substances in the body, psychoactive medications have a history of being inappropriately and excessively prescribed for elderly persons (e.g., Garrard et al., 1991).

In summary, the research reviewed concerning the influence of common health conditions on cognitive functioning in old age indicates that such conditions may indeed exert negative effects on cognitive performance. Although it may not be realistic to implement a comprehensive assessment of vascular status, thyroid function, vitamin status, and so forth as a standard in cognitive aging research, we should be aware of the fact that these and other conditions contribute to performance variation. Given that health conditions increase in very old age, the failure to assess these conditions will inevitably overestimate the size of normal age-related changes in late-life cognitive performance.

Genetic Factors

There has been growing interest in recent years in the role that genetics play in affecting cognitive functioning in both normal (e.g., McClearn et al., 1997; Pedersen, Reynolds, & Gatz, 1996) and pathological (e.g., Gatz, Lowe,

Berg, Mortimer, & Pedersen, 1994; Levy-Lahad & Bird, 1996) elderly populations. However, there is debate as to whether the relationship between these two factors is as great in very old adults as it is in younger cohorts. The strength of the link between genetics and cognition across the adult life span could be described by three performance functions. On the one hand, it could be argued that the influence of genotype should be reduced in very old age because of the accumulation of lifelong exposure to varied and complex environmental demands (Baltes, 1987). On the other hand, because of the association between genetics and late-life diseases known to exert an influence on cognitive functioning (Elias et al., 1990), such as heart disease (van Bockxmeer & Mamotte, 1992) and stroke (Basun et al., 1996), the impact of genotype may grow stronger as we get older. Finally, changing environmental demands and changes in the expression of genotypic variability may counteract one another and result in a maintained level of importance for genetic factors across the life span.

One class of studies that has examined the link between genotype and cognitive functioning in old age are those that focus on a particular gene. For example, there has been a great deal of interest in the gene coding for apolipoprotein E (ApoE), a plasma protein involved in the transportation of cholesterol. This gene is located on the long arm of chromosome 19 and has three alleles, ε2, ε4, and ε3, the last of which is the most common variety (Wahley, 1988). In general, there is consensus that the presence of the ε4 variant of ApoE conveys an increased risk of developing AD. For example, Peterson et al. (1995) found that ε4 carriers had a four times increased risk for becoming demented over a 4-year follow-up interval as compared with noncarriers in their sample of individuals with mild cognitive impairment (see also Strittmatter et al., 1993; Tierney, Szalai, Snow, Fisher, Tsuda, et al., 1996b).

The role of ApoE for cognitive functioning in normal aging has also received a lot of attention recently. The available evidence suggests slight decrements in cognitive performance among nondemented older adults with the ε4 allele (Helkala et al., 1995, 1996; Hyman et al., 1996). However, whether these changes reflect a direct influence of the specific genotype or are related to an overrepresentation of persons in a preclinical phase of dementia among ε4 carriers is yet unresolved (Bondi et al., 1995; Small, Basun, & Bäckman, 1998).

Although ApoE is an important risk factor for the development of AD and may be related to cognitive performance in persons without dementia, some authors have argued that the potency of its influence may diminish in very old age (Corder et al., 1994; Peterson, Waring, Smith, Tangalos, & Thibodeau, 1996). For example, Peterson et al. reported that the majority of risk associated with being an ε4 carrier was manifested in those participants who developed AD before age 75. Thus, for this specific gene, very advanced age may result in an attenuation of the impact of the ε4 allele as a predictor of the development of AD.

An additional class of studies examining the relationship between genotype and cognitive functioning has compared the performance of monozygotic and dizygotic twins. With these groups, the relative impact of genetics versus environmental factors can be determined. Although the number of studies that have examined this issue exclusively among very old adults is sparse, there is initial evidence to suggest that the contribution of genetics to cognitive performance remains strong in very old age. Finkel, Pedersen and McGue (1995) reported no significant differences in the contribution of genetic factors to memory performance among middle-aged (50–64 years) and older (65–88 years) adults, although there was a trend toward decreased genetic contribution in the older group.

In a recent study that focused exclusively on very old adults, McClearn et al. (1997) reported results from groups of twins who were 80 years and older. They found that the influence of heritability was uniformly high, on average accounting for approximately 50% of the variance in tests of general cognitive ability, verbal ability, spatial ability, processing speed, and memory in this group of very old adults. Taken together, although no studies have systematically contrasted the relative contribution of genotype to cognitive performance in very old adults versus adults from earlier cohorts, the relevant evidence suggests that genetic factors remain as powerful determinants of cognitive functioning in very old age.

As a final note, it is possible that different results may be derived from studies that examine the influence of a particular gene versus those that focus on the broad influence of genotype by examining twins. For example, the ε4 variant of ApoE is also related to increased rates of mortality (Corder et al., 1996). Thus, the relative importance of ε4 may be reduced in very old age because surviving ε4 carriers may be at an advantage in terms of other genetic as well as environmental factors. By contrast, examining the broad influence of genotype involves the interaction of many genetic factors. Thus, unless very old adults become increasingly select in terms of multiple genetic factors, the contribution of genotype to performance seen in these studies is more likely to remain invariant into very advanced age. Until more studies are completed that examine the specificity of the genetic influence (e.g., one particular gene versus the general influence of genetics) from early adulthood to very old age, definite conclusions regarding the potency of genetic factors in cognitive functioning across the life span must be postponed.

Selective Attrition and Terminal Decline

The study of cognitive functioning in very old age poses some special interpretive difficulties associated with mortality. Depending on whether deaths of some of the group occur before or after the cognitive assessment takes place, this factor can act either to underestimate the decline that is demonstrated or to overestimate the magnitude of normal age-related changes in performance.

One way in which mortality can affect the results is by underestimating the age-related performance decline because of selective attrition. Typically discussed in the context of longitudinal studies, selective attrition refers to the fact that persons who return to be retested are often superior, in terms of both demographic characteristics and baseline cognitive functioning, than those who fail to return (e.g., Hultsch et al., 1998; Lindenberger et al., 1999; Schaie, 1996). This positive selection may lead to the increasing presence of an elite group of participants, resulting in underestimation of the rate of decline.

The presence of selective attrition is of great concern for studies that examine performance patterns in very old age. In this case, selective attrition may be related to the fact that individuals who survive into very old age, and are able to participate in studies, may be somehow different from their counterparts who do not reach such an advanced age. For example, Perls, Morris, Ooi, and Lipsitz (1993) examined the influence of selective survival on cognitive functioning in a sample of very old adults. They reported that a group of 90- to 99-year-old men actually performed better than a group of 80- to 89-year-old men. As it is unreasonable to expect cognitive performance to improve from the 9th to the 10th decade of life, this difference likely reflects the select nature of the 90-year-olds. Similar results were reported by Siegler and Botwinick (1979). They observed that those very old individuals who were able to complete five longitudinal test sessions were almost 15 points higher on baseline WAIS intelligence scores than the remaining sample. Siegler and Botwinick suggested that the limited longitudinal decline in intelligence that was observed in their study may be due to the elite nature of the longitudinal sample.

A factor that works in the opposite direction, leading to an overestimation of true age-related differences in cognitive performance, is labeled *terminal decline* (see Berg, 1996, and Siegler, 1975, for a review). First introduced by Kleemeier (1962), terminal decline refers to a hypothesized condition whereby there is an accelerated trajectory of cognitive decline that is related to the proximity to death. Kleemeier argued that some of the individual differences in cognitive performance that accompany old age may be due to the fact that a portion of these individuals are in a terminal decline phase.

The effect of terminal decline on cognitive performance may be expected to be especially salient in studies that include very old individuals because of the increases in mortality rates in this population. However, some authors have questioned whether the effect of impending death on cognitive functioning is present in all age groups. For example, Riegel and Riegel (1972) argued that terminal decline should be evident in middle-aged and young-old adults because those who die in these cohorts of individuals are different, in a variety of capacities, from those who survive. On the other hand, they suggested that because death is more expected among old-old adults, there should be less evidence for terminal decline in this segment of the population.

However, several studies have reported findings contrary to Riegel and Riegel's (1972) contention. Deeg, Hofman, and van Zonneveld (1990) found evidence for terminal decline in adults who were over 70 years of age but not for those aged 65 to 69 years. Similarly, Johansson and Berg (1989) reported terminal decline effects on cognitive performance in adults between 70 and 80 years of age. Finally, Small and Bäckman (1997) observed significant cross-sectional group differences across a variety of cognitive measures between persons in the 80s who would or would not survive across a 3-year follow-up interval. Taken together, these results suggests that mortality-related effects on cognitive functioning do generalize to individuals who are very old.

Obviously, the effects of selective attrition and terminal decline are related. One reason why individuals who return for retesting are superior at the initial assessment may be that those who did not return are deceased. That is, the differences in cognitive functioning between the two groups may result from the joint contribution of the select nature of the returnees, coupled with the impaired functioning of the dropouts that may partly stem from terminal decline effects. For example, in the study by Perls et al. (1993), the significant group difference in cognitive performance between men in the 80s and 90s may be related to the fact that in the 80-year-old group impaired cognitive performance was associated with increased rate of death across the follow-up interval. Thus, it is unclear whether the age-related performance increase observed in this study reflects selective attrition, terminal decline, or some combination of the two.

Dementia

Perhaps the most powerful individual-difference variable in cognitive aging research is dementia. Dementia disorders are especially relevant in studies examining very old adults because of the increased occurrence in late life. AD and VaD are the two most common dementia diseases. Epidemiological research indicates that AD accounts for approximately 60% of all dementia cases, whereas around 25% of the population of demented patients are diagnosed with VaD (e.g., Ebly, Parhad, Hogan, & Fung, 1994; Graves et al., 1997; Hendrie et al., 1995). The prevalence of both AD and VaD increases exponentially with increasing age (roughly a doubling every 5 years from age 65), although the size of the increase is somewhat larger in AD than in VaD (e.g., Fratiglioni et al., 1991; Hébert & Brayne, 1995). Approximately 1% of the population between 65 and 69 years of age are diagnosed with dementia; the corresponding figure for the 90+ population is around 50% (e.g., Fichter, Meller, Schröppel, & Steinkirchner, 1995; Ott, Breteler, van Harskamp, Grobbee, & Hofman, 1995). For AD, the slope of the incidence function across age resembles closely that of the corresponding prevalence function, although incidence rates are considerably lower and do not show the same strong age dependency in VaD (e.g., Fratiglioni et al., 1997; Letenneur, Commenges, Dartigues, & Barbeger-Gateau, 1994). This likely reflects differential mortality effects in the two diseases.

Although the etiologies of VaD and AD are different, the pattern of cognitive deficits are strikingly similar in the two diseases (e.g., Almkvist, Bäckman, Basun, & Wahlund, 1993; Erker, Russel Searight, & Peterson, 1995; Ricker, Keenan, & Jacobson, 1994). Here, the focus is on AD because most of the relevant cognitive research has focused on this disease. AD results in a global cognitive dysfunction affecting perception, attention, memory, visuospatial skill, language, and intelligence, and no form of memory appears to be completely spared from the neurodegenerative process (for a review, see Morris, 1996; Nebes, 1992). Despite the fact that AD influences cognitive functions in a global manner, there is a predictable pattern of decline across the pathogenesis. Specifically, episodic memory appears to deteriorate very early, visuospatial skill and verbal ability somewhat later, and primary memory still later in the disease process (e.g., Almkvist & Bäckman, 1993; Grady et al., 1988; Small & Bäckman, 1998). This trajectory of cognitive deterioration in AD is reasonable, given that some of the earliest AD-related brain changes occur in regions known to be critical to episodic memory, such as the hippocampus and neighboring regions (H. Braak & Braak, 1995; Fox et al., 1996; Killiany et al., 1993; M. J. West, Coleman, Flood, & Troncoso, 1994).

Considerable research effort has been directed at examining whether onset age (which, of course, is highly related to chronological age) influences performance at a given point in time, as well as rate of cognitive decline in AD. Although it has been suggested that early-onset patients may be more impaired and exhibit a faster rate of decline than late-onset patients because of more severe and widespread brain lesions (e.g., Hansen, De Teresa, Davies, & Terry, 1988; Mann, 1994; Weinstein et al., 1991), the bulk of empirical evidence indicates that onset age has a negligible effect on cognitive functioning in AD (e.g., Bäckman, Hill, Herlitz, Fratiglioni, & Winblad, 1994; Heston, Mastri, Anderson, & White, 1981; Hill, Bäckman, Wahlin, & Winblad, 1995; Katzman et al., 1983; Rubin et al.,

1993; Small & Bäckman, 1998; Small, Viitanen, Winblad, & Bäckman, 1997; Teri, McCurry, Edland, Kukull, & Larson, 1995).

The fact that most research has failed to document a systematic relationship between onset age and different aspects of cognitive functioning in AD indicates that onset age acts much like many other potentially relevant individual-difference variables in this disease. Several studies have demonstrated that variables known to influence cognitive performance in normal aging have little or no influence on performance in AD, once severity of dementia is controlled. This includes education (Bäckman et al., 1994; Burns, Jacoby, & Levy, 1991; Katzman et al., 1983) and gender (e.g., Buckwalter, Sobel, Dunn, Diaz, & Henderson, 1993; Teri, Hughes, & Larson, 1990), as well as a variety of biological variables (e.g., blood pressure, vitamin B_{12}, folic acid, and TSH; Bäckman et al., 1994; Hill, Bäckman, et al., 1995; Small & Bäckman, 1998; Small, Viitanen, et al., 1997). A likely reason for the lack of association between these variables and cognitive functioning in AD is that the influence of demographic and other participant characteristics may be overshadowed by the pathogenetic process itself.

As noted, a pronounced episodic memory deficit is a cardinal symptom of AD. Much research on episodic memory in AD has examined whether these patients, like their healthy aged counterparts, are able to utilize cognitive support for improving memory. In general, the early work addressing this issue revealed AD-related failures in making effective use of supportive conditions for remembering. Thus, when performance in a supportive condition (e.g., cued recall) was contrasted to that in a control condition (e.g., free recall), the normal old individuals, but not the AD patients, demonstrated memory facilitation (see Bäckman et al., 1990, for a review).

Such a pattern of outcome suggests a qualitative difference between normal old adults and AD patients with regard to the relationship between cognitive support and episodic memory (Dick, Kean, & Sands, 1989; A. Martin, Brouwers, Cox, & Fedio, 1985). However, more recent work reveals a rather different picture concerning the potential for memory improvement in AD (for a review, see Bäckman & Herlitz, 1996). This work differs from the early research in two main ways. First, patients in an early phase of the disease have a greater representation in the recent work. Conceivably, the probability of obtaining performance gains from cognitive support in AD may decrease across the pathogenesis. Second, in the early studies, support was typically provided at either encoding or retrieval rather than at both. The gross deterioration of episodic memory in AD, along with concomitant deficits in semantic memory (e.g., Chertkow & Bub, 1990; Hartman, 1991; Hodges, Salmon, & Butters, 1992; Nebes, 1989), may necessitate provision of cognitive support at both stages of remembering for performance gains to occur.

In addition to involving patients in an early phase of the disease and providing cognitive support at both stages of remembering, research demonstrating performance gains in AD from cognitive support is characterized by (a) task demands that direct participants to engage in elaborative cognitive activities at encoding and (b) the context prevailing during encoding being reinstated at retrieval. Thus, when retrieval support has been provided (e.g., category cues and copy cues), AD patients have profited from encoding support in the form of a rich stimulus input (Herlitz, Adolfsson, Bäckman, & Nilsson, 1991), guidance to engage in categorical processing (Bird & Luszcz, 1991, 1993; Lipinska & Bäckman, 1997), organizational structure in the materials (Herlitz & Viitanen, 1991), and activation of appropriate preexperimental knowledge (Lipinska, Bäckman, & Herlitz, 1992).

The findings from these studies indicate that AD patients are able to utilize cognitive support in episodic memory, although they typically require more support than their healthy aged counterparts to exhibit memory improvement. Thus, contrary to previous beliefs, there is a demonstrable link between knowledge and remembering in AD, although the disease process obviously weakens this link. In general, then, this research suggests that differences between normal old adults and AD patients regarding the relationship between cognitive support and memory are quantitative rather than qualitative. This conclusion is in agreement with other current experimental work addressing various aspects of cognitive functioning in AD (e.g., Becker & Lopez, 1992; Nebes, 1992)

The issue of whether the cognitive differences between normal old and demented adults should be conceptualized in dimensional or dichotomous terms has also been addressed in a series of studies by Huppert and colleagues (e.g., Brayne, Gill, Paykel, Huppert, & O'Connor, 1995; Huppert, 1994; Huppert & Brayne, 1994). These investigators have been interested in the distribution of cognitive performance scores in normal aging and dementia. A robust finding in their research, and one that has been demonstrated by several other groups as well (Storandt, Botwinick, Danziger, Berg, & Hughes, 1984; Welsh, Butters, Hughes, Mohs, & Heyman, 1992), is that the distribution of cognitive scores of normal old and demented persons is essentially nonoverlapping when the control group is composed of volunteers. This would suggest a dichotomy between normal aging and dementia. However, when population-based samples of normal and demented persons are examined, the near-to-perfect discrimination breaks down completely. The latter pattern of results suggests that (a) the self-selected volunteer group typically used in this type of research may not represent accurately the level of cognitive functioning in the population at large and (b) population differences in cognitive functioning between normal and demented persons are more subtle than previously thought.

Moreover, these data indicate that the transition from normal aging to dementia may be continuous in nature. Particularly intriguing are longitudinal data on cognitive change scores reported by Brayne et al. (1995). These data showed a normal and unimodal distribution of change scores (i.e., decline) across a 3-year interval in a sample of very old adults, irrespective of whether or not prevalent AD cases were included. This is certainly not the kind of pattern that would be expected if there is a clear demarcation between normal aging and dementia. Rather, these data suggest a dimensional view of normal aging and dementia.

Other research that speaks directly to the transition between normal aging and AD involves studies that attempt to determine preclinical cognitive markers of dementia. Recent evidence indicates that AD-related cognitive deficits may occur several years before a diagnosis is possible using available clinical criteria. Although some studies report that those who will develop AD across the retest interval show impairment in verbal ability and reasoning, it is clear that the largest and most consistent deficits in preclinical AD are found in tasks assessing episodic memory (e.g., Grober & Kawas, 1997; Howieson et al., 1997; Jacobs et al., 1995; Linn et al., 1995; Masur, Sliwinski, Lipton, Blau, & Crystal, 1994; Small, Herlitz, Fratiglioni, Almkvist, & Bäckman, 1997; Tierney, Szalai, Snow, Fisher, Nores, et al., 1996).

In a recent study of a population-based sample of individuals older than 74 years, Bäckman and Small (1998) addressed the nature of the episodic memory impairment in preclinical AD in terms of the influence of cognitive support on memory. Bäckman and Small reasoned that if the size of the memory deficit in preclinical AD is greater in more supported tasks (e.g., cued recall) than in less supported tasks (e.g., free recall), this would indicate that a reduction in cognitive reserve capacity is a salient feature of preclinical AD. By contrast, a result indicating that persons in a preclinical phase of AD show greater deficits in less supported tasks than in more supported tasks would suggest that these individuals are able to compensate for episodic memory deficits through the provision of cognitive support. Finally, an outcome indicating that the magnitude of the episodic memory impairment for persons in a preclinical phase of AD is invariant across different levels of cognitive support would indicate that a general impairment of episodic memory may precede a reduction of reserve capacity in the early development of AD.

The data were in agreement with the last-named proposition. Specifically, although persons who developed AD across a 3-year interval showed a clear overall performance deficit at baseline, their performance profile was indistinguishable from that of normal old adults at the initial time of measurement: Like the normal old adults, the incident AD patients showed performance gains from more study time, organizability, and retrieval cues at baseline. However, when these patients were diagnosed with AD at follow-up, they showed negligible gains from the encoding support in free recall, although performance was enhanced with the provision of retrieval cues; this pattern resembled closely that seen in a group of prevalent AD patients at both measurement occasions.

These results indicate that neither losses in reserve capacity nor compensation are characteristic features of the episodic memory deficit in preclinical AD. Rather, this deficit appears to generalize across important dimensions of episodic memory (i.e., presentation rate, item organizability, and testing conditions). In other words, deficits in cognitive reserve capacity may occur somewhat later in the pathogenesis of AD than a general episodic memory impairment. In addition, these results provide no evidence that persons in a preclinical phase of AD are able to compensate for their memory problems through the provision of cognitive support.

The bulk of research on episodic memory in clinical AD indicates that difficulties in engaging in elaborative cognitive operations at encoding constitute a major source of the performance deficit (see Morris, 1996, and Nebes, 1992, for a review). The Bäckman and Small (1998) study extended this notion to preclinical AD by demonstrating that incident AD patients had particular difficulties in transferring information from consciousness to some form of permanent storage. The notion that deficient encoding processes may largely determine the preclinical episodic memory deficits is supported by recent histopathological and brain imaging evidence. Postmortem examinations (H. Braak & Braak, 1995; H. Braak et al., 1996; Simic, Kostovic, Winblad, & Bogdanovic, 1997; M. J. West et al., 1994) and magnetic resonance imaging research (Deweer et al., 1995; Fox et al., 1996; Killiany et al., 1993; Lehericy et al., 1994) indicate that the hippocampal formation and related cortical structures are affected several years before diagnosis; only much later does the disease process appear to radiate into the neocortical association areas (e.g., H. Braak & Braak, 1995; H. Braak et al., 1996).

These findings provide a neurobiological basis for the episodic memory impairment seen in preclinical AD. In particular, because the hippocampal formation has been linked primarily to acquisition and consolidation processes rather than to retrieval processes (e.g., Grady et al., 1995; Squire, 1986), the finding of hippocampal lesions in preclinical AD is consistent with the view that the episodic memory deficit at this early stage of the disease process is largely due to encoding problems.

Depression

Prevalence estimates of clinical depression in old age vary widely, with figures typically ranging from 3% to 10% (e.g., Ben-Arie, Swarte, & Dickman, 1987; Blazer & Williams, 1980; Kivelä, Pahkala, & Laippala, 1988;

O'Connor, Pollitt, & Roth, 1990). Some research suggests that clinical depression may decrease in very old age (e.g., Reiger et al., 1993; Wittchen, Knäuper, & Kessler, 1994). However, the issue of potential age-related changes in the prevalence of depression is complicated by a variety of factors. This includes the fact that many elderly adults report more somatic complaints than depressed mood (e.g., Crum, Cooper-Patrick, & Ford, 1994; National Institutes of Health Consensus Conference, 1992). Moreover, comparisons of prevalence rates across the adult life span may be obscured by the unwillingness of depressed older adults to participate and the underreporting of symptoms, as well as by increased mortality rates among depressed older adults (Henderson, 1994; Lyness et al., 1995; Thompson, Heller, & Rody, 1994). Finally, some of the symptoms of clinical depression (e.g., sleep disturbance and loss of energy) are associated with the normal aging process. Indeed, Blazer (1989) argued that although the prevalence of clinical depression may decrease in old age, there may be an increase in the number of depressive symptoms in late life.

Research also suggests that old age depression may be more chronic in nature compared with what is true in younger cohorts. Elevated depressive symptomatology may occur several years before the time of diagnosis in older adults (Berger, Small, Forsell, Winblad, & Bäckman, 1998; Henderson & Jorm, 1997; Kivelä, Kongäs-Saviaro, Pahkala, Kesti, & Laipala, 1996). This lengthy development of depression may be contrasted to the relatively short clinical onset expected in cohorts of younger adults (American Psychiatric Association, 1994).

Although there is unequivocal evidence that subjective memory complaints are more common among depressed older adults than among nondepressed older adults (e.g., Albert, 1981; Feehan, Knight, & Partridge, 1991; Popkin, Gallagher, Thomson, & Moore, 1982; Williams, Little, Scates, & Blockman, 1987), a consensus has been more difficult to reach as to whether old age depression causes objectively verifiable memory impairment. Some investigators (e.g., Derry & Kuiper, 1981; O'Hara, Hinrichs, Kohout, Wallace, & Lemke, 1986; Rohling & Scogin, 1993) have observed similar levels of memory performance in depressed and nondepressed older adults, whereas others (e.g., Bäckman & Forsell, 1994; Gainotti & Marra, 1994; Hart, Kwentus, Hamer, & Taylor, 1987; King, Caine, Conwell, & Cox, 1991; La Rue, Goodman, & Spar, 1992; Lichtenberg, Manning, & Turkheimer, 1992; Rubin, Kinscherf, Grant, & Storandt, 1991) have documented depression-related memory deficits.

These discrepant findings may be due to several factors, including the severity of depression in the study samples, that is, whether symptoms are severe enough and sufficient in number to reach a clinical diagnosis of depression. In addition, the mixed results may be related to differences across studies with regard to the cognitive requirements in the tasks used to assess memory functioning. There is evidence that depression-related memory deficits are most likely to occur when there are high demands on effortful, elaborative activities at encoding (Cohen, Weingartner, Smallberg, Pickar, & Murphy, 1982; Weingartner, Cohen, Murphy, Martello, & Gerdt, 1981). Depressed older persons also tend to benefit less than normal old adults from the provision of cognitive support in the form of visual imagery (Hart et al., 1987), more study time (Bäckman & Forsell, 1994), and an inherent organizational structure (Bäckman & Forsell, 1994).

Even though the empirical picture concerning the effects of old age depression on memory is not entirely clear, the bulk of evidence suggests that depression has detrimental effects on memory performance among older adults. This conclusion was reached in two extensive meta-analyses, one targeting adults across the life span (Burt, Zembar, & Niederehe, 1995) and the other focusing on older adults (Kindermann & Brown, 1997).

Indeed, memory deficits are to be expected in depression, given that some of the symptoms of this disorder (e.g., concentration difficulties, loss of energy, and lack of interest) are linked to attentional processes known to be critical to memory functioning (e.g., Craik & Byrd, 1982; Plude, 1992; Salthouse, 1991). Changes in several cognitively relevant biological parameters have also been observed in older depressives. For example, reduced blood flow in the frontal cortex, the temporal cortex, and the anterior cingulate gyrus has been reported in elderly adults with depression (Beats & Levy, 1992; Bench et al., 1992). In addition, white matter hyperintensities and lesions in subcortical grey nuclei (Coffey et al., 1988; Figiel et al., 1991; Rabins, Pearlson, & Aylward, 1991), as well as ventricular enlargement and decreased brain density (Jacoby & Levy, 1980; Pearlson et al., 1989), are more often found in depressed older adults than in nondepressed older adults. Note, however, that the causal relationship between these biological alterations and the depressive disorder remains unknown.

A striking finding in the meta-analyses conducted by Burt et al. (1995) and Kindermann and Brown (1997), and one that is directly relevant to the present chapter, is that the negative effects of depression on memory performance were greater in younger and middle-aged samples than in samples of older adults. The observation that the effects of depression on memory may decrease gradually with advancing age was extended to very late life in recent work using population-based samples between 75 and 100 years of age (Bäckman & Forsell, 1994; Bäckman, Hassing, Forsell, & Viitanen, 1996). Specifically, although reliable decrements in both episodic memory and global cognitive functioning were seen among depressives in the late 70s and 80s compared with control participants (Bäckman & Forsell, 1994), there were no differences in cognitive performance between depressed and nondepressed participants in a sample of nonagenarians (Bäckman, Hassing, et al., 1996).

An interesting issue concerns which specific aspects of depression are particularly detrimental to memory functioning. This issue was addressed by Bäckman, Hill, and Forsell (1996), who used a classification taxonomy that identified mood-related (i.e., dysphoria, appetite disturbance, feelings of guilt, and suicidal ideation) and motivation-related (i.e., concentration difficulties, loss of energy, lack of effort, and psychomotor disturbance) symptoms of depression (Forsell, Jorm, Fratiglioni, Grut, & Winblad, 1993). In a sample of clinically nondepressed very old adults, it was found that the number of motivation-related, but not mood-related, symptoms were negatively related to both overall episodic memory performance and the ability to benefit from cognitive support. This data pattern likely reflects the fact that motivational symptoms of depression influence the individual's basic processing resources, whereas the mood symptoms may be more easily displaced in a cognitive testing situation. The fact that subclinical variations in depressive symptomatology may be related to memory performance in old age is interesting in light of research indicating that old age depression may have a rather long preclinical period (Berger et al., 1998; Henderson & Jorm, 1997; Kivelä et al., 1996).

Importantly, the observed relationship between motivation-related symptoms and memory may be relevant in understanding why the influence of depression on memory decreases in late life. As noted by many investigators (e.g., Blazer, 1989; Girling et al., 1995; Livingston, Hawkins, Graham, Blizard, & Mann, 1990), symptoms such as loss of energy, lack of effort, and concentration difficulties may be seen in many older adults who do not meet the clinical criteria for a major depressive episode. Given that these symptoms are particularly crucial for the existence of depression-related memory deficits, it follows that a reduction of the deficit should be expected with advancing age. This is because depressed and nondepressed persons from earlier cohorts are likely to differ greatly in the existence of motivation-related symptoms, whereas the normal age-related increase in these symptoms makes nondepressed very old persons more similar to their depressed counterparts with regard to motivational symptoms of depression (Bäckman, Hassing, et al., 1996). Thus, depression-related memory deficits may become less salient in advanced age because those symptoms of depression that are most critical to memory functioning are often present in clinically nondepressed individuals.

Methodological Issues

From the tone of this chapter, it is clear that we are advocating a more complete description of cognitive functioning in late senescence. However, the examination of individuals of very advanced age poses some unique methodological challenges regarding the generality of the conclusions that are derived, as well as the statistical treatment of the data. In this section, we highlight several potential pitfalls that investigators may encounter when conducting research with this particular participant population.

The problems associated with investigating very old adults may be viewed in relation to the concepts of internal and external validity. Although issues related to these types of validity are of concern for all age-comparative research, they may be especially salient when examining the functioning of very old adults. For example, one issue is the appropriate selection of research participants. With the increased prevalence of conditions that may impact cognitive functioning in very old age (e.g., CD; Elias et al., 1990), the inclusion of completely disease-free individuals may be problematic. Consequently, interpretative difficulties may emerge when trying to distinguish the effects of age from those resulting from disease on a particular outcome variable. One solution to this problem is routine assessment of the relevant conditions and either screening research participants who are positive or partialing out statistically the influence of the conditions. Unfortunately, however, the resources required to undertake such assessments may be lacking in most cognitive aging laboratories. In addition, a potential increase in internal validity may come at the expense of decreased generalizability of the results.

Although conditions such as high blood pressure may exert some influence on cognitive functioning, of greater concern are dementia disorders that have substantial effects on cognitive functioning and also increase dramatically in prevalence among those who are very old (e.g., Small, Herlitz, & Bäckman, 1998). One solution is to undertake an extensive dementia-screening process and eliminate those with AD or other dementias. However, this too can be a relative expensive proposition, and it is clear that the diagnosis of dementia is far from an exact science (e.g., Herlitz, Small, et al., 1997). In fact, some investigators have actually advocated combining demented and nondemented older adult samples in order to maintain high external validity (Lindenberger & Baltes, 1997).

Even in situations in which an individual can be accurately diagnosed as being demented, it may be the case that cognitive deficits are present among nondemented individuals beause of the long preclinical phase of the disease (e.g., Small, Herlitz, et al., 1997; Tierney, Szalai, Snow, Fisher, Nores, et al., 1996). This point was illustrated nicely by Sliwinski, Lipton, Buschke, and Stewart (1996) in a recent longitudinal study of older adults. Sliwinski et al. observed that the failure to eliminate preclinical cases of dementia resulted in the underestimation of mean-level cognitive performance, the overestimation of the variability, and the magnification of the age-related decline. Thus, even when diagnostic procedures are followed, the incipient nature of dementia may influence the results in research on normal cognitive aging. Of course, this is particularly likely to happen when the sample is composed of very old adults.

Another concern is related to the most appropriate statistical treatment of data from very old participants. As we have outlined, the performance patterns of some abilities do not necessarily follow a trajectory of linear decline from young-old to very old age (e.g., semantic memory). As a result, treating persons ranging in age from 60 to 90 or more years as a homogeneous group in mean-level analyses may be inappropriate. By so doing, investigators may overlook potentially interesting patterns of results, as well as contribute to increased error variance in their designs. A straightforward solution is to routinely divide the sample into subgroups depending on their age. Although this requires additional participants in order to have large enough samples in the age groups, one can determine whether the results that are observed in younger adults generalize to those who are much older.

When cognitive performance is assessed with age as a continuous variable, this may necessitate the inclusion of quadratic age terms, as well as interactions of age and other predictor variables, into the regression models. With quadratic terms, one is able to determine whether the age–cognition relationship is linear or whether the function changes direction at some point, possibly because of accelerated decline in very old age. The inclusion of interaction terms also enables researchers to determine directly whether age moderates the predictive relationship with a particular individual-difference variable. Although desirable, quadratic and interaction terms in regression analyses often suffer from problems associated with low statistical power, especially when correlational analyses are used (McClelland & Judd, 1993). One solution to this problem is oversampling of persons at the extreme ends of the age distribution. However, this practice may result in problems regarding the generalizability of the results that are obtained because the age composition of the study sample will not match that of the population at large.

In summary, assessing the cognitive functioning of very old adults is an interesting yet challenging endeavor. Investigators must balance methodological rigor with achieving generalizibility. Although these choices must also be made by those studying younger cohorts of older adults, the increase in late-life diseases, as well as the potential for cognitive functioning to demonstrate accelerated decline, makes this balance especially critical in very old age.

CONCLUDING COMMENTS

The research reviewed in this chapter indicates that there is a rather global deterioration of cognitive functioning in very old age. For some cognitive abilities (e.g., fluid intelligence, episodic memory, and working memory), the onset of decline occurs relatively early and continues into late life; for other abilities (e.g., crystallized intelligence and semantic memory), noticeable decline may not be evident until late adulthood. However, from the mid-70s and onward the magnitude of age-related decline appears to be rather similar across different forms of memory and cognition. Two important exceptions to this pattern are primary memory and implicit memory. For these forms of memory, relative preservation appears to be the empirical rule, even in very old age.

The patterns of cognitive deterioration described above are interesting in light of recent advances regarding the effects of aging on the human brain. Of particular interest is the finding that those brain structures thought to be especially critical to episodic memory and speeded performance in fluid-intelligence tests show gradual changes that start in early adulthood. The importance of the hippocampus and neighboring regions for successful episodic remembering has been documented in both lesion (e.g., Squire, 1986) and imaging (e.g., Nyberg, McIntosh, Houle, Nilsson, & Tulving, 1996) research. There is also strong evidence that the striatum plays a critical role in speeded cognitive performance (e.g., R. G. Brown & Marsden, 1988; Cummings, 1986). Hippocampal neurons begin to decrease in the hippocampus (e.g., Simic et al., 1997) and cytoskeletal changes emerge in the transentorhinal cortex (e.g., E. Braak, Braak, & Mandelkow, 1993) already in early to middle adulthood. Likewise, a decrease of various dopaminergic markers in the striatum is seen from the third decade of life; the average loss per decade across the adult life span is estimated to be just below 10% in both postmortem (e.g., Fearnley & Lees, 1991) and imaging (e.g., W. R. W. Martin, Palmer, Patlak, & Caine, 1989) research. By contrast, age-related changes in the neocortical association areas that may be especially critical to the use of stored knowledge appear to have a later onset and to be less systematic (e.g., Pietrini & Rapoport, 1994; M. J. West et al., 1994). Thus, the different patterns of age-related decline seen for these forms of cognition is consistent with current histopathological and brain imaging research.

The fact that cognitive functioning deteriorates in very old age should not conceal the fact that there is substantial variability among studies with regard to the slope of the age–performance function. Although our reading of the literature suggests that cognitive decline typically progresses gradually from earlier to later portions of the late adult life span, there is research indicating both accelerated and attenuated deterioration in very late life. Accelerated decline is certainly not unexpected, considering that many health conditions that have detrimental effects on cognitive functioning increase dramatically in very old age.

Even though most cognitive aging researchers may attempt to exclude individuals with dementia, depression, stroke, and so on, in many cases successful elimination may be impossible and in other cases perhaps not even desirable. With respect to the former case, consider the phenomenon of terminal decline, which, for obvious reasons, is highly relevant in very old age. Inclusion of participants who are going to die some time after the assessment will increase the size of the age-related decline as (a) impending death is associated with cognitive deficits and (b) the likelihood of dying increases with advancing age. AD and depression represent similar, albeit less extreme, cases in point. Both AD and depression may have long preclinical periods in late life during which cognitive deficits are detectable. Thus, following the same logic, including participants in a preclinical phase of AD or depression (which, in the case of AD, may be impossible to avoid in a sample of very old adults) will overestimate the size of the age-related deterioration in cognitive performance.

Another aspect of this problem concerns the fact that some conditions with known effects on cognitive functioning (e.g., sensory deficits and CD) are so common in very old age that eliminating participants on the basis of suboptimal status may result in a rather biased study sample. The issue of what constitutes "normal aging" in the late 80s and 90s is tricky, and one that requires much more careful analysis than in earlier cohorts. Of course, the problem is easier to deal with for conditions in which diagnostic criteria are well established (e.g., AD) than for conditions in which such criteria are fuzzy or lacking (e.g., sensory deficits and vitamin deficiency).

Findings of stability of cognitive performance from early to late senescence are rare but do exist, and some research even demonstrates increases of performance in very old age. Such results most likely reflect selective survival effects; that is, those individuals who are surviving into very late life and willing to participate in studies of cognitive functioning may constitute an elite group in terms of various biological, cognitive, and other characteristics. When rigorous health-screening criteria are used, these effects may be reinforced. Thus, we are dealing with two opposite trends, one resulting in an acceleration of decline due to preclinical AD, impending death, and so forth and the other resulting in attenuated decline because of participants being in optimal health. Perhaps these two trends cancel each other out in most research on cognitive functioning in very old age, the net effect being a gradual performance decrease.

Thus, the trivial yet often neglected point is that sample composition largely determines (and perhaps more so than in any other age group) the size of the estimated age-related deficit in cognitive functioning when participants are in very advanced age. Schematic illustrations of the influence of sample characteristics on performance on tasks that show gradual decline across the adult life span (e.g., episodic memory and fluid intelligence) and those that show relative stability until late adulthood (e.g., semantic memory and crystallized intelligence) are shown in Fig. 9.1. Note that in very old age the effects of the nature of the study samples are expected to have relatively similar effects on performance in the two categories of tasks.

An interesting issue concerns whether age modifies the effect of various individual-difference variables on cognitive performance. Although few studies have examined this issue in a systematic manner, the available evidence indicates that the magnitude of the influence of cognitively relevant participant characteristics changes relatively little in very old age. This pattern can be seen for demographic variables (e.g., gender and education), cognitive variables (e.g., processing speed and working memory), and lifestyle variables (e.g., social activity and exercise habits), as well as for a variety of health conditions (e.g., CD, diabetes, vitamin deficiency, and AD).

Although the relative impact of various health conditions may not change in very old age, it is important to note that the proportion of persons affected changes because of age-related increases in prevalence rates. A further point to note is that, although sociodemographic variables (e.g., education) typically remain strong predictors of cognitive performance in late life, there is some evidence that they may be successively replaced by health-related and biological variables in very old age. One possible reason for this changing influence of predictors across later adulthood is that health-related variables show relatively little variation earlier in life, whereas health-related problems and variability in health increase dramatically in old age. Thus, although education and health are correlated in late life, health-related variables tend to overshadow educational background as predictors of cognitive performance in old age.

With regard to AD, it is noteworthy that onset age has a limited impact on cognitive impairment and that most individual-difference variables known to exert an influence on cognitive performance in normal old adults lose their importance when faced with the neurodegenerative process.

There are some notable exceptions to the pattern of age invariance in predictors of cognitive performance. There is partial support for the view that measures of sensory functioning may increase in importance in late life. There is also suggestive evidence that specific genetic markers, such as ApoE, may be less important to cognitive functioning in very old age compared with earlier portions of late adulthood. This is also true for clinical depression, where the detrimental effects on cognitive performance decrease gradually from middle age through very old age.

Finally, the cognitive deficits seen in very old age are accompanied by a concomitant decrease in cognitive reserve capacity, as indicated both in experimental work on the effects of cognitive support on memory and in cognitive intervention research. In this way, very old age is one among

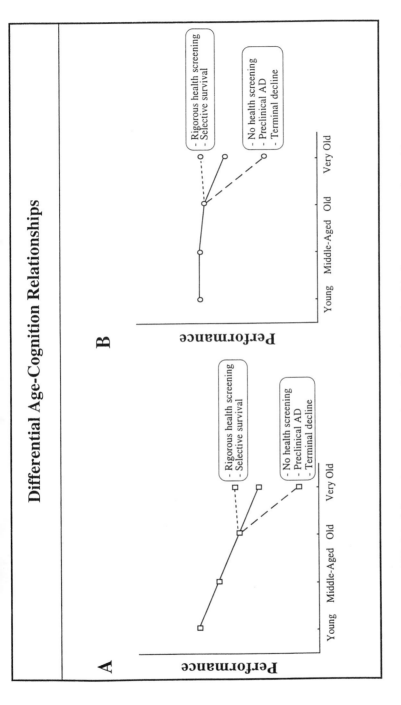

FIG. 9.1. Schematic representation of how the relationship between age and cognitive performance may be modified by factors working in the direction of attenuated and accelerated decline. Panel A depicts performance trajectories for domains that show an early onset of age-related decline (e.g., episodic memory and fluid intelligence), and panel B portrays performance trajectories for domains that show a late onset of decline (e.g., semantic memory and crystallized intelligence). AD = Alzheimer's disease.

several conditions that could be arranged on a continuum of cognitive ability. The continuum progresses from the very advantaged (e.g., young, well-educated, and socially active) to those with moderate cognitive skills (e.g., young-old, clinically depressed, and vitamin deficient) to those who are most disadvantaged (e.g., very old, sensory deficient, and demented). Progressing along this continuum results not only in a gradual deterioration of cognitive functioning but also in gradual losses of cognitive reserve capacity. This lawfulness should not conceal the fact that even very old demented persons possess the ability to improve cognitive performance when task conditions are highly supportive.

ACKNOWLEDGMENTS

Writing of this chapter was supported by grants from the Swedish Council for Research in the Humanities and the Social Sciences and from the Swedish Council for Social Research to Lars Bäckman.

REFERENCES

Abrahams, J. P. (1976). Health status in aging research. *Experimental Aging Research*, 2, 63–71.
Albert, M. S. (1981). Geriatric neuropsychology. *Journal of Consulting and Clinical Psychology*, 49, 835–850.
Albert, M. S., Heller, H. S., & Milberg, W. (1988). Changes in naming ability with age. *Psychology and Aging*, 3, 173–178.
Albert, M. S., Jones, K., Savage, C. R., Berkman, L., Seeman, T., Blazer, D., & Rowe, J. C. (1995). Predictors of cognitive change in older persons: MacArthur studies of succesful aging. *Psychology and Aging*, 10, 578–589.
Almkvist, O., & Bäckman, L. (1993). Progression of Alzheimers disease: Sequencing of neuropsychological decline. *International Journal of Geriatric Psychiatry*, 8, 755–763.
Almkvist, O., Bäckman, L., Basun, H., & Wahlund, L. -O. (1993). Patterns of neuropsychological performance in Alzheimer's disease and vascular dementia. *Cortex*, 29, 661–673.
American Psychiatric Association. (1994). *Diagnostic and statistical manual of mental disorders* (4th ed.). Washington, DC: Author.
Ashton, H., & Golding, J. F. (1989). Tranquilisers prevalence, predictors, and possible consequences. Data from a large United Kingdom survey. *British Journal of Addiction*, 84, 541–546.
Au, R., Joung, P., Nicholas, M., Obler, L. K., Kass, R., & Albert, M. L. (1995). Naming ability across the adult life span. *Aging and Cognition*, 2, 300–311.
Bäckman, L. (1991). Recognition memory across the adult life span: The role of prior knowledge. *Memory and Cognition*, 19, 63–71.
Bäckman, L., & Forsell, Y. (1994). Episodic memory functioning in a community-based sample of old adults with major depression: Utilization of cognitive support. *Journal of Abnormal Psychology*, 103, 361–370.

Bäckman, L., Hassing, L., Forsell, Y., & Viitanen, M. (1996). Episodic remembering in a population-based sample of nonagenarians: Does major depression exacerbate the memory deficits seen in Alzheimer's disease? *Psychology and Aging, 11,* 649–657.

Bäckman, L., & Herlitz, A. (1996). Knowledge and memory in Alzheimer's disease: A relationship that exists. In R. G. Morris (Ed.), *The cognitive neuropsychology of Alzheimer-type dementia* (pp. 89–104). Oxford, England: Oxford University Press.

Bäckman, L., Hill, R. D., & Forsell, Y. (1996). The influence of depressive symptomatology on episodic memory among clinically nondepressed older adults. *Journal of Abnormal Psychology, 105,* 97–105.

Bäckman, L., Hill, R. D., Herlitz, A., Fratiglioni, L., & Winblad, B. (1994). Predicting episodic memory performance in dementia: Is severity all there is? *Psychology and Aging, 9,* 520–527.

Bäckman, L., Hill, R. D., Herlitz, A., Robins Wahlin, T. -B., Wahlin, Å., & Winblad, B. (1998). Predictors of change in verbal and nonverbal episodic memory performance in a 2-year longitudinal study of optimally healthy very old adults. *Journal of Mental Health and Aging, 4,* 139–154.

Bäckman, L., & Larsson, M. (1992). Recall of organizable words and objects in adulthood: Influences of instructions, retention interval, and retrieval cues. *Journal of Gerontology: Psychological Sciences, 47,* 273–278.

Bäckman, L., Mäntylä, T., & Herlitz, A. (1990). The optimization of episodic remembering in old age. In P. B. Baltes & M. M. Baltes (Eds.), *Successful aging: Perspectives from the behavioral sciences* (pp. 118–163). New York: Cambridge University Press.

Bäckman, L., & Nilsson, L. -G. (1996). Semantic memory functioning across the adult life span. *European Psychologist, 1,* 27–33.

Bäckman, L., & Small, B. J. (1998). Influences of cognitive support on episodic remembering: Tracing the process of loss from normal aging to Alzheimers disease. *Psychology and Aging, 13,* 267–276.

Bäckman, L., Small, B. J., & Larsson, M. (in press). Memory. In J. G. Evans, T. F. Williams, B. L. Beattie, J. -P. Michel, & G. K. Wilcock (Eds.), *Oxford textbook of geriatric medicine* (2nd ed.). Oxford, England: Oxford University Press.

Bäckman, L., & Wahlin, Å. (1995). Influences of item organizability and semantic retrieval cues on word recall in very old age. *Aging and Cognition, 2,* 312–325.

Baddeley, A. D. (1986). *Working memory.* Oxford, England: Clarendon.

Baltes, P. B. (1987). Theoretical propositions of life-span developmental psychology: On the dynamics between growth and decline. *Developmental Psychology, 23,* 611–623.

Baltes, P. B., Dittmann-Kohli, F., & Kliegl, R. (1986). Reserve capacity of the elderly in aging-sensitive tests of fluid intelligence: Replication and extension. *Psychology and Aging, 1,* 172–177.

Baltes, P. B., & Lindenberger, U. (1997). Emergence of a powerful connection between sensory and cognitive functions across the adult life span: A new window to the study of cognitive aging? *Psychology and Aging, 12,* 12–21.

Baltes, P. B., & Mayer, K. U. (Eds.). (1999). *The Berlin Aging Study: Aging from 70 to 100.* New York: Cambridge University Press.

Basun, H., Corder, E. H., Guo, Z., Lannfelt, L., Corder, L. S., Manton, K. G., Winblad, B., & Viitanen, M. (1996). Apolipoprotein E polymorphism and stroke in a population sample aged 75 years or more. *Stroke, 27,* 1310–1315.

Bazargan, M., & Barbre, A. R. (1994). The effects of depression, health status, and stressful life-events on self-reported memory problems among aged Blacks. *International Journal of Aging and Human Development, 38,* 351–362.

Beats, B., & Levy, R. (1992). Imaging and affective disorders in the elderly. *Clinics in Geriatric Medicine, 8,* 267–274.

Becker, J. T., & Lopez, O. L. (1992). Episodic memory in Alzheimer's disease: Breakdown of multiple memory processes. In L. Bäckman (Ed.), *Memory functioning in dementia* (pp. 27–43). Amsterdam: North-Holland.

Bell, I. R., Edman, J. S., Marby, D. W., Satlin, A., Dreier, T., Liptzin, B., & Cole, J. O. (1990). Vitamin B_{12} and folate status in acute geropsychiatric inpatients: Affective and cognitive characteristics of a vitamin nondeficient population. *Biological Psychiatry, 27*, 125–137.

Ben-Arie, O., Swarte, L., & Dickman, B. J. (1987). Depression in the elderly living in the community: Its presentation and features. *British Journal of Psychiatry, 150*, 169–174.

Bench, C. J., Friston, K. J., Brown, R. G., Scott, L. C., Frackowiak, R. S., & Dolan, R. J. (1992). The anatomy of melancholia-focal abnormalities of cerebral blood flow in major depression. *Psychological Medicine, 22*, 607–615.

Berg, S. (1996). Aging, behavior, and terminal decline. In J. E. Birren & K. W. Schaie (Eds.), *Handbook of the psychology of aging* (4th ed., pp. 323–337). New York: Academic Press.

Berg, S., & Dellasega, C. (1996). The use of psychoactive medications and cognitive function in older adults. *Journal of Aging and Health, 8*, 136–149.

Berger, A. -K., Small, B. J., Forsell, Y., Winblad, B., & Bäckman, L. (1998). Preclinical symptomatology of major depression in very old age: A prospective longitudinal study. *American Journal of Psychiatry, 155*, 1039–1043.

Bird, M., & Luszcz, M. (1991). Encoding specificity, depth of processing, and cued recall in Alzheimer's disease. *Journal of Clinical and Experimental Neuropsychology, 13*, 508–520.

Bird, M., & Luszcz, M. (1993). Enhancing memory performance in Alzheimer's disease: Acquisition assistance and cue effectiveness. *Journal of Clinical and Experimental Neuropsychology, 15*, 921–932.

Blass, J. P., & Plum, F. (1983). Metabolic encephalopathies in older adults. In R. Katzman & D. Terry (Eds.), *Neurology of aging*. Philadelphia: Davis.

Blazer, D. (1989). Depression in the elderly. *New England Journal of Medicine, 320*, 164–166.

Blazer, D., & Williams, C. D. (1980). Epidemiology of dysphoria and depression in an elderly population. *American Journal of Psychiatry, 137*, 439–444.

Bodnar, A. G., Ouellette, M., Frolkis, M., Holt, S. E., Choy-Pik, C., Morin, G. B., Harley, C. B., Shay, J. W., Lichtsteiner, S., & Wright, W. E. (1998). Extension of life-span by introduction of Telomerase into normal human cells. *Science, 279*, 349–352.

Bohnen, N., Jolles, J., & Degenaar, C. P. (1992). Lower blood levels of vitamin B_{12} are related to decreased performance of healthy subjects in the Stroop Color-Word Test. *Neuroscience Research Communications, 11*, 53–56.

Bondi, M. W., Salmon, D. P., Monsch, A. U., Galasko, D., Butters, N., Klauber, M. R., Thal, L. J., & Saitoh, T. (1995). Episodic memory changes are associated with the APOE-ε4 allele in nondemented older adults. *Neurology, 45*, 2203–2206.

Bots, M. L., Grobbee, D. E., & Hofman, A. (1991). High blood pressure in the elderly. *Epidemiologic Reviews, 13*, 294–314.

Botwinick, J., & Storandt, M. (1974). *Memory, related functions, and age.* Springfield, IL: Thomas.

Bowler, J. V., Hadar, U., & Wade, J. P. H. (1994). Cognition in stroke. *Acta Neurologica Scandinavica, 90*, 424–429.

Braak, E., Braak, H., & Mandelkow, E. M. (1993). Cytoskeletal alterations demonstrated by the antibody AT8: Early signs for the formation of neurofibrillary tangles in man. *Society for Neuroscience Abstracts, 19*, 228.

Braak, H., & Braak, E. (1995). Staging of Alzheimer's disease–related neurofibrillary tangles. *Neurobiology of Aging, 16*, 271–284.

Braak, H., Braak, E., Yilmazer, D., de Vos, R. A. I., Jansen, E. N. H., & Bohl, J. (1996). Pattern of brain destruction in Parkinsons and Alzheimer's disease. *Journal of Neural Transmission, 103*, 455–490.

Brayne, C., Gill, C., Paykel, E. S., Huppert, F., & O'Connor D. W. (1995). Cognitive decline in an elderly population—A two wave study of change. *Psychological Medicine, 25*, 673–683.

Brébion, G., Ehrlich, M. -F., & Tardieu, H. (1995). Working memory in older subjects: Dealing with ongoing and stored information in language comprehension. *Psychological Research, 58*, 225–232.

Breteler, M. M. B., Claus, J. J., Grobbee, D. E., & Hofman, A. (1994). Cardiovascular disease and distribution of cognitive function in elderly people: The Rotterdam Study. *British Medical Journal, 308*, 1604–1608.

Brody, J. A., & Schneider, E. L. (1986). Disease and disorders of aging: A hypothesis. *Journal of Chronic Disorders, 39*, 871–876.

Brown, G. M. (1980). Psychiatric and neurologic aspects of endochrine disease. In D. T. Krieger & J. C. Huges (Eds.), *Neuroendocrinology* (pp. 185–193). Sunderland, England: Sinauer.

Brown, R. G., & Marsden, C. D. (1988). Subcortical dementia: The neuropsychological evidence. *Neuroscience, 25*, 363–387.

Bryan, J., & Luszcz, M. A. (1996). Speed of information processing as a mediator between age and free-recall performance. *Psychology and Aging, 11*, 3–9.

Buckwalter, J. G., Sobel, E., Dunn, M. E., Diaz, M. M., & Henderson, V. W. (1993). Gender differences on a brief measure of cognitive functioning in Alzheimer's disease. *Archives of Neurology, 50*, 757–760.

Burke, D. M., & Light, L. L. (1981). Memory and aging: The role of retrieval processes. *Psychological Bulletin, 90*, 513–546.

Burns, A., Jacoby, R., & Levy, R. (1991). Progression of cognitive impairment in Alzheimer's disease. *Journal of the American Geriatrics Society, 39*, 39–45.

Burt, D. B., Zembar, M. J., & Niederehe, G. (1995). Depression and memory impairment: A meta-analysis of the association, its pattern and specificity. *Psychological Bulletin, 117*, 285–305.

Bush, T. L. (1991). The epidemiology of cardiovascular disease in older persons. *Aging and Clinical Experimental Research, 3*, 3–8.

Busse, E. W., & Maddox, G. L. (1985). *The Duke Longitudinal Studies of normal aging: 1955–1980.* New York: Springer.

Chertkow, H., & Bub, D. (1990). Semantic memory loss in dementia of Alzheimer's type: What do various measures measure? *Brain, 113*, 397–417.

Christensen, H., Korten, A., Jorm, A. F., Henderson, A. S., Scott, R., & Mackinnon, A. J. (1996). Activity levels and cognitive functioning in an elderly community sample. *Age and Ageing, 25*, 72–80.

Christensen, H., Mackinnon, A., Jorm, A. F., Henderson, A. S., Scott, L. R., & Korten, A. E. (1994). Age differences and interindividual variation in cognition in community-dwelling elderly. *Psychology and Aging, 9*, 381–390.

Closser, M. (1991). Benzodiazepines and the elderly: A review of potential problems. *Journal of Substance Abuse and Treatment, 8*, 35–41.

Cockburn, J., & Smith, P. T. (1991). The relative influence of intelligence and age on everyday memory. *Journal of Gerontology: Psychological Sciences, 46*, 31–36.

Coffey, C. E., Figiel, G. S., Djang, W. T., Cress, M., Saunders, W. B., & Weiner, R. D. (1988). Leukoencephalopathy in elderly depressed patients referred for ECT. *Biological Psychiatry, 24*, 143–161.

Cohen, R. M., Weingartner, H., Smallberg, S. A., Pickar, D., & Murphy, D. L. (1982). Effort and cognition in depression. *Archives of General Psychiatry, 39*, 593–597.

Colsher, P. L., & Wallace, R. B. (1991). Longitudinal application of cognitive function measures in a defined population of community-dwelling elders. *Annals of Epidemiology, 1*, 215–230.

Corder, E. H., Lannfelt, L., Viitanen, M., Corder, L. S., Manton, K. G., Winblad, B., & Basun, H. (1996). Apolipoprotein E genotype determines survival in the oldest old (85 years or older) who have good cognition. *Archives of Neurology, 53*, 418–422.

Corder, E. H., Saunders, A. M., Risch, N. J., Strittmatter, W. J., Schmechel, D. E., Gaskel, P. C., Rimmler, J. B., Locke, P. A., Conneally, P. M., Schmader, K. A., Small, G. W., Roses, A. D., Haines, J. L., & Pericak-Vance, M. A. (1994). Protective effect of apolipoprotein E type 2 allele for late onset Alzheimer's disease. *Nature Genetics, 7*, 180–183.

Corey-Bloom, J., Wiederholt, W. C., Edelstein, S., Salmon, D. P., Cahn, D., & Barett-Connor, E. (1996). Cognitive and functional status of the oldest old. *Journal of the American Geriatrics Society, 44*, 671–674.

Costa, P. T., Jr., & McCrae, R. R. (1985). Hypochondriasis, neuroticism, and aging: When are somatic complaints unfounded? *American Psychologist, 40*, 19–28.

Craik, F. I. M., & Byrd, M. (1982). Aging and cognitive deficits: The role of attentional resources. In F. I. M. Craik & S. E. Trehub (Eds.), *Aging and cognitive processes* (pp. 191–211). New York: Plenum.

Craik, F. I. M., Byrd, M., & Swanson, J. M. (1987). Patterns of memory loss in three elderly samples. *Psychology and Aging, 2*, 79–86.

Craik, F. I. M., & Jennings, J. M. (1992). Human memory. In F. I. M. Craik & T. A. Salthouse (Eds.), *Handbook of aging and cognition* (pp. 51–110). Hillsdale, NJ: Lawrence Erlbaum Associates.

Craik, F. I. M., & McDowd, J. M. (1987). Age differences in recall and recognition. *Journal of Experimental Psychology: Learning, Memory, and Cognition, 13*, 474–479.

Craik, F. I. M., & Rabinowitz, J. C. (1984). Age differences in the acquisition and use of verbal information. In H. Bouma & D. G. Bouwhuis (Eds.), *Attention and performance* (Vol. 10, pp. 471–500). Hillsdale, NJ: Lawrence Erlbaum Associates.

Crook, T. H., & Larrabee, G. J. (1992). Changes in facial recognition memory across the adult life span. *Journal of Gerontology: Psychological Sciences, 47*, 138–141.

Crook, T. H., & West, R. L. (1990). Name recall performance across the adult life-span. *British Journal of Psychology, 81*, 335–349.

Croxon, S. C. M., & Jagger, C. (1995). Diabetes and cognitive impairment: A community-based study of elderly subjects. *Age and Ageing, 24*, 421–424.

Crum, R. M., Cooper-Patrick, L., & Ford, D. E. (1994). Depressive symptoms among general medical patients: Prevalence and one-year outcome. *Psychosomatic Medicine, 56*, 109–117.

Cummings, J. L. (1986). Subcortical dementia: Neuropathology, neuropsychiatry, and pathophysiology. *British Journal of Psychiatry, 149*, 682–697.

Davis, H. P., & Squire, L. R. (1984). Protein synthesis and memory: A review. *Psychological Bulletin, 96*, 518–559.

Dealberto, M. -J., Mcavay, G. J., Seeman, T., & Berkman, L. (1997). Psychotropic drug use and cognitive decline among older men and women. *International Journal of Geriatric Psychiatry, 12*, 567–574.

Deeg, J. H., Hofman, A., & van Zonneveld, R. J. (1990). The association between change in cognitive function and longevity in Dutch elderly. *American Journal of Epidemiology, 132*, 973–982.

Denicoff, K. D., Joffe, R. T., Lakshmanan, M. C., Robbins, J., & Rubinow, D. R. (1990). Neuropsychiatric manifestations of altered thyroid state. *American Journal of Psychiatry, 147*, 94–99.

Derry, P. A., & Kuiper, N. A. (1981). Schematic processing and self reference in clinical depression. *Journal of Abnormal Psychology, 90*, 286–297.

Deweer, B., Lehericy, S., Pillon, B., Baulac, M., Chiras, J., Marsault, C., Agid, Y., & Dubois, B. (1995). Memory disorders in probable Alzheimer's disease: The role of hippocampal atrophy as shown with MRI. *Journal of Neurology, Neurosurgery, and Psychiatry, 58*, 590–597.

Dick, M. B., Kean, M. L., & Sands, D. (1989). Memory for action events in Alzheimer-type dementia: Further evidence of an encoding failure. *Brain and Cognition, 9*, 71–87.

Dornan, T. L., Peck, G. M., Dow, J. D. C., & Tattersall, R. B. (1992). A community survey of diabetes in the elderly. *Diabetic Medicine, 9*, 860–865.

Earles, J. L. K., Connor, L. T., Smith, A. D., & Park, D. C. (1997). Interrelations of age, self-reported health, speed, and memory. *Psychology and Aging, 12,* 675–683.

Earles, J. L. K., & Salthouse, T. A. (1995). Interrelations of age, health and speed. *Journal of Gerontology: Psychological Sciences, 50,* 33–41.

Ebly, E. M., Parhad, I. M., Hogan, D. B., & Fung, T. S. (1994). Prevalence and types of dementia in the very old: Results from the Canadian Study of Health and Aging. *Neurology, 44,* 1593–1600.

Elias, M. F., D'Agostino, R. B., Elias, P. K., & Wolf, P. A. (1995). Neuropsychological test performance, cognitive functioning, blood pressure, and age: The Framingham Heart Study. *Experimental Aging Research, 21,* 369–391.

Elias, M. F., Elias, J. W., & Elias, P. K. (1990). Biological and health influences on behavior. In J. E. Birren & K. W. Schaie (Eds.), *Handbook of the psychology of aging* (pp. 79–102). San Diego, CA: Academic Press.

Elias, M. F., & Elias, P. K. (1993). Hypertension affects neurobehavioral functioning: So what's new? *Psychosomatic Medicine, 55,* 44–50.

Elias, M. F., & Robbins, M. A. (1991). Cardiovascular disease, hypertension, and cognitive function. In A. P. Shapiro & A. Baum (Eds.), *Behavioral aspects of cardiovascular disease* (pp. 249–285). Hillsdale, NJ: Lawrence Erlbaum Associates.

Elias, M. F., Wolf, P., D'Agostino, R., Cobb, J., & White, L. (1993). Untreated blood pressure is inversely related to cognitive function: The Framingham Study. *American Journal of Epidemiology, 138,* 353–364.

Erker, G. J., Russel Searight, H., & Peterson, P. (1995). Patterns of neuropsychological functioning among patients with multi-infarct dementia and Alzheimer's disease: A comparative analysis. *International Psychogeriatrics, 7,* 393–406.

Erngrund, K., Mäntylä, T., & Nilsson, L. G. (1996). Adult age differences in source recall: A population-based study. *Journal of Gerontology: Psychological Sciences, 51,* 335–345.

Erngrund, K., Mäntylä, T., & Rönnlund, M. (1996). Acting or listening: Age differences in source recall of enacted and nonenacted statements. *Journal of Adult Development, 3,* 217–232.

Falconer, J. A., Naughton, B. J., Strasser, D. C., & Sinacore, J. M. (1994). Stroke inpatient rehabilitation: A comparison across age groups. *Journal of the American Geriatrics Society, 42,* 39–44.

Fearnley, J. M., & Lees, A. J. (1991). Aging and Parkinson's disease: Substantia nigra regional selectivity. *Brain, 114,* 2283–2301.

Feehan, M., Knight, R. G., & Partridge, F. M. (1991). Cognitive complaint and test performance in elderly patients suffering depression and dementia. *International Journal of Geriatric Psychiatry, 6,* 287–293.

Fichter, M. M., Meller, I., Schröppel, H., & Steinkirchner, R. (1995). Dementia and cognitive impairment in the oldest old in the community: Prevalence and comorbidity. *British Journal of Psychiatry, 166,* 621–629.

Figiel, G. S., Krishnan, K. R., Deraiswamy, P. M., Rao, V. P., Nemeroff, C. B., & Boyko, O. B. (1991). Subcortical hyperintensities in brain magnetic resonance imaging: A comparison between late age onset and early age onset elderly depressed subjects. *Neurobiology of Aging, 26,* 245–247.

Finkel, D., Pedersen, N., & McGue, M. (1995). Genetic influences on memory performance in adulthood: Comparison of Minnesota and Swedish twin data. *Psychology and Aging, 10,* 437–446.

Forsell, Y., Jorm, A. F., Fratiglioni, L., Grut, M., & Winblad, B. (1993). Application of DSM–III–R criteria for major depressive episode to elderly subjects with and without dementia. *American Journal of Psychiatry, 150,* 1199–1202.

Fox, N. C., Warrington, E. K., Freeborough, P. A., Hartikainen, P., Kennedy, A. M., Stevens, J. S., & Rossor, M. N. (1996). Presymptomatic hippocampal atrophy in Alzheimer's disease: A longitudinal MRI study. *Brain, 119,* 2001–2007.

Foy, A., O'Connell, D., Henry, D., Kelly, J., Cocking, S., & Halliday, J. (1995). Bensodiazepine use as a cause of cognitive impairment in elderly hospital inpatients. *Journal of Gerontology: Medical Sciences, 50*, 99–106.

Fozard, J. L., Metter, E. F., & Brant, L. J. (1990). Next steps in describing aging and disease in longitudinal studies. *Journal of Gerontology: Psychological Sciences, 45*, 116–127.

Fratiglioni, L., Grut, M., Forsell, Y., Viitanen, M., Grafström, M., Holmén, K., Ericsson, K., Bäckman, L., Ahlbom, A., & Winblad, B. (1991). Prevalence of Alzheimer's disease and other dementias in an elderly urban population: Relationship with age, sex, and education. *Neurology, 41*, 1886–1891.

Fratiglioni, L., Viitanen, M., Bäckman, L., Sandman, P. -O., & Winblad, B. (1992). Occurence of dementia in advanced age: The study design of the Kungsholmen Project. *Neuroepidemiology, 11*(Suppl. 1), 29–36.

Fratiglioni, L., Viitanen, M., von Strauss, E., Tontodonati, V., Herlitz, A., & Winblad, B. (1997). Very old women at highest risk of dementia and Alzheimer's disease: Incidence data from the Kungsholmen Project, Stockholm. *Neurology, 48*, 132–138.

Fries, J. F., & Crapo, L. M. (1981). *Vitality and aging*. New York: Freeman.

Gainotti, G., & Marra, C. (1994). Some aspects of memory disorders clearly distinguish dementia of the Alzheimer type from depressive pseudodementia. *Journal of Clinical and Experimental Neuropsychology, 16*, 665–678.

Garrard, J., Makris, L., Dunham, T., Heston, L., Cooper, S., Ratner, E., Zelterman, D., & Kane, R. (1991). Evaluation of neuroleptic drug use by nursing home elderly under proposed Medicare and Medicaid regulations. *JAMA: Journal of the American Medical Association, 265*, 463–467.

Gatz, M., Lowe, B., Berg, S., Mortimer, J., & Pedersen, N. (1994). Dementia: Not just a search for the gene. *The Gerontologist, 34*, 251–255.

Giambra, L. M., Arenberg, D., Kawas, C., Zonderman, A. B., & Costa, P. T. (1995). Adult life span changes in immediate visual memory and verbal intelligence. *Psychology and Aging, 10*, 123–139.

Gilinsky, A. S., & Judd, B. B. (1994). Working memory and bias in reasoning across the adult life span. *Psychology and Aging, 9*, 356–371.

Girling, D. M., Huppert, F. A., Brayne, C., Paykel, E. S., Gill, C., & Mathewson, D. (1995). Depressive symptoms in the very elderly—Their prevalence and significance. *International Journal of Geriatric Psychiatry, 10*, 497–504.

Grady, C. L., Haxby, J. V., Horwitz, B., Sundaram, M., Berg, G., Schapiro, M., Friedland, R. P., & Rapoport, S. I. (1988). Longitudinal study of the early neuropsychological and cerebral metabolic changes in dementia of the Alzheimer type. *Journal of Clinical and Experimental Neuropsychology, 10*, 576–596.

Grady, C. L., McIntosh, A. R., Horwitz, B., Maisog, J. M., Ungerleider, L. G., Mentis, M. J., Pietrini, P., Schapiro, M. B., & Haxby, J. V. (1995). Age-related reductions in human recognition memory due to impaired encoding. *Science, 269*, 218–221.

Graf, P., & Masson, M. E. J. (Eds.). (1993). *Implicit memory: New directions in cognition, development, and neuropsychology*. Hillsdale, NJ: Lawrence Erlbaum Associates.

Graves, A. B., Larson, E. B., Edland, S. D., Bowen, J. D., McCormick, W. C., McCurry, S. M., Rice, M. M., Wenzlow, A., & Uomoto, J. M. (1997). Prevalence of dementia and subtypes in the Japanese American population of King County, Washington State. *American Journal of Epidemiology, 144*, 760–771.

Greenspan, S. L., & Resnick, N. M. (1991). Geriatric endocrinology. In F. S. Greenspan (Ed.), *Basic and clinical endocrinology* (3rd ed., pp. 741–756). Norwalk, CT: Appleton & Lange.

Greveson, G. C., Gray, C. S., French, J. M., & James, O. F. W. (1991). Long-term outcome for patients and carers following hospital admission for stroke. *Age and Ageing, 20*, 337–344.

Griffin, M. A., & Solomon, D. H. (1986). Hyperthyroidism in the elderly. *Journal of the American Geriatrics Society, 34*, 887–892.

Grober, E., & Kawas, C. (1997). Learning and retention in preclinical and early Alzheimer's disease. *Psychology and Aging, 12*, 183–188.

Guo, Z., Viitanen, M., & Winblad, B. (1997). Clinical correlates of low blood pressure in very old people: The importance of cognitive impairment. *Journal of the American Geriatrics Society, 45*, 701–705.

Gur, R. C., Mozley, P. D., Resnick, S. M., Gottlieb, G. E., Kohn, M., Zimmerman, R., Herman, G., Atlas, S., Grossman, R., Berretta, D., Erwin, R., & Gur, R. E. (1991). Gender differences in the age effect on brain atrophy measured by magnetic resonance imaging. *Proceedings of the National Academy of Sciences, 88*, 2845–2849.

Hall, S., Pinkston, S. L., Szalda-Petree, A. C., & Coronis, A. R. (1996). The performance of healthy older adults on the Continous Visual Memory Test and the Visual–Motor Integration Test: Preliminary findings. *Journal of Clinical Psychology, 52*, 449–454.

Halpern, D. F. (1992). *Sex differences in cognitive abilities*. Hillsdale, NJ: Lawrence Erlbaum Associates.

Hansen, L. A., De Teresa, R., Davies, P., & Terry, R. D. (1988). Neocortical morphometry, lesion counts, and choline acetyltransferase levels in the age spectrum of Alzheimer's disease. *Neurology, 38*, 48–54.

Hart, R. P., Kwentus, J. A., Hamer, R. M., & Taylor, J. R. (1987). Selective reminding procedure in depression and dementia. *Psychology and Aging, 2*, 307–317.

Hartley, J. T. (1986). Reader and text variables as determinants of discourse memory in adulthood. *Psychology and Aging, 1*, 150–158.

Hartman, M. (1991). The use of semantic knowledge in Alzheimer's disease: Evidence for impairments in attention. *Neuropsychologia, 29*, 213–228.

Hashtroudi, S., Johnson, M., & Chrosniak, L. D. (1989). Aging and source monitoring. *Psychology and Aging, 4*, 106–112.

Hashtroudi, S., Johnson, M., & Chrosniak, L. D. (1990). Aging and qualitative characteristics of memories for perceived and imagined complex events. *Psychology and Aging, 5*, 119–126.

Hassing, L., Wahlin, Å., & Bäckman, L. (1998). Minimal influence of age, education, and gender on episodic memory functioning in very old age: A population-based study of nonagenarians. *Archives of Gerontology and Geriatrics, 27*, 75–87.

Hassing, L., Wahlin, Å., Winblad, B., & Bäckman, L. (1999). Further evidence on the effects of vitamin B_{12} and folate levels on episodic memory functioning: A population-based study of very old adults. *Biological Psychiatry, 45*, 1472–1480.

Hébert, R., & Brayne, C. (1995). Epidemiology of vascular dementia. *Neuroepidemiology, 14*, 240–257.

Helkala, E. -L., Koivisto, K., Hänninen, T., Vanhanen, M., Kervinen, K., Kuusisto, J., Mykkänen, L., Kesänjumi, Y. A., Laakso, M., & Riekkinen, P., Sr. (1995). The association of apolipoprotein E polymorphism with memory: A population-based study. *Neuroscience Letters, 191*, 141–144.

Helkala, E. -L., Koivisto, K., Hänninen, T., Vanhanen, M., Kervinen, K., Kuusisto, J., Mykkänen, L., Kesänjumi, Y. A., Laakso, M., & Riekkinen, P., Sr. (1996). Memory functions in human subjects with different apolipoprotein E phenotypes during a 3-year population-based follow-up study. *Neuroscience Letters, 204*, 177–180.

Henderson, A. S. (1994). Does aging protect against depression? *Social Psychiatry and Psychiatric Epidemiology, 29*, 107–109.

Henderson, A. S., & Jorm, A. F. (1997). Some contributions to the epidemiology of dementia and depression. *International Journal of Geriatric Psychiatry, 12*, 145–154.

Hendrie, H. C., Osuntokun, B. O., Hall, K. S., Ogunniyi, A. O., Hui, S. L., Unverzagt, F. W., Guereje, O., Rodenberg, C. A., Baiyewu, O., & Musick, B. S. (1995). Prevalence of

Alzheimer's disease and dementia in two communities: Nigerian Africans and African Americans. *American Journal of Psychiatry, 152,* 1485–1492.

Herlitz, A., Adolfsson, R., Bäckman, L., & Nilsson, L. -G. (1991). Cue utilization following different forms of encoding in mildly, moderately, and severely demented patients with Alzheimer's disease. *Brain and Cognition, 15,* 119–130.

Herlitz, A., Nilsson, L. -G., & Bäckman (1997). Gender differences in episodic memory. *Memory and Cognition, 25,* 801–811.

Herlitz, A., Small, B. J., Fratiglioni, L., Almkvist, O., Viitanen, M., & Bäckman, L. (1997). Detection of dementia in community surveys: Is it possible to increase the accuracy of our diagnostic instruments? *Archives of Neurology, 54,* 319–324.

Herlitz, A., & Viitanen, M. (1991). Semantic organization and verbal episodic memory in patients with mild and moderate Alzheimer's disease. *Journal of Clinical and Experimental Neuropsychology, 13,* 559–574.

Heston, L. L., Mastri, A. R., Anderson, V. E., & White, J. (1981). Dementia of the Alzheimer type: Clinical genetics, natural history, and associated conditions. *Archives of General Psychiatry, 38,* 1085–1090.

Hill, R. D., Bäckman, L., Wahlin, Å., & Winblad, B. (1995). Visuospatial performance in very old demented persons: An individual difference analysis. *Dementia, 6,* 49–54.

Hill, R. D., Grut, M., Wahlin, Å., Herlitz, A., Winblad, B., & Bäckman, L. (1995). Predicting memory performance in optimally healthy very old adults. *Journal of Mental Health and Aging, 1,* 57–67.

Hill, R. D., Stigsdotter Neely, A., & Bäckman, L. (1997). Predictors of change on the Fuld Object Memory Evaluation in a two-year longitudinal study of optimally healthy very old adults. *Aging and Mental Health, 1,* 140–148.

Hill, R. D., Wahlin, Å., Winblad, B., & Bäckman, L. (1995). The role of demographic and life style variables in utilizing cognitive support for episodic remembering among very old adults. *Journal of Gerontology: Psychological Sciences, 50,* 219–227.

Hodges, J. R., Salmon, D. P., & Butters, N. (1992). Semantic memory impairment in Alzheimer's disease: Failure of access or degraded knowledge. *Neuropsychologia, 30,* 301–314.

Howard, D. V., Heisey, J. G., & Shaw, R. J. (1986). Aging and the priming of newly learned associations. *Developmental Psychology, 22,* 78–85.

Howieson, D. B., Dame, A., Camicioli, R., Sexton, G., Payami, H., & Kaye, J. A. (1997). Cognitive markers preceding Alzheimer's dementia in the healthy oldest old. *Journal of the American Geriatrics Society, 45,* 584–589.

Howieson, D. B., Holm, L. A., Kaye, J. A., Oken, B. S., & Howieson, J. (1993). Neurologic function in the optimally healthy oldest old: Neuropsychological evaluation. *Neurology, 43,* 1882–1886.

Hultsch, D. F., Hammer, M., & Small, B. J. (1993). Age differences in cognitive performance in later life: Relationships to self-reported health and activity life style. *Journal of Gerontology: Psychological Sciences, 48,* 1–11.

Hultsch, D. F., Hertzog, C., & Dixon, R. A. (1990). Ability correlates of memory performance in adulthood and aging. *Psychology and Aging, 5,* 356–368.

Hultsch, D. F., Hertzog, C., Dixon, R. A., & Small, B. J. (1998). *Memory change in the aged.* Cambridge, England: Cambridge University Press.

Hultsch, D. F., Hertzog, C., Small, B. J., McDonald-Miszczak, & Dixon, R. A. (1992). Short-term longitudinal change in cognitive performance in later life. *Psychology and Aging, 7,* 571–584.

Hultsch, D. F., Masson, M. E. J., & Small, B. J. (1991). Adult age differences in direct and indirect tests of memory. *Journal of Gerontology: Psychological Sciences, 46,* 22–30.

Huppert, F. A. (1994). Memory function in dementia and normal aging—Dimension or dichotomy? In F. Huppert, C. Brayne, & D. W. O'Connor (Eds.), *Dementia and normal aging* (pp. 291–330). Cambridge, England: Cambridge University Press.

Huppert, F. A., & Brayne, C. (1994). What is the relationship between dementia and normal aging? In F. Huppert, C. Brayne, & D. W. O'Connor (Eds.), *Dementia and normal aging* (pp. 3–11). Cambridge, England: Cambridge University Press.

Hyman, B. T., Gomez-Isla, T., Briggs, M., Chung, H., Nichols, S., Kohout, F., & Wallace, R. (1996). Apolipoprotein E and cognitive change in an elderly population. *Annals of Neurology, 40,* 55–66.

Inouye, S. K., Albert, M. S., Mohs, R., Sun, K., & Berkman, L. F. (1993). Cognitive performance in a high-functioning community-dwelling elderly population. *Journal of Gerontology: Medical Sciences, 48,* 146–151.

Isingrini, M., Vazou, F., & Leroy, P. (1995). Dissociation of implicit and explicit memory tests: Effect of age and divided attention on category exemplar generation and cued recall. *Memory & Cognition, 23,* 462–467.

Jacobs, D. M., Sano, M., Dooneif, G., Marder, K., Bell, K. L., & Stern, Y. (1995). Neuropsychological detection and characterization of preclinical Alzheimer's disease. *Neurology, 25,* 317–324.

Jacoby, R. J., & Levy, R. (1980). Computed tomography in the elderly: Affective disorder. *British Journal of Psychiatry, 136,* 270–275.

Jelicic, M., Craik, F. I. M., & Moscovitch, M. (1996). Effects of ageing on different explicit and implicit memory tasks. *European Journal of Cognitive Psychology, 8,* 225–234.

Jenkins, J. J. (1979). Four points to remember: A tetrahedral model of memory experiments. In L. S. Cermak & F. I. M. Craik (Eds.), *Levels of processing in human memory* (pp. 429–446). Hillsdale, NJ: Lawrence Erlbaum Associates.

Johanson, B., Zarit, S. H., & Berg, S. (1992). Changes in cognitive functioning of the oldest old. *Journal of Gerontology: Psychological Sciences, 47,* P75–P80.

Johansson, B., & Berg, S. (1989). The robustness of the terminal decline phenomenon: Longitudinal data from the Digit Span Memory Test. *Journal of Gerontology: Psychological Sciences, 44,* 184–186.

Jones, H. E., & Conrad, H. (1933). The growth and decline of intelligence: A study of a homogenous group between the ages of ten and sixty. *Genetic Psychological Monographs, 13,* 223–298.

Jongbloed, L. (1986). Prediction of function after stroke: A critical review. *Stroke, 17,* 765–776.

Kalmijn, S., Feskens, E. J. M., Launer, L. J., Stijnen, T., & Kromhout, D. (1995). Glucose intolerance, hyperinsulinaemia and cognitive function in a general population of elderly men. *Diabetologia, 38,* 1096–1102.

Karlsson, T., Bäckman, L., Herlitz, A., Nilsson, L. -G., Winblad, B., & Österlind, P. -O. (1989). Memory improvement at different stages of Alzheimer's disease. *Neuropsychologia, 27,* 737–742.

Katzman, R., Brown, T., Thal, L. J., Fuld, P., Aronson, M., Butters, N., Klauber, M. R., Wiederholt, W., Pay, M., Renbing, X., Ooi, W. L., Hofstetter, R., & Terry, R. D. (1983). Comparison of annual change of mental status scores in four independent studies of patients with Alzheimer's disease. *Annals of Neurology, 24,* 384–389.

Kaufman, A. S., Reynolds, C. R., & McLean, J. E. (1989). Age and WAIS–R intelligence in a sample of adults in the 20–74-year age range: A cross-sectional analysis with educational level controlled. *Intelligence, 13,* 235–253.

Kausler, D. H. (1991). *Experimental psychology, cognition, and human aging* (2nd ed.). New York: Springer-Verlag.

Kausler, D. H. (1994). *Learning and memory in normal aging.* San Diego, CA: Academic Press.

Kent, S. (1976). Is diabetes a form of accelerated aging? *Geriatrics, 31,* 140–151.

Killiany, R. J., Moss, M. B., Albert, M. S., Sandor, T., Tieman, J., & Jolesz, F. (1993). Temporal lobe regions on magnetic resonance imaging identify patients with early Alzheimer's disease. *Archives of Neurology, 50,* 949–954.

Kindermann, S. S., & Brown, G. G. (1997). Depression and memory in the elderly: A meta-analysis. *Journal of Clinical and Experimental Neuropsychology, 19,* 625–642.

King, D. A., Caine, E. D., Conwell, Y., & Cox, C. (1991). The neuropsychology of depression in the elderly: A comparative study of normal aging and Alzheimer's disease. *Journal of Neuropsychiatry and Clinical Neurosciences, 3,* 163–168.

Kinsbourne, M. (1980). Attentional dysfunctions and the elderly: Theoretical models and research perspectives. In L. W. Poon, J. L. Fozard, L. S. Cermak, D. Arenberg, & L. W. Thompson (Eds.), *New directions in memory and aging* (pp. 113–129). Hillsdale, NJ: Lawrence Erlbaum Associates.

Kivelä, S. -L., Kongäs-Saviaro, P., Pahkala, K., Kesti, E., & Laipalla, P. (1996). Health, health behavior, and functional ability predicting depression in old age: A longitudinal study. *International Journal of Geriatric Psychiatry, 11,* 871–877.

Kivelä, S. -L., Pahkala, K., & Laippala, P. (1988). Prevalence of depression in an elderly population in Finland. *Acta Psychiatrica Scandinavica, 78,* 401–413.

Kleemeier, R.W. (1962). Intellectual changes in the senium. *Proceedings of the American Statistical Association, 1,* 290–295.

Kliegl, R., Smith, J., & Baltes, P. B. (1990). On the locus and process of magnification of age differences during mnemonic training. *Developmental Psychology, 26,* 894–904.

Korten, A. E., Henderson, A. S., Christensen, H., Jorm, A. F., Rodgers, B., Jacomb, P., & MacKinnon, A. J. (1997). A prospective study of cognitive function in the elderly. *Psychological Medicine, 27,* 919–930.

Koss, E., Haxby, J. V., DeCarli, C., Schapiro, M. B., Friedland, R. P., & Rapoport, S. I. (1991). Patterns of performance preservation and loss in healthy aging. *Developmental Neuropsychology, 7,* 99–113.

Kruse, W. H. (1990). Problems and pitfalls in the use of bensodiazepines in the elderly. *Drug Safety, 7,* 328–344.

Kurlan, R., & Como, P. (1988). Drug-induced Alzheimerism. *Archives of Neurology, 45,* 356–357.

LaBarge, E., Edwards, D., & Knesevich, J. W. (1986). Performance of normal elderly on the Boston Naming Test. *Brain and Language, 27,* 380–384.

Lachman, M. E. (1983). Perception of intellectual aging: Antecedent or consequence of intellectual functioning. *Developmental Psychology, 19,* 482–492.

Langton-Hewer, R. (1990). Rehabilitation after stroke. *Quarterly Journal of Medicine, 76,* 659–674.

Larabee, G. J., & Crook, T. H. (1993). Do men show more rapid age-associated decline in simulated everyday verbal memory than do women? *Psychology and Aging, 8,* 68–71.

Larsson, M., & Bäckman, L. (1998). Modality memory across the adult life span: Evidence for selective olfactory deficits. *Experimental Aging Research, 24,* 63–82.

La Rue, A., Goodman, S., & Spar, J. E. (1992). Risk factors for memory impairment in geriatric depression. *Neuropsychiatry, Neuropsychology, and Behavioral Neurology, 5,* 178–184.

Launer, L. J., Masaki, K., Petrovitch, H., Foley, D., & Havlik, R. J. (1995). The association between midlife blood pressure levels and late-life cognitive function: The Honolulu–Asia Aging Study. *JAMA: Journal of the American Medical Association, 274,* 1846–1851.

Lazarus, J. H. (1997). Hyperthyroidism. *The Lancet, 349,* 339–343.

Lehericy, S., Baulac, M., Chiras, J., Pierot, L., Martin, N., Pillon, B., Deweer, B., Dubois, B., & Marsault, C. (1994). Amygdalaohippocampal MR volume measurements in the early stages of Alzheimer's disease. *American Journal of Neuroradiology, 15,* 927–937.

Letenneur, L., Commenges, D., Dartigues, J. F., & Barbeger-Gateau, P. (1994). Incidence of dementia and Alzheimers disease in elderly community residents of south-western France. *International Journal of Epidemiology, 23,* 1256–1261.

Levy, E. G. (1991). Thyroid disease in the elderly. *Medical Clinics of North America, 75,* 151–167.

Levy-Lahad, E., & Bird, T. D. (1996). Genetic factors in Alzheimer's disease: A review of recent advances. *Annals of Neurology, 40,* 829–840.

Lichtenberg, P. A., Manning, C. A., & Turkheimer, E. (1992). Memory dysfunction in depressed spousal caregivers. *Clinical Gerontologist, 12,* 77–80.

Light, L. L., & Singh, A. (1987). Implicit and explicit memory in young and older adults. *Journal of Experimental Psychology: Learning, Memory, and Cognition, 13,* 531–541.

Lindenberger, U., & Baltes, P. B. (1994). Sensory functioning and intelligence in old age: A strong relation. *Psychology and Aging, 9,* 339–355.

Lindenberger, U., & Baltes, P. B. (1997). Intellectual functioning in old and very old age: Cross-sectional results from the Berlin Aging Study. *Psychology and Aging, 12,* 410–432.

Lindenberger, U., Gilberg, R., Nuthmann, R., Pötter, U., Little, T. D., & Baltes, P. B. (1999). Sample selectivity and generalizability of the Berlin Aging Study. In P. B. Baltes & K. U. Mayer (Eds.), *The Berlin Aging Study: Aging from 70 to 100* (pp. 56–82). New York: Cambridge University Press.

Lindsay, R. S., & Toft, A. D. (1997). Hypothyroidism. *The Lancet, 349,* 413–417.

Linn, R. T., Wolf, P. A., Bachman, D. L., Knoefel, J. E., Cobb, J. L., Belanger, A. J., Kaplan, E. F., & D'Agostino, R. B. (1995). The "preclinical phase" of probable Alzheimer's disease. *Archives of Neurology, 52,* 485–490.

Lipinska, B., & Bäckman, L. (1997). Encoding-retrieval interactions in mild Alzheimer's disease: The role of access to categorical information. *Brain and Cognition, 34,* 274–286.

Lipinska, B., Bäckman, L., & Herlitz, A. (1992). When Greta Garbo is easier to remember than Stefan Edberg: Influences of prior knowledge on recognition memory in Alzheimer's disease. *Psychology and Aging, 7,* 214–220.

Livingston, G., Hawkins, A., Graham, N., Blizard, B., & Mann, A. (1990). The Gospel Oak Study: Prevalence rates of dementia, depression, and activity limitation among elderly residents in inner London. *Psychological Medicine, 20,* 137–146.

Luszcz, M. A., Bryan, J., & Kent, P. (1997). Predicting episodic memory performance of very old men and women: Contributions from age, depression, activity, cognitive ability, and speed. *Psychology and Aging, 12,* 340–351.

Lyness, J. M., Cox, C., Curry, J., Conwell, Y., King, D. A., & Caine, E. D. (1995). Old age and the underreporting of depressive symptoms. *Journal of the American Geriatrics Society, 43,* 216–221.

Maccoby, E. E., & Jacklin, C. N. (1974). *The psychology of sex differences.* Stanford, CA: Stanford University Press.

Madden, D. J., & Blumenthal, J. A. (1998). Interaction of hypertension and age in visual selective attention performance. *Health Psychology, 17,* 76–83.

Mann, D. M. A. (1994). Pathological correlates of dementia in Alzheimer's disease. *Neurobiology of Aging, 15,* 357–360.

Mäntylä, T., & Bäckman, L. (1990). Encoding variability and age-related retrieval failures. *Psychology and Aging, 5,* 545–550.

Mäntylä, T., & Bäckman, L. (1992). Aging and memory for expected and unexpected objects in real-world settings. *Journal of Experimental Psychology: Learning, Memory, and Cognition, 18,* 1298–1309.

Martin, A., Brouwers, P., Cox, C., & Fedio, P. (1985). On the nature of the verbal memory deficit in Alzheimer's disease. *Brain and Language, 25,* 123–132.

Martin, D. C. (1988). B_{12} and folate deficiency dementia. *Clinics in Geriatric Medicine, 4,* 841–852.

Martin, W. R. W., Palmer, M. R., Patlak, C. S., & Caine, D. B. (1989). Nigrostriatal function in humans studied with positron emission tomography. *Annals of Neurology, 26,* 535–542.

Masur, D. M., Sliwinski, M., Lipton, R. B., Blau, A. D., & Crystal, H. A. (1994). Neuropsychological prediction of dementia and the absence of dementia in healthy elderly persons. *Neurology, 44,* 1427–1432.

McClearn, G. E., Johansson, B., Berg, S., Pedersen, N. L., Ahern, F., Petrill, S. A., & Plomin, R. (1997). Substantial genetic influence on cognitive abilities in twins 80 or more years old. *Science, 276,* 1560–1564.

McClelland, G. H., & Judd, C. M. (1993). Statistical difficulties of detecting interactions and moderator effects. *Psychological Bulletin, 114,* 376–390.

Meinz, E. J., & Salthouse, T. A. (1998). Is age kinder to females than to males? *Psychonomic Bulletin and Reviews, 5,* 56–70.

Meyer, J. S., Obara, K., Muramatsu, K., Mortel, K. F., & Shirai, T. (1995). Cognitive performance after small strokes correlates with ischemia, not atrophy of the brain. *Dementia, 6,* 312–322.

Mitchell, D. B. (1989). How many memory systems? Evidence from aging. *Journal of Experimental Psychology: Learning, Memory, and Cognition, 15,* 31–49.

Mitrushina, M., & Satz, P. (1995). Repeated testing of normal elderly with the Boston Naming Test. *Aging: Clinical and Experimental Research, 7,* 123–127.

Morrell, R. W., & Park, D. C. (1993). The effects of age, illustrations, and task variables on the performance of procedural assembly tasks. *Psychology and Aging, 8,* 389–399.

Morris, R. G. (Ed.). (1996). *The cognitive neuropsychology of Alzheimer's disease.* Oxford, England: Oxford University Press.

Mortimer, J. A., & Graves, A. B. (1993). Education and other socioeconomic determinants of dementia and Alzheimer's disease. *Neurology, 43,* 39–44.

National Institutes of Health Consensus Conference. (1992). Diagnosis and treatment of depression in late life. *JAMA: Journal of the American Medical Association, 268,* 282–291.

Nebes, R. D. (1989). Semantic memory in Alzheimer's disease. *Psychological Bulletin, 106,* 377–394.

Nebes, R. D. (1992). Cognitive dysfunctions in Alzheimer's disease. In F. I. M. Craik & T. A. Salthouse (Eds.), *Handbook of aging and cognition* (pp. 373–446). Hillsdale, NJ: Lawrence Erlbaum Associates.

Neugarten, B. L. (1974). Age groups in American society and the rise of the young-old. *Annals of the American Academy of Political and Social Sciences, 415,* 187–198.

Nilsson, L. -G., Bäckman, L., Erngrund, K., Nyberg, L., Adolfsson, R., Bucht, G., Karlsson, S., Widing, M., & Winblad, B. (1997). The Betula Prospective Cohort Study: Memory, health, and aging. *Aging, Neuropsychology, and Cognition, 4,* 1–32.

Norman, S., Kemper, S., & Kynette, D. (1992). Adults' reading comprehension: Effects of syntactic complexity and working memory. *Journal of Gerontology: Psychological Sciences, 47,* 258–265.

Nyberg, L., McIntosh, A. R., Houle, S., Nilsson, L. -G., & Tulving, E. (1996). Activation of medial temporal structures during episodic memory retrieval. *Nature, 380,* 715–717.

Nyberg, L., Nilsson, L. -G., Olofsson, U., & Bäckman, L. (1997). Effects of division of attention during encoding and retrieval on age differences in episodic memory. *Experimental Aging Research, 23,* 137–143.

O'Brien, M. D. (1994). Vascular dementia: Problems with nomenclature, definition, and classification. *Journal of Stroke and Cerebrovascular Disease, 4,* 52–56.

O'Connor, D. W., Pollitt, P. A., & Roth, M. (1990). Coexisting depression and dementia in a community survey of the elderly. *International Psychogeriatrics, 2,* 45–53.

O'Hara, M. W., Hinrichs, J. V., Kohout, F. J., Wallace, R. B., & Lemke, J. H. (1986). Memory complaint and memory performance in the depressed elderly. *Psychology and Aging, 1,* 45–53.

Ott, A., Breteler, M. M., van Harskamp, F., Grobbee, D. E., & Hofman, A. (1995). Prevalence of Alzheimer's disease and vascular dementia: Association with education. *British Medical Journal, 310,* 970–973.

Park, D. C., Cherry, K. E., Smith, A. D., & Lafronza, V. N. (1990). Effects of distinctive context on memory for objects and their locations in young and elderly adults. *Psychology and Aging, 5,* 250–255.

Park, D. C., Smith, A. D., Lautenschlager, G., Earles, J. L., Frieske, D., Zwahr, M., & Gaines, C. L. (1996). Mediators of long-term memory performance across the life span. *Psychology and Aging, 11,* 621–637.

Park, D. C., Smith, A. D., Morrell, R. W., Puglisi, J. T., & Dudley, W. N. (1990). Effects of contextual integration on recall of pictures by older adults. *Journal of Gerontology: Psychological Sciences, 45,* 52–57.

Parkinson, S. R. (1982). Performance deficits in short-term memory tasks: A comparison of amnesic Korsakoff patients and the aged. In L. S. Cermak (Ed.), *Human memory and amnesia* (pp. 77–96). Hillsdale, NJ: Lawrence Erlbaum Associates.

Pearlson, G. D., Rabins, P. V., Kim, V. S., Speedie, L. J., Moberg, P. J., Burns, A., & Bascom, M. J. (1989). Structural brain CT changes and cognitive deficits in elderly depressives with and without reversible dementia ("pseudodementia"). *Psychological Medicine, 19,* 573–584.

Pedersen, N. L., Reynolds, C. A., & Gatz, M. (1996). Sources of covariation among Mini-Mental State Examination scores, education, and cognitive abilities. *Journal of Gerontology: Psychological Sciences, 51,* 55–63.

Perlmuter, L. C., Hakami, M. K., Hodgson-Harrington, C., Ginsberg, J., Katz, J., Singer, D. E., & Nathan, D. M. (1984). Decreased cognitive function in aging non-insulin-dependent diabetic patients. *American Journal of Medicine, 77,* 1043–1048.

Perlmutter, M., & Nyquist, L. (1990). Relationships between self-reported physical and mental health and intelligence performance across adulthood. *Journal of Gerontology: Psychological Sciences, 45,* 145–155.

Perls, T. T., Morris, J. N., Ooi, W. L., & Lipsitz, L. A. (1993). The relationship between age, gender and cognitive performance in the very old: The effect of selective survival. *Journal of the American Geriatrics Society, 41,* 1193–1201.

Peterson, R. C., Smith, G. E., Ivnik, R. J., Tangalos, E. G., Schaid, D. J., Thibodeau, S. N., Kokmen, E., Waring, S. C., & Kurland, L. T. (1995). Apolipoprotein E status as a predictor of the development of Alzheimer's disease in memory-impaired individuals. *JAMA: Journal of the American Medical Association, 273,* 1274–1278.

Peterson, R. C., Waring, S. C., Smith, G. E., Tangalos, E. G., & Thibodeau, S. N. (1996). Predictive value of APOE genotyping in incipient Alzheimer's disease. *Proceedings of the New York Academy of Sciences, 802,* 58–69.

Pietrini, P., & Rapoport, S. I. (1994). Functional neuroimaging: Positron emission tomography in the study of cerebral blood flow and glucose utilization in human subjects at different ages. In C. E. Coffey & J. L. Cummings (Eds.), *The American Psychiatric Press textbook of geriatric neuropsychiatry* (pp. 196–213). Washington, DC: American Psychiatric Press.

Plude, D. J. (1992). Attention and memory improvement. In D. J. Herrmann, H. Weingartner, A. Searlman, & C. McEvoy (Eds.), *Memory improvement: Implications for memory theory* (pp. 150–168). New York: Springer-Verlag.

Poon, L. W., Sweaney, A. C., Clayton, G. M., & Merriam, S. B. (1992). The Georgia Centenarian Study. *International Journal of Aging and Human Development, 34,* 1–17.

Popkin, S. J., Gallagher, D., Thompson, L. W., & Moore, M. (1982). Memory complaint and performance in normal and depressed older adults. *Experimental Aging Research, 8,* 141–145.

Price, T. R., Manolio, T. A., Kronmal, R. A., Kittner, S. J., Yue, N. C., Robbins, J., Anton-Culver, H., & O'Leary, D. H. (1997). Silent brain infarction on magnetic resonance imaging and neurological abnormalities in community-dwelling older adults: The Cardiovascular Health Study. *Stroke, 28,* 1158–1164.

Prirart, J. (1978). Diabetes mellitus and its degenerative complications: A prospective study of 4,400 patients observed between 1947 and 1973. *Diabetes Care, 1,* 168–263.

Puglisi, J. T., & Park, D. C. (1987). Perceptual elaboration and memory in older adults. *Journal of Gerontology, 42,* 160–162.

Rabbitt, P., Donlan, C., Watson, P., McInnes, L., & Bent, N. (1995). Unique and interactive effects of depression, age, socioeconomic advantage, and gender on cognitive performance of normal healthy older people. *Psychology and Aging, 10*, 307–313.

Rabinowitz, J. C., Craik, F. I. M., & Ackerman, B. P. (1982). A processing resource account of age differences in recall. *Canadian Journal of Psychology, 36*, 325–344.

Rabins, P. V., Pearlson, G. D., & Aylward, E. (1991). Cortical magnetic resonance imaging changes in elderly patients with major depression. *American Journal of Psychiatry, 148*, 617–620.

Reiger, D. A., Farmer, M. E., Rae, D. S., Myers, J. K., Kramer, M., Robins, L. N., George, L. K., Karno, M., & Locke, B. Z. (1993). One-month prevalence of mental disorders in the United States and sociodemographic characteristics: The Epidemiologic Catchment Area Study. *Acta Psychiatrica Scandinavica, 88*, 35–47.

Ricker, J. H., Keenan, P. A., & Jacobson, M. W. (1994). Visuoperceptual–spatial ability and visual memory in vascular dementia and dementia of the Alzheimer type. *Neuropsychologia, 32*, 1287–1296.

Riegel, K. F., & Riegel, R. M. (1972). Development, drop and death. *Developmental Psychology, 6*, 306–319.

Riggs, K. M., Spiro, A., III, Tucker, K., & Ruh, D. (1996). Relations of vitamin B_{12}, vitamin B_6, folate and homocysteine to cognitive performance in the Normative Aging Study. *American Journal of Clinical Nutrition, 63*, 306–314.

Robinson, F. A. (1966). *The vitamin co-factors of enzyme systems.* New York: Pergamon.

Rohling, M. L., & Scogin, F. (1993). Automatic and effortful memory processes in depressed persons. *Journal of Gerontology: Psychological Sciences, 48*, 87–95.

Rovet, J. F., Ehrlich, R. M., & Hope, M. (1988). Specific intellectual deficits in children with early onset diabetes mellitus. *Child Development, 59*, 226–234.

Rubin, E. H., Kinscherf, D. A., Grant, E. A., & Storandt, M. (1991). The influence of major depression on clinical and psychiatric assessment of senile dementia of the Alzheimer type. *American Journal of Psychiatry, 148*, 1164–1171.

Rubin, E. H., Storandt, M., Miller, J. P., Grant, E. A., Kinscherf, D. A., Morris, J. C., & Berg, L. (1993). Influence of age on clinical and psychometric assessment of subjects with very mild or mild dementia of the Alzheimer type. *Archives of Neurology, 50*, 380–383.

Rudorfer, M. (1993). Pharmacokinetics of psychotropic drugs in special populations. *Journal of Clinical Psychiatry, 54*(Suppl.), 50–56.

Russo, R., & Parkin, A. J. (1993). Age differences in implicit memory: More apparent than real. *Memory & Cognition, 21*, 73–80.

Ryan, C. R., Vega, A., & Drash, A. (1985). Cognitive deficits in adolescents who developed diabetes early in life. *Paediatrics, 75*, 921–927.

Salthouse, T. A. (1991). *Theoretical perspectives on cognitive aging.* Hillsdale, NJ: Lawrence Erlbaum Associates.

Salthouse, T. A. (1992). Reasoning and spatial abilities. In F. I. M. Craik & T. A. Salthouse (Eds.), *Handbook of aging and cognition* (pp. 167–211). Hillsdale, NJ: Lawrence Erlbaum Associates.

Salthouse, T. A., & Babcock, R. L. (1991). Decomposing adult age differences in working memory. *Developmental Psychology, 27*, 763–776.

Salthouse, T. A., Hambrick, D. Z., & McGuthry, K. E. (1998). Shared age-related influences on cognitive and non-cognitive variables. *Psychology and Aging, 13*, 486–500.

Salthouse, T. A., Hancock, H. E., Meinz, E. J., & Hambrick, D. Z. (1996). Interrelations of age, visual acuity, and cognitive functioning. *Journal of Gerontology: Psychological Sciences, 51*, 317–330.

Sands, L., & Meredith, W. (1992). Blood pressure and intellectual functioning in late midlife. *Journal of Gerontology: Psychological Sciences, 47*, 81–84.

Schaie, K. W. (1985). *Manual for the Schaie-Thurstone Adult Mental Abilities Test (STAMAT).* Palo Alto, CA: Consulting Psychologists Press.

Schaie, K. W. (1996). *Intellectual development in adulthood: The Seattle Longitudinal Study.* Cambridge, England: Cambridge University Press.

Scherr, P. A., Hebert, L. A., Smith, L. A., & Evans, D. A. (1991). Relation of blood pressure to cognitive function in the elderly. *American Journal of Epidemiology, 134,* 1303–1315.

Schoenfeld, D. E., Malmrose, L. C., Blazer, D. G., Gold, D. T., & Seeman, T. E. (1994). Self-rated health and mortality in the high-functioning elderly—A closer look at healthy individuals. MacArthur field study of successful aging. *Journal of Gerontology: Medical Sciences, 49,* 109–115.

Schultz, R., Mittelmark, M., Kronmal, R., Polak, J. F., Hirsch, C. H., German, P., & Bookwala, J. (1994). Predictors of perceived health status in elderly men and women. *Journal of Aging and Health, 6,* 419–477.

Siegler, I. C. (1975). The terminal drop hypothesis: Fact or artifact? *Experimental Aging Research, 1,* 169–185.

Siegler, I. C., & Botwinick, J. (1979). A long-term longitudinal study of intellectual ability of older adults: The matter of selective subject attrition. *Journal of Gerontology, 34,* 242–245.

Simic, G., Kostovic, I., Winblad, B., & Bogdanovic, N. (1997). Volume and number of neurons of the human hippocampal formation in normal aging and Alzheimer's disease. *Journal of Comparative Neurology, 379,* 482–494.

Simon, E., Leach, L., Winocur, G., & Moscovitch, M. (1995). Intact primary memory in mild to moderate Alzheimer's disease: Indices from the California Verbal Learning Test. *Journal of Clinical and Experimental Neuropsychology, 16,* 414–422.

Sliwinski, M., Lipton, R. B., Buschke, H., & Stewart, W. (1996). The effects of preclinical dementia on estimates of normal cognitive functioning in aging. *Journal of Gerontology: Psychological Sciences, 51,* 217–225.

Small, B. J., & Bäckman, L. (1997). Cognitive correlates of mortality: Evidence from a population-based sample of very old adults. *Psychology and Aging, 12,* 309–313.

Small, B. J., & Bäckman, L. (1998). Predictors of longitudinal changes in memory, visuospatial, and verbal functioning in very old demented adults. *Dementia, 9,* 258–266.

Small, B. J., Basun, H., & Bäckman, L. (1998). Three-year changes in cognitive performance as a function of Apolipoprotein E genotype: Evidence from very old adults without dementia. *Psychology and Aging, 13,* 80–87.

Small, B. J., Dixon, R. A., Hultsch, D. F., & Hertzog, C. (1999). Longitudinal changes in quantitative and qualitative indicators of word and story recall in young-old and old-old adults. *Journal of Gerontology: Psychological Sciences, 54,* 102–115.

Small, B. J., Herlitz, A., & Bäckman, L. (1998). Cognitive development in Alzheimer's disease. In B. Edelstein (Ed.), *Comprehensive clinical psychology* (Vol. 7, pp. 231–245). Amsterdam: Elsevier.

Small, B. J., Herlitz, A., Fratiglioni, L., Almkvist, O., & Bäckman, L. (1997). Cognitive predictors of incident Alzheimer's disease: A prospective longitudinal study. *Neuropsychology, 11,* 413–420.

Small, B. J., Hultsch, D. F., & Masson, M. E. J. (1995). Adult age differences in perceptually based, but not conceptually based implicit tests of memory. *Journal of Gerontology: Psychological Sciences, 50,* 162–170.

Small, B. J., Viitanen, M., Winblad, B., & Bäckman, L. (1997). Cognitive changes in very old demented persons: The influence of demographic, biological, and psychometric variables. *Journal of Clinical and Experimental Neuropsychology, 19,* 245–260.

Spencer, W. D., & Raz, N. (1994). Memory for facts, source, and context: Can frontal lobe dysfunction explain age-related differences? *Psychology and Aging, 9,* 149–159.

Squire, L. R. (1986). Mechanisms of memory. *Science, 232,* 1612–1619.

Starr, J. M., Whalley, L. J., Inch, S., & Shering, P. A. (1993). Blood pressure and cognitive function in healthy old people. *Journal of the American Geriatrics Society, 41*, 753–756.

Statistics Canada. (1996). *Population projections by age groups and sex.* Ottawa, Ontario, Canada: Author.

Statistiska Centralbyrån. (1994). *Framskrivning för åren 1994–2050. Demografiska rapporter* [Predictions for the years 1994–2050. Demographic reports]. Örebro, Sweden: Author.

Steinhagen-Thiessen, E., & Borchelt, M. (1993). Health differences in advanced old age. *Ageing and Society, 13*, 619–655.

Stigsdotter Neely, A., & Bäckman, L. (1995). Effects of multifactorial memory training in old age: Generalizability across tasks and individuals. *Journal of Gerontology: Psychological Sciences, 50*, 134–140.

Stine, E., & Wingfield, A. (1990). The assessment of qualitative age differences in discourse processing. In T. M. Hess (Ed.), *Aging and cognition: Knowledge organization and utilization* (pp. 33–92). Amsterdam: North-Holland.

Storandt, M., Botwinick, J., Danziger, W. L., Berg, L., & Hughes, C. P. (1984). Psychometric differentiation of mild senile dementia of the Alzheimer type. *Archives of Neurology, 41*, 497–499.

Strittmatter, W. J., Saunders, A. M., Schmechel, D., Pericak-Vance, M., Enghild, J., Salvesen, G. S., & Roses, A. D. (1993). Apolipoprotein E: High avidity binding to beta-amyloid and increased frequency of type 4 allele in late-onset familial Alzheimer's disease. *Proceedings of the National Academy of Sciences, 90*, 1977–1981.

Sulkava, R., & Erkinjuntti, T. (1987). Vascular dementia due to cardiac arrythmias and systemic hypotension. *Acta Neurologica Scandinavica, 76*, 123–128.

Suzman, R. M., Willis, D. P., & Manton, K. G. (Eds.). (1992). *The oldest old.* New York: Oxford University Press.

Taeuber, C. M., & Rosenwaike, I. (1992). A demographic portrait of America's oldest old. In R. M. Suzman, D. P. Willis, & K. G. Manton (Eds.), *The oldest old* (pp. 17–49). New York: Oxford University Press.

Teri, L., Hughes, J. P., & Larson, E. B. (1990). Cognitive deterioration in Alzheimer's disease: Behavioral and health factors. *Journal of Gerontology: Psychological Sciences, 45*, 58–63.

Teri, L., McCurry, S. M., Edland, S. D., Kukull, W. A., & Larson, E. B. (1995). Cognitive decline in Alzheimer's disease: A longitudinal investigation of risk factors for accelerated decline. *Journal of Gerontology: Medical Sciences, 50*, 49–55.

Thompson, M. G., Heller, K., & Rody, C. A. (1994). Recruitment challenges in studying late-life depression: Do community samples adequately represent depressed older adults? *Psychology and Aging, 9*, 121–125.

Tierney, M. C., Szalai, J. P., Snow, W. G., Fisher, R. H., Nores, A., Nadon, G., Dunn, E., & St. George-Hyslop, P. H. (1996). Prediction of probable Alzheimer's disease in memory-impaired patients: A prospective longitudinal study. *Neurology, 46*, 661–665.

Tierney, M. C., Szalai, J. P., Snow, W. G., Fisher, R. H., Tsuda, T., Chi, H., McLachlan, D. R., & St. George-Hyslop, P. H. (1996). A prospective study of the clinical utility of APOE genotype in the prediction of outcome in patients with memory impairment. *Neurology, 46*, 149–154.

Uemura, K. (1988). International trends in cardiovascular diseases in the elderly. *European Heart Journal, 9*(Suppl. D), 1–8.

U.S. Bureau of the Census. (1996). *Current population reports, special studies, 65+ in the United States* (pp. 23–190). Washington, DC: U.S. Government Printing Office.

Vakil, E., Melamed, M. -D., & Even, N. (1996). Direct and indirect measures of contextual information: Older versus young adult subjects. *Aging, Neuropsychology, & Cognition, 3*, 30–36.

van Bockxmeer, F. M., & Mamotte, C. D. (1992). Apolipoprotein epsilon 4 homozygosity in young men with coronary heart disease. *The Lancet, 340*, 879–880.

van Goor, L. P., Woiski, M. D., Lagaay, A. M., Meinders, A. E., & Tak, P. P. (1995). Review: Cobalamin deficiency and mental impairment in elderly people. *Age and Ageing, 24,* 536–542.

Venkataraman, S., Walerych, W., & Johnson, B. C. (1967). Methylation of t-RNA: Effect of vitamin B_{12} deficiency in rats. *Proceedings of the Society for Experimental Biology and Medicine, 124,* 204–207.

Verhaeghen, P., Marcoen, A., & Goossens, L. (1992). Improving memory performance in the aged through mnemonic training: A meta-analytic study. *Psychology and Aging, 7,* 242–251.

Wade, D. T., Wood, V. A., & Hewer, R. L. (1988). Recovery after cognitive function soon after stroke: A study of visual neglect, attention span and verbal recall. *Journal of Neurology, Neurosurgery and Psychiatry, 51,* 10–13.

Wahley, R. W. (1988). Apolipoprotein E: Cholesterol transport protein with expanding role in cell biology. *Science, 240,* 622–630.

Wahlin, Å., Bäckman, L., Mäntylä, T., Herlitz, A., Viitanen, M., & Winblad, B. (1993). Prior knowledge and face recognition in a community-based sample of healthy, very old adults. *Journal of Gerontology: Psychological Sciences, 48,* 54–61.

Wahlin, Å., Bäckman, L., & Winblad, B. (1995). Free recall and recognition of slowly and rapidly presented words in very old age: A community-based study. *Experimental Aging Research, 21,* 251–271.

Wahlin, Å., Hill, R. D., Winblad, B., & Bäckman, L. (1996). Effects of serum vitamin B_{12} and folate status on episodic memory performance in very old age: A population-based study. *Psychology and Aging, 11,* 487–496.

Wahlin, Å., Robins-Wahlin, T. -B., Small, B. J., & Bäckman, L. (1998). Influences of thyroid stimulating hormone on cognitive functioning in very old age. *Journal of Gerontology: Psychological Sciences, 53,* 234–239.

Waldstein, S. R. (1995). Hypertension and neuropsychological function. A lifespan perspective. *Experimental Aging Research, 21,* 321–352.

Waldstein, S. R., Jennings, J. R., Ryan, C. M., Muldoon, M. F., Shapiro, A. P., Polefrone, J. M., Fazzari, T. V., & Manuck, S. B. (1996). Hypertension and neuropsychological performance in men: Interactive effects of age. *Health Psychology, 15,* 102–109.

Walker, A. E., Robins, M., & Weinfeld, F. D. (1981). Clinical findings in The Report on the National Survey of Stroke. *Stroke, 12*(Suppl. 1), 113–131.

Weingartner, H., Cohen, R. M., Murphy, D. L., Martello, J., & Gerdt, C. (1981). Cognitive processes in depression. *Archives of General Psychiatry, 38,* 42–47.

Weinstein, H. C., Hijdra, A., Van Royen, E. A., Derix, M. M. A., Walstra, G., & Jonker, C. (1991). SPECT in early- and late-onset Alzheimer's disease. *Annals of the New York Academy of Sciences, 640,* 72–79.

Welsh, K. A., Butters, N., Hughes, J. P., Mohs, R. C., & Heyman, A. (1992). Detection and staging of dementia in Alzheimer's disease: Use of the neuropsychological measures developed for the consortium to establish a registry for Alzheimer's disease. *Archives of Neurology, 49,* 448–452.

Wenger, N. K. (1988). Cardiovascular disease in the elderly. *Ciba Foundation Symposium, 34,* 106–128.

West, M. J., Coleman, P. D., Flood, D. G., & Troncoso, J. C. (1994). Differences in the pattern of hippocampal neuronal loss in normal aging and Alzheimer's disease. *The Lancet, 344,* 769–772.

West, R. L., Crook, T. L., & Barron, K. L. (1992). Everyday memory performance across the life span: Effects of age and noncognitive individual differences. *Psychology and Aging, 7,* 72–82.

Whybrow, P. C., Prange, A. J., Jr., & Treadway, C. R. (1969). Mental changes accompanying thyroid gland dysfunction: A reappraisal using objective psychological measurement. *Archives of General Psychiatry, 20,* 48–63.

Wiederholt, W. C., Cahn, D., Butters, N. M., Salmon, D. P., Kritz-Silverstein, D., & Barrett-Connor, E. (1993). Effects of age, gender and education on selected neuropsychological tests in an elderly community cohort. *Journal of the American Geriatrics Society, 41,* 639–647.

Wilkie, F. H. P. Streeten (Eds.), *Hypertension and cognitive processes* (pp. 71–82). Mount Desert, ME: Beech Hill.

Williams, J. M. G., Little, M. M., Scates, S., & Blockman, N. (1987). Memory complaints and abilities among depressed older adults. *Journal of Consulting and Clinical Psychology, 55,* 595–598.

Wittchen, H. U., Knäuper, B., & Kessler, C. (1994). Lifetime risk of depression. *British Journal of Psychiatry, 165,* 16–22.

Worrall, G., Moulton, N., & Briffett, E. (1993). Effect of Type II diabetes mellitus on cognitive function. *Journal of Family Practice, 36,* 639–643.

Yesavage, J. A., Sheikh, J. I., Freidman, L., & Tanke, E. D. (1990). Learning mnemonics: Roles of aging and subtle cognitive impairment. *Psychology and Aging, 5,* 133–137.

Zelinski, E. M., & Burnight, K. P. (1997). Sixteen-year longitudinal and time lag changes in memory and cognition in older adults. *Psychology and Aging, 12,* 503–513.

Zelinski, E. M., Gilewski, M. J., & Schaie, K. W. (1993). Individual differences in cross-sectional and 3 year longitudinal memory performance across the adult life span. *Psychology and Aging, 8,* 176–186.

Human Factors, Applied Cognition, and Aging

Wendy A. Rogers
Arthur D. Fisk
Georgia Institute of Technology

> *Applied psychology is much more than cleverness and common sense using the facts and principles found in standard texts. It is scientific work, research on problems of human nature complicated by the conditions of the shop or school or army, restricted by time and labor cost, and directed by imperative needs. . . . The secret of success in applied psychology . . . is to be rigorously scientific.*
> —Edward L. Thorndike (1919, p. 60)

Applied psychology has the potential to improve the life, work, and leisure of individuals as they grow older. In addition, it has much to offer in our understanding of cognitive aging. Contrary to some beliefs, applied psychology is not simply conducting a study to solve a specific problem. Moreover, as the Thorndike quotation implies, applied psychology is more than the direct application of basic psychological principles. Instead, applied psychology may be defined as practically relevant research that "derive[s] from real, practical problems with the intent to solve those problems, but . . . also . . . to incorporate, build on, and advance theory" (Fisk & Kirlik, 1996, pp. 2–3).

Applications of psychological research may enhance the lives of the older population (Fisk & Rogers, 1997; Howell, 1997). Efforts to reach older consumers are often hampered by lack of understanding of the requirements and preferences of this population. For example, automatic teller machines (ATMs) and other computer-based systems have been designed with little regard for the potential older adult users (e.g., Rogers & Fisk, 1997). In the area of transportation, it is crucial to consider the types of changes that should be incorporated into the design of vehicles, signs, and roadways to accommodate the older driver (Barr & Eberhard, 1991; Eberhard & Barr, 1992). Other critical transportation issues include use of public transportation and "wayfinding" (Rogers, Meyer, Walker, & Fisk, 1998). A third area that could benefit tremendously from applications of psychology involves the health care arena, including home-based medical tasks (Bogner, 1994; Czaja, 1996). For instance, as Gardner-Bonneau and Gosbee (1997) pointed out, we have designed devices for home medical care that are prone to being seriously misused by older adults.

One challenge is to design products and services so older adults can realize their maximal performance potential and are assisted in doing so. Proper age-related research conducted to advance both theory and practice can bring this to fruition (Fisk & Kirlik, 1996). One valuable source of data relevant to these age-related concerns is the area of human factors. The field of human factors is interdisciplinary, with psychology representing one of the major contributing disciplines. As illustrated in Fig. 10.1, research findings and theories from disciplines such as psychology, engineering, and computer science contribute to the knowledge base of human factors. Of course, each of these disciplines comprises a number of subdisciplines. For example, psychology includes more specific areas, such as clinical, developmental, and cognitive. The specialization of cognitive aging draws from the areas of developmental and cognitive psychology. The focus of the present chapter is on the highlighted components of Fig. 10.1. That is, we assess the current understanding of the areas of cognitive aging that are most relevant to issues studied under the umbrella of human factors. As such, we consider the following research contexts: technology and computers, transportation, and health. The overarching goal of the chapter is to illustrate how cognitive aging research has had, and will continue to have, practical relevance.

HUMAN FACTORS RESEARCH

The discipline of human factors can be defined as "the study of human beings and their interactions with products, environments, and equipment in performing tasks and activities" (Czaja, 1997a, p. 17). The term *human factors* is typically used in the United States, whereas in Europe the more common term is *ergonomics*; in this chapter, we consider these terms interchangeable.

As a science, the focus of human factors research is on the study of human capabilities, limitations, and other characteristics; as a practice, the focus is on the application of human factors knowledge to the analysis, design, evaluation, standardization, and control of systems (Hendrick, 1997). The potential of the discipline is illustrated in examples such as ensuring that pilots can safely and effectively perform in the cockpit of

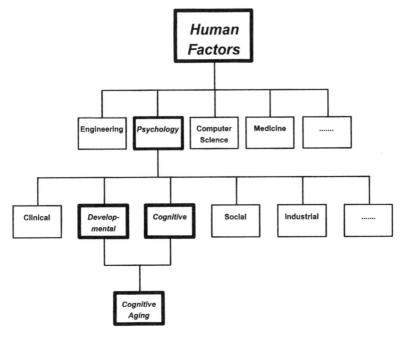

FIG. 10.1. The discipline of human factors.

high-performance jet fighters and that complex systems such as nuclear power plants can more effectively be controlled. Certainly, this discipline can be used to guide the design of tasks, devices, systems, and environments to better accommodate the aging user. Relevant applications include the interfaces between humans and other system components, such as complex hardware, computer software, environments, jobs, pill bottles, instructions, and warnings.

The underlying goal, we believe, of the field of human factors applied to aging was summed up eloquently by Rabbitt (1992):

> Demographic changes make it vital for designers to become aware of the nature and extent of age changes in physical, sensory, and cognitive abilities. The fact that these changes are complex, and interact with each other in subtle ways, make their study intellectually fascinating as well as humanely useful. The goal of helping each other to enjoy independence during the extra years that medical and social advances have won for us is surely as rewarding as concentrating on increasing sales and market penetration. Further . . . these goals are entirely compatible. (p. 137)

Rabbitt cogently pointed to the fact that the health, safety, and well-being of older adults are fundamental concerns of human factors. Although business practice may also be enhanced, this is a by-product of the main goal.

The specific steps required to advance the field of human factors and the older adult are straightforward but demanding. To paraphrase Czaja (1997b), these specific steps include (a) research to gather information concerning the types of problems encountered by older adults when interacting with products, devices, and systems; (b) data on specific aspects or demands of tasks that are problematic for older adults; (c) research on the capabilities and limitations of older adults in terms of implications for system design; (d) a principled approach to technology evaluation, from the perspective of the older adult; (e) specification of training programs designed to ensure that older adults can acquire the requisite skills to use systems.

Our view of human factors research as it relates to solving daily living problems for older adults is conceptualized in Fig. 10.2. Consistent with Czaja's (1997b) view, problem identification is the first step to problem resolution. Such identification occurs through the analysis of existing designs, technologies, and training procedures. Well-developed human factors techniques, such as task analysis, surveys, focus groups, and systematic observation, are invaluable for problem identification.

As illustrated in Fig. 10.2, human factors research is conducted both to refine our understanding of the problem and to identify potential solutions. Such research draws from existing design solutions as well as from the knowledge base of cognitive aging research. Importantly, there is a symbiotic relationship such that the results of the human factors research also ontribute to the development of new design solutions and to the corpus of cognitive aging research. Major goals of human factors research

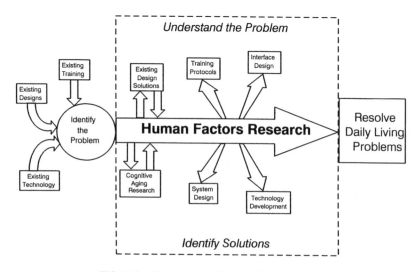

FIG. 10.2. The process of human factors research

are to develop training protocols, interface design solutions, general system design improvements, and ideas for future technology development.

The organization of the chapter follows the overview presented in Fig. 10.2 in conjunction with the basic research needs outlined by Czaja (1997b). First, we review the attempts to identify the needs and types of problems encountered by older adults. Next, within the context of technology and computers, transportation, and health-related issues, we examine the problematic aspects of tasks and identify solutions that may include specification of design improvements and training guidelines. The chapter concludes with a discussion of how to enable the usability of products and systems for older adults.

IDENTIFICATION OF NEEDS AND PROBLEMS

A driving force in our design efforts should be to enhance the daily lives of older individuals. Indeed, a primary goal of many older individuals is to maintain an independent lifestyle. What are the types of frustrations and difficulties that active older individuals encounter in their efforts to stay fully functional in a changing environment? How do we discover this information? The field of human factors provides valuable tools to address these two questions. One of the field's cornerstone tools is task analysis, which is a science-based procedure to determine the elements of a task and how these elements are arranged in time and space (Luczak, 1997). Task-analytic procedures may be used to understand the aspects of functional limitations, why these limitations exist, and ways to address the limitations.

Clark, Czaja, and Weber (1990) demonstrated the application of human factors techniques in their analysis of activities of daily living (ADLs) and instrumental activities of daily living (IADLs). ADLs include basic living tasks, such as bathing, dressing, and toileting, whereas IADLs involve more advanced tasks, such as cooking meals, housecleaning, and managing finances (Lawton & Brody, 1969). Clark et al. developed task-demand profiles as 60 older individuals (mean age = 72 years) performed a range of ADL and IADL tasks. The demand profiles provided detailed descriptions of the physical performance demands of each activity. Their data provide a rich database for the identification and prioritization of interventions. For each activity, they were able to specify the degree to which tasks required activities such as lifting, pulling, reaching, or precision grips. Those data may then be combined with the anthropometric and biomechanic data detailing the capabilities of older adults (e.g., Kroemer, 1997) to develop specific design guidelines for critical areas of the home environment, such as beds, kitchen cabinets, and appliances, as well as knobs, dials, and handles throughout the home.

Cognitive abilities play only a minor role in the successful performance of ADLs and IADLs. However, human factors methods may also be used to understand age-related difficulties in more cognitively demanding tasks. A recent analysis conducted by Rogers, Meyer, et al. (1998) included what they termed *enhanced activities of daily living* (EADLs). They defined such EADLs as the ability to adapt to new and sometimes complex technologies, a desire to learn throughout adulthood, the flexibility to adapt to declining functionality (e.g., vision or strength changes), and the willingness to accept new challenges. Such activities relevant to enhanced personal growth and leisure might include learning to use a computer, programming a videocassette recorder (VCR), or acquiring a new skill, such as playing bridge or tennis.

Rogers, Meyer, et al. (1998) assessed constraints on daily living in focus-group interviews of healthy, active adults aged 65 to 88. Individual comments about specific problems were coded along the dimensions of (a) locus of the problem (e.g., motor, visual, auditory, or cognitive), (b) the activity involved (e.g., transportation, leisure, housekeeping, or medication management), (c) whether the problem was due to task difficulty or the perception of risk, and (d) response to the limitations (e.g., persistence, cessation, compensation, or self-improvement). The data provided information about the types of difficulties experienced in everyday activities, as well as the way in which individuals responded to such difficulties. The focus-group methodology allowed participants to describe problems caused by changes in the environment and new technology. Such problems might not have been anticipated or detected in more structured processes, such as IADL-based assessments.

A common theme that emerged from the Rogers, Meyer, et al. (1998) data was the impact of new technology on the everyday lives of older adults. Participants reported encounters in their daily lives with a broad range of technologies, including home security systems, multiple-line telephones, credit card scanners, VCRs, computerized telephone menus, answering machines, entertainment centers, copy machines, cameras, microwave ovens, and fax machines. The variety of challenges that these participants faced from new technology as part of their normal activity was remarkable.

Many participants described transportation as one of the most important constraints on their activity, particularly those who could no longer drive. Many issues with driving had external sources, such as lack of a car, inadequate bus schedules, or problems in getting rides with other people. There were also problems with visual deficits in driving. Transportation was also affected by motor deficits, which caused problems getting in and out of cars and buses. The cognitive issues with transportation were largely concerned with wayfinding and to reaction time in

TABLE 10.1.
Potential Human Factors Interventions

Intervention	%	Issues	Examples
Training alone	7	Cognitive	Learning to drive, wayfinding, learning to cook, administering medical procedures, memory problems, time management, use of public transportation
Redesign alone	25	Sensory or motor	Lowering steps on buses, tools for grasping or scrubbing, lightweight garden tools, chair design, clothes fasteners, opening medicine bottles
Both training and design	21	Complex	Credit card scanners, exercise equipment, computers, home electronics, remote controls, kitchen appliances, insurance and income tax forms, security systems, banking technology, online library catalogues, cameras
Total problems remediable	53		

driving. A telling statement about the importance of transportation was made by one woman who said that "next to losing my husband, losing that car was the most important thing."

Most relevant to the present focus was the classification of whether problems raised by the participants could be addressed by human factors interventions. Each comment was coded in terms of whether it was remediable through training, design changes, or some combination of the two. Examples of these categories are presented in Table 10.1. More than half (53%) of the problems reported by the Rogers, Meyer, et al. (1998) sample of quite diverse older people (i.e., in terms of culture, socioeconomic status, and life history) had the potential to be improved by human factors intervention. Problems that were not directly remediable through human factors interventions were transportation problems (such as lack of a car), physical problems (such as fatigue or arthritis), and other general concerns (such as fear of crime or financial difficulties).

There is convergence between some areas for which older adults reported difficulties and important foci of age-related human factors research. Such areas include technology and computers, transportation, and health. These domains constitute the primary focus of the remainder of the chapter.

TECHNOLOGY AND COMPUTERS

Technological innovations occur at a rapid pace. In recent years, for example, the dominant audio technology involves compact disks, remote control televisions are common, and most individuals own VCRs. In the financial realm, credit card scanners in stores, direct deposits, telephone banking, and ATMs have revolutionized the transfer of money. However, new technologies are only as successful as they are easy to use by all members of the user population. The field of human factors must ensure that older adults are provided with the necessary information and training to successfully use current and future technologies (Fisk & Rogers, 1997).

Historically, the design of technology has been a responsibility of engineers, whereas the discovery of fundamental human capabilities and limitations has been a task for the behavioral scientist. The demands (both in terms of opportunities and risks) of designing technology for older adults are clearly pointing the way for the behavioral scientist to take a more active lead in developing design specifications for everyday and advanced technology.

To design effective systems and training programs in support of age-related performance capabilities, we must answer fundamental questions concerning aging and complex task performance. For example, knowing that older adults have working memory deficits, inhibitory problems, or slower information processing is very important and necessary; but it is not sufficient for motivating solutions for design-related problems. It is the understanding of the interactions of these age-related characteristics of cognition, manifested often in relatively complex activities, that can form the foundation of design principles. In other words, we need to know when there is need for design improvements versus training solutions and how that need should be fulfilled. Without answers to these questions, designs will likely be driven by technologies rather than by problems and principles, and solutions put forward may be ineffective or even worse, the source of new problems.

Input Devices

There is consensus that as people age, motor behaviors change such that, compared with younger adults, older adults take longer to make similar movements, their ability to maintain continuous movements declines, coordination is disrupted, and movements are more variable (for a review, see Vercruyssen, 1997). Age-related declines in movement control have direct relevance to the use of input devices, such that older adults have difficulty using a mouse to position a cursor on a computer. Walker, Philbin, and Fisk (1997; see also Walker, Philbin, & Spruell, 1996) assessed the ability of young (mean age = 22 years) and older adults (mean age = 70 years) to use a computer mouse to position a cursor over a target. They manipulated the distance to the target (100–500 pixels) and the size of the target (4–32 pixels squared). Walker et al. (1997) measured four factors as potential sources of age-related differences in movement control in the context of their mouse task: poorer perceptual feedback, increased "noise" in the motor pathway, strategy-related differences, and the ability to produce force. They were able to isolate these factors, and their results revealed increased motor noise for the older adults, slower verification times (suggesting poorer perceptual feedback), and more conservative movements (suggesting strategy differences). Interestingly, older adults were able to produce as much force as the young adults. Thus, the Walker et al. (1997) study suggests that the source of the age-related performance declines in mouse control is a combination of poorer perceptual feedback, increased noise in the motor pathway, and strategy-related differences with older adults.

Walker, Millians, and Worden (1996) applied the understanding of age-related declines in movement control to the development of an adaptive interface. Using a computer mouse, they manipulated the *gain adjustment*, which is the ratio of the pixels to the mouse movement. That is, with a high gain ratio, fast mouse movements result in relatively larger movements in space, whereas with a lower gain ratio, increasing the speed of movement has less influence on the amount of spatial movement. Walker et al. predicted that manipulating the gain adjustment might allow the older adults to compensate for their increased motor noise. Participants were required to use a mouse to move a cursor across a computer screen from a start box to a target. The distance to the target (50–400 pixels) and the size of the target (3–24 pixels squared) were varied across trials. They also compared four levels of gain ratio. The results showed that older adults did benefit from the adjusted mouse movement ratio: Their performance was best when the acceleration function had a medium slope. The benefits of mouse adjustment were especially evident for the smaller targets. The changes in the gain ratio had minimal effect on the performance of the younger adults. Walker et al. suggested that adjusting the acceleration of the mouse would be an easy way to improve computer usability for older adults.

Walker, Millians, and Worden (1996) also observed that for the very small target item (3 pixels squared), older adults had difficulty hitting the target: Their accuracy rate was only 75% for this target compared with over 90% for the other targets (6, 12, or 24 pixels squared). These data suggest that there may be a critical minimum target size below which older individuals will be unable to use a mouse to accurately position a cursor.

Worden, Walker, Bharat, and Hudson (1997) investigated other interface design solutions to compensate for age-related declines in movement control. They evaluated three primary independent variables:

1. *Icon stickiness.* The mouse-to-cursor gain (i.e., ratio of mouse movement to cursor movement) is dynamically adjusted when the cursor

moves over an icon or button. Thus, as the mouse approaches the item, the gain ratio is lowered, enabling fine control and allowing the user to more easily stop the mouse on the icon or button.

2. *Area cursor.* The cursor becomes a large square, which makes it easier to see and requires less movement precision. If the cursor covers two items or buttons, the default is the center of the square, where a crosshair is presented.

3. *Dynamic velocity-based gain adjustment.* The stickiness of the icons is adjusted when the cursor is moving below a set speed. Thus, an icon or button will only slow the movement of the cursor if the cursor is moving slowly.

Worden et al. found that a combination of these variables yielded the best performance for older adults. That is, for an area cursor with sticky icons with adaptive gain control, older adults' performance was improved by about 40%. An important by-product of attending to age-related issues was that this interface also improved young adults' performance by about 20%.

The research by Walker and colleagues is a prime example of the approach of identifying the source of age-related differences, implementing and evaluating potential design solutions, and, as a result, improving the performance of both older and younger adults (e.g., Walker, Millians, et al., 1996; Walker, Philbin, et al., 1996; Walker, Philbin, et al., 1997; Worden et al., 1997). Given the prevalence of point-and-click interfaces, age-related difference in the ability to use a mouse could be a major impediment to computer use by older adults. Walker and colleagues demonstrated how the understanding of age-related changes in human movement control could be applied to the design of an adaptive interface to allow easier and efficient computer input control across the adult life span.

Computers

Computers have the potential to improve the lives of older adults in a number of ways. Computers can increase access to services, provide alternative communication options, convert text into braille printouts, provide access to health information, handle banking needs, and facilitate social interactions (Czaja, 1997b; Meeks, 1994). Many older adults currently use computers, and often those that do not are interested in learning (Rogers, Cabrera, Walker, Gilbert, & Fisk, 1996; Rogers, Meyer, et al., 1998; Rousseau, Jamieson, Rogers, Mead, & Sit, 1998).

Studies of the acquisition of computer skills by older adults have revealed that older adults can successfully learn to use computers for a variety of tasks. Older adults have been trained to use electronic message systems (Czaja, Guerrier, Nair, & Landauer, 1993; Morrell, Park, Mayhorn, & Echt, 1996); text editing (Charness, Schumann, & Boritz, 1992; Czaja, Hammond, Blascovich, & Swede, 1989; Elias, Elias, Robbins, & Gage, 1987); and simulated work tasks, such as data entry, file modification, and inventory management (Czaja & Sharit, 1993).

The critical issues involved in training older adults to use computers have recently been reviewed by Czaja (1996, 1997b), Charness, Bosman, Kelley, and Mottram (1996), and Morrell and Echt (1996, 1997). Together, these reviews provide an excellent summary of the recent literature in this area. As such, we reiterate only briefly their main conclusions:

- Older adults are willing to use computers for routine tasks, such as correspondence, financial management, and information access.
- Older adults are capable of learning to use computers for a variety of tasks.
- Older adults are typically slower to acquire computer skills, with rates ranging from 1.2 to 2.5 times slower than younger adults.
- Computer systems should be designed to accommodate age-related cognitive and perceptual declines.
- Anxiety about use of computers is reduced as a result of computer experience.
- Computer manuals and instructional materials should be designed with the visual capabilities of older adults in mind.
- Learning appears to be better when trainees are paired with a partner or taught in small groups compared with learning alone or in large groups.
- Self-paced instruction enhances learning relative to fixed-paced instruction.
- Menu-based systems are easier to learn than command-based systems.

Morrell and Echt (1996) reviewed the computer-training studies for young and older adults and concluded that the most successful training appears to be that which reduces the cognitive (i.e., working memory) demands for the learner. Such training techniques tended to be beneficial for both young and older adults. They also suggested that cognitive mechanisms that have been shown to decline for older adults appear to be influential in the acquisition of computer skills, namely, working memory, text comprehension, spatial ability, and perceptual speed. As such, Morrell and Echt's general recommendation for optimizing training was to develop protocols that reduce demands on these cognitive mechanisms. This may be achieved through the development of instructional texts written in simple language, the addition of illustrations to text, and the development of online tutorials presented on the system to be trained.

ATMs

ATMs have provided a platform with which to test basic issues of training, transfer, and retention of skills for young and older adults. The system is relatively simple, yet using ATMs is more complex than many laboratory tasks used to study skills. One goal of human factors professionals is to ensure that, if individuals wish to interact with a system (e.g., use an ATM), sufficient analysis and design have been carried out to remove impediments to successful system interaction. Thus, studies of ATM systems are not designed to increase ATM use per se. Instead, the goal is to ensure that, if individuals wish to use an ATM, the system is designed to enable efficient interaction.

An extensive survey of adults aged 18 to 91 conducted by Rogers, Cabrera, et al. (1996) assessed the types of difficulties that ATM users have when using the system. Rogers et al. reported that more than 10% of all the respondents rated the following as problems that occurred frequently:

- Machine running out of money
- Remembering to record transactions
- Being unable to see the screen well
- Putting the card in the wrong way
- Having to wait in line to use the machine
- The machine working too slowly.

Along with the above problems, older ATM users (aged 65–91) also reported frequently having difficulty with the following:

- Getting the amount of money they wanted
- Understanding how to do what they wanted on the ATM.

A combination of design changes and the provision of ATM training could correct the majority of these problems. To comply with the Americans with Disabilities Act of 1990, larger screens, voice guidance, and braille indicators are also being incorporated into some recent models of ATMs (e.g., Fassett, 1991; Melia, 1991). Other new technologies currently being incorporated in the design of ATMs include touch screens, pen input, multimedia, and speech recognition (Henneman & Rubini, 1993), although these technologies may impose new problems for all users.

An important finding of the Rogers, Cabrera, et al. (1996) survey was that as many as 21% of the nonusers said that they would be interested in learning to use an ATM if they were provided with training. Thus, it was not the case that nonusers did not want to use ATMs. In their interviews with older adult nonusers, Rogers, Gilbert, and Cabrera (1997) reported comments such as "I don't know how to use it, and I don't want to embarrass myself" and "I don't like to feel rushed when I am trying to learn." Even the ATM users believed that "the bank should offer training or a chance to practice with the machine" (42% overall, 52% of adults over age 65; Rogers, Cabrera, et al., 1996). To provide new users with the opportunity to interact with ATMs, some banks have even developed mobile ATMs that can be transported to different areas and used to demonstrate the services of the system (Ferring, 1991).

The survey data suggest a clear need for ATM training. The critical question concerns the type of training that would be optimal. Rogers, Fisk, Mead, Walker, and Cabrera (1996) developed a computerized simulation of an ATM with which they investigated training protocols. They developed an online tutorial (step-by-step tutorial presented on the computer) based on the instructional design and cognitive aging literatures. The tutorial provided hands-on, interactive experience with the system. This type of active, self-paced training has proved to be particularly beneficial for older adults (e.g., Belbin, 1970; Czaja et al., 1989). The tutorial also provided specific practice on the consistent components of the task, and the skill acquisition literature has clearly demonstrated the importance of consistent practice (e.g., Schneider & Shiffrin, 1977). Lastly, the tutorial provided the equivalent of worked examples, thereby reducing the cognitive load of the trainee. Sweller and colleagues have shown the importance of reducing cognitive load for young adults (e.g., Sweller, Chandler, Tierney, & Cooper, 1990), although little research has investigated these effects for older adults.

Rogers, Fisk, et al. (1996) found that the online tutorial did enable the older adults to perform transactions on the ATM simulator. Their performance was significantly faster and more accurate compared with a control group that received only a general description of the ATM system. In addition, participants who had received training with the online tutorial were better able to transfer their learning to novel tasks on a novel ATM. These participants were also compared with two other training groups: one that had received step-by-step text-based instructions and another that had received text instructions accompanied by pictures of the ATM at each step of the transaction. For acquisition and transfer performance, the performance of the online tutorial group was more accurate and faster than these other groups, but these differences were not statistically significant.

The Rogers, Fisk, et al. (1996) data demonstrated that older adults could benefit from online training in learning how to use an ATM. Mead and Fisk (1998) manipulated the specific characteristics of the online tutorial to determine the optimal method and to compare training benefits across young and older adults (the Rogers, Fisk, et al., 1996, study tested only older adults). Mead and Fisk compared two online tutors (conceptual instructions vs. action instructions) that present instructional text super-imposed on the relevant system state. The concept training was analogous to providing declarative knowledge about the system, whereas the action training was designed to be consistent with the procedural aspects of the task (Anderson, 1983). Mead and Fisk found that for the young adults, type of training did not differentially affect performance. However, for older adults, action training was associated with faster and more accurate immediate performance and superior retention performance across a 1-month interval. Presenting the procedural information to the older adults during training was more beneficial than presenting the declarative information. These data suggest that it is more important to teach the older adults how to perform the transactions rather than to simply tell them what to do. The results clearly point to the need to evaluate different age groups when designing and evaluating computer-based training programs. The results also show the value of using cognitive aging theory in motivating the development of training design. The training intervention must still be tested, but theory focuses the application by reducing the number of plausible alternative design choices.

One benefit of using the ATM to study issues of training, transfer, and retention is that it is representative of many current technologies. That is, most ATMs are hierarchically organized, require selection of information from multiple choices, and do not offer the opportunity to go backward in the system. Consequently, training principles derived from this system are applicable to other categories of technology with similar requirements.

Computerized Information Retrieval

One increasingly pervasive technological tool is the computerized card catalogue system used by libraries. In fact, many libraries are completely doing away with their old-fashioned card catalogue files. An assumption by some libraries is that anyone can learn to use these systems. However, older adults who have not been exposed to similar technologies, including computers, may have difficulty learning to use such systems. Rousseau, Jamieson, et al. (1998) conducted a survey of over 1,000 individuals to evaluate the characteristics of a sample of people who have access to such a system on a university campus. Their data provide valuable information about the users of the system and the difficulties that they encounter.

Quantitative and qualitative analyses revealed that even respondents with a basic level of knowledge about how to use the system still experienced problems (e.g., not finding a book) when using advanced commands. Findings from the survey highlight the importance of training and online help with regard to information systems.

To directly examine age-related differences in online search performance, Mead, Sit, Rogers, Rousseau, and Jamieson (1999; see also Mead, Jamieson, Rousseau, Sit, Rogers, 1996) measured the performance of younger and older adults who were novice-level users of such systems. Participants were provided with a brief overview of the system and then asked to complete 10 search tasks of varying levels of difficulty. For example, a simple author search was "Look for two books by John Grisham," whereas a complex disjunctive search was "Look for two books by Susan Faludi or Naomi Wolf." None of the participants had experience with computerized library searches, but some participants did have computer experience; hence, level of computer experience was assessed as a variable. Analysis of the transaction logs (i.e., every keystroke entered by the participant) yielded the following measures: success in searching, types of errors made in database query-construction, and subsequent error recovery. Overall, the young adults' performance was superior for the more complex searches. In addition, for all searches, older adults entered more search commands per task, made more query-construction errors, and recovered from their errors less efficiently. As mentioned, Mead et al. were able to compare online search performance while equating for general computer experience for young and older adults. Performance comparisons were made for young and older adults with similar levels of computer experience. The age differences in performance remained. Thus, differential training needs for older adults cannot be dismissed as being solely due to differences in experience. However, within the older adult group, performance was superior for those older adults who had computer experience compared with older adults who did not. These data demonstrate the benefits of general computer experience for the acquisition of system-specific skills.

Westerman, Davies, Glendon, Stammers, and Matthews (1995) conducted a study to determine if age-related differences in computer performance could be minimized through the manipulation of the network structures and menu characteristics. They found that both young and older adults performed faster and more accurately on an information retrieval task when a linear structure was used (i.e., a list of files vs. hierarchical, multilevel organization). In addition, performance was better when the menu for the system was explicitly provided. The linear structure places fewer demands on working memory, and the explicit menu provides a memory aid. Both of these manipulations provide environmental support for the task and improved performance. Although the manipulations used in the Westerman et al. study did not reduce age-related differences in performance, their data do provide suggestive evidence for methods to improve information retrieval performance for both young and older adults.

In summary, the research reviewed on technology and computers has demonstrated that older adults are interested in using new technologies (contrary to some popular stereotypes). As important, the research has documented the importance of understanding the capabilities of the user population for the development of training and design solutions to overcome age-related declines in cognitive, speed, and motor abilities. Clearly, the age (and the abilities) of the user must be considered. Moreover, the features of the system will be influential. One must consider the characteristics of the interface, the information-processing requirements, and the goals of the user. Together, these variables will determine the degree to which there will be age-related differences in task performance. In addition, knowledge of such variables, and their interactions, will enable the development of interventions through training and design.

TRANSPORTATION

In the minds of some older adults, mobility is equated with independence: As long as they can get to the grocery store, the physician's office, and the bank, for example, they can continue to function as an independent. For many individuals, especially those in rural areas, driving may be their only option. Others may have the option of using public transportation. In either case, human factors research, led by attention to cognitive aging theory, is necessary to ensure the safety and mobility of older adults.

Driving

According to the U.S. Department of Transportation, for 1994, there were 15.7 million older (over age 70) licensed drivers, which was a 45% increase from the number in 1984. Moreover, although older people compose only 9% of the population, they account for 13% of all traffic fatalities and 18% of all pedestrian fatalities. Consequently, ensuring the safety of older drivers must be a high priority of human factors research. Efforts toward minimizing the risks to older drivers are discussed in two special issues of *Human Factors* devoted to the Safety and Mobility of Elderly Drivers (Barr & Eberhard, 1991; Eberhard & Barr, 1992).

A critical question involves the determination of which older drivers should continue to drive and which should not. One approach would be to disallow anyone over age 65 or 70 from driving. Obviously, this is not a reasonable solution, given the fact of individual differences. Instead, researchers have attempted to try to understand the individual-difference variables that are predictive of driving success. One such variable is the visual field that can be processed during a brief glance—the useful field of view (UFOV). The UFOV varies as a function of the duration, salience, and eccentricity of the target, as well as the degree of competing attentional demands (Ball & Owsley, 1991). Ball and Owsley have demonstrated that aging can bring with it a dramatic restriction in the UFOV such that, conceptually speaking, the driver may be looking out of a peephole (see also Owsley, Ball, Sloane, Roenker, & Bruni, 1991).

As reviewed by Ball and Owsley (1991), visual tests alone, such as static or dynamic visual acuity, typically account for less than 5% of the variance in accident rates and thus are not very useful for identifying at-risk drivers. However, Ball and Owsley reported that a measure of UFOV accounted for 13% of the variance of all accidents in a sample of older drivers and 21% of the variance of intersection accidents in the same sample. The UFOV measure provides an index of preattentive visual attention. It is at this stage of attention that visual events, such as the approach of vehicles in peripheral vision, are first noticed. The greater predictability of UFOV compared with strictly visual measures illustrates the importance of attentional components for driving.

Although older adults may have severely restricted UFOVs, preattentive attention (and hence UFOV) can be improved through training by as much as 133% after only 5 days of training (Ball, Beard, Roenker, Miller, & Griggs, 1988). Importantly, these improvements were maintained over a 6-month period without additional training. Thus, the construct of UFOV provides a potentially valuable technique for identifying at-risk drivers and for providing training to potentially minimize such risks.

Perceptual style (i.e., field dependence or independence) also plays a role in driving behavior (e.g., Gilmore, Wenk, Naylor, & Stove, 1992; Panek, Barrett, Sterns, & Alexander, 1977). For example, Shinar, McDowell, Rackoff, & Rockwell (1978) showed that field dependence or independence was an important factor in the ability of drivers to adjust their searching pattern. Lambert and Fleury (1994) demonstrated that performance on the Embedded Figures Test (a measure of perceptual style) accounted for more than 53% of the variance in a task wherein participants were required to recognize road signs in contexts of varying perceptual complexity. Field-dependent individuals, especially older adults, were much slower to recognize and respond to familiar traffic signs (e.g., stop signs or yield signs) presented against complex backgrounds. An encouraging fact is that Lambert and Fleury improved the performance of the older, field-dependent individuals by increasing the readability of the traffic signs. Readability was improved by a reduction in the spatial frequency (i.e., reducing fine details) of the information on the signs and an increase in the color contrast. Awareness of potential difficulties for older adults reading signs might lead to improvements in sign visibility that would benefit all drivers.

The provision of additional information signs may also be beneficial for older drivers. For example, left-turn intersections are a frequent site of traffic accidents for all drivers, but particularly for older adults. According to the U.S. Department of Transportation statistics for 1994, older drivers were nine times more likely than younger drivers to be turning left when involved in an accident. Staplin and Fisk (1991) assessed the benefits of providing precuing signs to prime drivers about an upcoming left-turn intersection. Young and older drivers were tested in a simulated driving context wherein they were required to make a decision to either make a left turn or wait. Older adults made the wrong decision (elected to make the turn when they did not have the right-of-way) significantly more frequently than did young adults. These age differences were especially striking when the traffic signal consisted only of a green light. Older adults may have had difficulties inhibiting the automatic process to go in the presence of a green light. Data in other contexts suggest that inhibiting well-learned automatic processes is particularly difficult for older adults (Rogers & Fisk, 1991). Age differences in incorrect response were minimized when a red light was presented along with a sign to wait for the left-turn signal. Both young and older drivers benefited from the provision of signs in advance that provided right-of-way information. Priming the drivers about the proper behavior for the intersection improved decision-making accuracy as well as latency. However, it is crucial that the additional sign corresponds directly to the meaning of the signal. Szymkowiak, Fisher, and Connerney (1997) showed that both young and older adults will make more errors if there is any incompatibility between the sign and signal information.

Additional evidence that older adults can benefit from environmental cues comes from a recent study by Walker, Fain, Fisk, and McGuire (1997). They assessed the decision-making capabilities of young and older experienced drivers in response to information about road conditions (e.g., congestion) and alternative route choices. Walker et al. found that older and younger adults made the same route decisions with equivalent optimality. These data suggest that task familiarity helps to maintain the quality of decision making as individuals age. In addition, these data demonstrate that older experienced drivers will benefit from new highway information systems that provide real-time information about traffic conditions.

Driver education has also proved to be a successful means of improving the driving skills of older individuals. Ashman, Bishu, Foster, and McCoy (1994) conducted a 2-year study of older drivers to evaluate methods of improving driving performance. In their initial analysis, they found that older adults' (aged 66 to 81) driving knowledge was deficient in the following areas: "(a) right-of-way rules and procedures for crossing and turning left at intersections, (b) safe following distances, (c) correct lane positioning and selection, and (d) proper procedures for backing and parking maneuvers" (p. 569). Ashman et al. also conducted a field test of driver performance wherein they measured maneuvers most typically related to older driver accidents, such as left turns and approaches to uncontrolled intersections. They compared the benefits of physical therapy to improve posture, perceptual therapy to improve visual discriminations, a general driver education course, and combinations of the education course and either physical or perceptual therapy. After the 8-week intervention, all of these groups showed improved driving performance compared with a control group. There was a trend for the combined perceptual therapy and driver education group to improve the most. Future efforts to understand the benefits of such interventions should focus on determining the aspects of the therapy and education programs that were most effective.

Waller (1991) has suggested that there are four primary areas in which modifications can be made to improve the safety of older drivers: "driver assessment, driver modification, vehicle modification, and highway modifications" (p. 503). Advances have been made in three of these areas, as is evidenced by the human factors research we have reviewed. Driver assessment programs may be improved tremendously through the inclusion of measures of UFOV (e.g., Ball & Owsley, 1991). Driver modification has involved training programs to increase UFOV (Ball et al., 1988) as well as more general driver training programs (e.g., Ashman et al., 1994). Highway modification suggestions include increasing the contrast of signs to improve readability (Lambert & Fleury, 1994) and the provision of additional signs to prime drivers with advance cues (Staplin & Fisk, 1991). In addition, research suggests that older adults will be able to benefit from novel highway technology that relies on well-learned decision-making ability (Walker, Fain, et al., 1997).

Vehicle modification represents an area in which there has been little published research designed to improve the driving capabilities of older adults. There are some efforts to develop smart vehicle technologies, known as intelligent vehicle highway systems (IVHS), which incorporate communication technology and displays within the vehicle to allow the transmission of information about roadway and traffic conditions (Lerner, 1994). Some technologies may even provide perceptual enhancements, such as infrared images, to improve night vision. Other technologies focus on providing navigational aids. While these technologies may aid the older driver (as demonstrated by Walker, Fain, et al., 1997), the needs and capabilities of the older individual must be considered in the development of such systems. For example, Sixsmith and Sixsmith (1993) reported that older drivers may be somewhat ambivalent about these supposed improvements. That is, they recognize the potential benefits but are concerned about potential problems as well. Such problems may include alarms that are startling or distracting, unwillingness to relinquish control of the vehicle (as required by some anticollision devices), and skepticism about devices that may make driving even more complicated. Thus, although IVHS may have some potential in the future for improving driving for adults of all ages, further research is clearly needed to refine such systems.

Public Transportation

The ability to make use of public transportation may be an important determinant of the independence of an older adult. Many older adults no longer feel competent to drive or have lost their driver's license. For some, previous access to a private automobile may have minimized contact with public transportation. In addition, older adults often relocate during retirement. These factors illustrate the need for easy access to public transportation systems. As driving skills decline, many older individuals may come to rely more on public transportation, such as buses and subways. Pushkar, Arbuckle, Conway, Chaikelson, and Maag (1997) found that 86% of the nearly 300 individuals they asked reported using some form of public transportation and 61% reported using public transportation at least monthly. Although the use of public transportation obviates age-related problems due to driving abilities, new issues arise that may impede successful use of public transportation modes. Such issues comprise both physical and cognitive components.

In the Rogers, Meyer, et al. (1998) focus-group study, older adults reported difficulty getting on and off buses and subways because of the design of the vehicles. Problematic aspects included high stairs, minimal handholds, and insufficient time. Rittner and Kirk (1995) questioned 1,083 older individuals about their use of public transportation. Their participants reported the following difficulties they encountered with public transportation: "Lack of shelter at many bus stops, dirty windows that compromise failing eyesight, problems entering and exiting most buses, fear of injury in crowded buses, and unsympathetic drivers" (Rittner &

Kirk, 1995, p. 366). Rittner and Kirk also investigated the ramifications of problems with public transportation. In their sample, availability of transportation was a significant predictor of health care use.

The difficulty in learning route systems is often a major impediment to public transportation use. There is a variety of passenger information that can aid the use of public transportation—for example, bus stop and terminal signage, route maps, brochures, and timetables. However, there has been very little research to determine whether such passenger information is appropriate for older adults. By appropriate, we mean whether the information transmission enables older adults to see it well (encoding), understand the meaning (comprehension), and remember the information until it is needed (retention). There are substantial data in the cognitive aging literature to suggest that there are age-related declines in encoding, comprehension, and retention of information (for a review, see Kausler, 1991).

Although there has been no direct measurement of how older adults can use such information systems, there is evidence to suggest that older adults do not show the same benefit from different types of information presentation. For example, Lipman and Caplan (1992) demonstrated that older adults were actually hindered by an accompanying diagram during the acquisition of route knowledge based on a slide presentation. The requirement for an abstraction from the map to the actual environment depicted on the slides was difficult for the older adults. However, in a later study, Caplan and Lipman (1995) did find that older individuals benefited from learning aids for the acquisition of route knowledge. Age differences were eliminated for older men (compared with younger men) when the aids provided landmark information. Interestingly, age-related differences for women were found only when landmark information was provided (i.e., younger women benefited from the additional information, whereas the additional information interfered for the older women). These data suggest the need for more understanding of optimal information presentation for younger and older adults and for men and women.

Given the prevalence of public transportation in cities today (as well as in large metropolitan airports), and the increased reliance of older adults on such methods of transportation, the physical and cognitive components of the reported difficulties deserve more attention. The physical problems can most effectively be dealt with through improved design of the buses and subway systems and the development of aids such as step stools or handholds. The cognitive issues of interpreting schedules and maps will require the input of cognitive psychologists. Additional research is necessary to identify the optimal methods for information presentation for adults of all ages. Access to public transportation may improve the quality of life for older adults, as it has been suggested that the "elderly can benefit from community mobility skills training which ultimately expands their social horizons" (Taylor & Taylor, 1989, p. 466).

HEALTH-RELATED ISSUES

A review of the literature indicates that very little research effort has gone into addressing human factors, aging, and health care. The research that has been conducted is in specific topic areas such as, medication adherence (e.g., Park & Jones, 1997) and general assistive technology (e.g., Fernie, 1997). Although some efforts have been undertaken to develop device usability requirements within the medical device area (e.g., Koncelik, 1982; Wiklund, 1992), a systematic human factors attack with the goal to guide design is needed. Two exemplar problem domains where vigorous research efforts are needed are telemedicine and warnings.

Video-Mediated Remote Health Care

Telemedicine is defined as "the electronic transmission of patient information to a clinician at a remote site" (Gardner-Bonneau & Gosbee, 1997, p. 234). Because of the advent of videoconferencing, telemedicine has the potential to greatly expand health care capabilities. Hubble, Pahwa, Micalek, Thomas, and Koller (1993) provided a demonstration of the promise of this technology. In their study, physicians assessed patients with Parkinson's disease through videoconferencing or with the patient in the clinic. The results of their study showed no differences in live versus remote patient evaluation. Further, the patients reported liking the video system and subjectively felt that it improved their access to care. Many of the elderly patients in this study lived miles away from the nearest neurologist; thus, it is not surprising that they perceived an improvement in access to care with the remote system. The promise of video-mediated remote care is enhanced by the dramatically decreasing cost of such systems (Internet access, low-priced personal computers, and inexpensive video units). Such systems also hold promise for improved "self-care" and on-demand aid for home-care providers. Unfortunately, numerous design-related issues must be addressed for this technology to deliver on its promises.

The videoconferencing system is an exemplar of a complex human–computer interface. The system can be subdivided into five components: communication technology, conferencing technology, the physical environment, the social environment, and the task environment. Successful interaction of these components can lead to effective communication and system use. Weak links in any of the components degrade system effectiveness. Major issues involve ease of instruction for use, visual capabilities and quality (for mimicking face-to-face visual cues), effects of audio and video synchronicity, compression and frame rate, image resolution, and communication issues. One also must consider a rather diverse user population, including physicians, older patients, and other professional and lay health care providers. Furthermore, it is not clear what tasks are appropriate for videoconferencing, especially from an age-related medical perspective. Understanding tasks and devising useful classification schemes is critical to future development of this technology. For example, research is needed to determine which aspects of tasks are supportable with this technology as well as which aspects of tasks are influenced by videocommunications. Certainly, an understanding of how the video medium acts as a filter to alter task performance is needed.

The study of video-mediated communication has been ongoing in one form or another for quite some time (e.g., Chapanis, 1971; Short, Williams, & Christie, 1976), yet examination from an age-related perspective is quite limited. Early work in this area was limited by the then-current technology and focused mainly on collaborative work groups. Research intensified as desktop videoconferencing systems became more viable products. Unfortunately, age-related design specifications have yet to be determined. Moreover, a body of work specifically examining the combined influence of system characteristics, task requirements, and age-related person characteristics (perceptual, cognitive, and movement control) has yet to emerge. Often those involved with the development of these systems wrongly equate clinical efficacy with viability and usability across the diversity of users of the systems (Gardner-Bonneau & Gosbee, 1997). Research addressing issues of video-mediated remote health care will provide answers to questions specifically related to this technology. However, because of the richness of the problem domain, coupled with the ability to constrain the research environment for experimental control, the results should generalize to human–computer interaction issues.

The Warning Process

Consumers face an array of products, medications, and tools that may be hazardous to their health or safety. Potential dangers are typically conveyed through warning labels. The costs of misunderstanding warning information may be particularly problematic for older adults. For example, 75% of older adults report using prescription drugs and 82% report using over-the-counter drugs. Approximately 15% of acute hospital admissions for patients over age 70 have been attributed to adverse drug reactions, indicating that warnings may be going unheeded for this population (Kart, Dunkle, & Lockery, 1994).

Understanding how best to present warning information is a complex undertaking. There are a large number of variables that can affect the degree to which a warning is ultimately complied with (Rogers, Lamson, & Rousseau, in press). Changes in cognition with age may exacerbate the effects of particular variables on the warning process. For example, symbols are frequently used to convey information. However, although the results are somewhat mixed, the preponderance of evidence suggests that symbol comprehension is impaired for older adults. Age-related differences favoring young adults have been found for information on a prescription medication label (Morrell, Park, & Poon, 1989), fire safety symbols (Collins & Lerner, 1982), traffic signs (Lambert & Fleury, 1994), mine safety symbols (Collins, 1983), and hazard symbols for household products (Easterby & Hakiel, 1981).

In one study of symbol comprehension, Hancock, Rogers, and Fisk (1998) surveyed 82 adults over age 60. Participants were queried about their experiences with warning information on household products and medicines. Only 22% of the sample reported ever having difficulty interpreting symbol information presented on warning labels. However, when presented with various symbols and asked to explain the meaning of the symbols, these older adults were quite inaccurate for some of the symbols. For example, the percentage of participants who were completely or partially incorrect in their interpretation of symbols was 76% for "flammable," 29% for "no open flame," 75% for "eyewash," and 76% for the generic warning symbol that is meant to attract attention (i.e., an exclamation point inside of triangle). Consequently, although the use of symbols in warning communication may have tremendous potential, symbols must be chosen that successfully convey information to all age groups.

Additional information about the effects of aging on the warning process may come from the cognitive aging literature. For example, selective attention involves choosing the information from the environment that will receive further processing. Thus, product users must be able to selectively attend to warning information in sometimes cluttered environments (Wogalter & Laughery, 1996). Age differences have been reported for laboratory-based selective attention tasks (for a review, see Hartley, 1992). However, Hartley also reported the encouraging finding that older adults are able to benefit from cues to the relevant information. Thus, cues to warnings, such as color or highlighting, might prove especially beneficial for older adults.

Working memory declines for older adults have been frequently documented (e.g., Salthouse, 1991). Reading warning labels can be working memory intensive if they are very complex. Also, if part of the warning process requires step-by-step directions, the need to maintain the steps in working memory may cause difficulties for older adults. Future research studies should investigate the importance of age-related working memory declines for the effectiveness of the warning process.

Prospective memory involves remembering to perform actions in the future. At least for some types of tasks, prospective memory declines with age (see A. D. Smith, 1997). There has been remarkably little research conducted on the importance of prospective memory to the warning process. However, it would seem to be of tremendous importance for warnings about medications. Individuals might read the warnings associated with a particular medicine the first time they take it. Every time thereafter, however, they would have to remember the instructions and warning-related information, such as not to consume alcohol while taking the product or to take with food or milk. The importance of this variable remains to be empirically determined.

Rousseau, Lamson, and Rogers (1998) provided recommendations for the design of warnings on the basis of documented changes in age-related perceptual and cognitive abilities. Their recommendations also compensate for age related changes in color vision, contrast sensitivity, glare sensitivity, temporal resolution, visual acuity, visual search, and changes in auditory perception. They also made some initial recommendations about designs that may compensate for age-related declines in working memory, language comprehension, prospective memory, and symbol comprehension. Briefly, these recommendations are to provide cues to aid memory for warning information; to use simple, explicit sentences; to provide interactive warnings that are available when needed, and to include older adults in the evaluation samples for symbol development.

ENABLING USABILITY

Vanderheiden (1997) has provided an excellent tutorial on three primary approaches available within the human factors' arsenal to address usability problems: changing the person, developing assistive tools, and designing for better usability. Each of these approaches clearly demonstrates the symbiotic relationship that exists between basic, fundamental scientific knowledge and solving fundamental applied problems.

Consider changing the individual. Certainly medical approaches such as medication or surgery may come to mind when this approach is mentioned. In addition, knowledge gained from cognitive aging researchers can be critically applied to design educational programs, design skill development techniques, or refresher courses to change the individual through improved knowledge or skills.

The development of assistive tools (or devices) suggests technologies such as eyeglasses or wheelchairs. These are certainly important. However, creating new interfaces to better meet needs of older computer users or capitalizing on basic cognitive data to better develop devices to remind individuals to take their medications on time are equally important and closely in line with the work of those conducting cognitive aging studies in the laboratory.

Finally, changing the way the world is designed leaves open numerous opportunities. For example, capitalizing on our basic knowledge of the value of environmental support offers the opportunity to understand how to build better system interfaces.

The Center for Applied Gerontology at the University of Birmingham in the United Kingdom has developed a unique approach to involving older adults in all stages of the development of consumer goods (Nayak, 1995). They have established a nationwide panel of over 4,000 older adults (aged 55 and over) of varying socioeconomic backgrounds. Subsets of this group are available to participate in focus groups, questionnaires, and product evaluations. Manufacturers may submit existing products or ideas for products to be evaluated by older adults. This approach has enabled the companies to address a basic tenet of human factors to "know thy user." Specific examples of similar efforts to involve older adults in the design process may be found in the special issue of *Applied Ergonomics* entitled "Designing for Our Future Selves" (Coleman & Pullinger, 1993).

The science and practice of human factors related to older adults is involved at some level in all three of the above-mentioned approaches. However, without a solid foundation gleaned from research in the domains encompassed by the field of cognition and aging, the human factors effort would be at a great disadvantage.

The goal of product and system design should be to achieve universal design. We echo Vanderheiden's (1997) view of universal design:

> *Universal design* is a term that has been given to the practice of designing products or environments that can be effectively and efficiently used by people with a wide range of abilities operating in a wide range of situations. . . . An ideal design is one that is attractive, easy to learn, effective and whose functions can be efficiently accessed and used by everyone across the full range of circumstances that may occur for its intended use. (pp. 2014–2015)

To truly achieve universal design, scientists must deliver fundamental research that is meaningful to designers and designers must attend to the fundamental knowledge derived from cognitive aging research.

CONCLUSIONS

Much work with allegiance to the broad field of cognition and aging has advanced our theoretical understanding of age-related performance in complex environments as well as set the stage for worthwhile practical advancement. A broad review of the literature is beyond the scope of this chapter. However, it is quite apparent that research within the domain of cognition and aging conducted by individuals driven to resolve both theoretical and pragmatic issues has had a major impact on the field of human factors and the older adult. Major findings of most relevance to the present review include the following:

- Human factors interventions are crucial to improving older and younger adults' interactions with a wide range of technologies; such improvements enhance the quality and safety of daily living activities.
- Even seemingly simple systems (e.g., ATMs) designed without systematic regard for the older user are prone to lack of use, high error rates, and user frustration.
- There is a need for age-specific training; researchers have uncovered techniques for developing such training and have tested the benefits of that training.
- Research has demonstrated the importance of attending to age-related issues in system design; in some systems, design improvements led to substantial performance gains even without training.
- As the scale of complexity of the system increases, so too does the need for training and proper design.

Research in the area of human factors and aging also contributes to the knowledge base of cognitive aging by assessing age-related differences in a broader task space, assessing the benefits of experience on learning new tasks, and testing the limits of cognitive theories in complex, real-world environments. What we have tried to do in this chapter is to show the linkage between cognitive aging research and human factors efforts and to demonstrate that both fields can contribute to the improved quality of daily living, safety, and well-being of older adults. Indeed, it is through a joint effort that much progress on all fronts will be made.

We did not intend this chapter to serve as a "design compendium" that a reader could access to solve a specific problem on a specific day. Although sufficient data exist in the physical and sensory areas for the beginnings of such a compendium (e.g., see Fisk & Rogers, 1997), the cognitive side of the house is less mature. When such compendiums are attempted from a cognitive perspective, the design guidelines often offer well-worn aphorisms that, although correct, are typically too general to be of much value to designers. These guidelines lack theoretical specificity. For example, recommendations in the general human factors literature include strive for consistency (Schneiderman, 1992), display data in usable forms (S. L. Smith & Mosier, 1986), avoid unnecessary details (Tullis,

1988), minimize ambiguity (Vanderheiden, 1997), reduce short-term memory (Schneiderman, 1992), and do not overuse colors (Murch, 1987). Within the aging literature, we see suggestions such as provide environmental support, simplify the task, or reduce working memory demands. The important questions really relate to more overarching, theoretically driven questions. For example, an important question is what it precisely means, cognitively, to provide environmental support. Another question concerns why display consistency is important and how it ultimately relates to transfer-specific learning. Answering this latter question is crucial if one wishes to design complex systems because it is impossible to completely meet the consistency guideline, per se, when one designs complex systems. The goal for the marriage of human factors and cognitive aging researchers should be *not* to provide a "good" design, *not* to provide a "better" design, but, rather, to provide the "best" design (Fisher, 1993). As Fisher pointed out, a principled approach to solving complex design questions must include theory. However, this theory must survive tests within rich, complex problem domains. We hope this chapter has provided insight into the challenges of human factors and the older adult, the important opportunities in the field, and the motivation for more cognitive aging research to assist in this crucially important endeavor.

ACKNOWLEDGMENTS

Work on this chapter was supported in part by Grants P50 AG-11715 and R01 AG-07654 from the National Institute on Aging. We acknowledge the helpful comments on an earlier version of this chapter from Gus Craik, Tim Salthouse, Nandita Amin, Monica Huff, Amber Robinson, and Kelly Shea.

REFERENCES

Anderson, J. A. (1983). A spreading activation theory of memory. *Journal of Verbal Learning and Verbal Behavior, 22,* 261–295.

Ashman, R. D., Bishu, R. R., Foster, B. G., & McCoy, P. T. (1994). Countermeasures to improve the driving performance of older drivers. *Educational Gerontology, 20,* 567–577.

Ball, K., Beard, B., Roenker, D., Miller, R., & Griggs, D. (1988). Age and visual search: Expanding the useful field of view. *Journal of the Optical Society of America, 5,* 2210–2219.

Ball, K., & Owsley, C. (1991). Identifying correlates of accident involvement for the older driver. *Human Factors, 33,* 583–595.

Barr, R. A., & Eberhard, J. W. (1991). Safety and mobility of elderly drivers: Part I [Special issue]. *Human Factors, 33,* 497–498.

Belbin, R. M. (1970). The discovery method in training older workers. In H. L. Sheppard (Ed.), *Toward industrial gerontology* (pp. 56–60). Cambridge, MA: Schenkman.

Bogner, M. S. (1994). *Human error in medicine*. Mahwah, NJ: Lawrence Erlbaum Associates.

Caplan, L. J., & Lipman, P. D. (1995). Age and gender differences in the effectiveness of map-like learning aids in memory for routes. *Journal of Gerontology: Psychological Sciences*, *50B*, P126–P133.

Chapanis, A. (1971). Prelude to 2001: Explorations in human communication. *American Psychologist*, *26*, 949–961.

Charness, N., Bosman, E., Kelley, C., & Mottram, M. (1996). Cognitive theory and word processing: When prediction fails. In W. A. Rogers, A. D. Fisk, & N. Walker (Eds.), *Aging and skilled performance: Advances in theory and application* (pp. 221–239). Mahwah, NJ: Lawrence Erlbaum Associates.

Charness, N., Schumann, C. E., & Boritz, G. M. (1992). Training older adults in word processing: Effects of age, training technique, and computer anxiety. *International Journal of Technology and Aging*, *5*, 79–106.

Clark, M. C., Czaja, S. J., & Weber, R. A. (1990). Older adults and daily living tasks profiles. *Human Factors*, *32*, 537–549.

Coleman, R., & Pullinger, D. J. (1993). Designing for our future selves. *Applied Ergonomics*, *24*, 3–4.

Collins, B. L. (1983). Evaluation of mine-safety symbols. In *Proceedings of the Human Factors Society 27th Annual Meeting* (pp. 947–949). Santa Monica, CA: Human Factors Society.

Collins, B. L., & Lerner, N. D. (1982). Assessment of fire-safety symbols. *Human Factors*, *24*, 75–84.

Czaja, S. J. (1996). Aging and the acquisition of computer skills. In W. A. Rogers, A. D. Fisk, & N. Walker (Eds.), *Aging and skilled performance: Advances in theory and application* (pp. 201–220). Mahwah, NJ: Lawrence Erlbaum Associates.

Czaja, S. J. (1997a). Systems design and evaluation. In G. Salvendy (Ed.), *Handbook of human factors* (2nd ed., pp. 17–40). New York: Wiley.

Czaja, S. J. (1997b). Using technologies to aid the performance of home tasks. In A. D. Fisk & W. A. Rogers (Eds.), *Handbook of human factors and the older adult* (pp. 311–334). San Diego, CA: Academic Press.

Czaja, S. J., Guerrier, J., Nair, S. N., & Landauer, T. K. (1993). Computer communication as an aid to independence for older adults. *Behavior and Information Technology*, *12*, 197–207.

Czaja, S. J., Hammond, K., Blascovich, J. J., & Swede, H. (1989). Age-related differences in learning to use a text-editing system. *Behavior and Information Technology*, *8*, 309–319.

Czaja, S. J., & Sharit, J. (1993). Age differences in the performance of computer-based work. *Psychology and Aging*, *8*, 59–67.

Easterby, R. S., & Hakiel, S. R. (1981). Field testing of consumer safety signs: The comprehension of pictorially presented messages. *Applied Ergonomics*, *12*, 143–152.

Eberhard, J. W., & Barr, R. A. (1992). Safety and mobility of elderly drivers: Part II [Special issue]. *Human Factors*, *34*, 1–2.

Elias, P. K., Elias, M. F., Robbins, M. A., & Gage, P. (1987). Acquisition of word-processing skills by younger, middle-aged, and older adults. *Psychology and Aging*, *2*, 340–348.

Fassett, W. S. (1991). New age ATMs. *Bank Management*, *67*, 63.

Fernie, G. (1997). Assistive devices. In A. D. Fisk & W. A. Rogers (Eds.), *Handbook of human factors and the older adult* (pp. 289–310). San Diego, CA: Academic Press.

Ferring, J. (1991). Seniors are prime ATM targets. *American Banker*, *156*, A8–A9

Fisher, D. L. (1993). Optimal performance engineering: Good, better, best. *Human Factors*, *35*, 115–139.

Fisk, A. D., & Kirlik, A. (1996). Practical relevance and age-related research: Can theory advance without practice? In W. A. Rogers, A. D. Fisk, & N. Walker (Eds.), *Aging and skilled performance: Advances in theory and application* (pp. 1–15). Mahwah, NJ: Lawrence Erlbaum Associates.

Fisk, A. D., & Rogers, W. A. (Eds.). (1997). *Handbook of human factors and the older adult*. San Diego, CA: Academic Press.

Gardner-Bonneau, D., & Gosbee, J. (1997). Health care and rehabilitation. In A. D. Fisk & W. A. Rogers (Eds.), *Handbook of human factors and the older adult* (pp. 231–255). San Diego, CA: Academic Press.

Gilmore, G. C., Wenk, H. E., Naylor, L. A., & Stove, T. A. (1992). Motion perception and age. *Psychology and Aging, 4*, 654–660.

Hancock, H. E., Rogers, W. A., & Fisk, A. D. (1998). *Product usage and warning symbol comprehension for older adults*. Paper presented at the Human Factors and Ergonomics Society 42nd Annual Meeting, Chicago, IL.

Hartley, A. A. (1992). Attention. In T. A. Salthouse & F. I. M. Craik (Eds.), *Handbook of aging and cognition* (pp. 3–49). Hillsdale, NJ: Lawrence Erlbaum Associates.

Hendrick, H. W. (1997). *Good ergonomics is good economics*. Santa Monica, CA: Human Factors and Ergonomics Society.

Henneman, R. L., & Rubini, D. M. (1993). New directions in transaction terminal interfaces. *AT&T Technical Journal, 72*, 50–56.

Howell, W. C. (1997). Foreword, perspectives, and prospectives. In A. D. Fisk & W. A. Rogers (Eds.), *Handbook of human factors and the older adult* (pp. 1–6). San Diego, CA: Academic Press.

Hubble, J. P., Pahwa, R., Micalek, D. K., Thomas, C., & Koller, W. C. (1993). Interactive video conferencing: A means of providing interim care to Parkinson's disease patients. *Movement Disorders, 8*, 380–382.

Kart, C. S., Dunkle, R. E., & Lockery, S. A. (1994). Self-health care. In B. R. Bonder & M. B. Wagner (Eds.), *Functional performance in older adults* (pp. 136–147). Philadelphia: Davis.

Kausler, D. H. (1991). *Experimental psychology, cognition, and human aging*. New York: Springer-Verlag.

Koncelik, J. (1982). *Aging and the product environment*. Florence, KY: Scientific & Academic Additions.

Kroemer, K. H. E. (1997). Anthropometry and biomechanics. In A. D. Fisk & W. A. Rogers (Eds.), *Handbook of human factors and the older adult* (pp. 87–124). San Diego, CA: Academic Press.

Lambert, L. D., & Fleury, M. (1994). Age, cognitive style, and traffic signs. *Perceptual and Motor Skills, 78*, 611–624.

Lawton, M. P., & Brody, E. M. (1969). Assessment of older people: Self-maintaining and instrumental activities of daily living. *Gerontologist, 9*, 179–185.

Lerner, N. (1994). Giving the older driver enough perception–reaction time. *Experimental Aging Research, 20*, 25–33.

Lipman, P. D., & Caplan, L. J. (1992). Adult age differences in memory for routes: Effects of instruction and spatial diagram. *Psychology and Aging, 7*, 435–442.

Luczak, H. (1997). Task analysis. In G. Salvendy (Ed.), *Handbook of human factors* (2nd ed., pp. 340–416). New York: Wiley.

Mead, S. E., & Fisk, A. D. (1998). Measuring skill acquisition and retention with an ATM simulator: The need for age-specific training. *Human Factors, 40*, 516–523.

Mead, S. E., Jamieson, B. A., Rousseau, G. K., Sit, R. A., & Rogers W. A. (1996). Online library catalogs: Age-related differences in query construction and error recovery. In *Proceedings of the Human Factors and Ergonomics Society 40th Annual Meeting* (pp. 146–150). Santa Monica, CA: Human Factors and Ergonomics Society.

Mead, S. E., Sit, R. A., Rogers, W. A., Rousseau, G. K., & Jamieson, B. A. (1999). *Novice users of on-line library systems*. Manuscript submitted for publication.

Meeks, C. B. (1994). Technological change and the elderly. *Advancing the Consumer Interest, 6*, 15–20.

Melia, M. (1991). The ATM agenda. *Savings Institutions, 112*, 38–42.

Morrell, R. W., & Echt, K. V. (1996). Instructional design for older computer users: The influence of cognitive factors. In W. A. Rogers, A. D. Fisk, & N. Walker (Eds.), *Aging and skilled performance: Advances in theory and application* (pp. 241–265). Mahwah, NJ: Lawrence Erlbaum Associates.

Morrell, R. W., & Echt, K. V. (1997). Designing written instructions for older adults: Learning to use computers. In A. D. Fisk & W. A. Rogers (Eds.), *Handbook of human factors and the older adult* (pp. 335–361). San Diego, CA: Academic Press.

Morrell, R. W., Park, D. C., Mayhorn, C. B., & Echt, K. V. (1996). *Electronic technology and older adults.* Paper presented at the International Conference on Memory, Albano Terme, Italy.

Morrell, R. W., Park, D. C., & Poon, L. W. (1989). Quality of instructions in prescription drug labels: Effects on memory and comprehension in young and old adults. *The Gerontologist, 29,* 345–354.

Murch, G. M. (1987). Color graphics: Blessing or ballyhoo? In R. M. Becker & W. A. Buxton (Eds.), *Readings in human computer interaction: A multi-disciplinary approach* (pp. 333–341). San Mateo, CA: Kaufmann.

Nayak, U. S. L. (1995). Elders-led design. *Ergonomics in Design, 3,* 8–13.

Owsley, C., Ball, K., Sloane, M. E., Roenker, D. L., & Bruni, J. R. (1991). Visual/cognitive correlates of vehicle accidents in older adults. *Psychology and Aging, 6,* 403–415.

Panek, P. E., Barrett, G. V., Sterns, H. L., & Alexander, R. A. (1977). A review of age changes in perceptual information processing ability with regard to driving. *Experimental Aging Research, 3,* 387–449.

Park, D. C., & Jones, T. R. (1997). Medication adherence and aging. In A. D. Fisk & W. A. Rogers (Eds.), *Handbook of human factors and the older adult* (pp. 257–287). San Diego, CA: Academic Press.

Pushkar, D., Arbuckle, T., Conway, M., Chaikelson, J., & Maag, U. (1997). Everyday activity parameters and competence in older adults. *Psychology and Aging, 12,* 600–609.

Rabbitt, P. M. A. (1992). Cognitive changes with age must influence human factors design. In H. Bouma & J. A. M. Graafmans (Eds.), *Gerontechnology* (pp. 113–140). Amsterdam: IOS Press.

Rittner, B., & Kirk, A. B. (1995). Health care and public transportation by poor and frail elderly people. *Social Work, 40,* 365–373.

Rogers, W. A., Cabrera, E. F., Walker, N., Gilbert, D. K., & Fisk, A. D. (1996). A survey of automatic teller machine usage across the adult lifespan. *Human Factors, 38,* 156–166.

Rogers, W. A., & Fisk, A. D. (1991). Age-related differences in the maintenance and modification of automatic processes: Arithmetic Stroop interference. *Human Factors, 33,* 45–56.

Rogers, W. A., & Fisk, A. D. (1997). Automatic teller machines: Design and training issues. *Ergonomics in Design, 5,* 4–9.

Rogers, W. A., Fisk, A. D., Mead, S., Walker, N., & Cabrera, E. F. (1996). Training older adults to use automatic teller machines. *Human Factors, 38,* 425–433.

Rogers, W. A., Gilbert, D. K., & Cabrera, E. F. (1997). An analysis of automatic teller machine usage by older adults: A structured interview approach. *Applied Ergonomics, 28,* 173–180.

Rogers, W. A., Lamson, N., & Rousseau, G. K. (in press). Warning research: An integrative perspective. *Human Factors.*

Rogers, W. A., Meyer, B., Walker, N., & Fisk, A. D. (1998). Functional limitations to daily living tasks in the aged: A focus group analysis. *Human Factors, 40,* 111–125.

Rousseau, G. K., Jamieson, B. A., Rogers, W. A., Mead, S. L., & Sit, R. A. (1998). Assessing the usability of on-line library systems. *Behavior and Information Technology, 17,* 274–281.

Rousseau, G. K., Lamson, N., & Rogers, W. A. (1998). Designing warnings to compensate for age-related changes in perceptual and cognitive abilities. *Psychology and Marketing, 15,* 643–662.

Salthouse, T. A. (1991). *Theoretical perspectives on cognitive aging.* Hillsdale, NJ: Lawrence Erlbaum Associates.

Schneider, W., & Shiffrin, R. M. (1977). Controlled and automatic human information processing: I. Detection, search, and attention. *Psychological Review, 84,* 1–66.

Schneiderman, B. (1992). *Designing the user interface: Strategies for effective human–computer interaction* (2nd ed.). Reading, MA: Addison-Wesley.

Shinar, D., McDowell, E. D., Rackoff, N. J., & Rockwell, T. H. (1978). Field dependence and driver visual search behavior. *Human Factors, 20,* 553–559.

Short, J., Williams, E., & Christie, B. (1976). *The social psychology of telecommunication.* New York: Wiley.

Sixsmith, J., & Sixsmith, A. (1993). Older people, driving, and new technology. *Applied Ergonomics, 24,* 40–43.

Smith, A. D. (1997). Memory. In J. E. Birren & K. W. Schaie (Eds.), *Handbook of the psychology of aging* (pp. 236–250). San Diego, CA: Academic Press.

Smith, S. L., & Mosier, J. N. (1986). *Guidelines for designing user interface software* (Report No. ESD-TR-86-278). Bedford, MA: The MITRE Corporation.

Staplin, L., & Fisk, A. D. (1991). A cognitive engineering approach to improve signalized left-turn intersections. *Human Factors, 33,* 559–571.

Sweller, J., Chandler, P., Tierney, P., & Cooper, M. (1990). Cognitive load as a factor in the structuring of technical material. *Journal of Experimental Psychology: General, 119,* 176–192.

Szymkowiak, A., Fisher, D. L., & Connerney, K. A. (1997). False yield and false go decisions at signalized left-turn intersections: A driving simulator study. In *Proceedings of the Europe Chapter of the Human Factors and Ergonomics Society Annual Conference* (pp. 226–235). Bochum, Germany: European chapter of the Human Factors and Ergonomics Society.

Taylor, B., & Taylor, A. (1989). Social casework and environmental cognition: Mobility training for community health services. *Social Work,* 463–467.

Thorndike, E. L. (1919). Scientific personnel work in the army. *Science, 49,* 53–61.

Tullis, T. S. (1988). Screen design. In M. Helander (Ed.), *Handbook of human computer interaction* (pp. 377–411). Amsterdam: Elsevier.

U.S. Department of Transportation (1994). *Traffic safety facts.* Washington, DC: National Center for Statistics and Analysis.

Vanderheiden, G. C. (1997). Designing for people with functional limitations resulting from disability, aging, or circumstance. In G. Salvendy (Ed.), *Handbook of human factors and ergonomics* (2nd ed., pp. 2010–2052). New York: Wiley.

Vercruyssen, M. (1997). Movement control and speed of behavior. In A. D. Fisk & W. A. Rogers (Eds.), *Handbook of human factors and the older adult* (pp. 55–86). San Diego, CA: Academic Press.

Walker, N., Fain, W. B., Fisk, A. D., & McGuire, C. L. (1997). Aging and decision making: Driving related problem solving. *Human Factors, 39,* 438–444.

Walker, N., Millians, J., & Worden, A. (1996). Mouse accelerations and performance of older computer users. In *Proceedings of the 40th Annual Meeting of the Human Factors and Ergonomics Society* (pp. 151–154). Santa Monica, CA: Human Factors and Ergonomics Society.

Walker, N., Philbin, D. A., & Fisk, A. D. (1997). Age-related differences in movement control: Adjusting submovement structure to optimize performance. *Journal of Gerontology: Psychological Sciences, 52B,* P40–P52.

Walker, N., Philbin, D. A., & Spruell, C. (1996). The use of signal detection theory in research on age-related differences in movement control. In W. A. Rogers, A. D. Fisk, & N. Walker (Eds.), *Aging and skilled performance: Advances in theory and application* (pp. 45–64). Mahwah, NJ: Lawrence Erlbaum Associates.

Waller, P. F. (1991). The older driver. *Human Factors, 33,* 499–505.

Westerman, S. J., Davies, D. R., Glendon, A. I., Stammers, R. B., & Matthews, G. (1995). Age and cognitive ability as predictors of computerized information retrieval. *Behaviour and Information Technology, 14*, 313–326.

Wiklund, M. E. (1992). Designing medical devices for older users. *Medical Device & Diagnostic Industry*, 78–83.

Wogalter, M. S., & Laughery, K. R. (1996). Warning! Sign and label effectiveness. *Current Directions in Psychological Science, 5*, 33–37.

Worden, A., Walker, N., Bharat, K., & Hudson, S. (1997). Making computers easier for older adults to use: Area cursors and sticky icons. In *Human Factors in Computing Systems '97 Proceedings* (pp. 266–271). Atlanta, GA: Association for Computing Machinery.

Emotion and Cognition

Derek M. Isaacowitz
University of Pennsylvania

Susan Turk Charles
Laura L. Carstensen
Stanford University

For hundreds of years, scholars have considered the possible relationship between emotion and cognition. Hippocrates speculated about the location of emotion and cognition in the brain. Buddha spoke about the interdependence of wisdom and compassion. Yet despite long-standing fascination with these concepts in philosophy and existential psychology, experimental psychology, by and large, has failed to consider seriously the interplay among the essential human processes involved in emotion and cognition.

Although cognitive psychologists studying processes of aging are certainly aware of the potential influences of emotion on cognition, this influence is often viewed as a confounding factor that must be controlled and, ideally, eliminated in order to study cognitive processes unfettered by emotional experience (e.g., Powell, 1994). Emotion researchers, in contrast, have paid considerable attention to cognition. In fact, many widely known theories of emotion embed emotional experience within cognitive frameworks, holding that emotions occur as a function of cognitive appraisals or goal interruptions (Lazarus, 1991). However, with some important exceptions (e.g., Blanchard-Fields, 1997), there have been few concerted attempts to better understand general cognitive processes through the understanding of emotional processes.

Debates about cognition among *emotion* researchers, where they remain, concern the causal role that cognition plays in emotion. Some theories about emotion assert explicitly that cognitions precede emotions (e.g.,

Stein & Trabasso, 1992). Other theoretical models downplay the role of cognition in emotion and instead focus on alternative pathways to subjective arousal, such as activation of the autonomic nervous system (Levenson, 1992) or facial efference (Zajonc, 1985; Zajonc, Murphy, & Inglehart, 1989). Zajonc (1997) took perhaps the strongest position against cognitive models of emotion, turning the tables on the traditional debate and maintaining that although emotion can occur in the absence of cognition, cognitive functioning relies essentially on emotion. Learning, Zajonc (1997) pointed out, cannot occur without hedonic discriminations about relevant and irrelevant stimuli and positive and negative reinforcement require valenced distinctions. In this view, emotion is a fundamental element of all cognitive functions, from classical conditioning to categorization.

Although interesting and theoretically important, such arguments have done little to persuade cognitive aging researchers of the need to consider emotion in cognitive processing. In this chapter, we attempt to show linkages between emotion and cognition and make the case that these connections are particularly important for research on cognitive aging. Our discussion focuses on the ways in which emotion may influence cognitive processing in older adults. We review evidence that emotional functioning is well maintained in later life and is highly salient in mental representations, memory, social judgments, and motivation among older adults. This strength and salience of emotions and emotional experiences may have implications for cognitive aging.

We begin with a brief overview of studies examining the influences of emotion on cognition. Next, we present relevant empirical findings about age differences in emotional experience and review theories that predict an increased prominence of emotion in cognitive processing across adulthood. Finally, we suggest ways that emotional changes may influence performance on traditional cognitive tasks and consider alternative explanations for observed age differences. We conclude that a comprehensive understanding of either cognitive or emotional functioning in old age must include consideration of the interplay between the two constructs.

COGNITION, MOOD, AND MEMORY

We approach this topic from findings indicating that emotional states and events influence cognitive processes. A review of research on memory for stressful situations indicates that central details of emotional events are better remembered than central details of neutral events and the reverse is true for peripheral details, suggesting that emotion influences attentional processes (Christianson, 1992). For example, in a study using eye tracking as a measure of attention, participants watching emotional slides fixated more often on central detail information compared with participants watching nonemotional slides (Christianson, Loftus, Hoffman, & Loftus, 1991). Although the results from studies examining memory for central and peripheral information of emotional and neutral events are somewhat complex, they provide some evidence that attentive and/or preattentive processing is influenced by the emotionality of the stimuli (e.g., Christianson, Goodman, & Loftus, 1992).

In addition to evidence for the attentional effects of emotional stimuli on cognitive processing, substantial evidence from clinical psychology research demonstrates that mood can influence, and interfere with, cognitions (see Sarason, Pierce, & Sarason, 1996). In two studies, Siebert and Ellis (1991) induced participants into happy, sad, or neutral mood states and then had them complete a memory task. In the first study, participants completed the memory task and then were asked to recall and list irrelevant thoughts experienced during the task. In the second study, participants were asked to "think aloud" during the task. In both studies, the valence of irrelevant thoughts was correlated with mood. In addition, negative irrelevant thoughts were found to interfere with task performance. Other studies have found that participants induced into negative moods perform more poorly on recall tests, particularly if the task is more difficult, which suggests that greater demands may increase group differences (Ellis, Thomas, & Rodriguez, 1984). In addition to studies using mood manipulations, investigations examining individuals who are moderately depressed find that they exhibit a variety of deficits on memory tasks (for a review, see Gotlib, Roberts, & Gilboa, 1996). Although this effect has been investigated primarily in younger adults, the handful of studies including older people suggests similar effects: In a sample of elderly men, La Rue, Swan, and Carmelli (1995) found that depressive symptoms were related to poorer cognitive performance on tasks involving both memory and psychomotor speed.

Like depression, anxiety also has been associated with cognitive interference on a wide range of cognitive tasks (MacLeod, 1996). As with depressed individuals, people experiencing anxiety also experience intrusive thoughts that interfere with cognitive processing of stimulus materials (MacLeod, 1996; Segal, 1996). For example, Blankstein, Toner, and Flett (1989) compared intrusive thoughts of students rated as either high or low test anxious while they were performing a demanding cognitive task. Compared with their low-test-anxious counterparts, high-test-anxious students listed more worry-laden thoughts that they specifically indicated had interfered with their performance on the test. These findings are consistent with other studies that have found a negative correlation between test-related worries and test performance (Nichols-Hoppe & Beach, 1990). Furthermore, anxiety influences task performance to a

greater extent when the task requires higher levels of cognitive organization. Indeed, Eysenck (1982) reviewed over 20 studies in which anxiety
influenced participants' performance minimally on simple tasks but significantly on difficult tasks.

On the basis of a meta-analysis of the literature on mood-congruent
recall, Matt, Vázquez, and Campbell (1992) concluded that there is a
robust asymmetric influence of mood on memory. Nondepressed people
remember more positive than negative material, whereas subclinically
depressed individuals exhibit no such asymmetry, being equally likely to
remember positive and negative stimuli. Clinically depressed participants,
as well as participants experimentally induced into sad mood states, show
clear evidence of mood-congruent recall, as do individuals induced into
elated mood states.

A major focus in cognitive psychology has been on ways in which
mood enhances the processing of mood-congruent material (Blaney, 1986;
Matt et al., 1992). Arguably, the most influential model in this area is that
formulated by Bower and colleagues. Bower (1981, 1992) maintained that
emotional states influence memory and learning. When people learn
information in a particular mood state, they disproportionately encode
and remember mood-congruent information. Thus, participants initially
exposed to both sad and happy information recall more positive information from the initial presentation when they are happy and more sad
information when they are subsequently sad. This bias in favor of mood-
consistent information generalizes to person perception. Forgas and
Bower (1987) showed that participants who were induced to feel happy
and soon thereafter were asked to recall attributes about a target person
were more likely to generate positive characteristics; participants induced
to be sad showed the opposite pattern of recall.

To account for these findings, Bower (1981) proposed an association
network model of spreading activation. In his model, concepts are represented by nodes. Activation of one node automatically activates related
nodes. Theoretically, distinct emotions are represented by specific nodes
in associative networks, each linked to related conceptual nodes. A specific
emotion node, for example, is connected to other nodes related to autonomic responsivity, cognitive appraisals, and memories for events that
occurred when the emotion was experienced. Activation of a specific
emotion node is distributed, thereby activating relevant physiology and
memory of related events. On the basis of this network model, Bower
(1981, p. 138) hypothesized that a participant's mood during cognitive
task performance influences associative processes, the interpretation of
ambiguous situations, and the salience of congruent emotional material.

Just as mood-congruent events are better remembered because of network elaborations, stimuli associated with strong emotional reactions tend

to be particularly well learned (Mineka, 1993; Wagner & Brandon, 1989). For example, in a study reported by Gilligan and Bower (1984), participants were hypnotized to experience low, medium, or high levels of happiness and then read either neutral or happy vignettes. Although the neutral vignettes were comparably well learned across levels of happiness, happy vignettes were better learned with increasing intensity of induced happiness.

Bower (1992) suggested that there may be costs to these processes, as people may "recall better the central idea of an emotional event but may so focus on this central feature that they fail to encode the peripheral details of the scene" (pp. 19–20). This assertion is supported by research on eyewitness testimony, which has found that attentional resources are allocated to the encoding of central information at the expense of encoding peripheral details of the emotional scene (Christianson et al., 1992). For instance, witnesses to a crime may accurately remember the crime weapon but may be inaccurate in their recall of the other people present (Christianson, 1992). Importantly, such peripheral details often constitute the information assessed in cognitive research.

In sum, emotion influences cognitive processing in a number of ways and affects attentional and memorial processes. First, emotions are associated with irrelevant thoughts. People induced to be unhappy and students who are high test anxious report more irrelevant thoughts while performing cognitive tasks compared with neutral participants. Second, negative irrelevant thoughts negatively influence cognitive performance. In addition, emotion is related to recall bias. Participants induced into particular mood states recall mood-congruent information more often than mood-incongruent information. Bias for mood-congruent information has been documented in people who are moderately depressed and those who are anxious as well. Finally, the influences of anxiety and depression on cognitive performance increase with the task difficulty.

EMOTION AND AGING

The evidence reviewed above suggests that emotions influence cognitive processing. To the extent that age is associated with changes in emotional salience and the frequency of particular mood states, these changes may impact the emotion–cognition relationship in everyday life differentially at different developmental stages. In this section, we review research that has examined the emotional experience of older adults. We summarize information about emotional intensity, control, and regulation, as well as the frequency of positive and negative mood states and general mental health. Following a review of theory and research concerning emotion in old age, we consider its potential implications for understanding cognitive aging.

Overall, emotional functioning appears relatively unscathed by the aging process. Below we review empirical evidence based on cross-sectional studies that suggests that (a) the basic component processes involved in emotion experience are similar for younger and older adults (Levenson, Carstensen, Friesen, & Ekman, 1991), (b) reports of emotional experience are equally if not more positive among older adults (Gross et al., 1997), and (c) descriptions of emotions are more complex in older adults than in younger adults (Labouvie-Vief, 1997). Furthermore, older adults report greater control over their emotions in self-report questionnaires (Gross et al., 1997; Lawton, Kleban, Rajagopal, & Dean, 1992), and the ability to solve emotionally charged social dilemmas is higher among older adults than among younger adults (Blanchard-Fields, 1997). In fact, the overall pattern of findings described in the following pages suggests that opposing trajectories characterize the course of cognitive and emotional functioning in the second half of life. Whereas findings from cognitive research suggest a clear downward trajectory for many processes, including increased response latencies, limited short-term memory capacity, and decreased attention span (see, e.g., Salthouse, 1991), the profile of findings about emotional functioning that we review below points to a modest upward trajectory (see also Carstensen, Gross, & Fung, 1997; Labouvie-Vief, 1997).

We should point out that empirical findings about emotion in later life published over the past decade contrast strikingly with early theoretical models that presumed deterioration in emotion that paralleled the declines in biological and cognitive functioning. For many years, old age was presumed to be a time in life when emotions were dampened and poorly regulated (e.g., Banham, 1951; Bromley, 1990; Cumming & Henry, 1961; Schulz, 1985). At this point, such characterizations are untenable, given empirical findings accrued over the past decade.

A wide variety of experimental methods have been used to assess emotional functioning in old age, and a broad spectrum of questions have been addressed, from those concerning potential changes in the autonomic architecture of specific emotions to the complexity of emotional understanding. Emotion researchers consider three component processes involved in emotion: expression, subjective experience, and physiological arousal. Expression refers to the facial and bodily displays of internal states, experience involves the subjective feelings of a person, and arousal involves the emotion's physiology and autonomic response. Levenson and colleagues (Levenson et al., 1991; Levenson, Carstensen, & Gottman, 1994) have examined all three concomitantly under controlled laboratory conditions using an older adult sample. Levenson et al. (1991) assessed facial configurations, physiological activity, and subjective intensity of emotion in a sample of elderly adults. Participants came to the laboratory, identified events that had elicited a range of strong emotional reactions in the past, and were instructed through imagery to reexperience the represented range of emotions while they were videotaped. Measures of heart rate, somatic activity, blood pressure, and respiration were simultaneously gathered. Ratings of subjective intensity obtained after each emotional induction and muscle-by-muscle coding of facial expressions were computed. Their findings suggest great similarity in subjective experience and expression of emotion in older and younger adults. In addition, the psychophysiological profile associated with specific emotions in younger adults were also observed in this sample of elderly adults, suggesting maintenance of emotion-specific differentiation in psychophysiological patterning. One important age difference, however, was that the magnitude of the autonomic response was relatively subdued in older participants. In other words, although emotion-specific patterns (e.g., heart rate increases more with anger than with disgust and somatic activity decreases more with fear than anger or surprise) are consistent for younger and older adults, the level of arousal is somewhat reduced in older adults, particularly in the cardiovascular response.

The above finding has now been replicated in older adults discussing marital conflicts with their spouses (Levenson et al., 1994) and in older European and Chinese Americans viewing emotion-eliciting films (Tsai, Levenson, & Carstensen, 1998). Whether the reduction in arousal reflects general age-related depression of the autonomic nervous system or a circumscribed dampening of emotional arousal remains unclear. In either case, this age difference may well facilitate the ability to control strong emotional reactions. In other words, particular age differences do not necessarily oppose, and may even contribute to, self-perceived maintained or improved emotional functioning and control with age.

Findings in the literature suggest few differences in the subjective intensity of emotional experience despite this reduction in arousal. On the basis of subjective reports, Malatesta and Kalnok (1984) reported no age differences in emotional experience. Older people did not report more negative affect or less positive affect, nor did they report any general decrease in emotional intensity with age. Similarly, in a study including over 1,000 participants, Lawton et al. (1992) found that the overall pattern of self-reported emotional experience was quite similar across adult age groups. Interestingly, the one difference they did identify relates to a reduction in surgency (i.e., excitability), which may well be related to the reduction in arousability reported by Levenson et al. (1991). In addition, Lawton et al. (1992) found no support for age-related increases in negative emotions.

One recent study reported by Carstensen, Pasupathi, and Mayr (in press) examined the frequency and intensity of emotion in everyday life by signaling 185 participants representing the adult age range (18–95 years) at 35 random times through electronic pagers. When participants were signaled, they recorded the degree to which they were experiencing each of 19 emotions. Their findings suggest that positive emotions are maintained in frequency and intensity across adulthood. Age does not distinguish the intensity of negative emotions, but the frequency of negative emotional experience is reduced in each successive age group until very old age (over 80 years) when a slight trend upward in frequency is observed. Even at this advanced age, however, frequency of negative affect is lower than in young adults. Thus, global evaluations about emotional experience are remarkably consistent with experiences monitored on a day-to-day basis.

Some of the above evidence may appear contradictory at first glance: Several findings point to no age differences in the experience of negative affect, whereas other studies point to decreased negative affect with age. However, what is importantly consistent among all the studies, including both self-report (Gross et al., 1997; Lawton et al., 1992; Malatesta & Kalnok, 1984) and naturalistic assessments (e.g., Carstensen, Pasupathi, & Mayr, in press) is that none provide any evidence for an increase in negative affect with age. There is simply no evidence in the literature to support the claim that negative affect dominates in old age.

Recent empirical evidence also suggests that when asked about the ability to control emotions, older adults report better regulation than do younger adults (Gross et al., 1997; Lawton et al., 1992). According to Gross et al. (1997), control is distinguished from the experience of emotion because, rather than referring to the intensity of the "feeling" of the emotion, control refers to people trying to influence what emotions they experience and how the experience unfolds. Self-reports about emotional control are often assessed with questionnaire items such as "I try to stay neutral." Lawton et al. (1992) analyzed questionnaire data about emotional experiences that included questions regarding emotional control from a large sample of young, middle-aged, and old adults. Compared with younger adults, older adults reported that they had better control and were more likely than younger adults to remain "calm and cool." Gross et al. (1997) found converging evidence across five highly diverse samples. In each, older adults responded more positively than younger adults to a question concerning how well they were able to control their emotions overall (Gross et al., 1997). In these data, the difference between older and younger adults in their self-reported emotional control was approximately 0.50 SDs across the three studies using diverse populations (Gross et al., 1997).

Additional evidence for improved emotion regulation was found in the experience sampling study mentioned above (Carstensen, Pasupathi, & Mayr, in press). Once a negative or positive emotion was recorded, its duration was examined as a function of age. The duration of positive states was comparable across the age range; however the duration of negative states was reduced in older adults. The decreased frequency of negative affect, even in the absence of increases in positive affect, is impressive evidence for increased emotional control with age, especially in light of shifts in the gain–loss ratio toward more losses with age (Heckhausen, Dixon, & Baltes, 1989).

Observational research examining age differences in emotional expression during social interactions suggests that older adults may be better than middle-aged adults at regulating their emotions as they interact socially, at least with intimate partners (Carstensen, Gottman, & Levenson, 1995; Levenson, Carstensen, & Gottman, 1993). In a study of long-term marriage, both happily and unhappily married couples completed questionnaires about possible areas of conflict and pleasure in their relationship and then were observed discussing an area of conflict. Couples were videotaped during their discussions, and their physiological activity was monitored. Outcome measures included both self-report and psychophysiological measures. On questionnaires, older adults reported lesser potential for conflict and greater potential for pleasure when discussing experiences and issues with their spouses (Levenson et al., 1993). Based on the observations of couples discussing an area of conflict, findings indicate that older spouses (even unhappily married ones) express less anger, belligerence, and disgust to one another during the session compared with middle-aged adults (Carstensen et al., 1995). Moreover, they express more affection during the sessions. Thus, older couples are not disengaged from the interaction: They display comparable levels of some negative emotions, such as tension, yet they manage to interject displays of affection into these otherwise difficult dialogues and resolve their conflicts with less negativity and more affection. Carstensen, Graff, Levenson, and Gottman (1996) interpreted this pattern in terms of social control of emotional experience. By expressing affection intermittently along with expressions of dissatisfactions, older couples are better able to regulate the emotional climate of the conflict discussion, thereby more effectively regulating their overall emotional state.

Finally, there is now convincing evidence that—with the exception of the dementias and other organically based brain syndromes—older adults experience lower levels of psychiatric disorders than do younger adults (Fisher, Zeiss, & Carstensen, 1993; Regier et al., 1988). Major affective disorders and anxiety and panic disorders appear at lower rates in older cohorts than in younger cohorts. Researchers were particularly surprised by the relatively low rate of major affective disorder, long suspected to increase linearly in prevalence across the life span (e.g., Gurland, 1976). However, the lifetime prevalence of depression in current cohorts of *adolescents* already matches the prevalence observed in the elderly (Klerman & Weissman, 1989). Although cohort (as opposed to age) differences in psychopathology are certainly plausible explanations for these findings, two points are worth noting: (a) Older people, despite disproportionate social losses, do not succumb disproportionately to mental disorders, an observation consistent with age-related improvements in emotion regulation, and (b) emotional responsiveness, even in later stages of dementia, is relatively well-preserved (Magai, Cohen, Gomberg, Malatesta, & Culver, 1996).

THEORIES OF EMOTIONAL DEVELOPMENT IN ADULTHOOD

Several life-span theories posit continued emotional development during adulthood. Each of these models considers cognitive processes critical to emotional development. We organize our review into two sections: First we consider theories rooted in a neo-Piagetian framework and then those embedded in a motivational one. As shown below, theoretical postulates about the nature and course of emotional change across the theories are not incompatible; indeed, all posit that emotions become more salient and better regulated with age. Below, we first describe the theories and then summarize findings testing their postulates.

Neo-Piagetian Theories of Adult Emotional and Cognitive Development

Emotional Complexity and Integration. Labouvie-Vief and colleagues applied a neo-Piagetian model to cognitive development in later life. They posited that, whereas the central cognitive task of early life is to learn that objects in the world exist independent of thoughts and feelings experienced by perceivers, the task of later adulthood is to "integrate an objective cognitive world with affect and value" (Labouvie-Vief, Hakim-Larson, DeVoe, & Schoeberlein, 1989, p. 284). Reintegration of affect and cognition continues to develop throughout adulthood, resulting in an increase in cognitive complexity related to experience and individual maturation in the form of ego development (Labouvie-Vief & DeVoe, 1991; Labouvie-Vief, DeVoe, & Bulka, 1989; Labouvie-Vief, Hakim-Larson, et al., 1989). To the traditional Piagetian stages of development, Labouvie-Vief and colleagues added new stages (viz., intrasystemic, intersystemic, and integrated), which reflect improved understanding of emotion and better integration of emotion and cognition in adulthood. At each stage, both cognition and emotion are present and perceived. However, in the earlier stages emotions more often interfere with cognitive processing, whereas in the later stages emotions enhance cognitive processing. At the intrasystemic level, emotions are understood as being mentally controlled and inner states are described in abstract terms. Cognitions related to emotions in this stage entail such mental strategies as forgetting or ignoring the problem. In contrast, the intersystemic level of cognitive development is characterized by an awareness that other people's feelings are distinct from those of the perceivers. According to the theory, at this stage individuals communicate more vividly about their emotions. At the highest level of cognitive development, the integrated stage, individuals are able to integrate objective knowledge about the world with both internal experiences and larger philosophical concerns, allowing them to explore the tension between the mental and physical realms (Labouvie-Vief, Hakim-Larson, DeVoe, & Schoeberlein, 1989). In this way, individuals acknowledge that multiple perspectives for a situation are possible and that there may not be one truth. In more recent work, this has been referred to as the "dynamic" stage (e.g., Labouvie-Vief, 1997).

Progression through these advanced stages of adult development is less strongly associated with chronological age than earlier Piagetian stages. Instead, cognitive development in this model is linked to ego development. In the absence of ego development, advanced stages of development are not likely to occur. Ego development is often positively correlated with age, possibly peaking in middle adulthood (Labouvie-Vief, 1997). Thus, although increased integration of emotion in cognitive processing is not considered an age effect per se, the theory suggests that these changes correlate positively with increasing age well into adulthood.

Postformal Reasoning. Closely related to Labouvie-Vief's theory is the postformal reasoning work of Sinnott (1996; see also the volume on postformal research by Sinnott & Cavanaugh, 1991). Heavily influenced by Perry (1970), this theory posits that the developmental tasks of middle and old age center on social and interpersonal domains and that cognitive resources are allocated to these tasks. In other words, a person's cognitive resources will be allocated differentially to those cognitive activities that are most related to the developmental tasks of their life stage. Thus, theoretically older adults allocate much of their increasingly limited cognitive resources to social and interpersonal tasks, preserving these highly prioritized activities in their lives. The model of postformal thought involves "cognitive qualities that are adaptive in everyday life because they regulate the integration of intellectual and emotional stimulation from events or people" (Sinnott, 1996, p. 363) and describes "the union of emotion and cognition in old age" (Sinnott, 1996, p. 363). Thus, adult cognitive development emphasizes emotional influence as a means of allowing the aging person to respond optimally to the social tasks of later adulthood.

Modal Logic. A third neo-Piagetian theory, modal logic (Chinen, 1984), contributes to the theoretical consensus that the subjective aspects of experience (including the emotional aspects of a person's response to stimuli) become more prominent with age, such that older adults are more concerned with the emotional aspects of experiences than are younger adults, who focus more on objective information. According to this theory, optimal aging involves revisiting earlier developmental modalities—that is, returning to ways of experiencing and of understanding what truths might be associated with certain propositions—with heightened self-awareness. Closely akin to the theories of Labouvie-Vief and Sinnott, this process culminates in subjective experiences associated with objects being incorporated into the perception of the object itself (Chinen, 1984). However, whereas Chinen suggested a return to previous stages with the possibility of a more mature experience of them, Labouvie-Vief posited that maturity requires a reorganization of a person's cognitive–affective life such that new stages are created.

Empirical Support. Research conducted by Labouvie-Vief and colleagues provides persuasive evidence that, with age, emotion becomes better integrated into reasoning and problem solving. In one line of research, adults of various ages described their own emotional experiences and evaluated written descriptions of conflict situations. Responses were classified according to both the postformal stages described above (Labouvie-Vief & DeVoe, 1991) and to ego level, as assessed by Loevinger's Sentence Completion Test (Loevinger, 1976). Findings indicate that relatively mature individuals (as indexed by increased age and ego level) experience emotions as more autonomous and less externally referenced. That is, they are able to describe their emotions as complex pheonomena, not just in mentalistic terms. A relationship was also found between verbal ability, emotional complexity, and emotional understanding (see also Labouvie-Vief, DeVoe, & Bulka, 1989). In this work, greater understanding of emotions, as predicted by age, greater verbal intelligence, and ego level, led to the use of different types of coping and defense mechanisms. Those who were older or who scored higher on ego level and verbal ability displayed greater flexibility and reported greater acceptance of the situation as compared with younger people and people who scored lower on ego level and verbal ability. Flexibility in this formulation involves the modulation of emotions. An openness to variation in emotion and feelings is characteristic of the highest integrated level and thus is a critical part of the coding system used to classify responses in this research paradigm. Labouvie-Vief contended that the most advanced levels of cognitive processing typify middle to early old age. We note that the assertion that integrated reasoning may develop in adulthood and may include greater flexibility in emotional understanding and experience in no way contradicts the literature on rigidity and aging, which has focused on very different notions of visual–motor flexibility (e.g., P. B. Baltes & Schaie, 1974), and egocentrism in social interactions and test performance (Looft, 1972).

Enhanced integration of emotion and cognition among older, as compared with younger, adults was also found by Sebby and Papini (1991) in research on everyday problem solving. When asked to solve problems that were syllogisms embedded in contexts that were crafted to be more or less relevant to participants, older adults were more likely to use an integrated level of reasoning, which involved accepting the inevitability of conflict and recognizing that logic and emotion cannot be separated. Their use of integration was particularly noticeable in problems older adults perceived as more relevant to their lives.

Although the above research demonstrates that cognition and emotion may indeed become better integrated with age in many people, it is still worth considering whether this increased integration is a positive change. Labouvie-Vief (1997) commented that emotion and cognition can function successfully as independent entities, but cognition tends to control emotion in earlier developmental stages. This control, according to Labouvie-Vief, often entails less adaptive forms of handling emotions in problem-solving situations. However, if they are linked, cognition does not just control emotion "but both informs it and is informed by it" (Labouvie-Vief, 1997, p. 231). With this integration, feelings and emotions that might be experienced as very scary or disruptive can instead be dealt with as mere parts of the complexities of human experience. Thus, a person who has integrated emotion and cognition has a better ability to balance aspects of their inner and outer worlds and may therefore be more wise.

Blanchard-Fields and colleagues have focused specifically on age differences in reasoning about social dilemmas. In one study, in which a postformal coding system[1] was used to assess reasoning, adolescents and young and middle-aged adults generated responses to social dilemmas that varied in emotional saliency (i.e., some of the dilemmas were emotionally salient, whereas others were not; Blanchard-Fields, 1986). Specifically, the coding system evaluated how much "the individual can differ-

---

[1]Blanchard-Field's (1986) coding system was based on Perry's (1970) stages of cognitive development, which also influenced and are similar to Labouvie-Vief's stages described above.

entiate the self as thinker from the product of the thinking self"(Blanchard-Fields, 1986, p. 327). For example, the lowest scores are given to responses that indicate an absolutist opinion with potential subjective biases going unrecognized. The highest level of reasoning acknowledges and validates multiple perspectives. On emotionally salient reasoning problems (e.g., conflict over an unwanted pregnancy), adolescents displayed lower levels of reasoning, as indicated by scoring their probed responses to these scenarios. They performed more poorly on emotional tasks than on nonemotional tasks (e.g., historical accounts of a fictional war), and reasoning scores on the emotional trials were lower than those of younger and middle-aged adults. Blanchard-Fields suggested that the age difference reflects the relative inability of adolescents to integrate cognition and emotion. Among relatively immature thinkers, emotional salience is disruptive to reasoning because their cognitive system is not as differentiated and flexible in its approach to reasoning and problem solving as the system is in older people. Emotion adds another complicated variable that needs to be integrated in the decision process. Postadolescent adults integrate emotion into cognition more successfully, thereby enabling them to consider more difficult and complex problems.

In other research, Blanchard-Fields included older adults in studies examining the interaction between emotional salience and problem solving. Older adults used more or less differentiated problem-solving strategies than did younger adults as a function of problem type. Specifically, older adults' performance depended on whether the problem was interpersonal or instrumental in nature (Blanchard-Fields & Camp, 1990). Whereas younger participants tended to use the same, problem-focused approach across situations, older adults were more likely to apply active problem-solving strategies to instrumental tasks (such as those related to home management) and avoidance or passive acceptance strategies to interpersonal problems high in emotional salience (such as conflicts with family members). Thus, older adults used a more differentiated approach to problem solving because they effectively changed their strategies in accordance with the demands of the problems; when problems had to do with emotions and emotional functioning, older adults were better able than younger adults to devise responses that dealt with the emotional aspects of the problem.

In another study (Blanchard-Fields, Jahnke, & Camp, 1995), participants wrote essays detailing how certain problems are best solved; participants in this study generated their own solutions to the problems presented to them. Again, older adults used more emotionally regulative problem-solving approaches than did younger adults in scenarios high in emotional salience. For instance, older adults tended to respond to highly emotionally salient problems by passivity or accepting the problem, focusing on the emotions related to the problem rather than with the problem itself. Older adults appear to use avoidant-denial strategies (i.e., managing their own emotional reaction) or passive-dependent strategies (i.e., doing nothing, avoidance) in emotionally salient situations. This is considered "adaptive problem solving" because it involves tailoring the problem-solving strategy to best fit the demands of the problem at hand. Younger adults, in contrast, tend to apply the same strategies across the board, even in situations in which active problem solving might be less successful (Blanchard-Fields et al., 1995). The findings are consistent with the assertion that emotions become increasingly central in cognitive processing as people age (see Blanchard-Fields, 1997).

A central message of Blanchard-Fields' program of research on problem solving is that emotional salience is disruptive to cognitive processing if emotion and cognition are not integrated. According to Blanchard-Fields (1997), adolescents and younger adults face emotionally salient problems by attempting to control or fix the problem without taking into account emotional information. They dislike the ambiguity inherent in many emotionally charged problems. In contrast, older adults are more willing to accept the problematic situation as it is, allowing them to focus on regulating their own emotions rather than on potentially futile attempts to "fix" a difficult, emotionally charged situation that may not have a controllable solution. Only when cognition and emotion are adequately integrated can such emotionally regulative problem solving occur effectively.

The role of emotion in cognitive processing also has been examined in recall of text material by Adams and colleagues (Adams, 1991; Adams, Labouvie-Vief, Hobart, & Dorosz, 1990; Adams, Smith, Nyquist, & Perlmutter, 1997). Findings across these studies indicate that older and younger adults recall different aspects of text and exhibit differences in the qualitative types of processes involved. Whereas older adults tend to offer more interpretive meaning of texts than do younger adults, younger adults recall more factual details. This adds further support to the assertion that subjective aspects of cognitive processing become more salient as people get older. In another recent study (Adams et al., 1997), participants read a story and later completed a recall task and interpreted or gave the meaning of the story, with the order of these tasks counterbalanced across participants and age groups. For the recall task, younger participants recalled more propositions in some conditions (recall first) but not in others (interpret first). On the interpretation task, older adults outperformed younger adults, regardless of condition, on the two 5-point rating scales used to analyze the responses. The first rating was composed of the depth scale, which evaluated how much the interpretation represented a deep underlying meaning of the story. Low scores were given to literal interpretations, whereas symbolic interpretations received high scores. The second was the synthesis scale; a high score was given on this scale only if participants unified conceptual elements into a complete whole. Response styles were then classified on the basis of the high–low dichotomy for each scale. Older adults preferred a deep-synthetic response style, characterized by holistic interpretations that reveal awareness of the symbolic themes of the stories.

Another study examined text recall among younger and older adults and found qualitative differences between the age groups (Gould, Trevithick, & Dixon,1991). In this study, Gould et al. presented a text to younger and older adults, either alone or in groups of 2 or 4. Participants were then asked to recall as much information as possible from the story in their own words; in the group conditions, the group worked on the recall task together, whereas participants recalled individually in the no-group condition. Elaborations were not encouraged, but many were found in the recall responses. Participants' recall was coded for two types of elaborations: denotative elaborations, which are very closely related to the text, and annotative elaborations, which involve evaluations of the characters and story, as well as interpretations and connections to personal experiences. Findings indicate that older adults use more annotative elaborations than do younger adults during the recall task, suggesting that they are interpreting the text as they recall it. Findings from these studies suggest that older adults may be motivated to produce different output from cognitive processes; in this case, output is consistent with goals of integrating knowledge gained over a lifetime and transmitting it within the culture (Adams, 1991; Adams et al., 1997).

Motivation and Emotion

The Meaning of Motivation. Links between emotion and motivation are undeniable because emotion is believed to "constitute a primary underlying motivational system that underlies memory, perception, thought, and action just as much as drives" (Filipp, 1996, p. 219). The two are also seen as having closely related neurological and endocrinological processes (Filipp, 1996). Therefore, any serious consideration of the bidirectional influences between emotion and cognition must address the potential role that motivation plays in task performance. Our definition of motivation contrasts with that traditionally used in cognitive psychology. In the cognitive literature, motivation is defined primarily in terms of need for achievement or mood states (e.g., anxiety; Leichtman, Ceci, & Ornstein, 1992). Conceptualized in this traditional way, motivation has been examined extensively and dismissed as largely uninformative in explaining age differences (Kausler, 1990; Salthouse, 1991; Smith, 1996). In other words, neither the desire to perform well nor mood accounts for observed age differences in performance on cognitive tasks.

In contrast to views that index motivation by variables that measure effort, however, the social cognitive literature considers motivation in terms of "processing goals" (Bargh, 1989; Hess, 1994), which are goals that presumably direct information-processing resources to specific aspects of a task based on the traits and concerns of the person. As shown in Fig. 11.1, processing goals are one of a number of hypothesized influences on cognitive processes, such as social event representations, which direct attention and effort to certain aspects of problems and away from others (Hess, 1994, p. 381).

Processing goals are influenced by personal values and experiences, which Hasher and Zacks (1988) argued may be applied broadly to information processing as people age. Hess (1994) also argued that age differences in cognition result in part from different experiences (knowledge) and processing goals, depicted in the left panel of Fig. 11.1. Both this model and the one offered by Hasher and Zacks, to which we return below, suggest that goals change with age as a function of experience and presumably change in idiosyncratic ways.

Socioemotional selectivity theory, described below, maintains that goals change in predictable ways as people move through adulthood and old age. Specifically, this theory predicts that emotional goals become increasingly salient as people age. This motivational model, proposed by Carstensen (1993, 1995; Carstensen, Isaacowitz, & Charles, 1999), posits that the construal of time as limited or expansive leads to the prioritization of

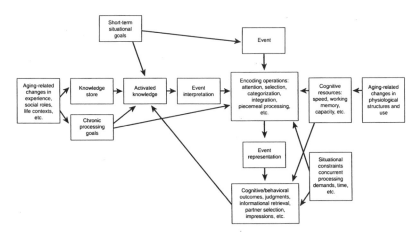

FIG. 11.1. Influences on the representation of social events. From "Social Cognition in Adulthood: Aging-Related Changes in Knowledge and Processing Mechanisms," by T. M. Hess, 1994, *Developmental Review, 14.* Copyright 1994 by the Academic Press. Reprinted with permission.

emotional or knowledge-seeking goals, respectively. Because age is inextricably and negatively associated with time left in life, age is associated with heightened emphasis on emotional goals in particular and emotional aspects of life more generally. Thus, socioemotional selectivity theory predicts that aging is associated with reduced motivation to acquire new knowledge and greater motivation to achieve emotionally satisfying states and to derive emotional meaning. The theory differs from other motivational theories in that the cognitive construal of the future, rather than acquired experience, accounts for goal changes throughout adulthood.

Socioemotional Selectivity Theory. A review of social interaction patterns across age is offered to clarify the increased importance of emotion in late life. Overall rates of social contact decline with age, and early theories in social gerontology presumed that emotional dampening or "turning inward" was at the core of this reliable social phenomenon. Disengagement theory (Cumming & Henry, 1961) postulates that older adults withdraw from others, especially intimates, in symbolic preparation for death. The theory also maintains that society engages in a simultaneous, motivated withdrawal from the older adult in order to prepare for the loss of its citizen. Thus, disengagement theory, widely influential in the field, suggests that older adults engage in proactive withdrawal from the social world, accompanied by emotional dampening or quiescence to protect themselves from emotional distress in the face of inevitable death.

Socioemotional selectivity theory was formulated in response to the same behavioral phenomenon (reduced social contact) and considers the approach of the end of life to be central in socioemotional changes in late adulthood. However, it differs importantly in its predictions about emotion. Socioemotional selectivity theory contends that emotional goals, emotional regulation, and emotional relationships grow increasingly important in the face of limited time. The reduction in social contact reflects a selective pruning process in which peripheral others are eliminated from the social network and only the most significant people are retained. According to the theory, the preference for familiar over rather novel social partners is an effective form of antecedent emotion regulation aimed at optimizing emotional experience (Carstensen et al., 1997).

The primary mechanism underlying the shift toward emotional goals is the cognitive appraisal of time (Carstensen et al., 1999). The theory maintains that a relatively stable constellation of goals (or motives) guides behavior throughout life. Goals are considered heuristically as involving one of two types: knowledge related (or information seeking) and emotional. Emotional goals involve successfully regulating one's emotions (Carstensen, 1993). These goals are pursued because of the feelings that accompany them, such as deriving meaning from life, verifying the self, and simply feeling good (Carstensen et al., 1997). Emotional and knowledge-related goals consistently compete throughout life. Sometimes information seeking entails emotional risks, for example, information seeking might be prioritized at the cost of emotion-related goals. An important determining factor in the activation of a particular goal is the perception of time. When time is perceived as open-ended, information-seeking goals are prioritized because information has immediate and long-term payoffs. Information is often banked for an expansive future. In contrast, when time is perceived as limited, goal hierarchies are reorganized and emotional goals are prioritized. Emotion, because it is experienced in the here and now, is highly salient in the face of limited time when future payoffs are far less likely.

Socioemotional selectivity theory predicts similar goal changes, regardless of age, when time is perceived as limited; and experimental evidence and field studies presented in the next section support the prediction (Carstensen & Fredrickson, 1998; Fredrickson & Carstensen, 1990; Fung, Carstensen, & Lutz, in press). However, because of the inextricable and negative association between chronological age and time left in life, emotional goals are increasingly important as people age. In youth, knowledge-related goals are presumed to take precedence over emotion-related goals. In old age, emotional goals are more important than informational goals (see Fig. 11.2). The theory predicts that emotion is generally more

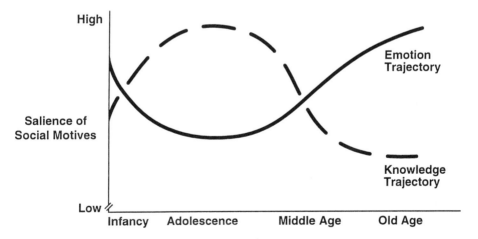

FIG. 11.2. Idealized life-span trajectories of emotion- and knowledge-related goal salience posited in socioemotional selectivity theory. From "The social context of emotion" by L. L. Carstensen, J. Gross, & H. Fung. In *Annual Review of Geriatrics and Gerontology* (p. 331), by K. W. Schaie & M. P. Lawton (Eds.), 1997, New York: Springer. Copyright 1997 by Springer Publishing Company. Reprinted with permission.

central in cognitive processing because of its increased relevance to the aging person. Whereas an adolescent might use his or her cognitive resources to pursue informational goals, an older adult expends cognitive resources primarily in the service of emotions and emotion regulation. Although there is some evidence for diminished magnitude of autonomic nervous system emotion responses with age (Levenson et al., 1991), there is substantial evidence that emotional functioning is maintained in old age, which speaks against the idea that endings such as death are accepted through affective flattening and withdrawal.

Empirical Support. The cardinal tenet of socioemotional selectivity theory is that when endings are salient, emotional goals are prioritized over others (Carstensen, 1993, 1995; Carstensen et al., 1997). A related prediction is that social partners are evaluated and preferred as a function of their emotional potential. In an early study, mental representations of social partners were investigated in a sample spanning adolescence to very old age. Research participants were presented with 18 cards, each of which described a potential social partner, and were asked to group them together according to how they would feel interacting with the people (Fredrickson & Carstensen, 1990). This task does not require participants to choose one person over another. Instead, participants are asked to sort these 18 cards into as many or as few piles as necessary to place people with whom they would feel similarly interacting with in the same pile. Multidimensional scaling techniques revealed three primary dimensions along which people classify social partners. One dimension reflects valenced (i.e., emotional) judgments of the social partners, and the remaining two were related, respectively, to future opportunities for contact and potential knowledge that could be derived from interaction with the person. Consistent with the theory, these dimensions suggest that people do consider affect, future prospects, and informational potential in mental representations of social partners.

Examination of dimension weights reveals age differences in the importance or salience of each dimension for each age group. As predicted by the theory, older adults place greater emphasis on emotion in their classification than do younger adults. Differences are also observed between age-matched subsamples of healthy and infirm elderly adults, presumably distinct in the amount of time they had left in life, such that the infirm older adults, in comparison with the healthy older adults, classified potential social partners increasingly along the affective dimension.

In an effort to further decouple age from place in the life cycle, another study was conducted in which subsamples of men were constructed based on HIV status (Carstensen & Fredrickson, 1998). In this study, all research participants were relatively young (mean age = 37 years) but varied in actuarial life expectancy. Using the same research paradigm described above, research participants completed the classification procedure. Just as the oldest age group in the initial study sorted primarily along the affective dimension, men who were HIV-positive and symptomatic also placed greatest weight on affect in their mental representations of others. The HIV-positive but asymptomatic subsample constructed similarity matrices similar to those of middle-aged people, and the HIV-negative subsample performed the task just as an age-matched subsample drawn from the general population performed the task, namely, using all dimensions comparably. Emotions, therefore, appear to become more salient in mental processing as people approach the end of life whether they are young or old.

The notion that emotions grow more salient as people age and face endings was supported by another study on social partner choice (Fredrickson & Carstensen, 1990). In this study, social preferences were assessed directly by presenting research participants of different ages (11 to 92 years) with three prospective social partners and asking them to select from among them. Social partner choices represented the dimensions revealed in the studies described above. They were (a) a member of your immediate family (affective potential), (b) a recent acquaintance with whom you seem to have much in common (potential for future contact), and (c) the author of a book you have just read (information seeking). Younger adults did not show a reliable preference for any of the three, but older adults showed a strong preference for the familiar social partner (the immediate family member). In a second condition, research participants were asked to imagine that they were about to move alone across the country but had "thirty minutes free" and wanted to spend it with another person. Under this experimental condition that limited time, younger participants also showed a bias for the familiar social partner. In another study, participants were asked to imagine that they had just received a telephone call from their physician telling them about a new medical advance that would add 20 years to their life. In this case, older participants changed their preferences such that the bias for the familiar social partner disappeared (Fung et al., in press).

Because socioemotional selectivity theory contends that emotion is more salient in later life, it predicts that emotional information should be better remembered. This prediction is consistent with Sinnott's (1996) assertion that cognitive resources are devoted to developmental tasks or, more generally, to what is most important at that developmental stage. In another study, an incidental memory paradigm was used to examine recall of emotional and nonemotional text (Carstensen & Turk-Charles, 1994). Participants aged 20 to 83 years each read a two-page selection from a popular novel. Names of the characters were changed to avoid association with the novel, and anyone who recognized the passage was not included in the analyses. The selection described a social interaction and contained comparable amounts of neutral and emotionally relevant information. At the end of the experimental hour, during which participants completed other unrelated questionnaires, they were asked to recall all that they could about the passage. Responses were transcribed and classified as emotional or nonemotional. Because age reductions in memory have been well established (Smith, 1996), this study did not focus on absolute levels of recall and the coding scheme was not formulated for the purposes of detecting small qualitative differences in recall. Instead, the study focused on age differences in the proportion of emotional material to the total material recalled. The coding scheme was organized around idea units and not on exact wording or correct number of words recalled. Although there were indeed age differences regarding absolute amount of information recalled, it appeared that the difference was related primarily to worse recall of neutral items by the older participants. Their recall of emotional items was relatively well maintained. When the proportion of emotional to nonemotional information was calculated and examined in relation to age, findings revealed that the proportion of emotional material recalled increased with each successive age group. Memory for emotional information may be relatively well preserved with age, spared possibly at the expense of other types of information; this suggests that recall deficits in cognitive aging may be circumscribed.

Similarities Among the Psychological Theories

All of the theories described above suggest a late-life shift toward greater emotional salience due either to changes in goals or to reorganizations of cognitive systems. Carstensen maintained that goals change as people approach endings, the ultimate of which is death, but that any ending increases the motivation to pursue emotional goals. In her view, goal shifts are highly malleable and depend importantly on the perception of time. Labouvie-Vief suggested that ego development is central and accounts for individual differences in cognitive and emotional development in adulthood. In all of the theoretical formulations and empirical work, however, emotion is considered ubiquitous in cognitive processing in old age. People mentally represent social partners along emotional dimensions, weight emotion heavily in problem solving, avoid emotionally charged situations, and prefer social partners who are emotionally meaningful to them.

Neurological Evidence of Emotional Changes With Age

Relatively recent neurological findings also inform discussions of emotion and aging. Myelination of certain regions of the hippocampus appear to continue well into middle age, with a substantial increase in myelination occurring between the fourth and sixth decades (Benes, Turtle, Khan, & Farol, 1994). Moreover, the amygdala is relatively spared from the predictable decrease in afferent fibers with age, despite experiencing some possible age-related neuronal loss (Scheibel, 1996). Because the hippocampus plays a role in complex emotional experiences, such as conditioned fear (LaBar & LeDoux, 1997), age-related changes in hippocampal structures and connections to the amygdala, which are involved in emotional stimulus evaluation (LaBar & LeDoux, 1997), are particularly relevant to discussions of emotion and aging. Scheibel described evidence pointing both to hippocampal atrophy and to hippocampal cell volume stability with aging.

Benes et al. (1994) speculated that these increases in hippocampal myelination may be related to increases in emotional maturity, which is thought to occur during this period of life. Certainly these findings fit nicely into the adult cognitive developmental literature, particularly the theoretical and empirical work of Labouvie-Vief and colleagues. Although it is impossible to know at this point whether any of the neurological evidence above precedes or results from changes in emotional experience, preliminary findings are consistent with the psychological theories described above, and as such are quite intriguing. Indeed, even decline in brain structures may be associated either with functional loss *or* with increased efficiency of that structure. Although Benes et al.'s view, which suggests a link between these neurological findings and enhanced emotional functioning, may seem optimistic, these findings suggest a means by which emotion-related cognitive functioning might be maintained despite other losses associated with age. Increased myelination in the hippocampus stands in contrast to neurological evidence examining overall changes in the brain that points to a degeneration of myelin with age (e.g., Dickson et al., 1992).

ALTERNATIVE INTERPRETATIONS
FOR EMPIRICAL STUDIES OF COGNITIVE AGING

Thus far, we have reviewed research suggesting that emotions become increasingly salient for older people and noted neurological findings consistent with the maintenance or improvement in emotional reasoning and emotional experience with age. In the following section, we review studies from cognitive psychology that explicitly or tacitly involve emotion. Heretofore, the findings from the following studies have been interpreted in terms of hard-wired changes resulting in deterioration of cognitive processes. In the following section, we suggest alternative explanations linked to findings about emotion in old age.

Empirical Findings That Link Emotion
and Cognition in Aging Research

Person Perception. Research by Hess and colleagues includes information about the influence of negative emotion on cognition, suggesting that older adults are particularly sensitive to affectively negative information about a target person. In his initial work, Hess found age differences in person perception that appeared to reflect reduced cognitive efficiency in revising social schemas (Hess & Tate, 1991). In this study, younger adults were found to show a consistency effect in their judgments of target people such that they recalled trait-inconsistent behaviors better than trait-consistent ones. Older adults, in contrast, showed no such effect. In a subsequent study, Hess and Pullen (1994) investigated the influence of positive and negative emotional stimuli in a study of impression formation. In this study, younger and older participants read a description of a target person. After reading the description, participants read additional information about the target person that was either consistent or inconsistent with the original description. It was hypothesized that older adults would be less likely to integrate new, inconsistent information about the target person and would therefore show less impression change from their initial opinions for the target person given the new information.

Contrary to their expectations, Hess and Pullen (1994) found no age-related differences in ability to integrate new information. Age differences were present, however, in impression change depending on the valence of the initial impression. Specifically, younger adults showed the consistency effect described above, regardless of whether the behaviors presented were positive or negative. Older participants showed the same consistency effects as did younger participants for positive information; however, older adults recalled more negative information, regardless of its consistency with the original information on the target person. Hess (1994) speculated that older adults differentially process negative behavioral information and have a stronger belief in the immutability of negative, as opposed to positive, person characteristics.

This finding could be interpreted as an age deficit related to older adults' inability to integrate new information into existing paradigms, as evidenced by their failure to integrate new positive information into initial first impressions (see also MacKay & Abrams, 1996, for a discussion of older adults' difficulty forming new connections). It could also be interpreted in terms of increasing rigidity with age or an inability to decenter processing from one aspect of a stimulus (Looft, 1972). However, differences by condition suggest a different interpretation, namely, that negative emotional material becomes more salient to older adults. Effective antecedent-focused emotion regulation demands that careful attention is paid to negative qualities of prospective social partners (Carstensen et al., 1997; Gross et al., 1997). That is, older adults appear to monitor the potential for negative emotional experiences and take active measures to avoid them. This interpretation is consistent with findings suggesting that older people better regulate affect (Lawton et al., 1992), experience less negative affect (Gross et al., 1997), and actively avoid arousing situations (Lawton et al., 1992). One aspect of antecedent-focused regulation appears to be monitoring the environment for possible sources of negative affect and avoiding them; that older adults appear to have a lower frequency of negative affective episodes (Carstensen, Pasupathi, & Mayr, in press) suggests that these attempts may be quite successful. In this way, attention to negative information can actually lead to less negative affect.

Subsequent studies have suggested the role of motivation in the consistency effect (Hess, Follett, & McGee, 1998). When older and younger participants were asked to evaluate a person for a job in their neighborhood (e.g., a police officer), age differences in inconsistency disappeared as long as the older adults scored above the mean on the reading span. Therefore, older adults with above-average reading span ability can integrate inconsistent information in a situation that is highly relevant to their lives in a manner similar to that of younger adults.

Source Memory. In a very different program of research, Johnson, Hashtroudi, and colleagues examined age differences in source monitoring and presented findings suggesting that attention to affect may play a role in source memory deficits among older adults. In an initial study, younger people, who were clearly superior at recalling the source of events, recollected more sensory and perceptual details about the original experience (Hashtroudi, Johnson, & Chrosniak, 1990). Interestingly, however, older people recalled *more* thoughts, feelings, and evaluative statements than did their younger counterparts. In addition, age differences in the correlates of participants' confidence ratings with recall accuracy were observed. Among younger participants, confidence ratings were associated with the amount of perceptual detail recalled, whereas among older adults confidence ratings were associated with the amount of emotional detail recalled. In other words, older adults rate their performance on the basis of emotional material.

In a subsequent study, Hashtroudi, Johnson, Vnek, and Ferguson (1994) experimentally manipulated participants' attention to either affective or factual aspects of the situation. As predicted, older participants in the absence of instructions performed more poorly on source-monitoring tasks. When instructed to focus on the factual component of the to-be-remembered events, younger adults still outperformed older adults, but the age difference was attenuated compared with the prior condition. Explicit instructions to focus on facts appears to enhance the older participants' performance. Also of interest, both younger and older participants performed worse in the affective focus condition. Affective focus appears to be associated with poorer performance on recall because it leads participants to make elaborative responses in their recall. Johnson (1995) speculated that older adults are more prone to focus on the affective details of an event and that this may worsen source memory because perceptual focus leads to better memory cues compared with affective focus.

Inhibition, Age, and Emotion. Hasher and Zacks (1988; Zacks & Hasher, 1997; chap. 5, this volume) interpret older adults' poorer performance relative to younger adults on many cognitive tasks as failures of inhibitory mechanisms. In this model, inhibitory mechanisms are hypothesized to become less effective as people get older. Because inhibitory mechanisms determine what enters working memory in the first place by excluding irrelevant stimuli, they promote efficient (and presumably faster) cognitive processing of target stimuli. Inhibition failures thus permit task-irrelevant material to receive more sustained activation than it would otherwise, resulting in heightened distractibility, increased forgetfulness, and longer response latencies (Hasher & Zacks, 1988; Stoltzfus, Hasher, Zacks, Ulivi, & Goldstein, 1993).

Hashtroudi et al. (1990) raised the interesting possibility that older adults' relatively good recall for thoughts and feelings may, in fact, represent failures of inhibitory mechanisms related to emotion. If so, emotional disinhibition could account for the apparent ubiquitousness of emotion in cognitive processing previously described. However, cognitive failures associated with an inefficient inhibitory mechanism are now thought to be fairly domain specific and not to generalize widely across stimuli (Connelly & Hasher, 1993; Kane, Hasher, Stoltzfus, Zacks, & Connelly, 1994). Thus, evidence for *emotional* disinhibition per se would be needed to make a compelling case that disinhibition accounts for heightened attention to emotion in older adults.

Concurrent with selective increases in disinhibition, according to Hasher and Zacks (1988; chap. 5, this volume), goals related to information processing change. Figure 11.3 illustrates their model. Essentially, personal values and experiences become more important and are applied more broadly to information processing as people age (Hasher & Zacks, 1988, p. 212); the left-most column of Fig. 11.3 should therefore represent what Hasher and Zacks conceived of as changes that occur with normal aging. Age changes in general goals, which subsequently affect processing goals, influence inhibitory mechanisms and generate information that extends well beyond the "objective" meaning of the stimulus to enter working memory. Reduced inhibition allows such information to leak into working memory and to receive more activation once in working memory than it would otherwise.

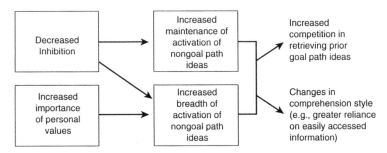

FIG. 11.3. Theoretical model of the effects of reduced inhibitory capacity. The left-most column represents changes hypothesized to take place with normal aging. From "Working memory, comprehension, and aging: A review and a new view," by L. Hasher & R. T. Zacks. In *The Psychology of Learning and Motivation*, by G. G. Bower (Ed.), 1988, San Diego, CA: Academic Press. Copyright 1988 by the Academic Press. Reprinted with permission.

Although we do not deny the possibility of inhibitory factors accounting for age differences, we also suggest that a possible alternative or even complementary explanation to the findings of Hashtroudi, Johnson, and colleagues is that shifts in goals and motivational processes lead to better memory for emotional, as opposed to objective, detail. A motivational role does not rule out the possibility of decreased inhibition. In fact, the two may work together to overdetermine age effects. As Hasher and Zacks (1988) argued, motivated attention to emotion may contribute directly to these findings. It is notable that older adults in Hashtroudi and Johnson's research appear to focus on the affective aspects of stimuli at the expense of factual aspect in contrast to younger adults' better factual focus. These findings are consistent with our assertion that older adults are motivated to allocate more cognitive resources to emotions and emotion regulation. Emotion regulation is especially a candidate for this specific resource allocation because by definition it involves a person's attempts to influence his or her emotional experiences, a process which may be under conscious control (Gross et al., 1997).

Related evidence consistent with the findings of Hashtroudi et al. (1990) is seen in research on collaborative storytelling and text recall, both studies providing more evidence that older people favor a more subjective approach to cognitive processing than do younger adults. In a study previously mentioned, Gould et al. (1991) found that older adults use more annotative elaborations (i.e., evaluations and interpretations) than do younger adults during a test recall task. When interpreting these results, annotative elaborations might be seen as intrusions if they interfered with recall. However, several interesting findings emerged from this study that are pertinent to the question of intrusions in this recall. Although older and younger adults did not differ in the generation of denotative elaborations (those closely related to the text), older adults did produce more annotative elaborations, which, by virtue of their personal relevance, implicate affect. Importantly, however, annotative elaborations were uncorrelated with recall, suggesting that focus on subjective material may not hinder performance on this type of memory task and thus were not intrusions per se. It appears that these more interpretive elaborations resulted from older people's different understanding of the meaning of memory, which is consistent with Labouvie-Vief and Blanchard-Fields' (1982) assertion that cognitive tasks may take on different meanings for older adults, as well as with the idea that changes in processing goals occur with age.

In a study of collaborative storytelling (Gould & Dixon, 1993), older and younger couples told stories related to a shared vacation experience. These experiences seemed to be comparable because types of vacations were fairly similar for the younger and older couples. The authors reported that 6 couples in both groups had gone to other countries and that most of the couples described fairly recent trips. Thus, the experiences themselves seem similar enough to warrant comparisons. Age differences in the content of the stories produced by younger and older couples were observed. Older couples' vacation stories were more subjective than the stories of younger couples; specifically, older couples provided more descriptions of people and places but less about the itineraries of the vacation than did younger couples. The authors speculated that there are two possible explanations for these findings. The processing-deficit view suggests that older adults may be unable to remember specific details about the vacation and thus report fewer items that are itinerary related, whereas the production-deficit view posits that older adults could simply have a different storytelling style and presume that the listener would rather hear this certain style. A motivational approach clearly favors the latter view, but it is indeed difficult to distinguish between the two alternatives (or to disentangle possible cohort effects) given the available data. The authors provide some anecdotal evidence in favor of the production-deficit view: specifically, some young adult couples acknowledged that they were being boring but felt they had to be thorough with details. In contrast, one older adult couple claimed that they were just giving highlights because other people do not want to hear all the details. There are also possible differences in cognitive processing at the encoding stage. Older adults' tendency to focus on (and process more deeply) emotions and subjective material may relate to the observed tendency to provide more subjective details of their vacation experience.

In summary, the studies reviewed above illustrate ways in which age-related differences in the efficiency of cognitive processing may be accounted for, in part, by changes in processing goals (Hasher & Zacks, 1988; Hess, 1994; Hess & Pullen, 1994). We have reviewed evidence suggesting that age differences in cognitive performance may result in part from different interpretations of the demands of the task (Gould & Dixon, 1993). This is consistent with earlier speculations that older adults may understand different reasons for cognitive task performance, which may be a confounding factor in age differences (Labouvie-Vief & Blanchard-Fields, 1982). Hess and Pullen (1994) argued that ignoring goal-based influences on cognitive processing can "lead to faulty conclusions about age differences" (p. 249). We add to this caveat that special concern is needed when information processing involves emotional material.

IMPLICATIONS FOR COGNITIVE AGING RESEARCH

So far, we have reviewed information about the intersection of cognition and emotion. Now we turn to a consideration of the possible implications these findings may hold for cognitive aging research. First, emotion appears to be sufficiently ubiquitous in the goals and thoughts of older adults that experimental stimuli may inadvertently prime emotions and subsequently place a potential confound in experiments. Special attention to experimental material, specifically to whether it explicitly (or even perhaps idiosyncratically) primes emotional response in older participants, bears consideration.

Second, we argue that motivational differences between younger and older adults continue to offer viable alternative explanations for some age differences in cognitive aging. Although we agree with Kausler (1990) that previous examinations of motivational effects in cognitive aging research explained little variance, we also agree with Filipp (1996) that the operational definitions of motivation in cognitive research have not been terribly informative and that "the conceptual meaning and scope of motivational constructs needs to be reformulated" (p. 232). Motivation, as defined in socioemotional selectivity theory, for example, does not concern individual differences in performance desire. Rather, processing goals—some of which may operate out of conscious awareness—may change with age such that the attentional focus of younger and older adults is systematically directed to different aspects of the task or stimulus. Specifically, socioemotional selectivity theory predicts that people who perceive their time as limited are motivated to focus on emotional content in all domains in order to most efficiently regulate their own emotions. Regulation will extend to cognitive processing insofar as it may contribute to effective emotion regulation.

Resource allocation is critical to any account of emotion–cognition dynamics. Bower (1992) suggested that emotional reactions may "soak up processing resources" (p. 17), leaving less capacity available for processing of other material. Findings reported by Johnson and colleagues (e.g., Johnson, Nolde, & De Leonardis, 1996) suggest that this may indeed be the case; in their research, focusing on affective aspects of a stimulus leads to poorer recall. This type of affective focus may represent the baseline means of encoding memories for older adults (Hashtroudi et al., 1990). Their findings are consistent with work in which older adults tend to focus on main ideas or themes in their recall and appear to remember the gist of a text or story better than details of the text (e.g. Adams et al., 1997; Gould et al., 1991), although other work has indeed found decreases in recall of high-level text information with age (see Cohen, 1988).

There may be an important gain–loss dynamic present across the life span involving resource allocation. A growing and consistent literature on emotion and aging points to maintained or improved functioning with age (Carstensen et al., 1997; Gross et al., 1997). Herein lies what has become known as "the paradox of aging": Although older adults report a greater proportion of losses than gains with age (Heckhausen et al., 1989), they also report greater satisfaction with close social relationships (e.g., Field & Minkler, 1988), less loneliness (Revenson, 1986), and enjoy better mental health than do younger adults (Regier et al., 1988). A consideration of emotion may be critical to deciphering this seeming paradox. When endings are salient and time is perceived as limited, emotion is prioritized over other goals and motivates social choices. It appears that older people place great value on social and emotional experience. Heightened focus on emotion may leave fewer resources available for processing information that older adults view as less relevant. Ironically, this is precisely the type of cognitive performance that is usually demanded in cognitive psychology experiments (e.g., attention to detail), so older adults may have fewer resources available for nonemotional tasks such as these and may therefore perform more poorly than younger adults. The apportioning of resources in such a manner may well be a motivated process.

It may also be the case that older adults are able to avoid more striking decrements in cognitive processing through their emphasis on the emotional aspects of stimuli. Extra emotion-related cues gained from a focus on subjective aspects of experience might allow them to maintain cognitive performance in some domains at the same time that performance in other domains is declining. Future research will need to address the issue of whether emotion focus results from reapportioning of cognitive resources and whether it allows maintenance of performance while other cognitive abilities might be showing some decline. Experimental designs need to be developed in which resources are held constant and then participants' allocation of processing resources to emotional or nonemotional stimuli are monitored to answer these types of questions. Eye-tracking techniques, such as those used by Christianson et al. (1991), might be useful in this endeavor.

Consistent with this argument are findings that cognitive processing tasks that rely on emotion improve with age (see Blanchard-Fields & Camp, 1990; Labouvie-Vief, 1997; Labouvie-Vief, DeVoe, & Bulka, 1989). Reasoning and social problem solving are tasks that require cognitive processing and that can often include emotional content. Studies suggest that older adults show more flexible reasoning about emotion-laden social dilemmas (Blanchard-Fields & Camp, 1990) and have a better understanding of emotional experience than do younger adults (Labouvie-Vief, DeVoe, & Bulka, 1989), a finding consistent with our above assertion. It is worth noting that nonemotional reasoning tasks do show age-related decline (e.g., Gilinsky & Judd, 1994), so improvement appears to be specific to tasks in which the stimuli specifically include emotional material. The development of key components of wisdom, such as compassion and empathy, requires reasoning beyond one's own thoughts and feelings to access the emotions of others (Kramer, 1990). In conjunction with Sinnott's (1996) theory that postformal thinking arises from a heightened concern for interpersonally oriented developmental tasks of late life, it appears that many of the cognitive tasks on which adults improve with age involve social problem solving (e.g., Blanchard-Fields & Camp, 1990).

An interesting implication of the theoretical and empirical work in social cognition is that some observed deficits in cognitive processing may be remediated by emotional framing. Research by Blanchard-Fields and colleagues (Blanchard-Fields, 1986, 1997; Blanchard-Fields & Camp, 1990) demonstrates, for example, that older adults perform better than younger adults on emotionally salient problems. When older and younger participants are asked to respond to hypothetical problem scenarios on a reasoning task, older adults appear to perform better on emotionally salient problems. On these problems, older adults demonstrate higher level reasoning (Sebby & Papini, 1991) and more differentiated responses (see Blanchard-Fields, 1997). For younger adults, emotional salience seems to interfere with cognitive processing and reasoning, whereas older adults seem not to have this disruption and therefore appear to better integrate emotional salience into their problem solving (Blanchard-Fields, 1986). Regardless of age, the central details of emotionally salient material are better recalled (Bower, 1992; Christianson et al., 1992). It is conceivable that emotional relevance facilitates better cognitive processing, from encoding to retrieval. Experimental instructions, for example, could be used to make experimental tasks more emotionally relevant. Adams (1990) reported a study in which instructions explicitly targeted emotional relevance. Participants were asked to memorize a story *in order to tell it to a child*, and in this case older adults' memory for propositional detail surpassed that of younger adults. Although this finding has yet to be replicated, it is still intriguing given our consideration of motivational links between emotion, cognition, and aging; thus, further research using this paradigm is clearly warranted.

CONCLUSION

Cavanaugh (1989) noted that there is "growing suspicion" (p. 604) among memory researchers that emotion and memory are more closely related in older adults than in younger adults. We concur. In this chapter, we have reviewed theories and empirical research on emotion, cognition, and their interactions across the life course. Emotional functioning remains intact well into old age (e.g., Carstensen et al., 1997; Gross et al., 1997; Lawton et al., 1992; Levenson et al., 1991; Malatesta & Kalnok, 1984). Socioemotional selectivity theory contends that older people regulate emotions better than younger people because the salience of emotion in many life domains increases as people age (Carstensen, Isaacowitz, & Charles, 1999).

There is considerable evidence that cognitive processing goals shift with age (Carstensen & Fredrickson, 1990; Hasher & Zacks, 1988; Hess, 1994), such that personal information and subjective aspects of the stimuli become more prominent. These changes in processing goals are evident in areas ranging from text recall (Adams et al., 1997; Carstensen & Turk-Charles, 1994) to social cognition (Hess & Pullen, 1994) to social preferences (Fredrickson & Carstensen, 1990). In each of these cases, there appear to be differences in what older adults understand as the meaning of the task and their motivation for performing it, such that subjective and affective aspects of the task are highlighted over more factual aspects. This shift in focus makes sense in light of goal changes favoring emotional regulation (Carstensen et al., 1997), as an explicit awareness of the affective nature of stimuli is necessary for effective regulatory responses.

Quite possibly, cognitive changes are overdetermined by experiential, maturational, neural, and motivational processes. As people get older and sense that their time is limited, there is also a simultaneous decrease in energy reserves available in all domains, including cognitive processing. Sinnott (1996) observed that middle-aged adults "must choose when (and why!) to deploy one's resources, newly aware of their limits" (p. 364). The decrease in energy capacity associated with a general slowing of cognitive processes surely accounts for an important part of the variance in age changes in cognition (Salthouse, 1991).

The increased salience of emotion and shifts in cognitive processing goals that occur as people age and mature appear to coalesce and produce an information-processing system that is increasingly emotion focused across adulthood. Increased focus on emotion in all life domains (Carstensen, Isaacowitz, & Charles, 1999) suggests that cognitive processing should not be spared from this emphasis on emotion and emotional regulation. Indeed, effective antecedent-focused emotion regulation requires a cognitive system that is attuned to emotional experience (Gross et al., 1997). Our assertion that information processing becomes more emotion focused with age is highly consistent with the neo-Piagetian approaches to adult cognitive development, which stress not only an increased awareness of subjective concerns but also, more important, an increased integration of emotional experience into reasoning, problem solving, and cognitive processing more generally (Blanchard-Fields et al., 1995; Sebby & Papini, 1991). This increased integration is adaptive because it allows people to accept the complexity of human experience rather than to experience certain emotions as too disruptive or to allow their emotions to be ruled by cognitive processes (Labouvie-Vief, 1997). As Labouvie-Vief's research shows, individual differences in cognitive–emotional abilities do exist. Not every individual achieves integration that is suggestive of high-level neo-Piagetian thought (Labouvie-Vief, 1997). However, increased focus on emotion does appear normative with age.

That emotion becomes more salient with age is hard to contest. The reasons for the effect are more controversial. On the one hand, older adults may be less able to inhibit irrelevant information from cognitive processing because of a decreasingly efficient inhibitory mechanism, which allows emotions to leak into cognitive processing (Hasher & Zacks, 1998; Hashtroudi et al., 1994; Zacks & Hasher, 1997). On the other hand, motivational changes appear to heighten the salience of emotional material. If the ubiquitous influence of emotion in cognitive processing among older adults was purely the result of disinhibition, one would not expect to see improved emotional regulation and superior mental health in older adults. Evidence of increased hippocampal myelination (Benes et al., 1994) also speaks against the disinhibition account.

We contend that under conditions in which energy and future time are limited, people focus on what is most salient in their lives. Furthermore, we contend that emotional aspects of life are most salient. The approach of endings directs attention specifically to emotional goals (Carstensen, Isaacowitz, & Charles, 1999; Fredrickson & Carstensen, 1990). Older adults' poorer performance on many cognitive tasks may therefore be an artifact of how they are choosing to apportion their energy in cognitive processing; this is a prediction of socioemotional selectivity theory (Carstensen, Isaacowitz, & Charles, 1999), and there is accumulating evidence to support this claim (e.g., Carstensen & Turk-Charles, 1994; Gould & Dixon, 1993; Hashtroudi et al., 1990, 1994).

The selective investment in particular goals in accordance with developmental changes is highly adaptive and may be a relatively unexplored aspect of successful aging, especially within a framework of selective optimization with compensation (M. M. Baltes & Carstensen, 1996; P. B. Baltes, 1997; P. B. Baltes & Baltes, 1990). The research reviewed in this chapter provides theoretical and empirical support for identifying the *nature* or direction that selections are likely to take in the later years of life. If older adults select emotion as an important aspect of their lives, they may indeed seek to optimize the processing of emotional material. This may be only one strategy they use to compensate for decreases in cognitive processing capabilities and may be one aspect of a more general focus on subjective factors (such as knowledge store) to maintain cognitive performances in the face of resource loss.

There is clearly much need for further research. We hope that investigators plan studies that directly explore the emotion–cognition relationship in different age groups and refine theoretical accounts of age differences to include consideration of findings about emotion and cognition. Additionally, it will be of interest to determine what adaptive function this relationship serves. Diverse methodologies should be used to investigate the role of emotion in age-related cognitive change: from traditional cognitive laboratory tasks, in which differential performance on emotional versus nonemotional tasks can be assessed, to newer neuroimaging technologies that can track areas of brain activation during task performance. Current research and theory does suggest, however, that motivational changes related to the emotion–cognition relationship in adulthood and old age appear to be important for understanding the nature of age differences in cognitive performance.

ACKNOWLEDGMENTS

Work on this chapter was supported by a National Science Foundation Graduate Research Fellowship to Derek M. Isaacowitz and by National Institute on Aging Grant R01-8816 to Laura L. Carstensen. We thank Turhan Canli and Matthew Prull for helpful comments on an earlier version of this chapter.

REFERENCES

Adams, C. (1990, November). *Age differences in story recall: Memory in the context of storytelling.* Poster session presented at the annual meeting of the Gerontological Society of America, Boston, MA.

Adams, C. (1991). Qualitative age differences in memory for text: A life-span developmental perspective. *Psychology and Aging, 6,* 323–336.

Adams, C., Labouvie-Vief, G., Hobart, C. J., & Dorosz, M. (1990). Adult age group differences in story recall style. *Journal of Gerontology: Psychological Sciences, 45,* P17–P27.

Adams, C., Smith, M. C., Nyquist, L., & Perlmutter, M. (1997). Adult age-group differences in recall for the literal and interpretive meanings of narrative text. *Journal of Gerontology: Psychological Sciences, 52,* P187–P195.

Baltes, P. B. (1997). On the incomplete architecture of human ontogeny: Selection, optimization, and compensation as foundation of developmental theory. *American Psychologist, 52*, 366–380.

Baltes, P. B., & Baltes, M. M. (1990). Psychological perspectives on successful aging: The model of selective optimization with compensation. In P. B. Baltes & M. M. Baltes (Eds.), *Successful aging: Perspectives from the behavioral sciences* (pp. 1–34). New York: Cambridge University Press.

Baltes, P. B., & Schaie, K. W. (1974). Aging and IQ: The myth of the twilight years. *Psychology Today, 7*, 35–40.

Baltes, M. M., & Carstensen, L. L. (1996). The process of successful ageing. *Ageing and Society. 16*, 397–422.

Banham, K. M. (1951). Senescence and the emotions: A genetic theory. *Journal of Genetic Psychology, 78*, 183.

Bargh, J. A. (1989). Conditional automaticity: Varieties of automatic influence in social perception and cognition. In J. S. Uleman & J. A. Bargh (Eds.), *Unintended thought* (pp. 3–51). New York: Guilford.

Benes, F. M., Turtle, M., Khan, Y., & Farol, P. (1994). Myelination of a key relay zone in the hippocampal formation occurs in the human brain during childhood, adolescence, and adulthood. *Archives of General Psychiatry, 51*, 477–484.

Blanchard-Fields, F. (1986). Reasoning on social dilemmas varying in emotional saliency: An adult developmental perspective. *Psychology and Aging, 1*, 325–333.

Blanchard-Fields, F. (1997). The role of emotion in social cognition across the adult life span. In K. W. Schaie & M. P. Lawton (Eds.), *Annual review of gerontology and geriatrics* (Vol. 17, pp. 238–265). New York: Springer.

Blanchard-Fields, F., & Camp, C. (1990). Affect, individual differences, and real world problem solving across the adult life span. In T. M. Hess (Ed.), *Aging and cognition: Knowledge organization and utilization* (pp. 461–497). Amsterdam: North-Holland.

Blanchard-Fields, F., Jahnke, H. C., & Camp, C. (1995). Age differences in problem-solving style: The role of emotional salience. *Psychology and Aging, 10*, 173–180.

Blaney, P. H. (1986). Affect and memory: A review. *Psychological Bulletin, 99*, 229–246.

Blankstein, K. R., Toner, B. B., & Flett, G. L. (1989). Test anxiety and the contents of consiousness: Thought listing and endorsement measures. *Journal of Research in Personality, 23*, 269–286.

Bower, G. H. (1981). Mood and memory. *American Psychologist, 36*, 129–148.

Bower, G. H. (1992). How might emotions affect learning? In S. -Ò. Christianson (Ed.), *Handbook of emotion and memory: Research and theory* (pp. 3–32). Hillsdale, NJ: Lawrence Erlbaum Associates.

Bromley, D. B. (1990). *Behavioural gerontology: Central issues in the psychology of ageing* (pp. 263–316). Chichester, England: Wiley.

Carstensen, L. L. (1993). Motivation for social contact across the life span: A theory of socioemotional selectivity. In J. Jacobs (Ed.), *Nebraska Symposium on Motivation: Vol. 40. Developmental perspectives on motivation* (pp. 209–254). Lincoln: University of Nebraska Press.

Carstensen, L. L. (1995). Evidence for a life-span theory of socioemotional selectivity. *Current Directions in Psychological Science, 4*, 151–156.

Carstensen, L. L., & Fredrickson, B. L. (1998). Influence of HIV status and age on cognitive representations of others. *Health Psychology, 17*, 1–10.

Carstensen, L. L., Gottman, J. M., & Levenson, R. W. (1995). Emotional behavior in long-term marriage. *Psychology and Aging, 10*, 140–149.

Carstensen, L. L., Graff, J., Levenson, R. W., & Gottman, J. M. (1996). Affect in intimate relationships: The developmental course of marriage. In C. Magai & S. McFadden (Eds.), *Handbook of emotion, adult development, and aging* (pp. 227–247). Orlando, FL: Academic Press.

Carstensen, L.L., Gross, J., & Fung, H. (1997). The social context of emotion. In K. W. Schaie & M. P. Lawton (Eds.), *Annual review of geriatrics and gerontology* (Vol. 17, pp. 325–352). New York: Springer.

Carstensen, L. L., Isaacowitz, D. M., & Charles, S. T. (1999). Taking time seriously: A theory of social selectivity. *American Psychologist, 54,* 165–181.

Carstensen, L. L., Pasupathi, M., & Mayr, U. (in press). Emotional experience in everyday life across the adult life span. *Journal of Personality and Social Pychology.*

Carstensen, L. L., & Turk-Charles, S. (1994). The salience of emotion across the adult life span. *Psychology and Aging, 9,* 259–264.

Cavanaugh, J. C. (1989). I have this feeling about everyday memory aging. *Educational Gerontology, 15,* 597–605.

Chinen, A. B. (1984). Modal logic: A new paradigm of development and late-life potential. *Human Development, 27,* 42–56.

Christianson, S. -Å. (1992). Emotional stress and eyewitness memory: A critical review. *Psychological Bulletin, 112,* 284–309.

Christianson, S. -Å., Goodman, J., & Loftus, E. F. (1992). Eyewitness memory for stressful events: Methodological quandaries and ethical dilemmas. In S. -Å. Christianson (Ed.), *Handbook of emotion and memory: Research and theory* (pp. 217–241). Hillsdale, NJ: Lawrence Erlbaum Associates.

Christianson, S. -Å., Loftus, E. F., Hoffman, H., & Loftus, G. R. (1991). Eye fixations and memory for emotional events. *Journal of Experimental Psychology: Learning, Memory, and Cognition, 17,* 693–701.

Cohen, G. (1988). Age differences in memory for texts: Production deficiency or processing limitations? In L. L. Light & D. M. Burke (Eds.), *Language, memory, and aging* (pp. 171–190). Cambridge, England: Cambridge University Press.

Connelly, S. L., & Hasher, L. (1993). Aging and the inhibition of spatial location. *Journal of Experimental Psychology: Human Perception and Performance, 19,* 1238–1250.

Cumming, E., & Henry, W. E. (1961). *Growing old: The process of disengagement.* New York: Basic Books.

Dickson, D. W., Crystal, H. A., Mattiace, L. A., Masur, D. M., Blau, A. D., Davies, P., Yen, S. H., & Aronson, M. K. (1992). Identification of normal and pathological aging in prospectively studied nondemented elderly humans. *Neurobiology of Aging, 13,* 179–189.

Ellis, H. C., Thomas, R. L., & Rodriguez, I. A. (1984). Emotional mood states and memory: Elaborative encoding, semantic processing, and cognitive effort. *Journal of Experimental Psychology, 10,* 470–482.

Eysenck, M. W. (1982). *Attention and arousal: Cognition and performance.* Berlin, Germany: Springer.

Field, D., & Minkler, M. (1988). Continuity and change in social support between young-old, old-old, and very-old adults. *Journal of Gerontology, 43,* P100–P106.

Filipp, S. -H. (1996). Motivation and emotion. In J. E. Birren & K. W. Schaie (Eds.), *Handbook of the psychology of aging* (4th ed., pp. 218–235). San Diego, CA: Academic Press.

Fisher, J. E., Zeiss, A. M., & Carstensen, L. L. (1993). Psychopathology in the aged. In P. B. Sutker & H. E. Adams, *Comprehensive handbook of psychopathology* (2nd ed., pp. 815–842). New York: Plenum.

Forgas, J. P., & Bower, G. H. (1987). Mood effects on person-perception judgments. *Journal of Personality and Social Psychology, 53,* 53–60.

Fredrickson, B. L., & Carstensen, L. L. (1990). Choosing social partners: How old age and anticipated endings make people more selective. *Psychology and Aging, 8,* 301–313.

Fung, H. H., Carstensen, L. L., & Lutz, A. (in press). Time perspective: A possible explanation for age differences in social preferences. *Psychology and Aging.*

Gilinsky, A. S., & Judd, B. B. (1994). Working memory and bias in reasoning across the life span. *Psychology and Aging, 9,* 356–371.

Gilligan, S. G., & Bower, G. H. (1984). Cognitive consequences of emotional arousal. In C. E. Izard, J. Kagan, & R. B. Zajonc (Eds.), *Emotions, cognition, and behavior* (pp. 547–588). Cambridge, England: Cambridge University Press.

Gotlib, I. H., Roberts, J. E., & Gilboa, E. (1996). In I. G. Sarason, G. R. Pierce, & B. R. Sarason (Eds.), *Cognitive interference: Theories, methods, and findings* (pp. 347–377). Mahwah, NJ: Lawrence Erlbaum Associates.

Gould, O. N., & Dixon, R. A. (1993). How we spent our vacation: Collaborative storytelling by young and old adults. *Psychology and Aging, 8*, 10–17.

Gould, O. N., Trevithick, L., & Dixon, R. A. (1991). Adult age differences in elaborations produced during prose recall. *Psychology and Aging, 6*, 93–99.

Gross, J. J., Carstensen, L. L., Pasupathi, M., Tsai, J., Skorpen, C. G., & Hsu, A. Y. C. (1997). Emotion and aging: Experience, expression, and control. *Psychology and Aging, 12*, 590–599.

Gurland, B. (1976). The comparative frequency of depression in various adult age groups. *Journal of Gerontology, 31*, 283–292.

Hasher, L., & Zacks, R. T. (1988). Working memory, comprehension, and aging: A review and a new view. In G. G. Bower (Ed.), *The psychology of learning and motivation* (Vol. 22, pp. 193–225). San Diego, CA: Academic Press.

Hashtroudi, S., Johnson, M. K., & Chrosniak, L. D. (1990). Aging and qualitative characteristics of memories for perceived and imagined complex events. *Psychology and Aging, 5*, 119–126.

Hashtroudi, S., Johnson, M. K., Vnek, N., & Ferguson, S. A. (1994). Aging and the effects of affective and factual focus on source monitoring and recall. *Psychology and Aging, 9*, 160–170.

Heckhausen, J., Dixon, R. A., & Baltes, P. B. (1989). Gains and losses in development throughout adulthood as perceived by different age groups. *Developmental Psychology, 25*, 109–121.

Hess, T. M. (1994). Social cognition in adulthood: Aging-related changes in knowledge and processing mechanisms. *Developmental Review, 14*, 373–412.

Hess, T. M., Follett, K. J., & McGee, K. A. (1998). Aging and impression formation: The impact of processing skills and goals. *Journal of Gerontology: Psychological Sciences, 53*, P175–P187.

Hess, T. M., & Pullen, S. M. (1994). Adult age differences in impression change processes. *Psychology and Aging, 9*, 237–250.

Hess, T. M., & Tate, C. S. (1991). Adult age differences in explanations and memory for behavioral information. *Psychology and Aging, 6*, 86–92.

Johnson, M. K. (1995). The relation between memory and reality. Paper presented at 103rd Annual Convention of the American Psychological Association, New York.

Johnson, M. K., Nolde, S. F., & De Leonardis, D.M. (1996). Emotional focus and source monitoring. *Journal of Memory and Language, 35*, 135–156.

Kane, M. J., Hasher, L., Stoltzfus, E. R., Zacks, R. T., & Connelly, S. L. (1994). Inhibitory attentional mechanisms and aging. *Psychology and Aging, 9*, 103–112.

Kausler, D. H. (1990). Motivation, human aging, and cognitive performance. *Handbook of the psychology of aging* (3rd ed., pp. 171–182). San Diego, CA: Academic Press.

Klerman, G. L., & Weissman, M. M. (1989). Increasing rates of depression. *Journal of the American Medical Association, 261*, 2229–2235.

Kramer, D. A. (1990). Conceptualizing wisdom: The primacy of affect–cognition relations. In R. J. Sternberg (Ed.), *Wisdom: Its nature, origins, and development* (pp. 279–313). Cambridge, England: Cambridge University Press.

LaBar, K. S., & Le Doux, J. E. (1997). Emotion and the brain: An overview. In T. E Feinberg & M. J. Farah (Eds.), *Behavioral Neurology and Neuropsychology* (pp. 675–689). New York: McGraw-Hill.

Labouvie-Vief, G. (1997). Cognitive–emotional integration in adulthood. In K. W. Schaie & M. P. Lawton (Eds.), *Annual review of gerontology and geriatrics* (Vol. 17, pp. 206–237). New York: Springer.

Labouvie-Vief, G., & Blanchard-Fields, F. (1982). Cognitive ageing and psychological growth. *Ageing and Society, 2*, 183–209.

Labouvie-Vief, G., & DeVoe, M. R. (1991). Emotional regulation in adulthood and later life: A developmental view. *Annual Review of Gerontology and Geriatrics, 11*, 172–194.

Labouvie-Vief, G., DeVoe, M., & Bulka, M. (1989). Speaking about feelings: Conceptions of emotion across the life span. *Psychology and Aging, 4*, 425–437.

Labouvie-Vief, G., Hakim-Larson, J., DeVoe, M., & Schoeberlein, S. (1989). Emotions and self-regulation: A life span view. *Human Development, 32*, 279–299.

La Rue, A., Swan, G. E., & Carmelli, D. (1995). Cognition and depression in a cohort of aging men: Results from the Western Collaborative Group Study. *Psychology and Aging, 10*, 30–33.

Lawton, M. P., Kleban, M. H., Rajagopal, D., & Dean, J. (1992). Dimensions of affective experience in three age groups. *Psychology and Aging, 7*, 171–184.

Lazarus, R. S. (1991). *Emotion and adaptation.* New York: Oxford University Press.

Leichtman, M. D., Ceci, S. J., & Ornstein, P. A. (1992). The influence of affect on memory: Mechanism and development. In S. -Ò. Christianson (Ed.), *Handbook of emotion and memory: Research and theory* (pp. 181–200). Hillsdale, NJ: Lawrence Erlbaum Associates.

Levenson, R. W. (1992) Autonomic nervous system differences in emotions. *Psychological Science, 3*, 23–27.

Levenson, R. W., Carstensen, L. L., Friesen, W., & Ekman, P. (1991). Emotion, physiology and expression in old age. *Psychology and Aging, 4*, 425–437.

Levenson, R. W., Carstensen, L. L., & Gottman, J. M. (1993). Long-term marriage: Age, gender, and satisfaction. *Psychology and Aging, 8*, 301–313.

Levenson, R. W., Carstensen, L. L., & Gottman, J. M. (1994). Marital interaction in old and middle-aged long-term marriages: Physiology, affect and their interrelations. *Journal of Personality and Social Psychology, 67*, 56–68.

Loevinger, J. (1976). *Ego development.* San Francisco: Jossey-Bass.

Looft, W. R. (1972). Egocentrism and social interaction across the life span. *Psychological Bulletin, 78*, 73–92.

MacKay, D. G., & Abrams, L. (1996). Language, memory, and aging: Distributed deficits and the structure of new-versus-old connections. In J. E. Birren & K. W. Schaie (Eds.), *Handbook of the psychology of aging* (Vol. 4, pp. 251–265). San Diego, CA: Academic Press.

MacLeod, C. (1996). Anxiety and cognitive processes. In I. G. Sarason, G. R. Pierce, & B. R. Sarason (Eds.), *Cognitive interference: Theories, methods, and findings* (pp. 47–76). Mahwah, NJ: Lawrence Erlbaum Associates.

Magai, C., Cohen, C., Gomberg, D., Malatesta, C., & Culver, C. (1996). Emotional expression during mid- to late-stage dementia. *International Psychogeriatrics, 8*, 383–395.

Malatesta, C. Z., & Kalnok, M. (1984). Emotional experience in younger and older adults. *Journal of Gerontology, 39*, 301–308.

Matt, G. E., Vázquez, C., & Campbell, W. K. (1992). Mood-congruent recall of affectively toned stimuli: A meta-analytic review. *Clinical Psychology Review, 12*, 227–255.

Mineka, S. (1993). Mechanisms involved in the observational conditioning of fear. *Journal of Experimental Psychology, 122*, 22–38.

Nichols-Hoppe, K. T., & Beach, L. R. (1990). The effects of test anxiety and task variables on predecisional information search. *Journal of Research in Personality, 24*, 163–172.

Perry, W. G. (1970). *Forms of intellectual and ethical development in the college years.* New York: Holt, Rinehart & Winston.

Powell, D. H. (1994). *Profiles in cognitive aging.* Cambridge, MA: Harvard University Press.

Regier, D. A., Boyd, H. J., Burke, J. D., Rae, D. S., Myers, J. K., Kramer, M., Robins, L. N., George, L. K., Karno, M., & Locke, B. Z. (1988). One-month prevalence of mental disorders in the United States. *Archives of General Psychiatry, 45,* 977–986.

Revenson, T. A. (1986). Debunking the myth of loneliness in late life. In E. Seidman & J. Rappaport (Eds.), *Redefining social problems* (pp. 115–135). New York: Plenum.

Salthouse, T. A. (1991). *Theoretical perspectives on cognitive aging.* Hillsdale, NJ: Lawrence Erlbaum Associates.

Sarason, I. G., Pierce, G. R., & Sarason, B. R. (Eds.). (1996). *Cognitive interference: Theories, methods, and findings.* Mahwah, NJ: Lawrence Erlbaum Associates.

Scheibel, A. B. (1996). Structural and functional changes in the aging brain. In J. E. Birren & K. W. Schaie (Eds.), *Handbook of the psychology of aging* (Vol. 4, pp. 105–128). San Diego, CA: Academic Press.

Schulz, R. (1985). Emotion and affect. In J. E. Birren & K. W. Schaie (Eds.), *Handbook of the psychology of aging* (2nd ed., pp. 531–543). New York: Van Nostrand Reinhold.

Sebby, R. A., & Papini, D. R. (1991). Perceived problem relevancy and its relationship to reasoning on everyday problems. In J. D. Sinnott & J. C. Cavanaugh (Eds.), *Bridging paradigms: Positive development in adulthood and cognitive aging* (pp. 153–168). New York: Praeger.

Segal, Z. V. (1996). Cognitive interference in depressive and anxiety-based disorders. In I. G. Sarason, G. R. Pierce, & B. R. Sarason (Eds.), *Cognitive interference: Theories, methods, and findings* (pp. 325–345). Mahwah, NJ: Lawrence Erlbaum Associates.

Siebert, P. S., & Ellis, H. C. (1991). Irrrelevant thoughts, emotional mood states, and cognitive task performance. *Memory and Cognition, 19,* 507–513.

Sinnott, J. (1996). The developmental approach: Post-formal thought as adaptive intelligence. In F. Blanchard-Fields & T. H. Hess (Eds.), *Perspectives on cognitive change in adulthood and aging* (pp. 358–383). New York: McGraw-Hill.

Sinnott, J. D., & Cavanaugh, J. C. (Eds.). (1991). *Bridging paradigms: Positive development in adulthood and cognitive aging.* New York: Praeger.

Smith, A. D. (1996). Memory. In J. E. Birren & K. W. Schaie (Eds.), *Handbook of the psychology of aging* (4th ed., pp. 236–250). San Diego, CA: Academic Press.

Stoltzfus, E. R., Hasher, L., Zacks, R. T., Ulivi, M. S., & Goldstein, D. (1993). Investigations of inhibition and interference in younger and older adults. *Journal of Gerontology: Psychological Sciences, 48,* P179–P188.

Stein, N. L., & Trabasso, T. (1992). The organization of emotional experience: Creating links among emotion, thinking, language, and intentional action. *Cognition and Emotion, 6,* 225–244.

Tsai, J. L., Levenson, R. W., & Carstensen, L. L. (1998). *Autonomic, expressive and subjective responses to emotional films in younger and older adults of European American and Chinese descent.* Manuscript submitted for publication.

Wagner, A. R., & Brandon, S. E. (1989). Evolution of a structured connectionist model of Pavlovian conditioning (AESOP). In S. B. Klein & R. R. Mowrer (Eds.), *Contemporary learning theories: Pavlovian conditioning and the status of traditional learning theory* (pp. 149–189). Hillsdale, NJ: Lawrence Erlbaum Associates.

Zacks, R. T., & Hasher, L. (1997). Cognitive gerontology and attentional inhibition: A reply to Burke and McDowd. *Journal of Gerontology: Psychological Sciences, 52,* P274–P283.

Zajonc, R. (1985). Emotion and facial efference: A theory reclaimed. *Science, 228,* 15–21.

Zajonc, R. (1997). Emotions. In D. Gilbert, S. T. Fiske, & G. Lindzey (Eds.), *Handbook of social psychology* (4th ed., 591–631). Cambridge, England: McGraw-Hill.

Zajonc, R., Murphy, S., & Inglehart, M. (1989). Feeling and facial efference: Implication of the vascular theory of emotion. *Psychological Review, 96,* 395–416.

12

Life-Span Perspectives on Self, Personality, and Social Cognition

Ursula M. Staudinger
Max Planck Institute for Human Development

Monisha Pasupathi
Max Planck Institute for Human Development

In this chapter, our goal is to provide a review of the evidence on developmental trajectories and adaptive functions of self, personality, and social cognition across adulthood. For this purpose, we first introduce a framework to organize and integrate theoretical and empirical evidence from these diverse areas.

For some years, researchers in the fields of personality, self, and social cognition have recognized the need for an integrative and overarching theoretical framework. This Zeitgeist is reflected in several recent integrative approaches (see also Sternberg & Ruzgis, 1994). Salovey and Mayer (1994), for instance, suggested the notion of "emotional intelligence," which focuses on the role of emotions in the link between intelligence and personality. They proposed that "the adaptive processing of emotionally relevant information is part of intelligence and, at the same time, individual differences in the skills with which such processing occurs constitute core aspects of personality" (Salovey & Mayer, 1994, p. 311). Higgins (1996) recently introduced the concept of a "self-digest," which combines and orchestrates self-knowledge and self-regulation, and used this concept to organize diverse work in the area of self-regulation. At even higher levels of aggregation, theoretical conceptions by Mischel and Shoda (1995; cognitive–affective system theory of personality), Kuhl (1994; volition and personality), Labouvie-Vief (1994), and Pascual-Leone (1990; life-engaged consciousness and vital reason), as well as attempts to build a psychology of action (Brandtstädter, 1998; Gollwitzer & Bargh, 1996), illustrate ways of integrating findings on stability and change, content and regulatory processes, self, personality and cognition, or motivation and emotion within one theoretical framework.

We take a somewhat different approach, adapting a dual-component model originating from the study of intellectual life-span development (Staudinger, Lindenberger, & Baltes, 1998). The dual-component model distinguishes between the mechanics and the pragmatics of the mind (e.g., P. B. Baltes, Dittmann-Kohli, & Dixon, 1984) and has been successful in organizing empirical efforts and promoting epistemological progress about cognitive development across the life span. It has been primarily our research on wisdom (for a summary, see Staudinger & Baltes, 1994) that suggested an extension of this dual-component model of intellectual development.

Our investigations of wisdom were originally motivated by the search for a prototypical example of cognitive pragmatics, or the experience-based and content-rich part of cognitive ability. Both theoretical work and empirical findings (e.g., P. B. Baltes, Smith, & Staudinger, 1992; Staudinger & Baltes, 1994; Staudinger, Lopez, & Baltes, 1997), however, demonstrated that even the broadly conceptualized notion of cognitive pragmatics was too cognition specific and failed to do complete justice to the holistic nature of wisdom. A better understanding of wisdom required the incorporation of personality, emotion, and motivation, as well as experiential contexts.

THE MECHANICS AND PRAGMATICS OF LIFE: AN INTEGRATIVE FRAMEWORK

The conception we have proposed elsewhere as an overarching framework for the study of self, personality, and social cognition across the life span (cf. Staudinger, Lindenberger, & Baltes, 1998), is grounded in this dual-process model of the mind (P. B. Baltes, 1997). The dual-component model differentiates between biology-based, content-poor mechanics and culture-dependent, content-rich pragmatics. We explicitly extend this basic distinction to encompass personality and self-related phenomena and their development, as well as intellect. For this purpose, we speak of the *mechanics and pragmatics of life*. Although this model comes from a cognitive research program, we do not assign cognition primacy over emotion and motivation. Rather, we take a systemic view of structural and dynamic relations between various areas and levels of psychological functioning (e.g., Barton, 1994).

Life Mechanics

As we develop, shape, and compose our lives, cognitive mechanics (e.g., information-processing speed and cognitive control processes) enable us to accumulate knowledge about and experiences with the "world," with our "self," and transactions between the two. The notion of *life mechanics*, in addition, allows us to describe how people differ in ways of engaging themselves with their selves and the world. Those differences arise not only because of their cognitive abilities but also because of the "basics" of personality, for example, differences in activity level, reactivity, basic emotional tone (positive vs. negative), or basic motivational tendencies (e.g., approach vs. avoidance). Thus, life mechanics include basic indicators of information processing (cognitive mechanics) but also basic dimensions of temperament (e.g., activity, reactivity, emotionality, and sociability; Bates & Wachs, 1994), which comprise basic emotional (e.g., Scherer, 1997) and motivational tendencies (e.g., Ryan, Sheldon, Kasser, & Deci, 1996). Adding the "mechanic" basis of emotion and motivation extends life mechanics beyond brain structures such as the cortex and the thalamus to involve the hypothalamus as well as enzymatic and hormonal regulation (e.g., Teitelbaum & Stricker, 1994). In sum, life mechanics reflect individual differences in biology-based patterns of perception, information processing, emotionality, and motivational expression.

Life mechanics and life pragmatics are by definition interrelated, and the investment theory proposed to describe the relation between fluid and crystallized intelligence (e.g., Cattell, 1971) may apply here. In this vein, life mechanics (involving cognition, emotion, and motivation) can be considered as the processual building blocks from which developmental progress in life pragmatics can emerge. We see below that research on life problem solving (e.g., everyday problem solving and professional expertise) and social cognition illustrates how important it is to consider *life* mechanics rather than only *cognitive* mechanics when exploring the investment of basic resources in different problem domains and contexts (e.g., Frensch & Funke, 1995).

Life Pragmatics

In contrast to life mechanics, which represent the power of biology-based patterns of perception, information processing, emotionality, and motivational expression, the *pragmatics of life* reveal the power of human agency and culture (e.g., Valsiner & Lawrence, 1997). In transactions with life contexts, we accumulate and construct (declarative *and* procedural, "hot" and "cold") knowledge about the *world* (i.e., knowledge about other people, events, circumstances, rules, places, and objects relevant for leading our lives) and about our *self*, as well as about transactions between ourselves and the world. Life mechanics provide the necessary "hardware" for these transactions.

Two facets of this conception warrant note. First, self and world are of course not necessarily mutually exclusive. We hope that our heuristic division allows a new way of organizing and integrating available evidence from relatively separate fields. Self-related knowledge may follow different rules than knowledge in general, though, lending support to this division (see, e.g., Carlston & Smith, 1996). Second, to conceive of life pragmatics as bodies of knowledge in the widest sense (see the notion of personal knowledge, Polanyi, 1958) implies the applicability of principles governing the acquisition, change, and activation of all knowledge. These rules, however, will probably provide only a partial account as "cognitive knowledge" is crossed with emotional and motivational influences into a new whole.

Having said this, we can use models of expertise development to learn something, although not everything, about the development of life pragmatics. In models of expertise, the accumulation of knowledge is not limited to declarative facts but also includes the emergence of domain-specific procedures and skill (Anderson, 1996). Acquisition of procedures can involve both conditioning and procedural learning. When applied to the domain "world," such procedures refer, for example, to behaviors with which we try to regulate or alter our environment. When applied to "our self," such procedures comprise ways of dealing with or regulating self-related knowledge, wishes, goals, and feelings.

In sum, life pragmatics comprise bodies of knowledge as well as regulatory functions and behaviors regarding the world and the self. The two distinctions we have proposed, between self and world on the one hand and between knowledge and regulatory functions and behaviors on the other, can be viewed as a 2 × 2 matrix, as shown in Table 12.1. Established

TABLE 12.1
Facets and Target Domains of Life Pragmatics
With Established Constructs as Illustrations

	Target Domain	
Variable	*World*	*Self*
Knowledge	Life problem solving	Personality dispositions (e.g.,
	Wisdom-related knowledge and judgment	Big Five)
	Professional expertise	Self-concept
	Knowledge about people and events	
	Beliefs and attitudes (e.g., just world)	
Regulatory functions and behavior	Skills (e.g., occupational, sports, and crafts)	Emotion-focused coping
		Secondary control
	Adaptive and maladaptive behavior (e.g., productivity, delinquency, and dependency)	Comparison processes (social and temporal)
		Goal selection and setting
	Problem-focused coping	Personal life investment
	Primary control	Emotion regulation

constructs in the study of self, personality, and social cognition provide examples for each of the four cells. Below, we organize our review using this matrix, but given the focus of the present chapter on aging and social cognition, we do not address actual behavior.

Our conceptualization of life pragmatics is still preliminary. However, we propose that the notion of life pragmatics provides a theoretical frame with the potential to consolidate cognition with emotion and motivation and trait personality with self-concepts, as well as self-regulation and the psychology of action. In the terminology of life pragmatics, personality is the well-organized and stable knowledge structure concerning our own behavior, experiences, goals, and usual reactions.[1] This conceptualization is completely in line with social–cognitive views on self and personality (e.g., Cantor, 1990; Markus, 1977; Mischel, 1973), as well as with work on self-concepts and self-schemas, which are described as a subset of a person's stored knowledge that concerns him- or herself as a distinct object in the world (cf. Bem, 1967). Finally, self-regulation constitutes the procedural part of our self-knowledge. Of course, people are more than their self-views, goals, and attributional styles, they also go out into the world and solve problems, work at jobs, and otherwise change and adapt to society. By making world-related knowledge and behaviors a part of life pragmatics, work on life insight, pragmatic reasoning, complex problem solving, and professional expertise is incorporated as well.

The framework offered here to conceptualize life pragmatics also integrates extant definitions of social cognition. For instance, Fiske and Taylor (1991, p. 19) defined social cognition as concerning how people make sense of themselves and of others; Hess (1994, p. 373) highlighted the importance of considering the interaction between knowledge structures and processing mechanisms in understanding social cognition; and Blanchard-Fields (1996, p. 454) focused on the adaptivity and growth aspect of social cognition in adulthood. All of these facets of social cognition are accommodated in the conceptualization of life pragmatics as introduced above.

The integrative framework offered by life mechanics and life pragmatics follows from a life-span approach to psychology (e.g., P. B. Baltes, 1997). First, life-span theory by definition aims at understanding the life

---

[1]Even after decades of nature–nurture discussions (see, e.g., Rutter, 1997), it is still unclear whether trait personality (e.g., the Big Five personality factors; McCrae & Costa, 1997) is more a part of life mechanics (i.e., are primarily biologically based structures) or life pragmatics. Until conflicting evidence arises, we include the Big Five (conceived of as knowledge and behavioral structures about one's self) as part of life pragmatics. Our decision receives some support from findings demonstrating that temperament, one of the constituent parts of life mechanics, seems to be the "precursor" of the Big Five rather than their equivalent (e.g., Caspi & Silva, 1995).

span as a whole. This extended time perspective brings into focus the complexity and interconnectedness of areas of psychological functioning usually considered in isolation, such as cognition and personality or self-concepts and temperament. Second, life-span theory emphasizes functionality. Whether characteristics and behaviors are adaptive is more important than whether they are cognitive, emotional, or motivational. Third, life-span theory is contextualistic and systemic in nature. All areas of functioning, such as cognition, emotion, and motivation, are subsystems of an overarching dynamic system and are considered in terms of their biological as well as cultural–historical components (see also Magnusson & Stattin, 1998).

In the following sections, we use the concept of life pragmatics to organize empirical evidence about self, personality, and social cognition across the life span. We begin by reviewing developmental trajectories of knowledge and regulation of the world and the self, and then turn to questions of functionality.

DEVELOPMENTAL TRAJECTORIES OF LIFE
PRAGMATICS: STABILITY, GROWTH, OR DECLINE?

What Constitutes Growth, and What Constitutes Decline?

In contrast to cognitive pragmatics, which present a rather homogeneous picture of increases until middle adulthood and stability thereafter (at least up to 75 years; Horn, 1994), the developmental pattern of life pragmatics is more complicated. First, as is evident below, there is less homogeneity in developmental trajectories. Second, determining what constitutes growth and what constitutes decline in life pragmatics (e.g., knowledge about life, personality, and self characteristics) is complex. It may seem obvious that the more words remembered or the faster the response, the better the performance. Even in intellectual functioning, however, more and faster may not always be gains in everyday life.

When it comes to knowledge and regulatory functions concerning ourselves and the world, the "best" direction of development is even less clear. Our solution was to use two approaches in labeling changes as growth or decline. First, changes that people view as subjectively valuable, on the basis of other research findings, were viewed as gains (e.g., Heckhausen, Dixon, & Baltes, 1989). Second, life-pragmatic characteristics were considered as gains in line with their theoretical valence as specified in growth models of development (e.g., ego maturity, integrity, and generativity) or in general conceptions of functionality and dysfunctionality (e.g., neuroticism and negative emotions). These two approaches often converged. However, characteristics contributing to adaptive fitness tend toward multidimensionality and multifunctionality, and with the complexity of the concept of adaptivity itself, categorizations of gains and losses are usually oversimplifications (see M. M. Baltes & Carstensen, 1996).

Developmental Trajectories in Knowing About the World

For our purposes, knowledge about the world includes any knowledge and beliefs that people hold about people, events, circumstances, rules, places, and objects (cf. Polanyi, 1958). Knowledge in this sense can concern matters of fact, such as the fact that a refrigerator can be repaired at a particular shop, as well as matters of belief, such as the opinion that the world is a fair place. Knowledge and beliefs about the world can accumulate and change across the life span. Consistent with this assumption, people typically (at least up to 75 years) show stability or even increases over time in crystallized intelligence (e.g., vocabulary), which is one common way to operationalize world knowledge (Camp, 1989; Horn, 1994; chap. 6, this volume). In our review, we focus on age changes in factual and procedural knowledge about difficult as well as mundane life problems, professional expertise, knowledge about other people, knowledge about events, and beliefs or attitudes.

The Development of Knowledge and Judgment About Life Problems

Life problems range from daily hassles, such as dealing with a broken refrigerator, or minor conflicts with the boss, friends, or family to existential issues, such as determining the meaning of one's life-as-lived. Researchers have addressed two features of such problems—knowledge and judgment about such problems and actual problem-solving behavior. We focus on the former.

Typical studies of life-problem knowledge (declarative and procedural) ask people of various ages to consider a problem and to identify potential solutions, issues to be considered, and other relevant aspects of their knowledge about the situation, often by generating strategies for solving the presented problem, but sometimes by evaluating a set of presented strategies or by reporting which of a set of strategies they personally endorse (see Berg, Klaczynski, Calderone, & Strough, 1994, for a review). These responses can be evaluated on the basis of quantitative (e.g., number of solutions generated) or qualitative (e.g., degree of match between participants' evaluations or endorsements and those of the experimenters) criteria. Age-related decline (Denney, Tozier, & Schlotthauer, 1992; Diehl, Willis, & Schaie, 1995; Marsiske & Willis, 1995), stability (Denney et al.,

1992; Heidrich & Denney, 1994), or increases in knowledge about life problems have been observed across various studies that have taken this general approach (Blanchard-Fields, Chen, & Norris, 1997; Cornelius & Caspi, 1987). Other studies suggest an inverted U curve, with problem knowledge increasing from young adulthood to middle age and decreasing thereafter (Denney & Pearce, 1989).

Research on life problems has also been done from a neo-Piagetian perspective, where the focus is on changes in cognitive structure, particularly in the level of complexity, abstraction, and differentiation people can use when reasoning about such problems. Here, researchers nearly always ask for free responses to problems elicited in interview settings. The resulting responses are then coded, using various schemes, for qualities like the representation and integration of multiple viewpoints. From this perspective, the sophistication of scientific and moral reasoning increases from childhood and adolescence through early adulthood (see Kitchener & King, 1990; Kramer, Kahlbaugh, & Goldston, 1992; Kuhn, 1989; Pratt, Pancer, Hunsberger, & Manchester, 1990). After early adulthood, there may be more stability in complex reasoning than change, according to cross-sectional studies (range = 35–85 years; e.g., Kuhn, 1989; Pratt et al., 1990). One longitudinal study (covering 4 years) showed declines in complexity or reasoning structure in the oldest group (range = 63–80 years; Pratt, Diessner, Pratt, Hunsberger, & Pancer, 1996). Unfortunately, these cross-sectional and longitudinal results are difficult to compare because of differences in variability and other methodological differences.

As just noted, life problems range from the mundane to the existential. The latter have been the focus of our work on wisdom, which brings together the knowledge and expertise emphasis of everyday problem-solving research and the relativistic or complexity elements of neo-Piagetian approaches. We define *wisdom* as expert knowledge and judgment in the domain "fundamental pragmatics of life" and have developed a paradigm for assessing adults' wisdom-related knowledge and judgment. The fundamental pragmatics of life entail insights into the quintessential aspects of the human condition and human life, including its biological boundaries, cultural conditioning, and intra- as well as interindividual variations. To assess wisdom-related knowledge and judgment, we ask people to think aloud about existential dilemmas faced by fictitious characters. Their responses are evaluated by trained raters for the depth, breadth, and quality of knowledge expressed according to five criteria. These criteria include two basic criteria, specifically, broad and deep factual and procedural knowledge about difficult life problems, and three metacriteria, namely, value relativism, life-span contextualism, and acknowledgment and management of uncertainty (see P. B. Baltes et al., 1992, for a review). People nominated by others as wise produce responses that are highly rated along all five criteria, supporting the validity of our paradigm for being also consistent with everyday conceptions of wisdom and wise people (P. B. Baltes, Staudinger, Maercker, & Smith, 1995).

Across an age range of 20 to 80 years, we find that wisdom-related performance is stable (for a review, Staudinger, in press). However, after age 80, declines in cognitive mechanics may become so strong that wisdom-related performance disintegrates (cf. P. B. Baltes et al., 1995). Consistent with out working model of the ontogenesis of wisdom, a complex pattern of person characteristics (e.g., openness to experience, personal growth, and creativity) and experiential contexts (e.g., extensive practice and guided training in fundamental life matters) need to interact in order for wisdom to emerge (Staudinger et al., 1997; Staudinger, Maciel, Smith, & Baltes, 1998). Fluid intelligence is rather unimportant for wisdom-related performance as long as it does not fall below a certain minimal level.

How can this quite heterogeneous pattern of findings concerning life knowledge be reconciled? Whether decline, stability, or gains in knowledge about life problems are found depends on several factors, including problem structure, time and motivation for responding, the age of the problem in conjunction with the age of the respondent, the age range covered in the study (middle age, old age, very old age), and more. Below, we consider some of these factors in more detail.

Age trajectories depend partly on the similarity between the logical structure of the problems presented and that of standard tests of fluid intelligence (see Labouvie-Vief, 1985). Measures of everyday problem solving that correlate highly with measures of fluid intelligence reliably show age-related decline. For example, everyday problem-solving measures that ask people to compute the amount of interest involved in a loan require performances similar to those assessed in traditional intelligence tests; thus, high correlations with fluid intelligence and reliable age declines are not surprising (e.g., Marsiske & Willis, 1995).

By contrast, gains in adulthood are reported for problems following a socio-logic (e.g., which involve other people and conflicts of interest). Such problems ask for the integration of emotions, motivation, and cognition. For example, when asked to explain the causes for interpersonal and complicated problems, older adults give more complex and multidimensional attributions and are more likely than younger adults to note the contributions of both personality and situational factors (see, e.g., Blanchard-Fields et al., 1997). One moral here is that selecting ecologically relevant *contents* (e.g., by exploring the ability to remember shopping list items rather than other frequently used words) does not do justice to age-related changes in cognitive pragmatics (see also Staudinger, 1989).

Other important factors, like motivation, processing time, evaluative criteria, and problem definitions, can be subsumed under contextualistic approaches to problem solving. These approaches highlight the importance of the situation in which problem solving occurs (e.g., time resources available); features of the problem solver, such as motivation and problem construal; and the relationship between the problem and the problem solver (e.g., whether the "age" of the problem matches the age of the respondent).

The relation between the problem's age and the participants' age matters. Adults of all ages appear to know more about difficult life problems related to their own age group (i.e., age-matched problems) than about problems related to other age groups (e.g., Smith, Staudinger, & Baltes, 1994; Staudinger, Smith, & Baltes, 1992). Knowledge for age-matched problems may be more frequently activated in everyday life and therefore more stably accessible, resulting in better performance for such problems (e.g., Staudinger et al., 1992). Thus, knowledge and judgment about the world does not just accumulate as we move through life. Rather, as suggested by a life-span view, people must adapt to sequentially ordered developmental tasks as well as to other changes, like cultural shifts or historical events. This means that some knowledge becomes less relevant, less important, or even incorrect over time, and adaptation requires that people lose or inhibit access to it. Depending on their developmental contexts, people at the same time acquire new and up-to-date bodies of knowledge.

Adults of different ages face different life problems, with small children reporting family problems, older children reporting school-related problems, and middle-aged adults focusing on work (Sansone & Berg, 1993). In addition, even seemingly similar problems may be differently defined by adults of different ages and thus require different solution strategies (e.g., Berg, Strough, Calderone, Sansone, & Weir, 1998; Blanchard-Fields et al., 1997). For example, older adults tend to see problems as more interpersonal than do younger adults (e.g., Berg & Calderone, 1994). Further, as noted above, older adults tend to interpret problems as more complex, giving more interactive (e.g., dispositional and situational together) explanations for problems (e.g., Blanchard-Fields et al., 1997). Not surprisingly, then, older adults choose different strategies than do young adults for solving their problems, as strategy choice is clearly related to problem definition (e.g., Berg et al., 1998). Without knowing how people define a life problem (their own or a hypothetical one), evaluating their strategy selection is difficult.

Motivation and processing time may also differ with age. Young adults may sometimes make less effort in a laboratory context and perform poorly relative to middle-aged and older adults. When motivated to give their best performance, they outperform other age groups (Denney et al., 1992). Offering older adults more time to think can also change age trajectories. When explaining an everyday problem, older adults use extra time to discount personality explanations and consider situational factors, typically viewed as an increase in attributional accuracy. Younger adults appear to do the opposite; given more time they endorse a personality-based explanation of a problem even more strongly (Chen & Blanchard-Fields, 1997). Whether positive age differences are identified or not may also be related to whether the response format demands recognition and selection of presented solutions (e.g., Cornelius & Caspi, 1987) or free production of solutions (e.g., Staudinger & Baltes, 1994).

So is it gains or losses? As we noted, it depends on features of the problem, features of the assessment situation, and features of the respondent's life context. One rather safe conclusion seems that for life problems structured like traditional intelligence tests, losses occur over adulthood. For life problems that are ill structured and follow a socio-logic requiring the integration of hot and cold knowledge of cognition, emotion, and motivation, age may lead to stability (e.g., Pratt et al., 1990) or improved performance (e.g., Berg et al., 1994; Blanchard-Fields et al., 1997; Labouvie-Vief, 1994).

On the basis of our review of the literature, we would like to point to one research caveat in this field. Currently, the difference between life problems of a fictitious "other" and personal life problems is not addressed. Usually, the theoretical distinction between performance changes due to a switch from formal logic to socio-logic and performance changes due to differences between general and self-related socio-logic is confounded. We know of only one study that compared (for different reasons) knowledge about one's own problems and hypothetical problems. This study found gender-differential effects of these two problem types (see Pratt et al., 1990). Until contradictory empirical evidence arises, we suggest these two aspects of socio-logic (self vs. general) should be treated separately. Provided that comparable assessment and evaluation procedures can be developed, our hypothesis is that high-level knowledge about personal problems is still more "difficult" to attain than high levels of performance on hypothetical problems following a socio-logic.

Acquiring Expertise in Fields of World Knowledge

Professional expertise provides another example of world knowledge developing over adulthood. Expertise in any domain is characterized by well-developed, elaborated knowledge structures that allow for fast and efficient problem definition, reasoning, and decision-making processes in domain-specific problem solving (e.g., Chi, Glaser, & Farr, 1991). Such knowledge structures (factual and procedural) take time, practice, and motivation to acquire and consequently are partly associated with increasing age within a specialization.

Expert managers, physicians, engineers, and academics know more about problems within their areas than do novices in their fields (Ericsson & Smith, 1991; Frensch & Funke, 1995; Patel & Groen, 1991). For example, older managers are better than younger managers in diagnosing the value of information (Taylor, 1975). Such managers also seek less information under simulated emergency conditions but perform as well as younger adults, further supporting notions of improved information selection (Streufert, Pogash, Piasecki, & Post, 1990). Similar findings can be shown in other domains, such as chess, bridge, or physics (Charness & Bosman, 1990; Chi et al., 1991). However, when age and experience are crossed such that young and old experts can be compared, old experts do not outperform young experts and may even perform less well in certain tasks despite their expertise (e.g., Lindenberger, Kliegl, & Baltes, 1992).

Findings from research on expertise in the domain of fundamental life pragmatics demonstrate that certain professionals, such as ministers, personnel managers, or clinical psychologists, receive extensive and guided practice, as well as mentoring and feedback, in dealing with difficult life problems. Not surprisingly, clinical psychologists, for instance, show better wisdom-related performance than do their age- and educationally matched peers. Older clinicians, however, do not outperform young clinicians (for a review, see Staudinger & Baltes, 1994).

Can we acquire expert-level knowledge at any age? The answer here is not simple. Some studies have explored intensive short-term training in cognitive skills as an analogy of expertise. Older adults can and do acquire such skills and the attendant performance benefits (e.g., Hertzog, Cooper, & Fisk, 1996; Lindenberger & Baltes, 1995); however, older adults often take longer to acquire the skills and seldom perform as well as younger adults with the same training. In contrast to these "age matters" findings, existing models of expertise argue that the age of beginning practice is less important for expertise development (except in relation to a person's remaining life span) than the fact that at least 10 years of deliberate and extensive practice are required (Ericsson, 1996). In fact, few studies have explored the acquisition of actual expertise as a function of the age at the beginning of training, perhaps because variability in age of starting is low. For example, for chess, the age at which a person begins is largely unrelated to the age at which they can perform at international levels. However, the participants of such studies typically began to play chess around the age of 10 (Charness, Krampe, & Mayr, 1996). From a life-span perspective, however, childhood and young adulthood offer a maximum in life mechanics resources, as well as maximum contextual support and time for investing in expertise development. Healthy old age may also be a period rich in time resources, but to our knowledge, there are no systematic explorations of older adults attempting to develop a new talent.

In sum, it may be increasingly difficult, but not impossible, to acquire expertise at later ages, although achieving the performance level possible for young adults (given the same amount of training and feedback) may well be impossible. Professional expertise continues to benefit individuals into middle age and later life in terms of decision making and job performance, provided it is maintained by practice.

Knowledge About Other People

There are several ways to think about knowledge of others. One approach is generally subsumed under the rubric "theory of mind," and research in this area focuses on knowledge and understanding of others' minds, predominantly in children. By the age of 5, most children understand that people have beliefs, that these beliefs are not always accurate, and that beliefs, desires, and goals can motivate actions and emotions; they can also engage in simple perspective taking (Flavell, Green, & Flavell, 1995). During middle childhood and adolescence, people come to view minds as constructive and agentic and to appreciate ambiguity and multiplicity of perspective (Schwanenflugel, Fabricius, & Noyes, 1996; Wellman & Hickling, 1994). Although researchers are only beginning to examine such knowledge in adults, knowledge about other people's minds and the causes of others' behavior may improve even into old age (Blanchard-Fields et al., 1997; Happé, Winner, & Brownell, 1998; Staudinger & Baltes, 1994). For example, when asked to provide explanations for the actions of characters in short vignettes, older adults, more often than younger adults, not only referred to the mental state of the target character but also took into consideration this target character's conception of the mental states of other characters involved in the vignette. Thus, they demonstrated a more complex theory of mind than did younger adults (Happé et al., 1998).

We also acquire knowledge about developmental norms and stereotypes through socialization. People within a culture show consensus about the normal course of adult development (e.g., Hagestad, 1990). Such beliefs do show changes during adolescence, with young adults believing that transitions occur at later ages than do adolescents (Green, Wheatley, & Aldava, 1992). From late adolescence to early middle age, people move from a stereotypical understanding of the typical biography (content and timing of life events) to a more differentiated view of between-person variation (Strube, Gehringer, Ernst, & Knill, 1985). Adult age differences in beliefs about how people develop are small, but older adults do hold more elaborate conceptions of adulthood development than do younger adults. When rating the degree and timing of life-span change in a large number of psychological attributes (e.g., wise, calm, anxious, depressed, and outgoing), older adults rated more attributes as changeable than did younger adults and gave more differentiated estimates of the timing of those changes (Heckhausen et al., 1989). Older people may also hold more differentiated and potentially more positive stereotypes about elderly people relative to younger adults (e.g., Brewer, Dull, & Lui, 1981; Hummert, Garstka, Shaner, & Strahm, 1994; Wentura, Dräger, & Brandtstädter, 1997). For example, older adults asked to group a broad set of terms describing elderly people into categories typically generate more categories than do younger adults (e.g., Hummert et al., 1994). People also appear to hold different conceptions of wise people and wisdom as they grow older—in particular, older people view wisdom as less associated with age (Clayton & Birren, 1980). Unfortunately, to our knowledge, this kind of work has not been thoroughly pursued for other social categories such as gender or ethnicity. Existing findings suggest there will be few age differences in *knowledge* about these social categories (for a review, see Hess, 1994).

Taken together, these findings suggest that older adults have more differentiated knowledge about human minds, adult development, and elderly people. Explanations of these findings usually emphasize knowledge and (self-related) experience as the source of these differences (e.g., Brewer et al., 1981; Heckhausen et al., 1989; Wentura et al., 1997).

Knowledge About Events

Mental representations of common activities and events are typically referred to as "scripts." Given the accumulation of idiosyncratic experience over the life span, older adults might have different event scripts than do younger adults. Early work by Light and Anderson (1983) showed no age differences in representations of common events, but as noted by Ross and Berg (1992), typical studies of scripts often emphasize widely shared features, thus obscuring age effects. Later studies confirmed age similarity in scripts but also provided evidence for idiosyncrasy. For example, Hess (1992) asked older and younger adults to describe the events involved in four common activities, namely, getting up in the morning, going grocery shopping, going out to eat, and going to the doctor for a minor ailment. In the resulting descriptions, a majority of named actions were shared across individuals and age groups. However, he also found evidence for age-related variability (older and younger adults elaborating on different subroutines) and unique variability (subroutines named by only one individual). These kinds of variability tended to covary across events, with getting up in the morning producing the most variability and going to a restaurant the least. More detailed content analyses suggested that changes in life contexts produce script variability; older adults' scripts about getting up in the morning were more elaborate about breakfast preparations (often shared with family members), whereas young adults' scripts were more elaborate regarding personal grooming (see also Ross & Berg, 1992).

Beliefs and Attitudes

In addition to what we know about life, people, and events, our knowledge of the world is constituted by a variety of beliefs and attitudes we hold, such as our opinions about feminism or attitudes toward ethnic groups. Three common assumptions in this area are (a) that older adults are more conservative than younger adults, (b) that people become more conservative as they get older, and (c) that people become less flexible in their attitudes and opinions as they get older. These assumptions receive relatively little empirical support. For example, in relation to the first, Danigelis and Cutler (1991b) noted in their literature review that older people sometimes express more liberal views than do younger people, sometimes more conservative views, and sometimes similar views. Their conclusion is that age differences in attitudes depend on the particular issues at stake. The second and third assumptions also seem to be wrong. Consider the attitudes of European Americans toward African Americans. A study of these attitudes, based on survey data collected from 1963 to 1985, explored changes over time within and across age cohorts (Danigelis & Cutler, 1991b). Example items asked for views about interethnic marriages or opinions about an African American presidential candidate. As expected, given sociopolitical shifts over this period, attitudes in general became more liberal. This was true for older adults as well as for younger adults, suggesting that the assumption that people become more conservative as they get older is wrong. Further, the trend toward more liberalism was just as strong among people in the oldest cohorts (those born between 1930 and 1938). These results, and others obtained for attitudes toward feminism (Cutler, 1983) and attitudes toward law and order (Danigelis & Cutler, 1991a), suggest that older adults are just as flexible as younger adults in responding to changes in sociopolitical climate. This flexibility in response to the sociopolitical climate, in turn, contradicts the third assumption above. These findings have been replicated in longitudinal studies (Alwin & Krosnick, 1991). The one exception to this rule may be that younger adults (below 30 years of age) are particularly susceptible to attitude change (Krosnick & Alwin, 1989). Prior work supporting the idea that older adults are more conservative or more rigid may have resulted from methodological artifacts. For example, because of cognitive limitations in working memory, older adults show a stronger recency effect in responding to spoken surveys and are more likely to select the last response provided. When this last response is the more conservative one, as has been the case in some past surveys, older adults appear more conservative than do younger adults (see Knäuper, 1999). Changes in beliefs and attitudes that do occur depend largely on the political climate of the time and the people we associate with (Roberts & Helson, 1997).

Schematic Processing

Perhaps related to the idea that older adults become more inflexible is the hypothesis that older adults depend more than younger adults on their existing knowledge to process novel information (see Hess, 1994, for a review). Results are somewhat equivocal and seem to vary according to, for instance, whether the processed information bears socioemotional relevance or not or whether recall or judgment is used to assess cognitive functioning. Older adults have been shown in some studies to focus more than younger adults on novel, emotionally relevant information about a person, particularly negative information when making a judgment about this person (Hess & Tate, 1991; Rankin & Allen, 1991). In other cases, older adults are more schema driven. For example, when asked to recall images of familiar scenes, such as pictures of kitchens, older adults do rely more than young adults on their existing knowledge about how such scenes are organized (Hess & Slaughter, 1990). A further dimension of age-relevant differentiation seems to be whether the processing of existing knowledge is automatic or not (e.g., Hess, McGee, Woodburn, & Bolstad, 1998). In general, however, it seems to us that there is not yet enough cumulative evidence available to reach overall conclusions in this field of study. More cumulative research is needed to systematically investigate how these three and perhaps more dimensions (i.e., domain, kind of cognitive process, and automaticity) relate to each other and to age.

Summary

With the possible exception of very old age (above 80 years), age is not the most critical predictor of performance in the area of world knowledge. Rather, person characteristics and experiential contexts are of greater importance. Across the adult life span, people can and do acquire new knowledge about the world (declarative and procedural), despite the fact that acquiring new knowledge or expertise may become increasingly difficult in later life because of declines in cognitive mechanics and reserve capacity (see P. B. Baltes, Lindenberger, & Staudinger, 1998; Salthouse, 1996). What people learn may depend on idiosyncratic factors, such as job choice, place of residence, chance events or historical times, and other life circumstances, rather than age alone. Practice is critical to maintaining the accessibility of world knowledge, and existing evidence suggests that when world knowledge is no longer practiced, as may be the case for problems experienced in earlier life periods, that knowledge becomes unavailable. Further, people of all ages may change their attitudes and beliefs in interaction with their social context. Finally, we may rely more on existing knowledge as we get older, sometimes with good results (as in decision making and expertise work), sometimes with ambiguous results (as in schematic-processing work). The processes by which world knowledge is maintained or transformed are largely unexplored.

The Development of Self-Related Knowledge and Structures

As is true for the world aspect of life pragmatics, a central feature of development of the self facet of life pragmatics is the emergence of *self-knowledge structures*. Beginning in later childhood, children show evidence of personality structure, a sense of coherence or identity, and some stable modes of adaptive behavior (e.g., Caspi & Bem, 1990). From a dynamic-systems model perspective (Lewis, 1995), a stable structure is necessary and functional, as the organization and coherence of self-related knowledge are necessary preconditions for adaptation and further growth. The importance of structure is shared between world- and self-related knowledge. The importance of coherence, in the sense of identity, may be more unique to self-related knowledge. Below, we review evidence on age changes in personality dispositions and self-definitions.

Self-Related Knowledge Structures: Personality Dispositions

There is evidence in personality research for stability and change of self-descriptions with regard to typical behaviors and experiences. For example, between 50% and 75% (depending on the calculation) of the interindividual variance in neuroticism, extraversion, openness to experience, agreeableness, and conscientiousness, or the so-called Big Five, is stable over the life span (e.g., Costa & McCrae, 1994). Clearly, this does not mean there are no changes in the Big Five. Small age-related decreases in neuroticism, extraversion, and openness to experience and moderate increases in agreeableness and conscientiousness are reported (Costa & McCrae, 1994). Growth perspectives on personality also provide evidence for change across different developmental periods. Between the ages of 30 and 50, people report increases in self-confidence, cognitive commitment, dependability, and warmth (e.g., Haan, Millsap, & Hartka, 1986;

Jones & Meredith, 1996). Costa and McCrae (1994, p. 145) suggested that one might call this an increase in maturity, to borrow language from the Eriksonian tradition.

This seemingly contradictory evidence can be reconciled—as we see below—if continuity and change are viewed as a necessary dialectic supporting the proactive–adaptive function of the self. In dynamic-system models of development, conflict and synergism between continuity and change are important ingredients (see also Mischel & Shoda, 1995). High levels of stability in personality structure should not be taken as evidence against personality development. Rather, such evidence indicates that people's self-related knowledge structures are organized in stable ways. But within this frame of a stable structure or a sense of coherence, individuals adapt to and compose their developmental contexts; that is, they change and provide for change in the way they view themselves. Thus, a life-span perspective on life pragmatics accounts for both structural stability and proactive–adaptive change in self- and world-related bodies of knowledge and regulatory functions.

One aspect of the interaction between structure and proactive adaptation is illustrated by research on the relationship between personality traits and coping behavior (Suls & Harvey, 1996). Broad dimensions of personality are associated with certain preferred modes of coping (i.e., ways of regulating one's self and the world). For example, when under stress, people high on neuroticism typically report engaging in more emotional venting, behavioral and emotional disengagement, and denial than people who are low on neuroticism (Watson & Hubbard, 1996). Self-related knowledge structures also constrain how we experience and evaluate the world. People working under objectively similar conditions perceive and evaluate these conditions differently, depending on how they view themselves (i.e., their personality characteristics; Schallberger, 1995).

Development of Self-Definitions

Self-knowledge is also investigated in terms of self-definition. Here, researchers have explored developmental changes in the content and structure of self-definitions. People's specific self-beliefs vary substantially over time, but structural features of people's self-organization (e.g., self-discrepancy and positivity) are more stable (e.g., Strauman, 1996). With increasing age, people define themselves increasingly in terms of health and physical functioning, life experiences, and hobbies (Dittmann-Kohli, 1991; Freund & Smith, 1997; McCrae & Costa, 1988). However, there is also substantial stability in the content of self-definitions across different age groups when it comes to central domains of life (e.g., health and social role domains; Filipp & Klauer, 1986; George & Okun, 1985). L'Écuyer (1994) found that self-definition development is characterized first by a stage of maturing selfhood (early to middle adulthood), in which people adapt to realities of adult life, and later by the longevous self (60 years and above), in which people adapt to the realities of aging. During the first stage, people's self-definitions hinge on aspirations, roles, competencies, adaptive strategies, social skills, and status. In later life, by contrast, other facets of self-definition reappear, particularly an emphasis on the physical self, whereas the emphasis on self-defining competencies wanes.

Developmental trajectories in the structure of self-definitions depend on which structural characteristics are investigated, but many theorists have argued for increased complexity and integration (Labouvie-Vief, 1994; Vaillant, 1993). Labouvie-Vief, Chiodo, Goguen, Diehl, and Orwoll (1995) have shown that adults' self-definitions move from those with little differentiation between self and other and heavy influence from social conventions toward definitions that emphasize contextual, process-related, and idiosyncratic features of selfhood. Older adults also report more synergy between their past, present, future, and ideal self-conceptions (Ryff, 1991).

The Development of Self-Regulatory Processes

There are multiple ways to view the organized abilities and skills, or self-regulatory processes that a person brings to bear on monitoring behavior and experience. From a life-span perspective, self-regulatory processes and behaviors that attempt to reach, maintain, or regain psychological equilibrium are of particular interest. Processes aimed at maintaining a coherent identity in the face of changing developmental contexts are an example. Below, we focus on the following social–cognitive processes: goal-related processes, self-evaluative processes, control beliefs, and coping mechanisms.

Goal-Related Processes Across the Life Span

Content and priorities of life goals and personal life investments are not arbitrary. Rather, they are embedded in subjective conceptions of the life course and also reflect the changing developmental tasks and themes of life (e.g., Cantor & Blanton, 1996). Across the life span (25–105 years), people report being most invested (in terms of time and effort) in domains that reflect the developmental tasks and themes of their respective life period (Staudinger, 1996a). From 25 to 35 years, work, friends, family, and independence are ranked highest in personal investment. From 35 to 45 years, family, work, friends, and cognitive fitness figure centrally. From

55 to 65, the top four ranks of personal life investment are held by family, health, friends, and cognitive fitness. For 70- to 85-year-olds, only friends and cognitive fitness reverse position. Finally, in very old age (85–105 years), health becomes the most important investment theme, followed by family, thinking about life, and cognitive fitness. Such findings illustrate the life-span developmental scripts and ecologies that regulate motivational investment over the life span (see Heckhausen, 1997, on the importance of life domains). Further, toward the end of life (70–105 years) the overall amount of "psychological" energy that people report to invest in central domains of life decreases slightly ($r = -.19$) but much less than biological markers of vitality would suggest (Staudinger, Freund, Linden, & Maas, 1999).

Life-Span Development of Self-Evaluative Processes

One of the most important features of self-evaluation processes is the standard by which the self is evaluated (e.g., temporal or social, e.g., Wood, 1996), and these standards may change with age. Theoretically, temporal comparisons, especially retrospective ones, become prominent in old age, whereas social comparisons decline (Suls & Mullen, 1982). Evidence to support this hypothesis is scarce and equivocal (e.g., Filipp, Ferring, Mayer, & Schmidt, 1997). When older adults are asked to explain self-evaluations provided earlier, they tend to report more temporal comparisons than social ones and specifically more prospective than retrospective comparisons (Filipp & Buch-Bartos, 1994). Other findings suggest that people of all ages prefer temporal comparisons to social comparisons (although not significantly for young adults). The endorsement of social comparisons appears stable across age groups, whereas temporal comparisons become increasingly preferred across the life span (Brown & Middendorf, 1996). However, the specific context and intended function of comparisons are more important determinants of which standard is used than age (Frey & Ruble, 1990). A further problem is that widely varying methods for assessing comparison practices make it difficult to integrate findings (Wood, 1996).

Social Cognitions That Regulate Oneself and the World
Across the Life Span: Coping and Control Strategies

Some authors have argued that with age the "changing landscape of stressors" (Pearlin & Skaff, 1996, p. 239) confronts us with more complex challenges, both in scope and temporal extension. Stressors in later life tend to involve more domains of life, as well as more relationships. Life complexity is also increased by accumulating history and experiences characterizing life domains and relationships. This complexity systematically increases until middle adulthood and decreases thereafter. Complexity of demand alone, however, does not determine the stressfulness of life; rather, it is the balance between demands and resources. On average, high life complexity at midlife is matched by rich resources. When considering both available resources and degree of challenges or stress, the net demand exerted by different life periods may be comparable. Smith and Baltes (1996) suggested that this may not be true for advanced old age. They offered the alternative speculation that the life-span challenge or stress curve follows the life-span mortality curve.

Evidence from research on control beliefs and on coping has demonstrated that old people are able to adapt to their landscape of stressors. Research on control beliefs (e.g., Brandtstädter & Greve, 1994; Heckhausen & Schulz, 1995; Lachman, Ziff, & Spiro, 1994), for instance, has shown that internal control beliefs (e.g., the belief that I control outcomes) stay relatively stable across the life span (e.g., Johnson & Barer, 1993; Sansone & Berg, 1993; Staudinger et al., 1999). However, beliefs about the power of others over one's life increase in conjunction with age-related changes in contingencies (e.g., Nurmi, Pulliainen, & Salmela-Aro, 1992; Welch & West, 1995).

For older adults, it is functional to place greater weight on external resources to compensate for decreases in internal resources (see also M. M. Baltes, 1996). Believing in the power of others over one's life is not synonymous with giving up responsibility and control. Rather, it may imply an explicit acknowledgment that others are part of one's resources. Further, acknowledging the role of powerful others or of chance does not necessarily diminish one's view of one's own agency, an interpretation consistent with the empirical findings.

With regard to age-related differences in coping (here, world- and self-regulation), the old regression hypothesis (Pfeiffer, 1977) has been contradicted. On the contrary, more and more recent evidence supports a stability and growth view of coping in adulthood and old age (e.g., Aldwin, 1991; Irion & Blanchard-Fields, 1987; Labouvie-Vief, Hakim-Larson, & Hobart, 1987; McCrae, 1989; Vaillant, 1993).

Older adults report that they are less likely to seek social support or use confrontive coping, that they are more likely to use distancing and positive reappraisal, and that they have greater impulse control (Diehl, Coyle, & Labouvie-Vief, 1996; Folkman, Lazarus, Pimley, & Novacek, 1987). Older adults also appear more flexible than younger adults in adapting their coping response to characteristics of the situation, such as its controllability (e.g., Aldwin, 1991). Based on a highly heterogeneous sample of 70- to 105-year-olds, findings from the Berlin Aging Study demonstrated that even very old people show high endorsement of problem-focused coping and rather low endorsement of "regressive" coping styles (Staudinger et al., 1999).

In addition, as with work on problem solving, individual differences in the endorsement of coping mechanisms seem more a function of the type of stressful event than of age (e.g., Aldwin, Sutton, Chiara, & Spiro, 1996; Lazarus, 1996; McCrae, 1989). For example, the type of stress in old age may change from acute to chronic, requiring different responses and also producing a different stress awareness on the part of the old person (Aldwin et al., 1996; Pearlin & Skaff, 1996).

Summary

Developmental changes in self-knowledge seem to be dominated by stability and growth (e.g., increases in ego strength, agreeableness, and decrease in neuroticism) rather than decline (e.g., decrease in openness to experience). Changes in the content of self-definitions and self-regulatory mechanisms may reflect changing developmental contexts and tasks and have been found to be adaptive (see below).

THE FUNCTIONS OF LIFE PRAGMATICS

In the previous section, we provided evidence that a dialectic between stability and change characterizes the life-span development of life pragmatics. Dynamic changes observed in life pragmatics may be strongly related to adaptive development across different contexts. In the following, we consider the functions of life pragmatics in more detail. Life pragmatics develop to serve three functions and by means of these three functions also contribute to development (see also Brandtstädter, 1998). The prime function is the proactive–adaptive one. Adaptation means both that people adapt to developmental contexts and that people "adapt the world to themselves," or produce developmental contexts. The term *proactive–adaptive* highlights the active aspect of this function.

Two other functions serve as subsidiaries to the proactive–adaptive function. One is a *reflective and evaluative function*. Human beings are unique in the ability to reflect on and evaluate the world and themselves. Reflection and evaluation contribute to the acquisition and elaboration of knowledge about self and world and serve as a precursor to effective action, thus, serving proactive adaptation. A second subsidiary function is an *integrative or executive function*. This function provides the link between reflection and evaluation of changes in the person and the world and the adaptation of either the person or the world. Integration also implies the coordination of different domains of psychological functioning (e.g., intelligence, personality, and social relations) in proactive adaptation. All aspects of the integrative function are essential for achieving proactive adaptation to changing circumstances.

Across the life span, life pragmatics "perform" these different functions in a landscape of change—in both the availability and allocation of internal and external resources (e.g., Staudinger, Marsiske, & Baltes, 1995). First, productive adaptation, reflection and evaluation, and integration are operating with less resources as people age. Second, more of those remaining resources must be invested in maintaining or recovering levels of functioning or managing losses, leaving fewer resources available for growth. Below, we review evidence on the proactive–adaptive function of life pragmatics. When available, we focus on life-span work. Unfortunately, for some very interesting areas of social cognition (or as we prefer to call it, "life pragmatics") such evidence is not yet available. In such cases, we report results from college samples to highlight the research gap and the potential usefulness of collecting life-span evidence on this question.

THE PROACTIVE–ADAPTIVE FUNCTION OF LIFE PRAGMATICS: EMPIRICAL EVIDENCE

We now turn to the ways that developmental changes in life pragmatics help individuals adapt to and produce their own development. For the world facet of life pragmatics, we address the adaptiveness of acquiring and using world knowledge. Self-conceptions and personality serve as examples when examining the adaptivity of self-knowledge. Comparison processes, life investment, control, and coping illustrate the adaptivity of self-regulatory aspects of life pragmatics.

Proactive–Adaptive Functions of World Knowledge

Are life-span changes of world knowledge adaptive or productive? In most cases, the adaptivity of knowledge about life problems, other people, and common events is obvious. It is difficult to solve a problem without knowing what the problem is or without knowing which potential solutions apply. Knowledge about problems is adaptive in problem-solving or decision-making contexts by reducing the amount of information that must be considered (Meyer, Russo, & Talbot, 1995; Streufert et al., 1990). Those with more knowledge of their professional domain often also have higher salaries, another adaptivity indicator (Colonia-Willner, 1998). Getting advice from a wise person will likely offer benefits for the managing, planning, and meaning-making of one's life, although this has not been empirically tested (e.g., Orwoll & Perlmutter, 1990). The perceived value of becoming wise is also high (Heckhausen et al., 1989). Understanding other people, and knowing about common events and social categories, is critical for making sense of experiences. Below, we elaborate on the adaptivity of greater complexity of knowledge and of using old knowledge to make sense of the new because in these cases the adaptivity of observed age changes is less obvious.

Complexity of Knowledge and Reasoning

Generally, greater complexity and abstraction in reasoning is viewed positively, perhaps because complex reasoning sometimes correlates with greater intelligence (e.g., Labouvie-Vief, DeVoe, & Bulka, 1989) and more education (e.g., Kitchener & King, 1990; Kuhn, 1989). Further, the association of increasing complexity with development in a theoretical sense may make it tempting to view complexity as generally adaptive (e.g., Siegler, 1996).

Complexity can be very adaptive. Experts have more complex and elaborated knowledge structures but also have automatized and intuitive ways of using this complexity. Consequently, in their domain of expertise, they can reason quickly and efficiently, make adaptive decisions, and compensate for age-related deficits in cognitive mechanics (e.g., Ericsson & Smith, 1991). Similarly, integrative complexity allows managers to take in more of the information in their environment and respond more appropriately to that information (see Stabell, 1978). However, too much complexity in reasoning, or "disintegrative" complexity, can lead to maladaptive inability to make decisions.

One key factor may be the "stage" in processing in which people apply complex reasoning about the world. At the information-gathering stage, greater complexity means more information is considered and incorporated into a judgment. At the decision-making stage, complexity needs to be integrated to make a final choice, not increased. Similar issues arise in self-knowledge and self-regulation (see below). Using case studies of Churchill and his major rival, Chamberlain, Tetlock and Tyler (1996) analyzed speeches and showed that being integratively simple in public speeches about major policy decisions was a strategy that worked sometimes in Churchill's favor and sometimes not. Had Churchill taken an integratively complex perspective on when to be simple and when to be complex (i.e., had he been integratively complex on a metalevel), he might have had more constant successes in terms of winning policy debates in the public forum. Other evidence comes from computerized simulations of decision making, in which models that consider only the "best" reasons for and against a course of action perform more adaptively than models that consider more information (Gigerenzer & Goldstein, 1996). The same may be true in many instances for modern humans. Of course, an emphasis on the adaptiveness of speed and frugality could be an artifact of focusing only on problems that require fast decision making. Whether most everyday problems are of that nature and require such speed is arguable.

Others also respond to the complexity of one's thinking, and not always positively. Managers who are complex in their reasoning are viewed both positively, in terms of their objectivity and initiative-taking, and negatively, in terms of their antagonism and narcissism (Tetlock, Peterson, & Berry, 1993). In contrast, other work has shown that Type A individuals (those who are more hostile, aggressive, and time-pressured) reason in less integratively complex ways and that higher integrative complexity is related to better established personal identities and more cooperative behavior in group problem-solving tasks (Bruch, McCann, & Harvey, 1991). Academics who, in interviews, reason about their research with integrative complexity are not very likeable but are highly cited, whereas those who demonstrate integratively complex thinking about teaching and teaching policy are well liked but not well cited (Feist, 1994). Thus, depending on the domain, the timing, and the perceiver, integratively complex reasoning may be associated with both positive and negative outcomes.

Adaptivity of Schematic Processing

As we noted above, world knowledge often functions to help us make sense of new information and can also help us to retain that information and conceive of new possibilities (see, e.g., Fiske & Taylor 1991; Hess, 1994). For example, we can use prior beliefs to narrow our search for information (for a recent study, see Trope & Thompson, 1997). Our prior knowledge also tells us what is new or unexpected about novel information (see Wyer & Carlston, 1994).

Knowledge can also help people transcend their usual errors in logical reasoning tasks. Given logical problems framed in terms of abstract principles, most adults do poorly. Given the same problems framed as social exchange or pragmatic-reasoning problems, they do well (Cheng & Holyoak, 1985; Cosmides, 1989; Gigerenzer & Hug, 1992). Whether such findings are best accounted for by specialized cognitive structures (e.g., mechanics) or accumulated world knowledge is not clear.

Using extant world knowledge is generally helpful; the world is vastly more complicated than the limited capacity our working memory can handle (e.g., Fiske & Taylor, 1991). However, there are associated costs for these benefits. We may be less than optimally flexible in representing events; we may hold erroneous beliefs far longer than evidence warrants because we fail to seek or to remember disconfirming evidence; and we may interpret mixed information as unrealistically supportive of our own beliefs and assumptions (in short, our prior knowledge; see, e.g., Trope & Thompson, 1997). Older adults may be more likely than young adults to rely on their prior knowledge, especially in automatic processing and with non socioemotional materials, although, as mentioned above, evidence here is still equivocal. Whether older adults' patterns of referring to prior knowledge optimizes the benefits over the costs of applying prior knowledge is still open to investigation.

More or Less Adaptive Beliefs?

Beliefs or knowledge about the world may also have long-term implications for successful adaptation, but this has not been adequately studied. As an example, consider beliefs about the fairness and predictability of the world. Belief in a just world means believing that the world is one in which people get what they deserve. People who have experienced uncontrollable negative events, such as violence, unemployment, or discrimination, are less likely to believe the world is just (e.g., Calhoun & Cann, 1994; Forest, 1995). In turn, believing that the world is fair (or not) could influence future development. Those who believe in a just world interpret difficult laboratory tasks as challenges rather than threats, have more adaptive emotional and physical responses to the tasks, and perform better (Tomaka & Blascovich, 1994). A stronger belief in a just world is also associated with better marital satisfaction (Lipkus & Bissonnette, 1996). Over the longer term, people who believe in a just world report higher well-being, particularly if the beliefs are assessed for the self rather than in general (Lipkus, Dalbert, & Siegler, 1996). As with rich desserts, however, there can be too much of a good thing. Those who believe in a just world tend not to perceive discrimination against themselves and thus fail to take appropriate action (Hafer & Olson, 1993). A general caveat is also important. Those with great faith in a just world are more advantaged by the world in which they live (see Calhoun & Cann, 1994); thus, it may be that their belief in a just world and their better long-term outcomes arise from the same source: social and economic advantage. Again, there is little work on how beliefs in a just world remain stable or change in adulthood; thus, it is hard to say whether individuals gain more of the benefits of this belief over their lifetimes. In the face of illness and other critical events more common in old age, it may be difficult to maintain such beliefs.

Summary

Developmental changes in world knowledge (declarative and procedural) are often, but not always, adaptive. The contextually appropriate nature of developmental changes in life knowledge and the increasingly complex structure of that knowledge in adulthood appear to be benefits of age. In other cases, like those we reviewed above, the picture is less simple, and these cases provide a cautionary note to a relatively optimistic picture. In general, there has been little attention to the adaptivity of many beliefs and even less attention to the ways in which knowledge and beliefs about the world serve to produce the world.

The Proactive–Adaptive Function of Self-Knowledge and Self-Regulatory Functions

There is little correlation between age and subjective indicators of adaptivity, such as self-esteem (e.g., Filipp, 1996), sense of personal control (e.g., Lachman et al., 1994), or happiness and subjective well-being (e.g., Diener & Suh, 1998). Only in advanced old age are such losses evident (P. B. Baltes & Smith, 1999; Martin, Poon, Kim, & Johnson, 1996). The discrepancy between an age-related increase in risks and maintenance of adaptive self-functioning has been labelled a "paradox." For us, the well-being paradox is an example of the self facet of life pragmatics at work.

There are many explanations for this discrepancy between an age-related increase in risks and age-related stability in subjective well-being (e.g., Staudinger & Fleeson, 1996). First, age is only a rough proxy of increasing risks; not everyone of a given age cohort will encounter age-associated risks. Second, as argued above, the self has a strong "interest" in continuity and growth (e.g., Brandtstädter & Greve, 1994). Over time, the self can adapt to adverse circumstances as if little change has occurred. For researchers interested in the "self at work," the time and method of assessment is crucial. For example, critical life events typically lose their effects on subjective well-being after 3 to 6 months (Suh, Diener, & Fujita, 1996). Stressors may also only affect domain-specific well-being rather than overall subjective well-being (Kahana et al., 1995; see also Smith, Fleeson, Geiselmann, Settersten, & Kunzmann, 1999). Third, many changes due to increasing risks are chronic rather than acute, producing gradual change. People may have difficulty recognizing and reporting such change. Below, we review findings on how various facets of self-knowledge and self-regulation serve proactive–adaptive functions and thus contribute to the well-being paradox.

The Proactive–Adaptive Function of Self-Knowledge

Adaptive Structures of Self-Related Knowledge. Dispositional ways of thinking about ourselves (i.e., personality traits) might serve a mediating function between age and indicators of self-related resilience, such as subjective well-being (Adkins, Martin, & Poon, 1996; Diener, Sandvik,

Pavot, & Fujita, 1992). Individuals with certain self-related knowledge structures (i.e., patterns of personality characteristics) do show higher levels of adaptation. Viewing oneself as emotionally unstable or outgoing (i.e., neuroticism and extraversion) is related to lower subjective well-being as measured by the Bradburn Affect Balance Scale. Over 10 years of middle adulthood, more neurotic individuals showed more negative affect, whereas more extraverted individuals showed more positive affect (Costa, McCrae, & Norris, 1981). Over 30 years of adulthood, higher extraversion predicted more social activity and greater perceived social support (Von Dras & Siegler, 1997).

The way we think about ourselves can also "produce" developmental contexts. In a 4-year study of young adults, those who viewed themselves as outgoing (i.e., extraverted) were more likely to experience positive events, whereas those who viewed themselves as neurotic were more likely to experience negative events (Magnus, Diener, Fujita, & Pavot, 1993). In that study, life events and personality characteristics were not independently assessed, but differentiating more "objective" from "subjective" events does not change the results. Events not only happen to people by chance, people may also seek out events according to their personality (e.g., Lerner & Busch-Rossnagel, 1981). Similarly, genetic influences on controllable life events for women are mediated by personality; thus, genetics influence personality, which influences controllable life events (Saudino, Pedersen, Lichtenstein, McClearn, & Plomin, 1997).

Adaptive life-span development is sometimes indexed by length of life. According to survival analyses from the longitudinal Terman study (covering 70 years), being more conscientious reduced mortality risk, whereas being cheerful increased risk (Friedman et al., 1993). These psychological risk and protection factors are similar in effect size to biological risk factors, such as systolic blood pressure or serum cholesterol.

The risk related to cheerfulness in childhood contradicts findings from short-term (e.g., 10 years) longitudinal studies in adulthood, in which optimism has been found to be highly protective (e.g., Cohen & Williamson, 1991; Scheier & Carver, 1987), a point acknowledged by the authors. This highlights the importance of distinguishing between short- and long-term predictions. Humor and optimism might be very effective coping mechanisms in particular situations rather than lifelong protective temperamental dispositions (see Friedman et al., 1993, for a discussion).

The protective power of conscientiousness obtained in the Friedman et al. (1993) work may be mediated by lifestyles that characterize highly conscientious people (e.g., less risk-taking behavior and leading a healthier life). Other personality concepts, such as ego strength, ego resilience, tough-mindedness, cognitive investment, competence, and maturity in the Eriksonian sense of wisdom, show benefits like those of conscientiousness. People with more ego strength, ego resilience, tough-mindedness, and so on, report greater well-being and adaptation, concurrently and longitudinally, as well as across various measures and study designs (e.g., Ardelt, 1997; Block, 1981; Haan, 1981; Helson & Wink, 1987; Klohnen, 1996).

In sum, individual differences in largely stable knowledge structures about the self contribute to successful adaptation. These adaptive patterns differ depending on whether short- or long-term predictions are considered. This applies especially to two traits widely assumed to function as risk or protective factors, that is, neuroticism and optimism or cheerfulness. Over shorter time spans (up to 10 years), neuroticism functions as a risk and cheerfulness as a protective factor. Over a lifetime, neuroticism becomes neutral and cheerfulness actually turns into a risk factor. Lifelong protective dispositions or general purpose mechanisms may differ from context-specific adaptive mechanisms. Because few lifetime studies are available, our knowledge about long-term protective personality profile (i.e., self-knowledge structures) is still limited.

Self-Definitions. As discussed above, self-definitions appear to increase in complexity over the life span and to become less conflicting. Evidence suggests that a multifocal and diversified structure of personal life priorities and self-definitions, or identity projects, makes it easier to productively adapt to developmental changes (e.g., Cross & Markus, 1991; Linville, 1987; Thoits, 1983). Adults who define themeslves with multiple and interconnected identities that are richly construed (i.e., "self-complexity"; Linville, 1987), positively evaluated, and anchored in the present retain their sense of well-being in the face of health declines (Freund & Smith, 1999). Similarly, a variety of sociologically oriented studies suggest that a greater number of identities (e.g., family and work) is related to better mental health (Coleman & Antonucci, 1982; Kessler & McRae, 1982). Note that the protective value of self-complexity depends on the positivity and consistency of self-descriptions. In fact, highly complex, negative, or inconsistent self-conceptions are related to more depression (Donahue, Robins, Roberts, & John, 1993; Woolfolk, Novalany, Gara, Allen, & Polino, 1995).

An additional issue in this vein is the importance that people attach to their various domain-specific self-conceptions. The personal importance that people place on their strengths and weaknesses is an important predictor of global self-esteem (e.g., Pelham, 1995). Recently, the interrelations between importance, positivity, and evaluative differentiation of self-concepts were investigated (Showers & Ryff, 1996). In a study of women who had relocated to a retirement home in the past year, perceived improvement predicted greater well-being only if the improvement was focused on important (and positive) domains of self-knowledge. When spread evenly across self-domains, perceived improvement was less adaptive. The authors argued that having a few highly positively evaluated self-domains supports resilience. A longitudinal study also involving relocation into a retirement home has shed some more light on this issue (Kling, Ryff, & Essex, 1997). In this study, if perceived health and relations with friends were viewed more negatively after the move, it was adaptive to downgrade their importance. In the case of economics, family, and daily activities, the reverse was the case; that is, when they were evaluated less positively after the move, it was adaptive to increase their centrality. It may be that participants felt less in control of health and friends and therefore "chose" to decrease their importance, whereas in economics, family, and daily activities, they felt more control over possible improvement or were unable to reduce the importance of these areas. Such social–cognitive mechanisms help us to adapt to changed environments.

Besides current self-definitions, research by Markus and others has demonstrated the adaptive value of "possible selves" (i.e., those identities that are either feared or hoped for in the present, in the past, or in the future, Cross & Markus, 1991). For example, in negotiating the changes and transitions of adulthood, possible selves are used as resources to motivate and defend the individual. In a study on possible selves and perceived health, the majority of older adults had hoped-for possible selves in the domain of health and also rated the most important possible self as being in the realm of health (Hooker, 1992). Older adults felt subjectively healthier if they simultaneously reported hopes for their health and believed that they had some control over their health.

In sum, recent work has shown that understanding the adaptivity of self-definitions is more complex than first thought. Combining dimensions like number, richness, positivity, and importance of self-definitions, as well as differentiation in self-evaluation and real and potential selves into one theoretical framework, will be an important step in capturing the adaptive life-span dynamics of self-knowledge.

The Proactive–Adaptive Function of Self-Regulatory Mechanisms

In this section, we provide examples for the proactive–adaptive function of self-regulatory mechanisms. As above, when we discuss developmental trajectories, we focus on goal-related processes, self-evaluative processes, control beliefs, and coping.

Adaptivity of Life Priorities and Personal Life Investments

Life-span theory emphasizes the critical importance of selection of domains and life priorities for effective regulation of developmental processes. The evidence on life-span *development* of life priorities and personal life investment patterns reported above points to selection into individual life contexts and the importance of internal and external contexts in defining salient features of the self across the life span (see also Brandtstädter & Rothermund, 1994; Cantor & Fleeson, 1994; Carstensen, 1995). Socioemotional selectivity theory, for instance, argues for systematic and adaptive life-span changes in social goals over the life span (e.g., Carstensen, 1995). In later adulthood, because of decreasing time, emotional regulation rather than information seeking becomes the driving and adaptive force for seeking social contacts. Older people, in contrast to younger adults, report preferring familiar over novel social partners and social relationships related to anticipated affect rather than information seeking or future contact (Fredrickson & Carstensen, 1990). So, temporal constraints like mortality may shift the criteria used for selecting social relationships, requiring a corresponding change in the criteria for judging a particular relationship adaptive (e.g., Carstensen, 1995).

Beyond the social realm, the adaptive value of life priorities in general seems to change. For example, older adults find meaning in life predominantly by searching for "contentment," whereas younger adults report searching for "happiness" (Dittmann-Kohli, 1991). Younger people tend to assess their subjective well-being in terms of accomplishments and careers, whereas older people associate well-being with good health and the ability to accept change (Ryff, 1989). These changes are highly adaptive and illustrate the importance of flexibility—giving up or reducing investment in those roles and commitments that are no longer available and investing in commitments that fit current conditions of living (e.g., Brim, 1992; Dittmann-Kohli, 1991; Lazarus & DeLongis, 1983). Flexibility in goals and investments (or priorities) is, of course, facilitated by a rich variety of self-defining concepts to select from and prioritize. In this sense, a rich variety of interrelated but well-articulated life goals is part of a person's developmental reserve capacity (cf. Staudinger et al., 1995).

In addition to the repertoire and selection of goals, other facets of goal pursuit also relate to adaptation. For instance, delay of gratification, or "willpower," is critical for successfully realizing goals (e.g., Mischel, 1996). Achieving a goal is usually adaptive, but the meaningfulness of the goal and the degree of commitment to it may enhance or limit that adaptivity (see also Brunstein, 1993; Emmons, 1996). Further, one must act; one study demonstrated that the relationship between people's goals and well-being was primarily mediated through doing more in the selected domain (C. K. Holahan, 1988; see also Harlow & Cantor, 1996). Recent evidence suggests that the pursuit of approach goals (or hoped-for selves) is related to greater well-being, whereas the pursuit of avoidance goals (or feared-for selves) relates to less well-being (e.g., Carver & Scheier, 1998; Coats, Janoff-Bulman, & Alpert, 1996; Elliot, Sheldon, & Church, 1997). Most of this research, however, is done with young adults, and little is known about changes over the life span. Because of reduced resources and increased risks, avoidance goals may increase in prevalence in later life, possibly changing in adaptive value. Alternatively, it may be adaptive to reformulate avoidance goals as approach goals at all ages.

The adaptiveness of goal investment is also altered by life circumstances. Given highly restrictive life circumstances, such as major health constraints, concentration on a few selected goals, rather than many, helps to sustain levels of subjective well-being (Staudinger & Fleeson, 1996). Further, the adaptiveness of goal patterns may depend on legal status or educational attainment (e.g., Rapkin & Fischer, 1992).

The Adaptive Value of Self-Evaluations

In addition to changes in content, ranking, and valence of self-concepts and goals, self-evaluative processes can be considered protective or risk factors. Three motives of self-evaluation (see Fiske & Taylor, 1991) can serve protective functions—self-verification (e.g., Swann, 1990), self-enhancement (e.g., Taylor & Brown, 1988), and self-improvement (e.g., Taylor, Neter, & Wayment, 1995).

Recent debate about the adaptiveness of self-enhancement versus self-verification has centered on the issue of when discrepancy between reality and attribution is adaptive and when it becomes maladaptive. Is it true that positive illusions always are more adaptive than veridical views (e.g., Baumeister, Smart, & Boden, 1996; Taylor & Brown, 1988)? Or does this relationship follow an inverted U-shaped function? Baumeister (1989) introduced the notion of the optimal margin of illusion, arguing that some discrepancy between reality and attribution is adaptive but that if that discrepancy becomes too large, the connection to reality is lost and maladaptive consequences result (e.g., Colvin & Block, 1994).

General statements such as "positive illusions are adaptive" are simplistic. It is important to know when positive illusions are adaptive (e.g., at which point in the action sequence; see, e.g., Schwarz & Bohner, 1996). It has been found, for instance, that people think relatively more realistically when setting goals than when implementing them (Taylor & Gollwitzer, 1995). The particular content of the illusions is also important. For example, positive expectations about behavior outcomes contrasted with negative fantasies about the same outcome can result in the best behavioral outcome (Oettingen, 1996). To our knowledge, however, there is no age-comparative work yet on optimal margins of illusions. Such unresolved recent issues qualify the existing literature on the adaptivity of self-evaluations, which we address next.

Self-Evaluation: Social Comparisons. Goals shift in any activity during the life span, and those shifts lead to shifts in the selection and weighting of comparative information (Bandura & Cervone, 1983; Frey & Ruble, 1990). Individuals also modify their self-evaluative standards within a given domain in order to adapt to decreases in their behavioral competence or negative changes in their health condition, thus maintaining stability in their self-views (Frey & Ruble, 1990).

Social comparison and other forms of interactive minds (P. B. Baltes & Staudinger, 1996) are one important social–cognitive mechanism of self-regulation (e.g., Wood, 1996). New reference groups are selected or sometimes even constructed to permit a reorganization of personal standards of evaluation (e.g., Buunk, 1994). For example, one compares oneself to specific subgroups, such as age, gender, and ethnic–cultural groups, rather than to the population at large. Three types of social comparisons (i.e., downward, lateral, and upward) can be distinguished and serve distinct and age-related self-regulatory functions. Downward comparisons, in which individuals compare themselves to people who are worse off in a relevant domain of functioning, may become more and more important with age, increasing levels of risk, or losses that cannot be remedied through instrumental action (e.g., Filipp, 1999; Heckhausen & Krueger, 1993; Heidrich & Ryff, 1993; Markus & Cross, 1990; Suls & Wills, 1991).

Selection of appropriate comparison groups is one of the protective life-pragmatic mechanisms (for a review, see Buunk, 1994) that allow people to manage the gains and losses of aging. Comparisons with better functioning groups (upward comparisons) help when the goal is to maintain and to improve, whereas comparisons with more poorly functioning groups (downward comparisons) can help in dealing with loss. Of course, little is known about the level of consciousness at which people make such comparisons in everyday life.

Downward comparisons can be very important. Women with breast cancer rated their postsurgery level of well-being as positive, sometimes as more positive than before they were diagnosed with cancer. The same women reported overwhelmingly that they were doing as well or better than other women with breast cancer by comparing themselves with subgroups of cancer patients (Taylor & Lobel, 1989; Wood, Taylor, & Lichtman, 1985). Similarly, older people who are relocating and use downward social comparisons show higher levels of some types of well-being, such as a sense of personal growth and self-acceptance (Ryff & Essex, 1992). People make downward social comparisons more often in domains in which they are experiencing problems, allowing them to maintain a sense of well-being even in the face of loss (e.g., Heckhausen & Brim, 1997).

The downward comparison story is not as simple as it seems, however (see also Wood, 1996). The operationalization of downward social comparisons, for instance, varies markedly between studies. Some studies evaluate spontaneous reasons for self-evaluations provided "online," which are later coded for comparison standards. Other studies ask in retrospect for the frequency with which social upward, downward, and lateral comparisons are made and relate this to measures of well-being (e.g., Filipp & Buch-Bartos, 1994; Taylor & Lobel, 1989). Still other studies have participants rate themselves and a generalized other on certain personality dimensions and then indirectly infer upward or downward comparisons (e.g., Heckhausen & Krueger, 1993). As suggested above, the most critical issue for adaptiveness may be the use of the most functional comparison at the appropriate time during the person–situation transaction, something seldom addressed in these studies.

Self-Evaluation: Lifetime Comparisons. Besides social comparisons, comparisons across one's own lifetime constitute an important resource for the self. As noted earlier, evidence on lifetime trajectories of social and lifetime comparisons remains scarce. In one study, higher frequency of future-oriented comparisons by older participants was related to lower well-being (Filipp & Buch-Bartos, 1994). In contrast, drawing on past successes in difficult situations can produce adaptive outcomes in old age (Aldwin et al., 1996; see also Staudinger & Fleeson, 1996). Obviously, it is critical to distinguish between upward and downward temporal comparisons, as past and future comparisons can involve standards of better or worse functioning. It is not the temporal comparison per se that is protective or damaging; rather, depending on the characteristic or domain, and on the point in the self-regulatory process, lifetime comparisons can result in an enhanced self-evaluation or a sense of loss and decline. Selectively attending to positive aspects of the self at different points in the lifetime can support a positive sense of self at the present. The endorsement of selective lifetime comparisons may contribute to the lack of age differences in concurrent self-evaluations.

Longitudinal work has demonstrated that self-perceived personality change may be biased by what one might call "time enhancement" (Woodruff & Birren, 1972). Participants perceive improvement as compared with their own past, whereas the actual ratings collected at the two occasions (25 years apart) did not reveal significant change (see Ross, 1997). Unfortunately, no interactions with age in this tendency to upgrade the past were tested. Other work on self-perceived personality change shows that discrepancies between ratings of past, present, future, and ideal personality are especially pronounced for young adults and hardly existent for older adults. It seems adaptive for young adults to strive for improvement, whereas for older adults, with decreasing resources, it seems adaptive to conceive of the future as being close to the present and the past (Ryff, 1991).

A person's current view of themselves may not be meaningful unless we also understand how he or she believes he or she once was and will become. Being moderately extraverted in the present when having been very extraverted in the past has different implications for well-being than being moderately extraverted in the present and introverted in the past. Fleeson and Baltes (1997) showed that past and future ratings of personality predicted well-being above and beyond present ratings. When only current personality is assessed, the absence of information about change may mask relationships between personality perceptions and well-being (see also Fleeson & Heckhausen, 1997). Similar cautions apply to goal assessments. Regrets about past, unattained goals predict lower subjective well-being over and above current goal ratings and general tendencies toward negative affect (Lecci, Okun, & Karoly, 1994).

In future social–cognitive work on life-span development of self and personality, it will be critical to introduce a stronger focus on subjective lifetime comparisons. Such work would be less aimed at assessing ontogenetic reality than at assessing people's ideas about lifetime change and continuity—their notions of who was I, who am I, who will I be?

The Adaptivity of Social Cognitions That Regulate Oneself and the World Across the Life Span: Coping and Control Strategies

In contemporary contextual models of coping (see Berg et al., 1994; Brandtstädter & Greve, 1994; Filipp, 1999; Heckhausen & Schulz, 1995; Lazarus, 1996; Staudinger et al., 1995), questions of adaptivity are conditioned on the particular situation, including all its inherent constraints and demands. Whether a coping behavior is adaptive depends entirely on who does it, in response to which stressor, and in which situation the behavior occurs.

Increasing evidence highlights the importance of context. For example, depending on a person's level of physical impairment, different coping styles are related to subjective well-being (Aldwin & Revenson, 1987; C. J. Holahan & Moos, 1987; Lazarus & Golden, 1981; Staudinger & Fleeson, 1996). What has been labeled "regressive" and thus dysfunctional coping under "normal" living circumstances (e.g., "I like someone to take over," "denial," and "I give up") is functional under conditions of physical impairment. Thus, older adults' regression in coping styles may be adaptive, given higher incidences of physical constraints. Of course, even normally adaptive behaviors are useless if not well executed (e.g., Suls & David, 1996).

Beyond the adaptivity of specific coping behaviors, it is important to have multiple coping options to choose from while retaining some selectivity. Those old individuals who report selective flexibility in coping (i.e., endorsing some coping styles very strongly and others not at all), also demonstrate high levels of well-being (Staudinger & Fleeson, 1996). Similar findings are reported for coping with depression in old age. Rather than any particular form of coping, better mental health means being able to choose from several different responses (Forster & Gallagher, 1986). In a similar vein, the integrated multiplicity and selectivity (with regard to importance) of self-definitions has protective value, and social relations with multiple functions are a richer resource than other types of relationships (for an overview, see Staudinger et al., 1995). This evidence suggests that access to, and flexible selection from, a repertoire of regulating functions or characteristics (e.g., coping, self-definitions, functions of a relationship, and life investments) may be a key resource used by individuals in proactive adaptation.

People obviously show highly adaptive coping behavior well into old age. In contrast to stereotypical views of elderly persons as rigid, the evidence based on social–cognitive processes of self-representation, self-regulation, and self-enhancement points to a substantial capacity for adjustment to and mastery of life's demands. Of course, this capacity for adaptation may find its limits in extreme situations, such as the challenges of advanced old age (Smith & Baltes, 1996).

Many facets of coping and control processes remain uninvestigated or poorly understood, however, including the microgenesis of coping processes (e.g., Lazarus, 1996). To outline one example, recent findings suggest that the critical factors in success at quitting cigarette smoking involve being reflective and thoughtful (e.g., emotion focused and self-focused) at a planning stage and then problem focused and behavioral during the actual quitting process (Perz, DiClemente, & Carbonari, 1996). As in the case of self-evaluative cognitions, it is also crucial to focus on the timing of coping.

Summary

These sections on the adaptive power of certain characteristics of self-knowledge and of self-regulation provide evidence in support of the proactive–adaptive function of life pragmatics and its specific value in adulthood and old age. Thinking of oneself as conscientious, extraverted, open to experience, and behaviorally flexible contributes to adaptive functioning across the life span. Similarly, defining oneself in multifaceted, integrated, positive, and present-oriented ways has adaptive value. But being is not all; doing (i.e., regulating) matters as well. Applying functional types of comparisons (social or temporal), selecting and reorganizing life priorities, and being selectively flexible in coping behaviors all promote higher levels of adaptation across adulthood.

LIFE PRAGMATICS: INTEGRATING SELF AND WORLD, KNOWLEDGE AND REGULATORY MECHANISMS

In closing, we hope to complicate the distinctions between self and world and between knowledge and regulatory mechanisms. We introduce such distinctions to show the comprehensive scope of life pragmatics and to integrate diverse areas of research. Of course, self and world, as well as knowledge and regulatory mechanisms, are inextricably intertwined in everyday human lives. Three perspectives illustrate this connectedness: narrative approaches to the study of self and personality, work on the inherent social nature of psychological functioning, and a recent model of successful development.

Narrative Approaches to Self, Personality, and Social Cognition

People tell stories that reflect self and world, and involve knowledge and regulation. They fulfill reflective, executive, and proactive–adaptive functions; unfold over time; and reflect on the current social context. Narrative approaches are not a unified theoretical or even empirical approach, but research using narrative methods complements mainstream work on self, personality, and social cognition (see Bruner, 1990; McAdams, 1996; Singer & Salovey, 1993).

Narrative approaches focus on stories people tell about themselves and their experiences (e.g., McAdams, 1996; Singer & Salovey, 1993), the functionality of reviewing the past (e.g., Webster & Cappeliez, 1993; Wong & Watt, 1991), and the role of social context in the ways people narrate (Fivush, 1991). Thus, when we refer to narratives we refer to studies of autobiographical recollection; storytelling; autobiography (narratives of the entire life); life-review processes; and any other research focusing on connections between personality, social cognition, and narratives. Unfortunately, to our knowledge, narratives about the future have not yet been explored. From our perspective, talking about the future is an important part of the temporal extension of human life as well (e.g., Neisser, 1988; Staudinger, in press). We not only (re)construct our past and present, but also our future and ideal worlds.

Self-knowledge in narrative form consists of what we remember of the past and how we conceive of the present, future, and ideal—what Neisser (1988) called the "extended self." Both autobiographical memory researchers and self researchers agree that this extended self-knowledge is organized in narrative structures (Fivush, 1991; Neisser, 1988; Schank & Abelson, 1995; Singer & Salovey, 1993). Such narratives not only document our past experiences and projections about the future or ideal but also reflect our self-knowledge (i.e., that we are generative, oriented toward others, or agentic; e.g., McAdams, 1996; Neisser, 1988). In fact, Singer and Salovey argued that individuals' reconstructions of past events not only express their explicit self-knowledge but also their subconscious motivations and conflicts. Narratives also serve purposes of self-regulation, as shown by life-review research (see Webster & Cappeliez, 1993). This work, focusing on the reconstruction and evaluation of our life-as-lived, shows that life review is a lifelong self-regulatory process used in coping with developmental tasks (e.g., Bluck & Levine, 1998; Staudinger, 1989; Webster & Cappeliez, 1993). Of course, self-knowledge and self-regulation is not the whole story: Narratives also reflect the proximal and distal social contexts in which they are told (e.g., Markus, Mullally, & Kitayama, 1997; Neisser & Jopling, 1997); cultures differ in the themes that govern members' self-narratives (e.g., Markus et al., 1997); and self-narratives differ depending on the proximal social context in which they occur (e.g., Staudinger, 1996b).

From a perspective that views language as action as well as representation (see Clark, 1996), narratives also regulate the world by defining what exists and what happened (e.g., Gergen, 1994). Such functions depend on the acceptance of a given narrative as true by the social group, reminding us of the next issue.

The Social Nature of Life Pragmatics

From a life-span perspective, development is always the simultaneous and complex outcome of nature and nurture, genes and environment, intra- and extrapersonal influences. This interaction has been further specified by distinguishing between three gradings of influences (P. B. Baltes, Reese, & Lipsitt, 1980): age graded, history graded, and nonnormative. Table 12.2 provides examples of the interplay between the two major developmental influences (biology and culture) and the three gradings of such influences. Of course, the three gradings also interact with

TABLE 12.2
Illustrating the System of Opportunities and Constraints Influencing
Self- and Personality Development Across the Life Span

Variable	Opportunities and Constraints of Self-Development	
	Biology	*Sociocultural Context*
Age	Neuronal maturation	Family of origin
	Physical growth	Teacher and mentors
	Pregnancy	Professional context
	Menopause	Financial context
	Increasing morbidity	Partnership and family
	Changes in level of energy	Social network
	Changes in sensory–motor function	Retirement
History	Altered ecologies	Value changes
	Nutrition	Role changes
	Medical system	War
	Cultural and biological coevolution	Economic depression
Idiosyn-	Specific physical strength and weaknesses	Orphanhood
crasies	Genetic risk	Unemployment
	Premature birth	Divorce
	Accidents	Widowhood
	Person-specific health stresses	

Note. Adapted from Baltes, Lindenberger, & Staudinger (1998).

each other. For example, the effect of a historical event might depend on the age and the idiosyncratic circumstances of an individual when it occurred (e.g., Elder, 1998; Little, Oettingen, Stetsenko, & Baltes, 1995).

Within this matrix of developmental influences, sociocultural contexts have been conceptualized as a system of interlocking frames ordered along a dimension of proximity, ranging from day-to-day interactions with our social and physical environment to the more distant world of institutions and constitutions (e.g., Bronfenbrenner, 1979; Lawton, 1988). Life-span developmental research has mostly focused on more distal social influences, but the facilitative and debilitative effect of social interaction in the most proximal sense has been an important topic of social and child developmental psychology (see Staudinger, 1996b). Recently, research on lifespan development has rediscovered the developmental opportunities and constraints posed by social interaction and interacting minds (Baltes & Staudinger, 1996; see also Levine, Resnick, & Higgins, 1993; Sternberg & Wagner, 1994). Understanding and optimizing the facilitative effect of social interactions and interacting minds is the major goal of such efforts.

In wisdom research, for instance, providing people with the opportunity to discuss a difficult life problem with a natural partner, followed by some individual thinking time, resulted in significantly better performances than those elicited under standard laboratory conditions in which an isolated individual responds. When discussion was not followed by individual thinking time, performance was not enhanced (Staudinger & Baltes, 1996). This finding highlights the complexity of conditions under which social interaction is beneficial. Older adults profited more from the interactive-minds condition than did younger adults, suggesting that we may become better at using social interaction as a resource as we get older. This is consistent with other findings suggesting that older adults are better at ignoring maladaptive social influence (e.g., Pasupathi, 1999; Reifman, Klein, & Murphy, 1989). With the exception of social support as a form of coping (for a review, see Staudinger et al., 1995), the study of social interaction and its effect with regard to self and personality functioning has only begun. One current focus is on collective instantiations of well-established constructs and mechanisms (e.g., self-efficacy [Bandura, 1997] and selection, compensation, and optimization [M. M. Baltes & Carstensen, 1998]), which have previously been studied in individuals.

Life Pragmatics and Current Theories of Successful Development

Finally, current theories of successful development also bring together self and world and knowledge and regulation. We take as an example the selection–optimization–compensation (SOC) model of Paul and Margret Baltes and colleagues (e.g., P. B. Baltes & Baltes, 1990; Freund & Baltes, in press). According to the SOC model, development is optimized by selection and compensation. *Selection* refers to the narrowing of the subset of domains in which energy is invested. *Optimization* pertains to increases in capacity within a given domain. *Compensation* means adaptation to changes in resources or situations that challenge the attainment or maintenance of competence. Processes of selection, optimization, and compensation are viewed as basic developmental mechanisms operating across multiple levels of analysis. Consider the mechanism of selection— "choosing" one option from an array of potential options. Selection operates at the level of cell proliferation in embryonic development in that cells are "selected" into various specializations and replicate as specialized cells, neurons or muscle fibers. This specialization optimizes the embryo's development into a functioning human being and the cell's development into an optimal component of the person. At a macroanalytic level, societies may select particular educational systems to fit their needs.

In our view, a model of life mechanics and life pragmatics and the SOC model complement each other. First, our framework provides elements on which SOC processes may operate. Mechanisms of selection, optimization, and compensation can apply to aspects of world knowledge, self-knowledge, and regulation, such as knowledge about life problems or coping with the emotions that accompany a stressful event. For example, knowledge about life problems seems to be selectively maintained and optimized to match the current life context; knowledge more pertinent for past contexts, such as childhood, appears less easily accessible (e.g., Denney et al., 1992; Staudinger et al., 1992). We select life priorities to fit our inner and outer life circumstances (e.g., Staudinger, 1996a). We also compensate for loss in one aspect of our self-definition (e.g., I have a good memory) by choosing another facet of that self-aspect (e.g., I have a good memory for the old times) or by dropping that self-aspect altogether and shifting to another one (e.g., I am a good storyteller; Brandtstädter & Greve, 1994; Freund & Smith, 1997).

In addition, SOC defines processes bridging life mechanics and life pragmatics. The performance of older experts shows how losses in life mechanics are compensated by gains in knowledge and experience (Salthouse, 1995). Life-pragmatics elements like coping strategies offer ways of managing physical constraints due to age (life mechanics). But life mechanics are not always the constraint; for example, physiological vigor and ability, part of life mechanics, make the acquisition of athletic skills easier for some people than for others (see Uttal & Perlmutter, 1989, for an extensive discussion of the logical relations between developmental gains and losses).

Summarizing Life-Span Perspectives on Self, Personality, and Social Cognition

In this chapter, we presented the theoretical framework of life mechanics and life pragmatics and reviewed a wide range of evidence about adult development in life pragmatics as it pertains to self, personality, and social cognition. Here, we summarize the evidence on age-related gains and losses and age-related adaptivity (i.e., reserves) and point to some important issues that crosscut much of the work we reviewed.

Over the life span, people demonstrate stability, increases, and, particularly, context-related changes in their knowledge about themselves and the world. Context-related changes cannot be easily labeled as gains or losses in a general sense but may be adaptive for the relevant context. People show a more consistent pattern of gains in their ability to regulate themselves and the world, and older people demonstrate particularly great resilience and reserve capacity in the face of very real losses in life mechanics. Our conclusion is that life pragmatics continue to serve proactive–adaptive functions despite age-related losses in life mechanics and physical functioning. This rather positive picture of development does require a minimal level of functioning of life mechanics. For example, cognitive mechanics are more likely to drop below this minimum level after age 80, and under such circumstances life pragmatics may not compensate (see P. B. Baltes et al., 1998).

One of the points of life pragmatics is to promote integration of work from separate subdisciplines. For example, problem- (or world-) focused coping behaviors are often viewed separately from everyday problem solving. However, both these areas address people's attempts to construct and alter their worlds. Further, different approaches used in different subdisciplines offer new ways to use established concepts, such as viewing everyday problem solving from an expertise perspective (an approach similar to that taken initially in research on wisdom, as noted above).

Our review also highlights consistencies across subdisciplines regarding features of successful adaptation. For example, multifacetedness and selectivity facilitated the adaptiveness of self-definitions, social relations, and coping behaviors. A selective choice from multiple options was always more adaptive than having too many or too few options. Or recall the importance of considering how processes unfold over time. The adaptiveness of using a self-evaluative mechanism, coping behavior, social interaction, or complex reasoning depends on timing. Complexity early, when information must be evaluated and integrated, is useful. Complexity too late, when a decision must be made, is maladaptive. Positive illusions at the outset may motivate action. Later, at the stage of action implementation, excessive positive illusions seem to impair necessary volitional processes.

In our attempt to be integrative, we did draw some distinctions, specifically between self and world and between regulatory processes and knowledge. We later noted that these are heuristic rather than real distinctions and reviewed research that offered reintegrations. First, narrative approaches to self and personality provide access to data that reflect knowledge of both self and world and also demonstrate the regulation of both self and world through narrative. Second, illustrations of the inherent social nature of human psychological functioning demonstrate how nature and nurture or self and world are inextricably intertwined in influencing psychological functioning. Finally, one of the prominent models of developmental regulation, the SOC model, complements the framework of life mechanics and life pragmatics by providing mechanisms that connect mechanics and pragmatics, as well as self and world and knowledge and regulation.

We also found several gaps in the adult developmental literature on life pragmatics. One is the consideration of the diachronic dimension when studying self, personality, and social cognition (see Staudinger, 1999). Understanding lives within temporal contexts (past, present, and future), viewing coping or problem-solving behaviors as they occur in time, and addressing how knowledge bases are updated or transformed across years are important and underresearched. Further, many facets of social cognition in our language of life-pragmatic knowledge or regulatory processes, such as beliefs in a just world, have not yet been studied developmentally. When comparing research on the various facets of life pragmatics in adulthood and old age with the research on the various facets of cognitive mechanics, the variability in measurement procedures—and sometimes also the lack of methodological precision—illustrates not only the youth of that field but also a dilemma facing research in life pragmatics, namely, the joining of experimental precision with ecological validity. We hope that more and more research in the future will attempt to be cumulative and to increase methodological rigor. Finally, our review itself certainly has gaps and is idiosyncratic, as we could not review all the literature relevant to the matrix in Table 12.1.

We hope that the model of life mechanics and life pragmatics sketched in this chapter may support and stimulate research that pursues these and other gaps. We also hope that we have demonstrated the utility and integrative potential of the life-mechanics and life-pragmatics framework. Finally, in the context of a handbook that has much to do with losses in later life, we hope to have identified some of the gains and resiliencies that are also part of human development, even in old age.

ACKNOWLEDGMENTS

We acknowledge the many valuable discussions with our colleagues from the Max Planck Institute for Human Development and Education, especially with Paul Baltes, Ulman Lindenberger, and Alexandra Freund, and with colleagues from the Berlin Aging Study and the Network on Successful Midlife Development of the Mac Arthur Foundation. We also thank Alexandra Freund, Bärbel Knäuper, Fergus I. M. Craik, and Timothy A. Salthouse for their comments on an earlier version of this chapter.

REFERENCES

Adkins, G., Martin, P., & Poon, L. W. (1996). Personality traits and states as predictors of subjective well-being in centenarians, octogenarians, and sexagenarians. *Psychology and Aging, 11*, 408–416.

Aldwin, C. M. (1991). Does age affect the stress and coping process? Implications of age differences in perceived control. *Journals of Gerontology: Psychological Sciences, 46*, 174–180.

Aldwin, C. M., & Revenson, T. A. (1987). Does coping help? A reexamination of the relation between coping and mental health. *Journal of Personality and Social Psychology, 53*, 337–348.

Aldwin, C. M., Sutton, K. J., Chiara, G., & Spiro, A., III (1996). Age differences in stress, coping, and appraisal: Findings from the Normative Aging Study. *Journals of Gerontology: Psychological Sciences, 51B*, P179–P188.

Alwin, D. A., & Krosnick, J. A. (1991). Aging, cohorts, and the stability of sociopolitical orientations over the life span. *American Journal of Sociology, 97*, 169–195.

Anderson, J. R. (1996). ACT: A simple theory of complex cognition. *American Psychologist, 51*, 355–365.

Ardelt, M. (1997). Wisdom and life satisfaction in old age. *Journals of Gerontology: Psychological Sciences, 52B*, P15–P27.

Baltes, M. M. (1996). *The many faces of dependency in old age*. New York: Cambridge University Press.

Baltes, M. M., & Carstensen, L. L. (1996). The process of successful ageing. *Ageing and Society*, 397–422.

Baltes, M. M., & Carstensen, L. L. (1998). Social psychological theories and their application to aging: From individual to collective social psychology. In V. L. Bengtson & K. W. Schaie (Eds.), *Handbook of theories of aging* (pp. 206–226). New York: Springer.

Baltes, P. B. (1997). On the incomplete architecture of human ontogeny: Selection, optimization, and compensation as foundation of developmental theory. *American Psychologist, 52*, 366–380.

Baltes, P. B., & Baltes, M. M. (1990). Psychological perspectives on successful aging: The model of selective optimization with compensation. In P. B. Baltes & M. M. Baltes (Eds.), *Successful aging: Perspectives from the behavioral sciences* (pp. 1–34). New York: Cambridge University Press.

Baltes, P. B., Dittmann-Kohli, F., & Dixon, R. A. (1984). New perspectives on the development of intelligence in adulthood: Toward a dual-process conception and a model of selective optimization with compensation. In P. B. Baltes & O. G. Brim (Eds.), *Life-span development and behavior* (Vol. 6, pp. 33–76). New York: Academic Press.

Baltes, P. B., Lindenberger, U., & Staudinger, U. M. (1998). Life-span theory in developmental psychology. In R. M. Lerner (Ed.), *Handbook of child psychology: Vol. 1. Theoretical models of human development* (5th ed., pp. 1029–1143). New York: Wiley.

Baltes, P. B., Reese, H. W., & Lipsitt, L. P. (1980). Life-span developmental psychology. *Annual Review of Psychology, 31*, 65–110.

Baltes, P. B., & Smith, J. (1999). Multilevel and systemic analyses of old age: Theoretical and empirical evidence for a fourth age. In V. L. Bengtson & K. W. Schaie (Eds.), *Handbook of theories of aging* (pp. 153–173). New York: Springer.

Baltes, P. B., Smith, J., & Staudinger, U. M. (1992). Wisdom and successful aging. In T. B. Sonderegger (Ed.), *Nebraska Symposium on Motivation 1991* (Vol. 39, pp. 123–67). Lincoln: University of Nebraska Press.

Baltes, P. B., & Staudinger, U. M. (1996). Interactive minds in a life-span perspective: Prologue. In P. B. Baltes & U. M. Staudinger (Eds.), *Interactive minds: Life-span perspectives on the social foundation of cognition* (pp. 1–32). New York: Cambridge University Press.

Baltes, P. B., Staudinger, U. M., Maercker, A., & Smith, J. (1995). People nominated as wise: A comparative study of wisdom-related knowledge. *Psychology and Aging, 10*, 155–166.

Bandura, A. (1997). *The exercise of control*. New York: Freeman.

Bandura, A., & Cervone, D. (1983). Self-evaluative and self-efficacy mechanisms governing the motivational effects of goal systems. *Journal of Personality and Social Psychology, 45*, 1017–1028.

Barton, S. (1994). Chaos, self-organization, and psychology. *American Psychologist, 49*, 5–14.

Bates, J. E., & Wachs, T. D. (Eds.). (1994). *Temperament: Individual differences at the interface of biology and behavior*. Washington, DC: American Psychological Association.

Baumeister, R. F. (1989). The optimal margin of illusion. *Journal of Social and Clinical Psychology, 8*, 176–189.

Baumeister, R. F., Smart, L., & Boden, J. M. (1996). Relation of threatened egotism to violence and aggression: The dark side of high self-esteem. *Psychological Review, 103,* 5–33.

Bem, D. J. (1967). Self-perception: An alternative interpretation of cognitive dissonance phenomena. *Psychological Review, 74,* 183–200.

Berg, C. A., & Calderone, K. S. (1994). The role of problem interpretations in understanding the development of everyday problem solving. In R. J. Sternberg & R. K. Wagner (Eds.), *Mind in context* (pp. 105–132). New York: Cambridge University Press.

Berg, C. A., Klaczynski, P. A., Calderone, K. S., & Strough, J. (1994). Adult age differences in cognitive strategies: Adaptive or deficient? In J. D. Sinnott (Ed.), *Interdisciplinary handbook of adult lifespan learning* (pp. 371–388). Westport, CT: Greenwood.

Berg, C. A., Strough, J., Calderone, K. S., Sansone, C., & Weir, C. (1998). The role of problem definitions in understanding age and context effects on strategies for solving everyday problems. *Psychology and Aging, 13,* 29–44.

Blanchard-Fields, F. (1996). Social cognitive development in adulthood and aging. In F. Blanchard-Fields & T. M. Hess (Eds.), *Perspectives on cognitive change in adulthood and aging* (pp. 454–487). New York: McGraw-Hill.

Blanchard-Fields, F., Chen, Y., & Norris, L. (1997). Everyday problem solving across the adult life span: Influence of domain specificity and cognitive appraisal. *Psychology and Aging, 12,* 684–693.

Block, J. (1981). Some enduring and consequential structures of personality. In A. I. Rabin (Ed.), *Further explorations in personality* (pp. 27–43). New York: Wiley.

Bluck, S., & Levine, L. J. (1998). Reminiscence as autobiographical memory: A catalyst for reminiscence theory development. *Ageing and Society, 18,* 185–208.

Brandtstädter, J. (1998). Action perspectives on human development. In R. M. Lerner (Ed.), *Handbook of child psychology: Vol. 1. Theoretical models of human development* (5th ed., pp. 807–863). New York: Wiley.

Brandtstädter, J., & Greve, W. (1994). The aging self: Stabilizing and protective processes. *Developmental Review, 14,* 52–80.

Brandtstädter, J., & Rothermund, K. (1994). Self-perceptions of control in middle and later adulthood: Buffering losses by rescaling goals. *Psychology and Aging, 9,* 265–273.

Brewer, M. B., Dull, V., & Lui, L. N. (1981). Perceptions of the elderly: Stereotypes as prototypes. *Journal of Personality and Social Psychology, 41,* 656–670.

Brim, O. G., Jr. (1992). *Ambition: Losing and winning in everyday life.* New York: Basic Books.

Bronfenbrenner, U. (1979). *The ecology of human development.* Cambridge, MA: Harvard University Press.

Brown, R., & Middendorf, J. (1996). The underestimated role of temporal comparison: A test of the life-span model. *Journal of Social Psychology, 136,* 325–331.

Bruch, M. A., McCann, M., & Harvey, C. (1991). Type A behavior and processing of social conflict information. *Journal of Research in Personality, 25,* 434–444.

Bruner, J. (1990). *Acts of meaning.* Cambridge, MA: Harvard University Press.

Brunstein, J. C. (1993). Personal goals and subjective well-being: A longitudinal study. *Journal of Personality and Social Psychology, 65,* 1061–1070.

Buunk, B. P. (1994). Social comparison processes under stress: Towards an integration of classic and recent perspectives. *European Review of Social Psychology, 5,* 211–241.

Calhoun, L. G., & Cann, A. (1994). Differences in assumptions about a just world: Ethnicity and point of view. *The Journal of Social Psychology, 134,* 765–770.

Camp, C. J. (1989). World-knowledge system. In L. W. Poon, D. C. Rubin, & B. A. Wilson (Eds.), *Everyday cognition in adulthood and late life* (pp. 457–482). New York: Cambridge University Press.

Cantor, N. (1990). From thought to behavior: "Having" and "doing" in the study of personality and cognition. *American Psychologist, 45,* 735–750.

Cantor, N., & Blanton, H. (1996). Effortful pursuit of personal goals in daily life. In P. M. Gollwitzer & J. A. Bargh (Eds.), *The Psychology of action: Linking cognition and motivation to behavior* (pp. 338–59). New York: Guilford.

Cantor, N., & Fleeson, W. (1994). Social intelligence and intelligent goal pursuit: A cognitive slice of motivation. In W. D. Spaulding (Ed.), *Integrative views of motivation, cognition, and emotion: Nebraska Symposium on Motivation* (Vol. 41, pp. 125–179). Lincoln: University of Nebraska Press.

Carlston, D. E., & Smith, E. R. (1996). Principles of mental representation. In E. T. Higgins & A. W. Kruglanski (Eds.), *Social psychology. Handbook of basic principles* (pp. 184–210). New York: Guilford.

Carstensen, L. L. (1995). Evidence for a life-span theory of socioemotional selectivity. *Current Directions in Psychological Science, 4,* 151–156.

Carver, C. S., & Scheier, M. F. (1998). *On the self-regulation of behavior.* New York: Cambridge University Press.

Caspi, A., & Bem, D. J. (1990). Personality continuity and change across the life course. In L. A. Pervin (Ed.), *Handbook of personality: Theory and research* (pp. 549–575). New York: Guilford.

Caspi, A., & Silva, P. A. (1995). Temperamental qualities at age three predict personality traits in young adulthood: Longitudinal evidence from a birth cohort. *Child Development, 66,* 486–498.

Cattell, R. B. (1971). *Abilities: Their structure, growth, and action.* Boston: Houghton Mifflin.

Charness, N., & Bosman, E. A. (1990). Expertise and aging: Life in the lab. In T. H. Hess (Ed.), *Aging and cognition: Knowledge organization and utilization* (pp. 343–385). Amsterdam: Elsevier.

Charness, N., Krampe, R., & Mayr, U. M. (1996). The role of practice and coaching in entrepreneurial skill domains: An international comparison of life-span chess skill acquisition. In K. A. Ericsson (Ed.), *The road to excellence* (pp. 51–80). Mahwah, NJ: Lawrence Erlbaum Associates.

Chen, Y., & Blanchard-Fields, F. (1997). Age differences in stages of attributional processing. *Psychology and Aging, 12,* 694–703.

Cheng, P. W., & Holyoak, K. J. (1985). Pragmatic reasoning schemas. *Cognitive Psychology, 17,* 391–416.

Chi, M. T. H., Glaser, R., & Farr, M. J. (Eds.). (1991). *Toward a general theory of expertise.* Hillsdale, NJ: Lawrence Erlbaum Associates.

Clark, H. H. (1996). *Using language.* Melbourne, Australia: Cambridge University Press.

Clayton, V. P., & Birren, J. E. (1980). The development of wisdom across the life span: A reexamination of an ancient topic. In P. B. Baltes & O. G. Brim (Eds.), *Life-span development and behavior* (Vol. 3, pp. 103–135). New York: Academic Press.

Coats, E. J., Janoff-Bulman, R., & Alpert, N. (1996). Approach versus avoidance goals: Differences in self-evaluation and well-being. *Personality and Social Psychology Bulletin, 22,* 1057–1067.

Cohen, S., & Williamson, G. M. (1991). Stress and infectious disease in humans. *Psychological Bulletin, 109,* 5–24.

Coleman, L. M., & Antonucci, T. C. (1982). Impact of work on women at midlife. *Developmental Psychology, 19,* 290–294.

Colonia-Willner, R. (1998). Practical intelligence at work: Relationship between aging and cognitive efficiency among managers in a bank environment. *Psychology and Aging, 13,* 45–57.

Colvin, C. R., & Block, J. (1994). Do positive illusions foster mental health? An examination of the Taylor and Brown formulation. *Psychological Bulletin, 116,* 3–20.

Cornelius, S. W., & Caspi, A. (1987). Everyday problem solving in adulthood and old age. *Psychology and Aging, 2,* 144–153.

Cosmides, L. (1989). The logic of social exchange: Has natural selection shaped how humans reason? *Cognition, 31,* 187–276.

Costa, P. T., & McCrae, R. R. (1994). Stability and change in personality from adolescence through adulthood. In C. F. Halverson, G. A. Kohnstamm, & R. P. Martin (Eds.), *The developing structure of temperament and personality from infancy to adulthood* (pp. 139–150). Hillsdale, NJ: Lawrence Erlbaum Associates.

Costa, P. T., McCrae, R. R., & Norris, A. -H. (1981). Personal adjustment to aging: Longitudinal prediction from neuroticism and extraversion. *Journal of Gerontology, 36,* 78–85.

Cross, S., & Markus, H. (1991). Possible selves across the life span. *Human Development, 34,* 230–255.

Cutler, S. J. (1983). Aging and changes in attitudes about the women's liberation movement. *International Journal of Aging and Human Development, 16,* 43–51.

Danigelis, H. L., & Cutler, S. J. (1991a). Cohort trends in attitudes about law and order: Who's leading the conservative wave? *Public Opinion Quarterly, 55,* 24–49.

Danigelis, H. L., & Cutler, S. J. (1991b). An inter-cohort comparison of changes in racial attitudes. *Research on Aging, 13,* 383–404.

Denney, N. W., & Pearce, K. A. (1989). A developmental study of practical problem solving in adults. *Psychology and Aging, 4,* 438–442.

Denney, N. W., Tozier, T. L., & Schlotthauer, C. A. (1992). The effect of instructions on age differences in practical problem solving. *Journal of Gerontology, 47,* P142–P145.

Diehl, M., Coyle, N., & Labouvie-Vief, G. (1996). Age and sex differences in strategies of coping and defense across the life span. *Psychology and Aging, 11,* 127–139.

Diehl, M., Willis, S. L., & Schaie, W. K. (1995). Everyday problem solving in older adults: Observational assessment and cognitive correlates. *Psychology and Aging, 10,* 478–491.

Diener, E., Sandvik, E., Pavot, W., & Fujita, F. (1992). Extraversion and subjective well-being in a U.S. national probability sample. *Journal of Research in Personality, 26,* 205–215.

Diener, E., & Suh, E. (1998). Subjective well-being and age: An international analysis. *Annual Review of Gerontology and Geriatrics, 17,* 304–324.

Dittmann-Kohli, F. (1991). Meaning and personality change from early to late adulthood. *European Journal of Personality, 1,* 98–103.

Donahue, E. M., Robins, R. W., Roberts, B. W., & John, O. P. (1993). The divided self: Concurrent and longitudinal effects of psychological adjustment and social roles on self-concept differentiation. *Journal of Personality and Social Psychology, 64,* 834–846.

Elder, G. H., Jr. (1998). The life course and human development. In R. M. Lerner (Ed.), *Handbook of child psychology: Volume 1. Theoretical models of human development* (5th ed., pp. 939–991). New York: Wiley.

Elliot, A. J., Sheldon, K. M., & Church, M. A. (1997). Avoidance personal goals and subjective well-being. *Personality and Social Psychology Bulletin, 23,* 915–927.

Emmons, R. A. (1996). Striving and feeling: Personal goals and subjective well-being. In P. M. Gollwitzer & J. A. Bargh (Eds.), *The psychology of action: Linking cognition and motivation to behavior* (pp. 313–337). New York: Guilford.

Ericsson, K. A. (Ed.). (1996). *The road to excellence: The acquisition of expert performance in the arts and sciences, sports, and games.* Hillsdale, NJ: Lawrence Erlbaum Associates.

Ericsson, K. A., & Smith, J. (Eds.). (1991). *Toward a general theory of expertise: Prospects and limits.* Cambridge, England: Cambridge University Press.

Feist, G. J. (1994). Personality and working style predictors of integrative complexity: A study of scientists' thinking about research and teaching. *Journal of Personality and Social Psychology, 67,* 474–484.

Filipp, S. H. (1996). Motivation and emotion. In J. E. Birren & K. W. Schaie (Eds.), *Handbook of the psychology of aging* (pp. 218–235). San Diego, CA: Academic Press.

Filipp, S. H. (1999). A three-stage model of coping with loss and trauma: Lessons from patients suffering from severe and chronic disease. In A. Maercker, M. Schützwohl, &

Z. Solomon (Eds.), *Posttraumatic stress disorder: A lifespan developmental perspective* (pp. 43–80). Seattle, WA: Hogrefe & Huber.

Filipp, S. -H., & Buch-Bartos, K. (1994). Vergleichsprozesse und Lebenszufriedenheit im Alter: Ergebnisse einer Pilotstudie. *Zeitschrift für Entwicklungspsychologie und Pädagogische Psychologie, 26,* 22–34.

Filipp, S. H., Ferring, D., Mayer, A. K., & Schmidt, K. (1997). Selbstbewertungen und selektive Präferenz für temporale vs. soziale Vergleichsinformation bei alten und sehr alten Menschen. *Zeitschrift für Sozialpsychologie, 28,* 30–43.

Filipp, S. -H., & Klauer, T. (1986). Conceptions of self over the life span: Reflections on the dialectics of change. In M. M. Baltes & P. B. Baltes (Eds.), *The psychology of control and aging* (pp. 167–205). Hillsdale, NJ: Lawrence Erlbaum Associates.

Fiske, S. T., & Taylor, S. E. (1991). *Social cognition* (2nd ed.). New York: McGraw-Hill.

Fivush, R. (1991). The social construction of personal narratives. *Merrill-Palmer Quarterly, 37,* 59–82.

Flavell, J., Green, F. L., & Flavell, E. R. (1995). Young children's knowledge about thinking. *Monographs of the SRCD, 60,* 1–96.

Fleeson, W., & Baltes, P. B. (1998). Beyond present-day personality assessment: An encouraging exploration of the measurement properties and predictive power of subjective lifetime personality. *Journal for Research on Personality, 32,* 411–430.

Fleeson, W., & Heckhausen, J. (1997). More or less "me" in past, present, and future: Perceived lifetime personality during adulthood. *Psychology and Aging, 12,* 125–136.

Folkman, S., Lazarus, R. S., Pimley, S., & Novacek, J. (1987). Age differences in stress and coping processes. *Psychology and Aging, 2,* 171–184.

Forest, K. B. (1995). The role of critical life events in predicting world views: Linking two social psychologies. *Journal of Social Behavior and Personality, 10,* 331–348.

Forster, J. M., & Gallagher, D. (1986). An exploratory study comparing depressed and nondepressed elders coping strategies. *Journal of Gerontology, 41,* 91–93.

Fredrickson, B. C., & Carstensen, L. L. (1990). Choosing social partners: How old age and anticipated endings make people more selective. *Psychology and Aging, 5,* 335–347.

Frensch, P. A., & Funke, J. (Eds.). (1995). *Complex problem solving: The European perspective.* Hillsdale, NJ: Lawrence Erlbaum Associates.

Freund, A. M., & Baltes, P. B. (in press). The orchestration of selection, optimization, and compensation: An action-theoretical conceptualization of a theory of developmental regulation. In W. J. Perrig & A. Grob (Eds.), *Control of human behavior, mental processes, and consciousness.* Mahwah, NJ: Lawrence Erlbaum Associates.

Freund, A. M., & Smith, J. (1997). Die Selbstdefinition im hohen Alter. *Zeitschrift für Sozialpsychologie, 28,* 44–59.

Freund, A.M., & Smith, J. (1999). Content and function of the self-definition in old and very old age. *Journals of Gerontology, 54,* P55–P67.

Frey, K. S., & Ruble, D. N. (1990). Strategies for comparative evaluation: Maintaining a sense of competence across the life span. In R. J. Sternberg & J. J. Kolligian (Eds.), *Competence considered* (pp. 167–189). New Haven, CT: Yale University Press.

Friedman, H. S., Tucker, J. S., Tomlinson-Keasey, C., Schwartz, J. E., Wingard, D. L., & Criqui, M. H. (1993). Does childhood personality predict longevity? *Journal of Personality and Social Psychology, 65,* 176–85.

George, L. K., & Okun, M. A. (1985). Self-concept content. In E. Palmore, E. W. Busse, G. L. Maddox, J. B. Nowlin, & I. C. Siegler (Eds.), *Normal aging: III. Reports from the Duke Longitudinal Studies, 1975–1984* (pp. 267–282). Durham, NC: Duke University Press.

Gergen, K. J. (1994). Exploring the postmodern: Perils or potentials? *American Psychologist, 49,* 412–416.

Gigerenzer, G., & Goldstein, D. G. (1996). Reasoning the fast and frugal way: Models of bounded rationality. *Psychological Review, 103,* 650–669.

Gigerenzer, G., & Hug, K. (1992). Domain-specific reasoning: Social contracts, cheating, and perspective change. *Cognition, 43,* 127–171.

Gollwitzer, P. M., & Bargh, J. A. (Eds.). (1996). *The psychology of action: Linking cognition and motivation to action.* New York: Guilford.

Green, A. L., Wheatley, S. M., & Aldava, J. F., IV (1992). Stages on life's way: Adolescents' implicit theories of the life course. *Journal of Adolescent Research, 7,* 364–381.

Haan, N. (1981). Common dimensions of personality development: Early adolescence to middle life. In D. H. Eichorn, J. A. Clausen, N. Haan, M. P. Honzik, & P. H. Mussen (Eds.), *Present and past in middle life* (pp. 117–153). New York: Academic Press.

Haan, N., Millsap, R., & Hartka, E. (1986). As time goes by: Change and stability in personality over fifty years. *Psychology and Aging, 1,* 220–232.

Hafer, C. L., & Olson, J. M. (1993). Beliefs in a just world, discontent, and assertive actions by working women. *Personality and Social Psychology Bulletin, 19,* 30–38.

Hagestad, G. O. (1990). Social perspectives on the life course. In R. Binstock & L. George (Eds.), *Handbook of aging and the social sciences* (3rd ed., pp. 151–168). New York: Academic Press.

Happé, F. G. E., Winner, E., & Brownell, H. (1998). The getting of wisdom: Theory of mind in old age. *Developmental Psychology, 34,* 358–362.

Harlow, R. E., & Cantor, N. (1996). Still participating after all these years: A study of life task participation in later life. *Journal of Personality and Social Psychology, 71,* 1235–1249.

Heckhausen, J. (1997). Developmental regulation across adulthood: Primary and secondary control of age-related challenges. *Developmental Psychology, 33,* 176–187.

Heckhausen, J., & Brim, O. G. (1997). Perceived problems for self and other: Self-protection by social downgrading throughout adulthood. *Psychology and Aging, 12,* 610–619.

Heckhausen, J., Dixon, R. A., & Baltes, P. B. (1989). Gains and losses in development throughout adulthood as perceived by different adult age groups. *Developmental Psychology, 25,* 109–121.

Heckhausen, J., & Krueger, J. (1993). Developmental expectations for the self and most other people: Age-grading in three functions of social comparison. *Developmental Psychology, 29,* 539–548.

Heckhausen, J., & Schulz, R. (1995). A life-span theory of control. *Psychological Review, 102,* 284–304.

Heidrich, S. M., & Denney, N. W. (1994). Does social problem solving differ from other types of problem solving during the adult years? *Experimental Aging Research, 20,* 105–126.

Heidrich, S. M., & Ryff, C. D. (1993). Physical and mental health in later life: The self-system as mediator. *Psychology and Aging, 8,* 327–338.

Helson, R., & Wink, P. (1987). Two conceptions of maturity examined in the findings of a longitudinal study. *Journal of Personality and Social Psychology, 53,* 531–541.

Hertzog, C., Cooper, B. P., & Fisk, A. D. (1996). Aging and individual differences in the development of skilled memory search performance. *Psychology and Aging, 11,* 497–520.

Hess, T. M. (1992). Adult age differences in script content and structure. In R. L. West & J. D. Sinnott (Eds.), *Everyday memory and aging* (pp. 87–100). New York: Springer.

Hess, T. M. (1994). Social cognition in adulthood: Aging-related changes in knowledge and processing mechanisms. *Developmental Review, 14,* 373–412.

Hess, T. M., McGee, K. A., Woodburn, S. M., & Bolstad, C. A. (1998). Age-related priming effects in social judgments. *Psychology and Aging, 13,* 127–137.

Hess, T. M., & Slaughter, S. J. (1990). Schematic knowledge influences on memory for scene information in young and older adults. *Developmental Psychology, 26,* 855–865.

Hess, T. M., & Tate, C. S. (1991). Adult age differences in explanations and memory for behavioral information. *Psychology and Aging, 6,* 86–92.

Higgins, E. T. (1996). The "self digest": Self-knowledge serving self-regulatory functions. *Journal of Personality and Social Psychology, 71,* 1062–1083.

Holahan, C. J., & Moos, R. H. (1987). Personal and contextual determinants of coping strategies. *Journal of Personality and Social Psychology, 52,* 946–955.

Holahan, C. K. (1988). Relation of life goals at age 70 to activity participation and health and psychological well-being among Terman's gifted men and women. *Psychology and Aging, 3,* 286–291.

Hooker, K. (1992). Possible selves and perceived health in older adults and college students. *Journal of Gerontology: Psychological Sciences, 47,* P85–P95.

Horn, J. (1994). Theory of fluid and crystallized intelligence. In R. J. Sternberg (Ed.), *Encyclopedia of intelligence* (Vol. 1, pp. 443–451). New York: Macmillan.

Hummert, M. L., Garstka, T. A., Shaner, J. L., & Strahm, S. (1994). Stereotypes of the elderly held by young, middle-aged, and elderly adults. *Journal of Gerontology, 49,* P240–P249.

Irion, J. C., & Blanchard-Fields, F. (1987). A cross-sectional comparison of adaptive coping in adulthood. *Journal of Gerontology, 42,* 502–504.

Johnson, C. L., & Barer, B. M. (1993). Coping and a sense of control among the oldest old: An exploratory analysis. *Journal of Aging Studies, 7,* 67–80.

Jones, C. J., & Meredith, W. (1996). Patterns of personality change across the life span. *Psychology and Aging, 11,* 57–65.

Kahana, E., Redmond, C., Hill, G. J., Kercher, K., Kahana, B., Johnson, J. R., & Young, R. F. (1995). The effects of stress, vulnerability, and appraisals on the psychological well-being of the elderly. *Research on Aging, 17,* 459–489.

Kessler, R. C., & McRae, J. A. (1982). The effects of wives' employment on the mental health of married men and women. *American Sociological Review, 47,* 216–227.

Kitchener, K. S., & King, P. M. (1990). The reflective judgment model: Ten years of research. In M. L. Commons, C. Armon, L. Kohlberg, F. A. Richards, T. A. Grotzer, & J. D. Sinnott (Eds.), *Adult development: Vol. 2. Models and methods in the study of adolescent and adult thought* (pp. 63–78). New York: Praeger.

Kling, K. C., Ryff, C. D., & Essex, M. J. (1997). Adaptive changes in the self-concept during a life transition. *Personality and Social Psychology Bulletin, 23,* 981–990.

Klohnen, E. C. (1996). Conceptual analysis and measurement of the construct of ego-resilience. *Journal of Personality and Social Psychology, 70,* 1067–1079.

Knäuper, B. (1999). Age differences in question and response order effects. In N. Schwarz, D. Park, B. Knäuper, & S. Sudman (Eds.), *Cognition, aging, and self-reports* (pp. 341–363). Washington, DC: Psychology Press.

Kramer, D. A., Kahlbaugh, P. E., & Goldston, R. B. (1992). A measure of paradigm beliefs about the social world. *Journal of Gerontology: Psychological Sciences, 47,* 180–189.

Krosnick, J. A., & Alwin, D. F. (1989). Aging and susceptibility to attitude change. *Journal of Personality and Social Psychology, 57,* 416–425.

Kuhl, J. (1994). A theory of action and state orientation. In J. Kuhl & J. Beckmann (Eds.), *Volition and personality: Action versus state orientation* (pp. 375–390). Göttingen, Germany: Hogrefe.

Kuhn, D. (1989). Children and adults as intuitive scientists. *Psychological Review, 96,* 674–689.

Labouvie-Vief, G. (1985). Intelligence and cognition. In J. E. Birren & K. W. Schaie (Eds.), *The handbook of the psychology of aging* (2nd ed., pp. 500–530). New York: Van Nostrand Reinhold.

Labouvie-Vief, G. (1994). *Psyche & eros: Mind and gender in the life course.* New York: Cambridge University Press.

Labouvie-Vief, G., Chiodo, L., Goguen, L., Diehl, M., & Orwoll, L. (1995). Representations of self across the life span. *Psychology and Aging, 10,* 404–415.

Labouvie-Vief, G., DeVoe, M., & Bulka, D. (1989). Speaking about feelings: Conceptions of emotion across the life span. *Psychology and Aging, 4,* 425–437.

Labouvie-Vief, G., Hakim-Larson, J., & Hobart, C. J. (1987). Age, ego level, and the life-span development of coping and defense processes. *Psychology and Aging, 2,* 286–293.

Lachman, M. E., Ziff, M., & Spiro, A. (1994). Maintaining a sense of control in later life. In R. Abeles, H. Gift, & M. Ory (Eds.), *Aging and quality of life* (pp. 116–132). New York: Sage.

Lawton, M. P. (1988). Behavior-relevant ecological factors. In K. W. Schaie & C. Schooler (Eds.), *Social structures and aging: Psychological processes* (pp. 57–78). Hillsdale, NJ: Lawrence Erlbaum Associates.

Lazarus, R. S. (1996). The role of coping in the emotions and how coping changes over the life course. In C. Magai & S. H. McFadden (Eds.), *Handbook of emotion, adult development, and aging* (pp. 284–306). San Diego, CA: Academic Press.

Lazarus, R. S., & DeLongis, A. (1983). Psychological stress and coping in aging. *American Psychologist, 38*, 245–254.

Lazarus, R. S., & Golden, G. Y. (1981). The function of denial in stress, coping, and aging. In J. L. McGaugh & S. B. Kiesler (Eds.), *Aging, biology and behavior* (pp. 283–307). New York: Academic Press.

Lecci, L., Okun, M. A., & Karoly, P. (1994). Life regrets and current goals as predictors of psychological adjustment. *Journal of Personality and Social Psychology, 66*, 731–741.

L'Écuyer, R. (1994, January). *The modifications of the hierarchical organizations of the self concept from ages 3 to 100.* Paper presented at the North Atlantic Treaty Organization Advanced Research Workshop, Chersonnissos, Crete.

Lerner, R. M., & Busch-Rossnagel, N. A. (1981). *Individuals as producers of their development: A life-span perspective.* New York: Academic Press.

Levine, J. M., Resnick, L. B., & Higgins, E. T. (1993). Social foundations of cognition. *Annual Review of Psychology, 44*, 585–612.

Lewis, M. D. (1995). Cognition–emotion feedback and the self-organization of developmental paths. *Human Development, 38*, 71–102.

Light, L., & Anderson, P. (1983). Memory for scripts in young and older adults. *Memory and Cognition, 11*, 435–444.

Lindenberger, U., & Baltes, P. B. (1995). Testing-the-limits and experimental simulation: Two methods to explicate the role of learning in development. *Human Development, 38,* 349–360.

Lindenberger, U., Kliegl, R., & Baltes, P. B. (1992). Professional expertise does not eliminate negative age differences in imagery-based memory performance during adulthood. *Psychology and Aging, 7*, 585–593.

Linville, P. W. (1987). Self-complexity as a cognitive buffer against stress-related depression and illness. *Journal of Personality and Social Psychology, 52*, 663–676.

Lipkus, I. M., & Bissonnette, V. L. (1996). Relationships among belief in a just world, willingness to accomodate, and marital well-being. *Personality and Social Psychology Bulletin, 22*, 1043–1056.

Lipkus, I. M., Dalbert, C., & Siegler, I. C. (1996). The importance of distinguishing the belief in a just world for self versus for others: Implications for psychological well-being. *Personality and Social Psychology Bulletin, 22*, 666–677.

Little, T. D., Oettingen, G., Stetsenko, A., & Baltes, P. B. (1995). Children's action-control beliefs about school performance: How do American children compare with German and Russian children. *Journal of Personality and Social Psychology, 69*, 686–700.

Magnus, K., Diener, E., Fujita, F., & Pavot, W. (1993). Extraversion and neuroticism as predictors for objective life events: A longitudinal analysis. *Journal of Personality and Social Psychology, 65*, 1046–1053.

Magnusson, D., & Stattin, H. (1998). Person–context interaction theories. In R. M. Lerner (Ed.), *Theoretical models of human development: Volume 1. Handbook of child psychology* (5th ed., pp. 685–759). New York: Wiley.

Markus, H. (1977). Self-schemata and processing information about the self. *Journal of Personality and Social Psychology, 35*, 63–78.

Markus, H., & Cross, S. (1990). The interpersonal self. In L. A. Pervin (Ed.), *Handbook of personality: Theory and research* (pp. 576–608). New York: Guilford.

Markus, H., Mullally, P. R., & Kitayama, S. (1997). Selfways: Diversity in modes of cultural participation. In U. Neisser & D. A. Jopling (Eds.), *The conceptual self in context* (pp. 13–61). New York: Cambridge University Press.

Marsiske, M., & Willis, S. L. (1995). Dimensionality of everyday problem solving in older adults. *Psychology and Aging, 10,* 269–283.

Martin, P., Poon, L. W., Kim, E., & Johnson, M. A. (1996). Social and psychological resources in the oldest old. *Experimental Aging Research, 22,* 121–139.

McAdams, D. P. (1996). Personality, modernity, and the storied self: A contemporary framework for studying persons. *Psychological Inquiry, 7,* 295–321.

McCrae, R. R. (1989). Age differences and changes in the use of coping mechanisms. *Journal of Gerontology: Psychological Sciences, 44,* 919–928.

McCrae, R. R., & Costa, P. T., Jr. (1988). Age, personality, and the spontaneous self-concept. *Journal of Gerontology: Psychological Sciences, 43,* P177–P185.

McCrae, R. R., & Costa, P. T., Jr. (1997). Personality trait structure as a human universal. *American Psychologist, 52,* 509–516.

Meyer, B. J. F., Russo, C., & Talbot, A. (1995). Discourse comprehension and problem solving: Decisions about the treatment of breast cancer by women across the life span. *Psychology and Aging, 10,* 84–103.

Mischel, W. (1973). Toward a cognitive social learning reconceptualization of personality. *Psychological Review, 80,* 252–283.

Mischel, W. (1996). From good intentions to willpower. In P. M. Gollwitzer & J. A. Bargh (Eds.), *The psychology of action: Linking cognition and motivation to behavior* (pp. 197–218). New York: Guilford.

Mischel, W., & Shoda, Y. (1995). A cognitive–affective system theory of personality: Reconceptualizing situations, dispositions, dynamics, and invariance in personality structure. *Psychological Review, 102,* 246–268.

Neisser, U. (1988). Five kinds of self-knowledge. *Philosophical Psychology, 1,* 35–59.

Neisser, U., & Jopling, D. A. (Eds.). (1997). *The conceptual self in context.* New York: Cambridge University Press.

Nurmi, J-E., Pulliainen, H., & Salmela-Aro, K. (1992). Age differences in adults' control beliefs related to life goals and concerns. *Psychology and Aging, 7,* 194–196.

Oettingen, G. (1996). Positive fantasy and motivation. In P. M. Gollwitzer & J. A. Bargh (Eds.), *The psychology of action: Linking cognition and motivation to action* (pp. 236–259). New York: Guilford.

Orwoll, L., & Perlmutter, M. (1990). The study of wise persons: Integrating a personality perspective. In R. J. Sternberg (Ed.). *Wisdom: Its nature, origins, and development* (pp. 160–177). New York: Cambridge University Press.

Pascual-Leone, J. (1990). An essay on wisdom: Toward organismic processes that make it possible. In R. J. Sternberg (Ed.), *Wisdom: Its nature, origins, and development* (pp. 224–78). New York: Cambridge University Press.

Pasupathi, M. (1999). Age differences in response to conformity pressure for emotional and non-emotional material. *Psychology and Aging, 14,* 170–174.

Patel, V. L., & Groen, G. J. (1991). The general and specific nature of medical expertise: A critical look. In K. A. Ericsson & J. Smith (Eds.), *Toward a general theory of expertise: Prospects and limits* (pp. 93–125). New York: Cambridge University Press.

Pearlin, L. I., & Skaff, M. M. (1996). Stress and the life course: A paradigmatic alliance. *Gerontologist, 36,* 239–247.

Pelham, B. W. (1995). Self-investment and self-esteem: Evidence for a Jamesian model of self-worth. *Journal of Personality and Social Psychology, 69,* 1141–1150.

Perz, C. A., DiClemente, C. C., & Carbonari, J. P. (1996). Doing the right thing at the right time? The interaction of stages and processes of change in successful smoking cessation. *Health Psychology, 15,* 462–468.

Pfeiffer, E. (1977). Psychopathology and social pathology. In J. E. Birren & K. W. Schaie (Eds.), *Handbook of the psychology of aging* (pp. 650–71). New York: Van Nostrand Reinhold.

Polanyi, M. (1958). *Personal knowledge.* Chicago: University of Chicago Press.

Pratt, M. W., Diessner, R., Pratt, A., Hunsberger, B., & Pancer, S. M. (1996). Moral and social reasoning and perspective taking in later life: A longitudinal study. *Psychology and Aging, 11,* 66–73.

Pratt, M. W., Pancer, M., Hunsberger, B., & Manchester, J. (1990). Reasoning about the self and relationships in maturity: An integrative complexity analysis of individual differences. *Journal of Personality and Social Psychology, 59,* 575–581.

Rankin, J. L., & Allen, J. L. (1991). Investigating the relationship between cognition and social thinking in adulthood: Stereotyping and attributional processes. In J. D. Sinnott & J. C. Cavanaugh (Eds.), *Bridging paradigms: Positive development in adulthood and cognitive aging* (pp. 131–152). New York: Praeger.

Rapkin, B. D., & Fischer, K. (1992). Framing the construct of life satisfaction in terms of older adults' personal goals. *Psychology and Aging, 7,* 138–149.

Reifman, A., Klein, J. G., & Murphy, S. T. (1989). Self-monitoring and age. *Psychology and Aging, 4,* 245–246.

Roberts, B. W., & Helson, R. (1997). Changes in culture, changes in personality: The influence of individualism in a longitudinal study of women. *Journal of Personality and Social Psychology, 72,* 641–651.

Ross, B. L., & Berg, C. A. (1992). Examining idiosyncracies in script reports across the life span: Distortions or derivations of experience. In R. L. West & J. D. Sinnott (Eds.), *Everyday memory and aging* (pp. 39–53). New York: Springer.

Ross, M. (1997). Validating memories. In N. L. Stein, P. A. Ornstein, B. Tversky, & C. Brainerd (Eds.), *Memory for everyday and emotional events* (pp. 49–82). Mahwah, NJ: Lawrence Erlbaum Associates.

Rutter, M. (1997). Nature–nurture integration. *American Psychologist, 52,* 390–398.

Ryan, R. M., Sheldon, K. M., Kasser, T., & Deci, E. L. (1996). All goals are not created equal. In P. M. Gollwitzer & J. A. Bargh (Eds.), *The psychology of action: Linking cognition and motivation to behavior* (pp. 7–26). New York: Guilford.

Ryff, C. D. (1989). In the eye of the beholder: Views of psychological well-being among middle-aged and older adults. *Psychology and Aging, 4,* 195–210.

Ryff, C. D. (1991). Possible selves in adulthood and old age: A tale of shifting horizons. *Psychology and Aging, 6,* 286–295.

Ryff, C. D., & Essex, M. J. (1992). The interpretation of life experience and well being: The sample case of relocation. *Psychology and Aging, 7,* 507–517.

Salovey, P., & Mayer, J. D. (1994). Some final thoughts about personality and intelligence. In R. J. Sternberg & P. Ruzgis (Eds.), *Personality and intelligence* (pp. 303–318). New York: Cambridge University Press.

Salthouse, T. A. (1995). Refining the concept of psychological compensation. In R. A. Dixon & L. Bäckman (Eds.), *Compensating for psychological deficits and declines* (pp. 21–34). Mahwah, NJ: Lawrence Erlbaum Associates.

Salthouse, T. A. (1996). The processing-speed theory of adult age differences in cognition. *Psychological Review, 103,* 403–428.

Sansone, C., & Berg, C. A. (1993). Adapting to the environment across the life span: Different process or different inputs? *International Journal of Behavioral Development, 16,* 215–241.

Saudino, K. J., Pedersen, N. L., Lichtenstein, P., McClearn, G. E., & Plomin, R. (1997). Can personality explain genetic influences on life events? *Journal of Personality and Social Psychology, 72,* 196–206.

Schallberger, U. (1995). Die Persönlichkeitsabhängigkeit von Beschreibungen der eigenen Arbeitssituation. *Zeitschrift für Experimentelle Psychologie, 42,* 111–131.

Schank, R. C., & Abelson, R. P. (1995). Knowledge and memory: The real story. *Advances in Social Cognition, 8,* 1–86.

Scheier, M. F., & Carver, C. S. (1987). Dispositional optimism and physical well-being: The influence of generalized outcome expectancies on health. *Journal of Personality, 55,* 169–210.

Scherer, K. R. (1997). Profiles of emotion-antecedent appraisal: Testing theoretical predictions across cultures. *Cognition and Emotion, 11,* 113–150.

Schwanenflugel, P. J., Fabricius, W. V., & Noyes, C. R. (1996). Developing organization of mental verbs: Evidence for the development of a constructivist theory of mind in middle childhood. *Cognitive Development, 11,* 265–294.

Schwarz, N., & Bohner, G. (1996). Feelings and their motivational implications: Moods and the action sequence. In P. M. Gollwitzer & J. A. Bargh (Eds.), *The psychology of action: Linking cognition and motivation to behavior* (pp. 119–45). New York: Guilford.

Showers, C. J., & Ryff, C. D. (1996). Self-differentiation and well-being in a life transition. *Personality and Social Psychology Bulletin, 22,* 448–460.

Siegler, R. S. (1996). *Emerging minds.* New York: Oxford University Press.

Singer, J. A., & Salovey, P. (1993). *The remembered self.* New York: The Free Press.

Smith, J., & Baltes, P. B. (1996). Profiles of psychological functioning in the old and oldest-old. *Psychology and Aging, 12,* 458–478.

Smith, J., Fleeson, W., Geiselmann, B., Settersten, R. A., Jr., & Kunzmann, U. (1999). Well-being in very old age: Predictions from objective life conditions and subjective experience. In P. B. Baltes & K. U. Mayer (Eds.), *The Berlin Aging Study: Aging from 70 to 100* (pp. 450–474). New York: Cambridge University Press.

Smith, J., Staudinger, U. M., & Baltes, P. B. (1994). Occupational settings facilitative of wisdom-related knowledge: The sample case of clinical psychologists. *Journal of Consulting and Clinical Psychology, 62,* 989–1000.

Stabell, C. B. (1978). Integrative complexity of information environment perception and information use: An empirical investigation. *Organizational Behavior and Human Performance, 22,* 116–142.

Staudinger, U. M. (1989). *The study of life review: An approach to the investigation of intellectual development across the life span.* Berlin, Germany: Sigma.

Staudinger, U. M. (1996a). Psychologische Produktivität und Selbstentfaltung im Alter. In M. M. Baltes & L. Montada (Eds.), *Produktivität und Altern* (pp. 344–373). Frankfurt, Germany: Campus Verlag.

Staudinger, U. M. (1996b). Wisdom and the social-interactive foundation of the mind. In P. B. Baltes & U. M. Staudinger (Eds.), *Interactive minds: Life-span perspectives on the social foundation of cognition* (pp. 276–315). New York: Cambridge University Press.

Staudinger, U. M. (1999). Social cognition and a psychological approach to an art of life. In F. Blanchard-Fields & T. Hess (Eds.), *Social cognition, adult development and aging* (pp. 386–423). New York: Academic Press.

Staudinger, U. M., & Baltes, P. B. (1994). The psychology of wisdom. In R. J. Sternberg (Ed.), *Encyclopedia of intelligence* (pp. 1143–1152). New York: Macmillan.

Staudinger, U. M., & Baltes, P. B. (1996). Interactive minds: A facilitative setting for wisdom-related performance. *Journal of Personality and Social Psychology, 71,* 746–762.

Staudinger, U. M., & Fleeson, W. (1996). Self and personality in old and very old age: A sample case of resilience? *Developmental Psychopathology, 8,* 867–885.

Staudinger, U. M., Freund, A. M., Linden, M., & Maas, I. (1999). Self, personality, and life management: Psychological resilience and vulnerability. In P. B. Baltes & K. U. Mayer (Eds.), *The Berlin Aging Study: Aging from 70 to 100* (pp. 302–328). New York: Cambridge University Press.

Staudinger, U. M., Lindenberger, U., & Baltes, P. B. (1998). *A lifespan framework for the study of self and personality.* Unpublished manuscript, Max Planck Institute for Human Development, Berlin, Germany.

Staudinger, U. M., Lopez, D. F., & Baltes, P. B. (1997). The psychometric location of wisdom-related performance. *Personality and Social Psychology Bulletin, 23,* 1200–1214.

Staudinger, U. M., Maciel, A., Smith, J., & Baltes, P. B. (1998). What predicts wisdom-related knowledge? A first look at personality, intelligence, and facilitative experimental contexts. *European Journal of Personality, 12,* 1–17.

Staudinger, U. M., Marsiske, M., & Baltes, P. B. (1995). Resilience and reserve capacity in later adulthood: Potentials and limits of development across the life span. In D. Cicchetti & D. Cohen (Eds.), *Developmental psychopathology* (Vol. 2, pp. 801–847). New York: Wiley.

Staudinger, U. M., Smith, J., & Baltes, P. B. (1992). Wisdom-related knowledge in a life review task: Age differences and the role of professional specialization. *Psychology and Aging, 7,* 271–281.

Sternberg, R. J., & Ruzgis, P. (Eds.). (1994). *Personality and intelligence.* New York: Cambridge University Press.

Sternberg, R. J., & Wagner, R. K. (Eds.). (1994). *Mind in context: Interactionist perspectives on human intelligence.* New York: Cambridge University Press.

Strauman, T. J. (1996). Stability within the self: A longitudinal study of the structural implications of self-discrepancy theory. *Journal of Personality and Social Psychology, 71,* 1142–1153.

Streufert, S., Pogash, R., Piasecki, M., & Post, G.M. (1990). Age and management team performance. *Psychology and Aging, 5,* 551–559.

Strube, G., Gehringer, M., Ernst, I., & Knill, K. (1985). *Knowing what's going to happen in life: II. Biographical knowledge in developmental perspective.* Unpublished manuscript, Max Planck Institute for Psychological Research, Munich, Germany.

Suh, E., Diener, E., & Fujita, F. (1996). Events and subjective well-being: Only recent events matter. *Journal of Personality and Social Psychology, 70,* 1091–1102.

Suls, J., & David, J. P. (1996). Coping and personality: Third time's the charm? *Journal of Personality, 64,* 993–1005.

Suls, J., & Harvey, J. H. (Eds.). (1996). Personality and coping [Special issue]. *Journal of Personality, 64.*

Suls, J., & Mullen, B. (1982). From the cradle to the grave: Comparison and self-evaluation. In J. N. Suls (Ed.), *Psychological perspectives on the self* (Vol. 1, pp. 97–128). Hillsdale, NJ: Lawrence Erlbaum Associates.

Suls, J., & Wills, T. A. (Eds.). (1991). *Social comparison: Contemporary theory and research.* Hillsdale, NJ: Lawrence Erlbaum Associates.

Swann, W. B. (1990). Bridge over troubled water. *Psychological Inquiry, 1,* 211–212.

Taylor, R. N. (1975). Age and experience as determinants of managerial information processing and decision making performance. *Academy of Management Journal, 18,* 74–81.

Taylor, S. E., & Brown, J. D. (1988). Illusion and well-being: A social psychological perspective on mental health. *Psychological Bulletin, 103,* 193–210.

Taylor, S. E., & Gollwitzer, P. M. (1995). Effects of mindset on positive illusions. *Journal of Personality and Social Psychology, 69,* 213–226.

Taylor, S. E., & Lobel, M. (1989). Social comparison activity under threat: Downward evaluation and upward contacts. *Psychological Bulletin, 96,* 569–575.

Taylor, S. E., Neter, E., & Wayment, H. A. (1995). Self-evaluation processes. *Personality and Social Psychology Bulletin, 21,* 1278–1287.

Teitelbaum, P., & Stricker, E. M. (1994). Compound complementarities in the study of motivated behavior. *Psychological Review, 101,* 312–317.

Tetlock, P. E., Peterson, R. S., & Berry, J. M. (1993). Flattering and unflattering personality portraits of integratively simple and complex managers. *Journal of Personality and Social Psychology, 64,* 500–511.

Tetlock, P. E., & Tyler, A. (1996). Churchill's cognitive and rhetorical style: The debates over Nazi intentions and self-government for India. *Political Psychology, 17,* 149–170.

Thoits, P. A. (1983). Multiple identities and psychological well-being: A reformulation and test of the social isolation hypothesis. *American Sociological Review, 8,* 174–187.

Tomaka, J., & Blascovich, J. (1994). Effects of justice beliefs on cognitive appraisal of and subjective, physiological, and behavioral responses to potential stress. *Journal of Personality and Social Psychology, 67,* 732–740.

Trope, Y., & Thompson, E. P. (1997). Looking for truth in all the wrong places? Asymmetric search of individuating information about stereotyped group members. *Journal of Personality and Social Psychology, 73,* 229–241.

Uttal, D. H., & Perlmutter, M. (1989). Toward a broader conceptualization of development: The role of gains and losses across the life span. *Developmental Review, 9,* 101–132.

Vaillant, G. E. (1993). *Wisdom of the ego.* Cambridge, MA: Harvard University Press.

Valsiner, J., & Lawrence, J. A. (1997). Human development in culture across the life-span. In J. W. Berry, P. R. Dasen, & T. S. Saraswathi (Eds.), *Handbook of cross-cultural psychology* (pp. 69–106). Boston: Allyn & Bacon.

Von Dras, D. D., & Siegler, I. C. (1997). Stability in extraversion and aspects of social support at midlife. *Journal of Personality and Social Psychology, 72,* 233–241.

Watson, D., & Hubbard, B. (1996). Adaptational style and dispositional structure: Coping in the context of the Five-Factor model. *Journal of Personality, 64,* 737–774.

Webster, J. D., & Cappeliez, P. (1993). Reminiscence and autobiographical memory: Complementary contexts for cognitive aging research. *Developmental Review, 13,* 54–91.

Welch, D. C., & West, R. L. (1995). Self-efficacy and mastery: Its application to issues of environmental control, cognition, and aging. *Developmental Review, 15,* 150–171.

Wellman, H. M., & Hickling, A. K. (1994). The mind's "I": Children's conception of the mind as an active agent. *Child Development, 65,* 1564–1580.

Wentura, D., Dräger, D., & Brandtstädter, J. (1997). Alternsstereotype im frühen und höheren Erwachsenenalter: Analyse akkommodativer Veränderungen anhand einer Satzpriming-Technik. *Zeitschrift für Sozialpsychologie, 28,* 109–128.

Wong, P. T. P., & Watt, L. M. (1991). What types of reminiscence are associated with successful aging? *Psychology and Aging, 6,* 272–279.

Wood, J. V. (1996). What is social comparison and how should we study it? *Personality and Social Psychology Bulletin, 22,* 520–537.

Wood, J. V., Taylor, S. E., & Lichtman, R. R. (1985). Social comparison in adjustment to breast cancer. *Journal of Personality and Social Psychology, 49,* 1169–1183.

Woodruff, D. S., & Birren, J. E. (1972). Age changes and cohort differences in personality. *Developmental Psychology, 6,* 252–259.

Woolfolk, R. L., Novalany, J., Gara, M. A., Allen, L. A, & Polino, M. (1995). Self-complexity, self-evaluation, and depression: An examination of form and content within the self-schema. *Journal of Personality and Social Psychology, 68,* 1108–1120.

Wyer, R. S., & Carlston, D. E. (1994). The cognitive representation of persons and events. In R. S. Wyer & T. K. Srull (Eds.), *Handbook of social cognition: volume 1. Basic processes* (pp. 41–98). Hillsdale, NJ: Lawrence Erlbaum Associates.

13

Closing Comments

Timothy A. Salthouse
Georgia Institute of Technology

Fergus I. M. Craik
University of Toronto

In this final chapter, we offer a few comments on the field of cognitive aging in light of the preceding reviews. The chapter is not intended as a summary of the work in the field, or even as an integration of the material from the preceding chapters, but more as a set of comments on issues raised in the earlier chapters, with a few speculations about the future.

In general, we are optimistic. Cognitive aging is a flourishing research field, as evidenced by the success of journals and conferences and by the fact that the area continues to attract researchers from related disciplines. Not only has there been an increase in the quantity and quality of research in the core areas of cognition (e.g., attention, memory, and language) over the past 10 to 15 years, but there has also been considerable interest in extending the boundaries of cognitive aging to related subdisciplines, such as neuroscience, sensory processes, motivation and emotion, and social cognition and personality, and various fields of application, such as human factors. Despite the optimism and excitement, not everything is perfect, of course, and in the following sections we comment on a few of the pluses and minuses in our field as we see them.

DESCRIPTION AND EXPLANATION
IN COGNITIVE AGING

In some respects the field of cognitive aging still appears to be struggling with conceptual frameworks to interpret age-related differences in cognitive functioning. One manifestation of the current confusion concerns the distinction between description and explanation because, as it currently stands, one person's explanation could be another's description, and vice versa. For example, what might be considered explanation in terms of localization of the age differences with respect to a parameter or process within a particular theoretical model might, from a different perspective, merely be considered a form of description, albeit more precise and refined than what is typically provided.

This ambiguity is particularly apparent with respect to the usage of the term *processing resources* in discussions of cognitive aging research. As an example, some researchers tend to use this term in an explanatory sense, as when the age-related differences in many different variables are attributed to a reduction in processing resources. The problem with this usage is that it may not be meaningful unless clarification is provided with respect to exactly what is meant by resources and how they are related both to age and to the cognitive variables one is attempting to explain. In fact, a number of authors have noted that the interpretations are clearly circular when the same empirical results that are "explained" by reduced resources also serve as the primary evidence for inferring the existence of an age-related reduction of resources (e.g., Light, 1991; Salthouse, 1991). Metaphors (e.g., time, energy, and space) and vague terms (e.g., controlled attention, inhibition, working memory, and processing speed) are frequently mentioned in discussions of processing resources, but they are not very informative unless they are made more precise, are linked to empirical data by means of explicit operational definitions, and ultimately are supplemented by a description of the mechanisms by which they operate.

From the present vantage point, we can see three different approaches that might be fruitful in examining the nature of the hypothesized processing resources. First, the resource in question could be conceptualized in terms of particular behavioral measures, perhaps as indexed by time or accuracy of performance in carefully described cognitive tasks. Variants of this approach have been used when measures of processing speed or working memory have served as indices of a processing resource postulated to mediate at least some of the age-related differences evident in cognitive variables. What has been lacking thus far in this approach is detailed specification of the relevant mechanisms.

A second approach might focus on resources not in terms of observable behavioral measures but as reflections of the efficiency or effectiveness of various types of attentional control processes. Versions of this effectiveness-of-control view of processing resources are represented in the discussions of resource allocation in the Wingfield and Stine-Morrow chapter (chap. 6, this volume); in the discussion of notions of attentional inhibition in the McDowd and Shaw (chap. 4, this volume) and the Zacks,

Hasher, and Li (chap. 5, this volume) chapters; and in the references to monitoring processes in the Hertzog and Hultsch chapter (chap. 7, this volume). As noted in those chapters, perspectives emphasizing the role of control processes tend to focus on hypothesized deficiencies in aspects of attentional control, such as allocation or distribution, coordination, switching, and suppression, which can be presumed to be involved in a wide range of cognitive tasks. This approach differs from the first approach in that there is greater emphasis on theoretical processes and mechanisms that might contribute to cognitive deficits than on observable indices of those mechanisms. Eventually, however, these speculations will need to be made sufficiently explicit to allow relevant empirical data to be brought to bear.

Finally, a third approach to the notion of processing resources might involve a search for neurophysiological analogs of some form of "mental energy." The term *mental energy* can be traced back to Spearman (1927), but it was introduced into the cognitive aging literature by Craik and Byrd (1982), who suggested that age-related cognitive inefficiencies may be attributable to a decline in the energy that fuels mental processes. Among the possible neurophysiological correlates of mental energy that might be examined are indices of neural activity in the form of glucose or oxygen metabolism and the quantity of particular neurotransmitters or the density of receptor sites. Because age-related declines in efficiency in some or all of these brain mechanisms are likely to result in behavior patterns that are impoverished, attenuated, or truncated relative to the patterns shown by younger adults, they might be considered analogous to resources needed for the adequate operation of particular processing operations. It may be some time before these types of brain–behavior linkages can be firmly established, but if they are successful, they might ultimately serve to eliminate some of the confusion currently associated with the processing-resources concept.

THE COGNITIVE NEUROSCIENCE APPROACH

The cognitive neuroscience approach is represented in the chapters by Raz (chap. 1, this volume) and by Prull, Gabrieli, and Bunge (chap. 2, this volume). Research in the area of cognitive neuroscience is booming at present, with new links between brain and behavior being discovered at a rapid rate. The area is also important for cognitive aging, given the apparent parallels between normal aging and certain types of brain impairment and, as just noted, the potential for revealing the biological bases of such ambiguous concepts as processing resources.

One of the major issues in the area of the cognitive neuroscience of aging at the present time is whether the cognitive inefficiencies associated with normal aging can be located in specific brain regions. A number of observers have noted intriguing parallels in the patterns of behavioral deficits associated with aging and with damage to the frontal lobes (e.g., West, 1996). Although the frontal-deficit hypothesis clearly warrants further investigation, we believe that it is important to have evidence for specificity as well as for sensitivity. That is, in addition to finding evidence that the frontal lobes are involved in at least some age-related cognitive deficits (i.e., exhibit sensitivity), it is desirable to determine if the behavioral deficits are limited to impairments of the frontal region (i.e., exhibit specificity) or if other regions also contribute to the observed age-related effects. It is generally acknowledged that the most valuable type of evidence for functional localization is a double-dissociation pattern. In the present context, this might consist of a demonstration that certain age-related behavioral deficits are restricted to damage in the frontal lobe and are not affected by damage in other regions, whereas other age-related behavioral deficits are restricted to damage in other neuroanatomical regions and are unaffected by damage to the frontal region. Another obvious site to explore as a source of age-related cognitive impairments is the hippocampus and medial-temporal regions because recent work has suggested that these regions are associated with the integration of aspects of an experienced event (the "binding" functions) prior to memory storage (Chalfonte & Johnson, 1996; Cohen & Eichenbaum, 1993; Johnson & Chalfonte, 1994). In addition, functional neuroimaging studies have implicated the cerebellum in some cognitive tasks, and Rubin (1999) has suggested that age-related damage to the caudate nucleus may play a major role in cognitive aging. In general, it is clear that various structures should be examined before concluding that a single neural structure or region is responsible for all age-related cognitive deficits.

Neuroimaging techniques have generated considerable interest recently because they appear to offer the potential for an online window into cognitive functioning. However, it appears to us that several issues still need to be addressed before age-comparative results based on these techniques can be fully interpreted. Many of these are mentioned in the chapter by Raz, but to our knowledge others have not yet been addressed by researchers in this area.

First, sample sizes are generally so small that the power to detect small or moderate age differences in activation patterns is very limited (see chap. 8, this volume). Significant differences (when they are established with direct contrasts between groups instead of when the values in each group are separately compared against zero) are informative about the presence of age differences, but nonsignificant results are not easily interpretable when there is a low likelihood of detecting even moderate-sized effects with small samples. Replications of the same pattern of results in several studies (preferably from different laboratories), ideally followed eventually by meta-analytic integrations of the findings, may provide the best solution to this particular problem.

Second, age-related shrinkage occurs throughout the brain, but it is not uniform across all regions (see chap. 1, this volume), and it is not yet clear how to adjust for selective distortions. For example, if older adults have less neural tissue in a particular region than do young adults, is it reasonable to expect them to exhibit the same amount of regional activation, or should the amount of activation somehow be expressed relative to the volume of relevant tissue?

Third, there is still uncertainty with respect to how to deal with global reductions in cerebral blood flow. The problem is that the results of subtractions between the measures of blood flow in two different conditions, which are the basis of most current neuroimaging procedures, may be dependent on the absolute level of blood flow in the baseline condition, and it is not yet obvious whether absolute or relative comparisons are the most meaningful in neuroimaging studies concerned with individual differences. This problem is similar to the controversy that exists in behavioral research when there are different baselines because the results of the condition comparisons can be quite different when based on absolute (difference score) comparisons versus relative (e.g., proportional) comparisons.

Fourth, how should we deal with the possibility of age differences in the time or amplitude of various transfer or coupling functions (e.g., hemodynamic response, transmissivity of signals through brain tissue and skull, and correspondence between level of blood flow and level of neural activity)? Very little is currently known about age-related effects on the sequence of transduction processes necessary to produce the signals that form the basis of neuroimaging, but interpretations of age differences in patterns of activation would obviously become quite complicated if the relation between what is observed and what is inferred differs across age groups.

Fifth, how should the elements (i.e., pixels, voxels, or regions of interest) that are subjected to analysis be selected? In studies with young adults or other age-homogeneous samples, these regions are often selected on the basis of significant condition differences (i.e., activation differences between experimental and control conditions that are significantly different from zero). However, if the researcher is interested in age differences in patterns of activation, then a more appropriate strategy might involve selecting regions on the basis of significant interactions of age and condition rather than significant main effects of condition. Unfortunately, because the number of age-comparative neuroimaging studies is still quite limited, the impact of these different types of selection criteria is not yet obvious.

Sixth, if there are age differences in the measures of behavioral performance, then the patterns of activation in the young and old groups may reflect differences in the level of performance that was achieved instead of, or in addition to, the ages of the individuals. There are no perfect solutions to this problem because, if the stimulus parameters are adjusted (or manipulations introduced, such as the amount of prior practice) to alter the level of performance in one group relative to the other, then the activation differences may reflect these factors as much as, or more than, factors associated with the individuals' ages. Moreover, if the participants are selected to be equivalent in their level of behavioral performance, then one could question whether the results represent typical aging because age differences are frequently found in many cognitive variables. One possible strategy might involve testing two groups of older adults: one that exhibits the typical pattern of behavioral deficit and another that is matched in performance to the young sample. Not only would this three-group design allow comparisons of performance-matched young and old adults, and likely more representative groups of young and old adults, but it would also allow a potentially informative contrast between "typical" and "superior" older adults.

Finally, it is not yet obvious how a pattern of lower activation among older adults relative to young adults should be interpreted. Among the possibilities are that with increased age the same total quantity of activation is distributed across a broader region and thus is lower at any local area, that there is less functional neural tissue available to support activation among older adults, that the older brain cannot work as intensely as the younger brain, or possibly even that the older brain does not have to work as hard as the younger brain because of greater cumulative experience with cognitive activities (on the basis of the finding that more experience with an activity is typically associated with lower levels of activation).

It is important to emphasize that we do not believe that the preceding questions and concerns imply that age-comparative research in functional neuroimaging is not valuable, interesting, or important. Instead, we are merely raising issues that, in our opinion, ultimately must be resolved before the full potential of this type of research will be realized.

APPLIED COGNITIVE AGING

Another active area of research at the boundary of traditional cognition is the field of applied cognitive aging. The chapter by Rogers and Fisk (chap. 10, this volume) provides an excellent review of research at the interface of aging and human factors. However, a question they did not address—but which ultimately may need to be addressed in the development of the field of applied cognitive aging and in its various branches, such as human factors—is whether the issues and problems are age-specific or whether the concerns are simply more relevant to older adults because they have a greater prevalence of the limiting conditions. Stated somewhat differently, should the research focus in these applied branches be on interventions that are specific to the elderly segment of the population, or should the interventions be designed to deal with problems that can occur among people at any age but are simply more frequent among elderly individuals?

We suspect that the answer to this question could have important implications for the future of applied cognitive aging research. The approach of focusing on aspects of processing presumed to contribute to the problems would probably be more appealing to investigators primarily interested in basic research because it might be more likely to contribute to advances in theory. This approach also seems to have the paradoxical implication that if it is possible to identify which characteristics are associated with particular limitations of functioning, then it may not be necessary to study elderly populations to investigate age-related impairments. Instead, greater generalizability might be possible by focusing on the characteristics that limit relevant aspects of performance rather than on a particular group of individuals in whom those characteristics are highly prevalent. Moreover, if the problems are not specific to elderly adults, then the ultimate solutions will presumably benefit broader segments of the population.

Another possible implication of this perspective is that it may no longer be meaningful to have subdisciplines of aging and human factors, industrial gerontology, or other age-specific subspecialities of applied areas. Instead, research concerned with basic processes of aging might serve to identify relevant characteristics, such as reduced dynamic visual acuity, slower processing, and impaired working memory; the task of the applied researchers in human factors, industrial psychology, and so on would then be to attempt to deal with these limitations, regardless of the particular segment of the population to which they apply.

However, we are not yet convinced that the elimination of subspecialities in applied fields concerned with aging is desirable. For example, it might still be useful to have a subdiscipline specialized to deal with the probability of multiple limitations occurring simultaneously and the possibility of interactions among those limitations that are unlikely to occur except in elderly populations. Even under these circumstances, however, it will still be desirable to emphasize generalizable principles rather than to focus only on pragmatic solutions to local and immediate problems.

Rogers and Fisk (chap. 10, this volume) clearly acknowledged these goals, but it is probably still the case that relatively few mainstream cognitive aging researchers are aware of contributions from the area of applications to the realm of theory and basic research.

MACRO- AND MICROAPPROACHES
TO COGNITIVE AGING

Two major approaches to the study of cognitive aging are evident in the work of researchers during the past 50 years or so. One, which may be designated as the "microapproach," stems from mainstream human experimental psychology and tends to focus on the nature of age-related effects on a single variable by attempting to decompose the hypothesized processes involved in that variable. This approach has been popular within the field of cognitive aging since the pioneering work of Welford and colleagues in Britain (Welford, 1958), and it is closely related to the information-processing perspective to cognition in that the researcher attempts to isolate the critical aspect of processing by careful design of experimental conditions. Primarily for reasons of efficiency, it is often used with small samples from extreme groups (e.g., young vs. old adults).

In contrast, "macroapproaches" to cognitive aging examine age-related effects on one variable in the context of age-related effects on other variables. This perspective is closely related to the psychometric tradition in the sense that the studies are multivariate in nature and typically involve moderately large samples of 100 or more adults across a wide age range. The macroapproach relies on correlational techniques to investigate patterns of relations among variables and as such is concerned with the formulation of coherent descriptive models of the correlational structure that exists among cognitive variables and individual difference characteristics, such as age. Structural equation modeling is one prominent technique in the current literature exemplifying this approach; factor analysis is another technique that has provided valuable insights into cognitive processes and their changes with age.

Thus, both approaches draw on large, well-developed literatures in cognitive psychology and psychometrics for concepts and inspiration (and, indeed, findings from cognitive aging have also enriched each of these literatures). One advantage of the microapproach is that its emphasis on the dissection and identification of specific processes leads naturally to a consideration of mechanisms, first at the level of behavior and possibly later at the level of brain correlates. The microapproach thus generates concepts and findings that might be translated relatively easily into the languages of neuropsychology and cognitive neuroscience. A corresponding disadvantage of the microapproach, however, is that overall behavioral patterns may ultimately be best understood in terms of interactions among processes and their underlying mechanisms; if this is so, then undue focus on single processes in isolation may miss some of the most important and interesting aspects of the phenomena of cognitive aging. The chapters in this volume dealing with basic cognitive processes are mostly written from the microperspective; so, in an attempt to partially restore the balance, we briefly describe a few interesting ideas and findings that have emerged from recent macroanalyses.

First, we wish to highlight the fact that mediational models, in which the age-related effects on one or more presumably simple variables are postulated to mediate at least some of the age-related effects on other more complex variables, have been found to be fairly successful in accounting for large proportions of age-related influences on many different types of cognitive variables (e.g., Park et al., 1996; Salthouse, 1993, 1994; Verhaeghen & Salthouse, 1997). Although currently quite popular, these methods do have certain limitations. For example, interpretation of the results of mediational models requires certain assumptions to be accepted, and explanations are still needed for the mechanisms responsible for any relations that are discovered. Furthermore, most of the studies have relied on measures of processing speed and working memory as the hypothesized mediators, and it is not yet known whether models with other types of mediators, such as those related to concepts of attentional control or neurophysiological indices of brain function, would be equally successful.

A second intriguing set of recent findings concerns the mounting evidence for "dedifferentiation" of abilities in older people, in the sense that the correlations between variables and factors are frequently higher among older adults than among young adults. The term *dedifferentiation* derives from the concept of differentiation in childhood, which refers to the gradual separation of a single general ability into distinct specialized abilities as the child matures. It has been hypothesized that this process might operate in reverse across the period of adulthood because specialized abilities have been found to be more highly correlated, or less differentiated, among older adults relative to young adults (e.g., Baltes, Cornelius, Spiro, Nesselroade, & Willis, 1980; Cunningham, 1980; Schultz, Kaye, & Hoyer, 1980).

It is still not clear why this "factor collapse" or dedifferentiation occurs, but there are at least two interesting possibilities. One is that there could be an age-related decrease in the degree of functional specialization and localization such that with increased age either a given brain region might be able to contribute to several different types of cognitive processes or the same cognitive process could be "controlled" by multiple neuroanatomical regions (e.g., Kinsbourne, 1980). Correlations between variables or factors might therefore increase because the neural substrates for different cognitive processes lose some of their specialized character and increase in their extent of equipotentiality in the sense that they contribute to a greater number of cognitive processes. A second possibility that could account for the dedifferentiation pattern is that with increased age there might be greater reliance of cognitive variables on a single critical structure or process. The nature of the critical structure or process is not yet obvious, but to the extent that its functioning is relevant to many different cognitive variables, if it then becomes impaired, it might affect performance in a wide range of cognitive tasks. The available data do not allow these possibilities to be distinguished at the present time, but they will eventually need to be distinguished because the phenomenon of larger interrelations among variables in samples of older adults than in samples of young adults now seems relatively well established.

A third phenomenon revealed from macrotype research that is likely to generate useful work over the next decade concerns the interrelations of cognitive and noncognitive variables, particularly in the period of later adulthood. The chapter by Bäckman, Small, Wahlin, and Larsson (chap. 9, this volume) reviews some of these interrelations among the oldest old, and relations between cognitive and sensory variables are discussed in the chapter by Schneider and Pichora-Fuller (chap. 3, this volume).

The phenomenon that sensory and cognitive variables may become more closely related to one another with increased age has been reported in assorted articles over the years (e.g., Farrimond, 1967; Granick, Kleban, & Weiss, 1976), but recent reports from Australia (Anstey, Lord, & Williams, 1997) and Germany (Baltes & Lindenberger, 1997; Lindenberger & Baltes, 1994) have stimulated renewed interest in this topic. Both of these projects focused on adults 65 years of age and older and found that cognitive variables shared considerable age-related variance with motor variables (Anstey et al., 1997) or with sensory variables (Baltes & Lindenberger, 1997). Even more recent research (Baltes & Lindenberger, 1997; Salthouse, Hambrick, & McGuthry, 1998; Salthouse, Hancock, Meinz, & Hambrick, 1996) has extended these findings and revealed that sensory and motor variables account for nearly the same proportions of age-related variance for adults under the age of 50 or 60 as for older adults.

The topic of sensory–cognitive relations is explored in some depth in the chapter by Schneider and Pichora-Fuller (chap. 3, this volume). Although there seems little doubt about the existence of a strong relation between sensory and cognitive functioning in older people, the interpretation of the various results is still under debate. One possibility is that age-related decreases in sensory efficiency reduce the quantity and quality of sensory information necessary for higher level cognitive functions.

Some support for this position comes from findings that certain age-related patterns of memory impairment can be simulated in young adults by adding noise to the sensory signal (e.g., Murphy, Craik, Li, & Schneider, 1999). This interpretation is obviously optimistic in that it suggests that some types of cognitive rehabilitation may be achieved by improving the quality and clarity of the sensory input. A second possibility, originally mentioned by Lindenberger and Baltes (1994; Baltes & Lindenberger, 1997), is that sensory and cognitive functions correlate highly in older adults as a reflection of some "common cause" that affects both sets of factors. More specifically, if the brain works less efficiently with increasing age, this decreasing efficiency may be reflected in a variety of sensory, motor, and cognitive functions, but none of these consequences may necessarily be more fundamental than the others. It is not yet clear which of these interpretations will ultimately prove most viable, but the available evidence seems fairly consistent in suggesting that age-related influences on many aspects of cognitive functioning are not independent of age-related influences on aspects of sensory and motor functioning.

We conclude this section by restating that micro- and macroapproaches are concerned with different levels of analysis because the microapproach focuses on age-related effects apparent in a single variable, whereas the macroapproach examines effects operating across multiple variables. It is therefore important to recognize that the two approaches are complementary rather than contradictory or in opposition. However, it is interesting that research from the microapproach or the process approach often seems to implicate highly specific age-related effects, whereas the macroapproach or the structural approach has tended to implicate broad and general age-related influences. That is, the microapproach has often been successful in distinguishing between processes with high and low degrees of age sensitivity (i.e., identifying differential deficits), and results of this type have been interpreted as evidence for specific age-related influences. In contrast, results from macroapproaches suggest that large proportions of the age-related effects on individual cognitive variables are shared and are not specific to a particular variable. Ultimately, results from the two approaches will need to be integrated to achieve a more complete understanding of the nature of age-related effects on cognition.

THE CONTEXT FOR COGNITION

A final issue that merits some reflection concerns the context within which cognition should be viewed and understood. The microapproach described in the previous section attempts to dissect complex cognitive processes into their constituent components and then to relate these components to their underlying neural correlates. The macroapproach, on the other hand, is more concerned with broad patterns of interaction and is thus more inclined to view mental experience and overall behavior in holistic terms. Proponents of this second approach argue that cognitive processes cannot be fully understood in isolation but must be viewed in conjunction with many other factors, not only other cognitive variables but also aspects of emotions, motivations, and a host of other social and personality characteristics. Most chapters in this volume take the former view, and substantial gains in understanding have been achieved in the past 20 years using micromethods. However, Isaacowitz, Turk Charles, and Carstensen (chap. 11, this volume) and Staudinger and Pasupathi (chap. 12, this volume) urged us to take a broader and more integrative view, and they made an excellent case for the reinterpretation of age-related cognitive changes after a careful consideration of age-related changes in such things as aspirations, goals, the self-concept, and the social context.

The history of psychology reflects this continuing interplay between what might be termed reductionist and contextualist points of view. The stimulus–response theorists sought to isolate the fundamental building blocks of learning and then to construct models of complex behavior from them, much as chemistry had done with atoms, molecules, and compounds. The Gestalt school then attacked the behaviorists on the grounds that combinations of behavioral elements typically resulted in emergent behaviors or experiences that were qualitatively quite different from their constituents. An implication of this latter position is that the valid interpretation of a mental process, an experience, a segment of behavior, or even of a specifically located patch of neural activity may vary as a function of its mental, experiential, behavioral, or neural context. Thus, as pointed out by Isaacowitz et al. (chap. 11, this volume), older adults appear to allocate more resources to emotions and emotional regulation than do younger adults, and this age-related shift in emphasis may be reflected in different patterns of recall of stories and events. Isaacowitz et al. also suggested that a further difference in this connection is that older adults place greater emphasis on integrating experiences within their own personal knowledge base and within the culture generally. That is, changing patterns of cognitive behavior should be interpreted within the framework of the older person's motivations and goals, which may well differ from those dominant in young adulthood.

Staudinger and Pasupathi (chap. 12, this volume) endorsed and extended these arguments. They distinguished between life mechanics and life pragmatics, with the former dealing with information-processing mechanisms viewed in the context of changing emotional, motivational, personality, and social variables and the latter dealing essentially with transactions between the self and the social–cultural environment. Their approach is rather optimistic, stressing as it does the adaptive functions of life pragmatics; as they said in their closing sentence, they hoped to have identified some of the "gains and resiliencies" that are also part of the aging process. Is there a necessary conflict between the optimistic view of the life-span development school and the "pessimistic" view that emerges from the traditional biological–cognitive perspective? We are inclined to think not. It seems to us perfectly possible to accept the fact that the brain (like most other bodily organs) becomes less efficient with age but also to endorse the flexibility of human cognition and the adaptability of people as they progress from youth to old age. It seems possible to draw a parallel here to changing views of aging in the realms of physical fitness and social and professional life. The concept of what it means to be 50 or 60 or 70 has changed radically over the past century, but this more positive set of cultural expectations coexists with an acceptance that the body does age, even if some of the effects of biological aging might be mitigated by paying due attention to diet and exercise.

In a similar way, it seems to us that cognitive aging researchers can accept the reality of declining cognitive powers stemming from the reduced efficiency of the brain but at the same time look for means by which older adults can best hold the negative effects of aging at bay and optimize the mental capacities they possess. Traditional experimental researchers should also pay greater attention to the changing contexts—emotional, motivational, attitudinal, and social—in which cognitive processes occur in older adults. We are hopeful that the next decade of research will see great progress, both in an understanding of the brain correlates of cognitive processes and in a greater understanding of how such processes are modified adoptively by the variety of contexts in which they take place.

In conclusion, although we believe that a number of issues remain to be addressed and that a great deal of information is still needed before a complete understanding of cognitive aging will be achieved, we are optimistic about the progress that is occurring in the field. One sign of this progress is the tremendous growth that is occurring in the relevant literatures, and we would once again like to express our sincere gratitude to the contributors of this volume for providing very informative and insightful reviews of these ever-expanding fields.

REFERENCES

Anstey, K. J., Lord, S. R., & Williams, P. (1997). Strength in lower limbs, visual contrast sensitivity, and simple reaction time predict cognition in older women. *Psychology and Aging, 12,* 137–144.

Baltes, P. B., Cornelius, S. W., Spiro, A., Nesselroade, J. R., & Willis, S. L. (1980). Integration versus differentiation of fluid/crystallized intelligence in old age. *Developmental Psychology, 16,* 625–635.

Baltes, P. B., & Lindenberger, U. (1997). Emergence of a powerful connection between sensory and cognitive functions across the adult life span: A new window to the study of cognitive aging? *Psychology and Aging, 12,* 12–21.

Chalfonte, B. L., & Johnson, M. K. (1996). Feature memory and binding in young and older adults. *Memory & Cognition, 24,* 403–416.

Cohen, N. J., & Eichenbaum, H. (1993). *Memory, amnesia, and the hippocampus.* Cambridge, MA: MIT Press.

Craik, F. I. M., & Byrd, M. (1982). Aging and cognitive deficits: The role of attentional resources. In F. I. M. Craik & S. Trehub (Eds.), *Aging and cognitive processes* (pp. 191–211). New York: Plenum.

Cunningham, W. R. (1980). Age-comparative factor analysis of ability variables in adulthood and old age. *Intelligence, 4,* 133–149.

Farrimond, T. (1967). Visual and auditory performance variations with age: Some implications. *Australian Journal of Psychology, 19,* 193–201.

Granick, S., Kleban, M. H., & Weiss, A. D. (1976). Relationship between hearing loss and cognition in normally hearing aged persons. *Journal of Gerontology, 31,* 434–440.

Johnson, M. K., & Chalfonte, B. L. (1994). Binding complex memories: The role of reactivation and the hippocampus. In D. L. Schacter & E. Tulving (Eds.), *Memory systems 1994* (pp. 311–350). Cambridge, MA: MIT Press.

Kinsbourne, M. (1980). Attentional dysfunctions and the elderly: Theoretical models and research perspectives. In L. W. Poon, J. L. Fozard, L. S. Cermak, D. Arenberg, & L. W. Thompson (Eds.), *New directions in memory and aging* (pp. 113–129). Hillsdale, NJ: Lawrence Erlbaum Associates.

Light, L. L. (1991). Memory and aging: Four hypotheses in search of data. *Annual Review of Psychology, 42,* 333–376.

Lindenberger, U., & Baltes, P. B. (1994). Sensory functioning and intelligence in old age: A strong connection. *Psychology and Aging, 9,* 339–355.

Murphy, D., Craik, F. I. M., Li, K., & Schneider, B. A. (1999). *Comparing the effects of aging and background noise on short-term memory performance.* Manuscript submitted for publication.

Park, D. C., Smith, A. D., Lautenschlager, G., Earles, J. L., Frieske, D., Zwahr, M., & Gaines, C. L. (1996). Mediators of long-term memory performance across the life span. *Psychology and Aging, 11,* 621–637.

Rubin, D. C. (1999). *The neural basis of cognitive aging: Could it be the caudate?* Unpublished manuscript.

Salthouse, T. A. (1991). *Theoretical perspectives on cognitive aging.* Hillsdale, NJ: Lawrence Erlbaum Associates.

Salthouse, T. A. (1993). Speed mediation of adult age differences in cognition. *Developmental Psychology, 29,* 722–738.

Salthouse, T. A. (1994). The nature of the influence of speed on adult age differences in cognition. *Developmental Psychology, 30,* 240–259.

Salthouse, T. A., Hambrick, D. Z., & McGuthry, K. E. (1998), Shared age-related influences on cognitive and non-cognitive variables. *Psychology and Aging, 13,* 486–500.

Salthouse, T. A., Hancock, H. E., Meinz, E. J., & Hambrick, D. Z. (1996). Interrelations of age, visual acuity, and cognitive functioning. *Journal of Gerontology: Psychological Sciences, 51B,* P317–P330.

Schultz, N. R., Kaye, D. B., & Hoyer, W. J. (1980). Intelligence and spontaneous flexibility in adulthood and old age. *Intelligence, 4,* 219–231.

Spearman, C. (1927). *The abilities of man: Their nature and measurement.* London: Macmillan.

Verhaeghen, P., & Salthouse, T. A. (1997). Meta-analyses of age-cognition relations in adulthood: Estimates of linear and non-linear age effects and structural models. *Psychological Bulletin, 122,* 231–249.

Welford, A. T. (1958). *Ageing and human skill.* London: Oxford University Press.

West, R. L. (1996). An application of prefrontal cortex theory to cognitive aging. *Psychological Bulletin, 120,* 272–292.

Author Index

Subject Index